A SPELLBINDING STORY

"A near-miracle; for the first time I think I understand not only *what* happened at Watergate but *how* it happened, and why. *Nightmare* seems the one indispensable Watergate book."
—Joe McGinness, author of
The Selling of the President, 1968

"A blockbuster that sheds new light on many dark corners and reads as smoothly as fiction."
—*Cleveland Plain Dealer*

"An investigative masterwork."
—*The New Republic*

"A massive, careful encyclopedia that sorts out all existing Nixon-era evidence . . . and puts it in order for the final judgment of a dispassionate reader, or of history itself. *The one book to have if you're having only one.*"
—*Time*

NIGHTMARE
THE UNDERSIDE OF
THE NIXON YEARS

J. ANTHONY LUKAS

BANTAM BOOKS
TORONTO · NEW YORK · LONDON

NIGHTMARE
*A Bantam Book | published by arrangement with
The Viking Press*

PRINTING HISTORY
Viking Press edition published February 1976
2nd printing .... May 1976
Bantam edition | March 1977

*Bantam Books are published by Bantam Books, Inc. Its trade-
mark, consisting of the words "Bantam Books" and the por-
trayal of a bantam, is registered in the United States Patent
Office and in other countries. Marca Registrada. Bantam
Books, Inc., 666 Fifth Avenue, New York, New York 10019.*

PRINTED IN THE UNITED STATES OF AMERICA

PREFACE

I didn't set out to write a book. Watergate and the fall of Richard Nixon engulfed me—as they engulfed the nation—by degrees.

In April 1973, *The New York Times Magazine* asked me to write a full issue on the Watergate scandal, which was just then cracking open. I went to Washington and spent three months assembling material for a lengthy account, which ran on July 22. That fall, after the Saturday Night Massacre, the magazine commissioned another full issue, which appeared on January 13, 1974. In May 1974, I began work on still a third issue, focusing on the impeachment struggle. That project aborted after Nixon abruptly resigned on August 9. But by then the story consumed me. Immersed for so long in the massive store of evidence, I wanted to draw from it a coherent narrative that would weave together the diverse strands and make fresh connections. As I worked my way through the welter of conflicting testimony, new puzzles confronted me, new areas which demanded to be explored. The result is a manuscript four times the length of the two published pieces combined.

The book, as the title suggests, is about that slice of our recent history which Gerald Ford described as "our long national nightmare." Although several commentators have construed that phrase narrowly to cover only the Watergate break-in and its aftermath, I have taken it to mean the whole story of Richard Nixon's abuse of his presidential powers. I believe that story properly begins in the early days of his first term and runs, like a fault in the marble, through his entire administration, weakening and ultimately bringing down the entire edifice. Yet this is not a book about the Nixon presidency. It does not deal with foreign policy, except as it directly intersects the story I have to tell. It does not deal with the bulk of Nixon's domestic programs and policies. These subjects need thorough examination—and undoubtedly will get it. I hope this effort will be of help to future historians who attempt more comprehensive studies.

To assist further research, I analyze the raw materials for this book in a "Note on Sources" at the end. It remains here merely to express my deepest gratitude to two wonderful women: Elisabeth Sifton, my wise and discerning editor; and Toby Wertheim, indefatigable researcher, scrupulous assistant, and valued friend.

J.A.L.

New York City
August 1975

CONTENTS

1

FEAR OF LOSING

Chief Newman, my coach, an American Indian, produced some very fine teams at that small, little college at Whittier. . . . There were no excuses for failure. He didn't feel sorry for you when you got knocked down. He had a different definition of being a good loser. He said: "You know what a good loser is? It's somebody who hates to lose . . ."

—Richard M. Nixon,
Pro Football Hall of Fame Dinner,
July 30, 1971

In the raw winter of 1970 Richard Nixon looked like a loser. From balmy San Clemente and Key Biscayne, he and his aides strove earnestly to put the best possible face on the returns in the midterm elections. "We have increased our majority now," Nixon told reporters at San Clemente on November 4. "I hope all the American people realize that now the majority has spoken, the real majority in this country." Later that week, in Key Biscayne, his assistants said the President thought that "the election, ideologically, was enormously successful." But realists in both parties knew better. Back in Washington, a consensus was hardening, like ice on the Mall's reflecting pool, that the election constituted a serious setback for Nixon and an ominous portent for 1972.

The Republicans gained two seats in the Senate, and lost twelve in the House—less than the party in power generally does at midterm. But this was misleading because a midterm defeat generally follows a Presidential victory which carries into office many marginal congressmen who become vulnerable when they run on their own. Nixon, however, was the first President since Zachary Taylor in 1849 to start his term without a majority in either chamber. The 1970 midterm election did not pare his overblown majority; it deepened his deficit in the House and failed to improve it much in the Senate.

Even more important, the GOP lost eleven governorships and some key state legislatures. Except for Tennessee, the ballyhooed "Southern Strategy" failed to gain the Republicans any ground below the Mason-Dixon Line. And they did badly in the large, populous states—notably Pennsylvania, Ohio, Wisconsin, Minnesota, Michigan, Texas, and Florida—in which the 1972 election would almost certainly be decided. In December, when the Republican governors and governors-elect gathered beneath the snowy peaks of Sun Valley, Idaho, their standing joke was that they should have met at Death Valley. One prominent party worker said his analysis showed that if the election were held that week, Nixon would not carry any of the ten largest states, with the possible exception of Florida. Governor Edgar D. Whitcomb of Indiana, which had given Nixon his biggest majority in 1968, said the President was in trouble even there. Governor Francis W. Sargent of Massachusetts said: "The storm clouds are gathering for Mr. Nixon in 1972."

The election results were particularly devastating because of the extravagant expectations harbored at the White House, and because of the unprecedented Presidential intervention designed to achieve them. Curiously, for an administration hardly given to bookishness, its overblown objectives that fall had been nurtured in part by two recent political books: Kevin Phillips's *The Emerging Republican Majority* and Richard M. Scammon's and Ben J. Wattenberg's *The Real Majority*. Phillips, a young conservative from New York, who had worked for John Mitchell during the 1968 campaign and later at the Justice Department, had absorbed Mitchell's Southern Strategy—a simple tactic aimed at adding the 13.5 per cent of the vote which Governor George C. Wallace of Alabama had garnered in 1968 to Nixon's 43.4 per cent to build a powerful new majority in 1972. Phillips elaborated this strategy into a grand thesis: that Americans (except for pockets of liberals, blacks, and Latins) were fed up with the New Deal-Fair Deal-New Frontier brand of Liberalism and craved a New Conservatism. Looking particularly to the South, the suburbs, and the white ethnic workingman, Phillips foresaw an emerging Republican majority that would replace the old Democratic coalition of big cities, unions, and minorities forged by Franklin D. Roosevelt in the 1930s.

Phillips's work was the most talked about political book of 1969. Its argument was complemented the next year by the Scammon-Wattenberg volume, which pictured the electorate as largely unblack, unyoung, unpoor, and preoccupied with the Social Issue—an amalgam of attitudes toward violence, race, students, dissent, crime, promiscuity, and drugs. The authors, both Democrats, directed their argument chiefly to their own party, but its implications seemed to buttress hopes for the new majority envisioned by Phillips.

The President grasped hungrily at such projections. For, after a propitious start in 1969, the spring of 1970 had been a sour, frustrating time for him. First, the Senate had refused to confirm his appointment of G. Harrold Carswell to the Supreme Court, the second rejection of a court appointee in six months. And then in May many Americans refused to accept his rationale for the invasion of Cambodia, and this set off a tumult across the country which culminated in the deadly fusillade that killed four students at Kent State University in Ohio. These twin uprisings by the President's "enemies" marked a turning point in the Nixon administration. According to some White House officials, the President's tone shifted markedly as he moved toward a policy of "positive polarization"—punishing his enemies and trying to capture the crushing majority which Phillips and Scammon-Wattenberg assured him was out there waiting to be mobilized.

The goal was nothing less than a reversal of history. Not only would the Republicans try to avoid losing congressional seats at midterm—as virtually every party in power had during the twentieth century—but they were determined to win a few more seats in the House and wrest control of the recalcitrant Senate from its heavy Democratic majority. That would require a gain of at least seven Senate seats (to create a 50–50 tie, which could then be broken by Vice President Spiro T. Agnew, the Senate's presiding officer). Nixon hand-picked certain Republican candidates to spearhead that assault—among them George H. W. Bush in Texas, William E. Brock III in Tennessee, and William C. Cramer in Florida; and he passed the word to go easy on certain opponents (notably the Conservative candidate, James L. Buckley, in New York and Democrat Henry M. Jackson in Washington) who might serve his purposes. For the majority he sought needed not be entirely Republican. An "ideological majority" would suffice.

Moreover, Nixon concluded that such a victory could be gained only with a freewheeling, bareknuckled campaign that would carry the fight aggressively to the Democrats. At conferences during August, White House political operatives mapped out such tactics and even came up with a term—"Radical-Liberal"—with which to brand the Democrats as left-leaning, big-spending, permissive, and immoral. On September 10 Nixon dispatched his ever-willing Vice President on the campaign circuit with specific instructions to hit their opponents hard and often. Mr. Agnew eagerly obliged, flailing away at the "disruptive and militant minority," "rotten apples," and "radiclibs."

But even this didn't satisfy the impatient President. Over the weekend of October 10–11 he suddenly reversed his earlier decision against involving himself in personal campaigning. Eager for the taste of battle, convinced he could win a historic victory, Nixon decided to put his prestige on the line in every state where he thought Republican senatorial candidates might have a chance—twenty-three in all. For the next three weeks—in what Hugh Sidey of *Life* magazine called "an eleventh-hour orgy of tawdry histrionics" —Nixon crisscrossed the country in Air Force One, delivering a standard law-and-order speech that decried "the small group which always tears America down" and called on "the Great Silent Majority" to "speak up for America."

Throughout the tour, Nixon instructed his Secret Service men to allow just enough hecklers to provide a foil for his denunciations. This policy reached its logical climax on October 29 in San Jose, California, where, confronted with a large, hostile crowd outside the auditorium, Nixon clambered onto the hood of his limousine and raised his fingers in the familiar V-sign, seemingly inviting the stones and epithets that followed. And the next day, in Phoenix, he gleefully exploited the incident: "No band of violent thugs is going to keep me from going out and speaking with the American people." His strident Phoenix speech was rebroadcast on election eve—only to be followed by Senator Edmund S. Muskie, measured and calm in a Maine living room, asking the voters to repudiate the Republicans' "politics of fear."

Once the returns were in, many Republicans felt the voters had done just that. Governor David F. Cargo of New Mexico warned that his party had "lost the election because the strategy was completely negative." Senator Robert W. Packwood of Oregon called the campaign a "disaster." And John Mitchell—miffed that he had not called the shots as he had in 1968 —told a friend that the President had behaved as if he were "running for sheriff."

If the President was the sheriff, then in those early years of the administration John N. Mitchell was his chief deputy. Richard Whalen, a former Nixon aide, writes: "Mitchell was Number 1, tied to the White House by a direct line, the uniquely intimate counselor to whom Nixon turned on every subject from minor political matters to Supreme Court appointments." This relationship has been compared to that of President John F. Kennedy and Attorney General Robert F. Kennedy, but it was less fraternal than paternal—with Mitchell, the younger man by a year, often seeming to be the President's father figure. It all began in 1963, when Nixon came to New York to launch his new career as a Wall Street lawyer. He had never felt secure in the Big Apple—whether as a young man fresh from Duke Law School and unable to find a job, or as a candidate rebuffed by the starchy patriarchs who frequented Le Pavillon and Carnegie Hall. A friend from those days recalls him railing at the "Ivy League bastards" who snubbed him. "He felt he was as good as anyone, but here he'd been Vice President for eight years and all that, and he wasn't quite an equal. . . . Maybe that's why he was drawn to John Mitchell, who never snubbed him. It was a class thing." Mitchell took him under his pin-striped wing, showed him where the levers of power were, and—perhaps most important —listened to his myriad problems with that calm, impassive, jowly face hidden behind the perpetual screen of pipe smoke. Nixon was impressed. "I've found the heavyweight," he told the speechwriter William L. Safire in 1967. That year, Nixon, Mudge, Rose, Guthrie & Alexander became Nixon, Mudge, Rose, Guthrie, Alexander & Mitchell. But Nixon absorbed not only his friend's law firm but much of his style. For Mitchell was a state- and municipal-bond lawyer, that special breed of practitioner who operates best behind closed doors in city halls and statehouses across the land, clinching deals with a handshake and a wink. Unaccustomed to the give-and-take of hustings politics, he brought his back-room manner into his role as Nixon's 1968 campaign manager—and thence into the administration. At first he was reluctant to leave his lucrative law practice ($300,000 a year) and his rambling house overlooking a golf course in Rye, New York. But after Robert H. Finch, Nixon's old California associate, turned the job down, the President prevailed on Mitchell to become attorney general. Once transplanted to Washington, Mitchell took the job with deadly seriousness. "I am first and foremost a law-enforcement officer," he said. Mitchell became— in Nixon's words—"our leader against crime and lawlessness": the prime advocate of no-knock laws, wiretapping, stop and frisk, preventive detention, and a "restructured" Supreme Court. He could sound deep-

ly conservative, warning that "this country is going so far right you won't recognize it." But above all he was a steely-eyed practitioner of the old politics. Some people found him cold, even ruthless, but his ebullient wife, Martha, called him "a cute, cuddly, adorable fellow."

After the 1970 election the Southern White House stuck publicly to its upbeat appraisal, but behind the palm fronds Nixon and his aides began reassessing their strategy. On November 7 the President met with seven senior assistants to "go over the game films." The conclusion was unanimous: unless Nixon quickly transformed his campaign style he might well be a one-term President.

Eight months before—in his April 30 speech announcing the invasion of Cambodia—Nixon had shown how, even then, this prospect preyed on his mind. "I would rather be a one-term President and do what I believe was right," he said, "than to be a two-term President at the cost of seeing America become a second-rate power and to see this nation accept the first defeat in its proud hundred-and-ninety-year history." If this was the ultimate proof of his devotion to the national interest, it also proved how deep was his fear of another repudiation by the voters. Indeed, this fear of humiliation at the polls may have been on his mind when he spoke in that same speech of a national humiliation that would occur if "the world's most powerful nation, the United States of America, acts like a pitiful, helpless giant." The world's most powerful political leader, the President of the United States, feared that he too might soon be brought to his knees.

That was a devastating prospect to a man who had all too often been a loser. The campaign losses (to John Kennedy in 1960, Edmund G. "Pat" Brown in 1962), the humiliations (from Dwight D. Eisenhower), the barbs (from columnists and television commentators), and all the quiet little snubs (from Park Avenue ladies and Georgetown gentlemen) had left a battered psyche that could not tolerate another defeat.

Richard Nixon needed a victory in 1972—if possible, a big one—far more than most politicians need victory. He craved it in the way an exhausted athlete craves a drink of water, the way an aging movie star craves applause.

In mid-November a smaller group headed by John Mitchell closeted with Nixon again. From this session emerged another unanimous conclusion: Nixon must drop his partisan image and henceforth be the President. Four days into the new year, Nixon publicly proclaimed his new persona in a televised interview with four network correspondents. "This is a noncampaign year," he told his interlocutors, "and now I am going to wear my hat as President of the United States."

But if the President was to assume an air of statesmanlike high-mindedness for the next two years, then others would have to carry on the tough partisan brawl building for 1972. The two-tiered game plan called for a posture of unusual conciliation on the President's part and a stance of extra combativeness by his political operatives.

In January the President handed the chairmanship of the Republican National Committee to Senator Robert J. Dole of Kansas, known for his hard-nosed partisanship. But nobody expected the real reins of the campaign to be held at the National Committee. "We knew we had a damn tough fight," one Presidential aide recalls, "and we weren't going to entrust it to the bunch of cautious old hacks down at the committee." Moreover, the President made increasingly clear that he cared little about the election of other Republican candidates per se or the success of the party as an organization. He wanted his campaign run by people who owed their loyalty not to the Grand Old Party but to Richard Nixon.

Those people became the Citizens Committee for the Re-election of the President, later simply the Committee for the Re-election of the President (known to friend and foe alike as CREEP). In March 1971 the committee opened its offices in the First National Bank Building, a glass and steel tower at 1701 Pennsylvania Avenue. The CREEP offices—replete with burnt orange carpeting, color-coordinated décor, and new electric typewriters—were nothing if not convenient to the White House. Barely a hundred and fifty yards from the big iron gates, it was an easy stroll for the brisk young men in double-knit suits who began shuttling back and forth along the fringes of Lafayette Park that spring. One floor up were the offices of Murray Chotiner, one of the President's key political operatives, and right down the fourth-floor hallway from CREEP were the Washington offices of Mudge, Rose, Guthrie & Alexander, which Mitchell would soon use as a base for running the 1972 campaign.

But even while attorney general, Mitchell was already the *de facto* boss of the campaign. "John Mitchell runs this committee with an iron hand," said DeVan L. Shumway, the CREEP spokesman. "We are only the input." When the CREEP office opened in March he placed one of his protégés, Harry S. Flemming, in a key position. Then in May H. R. "Bob" Haldeman, the President's chief of staff, who headed a rival faction jockeying for supremacy in Nixon's inner circle, sent over one of his own lieutenants, Jeb Stuart Magruder. Magruder established a surprisingly close working relationship with Mitchell and within a few months was virtually running CREEP for the attorney general. But his prime loyalty remained to Haldeman at the White House.

Named by his father, a Civil War buff, after the dashing Confederate cavalry general, Jeb Magruder hardly cut a dashing figure in the mid-1960s when he was a merchandiser of cosmetics, facial tissues, and women's hosiery. But he had high aspirations. Magruder's grandfather had been a wealthy, prominent shipyard president, who was convicted in 1921 of misapplication of funds and went to jail for six months. In the wake of that debacle, young Jeb grew up in somewhat straitened circumstances on Staten Island. The gap between the family's once-considerable social standing and its current realities largely formed his view of the world. Magruder recalls that his parents tried to give him and his brother "a taste of upper-class living," doing things the rich did that weren't expensive, such as going over to Forest Hills for the tennis matches or down to Princeton for the football games. But they weren't rich and they knew it. In high school, Jeb found echoes of his own life in F. Scott Fitzgerald's stories about ambitious young men who yearned for the world of the wealthy. He sold Prince Matchabelli perfume to work his way through Williams College, yet tried assiduously to match the poise, sophistication, and grooming of his "preppie" classmates. After graduation, he went to work for IBM, attracted by its "aura of power and prestige." But he jumped quickly from corporation to corporation—Crown Zellerbach; Booz Allen and Hamilton; the Jewel Tea Company—finally becoming president of two small cosmetics companies in California. Meanwhile, he faithfully put in time as a Republican worker, "coordinated southern California" for Nixon in 1968, and eagerly moved with him to Washington the next year. Haldeman, seeking full control of Herbert G. Klein's press operation, installed Magruder as deputy director of communications. That was the right place for him, most of his associates agreed. "He was a PR man one hundred per cent," one of them said later. A self-styled "Nixonian Republican," Magruder developed a reputation for loyalty. "He'll do what he's told to do, maybe even to the point of sublimating his own judgment," says a former associate. (Nixon surrounded himself with young men like Magruder, in part because they had no independent judgment, no autonomous will. "Young people will do things that older people won't do in campaigns," one of Nixon's older—and former—aides once said. "They also won't do things that older people will do, like telling you to go fuck yourself. Nixon wanted people around him who would do what he wanted them to do. That's what he got.") Magruder had an open, friendly manner. ("If he had a tail, he would wag it," quipped Theodore White.) His easy informality—riding his ten-speed bike to work, showing up on Saturdays in a sport shirt—helped him earn the loyalty of others. One colleague calls him "a master seducer."

Another says, "I performed things for Jeb I wouldn't have done for anyone else."

There was a lot to do. As the spring wore on, it looked increasingly as though Nixon might indeed be a one-term President. In February the Harris Poll showed Muskie leading Nixon 43 to 40. In March, it was 44 to 39; in May, 47 to 39.

2

STATE OF SIEGE

Everything is valid, everything is possible.
—Tom Charles Huston,
June 9, 1970

May 1971 was a time of torment in Washington. After weeks of orderly antiwar protests, the May Day Tribe descended on the city determined to "stop the government" with an unprecedented wave of civil disobedience and disruption. For days, the motley legion of young demonstrators blocked streets and bridges with automobiles, trash cans, lumber, and their own bodies. The government responded with new "get tough" tactics, flying in the National Guard and Marines to augment police, arresting some 13,500 demonstrators, and holding them for hours in large outdoor stockades. As tear gas swirled around some of the nation's most revered shrines and demonstrators blocked entrances to major government buildings, the capital was in a virtual state of siege.

The events of May fulfilled the worst fears of the men in the White House, fears that had been building for two years. As the Vietnam war dragged on and racial tensions persisted, the late 1960s and early 1970s had been a period of nearly perpetual protest in America. Campus unrest, intensifying through the decade, reached a peak in 1969–70 with nearly 1800 demonstrations, many of them accompanied by bombings and other violence. The disorders culminated after the Cambodian invasion and the killing of students at Kent State and Jackson State in May 1970, with more than

440 colleges closed down or otherwise disrupted. Sporadic gun battles continued in communities across the country between militant blacks and police.

The President did his best to project an air of lofty disdain for such activities, letting word leak out that he had been watching football on television during one protest march. But it now appears that he and the men around him were far more concerned, even desperate, than they let on. Nixon—who often felt powerless in the world's most powerful office—was increasingly obsessed by real or imagined threats to his own authority.

The policy of mass arrests for the May Day demonstrations was established at meetings attended by John Mitchell; John D. Ehrlichman, assistant to the President for domestic affairs; and John W. Dean 3d, counsel to the President. According to notes taken at the meetings, Ehrlichman, in particular, took a hard line. When Lieutenant General Hugh M. Exton, director of military support for the Army Department, urged a delay in committing troops, Ehrlichman said he was "amazed at the general's attitude." He said that "the President wanted the city kept open if it took a hundred thousand" soldiers, that "no fine tuning was needed," and "if we were short on troops someone will be in big trouble." A few minutes later, Ehrlichman said that "a lot of questions were being raised as to why the government was permitting pot and violations of the law" in the demonstrators' encampments and "the President was ready to go further than had been discussed up to now in this meeting." *

Jeb Magruder recalls that the White House in 1970–71 existed in "a state of permanent crisis." When there was no major calamity, "there were always a dozen or so smaller crises brewing." John Dean says that "advance men" who prepared Presidential trips were instructed to insure that demonstrators remained "unseen and unheard" by Nixon, and for that purpose

---

*A Washington jury later determined that Nixon's hard-line tactics had violated the demonstrators' constitutional rights and awarded them $10,000 apiece in damages.

Haldeman authorized "any means—legal or illegal." One day the President looked out his window and saw a man (later identified as Monroe Cornish, a Maryland schoolteacher and perennial candidate for office) with a ten-foot banner stretched out in front of Lafayette Park. Dean says that one of Haldeman's assistants told him of the President's "displeasure" and of Haldeman's decision that "the sign had to come down." Dean says he ran into Dwight L. Chapin, the President's appointments secretary, who said he was going to get some "thugs" to remove the man. Instead, Dean called the Secret Service, who got the park police to convince the man that he should move across the park, where the sign would be out of the President's sight.

Nixon's sense of emergency was reinforced by his advisers. According to Magruder, "Haldeman contributed to the constant state of emergency by his administrative style. He never said 'Get me this by next week'; it was always 'Get me this by three p.m.' Everything was important, every detail, and the result was a highly charged atmosphere, one that encouraged a siege mentality." One official recalls a feeling at the White House that "we were faced with one of the most serious domestic crises we've had." There is little doubt that in this superheated atmosphere the President and the men around him perceived the unrest as a genuine threat to "national security." But, apparently, they felt another kind of security was at stake too—Nixon's political security.

During the October 1969 antiwar moratorium, David Broder had written a column in *The Washington Post* which said: "It is becoming more obvious with every passing day that the men and the movement that broke Lyndon B. Johnson's authority in 1968 are out to break Richard M. Nixon in 1969. The likelihood is great that they will succeed again. . . ." According to a White House aide, Broder's column was "read and discussed very thoroughly in the circles around the President and had quite an impact. We took the warning very seriously." A Justice Department memo reinforced this fear by contending that antiwar leaders had devised "a three-phase program designed to defeat President Nixon in the 1972 Presidential election."

By the spring of 1970 the White House was pervaded by what one aide calls the "us vs. them" outlook. "It didn't matter who you were or what ideological positions you took," he recalls. "You were either for us or against us, and if you were against us we were against you. It was real confrontational politics and there were a number of men around the White House who clearly relished that sort of thing." One of those men was Charles W. "Chuck" Colson, special counsel to the President.

"When you've got 'em by the balls, their hearts and minds will follow," read the Green Beret slogan over the bar in Chuck Colson's den. Described by his father as "viciously loyal," by one colleague as "a cobra," by another as an "evil genius," by still another as an "operator in expediency," and by his former assistant as "an unguided missile," Colson called himself "the chief ass-kicker around the White House" and a "flag-waving, kick-'em-in-the-nuts, anti-press, anti-liberal Nixon fanatic." His combativeness was probably bred in the ethnic and social warfare of Boston. Coming of age as an upwardly mobile middle-class Yankee, he deeply resented both the Brahmin aristocracy which ruled the Commonwealth and the Irish Catholic oligarchy which dominated his native city. He was granted a scholarship to Harvard and told by the dean of admissions that nobody had ever turned one down, so he did just that and stamped off to Brown University, where he was active in student government, debating, and the Young Republicans. Commissioned in 1954 as the youngest company commander in the Marines, he was deeply influenced by the Corps' "can do" spirit, and the Marine Hymn remained his favorite tune. After a stint on the staff of Senator Leverett Saltonstall, Colson practiced law in Washington for nine years until he joined the White House staff as a special counsel in November 1969. At the beginning he was an obscure new-

comer, clearly outside the White House inner circle, and this gnawed at his aggressive gut. Jeb Magruder recalls Colson coming into his office one Monday morning in a state of great agitation. "I went to church services yesterday," he said. "I went through the receiving line and shook hands with the President. Damn it, Magruder, he doesn't know who I am." But it didn't take Colson long to make his presence felt. He soon persuaded Haldeman that he was a master of precisely the gritty, precinct-level, interest-group politics that the President needed to assure his re-election. The air of political disaster around the White House in 1970 only strengthened his hand. Colson was one of only seven aides summoned to the first Key Biscayne strategy session following the midterm election. When the second session was convened a week or so later, only Colson, Mitchell, and Haldeman joined the President. Colson had penetrated the inner circle with astonishing speed. He could be a compelling talker, and Nixon began inviting him into his office to sit and jaw. Colson's new influence was symbolized by his new office adjacent to the President's "hideaway" in the Executive Office Building. He intrigued Nixon with his Northern version of Mitchell's Southern Strategy which saw the potential heart of the "new majority" not in the Carolina farmlands or Louisiana bayous but among the ethnic "hard hats" in the big industrial states with the bulk of the electoral votes. With his own hard-hat eagerness for combat, Colson quickly became the point man for the President's search-and-destroy missions: feeding damaging information on Senator Joseph D. Tydings of Maryland to a Life *reporter, forming an "attack group" to assail Democratic candidates, orchestrating a campaign against AFL-CIO President George Meany as "sadly out of step" with the workingman. His three heroes were Lieutenant General Lewis B. "Chesty" Puller ("the greatest blood-and-guts Marine who ever walked"), John Wayne, and Richard Nixon. And there was just about nothing Chuck Colson wouldn't do for one of his heroes. "Colson would do anything," Nixon once said. "He's got the balls of a brass monkey." And one White House*

aide said later, "If you think what Colson did was bad,
you should have heard what he wanted to do, what he
was kept from doing."

Colson played a major role in developing the administration's "enemies list." This list was continually updated in a series of memoranda called "Opponents
List, Political Enemies Project," most of them prepared
by Joanne Gordon and George Bell in Colson's office.
Eventually it contained the names of some two hundred
individuals and eighteen organizations. A few of the
names—Jane Fonda, Dick Gregory, Ramsey Clark,
Bella Abzug, Shirley Chisholm, the Black Panthers,
and the Institute for Policy Studies—could be regarded
as "enemies" of Richard Nixon. Others—Edward Kennedy, Edmund Muskie, Harold Hughes, Walter Mondale, William Proxmire, Birch Bayh—were at least political enemies. Most of the rest were drawn from the
mainstream of American life, indeed from some of its
pre-eminent institutions (for, even as President, Nixon
felt terribly threatened by those institutions, at war with
the Establishment which had long ruled the nation
from its power centers in Wall Street, Cambridge, and
Georgetown). There were the presidents of Yale, the
Harvard Law School, the Massachusetts Institute of
Technology, the World Bank, the Ford Foundation, the
Rand Corporation, the National Education Association,
Philip Morris, and National Cleaning Contractors.
There were four ex-cabinet members; two ex-ambas-
sadors; a Nobel prizewinner; and such favorites of
Middle America as Gregory Peck, Steve McQueen,
Carol Channing, and Joe Namath. By far the largest
category were media figures: there were fifty-seven,
among them such titans of the press establishment as
James Reston of *The New York Times;* Julian Good-
man of NBC; Marvin Kalb of CBS, and syndicated
columnists Rowland Evans and Joseph Kraft—none of
them previously considered particularly hostile to Nixon. Some people got on the enemies list for doing no
more than contributing to Democratic candidates.
Professor Hans Morgenthau got on because he was

confused with Robert Morgenthau, the former U.S. attorney in New York City.

To deal with such enemies, the White House needed some undercover operatives. In March 1969, barely two months after the inauguration, John Ehrlichman, who was then counsel to the President, called John Caulfield, a New York City policeman, and asked him—according to Caulfield—whether he would set up a "private security entity in Washington for the purposes of providing investigative support for the White House." Caulfield proposed instead that he join Ehrlichman's staff, and on April 8, 1969, he entered the White House.

"My father has never gotten over that," John J. Caulfield says of the 1958 Meritorious Police Award he won for his seizure of contraband weapons destined for Ireland. John Caulfield is an Irish cop. He comes, in his own words, "from a humble background" in the Bronx. His basketball exploits at Rice High School won him a partial athletic scholarship to Wake Forest, but he had to leave after two years for lack of money. Later he spent some time at John Jay College of Criminal Justice and at Fordham University, without getting a degree from either of them. After military service and a stint as a draftsman with the New York Telephone Company, Caulfield joined the New York City Police Department in June 1953. Walking a patrolman's beat in the Bronx he helped uncover a robbery ring and won promotion to detective, serving from 1955 to 1966 in the Bureau of Special Services and Investigations (BOSS), which gathers intelligence and protects visiting dignitaries. One of the dignitaries who visited New York during that period was Vice President Richard Nixon. During the 1960 Presidential campaign Caulfield was assigned to help protect the Republican candidate while he was in the city. He became very friendly with Jack Sherwood, the Secret Service agent in charge of the Vice President's detail, and, if Nixon had won, Caulfield would probably have moved into the White House in some security job.

But Nixon lost, so Caulfield went back to his job with BOSS, "monitoring the activities of terrorist organizations." During his ten years with this undercover squad, Caulfield helped break some major cases. He proudly boasts of his role in arresting "the prime Castro agent" in the "bazooka attackers" at the United Nations, and the "Black Liberation Front," which planned to blow up the Statue of Liberty and other national monuments in 1965. (BOSS's tactics in such cases often came under attack from civil libertarians. The Statue of Liberty case, in particular, stirred doubts when one of the defendants testified that the plan to blow up the statue was originally proposed by the undercover cop who had insinuated his way into the black group. BOSS specialized in "penetration" and "surveillance." According to one policeman who served with the bureau, "We surveilled people, went to their meetings, took their photographs, the plate numbers of their cars. . . . We had guys with beards down to their knees to infiltrate the hippies, and guys who wore thin ties to mingle with the conservative hard-hat groups.") During the 1960s Caulfield maintained his ties with the Nixon camp. Although Nixon as a private citizen and Wall Street lawyer was no longer entitled to Secret Service protection, he could still get some security from the New York police, and Caulfield sometimes drew that duty. Always on the watch for useful connections, the ruggedly handsome black-haired cop became especially close to Nixon's longtime personal secretary, Rose Mary Woods. Miss Woods, in turn, introduced him to Lilburn "Pat" Boggs, then the agent in charge of the Secret Service office in Chicago, where he was a close friend of her brother, Joe Woods, the sheriff of Cook County. With all these connections, Caulfield was a natural to move into a security job with the 1968 Nixon campaign. After the election, Caulfield was interviewed but rejected by John Mitchell for the job of chief U.S. marshal.

Caulfield brought with him another member of the New York Bureau of Special Services, Anthony T.

Ulasewicz (allegedly the man in charge of running the undercover operation in the Statue of Liberty case). Ulasewicz was hired by Ehrlichman in May 1969, after a clandestine meeting in the American Airlines VIP lounge at La Guardia Airport, but he was not placed on the White House payroll. Instead, Ehrlichman arranged for him to be paid $22,000 a year (out of surplus 1968 campaign funds) by Herbert W. Kalmbach, the President's private lawyer. On June 29, 1969, Caulfield, Ulasewicz, and Kalmbach met at the Madison Hotel in Washington and Ulasewicz told Kalmbach he would use the alias "Edward T. Stanley." (He even got an American Express card in that name.)

Although Ulasewicz was paid through this circuitous route, he worked directly for Caulfield, and during the next few years the two ex-New York cops kept busy on a variety of assignments, first from Ehrlichman and then, after July 1970, from John Dean. Among other things, Ulasewicz investigated the background of Richard M. Dixon, a comic imitator of the President; a group in New York City who sold Presidential emblems on walnut plaques "without appropriate authorization"; a water-purification controversy in New Mexico; the House of Mercy Home for Unwed Mothers in Washington; a drinking incident involving Speaker of the House Carl Albert at a Washington night club called the Zebra Room; allegations that a White House official was visiting call girls; a group of Quakers who held a vigil in front of the White House; and an unnamed politician who rented an intriguing hotel suite. For a time, in the winter of 1969–70, Ulasewicz and Caulfield hired another former New York City policeman—Anthony LaRocco—for several "special projects" in the Big Apple.

If "us vs. them" was the White House battle plan, then the first of the "them" was almost certainly Senator Edward M. Kennedy of Massachusetts. Ever since Nixon had lost the Presidency by a heartbreaking

sliver to John Kennedy in 1960, he had been preoccupied—even obsessed—with this wealthy, glamorous,
powerful clan. "If there's one word which drove the
President up the wall, it was 'Kennedy,' " says a veteran
White House observer. "He never quite got over his
loss to Jack in 1960, geared up to face Bobby in 1968,
saw Teddy as his major threat in 1972 and as the major rebuff to his legacy in 1976." This fixation quickly
spread to his aides, who saw, in John Dean's words,
"the fine hand of Kennedy" behind almost every adverse development. But Nixon's attitude toward the
Kennedys was by no means pure hostility. In many
respects, Nixon had liked John Kennedy. Certainly he
admired him—his professionalism, his toughness, his
will to win. Above all he envied him—his good looks,
his beautiful wife, his natural charm and style. Great
opponents are often as inextricably linked as great
lovers. From 1960 on, Kennedy and Nixon were two
sides of a political coin, and that rivalry left its indelible
stamp on Nixon. The Kennedys were the standard
against which he measured himself, the model for much
of his behavior. But they were also the chief threat to
his most cherished ambitions, the stunning rebuke to
his lack of "class," the private demons who haunted
him down through the years.

Not surprisingly, Nixon reacted with scarcely disguised glee to the news from Chappaquiddick, Massachusetts, on July 19, 1969. That weekend, the President,
like most other Americans, had been riveted to
the astronauts' imminent landing on the moon. But
William Safire recalls that when Nixon heard the news
from Chappaquiddick he exclaimed, "This is quite a
day on another front too! It'll be hard to hush this one
up; too many reporters want to win a Pulitzer Prize."

Hours after Mary Jo Kopechne's body was pulled
from the car driven by Senator Kennedy, Ehrlichman
told Caulfield to send the newly hired Ulasewicz to the
scene. The White House sleuth spent four days on the
island, where he posed as a newspaperman, frequently
asking the most embarrassing questions at news conferences, and reported back to Caulfield by phone.
And he spent more time during the summer and fall

at Chappaquiddick trying to dig up dirt on Kennedy. "He talked to everybody in that town," Dean later told the President. "The guy did a masterful job."

That fall the three girls with whom Miss Kopechne had shared a house in Washington thought their telephone was being tapped and Senate investigators for a time believed that Caulfield and Ulasewicz had installed a tap, although this has never been proved. That winter the two ex-cops apparently did set up an apartment on New York's East Side in an attempt to entrap one of the women who had attended Kennedy's Chappaquiddick party. According to one secondhand account, Caulfield hired another ex-cop to get the woman into bed. Cameras hidden behind a partition would whirl and she would presumably be blackmailed into revealing all she knew about Chappaquiddick. One White House operative who saw the apartment said, "It was a cop's idea of an East Side bordello in the 1880s—secondhand furniture, red plush sofas." The plan was ultimately abandoned.

Meanwhile, the White House surveillance began zeroing in on Senator Kennedy himself. On the weekend of August 17–19, 1969, Caulfield followed Kennedy during his stopover in Hawaii on the way back from India. His report notes that the senator stayed at the estate of one "J. Otani, a wealthy Japanese industrialist," and that he played tennis one afternoon at the estate of Lloyd Martin, a Honolulu contractor: "partners in the tennis match were Mrs. Warnecke, Mrs. Martin, Lloyd Martin, and EMK." Caulfield added, "An extensive survey of hotels, discreet cocktail lounges, and other hideaways was conducted with a view toward determining a covert EMK visit. The results were negative. . . . No evidence was developed to indicate that his conduct was improper."

Ulasewicz checked out at least three other reports of "wild parties" involving the senator, and in each case the rumors proved unfounded. But none of this satisfied the President. On September 22, 1969, Nixon sent a memo to Haldeman demanding a more powerful response to Kennedy's criticism of his Vietnam policy: "one senator with plenty of guts should hammer him,"

and "one of our best people" should be assigned to
what Nixon called "the Teddy Kennedy fight." Apparently in response to that memo, Haldeman ordered a
"24-hour surveillance of Kennedy" that fall, but Dean
says he talked him out of it. (If anyone specialized in
the Kennedy "fight" around the White House it was
Colson, the administration's own man from Massachusetts who had battled the senator in their home state.
Colson grasped at every opportunity to embarrass Kennedy. Once, he came up with a picture of him with a
beautiful woman not his wife. Colson asked Magruder
to peddle it to a magazine. Magruder placed it in the
scandal-mongering *National Enquirer* and later a news
magazine picked it up.)

Another "enemy" investigated was Daniel Schorr, a
veteran CBS newsman. Schorr's hard-nosed reporting
had frequently irritated administration officials—and
Nixon himself, who publicly accused Schorr of "telling
a little lie" and privately called him "that son-of-a-
bitch." On August 19, 1971, officials summoned
Schorr to the White House to complain about his report
on the CBS *Evening News* two nights before which
had raised doubts about the actual effects of the President's promise to assist Catholic parochial schools (one
of Colson's pet projects). A few hours afterward,
Haldeman, flying with the President to Jackson Hole,
Wyoming, found time to instruct his assistant, Lawrence M. Higby, to call FBI Director J. Edgar Hoover
for information on Schorr. (There was a rumor around
the White House that Schorr's wife had some "Marxist"
associations in her background.) The next morning an
FBI agent approached Schorr—who protested the investigation—and within the next seven hours other
agents interviewed twenty-five of his relatives, friends,
and associates. When the investigation was disclosed
publicly, the White House said Schorr was being
screened for a job as assistant to the chairman of the
Environmental Quality Council. Colson later conceded
that the President had come up with this story as "the
best way to work ourselves out of a situation that could
have been embarrassing," and he told Colson to have
his press secretary, Ronald L. Ziegler, put it out. Need-

less to say, Schorr was never appointed to anything.
(A subsequent FBI memo revealed that Haldeman
frequently asked the bureau for background information—though not such a "full field" investigation—on
other "news personalities.")

Schorr ("a real media enemy") was on a special
twenty-name version of the "enemies list," apparent
targets for specific and immediate reprisals. Others on
the short list included Edwin O. Guthman, national
editor of the *Los Angeles Times* (the "former Kennedy aide was a highly sophisticated hatchetman
against us in '68. . . . It is time to give him the message"); John R. Conyers, Jr., congressman from
Detroit ("emerging as a leading black anti-Nixon
spokesman. Has known weakness for white females");
Sidney Davidoff, aide to New York Mayor John V.
Lindsay ("a first class s.o.b., wheeler-dealer and suspected bagman"); Allard Lowenstein ("guiding force
behind the eighteen-year-old 'dump Nixon' vote
drive"); Stewart Mott ("nothing but big money for
radic-lib candidates"). What the White House had in
mind is suggested in a memo, written by John Dean
in August 1971, which showed "how we can maximize
the fact of our incumbency in dealing with the persons
known to be active in their opposition to our administration. Stated a bit more bluntly—how we can use
the available federal machinery to screw our political
enemies." Dean said the "project coordinator" should
"determine what sorts of dealings these individuals
have with the federal government and how we can best
screw them (e.g., grant availability, federal contracts,
litigation, prosecution, etc.)." Finally, the coordinator
should have "the full support of the top officials of the
agency or department in proceeding to deal with the
individual."

People on the enemies list weren't the only "enemies"
Nixon worried about. Many of them were right there in
his own administration. Although Nixon had at last attained the position generally regarded as the most powerful in the world, he retained his lifelong sense of
powerlessness. Years later, Haldeman tried to explain

why Nixon felt this "lack of power" when he entered the White House: "We came in to a government populated by people who had been placed there by previous administrations, most of them Democratic, one of them for eight years, [and] the Eisenhower administration, a basically apolitical Republican administration. And we were dealing with a bureaucracy throughout the government peopled with individuals whose political philosophies were alien to ours." Nixon could be much blunter. Talking with his assistants on April 19, 1971, he railed, "We have no discipline in this bureaucracy. We never fire anybody. We never reprimand anybody. We never demote anybody. We always promote the sons-of-bitches that kick us in the ass. . . . We are going to quit being a bunch of goddamn soft-headed managers. . . . When a bureaucrat deliberately thumbs his nose, we're going to get him. . . . The little boys over in State particularly, that are against us, will do it. Defense, HEW—those three areas particularly. . . . There are many unpleasant places where civil service people can be sent. . . . When they don't produce in this administration, somebody's ass is kicked out. . . . Now, goddamnit, those are the bad guys—the guys down in the woodwork."

So Nixon and his men went after "the guys down in the woodwork." They made sure that the bureaucrats knew whom they were working for. And they tried to harness them into the White House efforts to "take maximum advantage of the incumbency"—that is, to use Nixon's seat in the saddle to make sure he stayed in the saddle. Although the Hatch Act prohibits federal civil-service employees from taking part in partisan political efforts, all Presidents have tried to make the bureaucrats march to their political tune. The Nixon effort was unusual both in its scope and in the fierce determination with which it was enforced.

On January 12, 1971, Magruder wrote to Mitchell, "Our administration has not made effective political use of the resources of the federal government, the RNC [Republican National Committee], the White House. . . ." That summer, Dean says, Haldeman told him "the White House would reshift itself from the current duties to focus very much on the re-election of the President."

In late 1971 Haldeman assigned Frederic V. Malek, a special assistant to the President, to develop a program for using the resources of the federal bureaucracy to assist in the President's re-election. Malek, a tough West Point graduate and former Green Beret, took the assignment seriously. On December 23, 1971, he wrote to Haldeman, "As you have pointed out, the President's unique asset in the forthcoming campaign is his control of the executive branch. The White House must insure that the President is able to capitalize fully upon this asset. . . . As you know, we have already initiated programs to derive greater political benefit from grants, communications, and personnel. . . . In addition, we should take action to insure that the day-to-day departmental operations are conducted as much as possible to support the President's re-election." To achieve this end, he brought to bear an elaborate system of rewards and punishments ("We've corralled all the goodies that are available"). Malek warned that there was a "substantial risk" that the program could become public and embarrass the administration. Therefore, he urged that no directions should be issued in writing. "In fact," he added, "as this concept is refined further, I propose we stop calling it 'politicizing the executive branch,' and instead call it something like strengthening the government's responsiveness." The euphemism caught on, and from then on the operation was known as the Responsiveness Program.

The program was used most vigorously to corral the votes of minority groups that had traditionally voted Democratic, particularly the Spanish-speaking minority. In early 1972 Alex Armendariz, head of CREEP's Spanish-speaking voters division, wrote in a memo, "Use the incumbency to the greatest extent possible to stroke this community over the next several months through appointments, grants, program development, accelerated program implementation, and publicity of the President's records through the departments and agencies."

A striking application of this principle was the treatment accorded Joseph A. Reyes, an active supporter of the President. Reyes was chairman of the District of Columbia, Maryland, and Virginia section of the National Hispanic Finance Committee, an authorized fund-raising arm of the Nixon campaign. He was also a consultant whose firm—J. A. Reyes & Associates—did most of its business under section 8(a) of the Small Business Administration Act. During 1971 Reyes's firm grossed between $400,000 and $500,000. In 1972, as he actively raised money for the President's re-election, his business doubled to $1 million, all of it under the 8(a) program. Reyes says he received seven or eight contracts and one grant during 1972. One contract was a $200,000 noncompetitive agreement with the Office of Economic Opportunity, awarded in July 1972. Arnold Baker, an OEO official, said the contract —for evaluation of the agency's emergency food and medical services program—was totally unnecessary and was awarded over the objections of the OEO staff.

The Responsiveness Program cut the other way for Leveo Sanchez, head of Development Associates, Inc., another Washington-based consulting firm. In the spring of 1972 Reyes approached Sanchez and told him he was "expected" to make a $1000 contribution to the President's re-election through the National Hispanic Finance Committee. Sanchez declined. On July 17, 1972, William Marumoto, a staff assistant to the President for Spanish-American affairs, invited Sanchez to a White House luncheon with David Wimer, special assistant to the assistant secretary of labor for administration and management. According to Sanchez, Marumoto and Wimer told him that "they" had been very good to his firm, that he was about to be awarded a $400,000 contract from the Department of Labor, and that he would be expected to show his appreciation in a substantial manner to the President's campaign. Sanchez again declined. Marumoto and Wimer deny that they linked the Labor Department contract to a campaign contribution. But two days later, Marumoto wrote a memo to Armendariz at CREEP noting that Sanchez had close relations with such

Democrats as Sargent Shriver and Frank Mankiewicz, but that during the first years of the Nixon administration his firm had nevertheless received government contracts worth $1–2 million, and that he was now under consideration for new contracts from the Labor Department and the Department of Housing and Urban Development. "This is a classic example of a firm, not necessarily on our team, which is making a comfortable living off of us. . . . I would recommend if it's not too late, we stop the proposals at DOL and HUD." Five days later Armendariz wrote back, "We have inquired about Development Associates and have learned of their close ties with the DNC [Democratic National Committee] and Cesar Chavez. We fully concur with Bill Marumoto's memo of July 19." On September 25 Sanchez's company was "graduated" from the 8(a) program, which meant that Development Associates could no longer qualify for contracts under the Small Business Administration Act. Marumoto concedes there was a "political input" into this decision. He could not recall any other Spanish-speaking "graduate" from the 8(a) program.

Similar efforts were made to encourage and pressure blacks into supporting the President's re-election. A plan was developed by Paul Jones, director of CREEP's black vote division, and Robert J. Brown, special assistant to the President, for "a selective funding approach [which] will furnish encouragement incentives for black individuals, firms, and organizations whose support will have a multiplier effect on black vote support for the President."

Among the leaders whom Jones and Brown sought to bring into the President's camp was the Reverend Jesse Jackson, the Chicago civil-rights leader, who in 1972 was forming People United to Save Humanity (PUSH). A memo from Jones noted that federal funding might be useful here: "Jackson is now seeking financial support for the new group . . . and is also anxious to meet with the President. His support and/ or 'neutrality' could go far in favorably swinging black votes to R.N." Another Jones memo reported on a meeting he and Brown had with James Farmer, former director of the Congress of Racial Equality (CORE), who had been an assistant secretary of HEW during Nixon's first term. The memo said Farmer expressed a "willingness to work in support of the President—it was agreed he might better serve at this time by maintaining a nonpartisan posture." Jones noted that Farmer wanted "funding for his think-tank proposal; he's seeking $200,000 seed money from HEW (This should be moved on but should allow for a final Brown-Jones checkoff in order to reinforce Farmer's involvement.)" Farmer got a $150,000 HEW grant for his think tank and Malek, reporting the grant, wrote, "He will now be able to spend a major part of his time on the above project while also making time available to the re-election efforts. He has agreed to do speaking on our behalf and also to talk to key black leaders in an effort to gain their loyalties."

But Malek disapproved of grants to black communities in which he anticipated a low "political payoff." For example, he noted that a Cleveland recreation program would receive only $164,000 out of a requested $354,000 because "the program is designed to impact inner-city residents, and this does not fall within our political guidelines."

Another target of the Responsiveness Program was the elderly. In 1972 the White House helped to form a new organization called the Federation of Experienced Americans which was largely designed to mobilize the elderly for Nixon's re-election. Within months, the new group got a $1,540,000 grant from the Labor Department and $399,839 from OEO. Meanwhile, the White House brought heavy pressure on the Labor Department to cease funding two other organizations for the elderly—the National Council on the Aging and the National Council of Senior Citizens—which were regarded as "enemies" of the President. They continued to get grants, but their funding was substantially reduced.

The agency from which the White House most desperately wanted "responsiveness" was the Internal Revenue Service. John Dean says the President specifically urged "the use of the Internal Revenue Service to attack our enemies" and, in the summer of 1969, the White House began trying to use the IRS for such purposes. On July 16 Dr. Arthur F. Burns, then counselor to the President, met with IRS Commissioner Randolph W. Thrower. According to Thrower's memo for the files, Dr. Burns said, "The President had expressed to him great concern over the fact that tax-exempt funds may be supporting activist groups engaged in stimulating riots both on the campus and within our inner cities." Later, Burns "raised the question as to whether there possibly might be some ideological bias within the IRS toward the more liberal organizations." Eight days later, the service established the Activist Organizations Committee to "collect relevant information on organizations predominantly dissident or extremist in nature and on people prominently identified with these organizations. Many of the organizations are controversial, all are newsworthy and a large number are known to be militant, revolutionary, and subversive." The committee, operating under "Red Seal Security" out of Room 3049 of IRS headquarters, was later renamed the Special Services Staff (SSS) to disguise its purpose.

But differences soon developed between the White House and the IRS over just what that purpose was. A White House memo said: "What we cannot do in a courtroom via criminal prosecutions to curtail the activities of some of these groups, IRS could do by administrative action. Moreover, valuable intelligence-type information could be turned up by IRS as a result of their field audits." But an IRS memo on the group's activities up to September 1970 stressed that the service must "administer taxing statutes without regard to the social or political objectives of individuals or organizations." It contended: "the sole objective of the Special Services Group is to provide a greater degree of assurance of maximum compliance with the Internal Revenue laws by those involved in extremist activities and those providing financial support to these activities." Up to that time, the memo said, the group had mainly been compiling information—on 1025 groups and 4300 individuals. Criminal investigations were under way on four individuals and one group. A White

House aide forwarded the memo to Haldeman, noting that it was "long on words and short on substance."

Later, under continued White House pressure, the SSS threw its net wider—using computerized lists of alleged "radicals" provided by the Justice Department; other information supplied by the FBI, Secret Service, Army and Air Force intelligence; and sometimes even press clippings. Its files eventually held information on 2873 organizations and 8585 individuals. Among the persons on whom files were maintained were Kareem Abdul Jabbar, the basketball star; Jimmy Breslin, Seymour Hersh, and Nat Hentoff, journalists; Tony Randall, Elizabeth Taylor, Mrs. Burt Lancaster, Julie Andrews, and Connie Stevens. A list of ninety-nine "ideological, militant, subversive, and radical organizations" included the Americans for Democratic Action, the Urban League, the National Council of Churches, the American Civil Liberties Union, the American Jewish Committee, and the National Organization of Women. Some 78 per cent of the files were ultimately found to have "no apparent revenue significance or potential." About 225 audits were ordered on the remaining files and very few prosecutions resulted. The SSS was ordered dismantled in August 1973, after details of its operations came to light.

Thrower, a soft-spoken Atlanta lawyer and former FBI man, insists he knows little about the unit's functions and cannot explain how so many benign groups and harmless individuals got into its files on "radicals" and "subversives." Indeed, the SSS seems to have hit full stride only after Thrower left office. Moreover, there is ample evidence that Thrower did not buckle easily under White House pressure. In the summer of 1970 the White House pushed him hard to appoint John Caulfield as director of the Alcohol, Tobacco and Firearms Division of the IRS, a division which John Mitchell later noted had "a very competent intelligence capacity." When Thrower resisted, the White House switched its tactics. It urged Caulfield's appointment to a less important post—chief of the enforcement branch of ATF—but suggested that the branch be established as a quasi-autonomous body within the IRS.

Thrower balked again, fearing that some attempt was being made to install Caulfield as head of a "personal police force." When the White House ordered him to make the appointment, Thrower threatened to resign. The White House backed down.

But Thrower was fed up. In January 1971 he told Secretary of the Treasury David M. Kennedy that he was resigning, but asked to see the President to tell him that the "introduction of political influence into the IRS would be very damaging to him and his administration, as well as to the revenue system and the general public interest." Nixon refused to see Thrower, so the commissioner gave up.

The next commissioner, former Assistant Attorney General Johnnie McK. Walters, ultimately had his confrontation with the White House too. But for a while the President's men simply bypassed him. Dean told Nixon, "We have a couple of sources over there that I can go to. I don't have to fool around with Johnnie Walters or anybody, we can get right in and get what we need." One "back-door channel" is thought to have been Roger Barth, who had served during the 1968 campaign as an advance man for Nixon's daughters and David Eisenhower, and was then moved to IRS —first as special assistant to the commissioner and then as deputy counsel. (Walters says Barth was widely "thought to be a White House spy.") The other channel ran from Caulfield to his friend Vernon "Mike" Acree, the assistant commissioner for inspection. Caulfield proved particularly adept at getting information out of the IRS. For example, in July 1971, the White House became agitated about The Brookings Institution, a research organization in Washington largely staffed by Democrats. So Caulfield obtained a copy of Brookings' tax returns which disclosed that the institution got "a number of large government contracts." Haldeman scrawled on the memo: "These should be turned off." (Curiously enough, a Brookings spokesman says, they never were.)

In early October 1971 the Long Island newspaper *Newsday* published an investigative series on Charles G. "Bebe" Rebozo, one of the President's closest friends. Shortly thereafter, Haldeman instructed Dean that Robert W. Greene, the senior editor who headed the *Newsday* team, "should have some [tax] problems." Caulfield spoke with his contact, Acree, who arranged for an anonymous letter to be written to the IRS requesting an audit on Greene. Later, Greene's taxes were audited by the New York State Department of Taxation under the federal-state exchange program, but there is no firm evidence that the audit had anything to do with his unpopularity at the White House. In a similar case, the White House apparently obtained confidential tax information on James Polk, a reporter who had written investigative articles on the activities of Herb Kalmbach, the President's lawyer.

That same fall Caulfield recommended that a "discreet IRS audit" be conducted on Emile de Antonio, producer of *Millhouse: A White Comedy,* a satirical film about the President. Caulfield did run an FBI "name-check" on Antonio and sent Tony Ulasewicz to New York to interview the film's distributor, but it is unclear whether any action was ever initiated through the IRS. On several other occasions, Haldeman apparently asked Dean for tax audits on individuals, and once Dean asked Caulfield to bring Acree to his office, where he asked the IRS man for three or four audits. Colson asked Dean to initiate an audit on Harold J. Gibbons, a Teamsters Union vice president whom Colson described as "an all-out enemy," but no audit was made.

If harassment of "enemies" was half the White House strategy, the other half was succor for friends. Dean says the President asked that tax troubles "be turned off on friends of his," and Caulfield looked into IRS audits on Billy Graham and John Wayne. Caulfield's report on Graham was forwarded by one of Haldeman's aides with the query, "Can we do anything to help?" Haldeman replied, "No, it's already covered."

But the IRS wasn't covering half of what the White House had in mind, for Commissioner Walters—a stubborn South Carolina lawyer—had proved not much more cooperative than his predecessor. In November 1971 Dean and Caulfield prepared a "talking paper" for Haldeman's use when he took this matter up with Secretary of the Treasury George P. Shultz. It read in part, "IRS is a monstrous bureaucracy which is dominated and controlled by Democrats. The IRS bureaucracy has been unresponsive and insensitive to both the White House and the treasury in many areas. . . . Walters appears oversensitive in his concern that the IRS might be labeled 'political' if he moves in sensitive areas [e.g., audits, tax exemptions]. During the Democrat administration, the IRS was used discreetly for political purposes, but this has been unavailable during this administration."

Haldeman denies that he ever discussed this with Shultz. But in the summer of 1972, Walters says, Shultz asked him to check on a report from Ehrlichman that Lawrence F. O'Brien, chairman of the Democratic National Committee, had large amounts of income which he might not have reported properly. Walters looked into the matter and found that O'Brien had indeed reported large incomes for 1970 and 1971, evidently fees from his public-relations work for multimillionaire Howard R. Hughes. But Shultz said Ehrlichman was dissatisfied with the report, so Walters ordered his agents to interview O'Brien. Still dissatisfied with the results, Ehrlichman, according to Walters, shouted through the phone at him, "I'm goddamn tired of your foot-dragging tactics." Later, Ehrlichman conceded, "I wanted them to turn up something and send him [O'Brien] to jail before the elections." In September, weeks after the IRS had resolved the question, Ehrlichman tried to get a story leaked to the press that O'Brien was in serious tax trouble.

The White House kept up the pressure on Walters. On September 11, 1972, Dean called the commissioner to his office and asked for an investigation of 490 staff members and contributors to George S. McGovern's Presidential campaign. Walters says he balked, warning that this would be "disastrous for the IRS." Two days later he took the matter up with Shultz, who told him to "do nothing." Walters put the list in a sealed envelope and placed it in his office safe. White House hostility then shifted to Shultz for shielding the IRS from political pressures. On September 15 the President told Haldeman and Dean, "I don't want George Shultz to ever raise the question because it would put me in the position of having to throw him out of the office. He didn't get secretary of the treasury because he has nice blue eyes. It was a goddamn favor to him to get that job." Nixon was determined to make the IRS more "responsive"—by manipulating the agency before the elections, and, if necessary, through a wholesale ouster of uncooperative officials afterward. Before the election he said, "We have to do it artfully so that we don't create an issue that we are using the IRS politically. And there are ways to do it, goddamnit. Sneak in one of our political appointees." But after the election, ". . . the whole goddamn bunch go out and if he [Shultz] doesn't do it he is out as secretary of the treasury and that is the way it is going to be played. . . . I look forward to the time that we have the agents in the Department of Justice and the IRS under our control after November 7."

In the same conversation, Dean told Nixon he was keeping notes "on a lot of people who are emerging as less than our friends." The President said, "They are asking for it and they are going to get it. We have not used this power in this first four years as you know. We have never used it. We have not used the bureau and we have not used the Justice Department, but things are going to change now. And they are either going to do it right or go."

"What an exciting prospect!" Dean exclaimed.

All the while, the White House kept talking in lofty terms of "national security." From the beginning of his term the President and the men around him seemed convinced that much of the domestic disorder was being financed or fomented from abroad. Specifically, the White House and some intelligence analysts believed that many Black Panthers were getting ideological indoctrination in Algeria and Moscow and sabotage and guerrilla training in North Korea. They believed that the Weathermen and other young radicals were being aided—even directed—by Cuban and Soviet-bloc regimes.

The CIA carefully examined these contentions and in two lengthy reports to the President—in 1967 and 1968—largely dismissed them. It concluded that while the Communists encouraged such movements through propaganda, there was little evidence that they funded or trained them and no evidence at all that they controlled or directed them. One official who worked on the studies recalls, "We tried to show that the radical movements were home-grown, indigenous responses to perceived grievances and problems that had been growing for years."

But the White House discounted these reports and this, in turn, fueled the growing mistrust between Nixon and the director of the CIA, Richard McG. Helms. Part of this was purely visceral. From the start, Nixon had been unable to establish any rapport with Helms, an elegant patrician who had been schooled in Switzerland, had graduated Phi Beta Kappa from Williams, and had entered the intelligence community through wartime service in the Office of Strategic Services. Haldeman recalls, "I don't believe he [Nixon] had much confidence in him [Helms] and his overall direction of the agency. . . . There was a feeling that there was an old-school-tie atmosphere within the CIA that led to some nonuseful personnel and some less-than-most-effective operations."

There were real differences over policy, too. Haldeman recalls that Nixon thought "what he got from the CIA wasn't particularly useful in many cases and was often not correct." The sticking points were the CIA's intelligence assessments on Vietnam and the Soviet Union which in each case differed with those prepared by the Defense Intelligence Agency. While the DIA stressed the importance of Cambodia as a staging area and supply route for the Viet Cong, the CIA said most supplies were coming down the Ho Chi Minh Trail in Laos. For an administration that was secretly bombing

Cambodia and preparing a limited invasion of that country, this was a critical difference and caused severe tension between the White House and the agency. Similarly, CIA estimates of Soviet nuclear-missile development were substantially lower than the DIA's and the White House preferred to believe the DIA.

So the White House was not inclined to accept the CIA's insistence that domestic radicals weren't getting foreign support. As protests against the war in Indochina intensified during the first years of the administration, the White House brought increasing pressure on the agency to change those assessments and to get more involved in domestic intelligence and surveillance activities.

The 1947 act establishing the CIA forbids it to have "police, subpoena, law-enforcement or internal-security functions" inside the United States. But very quickly the anti-Communist hysteria of the late 1940s and early 1950s pulled the agency into apparently illegal domestic activities. At first, these activities—wiretapping, break-ins, and the interception and reading of mail— were almost entirely directed at Americans suspected of being agents for foreign powers.

Then, in the early 1960s, the CIA established a new branch called the Domestic Operations Division (DOD). The division had some functions that were entirely legal: to coordinate with American corporations supplying "cover" for CIA agents abroad and to aid in the interrogation of American travelers after their return from foreign countries. The division ultimately established offices in fifteen American cities. But very early, DOD established a "covert section" which engaged in some activities apparently targeted at a domestic audience. It ran a press service in Washington called Continental Press, financed and devised book projects for Frederick A. Praeger, a publishing company in New York, and largely funded the popular *Fodor's Travel Guides* (in part to provide a cover for agents abroad).

With the expansion of the antiwar movement in 1967, the CIA came under increasing pressure from Lyndon Johnson's White House to get into the surveillance of domestic radicals. That year, the DOD began a limited surveillance program against the Black Panthers, justified on the assumption that the black activists had ties to foreign powers. That year, and particularly the next, the surveillance was extended to white radicals in the universities. According to one agent, it was a "low-key operation" at first, with agents observing and photographing demonstrators at Columbia, Cornell, and other universities.

In 1967 and 1968, another domestic intelligence operation was undertaken by another branch of the CIA—the Office of Security. Normally the office provides physical protection for agency facilities at home and abroad, conducts lie-detector tests, and carries out background investigations of personnel and others with whom the CIA contemplates doing business. But then —allegedly to protect the agency's facilities, personnel, and operations—it infiltrated up to twelve agents into dissident groups in the Washington area. The agents gathered information on planned demonstrations, leadership and organization of such groups as Women Strike for Peace, the Washington Peace Center, the Student Non-Violent Coordinating Committee, Congress of Racial Equality, the Washington Ethical Society, and the Washington Urban League.

The biggest step over the line came in August 1967, when the agency established a Special Operations Group within its counterintelligence staff to investigate foreign links to domestic radicals. The group's activities came to be known as Operation CHAOS.

The counterintelligence staff, charged with preventing foreign agents from penetrating the CIA, was headed by James Angleton, an accomplished botanist and amateur poet who was for years one of the most powerful figures in the agency. The new special unit was entrusted to Richard Ober, a longtime counterintelligence official. According to Seymour Hersh of *The New York Times*—whose reporting uncovered these activities—the officials who drew up the CIA's assessments that found no ties between domestic radicals and foreign powers were unaware of the new unit. Angleton and Ober—both unreconstructed cold warriors—disagreed with those assessments and investigated the radicals as if they were virtually foreign agents themselves. According to one official familiar with the unit's activities, "It started as a foreign intelligence operation and it bureaucratically grew. They simply began using the same techniques for foreigners against new targets here."

If the Johnson administration had cautiously prodded the CIA into the domestic arena, the Nixon White House lashed it into a vast program of spying on private American citizens. Operation CHAOS became the spearhead of that effort. Working in supersecrecy from a vaulted basement area of the Langley headquarters, the special unit soon achieved virtual autonomy. Although Angleton was nominally responsible, a Presidential commission later concluded that he had little connection with its actual performance. Ober reported directly to Helms, but nobody seems to have exercised effective control or review of CHAOS. Not surprisingly, it soon ran far beyond its original charter.

Starting with only a handful of officers, it grew to a staff of fifty-two. At first, it gathered most of its information from other government agencies or CIA field stations abroad. But in October 1969 it began recruiting some thirty of its own agents. Most of these eventually reported from abroad on foreign connections to the domestic radical movement. Some, however, operated within the United States, and three, in particular, infiltrated and spied on New Left or black militant groups. CHAOS also made use of a large CIA "mail intercept" program which for some twenty-four years had opened and examined mail between American citizens and Communist countries.

Helms and his associates knew they were violating the law. In a covering memorandum on one report to the White House, the director wrote: "This is an area not within the charter of this Agency, so I need not emphasize how extremely sensitive this makes the paper. Should anyone learn of its existence, it would prove most embarrassing for all concerned." He bluntly lied to the public, as in a 1971 speech to the American Society of Newspaper Editors, in which he declared: "I can assure you that except for the normal responsibilities for protecting the physical security of our own personnel, our facilities, and our classified information, we do not have any such powers and functions [in the area of domestic intelligence]. We have never sought any; we do not exercise any. In short, we do not target on American citizens." And he lied to the agency's own employees. In his annual "State of the Agency" speech, in September 1971, he told the staff: ". . . we're not trying to do espionage on American citizens in the United States, and we're not tapping telephone lines, and we're not doing a lot of other things which we're accused of doing. One of the things that tends to perpetuate some of these silly ideas are jokes that are made about them, particularly about domestic espionage. Although the jokes have no basis in fact, they nevertheless give us a name which we don't deserve."

The Nixon White House justified its pressure on the CIA by pointing to the lethargy and ineffectiveness of the FBI. If Richard Helms was a thin-blooded aristocrat not likely to get along with a President so sensitive to class distinctions, J. Edgar Hoover was an earthy, profane ruffian who fit in easily with Nixon's lockerroom crowd. Before he became President, Nixon and Hoover had established a joke-swapping cordiality. But despite this personal rapport, the President and his aides became increasingly irritated with Hoover. The White House was particularly agitated because of Hoover's cancellation in 1966 of the domestic espionage program, which the bureau had carried out since the start of World War II, against suspected foreign agents and some domestic radicals. With the formal or tacit approval of successive administrations, the bureau had tapped phones, bugged rooms, read mail, infiltrated organizations, and carried out "black-bag jobs" against foreign embassies and subjects' homes (the bureau's burglars carried their picks and prods in little black bags). The bureau even planted bugs in two Washington houses of prostitution, ostensibly to blackmail foreign diplomats (but they also picked up some embarrassing material on U.S. congressmen and other public figures). "The boys would do what they had to," recalls one FBI man. "And if they got caught, Hoover would disavow them." But in 1966 Hoover had had enough. Increasingly cautious and unwilling to risk embarrassment to himself or the bureau, Hoover abruptly dropped these programs and even ruled out recruitment of campus informers under the age of twenty-one, a policy which severely hampered the bureau's capacity to infiltrate young dissidents.

Then in February 1970 Hoover compounded the bureaucratic paralysis by cutting off all but formal written communications between the FBI and CIA. He had always resented any agency with which the bureau shared responsibility for intelligence-gathering. But his sudden break with the agency sprang from a ridiculously small incident. In March 1969 Thomas Riha, a Czech defector-turned-professor, disappeared from the University of Colorado. An FBI agent told the CIA that Riha had gone to Montreal after a domestic squabble. When Hoover demanded to know which of his agents had talked, the CIA refused to reveal its source, so Hoover shut off liaison with the agency. Shortly afterward, he cut off contact with other intelligence agencies. "My God," said one official, "we've got to do something about this!"

What the White House did was to devise a cumbersome bureaucratic mechanism for dislodging the obstinate Hoover from his central responsibility for domestic intelligence. In the spring of 1970 staff assistant Tom Huston was told to start preparing studies looking toward a new domestic security program.

Indiana is a stronghold of "libertarianism," that brand of intense individualism which can serve as an ideological underpinning for everything from freewheeling radicalism to rigid conservatism. Tom Charles Huston of Logansport, Indiana, began as a Stevensonian Democrat but in high school became a "Jeffersonian Republican" who admired Cato, the Roman moralist, and John C. Calhoun, the Southern theorist of states' rights. At Indiana University, where he gained bachelor's and law degrees, he founded the local chapter of Young Americans for Freedom and quickly moved up the organization's ladder—to state chairman, national vice chairman, and in 1965 national chairman. In 1966 he organized the World Youth Crusade for Freedom, which tried to build support for the war in Vietnam. That same year he endorsed Nixon for President—a maverick move at a time when many young conservatives preferred Ronald Reagan—and while serving in Army intelligence he found time to work in Nixon's campaign. The White House remembered: when he left the Army in January 1969 a low-ranking speechwriter's job was waiting for him. But when the New Mobilization Committee to End the War in Vietnam and its more violent allies descended on Washington for massive antiwar demonstrations that November, Huston was recruited to serve on the White House domestic-security committee, whose function, he recalls, was to "make sure we were ready for the various contingencies, keep in touch with the police, that sort of thing." Beyond his service in Army intelligence, the twenty-nine-year-old Huston brought no experience to his new security post. But he took to it with gusto; John Dean recalls that Huston kept a scrambler phone locked in a safe beside him and used it for a lot of calls. He made so many calls to various intelligence agencies that one White House secretary began calling him "X-5." Huston pushed for a tough line against dissenters. "Perhaps lowered voices and peace in Vietnam will defuse the tense situation we face," he argued in a top-secret memo, "but I wouldn't want to rely on it exclusively." He justified his tough stand in terms of "libertarian" doctrine. "The real threat to internal security—in any society—is repression. A handful of people can't frontally overthrow the government; but if they can engender enough fear, they can generate an atmosphere that will bring out of the woodwork every repressive demagogue in the country." This stance—abridging freedom to preserve freedom—was not casually arrived at. Huston called it "a principled decision." Indeed, Huston reserved his worst scorn for those "technocrats" and "pragmatists," like Chuck Colson, who had no firm ideological principles. To his White House colleagues, Huston often seemed an almost eighteenth-century figure. He proudly displayed an oil portrait of his hero, Calhoun, on his office wall; he prowled through Washington's secondhand bookstores to add to his collection of antique volumes; and he cherished his house full of period furniture. Most of all, he loved philosophical dispute. When William Safire wrote a nineteen-page tract entitled "New Federalist Paper No. 1 by Publius"—in imitation of the Federalist Papers, *which were signed "Publius" by Hamilton, Madison, and Jay—Huston fired back with a missive he called "Federalism Old and New or, the Pretensions of New Publius Exposed, by Cato." After arguing that Safire would curtail states' rights, Huston went on, "If the government in Washington is free to determine the national conscience it is free to force adherence to it. In the name of 'national conscience' (which has a striking similarity to 'the general will') it can ignore state lines and private rights, extending its power into every corner of the land and imposing it directly on every individual. It thus becomes a total government, bound by no restraints other than those voluntarily assumed by the man temporarily in command." A warning which Huston himself might well have heeded.*

On June 5, 1970, the President called a meeting in the Oval Office attended by Hoover; Helms; Lieutenant General Donald V. Bennett, director of the Defense Intelligence Agency; Admiral Noel Gayler, director of the National Security Agency; Haldeman; Ehrlichman; Robert Finch, counselor to the President; and Tom Huston. Nixon expressed concern that the government was not getting adequate domestic intelligence, partly because the intelligence services were not cooperating with each other. He instructed the service directors to prepare a "threat assessment," an "analysis of the gaps in intelligence-gathering efforts," and a "range of options" on steps to deal with those gaps. The President named Hoover as chairman of an Interagency Committee on Intelligence (ICI) to prepare that report.

It was a shrewd maneuver. For while Hoover held the nominal leadership, the real cards were held by

Huston, whom the President designated as White House liaison to the committee. And Huston, in turn, stayed in close touch with William C. Sullivan who, as assistant to Hoover, served as the director's representative on the working group which prepared the report and thus was its effective chairman. Formerly in charge of the bureau's domestic intelligence division, Sullivan had frequently complained that Hoover's abandonment of domestic espionage activities were severely hampering the FBI's efforts in the security field. Known as "Crazy Billy," the flamboyant, opinionated Sullivan had often criticized Hoover for devoting too much attention to the virtually moribund Communist party instead of such potent new forces as the New Left and the Black Panthers. So Nixon's initiative presented him with just the opportunity he had been looking for. Working closely with Huston, Sullivan played a major role in drafting the new program. James Angleton was designated as the CIA's representative on the working group; Richard Ober was an "observer."

At the ICI's first meeting, on June 9, Huston told the committee that, in considering obstacles to intelligence-gathering, the President wanted them to recognize that "everything is valid, everything is possible."

After less than three weeks of deliberation, the working group submitted a forty-three-page report which began with a grave assessment of the current threat: "The movement of rebellious youth known as the 'New Left,' involving and influencing a substantial number of college students, is having a serious impact on contemporary society with a potential for serious domestic strife. The revolutionary aims of the New Left are apparent when their identification with Marxism-Leninism is examined. . . ." The report went on to describe the current restraints on intelligence collection and to set forth the arguments for and against relaxing them.

At almost every point in the report, Hoover insisted on footnoting his objections to lifting restraints. According to Huston, the FBI director never said such steps were wrong or unconstitutional, but seemed more concerned about public-relations problems. "He'd just sit there and moan about the 'jackals of the press,' "

Huston recalls, "and how you had to be careful because, if you weren't, the 'jackals of the press' and the civil liberties people would jump down your back and raise hell."

During the first week of July Huston wrote his own top-secret memorandum to accompany the report. In it, he recommended that in virtually every area the President select the option providing for the maximum relaxation of existing restraints. Huston's proposals, which came to be known as "the Huston Plan," called for: (1) intensified electronic surveillance of both "domestic security threats" and foreign diplomats; (2) the monitoring of American citizens using international communications facilities; (3) increased legal "mail coverage" (the examination of envelopes to determine sender, postmark, etc.) and a relaxation of the restrictions on illegal mail coverage (opening and reading); (4) more informants on college campuses; (5) the lifting of restrictions on "surreptitious entry"; (6) the establishment of an Interagency Group on Domestic Intelligence and Internal Security, with representatives from the White House, FBI, CIA, NSA, DIA, and the three military counterintelligence agencies.

Huston's memo noted that some of the proposed steps were hazardous, but it dismissed most of the risks out of hand. The only argument against legal mail coverage, it noted, was "Mr. Hoover's concern that the civil liberties people may become upset [and] this risk is surely an acceptable one." On electronic surveillance, Huston wrote, "Everyone knowledgeable in the field, with the exception of Mr. Hoover, concurs that existing coverage is grossly inadequate. CIA and NSA note that this is particularly true of diplomatic establishments, and we have learned at the White House that it is also true of New Left groups." On campus informers, he declared, "The campus is the battleground of the revolutionary protest movement. It is impossible to gather effective intelligence about the movement unless we have campus sources. The risk of exposure is minimal, and where exposure occurs the adverse publicity is moderate and short-lived. It is a price we must be willing to pay. . . ."

The only danger which Huston seemed to take seriously was that involved in "surreptitious entry." He warned, "Use of this technique is clearly illegal: it amounts to burglary. It is also highly risky and could result in great embarrassment if exposed. However, it is also the most fruitful tool and can produce the type of intelligence which cannot be obtained in any other fashion. . . . This technique would be particularly helpful if used against the Weathermen and Black Panthers."

As for the interagency group, Huston said, "The need for increased coordination, joint estimates, and responsiveness to the White House is obvious to the intelligence community. There are a number of operational problems which need to be worked out since Mr. Hoover is fearful of any mechanism which might jeopardize his autonomy."

But no one yet realized the depth of Hoover's resistance to the plan. On July 14 Haldeman notified Huston that the President had approved his proposal in its entirety and asked him to prepare a formal "decision memorandum" notifying the intelligence directors. Huston sent such a memorandum to the four directors on July 23. On July 27 Hoover went to John Mitchell's office and told the attorney general of his strong objections. The director—who was accompanied by his assistant director, Cartha D. DeLoach—may also have weighed in with some threats, perhaps to uncover some of the bodies buried around the administration, for Mitchell was quickly persuaded. The attorney general communicated his feelings on the matter to the President—either directly or through Haldeman—and within twenty-four hours Haldeman notified Huston that the decision memorandum should be withdrawn. Huston instructed the four directors to return their copies of the memo to the White House, which they did.

Once Huston had idolized Hoover as the quintessential "100 per center," but now he too saw him as a crotchety, stubborn old man. "He wouldn't cooperate with anybody," he recalls. "He wanted to do things his own way and to hell with everybody else. It was an extremely serious situation."

For a time Huston lobbied vigorously for his baby. On August 5 he wrote a memorandum to Haldeman arguing, "At some point, Hoover has to be told who is President. He has become totally unreasonable. . . . All of us are going to look damn silly in the eyes of Helms, Gayler, Bennett, and the military chiefs if Hoover can unilaterally reverse a Presidential decision." Huston said Hoover would undoubtedly argue that "our present efforts are adequate"; to which, he said, "the answer is bullshit!" Warning that the country faced increasing unrest, he said, "I believe we are talking about the future of this country, for surely domestic violence and disorder threaten the very fabric of our society." And he closed on a theme well calculated to underscore the deep distrust of the bureaucracy—whether FBI, CIA, IRS, or others—which then infected everyone at the White House: "For eighteen months we have watched people in this government ignore the President's orders, take actions to embarrass him, promote themselves at his expense, and generally make his job more difficult. It makes me fighting mad. . . ."

The only real alternative for Nixon at that point would have been to fire Hoover and install a new FBI chief more amenable to White House direction. Perhaps if he had, the White House might not have found it necessary to get so deeply involved in its own domestic intelligence program. But Hoover was a Washington institution, as much part of the capital scene as Woodward & Lothrup and the National Gallery of Art. Rightly or wrongly, every President since Franklin Roosevelt had believed that the American voter would not tolerate his removal from office. And any President who might be tempted would be deterred by the knowledge that Hoover had enough dirt on most public figures to tar their reputations irredeemably if not put them in jail. Hoover kept some sixty-one "OC" (Official and Confidential) files in his private office which detailed the private lives of Presidents, members of Congress, federal officials, and those who merely tried to oppose him and his policies. Many of the files, uncovered after his death, contained highly derogatory information on the sex lives, drinking habits, and other indiscretions of these people. And Hoover made sure that Nixon—like other Presidents before him—knew of his store of information by sharing some of the juicier tidbits with him from time to time.

Richard Nixon was not going to risk that kind of retaliation. So, for the time being, he gave in to Hoover. In August Tom Huston learned just how costly it could be to tangle with a national institution. Abruptly, Haldeman took away Huston's staff responsibility for domestic intelligence and internal security, transferring it to John Dean, who had just come over to the White House from the Justice Department.

But the White House didn't give up on its efforts to bring about more coordination among the intelligence agencies—and one of its chief allies proved to be the CIA. On September 17 Mitchell went to CIA headquarters for lunch with Helms; Thomas Karamessines, the agency's deputy director for plans; Angleton; and Ober. Gathered around a table covered with sparkling crystal and gleaming silver, the five men talked about the FBI's failure to develop an adequate organization for "evaluation of domestic intelligence." They agreed that an interagency unit should be established to "provide evaluated intelligence from all sources" and to permit adequate time for "preventive action."

Several hours after this luncheon, Mitchell conferred with John Dean. In a memo summarizing their conversation, Dean wrote, "A key to the entire operation will be the creation of an interagency intelligence unit for both operational and evaluation purposes." The President's counsel was still pressing for the lifting of at least some of the restraints on intelligence-gathering. "I believe we agreed that it would be inappropriate to have any blanket removal of restrictions; rather, the most appropriate procedure would be to decide on the type of intelligence we need, based on assessment of the recommendations of this unit, and then to proceed to remove the restraints as necessary to obtain such intelligence." In other words, what could not be swallowed in a gulp would be taken in nibbles.

To accomplish these purposes, the White House reconstituted a moribund outfit in the Department of Justice known as the Intelligence Evaluation Committee (IEC). On December 3, 1970, a new committee was formed, composed of representatives of the White House, FBI, CIA, NSA, Secret Service, and the Departments of Justice, Treasury, and Defense. Robert C. Mardian, assistant attorney general in charge of the Internal Security Division, was the committee's chairman; Dean was the White House representative; Angleton represented the CIA, with Ober as his alternate. Ober also served as the CIA member of the Intelligence Evaluation Staff, the committee's working level. The very existence of both groups was held tightly secret, with "cover" provided by the Interdivision Information Unit, an earlier coordinating group lodged in the Justice Department's Internal Security Division. During the next two and a half years, the committee itself met only 7 times, but the staff met 117 times to prepare some 30 intelligence studies and 55 "calendars" of future demonstrations, protests, or other New Left, black militant, or peace-movement activities. The studies sought to predict the size of the demonstrations and their potential for violence.

Angleton's notes from one IEC meeting make clear that the committee was intended as an "implementation" of the Huston Plan. Although John Dean has said the unit had "both operational and evaluation purposes," there is no evidence that the committee or staff became directly involved on the operational side. One member of the staff insists, "We were paper shufflers." But, during the next few years, the agencies that made up the committee were very operational indeed, strongly suggesting that the Huston Plan was implemented piecemeal:

• The CIA intensified its domestic surveillance program. By 1974, CHAOS had compiled 13,000 files—including individual folders on 7200 Americans. The documents in these files and related materials included the names of more than 300,000 persons and organizations, all of which were entered into a computerized index. The agency conducted physical surveillance, installed wiretaps, opened mail, and carried out at least two break-ins against American citizens during the Nixon administration (the CIA claims that most of these techniques were used against agency employees or former employees suspected of dealing with foreign agents). It trained and advised local police departments in intelligence and communications, and its domestic agents operated in several cities with credentials provided by police forces there.

• The FBI used its so-called COINTELPRO (Counterintelligence Program) against a wide variety of radical groups on both the left and right. Under the program—initiated in 1956—bureau agents faked documents, made phone calls under false pretenses, leaked bogus stories to the press, and carried out a wide variety of other "dirty tricks" designed to disrupt and confuse organizations they were "investigating." Hoover officially discontinued the program on April 28, 1971, after documents disclosing some aspects of it were stolen from the bureau's office in Media, Pennsylvania; but there is evidence suggesting that the FBI went on using many of the same techniques against radical groups.

• The Secret Service accumulated intelligence files on some 47,000 persons considered to be potential "threats" to the President. David R. MacDonald, head of the service, has said that the files "are not created to list political dissidents, nor are political dissidents included in it simply because they are political dissidents." But a House committee submitted twenty randomly selected "household names" connected with the antiwar movement and found that the Secret Service maintained files on each of them.

And there are other, more obscure signs that some elements of the Houston Plan were implemented. Between 1970 and 1972 radicals and dissident groups reported a rash of burglaries which followed a similar *modus operandi:* the robbers generally did not touch cash or valuables but concentrated on files, correspondence, or other documents; the break-ins almost always occurred when the victims were away, and the burglars seemed to know not only their targets' schedules but the location of the documents they sought.

Among those who reported such burglaries were

Gerald Lefcourt, a New York lawyer who represented the Black Panthers, Students for a Democratic Society, and Mark Rudd (a prominent SDS leader at Columbia University); Charles Garry, a California attorney for Huey Newton, Bobby Seale, and Angela Davis; Carol Scott, a Florida lawyer who says someone stole the file on her client Scott Camil, an indicted member of Vietnam Veterans Against the War; Eqbal Ahmed, a Pakistani scholar who has been a leading opponent of the Vietnam war; Potomac Associates, a policy research group based in Washington; the United States Servicemen's Fund, a group which supported dissident members of the armed forces; the National Welfare Rights Organization, a poor people's lobby; Common Cause, a citizens' gadfly organization; Dan Rather and Marvin Kalb, both reporters for CBS; and Louis Harris, the pollster. Many of these reports remain unverified and the perpetrators unidentified.

There are indications that some of these burglaries may have been carried out by "contract" operatives hired by the CIA or by agents whose relationship to the agency was obscured by layers of corporate camouflage. The CIA has long operated abroad through companies which provide a "cover" for its operations. Sometimes these companies are owned outright by the CIA and are known in the trade as "proprietaries." Sometimes legitimate corporations with overseas offices merely agree to fabricate positions and fill them with CIA agents. Occasionally they are something in between: a privately owned company which devotes much of its time and energy to serving the agency. These are often known as "fronts."

One company which served as a CIA "front" during the 1960s and early 1970s was Robert R. Mullen & Company, a Washington public-relations firm. Its founder, Robert R. Mullen, was a former journalist (*Christian Science Monitor, Life, Kiplinger Washington Letter*) who in the late 1940s became director of information at the Economic Cooperation Administration in Paris, where he became friendly with General Dwight D. Eisenhower, then serving as Supreme Allied Commander in Europe. In 1952 Mullen served as public-relations director of Citizens for Eisenhower, and when his candidate won he expected to be named Ike's press secretary but lost out to James C. Hagerty. In the mid-1950s Mullen got to know several high-ranking CIA officials, among them Richard Helms, who lived near him in Rockville, Maryland. In 1956 Mullen established his public-relations firm, which quickly picked up clients on the strength of his good connections in government and in the Republican party. He got a big hand from one prominent Republican—Samuel W. Meek, board chairman of the major advertising firm J. Walter Thompson—who arranged to set up joint Mullen-Thompson offices in Paris, London, and Tokyo.

There may have been a third partner in the Mullen-Thompson relationship. J. Walter Thompson has long been rumored to enjoy good relations abroad with the CIA, and it may have initiated Mullen into that cozy alliance. In any case, when Mullen established its "own" office in Stockholm in 1962, it was staffed by two CIA men—James Everett and Jack Kindschi—who pretended to be working on a study for General Foods, one of Mullen's earliest clients, while they were actually debriefing Soviet and Chinese defectors. After scoring a major coup—the defection of a ranking KGB official—the Stockholm office closed in 1967. Kindschi moved for a time to Mexico City, again under Mullen cover, while Everett established a Mullen office in Amsterdam. In 1970 Mullen opened still another foreign office, this time in Singapore. Another CIA agent—Arthur Hochberg—ran this operation out of Suite 306 of the Cathay Building.

These offices were eventually closed after Philip Agee, a former CIA agent, revealed Mullen's cover role. Later, Richard Helms conceded, "Mr. Mullen did us the patriotic favor of allowing us to put some of our agents abroad under his company." But there is evidence that Mullen & Company may have served a similar role at home.

Just prior to the Bay of Pigs invasion in 1961, the CIA established an organization called the Cuban Freedom Committee, based in Washington. This propaganda outlet for the agency, which operated a station called Free Cuba Radio broadcasting anti-Castro material into Cuba, was financed by $2 million in CIA money funneled through various foundations. The committee's board of directors included Samuel Meek of J. Walter Thompson; General Albert C. Wedemeyer (ret.); and Mrs. Oveta Culp Hobby, then the publisher of the *Houston Post*. But, according to a CIA memo, Robert Mullen was "instrumental in the formation" of the committee and prepared some of its material. In more recent years, many of Mullen & Company's employees in Washington—including two successive accountants—were "retired" CIA officials.

Then, in January 1971, another kind of man joined the staff at Mullen & Company. He wasn't a CIA man. He had other interests.

Robert Foster Bennett was a friend of Chuck Colson's. They had first met during the 1968 campaign, when Bennett, on leave from his job as Washington representative of J. C. Penney & Company, was managing the re-election campaign of his father, Senator Wallace F. Bennett, Republican of Utah. Bennett says Colson's name was given to him as someone who could raise money. Colson, then a Washington lawyer, raised about $15,000 for the senator and Bob Bennett was very grateful. In 1969 both men joined the Nixon administration: Colson as a White House assistant, Bennett as director of Congressional Relations at the Department of Transportation. But they had no further dealings until early in 1970 when Colson invited Bennett to lunch. One of Colson's jobs at the White House was to deal with interest groups—like the American Truckers Association—and he needed a man in each department to help expedite problems for such groups. Colson asked Bennett if he would perform that role for him at Transportation. Bennett was flattered and delighted to be of service to his friend at the White House. Through 1970 Bennett and Colson stayed in touch. In July Bennett got a call from William Gay, senior vice president of the Hughes Tool Company and *a top aide to Howard Hughes. Gay and Bennett were both Mormons (Bennett, in fact, was a member of the three-man bishopric of the Church of Jesus Christ of Latter-day Saints near his home in Arlington, Virginia), and Hughes had increasingly surrounded himself with that steady, straight-living, efficient breed of men. Gay asked Bennett to find out whether anything could be done to stop the government's plans to dump tons of nerve gas on the ocean floor near the Bahamas. Evidently Hughes was already contemplating a move from Las Vegas to the Bahamas and was worried lest the deadly fumes contaminate his island retreat. Bennett called Colson and Colson called the President's friend Bebe Rebozo. Eventually, Bennett reported that nothing could be done about the nerve-gas plan. But apparently Gay had been impressed by his fellow Mormon, for, one day in December, he called again. Hughes had just dismissed Robert Maheu, his chief lieutenant, and this meant that Maheu's hand-picked Washington representative—Larry O'Brien—would soon be out of a job too. Hughes was looking for a new man in Washington, somebody well plugged into the Nixon administration. Would Bennett like the job? Bennett would. "Get set then," Gay said. "Get a base." At about this same time, Colson called Bennett to say that Robert Mullen wanted to sell his company. Colson urged Bennett to buy the company and said he would help him find clients. Some investigators believe that, indeed, it was Colson who first suggested Bennett to Hughes. In any case, Bennett left the Department of Transportation in January 1971 and joined Mullen & Company as executive vice president. A month later he became president. In September he completed the acquisition of the company. He says he paid $50,000 to Mullen and two other stockholders and owed them an additional $25,000. (He also paid them $1 million more in "company funds" and owed them $125,000 more.) Sometime during his first few months with the company, Bennett says, Robert Mullen told him about the company's relationship with the CIA. He was soon introduced to the company's CIA "case officer"—Martin J. Lukasky. By mid-1971 Bennett was the fulcrum* *where three powerful forces met: the White House, the CIA, and Howard Hughes. With that kind of power rattling around, important things were bound to happen at Mullen & Company.*

Jeb Magruder, who was at the White House during this period, has suggested that the administration's willingness to engage in illegal acts was related directly to the illegality of acts undertaken by radicals and antiwar demonstrators. For Magruder, the most telling exemplar was William Sloane Coffin, under whom he had studied ethics at Williams College. "We saw continuing violations of the law by men like William Sloane Coffin. He tells me my ethics are bad. Yet he was indicted for criminal charges. He recommended on the Washington Monument grounds that students burn their draft cards and that we have mass demonstrations, shut down the city of Washington. . . . We had become somewhat inured to using some activities that would help us in accomplishing what we thought was a cause, a legitimate cause."

3

LEAKS AND TAPS

I don't find wiretapping a particularly attractive procedure. I similarly don't find the leakage of documents a particularly attractive procedure.

—Henry Kissinger,
news conference,
May 23, 1973

"The gap between you and your enemies is the largest in Washington," Henry A. Kissinger once told Morton H. Halperin, chief of the National Security Council planning group. By that, Kissinger meant that the government officials who suspected Halperin's political views and his loyalty to the administration were very "senior people" while Halperin was relatively junior. Indeed, at thirty-one, Halperin was a rather low-ranking official to be drawing the fulminations of cabinet members, Presidential assistants, apparently even the President himself. But he was a staff man in a very sensitive body—the NSC—which, under Kissinger, had assumed the central role in the formation and conduct of American foreign policy. And he brought to that job a background which was certain to make H. R. Haldeman's crew cut stand up straight and quiver: a B.A. from Columbia; a Ph.D. from Yale; an assistant professorship of government at Harvard; and then he had become deputy assistant secretary of state in the Johnson administration. In other words, Halperin was a full-blooded Ivy League intellectual, who had written several books, hobnobbed with Democrats in Cambridge, served them in Washington, and even begun to voice

doubts about the wisdom of U.S. military intervention
in Southeast Asia. To top it all off, the FBI discovered
that he had once participated in a Vietnam sit-in and
had subscribed to the *World Marxist Review,* the
North American edition of the Communist periodical
Problems of Peace and Socialism published in Prague.
(Halperin now notes with a smile that he reluctantly
agreed to take part in the 1965 sit-in because the
organizers could find nobody else willing to defend the
government's position; and he subscribed to the *World
Marxist Review* as part of his Harvard research on
Sino-Soviet relations under a contract with the Arms
Control and Disarmament Agency.) Small wonder
then that his selection by Kissinger stirred apprehension both in the White House and at the FBI.

At least two other men Kissinger brought to the
NSC in early 1969 aroused similar suspicions among
Nixon loyalists. One was Daniel I. Davidson, a Colum-
bia-trained lawyer who had served with the Wall Street
firm of Cravath, Swaine & Moore, then had become
personal assistant to Ambassador-at-large W. Averell
Harriman, chief American negotiator on Vietnam in the
Johnson administration. The FBI reported that while
serving with Harriman at the Vietnam peace talks in
Paris, Davidson was suspected of leaking information
to reporters there, but stopped when warned by superiors. (Davidson heatedly denies that he ever leaked
"classified" information or was "reprimanded" for it.
But he concedes that he had back-to-back rooms at the
Hotel Crillon with Hedrick Smith, who was covering
the Paris talks for *The New York Times,* and that they
sometimes shared the same bathroom mirror while
shaving in the morning. Others say that Davidson was
undoubtedly the source for many of Smith's best
stories and that, indeed, his superiors were not at all
happy with the cordial relationship between the two
men.)

The third NSC staff member who fell under suspicion was Helmut Sonnenfeldt, a German-born career
diplomat who had risen through the State Department's
ranks to become director of research and analysis for
the Soviet Union and Eastern Europe. Although a reg-

istered Democrat, he was a conservative on domestic issues, a hawk on Vietnam, and—within the context of Kissinger's détente policy—a hard-liner on relations with the Communist bloc. But during the 1950s he had been regarded with deep suspicion by several State Department security officers, notably Otto F. Otepka, who had put him under surveillance, which apparently included wiretapping. Otepka charged that Sonnenfeldt had leaked information to many members of the Washington press corps during the mid-1950s, and to John Kennedy's aides during the 1960 Presidential campaign. Although he was eventually cleared in a departmental investigation, Sonnenfeldt's reputation as a "leaker" and particularly his supposed ties to the Kennedys pursued him down the corridors of power.

According to Kissinger, J. Edgar Hoover objected to the appointment of Halperin, Davidson, and Sonnenfeldt to the NSC's staff. But Kissinger "thought the charges against them were unjustified" and he overrode the director's objections. Kissinger says that doubts were also raised about the appointments by some members of the White House staff—among them, Bob Haldeman and John Ehrlichman. "There is no doubt that some of my colleagues in the White House were very upset about the fact that I alone of the senior officials in the White House brought on my staff individuals who had been closely identified with the previous . . . administrations." Nixon too jibed at Kissinger for the number of liberals and Democrats he had serving on his staff. But Nixon's attitude toward that nest of expertise centered on Harvard was as ambivalent as his stance toward John Kennedy. (When he was graduated from high school, Nixon won a Harvard Club of California prize—a biography of Dean LeBaron Briggs—but his family couldn't afford to send him to the Mecca-on-the-Charles, so he worked his way through Whittier instead.) Many Cantabrigians had served the Kennedys over the years and to that extent Nixon distrusted them. Yet he envied Kennedy's ability to draw on the best brains in the country and felt he was entitled to no less. Though he packed his cabinet with wealthy businessmen from the Middle West and California, he allocated two key positions on his own staff to Harvard professors (one of them—Daniel Patrick Moynihan—a Kennedy Democrat). And he gave the other, Professor Kissinger, a free hand in assembling his own staff.

The suspicions directed at Kissinger's staff lingered on—particularly in J. Edgar Hoover and Bob Haldeman—only to surface again a few months into the administration. The trigger this time was several newspaper stories that disclosed aspects of the emerging Nixon foreign policy. These stories were believed to flow from "leaks" by government officials.

"Leaks"—the surreptitious release of sensitive information—have long been an essential ingredient of the Washington stew. Without them, newsmen would get very little reliable news about what was happening inside the bureaucracy. But leaks are as important to the bureaucrats and politicians as they are to reporters. Thomas J. Smith, an inspector in the FBI's intelligence division, was later to draw a distinction between what he called "controlled" and "uncontrolled" leaks. A "controlled" leak, he suggested, was one undertaken by the government for good and proper purposes of its own. An "uncontrolled" leak was one undertaken by a government official for purposes deemed to be improper. The FBI, Smith said, had decided to investigate only "uncontrolled" leaks.

This distinction is artificial, very difficult to draw in practice. The motivations for Washington leaks are far more tangled. Officials frequently tell newsmen certain facts in order to advance their own careers. Others do so to damage an enemy. Trial balloons are sent up to see if they will float. Other projects are prematurely disclosed in hopes that they will sink. Politicians pop tidbits into the mouths of chosen reporters to curry favor for future exigencies. Congressmen leak stories about secret testimony to build up—or undermine—the witness. The FBI hands out privileged information to discredit "subversives." The CIA leaks to cover its own operations. Often it seems that Washington is one great sieve artfully constructed to water everybody's garden.

The men brought in to staff the upper levels of Richard Nixon's administration that winter had little experience with the Washington leaks game. Many were businessmen accustomed to dealing with the public through corporate public-relations departments which fed bland releases to docile financial-page writers. Others were Midwest or California provincials serving in the capital for the first time. Still others were Republican ideologues who had not served in Washington since the Eisenhower administration and felt themselves surrounded by entrenched Democratic bureaucrats ready to show their every memo to the press.

Finally, there was Kissinger himself—who had written his Ph.D. thesis on Metternich and accepted the traditional European view that successful diplomatic negotiations must be carried out in absolute secrecy. Later, Kissinger was to say, "chasing down leaks was not my central preoccupation." But some of those who served with him during his years as Nixon's special assistant for National Security Affairs are inclined to disagree. They recall a Kissinger often obsessed with what the press wrote about him and his foreign-policy initiatives. "Henry must have spent close to half his time either dealing with the press or worrying about how to deal with them," recalls one former assistant. It was not so much that he opposed leaks as that he insisted on controlling them. His staff members on the NSC were strictly forbidden to talk with the press. "If anybody leaks anything, I will do the leaking," he told his first staff meeting in January 1969. And Kissinger did leak—to favored powers in the Washington press corps like Max Frankel of *The New York Times,* Chalmers Roberts and Murray Marder of *The Washington Post,* and Marvin Kalb of CBS. Indeed, he played the press like a glockenspiel—dazzling them with his secret missions, beguiling them with his Central European charm, fascinating them with his glamorous dinner companions. "I attach great importance to being believed," he told Oriana Fallaci.

Kissinger later told a Senate committee that the spring of 1969 was a "particularly sensitive time with regard to the formulation of this country's foreign policies and the establishment of our future relations with other nations. During this period, policies were being considered which would establish the fundamental approach to major foreign-policy issues such as the United States' strategic posture, Strategic Arms Limitation Talks (SALT), Vietnam and many other national security issues. Because of the sensitive nature of these matters, the secrecy of each was of vital importance, and the success or failure of each program turned in many instances upon the maintenance of necessary security. However, notwithstanding the critical need for such security during this period, we were confronted with leaks to the press of information of the greatest importance to the national security."

Kissinger points to half a dozen press reports published in the spring of 1969 which he says compromised the government's foreign-policy initiatives— most of them written by members of the Washington bureau of *The New York Times*. One was by bureau chief Max Frankel, who reported on April 1 that the United States was moving toward unilateral withdrawal from Vietnam. Another was a May 1 story by William Beecher, the *Times*' Pentagon correspondent, reporting five strategic options being considered for the U.S. position at the SALT conference. Beecher followed several days later with a story about deliberations over U.S. response to the shooting down of a EC-121 reconnaissance plane off the shores of North Korea. Other reports on troop withdrawals from Vietnam, the return of Okinawa to Japan, and intelligence on Soviet military capabilities followed later in the spring.

Such stories were no more frequent in early 1969 than they were in other administrations and the *Times* articles appear to reflect digging by vigorous, able reporters, not a bureaucratic conspiracy to sabotage government initiatives. Yet Nixon and his closest advisers on such matters preferred to see a conspiracy—or at least a determined effort by one or more individuals to leak national security data.

On April 25 a meeting took place at the White House which may have set the policy for later efforts to uncover such leaks. According to Kissinger, he was called into the Oval Office that day to find the President already with Mitchell and Hoover. The subject was leaks and how to stop them. Kissinger says someone— he does not remember who—told him that "wiretapping was necessary, that the practices and procedures were well established." The meeting established four categories of people to be tapped: people with access to the leaked information (and Kissinger says he was instructed to supply the names of such people), newsmen who had printed leaked information, people with "adverse information" in their security files, and people discovered from the taps themselves to be involved in leaks. Then they discussed "specific individuals," and (according to Kissinger) Hoover mentioned four men—Halperin, Davidson, and Sonnenfeldt whom he had labeled as security risks months before, and Henry Brandon, the Czech-born Washington correspondent of the London *Sunday Times* whom Hoover had long suspected of maintaining close ties with Soviet-bloc representatives. Indeed, Hoover seems to have been obsessed with the erudite, well-connected Brandon, who numbered Kissinger among his close friends.

Kissinger has given several different versions of this April 25 meeting. Some skeptics do not accept his accounts, and suspect that the program was really launched when Kissinger met with Hoover at FBI headquarters on May 5. Nixon has admitted publicly that he "authorized the entire program," but he told John Dean privately that Kissinger "asked that it be done." Kissinger insists, "I did not recommend the program," but he clearly played a central role.

Even if Nixon or Hoover took the initiative, Kissinger was being asked to help tap three of his staff members and one of his close friends and he raised no objection. Kissinger says he was reacting to the spate of dangerous "leaks," but the leaks which had occurred up to April 25—or May 5—were relatively harmless. The real reason may be suggested in Kissinger's later testimony: "In May 1969 . . . I was an outsider who had not known the President or any of his associates prior to his appointment, and, therefore, when the director of the FBI and the attorney general both asserted that this was a program that had been carried on previously, it did not occur to me to question it."

In the Nixon White House, Henry Kissinger was an outsider. So he did what awkward, pudgy, bespectacled Jewish kids generally do when snubbed by the tough guys in the neighborhood. He proved he could be just as tough as they were. Kissinger knew that he would always be suspect in the White House because of his foreign accent, his ties to Harvard and to Nelson Rockefeller, his friends on the Georgetown social circuit, not to mention his liberal staff members, unless he showed Hoover, Mitchell, Haldeman—and Nixon— that he was just as security-conscious, just as tough-minded, just as ruthless as they were. But Kissinger had long had a knack for gaining the respect of men who could do something for him. In the Army, which he entered as a clumsy nineteen-year-old, it was Fritz Kraemer, a monocled double Ph.D., who recognized "historical musicality" in the young émigré and recommended him as a German interpreter at division headquarters. As a graduate student at Harvard, Kissinger formed a similar relationship with William Yandell "Wild Bill" Elliott, a political science professor who spent more time consulting with the powerful men in Washington than he did with his students. But Elliott found plenty of time for Kissinger, getting him scholarships and finally naming him director of the Harvard International Seminar. For a while he hobnobbed with bankers and Wall Street lawyers at the Council on Foreign Relations, where Kissinger reveled in "a human environment I find attractive." Through the council he met Nelson A. Rockefeller, a munificent patron whom he served as director of a family-financed project on national security and then as foreign-policy adviser when Rockefeller tried for the Republican Presidential nomination. But never one to let personal loyalty or ideological consistency stand in the way of his advancement, Kissinger was ready and willing when Rockefeller's archrival offered him the White House job. Though some were puzzled over this selection of a man who had once called Nixon "not fit to be President," it made sense for Nixon. As Ronald Steel has noted, "Nixon needed someone with ties to the Eastern liberal establishment, who was not sullied by intimate association with the Democrats, who had no independent political base and who shared his cold war views." And from Kissinger's point of view, Nixon was the ultimate patron—the one who could provide him with the world stage on which to perform his dazzling Realpolitik.

The April 25—or May 5—meeting merely established the administration's policy on wiretapping. No taps were installed until *The New York Times* published another revealing story about the emerging Nixon-Kissinger foreign policy—this one more sensational and probably more significant than its predecessors. On May 8 Bill Beecher wrote, "American B-52 bombers in recent weeks have raided several Viet Cong and North Vietnamese supply dumps and base camps in Cambodia for the first time, according to Nixon administration sources, but Cambodia has not made any protest." It was the first report here about the Cambodian bombing and the first indication of the administration's decision to assault Viet Cong "sanctuaries" in Cambodia—which was to lead one year later to the brief invasion of Cambodia. Beecher's story is said to have caused "dismay and outrage" at the White House. One official says it was regarded as "a serious security breach."

It is difficult to see why. The bombing was no secret to the Communist forces in Cambodia, nor to the villagers on whom some of those bombs were falling. Kissinger claimed later that the secrecy was necessary to preserve the "tacit support" for such bombing by Cambodia's Prince Norodom Sihanouk. Yet the Sihanouk government had repeatedly protested American ground incursions into Cambodia and helicopter strafings along the border, with no visible response from Washington. If Beecher's story had forced Sihanouk to protest the bombing, the B-52s would probably have kept right on dropping their deadly loads.

A curious debate has developed concerning Beecher's source. According to an FBI memo, Beecher conceded at the time that he got the story from someone in the Air Force, a plausible explanation, since no such massive raids could have been mounted without many Air Force officers knowing about them. But Melvin R. Laird, who was then the secretary of defense, told newsmen several years later that he didn't believe the story was based on a leak at all: "The Beecher story was written on the basis of a story that appeared in the London *Times* some forty-eight hours before he wrote. A correspondent had flown over the border and he saw certain craters in Cambodia and the London *Times* came out with this particular story. Bill Beecher, being an enterprising young reporter, went out and started checking this out and he couldn't get denials because I wouldn't deny it." Yet the London *Times* printed no such story. Fred Emery, its man in Vietnam in those days, says he did take an aerial photo which showed bomb craters along the Cambodia-Vietnam border. But the caption made clear that these craters were in Vietnam, and Emery says he did not know at the time that the B-52s were also dropping bombs across the border in Cambodia. Moreover, Beecher has told colleagues privately that he did not get his story from the London *Times*.

In any case, Henry Kissinger clearly thought the story stemmed from a leak. For at 10:35 a.m., only minutes after he opened his *New York Times* on some sun-splashed patio in Key Biscayne, Kissinger telephoned Hoover in Washington. According to Hoover's memo for the files, Kissinger said the story used "secret information" and was therefore "extraordinarily damaging." Hoover recalled that Kissinger "wondered whether I could make a major effort to find out where that came from . . . and to put whatever resources I need to find who did this." Hoover said he would "take care of it right away."

Evidently Hoover's assurances did not fully satisfy Kissinger. Thirty minutes later he called back to tell the director that Beecher had written two previous stories apparently based on high-level leaks—presumably the articles on the SALT options and on the shooting down of the reconnaissance plane. Kissinger asked that these stories be included in the FBI "inquiry." Hoover assured him they would be.

Then Kissinger started stewing about what would happen if word of Hoover's "inquiry" reached the press. At 1:05 p.m. he called the director a third time, to urge that the investigation be handled discreetly "so no stories will get out." Hoover told him that the agents in charge had decided not to contact Beecher directly but were checking with other reporters "to see if they can find out where it came from."

Finally—at 5:05 p.m.—Hoover telephoned Kissinger in Key Biscayne to relay the first results of the bureau's investigation. In this, their fourth conversation of the day, Hoover reported that "a strong possibility" existed that Beecher "may have gotten some of his information from the Southeast Asian Desk, Public Affairs Office of the Department of Defense, as the Public Affairs Office is constituted of employees who are pronounced anti-Nixon. I continued that Beecher frequents this office as well as the National Security Council, and the employees freely furnish him information inasmuch as they are largely Kennedy people and anti-Nixon. I said that also in the Systems Analysis Agency, in the Pentagon, there are at least 110 of the 124 employees who are still McNamara people and express a very definite Kennedy philosophy."

But, according to Hoover's file memo, he told Kissinger that most of the bureau's contacts agreed that the story probably came from Mort Halperin. (Hoover had warned Kissinger about Halperin months before, of course, and now it must have given him pleasure to run through the evidence again for the disconcerted Kissinger.) He said Halperin and another man who worked in the Systems Analysis Agency were both "so-called arrogant Harvard-type Kennedy men who would not hesitate to do anything to save their jobs . . . both men know Beecher and consider him a part of the Harvard clique, and, of course, of the Kennedy era. . . ." The FBI had conducted an applicant investigation of Halperin in February 1969 which showed that he was "of the opinion that the United States leadership erred in the Vietnam commitment as we did not possess the interest or capabilities to obtain the original objectives."

According to Hoover, Kissinger said he had heard Halperin suggested as Beecher's source, "but there is no proof. . . . He hoped I would follow it up as far as we can take it and they will destroy whoever did this if we can find him, no matter where he is."

That very day, between all the telephone calls to and from Hoover, Kissinger summoned Halperin, who was with the Presidential party in Florida. Kissinger never mentioned this conversation to Hoover; apparently, he was employing the old diplomatic technique of telling both sides what they wanted to hear. According to Halperin's affidavit, Kissinger told him he was suspected of leaking the story to Beecher. "I assured him that I had not. I pointed out that I could not have been the source of most of the information and did not know whether the story was accurate or not. . . . Kissinger indicated that he accepted my assurance but that others would not." But four years later, in his own affidavit on the matter, Kissinger said that Halperin was "unquestionably one of several persons who had had access to such information. . . . During the period from January until May 1969, Dr. Halperin regularly participated, in conjunction with the responsible staff area specialists, in sensitive National Security Council studies. In addition, he also frequently attended National Security Council Review Group meetings which I chaired, and which considered a variety of subjects, including the United States strategic posture, strategic arms negotiations, Vietnam, the Middle East and United States trade policies, to name only a few. . . . To maintain his currency in each of these areas, Dr. Halperin received cables to and from our embassies, including limited-distribution cables on Vietnam and the Paris negotiations, as well as daily intelligence reports and sensitive intelligence publications."

On that afternoon of May 9 Kissinger told Halperin that, though he believed him, he was cutting off his future access to such sensitive materials. That way, he said, if any information leaked Halperin could not be blamed.

What Kissinger did not tell his young aide was that the very next day, his deputy, Colonel Alexander M. Haig, Jr., would go to FBI headquarters to see Assistant Director William Sullivan, and ask that wiretaps be installed on four persons. The Haig-Sullivan channel had already been established—presumably at the April 25 or May 5 meetings—as the route through which Kissinger would supply the names of people with access to leaked materials. But it was only a channel of communication. Haig emphasizes, "I never viewed myself as anything but an extension of Dr. Kissinger. . . . I would never presume to do anything in this area that I had not discussed with him or had specific authority for." According to Haig, Kissinger gave him the four names to take to Sullivan. But Haig says he understood that the names had already been approved at a higher level. Indeed, three of the names Haig supplied to Sullivan that day were among those which Hoover had listed—Halperin, Davidson, and Sonnenfeldt. But the fourth was different. In place of Brandon—Hoover's nemesis—somebody, presumably Kissinger, had substituted Air Force Colonel Robert E. Pursley, senior military assistant to Defense Secretary Laird.

Kissinger's precise intentions in this early wiretapping are still subject to intense debate. His allies have suggested that in urging the wiretapping of his own aides, Kissinger was really seeking to exonerate them. Haig has testified, "Dr. Kissinger at the outset of the program was very concerned that he and we were suspect because of the character of the staff that we had put together, and I feel quite frankly that part of Henry's own mental comfort with proceeding with this thing was an effort to vindicate these men and to assure those who had suspicions, [including] the director. It was a means of showing that there was no justification for it." There is probably an element of truth in that, but Kissinger's strategy—as befitted a master diplomat—was almost certainly shrewder and more subtle. By supplying names of close associates on his own staff, he not only demonstrated that he was just as tough as anybody else in the White House but set up a situation in which, whatever happened, he would win. If his aides were exonerated by the wiretaps, he was shown to have been right all along. If they were found to be leaking information, he had taken the lead in uncovering them. The addition of Colonel Pursley was a deft grace note. Pursley was widely considered one of the most discreet men in the national security establishment, an unlikely leaker. But he was a close confidant of Laird's and saw most of what crossed the secretary's desk. Since many of the leaks which so distressed the White House that spring involved military affairs, the Defense Department was as likely a source as the National Security Council. (Beecher, after all, was the *Times'* Pentagon correspondent, and insisted he had gotten the bombing story from the Air Force.) A rivalry was already beginning to spring up between Kissinger and Laird for primacy in military policy. The tapping of Pursley was a chessplayer's gambit—the advance of a pawn into enemy territory to see what it might stir up.

According to Sullivan's memo on his May 10 conversation with Haig, the colonel told him the wiretaps were being requested "on the highest authority and involves a matter of most grave and serious consequences to our national security." According to another source, Haig warned that the leaks, if continued, were "going to destroy Mr. Kissinger's foreign policy." In going over the ground rules with Sullivan, Haig stressed that the matter was so sensitive that "no record" should be maintained. And indeed, unlike previous national security wiretaps, no record of these taps was retained in the regular FBI files. The logs and other documents were kept first in Hoover's office and later in Sullivan's.

Like other wiretaps, these required approval from Attorney General Mitchell. Mitchell was present at the April 25 meeting, but he has persistently denied that he knew of the wiretap program and says he did not sign the requisite approvals. Yet his name is on each of the forms and the FBI analysts say it is his signature. (He did not, however, review the taps every ninety days, as required by law.)

If Mitchell gave his approval, though, it seems to have been *pro forma*. For although the approvals for the first four wiretaps were signed on Monday, May 12, at least one tap was installed before Mitchell could ever have set pen to paper. The tap on Halperin's phone, in fact, was installed even before Haig arrived on May 10 to see Sullivan. It was working by 6:20 p.m. on Friday, May 9—the very day Beecher's story appeared in the *Times.* Hoover, who had long waited for a chance to tap Halperin's telephone, wasted no time now in getting this one started (although he apparently didn't tell Kissinger that, just as Kissinger didn't tell him he had met with Halperin. Nobody was quite leveling with anybody that day). Moreover, a Justice Department memo suggests that several of the other taps may have been installed over the May 10–11 weekend.

The tapped conversations were tape-recorded and then transcribed by clerks in the FBI's Washington field office. The clerks took the conversations down verbatim, and at the end of the day sent these logs over to Sullivan's office at FBI headquarters. Each morning, Sullivan would flip through the batch that had come in overnight and give them to Bernard Wells, a supervisor in the domestic intelligence division whom he had assigned to handle all paperwork on the taps. Frequently, Sullivan would designate sections of the logs which he deemed important and Wells would type these and his own selections into "summaries." Each summary would be sent in a memorandum to Hoover, enclosing letters for his signature to Kissinger and to the President. Delivered by Robert Haynes, the FBI liaison officer to the White House, these letters disguised the source of the information, invariably referring to it as from "our most sensitive sources," an FBI euphemism for wiretaps. Much of the paperwork also contained the FBI code word "June," which indicated to knowing eyes that these were the fruits of wiretaps.

Bernard Wells says Sullivan told him to look out for "loose talk and leaks" and to watch particularly for anything on the Paris peace talks or SALT. Wells says he also looked for homosexuality, heavy drinking, or other unorthodox behavior which might make the individual subject to blackmail. But Wells recalls little of this sort of thing on the logs. Indeed, he says most of the conversations contained nothing at all of interest. At the height of the wiretapping program, the summaries took him only about two hours a week. "It was routine work," he says. "They were all boring."

The tap on Halperin's telephone at his home in Bethesda, Maryland, for example, produced plenty of information on the family's personal lives: Mort and Ina Halperin's anxious calls to New York about a relative's surgery; their sons—David, Mark, and Gary—asking their friends out to play; and probably those obscenities whispered by an unknown voice in the middle of the night. Halperin was overheard talking to journalists from time to time, but he was never caught disclosing any confidential data. Indeed, once he flatly refused to leak a Kissinger statement to a reporter. The FBI noted that Mrs. Halperin, like some of the other tapped wives, talked about her husband's work "unnecessarily." For example, she was overheard telling a salesman that her husband had been working long hours preparing a speech for Nixon to deliver. The tap also picked up fifteen conversations involving Daniel Ellsberg, a friend of the Halperins—some, while he was staying with them in late 1969 and early 1970; others, in calls that the Halperins made to Ellsberg or vice versa. One of these calls, the bureau reported, "perhaps established a rationale for Ellsberg's antiwar posture." Some, the FBI said, "related to drugs such as LSD and marijuana."

The Halperin wiretap produced so little of value that within a few weeks Sullivan began urging that it be removed. And the taps on Sonnenfeldt and Pursley were no more productive. Pursley was overheard voicing "dissatisfaction with his job and its emotional effect upon him." Sonnenfeldt was reported to be in contact with a newspaper reporter who had "numerous contacts with individuals assigned to Soviet-bloc embassies."

The only one of the four taps which may have produced something was the one on Dan Davidson. On May 29, 1969—less than three weeks after the tap was installed—Davidson resigned from the National Security Council and joined a Washington law firm. That day Sullivan wrote to Hoover: "They are releasing Davidson today. At least this is one leak that will be stopped." Davidson insists he was not caught leaking and was not removed for that. He says he left the NSC by "mutual consent" with Kissinger because he was unhappy with many of the Nixon-Kissinger policies and they were unhappy with the good relationships he maintained with reporters. "I never gave a reporter classified information, never passed them secret documents, never violated security regulations," he says. "I did see reporters, I talked with them. I gave them nonclassified information." Indeed, Davidson was gregarious, voluble, and liked to talk to the press. He recalls chatting for two hours one day with Joseph Kraft about one of Nixon's Supreme Court appointments. Moreover, his friendship with Averell Harriman undoubtedly did him no good. He recalls that one weekend he was going off to visit Harriman and a senior colleague on the NSC said confidentially, "I won't tell anybody where you're going." But Davidson's rapid departure from the NSC that month remains something of a puzzle. Although Kissinger has said that "nobody was penalized" as a result of the wiretapping, he has also said that Davidson's wiretap was "the one instance where ambiguous information was developed." Sullivan, urging that Halperin's tap be lifted on July 8, told Hoover, "Since Davidson was removed, Halperin has said almost nothing on the telephone. My guess is that he assumes it is tapped." (Halperin says he never knew why Davidson left, never guessed that his phone was tapped, and never consciously changed his telephone habits.) Not only was the tap retained on Halperin's telephone but Davidson's tap also remained in place for three and a half months after he left the NSC staff—or until September 15, 1969.

Meanwhile, other taps were being placed. On May 20 Haig brought two more names of NSC staff members over to Sullivan: Richard L. Sneider and Richard Moose. Unlike Halperin, Sonnenfeldt, and Davidson—whose access to material on Cambodia was at best limited—Moose and Sneider were among those on the staff who dealt directly with the Cambodia bombing and who had the most direct access to relevant documents. If—as many suspect—the first four men were tapped for reasons that had little to do with Beecher's story about Cambodia, the taps on Moose and Sneider may have been Kissinger's pass at doing what he had claimed to be doing eight days before.

On May 29 Hoover finally got around to tapping the last of his original targets, Henry Brandon. This tap too was attributed to a request from Haig-representing-Kissinger, but Hoover seems to have merely used Haig's name to justify the tap he had wanted to place on Brandon all along. Indeed, Kissinger denies giving Brandon's name to the FBI, noting that Brandon fit none of the categories for those to be tapped—particularly since his stories rarely included leaked material. Hoover's memo said that Haig, in asking for the tap, had noted that Brandon had recently been overheard on Halperin's wiretap, but it cited no evidence that he had received any information compromising "national security." Kissinger was friendly with Brandon, who was about to start work on a biography of him. In fact, Brandon says Kissinger once told him that he lied to every reporter in Washington except Brandon. The tap produced many conversations with high-ranking officials, but the only tidbit worth much notice was a remark which Brandon managed to extract from a White House official and read over the phone to a friend: "The President is weak. He has difficulty saying no. He wants to please all and he dislikes having to make a choice. . . . With a man like this, Henry Kissinger, of course, has great influence." Later, an FBI agent reported that Brandon and Halperin had lunched on August 6, 1969, at the Occidental Restaurant, "where they engaged in a continuing conversation" for an hour and thirty-five minutes. (The agent photographed the two men as they came out of the restaurant.)

Six days after the wiretap was installed on Brandon's telephone, Haig requested and Hoover ordered a tap placed on Hedrick Smith, the *New York Times* reporter then serving as a diplomatic correspondent in Washington. This was on June 4, hours after the *Times* appeared with a page-one story by Smith reporting that Nixon and President Thieu of Vietnam were preparing to announce plans for the first unilateral reduction of American troops in Vietnam. Nixon later identified this article as one of those based on serious "leaks." FBI reports say that Smith's telephone was tapped because he had been overheard talking with one of the officials already tapped—his old Paris shaving partner, Dan Davidson.

Still another newsman—Marvin Kalb—was tapped on September 10. Kalb, who had once served as CBS's correspondent in Moscow, was reported by the FBI to have "close contacts with Soviet-bloc personnel" in Washington. But this does not seem to have been the basis for the tap. Indeed, the Kalb tap involved several peculiar features. First, it was requested not by Haig but by John Mitchell, directly on behalf of the President. Second, Mitchell asked for both a wiretap and around-the-clock physical surveillance, abandoning the surveillance request only when told that it would tie up six men every day. Third, memos reporting the fruits of the tap were to go not to Kissinger and the President, as the others did, but to the President and Ehrlichman. This suggests that the wiretap may have been directed chiefly at Kissinger. Kalb was one of Kissinger's closest confidants in the press corps and, like Brandon, was writing a book about him. If Kissinger himself was leaking, Kalb would be among the first to catch the drops.

From the start, Haldeman and Ehrlichman had distrusted Kissinger as much as they did some of his staff members. Haldeman in particular regarded him as a suspect recruit from the alien Eastern world of Harvard, the Council on Foreign Relations, and Rockefeller. They may well have suspected that some of the leaks that spring were coming from Henry himself. The request for physical surveillance on Kalb strongly suggests that they were very much after hard evidence that someone knowledgeable was talking to him. Most sophisticated government officials who want to leak something to a reporter don't do so over the telephone. They meet him in a restaurant, a bar, or, better yet, a more private place. Only close physical surveillance would turn this up.

Yet, by then, the wiretapping program was plainly straying rather far from its original purposes. One former NSC official cites what he calls the *"Des Moines Register* syndrome" in explaining how the wiretapping became institutionalized. "If you're a government official and you want to subscribe to the *Register,"* he says, "you'll have a hell of a time. Your office has never subscribed to the paper and your superiors simply won't see why you need it. But if you persuade them, then the *Register* will simply become part of the office equipment. It will come forever. You won't be able to get rid of it." So with the wiretaps. Their introduction in the spring of 1969 required a high-level policy decision. Haig told Sullivan in early May that taps would "only be necessary for a few days to resolve the issue." He was kidding either himself or the FBI. The tapping program lasted twenty-one months. Once they were undertaken, they became part of the executive's equipment and were used promiscuously by several different factions, each for its own purpose.

Perhaps the best evidence of that was the wiretapping of three members of the White House staff who had responsibilities largely or wholly in the domestic arena and little or no access to "national security" information.

The first was John P. Sears, deputy Presidential counsel, who was tapped and placed under twenty-four-hour surveillance on July 23, 1969, at Mitchell's request. A former associate in the Nixon-Mitchell law firm, Sears once appeared to have a bright future at the White House. He had briefly been a candidate for a job as political adviser to the President, but he lost out to Harry S. Dent, a South Carolina politician who had once worked for Senator Strom Thurmond. As early as the 1968 campaign, Sears had been friendly with political reporters, often chatting with them until late in the night. This did not endear him to Mitchell, Haldeman, and Ehrlichman, and when political information began to seep into the press, the "inner circle" naturally thought of Sears. Mitchell, in particular, disliked and distrusted his former law associate. On July 22 Mitchell told Cartha DeLoach of the FBI that the President was "extremely exercised and very aggravated" about a news leak he attributed to Sears. Mitchell said the President wanted to "set Sears up" and planned to send material that week from Guam which Sears would definitely see and, it was hoped, pass on to his contacts in the press. The ploy evidently did not work.

The second White House aide to be tapped was William Safire, the urbane Presidential speechwriter. FBI records show that Haig requested a tap on Safire on August 4, 1969, citing "the highest authority," a euphemism frequently used in the wiretap requests and apparently meaning the President. But Haig has denied making any such request. According to an FBI memo, Haig said the tap was needed because Safire had been overheard talking with Brandon on *his* tapped telephone—the last link in an ill-fated chain, since Brandon was allegedly tapped for talking to Halperin on his tapped telephone. But Safire was probably tapped less for any specific conversation than for his tendency to tramp the Georgetown social circuit, much disdained among Nixon's super-loyalists.

The third tap in this series was placed on James W. McLane, head of the Domestic Council's Committee on Aging. It was installed on December 14, 1970, at Haldeman's request. McLane was the son-in-law of Governor Francis Sargent of Massachusetts, for whom he had worked as deputy campaign manager that fall. Before that, McLane had been executive assistant to Robert Finch when he was secretary of health, education, and welfare. (Finch was once one of Nixon's closest friends and political allies, but he was gradually edged out by Haldeman and Ehrlichman.) Both Finch and Sargent were members of the so-called liberal wing of the Republican party, which had not always been enamored of Nixon. The tap on McLane may have been designed to see if he was still loyal.

Meanwhile, if the taps were ever truly intended to uncover national security leaks, they failed to turn up much of anything. Haig came to Sullivan's office several times to examine the summaries and logs. According to an FBI report, Kissinger came with him on May 20, 1969—barely ten days after the first taps were installed —to read through the logs. Afterward, Kissinger is said to have remarked, "It is clear that I don't have anybody in my office I can trust except Colonel Haig." Kissinger, Sullivan, and Haig now all insist they have no memory of such a meeting. Kissinger says that if he made the remark at all, he meant it sarcastically. Given the paucity of material turned up on the taps, it is difficult to imagine what he might have meant. The only one of his aides implicated in any way at that time was Davidson, and Kissinger himself has described the material on him as "ambiguous."

In the months to come, little of any value was uncovered. Haig recalls that one day Sullivan summoned him to look at the report of one tapped conversation. "He was quite excited about it and said it was a very serious matter," Haig recalls. "I went over and looked. . . . I felt it did not involve a national security matter but rather a criminal matter and I told Henry about it."

On another occasion, Kissinger and Haig went to Hoover's office for a broad review of the security problem. Haig recalls Hoover warning them about "an espionage agent who had been very successful here in Washington with a number of highly placed people . . . a very attractive gal who I guess spread her favors around rather loosely. . . . I think it [the warning] was directed at Dr. Kissinger."

Gradually, Haig says, he became concerned about the scope of the wiretapping program. "I had seen a program which I initially was told would be very brief and very informal, and was designed to cope with a severe immediate problem, going on. I had growing personal reservations about it and our role in it and my role in it." He says he "urged Henry to disassociate the National Security Council staff, meaning me or anybody else, from what was essentially an internal security matter," in fact to get out of what he called "the mucky business." But for a full year, through the fall and winter of 1969 and the spring of 1970, the summaries kept flowing from Sullivan's office to Kissinger's—thirty-seven in all between May 1969 and May 1970.

Then, on May 2, 1970, the ubiquitous Beecher wrote still another story which raised hackles at the White House. Two days after Nixon went on nationwide television to announce the invasion of enemy "sanctuaries" in the Parrot's Beak and Fishhook sections of Cambodia, Beecher disclosed that U.S. bombers had carried out heavy raids against North Vietnamese supply dumps and other targets north of the demilitarized zone. Quoting "well-placed administration sources," Beecher said the raids were far greater than any carried out since November 1968, when the United States announced the end of most bombing of North Vietnam. Again, the story could hardly have come as news to the enemy on whom the bombs had fallen, but the White House seized on Beecher's piece to launch a new round of wiretaps.

Haig telephoned the FBI to say that the President had told him that Beecher's story was based on "a serious security violation" and that the source had been "nailed down to a couple of people." He said the President urgently wanted four taps installed: on Beecher; Richard F. Pedersen, State Department counselor; William H. Sullivan, deputy assistant secretary of state for East Asia and Pacific affairs; and a new tap on Colonel Pursley at the Pentagon. (Pursley's first tap, the year before, had lasted for only fifteen days.)

These four taps all have curious features. First, if Bill Beecher's story in May 1969 really triggered the wiretapping program, it seems strange that the White House did not order his telephone tapped until nearly a year later. Perhaps Kissinger felt that the rationale for the program would lose credibility if he did not tap Beecher this time. The rationale was indeed shaken by the identity of the people targeted in this second round of "national security" wiretaps. Pedersen, like Pursley, was a highly discreet career official and most unlikely to leak anything to the press. Sullivan too does not seem a likely source for Beecher's article. One former NSC official describes these taps as "Henry feeling his oats," reaching out to tap high-ranking officials in the Defense and State departments.

By this time, Kissinger was increasingly at odds with both Secretary of Defense Laird and Secretary of State William P. Rogers, both of whom had serious reservations about the Cambodian invasion. Kissinger was gradually encroaching on the two men's authority in foreign affairs and defense policy. In the happy phrase coined by Dan Rather and Gary Gates, Laird and Rogers were "destined to play Poland and Czechoslovakia to Henry Kissinger's blitzkrieg." If he coveted their powers—and, in Rogers' case, his job—Kissinger needed intelligence. Pedersen and Pursley, in particular, were well-placed pipelines into the thinking of their bosses. Perhaps significantly, Haig not only asked for wiretaps on their home telephones but, for the first time, requested that their office telephones be tapped too. This was technically difficult, and it is not clear whether it was accomplished.

Suspicions that these taps were motivated more by political than security considerations are strengthened by the nature of the next two wiretaps. On May 13 Haig asked for taps on the telephones of Anthony Lake and Winston Lord, two more members of the NSC's staff. Both Lake and Lord had voiced strong opposition to the Cambodian invasion. Indeed, Lake had resigned in protest the week before he was tapped, although for financial and other reasons, he did not leave the staff until the end of June.

Kissinger has expressed his high admiration for Lake, who served as his personal assistant. He said Lake was someone who "knew everything in my office, who had been with me on secret negotiations with Le Duc Tho, and before whom I had no secrets, a man for whom I had then, for whom I continue to have the highest personal regard. . . ." But he noted that because Lake stayed on for a while after his resignation, "We had a potential security problem here in the sense that a man had resigned in strong opposition to the President's policy but was still continued on the staff in a sensitive position and, moreover, still had all the files."

But if Lake and Lord were tapped because it was feared they would disclose secret material from Kissinger's office, then it is hard to understand why on the very day their taps were installed Nixon, Hoover, and Haldeman decided that reports on the taps would no longer be sent to Kissinger and the President but only to Haldeman. It is difficult to suppress the suspicion that Lake and Lord were tapped primarily because of their opposition to the Cambodian invasion at a time when the White House was deeply embattled on this subject and all internal opposition was viewed as virtual treason.

Finally, suspicions about the political nature of these and other taps are reinforced by their duration. The tap remained on Lake's telephone for some seven months after he left the NSC in June to join Senator Muskie's staff as a foreign affairs adviser. Summaries of FBI logs note that Lake's tap then produced data on "the activities of certain potential Democratic candidates for national office." By that time, Mort Halperin was also working as an unpaid foreign policy adviser to Muskie and his tap too was continued long after he left the NSC on September 19, 1969, to become a relatively inactive consultant to Kissinger, and after he resigned as a consultant on May 4, 1970, in protest against the Cambodian invasion. From the spring of 1970 until early 1971 the taps on Halperin and Lake were, in fact, taps on the Muskie Presidential campaign—in a period when Muskie was considered the front-runner for the Democratic nomination.

The White House was particularly sensitive to contacts between government officials—especially "holdovers" from previous administrations—and leaders of the Democratic party. Once, Assistant Secretary of State Sullivan was overheard talking with a former official in a prior administration who inquired about

"Sullivan's position on the Cambodia situation and advised Sullivan of a meeting of individuals opposing the present administration's policies." This apparently was a reference to a meeting held at the Georgetown home of Averell Harriman on May 18, 1970, attended by State Department personnel opposed to the Cambodian invasion. Harriman, of course, was a prominent Democrat with multifarious ties in that party's leadership. Bernard Wells has testified that the FBI put the meeting under surveillance. "They wanted to identify the people who came," Wells said. Agents lurked in the shadows outside photographing those who entered and taking down their license-plate numbers. Later, Hoover scrawled a note on the report, "An excellent job. I talked to Haldeman at Key Biscayne."

In December 1969 Hoover had informed Nixon that Halperin was in touch with former Secretary of Defense Clark M. Clifford, who, like Harriman, was an important figure in the Democratic party. The wiretapped telephone call had revealed that Clifford was "sharpening up his attack on Nixon," and that he had collected several "old Nixon statements" for use in a major article he planned to write on the President's Vietnam policy, probably for *Life* magazine. On January 8, 1970, Alexander P. Butterfield, one of Haldeman's aides, sent Hoover's letter to Jeb Magruder urging him to "get ourselves springloaded to a position from which we can effectively counter whatever tack Clifford takes." A week later Magruder responded that Clifford was indeed doing an article for *Life,* that it would be published "within the next month," and that it would be "a very strong article against our policy in Vietnam, utilizing quotes and information he has regarding the President, and probably suggesting complete troop withdrawal by the end of 1970." Magruder suggested that Clifford's article be met with a counterattack from Dean Acheson or some other defender of Nixon's policy in *Look* magazine; or the White House could respond by "utilizing administration spokesmen on television, by letters to *Life* relating the true context of the President's remarks, or by relating some of Clifford's activities to the press that would indicate the hypocrisy of his position." Ehrlichman forwarded Magruder's memo to Haldeman saying, "This is the kind of early warning we need more of. Your game planners are now in an excellent position to map anticipatory action." Haldeman wrote to Magruder, "I agree with John's point. Let's get going."

Apparently with this sort of political action in mind, Haldeman received some fifty-two summaries of wiretap materials during the following months. On October 19 he ordered still another tap—a resumption of the discontinued tap on Helmut Sonnenfeldt. A Hoover memo several days before said that Haldeman felt "they may have a bad apple and have to get him out of the basket." Sonnenfeldt was an old apple, of course, one that had been probed and poked in every administration—but no rotten spots were found this time.

Indeed, it appears, most of the new wiretaps, like most of the old ones, produced nothing at all. They picked up a few grumbles—Winston Lord making "uncomplimentary remarks about Mr. Kissinger and the President"—but no leaks. Seventeen persons in all had been tapped: seven on Kissinger's NSC staff (Halperin, Sonnenfeldt, Davidson, Moose, Sneider, Lake, and Lord); three elsewhere on the White House staff (Safire, Sears, and McLane); two in the State Department (Pedersen and Sullivan); one at the Defense Department (Pursley); and four newsmen (Brandon, Smith, Kalb, and Beecher). The taps were maintained for periods varying from one month (Moose and Sneider) to twenty-one months (Halperin). But with the possible exception of Davidson's, they were all dry holes. Later, the President told John Dean, "The tapping was a very, very unproductive thing. . . . They never helped us. Just gobs and gobs of material: gossip and bullshitting."

The wiretapping program ended on February 10, 1971. As with almost everything about it, there are at least two explanations for the cessation. According to one group of sources, Haig called Sullivan on February 8, 1971, and ordered the last eight taps discontinued, saying they had "served their purpose." According to others, Hoover ordered the remaining taps removed because he was about to testify before a subcommittee of the House Appropriations Committee on the FBI budget. The director generally liked to discontinue as many wiretaps as possible before congressional appearances so that, if questioned, he could report a minimum number of taps in effect.

Within the next few weeks, Robert Haynes, the FBI liaison officer to the White House, collected all the summaries of wiretap material from Haig, Kissinger, Haldeman, Ehrlichman, and the President. They were returned to Sullivan's office and, with the original logs and memoranda, were put in his safe.

The wiretap material was still in Sullivan's safe in late June 1971, when Daniel Ellsberg was indicted for violation of the espionage statutes in handing the Pentagon Papers over to *The New York Times* and other newspapers. On July 2 Assistant Attorney General Robert Mardian, who was supervising the Ellsberg case in the Justice Department, asked the FBI for any "electronic surveillance information" regarding Ellsberg—a routine request, designed primarily to prepare for the inevitable demand from Ellsberg's lawyers that any wiretap material be supplied prior to trial. A week later, another request went to the FBI for wiretap records on a number of individuals involved in the Ellsberg case, including Morton Halperin. The data in Sullivan's safe included, of course, the logs of the tap on Halperin's telephone, among them the logs of fifteen conversations to and from Daniel Ellsberg.

At about the time of Mardian's two inquiries, Sullivan paid a call on the assistant attorney general. Sullivan, who was feuding with Hoover at this time, said he wanted to turn the logs over to Mardian. According to Mardian, Sullivan told him, "Mr. Hoover had used wiretap information to blackmail other Presidents of the United States and [Sullivan] was afraid that he could blackmail Mr. Nixon with this information." Mardian reported the conversation to John Mitchell, who said he would take care of it.

On July 10 Ehrlichman's notes of a Presidential meeting in San Clemente include the entry, "Re: grand jury—don't worry re tapes on discovery—re White

House." In legalese, "discovery" is the process by which the prosecution and defense seek material related to their case before a trial begins. Clearly, what was worrying the White House was not so much Hoover's blackmail as the danger that the wiretapping program might be revealed during Halperin's appearance before the grand jury investigating the Pentagon Papers case.

That same day, July 10, Mardian was summoned to the Western White House, and he took the regular courier plane from Andrews Air Force Base to California. There, on July 12, he met with Nixon. Mardian has testified that most of their conversation dealt with the Ellsberg case, but the President also instructed Mardian to get the wiretap materials from Sullivan and deliver them to the White House. Back in Washington, Mardian relayed these instructions to Sullivan, and a few days later an FBI official appeared in his office bearing an old "beat-up" satchel. Two days later, Mardian took it to the White House, where he delivered it first to Kissinger, who quipped, "Do you have what I said on the phone?"—a remark which Mardian considered in "extremely poor taste." After Kissinger, Haig, and Haldeman had verified the materials, Mardian was ushered into the Oval Office, where he handed over the satchel. Asked later by an FBI agent, "Did you give the bag to Mr. Nixon, the President of the United States?" Mardian said, "I cannot answer that question." Ehrlichman has testified that the President ordered him to "take custody" of the wiretap materials, and from then on they were held in a safe in Ehrlichman's outer office.

The greatest moment of John Ehrlichman's youth was the day he became an Eagle Scout. Growing up in Santa Monica, California, he loved to hike and camp and tie knots. And he has retained his love of the great outdoors. After studying political science at UCLA, serving three years as a B-24 navigator during World War II, and getting a law degree from Stanford, he was offered a job with a Los Angeles firm. But he and his new wife—a UCLA classmate—opted instead

*for Seattle, where "the sun was shining and the straw-
berries were big and fat." And, appropriately enough,
Ehrlichman's law practice there focused primarily on
land-use, a major subject in the conservation-minded
Northwest. By the early 1960s he was Seattle's foremost zoning lawyer. Another Seattle attorney recalls:
"He had a passion for detail and was indefatigable.
And that's what made him good. Land-use tends to be
boring, but he could just outwait you. He never let up."
Earning $50,000–60,000 a year, Ehrlichman might
have gone on leading the good Northwest life forever
had it not been for his old UCLA friend Bob Haldeman, who was serving as Richard Nixon's chief advance man in the 1960 campaign. Haldeman induced
Ehrlichman to serve as a kind of political espionage
agent in Nelson Rockefeller's abortive effort to gain the
Republican nomination. Once, during a cavalcade
through North Dakota, Ehrlichman actually drove one
of the Rockefeller cars. "The Rockefeller people
thought I was from North Dakota and the North
Dakota people thought I was from Rockefeller," he
said. Later he was sent as a secret observer to the
Democratic National Committee, where he prepared
a dossier on John Kennedy's campaign apparatus.
After Nixon lost, Ehrlichman went back to his law
practice. He worked briefly in Nixon's 1962 campaign
for the California governorship, but for the next six
years he seemed convinced that his man's political
career was finished. Not until June 1968 did he and
Haldeman get fully back into Nixon politics. At the
White House, Ehrlichman served first as counsel to the
President, then as the President's chief assistant for
domestic affairs. In this latter job, Ehrlichman played
much the same role for the domestic arena that Henry
Kissinger played for foreign affairs (although, increasingly, he shared that role with Secretary of Labor
George Shultz). All major domestic programs and
legislation—revenue sharing, welfare reform, drug control—funneled through his office. White House staffers
differed widely in their assessments of Ehrlichman.
Some saw him as a martinet, a stiff, humorless ascetic,
who neither smoked nor drank, and who had little*

*sympathy with other men's failings ("Your Nixon pin is
upside down," he once snapped at a hapless speechwriter). Others found him a force for moderation in
the ruling councils, even a "closet liberal." (One genuine liberal on the staff said, "John is a humanist. He
sees the absurdities, the suffering in life. He is interested
in people.") But, whatever his essential nature, all
agreed that he was a cool, efficient executor of the
Presidential will. One colleague said, "He leaves no
more blood on the floor than he has to."*

The President's fear that the wiretapping might be
disclosed in the Pentagon Papers grand jury was undoubtedly accentuated by his knowledge that some of
the taps had been used to gain domestic political information—a clear violation of law. But he may also
have been nervous about the legal underpinning even
for the so-called "national security" wiretaps. Whether
such taps are legal is still a matter of some dispute,
and the final answer will depend on a judicial determination of just what "national security" means in such
cases.

The federal government has wiretapped for decades
—beginning with Prohibition bootleggers—but the first
taps for "national security" purposes came in 1940,
when President Roosevelt ordered the FBI to use them
against the "Fifth Column," limiting its targets "insofar as possible to aliens." In 1946 Attorney General
Tom Clark persuaded President Harry S. Truman to
broaden this category to include domestic subversives.

Efforts to curb the government's use of telephone
taps began in 1967, when the Supreme Court held that
the practice came under the Fourth Amendment's stric-
ture against unreasonable search and seizure, and thus
required a court-ordered warrant. In 1968 Congress
specifically authorized law-enforcement officers to seek
warrants for wiretaps in the fight against crime, notably
against gambling and the narcotics trade. But neither
Court nor Congress limited the President's constitutional power "to protect national security information
against foreign intelligence activities." Then, in June

1969, Attorney General Mitchell proclaimed an auda-
cious doctrine. He claimed that these Presidential
powers permitted wiretapping of any domestic group
"which seeks to attack and subvert the government by
unlawful means." In June 1972 the Supreme Court
rejected this doctrine, holding that no such domestic
group or individual could be tapped without a warrant.
But the Court still did not touch the President's right
to tap, without warrants, when the case involved foreign intelligence. Some officials therefore contend that
the 1969–71 taps were legal because they were designed to prevent "national security" information from
falling into the hands of the press and then of foreign
agents. Others are convinced that the Court would never construe the President's power that broadly, and
thus argue that the 1969–71 taps were illegal from the
start.

If Nixon was worried about the grand jury uncovering the taps placed by the FBI, he was even more concerned about two clearly illegal taps placed through the
resources of the White House: one on Joseph Kraft, the
other on the President's brother F. Donald Nixon.

In June 1969, just a month after the first FBI taps
were installed, Ehrlichman told John Caulfield that he
wanted a tap on Kraft, a member in bad standing of the
White House "enemies list." Ehrlichman said the tap
was needed because of "the Cambodian situation," presumably the same news reports on the bombing in
Cambodia which had allegedly precipitated the other
taps. Caulfield replied that "since it was a national
security matter it would properly be within the purview of the FBI." But Ehrlichman said no, because
the FBI was a "sieve"—a curious assessment, since the
White House had just entrusted the other supersecret
wiretap program to the bureau. Nixon later told Dean,
"Hoover didn't want to do Kraft."

The explanation may simply be that a wiretap on
Joe Kraft—even more than on Brandon and Kalb—was
a tap on Henry Kissinger. All three newsmen were close
to Kissinger. Other reporters were close to him too,
notably Chalmers Roberts of *The Washington Post,*
who got more good material out of Kissinger's office

than anyone else. But Roberts was a blunt, newsroom type who didn't spend much time on the Georgetown social circuit, the social-political milieu that made the Nixon loyalists so uneasy. They didn't seem to mind so much when an administration official talked with a man like Chal Roberts, but they shuddered at the thought of one of their own people consorting with the likes of Brandon or Kraft over a punchbowl at a Q Street garden party. That was trafficking with the enemy.

Ehrlichman—and the President—probably wanted to know just how often Kissinger was trafficking with Kraft. Kissinger was deeply involved in the FBI wiretap program and it would be difficult to get a tap on Kraft through that channel without his hearing about it. So Ehrlichman said he wanted Caulfield to handle the tap. Caulfield got in touch with John Ragan, a former FBI man and at the time chief of security for the Republican National Committee. The two men had become friendly during the 1968 campaign, when Ragan was a Republican "counter-measure security expert," responsible for insuring that Nixon's traveling campaign staff was neither tapped nor bugged. Caulfield told Ragan that he had a "high priority national security assignment" from the White House, and Ragan, suitably impressed, agreed to help him. One night they cased Kraft's residence in what Caulfield describes as "a very prestigious area of Georgetown," reporting back to Ehrlichman that it was "a very difficult matter to handle."

But Ehrlichman said "it had to be done." Ragan needed the "parent cable numbers" for the line leading into Kraft's home, so Caulfield arranged to get them through a friend in the Secret Service, telling him only that it was needed for a vital "national security" operation. Ragan also asked for telephone company credentials and Caulfield got these through John Davies, the White House tour director, who had once worked for A.T.&T. According to Caulfield, Ragan and "an individual from New York whom I don't know" installed a tap on "the rear pole [outside] of Mr. Kraft's residence." John Dean gave a third-hand version of the operation as "a rather harrowing experience when he [presumably Ragan] was holding the ladder in a back alley of Georgetown while also trying to keep a lookout as another member of the group was working at the top of the ladder."

Shortly thereafter, Caulfield recalls, Ehrlichman called him in again and said that he "was to desist in the matter; they had decided that the FBI was going to take care of [it]." But the tap was already producing tapes, one of which Ragan gave him. Caulfield took it home, but insists he never played it. If he had, he wouldn't have heard Kraft—the family was on vacation in Europe (indeed, an FBI man later told Kraft that the only thing overheard was a woman speaking in a foreign language; the Krafts employed an Argentine maid). Caulfield says he burned the tape in the White House "burn bag" and ordered Ragan to remove the tap.

The FBI never did tap Kraft's phone in Washington. Hoover recommended it, but for some reason John Mitchell declined to sign the necessary authorization. In June 1969, though, Sullivan trailed Kraft to Paris, where the columnist was interviewing Communist delegates to the Vietnam peace talks (he planned to go on to the Soviet Union). Through French authorities, Sullivan placed a microphone in Kraft's hotel room. Later, the legal attaché at the American embassy in Paris, an FBI man, shipped nineteen pages of material from this bug back to Washington in the diplomatic pouch. French intelligence officials put their own watch on the columnist. Jean-Paul Maurist, deputy director of the Bureau of Territorial Security, told *Newsweek* that such surveillance is carried out "if a foreigner is susceptible to having contacts with a foreign government."

Late that fall, Mitchell asked the FBI to recommend other forms of surveillance on Kraft. The bureau advised that "close physical surveillance" of the columnist would be too dangerous and suggested instead a "selective spot surveillance" of his evening social contacts. After only a few weeks Sullivan reported that the spot surveillance had proved unproductive and it was dropped on December 12.

The tap on the President's brother has a longer and murkier history. Donald Nixon—a likable, loquacious wheeler-dealer—had been something of an embarrassment to his older brother for a decade. In 1960 it was disclosed that four years before, while his brother was Vice President, Donald Nixon had taken a $205,000 "loan" from the Howard Hughes organization to help him rescue a failing fast-food business that specialized in triple-decker sandwiches called "Nixonburgers." (The loan, which was never repaid, was secured by a $13,000 family plot that no bank would have accepted as security for a loan that size.) Reports of this transaction helped to defeat Nixon in his 1960 Presidential campaign and in his 1962 race for the governorship of California—and, ever since, he had been extremely sensitive about his brother's ties with the Hughes organization or other questionable enterprises.

Shortly after his brother Richard moved into the White House in 1969, Donald Nixon moved to Las Vegas. Haldeman and Ehrlichman asked the CIA to keep a watch on him to make sure he didn't fall under the influence of criminal figures there. The agency refused, noting that it had no jurisdiction to engage in domestic law enforcement or surveillance.

But a year later the Secret Service was ordered to install a tap on Donald Nixon's phone in Newport Beach, California. Ehrlichman assigned Caulfield to monitor the tap, in order to ascertain "whether or not persons of unsavory character might be attempting to embarrass the President through his brother." After about three weeks the tap had turned up no such evidence. The Secret Service recommended that it be terminated and Ehrlichman agreed.

The Secret Service also carried out some physical surveillance of the President's brother. Caulfield recalls being shown a photograph, apparently taken by Secret Service men in July 1969, of Donald Nixon and three other men at the Orange County Airport. One of the men was John Meier (then a "scientific adviser" to Hughes), who is now under indictment for income-tax evasion and for an alleged $8-million mining swindle. Another was Anthony Hatsis, who is suspected by congressional investigators of having connections with organized crime. The President had apparently been concerned about these associations and had asked his friend Bebe Rebozo to help keep Donald out of trouble. In early 1969 Rebozo had approached Richard Danner, an old friend who had once headed the FBI office in Miami, then had taken a leave of absence from his Washington law practice to work full time in the Nixon campaign, and had ended up that spring as manager of Hughes's Frontier Hotel in Las Vegas. Rebozo had asked Danner to keep Meier away from Donald Nixon. Now, in July, Danner got a phone call from Rebozo. "I thought I told you to keep Johnny Meier away from Don Nixon," Rebozo said. Danner said it had been taken care of. "The hell it has," replied Rebozo. "They're meeting right now." The Orange County Airport meeting was apparently taking place that very day—and Rebozo must have been tipped off through the Secret Service men trailing Donald. Three months later Meier left his job with Hughes, and some sources insist he was fired as a direct result of these events.

But a few weeks after the airport meeting, Meier was still with Don Nixon and Tony Hatsis, this time on a trip to the Dominican Republic to see President Joaquin Balaguer. Everybody involved in this curious meeting was trying to use someone else for his own purposes. Meier and Hatsis hoped that the President's brother could help persuade Balaguer to lease them mining rights for their Toledo Mining Company. Donald Nixon wanted Balaguer to let him construct apartment buildings on oceanside property owned by the Dominican Republic. And Balaguer thought Donald Nixon could persuade his brother to increase the Dominican sugar quota and thus help him in an upcoming election. The three visitors took over the entire floor of a hotel. President Balaguer assigned thirty armed guards to insure their safety and privacy, and their trip got a lot of attention in the Dominican press. (The three men presented Balaguer with a gift which Donald Nixon said was from his brother the President: ironically, it turned out to be a bust of Nixon's old archenemy, John Kennedy.) James Juliano, a Dominican sugar lobbyist who was one of Caulfield's prime sources, gave his friend at the White House a picture of the eminent visitors as clipped from a Dominican paper. Caulfield passed it on to Ehrlichman, intensifying the concern about Donald Nixon's curious behavior.

4

PLUMBERS

Anyone who opposes us, we'll destroy. As a matter of fact, anyone who doesn't support us, we'll destroy.

—Egil Krogh, Jr.,
to Daniel X. Freedman, chairman of the Psychiatry Department,
University of Chicago, July 27, 1971

On the morning of June 13, 1971, the Sunday edition of *The New York Times* plunked down on doorsteps along the East Coast bearing a laconic headline at the top of page one: "Vietnam Archive: Pentagon Study Traces 3 Decades of Growing U.S. Involvement." Inside were three more pages of stories and three pages of documents—the first installment of what were to become known as the Pentagon Papers.

Nixon's early reaction to the Papers' publication was remarkably relaxed. He told Republican congressional leaders at the White House the next Tuesday that since the massive Defense Department study of policy-making on Vietnam covered a period ending in early 1968, it was far more likely to embarrass former President Johnson and his aides than anyone in the Nixon administration. But a different attitude was emerging elsewhere in the White House, particularly in the office of Henry Kissinger.

Kissinger argued that unhindered publication of the papers could damage two sets of secret negotiations then under way: the highly sensitive feelers being put out through Pakistan to arrange Kissinger's trip to Peking (which, in turn, was to pave the way for the President's visit and the historic rapprochement with China); and, second, the secret negotiations which had been going on for nearly two years with North Vietnamese officials in Paris seeking an end to the Vietnam war. Kissinger argued that the Chinese and the North Vietnamese might back out of these negotiations because they feared the United States could not be counted on to negotiate secretly and keep confidences with other nations.

At the start, Chuck Colson recalls, Kissinger was clearly "more alarmed" than Nixon, but he quickly communicated his distress to the President. In the weeks following the Pentagon Papers' publication, Nixon and his chief aides held a series of meetings that Colson describes as "panic sessions." Kissinger took the lead at these meetings, demanding that further disclosure of classified information must be stopped "at all costs."

Within a few days the FBI identified Daniel J. Ellsberg as the "thief," and this seemed to provoke Kissinger even further. For Kissinger knew Ellsberg well and had dealt with him on Vietnam more than once. After the 1968 election, Kissinger had asked the Rand Corporation for a study of U.S. options in Vietnam and Rand had put Ellsberg to work on it. Ellsberg spent four days at Nixon's transition headquarters in New York's Hotel Pierre going over the options with Kissinger. He proposed as one option a unilateral and total U.S. withdrawal from Vietnam, but Kissinger deleted that one when he submitted the report to the National Security Council. (During this period, Ellsberg says, he warned Kissinger not to be seduced by classified information which was "a magic potion that turns ordinary human beings into arrogant, contemptuous menaces to democracy," but when he saw him some time later he concluded that Kissinger was "eating the secret honeydew".) In August 1970 Ellsberg had lunch with Kissinger and Lloyd Shearer of *Parade* magazine, and Kissinger told Ellsberg he would like to talk with him alone about the war. Several appointments were made and canceled (by Kissinger, Ellsberg says). In September 1970 Ellsberg and Kissinger met for a half hour in San Clemente, at which time, Ellsberg says, he urged Kissinger to study the then secret Pentagon Papers for their lessons on current policy formulation. Finally, in January 1971, Ellsberg and Kissinger had a tense confrontation at a weekend conference sponsored by MIT on an estate outside Boston. Following a speech by Kissinger, Ellsberg rose from the audience and asked him to estimate the Asian dead and wounded that would result from "Vietnamization" of the war. When Kissinger said one had to "consider the options," Ellsberg interrupted, "I know the option game, Dr. Kissinger. Can't you just give us an answer?" The two men glared angrily at each other, and the student moderator hastily ended the meeting.

Now, barely five months later, Kissinger apparently felt betrayed by a man he had once trusted. Ellsberg was a Harvard man, a graduate student at Cambridge University, a full-fledged "cold war intellectual," a Defense Department "whiz kid"—in short, a man out of the same mold as Kissinger and many of his staffers. (In many ways, Ellsberg's career had paralleled that of Mort Halperin's since their days at Harvard.) The intensity of Kissinger's feeling against Ellsberg may have reflected his sense that this association was now tainted and his eagerness to clear himself.

According to Ehrlichman, who met several times with Kissinger and Nixon to discuss the Pentagon Papers matter, Kissinger said Ellsberg was "a fanatic" and was "known to be a drug abuser," but he also had "knowledge of very critical defense secrets of current validity, such as nuclear deterrent targeting." Ehrlichman, "having never heard of Ellsberg before the theft of the papers," gathered from Kissinger's description "that the nation was presented with a very serious potential security problem."

On July 6 the President, John Ehrlichman, and John Mitchell met at the White House and, according to Ehrlichman, the attorney general said he believed Ellsberg had "Communist ties and was part of a conspiracy." The concern about a conspiracy was also fed by an FBI report which said that "a group in Massachusetts," had duplicated the Pentagon Papers in Cambridge. And there was further consternation when Robert Mardian reported that some of the papers had

been delivered to the Soviet embassy on June 17—
several days after the *Times* began publication—by a
man who also handed over a letter signed with an alias.
(The FBI's Washington field office maintained a
twenty-four-hour-a-day physical surveillance of the Soviet embassy on 16th Street, N.W., and filmed all persons who came and went. But the report on the Pentagon Papers' delivery more likely came from an informer
within the embassy. It has aroused much skepticism. Even CIA Director Richard Helms later told the
White House, "We know the fellow who is giving us
these reports and we have our doubts about them.")
Finally, some officials initially believed that thirty-one
of the forty-five documents appearing in the *Times* had
come not from the Pentagon Papers at all but from
other secret government sources. They were wrong, although the *Times*' first installments did include material
from the "Wheeler Report," a memorandum on the
Vietnam situation after the 1968 Tet offensive, prepared by General Earle C. Wheeler, chairman of the
Joint Chiefs of Staff.

White House assessments shifted almost daily during
this period, but after the initial uncertainty, Nixon and
his aides were not genuinely concerned about the damage done by actual publication of the papers. None of
Ehrlichman's notes from the midsummer meetings suggests any fear that vital secrets had been compromised.
And barely a month later, following another leak, the
President told his assistants: "This does affect the national security—this particular one. This isn't like the
Pentagon Papers."

Yet there were at least three genuine fears rampant
at the White House in those weeks. One was that Ellsberg—and his possible "co-conspirators"—might be
planning to release some really damaging secrets or pass
them along surreptitiously to the Soviets. Second, there
was fear that Ellsberg's action would inspire other radicals or liberals within the government bureaucracy to
leak further classified information to the press. (Nixon
believed that thousands of hostile bureaucrats were
waiting to do him in.) The last was a corollary concern—that conservatives might leak information about

the as yet secret Nixon-Kissinger plans for rapprochement with Moscow and Peking in an effort to sabotage them.

In part to discourage these possibilities, Nixon ordered the Justice Department to go into court seeking an unusual "prior restraint" on continued publication of the Pentagon Papers. On June 15 and 19 the government got temporary restraining orders against the *Times* and *The Washington Post,* but the Supreme Court permitted the newspapers to resume publication of the papers on June 30.

And the President demanded that further steps be taken to counteract what he called "the counter-government." Colson recalls that at a meeting in late June the President said, "I don't give a damn how it is done, do whatever has to be done to stop these leaks and prevent further unauthorized disclosures; I don't want to be told why it can't be done. This government cannot survive, it cannot function if anyone can run out and leak whatever documents he wants to. . . . I want to know who is behind this and I want the most complete investigation that can be conducted. . . . I don't want excuses. I want results. I want it done, whatever the cost."

But clearly the White House saw as much opportunity as threat in the Pentagon Papers flap. Ehrlichman's notes from a meeting with the President on June 17— just four days after the *Times* began publishing the papers—include a notation: "Win PR, not just court case." On June 25 Colson sent Haldeman a memo, noting that prosecution of Ellsberg would present a great opportunity. "He is a natural villain to the extent that he can be painted evil. We can very effectively make the point of why we [had] to do what we did with *The New York Times;* we can discredit the peace movement and we have the Democrats on a marvelous hook because thus far most of them have defended the release of the documents. . . . I have not yet thought through all of the subtle ways in which we can keep the Democratic party in a constant state of civil warfare, but I am convinced that with some imaginative and creative thought it can be done." And on July 1 Colson said in a telephone conversation, "This thing could go two ways. Ellsberg could be turned into a martyr of the New Left. He probably will anyway. Or it could be another Alger Hiss case, where the guy is exposed, other people were operating with him, and this may be the way to really carry it out. We might be able to put this bastard into a helluva situation and discredit the New Left."

Nixon also saw the Hiss case as a precedent for the Ellsberg case. Ehrlichman's assistant, Egil Krogh, recalls, "The President had directed that I read his book, *Six Crises,* and particularly the chapter on Alger Hiss, in preparation for this assignment." Nixon urged his book—and particularly the Hiss chapter—on his other aides too. The zealous Colson says he read it fourteen times.

Hiss and Ellsberg bear a certain surface similarity, enough to have intrigued Nixon, who came from such a different background. Both were privileged young men who studied at the best universities, traveled in the best circles, rose to prominence in Washington, and, though accused of treason, continued to draw fierce support from many of the "best people" in government, the universities, and the press.

In *Six Crises,* Nixon pictures Hiss as both a danger and an opportunity. (The intimate relationship between danger and opportunity is Nixon's main point about crisis. Drawing on a metaphor which William Safire lifted from a James Reston column, Nixon frequently talked about this in public and private: "The Chinese have a symbol for the word 'crisis.' One brush stroke stands for danger. The other brush stroke stands for opportunity. We must recognize the danger, but we must seize the opportunity. . . .") Nixon wrote, "The Hiss case, for the first time, forcibly demonstrated to the American people that domestic Communism was a real and present danger to the security of the nation." But he also wrote, "The Hiss case brought me national fame. I received considerable credit for spearheading the investigation which led to Hiss's conviction. Two years later I was elected to the United States Senate and two years after that, General Eisenhower introduced me as his running mate to the Republican National Convention as 'a man who has a special talent and an ability to ferret out any kind of subversive influence wherever it may be found and the strength and persistence to get rid of it.' "

In Dan Ellsberg, Nixon recognized the danger of Hiss and the opportunity of Hiss (and perhaps, as Gary Wills has suggested, the curse of Hiss, which threatened to destroy him just as it had Whittaker Chambers and Hiss himself). The danger was that the Chinese and the Russians—with whom he was seeking to negotiate—might now conclude that America couldn't keep secrets. The opportunity was that Ellsberg could be used to discredit Nixon's domestic opposition and to help assure his re-election.

To meet the danger and seize the opportunity, Nixon needed someone to "handle" Ellsberg the way he had handled Hiss. As early as June 25 Nixon told Colson, Haldeman, and Ehrlichman to find someone to supervise all aspects of the Pentagon Papers case. This time it was not to be the New York cop contingent which had handled most of the White House investigations so far. Sometime in the spring of 1971, John Caulfield noticed that he and Tony Ulasewicz were getting fewer assignments. "For some reason," a former White House aide recalls, "it was decided that Caulfield couldn't handle the really heavy stuff." Ellsberg and the Pentagon Papers were "heavy stuff."

At first, Haldeman and Ehrlichman wanted to give the job to Patrick J. Buchanan, a tough former newspaperman who was one of Nixon's speechwriters. But Buchanan declined in a July 8 memo which said, "There are some dividends to be derived from Project Ellsburg [*sic*]—but none to justify the magnitude of the investment recommended." Several other names were considered—among them, Richard V. Allen, a former member of Kissinger's staff who had been Nixon's first national security adviser during the 1968 campaign (ironically, Allen himself had been the target of a covert CIA investigation in 1968). In early July, with the selection still hanging fire, Nixon went to San Clemente. There, on July 12, he got a report on the Ellsberg investigation from Assistant Attorney General Mardian, who was still supervising the case. According to Ehrlichman, Nixon was "not satisfied with Mr. Mardian's report and insisted upon an early designation of a White House man-in-charge." Finally, on July 17, Ehrlichman gave the assignment jointly to David R. Young, Jr., a thirty-two-year-old lawyer whom he plucked from Kissinger's staff, and Egil Krogh, Jr., thirty-one, one of his own top assistants.

Many a noon those past few years, a lone figure in a gray sweatsuit could have been seen jogging around the Ellipse behind the White House. The runner was Egil "Bud" Krogh, Jr., who jogged five miles a day to keep in shape (twice he won the D.C. Roadrunners annual race). He was also a regular user of the Executive Office Building gym and the White House tennis courts. Krogh maintained a similar regimen in the rest of his life. One acquaintance described him as "a brisk, polite, dynamic young executive—he had all the facts, he'd done his homework. Never mussed, never damp, absolutely spic and span." Others called him "straight as an arrow" and "a very spiritual guy" (like Haldeman and Ehrlichman he was a Christian Scientist), and some liked to call him "Evil Krogh" because he was so patently the opposite. Born in Chicago, Krogh graduated in 1961 from Principia College, a Christian Science institution in Elsah, Illinois. From 1962 to 1965 he served as a communications officer in the Navy, then entered law school at the University of Washington, working part time in the Seattle law firm of Hullen, Ehrlichman, Roberts & Hodge. When he got his law degree in 1968, he joined a Stanford Research Institute team studying Vietnamese land reform for the Agency for International Development. But the next spring he accepted eagerly when his old boss, John Ehrlichman, then counsel to the President, invited him to become his deputy—an impressive post for a twenty-nine-year-old barely a year out of law school. As Ehrlichman rose in the White House hierarchy so did his protégé—to assistant director of the Domestic Council staff and executive director of the Cabinet Committee on International Narcotics Control. His specialties were transportation, narcotics, crime prevention, and corrections. Krogh was also the White House liaison with the District of Columbia, seeking to create "a new psychological climate" in the nation's capital. (Partly that meant law and order, he said, "but it doesn't mean repression. We're trying to create a respect for authority, not necessarily for power.") In that capacity, he was in the Secret Service command post on the White House lawn in the predawn hours of May 10, 1970, when the President suddenly appeared on his nighttime ramble to the Lincoln Memorial for a talk with the young people demonstrating against the Cambodian invasion. Krogh tagged along. Profoundly impressed by the President's earnest efforts to communicate with the demonstrators, he was ready to do anything Nixon asked him to do.

Now Krogh and Young headed an operation known cryptically as the Special Investigations Unit. Everything about the unit was studiedly covert. It was hidden away in Room 16 on the partially subterranean first floor of the Executive Office Building, next door to the White House. Room 16 was actually a warren of offices and a conference room, equipped with a special alarm system, a three-way combination safe, "sterile" telephones, and a "war room" with a cork bulletin board listing all their projects, the status of each, and the man responsible for its completion. Room 16 documents were stamped "ODESSA" to distinguish them from other classified papers at the White House. To insiders, the outfit was often known as "the Room 16 project," but soon it acquired another nickname. Kathleen Chenow, the twenty-three-year-old project secretary brought down from Capitol Hill, where she had worked for a Republican senator, recalls, "David Young's mother-in-law or grandmother or somebody saw in *The New York Times* that Krogh and Young were working on leaks. She called the story to his attention, saying, 'Your grandfather would be proud of you, working on leaks at the White House. He was a plumber.' So David put up a sign on the door which said 'Mr. Young—Plumber.' "

New urgency was attached to the Plumbers' work as a result of several other developments besides the Pentagon Papers. One was a story by Tad Szulc in *The New York Times*. An aggressive and resourceful reporter, Szulc had broken many stories based on classified information, so many that Ehrlichman referred to the "Szulc group" of stories. But one on August 13, 1971, was of special concern to the CIA because it was based on a report from one of its agents. That day, citing "intelligence reports," Szulc wrote, "Authoritative United States officials said today that they understood the Soviet Union succeeded in dissuading India from formally recognizing East Pakistan as an independent nation three days ago by quickly signing a friendship treaty with India." Some CIA officials apparently feared that Szulc's story could jeopardize a high-level CIA informant in the Indian government. Krogh was even told that the report had put the informant's life in danger, though this seems unlikely.

But the most significant news leak came three weeks before, when, on July 23, Bill Beecher had produced another of his annoying scoops. This one began, "American negotiators have proposed to the Soviet Union an arms control agreement that would halt construction of both land-based missiles and missile submarines," and went on to spell out the American proposals at the U.S.-Soviet SALT meetings under way in Helsinki. The story stirred rage in the White House. The Americans and Russians had a firm agreement not to release details of their proposals to the press. Not only was Beecher's article full of such details but it came out the morning before the U.S. delegation was to make its first presentation of the proposal to the Russians. Worse yet, it disclosed one of the American fall-back positions. Nevertheless, some observers believe the administration was worried less about the Soviet reaction than about domestic considerations, fearing that the proposal would now become the subject of political pulls and counterpulls at home.

The day after Beecher's SALT story appeared, Nixon, Ehrlichman, and Krogh met at the White House. Already, Krogh reported, they had a "prime suspect" —William Van Cleave, special assistant to the assistant secretary of defense for international security affairs, specializing in SALT and nuclear affairs matters. "He spent two hours with Beecher, apparently this week," Krogh told the President. "He had access to the document. He apparently had views very similar to those which were reflected in the Beecher article."

"I don't care whether he's a hawk or a dove or a—" the President exploded. "If the son-of-a-bitch leaked, he's not for the government . . . little people do not leak . . . this crap to the effect: well, a stenographer did it, or the waste pap—paper basket did it. It's never that case. I've studied these cases long enough, and it's always a son-of-a-bitch that leaks."

The three men agreed that some way had to be found to screen the "sons-of-bitches" out of the upper bureaucracy—probably through a new classification, for which officials would have to submit to a lie-detector test. The old classifications, they agreed, had been abused so often they were nearly meaningless.

NIXON: . . . Don't use TOP SECRET for me ever again. I never want to see TOP SECRET in this goddamn office. I think we just solved—shall we call it— Uh, John, what would be a good name? "President's Secure—" or, uh—"Eyes Only" is a silly thing, too. It doesn't mean anything any more. Uh—

KROGH: We used "Presidential Document" before with one of the counsel we were working with, but that didn't— There's some—

EHRLICHMAN: How about— Uh, uh, looking forward to the court case, I wonder if we could get the words "national security" in it.

NIXON: Yeh. . . .

EHRLICHMAN: How about "Privilege"?

NIXON: "Privilege" is, is not strong.

EHRLICHMAN: Too soft. Too soft.

NIXON: "National Security—" uh, "National Security—" uh—

EHRLICHMAN: "Restricted." "Restricted."

NIXON: Right. "National Security—" and, uh— I agree to "National, Na—, National Security—"

EHRLICHMAN: "Restriction"?

NIXON: "Priority."

EHRLICHMAN: "Controlled"?

NIXON: Or "National Security"—"Priority"—"Restricted"—"Controlled."

EHRLICHMAN: Oh, well—let us work on it.

In subsequent statements, White House officials have given the impression that Beecher's story and others based on classified information were part of a plot orchestrated by the radical left and abetted by its allies in government. But the known facts do not support that premise. The precise identity of Beecher's sources has never been revealed. The Plumbers grilled Van Cleave and gave him two lie-detector tests, administered by the CIA in apparent violation of the statute that bars the agency from domestic operations. (Van Cleave says he passed both. Three months later, he returned to his job as professor of international relations at the University of Southern California. He says his departure was on schedule after two years of leave at the Pentagon, but there is some evidence that the White House still blamed him for the SALT leak and was by no means unhappy to see him go.) The CIA also administered lie-detector tests to three State Department officials known to have talked to Beecher during this period, but a department spokesman said in June 1973 that the officials still occupied "positions of responsibility." Some believe Beecher's story came from Pentagon officials who wanted to sabotage the SALT meetings because they disapproved of any rapprochement with Russia; others think it came from those who wanted to "freeze" the U.S. negotiating position. But it almost certainly came from government officials with no current ties to Dan Ellsberg or to the Weathermen.

By then, it hardly mattered where it came from. Many men in the White House apparently felt events closing in, as if somehow all the people on their "enemies list" had joined hands to destroy them. In part, their fears involved national security considerations, but plainly there were political considerations, too. The President knew that he was going to be campaigning for re-election largely in Peking and Moscow. Any obstacles on the road to those two capitals also blocked his parallel campaign trail. Part of the problem in succeeding months may have been the inability of Nixon and the men around him adequately to distinguish between those two thoroughfares.

Not surprisingly as Chuck Colson sought more skilled hands to plug the leaks during that summer of 1971, he turned to an outfit which curiously intermingled the Nixon administration's political and national security interests—Robert R. Mullen & Company. Specifically, he approached a man whom he had first come to know at the Brown University Club of Washington during the late 1960s when, for a year, he was president and his friend was vice president. That friend was E. Howard Hunt.

"We become lawless in a struggle for the rule of law —semi-outlaws who risk their lives to put down the savagery of others," says Peter Ward, a CIA agent in the novel Hazardous Duty *by David St. John—also known as John Baxter, Gordon Davis, Robert Dietrich, and Howard Hunt. The forty-six published novels that Hunt has written under these names reflect the curious amalgam of luxuriant fantasy and actual skullduggery to be found in the life of Everette Howard Hunt, Jr. In part his books are based on his own twenty-three years as a CIA agent in Mexico City, Madrid, Tokyo, and Montevideo. A specialist in "dirty tricks," he was assigned as "chief of political action" in the 1954 overthrow of the left-wing Guatemalan government. And in 1960, operating under the code name "Eduardo," he helped forge Cuban exile leaders into a provisional government which would take over after the Bay of*

Pigs operation. But Hunt, who identified strongly with the old-line Batista forces, regarded many of the exiles assigned to him as dangerous "leftists." Ultimately, he was forced out of this job and followed the abortive invasion from a CIA "war room" in Virginia. Hunt says that he, like others who had participated in the Bay of Pigs debacle, were "made to feel like pariahs and were discriminated against with regard to subsequent assignments." When the CIA established its Domestic Operations Division, Hunt was named its chief of covert action and thus, he recalls, was forced to handle projects not wanted by others in the agency. During 1964, he contends, he was ordered to have some of his agents collect information from the campaign headquarters of the Republican Presidential candidate, Barry Goldwater, and deliver it to the CIA liaison man in Lyndon Johnson's White House. An ardent Goldwater man, Hunt says, "I allowed my subordinates to carry out this domestic political mission, seeing myself not as a partisan political appointee but rather as a career officer of the CIA whose professionalism required that he respond to the orders of whatever administration might be in power." But his institutional loyalty won him few points. Increasingly regarded as a "burnt-out case," he was blocked from further promotions and apparently given tedious assignments to nudge him into early retirement. Hunt began looking for a job. Through Frank O'Malley of the agency's External Employment Assistance Branch, he got in touch with Robert Mullen, whom Hunt had known when they were both with the ECA in Paris in the late 1940s. On April 30, 1970, Hunt "retired" from the agency and the next day he went to work for Mullen & Company. But the circumstances are curious. Hunt knew of the company's CIA connections; Mullen understood that Hunt's new job had Richard Helms's "blessing"; and, oddest of all, Hunt's "covert security clearance" was continued after he joined Mullen. But for the time being, his assignments were pedestrian public relations and Hunt missed the old life desperately. "You see, our government trains people like myself to do these things and do them successfully," he explained later.

"It becomes a way of life for a person like me." In retirement, he lived out the riper reveries from his own book: French food, wine, and the elegant life *("The service plates were Revere gadroon, the crystal was an opaline much favored by the Sun King's sycophants. . . ."),* exciting women *("Oh, Jake,"* breathes the senator's wife in The Coven, *"oh, you bastard. You brutal goddamn woman killer"),* and truly uninhibited espionage *(the former agent in* The Berlin Ending *thinks the CIA has "grown old and cautious. Prim. Reliant on technology far more than human beings").* He yearned for some action.

Hunt had a nose for power and he could smell it on Chuck Colson (whom he regarded as "a dynamo around which spun large and powerful wheels"). So he cultivated Colson carefully. The two families lived near each other and they sometimes dined together or visited on weekends. Sometimes they were joined by Bob Bennett, whom Colson had helped take over Mullen & Company, and the three men would talk about Republican politics. Colson was impressed by Hunt's hard-nosed style and began recommending him for administration jobs. In early 1970 the White House was thinking of organizing something variously called the Institute for an Informed America or the Silent Majority Institute, a conservative think tank that would do for the Republicans what The Brookings Institution did for the Democrats. Colson thought Hunt might make a good director of the institute and sent him to see Jeb Magruder, who was coordinating the project. Hunt struck Magruder as "bright, articulate, and highly conservative," but Hunt then followed up by sending Magruder an outline for turning the institute into a base for covert political activity. Magruder told Colson he didn't think Hunt was right for the job because he had "a cloak-and-dagger orientation."

That never struck Colson as a serious drawback. Indeed, when the White House was looking for someone to head up the Pentagon Papers investigation, Colson called Hunt to sound him out for the job.

COLSON: Let me ask you this, Howard, this question. Do you think, with the right resources employed, that this thing could be turned into a major public case against Ellsberg and co-conspirators?

HUNT: Yes, I do, but you've established a qualification here that I don't know whether it can be met.

COLSON: What's that?

HUNT: Well, with the proper resources.

COLSON: Well, I think the resources are there.

HUNT: Well, I would say so absolutely.

COLSON: Then your answer would be we should go down the line to nail the guy cold?

HUNT: Go down the line to nail the guy cold, yes. . . .

Colson transcribed the conversation and sent it on to Ehrlichman with a note: "The more I think about Howard Hunt's background, politics, disposition, and experience, the more I think it would be worth your time to meet him. I had forgotten when I talked to you that he was the CIA mastermind on the Bay of Pigs. He told me a long time ago that if the truth were ever known, Kennedy would be destroyed."

On July 7 Colson took Hunt in to meet Ehrlichman, who didn't think the former agent was the man to head up the operation but agreed to hire him as a White House "consultant." He was engaged effective the day before at $100 a day. Hunt was assigned Room 338, a small office on the third floor of the Executive Office Building (although he retained his job at Mullen & Company, where he worked, among other things, on a HEW project on handicapped children and produced a television spot on the subject featuring Julie Nixon Eisenhower). Colson says Hunt was assigned to his staff for "internal budget" reasons only. But Hunt says he worked under Colson's direction for the next year on a wide variety of matters, most of which had nothing to do with the Pentagon Papers.

Colson had already been placed in charge of the public-relations end of the Pentagon Papers operation —the effort to discredit Ellsberg and link him with Democratic politicians. For that purpose, he told Hunt he wanted him to become "the resident expert on the origins of the Vietnam war," and told him he should interview people who might throw light on the war. Since Hunt was told that such interviews should be on a "quasi-covert basis," he asked the White House to arrange CIA disguises.

Colson relayed the request to Ehrlichman who, on July 7, called Marine General Robert E. Cushman, Jr., then the CIA's deputy director, to say: "I want to alert you that an old acquaintance, Howard Hunt, has been asked by the President to do some special-consultant work on security problems. He may be contacting you sometime in the future for some assistance. I wanted you to know that he was in fact doing some things for the President. He is a longtime acquaintance with the people here. You should consider he has pretty much carte blanche. . . ."

From Ehrlichman's description, Cushman could not be sure just what Hunt's mission was—whether, for example, it would violate the law (already honored in the breach) prohibiting the CIA from engaging in, or assisting, domestic intelligence-gathering. But there is no indication that he asked for further clarification. From the general's point of view, he had several good reasons to accede to the request on faith. First, he assumed that Ehrlichman was speaking on behalf of the President. Second, Cushman had great personal loyalty to the President, having served as his military aide when Nixon was Vice President and evidently owing his high CIA post to that tie. Finally, he knew Howard Hunt well, from the time they had shared an office during the spring of 1950 in the CIA's clandestine division, and regarded him as "a highly respected and honorably retired CIA employee." (There are those who believe that Hunt had never really resigned from the CIA and was still acting more or less on behalf of the agency.)

On July 22 Hunt went to see Cushman in his office at the CIA's secluded Langley, Virginia, headquarters. Hunt told his old friend, "I've been charged with quite a highly sensitive mission by the White House to visit and elicit information from an individual whose ideology we aren't entirely sure of, and for that purpose they asked me to come over here and see if you could get me two things: flash alias identification, which wouldn't have to be backstopped, and some degree of physical disguise, for a one-time op—in and out."

And Cushman replied, "I don't see why we can't."

The two men chatted for another few minutes about how they kept their weight down—Hunt missed his daily workouts at the CIA gym—and the general promised to have somone call Hunt at the White House the next day. On July 23 he was summoned to a "safe house"—a clandestine CIA meeting place—on upper Wisconsin Avenue near the National Cathedral where Stephen C. Greenwood, a representative of the CIA's Technical Services Division, furnished him with a red wig, thick glasses, and a speech-alteration device (a plate which fits into the mouth and produces a lisp) as well as a Social Security card, a driver's license, and several association cards and other "pocket litter" in the name of Edward Joseph Warren. (From his active days with the agency, Hunt retained the alias Edward J. Hamilton. In September 1960 he had obtained a District of Columbia driver's license with the name erroneously recorded as Edward V. Hamilton. He later opened a post office box in that name and was issued several club and association cards which he used as identification in future years.) Two weeks later, Hunt —who called himself merely "Mr. Edward"—asked for a tape recorder. Cleo Gephart of Technical Services met him at the safe house and gave him a Uher stereo recorder and two Sony microphones, all concealed in a used portable typewriter case. (Gephart says he had been told by his superiors to provide "all possible assistance" to the man called "Mr. Edward" who he assumed was a CIA staff officer assigned to the executive branch or some other area of the agency's domestic division.)

Hunt used his disguise and the tape recorder to investigate Senator Ted Kennedy. Those summer months of 1971 were a boom time for Kennedy. A Gallup Poll released on May 16 had shown that 29 per cent of registered Democrats favored him for the 1972 nomination, with only 21 per cent for Edmund Muskie, the previous front-runner. Rumors circulated in Washington that the Kennedy clan was already charting campaign strategy at Hyannis Port. So the White House—which had earlier assigned Caulfield to dog the senator's steps—reactivated the Kennedy watch and actively sought ways to discredit him.

After boning up on Jack Olsen's *The Bridge at Chappaquiddick* and other Kennedy books taken from the White House library, Hunt traveled to Providence, Rhode Island, where he met for two hours at a motel near the airport with Clifton DeMotte, a General Services Administration employee, who was also known to be a Kennedy watcher by avocation, having followed the family's activities closely ever since he worked as a "public-relations man" in a Hyannis Port hotel in 1960. Hunt asked him about Chappaquiddick, about any "woman-chasing by the Kennedy boys," "any scandal-type material." DeMotte passed along some hearsay on "real swinging parties" and "booze" and some harder information on "hell-raising" by Kennedy staffers. But when Hunt asked him to do some research on Chappaquiddick, DeMotte turned him down, partly because Hunt refused to say who he was working for.

Although Bob Bennett had suggested the DeMotte interview, in his Kennedy investigations Hunt was clearly working for Chuck Colson. Colson harbored an intense dislike of Ted Kennedy—he has said that if he had run into the senator after his 1970 denunciations of Nixon "I might have attacked him physically." Like Colson, Hunt was a Brown man who resented the rich prigs from Harvard. "JFK and I were college contemporaries," he writes, "and I had met him at a Boston debut where he was pointed out to me as the son of a leading importer of Scotch whisky. The young man was dozing in a corner chair and I freely confess not having discerned in his relaxed lineaments the future naval hero, Pulitzer laureate, senator and President." Hunt's book *The Coven*—which he wrote during the early 1970s—features a Senator Newbold Vane who is certainly patterned after one or all of the Kennedys: "The Vanes were nonserious people who demanded to

be taken seriously. . . . The Vanes are legally married
to each other and that's about all. He's a terror among
the chicks and she gets her jollies from the artists,
writers, and beach-boy types Vane gets public grants
for. . . . Their whole imperious life-style was preposterous. Vane was about as qualified to be President as
I was to practice open-heart surgery." But Hunt's grievance against Kennedy stemmed chiefly from the President's role in the Bay of Pigs. When the invasion
foundered on the beach, partly for lack of air support,
Hunt was "sick of lying and deception, heartsick over
political compromise and military defeat." Kennedy,
he says, "rightfully assum[ed] sole blame for the
fiasco," but then began a subterranean campaign "to
whitewash the New Frontier by heaping guilt on the
CIA." In his book on the operation, Hunt exclaims,
"How ironic it seemed that Kennedy's successful campaign against Nixon had been largely waged—and won
—on his promise to aid the Cuban exiles in their
struggle against communism." (Indeed, Hunt's admiration of Nixon often seems to be the flip side of his
hatred of Kennedy. He had admired Nixon's pursuit of
Alger Hiss and told him so at a brief meeting in a
Washington restaurant in the 1960s. They met again
when Nixon, as Vice President, visited Montevideo,
where Hunt was then CIA station chief. But his particular loyalty to Nixon stemmed from the days when
the Vice President served as secret White House "action officer" for the Bay of Pigs and showed himself,
so Hunt believes, "determined that it should not fail."
Clearly, Hunt believed that if Nixon had beaten Kennedy in 1960 the Cuban invasion the next year would
not have failed and Hunt would not have become an
outcast in his own agency.)

Nixon too thought John Kennedy's memory was vulnerable on the Bay of Pigs. All summer he pressed his
aides to get out the story of that debacle. Six days after
Hunt was hired—in part because Colson had said he
was "the CIA mastermind on the Bay of Pigs"—the
President suggested that they arrange to have "Hunt's
memoirs" published in *Look* magazine. Later, the CIA

was told to deliver the "full" Bay of Pigs file to the White House "or else."

But for some reason Nixon then largely abandoned the Bay of Pigs gambit to focus on another of Kennedy's foreign-policy "blunders"—the 1963 coup against President Ngo Dinh Diem of South Vietnam. Hunt was instructed to mine the Pentagon Papers—his nominal concern—for material on this. During much of July he combed through the papers, which clearly showed that Kennedy had known of, approved, and—through the CIA—actively supported the coup against Diem. Soon Hunt, under Colson's direction, attempted to go one step further—to show that the Kennedy administration had some direct complicity in the murder of Diem and his brother Ngo Dinh Nhu, an allegation the papers did not seem to support.

To dig up more information, Hunt interviewed retired General Paul D. Harkins, who had been commander of U.S. forces in Vietnam at the time. He also called an old friend, Lieutenant Colonel Lucien Conein, who had been the CIA's liaison man with the Vietnamese plotters. On July 8 Conein came down to the White House and he and Hunt had a long talk over drinks in Ehrlichman's office, which Hunt had bugged for the occasion. The tape recorder malfunctioned and Hunt drank so much that he forgot the pertinent details, so they did it all over again the next day by telephone, with Colson participating this time in the guise of a White House security man named "Fred Charles."

At the President's news conference on September 16, Peter Lisagor of the Chicago *Daily News* asked about a statement by Senator Henry Jackson that the President possessed great leverage in Vietnam because of the U.S. aid program. Nixon replied, "If what the senator is suggesting is that the United States should use its leverage now to overthrow Thieu, I would remind all concerned that the way we got into Vietnam was through overthrowing Diem, and the complicity in the murder of Diem." This answer puzzled White House and State Department officials who say they do not know where the President got such information. They say there was nothing to support it in the briefing book prepared for that press conference, nor in any position paper or research document they know of.

Two days later, at a meeting with Haldeman, Ehrlichman, and Mitchell, the President discussed a political strategy which would keep the origins of the Vietnam war "front and center" so that the Democrats would "squabble about it." They agreed that the "Diem incident" was the "best ground" for attack because it involved both Averell Harriman—a Muskie supporter—and Ted Kennedy. Nixon suggested that several Republican senators might pick up his accusation of September 16 and "demand that Conein be released from the silence" required by CIA regulations. "Let the CIA take a whipping on this," Nixon said, demanding that the agency deliver its "entire Diem file" immediately.

The CIA handed over some documents, but Helms refused to turn over the full file without talking with Nixon personally. So Ehrlichman renewed a request made by David Young a month before for access to all cables between the State Department and the American embassy in Saigon for the period April–November 1963. This time the request was granted in twenty-four hours. On September 20 Hunt went to the file room at the department and had some 240 cables photocopied. He says his suspicions were aroused because "the closer one approached the assassination period, the more frequently were cables missing from chronological sequence."

After about a week, Colson asked him, "What kind of material have you dug up in the files that would indicate Kennedy complicity in Diem's death?" Hunt said that nobody who read the cables could have any doubt about it, but no single cable would establish it. "You'd have to take a sequence of three or four cables, be aware of their context, and speculate on what was contained in the cables missing from the sequence." According to Hunt, Colson asked, "Do you think you could improve on them?" Hunt said he would need technical assistance, particularly in finding the original typewriters on which the cables had been typed. "Well, we won't be able to give you any technical help," Hunt recalls Colson saying. "This is too hot. See what you can do on your own."

Using a razor blade and a White House Xerox machine, Hunt pieced together two fake cables. One purported to be a query from the American embassy in Saigon asking what it should do if Diem and his brother should seek asylum there. The other was a response from the State Department dated October 29, 1963—three days before Diem's death. It began, "At highest level meeting today, decision reluctantly made that neither you nor Harkins should intervene in behalf of Diem or Nhu in event they seek asylum." (Not only did no such cable exist but the Pentagon Papers suggest that the American embassy on the contrary was concerned about Diem's safety. In a telephone conversation Ambassador Henry Cabot Lodge told Diem, "If I can do anything for your physical safety, please telephone me." Senate investigators later concluded that the assassination of Diem was considered by U.S. officials at one time, but "specifically rejected at high levels as a means of implementing national policy.")

Hunt says he and Colson were trying to "demonstrate that a Catholic U.S. administration had in fact conspired in the assassination of a Catholic chief of state of another country" or—to quote a Hunt memo of that summer—"as Madame Nhu said at the time, the blood of Diem and Nhu is on Kennedy's hands." This, Colson felt, would hurt Ted Kennedy with Catholic voters in 1972.

Hunt says he showed the fake cable to Colson, who said he would try to get it into the hands of a reporter. The reporter he had in mind was William Lambert of *Life* magazine, to whom Colson had fed information on Senator Tydings in 1970. Sometime during the week of September 19–25, Lambert stopped by to see Colson, who told him there was more to the Diem assassination than showed up in the Pentagon Papers. He suggested that Lambert look at Nixon's response in the news conference the week before.

On September 24 Colson sent Ehrlichman a memo saying that if the White House gave Lambert access to government officials and "certain documents which have not been published" Lambert would "make it a major *Life* exposé—the true story behind the Diem coup. He would also put someone else's by-line on the story (the press would surely recall that Lambert was the author of the Tydings story). . . . The *Life* operation could be run completely by Howard Hunt working out of his home or his private office. Lambert would further construct an elaborate cover and slant the story in such a way that it would appear to be the product of Conein and/or State."

Colson soon sent Lambert to see Hunt, who showed him the fake cables. According to Hunt, "Mr. Lambert was quite exultant over the find," but the reporter kept asking to borrow the cables long enough to photograph them. This Hunt and Colson refused to permit—for fear that the bogus typewriter face would be discovered. Lambert was never able to satisfy himself of the cable's authenticity before *Life* folded in December 1972. Only in May 1973 did Colson tell Lambert that the cable was a fake, although he said he had learned that by February 1972. Colson emphatically denies ordering Hunt to fabricate the cable, but he concedes, "It is entirely possible that Hunt misunderstood something I said to him at the time he was reviewing Pentagon Papers cables with me."

On September 22 Ehrlichman met with Helms and told him the President wanted CIA files not only on Vietnam and the Bay of Pigs but also on the Cuban missile crisis of 1962 and the 1958 landing of U.S. troops in Lebanon. On October 1 Helms turned over most of the requested materials, but declined to provide the file on the Diem coup. On October 8 the President summoned Helms to the White House to forcefully renew his demand for the Vietnam file. He explained his unusual command by saying that he needed to be fully informed on this matter so he could "duck" embarrassing issues at international negotiations scheduled for 1972. Nixon promised to neither "hurt the agency nor attack [his] predecessors." At this, Helms conceded, "There is only one President at a time. I only work for you." Then he handed over the Vietnam file, which

Nixon slipped into his desk drawer. Ehrlichman, who
sat in on the meeting, said he would be "making requests for additional material" and the compliant
Helms said, "Okay, anything."

But the White House had largely dropped the Diem
project by then. Ultimately, Hunt did manage to foist
the bogus cables on someone—his friend Lucien
Conein, who had been invited to appear on an NBC
News *White Paper: Vietnam Hindsight*. When Hunt
showed him the cables, Conein said, "Funny, the things
you don't know about when you're working in the
field." By that time, he had already been interviewed
for the show, but the White House persuaded the network that Conein had vital new information to provide
and the interview was filmed over again. The documentary was shown in two parts on December 22 and 23,
1971. Reviewing the second part, "The Death of Diem,"
for *The New York Times,* Neil Sheehan remarked particularly on Conein's interview, saying that Conein
"leaves the viewer with little doubt about the extent of
United States implication" in Diem's death.

By midsummer 1971 Hunt was spending much of
his time with the Plumbers. Colson says Ehrlichman instructed him that Hunt should work with Krogh,
and on July 22 he introduced the two men and told
Hunt of his new assignment. Meanwhile, two other investigators had been added to the squad. One was Walter Minnick, who worked for the Cabinet Committee on
International Narcotics Control, of which Krogh was
the executive director. As a temporary Plumber, Minnick continued to work on drug matters for Krogh. The
other new man, G. Gordon Liddy, had been forced
out of the Treasury Department only weeks before, after he had vigorously lobbied against the administration's gun-control legislation and had even delivered
a rousing speech against such controls before the hun-
dredth-anniversary convention of the National Rifle
Association. But all that was no disqualification for

work with the Plumbers. He was recommended by Egil Krogh and hired (at $26,000 a year) by Ehrlichman on July 19.

Gordon Liddy loves guns. An FBI man in the early 1960s, he recalls that he "bailed out of a moving car and outdrew" a most-wanted fugitive. (By the mid-1960s he had bailed out of the FBI too, and some people say he was "encouraged" to leave because his superiors feared what he might some day do with a gun. One former FBI official described him as "a wild man" and "a superklutz.") As an assistant district attorney in Dutchess County, New York, he rode around with a gun strapped to his shoulder, and once, while summing up a robbery case to the jury, he pulled a pistol out of his pocket and fired it at the ceiling. Liddy had a knack for publicity: "He could turn the most routine case into an earth-shattering event when it hit the papers," a former colleague recalls. In 1966 Liddy took public credit for a drug raid on Timothy Leary which, according to a Poughkeepsie lawyer, "he had very little to do with." "Gordon's a cowboy," says a former political rival. "He wanted to go back to the days when men were men and life was simpler." Liddy liked to keep things simple, even elemental. "He hates the other side," Nixon said of him. His view of life was almost Nietzschean: the Triumph of the Will. "The master who instructed me in the deadliest of the Oriental martial arts taught me that the outcome of a battle is decided in the minds of the opponents before the first blow is struck," Liddy wrote. "Nature is elitist. By definition, not everyone can be a member of an elite, but it is of the nature of men to try." His motto was "duty, loyalty, patriotism." In 1968 Liddy ran in a Republican primary against the district's incumbent Congressman Hamilton Fish, Jr. His campaign literature featured a larger-than-life picture of him shining a police spotlight at a crowd of angry blacks: "He knows the answer is law and order, not weak-kneed sociology. Gordon Liddy doesn't bail them out—he puts them in." (Liddy would give a poster-size copy of the picture to any woman who would take one.) Although he lost the primary, Liddy had the Conservative party nomination. This put him in an ideal position to deal—and deal he did. Although his name remained on the ballot, as state law required, he did not campaign, enabling Fish to win by 5000 votes. Grateful Republicans helped him to get a job with the Treasury Department, where he became a special assistant to the secretary for Organized Crime and where he helped to administer Operation Intercept, an inept blockade of the Mexican border ostensibly intended to halt drug traffic. Liddy brought his gun collection and his macho style with him to Washington. Once he burned his hand badly when he held it over a candle flame to impress some friends. And he liked to demonstrate how you could kill someone with a pencil. This involved bracing the eraser end in your palm and ramming the point into the victim's neck, just above the Adam's apple. He recommended that the pencil be freshly sharpened.

Hunt liked Liddy immediately because he was "decisive and action-oriented, impatient with paperwork and the lucubrations of bureaucracy." They began lunching together in the White House cafeteria and having an afternoon drink or two at one of Hunt's cherished social clubs—the Army and Navy Club or the Tavern Inn. Hunt was also impressed by Krogh's "skill" and "decisiveness," but regarded Young as a "paperpusher" with a passion for tennis.

While Hunt continued to work on several projects (including the Kennedy investigations) for Colson, as Plumbers he and Liddy quickly turned their attention to Ellsberg. For if Ted Kennedy was the first of the "them," by midsummer 1971 Dan Ellsberg was a very close second.

Nixon has said he told Egil Krogh that "as a matter of first priority the [Special Investigations] unit should find out all it could about Mr. Ellsberg's associates and his motives." Ehrlichman and Krogh have both testified that the White House began its own investigation of Ellsberg because the FBI was dragging its feet. White

House aides complained that the bureau had not even designated the Ellsberg case as a "primary," or priority, one. The White House may also have been suspicious when it learned that the FBI had known that Ellsberg was copying classified papers at the Rand Corporation as early as January 1970. But knowledgeable sources suggest that this original investigation was a routine one, produced no evidence of espionage, and was dropped.

The bureau's lack of enthusiasm for the Ellsberg case was often attributed at the White House to Hoover's friendship with Louis Marx, the wealthy toy manufacturer who was the father of Ellsberg's second wife, Patricia. On several counts this seemed improbable. Hoover and Marx were only casual race-track acquaintances (though every Christmas Marx sent Hoover a load of toys for his friends' children and favorite charities). Moreover, it seems doubtful that the ultraconservative millionaire would have resisted an FBI interview or tried to protect his son-in-law whose politics he despised (Marx refused to contribute to the Ellsberg defense fund).

But Hoover often acted improbably and he did try to shield Marx from an interview. Charles D. "Chick" Brennan, the new assistant director for domestic intelligence, sent Hoover a memo in June 1971 recommending that Marx be interviewed. Hoover rejected it, but his response did not reach Brennan until agents had already conducted the interview (which produced little of value). Hoover flew into a rage, demoted Brennan to inspector, then reassigned him as agent-in-charge of the Alexandria, Virginia, office.

The FBI foot-dragging evidently stemmed not only from the Hoover-Marx friendship but from the director's characteristic effort to protect himself from criticism by press and public. According to reliable information from within the bureau, Hoover realized quickly that the Ellsberg case did not involve espionage. Instead, he saw it as a political battle between the administration and the press—a battle in which he could only get hurt. Therefore, he reportedly told his subordinates to do only what they had to do on the matter.

White House dissatisfaction with the FBI's performance had still another focus: the bureau was unwilling or unable to find the grand conspiracy which the President's men kept seeking in the case. An August memo from Young to Ehrlichman reported that the FBI alone still regarded Ellsberg as "the sole prime mover." Justice and Defense Department investigators—and apparently the Plumbers themselves—were said to feel that "substantial evidence is being developed for the criminal prosecution of individuals other than Ellsberg," and that such individuals might be in touch with "still another and even larger network." The prime targets of the investigation were identified then as Paul Warnke, a former assistant secretary of defense for international security affairs, who once exercised some remote supervision over the Pentagon Papers project; Mort Halperin, who had been Warnke's deputy; Leslie Gelb, director of the Vietnam History Task Force, which produced the Papers; and certain officials of the Rand Corporation. The White House also wanted to implicate Clark Clifford, President Johnson's last secretary of defense. Not coincidentally, Clifford, Warnke, Halperin, and Gelb were by then all serving as advisers to Senator Muskie.

Gelb and Halperin were then at The Brookings Institution. In early July Colson obtained an outline of the "foreign-policy studies" under way at Brookings, and found one of them particularly intriguing: "U.S. Policy and Vietnam—the Lessons Learned" was described in the prospectus as "a balanced and accurate history of our Vietnam experience, written with fidelity and judiciousness, while memories of the principal actors are still fresh." The study was being conducted by Gelb—who had left the Pentagon in May 1969—and his work would occasionally be reviewed by an advisory committee including both Halperin and Ellsberg. (For balance, the committee also included such establishment figures as John J. McCloy, former president of the Council on Foreign Relations.) On July 6 Colson sent the prospectus to Ehrlichman with a memo saying, "It looks to me like we may soon expect another installment in the Pentagon Papers written by the same authors but doubtless more up to date. You will note that this report is dated August 1969 and the indication is a two-year study was to be conducted which would mean that we could expect something dropping on us this fall. In my opinion, this should be promptly investigated. . . ."

A few days later, John Caulfield recalls, Colson called him into his office and said he had talked with people in the Presidential party, then at San Clemente, who felt there was "a high priority need to obtain papers from the office of a gentleman named Leslie Gelb" at Brookings. According to Caulfield, Colson suggested that the papers could be obtained through a rather ingenious scheme: "The suggestion was that the fire regulations in the District of Columbia could be changed to have the FBI respond to the scene of any fire in the District and that if there were to be a fire at the Brookings Institute [sic] that the FBI could respond and obtain the file in question from Mr. Leslie Gelb's office." Caulfield felt the implication was clear that he should start the fire, perhaps with a fire bomb.

Caulfield says he quickly excused himself and "literally ran" to John Dean's office, where he pleaded for Dean to get him out of the "asinine" assignment. Dean says Caulfield told him that Tony Ulasewicz had already "cased" Brookings, made "friendly contact" with a security man, and found the security system "extremely tight." According to Gelb, the truth was quite the contrary: "There was only one guard downstairs and you could usually get by him by saying you were on your way to see so-and-so. Or you could certainly have waited in the garage for somebody to come down and then slip right past him and go up the elevator. Once you got to the fifth floor, you would have found my office unlocked and all my papers right on the desk or in the bookcases. But I'm afraid they would have been pretty disappointed with what they found there: three bookcases full of books on Vietnam, some card files, and drafts of chapters on Vietnam during the Roosevelt and Truman administrations."

Dean says he told Caulfield to "do nothing further." He caught a courier flight to California, sitting next to Robert Mardian, who was on his way to see the President about the secret wiretapping logs and the Ellsberg case. (Mardian told Dean he was involved in "a highly important matter" which he could not even discuss with the counsel to the President.) At San Clemente, Dean says, he persuaded Ehrlichman that the Brookings burglary was "insane" and Ehrlichman called Colson to cancel it. Colson denies the whole story, although an associate says he may have suggested the fire-bomb burglary as a "joke."

All that summer, Colson has testified, Nixon put pressure on him to spread damaging reports about Ellsberg and tie him in to a grand conspiracy with the New Left and the Democrats.* In August, for example, Colson assigned Hunt to write an article about Leonard Boudin, Ellsberg's attorney, which Hunt did in his most electric spy-novel style: "The art of espionage, of course, is seldom conducted in the open, for its very success depends upon those involved remaining hidden from public view. Nevertheless, it has been said with some certainty that over the years Leonard Boudin has been a contact of both the Czech and Soviet espionage organizations, the latter best known by its initials, KGB. . . ." The handout was passed on to J. F. ter-Horst, Washington correspondent of the *Detroit News.* Hunt says it "formed the second half of a story" that terHorst wrote about the Ellsberg defense fund. (terHorst denies this and, although his story uses some of the same material, Hunt's claim seems wildly exaggerated.)

Meanwhile, the Plumbers were zeroing in on Ellsberg himself. Colson and Ehrlichman pressed for information that could damage Ellsberg's public standing. This would be helpful in preparing for the trial, for a congressional investigation which Colson was trying to stimulate, and, naturally, for the broad publicity campaign being organized against Ellsberg and his collaborators. In a memorandum to Ehrlichman on July 14 Colson said, "I think what is urgently needed is an as-

---

*Later, Colson pleaded guilty to obstruction of justice in this propaganda campaign against Ellsberg and was sentenced to one to three years in prison. He was released after serving only seven months because of "severe family difficulties."

sessment of how good our information is and how effective we can be in putting our case together."

Colson asked Hunt to study the matter and, on July 28, Hunt sent a memo entitled "Neutralization of Ellsberg," listing a series of steps designed to build a file on Ellsberg that would contain "all available overt, covert, and derogatory information." The recommended steps included collection of all press material on Ellsberg; an interview with his first wife, who was known to be hostile toward him; an interview with a Corsican restaurant owner in Saigon named Nicolai and his Eurasian mistress, Germaine, whom Ellsberg was said to have "coveted"; and collection of data on Ellsberg from the CIA, FBI, military counterintelligence agencies, and Rand. These were relatively easy matters to arrange, but Hunt also proposed two more difficult ones: "Request CIA to perform a covert psychological assessment/evaluation on Ellsberg" and "obtain Ellsberg's files from his psychiatric analyst."

Both Hunt and Young knew that the CIA's Office of Medical Services prepared psychological profiles on world figures in order to guide the government in dealing with them; Young had been particularly impressed by a profile of Fidel Castro. In mid-July he called Howard J. Osborn, the CIA's director of security, who had been established as the agency's liaison with the Plumbers. Osborn—a classmate of Hunt's at Hamburg High School in Hamburg, New York—had become involved in the CIA's domestic surveillance activities in 1967–68, infiltrating agents into dissident organizations in Washington. But now he was hesitant and said he would have to check with Helms. Helms too was said to be reluctant. (Later the CIA claimed that it had prepared only one previous profile of an American, Commander Lloyd Bucher of the USS *Pueblo* after he and his crew were captured by the North Koreans in 1968. But a former agent insists the agency routinely prepared psychological "assessments" of American radicals during the late 1960s and early 1970s.) When Young stressed that Ehrlichman—and therefore presumably the President—regarded the study as most important, Helms said, "All right, let's go ahead and try it." The chief of medical services turned the project over to Dr. Bernard Malloy, the chief of the psychiatric staff. Dr. Malloy recalls, "There was general reservation and concern expressed about such an effort involving as it did potentially controversial and highly speculative efforts. It was felt that such activity, involving as this did an American citizen, might be outside of the agency's purview." But under Dr. Malloy's direction, another staff psychiatrist—relying chiefly on newspaper and magazine articles, television interviews, and a few State Department and FBI memos—prepared what was called an "indirect personality assessment." It was delivered to Young by special courier on August 11 and read, in part:

"There is nothing to suggest in the material reviewed that Subject suffers from a serious mental disorder in the sense of being psychotic and out of contact with reality. There are suggestions, however, that some of his long-standing personality needs were intensified by psychological pressures of the mid-life period and that this may have contributed significantly to his recent actions. . . . An extremely intelligent and talented individual. . . . There has been a notable zealous intensity about the subject throughout his career. . . . He had a knack for drawing attention to himself and at early ages attained positions of considerable distinction, usually attaching himself as a "bright young man" to an older and experienced man. . . . But one can only sustain the role of "bright young man" so long. Most men between the ages of 35 and 45 go through a period of re-evaluation. . . . The evidence reviewed suggests that this was so for Ellsberg, a man whose career had taken off like a rocket, but who found himself at mid-life not nearly having achieved the prominence and success he expected and desired. Thus it may well have been an intensified need to achieve significance that impelled him to release the Pentagon Papers. There is no suggestion that Subject saw anything treasonous in his act. Rather, he seemed to be responding to what he deemed a higher order of patriotism. . . ."

This sort of stuff was, of course, not what the White House was looking for. Within a few hours, Krogh and

Young informed Ehrlichman that they were "disappointed" with the profile, which they considered "very superficial." The next day Dr. Malloy was summoned to meet with Young, Liddy, and Hunt in Room 16. According to Malloy, Liddy said the Plumbers wanted "to render Dr. Ellsberg ineffective or to make him the object of pity as a broken man." Hunt said that in order to "try Dr. Ellsberg in public," they needed material similar to that which "psychiatrists found out about Barry Goldwater in 1964"—data which would allow them to refer knowledgeably to Ellsberg's "oedipal conflicts or castration fears."

The "best instant source" for such material, the Plumbers realized, would be Ellsberg's psychiatric records, and, even before the CIA's profile proved unsatisfactory, they had been seeking them. During his first days in Room 16, Hunt says, he discovered through reading FBI reports that Ellsberg had been seeing a California psychiatrist. And the same FBI reports indicated that shortly after his last delivery of the Pentagon Papers to the newspapers, Ellsberg called his psychiatrist and said, in effect, "Now I am free." Kissinger and others had mentioned Ellsberg's experimentation with drugs and sex, what Hunt called his "rather peculiar background." By then, the Plumbers had reports about a "bizarre" sex life between marriages, including Swedish and Indonesian "mistresses" and participation in weekly "orgies" under the alias "Don Hunter." And they had heard rumors that Ellsberg and his new wife, Patricia, had attended group-sex sessions at the Sand Stone Club in Los Angeles. There was every reason to expect that the psychiatric records—if they could be obtained—would be useful. Indeed, Krogh testified later, they believed that the records might "hold the key to breaking the impasse," unlocking the secrets not only of Ellsberg's psyche but of the wider "conspiracy."

On July 20, 1971, two FBI agents appeared at the door of Dr. Lewis J. Fielding's office at 450 North Bedford Drive in Beverly Hills. The agents said they wanted to talk to Dr. Fielding about Ellsberg, who had been his patient until July 1970, but the analyst refused to talk until he consulted his lawyer. Two days later,

Dr. Fielding and his lawyer decided that he should not violate the confidential doctor-patient relationship and this decision was passed on to the FBI. On July 26, an agent called Dr. Fielding again and the doctor referred him to his lawyer, who reiterated the decision. This rebuff was reported to the Plumbers on July 27, and, over the next three days, Krogh, Young, Liddy, and Hunt began some "low-key conversations" about a possible "bag job" on the psychiatrist's office.

Hunt asked, "If this material is required, why can't we simply request the bureau to acquire it for us?" Liddy recalled that when he was an agent the FBI had conducted such "surreptitious entries" in national security investigations—he boasted of having done one himself in Denver—but five years before Hoover had banned such burglaries and disbanded the special cadres used for them. (Hunt too had some experience in this field. While serving in Mexico City he helped supervise a break-in—by an itinerant team of CIA specialists —at the embassy of a Soviet-bloc country. And some years later, as station chief in Montevideo, he directed several other "penetrations" of Communist embassies, including one in which the "entry team" spent three days vainly trying to break into an ancient but impregnable safe.) Hunt asked why the Secret Service couldn't pull the Fielding job. Liddy said the White House didn't trust it for such operations. Finally, Hunt suggested that he might have some former colleagues who could be called on in a pinch.

On August 5 Krogh and Young reported to Ehrlichman that the FBI had been unable to get Fielding's files and that if they were wanted "something other than the regular channels through the FBI or through the ongoing agencies would have to be undertaken." Krogh indicated that "we did have individuals in the unit and individuals available who had professional experience in this kind of thing." As Young recalls it, Ehrlichman listened quietly and then said, "Let's think about it."

Ehrlichman says he kept the President up to date on Plumbers' activities and "invariably when they made recommendations, jointly or severally, the President concurred. His only criticism of their effort was that it was not vigorous enough." After Krogh recommended that some Plumber personnel be sent out to "complete the California investigation of Ellsberg," Ehrlichman says he told the President about this. Nixon—after discussing it with Hoover—said that "Krogh should, of course, do whatever he considered necessary to get to the bottom of the matter—to learn what Ellsberg's motives and potential further harmful action might be." So Ehrlichman told Krogh he should do "whatever he considered necessary."

On August 11—in the same memo in which they reported that the CIA profile had proved unsatisfactory—Krogh and Young wrote, ". . . we would recommend that a covert operation be undertaken to examine all the medical files still held by Ellsberg's psychoanalyst covering the two-year period in which he was undergoing analysis." The memo left spaces for Ehrlichman to "approve" or "disapprove." Ehrlichman initialed "approve," adding, "if done under your assurance that it is not traceable."

This was a quantum leap in White House tactics. Originally, Ehrlichman recalls, the Plumbers were established "for the purpose of getting the security people in the departments and agencies to do a better job." Now it was about to become "an investigative unit," to engage in a "first-party investigation." Caulfield and Ulasewicz, to be sure, had done plenty of first-party investigations, but they were free-lance gumshoes working on a long leash, usually handling relatively minor matters. As early as July 7 Ehrlichman had asked Cushman to provide Hunt with disguises and equipment, but at first he used these only on his separate investigations for Colson. Now, the Special Investigations Unit—an official body established by the President—was about to go "operational." Ehrlichman says this was "a fallback, a last resort." He insists that he did not know precisely what kind of "covert operation" was contemplated and assumed that the Plumbers were going to carry out merely "a quiet investigation of facts." But, in retrospect at least, it seems that at this point the White House moved across the line from jittery prodding of other agencies into direct operations more appropriate to a secret-police force. It was, indeed, the ultimate step in applying the techniques developed for foreign intelligence operations to the domestic political scene.

Krogh and Young had warned Hunt and Liddy that "no one with any association with the White House could be involved in any way directly with such an operation." So, Hunt recalls, "I was asked whether or not, as a result of my old CIA contacts, I could come up with a team capable of making such an entry."

He immediately thought of an old friend, Bernard L. Barker, who—under the code name "Macho"—had been his principal assistant in the Bay of Pigs operation. For the past decade, they had largely lost touch. Then, on April 16, 1971, Hunt and his wife, Dorothy, went to Miami to attend a tenth-anniversary reunion of Bay of Pigs veterans. He called the only Bernard L. Barker listed in the phone book and, getting no answer, stopped by his house and pinned a note on the door, "If you are the Bernie Barker who worked for me in 1960–61, call me at the Singapore Hotel in Miami Beach. Howard." That evening, Barker called him at the hotel and they made plans to go to the reunion together in Miami's Little Havana district. In a ceremony the next day, at Thirteenth Avenue and S. W. 8th Street, the veterans dedicated a memorial to "the martyrs of Assault Brigade 2506"—a marble obelisk topped by an eternal flame to commemorate those who died for the liberation of their homeland. At the ceremony, which was addressed by Senator Lawton Chiles, Barker and Hunt had their own private reunion. Then Barker introduced his old commander to other veterans under his Bay of Pigs code name, "Eduardo." Hunt was delighted to find that the name still guaranteed him a warm welcome there. (Barker has said that "E. Howard Hunt, under the name of Eduardo, represents to the Cuban people their liberation.") Afterward, the two "freedom fighters" and their wives had dinner in a "stone crab" restaurant and talked about "old times."

Miami's Little Havana lived off "old times." Most of the 300,000 Cuban refugees who had flooded into the city since Castro's seizure of power were awash in nostalgia for the good times when many of them had formed the middle class of the *ancien régime,* living well from small businesses, hotels, factories, or—in some cases—gambling and racketeering, which flourished under Fulgencio Batista. Although some of these exiles had made it big in their adopted land—becoming bank presidents, contractors, or newspaper publishers—few could forget that their roots were sunk deep in the cane fields of that lovely island. In the decade of exile, those old loyalties had festered into a virulent right-wing extremism. One émigré calls Dade County, in which Miami is located, "the number-one stronghold of radical anticommunism in the United States today."

The CIA had long exploited the resentment which seethed in the hearts of so many Miami Cubans. The Company easily recruited thousands of them for the Bay of Pigs operation and, when that failed, recruited thousands more for the "secret war" which the Kennedy and Johnson administrations waged against Cuba during the next four years. From 1963 through 1966, the CIA station in Miami—known by its code name JM WAVE—ran an immense campaign of propaganda, infiltration, sabotage, and outright armed attack designed to bring down the Castro government and return Cuba to the "free world." Operating at a former Navy blimp center on the south campus of the University of Miami—under cover of a CIA proprietary company called Zenith Technical Enterprises—the three hundred American employees of JM WAVE controlled a few thousand more Cuban agents. A clandestine Navy ferried many of them into Cuba and out again and launched a series of commando raids designed to damage Cuba's infrastructure so badly that the Cuban people would rise up in revolt against their economic deprivation.

This vast operation had ramifications throughout southern Florida, particularly in the Cuban exile community which was shot through with Company spies, agents, double agents, and informers. Since JM WAVE's activities involved breaking many American laws, Company officials had worked out a *modus vivendi* with local, state, and federal law-enforcement officials, judges, newspapers, and political leaders. If an agent was arrested with explosives or weapons in his car, or if a boat was stopped by the Coast Guard on its way to Cuba, a code word or a telephone call was sufficient to speed them on their way. The agents soon discovered that they lived above the law. If they were caught in Cuba, the Company spared no effort to get them out. If they were killed, their families were to be supported for life.

Moreover, it was only a small step from this extra-legal activity directed at Cuba to outright illegal activity inside the United States. There is substantial evidence to indicate that the CIA used many of these same Cuban agents in actions which, though they related to foreign affairs, were essentially domestic in nature. By the late 1960s there were some hundred and fifty Cuban informants of a special CIA counterintelligence office in Miami. At first, they organized picketing of foreign consulates or boycotts of products manufactured in countries which traded with Cuba. Others "de-briefed" Cuban refugees arriving in Miami. But, later, they began spying on other exiles living in South Florida, many of them now U.S. citizens. The informers turned in detailed reports to the chief operator—a man named José Joaquin Sangenis Perdomo—who, in turn, re-ported to a CIA case officer named Felix. These domes-tic operations were as protected as the agency's foreign activities. "There was never a problem," one partici-pant says. "We were detained once or twice, but each time someone would call the Miami police and we would be immediately released with no charges." An-other recalls, accurately enough, "It was like a small secret army."

Like an army, its discipline and loyalty remained in-tense. Four months after their reunion, Hunt got in touch with his old comrade in arms again. (Barker says Hunt flew to Miami but Hunt says the conversa-tions took place on the telephone.) Hunt asked whether Barker would "be willing to help out in a matter of national security." Barker says Hunt contended that the "national security organization" to which he then belonged was "above both the CIA and the FBI." He was vague about the specific mission, saying only that it involved "a traitor to this country who had given information to a foreign embassy." Barker eagerly signed on, believing that "Mr. Hunt's position in the White House would be a decisive factor at a later date for obtaining help in the liberation of Cuba."

Hunt then asked him to recruit two others. Barker chose two of his own real-estate salesmen. One was Felipe DeDiego, forty-three, a Bay of Pigs veteran, who once took part in a successful raid to capture Castro government documents, and later served for four years as an officer in U.S. Army Intelligence. The other was Eugenio R. Martinez, forty-eight, who had a far longer record of covert activity. For years, he had been one of the most daring of the CIA's boat captains, with 354 missions to Cuba on his record. Sometimes he would pilot his boat all the way from the Florida Keys to Cuba, but most of the time a "mother ship" would tow him to within fifty miles of shore. Starting with a twenty-six-foot motorboat, then graduating to somewhat larger craft, he would thread his way past the Cuban coastal defenses to deliver agents, arms, and ammunition to the beaches of his beloved homeland. Some time before Hunt and Barker recruited him in the summer of 1971, Martinez had left the agency's direct employ and gone on "retainer status," getting $100 a month to report on maritime movements and the activities of Cuban exile groups. Martinez remained in close touch with his CIA "case officer" in Miami, seeing him at least once a month and frequently talking with him on the telephone. In midsummer Hunt asked Young to run a regular Civil Service check on Barker, DeDiego, and Martinez, then called Barker to tell him they were clear.

On August 25 Hunt got a Tessina camera concealed in a tobacco pouch from Steve Greenwood, his contact in the CIA's Technical Services Division. He also arranged for Liddy to be outfitted with false identification and "pocket litter" in the name of "George F. Leonard," a black wig, and a heel-lift device to make him limp. That afternoon the two men flew to Los Angeles and registered under their aliases at the Beverly Hilton

Hotel. The next morning they donned their disguises and conducted what Hunt called "a preliminary vulnerability and feasibility study" of the doctor's office. They rented a car and drove to North Bedford Drive. Wearing dark glasses, Liddy posed by some bright flowering bushes outside the office while Hunt snapped some pictures of the building, a nondescript three-story structure decorated with blue panels around the windows. They also photographed all "access and escape routes" and even Dr. Fielding's Volvo in the parking lot. Then they drove to Fielding's residence and photographed it from three sides.

After a nap and a late dinner in their room, they set out for the second stage of their reconnaissance. They photographed the office building again, noting which windows were lighted, then walked through the large glass doors and down the wood-paneled hallways toward Dr. Fielding's office in Room 212. As they approached the office, Maria Martinez, the cleaning man's mother, stepped out of a nearby doorway. Hunt coolly addressed her in Spanish, "Señora, we are doctors and friends of Dr. Fielding. With your permission, we would like to go into his office for a moment and leave for him something he has been expecting."

"Very well, *caballeros,*" she said, opening the door with a pass key. Hunt engaged the woman in conversation, while Liddy, a corncob pipe stuck jauntily in his mouth, snapped pictures of Fielding's office with the photographic tobacco pouch. During the next three hours, they checked the building at fifteen-minute intervals, noting that both the front and rear doors stayed open even after Mrs. Martinez left at midnight. Hunt called Steve Greenwood in Washington and asked him to meet their "red-eye special" at Dulles Airport at 6:30 a.m. There Hunt handed a roll of film to Greenwood, who got it developed and—after making photocopies for the CIA files—returned the negatives and prints to Hunt.

The next day Hunt and Liddy presented the results of their trip at a meeting in Room 16. They showed Krogh and Young photographs and diagrams of Dr. Fielding's office.

"I think we have a perfect situation here for a clandestine entry," said Hunt.

"Good," said Young.

Hunt and Liddy recommended Labor Day as the optimum time for the burglary, since the doctors in the professional building would almost certainly be away for the three-day weekend and all cleaning would probably be finished Friday night or early Saturday.

With the operation imminent, Young sent Ehrlichman a memo on August 26, asking, among other things, "How quickly do we want to try to bring about a change in Ellsberg's image? . . . If the present Hunt/Liddy Project #1 is successful, it will be absolutely essential to have an overall game plan developed. . . ." The next day Ehrlichman passed on the word to the chief strategist for such matters, Chuck Colson: "On the assumption that the proposed undertaking by Hunt and Liddy would be carried out and would be successful, I would appreciate receiving from you by next Wednesday a game plan as to how and when you believe the materials should be used."

But Hunt/Liddy Project #1 needed funds. Until then, the White House agents had traveled on government vouchers; but Krogh recalls, "It was felt there shouldn't be any way to trace the money that was used"—which meant cash. The week before Labor Day, Colson called Joseph Baroody, a Washington public-relations man. At Colson's virtual insistence, Baroody had been retained by Associated Milk Producers, Inc., a lobby eager to please the White House, and over fifteen months had been paid $40,000 for no visible services. Colson now said the White House had an urgent need for $5000. Baroody got the cash and—on Colson's instructions—delivered it to Krogh. In September Colson arranged for TAPE—one of the milk lobby trusts—to make an additional $5000 contribution to one of the recipient committees—People United for Good Government. Then, he told the committee treasurer to write a $5000 check to Baroody—completing a neat little money-"washing" operation.

Minutes before Hunt and Liddy were scheduled to leave on their mission, they were still in Room 16 waiting for their money. As Hunt describes the scene in his book *Undercover: Memoirs of an American Secret Agent:*

". . . at the last minute Krogh appeared, handed Liddy an envelope and said, 'Here it is. Now for God's sake, don't get caught.'

"Liddy said, 'We won't.'

"Krogh shook his head. 'I'm going to give you my home phone number,' he told Liddy. 'As soon as the operation's over—whatever happens—call and let me know. I'll be waiting.' He wrote down a number and handed it to Liddy, who tucked it in his pocket.

" 'I'll call from a pay station,' Liddy told him. 'I'll be George—honest George Leonard.' He smiled. 'What'll I call you?'

"Krogh grimaced. 'Just call me Wally,' he told Liddy.

" 'Wally?'

" 'Yeah—Wally Fear.' "

On September 1 the two branches of the burglary team began converging on Los Angeles. Liddy and Hunt flew via Chicago, stayed overnight there to pick up a Minolta camera and four walkie-talkies, then went on to the coast. When they checked into the Beverly Hilton, they found Barker, Martinez, and DeDiego, who had arrived earlier that day from Miami. That night Hunt gave the three Cubans a "visual reconnaissance" of the target. The next day, at widely separated stores, the team purchased deliverymen's uniforms, a large green suitcase, surgical gloves, a glass cutter, a crowbar, black muslin to cover the windows, and a length of nylon rope to serve as an emergency escape route from the doctor's second-floor window. At 9:00 p.m., two of the Cubans went to Dr. Fielding's office in the deliverymen's uniforms, carrying the suitcase addressed to the doctor and marked with "Air Express" and "Rush" stickers. The cleaning man let them into the doctor's office, where they placed the suitcase on the floor. As they left, one of the Cubans punched the inside doorknob lever to leave the door unlocked.

A few minutes past midnight, the team swung into

action. Hunt drove a rented car to Dr. Fielding's home and kept watch there until the lights went out. Liddy cruised the area in another rented car, watching for police. When Barker, Martinez, and DeDiego got the go-ahead, they checked the front and rear doors of the office building and, finding them locked, broke through a window on the ground floor. Snaking their way through the darkened corridors to Room 212, they found its door locked too and pried it open with the crowbar. Inside, Barker finally told his two compatriots what their mission was. "We are here because we are doing a great job for the country," he said. "We have to find some papers of a great traitor to the United States, who is an s.o.b., and who will help enemies of this country." The two salesmen asked who this was, and Barker said, "Daniel Ellsberg." He showed them a scrap of paper on which Liddy had scrawled in big letters "E-L-L-S-B-E-R-G," so that they would know what files to look for.

The burglary was to have been a "clean" one which left no trace of entry. The Cubans were equipped with a Polaroid camera, so that they could tell how to restore a drawer or cabinet to the condition in which they had found it. But the wooden cabinet and steel file drawers in the office were so securely locked that they had to pry them open; they therefore abandoned the "clean burglary" concept, messed up the office, and Martinez even took some pills from Dr. Fielding's briefcase—vitamin C, he thinks—and scattered them on the floor to make it look like a "drug rip-off" by addicts. Opening the green suitcase, they took out the Minolta camera and some high-powered lights to photograph any papers they found on Ellsberg. But, the Cubans insist, they found nothing except his name in a pop-up address file on the doctor's desk. Martinez photographed the file "just to have something," and he also photographed some of the open desk and file drawers to show they had made a thorough search. (The Cubans' version is difficult to reconcile with Dr. Fielding's description of his office when he saw it the next day. He says the bottom drawer of his filing cabinet, where he kept his file on Ellsberg, had been opened and papers strewn all over the floor. Two batches of notes on Ellsberg—one of about twenty-five pages, the other of forty pages—were outside the envelope in which he recalls leaving them and looked as if they had been "fingered.")

Meanwhile, Hunt, making a final check at Dr. Fielding's home, noticed that the doctor's Volvo was missing from the driveway where it had been parked earlier in the evening. Fearing that Dr. Fielding might have gone to his office, Hunt sped through the darkened streets toward the office building where Liddy, in the other car, was keeping his own watch. Hunt breathlessly explained the situation and asked, "Where are the boys?"

"Hell, they're inside!" exclaimed Liddy.

Liddy picked up his walkie-talkie and croaked, "George to Leader. George to Leader. Come in. Come in." But just then the three Cubans came tumbling out of a ground-floor window—Barker and DeDiego wearing the disguises issued to Hunt and Liddy.

Back at the hotel, the five men drank champagne to celebrate their safety. (Although the mission had apparently failed, Hunt was clearly exhilarated. In his novel *The Berlin Ending*—written about this time—, Hunt described the feelings of a former CIA agent as he became caught up once more in intrigue and espionage: "Whatever had been lacking from his life before —danger, romance—was more than filling the void. He was alive again.") At 4:00 a.m. Liddy reported by phone to "Wally Fear" in Washington. The Cubans then flew almost immediately to Miami, but there was no flight to Washington until much later in the day. So Hunt and Liddy caught a morning plane to New York, boasting to two stewardesses that they had just pulled a "big national security job." In New York, they spent the night at the Pierre Hotel, registering under their own names and flashing their White Houses passes to get discounts.

On Tuesday, September 7—the first working day after the Labor Day weekend—Hunt and Liddy reported in more detail to Krogh and Young in Room 16, showing them Polaroid shots of the office. Believing that after the FBI visits Dr. Fielding might have taken his Ellsberg file home, they proposed a burglary there. Krogh and Young say they did not favor any more burglaries, but they discussed the suggestion with Ehrlichman, who flatly rejected it. Ehrlichman says he felt the burglary went far beyond the covert activity he had approved and told Krogh, "The thing should be terminated, discontinued, finalized, stopped."*

Apparently it was, but one other burglary took place that fall which may have been the work of the Plumbers. Early in November the penthouse office of Dr. Robert U. Akeret, a Manhattan psychiatrist who had once treated Patricia Ellsberg, was broken into, searched, and left in considerable disarray. The thieves apparently rifled an unlocked cabinet containing a file on Mrs. Ellsberg, but only some blank checks were missing. The doctor recalls that the day after the first publication of the Pentagon Papers, two FBI agents had come to his office seeking information on Mrs. Ellsberg, who was often credited with helping to transform her husband's views on the war. Dr. Akeret, like Dr. Fielding, refused to talk to the FBI.

Meanwhile, others besides Ehrlichman were pulling in the reins on the White House agents. In late August Hunt had intensified his requests for assistance from the CIA. On August 18 he asked Carl Wagner, General Cushman's assistant, to assign to him one of the agency's secretaries in Paris—he had apparently known her during his service there—for a period of thirty to ninety days. Hunt said he needed this particular secretary, because of her "loyalty," to work on a highly sensitive assignment, but did not want her division chief to know that the White House was involved in

---

*Seven people were indicted in connection with the break-in at Fielding's office. Ehrlichman was convicted on a three-count charge of violating Fielding's civil rights and lying to a grand jury; he was sentenced to concurrent prison terms of twenty months to five years. Liddy, also found guilty of conspiring to violate Fielding's rights, got one to three years in prison. Colson pled guilty to obstructing justice by disseminating damaging information about Ellsberg; he was fined $5000 and served nearly seven months of a one-to-three-year prison term. Krogh pled guilty to violating Fielding's civil rights and received a three-to-six-year prison term, of which all but six months was suspended. Barker and Martinez were also found guilty of violating Fielding's civil rights and each received a suspended sentence and three years' probation. The indictment against De-Diego was dismissed.

the request. Then Hunt asked the agency to help him set up a fake New York address and a telephone covered by an answering service. He also wanted "fully back-stopped" identification, including a driver's license and car-rental credit cards under his false identity. Meanwhile, top-ranking agency officials learned for the first time that Hunt had been given false identification and a disguise for Liddy. And after the Fielding reconnaissance photos were developed, they may have learned what the target of the action was, for the name "Dr. Fielding" was prominently displayed on the wall over the doctor's parking space in one photo. One official speculated that they were "casing" photographs. These developments all contributed to increasing fear at the CIA that Hunt might draw the agency even further into the sensitive area of domestic clandestine operations against Americans. The acting chief of the Technical Services Division became concerned at Hunt's failure to return the alias identification which had been issued with the understanding that it was to be used for a "one-time operation." On August 27 Wagner recommended to Cushman that "the agency terminate its support to Mr. Hunt because he was drawing us into a compromising and dangerous situation." That very day Cushman told Ehrlichman that "Hunt was becoming a pain in the neck" and the agency could no longer support him. Ehrlichman agreed to "call a halt to this."

Nevertheless, contacts between Hunt and the agency continued. In mid-October Hunt had lunch with Thomas Karamessines, the CIA's deputy director for plans. The official explanation is that Hunt had come to ask Karamessines to continue the existing Mullen & Company "cover" arrangements in Europe. But this does not seem to be a matter which would require the personal attention of Karamessines, one of the CIA's most powerful figures.

Meanwhile, the psychiatric staff went back to work on the Ellsberg profile. On October 12 the Plumbers supplied Dr. Malloy with copies of some classified FBI reports and State Department documents. The memos indicated, among other things, that Ellsberg might have revealed "quasi-secret" information about his military units while applying for a Ph.D. fellowship at Harvard; that he had volunteered for State Department service in Vietnam while "under the stress of obtaining a divorce from his first wife"; and that "he may have been involved in leaking information about a South Vietnamese in 1970 while he was actually in psychoanalytic treatment." On October 27 Dr. Malloy met again with Hunt, Liddy, and Young in Room 16 and summarized his findings. He was reluctant to put them on paper, for fear that they would be misused or traced to the CIA, but the Plumbers insisted. So on November 12 Dr. Malloy brought them a new profile of Ellsberg. From the Plumbers' point of view it was something of an improvement, delving more deeply into the psychic forces which allegedly drove Ellsberg to release the Pentagon Papers.

"Very little is available about his early background, but at 15 he did an about-switch when he gave up the piano at which he had been very proficient, and by his senior high school year he was captain of the basketball team. The loss of interest in the piano, and the subsequent concentration on a sport were associated with an automobile accident which led to his wearing a cast for a year because of a broken knee. His father was driving and his mother and sister were killed. His father subsequently remarried. It is possible that strong feelings of resentment and rage and frustration stirred up by death and personal illness or injury are associated with his apparently sudden and extreme shifts in loyalty and enthusiasm.

"In April 1967, the subject was ill with hepatitis in Bangkok. That summer he returned from Vietnam. He had vigorously favored and participated in the pacification efforts of the Vietnam countryside as espoused by General [Edward G.] Lansdale, and he had not been ostensibly distressed at that time by taking part in search-and-destroy missions in which it is quite possible that he actually killed the enemy himself. In 1967, John McNaughton, for whom he had worked in 1964–65, was killed in an airplane accident. It was in these circumstances, and on returning to the United States, that he retrospectively first speaks of feeling more and more the US should get out of Vietnam. It is possible that the anger and frustration engendered by his hepatitis (and immobilization by bedrest) combined with the loss by an accident of an erstwhile mentor (McNaughton), mobilized a shift in his views. . . .

"His central theme for leaking the Pentagon Papers has been that 'the Executive' should not alone have so much unshared power as to plunge the country into war and the misery and death that it brings. It is probable that the Subject is not only referring here to the various Presidents, but also to his own father whom, after all, he saw as responsible for the death of his mother and sister, injuring him to boot. . . .

"And yet, there is also an element of desiring to please, to be influenced by, and to placate an important man, through the use of his natural gifts. . . . In the opinion of the writer, the intense injury to his pride, the rage and murderous anger which is stirred up when his gifts and abilities are not given proper recognition as he wishes is the motivating force for his shifting enthusiasms and for his search for another who will give him his proper due . . . to an important degree the leaking of the Pentagon Papers was also an act of aggression at his analyst, as well as at the President and his father. . . . It is of course possible that the Subject has more documents with which he will seek to continue to pursue his odyssey of being appreciated (and disappointed) by a senior personage. . . ."

Yet the next—and last—leak the Plumbers had to plug came not from Ellsberg but from a source within the White House itself. In mid-December Jack Anderson wrote several columns containing material from the minutes of the Washington Special Action Group, a top-level crisis-management outfit then dealing with the India-Pakistan war. The minutes contradicted Nixon's public insistence that the United States was remaining neutral in that conflict and clearly demonstrated that the President and Kissinger were doing what they could to aid Pakistan. For example, in his December 14 column, Anderson quoted Kissinger as saying at the December 3 meeting, "I'm getting hell every half-hour from the President that we're not being tough enough on India. He has just called me again. He doesn't believe we're carrying out his wishes. He wants to tilt in favor of Pakistan."

These Anderson columns aroused predictable fury at the White House, and the Plumbers were directed to investigate. But the plumbing force had been largely dissipated by then. Ehrlichman recalls that by early fall "the President had sufficiently stimulated Mr. Hoover and the attorney general had sufficiently stimulated the Justice Department that they were very much back in business." Specifically, he says, the White House had pretty well turned the "whole Pentagon Papers business back to the Justice Department" (perhaps out of a nervous reaction to the bungled Fielding burglary). Now the Anderson columns briefly galvanized the Plumbers again.

To some in the White House, Anderson's revelations seemed even more heinous than Ellsberg's because they dealt, not with historical "secrets," but with current ones.

The Plumbers then reverted to more traditional methods. Egil Krogh, who had turned his attention back to stemming international drug traffic, was recalled to duty, and he and Young went off in search of the columnist's source.

Rather quickly, they focused on Yeoman First Class Charles E. Radford, a thirty-year-old clerk in the Joint Chiefs of Staff liaison office with the National Security Council. The liaison office, established in the early days of the Kennedy administration, was designed to coordinate the flow of information between the Pentagon and the NSC. Radford would have had access to minutes of the Action Group's deliberations taken by a civilian Pentagon official, and the Plumbers believed that Radford—who like Anderson was a Mormon—had passed copies to the columnist. Radford was quietly banished to a reserve recruiting station in Oregon where he had no access to classified data.

But the Plumbers' investigation turned up far more than that: evidence that Radford had taken other highly sensitive documents, never intended for transmittal to the Pentagon, and funneled them through the liaison office to Admiral Thomas H. Moorer, chairman of the Joint Chiefs of Staff. The Plumbers' evidence indicated that he had rifled files, briefcases, and "burn bags" for documents, which included the verbatim record of a conversation between Kissinger and Chinese Premier Chou En-lai during Kissinger's first secret trip to Peking in July 1971—at that time perhaps the government's most sensitive classified document. Radford contended that he was carefully trained and instructed by his immediate superiors—including Admiral Robert O. Welander—to take "anything I could get my hands on."

This interagency spying was almost certainly not real espionage but a natural response to the increasing concentration of national security decision-making in Kissinger's NSC. Pentagon officials evidently felt they had to know what was going on in "Henry's shop." Kissinger concedes he was "beside myself" and "outraged" at the betrayal and ordered the liaison office closed down. Admiral Welander was transferred to command of a cruiser flotilla. But, curiously enough, nobody was punished—not even Yeoman Radford. The White House may have feared that its effort to prosecute and defame Ellsberg for "stealing" the Pentagon Papers might suffer if the public learned that the highest military officers in the land were also reading documents purloined in the name of "national security." And it may also have feared that public disclosure of the affair could bring the rest of the Plumbers' activities to light.

The Plumbers had reverted to secret wiretapping for the Radford investigation. Egil Krogh says Ehrlichman dismissed him from the Plumbers once and for all in late December because he refused to authorize a wiretap in this connection. But the FBI subsequently disclosed that on John Mitchell's instructions it placed four taps during this investigation: on Radford, both in Washington and in Oregon; on a "close associate" of Radford's who was said to have "been in contact with the

Soviet attaché in New Delhi"; and on a State Department employee, also close to Radford, who had served in embassies abroad.

(The CIA evidently got into the act too. The agency tapped the phones of several people suspected of receiving classified information during this period. Among the targets were Jack Anderson; Michael Getler, the *Washington Post*'s Defense Department correspondent; and Victor Marchetti, a former CIA agent who was writing a book on the agency.)

There have been unverified reports of other wiretaps instigated or carried out directly by the Plumbers. At one point, Ehrlichman testified ambiguously that he authorized Gordon Liddy to install several wiretaps, but these have never been identified. Among those at one time believed to have been tapped by the Plumbers are Neil Sheehan, the *New York Times* reporter who obtained the Pentagon Papers from Ellsberg; Tad Szulc, the *Times* reporter who had broken several sensitive stories during this period, in addition to the one which allegedly jeopardized the life of a CIA informant in India; and Marcus Raskin and Richard Barnet, co-directors of the Institute for Policy Studies, a research organization in Washington which had examined Vietnam policy-making.

By the end of 1971 the Plumbers were largely out of business. Hunt did occasional work in the narcotics field for Krogh and Young, and he maintained a clandestine telephone in Room 16 until March 1972, for which bills were sent to Kathy Chenow's home in Alexandria and paid by John Campbell, staff secretary to the President. (The phone was used chiefly for calls to and from Bernard Barker in Miami.) But with the approach of election year, most of the Plumbers were moving on to more overtly political activities.

In planning their intelligence program for the 1972 campaign, Nixon's men briefly considered working through a private detective agency. The plan originated with John Caulfield who, noting the decline in his own assignments, decided to strike out on his own. During the spring and summer of 1971 he had discussed the idea with Commissioner of Customs Myles Ambrose and Mike Acree, the IRS assistant commissioner who had proved so helpful in providing him with access to income-tax returns. The three men spoke about a project Caulfield called "Operation Sandwedge," which would provide "security services" to large corporations and, fueled by big corporate fees, would carry out free investigating and covert activities for the White House and the Republican campaign.

That summer Caulfield tried to get a commitment of White House support from John Dean. In September he drafted a memo to Dean which began, "The 1972 Presidential Campaign strongly suggests a definitive need for the creation of a political intelligence-security entity to be located within the private sector. This entity, surfacely disassociated from the Administration by virtue of an established business cover, would have the capability of performing in a highly sophisticated manner designed to ensure that the major offensive intelligence and defensive security requirements of the entire campaign would be professionally programmed and implemented. In the author's judgment, this effort would make a significant and perhaps crucial contribution towards the re-election of Richard Nixon. . . ."

Caulfield described Sandwedge as a Republican equivalent of Intertel, the Washington-based private investigating firm. The memo outlined a complex, nation-wide structure for Sandwedge. Caulfield would run the overt Washington office and handle liaison with the White House and CREEP. Joe Woods, former sheriff of Cook County and brother of Rose Mary Woods, would run the Chicago office and supervise private security forces at the Republican National Convention. Mike Acree would provide "IRS information input," supervise financial investigations, and maintain liaison with law-enforcement agencies. And Tony Ulasewicz would direct the covert New York office which would place informers in Democratic campaigns, conduct "surveillance of Democratic primaries, conventions, meetings, et cetera," and have a "black-bag capability" (apparently a reference to surreptitious breaking and entry). Caulfield stressed that Ulasewicz's New York operation would be conducted in "extreme clandestine fashion."

In the fall of 1971 Caulfield explored Sandwedge further with Dean, Magruder, and Ehrlichman. Ehrlichman was not impressed. Dean mentioned it to John Mitchell, who talked about it with Haldeman. According to Mitchell, Haldeman disapproved of it because of the "lack of experience" of the individuals involved. Clearly, everybody was intrigued by the plan, but nobody felt Caulfield was the man to run it.

By November Caulfield seems to have recognized that Sandwedge was dead. But it lingered on for a while and its death spasms are peculiar. Although Ehrlichman turned down the comprehensive plan, he wanted to keep Tony Ulasewicz around through the 1972 campaign. Indeed, Kalmbach gave Caulfield $50,000 that fall to finance Ulasewicz's efforts through 1972. On November 18 Caulfield sent Ulasewicz to New Hampshire to investigate the campaign of California Congressman Paul N. "Pete" McCloskey, who was running against Nixon in the Republican primary there. As late as December 12 Caulfield described a Ulasewicz visit to McCloskey volunteer headquarters as "a Sandwedge-engineered penetration." In late December and early January Dean and Mitchell were still talking about Caulfield-Ulasewicz projects. On January 12 Dean wrote Mitchell that "Sandwedge will be in need of refunding at the end of this month," suggesting that the $50,000 had been consumed in scarcely five months. Ulasewicz continued working for the White House until late that spring, although his assignments dropped off sharply.

Yet, as early as October 1971, Mitchell told Dean that the principal security problem of the coming campaign would be dealing with demonstrators and he wanted a lawyer to handle any such operation. Magruder and one of Haldeman's assistants, Gordon C. Strachan, asked Dean to find a lawyer who could serve as CREEP's general counsel and also direct an intelligence-gathering program. Dean says Magruder first wanted his assistant, Fred F. Fielding, but Dean refused, saying he'd "look around" for someone else. Dean asked Krogh whether David Young could take on the job, but Krogh said no and suggested Liddy, reporting, "he has written some wonderful legal opinions over here for me." But legal talent wasn't really what CREEP was looking for and it was almost certainly Liddy's FBI and Plumber experience which got him the job.

In November Caulfield decided he wanted to work for John Mitchell as a scheduling aide. He asked Dean to get him an appointment. Caulfield discussed possible employment with Mitchell on November 24. On the way out of the attorney general's office, he saw Dean and Liddy waiting to go in. That afternoon, Mitchell hired Liddy and on December 13 the former Plumber reported to work at CREEP.

In February 1972 Magruder got a telephone call from Richard Howard, one of Colson's assistants, who told him that Hunt had "completed his assignments at the White House" and might prove "very valuable" in CREEP's intelligence-gathering effort. Magruder had met Hunt only once—when he interviewed him some two years before for the Silent Majority Institute—and he wasn't quite sure how Hunt could be valuable. But he told Howard to "refer Mr. Hunt to Mr. Liddy."

5

DIRTY MONEY

I have often thought we had too much money.
—Herbert L. Porter,
testimony to the Senate Select Committee
on Presidential Campaign Practices, June 7, 1973

From the top floor of Irvine Towers, where Herbert W. Kalmbach had his office, one could watch the sparkling white yachts bobbing in the Pacific along "Millionaire's Row" in Newport Beach, California. Within a silver dollar's throw of the twin office towers, some ten or twelve millionaires lived in walled, well-guarded beachfront compounds. And many of those men belonged to the Lincoln Club, an exclusive group of about a hundred and sixty businessmen that over the years had given vast sums of money to Richard Nixon—much of it funneled through the President's personal lawyer, Herb Kalmbach.

In 1970 Kalmbach opened an account in the Bank of America's Newport Beach branch, which has offices in Irvine Towers East. The account ultimately held $105,340—many of the deposits coming in cashier's checks which he purchased with cash at a branch of the Security Pacific National Bank, whose office is in Irvine Towers West. Money was transferred back and forth between Irvine Towers East and Irvine Towers West in an apparent effort to blur its trail.

Kalmbach was the chief fund-raiser for Nixon's Presidential campaign until February 1972, and thereafter he was second only to Maurice H. Stans, the campaign's official finance chairman. His secret fund, established nearly four years before the election, set the tone for the financial side of Nixon's re-election campaign.

In 1968 Nixon offered to make Herb Kalmbach undersecretary of commerce, but Kalmbach preferred to stay in California to build up his law practice. It was a shrewd decision, which looked even shrewder the following spring when Nixon asked him to serve as his personal lawyer. Starting in 1969, the Los Angeles firm of Kalmbach, DeMarco, Knapp & Chillingworth began to rise in the world: from the eighth floor of Century City to the nineteenth floor of a downtown office building to the forty-fourth floor of the city's newest skyscraper. (The firm maintained a separate office in Newport Beach.) In 1968 the firm had only three lawyers; by 1970 it had fourteen, and by 1973 the total had jumped to twenty-four. And the firm's clientele was similarly transformed. In 1968 it had represented the likes of Pacific Lighting and the Newport National Bank, but then a host of national companies began flocking to its doors: among them, the Marriott Corporation, United Air Lines, Travelers Insurance, Dart Industries, and Music Corporation of America. The main attraction did not appear to be Kalmbach's legal wizardry. William King, a former Nixon campaign finance chairman, says, "He [Kalmbach] isn't especially known for his practice of law." Indeed, Nixon told Dean that Kalmbach "isn't a lawyer in the sense that most people have a lawyer. . . . I don't need a lawyer. He handles that property out there [San Clemente]. . . . I see Herb once a year when he brings the income-tax returns." But evidently a lot of powerful clients thought they would be well served by the man who represented the President. A Newport businessman said, "If you have business with Washington and you want a lawyer, you can get to Herb, but you can't talk to him for less than ten thousand dollars." For years, Kalmbach's career has benefited from political friendships. He was a classmate of Robert Finch at the University of Southern California Law School, from which they graduated in 1951. Seven years later, he headed the Orange

County campaign in Finch's successful race for lieuten-
ant governor. In 1968, he served as Stans's deputy on
the Nixon campaign finance committee and distin-
guished himself by raising $6 million through his own
efforts. Rather quickly he emerged as the chief strategist
of the formidable Lincoln Club. He could often be seen
drinking with John "Duke" Wayne or lunching with F.
Donald Nixon at a restaurant called the Quiet Woman.
He and his wife, Barbara—a former Rose Bowl Prin-
cess—lived in a $100,000 house overlooking the yacht
basin.

Kalmbach's secret fund came largely from a surplus
in Nixon's 1968 campaign monies. In mid-January
1969 Maurice Stans asked Kalmbach to become trustee
of the surplus, then at $1,668,000. Of this, $1,098,000
was in cash, held in safe-deposit boxes at the Chase
Manhattan Bank in New York and the Riggs National
Bank in Washington, and the remaining $570,000 was
in a checking account at the National Bank of North
America in New York. Kalmbach became the trustee of
all three accounts, with the right to withdraw funds at
any time if joined by one of two designated co-signa-
tories: Thomas W. Evans, managing partner of Mudge,
Rose, Guthrie & Alexander, and France M. Raine, Jr.,
a Los Angeles real-estate operator and Bob Haldeman's
brother-in-law.

Over the next few years the $570,000 remained in
the New York checking account, but much of the cash
was moved from the Chase and Riggs banks to new
safe-deposit boxes in southern California: one in the
Security Pacific National Bank in Newport Beach and
one in the Crocker Citizens Bank in Los Angeles. And
the funds were shuffled around between those boxes
and checking accounts at Security Pacific and the Newport Beach branch of the Bank of America. Meanwhile,
$300,000 in cash from several contributors was
added to the secret fund, bringing it to nearly $2
million. Kalmbach says the fund was designated for "political purposes" and could be spent only on the instruc-

tions of Haldeman or others clearly acting on his behalf.

This fund must be distinguished from still another secret fund that Kalmbach helped to raise for the 1970 congressional campaign. In March 1970 Haldeman; Harry Dent, a White House political adviser; and Dent's assistant, Jack A. Gleason, decided that a special fund was needed for that fall's Senate and House races. Haldeman asked Kalmbach to do the bulk of the fundraising, urging him to "get cash whenever you can get it." And "old reliable" Herb did raise some $2.8 million of the $3.9 eventually garnered for the fund. According to a confidential memo from Kalmbach to Haldeman, two of the President's friends—W. Clement Stone, a Chicago insurance executive, and Donald McI. Kendall, board chairman of PepsiCo, Inc.—each pledged $250,000. H. Ross Perot, a Texas millionaire, also came in with $250,000. Claude C. Wild, Jr., Gulf Oil's Washington vice president, was listed for $25,000. Edward J. Gerrity, Jr., International Telephone and Telegraph's vice president for public relations, was listed for $50,000 (although Gerrity says he never paid it). The money was collected and the funds disbursed by Jack Gleason out of a back-room office in the basement of a town house at 1310 19th Street, N.W., and thus the operation was known as the Town House Project. The contributions were siphoned into congressional campaigns in at least nineteen states, including crucial contests in Maryland, Tennessee, Florida, Indiana, and North Dakota. The whole project was illegal because Dent, Gleason, *et al.* were functioning as a political committee and such committees could not support candidates in two or more states without having a treasurer who filed public reports to Congress.*

But in late 1970 Kalmbach was ordered to start focusing immediately on the 1972 Presidential election. While White House aides absorbed the disappointing

---

*Kalmbach, Gleason, and Dent were all convicted for their activities in the project. Kalmbach served six months of a six-to-ten-month sentence and was fined $10,000. Dent was sentenced to one month of unsupervised probation. Gleason received a suspended sentence.

off-year results and plotted their political strategy for the next two years, Haldeman told Kalmbach to go out and raise as much money as he could. Nixon had always recognized the central importance of campaign contributions. "Get to know the big finance men, that's the key," he told Representative John H. Rousselot of California in 1957. But he had been particularly obsessed with political money since 1960, when he felt John Kennedy had beaten him, in large part, by outspending him. "Remember Nineteen Sixty," he would tell Haldeman, "I never want to be outspent again." The embattled White House feared it was in for a life-and-death struggle, and it wanted all the money—particularly all the untraceable cash—it could get.

The major coup in this early fund-raising effort came at a White House dinner in mid-November 1970. Present were the President, John Mitchell, Kalmbach, and five potential contributors. There was no discussion of money in the presence of the President, but after dinner Kalmbach asked the guests what they could be expected to contribute to the 1972 campaign. According to the lawyer, he got pledges of $3 million from Clement Stone and from John Mulcahy, president of a firebrick subsidiary of the Pfizer pharmaceutical firm and once Nixon's host during a Presidential trip to Ireland. Kalmbach also got a $1-million pledge from Richard Mellon Scaife, a Pittsburgh banker. The other two at the dinner—Kent Smith and John Rollins—each pledged $250,000. A plump $7.5 million for four hours' work.

Another major contributor in those years was one of America's wealthiest and most mysterious men —Howard Hughes. The multimillionaire had long given heavily to politicians of both parties, believing that this would assure him access and influence for his extensive interests. And he had long used healthy dollops of his vast wealth to buy influence with Richard Nixon. Years before, while Nixon was still Vice President,

Hughes had loaned Donald Nixon the $205,000 which, ironically, had helped cost brother Richard the Presidency in 1960. On March 14, 1968, with Nixon again a candidate, Hughes sent his Nevada lieutenant Robert Maheu a memo which said in part, ". . . I want you to go see Nixon as my special confidential emissary. I feel there is a really valid possibility of a Republican victory this year . . . that could be realized under our sponsorship and supervision every inch of the way. . . ."

If such a meeting took place, we have no record of it. But Hughes would have had many reasons for seeking a close relationship with Nixon. Preoccupied with germs and contamination, he had long sought to force an end to underground nuclear testing in the Nevada desert. Much of his empire was subject to federal regulation and many of his companies depended on federal —particularly defense—contracts. (In one memo, allegedly sent in late 1968 or early 1969, Hughes urged Maheu to press for continuation of the Vietnam war, so that one of his companies making light observer helicopters could recoup its losses.) Hughes had a particularly lengthy and complex relationship with the CIA, in which many of his ranking executives had served. It has long been believed that Hughes offices abroad— and at home—function as fronts for certain agency activities. (In late 1972 Hughes got a $350-million contract to build the *Glomar Explorer* and then provide elaborate cover for the CIA's use of the ship to raise a Soviet submarine off the Pacific floor.)

But in the late 1960s Hughes's most pressing problems were more parochial. He was hard at work buying up the "Strip," the hotel and gambling Prunkstrasse of Las Vegas, where he had installed himself on Thanksgiving Eve 1966 in a penthouse bastion at the Desert Inn. By early 1968 he had acquired four hotels (the Desert Inn, the Sands, the Castaways, and the Frontier); a casino (the Silver Slipper); and a lot of vacant land on the Strip—not to mention KLAS-TV, Alamo Airways, and the 518-acre Krupp Ranch. People said he was going to buy up the whole town. Certainly, he was already the dominant economic force in the state of Nevada.

Not surprisingly, such grandiose schemes had attracted the attention of the Justice Department. In April 1968, aware that Hughes was eyeing the Stardust and several other hotel-casinos, the department's Antitrust Division began a preliminary investigation of his holdings. Concluding that acquisition of the Stardust would violate its guidelines on corporate mergers, the division prepared a complaint. Hughes dropped his plans to purchase the hotel.

This was the context in which Hughes's representatives began to discuss a campaign contribution to Nixon which would eventually total at least $100,000. (It should be distinguished from the $150,000 which Hughes legally contributed to Nixon's official committees over the next few years, some of it with blank checks signed by Robert Bennett of Mullen & Company, with the sums filled out by Sally Harmony, Gordon Liddy's secretary.) This $100,000 contribution has become the subject of labyrinthine dispute and conjecture. Almost everything about it—including its exact source, timing, purpose, and use—are still in some doubt. But a Senate inquiry has pieced together the following story:

Sometime during the late summer of 1968 Nixon's close friend Bebe Rebozo met with Richard Danner, the ex-FBI man then on leave from his Washington law practice to work full time in the Nixon campaign. They discussed the possibility of a Hughes contribution to Nixon's campaign. (Danner says that Nixon was also present at the meeting; Rebozo and Nixon deny this. Danner says that either Nixon or Rebozo initiated the talk about a Hughes contribution; Rebozo insists Danner brought it up.) Danner raised the matter with Edward P. Morgan, a Washington attorney who had represented several Hughes interests, but the negotiations foundered. (Rebozo says Morgan "wanted to hand the money to the President himself"; Morgan says he merely asked for assurances that Hughes would get an explicit acknowledgment of his contribution. When neither Rebozo nor Danner could give him such an assurance, Morgan called the Hughes representatives and recommended against contributing to Nixon.)

A few months later Hughes and his lawyers found a way around the antitrust regulations. Hughes fixed his eyes on the unfinished shell of the Landmark Hotel which had, indeed, become something of a Strip landmark—or eyesore. His lawyers argued to the Justice Department that the Landmark was a "failing company" that could be saved from bankruptcy only by Hughes's takeover. The department reluctantly approved the purchase three days before Nixon's inaugural in January 1969.

In February 1969 Dick Danner went to work for Hughes—with special responsibility for liaison between Hughes's interests and the Nixon administration. In that role, he kept up negotiations with Rebozo over the promised contribution. Finally, $50,000 in $100 bills was removed from the safe-deposit box at the Frontier. Danner delivered it to Rebozo in Key Biscayne, probably on September 11 or 12, 1969.

In early 1970 Hughes moved once more to expand his Las Vegas empire, instructing Maheu to buy the Dunes Hotel. It was clear to all that the Antitrust Division would oppose this purchase, too—particularly since acquisition of the Landmark had given Hughes even more hotel rooms in Las Vegas than he had when the Justice Department had blocked the Stardust purchase. So Hughes sought to bypass the Antitrust Division altogether. He told Maheu to send Danner to the very top —to Attorney General John Mitchell.

Danner, who knew Mitchell from the 1968 campaign, met with the attorney general on the Dunes matter three times that winter—in January, in February, and in March. After the February meeting, Mitchell called Assistant Attorney General Richard W. McLaren, head of the Antitrust Division, and, according to McLaren, told him that Governor Paul Laxalt of Nevada was pressing for approval of the Dunes purchase. Mitchell reportedly said Laxalt wanted the Dunes bought because it was hoodlum-owned and Hughes would "clean it up." (Laxalt says this was a phony story concocted to cover up some other reason for favoring Hughes. "Hell," he told *The Wall Street Journal,* "Mitchell never even talked to me about the Dunes deal, and I would have opposed it if he had because we'd already drawn the line on no more acquisitions by Hughes.")

On March 12, after consulting his staff, McLaren told Mitchell that purchase of the Dunes by Hughes would violate the merger guidelines and make the department look bad, given its previous position on the Stardust. He suggested that criminal elements in Las Vegas should be dealt with by Nevada authorities, not by making exceptions to antitrust regulations. Yet, just one week later, at their third meeting, Danner says Mitchell told him, "From our review of these figures, we see no problem. Why don't you go ahead with the negotiations?" (Mitchell, through his lawyer, has denied giving any go-ahead for the Dunes purchase.) Later that day Danner told Maheu that the Dunes matter "was taken care of in Washington and there would be no interference beyond that." That evening Danner flew to Florida and met with Rebozo the next day. Both men concede they discussed certain Hughes business matters, but Danner insists that he never mentioned Mitchell's go-ahead for the purchase of the Dunes.

After one of Danner's trips to see Mitchell, Maheu recalls, he told Tom Bell, then a Hughes lawyer in Las Vegas, that "certain political obligations had to be met as the result of the trip which Mr. Danner has made," and he asked Bell to "make those funds available to Mr. Danner." (Bell says he gave Danner $50,000 in $100 bills from the Silver Slipper, the casino which Hughes organized as a proprietorship, so that political contributions from it would not be illegal corporate gifts.) Later in 1970, at either Key Biscayne or San Clemente, Danner delivered this second installment of $50,000 to Rebozo.

Ultimately, Hughes's purchase of the Dunes fell through for financial reasons. But Rebozo had Hughes's $100,000. What he did with it remains a matter of great debate.

The largest contributor of "early money" to Nixon's campaign was the dairy industry, which was trying hard to ingratiate itself with the new Republican administration. In the late 1960s the dairy farmers were becoming the country's most determinedly organized agricultural lobby—and the most politically active. In part, this was because of their heavy dependence on government decision-making. For most other farmers, support prices are well below market prices and serve as little more than insurance against a catastrophic market collapse. But in dairy foods, federal policy—on price supports, tariffs, and import quotas—directly affects prices.

The organization of the dairy industry was spearheaded by Harold S. Nelson and David L. Parr, who began twenty-five years ago as farm organizers in Texas and Arkansas. By 1969 they had pyramided their small outfits into Associated Milk Producers, Inc. (AMPI), the largest milk cooperative in the nation, with 40,000 members spread across the Midwest and Southwest producing 12.4 per cent of America's milk. The next largest co-ops—Mid-America Dairymen and Dairymen, Inc.—grew by imitating the Nelson-Parr techniques. All three groups have been sued by the Justice Department for allegedly using illegal methods to enroll members. Parr conceded that AMPI was after "political power." Even Secretary of the Treasury John B. Connally, Jr., AMPI's most fervent supporter in the administration, told the President, "They're doing some things that I think are a little strong-armed tactics. . . ."

Nelson and Parr were working toward a single national milk cooperative that could compel attention from the federal government. In the meantime, though, they operated through more traditional means. AMPI formed the Trust for Agricultural and Political Education (TAPE), modeled after the AFL-CIO's Committee on Political Education (COPE), to funnel funds into political campaigns. In turn, Mid-America

Dairymen established the Agricultural and Dairy Educational Political Trust (ADEPT), and Dairymen, Inc., set up the Trust for Special Political Agricultural Community Education (SPACE). Like COPE, these trusts supported whichever party was in power.

But most of the AMPI leaders were Democrats. During the mid-1960s the San Antonio–based association enjoyed close ties to Lyndon Johnson, himself a Texas rancher (AMPI rented partial use of an airplane based at the LBJ ranch for a minimum of $94,000 a year). As its attorney, it hired Jacob "Jake" Jacobsen, a former special assistant to Johnson, and now an Austin, Texas, lawyer who wheeled and dealed in political circles, invariably attired in raw silk suits and Countess Mara ties. And in 1968 it backed a losing horse, giving more than $150,000 to Hubert H. Humphrey. As Nelson conceded later, "We were Democrats who had a track record that, you know, couldn't be denied . . . that is a cross you had to bear."

So in early 1969 AMPI set out to woo the new Republican administration. At first, it went about the job rather clumsily. Nelson purchased five tickets to the Republican victory dinner with a $5000 personal check, for which he was illegally repaid out of corporate funds. And to win the friendship of White House aide Bryce N. Harlow he sent two tickets to "Mr. and Mrs. Bryce Barlow." But then, after consultation with Jake Jacobsen, AMPI asked Jacobsen's Washington law partner, Milton Semer, to make a more judicious approach. When Semer contacted the White House he was put in touch with Herb Kalmbach, who told him that "contributions would be appreciated." On August 1, 1969, Semer flew to Dallas, picked up an attaché case containing $100,000 in cash, and the next day delivered it to Kalmbach at his Newport Beach office. Kalmbach put it in his safe-deposit box at the Security Pacific National Bank, where it formed part of his secret fund for the 1972 campaign.

Kalmbach says Semer made clear to him that AMPI hoped the money would help clear the way to three specific goals: milk price supports at 90 per cent of parity; a Presidential address to the AMPI convention the following year; and some access to President Nixon and the men around him. Nelson testified later, "It seemed to us then that nothing was happening as a result of that." But the money did serve as a door opener. On August 19 Nelson, Semer, and Parr were granted an audience with Harry Dent during which they outlined some of their problems. (Dent says that the meeting was a routine "massage" session.) Nelson told Dent, "We want to support the President," but he says that, in retrospect, "I am quite sure that at that point they didn't consider us to be supporters." So the relentless AMPI came up with still more concrete evidence. It contributed $135,000 to the Town House Project and pledged $2 million for Nixon's 1972 campaign. (At one point, Chuck Colson merrily told them, "This is a $2-million package.") All this got them was a nine-minute "photo opportunity" with the President on September 9, 1970.

At about that time, AMPI ditched Semer and hired the law firm of Harrison & Reeves, whose senior partner, Marion Harrison, had been co-chairman of the 1968 Nixon campaign in Virginia. But even that didn't do them much good. For that fall, TAPE made some contributions to unopposed Democratic candidates. This enraged Chuck Colson, who on November 3 sent a memo to Murray Chotiner, special counsel and political adviser to the President, asking him to tell Harrison, "If he wants to play both sides, that's one game; if he wants to play our side, it is entirely different. This will be a good way for you to condition him before we put the screws on him on imports, which we are about to do."

The import question aroused the dairymen greatly at that time. The Tariff Commission had recommended in September 1970 that the President offer additional protection to the domestic dairy industry—by closing off all imports on ice cream, certain chocolate products, and animal feeds containing milk derivatives, and by sharply reducing import quotas on low-fat cheese. On December 16 Patrick J. Hillings, a Republican lawyer who had once served as congressman from Nixon's old California district and was now "of counsel" to Harrison & Reeves, wrote President Nixon a letter raising what he called "a matter of some delicacy and of significant political impact." Stressing AMPI's contributions to date and its $2-million pledge for 1972, Hillings urged quick action on the new import quotas. "We write you both as advocates and as supporters," he noted. Two weeks later, Nixon set import quotas on the dairy products—but not quite as low as the dairymen had wanted. Apparently, the President was "putting the screws" on the farmers—giving them some *quo* for their *quid* but punishing them for their attempt to play both sides of the political fence and indicating that future favors would be conditioned on more unequivocal support.

This lesson was not lost on the dairymen when they made their big push the following spring. As the 1971–72 marketing season approached, the Agriculture Department had to decide whether to maintain the milk support price at $4.66 per 100 pounds—the same as the previous year—or raise it, as the dairy farmers wanted. Because of a grain shortage and increased production costs, maintenance of the $4.66 price would lower the parity rate from 85 to about 80 per cent. The dairymen wanted an increase to $5.21 per 100 pounds (90 per cent of parity) or, at the very least, $4.92 (85 per cent). The Agriculture Department feared that such price increases would not only raise the prices of dairy products for the consumer but encourage excess production.

In early 1971 AMPI and other dairy representatives began an intense lobbying effort in Congress to get legislation requiring milk price supports at between 85 and 90 per cent of parity. During late February and March, a hundred and eighteen representatives and twenty-nine senators sponsored bills to raise milk supports.

But on March 12—after consultation with the President—Secretary of Agriculture Clifford M. Hardin announced that the price would be maintained at $4.66 —approximately 79 per cent of parity.

This merely galvanized AMPI into more strenuous efforts. The first thing it did was to hire—on a

$60,000-a-year retainer—still another lawyer close to the President: Murray Chotiner, who had resigned his White House job only a few days before. Within a few weeks Chotiner had spoken about the milk problem with Ehrlichman; Colson; Colson's assistant, Harry Cashen; and John Whitaker, Ehrlichman's assistant on agricultural matters—arguing, in effect, that "what was good for the dairy farmers was good for the country and what was good for the country was good for the dairy farmers."

And Jake Jacobsen talked with his friend of twenty-five years' standing—John Connally. According to Jacobsen, Connally said he would "do what he could to be helpful." Bob Lilly, secretary of TAPE, has testified that sometime in March, Connally told him the increase was "in the bag."

Shortly after John Connally became treasury secretary in December 1970, some leading Democrats dined secretly with him and one former cabinet member emerged asking, "Can this country stand another Lyndon Johnson?" The columnist Pete Hamill has called Connally "Lyndon Johnson with small ears." And, indeed, he often seemed to be following in the dinosaur tracks of his longtime mentor. After service in the Navy during World War II and a stint with an Austin radio station, he went to Washington as administrative assistant to Johnson, then in his first Senate term. Later he managed most of LBJ's political campaigns, nominated him for President three times, and functioned as an intimate White House adviser while serving as three-term governor of Texas. One of seven children of a dirt-poor farmer, Connally had LBJ's country-boy earthiness and stupefying ego. (When his aides permitted him to be scheduled as the second speaker at a campaign dinner some years ago, he railed, "I don't speak second to anybody but the President, and you all better get that goddamn clear right now.") But, with his steel-gray hair impeccably waved, a knife-edge crease on his tailored trousers, and a hand-rubbed gloss on his white Mercedes, he had a suave polish Johnson never achieved. Though Connally called himself a "liberal in social affairs," his policies as governor were generally favorable to the Texas rich —like the oil billionaire Sid Richardson, whose lawyer he was for many years. And, skillfully pyramiding borrowed money, he became a rich man himself—with three ranches, membership in a prestigious Houston law firm, several company and bank directorships. Connally had the imperious style of the sun-belt aristocracy. When Haldeman once told him, "I'll convey your wishes to the President," Connally snorted, "I will convey my wishes to the President." But it was precisely this masterful air which Nixon, who lacked it himself, so admired in others. "Connally seemed so sure of himself," says one White House aide. "The old man liked that. He wanted to be like Connally." By early 1971 Washington was seething with rumors that the administration's new "strong man" would move first into the Republican party and then into position as Nixon's heir apparent.

On March 23, 1971, Nelson, Parr, and about fifteen other dairy representatives were scheduled to meet with President Nixon at 10:30 a.m. to protest Hardin's price-support decision. At 10:16, Connally spoke with the President and—according to a memo by Whitaker—recommended that he accept the farmers' demands for at least 85 per cent of parity. (This ran counter to a recommendation that he hold the line, endorsed by George Shultz, Ehrlichman, and most other White House aides.) At ten-thirty the dairymen filed into the Cabinet Room along with Hardin, Shultz, and Whitaker. Nixon welcomed them with long, rambling but occasionally rather frank remarks:

". . . I first wanted to say that I have been very grateful for the support that we have had in this administration from this group. . . . Uh, I know too that you are a group that are politically very conscious. Not in any partisan sense, but that you realize that what happens in Washington, not only affecting your business but affecting the economy, our foreign policy, and the rest, affects you. And you're willing to do something about it. And I must say a lot of businessmen and others that I get around this table they'll yammer and talk a lot but they don't do anything about it. And you do and I appreciate that. And I don't have to spell it out. Uh, my friend, uh and some others keep me posted as to what you do. . . ."

HARDIN (perhaps feeling the political winds blowing in his face): . . . uh, there is a point in these agricultural commodities where we don't control supply, where you can push over the hill, where total returns start reducing if you push the price up. . . . I think we have to be statesmen. We have to look at what's best for the man that's pulling the teats out on the farm, if I can use that old expression.

DAIRYMAN: You do it with machines.

PRESIDENT: I know something about that.

And they all guffawed at the President's barnyard humor.

Later, as they debated the economics of milk production, Nixon broke in again: ". . . not to get into your business at all, but, in your promotion, everybody is going for gimmicks these days, you know . . . take sleep-inducers. Now, uh, an article in *Reader's Digest* a couple of months ago in regard to sleeping pills—enormous use of them—but almost any person who really studies sleep will tell you probably that lacking a pill . . . the best thing you can do is milk . . . it could be warm. It could be, uh, tepid, or it could be cold. But it has a certain soothing effect . . . sometimes you've just got so many problems you're not going to sleep. But that's all psychological too. If you get people thinking that a glass of milk is going to make them sleep, I mean, it'll do just as well as a sleeping pill. It's all in the head."

At the end of the fifty-five-minute meeting, Nixon launched into a peroration on the virtues of farmers: "The cities are all corrupt. . . . Show me a country that loses its rural heartland . . . it almost always follows that it loses its character. . . . The new frontier basically is now in the center of the country, not on either coast." And finally: ". . . I have some Presidential cuff-links for everyone here, with the Presidential seal. . . . And since your wives will wonder where you really were today, uh, you can . . . it's a little bow that she can wear if she likes, and the Presidential seal."

At 12:18 p.m. the President met with Ehrlichman and Shultz and later talked by phone with Colson. And at 5:05 he convened a full conference to resolve the price-support issue attended by Ehrlichman, Connally, Hardin, Whitaker, Shultz, Under Secretary of Agriculture J. Phil Campbell, and Assistant Director of the Office of Management and Budget Donald Rice. Connally began the meeting with a frank exposition of the political realities: "It appears very clear to me that you're going to have to move, uh, strong in the Midwest. You're going to have to be strong in rural America. . . . These dairymen are organized; they're adamant; they're militant."

And he stressed the money the farmers had to contribute: "They, uh, very frankly, they tap these fellows —I believe its one-third of one per cent of their total sales or ninety-nine dollars a year. . . . They have them a Sabreliner airplane and they just travel from one part of the country to another part of the country to get these fellows in. . . . And they're amassing an enormous amount of money that they're going to put into political activities. And, uh, uh, I think the purpose—I think they've got a legitimate cause. I wouldn't recommend that you do, you take—do that if it didn't have any merit to it. . . . I don't think there's a better organization in the United States. If you can get it, uh, if you can get more help for 'em that will be more loyal to you . . . I just think you ought to stretch the point. . . ."

The President and his advisers agreed that, in any case, Congress was almost certain to pass a bill setting milk price supports at 85 or 90 per cent of parity. And Nixon said, "I could not veto it. Not because they're milkers, but because they're farmers. And it would be just turning down the whole damn Middle America, uh, where we need support. And under the circumstances I think the best thing to do is to just, uh, relax and enjoy it."

Connally quickly assented: ". . . you're in this thing for everything you can get out of it."

The decision for increased supports was made. They got up to leave.

Ehrlichman quipped, "Better go get a glass of milk. (*Laughter*.) Drink it while it's cheap."

Connally stayed behind to chat a few minutes more with the President (making an unexplained reference to "a very substantial allocation of oil in Texas that you, that will be at your, at your discretion"). Ehrlichman talked later with Colson, who then immediately met with Chotiner. At these meetings, a White House strategy evidently evolved: notify the dairy trusts that a favorable decision on price supports was imminent but hold up any announcement until they made firm commitments of the $2 million already promised for the 1972 campaign. Connally may have passed this message in a phone call to Jacobsen that afternoon. According to Parr, Connally on this or another occasion said that to get the increased supports "new money should be committed." And Chotiner hinted as much to Nelson, telling him that afternoon that prospects for the 85 per cent of parity looked favorable, but "not to count on it until it was absolutely done." Chotiner also warned that the dairymen should by no means boycott the Republican fund-raising dinner scheduled for the next evening in Washington. Before Hardin's March 12 decision, the three dairy groups had planned to buy as many as one hundred tickets at $1000 each—a form of political contribution. But when the secretary's decision went against them, they had canceled those plans and talked of a virtual boycott. On March 22, when the meeting with the President was scheduled, TAPE made a tentative gesture of support by purchasing ten dinner tickets.

Now Chotiner's message to Nelson set off a frantic series of moves to funnel more dairy money into the dinner within the remaining twenty-four hours. After the dairymen's meeting with Nixon, Paul Alagia, executive director of Dairymen, Inc., had had to go to Chicago on business. But that evening he got a call from his wife in Louisville, Kentucky, saying that AMPI officials wanted to see him that very night and would meet him at the Louisville Airport. When he landed there at about 4:00 a.m., he found Nelson, Parr, Lilly, and Gary Hanman, senior vice president of Mid-America Dairymen, who had flown in on AMPI's private plane only minutes before. They sat down on some benches in the airport lobby, where the AMPI officials told Alagia that things were going their way. Alagia recalls, "They had either been to see Connally or they were on their way to see Secretary Connally . . . [and] they were trying to tell me what kind of a forceful fellow Mr. Connally was." Then, Alagia says, "They indicated to me they wanted two or three hundred thousand dollars." Alagia replied, "What are you guys talking about? You have to be kidding!" So the AMPI officials reduced their request. They explained that in light of the administration's decision to raise price supports it was very important that all three dairy groups attend the Republican dinner in force. Mid-America Dairymen and its political trust, ADEPT, could not afford a major contribution, so the AMPI people were asking Alagia to arrange for SPACE to loan ADEPT about $100,000. Alagia was very tired and very ill at ease. "I would have done anything within limits to politely excuse myself and get out of there," he recalls. "I didn't appreciate them descending on me, you know." But he said he would see what he could do.

Alagia went home, got a couple of hours' sleep, and then went to the Dairymen, Inc., office, where he informed his colleagues about the airport meeting. James Mueller, the SPACE trustee, wrote five checks, each for $5000, to five Republican committees, and a Dairymen employee took them to Washington just in time to buy tickets for the "Kick-Off 1972" Republican bash. (Later, TAPE loaned ADEPT $50,000 to contribute to Republican committees.)

That evening, some 1500 contributors gathered at the Washington Hilton for the dinner to benefit the Republican National Committee and the Senate and House Republican campaign committees. Executives from U.S.

Steel, General Motors, Jersey Standard, United Aircraft, and other major corporations were there. (One executive said Republican fund-raisers had "bombarded" his company with "invitations" from some sort of Washington "boiler-room operation.") For his $1000 the contributor got cocktails, a seafood coquille, filet mignon, tomato stuffed with cauliflower, potatoes sprinkled with almonds, and *"Vacherin Glacé Chantilly GOP,"* a dessert consisting of ice cream, meringue, whipped cream, and strawberries soaked in Grand Marnier. They also got a series of one-liners from Vice President Agnew and a speech by President Nixon in which he quoted Rutherford B. Hayes's dictum, "He serves his party best who serves his country best."

The dinner ended around midnight and afterward Chotiner and Nelson went over to the nearby Madison Hotel, where Kalmbach was staying. Kalmbach had been alerted beforehand by Ehrlichman that they were coming to see him, but he had evidently forgotten and was already in bed. When the two men called from the lobby, Kalmbach received them in his pajamas. Nelson reaffirmed the dairy industry's pledge of $2 million for Nixon's re-election campaign and Kalmbach said he would set up the necessary machinery. Kalmbach has testified that he knew an announcement of increased milk supports was scheduled for the next day and that this was "linked to the reaffirmation of the $2-million pledge."

On March 25 Secretary Hardin announced an "upward adjustment" of the milk support price from the $4.66 announced only twelve days before to $4.93 (about 85 per cent of parity). Hardin has since testified that the decision was "based entirely on a reconsideration of the evidence." But shortly thereafter dairy funds began to flow in earnest into the Nixon campaign coffers —rising eventually to a total of $632,500.

John Connally had played a key role in obtaining the new price supports, which, a Senate report says, was worth "tens of millions of dollars" to dairy farmers (and cost the American consumer corresponding millions). The dairymen were very grateful. According to Bob Lilly, Jake Jacobsen called him on April 28 and said he needed $10,000 for Connally, who had been "helpful to us in the price support thing." (Connally was, of course, a millionaire, although Jack Anderson says he had been telling friends around this time that he had to borrow money to avoid selling off investments.) On May 4 Lilly borrowed $10,000 from the Citizens National Bank in Austin and gave it to Jacobsen. According to a later indictment handed down against Connally and Jacobsen, the lawyer took the cash to Washington on May 14 and presented $5000 of it to the treasury secretary in his office. One official source says, "Jacobsen apparently figured, 'Why blow it all at once?' when he could come back and get another thank you." According to the indictment, Jacobsen came back to Washington on September 24, retrieved the remaining $5000 from a safe-deposit box in the Riggs National Bank, and presented it to Connally. Lilly has testified that he gave still a third $5000 installment to Jacobsen for Connally in November 1971.*

The White House was delighted with the dairymen's $2-million pledge—one of the three largest made to Nixon's re-election campaign. The money was scheduled to come in regular monthly installments of $90,000 a month beginning April 1, 1971—five days after the price supports were raised. On May 18 Haldeman and Dean decided that the "milk money" could pay for all of CREEP's activities until the summer of 1972. But several days later, Kalmbach and others persuaded Haldeman that the money should not be used for official campaign expenses because of the "risk of discovery."

The White House wanted to avoid any publicity about the dairymen's contribution for fear that the public might regard it as a *quid pro quo* given for the increased price supports. The milk trusts thought they had to report their contributions to the clerk of the

---

*Jacobsen has pleaded guilty to bribery in these transactions and is awaiting sentencing. But Connally was acquitted of receiving bribes after thirty-five government witnesses at his trial could not directly corroborate Jacobsen's testimony. Several other criminal indictments stemmed from the milk affair. AMPI pleaded guilty to making illegal campaign contributions in 1968, 1970, and 1972, and was fined $35,000. Parr and Nelson pleaded guilty to conspiring to bribe government officials and making illegal corporate campaign contributions. They were fined $10,000 each and sentenced to three years in jail. All but four months of their sentences were suspended.

House, as required by law, but in a series of meetings, Kalmbach recalls, "We were trying to develop a procedure . . . where they could meet their independent reporting requirements and still not result in disclosure." The solution was for the milk trusts to give their money in small amounts to a network of committees set up in the District of Columbia and for those committees then to pass the money on to the President's campaign without reporting the transfer.

This formula took advantage of several supposed "loopholes" in campaign finance law. At that time, Illinois, Delaware, and the District of Columbia had no laws requiring a political committee to report its contributions and expenditures, and many senators and congressmen set up committees in those areas to keep their financial transactions anonymous. Federal law required reporting of all contributions and expenditures by a political committee "organized for the purpose of influencing the outcome of the general election in two or more states." But the Nixon fund-raisers reasoned that this would not apply to the milk money if the committees operated only in the District and nominally worked for the renomination, not the election, of the President. (Common Cause has challenged this rationale, arguing that the law speaks not of operating but of influencing the outcome in two or more states, which the milk money would certainly do, and that the President was under no serious challenge from his opponents in the primaries—Representatives Pete McCloskey of California and John M. Ashbrook of Ohio —so that, from the start, the money was raised for his re-election campaign.)

At Colson's suggestion, the job of forming the milk committees was handed over to Robert Bennett, who only recently had taken over Mullen & Company. John Dean drafted the basic charter for the committees and Bennett began forming them. He and others often stayed up late into the night thinking of names—the sole criterion being that they make no mention of Richard Nixon. Some of the names showed great imagination: Organization of Sensible Citizens, Americans United for Objective Reporting, Committee for Political

Integrity, Association of Americans for Retention of Sound Ideals, Americans United for Safer Streets, and Supporters of the American Dream. (Each committee was to receive only $2500, to take advantage of an IRS rule eliminating the gift tax for contributions under $3000.)

To insure maximum anonymity, Bennett enlisted employees of the Union Trust Company of Washington and the National Savings and Trust Company—the two banks where the committees' accounts were to be held—to serve as committee treasurers. The committee chairmen were generally loyal partisans who agreed to serve, often without the faintest idea of what the committees were set up to do. The Organization of Involved Americans, for example, listed its address at the office of John Y. Merrell, a Washington attorney. Americans United for Political Awareness was listed at Merrell's home in Arlington. He was chairman of one, his wife of the other, but Merrell couldn't remember which was which. The Merrells say Bennett asked them to lend their names and addresses to the cause.

Other chairmen knew even less. Two men originally recruited by Bennett, then replaced, were inadvertently listed by the dairymen in their reports to the clerk of the House. This and other goofs led to disclosures that the committees had indeed been set up by Bennett as conduits for the milk money to flow into Nixon's campaign. By September 1971 newspapers—notably the *Minneapolis Tribune, The Washington Post* and *The Wall Street Journal*—began linking this to the price-support increases. Both the White House and the dairymen were embarrassed and late that fall the dairy trusts put a "hold" on further contributions. That winter, after receiving $237,000, the committees were abolished and the milk producers began looking for other ways to meet their commitment to Nixon's campaign.

But before new channels could be opened, friction developed between the milk producers and the government. On February 1, 1972, the Justice Department filed a civil antitrust suit against AMPI, based on a long investigation of methods which the association allegedly used to squeeze smaller cooperatives out of their markets. At first, this suit sharply reduced the dairymen's interest in making further contributions to Nixon. But in the spring interest suddenly revived. George Mehren, a former assistant secretary of agriculture who had replaced Harold Nelson as AMPI general manager on January 12, met first with Connally and then with Kalmbach in an apparent effort to use further contributions to get the antitrust suit dropped. According to Kalmbach, Mehren told him on April 4 that AMPI was ready to make a substantial contribution ($150,000 according to other sources) but wanted Kalmbach in turn to call the White House about the suit. Kalmbach says he flatly refused and Mehren complained, "Here you're asking for contributions and you're not willing to help." Later, the milk producers did cough up another $295,000 for the Nixon campaign—$200,000 channeled through the congressional campaign committees. (That fall, the milk trusts also gave substantial contributions to Democrats—$185,000 to Representative Wilbur D. Mills of Arkansas, chairman of the House Ways and Means Committee; $39,000 to Representative James Abourzek of South Dakota; at least $25,000 to Senator Hubert Humphrey of Minnesota, and lesser sums to thirty other Democratic senators and congressmen. Some of the contributions came illegally from corporate funds.)

The milk industry was not the only one that depended heavily on government regulation. Others—notably the airlines, oil companies, and defense industries—looked with hope and apprehension to Washington. There have been rumors that Nixon campaign officials drew up a list of corporations that had particular "problems with the government," but investigators have been unable to find it. However, Kalmbach and other Nixon fund-raisers managed to find their way to many such industrialists.

Political contributions out of corporate funds are strictly prohibited, but in addition to AMPI, eighteen corporations contributed a total of $754,540 to Nixon's re-election campaign. They were: American Airlines ($55,000); American Ship Building ($25,000); Ashland Oil ($100,000); Braniff Airways ($40,000); Carnation ($7900); Diamond International ($5000); Goodyear Tire & Rubber ($40,000); Gulf Oil ($100,000); HMS Electric ($5000); Lehigh Valley Cooperative Farmers ($50,000); Minnesota Mining and Manufacturing ($36,000); Northrop ($150,000); Phillips Petroleum ($100,000); Greyhound ($16,040); National By-Products ($3000); LBC & W, an architectural firm in Columbia, South Carolina ($10,000); Time Oil, a Seattle gasoline distributor ($6600); and Ratrie, Robbins & Schweitzer, a Baltimore construction company ($5000). (Seven of the companies have also admitted giving $44,864 in corporate funds to Democratic Presidential candidates—Senators Humphrey, Jackson, McGovern, Muskie and Representative Wilbur Mills—in 1972 and $50,000 to the Democratic National Committee.)*

The 1972 contributions which have surfaced so far are only a small part of a huge corporate kitty which every year clatters into the pockets of candidates for local, state, and national office. Several companies that made corporate contributions in 1972 have now conceded that their gifts came from large political "slush funds" which in some cases had been in existence for more than a decade. The largest discovered so far— $10.3 million—belonged to Gulf Oil, which acknowledged that it used the money for political contributions and "related activities" here and abroad between 1960 and 1974 ($5.4 million was spent in the United States). Minnesota Mining and Manufacturing conceded that between 1963 and 1972 it doled out at least $634,000 in 390 contributions to politicians of both

---

*Sixteen of these corporations pleaded guilty to violations of laws governing campaign contributions. They paid fines ranging from $1000 to $25,000. The American Ship Building Company was also charged with one count of conspiracy and fined $20,000. In many cases, corporate executives pleaded guilty to similar violations of campaign laws. While three executives received suspended sentences, thirteen of them were fined between $500 and $2000. George-Steinbrenner of American Ship Building pleaded guilty to charges of conspiracy to violate the campaign-contributions laws and devising a cover story to explain the contributions. He was fined $15,000.

parties. Northrop spent $476,000 since 1961, Phillips Petroleum spent some $585,000 in ten years, and Ashland Oil $801,165 in eight years—both excluding their 1972 contributions to Nixon. The Civil Aeronautics Board has charged Braniff with diverting $641,285 into a secret political fund and American Airlines of concealing a cash fund of "at least $275,000."

Candidates of both parties have eagerly dipped their fists into these corporate cash drawers—and presumably repaid the kindness with governmental favors. What distinguished Nixon's 1972 campaign from others was both the amount of corporate money collected and the strategy that seemed to zero in on large companies with problems in Washington. A Senate committee later concluded that although Nixon fund-raisers may not have directly solicited corporate contributions, "there is evidence that a number of them either were indifferent to the source of the money or, at the very least, made no effort whatsoever to see to it that the source of the funds was private rather than corporate." Some of the executives who were solicited believed that the fund-raisers were willing to take corporate money because the sums they asked for were far beyond the capacities of the executives themselves.

Nixon's campaign pitch to businessmen was finely calibrated, depending on who they were and how much his fund-raisers thought they could extract. The run-of-the-mine executive got a slick, folder-type kit with a large, friendly shot of the President on the cover under the legend: "The responsibility of every American . . . support the candidate of your choice." Bigger fish got a personal visit from one of Nixon's fund-raisers, which in the early days usually meant Kalmbach. The President's lawyer was generally low-key and discreet. In his first contact he rarely asked for a firm commitment but would suggest a "goal figure," returning later to nail down a contribution. He talked of different classes of contributors—$25,000, $50,000, and $100,000—often suggesting that, since there were so many people at $25,000, those who wanted to be known as "major contributors" should give more. Sometimes he referred to a "100 Club"—people or corporations that gave $100,000. He told some executives that this was the sum expected from "major corporations" and that it would put them in a "special class." Occasionally, he overdid it. Once he antagonized a seasoned contributor by telling him that with $100,000 he could join "the privileged few that would have the honor of raising funds for the President."

One man who got the full Kalmbach treatment was George A. Spater, chairman and chief executive officer of American Airlines. At a dinner in New York on October 20, 1971, Kalmbach asked Spater for $100,000. Spater said he might be able to produce $75,000. Kalmbach said he hoped Spater could do better than that. American Airlines was susceptible to such pressure because the company had at least twenty important matters pending before various federal agencies, among them a proposed merger between American and Western airlines. Spater says he and Kalmbach never discussed the merger or other airline business. But he was apprehensive: he knew that Kalmbach represented not only the President—who at that very moment had the merger matter on his desk—but also United Airlines, American's major competitor and a determined opponent of the merger. Spater worried that if American didn't come up with $100,000 it would be declared *persona non grata* at the White House. He has testified, "There were two aspects: would you get something if you gave it, or would you be prevented from getting something if you didn't give it? . . . Most contributions from the business community are not volunteered to seek a competitive advantage but are made in response to pressure, for fear of the competitive disadvantage that might result if they are not made. . . . It is something like the old medieval maps that show a flat world and then what they called 'terra incognita,' with fierce animals lying around the fringes of this map. You just don't know what is going to happen to you if you get off it. I think sometimes the fear of the unknown may be more terrifying than the fear of the known."

These terrors proved compelling and American paid

its tithe. First, $20,000 was paid out of personal funds. Then $100,000 was drawn on the airline's account at the Chemical Bank in New York and transmitted to the Swiss account of a Lebanese agent, André Tabourian (American had used him for other more legitimate transactions). The money was charged on American's books as "a special commission to André Tabourian in connection with used aircraft sales to Middle East Airlines." From Switzerland the money was transferred back to an account at the Chase Manhattan Bank in New York. Later, Tabourian came to New York, withdrew the $100,000 in cash, and gave it to an American Airlines official who put it in an office safe. In March 1972 Spater arranged for $55,000—now "washed" of corporate contamination—to be removed from the safe, placed in an envelope, and delivered to the Nixon fund-raisers.

But that was nothing compared to the washing Braniff gave to its contribution. On March 1, 1972, Harding L. Lawrence, Braniff's chairman, gave Maurice Stans an unsolicited $10,000 in cash ($5000 of his own money and $5000 from the company president). Stans thanked him for the money, but said he felt Braniff could do more because the company was "doing much better than the rest of the industry." He suggested that $100,000 would be appropriate. Lawrence decided the company could manage another $40,000. His executives came up with an ingenious scheme for producing the money out of corporate funds without leaving a telltale trail. Camilo Fabrega, Braniff's manager in Panama, owned a firm called Camfab. Braniff issued a voucher, dated March 29, 1972, approving payment of $40,000 to Camfab for "expenses and services," and the check was entered on Braniff's books as an account receivable due from Camfab. The check was forwarded to Fabrega, who endorsed it on behalf of Camfab and cashed it at a bank in Panama, returning the proceeds in U.S. currency to Braniff officials in Dallas. Subsequently, Lawrence and others delivered the $40,000 in cash to Stans. Now Braniff had to pay off the account receivable. This it did by issuing a supply of special ticket stock to Fabrega. Tickets written on that stock were sold only by the supervisor at Braniff's Panama office and only for cash (if a customer wanted to pay by check regular tickets were used). Receipts for these cash sales were not accounted for as ticket receipts but were applied to the liquidation of the Camfab account receivable. Then, on his trips from Panama to the Dallas office, Fabrega would take several thousand dollars in cash and deliver it to Braniff. By December 1972, when Braniff wanted to liquidate the account, the ticket sales had brought in only $27,000. So Fabrega got a $13,000 loan from a Panamanian bank, then recouped it on further ticket sales. (Northrop, Goodyear, and Ashland Oil also laundered their contributions through foreign subsidiaries or agents.)

Some companies—among them Carnation and American Ship Building—attempted to disguise their corporate contributions by giving fake bonuses to their executives, who, in turn, passed them on to the Nixon campaign. George Steinbrenner III, chairman and chief executive officer of American Ship Building, wanted an "input into the administration"—presumably because of a cost-overrun problem with the Commerce Department and an antitrust suit against it filed by the Justice Department. According to Steinbrenner, Kalmbach said such input would cost him $100,000. At least $25,000 of that was laundered through bonuses that Steinbrenner gave to six trusted employees.

George Spater of American Airlines noted that one reason some companies gave corporate funds was that their salaried managers could not afford to keep pace with the wealthy "old money" executives of other companies. Indeed, corporate executives gave heavily to the Nixon campaign. Of 334 corporate officials who responded to a survey by a Senate committee, 164 individuals from 112 different corporations contributed more than $100 to a Presidential candidate in 1972, for a total of $1,896,322. Of this, $1,433,830—or about 80 per cent—went to the Nixon campaign.

The companies that got caught making corporate contributions often simply didn't have the political know-how to circumvent the regulations. One company that did have the know-how was International Telephone and Telegraph, a vast multinational corporation which ranked in 1970 as the twelfth largest company in America. ITT had grown rapidly during the 1960s—largely through acquisitions and mergers—and thus began attracting the attention of the Justice Department's Antitrust Division. In 1969 the department filed suits seeking to divest the corporation of three recent acquisitions: Canteen Corporation, which specialized in vending and industrial food-service; Grinnell Corporation, the nation's largest manufacturer of automatic-sprinkler systems; and the Hartford Fire Insurance Company, America's fourth largest property and liability insurance company.

To this three-pronged challenge, ITT responded with a dogged and determined lobbying campaign that reached time and again into the highest levels of the Nixon administration. The corporation, which depended heavily on government regulation, had long since developed a cadre of skilled "public affairs" officers who specialized in making the ITT case persuasive to government. Most of them were on a first-name basis with the highest officials in the land, men who did not allow themselves to be first-named by any old Sam or Ralph in a corporate suite. Edward Gerrity, ITT's vice president for public relations, was on a "Ned-Ted" basis with Vice President Spiro Agnew. In a memo describing a meeting between Harold S. Geneen, ITT's president, and Attorney General Mitchell, Gerrity could write: "Hal had a very friendly session with John whom, as you know, he admires greatly. . . ." Nobody called the President "Dick," but sometimes all the chumminess could get embarrassing. In a letter from "Bill" Merriam, director of ITT's Washington relations, to "John" Ehrlichman, Merriam wrote, "Incidentally, after leaving your office Hal was upset with himself for having called you 'Chuck' on several occasions during the meeting with you. We have previously discussed our contacts with Chuck Colson and apparently that stuck in his mind. I hope I rightly assured him that you would understand."

And the administration did understand. There often seemed to be remarkable understanding between ITT lobbyists and the White House. On more than one occasion, Nixon made clear to his subordinates that he abhorred the idea of breaking up large, acquisitive corporations simply because they were big—a view which both ITT and he attributed to Richard McLaren, the head of the Antitrust Division. Thus, when the government lost its suit on ITT's acquisition of Grinnell, the President adamantly opposed the appeal McLaren was pursuing. On April 19, 1971, he met with Ehrlichman and George Shultz, director of the Office of Management and Budget, to discuss, among other things, the proposed Grinnell appeal. The conversation went like this:

NIXON: They're not going to file [an appeal].
EHRLICHMAN: Well, I thought that was your position.
NIXON: Oh, hell.
EHRLICHMAN: I've been trying to give . . . them signals on this, and, uh, they've been horsing us pretty steadily. . . .
NIXON: . . . I don't know whether ITT is bad, good, or indifferent. But there is not going to be any more antitrust actions as long as I am in this chair. . . . Goddamn it, we're going to stop it.

Then, Nixon put through a call to Richard G. Kleindienst, the deputy attorney general who was supervising the ITT suits because John Mitchell's former law firm had once represented an ITT subsidiary. After some perfunctory preliminaries, the conversation went like this:

NIXON: . . . I want something clearly understood, and, if it is not understood, McLaren's ass is to be out within one hour. The ITT thing—stay the hell out of it. Is that clear? That's an order.

KLEINDIENST: Well, you mean the order is—

NIXON: The order is to leave the goddamn thing alone. Now, I've said this, Dick, a number of times, and you fellows apparently don't get the me—the message over there. I do not want McLaren to run around prosecuting people, raising hell about conglomerates, stirring things up at this point. Now you keep him the hell out of that. Is that clear?

KLEINDIENST: Well, Mr. President—

NIXON: Or either he resigns. I'd rather have him out anyway. I don't like the son-of-a-bitch. . . .

After the President's call, Kleindienst ordered Solicitor General Erwin Griswold to seek an extension of time for the Grinnell appeal, and the next day the Supreme Court granted an extension until May 20. But Kleindienst evidently told Mitchell about the President's tirade, because Mitchell soon warned Nixon that an attempt to stop the appeal could be "political dynamite." "You just can't stop this thing up at the Supreme Court," Mitchell told him on April 21, "because you will have Griswold quit, you will have a Senate investigation. . . . We don't need it. There are other ways of working this out."

The President agreed to let Mitchell work it out his way. And he, or his subordinates, did. For during the month-long extension of the Grinnell appeal, ITT and government negotiators began exploring a settlement of the three cases. The settlement, announced on July 31, allowed ITT to retain its prize acquisition, the Hartford Fire Insurance Company, in exchange for divesting itself of Grinnell, Canteen, and two other subsidiaries, Avis and Levitt.

But there may have been more to the deal. At the very time the Justice Department and ITT were working out this settlement, ITT was also committing a large amount of money to underwrite the 1972 Republican National Convention, then planned for San Diego.

According to Jeb Magruder, Nixon had told Haldeman he wanted the convention in San Diego. "One reason for the President's choice was simply convenience," Magruder has written. "He could stay at his San Clemente estate and fly over to the convention by helicopter when he was needed. But the more important reason was political. California was a crucial state, the state with the biggest bloc of electoral votes, and a state we had carried by a relatively narrow margin in 1968. The publicity that would surround a Republican convention in California might be enough to lock up California for the President before the campaign had even begun."

This strong Presidential interest gave ITT a special leverage on the White House. When William E. Timmons, Nixon's assistant for congressional relations, went to San Diego in early May to study the possibility of holding the convention there, he concluded that one of the major drawbacks was the city's low financial "bid"—only $200,000 compared to the $800,000 the Republican National Committee estimated it would need to run the convention. All other cities in the running had offered more. (It is customary for cities to bid cash and services for a political convention just as they do for major commercial gatherings.)

Haldeman had already spoken with California's Lieutenant Governor Ed R. Reinecke about the San Diego situation in April. Reinecke and Bill Timmons also conferred. Then, in mid-May, ITT's hierarchy descended on San Diego for the annual stockholders' meeting which was being held there that year. (ITT owned three hotels in San Diego, was building a cable plant there, and regarded itself as a "booster" of the city.) At a dinner on May 12 at the Sheraton Half Moon Inn, Representative Bob Wilson, a prominent Republican congressman from San Diego, told ITT president Geneen that the city could probably get the convention for $800,000 in cash. According to Wilson, Geneen "showed great interest" and said he would "see that they backed me personally for half the total amount needed, which would be $400,000. There was no written agreement, not even a handshake, but my personal knowledge of Mr. Geneen satisfied me as to the integrity of his guarantee."

On May 21—as discussions continued between ITT and government officials—Reinecke called John Mitchell in Washington and told him about the ITT guarantee. Reinecke recalls that Mitchell was "encouraging, tolerant, and fatherly . . . [but] he was like most of those fellows in the White House. They all say the same thing, which is very little." Reinecke talked with Mitchell about the ITT money once more in June, and the $400,000 figure was mentioned several more times in memos circulating among Timmons, Magruder, and Mitchell. Ultimately, ITT gave a written pledge for only $200,000, of which $100,000 was contingent on other fund-raising; the whole pledge was contingent on the selection of ITT's Harbor Island Hotel as Presidential headquarters.

ITT officials have since insisted that the only motive in making this enormous commitment was to promote their new hotel, scheduled to open in June 1972, just before the convention. Moreover, ITT carefully covered itself against any possible charge that it was making an illegal corporate contribution to the Republican party. It got an opinion from its own counsel that it was not making a corporate contribution to a party or candidate, since the money was to go first to the San Diego County Tourist and Convention Bureau.

But the effect was much the same. The corporation promised a very substantial contribution in cash or services to the party's convention and simultaneously got the government's permission to keep the Hartford insurance company. If a direct relationship could be proved between one and the other, the company could be prosecuted for bribery. But if there was a *quid pro quo* it was shrewdly disguised. As yet, despite years of probing by investigators, no prosecutions have been brought arising out of the settlement itself.

nother group of wealthy individuals sought out
by Nixon's fund-raisers were the investment
bankers, Wall Street lawyers, and corporation presidents
who dreamed of becoming ambassadors. For decades
these men have been a major source of campaign funds
for both political parties, but Nixon probably set some
kind of record for squeezing money out of aspiring
diplomats. More than $1.8 million poured into the
Nixon campaign chest in 1968 and 1972 from people
who later became ambassadors, and this amount does
not include some substantial contributions from those
who hoped for such appointments but never got them.
(In 1972, John Safer, a Washington developer and
sculptor, gave $250,000, and Roy Carver, board chair-
man of Bandag, Inc., gave $257,000 in hopes that the
gifts would get them embassies somewhere, but they
never did.) After his re-election in 1972, Nixon appointed thirteen noncareer ambassadors, eight of whom
had donated at least $25,000; together they had con-
tributed more than $706,000 to his campaign.

Sometimes a contribution would "buy" only a small,
out-of-the-way embassy in a steamy equatorial country
where the water had to be boiled before you could
drink it. Ambassadors assigned to such countries often
would do almost anything to get to a more salubrious
spot.

Consider the case of J. Fife Symington. A longtime
Republican partisan in Maryland, Symington had served
for a while as the state's Republican finance chairman
and had run for Congress three times without success. In
the mid-1960s, he had retired to his estate in the rolling
farmland of Baltimore County, but—as his lawyer later recalled—he was "very anxious to serve his country
as an ambassador in an area where his background
would help." In 1968 he gave a modest $5500 to
Nixon's campaign and was rewarded with the ambassadorship to one of the smallest and newest countries anywhere—Trinidad and Tobago. In September 1970,

after only fifteen months on the job, Symington called Kalmbach and then flew to Los Angeles to see him. Over lunch at the California Club, Kalmbach recalls, the ambassador told him "the humidity was terrible in Trinidad and it was affecting his wife in such a manner that he was giving serious consideration to resigning and coming back home." But, he said, he "liked being an ambassador" and felt he was now entitled to a "European post."

Sensing his opportunity, Kalmbach reminded the ambassador that he was then "involved" in a "senatorial campaign program [the Town House Project]." He said "Fife . . . I'm soliciting funds. . . . I've talked to you about this before, but I would like to talk to you about your financial help for this program."

Symington was a prime prospect. His wife, Marsie, was the granddaughter of Henry C. Frick, the fabulously wealthy steel magnate, and her dowry had been generous. So, Kalmbach says, Symington quickly told him: "Herb—Marsie and I will contribute a hundred thousand dollars to the President and the 1972 program. Now, if you want to split it up [half for the Town House Project, as Kalmbach had proposed] that is your decision . . . but before I make this pledge firm, Herb, I would like to be certain . . . that I will receive an appointment to a European post."

"Well, Fife, I just don't have the authority to do more than I've done before, and this is give you my word I'll act as a reference and I'll support your candidacy for a major post," Kalmbach says he replied.

"Herb, with all respect . . . that isn't good enough. I've got to have the assurance from Bob Haldeman."

"Fife, I can't do that, you know."

"Why don't you call him?"

"Okay, I will."

Kalmbach says he reached Larry Higby, Haldeman's assistant, in Chicago, where he was traveling with the President and Haldeman. Higby called him back in fifteen or thirty minutes and, according to Kalmbach, said, "Herb, the answer is go." Kalmbach went back to the lunch table and wrote out the agreement on a slip of paper—listing Symington's preference for Spain or Portugal—which the ambassador put in his wallet.

Shortly after their luncheon, Symington gave Kalmbach the first $50,000—earmarked for the Town House Project. Early the next year, he resigned the Trinidad and Tobago post, convinced that he had an Iberian job in the bag. But he didn't. Kalmbach talked repeatedly with Haldeman; with Gordon Strachan, another one of Haldeman's assistants; and with Peter M. Flanigan, the White House official directly charged with screening ambassadorial candidates, but he could never get them to honor the commitment.*

Kalmbach was involved in a similar arrangement with Vincent de Roulet, a New York socialite, yachtsman, and race-horse breeder. De Roulet owned Towne-Oller & Associates, a company that provides marketing information to manufacturers of health and beauty aids. He was also the son-in-law of Mrs. Joan Whitney Payson, owner of the New York Mets. And he was an avid clubman, proud of his membership in the New York Yacht Club, the Links Club, the Links Golf Club, the Turf and Field Club, the Jockey Club, the Twenty-Nine Club, Deepdale and the Madison Square Garden Club. Feeling "a certain noblesse oblige," he had grown "sick of sitting around the club simply complaining about things." He was "seeking some position in government for which I considered myself qualified and I knew that there were only three or four ways to get it, one of which was money." In 1968 he and his wife contributed $75,000 to the Republican campaign (his mother-in-law was also a major contributor), and shortly after Nixon's election De Roulet was named ambassador to Jamaica. In his four stormy years there, De Roulet was a controversial diplomat: he refused visas to Miriam Makeba and Mick Jagger because he didn't like their life-styles; called the Jamaicans "niggers," and closed off the embassy toilet facilities to visa applicants, explaining publicly that the Jamaicans used too much toilet paper and clogged the plumbing. And

*Kalmbach pled guilty to a charge of promising federal employment—to Symington—in return for support of a candidate. He served six months of his six-to-eighteen-month sentence concurrently with his sentence for the Town House Project.

almost from the start he was trying to move on to better things. In May 1970 for his wife's birthday party he invited Kalmbach to Jamaica and told him he was willing to contribute $100,000 to Nixon's 1972 campaign. In early summer Kalmbach returned to Jamaica to nail down the contribution, but the ambassador said that before he made it firm he wanted to be sure he wasn't being "blackballed" for the European post he was after. Kalmbach spoke with Haldeman and Stans about the problem and says he understood that De Roulet later got a firm "commitment" from Haldeman for the European embassy (said to be Italy, Spain, or Portugal). De Roulet evidently thought so too. He contributed $50,000 for the Town House Project and eventually $53,500 more to Nixon's campaign. In July 1973 he was declared *persona non grata* by the Jamaican government after he testified publicly that he had made a deal with Prime Minister Michael Manley to keep the CIA from intervening in Jamaican elections if the Jamaican government would not seek to nationalize American bauxite interests. He never got the European appointment.

But Dr. Ruth B. Farkas got to Luxembourg. Mrs. Farkas, whose family owns Alexander's department store in New York City, wanted to be an ambassador; but, like Symington and De Roulet, she wasn't captivated by the Caribbean. In the summer of 1971, Kalmbach recalls, Peter Flanigan called him to say, "Herb, we would like to have you contact a Dr. Ruth Farkas in New York. She is interested in giving two hundred and fifty thousand dollars for Costa Rica." Kalmbach says he met with Mrs. Farkas, who said, in effect, "Well, you know, I am interested in Europe, I think, and isn't two hundred and fifty thousand dollars an awful lot of money for Costa Rica?" Mrs. Farkas and her husband, George, say they were then "tricked" into purchasing the ambassadorship by Representative Louis C. Wyman, a New Hampshire Republican whom they met through a mutual friend. According to the story which the Farkases have told a grand jury, they met with Wyman at Palm Beach in late 1971. When Mr. Farkas said he wanted an embassy for his wife—preferably in Europe and ideally in Luxembourg—Wyman said that would cost $300,000 and Farkas replied, "Done!" The agreement was allegedly confirmed in a meeting between Mrs. Farkas, Wyman, and Maurice Stans in March 1972. (Wyman concedes that he was the middleman but insists there was nothing illegal in all this because there was never an explicit agreement. "You establish your eligibility" with a large campaign contribution, he explains.) On August 15, 1972, the White House sent the Senate Foreign Relations Committee a letter of intent to nominate Mrs. Farkas as ambassador to Luxembourg, pending an FBI clearance. But the appointment was held up. In late September Mrs. Farkas began making a $300,000 contribution to the Nixon campaign. The final check—for $5000—was received on February 21, 1973. Six days later, her nomination went to the Senate.

Much of Nixon's fund-raising strategy centered on the need to get contributions into the campaign kitty before Congress passed a new campaign-finance law with more stringent reporting requirements. There had long been recognition of the need for a new law to replace the Federal Corrupt Practices Act of 1925, which Lyndon Johnson once called "more loophole than law." But as the new bill moved through congressional committees in the fall of 1971, Republican leaders (and some Democrats, too) were in no rush to get it passed. Clark MacGregor, then White House chief of congressional liaison, recalls a high-level meeting at which Maurice Stans argued that the bill had to be "slowed down" to give the Republican fund-raisers "more time to raise money anonymously." MacGregor says Stans's position was supported at the meeting by Mitchell, Haldeman, and Ehrlichman. The message, in turn, was relayed to Nixon's friends in Congress.

Although Congress sent the bill to the White House on January 26, 1972, Nixon waited the full limit of ten working days before he signed it on February 7. In his statement that day, the President said the bill would "work to build public confidence in the integrity of the electoral process." Since the bill did not take effect until sixty days after signing, Nixon's delay created a legal no man's land between the expiration of the old law, on March 10, and the effective date of the new one, April 7—a period in which literally no disclosure of contributors' names was required.

With this transition period artfully maneuvered into the very heart of the political giving season, the Republican fund-raisers went all-out to exploit it. And they were in a perfect position to do so. While half a dozen Democratic contenders were still slugging away in the primaries, the Republicans had the President-as-Candidate ready to accept any and all contributions. A CREEP memo to John Dean made the strategy clear: seek maximum giving during the March 10–April 7 period, during which the identity of contributors could be absolutely protected.

To handle this tricky operation, the Republicans brought in their first team. On February 15 Maurice Stans resigned as commerce secretary and resumed his 1968 role as finance chairman (officially, chairman of the Finance Committee for the Re-election of the President). That same day, Herb Kalmbach, who had been raising money since 1969 without a title, once more became Stan's associate chairman. (On February 3 Kalmbach had closed out his secret trust fund, transferring $915,037.68—$233,802.86 in cash and $681,234.82 in checking-account balances—to Hugh W. "Duke" Sloan, Jr., treasurer of the finance committee.) And on March 1, John Mitchell resigned as attorney general to take charge officially at CREEP.

As finance committee chairman, Stans crisscrossed the country beating the corporate-financial thickets for "pre-April 7" funds. On February 28 he met thirty-five wealthy contributors at the Casino Restaurant in Chicago. On March 31 he met with Midwestern executives at the Olin Corporation's hunting and game preserve near Brighton, Illinois.

Maury Stans undoubtedly felt at home at the preserve, for he is an avid big-game hunter known as "the first American to bag a bongo in the Congo." To get his bongo—a red-and-white-striped antelope—Stans, a Belgian plantation owner, and thirty Congolese porters stalked through the brush for ten days. When Stans's gunbearer fired too soon, the bongo charged, but Stans felled it with one shot. A later African safari caused him more trouble. In 1966, while hunting in Chad, he shot a film of his experience which was later shown publicly. Its script, approved by Stans, referred to "boys" and "natives," and the film showed the white hunters giving an African his first cigarette and guffawing when he chewed it rather than smoked it. When a USIA official denounced it as "an Amos 'n' Andy show," Stans took the film off the exhibition circuit. The future big-game hunter began life as the son of a Belgian immigrant housepainter in Shakopee, Minnesota. "We had very rough times," he recalls, "living on the credit of the corner store which my father worked off by painting the store." Starting as a stenographer in a sausage factory, young Stans worked his way through three years of night school at Northwestern University in Chicago before landing a job as an office boy and, eventually, becoming managing partner in the firm of Alexander Grant & Company, certified public accountants. (Later, he was elected to the Accounting Hall of Fame.) He first came to Washington in the spring of 1953 as one of forty consultants to the House Appropriations Committee in its study of the budget. Assigned to examine post office operations, he produced a hundred-page memo recommending increased research and shortly thereafter he was named financial consultant to the postmaster general. Stans impressed his colleagues in the Eisenhower administration as a meticulous "numbers man," and he rose quickly: to deputy postmaster general in 1955, deputy budget director in 1957, and budget director in 1958. Leaving government in 1961 he became president of Western Bancorporation of Los Angeles and later of Glore Forgan, William R. Staats, Inc., an investment-banking and brokerage house. When Nixon took office, Stans *sought to become secretary of the treasury and some-what reluctantly agreed to take the commerce post in-stead. He was a fervent Nixon loyalist and, according to Jeb Magruder, set up a "discretionary fund" from public monies in his office which he used for "activities that will be beneficial to the President's re-election." Stans and his wife lived in a luxury apartment building called the Watergate.*

Stans's thicket-beating produced an enormous out-pouring of anonymous contributions those last few weeks before April 7. In one two-day period, Hugh Sloan personally handled about $6 million. Much of this last-minute money was in cash, the least traceable medium. The committee had a squad of four to six "pickup men" roving the country collecting the cash. But the flow was greater than they could handle. In one city, Sloan says, "we couldn't even pick up a $50,000 contribution." A secretary recalls that the torrent of cash and checks those last few hours turned the com-mittee's office into a madhouse.*

Although no public record was maintained of those contributions, Rose Mary Woods, the President's pri-vate secretary, kept a list—later known irreverently as "Rose Mary's Baby"—of the pre-April 7 contributors. She claims the list was used to draw up invitations to Presidential dinners, prayer meetings, and other social functions. But there is some evidence that it was used to dispense more tangible favors. For example, the list shows $250,000 in contributions from executives of Amerada Hess, a New York oil company which at the time was facing an Interior Department investigation of its refinery operations in the Virgin Islands. Several weeks after the large contribution, that investigation was dropped. Another major contributor in the pre-April 7 period was Armand Hammer, chairman of Oc-cidental Petroleum, who gave $46,000. About a year

---

*Three years later, Stans pleaded guilty to five charges of violating campaign finance laws—three for failing to make accurate reports of these transactions and two for accepting corporate contributions; he was fined $5000.

later, Occidental announced it had worked out an $8-billion, twenty-year fertilizer agreement with the Soviet Union, the largest commercial transaction ever made between the Soviet Union and the United States and one in which the Nixon administration may have been helpful. That fall, Hammer funneled another $54,000 into the Nixon campaign through Tim M. Babcock, a former governor of Montana, who was then serving as Occidental's senior executive vice president—a device which disguised the source of the money.* The two secret contributions from Hammer added up to $100,000, the figure Kalmbach and Stans were asking from corporations seeking "special class" status.

Some of the money didn't make the deadline at all. In early March 1972 Robert L. Vesco, a New Jersey financier, went to Washington to see Stans in his office at the finance committee. The Securities and Exchange Commission was then investigating Vesco's "looting" of his mutual-fund complex, and the financier told Stans he wanted to be a "front-row contributor" to the Nixon campaign. He said he was prepared to give $500,000 and, according to one eyewitness, linked this to getting the SEC "off his back." Stans said he would like to have $250,000—in cash—before April 7.

Despite Vesco's best efforts, he could not get the money to Washington before April 10. At eleven that day, Laurence B. Richardson, Jr., president of Vesco's International Controls Corporation, and Harry L. Sears, ICC's associate counsel, walked into Stans's office and placed on his desk a worn, brown attaché case loosely packed with $200,000 in $100 bills. According to Sears, Richardson then said, "Mr. Vesco wants me to deliver you a message. He'd like to get some help." And (still according to Sears) Stans said rather quickly, "That's not—tell him that's not my department. That's John Mitchell's department." (Stans put the money, coded "J.M." for John Mitchell, in his safe and later told Hugh Sloan that it was to be regarded as "pre-

---

*Babcock pleaded guilty to concealing the source of the contribution and was fined $1000. Armand Hammer was sentenced to a year's probation and fined $3000 for making illegal campaign contributions.

April 7 funds because it had been committed to us before that date.")

A few hours later, Sears met with his old friend Mitchell. (Indeed, Vesco had hired Sears, a former Republican majority leader of the New Jersey Senate, precisely because of this impressive "Mitchell connection.") Sears says they discussed Vesco's problems with the SEC and Mitchell picked up the phone and called William J. Casey, the SEC chairman whom Sears had been trying to see for months. While he does not dispute Sears's testimony, Mitchell has said he cannot recall either the meeting or the telephone call. If he did participate in them, he said, he was doing no more than any congressman would do for a constituent.

But of course John Mitchell was not a congressman. He was one of the most powerful men in Washington. And within hours after that telephone call, Sears got his long-awaited meeting with Casey and Bradford Cook, the SEC counsel. After Vesco contributed still another $250,000 to Nixon's campaign, Sears had several more meetings with Casey and Cook in an effort to water down the SEC investigation.*

Another major contribution that spring was arranged by Robert H. Allen, the Republican finance chairman for Texas and president of Gulf Resources and Chemical Corporation in Houston. (At the time, a Gulf Resources mining subsidiary was under pressure from the Environmental Protection Agency to correct water and air pollution in Idaho.) In late 1971 or early 1972 Allen and some other prominent Houston-area businessmen formed a loosely knit organization called Texas Ad Hoc Fund-Raising Committee to collect pre-April 7 funds. Among those in the group were William C. Liedtke, Jr., president of Pennzoil United, Inc., and Roy Winchester, Pennzoil's vice president in charge of public relations.

A report by investigators for the House Banking and

---

*Sears's efforts failed, but a federal indictment later portrayed the $250,000 as Vesco's attempt to buy his way out of the SEC investigation. And it charged Mitchell, Stans, and Sears with participating in a conspiracy to that end. A federal jury, after a long trial in New York ending in April 1974, acquitted all three men.

Currency Committee tells the following story: On April 3, $100,000 was withdrawn from the corporate account of Gulf Resources in the First National City Bank of Houston. The money was transferred to the account of Compañía de Azuere de Veracruz, S.A. (CAVSA), an inactive Gulf Resources subsidiary, in the Banco Internacional of Mexico City. The subsidiary turned the money over to Manuel Ogarrio Daguerre, who for years had been labor counsel for CAVSA. An associate converted $89,000 into four cashier's checks for $15,000, $18,000, $24,000, and $32,000. (Allen insists that the money was not a corporate contribution. He says CAVSA owed Ogarrio a fee for work done in connection with the company's shutdown. He says he went to Mexico on March 21, 1972, to negotiate the fee and agreed on $100,000. Then, he says, as a separate transaction he negotiated a $100,000 loan from Ogarrio for the Nixon contribution and gave the lawyer a promissory note for it. Senate investigators are skeptical of Allen's explanation, but have been unable to disprove it.)

On the afternoon of April 5 José Díaz de León, president of CAVSA, brought the four checks and $11,000 in cash in a large pouch to the Pennzoil offices in the Houston Southwest Tower. Díaz de León asked for a receipt but Liedtke says he told him that "we didn't want to give him a receipt, he could get a receipt from Washington, that we were merely agreeing to transmit the funds to Washington."

The $100,000 was placed in a suitcase, along with $140,000 more in cash and $460,000 in checks and stock certificates which had already been collected by the ad-hoc committee's members. Winchester and Peter Mark, a "young and strong" Pennzoil employee designated to ride shotgun on the money, took the suitcase to the Houston airport, where they boarded a waiting Pennzoil company plane (according to congressional sources, it may be the executive jet that was used in the James Bond movie *Goldfinger*). The plane landed at Washington's National Airport at about 9:00 p.m. Winchester and Mark took the suitcase to the finance committee's office and delivered it to Sloan.

Four days later, another $25,000 trickled in. It came from Dwayne O. Andreas, president of the Archer-Daniels-Midland Company, processors of agricultural commodities. Andreas was a longtime backer of Hubert Humphrey, but like many businessmen he liked to maintain amicable relations with both parties. On April 5 Andreas called Kenneth H. Dahlberg, the Midwest finance chairman of Nixon's campaign, and told him he wanted to contribute $25,000 in cash. Andreas was spending the winter in Florida and invited Dahlberg to come down and pick up the money. In the meantime, he placed it in a safe-deposit box at the Sea View Hotel in Bal Harbour. Dahlberg arrived on the night of April 7, but the hotel's vaults were closed. The next day Andreas took Dahlberg and his wife to play golf and passed the cash to him on the golf course. For security, Dahlberg had a cashier's check made out to himself at the First Bank and Trust Company of Boca Raton. On April 11 he handed the check to Stans during a coffee break at the finance committee meeting at the Washington Hilton Hotel. Stans passed the check on to Sloan. (On August 22 Andreas, Dahlberg, and three associates were granted a federal bank charter for a bank in a Minnesota shopping center. Of 424 charters granted in the previous five years, only 13 had been approved more quickly.)

Hugh Sloan recalls that he and Stans talked about how to deal with the Mexican and Dahlberg checks. Stans asked, "Do we have any problem in handling these?" and he replied, "I don't know; I'll check with counsel." Counsel was Gordon Liddy, who, as Sloan recalls, recommended "a diversion to cash" and offered to "handle the transaction." On April 12 or 13 Sloan gave Liddy the five checks totaling $114,000.

Howard Hunt recalls that early in April Liddy came to his office at Mullen & Company and showed him checks for large amounts of money. "He asked me if I thought that Barker would be able to negotiate them through his business in Miami and return the cash. I telephoned Barker and found that Bernie foresaw no difficulties." Liddy carried the checks to Miami, and on April 19 Barker walked into the Republic National

Bank in Miami's Little Havana section and deposited them in the trust account of Barker Associates, Inc., his real-estate firm. Over the next three weeks, he withdrew the $114,000 in cash. In mid-May Liddy gave Sloan his money back—minus $2500 in unexplained "expenses."

The first phase of Nixon's fund-raising effort had been a stunning success. By April 7, the finance committee later reported, it had $10.2 million on hand. Actually, it had raised about $20 million. But it spent $5 million and "prespent" another $5 million. (That is, it paid out money for future campaign services, so that it would not have to report the money. For example, a few days before the April 7 deadline, the committee gave $1 million to the November Group, the advertising agency set up in New York to handle media work for the campaign. One reason for such prepayments, a Republican official says, was "to avoid looking like we had a lot of money, which would make further fund-raising difficult.")

But the Republicans didn't have much difficulty raising more money. To the $20 million gathered before April 7, they added about $40.2 million—producing a total of about $60.2 million (including about $2 million carried over from 1968). It was, as Maury Stans later proudly proclaimed, "the largest amount of money ever spent in a political campaign."

All that money made some Republicans nervous. Even Stans, the master fund-raiser, says now that he originally thought the President could be re-elected for $25 or $30 million. He says he objected to budgetary "overkill" and once urged Haldeman, "Let's just run this campaign with less money."

Those who worried about the money worried particularly about all the cash that flowed through the committee's offices during that spring of 1972. According to Sloan, about $1.7 million in cash came in before April 7. Of that, he says, about $700,000 ultimately found its way into bank deposits. But for weeks and months, $1 million or so in crisp, freshly minted $100 bills piled up in safes and deposit boxes. At first, much of it lay in a safe in the office of thirty-one-year-old Hugh Sloan.

When Duke Sloan was a student at the Hotchkiss School, the student elections were rigged by a clique of upperclassmen. Sloan told a teacher about it, and some of the conspirators were punished. "That's the way he always was," a Princeton classmate says. "He stood for honesty and integrity and doing the right thing, no matter what." When Sloan got out of the Navy in 1966, his father—a vice president of the St. Regis Paper Company—suggested a diplomatic career, so his son dutifully enrolled in the Georgetown School of Foreign Service. But he didn't care for it and after only three months quit to work for the Republican Congressional Campaign Committee, handling direct-mail projects, raising funds, and "enjoying the hell out of it." His earnest dedication brought steady promotions: assistant finance director for the 1968 campaign, personal aide to the President, assistant to Appointments Secretary Dwight Chapin. "It was great," he recalls. Sloan met his wife while she was working as a White House assistant social secretary; they have a photograph showing them with Nixon on the day they were engaged. In May 1970, when students disrupted Columbia University, the President sent Sloan to find out why he had a "problem" with the academic community. After talking with students who had "occupied" Low Library, he emerged to say, "The depth of feeling is considerably stronger than I personally imagined." In early 1971 he left the White House for CREEP, and by the next February he was its treasurer. Sloan awakened confidence in men, like his father, who had money. He looked like a trust officer at a good New York bank—a year later a Washington Post reporter described him as "slim, hair nicely trimmed, just long enough, blue blazer, muted shirt, rep tie, quite handsome, maybe too thin." Not everyone had confidence in him. Jeb Magruder, for example, thinks Sloan was self-serving and malicious. "Sloan felt he had been *shunted aside by the White House, resented the fact that Mitchell wouldn't deal with him directly and seemed to resent me and the authority I had in the campaign," Magruder says in his book* An American Life. *"He seemed bitter that he didn't have a bigger role, but the fact was that he hadn't sufficient experience." Sloan did lack experience in the world of politics. Later, he was ruefully to recall his father's warning when he joined the Republican campaign committee, "Take care of number one, old man, because that's what everybody else in that crowd will do."*

Although he was the finance committee's second-ranking official, Sloan had no real control over the money. A whole panoply of Nixon's people could instruct him to hand out cash: Kalmbach, Mitchell, Stans, Magruder, even Liddy and Porter, to whom Magruder had given blanket "drawing authority." And soon the demands for cash began.

• The first was in April 1971, when Sloan was told to give $25,000 in cash to Robert Hitt, executive assistant to Interior Secretary Rogers C. B. Morton. Hitt passed the money on to William Mills, the Republican candidate in a special election for the congressional seat vacated by Morton on Maryland's Eastern Shore (when the unreported donation became known in the spring of 1973, Congressman Mills committed suicide).

• Between April 1971 and April 7, 1972, Sloan gave Kalmbach cash totaling $250,000.

• In February 1972 Magruder himself asked for $22,000. Sloan went to his safe and gave him the money without asking why he needed it. Magruder didn't volunteer the information.

• Starting in early 1972 Liddy drew a total of $199,-000 in cash.

• In February 1972 Haldeman directed that $350,-000 in 1968 surplus funds be placed under his personal control. In early April, Sloan took the cash from his safe, put it in a briefcase, and gave it to Kalmbach, who passed it on to Gordon Strachan. On April 6 Strachan asked Alexander Butterfield, deputy assistant to the President, if he knew someone "outside of government," "free to travel," "very, very honest," "deeply loyal to the President," and with "impeccable references" who could make himself available at a moment's notice to deliver funds from a cash "reserve fund." Butterfield said he did know such a person—Leonard W. Lilly, an old friend who was president of a northern Virginia management-consulting firm. He telephoned Lilly, who readily agreed to take custody of the cash. On the afternoon of April 7 Butterfield drove to the Key Bridge Marriott Motor Hotel, where he delivered the briefcase full of cash to his friend. Lilly placed it in a safe-deposit box in an Arlington bank—thus establishing a secret cache of money under White House control.

• Starting in December 1971 Herbert Porter drew batches of cash that he recalls added up to $69,000 and Sloan thinks totaled $100,000. In January 1972 Sloan recalls he asked Porter what one $15,000 withdrawal was for. He says Porter replied, "I can't tell you. You are going to have to go over my head if you want to find out." Porter says he really didn't know much about what the money was used for, except that he'd been told it would finance "Dick Tuck-type pranks and dirty tricks."

6

DIRTY TRICKS

> Haldeman: *You s.o.b., you started this.*
> Tuck: *Yeah, Bob, but you guys ran it into the ground.*
> —Exchange between Dick Tuck and H. R. Haldeman
> in the Dirksen Senate Office Building, May 5, 1973

During the 1960 Presidential campaign, a beaming Richard Nixon posed in San Francisco's Chinatown with children holding a large campaign banner. Only later did he learn that the Chinese characters on the banner spelled out, "What About the Hughes Loan?" —a reference to the disputed loan from multimillionaire Howard Hughes to Nixon's brother Donald. And at the postrally luncheon, attended by Chinese political leaders and the national press, every fortune cookie contained the same message—this time in plain English —"Ask him about the Hughes Loan."

The Chinatown Caper was the work of Dick Tuck, a Democrat whose name has since become something of a trade-mark for political mischief. Though wittier than most of his imitators, Tuck is by no means unique. During California's 1962 gubernatorial campaign, 500,000 Democrats throughout the state received postcards from a group called The Committee for the Preservation of the Democratic Party. In the guise of an opinion poll, the cards asked whether the Democrats were aware how their party—and their candidate, Governor "Pat" Brown—had fallen under the domination of the California Democratic Council, which the cards pictured as virtually a Communist front. Two years later, Judge Byron Arnold found that the Committee for the Preservation of the Democratic Party was actually a committee to enhance the political future of Richard Nixon and that the postcard poll, purporting to be a communication among concerned Democrats, was prepared under the supervision of H. R. Haldeman, Nixon's campaign manager, and "approved by Mr. Nixon personally."

In the White House, Nixon and his lieutenants showed a continued penchant for political dirty tricks. Even before the 1970 election returns drove them to more extreme measures, the President's men were using such tricks to guarantee Nixon's re-election in 1972.

The political Bible of the Nixon administration—Kevin Phillips's *The Emerging Republican Majority*—stressed the vital role of George Wallace in Republican calculations for 1972. "Although most of Wallace's votes came from Democrats," Phillips wrote, "he principally won those in motion between a Democratic past and a Republican future. . . . Three-quarters or more of the Wallace electorate represented lost Nixon votes. . . . The appeal of a successful Nixon Administration and the lack of a Wallace candidacy would greatly swell the 1972 Republican vote in the South, West, Border and the Catholic North."

Sometime during 1970 the White House began its drive to stop Wallace from running. The *Atlanta Constitution* had reported that James D. Martin, Republican national committeeman from Alabama, paid a visit to Wallace that spring and, calling himself an emissary from the President, demanded that Wallace sign an agreement not to run as an Independent in 1972. Martin has denied this. In any case, when it became clear that Wallace's ambitions were as grandiose as ever, the White House set out with determination to throw some roadblocks in his way.

On Haldeman's instructions, Herb Kalmbach channeled $400,000 into the campaign of Albert Brewer, who was running against Wallace in Alabama's Democratic gubernatorial primary that year. This was among the first disbursements from Kalmbach's secret fund, and it was carried out in characteristically surreptitious fashion. At the time, not even Kalmbach knew where the money was headed. First, he flew to New York, withdrew $100,000 from the safe-deposit box at the Chase Manhattan Bank, and gave it to a man Haldeman instructed him to meet in the lobby of the Sherry-Netherland Hotel. Later, France Raine, Haldeman's brother-in-law, withdrew $200,000 from the same safe-deposit box and delivered it to another man in the Sherry-Netherland. The final $100,000 was withdrawn by Kalmbach from the Bank of America in Los Angeles and a courier went there to pick it up. Primed with this unusual infusion of Yankee money, Brewer led in the first primary; but he failed to gain a clear majority and Wallace won the runoff.

Simultaneously, the White House was doing its best to embroil Wallace in a tax scandal. In early 1970 the Internal Revenue Service had begun to investigate irregularities in the taxes of Gerald Wallace, George's brother, former law partner, and political confidant. A brief mention of this was made in an IRS "sensitive case report," a document with limited and carefully controlled distribution within the IRS and the Treasury Department. Haldeman learned of the report—probably through Roger Barth or through John Caulfield's pipeline to Mike Acree—and he asked Clark Mollenhoff, the former *Des Moines Register* correspondent who had joined the White House staff as a special counsel, to get a full report from the IRS on the status of the investigation. Mollenhoff says he initially expressed some reluctance, but went ahead after Haldeman assured him that the request came from the President himself. Commissioner Randolph Thrower supplied the report, and Mollenhoff turned it over to Haldeman on March 21, noting that "there is a possibility of a rather large criminal case." Within the next few days, someone turned an account of the matter over to the columnist Jack Anderson, who published detailed information on it in his column of April 13 —three weeks before the Alabama primary. Anderson said the IRS was investigating charges that Gerald Wallace and Rankin Fite, speaker of Alabama's House of Delegates, collected kickbacks on state and federal highway contracts. "Part of the money is alleged to have been turned over to George Wallace to fuel his 1968 Presidential campaign, in which he promised to restore 'law and order' to the nation," wrote Anderson. He said the investigation also embraced alleged kickbacks on textbook sales, engineering contracts, and misuse of funds at the state docks in Mobile. Now when Commissioner Thrower saw the Anderson account he felt sure it came "directly out of my memorandum." He called Mollenhoff, who denied leaking it. Mollenhoff believes the leak came at "the highest White House level."

When Brit Hume, then one of Jack Anderson's assistants, questioned Gerald Wallace about this tax investigation, Wallace exploded: "They have got forty-seven agents on me right now. You all are trying to beat George Wallace. You're not interested in my tax returns." He had a point.

But the White House failed in this many-pronged effort to destroy Wallace's political base in Alabama. By late 1970 he was back in the governor's seat and talking more confidently than ever of a run for President in 1972. The best the White House could hope for now was to divert Wallace's bombastic energies from his crusade to mobilize the independent conservative forces in the South into a series of bruising Democratic primaries (in which, the White House concluded, he would be "an excellent vehicle for surfacing and hardening the divisions within the Democratic party"). In May 1971 Nixon was visiting Alabama and he invited Wallace to fly with him from Mobile to Birmingham. On the brief flight, a deal may have been made. For shortly afterward the tax case against Gerald Wallace was dropped and the governor announced he would run as a Democrat, not as an Independent, in 1972.

Still, Nixon and his men knew that eventually Wallace would lose out in the Democratic primaries and would decide to run as the standard-bearer of his own American Independent party. So they were ready when an opportunity presented itself to push the AIP off the ballot in California. The particular scheme was the brainchild of Robert J. Walters, a California businessman and former Wallace supporter who had become disenchanted with the AIP after the 1968 election. Concerned that the AIP would draw votes away from conservative candidates in the two major parties, Walters wrote to many conservative groups asking for their support in his plan. One letter reached CREEP, and in mid-September 1971 Jeb Magruder called Walters from the Beverly Hills Hotel. Over a drink at the Polo Lounge, Walters explained his scheme to take advantage of the requirement that a party have at least one-fifteenth of 1 per cent of the state's registered voters in order to get on the ballot. "All we've got to do is to get our people who are disgruntled to go around and talk to their friends and get them to switch parties," Walters explained. "Then Wallace is off the ballot and your problem is solved." Walters needed $10,000 to carry out the plan. Jeb Magruder was intrigued and got John Mitchell's approval to spend the money. To insure secrecy, the $10,000 was channeled through Lyn Nofziger, a veteran California Republican who was then director of communications for the Republican National Committee, and his friend John Lindsey, a Los Angeles businessman. Joseph Tommassi, the twenty-two-year-old head of the Southern California Nazi party, got half the money to supply twenty Nazis to do the canvassing. But they were evidently not very persuasive. AIP registration during this period actually increased 6500. (Even if the canvassers had been more successful, Wallace and his AIP would have stayed on the ballot. For Magruder and Mitchell failed to check another provision of California election law, which automatically puts on the ballot any party which received more than 2 per cent of the vote in the previous gubernatorial election, as the AIP did.)

By the spring of 1972 Wallace had bulled through all the flimsy barriers erected by the White House and seemed ready to fulfill his campaign slogan, "Send Them a Message." In mid-May he was second only to George McGovern in committed delegates (560 to 324) and was running ahead of both McGovern and Humphrey in primary votes. Although Wallace still seemed unlikely to win the Democratic nomination, he might well get enough votes on the Independent ticket to cost Nixon the election. So Nixon reinforced his political maneuvers with a parallel evolution of his stands on public issues. Since Wallace fed off deep currents of racial animosity, Nixon toughened his positions on such questions—particularly his opposition to busing for racial integration—in an effort to catch the Alabamian on the right. Meanwhile, CREEP staffers worked into the balmy Washington night looking for legal ways to remove Wallace from various state ballots.

There has been widespread speculation that, given this obsession with Wallace, the Nixon forces had some hand in the attempted assassination of the Alabama governor at Laurel, Maryland, on May 15, 1972. Rumors circulated that Arthur Bremer, the would-be assassin, had been seen talking with Tony Ulasewicz on a ferryboat days before the shooting. Indeed, it would have been the ultimate dirty trick—but no hard evidence has ever been adduced to connect Bremer with the White House.

The day after Wallace was shot, Charles Colson asked Howard Hunt if he would fly to Milwaukee and "take a look" at Bremer's apartment. Hunt says he objected that the press had already been tramping through the place and the FBI probably had it sealed off, but Colson shouted, "I know, goddamn it. That's the trouble. Every time there's an assassination in this country the press blames the political Right. Weeks later the truth seeps out—like Oswald and Sirhan Sirhan, who were lefties. Just once I'd like the truth to come out —if Bremer's a Marxist himself." Hunt demurred, but Colson persisted, arguing that Hunt could "bribe the janitor" or get in with his "CIA experience." Hunt reluctantly packed a bag, including his shaving kit that held the CIA disguise and false identification. A few hours later, Colson's secretary telephoned him to say, "You don't have to travel, Howard." (Hunt's version of this episode inspires some disbelief among investigators who suspect that Colson asked Hunt not merely to look through the apartment but to plant literature there which would link Bremer to the Democrats.)

For, ultimately, the Democrats were the enemy. By the spring of 1971 a formidable array of Democratic challengers had pitched their tents on the 1972 battlefield: Kennedy, Muskie, Humphrey, McGovern. With the Republican nomination in the bag, Nixon's strategists could devote most of their time to plotting disruptions in the Democratic camp. One of these strategists was Presidential speechwriter, Pat Buchanan, who wrote in one memo, ". . . our great hope for 1972 lies in maintaining or exacerbating the deep Democratic rift between the elite, chic, New Left, intellectual, avant-garde, isolationist, bell-bottomed, environmentalist, new-priorities types on the one hand —and the hard hat, Dick Daley, Holy Name Society, ethnic, blue collar, Knights of Columbus, NYPD, Queens Democrats on the other. The Liberal Democrats should be pinioned to their hippie supporters. The Humphrey Democrats should be reminded of how they were the fellows who escalated and cheered the war from its inception."

Buchanan urged his colleagues to focus their attacks on "issues that divide Democrats, not those that unite Republicans." Everything was grist for this "divide and rule" strategy—even the nation's most fundamental moral issues. Buchanan urged Nixon to use "the race issue" to split the opposition by assailing liberal Democrats who supported forced busing; and to exploit the Vietnam war by praising any Democrat who supported it, thus going "far toward making them 'Establishment' and driving a wedge between them and the ideological hard core of their party." At other times, Buchanan suggested supporting the Democratic left—"saying we disagree with them, but that they have a just cause and the Power Elite within the Party is denying them effective participation." In short, any policy was useful, any stand effective, if it heightened national tensions and pitted one potential opponent against another.

Beyond sowing dissension in Democratic ranks, the

Nixon strategy was to help get the weakest Democratic candidate nominated. That meant knocking off the stronger front-runners at any given time. Until Chappaquiddick that was Kennedy. But after Muskie's Lincolnesque address on election eve of 1970 and his impressive showing in the polls the following spring, the prime threat was the senator from Maine. In the summer of 1971 Buchanan wrote another memo, noting, ". . . Senator Muskie is target A as of midsummer for our operation. Our specific goals are (a) to produce political problems for him, right now, (b) to hopefully help defeat him in one or more of the primaries (Florida looks now to be the best early bet, California, the best later bet), and (c) finally, to visit upon him some political wounds that would not only reduce his chances for nomination—but damage him as a candidate, should he be nominated."

Two other White House aides were thinking along similar lines: Gordon Strachan, Haldeman's assistant, and Dwight Chapin. Together, they discussed the need for a "non-Colson dirty-tricks operation in the field" for 1972. According to Strachan, Chapin and Buchanan had been involved in some 1968 campaign pranks, such as a false mailing in the New Hampshire primary. Chapin seemed fascinated by such pranks.

Chou En-lai was impressed. The thirty-year-old advance man for Nixon's trip to China had handled all the details so efficiently that the premier went out of his way to congratulate him. "This is the way our young people should be used in government," he told the President. Dwight Chapin was the master detail man for Richard Nixon even before they reached the White House. In 1966 he quit a promising career at J. Walter Thompson to become Nixon's personal aide, "responsible for getting him up in the morning, putting him to bed at night, and looking after his wardrobe, meals, and schedules." Hollywood handsome—he was known to his colleagues as "Valentino" and "Slick" because of his carefully groomed hair—Chapin was the perfect batman, a "superloyalist" who was proud to work for the man he was sure would become "the greatest President in history." During the 1968 campaign, the writer Joe McGinniss watched Chapin applauding after Nixon answered each question in his taped discussions with "common people," which were actually meticulously staged television commercials. And Chapin expected others to be as unequivocally admiring as he was. On a Presidential trip to Rome, Chapin was with Nixon in a helicopter rising from St. Peter's Square when he looked down and saw the Pope at a window in the Vatican. "The Pope was clearly blessing the helicopter as it took off," he concluded. "It was wonderful." Born in Wichita, Kansas, Chapin's family moved to California's San Fernando Valley when his father was transferred there. He began working for Nixon in 1962 while still an undergraduate at USC. During that campaign he got to know Haldeman and afterward went to work for him at J. Walter Thompson. He remained as loyal to Haldeman as to Nixon; he regarded Haldeman as his "best friend" and the two men shared a limousine to work each morning. Haldeman returned the faith, praising Chapin's "very sharp, creative, facile mind," making him the man who "processed the input" to the Oval Office, giving him control of the dazzling array of twenty-five telephone lines in and out of the President's lair. (Every day, Chapin turned down in writing 125 to 175 requests to see the President.) Chapin was also close to another old California friend, Ron Ziegler, the President's press secretary, who recalled, "When we were young marrieds in California, they [Chapin and his wife, Suzie] were a lot of fun to go out with; he's a very humorous guy."

They were all humorous back in those days. USC in the early 1960s was a lighthearted place devoted to sports, fraternity life, practical jokes, and campus politics. Chapin and many of his friends belonged to the Squires and the Knights, honorary societies which guarded the USC Trojan Sword and otherwise upheld "Troy Traditions." They also belonged to Trojans for

a Representative Government, a group from the large
fraternities that tried to oust a small fraternity clique
from control of campus government. USC's relentlessly
Republican politics produced a whole pep squad of Nixon aides including Chapin, Ziegler, Porter, Strachan,
Tim Elbourne (one of Ziegler's assistants), and
Mike Guhin (a member of Kissinger's staff)—not to
mention an older generation of Trojans: Herb Klein,
Bob Finch, and Herb Kalmbach. And the politics could
get rough. An alumnus recalls, "There were secret
organizations that engaged in all kinds of espionage
. . . one guy infiltrated another person's campaign for
class president to the extent that he became the opposition guy's campaign manager. Needless to say, nothing
ever quite went right." *Newsweek* says the Trojans for
a Representative Government also ripped down opposition campaign posters, stole leaflets, stuffed ballot
boxes, and packed the student court in order to quash
any complaints brought against them. So when Chapin
began thinking of someone to head up the White
House's "dirty tricks" squad for 1972 he naturally
thought of a former Squire, Knight, and Trojan for a
Representative Government.

In June 1971 he got in touch with his old friend
Donald H. Segretti, a lawyer then serving as a captain
in the Judge Advocate General Corps at Fort Ord, near
San Francisco. Earlier that month Segretti had been in
touch with Strachan to ask about the possibility of a
job in the executive branch. Chapin and Strachan discussed their old college chum and decided he would be
perfect for what they called the "black advance" program of spying and sabotage. In late June Segretti
flew to Washington and met with Chapin and Strachan
twice—once over dinner at Chapin's house and then at
lunch the next day. At that and subsequent meetings,
they told him that they wanted a "Republican Dick
Tuck" who would harass and confuse the Democrats
without doing anything illegal, that he should try to
foster hostility between the Democratic candidates, and
should, at the start, focus his attention on Muskie.
Segretti thought the job sounded exciting and wanted
it. Strachan and Chapin got Haldeman's approval for

the project. (Haldeman later took credit for toning down their plans. "They were gonna cut cars, cut tires on press buses, you know, and take the keys out of cars in motorcades, and that sort of stuff," he told the President. "I said that's ridiculous, it's childish and doesn't do us any good.") They arranged to have Segretti paid from Kalmbach's secret fund. In late August, on Strachan's instructions, Segretti drove down to Newport Beach to see the President's lawyer, who offered him $16,000 a year plus expenses. (Over the next eight months, he got $45,336, but $22,000 of this was for expenses and $9000 of that went to various agents he hired.)

Segretti began using his accumulated leave-time for mysterious trips around the country. On June 27 he came to Washington and asked Alex B. Shipley, a judge advocate officer based there, if he wanted to engage in "a little political espionage." According to Shipley, Segretti explained, "The Democrats have an ability to get back together after a knock-down, drag-out campaign. What we want to do is wreak enough havoc so they can't." Segretti reportedly told Shipley that everything would have to be carried out in great secrecy and under assumed names, but that "Nixon knows that something is being done. It's a typical deal: Don't-tell-me-anything-and-I-won't-know." Finally, Shipley says, Segretti "stressed what fun we could have." For example, they might set up a "Massachusetts Safe Driving Committee" and award a gold medal to Ted Kennedy. Shipley says he turned Segretti down.

Segretti was discharged from the Army on September 13. Shortly afterward, he got a telephone call from Chapin, who told him that Strachan would no longer be involved in the operation, and warned him that his activities must be carried out with the utmost secrecy and with no visible connection to the White House, the Republican party, or CREEP. In their contacts, Chapin was to operate under the alias "Bob Duane" and Segretti as "Don Morris" (he also used the names "Don Simmons" and "Don Durham"). Later, at a meeting at the Hay-Adams Hotel in Washington, Chapin told Segretti to get a post-office box and a telephone-answering service, so that he could be reached at all times. Segretti says Chapin gave him a list of 1968 advancemen as "contacts" in the primary states. On September 24 Segretti flew to Portland, Oregon, and checked into the Benson Hotel the night before the President's party was due to arrive there on the way to meet Emperor Hirohito in Anchorage. On Chapin's instructions, he learned the President's advance operation and methods used to handle demonstrators.

Then, in October, Segretti settled down in an adults-only apartment colony in Marina del Rey, a shiny new community built around a boat basin in Venice, near Los Angeles, which the *Los Angeles Times* had called "a highly desirable residential-social-recreational area for the affluent single set."

In late 1971 a $6000 white Mercedes sports car replaced the aging Mustang in Segretti's reserved parking space. The tanned young veteran, whose neighbors thought he worked for a Los Angeles law firm, led the Southern California version of the good life: bicycling around the marina, sailing, swimming, throwing Sunday "open houses" with lots of California red wine, and dating several attractive young women. Segretti—whose name means "secrets" in Italian—projected an air of brisk self-confidence, but friends say he was very sensitive about his size (5 feet, 4 inches and 135 pounds). After graduating from USC in 1963, he attended one of the nation's best law schools—Boalt Hall at Berkeley —then worked briefly for the Treasury Department in Washington. About to be drafted, he volunteered for the Judge Advocate General's Corps of Army lawyers and served for a year with the JAG group at the Long Binh Army base outside Saigon. Back at Fort Ord, he developed a reputation as a liberal, printed a peace symbol on his checks, hung a "Free Huey" poster on his wall, and specialized in representing soldiers seeking conscientious-objector status. This may have been merely protective coloration for his undercover role in the campaign. Later Segretti described himself as essentially "apolitical." And by the time Chapin contacted *him, he says, "I really believed in Richard Nixon. I believed in the election of Richard Nixon." Above all, Segretti was fiercely ambitious. The son of a hotel bellhop, he was determined to make a splashy career for himself. Eight years out of college, he wanted badly to catch up with his USC friends like Chapin and Strachan. A former girl friend says Segretti was aiming for a job at the White House. "He would hate most being stowed away doing some monotonous, unglamorous job," she says. "He was looking for excitement, challenge, big stakes." But Segretti would have been disconsolate if he had known that several years later Richard Nixon would describe him as a "clownish figure."*

In the fall of 1971 and the spring of 1972 Segretti traveled to more than sixteen states. Ultimately, he concentrated on eleven, most of which had key Presidential primaries: New Hampshire, Florida, Illinois, Wisconsin, Pennsylvania, Ohio, Indiana, California, New Jersey, New York, and Texas. His first task was to recruit a network of agents, and during his travels he talked with at least eighty people. Having failed to sign up Shipley and other Army lawyers the summer before, he turned his attention to current and former Young Republicans, College Republicans, and Young Voters for the President. Among those he recruited through the national "old boy" network of former College Republicans were Thomas J. Visney, a twenty-four-year-old aide to the then governor, Richard B. Ogilvie of Illinois, and Charles Svihlik, who had worked as an aide to several major Indiana Republicans (Svihlik signed on "for the fun of it"). Segretti also recruited James Norton for work in California, Skip Zimmer and Bob Nieley in Pennsylvania, Michael Martin, Jr., in New York, and Bobby Garner in Texas.

But some of the people Segretti contacted that winter became suspicious. Reports began pouring into CREEP about a short fellow in rimless glasses who would walk into state Republican headquarters claiming to be from "the highest levels" in Washington and proposing to show the locals how they could win the election in their areas. Some state party officials feared that the fellow—who often identified himself as "Don Simmons"—might be a Democratic plant or some other kind of troublemaker. One such complaint came from Allan Walker, chairman of the New Hampshire Committee to Re-elect the President, whom Segretti had approached rather bluntly, even giving his real name. (This caused Chapin to yank Segretti abruptly out of New Hampshire with a stern warning to be more careful in the future.) In January 1972 Tony Ulasewicz was dispatched to Wisconsin to investigate reports of a strange figure recruiting college students there to pull pranks during the primary. When the New Hampshire and Wisconsin complaints crossed Jeb Magruder's desk, he called Strachan and asked for an explanation. Strachan claimed to know nothing about the mysterious prankster. So Magruder sent a memo to Mitchell, entitled "Matter of Potential Embarrassment," in which he told of the agent's activities and speculated that someone at the White House was directing him. As was customary, Magruder sent a copy of the memo through Strachan to Haldeman, and this forced Haldeman to confess responsibility for Simmons-Segretti.

Gordon Liddy talked about the suspected Democratic agent with Howard Hunt, who by then was beginning to work with Liddy at CREEP, and told Hunt that he had been ordered to locate and "neutralize" the infiltrator. A warning memo was sent to all Republican state chairmen and Liddy waited for "Simmons" to surface again. But when Haldeman identified Segretti, Hunt and Liddy were ordered to meet with him and evaluate his potential.

On February 11, 1972, the two men flew to Florida and—using their customary aliases, "Ed Warren" and "George Leonard"—met with Segretti in his room at the Frolics Motel on Miami Beach. Hunt immediately turned on the television set to disrupt any bugs that might have been planted in the room. In his book, Hunt recalls that he and Liddy had decided to play the "good-cop-bad-cop-routine," with Hunt designated as the heavy. When Hunt left the room to use a pay phone, Liddy told Segretti:

"There's one thing about Warren you ought to know. We have trouble with him."

"Trouble?" asked Segretti. "What kind of trouble?"

"Well," said Liddy, lowering his voice. "Warren tends to kill without orders."

Segretti was impressed. But Hunt and Liddy were not —or at least Hunt says they found Segretti's pranks "sophomoric" and agreed that "his unbounded enthusiasm could become a campaign liability." When they got back to Washington, Hunt says, they made a joint recommendation that Segretti's operation be terminated, but were overruled in the White House. (Segretti says Hunt gave no sign of such disapproval at the motel meeting. On the contrary, he says, Hunt referred him to a printer in the Miami area, gave him his own telephone number in Washington, and told him to "keep in touch.") In any case, Liddy was ordered to monitor Segretti's activities and try to keep him out of trouble. Liddy turned the assignment over to Hunt, who met with Segretti several times over the next few months and called him from time to time with ideas or instructions, speaking in a "whispery, conspiratorial voice." Segretti later told John Dean that Hunt "scared" him.

Segretti's most efficient operation, by far, was in Florida—one of the two states in which Pat Buchanan had said Muskie was most vulnerable. On December 15 Segretti called Robert Melton Benz, the former chairman of the Hillsborough County Young Republican Club, and asked if he was interested in a "voter-research project." Over draft beer at a motel, he was more frank and found Benz bursting with enthusiasm to "screw up" the Democrats. Over the next few weeks, Benz hired seven assistants at $75 a week. He placed Peg Griffin, a Tampa secretary, in the Muskie headquarters, where she tapped a steady stream of memos, stationery, contributors' lists, and scheduling data. Eselene Frolich supplied similar data from Senator Henry Jackson's campaign. Douglas Kelly became Benz's assistant, and from December through the March 14 primary, Segretti's "gang"—as he called them—set off a pyrotechnic display of dirty tricks.

Some were merely impish. Doug Kelly walked into a Muskie press conference in a long overcoat and dropped two white mice with blue ribbons on their tails reading "Muskie is a rat fink," and a small finch which darted around the conference room causing great commotion. In Gainesville, Kelly gave a girl $20 to run naked outside Muskie's hotel room shouting, "I love Ed Muskie."

Some of the tricks were noxious. A chemist friend of Kelly's mixed up a batch of butyl percaptain, a foul-smelling substance, which Segretti's gang fashioned into stink bombs. On at least four occasions, these bombs were used against the Muskie campaign: twice at his Tampa headquarters and twice at picnics, where, Kelly reported, "everybody thought the food was bad."

Some were divisive. Segretti had Howard Hunt's Miami printer turn out 300 Day-Glo red posters reading, "Help Muskie in busing more children now" and signed by the fictitious "Mothers Backing Muskie Committee." (Muskie's pro-busing position was very unpopular in Florida.) At a Wallace rally in Tampa, Benz distributed a thousand cards reading, "If you liked Hitler, you'll just love Wallace" on one side, and "Cast your vote for Senator Edmund Muskie" on the other. Fliers attacking Muskie's stand on Israel and purporting to come from Mayor John Lindsay of New York were placed under the windshield wipers of cars parked outside Miami Beach synagogues.

And at least one trick was downright malicious. In early March Segretti sent Benz a packet containing about two hundred pieces of Citizens for Muskie stationery and envelopes plus a typewritten letter. Benz gave the materials to George Hearing, an accountant, who duplicated the letter and mailed it to supporters of Senator Jackson on March 11, three days before the Florida primary. It began, "We on the Sen. Ed Muskie staff sincerely hope that you have decided upon Senator Muskie as your choice. However, if you have not made your decision you should be aware of several facts." The "facts" were that Senator Jackson, while a high-school senior in Everett, Washington, in 1929, had become involved with a seventeen-year-old girl and fathered an illegitimate child, and that in May 1955 and October 1957 he had been arrested on homosexual charges in Washington, D.C. The letter also alleged that Senator Humphrey had been arrested for drunken driving in Washington on December 3, 1967, after hitting two cars and a mailbox and that in the car was a "well-known call girl" who had been paid by a lumber lobbyist to entertain the senator. Senators Jackson and Humphrey have denied these allegations and there is nothing in police files to substantiate them.

The phony letter pleased Chapin. According to Segretti, the President's appointments secretary was delighted when he learned that it had cost only $20, remarking that it was worth $10,000 or $20,000 to the Nixon campaign.* One strategy underlay all the tricks. As Kelly later testified, "These things . . . were not done to influence votes, necessarily, at all. . . . You are not going to affect the primary by sending fifty letters out. . . . The idea was to get the candidates backbiting each other and possibly starting doing it to each other outside of our activities."

Following the Florida primary—in which Muskie finished a poor third behind Wallace and Humphrey—Segretti and Benz took their bag of tricks to Wisconsin. As in Florida, most of the tricks were directed at Muskie, who was still regarded as the leading candidate. They distributed bumper stickers with derogatory sexual slogans about Muskie, and they ordered several dozen flowers, fifty pizzas, fifty buckets of fried chicken, and two limousines in the name of George Mitchell, Muskie's advance man, and had them sent to Muskie's hotel. But Humphrey also came in for some attention. Segretti printed up a fake invitation to an April Fool's Day lunch with Humphrey and distributed it in Milwaukee's black ghettos. It read: "FREE—All you can

---

*Whatever it was worth, it led to Segretti's indictment on three counts of distributing illegal campaign literature. He pleaded guilty and served four and a half months in prison. George Hearing was also convicted and served nine months. Chapin was convicted of making false statements to a grand jury about his relationship with Segretti and sentenced to ten to thirty months in prison. He was released after serving nearly eight months.

eat lunch with beer, wine or soda! With Senator Hubert H. Humphrey. Lorne Greene. Mrs. Martin Luther King." Of course, there was no lunch, no free drinks, but plenty of disappointed and thirsty voters. (The fake invitation gambit—which Segretti used in several other states—may have been suggested by Hunt, for it was strikingly similar to a trick he pulled on the Chinese Communists while based in Tokyo during the mid-1950s. At Hunt's suggestion, thousands of leaflets were dropped over the city inviting people to the Chinese trade fair. On the back was printed an admission ticket and other coupons which purported to guarantee as much free beer, rice, and raw fish as the bearer could consume or carry away. The exhibition hall was stormed by thousands of Japanese incensed over the Chinese failure to honor the coupons.)

The Wisconsin primary on April 4 badly damaged Muskie's prospects: he finished a dismal fourth, far behind McGovern, Wallace, and Humphrey. But Segretti was not through with the senator from Maine. On Hunt's suggestion, he transferred his operations to the District of Columbia, where a primary was scheduled for May 2. Joined there by the resourceful Doug Kelly, Segretti pulled off his most elaborate single stunt of the campaign.

On April 17 the Muskie forces threw a fund-raising dinner for 1300 people at the Washington Hilton. Segretti and Kelly ordered a $300 supply of liquor, a $50 floral arrangement, two hundred pizzas, and some pastries for delivery to the hotel. They also hired two magicians, who said they had come all the way from the Virgin Islands to "perform for the children," and warned the Muskie staff, "If you don't let us in, we'll turn you into something terrible." The morning of the dinner, the embassy of Niger called to say that the chargé d'affaires was coming and asking when the limousine would pick him up. Madalyn Albright, the dinner's organizer recalls, "We hadn't invited anybody from foreign embassies. This was an internal thing for Democrats, but you can't offend foreign dignitaries, so we said come ahead, but that there would be no limousine. . . . The evening started out with a small VIP cocktail party. I was there when I saw a couple arriving. They were dressed in batik, so I went up and said, 'You must be the chargé from Niger.' But it wasn't. He said he was the ambassador from Kenya. Upstairs we got a call that the ambassador from Afghanistan was arriving. Finally, sixteen ambassadors showed up, all from African and Middle Eastern countries. Since this was a seated dinner, it caused us a little bit of pain trying to seat them without causing embarrassment. . . . Later on we discovered that they had all come in rented limousines. We were presented with the bill for the limousines." Naturally, the organizers told the chauffeurs that they had not ordered the cars and sent them away, but Segretti and Benz kept calling the limousine companies and telling them to come back and get paid. It could have been worse. "We also made inquiries about renting an elephant," Segretti recalls, "but were unable to make the necessary arrangements."

Segretti's operation was not the only infiltration and harassment campaign waged against Muskie. Every faction in the White House and CREEP seemed determined to have its own undercover network. There were at least four other parallel operations.

The first was directed by Jeb Magruder. In the summer of 1971, as Muskie appeared increasingly strong, White House people kept asking Magruder, "Why can't you guys find out what Muskie is up to?" Magruder spoke with Mitchell, who agreed they ought to do something. He then asked Ken Rietz, CREEP's youth director, if he could plant a young volunteer in Muskie's headquarters. Rietz approached a friend—John Buckley, a former private investigator who was then director of the inspection division in the Office of Economic Opportunity. In September Buckley told Rietz that, inspired by an article in the Washington *Evening Star* about a free taxi ride offered to Humphrey, he had devised a plan to plant a taxi driver in the Muskie campaign. Magruder and Mitchell approved the plan, including a $1000-a-month salary for the driver. On September 18 Strachan reported to Haldeman in one of his regular "political matters" memos that "a plant will be in Muskie headquarters beginning October 1."

Buckley had already secured the services of his friend Elmer Wyatt, a retired Maryland taxi driver, and now he told him to volunteer for work at Muskie headquarters. At first, Wyatt and his cab were used for the most mundane errands—picking up dry cleaning and mailing campaign literature to other Muskie offices. Eventually, though, he was asked to carry documents between Muskie's Senate office and his campaign headquarters.

For the next seven months, Wyatt and Buckley obtained and copied hundreds of Muskie's interoffice memos, itineraries, drafts of speeches, and position papers. At first, before leaving to deliver documents, Wyatt would call Buckley and arrange to pick him up on a street corner. While riding in the back seat, Buckley would photograph the most interesting papers. This procedure proved cumbersome, so Buckley rented an office at 1026 17th Street, equipped it with more sophisticated photographic equipment, and copied the documents there during his lunch hour. In prearranged meetings on Pennsylvania Avenue, Buckley would hand the developed film to Rietz, who would pass it on to Magruder. Magruder assigned Porter to pay Wyatt's monthly retainer, review his film on a .35 mm viewer, and bring anything interesting to Magruder's attention. Porter, who claims he did not know the source of the film, had his secretary type up the most interesting material. (Copies were sent to Strachan at the White House.) A twenty-page speech which Muskie was planning to deliver against the nomination of William H. Rehnquist to the Supreme Court was typed up in advance and forwarded to Mitchell. Two memos were considered so damning that they were sent to Rowland Evans and Robert Novak, who used the material in their newspaper column. A memo from Muskie's foreign-policy advisers formed the basis of a column which argued that Muskie was surrounding himself with left-wing counselors. Another memo suggested that the senator, as chairman of the Senate Intergovernmental Relations Subcommittee, hold tax hearings in California, where the issue was a live one and "take advantage of free TV time before it is too late." Evans and Novak printed portions of this memo; the hearings were never held. In the Muskie camp these leaks were blamed on Cynthia Johnson, a researcher who had once been Novak's secretary, and despite her protestations of innocence she was exiled to run Muskie's office in Harrisburg, Pennsylvania.

In early 1972 Howard Hunt took over responsibility for this operation. Twelve or fifteen times, he met Buckley on various corners of Pennsylvania Avenue to pick up the film and give Buckley plain envelopes containing cash. Buckley used the alias "Jack Kent," but Hunt called him "Fat Jack" and later "Ruby I."

The second anti-Muskie operation, dubbed "Ruby II," was also directed by Hunt. In February 1972 Bob Bennett at Mullen & Company asked Hunt if his nephew, Robert Fletcher, could work at CREEP during the summer vacation. Hunt and Liddy were trying to hire young volunteers to infiltrate Muskie's campaign, but Fletcher wasn't interested in undercover work and suggested a friend, Thomas J. Gregory, a twenty-five-year-old history student at Brigham Young University in Provo, Utah. Using the alias "Ed Warren," Hunt called Gregory and invited him to Washington for an interview. Hunt found Gregory a "slack-mouthed, disheveled youth" and thus, he thought, perfectly suited for the Muskie campaign. He agreed to pay him $175 a month for whatever information he could supply. Gregory went back to Provo and arranged to receive credit for "off-campus study," and then returned to Washington. On March 1 he went to Muskie headquarters and was promptly assigned to the foreign affairs section under Anthony Lake, one of the former Kissinger staffers who at this time was being wiretapped by the FBI. Over the next two months, Gregory typed reports on documents he read or conversations he overheard and handed them to Hunt every Friday at a Drug Fair at 17th and K Streets. Hunt turned the information over to Liddy.

The third operation belonged to Murray Chotiner. It was a sequel to a similar scheme he had directed in 1968. Chotiner hired two writers to pose as reporters with the Democratic campaigns and send back reports to him under the code name "Mr. Chapman's

Friends." (The name, Chotiner later disclosed, originated with former New York Governor Thomas Dewey, who would always use the name "Chapman" when he made a long-distance call on a telephone outside his office because he feared the operator would listen in if he gave his real name.) The first of Mr. Chapman's Friends was Seymour K. Freidin, a veteran journalist then working as a free-lance writer. Freidin had supplied intelligence on the Humphrey campaign for Chotiner in 1968. In March 1971 Chotiner hired Freidin again —at $1000 a month—and he reported on the Muskie campaign and others intermittently until August 1972. Freidin denies that he was spying: "I'm not really the James Bond type," he says. In August 1972 he was replaced by another writer, Lucianne Goldberg, who reported on the McGovern campaign that fall. "They were looking for really dirty stuff," she says. "Who was sleeping with whom, what the Secret Service men were doing with the stewardesses, who was smoking pot on the plane—that sort of thing."

The fourth operation was Magruder's. According to Porter, Magruder decided in the fall of 1971 that he needed someone to carry on "dirty tricks" against the Muskie campaign. At that time, he didn't know that Chapin had hired Segretti, and his own Buckley-Wyatt team was merely gathering intelligence. Porter says Magruder's concept of dirty tricks involved stealing car keys from motorcades, scheduling fake meetings, or taking shoes that campaign workers left in hotel hallways to be polished. Porter asked Ronald Walker, then the President's chief advance man, if he knew someone who would be good at this sort of thing. Walker suggested a California friend named Roger Greaves, and shortly thereafter Magruder and Porter engaged Greaves under the code name "Sedan Chair I" (after a Marine Corps operation that Porter had once been in). Greaves was to get only expense money for the first few months but if he proved adept he would be hired full time. Porter, the CREEP contact for the operation, passed several instructions to Greaves that fall: chiefly to arrange for pickets at Muskie appearances in California (blacks and hippies preferred). In January 1972

Porter hired Greaves to work for $2000 a month in the primary states, starting with New Hampshire. Before Greaves left for the frozen north he was photographed, at Gordon Liddy's suggestion, because Liddy said some of his agents would be pulling some "rough stuff" in New Hampshire and he didn't want Greaves injured. According to most accounts, Greaves did very little in New Hampshire except go to bars and try to over-hear conversations among Muskie staffers. (Soon after-ward he resigned and was replaced by Michael W. Mc-Minoway, a young private detective from Louisville, Kentucky, who was dubbed "Sedan Chair II.") Por-ter says Greaves did arrange for voters to get calls late at night from representatives of the "Harlem for Muskie Committee" who, in plainly black accents, promised "full justice for black people." Other people, identifying themselves as "Muskie sympathizers," would call a vot-er's phone repeatedly asking for voter information. Tony Podesta, Muskie's campaign manager in the state, said, "People are getting furious."

And then on February 24—less than two weeks be-fore the primary—came the clincher. On that day, the *Manchester Union Leader,* William Loeb's virulently right-wing paper, published a letter from a "Paul Mor-rison" of Deerfield Beach, Florida, which said that Muskie, campaigning in Florida, had been asked what he knew about blacks. "He didn't have any in Maine, a man with the senator said. No blacks, but we have 'Cannocks [*sic*].' What did he mean? We asked—Mr. Muskie laughed and said come to New England and see." Together with the letter, Loeb ran a signed, front-page editorial entitled "Sen. Muskie Insults Franco-Americans." The next day, he reprinted a *Newsweek* magazine item about Jane Muskie, the senator's wife, which quoted her as telling reporters on a campaign bus, "Let's tell dirty jokes," and "Pass me my purse—I haven't had my morning cigarette yet." The article, condensed from a Kandy Stroud piece in *Women's Wear Daily,* said Mrs. Muskie confessed "to a pref-erence for two drinks before dinner and a *crème de menthe* afterward." These articles enraged the ex-hausted Muskie and on the morning of February 26 he exploded. Standing on a flatbed truck before the *Union Leader* building, he denounced Loeb as a "gutless coward" for his article about Mrs. Muskie and strenuously denied the story about his slur on Canucks. Three times during the speech he broke down in tears. David Broder of *The Washington Post* described him as "standing silent in the near blizzard, rubbing at his face, his shoulders heaving, while he attempted to regain his composure sufficiently to speak." Broder quoted Loeb as saying later, "I think Senator Muskie's excited and near-hysterical performance this morning again indicates he's not the man that many of us want to have his finger on the nuclear button." Many voters apparently agreed. Muskie, the overwhelming favorite in the primary, did much worse than anyone expected.

The Paul Morrison letter was almost certainly bogus and very probably part of the Nixon dirty-tricks campaign against Muskie. Reporters searched Deerfield Beach and neighboring communities in Florida and were never able to find anybody by that name. Seven months later, Marilyn Berger, a diplomatic reporter for *The Washington Post,* wrote a memo to her editors saying that Kenneth Clawson, a one-time *Post* reporter who was then deputy director of communications at the White House, had told her over a drink at her apartment, "I wrote the . . . letter." Berger said she asked him why and he said, "Because Muskie was the candidate who would represent the strongest opposition and they wanted him out." Clawson has repeatedly denied saying this. He told Nora Ephron of *New York* magazine that what he really said was, "Jesus, I wish I'd written that!" To which Berger replied, "You don't mean that?" And he said, "Yeah, that's politics." And he told Ben Bradlee, the *Post*'s editor, "I didn't do it, and when you know who did, you're going to be sick, Ben, just sick."

Some thought it bore the stamp of Pat Buchanan or his assistant, Kenneth L. Khachigian, who had already proved adept at fakery. Khachigian was the author and Buchanan the editor of a bogus pamphlet widely distributed during the Muskie campaign. Purporting to come from "Citizens for a Liberal Alternative" (a fictitious group of liberal Democrats), it attacked Muskie's positions as overly cautious and conservative. The pamphlet was mailed to some four hundred "liberals" across the country, distributed by Segretti's agents in Florida, and kept cropping up throughout the New Hampshire primary.

And others thought they detected Chuck Colson's fine hand in the Morrison letter. Colson too had a penchant for fabrication. He urged Porter to send someone into New Hampshire to make a contribution from a radical group to the Republican primary campaign of Representative Pete McCloskey. Porter gave $135 to Roger Stone, a young scheduler in his office, and told him to contribute the money to McCloskey on behalf of the Gay Liberation Front. Stone says he persuaded Porter to let him make the contribution instead from the Young Socialist Alliance. Porter and Stone then drafted an anonymous letter to the *Manchester Union Leader,* enclosing a receipt for the contribution. Colson also devised a scheme for siphoning off Muskie votes in New Hampshire by orchestrating a Kennedy write-in campaign there. Some 150,000 letters urging such write-ins were sent into New Hampshire over the signature of Robin Ficker, a Maryland Democrat, who evidently thought he was acting on behalf of Kennedy's aides. Colson's suggestions, though often ingenious, frequently caused friction with the CREEP aides who were called on to carry them out. They particularly annoyed Magruder, who says he felt Colson's suggestions were "too hard-line," "too heavy-handed," and "counterproductive." One CREEPster recalls Magruder complaining, "That goddamn Colson, he just sits there and dreams up this crap!"

Although some of the dirty tricks may have been counterproductive, on the whole they seemed to have worked rather well. Berl I. Bernhard, who was Muskie's campaign manager, says the tricks "took a toll in the form of diverting our resources, changing our schedules, altering our political approaches, and being thrown on the defensive." Bernhard cites, in particular, the theft of "the most vital document we had put together," the advance and scheduling program for late 1971 and early

1972. This theft—probably by the Buckley-Wyatt team—caused some major revisions in the senator's plans. Bernhard also cites the theft of some raw polling data and the entire New Jersey and New Hampshire polls as particularly damaging. The dirty tricks also exacerbated Muskie's natural tendency to fly off the handle at critics and questioners, particularly reporters. In late 1971 Chapin sent Segretti a report on some sharp questioning directed at Muskie during an appearance at Whittier College. "Big Ed proved that he can keep his cool," the report said. Chapin penciled in next to it: ". . . we really missed the boat on this—obviously the press now wants to prove EM can keep his temper—let's prove he can't." One reporter who followed Muskie during his primary campaigns recalls, "You could see him losing his cool progressively week by week. Part of it was just fatigue and his increasingly bad showing in the primaries. But I'm sure part of it was all these incredible things that kept happening and that we now know were orchestrated by CREEP. In the best of times, Muskie has a hair-trigger temper. In the worst of times, it could be volcanic."

And mid-April was the worst of times for Muskie. Following his dismal showing in the Wisconsin primary on April 4, Buchanan and Khachigian wrote to Haldeman and Mitchell, "Our primary objective, to prevent Senator Muskie from sweeping the early primaries, locking up the convention in April and uniting the Democratic Party behind him for the fall, has been achieved." They had achieved even more than they hoped. On April 24 Muskie finished last in the Pennsylvania primary—behind Humphrey, Wallace, and McGovern. That was the *coup de grâce*. Two days later, he withdrew from the race.

Even before the formal withdrawal—sometime in mid-April—Haldeman ordered Liddy to "transfer whatever capability he had from Muskie to McGovern, with particular interest in discovering what the connection between McGovern and Senator Kennedy was." Until the convention, though, CREEP's McGovern operation was to be chiefly intelligence-gathering rather than dirty tricks. For the White House had found the

Democrat it wanted to run against. That same month Buchanan noted in a memo, "We must do as little as possible at this time to impede McGovern's rise."

With Muskie officially out of the race, CREEP completed the shift in its "capability." Elmer Wyatt was unable to transfer his taxi shuttle service and simply went out of business. But on Hunt's instructions Tom Gregory easily moved from the Muskie campaign to McGovern's headquarters. And Stone and Porter ordered Sedan Chair II, Michael McMinoway, to go to California and infiltrate the McGovern and Humphrey campaigns in the June 6 primary there. McMinoway was soon sending back reports from both camps.

Donald Segretti was in California too. The battle for the Democratic nomination had now come down to a head-on scrap between McGovern and Humphrey. Ill feeling was developing naturally, but Segretti fed the fires of distrust by sending out bundles of bogus leaflets and letters attacking one candidate on behalf of the other. Trying to help McGovern, he focused his attack on Humphrey. Segretti distributed thousands of bumper stickers which proclaimed "Humphrey: He started the war. Don't give him another chance!" and were signed "Democrats for a Peace Candidate." He also prepared a pamphlet which showed Humphrey holding up a large fish with a caption, "Humphrey: A Fishy Smell for the White House?" and then spread rumors that it had been sent out by McGovern. He distributed a letter over the forged signature of Barbara Barron, Minnesota Senator Eugene J. McCarthy's campaign coordinator, urging McCarthy delegates and Shirley Chisholm supporters to shift their support to Humphrey. And he sent out a press release on Humphrey stationery saying that Representative Chisholm had been committed to a private home for the mentally ill from February 1951 to April 1952 (at the bottom were the initials "HHH"). Frank Mankiewicz, McGovern's campaign director, has testified that such tricks created "a strong sense of resentment among the candidates and their followers." McGovern and Humphrey "were no longer opponents; we had become enemies and I think largely as a result of this activity."

On May 8—the day the President announced that Haiphong harbor had been mined and the bombing of North Vietnam resumed—Howard Hunt called Donald Segretti in Los Angeles and asked him to organize support for Nixon's actions. Segretti in turn called Bob Benz and Doug Kelly in Florida and told them to set up tables at which people could sign telegrams to the White House. And he sent two telegrams to the President signed with several hundred false names.

Bogus letters and telegrams to newspapers, congressmen, and the White House had long been used by Nixon's men to demonstrate alleged public support for the President's actions—notably at the time of the Carswell nomination to the Supreme Court and after the Cambodian invasion in 1970. While still in the White House Communications Office, Jeb Magruder had organized an efficient letter-writing procedure: his staff would feed ideas to Betty Nolan, at the Republican National Committee, who would write the letters and forward them to volunteers around the country for signing and mailing. Later Ron Baukol, a White House Fellow, took responsibility for the program and proudly described it in a memo to Chuck Colson as "a true undercover operation." In February 1972 Betty Nolan began to organize CREEP's letter-writing operation and soon at least fifty bogus letters a week were going out to the press or Capitol Hill.

As expected, the President's May 8 announcement ignited fires of protest across the nation. So White House and CREEP staffers swung into high gear. "We felt the Haiphong decision could make or break the President," a CREEP official explained. Robert C. Odle, Jr., CREEP's director of administration, recalls, "The entire campaign apparatus that week went to work in support of what happened." Many letters were generated through hurried phone calls to such organizations as the American Legion and the Veterans of Foreign Wars. Betty Nolan and her staff produced many more. On May 10 Ron Ziegler could announce that telegrams and phone calls were running five or six to one in favor of the President's action. At the same time, CREEP sent 2000–4000 phony ballots into a poll conducted by television station WTTG in Washington (the station's final count showed 5157 for the President's decision and 1158 against). James Dooly, the head of CREEP's mail room, recalls that "work ground to a halt in the press office while everybody filled out fifteen postcards [apiece]. Ten people worked for several days buying different kinds of stamps and postcards and getting different handwriting to fake the responses."

One protest against the President's action was contained in a *New York Times* editorial of May 10 which said the mining of the harbor was "counter to the will and conscience of a large segment of the American people." A week later an ad appeared in the *Times* entitled "The People vs. The New York Times." It cited polls showing that anywhere from 59 to 76 per cent of the American people supported the President. The ad was signed by fourteen private citizens, but it was in fact prepared by the November Group, the special New York agency which handled advertising for Nixon's campaign; edited by Chuck Colson at the White House; and paid for with forty-four crisp new $100 bills sent up to New York by Bart Porter at CREEP.

F inally the focus of the dirty-tricks campaign turned to the Democratic National Convention in Miami. In early June Hunt met with Segretti at the Sheraton Four Ambassadors Hotel in Miami and instructed him to assemble peaceful demonstrators to picket the Doral

Hotel, where McGovern would have his headquarters during the convention. Hunt told Segretti that his group would be confronted by an unruly group who would create a "disruption" that would be blamed on McGovern. (Segretti never got around to arranging that demonstration, although he and Doug Kelly did hire an airplane to fly over the convention site with a trailer reading: "Peace, Pot, Promiscuity, Vote McGovern.")

Hunt assigned Bernie Barker to provide the unruly demonstrators at the Doral. Barker passed the assignment on to Eugenio Martinez, who in turn asked Pablo Fernandez to handle it. Fernandez says Martinez offered him $700 a week to hire "hippies" who were to throw rocks, break glass, defecate, and urinate outside the Doral, "and all that sort of thing, to give the voters a bad impression of people supporting McGovern." Fernandez says he refused because he "did not want to get involved" and because he suspected that, at $700 a week, Martinez and his superiors "would want more for their money" than just disruption of the McGovern headquarters.

Indeed, they did want more. In subsequent telephone calls Martinez urged Fernandez to infiltrate protest groups and to spy on McGovern's movements around Miami Beach. Fernandez says he turned this proposal down because he was already spying for law-enforcement bodies. A former CIA operative in South America, Fernandez was then serving as a volunteer informer for the FBI and the Miami City police department inside the Vietnam Veterans Against the War, a group planning demonstrations at the Republican convention.

Vincent J. Hanard, who had earlier worked as an informer for the CIA, FBI, and local police forces, says that a man who called himself "Eduardo"—almost certainly Hunt—called that spring to offer him $1500 a week to infiltrate the VVAW and cause trouble. "Basically," he said, "we had to expose the VVAW being pink and Communist and all this stuff."

In May John Dean had tried to set up still another undercover operation to infiltrate protest groups in Miami. He approached Kenneth Tapman, an Interior

Department official who had handled negotiations with demonstrators during antiwar marches in 1969 and 1970. But Tapman refused to work underground.

Michael McMinoway got a job as a security guard at McGovern headquarters at the Doral and relayed information to CREEP. According to the St. Louis *Post-Dispatch*, McMinoway overheard Frank Mankiewicz discussing Missouri Senator Thomas F. Eagleton's health before he was nominated for Vice President. There have been other reports that Eagleton's health records arrived in Ehrlichman's office before they were leaked to the press. McGovern's campaign was so badly damaged by the reports that his running mate had a history of serious depressions that he replaced Eagleton with Sargent Shriver. If McMinoway knew this in advance, it raises the intriguing possibility that Nixon's men may have had something to do with getting the story out.

And one day, Robert Reisner, Magruder's administrative assistant recalls, Gordon Liddy burst into his office exclaiming, "I have this great idea!" The idea was for a woman to "disrobe at the Democratic National Convention."

Gordon Liddy had some other great ideas, too.

7

BREAK-IN

Any old retired man in the New York City Police Department who would have become involved in a thing like that . . . he would not have walked in with an army, that is for sure.
—Anthony Ulasewicz,
testimony to the Senate Select Committee
on Presidential Campaign Pactices, May 23, 1973

Gordon and Frances Liddy spent New Year's Eve 1971 with Howard and Dorothy Hunt at Witches Island, the Hunts' green ranchhouse in Potomac, Maryland. During the previous six months, the two ex-Plumbers had become "almost inseparable." The Hunts were "the only ones we ever saw socially," Frances Liddy recalls. "We would go there for dinner and the men would sit around talking for hours." Mrs. Liddy thought that Hunt was consciously or unconsciously "intending to make Gordon a character in a future book." Late that New Year's Eve, while their wives chatted in the living room, the two former agents withdrew to Hunt's office in the basement and there, beneath the rifles, hunting knives, pistols, and swords, they talked about the intelligence-gathering plan that Liddy was preparing for John Mitchell. At midnight they rejoined the ladies and hoisted glasses of champagne to what promised to be an exciting new year.

As CREEP's general counsel, Liddy had several important duties—to keep abreast of filing requirements in the twenty-three states where Nixon was entering primaries, and to make sure the campaign did not run afoul of the complex new campaign finance law. But it quickly became clear that Liddy felt much more comfortable wearing his other dashing new hat: as chief of CREEP's intelligence system. In his first meetings with Jeb Magruder, he boasted that White House officials had talked with him about a "broad-gauged intelligence plan" and promised him a million dollars to carry it out. (He told Hunt that Mitchell wanted him to use "every available method" to obtain intelligence, because "we don't want to be caught with our pants down.") But when Magruder introduced him at a staff meeting as the committee's "supersleuth," Liddy angrily rebuked him: "I can't do this job unless I have my anonymity. Are you trying to blow my cover?"

Magruder told Liddy that a $1-million program would require Mitchell's approval and instructed him to prepare detailed "background documents" to justify the scheme. So, during the first weeks of 1972, Liddy began drafting his plans. He told Hunt that he planned extensive electronic surveillance and asked him to find a former CIA agent skilled in "electronics and physical entries." Calling the agency's External Employment Assistance Branch—which one investigator has described as "the switchplate of an old boy network of former CIA agents"—Hunt asked for men whose background fitted them for the job. One man referred to him was Thomas C. Amato, for ten years a CIA photographer, photoengraver, and locksmith; but for some reason Amato did not fit the bill. Hunt had received a Christmas card that winter from Jack Bauman, the security officer for the CIA's Guatemala operation, who had retired early after a heart attack. He wrote Bauman in Winterhaven, Florida, asking if he would be available for "some work." Hunt and Bauman met on December 28, 1971, and later in Washington. Bauman received four $100 bills for his expenses, but ultimately he turned down the job. At Hunt's request, Bauman interviewed one candidate the CIA had suggested, but he wasn't interested, either. Hunt then approached a man later identified only as "Mr. Stewart," who spent February 1 with Bernard Barker in Miami discussing various "operations" against the Democrats. Stewart too turned down the job.

Early that year, Liddy met another man who had been brought into CREEP the fall before on the recommendation of John Caulfield and Alfred Wong, special agent in charge of the technical services division. He was James W. McCord, Jr., who became a part-time "security coordinator" for the committee on October 1 and full-time chief of security on January 1, 1972. Meanwhile, his firm—McCord Associates, Inc.—was given a contract to provide "security services" for the Republican National Committee.

In the spring of 1971 Montgomery College in Rockville, Maryland, offered a course called Criminal Justice 234, Industrial and Retail Security, described in the catalogue as an "introduction to historical, philosophical and legal basis of government and industrial security programs in a democratic society." (Before taking the course, students were required to take C.J. 102, Administration of Justice.) The instructor in Criminal Justice 234 was James McCord, who had become a teacher and "security consultant" in 1970 after twenty-five years in government service. Born in Waurika, Oklahoma, McCord joined the FBI in 1942, serving in "radio intelligence" until late 1943. After two years as an Army Air Corps officer, he earned a bachelor's degree in business administration from the University of Texas. Rejoining the bureau in 1948, he served as a special agent in San Francisco and San Diego until 1951, when he moved over to the CIA, where he remained for the next nineteen years. He is believed to have played a role in the 1961 Bay of Pigs invasion, served in 1962–64 as the agency's senior security officer in Europe, and ultimately became chief of the CIA's physical security division, with responsibility for guarding the agency's facilities from other people's spies. (He worked under Howard J. Osborn, the agency's director of security and an old acquaintance of Howard Hunt's.) McCord won a reputation as a brilliant interrogator for his work in debriefing pilots shot down over the Soviet-Iranian border in 1959. Allen W. Dulles, then the CIA director, once described him as *"my top man." On retirement, he was given the Distinguished Service Award for "outstanding performance." But even after retirement he dabbled in intelligence as a member of the Office of Emergency Preparedness's "special analysis unit," a fifteen-member reserve unit that helped to develop a list of radicals and also worked on contingency plans for censorship of the news media and the mails in event of war. (McCord was a lieutenant colonel in the Air Force reserve.) He also plunged into community work: helped raise money for a new wing at the Kennedy Institute, a special school attended by his retarded daughter, Nancy; and spent half a day each week at the Rockville United Methodist Church, running a "social fellowship" for older members. But he and his wife, Sarah, didn't mix much with the neighbors around their $38,000 colonial brick house. The stocky, balding McCord was reserved and quiet. According to one neighbor, "He often seemed as though he had some very important secret weighing on his mind."*

As the only former FBI agents at CREEP, McCord and Liddy naturally fell into a nostalgic sort of friendship, swapping "war stories" around the water cooler. Soon, Liddy started inviting McCord into his office to talk about the dangers posed by demonstrators at the Republican National Convention in San Diego: "Well, what is the latest estimate?" one would ask, "what do you hear?" Once Liddy said he expected 250,000 demonstrators. Later, he upped that to 500,000. He seemed very worried.

Liddy began asking McCord about "listening devices." McCord regarded this as "a normal professional interest, to find out what was the state of the art." But gradually, as Liddy inquired about the capacity and cost of specific bugging devices, "it became apparent that Liddy had an interest in several areas of intelligence-gathering pertaining to the Democratic party and the Democratic convention." In late January Liddy showed McCord several charts wrapped in brown paper in his office. He said he was going to use them for a "presentation" to the attorney general.

At eleven-fifteen on January 27, Liddy carried his brown paper packages into the Justice Department, past a mural showing a stern black-robed figure facing an aroused mob, through the attorney general's seventy-five-foot, blue-carpeted ceremonial office, and into the private office beyond. He stripped off the paper and set the six professionally drawn color charts on a chair. The overall project was called "Gemstone," and each chart dealt with a different activity, code-named "Diamond," "Ruby," "Sapphire," "Opal," "Crystal," and so on. (The precious-stone code was developed by Howard Hunt, who says it was "in keeping with clandestine practice" and therefore "charmed" Liddy.) A summary chart pictured the entire project and its budget—which came to $1 million.

With Mitchell, Magruder, and Dean gathered before him, Liddy launched into a well-prepared thirty-minute "show-and-tell" presentation. Pointing to various charts as he went along, he outlined a vast intelligence-gathering and dirty-tricks scheme which included:

• Electronic surveillance and wiretapping of the Democratic National Convention, candidates' headquarters and hotel rooms, including use of a "chase plane" that could intercept radio-telephone communications between the Democratic candidate and people on the ground.

• Break-ins to obtain and photograph documents.

• Kidnaping squads which would capture radical leaders such as Jerry Rubin and Abbie Hoffman planning to demonstrate at the Republican National Convention in San Diego. The radicals would be drugged and taken to a "safe house" in Mexico until the convention was over. "They'd never even know who had them or where they were," Liddy promised.

• Mugging squads to rough up hostile demonstrators at the convention.

• Call girls to compromise Democratic politicians in Washington and at the convention in Miami Beach. A yacht would be rented in Miami and equipped with hidden cameras and recording devices to blackmail Democrats lured there by the girls. "These would be high-class girls," Liddy said. "The best in the business."

• Sabotage of the air-conditioning system at the Democratic convention. "Can't you see all those delegates sitting there dripping wet in a hundred-and-twenty-degree heat on national television," Liddy chortled.

His audience was stunned. Magruder says he was "appalled." Dean found much of it "mind-boggling." Dean recalls that once he gave Mitchell a "bewildered" look and the attorney general winked. When the sales pitch was over, Mitchell took a few long puffs on his pipe and told Liddy, "That's not quite what I had in mind." He said the budget in particular was out of the question and suggested that Liddy should "go back to the drawing boards and come up with a more realistic plan."

Liddy was "despondent" when he left Mitchell's office, and both Magruder and Dean tried to raise his spirits.

"Cheer up, Gordon," said Magruder. "You just tone the plan down a little and we'll try again."

"I thought that was what he wanted," said Liddy.

"It was just a little too much, Gordon," Magruder said soothingly.

According to Hunt, Liddy was furious at Dean and Magruder for not backing him up at the meeting: "There they sat like two bumps on a log. All they are, for Christ's sake, is yes-men."

But Liddy quickly regained his natural ebullience. A few days later, he told McCord that he had talked with Dean, who said that things "looked good" for the plan but that "some means would have to be found for deniability for Mr. Mitchell" and "a method of funding should be arranged so that the funds would not come through the regular committee." At about this time Liddy asked McCord whether he would be willing to join an operation to bug Democratic headquarters if it was approved. Impressed by the high-level names being bandied about—and convinced that Mitchell would consult the President as he did about all major and many minor campaign decisions—McCord readily agreed.

Over the next week, Liddy retooled his plan. That weekend he flew to San Diego to examine the site for the Republican convention, and concluded that it could not be defended against the horde of expected demonstrators. Convinced that the convention would be moved to Miami Beach—as it eventually was—he scaled down some of the costs for "protective security" there. He also discarded the chase plane, the abduction scheme, the mugging squad, and the Miami bordello-yacht (although he retained the call girls in Washington). His new plan focused on electronic surveillance, wiretapping, and surreptitious photography, and the budget was cut in half to $500,000.

Liddy also discarded his charts, reducing the presentation to a couple of eight-by-eleven-inch sheets of paper—which he distributed to the same group when it trooped back into Mitchell's office at four o'clock on February 4. This time, according to everyone but Mitchell, they discussed specific targets.

Magruder and Dean agree that the targets were Larry O'Brien's office at the Democratic National Committee; O'Brien's hotel suite in Miami Beach during the convention; the rooms of other prominent Democrats at the Fontainebleau Hotel in Miami Beach; and, ultimately, the campaign headquarters of whichever Democrat emerged as the Presidential nominee.

Finally, Magruder says, Mitchell mentioned another possible target: the office of Hank Greenspun, publisher of the *Las Vegas Sun*. A combative Brooklyn Jew transplanted to the gaudy playpen of the Northern Plains, Greenspun was a legendary figure in American journalism. In the 1950s he had become a darling of the liberals for tangling with Senators Joseph R. McCarthy of Wisconsin and Patrick A. McCarran of Nevada; and over the years he had raked gamblers and judges, sheriffs and government agencies with his lethal prose ("crawling and sniveling jackals," "vicious, disreputable, drunken, scurvy, lying cowardly traitor"). But when Howard Hughes breezed into town in 1966, the fighting frontier editor struck up a self-serving alliance with the millionaire recluse: extolling him editorially, urging the rest of the press to leave him alone, selling him his television station, and, finally, hitting him for a substantial loan. Yet the alliance was maintained chiefly through Robert Maheu, Hughes's chief lieutenant in Nevada, and when Maheu and Hughes had their pyrotechnic falling-out in November 1970, Greenspun sided with Maheu and began training his editorial six-shooter on Hughes (now fled to the Bahamas and thence to Nicaragua). Indeed, Maheu was known to have given Greenspun copies of the multifarious memos through which Hughes had passed him orders over the years. Greenspun kept the memos in the huge green Meilink safe that squatted in the corner of his office under the autographed picture of Richard M. Nixon.

According to Howard Hunt, the Greenspun caper began several days *before* the February 4 meeting, when Robert Bennett returned from Las Vegas where he had been consulting on his contract with the Hughes Tool Company. Hunt says Bennett summoned him into his office and told him he had picked up an intriguing rumor: that Greenspun was going around Las Vegas saying that if Muskie received the nomination, he had enough information on the senator to "blow him out of the water." Hunt said that was "very interesting," and Bennett replied, "I thought it might be. And you might want to pass it along to your friends." (Bennett offers a totally different version. He says Hunt came to him with the report about Greenspun's boast and asked the help of the Hughes organization in checking it out.)

Hunt says he typed up a two-sentence memo summarizing Bennett's information, stuck it in an envelope, and took it across the street to Liddy's office. That evening or the next morning Liddy came to him in a "euphoric state" because the information had been "well received" by his superiors, who wanted him to investigate further. (It is unclear whether this approval came at the February 4 meeting or an earlier conference.) Liddy "indicated that it would be a marvelous opportunity for us to travel jointly to Las Vegas and spend a number of days and nights there under luxurious circumstances. And that, as far as he was concerned, would be the high point of the mission." (Liddy was always "horny." Hunt has told friends that as soon as they got on a plane to go on any of their missions, Liddy would ask, "Can you get me laid?" Once in Miami, Hunt recalls, he found a beautiful Cuban prostitute and brought her up to their suite, "but do you know that Liddy is such a racial bigot he wouldn't touch her!")

At that stage, apparently, neither Hunt nor Liddy took the Las Vegas caper too seriously—not being sure just what Greenspun's information was and where it was stored. But, Hunt says, he reported Liddy's reaction to Bennett and suggested that perhaps he could "go back to his sources and attempt to nail it down." A few days later, Bennett summoned Hunt to his office again and introduced him to Ralph Winte, chief of security for the Summa Corporation (the successor to Hughes Tool), who was in Washington in connection with Clifford Irving's bogus biography of Hughes. Bennett said he had told Winte about the project and felt that the two of them might have a "commonality of interest." With that, Hunt and Winte went into Hunt's office to continue the discussion.

Winte was an ex-FBI agent, and he and Hunt established a rapport as "two former professionals of government investigative agencies." They quickly recognized that it could be useful for them to cooperate on a joint operation to obtain whatever Greenspun might have squirreled away. Hunt says he was still thinking only of the information which could "blow Muskie out of the water." Winte talked of all the problems Hughes was having with Maheu, in part because of the "Maheu-Greenspun alliance," and said that "anything that could be done against Greenspun, in fact, would be a blow against Maheu." According to Hunt, Winte also said that Maheu had "bought off" one or more of the judges presiding over his litigation with Hughes, that Greenspun knew about this, and that of course any evidence on this would be particularly valuable to Hughes. Hunt suggested that Winte try to find out more about where Greenspun kept his confidential papers and also get a floor plan of Greenspun's office. They talked about a possible reconnaissance trip by Hunt and Liddy, for which Winte would provide rooms, limousines, and "a good time in Las Vegas at company expense."

On the weekend of February 20–21 Hunt and Liddy made one of their periodic trips to Los Angeles (during which they provided their own good time with a receptionist and a secretary who worked for one of Hunt's old CIA colleagues). Saturday morning Winte came to their suite at the Beverly Wilshire Hotel and, according to Hunt, showed them a rough floor plan of the *Las Vegas Sun* offices which had been provided by one of his operatives. It had most of what they needed to know, with one major omission—the location of the safe. Hunt says they then discussed a possible burglary attempt—not a simple photographic mission but an "all-out forced entry"—in which they would empty the safe and later "divide the spoils" on the basis of "who had primary interest in what information." Hunt says he was still interested in the Muskie data, "and we assumed that the Hughes Tool Co. would be interested in everything else."

Hunt says it was agreed that he would provide the burglars—Barker's team—and Winte would take care of the logistics. Liddy, whom Hunt describes as "something of a hot-car buff" and who had been "involved with the FBI in many high-speed chases," expressed a particular interest in getaway vehicles. He and Winte discussed "the availability of certain horsepower engines and certain kinds of cars in the area, whether rental or on a loan basis." And they also discussed a getaway plane. Liddy, who was a pilot, said, "If we could have a waiting plane, that would be great. We could pull in at some airfield across the border . . . and make our ways separately back to the United States." Hunt says Liddy and Winte discussed the various aircraft available to Hughes Tool and agreed on an "executive jet" appropriate to the mission. He says he and Liddy envisioned a landing in Baja California or elsewhere in Mexico, and denies McCord's testimony that they were considering landing in some "Central American country." Hughes was then in Nicaragua, but Hunt says a landing there would have been impractical because it is much more difficult to re-enter the United States from Nicaragua than from Mexico. According to Hunt, Winte said the loan of the aircraft—particularly for a cross-border operation—would require approval from higher levels in the Hughes organization.

Winte denies ever seriously discussing a burglary with Hughes and Liddy. He denies supplying a floor plan for Greenspun's office. At the Beverly Wilshire meeting, he says, Hunt outlined the burglary plan and then the conversation went something like this:

WINTE: Gee! I don't know what you mean. Suppose you get caught?

HUNT: We'll take care of the guards; there's no possibility of getting caught!

WINTE: Do you know anything about Hank Greenspun's office?

HUNT: We're professionals! Don't worry about that.

WINTE: Let me talk this over with my boss.

Winte says he reported Hunt's plans to Bill Gay, by then Hughes's chief administrative aide, observing, "These guys are wild, man!" Gay says he got angry, criticized Winte for even talking to Hunt and Liddy, and said, "We have nothing to gain, and it would be wrong to do it." Then, several weeks later, Bennett told Hunt that Gay had turned down the request for a plane (and, by inference, the whole plan). Hunt and Liddy never saw or heard from Winte again.

Hunt says they were disappointed—Liddy expressed regret that they "wouldn't be able to have those great times in Las Vegas"—but by then they were deeply involved in other aspects of the Gemstone plan. (McCord has testified that Liddy was still talking about a burglary of Greenspun's office as late as April or May 1972 and that Liddy told him he had actually gone to Las Vegas to "case" the situation. In 1973 John Ehrlichman told Nixon that the Hunt-Liddy team "flew out, broke his safe, got something out." Greenspun says that somebody tried to break into his safe in August

1972 but only succeeded in tearing the front cover plate. A window in Greenspun's office also shows marks of a forced entry, but nobody at the *Sun* is sure exactly when the damage occurred.)

The mystery remains: just what were Hunt and Liddy —and beyond them, Mitchell, Magruder, and Dean —after in Greenspun's safe? McCord testified that Liddy said it was "blackmail-type information" on Muskie, it was related to "racketeering," and it might show that the national crime syndicate would have influence over Muskie if he became President. Greenspun says the only information he had linking Muskie to any kind of crime was data on a 1965 conviction of Muskie and the then Senator Eugene J. McCarthy of Minnesota for illegally hunting ducks on a federal reserve, for which both men had been given a small fine (the violation apparently involved spreading grain on the ground and then shooting the ducks as they landed to eat it); he checked this out through his friend Jack Anderson but didn't use it because it was "trivial"; and indeed, he thought so little of it that he kept it not in his safe but in a cubbyhole of his roll-top desk.

Were the ex-Plumbers on a wild-duck chase? Or were they, in fact, after something entirely different? Greenspun believes their real target was the mound of Hughes-Maheu memos he kept in his safe—the same memos that the Hughes people were evidently after. Certainly the evidence suggests a strong, continuing White House interest in those memos. On February 3, 1971, Caulfield wrote to John Dean suggesting that he view the last half of the CBS *Sixty Minutes* show—on "the ongoing Hughes controversy"—that had aired the night before. Two days later Dean asked Caulfield to set up a screening "as soon as possible." The segment contains the following exchange:

MORLEY SAFER: Hughes has a knack for playing one side off against the other with letters. Hank

Greenspun has a knack for finding copies of the letters.

GREENSPUN: I have a document in my pocket. I don't know if I can show you. I have friends in very low places so I can get lots of information. I'm not going to read this document to you, but this is in his own handwriting.

And, perhaps significantly, on February 3, 1972—the day before Mitchell instructed Liddy to see if Greenspun's office could be burglarized—*The New York Times* reported that Greenspun had Hughes memos in his safe. The *Times* article, by its well-informed investigative reporter Wallace Turner, said Greenspun claimed to have "about 200 individual items" in his collection of Hughes communications. Many of these were memos in Hughes's own handwriting, but some were memos from Hughes's employees in response to various assignments.

If the President's men were after these memos, what did they hope to learn from them? Several possibilities have been suggested. First, given the President's extreme sensitivity about his brother, they may have hoped that the memos would reveal more about the relationship between Donald Nixon and the Hughes interests. More likely, though, they wanted to know what the memos contained about dealings between Hughes and Richard Nixon, particularly the $100,000 funneled through Bebe Rebozo. Nixon probably feared that disclosure of that payment could greatly harm his re-election chances—especially if it were tied to Mitchell's about-face on the Dunes antitrust case.

The President would have been eager to find out who else knew about the Hughes money and how such persons might plan to use it against him. Obviously, one man who knew was Bob Maheu, who had been involved in the negotiations for the contribution. Since his split with Hughes, Maheu had become a walking repository of explosive information potentially damaging to both the Hughes and Nixon interests. (In Ron Rosenbaum's apt phrase, he had developed into "a kind of wild card Ellsberg-at-large.") Both the Washington

White House and the Nicaraguan Penthouse were presumably wondering just how widely Maheu had distributed his data.

One man Maheu had almost certainly told was Hank Greenspun. On September 24, 1971, while the President was stopping off in Portland, Oregon, Greenspun warned Director of Communications Herb Klein that he had heard that $100,000 from Hughes had been used to furnish Nixon's San Clemente estate. Greenspun's notes of this conversation show that he told Klein that if the story got out, it could "sink Nixon." (Greenspun was a fervent Nixon supporter, chiefly because of the President's support for Israel, Greenspun's single greatest enthusiasm.) When word of Greenspun's inquiry reached John Ehrlichman, he assigned Herb Kalmbach to fly to Las Vegas and talk with the publisher. On October 12 Kalmbach checked into Del Webb's suite at the Sahara Hotel and talked with Greenspun for nearly four hours, scribbling notes on page after page of his yellow legal pad. According to Greenspun, the lawyer began by asking him about Donald Nixon's activities. Only later did he slide into discussion of the Hughes money—as if he didn't want Greenspun to realize that's what he was concerned about. Then he vehemently reassured Greenspun that no Hughes money had gone into San Clemente. "I'll be glad to open our books and show you," he said. "I know where every nickel came from and I can assure you none of it came from Hughes." Then Kalmbach began asking questions, most of them about Larry O'Brien: what were O'Brien's relations with Hughes? with Maheu? with Greenspun? Finally, the lawyer asked, "Do you mind if I grind all of this into our computer?" Greenspun didn't mind.

Nixon's men were particularly suspicious of Greenspun because he was known to be very friendly with Jack Anderson; Anderson even owned a small piece of the *Las Vegas Sun;* and Anderson had published the first story about money, siphoned off from the Silver Slipper Casino, being passed from Hughes through Rebozo to Richard Nixon. Then, on January 24, 1971— twelve days before the second Gemstone planning session—Anderson had published the story again, this time claiming he had "documentary evidence" to back it up. This must have aroused something approaching panic in the White House—visions of Anderson getting memos or other documents about the contribution either directly from Maheu or through their mutual friend Greenspun.

Finally, still another man was known to have close ties with Maheu, a man who would have the most compelling reasons of all to want information on the Hughes-Rebozo contribution and the greatest motive to use it. This was Larry O'Brien—the other main target selected by John Mitchell at the second Gemstone planning session.

The White House had long been obsessed with gathering damaging material about Larry O'Brien, in much the same way as it had sought information on Ted Kennedy, Dan Ellsberg, and Edmund Muskie. John Dean recalls that from very nearly the start of the Nixon administration, Haldeman, Ehrlichman, and Colson had pressed for "politically embarrassing information" on O'Brien. Magruder says the White House regarded O'Brien as the Democrats' "most professional political operator," who could be "very difficult in the coming campaign," and that they were constantly looking for "information that might discredit him."

For example, on August 5, 1970, Haldeman asked Dean to look into O'Brien's participation in an international consulting firm called Public Affairs Analysts to see if there might be embarrassing material there. Caulfield examined the company, in which O'Brien had joined with Republican F. Clifton White, Democrat Joe Napolitan, and others to offer political consulting services to foreign clients. The investigation turned up nothing embarrassing and was dropped.

Likewise, Magruder recalls, he got a tip early in 1972 from Kevin Phillips, the former Mitchell aide and now a syndicated columnist who remained close to the administration. Phillips told him that O'Brien might be involved in a kickback scheme involving a commercial exposition at the Democratic National Convention. The plan, offered to both the Republicans and the Democrats by Walter Scott, president of the Columbia Exposition Company of New York, called for an Exposition of the American Economy to be held simultaneously with each party's convention. Participating companies would purchase booths and the proceeds would be divided, 80 per cent for the party and 20 per cent for Columbia—an arrangement that Scott describes as quite standard for such expositions. The plan was turned down by both parties. But Phillips's report greatly interested CREEP. Liddy was dispatched to Miami to "take a look at the situation." Magruder says Liddy persuaded a businessman friend to telephone Richard Murphy, the Democrats' convention manager, and then taped the ensuing conversation. The tape was ambiguous but merited further investigation, so Magruder said, "Fine, Gordon, find out some more." But Liddy never produced any more evidence on the alleged kickback.

But the White House obsession with O'Brien focused chiefly on his relationship with Hughes and Maheu. After the June 1968 assassination of Robert Kennedy—whom O'Brien had served as campaign manager—Hughes had instructed Maheu to see if he could hire O'Brien. In October 1969, after lengthy negotiations with Maheu and others, O'Brien formed a Washington consulting firm, O'Brien Associates, and immediately received a $15,000-a-month contract with Hughes. Operating as Hughes's chief Washington representative, O'Brien performed a number of tasks, including seeking to mediate an out-of-court settlement between Hughes and TWA, and devising public-relations programs for Hughes and his companies. But when Maheu and Hughes had their massive falling out, O'Brien was regarded as an ally of Maheu's and gradually eased out—being replaced in January 1971 by the ubiquitous Bob Bennett of Mullen & Company.

From that time forward, Nixon and his men intensified their efforts to investigate O'Brien's relationship with Maheu and Hughes. This apparently began on January 18, 1971, with a memo from Haldeman to Dean requesting any or all information on the subject. On or about that date, Colson asked his friend Bob Bennett about it—remarking that it could be embarrassing to O'Brien if it were revealed that he had been on a Hughes retainer while serving as Democratic National Chairman (a post O'Brien had resumed in February 1970). Bennett talked with Bill Gay about O'Brien's job and relayed what little he found out to Colson. Dean, in turn, talked with Colson, Bennett, Caulfield, and Bebe Rebozo, and reported on these conversations to Haldeman in a January 26 memo. He said a source of Caulfield's had indicated that "O'Brien and Maheu are longtime friends from the Boston area, a friendship which dates back to early or pre-Kennedy days. During the Kennedy administration there apparently was continuous liaison between O'Brien and Maheu." On January 28 Haldeman instructed Dean to "keep in contact with Bob Bennett, as well as looking for other sources of information on this subject. . . . You and Chuck Colson should get together and come up with a way to leak the appropriate information. . . . Please keep me advised of your progress on this and any plans you decide on."

Gradually, however, the White House recognized that leaks on the O'Brien-Hughes relationship might spring other leaks embarrassing to Nixon. In his January 26 memo Dean reported that Rebozo "requests that if any action be taken with regard to Hughes that he be notified because of his familiarity with the delicacy of the relationship as a result of his own dealings with the Hughes people" (an apparent reference to the Hughes-Rebozo-Nixon contribution). And on February 1 Caulfield wrote to Dean, "Mayhew's [*sic*] controversial activities and contacts in both Democratic and Republican circles suggests the possibility that forced embarrassment of O'Brien in this matter might well shake loose Republican skeletons from the closet."

Finally, the Operation Sandwedge proposal drafted by Caulfield in the summer of 1971 reveals a deep concern about what information O'Brien could gather and how he might use it against Nixon. "The presence of Lawrence O'Brien as Chairman of the Democratic National Committee unquestionably suggests that the Democratic nominee will have a strong, covert intelligence effort mounted against us in 1972," Caulfield wrote. "We should be particularly concerned about the new and rapidly growing Intertel organization. . . . Should this Kennedy mafia dominated intelligence 'gun for hire' be turned against us in '72, we would, indeed, have a dangerous and formidable foe."

Intertel—International Intelligence, Inc.—is a private intelligence and security group founded in early 1970 by several former high-ranking Justice Department officials, among them Robert Peloquin, former top attorney in the Organized Crime and Racketeering Section, and William Hundley, former chief of the section and special assistant to Attorney General Robert Kennedy. Intertel specialized in protecting corporations against underworld infiltration. Probably its best-known client was Howard Hughes, who called on it to provide security for his Las Vegas hotels and casinos when Maheu was forced out. Intertel almost certainly knew about Hughes's payments to Rebozo. (Caulfield, for his own reasons, exaggerated Intertel's connections to Kennedy and ignored the Nixon connections.) The company's owner, James M. Crosby, was an old friend of Bebe Rebozo's and a new friend of Richard Nixon's. He had donated $100,000 to Nixon's 1968 campaign, placed a yacht at his disposal, and become an occasional guest at the White House. Six months after the election, evidently at Nixon's request, Crosby hired James O. Golden, Nixon's personal attaché during the Eisenhower administration and then a member of the Secret Service, as Intertel's vice president. Nevertheless, Peloquin, Hundley, and other leading Intertel figures did have close ties with O'Brien and Kennedy, and anything they might have passed on about the Hughes-Rebozo dealings would have proved most embarrassing to Nixon in 1972.

For all these reasons, the Nixon White House may well have decided that it should burglarize Hank Greenspun and Larry O'Brien to find out just what each man knew about "Republican skeletons" in the closet—specifically, the $100,000 Hughes payment through Rebozo to Nixon. But the February 4 meeting at which John Mitchell authorized both these targets ended somewhat equivocally. According to Magruder and Dean,

Liddy's plan still did not have Mitchell's approval. Magruder says Mitchell "didn't feel comfortable" with it, even at the $500,000 level, and wanted Liddy to cut it still further. Dean says he strenuously objected to discussing such matters in the office of the attorney general, and he says that after the meeting he sought out Haldeman and told him what Liddy proposed, calling it "incredible, unnecessary, and unwise." Haldeman agreed with this assessment, Dean says, and told him he should have "no further dealings on the matter." Haldeman does not recall this conversation.

Meanwhile, White House attention was abruptly diverted to more urgent matters. On February 29 Jack Anderson's column quoted from a confidential ITT interoffice memo admitting that the $400,000 it had committed for the Republican convention had been part of a deal for settlement of the Justice Department's antitrust suit against it. The memo was allegedly written on June 25, 1971, by Dita Beard, an ITT lobbyist, to William Merriam, head of the corporation's Washington office. "I am convinced," she wrote, ". . . that our noble commitment has gone a long way toward our negotiations on the mergers eventually coming up as Hal [Geneen] wants them. Certainly the President has told Mitchell to see that things are worked out fairly." Anderson charged bluntly that the antitrust case had been "fixed," and "the fix was a payoff for ITT's pledge of up to $400,000." Mitchell and ITT immediately denied this, but the furor it and subsequent Anderson columns caused led to renewed Senate Judiciary Committee hearings on the confirmation of Richard Kleindienst to replace Mitchell as attorney general.

The President's men regarded Anderson's revelations as the most serious threat yet to Nixon's re-election, and responded with all the single-minded determination that they had brought to such threats in the past. A "task force"—including Ehrlichman, Colson, Dean,

Mardian; Fred Fielding, Dean's assistant; Richard A. Moore, a special counsel to the President; and Wallace Johnson, special assistant to the President for legislative affairs—began meeting regularly in Ehrlichman's office to monitor the resumed Kleindienst hearings, coordinate activities with ITT, and generally try to limit the damage caused by the disclosure.

Meanwhile, ITT did its best to seal off the leaks. Not surprisingly, it hired Intertel, whose agents were soon scurrying around the corporate offices. The very day Anderson's column appeared, Ned Gerrity, ITT's vice president for public relations, summoned Mrs. Beard to New York. She spent that day and the next there, went briefly back to Washington, and left on March 2 for what she says was to have been a vacation in West Yellowstone, Montana. She caught a flight for Bozeman, Montana, through Denver, but on the plane she became ill. A United Airlines stewardess report says she "started turning gray and blue around the mouth," and was revived with pills from her purse and some whisky; she left the plane in Denver without assistance. The next evening, she was admitted to the Rocky Mountain Osteopathic Hospital in Denver, complaining of chest pains. A doctor who later examined her for the Senate Judiciary Committee concluded that she may have been suffering from "coronary artery disease with angina pectoris." But the effect of the illness—real or feigned—was to keep Dita Beard incommunicado during the new Senate hearings.

On March 15, Howard Hunt says, he was summoned to Chuck Colson's office, where he found members of the ITT "task force" in deep and urgent conversation. Colson asked him, "Would you be able to fly to Denver and interview Dita Beard?" Colson says the trip was, in effect, Hunt's idea, proposed in a memo a few days earlier, and that he told Hunt "to urge her [Mrs. Beard] to tell the truth with respect to the memorandum and to reassure her if she told the truth, her many friends back here in Washington would not hold against her the fact that she had contrived this memorandum if, in fact, that was what she had done." Wallace Johnson then arranged for Hunt to meet with Dita Beard's daughter, Lane, with whom the White House had already arranged Hunt's Denver trip.

"Who exactly do you represent?" Lane asked nervously.

"High Washington levels who are interested in your mother's welfare," Hunt replied. When she pressed him, he showed her his CIA identification in the name of Edward J. Hamilton. Lane said she would tell her mother's doctor to expect a visit from Mr. Hamilton.

Arriving in Denver—wearing the red wig provided by the CIA—Hunt telephoned Dr. David Garland, who arranged for him to talk with Mrs. Beard that night and again on the following day. Working from an *aide-mémoire* given him by Johnson and consulting frequently with Colson by telephone, Hunt questioned Mrs. Beard. "After some disjointed exchanges she asked me what it was I wanted her to do. I told her the most useful action would be to have her return to Washington as soon as possible, making a brief statement, denying authorship of the memorandum—if she was able to in good faith—and then collapse." Mrs. Beard said she was unable to travel, but Hunt did extract from her a fairly firm denial that she had written the memorandum. Before he left the hospital, he ran into Mrs. Beard's son, David, who recalled, "[Hunt] was very eerie, with this huge red wig on cockeyed, like he put it on in a dark car."

Arriving back in Washington, Hunt found Bob Bennett coordinating a rush effort to get Mrs. Beard's denial out to the press. Bennett drafted her statement, then checked it with her lawyers, officials at ITT, and Senator Hugh Scott of Pennsylvania, the Senate minority leader. Drafts were transmitted back and forth between Washington and Denver by facsimile copier. Finally the statement—branding the memo a "hoax," a "forgery," and a "cruel fraud"—was issued simultaneously by Senator Scott in Washington and by Mrs. Beard's lawyer in Denver, David W. Fleming (a longtime Republican activist whose fees for this case were paid by ITT).

ITT and the White House had also joined forces on another front: to round up all potentially incriminating documents on the matter. As early as February 24—the

day after Brit Hume, of Anderson's staff, first spoke
with Mrs. Beard—ITT's Washington office began shred-
ding papers. And soon afterward the White House "task
force" began frantically collecting every memo and
letter it could lay its hands on. (John Dean remembers
that Fred Fielding, who had been designated custodian
for the collected documents, came into one meeting
saying, "Boy, you ought to see the one we caught today!") But they faced special problems here. For about
two years, the Securities and Exchange Commission had
been investigating irregularities—such as insider trading—in the ITT-Hartford merger, and months before,
the SEC had subpoenaed all documents relating to the
merger. Thus, when SEC attorneys read Dita Beard's
memo in the press, they asked ITT why the document
had not been turned over in the first place and whether
any similar memos were lying about in the company's
files. Neither ITT nor the White House wanted such
documents in the hands of investigators; but to destroy
documents under subpoena is a criminal act. So in early March lawyers representing ITT handed over to the
White House thirteen "politically sensitive" documents
dealing with meetings between ITT and government officials (some of them were delivered to Wallace Johnson
at a room in the Sheraton-Carlton Hotel). On March 6
Ehrlichman summoned William Casey, chairman of the
SEC, to the White House and asked him "why the
commission was chasing after additional ITT documents" and "whether this was necessary." Casey says he
told Ehrlichman that he supported his enforcement
officials. (Ultimately, the White House turned its documents over to the SEC. But for months Casey frustrated
attempts by congressional committees to get a look at
them.)

Even such strenuous efforts to blur the trail did not
satisfy some zealots in the administration. On March
30 Colson warned Haldeman that Kleindienst's nomination should be withdrawn because of the risk of "serious
additional exposure." He warned that some memos
were still drifting around town that could undermine
the testimony of Mitchell, Erwin Griswold, and, of
course, Kleindienst; outline "the $400,000 arrangement

with ITT"; and "lay this case on the President's door-step."

But Nixon refused to withdraw the nomination. Mitchell, Kleindienst, and Ed Reinecke stuck to their stories as they trooped up to testify before the committee. Kleindienst, for example, told the committee, "I was not interfered with by anybody at the White House. I was not importuned. I was not pressured. I was not directed. I did not have conferences with respect to what I should or should not do." On June 8 Kleindienst was confirmed by the Senate.*

T he ITT affair preoccupied high-ranking administration officials throughout March, as Gordon Liddy was putting the final touches to his Gemstone plan. It may also have intensified some people's desire to get dirt on Larry O'Brien, who became by far the most effective critic of Kleindienst's nomination and the whole ITT settlement.

But Gemstone was hampered by deteriorating relations between Liddy and Magruder. At the age of forty-two, Liddy resented working for a man four years his junior. From the beginning, they clashed on matters of privilege and prerogative. Magruder tried unsuccessfully to block Liddy's salary increase from $26,000 to $30,000, which he regarded as a violation of the principle that CREEP aides should make the same salary they earned at the White House. Then Liddy exploded when his office was moved from the fourth floor— where most of the top CREEP officials were lodged— to the eighth. "If I'm the general counsel of this committee, I've got to be where the important people are," he roared at Magruder. And Magruder was annoyed because he felt Liddy was so preoccupied with his

---

*A year later, Kleindienst pleaded guilty to failing to respond fully to questions and was sentenced to one month in jail and a $100 fine, but the sentence was suspended. Reinecke was also found guilty of perjury and given a suspended eighteen-month sentence. His conviction was overturned on appeal.

"cloak-and-dagger" missions that he was neglecting his meat-and-potatoes duties as CREEP's lawyer. One day in mid-March they met in the third-floor reception area. According to Magruder, the conversation went something like this:

"Gordon, where are those reports you promised me?"

"They're not ready," said Liddy.

"Well, the delay is causing me problems," said Magruder, putting his hand on Liddy's shoulder. "If you're going to be our general counsel, you've got to do your work."

"Get your hand off me," Liddy shouted. "Get your hand off me or I'll kill you." (Liddy recalls a more colorful version. He says he snarled: "Jeb, if you don't take your arm off me I'm going to break it off and beat you to death with it.")

In his book, Magruder dismisses this as "just Liddy's tough-guy talk," but at the time he was angry and probably a bit frightened of the violent, impulsive man he had working for him. A few minutes later, he called Liddy into his office and told him, "This isn't working out, Gordon." They quickly agreed that Liddy should leave the committee. But Frederick C. LaRue, Mitchell's special assistant, who was sitting in, warned that Liddy's departure could destroy the intelligence-gathering network. Afterward, Liddy asked Dean for his support, and Dean told Magruder, "Jeb, you don't want to let your personal feelings about Liddy get in the way of an important operation." During the next few days, Gordon Strachan and Egil Krogh also talked with Magruder about Liddy. (Strachan told Magruder, "Liddy's a Hitler, but at least he's our Hitler.") Eventually, it was decided that Liddy should move his base of operations down to the second floor and become counsel to Maurice Stans's finance committee but continue to report to Magruder as CREEP's intelligence chief.

Hunt and Liddy were champing at the bit. One day, after making his usual disparaging remarks about Magruder's "youth, inexperience, and obstructionism," Liddy asked Hunt to introduce him to Colson. Hunt took Liddy to Colson's office and then, he insists, went to the back of the large room, where he smoked his pipe and leafed through magazines while Colson and Liddy talked. Colson says Liddy told him only that they had some intelligence-gathering plans which they couldn't get Mitchell to approve. Colson picked up the phone and spoke with Magruder.

"Why don't you guys get off the stick and get Liddy's budget approved? We need the information, particularly on O'Brien," Magruder says Colson told him.

Magruder says he replied, "It's under consideration. We'll get to it as fast as we can. You know the problems with Mitchell."

As they left Colson's office, Liddy told Hunt, "I think I may have done us some good."

Strachan was also pushing Magruder on the plan—"tickling" him, as Dean put it. One day he called Magruder and said Haldeman had told him to "get this going" and "the President wants it done and there's to be no more arguing about it." Dean says these calls made Magruder go to Mitchell and say, in effect, "they are pushing us like crazy for this from the White House."

One night, Gordon Strachan was awakened by a telephone call from his outraged boss, Bob Haldeman, who "chewed him out royally" for some minor slip. When Strachan woke up the next morning, he thought the call had been a nightmare—until he checked with the White House switchboard and discovered that Haldeman had indeed called his home shortly after three. Strachan was terrified of Haldeman. He traveled through the White House corridors with shoulders slightly hunched in anticipation of a sudden bellow from behind, "Strachan, where the hell is that report you promised me!" Haldeman made him carry a "beeper" in his breast pocket, so he could be reached wherever he might be—walking down the street, at a restaurant, in a movie (not that he had any time to go to movies). Strachan hated that damned beeper. People called him "Haldeman's gofer" (Haldeman himself told the President that Strachan was no more than "an office boy . . . a conference boy"). But he bore their

*jibes with wry good humor. For even if he was some-
thing of a flunky, he was a flunky at the fulcrum of
power and he liked it there. His dalliance with power
began when he was elected president of his kindergarten class in Santa Rosa, California. At USC—
where his classmates included Donald Segretti and
Dwight Chapin—he made class president in his junior
year and moved easily into the right organizations on
campus: the Trojan Knights, the Squires, and Phi Kappa Sigma. His fraternity brothers remember a big blond
guy, bright, popular, and "with it" (he taught them the
current dance craze, the "stomp"). After graduating in
1965 with a degree in international relations, Strachan
entered law school at Boalt Hall in Berkeley. His bride,
Kristine, proved to be a better law student, making the
Law Review; but they were an active, engaging couple,
who spent their weekends skiing at Lake Tahoe or Sun
Valley. After law school, the couple went to Wall Street,
where Kristine got a job with one prestigious law firm
and her husband went to work for another—Mudge,
Rose, Guthrie & Alexander. Strachan soon found himself mixing his trusts and estates work with a soupçon
of politics. Through Chapin and Ziegler—and also
perhaps through Jeffrey Donfeld (a fellow lawyer at
Mudge, Rose), who was dating Tricia Nixon at the
time—Strachan got some "advance" work from the
White House in 1970. That fall he met several times
with the younger men on the White House staff and,
duly impressed, Magruder hired him to help out on the
advertising for the congressional elections. After a few
months, Strachan left to become Haldeman's political
aide, a move Magruder attributes to his "blatant ambition." He found Strachan "one of those people, like
John Dean, who was capable and could be engaging,
but who was obviously always studying all the angles
and trying to manipulate events to his own advantage."
Yet sometimes Strachan found himself being manipulated to other people's advantage. As the aide chiefly
responsible for White House liaison with CREEP, he
did his job well. (Dean once called him "tough as
nails," a man who "can go in and stonewall and say*

'Don't know anything about what you are talking about,'" and Nixon said "He's a good man, good man.") But Strachan felt badly used, and later, looking back at his White House experience, he had only one message for young people considering a career in government: "Stay away."

In late March the Mitchells (John, Martha, and their daughter, Marty) left for an Easter vacation in Key Biscayne, where they stayed at a house loaned to them by Bebe Rebozo, adjacent to the Presidential compound. For a few days they lolled in the sun and went out fishing on Bebe's boat. Then Mitchell summoned Magruder and Harry Flemming down to discuss various campaign decisions which had been piling up for weeks. (Even the President was getting impatient; he told Mitchell around this time to "get the hell off of the ITT and then get on to politics which is more interesting.") Magruder flew to Miami on March 29, checked into the Key Biscayne Hotel, and that afternoon, gave Fred LaRue, who was staying with the Mitchells, two briefcases filled with about thirty decision papers. LaRue arranged the papers in "priority" order, putting Liddy's proposal at the bottom of the pile because Magruder wanted to discuss it only after Flemming had been maneuvered out of the room on some pretext.

The next morning, Mitchell, Magruder, Flemming, and LaRue—changed now into tropical slacks and polo shirts—gathered in Mitchell's big, comfortable den overlooking Biscayne Bay. One after another, they took up the major matters that had been awaiting Mitchell's approval: the campaign's advertising strategy, the direct-mail program, Pat Buchanan's plan for "truth squads" to counter the Democratic candidate. At midday, they munched sandwiches brought in by the Mitchells' maid, Julia, and kept on talking. The telephone rang frequently—often with calls about the ITT matter—and LaRue took most of the messages on an extension at the other end of the den. Martha Mitchell was on the rampage that week, deeply resentful at the interruption of their vacation, but she generally left them alone as they moved quickly through the papers.

Finally they reached Liddy's proposal. Flemming was excused from the room and Magruder handed Mitchell the eight-by-eleven sheets on which Liddy had outlined the third version of his plan: the number of people he would have to hire, the electronic equipment he would have to purchase, the total cost ($250,000). Magruder recalls that they discussed "the pros and cons" and that "no one was particularly overwhelmed with the project." LaRue says he voiced outright opposition, warning, "I don't think it's worth the risk." Magruder says that all of them had doubts about Liddy's "stability" (though none about his competence); but, on the other hand, they were all aware of "the atmosphere at the White House," particularly the pressure from Colson and Haldeman to obtain maximum intelligence on the Democrats. And they too believed that "the information could be useful." Ultimately, Magruder writes, "after starting at the grandiose sum of $1 million, we thought that probably $250,000 would be an acceptable figure . . . feeling that we should leave Liddy a little something—we felt we needed him and we were reluctant to send him away with nothing." So, he says, Mitchell "signed off on it in the sense of saying 'Okay, let's give him a quarter of a million dollars and let's see what he can come up with.'" Magruder says it was agreed that Liddy should go ahead first and wiretap O'Brien's office telephone at the Watergate, and then, if funds were available, they would consider other targets. The two other participants at the meeting recall the conclusion differently. LaRue says Mitchell ended by saying, "Well, this is not something that will have to be decided at this meeting." As for Mitchell, he says he flatly rejected the plan with a phrase like "We don't need this. I'm tired of hearing it; out—let's not discuss it any further." But most investigators have been unwilling to accept these disclaimers. Because of the events that followed, they largely accept Magruder's version of the meeting.

After the meeting, Magruder says, he telephoned Strachan at the White House and told him of all the decisions taken that day. Strachan says Magruder told him very little about Liddy's project but that he relayed what he had to Haldeman the next day in a "Political Matters Memorandum" which noted that CREEP "now has a sophisticated intelligence-gathering system including a budget of $300[000]." Strachan also prepared a "talking paper" (with an item about the intelligence system) for a meeting Haldeman and Mitchell were to have on April 4, but Haldeman denies talking with Mitchell about Liddy's project.

When Magruder got back to Washington on April 4, he walked into the office of his administrative assistant, Robert Reisner, and said, "Call Liddy. Tell him it is approved and that we need to get going in the next two weeks."

Reisner called Liddy, who told him, "I can't do it. It's going to be hard. I've got to talk to Magruder."

The next day he came rushing into Magruder's office and said, "I can't do it. There's not enough time. We've waited too late to put it together."

Magruder says he replied, "It's your decision. If you can do it, do it; if you can't, don't."

Liddy could and did. He told Hunt, "The big man's given his okay to it." And he called McCord in "high spirits," telling him "the operation has been approved."

One day that week, Liddy went to Hugh Sloan with a budget of $250,000. "He did not release it from his hand," Sloan recalls. "He merely showed me the figure and said, 'I will be coming to you for substantial cash payments. The first will be for eighty-three thousand dollars and I would like to pick that up in a day or two.'" Startled by the size of the demand, Sloan called Magruder, who said this was the "front-end load" (a mutual-fund term) and told Sloan to pay it. Still disconcerted, Sloan went to Stans and said the single payment of $83,000 was "totally out of line with anything we had done before." Stans said he would check with Mitchell. A few days later, Sloan says, Stans told him he had talked with Mitchell, who had said Sloan should take his orders from Magruder. But when Sloan asked what the money was for, Stans told him, "I do not want to know; you do not want to know."

Reaching into his office safe for $83,000 in ready cash, Sloan's hands fell—apparently by utter coincidence—on some of the very packets of crisp new $100 bills which Liddy had laundered through Barker's Miami bank a few weeks before. The circle was complete.

When Liddy and McCord met at the finance committe on April 12 Liddy pulled a manila envelope from his desk and began to count out a stack of $100 bills totaling $65,000. "This is for the electronic equipment and related expenses," he said. "Get the equipment as quickly as you can, there's pressure to get the project under way immediately and I've told them that it would take at least thirty days." Liddy then took McCord across the street to Mullen & Company, where he introduced him to Hunt for the first time (although they had served simultaneously in the CIA for years, their paths had apparently never crossed), and the three exagents chatted for about half an hour. Liddy said McCord was purchasing some small but highly effective walkie-talkies: "Not like those Mickey Mouse monsters we used in L.A." And for the first time, Liddy told them that their target would be the Democratic National Committee office at the Watergate.

I ts critics have called it a "Republican Bastille," and, indeed, to many of the Republicans who poured into Washington at the start of the Nixon administration, the crenelated fortress on the Potomac seemed a welcome alternative to a town house in crime-ridden and Kennedy-tainted Georgetown. At one time or another, Watergate's tenants included three cabinet members (Mitchell, Stans, and Volpe), three Republican senators (Jacob K. Javits, Robert J. Dole, and Gordon L. Allott), the chairman of the Federal Reserve Board, the treasurer of the United States, the chief White

House speechwriter, President Nixon's personal secretary, a swarm of judges and other high-ranking officials, and a leading Republican hostess, Mrs. Anna Chennault. Radicals chose the Watergate as the site of a 1970 demonstration against the administration, hurling angry epithets—"Pigs" "Fascists!" "Sieg Heil!"—at the Nixonian citadel. Tenants on their balconies cheered as Washington police, armed with tear gas and billy clubs, drove the demonstrators back toward George Washington University. Promotional literature calls the Watergate "one of the most distinctive private real-estate developments in the nation." It is also the most valuable piece of privately held real estate in Washington: a ten-acre site crammed with a hotel, two office buildings, and three apartment cooperatives ("East," "South," and "West") in which units sold for $40,000 to $250,000. Although it is only two blocks from the State Department and eight from the White House, the Watergate turns its face away from the black slums and crumbling tenements toward the river, the white marble Kennedy Center, and the majestic vistas to the south. Indeed, the Watergate is a redoubt for those who shun the city. A tenant who never wished to leave its sawtoothed façade could live forever amid its four swimming pools, two restaurants, health club, liquor store, florist, drugstore, hairdresser, and posh boutiques (Pierre Cardin, Gucci, Yves St. Laurent, Enzo)—all linked in a labyrinth of "malls," twisting through arcades, underground passageways, and landscaped courtyards. And there, on the sixth floor of one of the office buildings, was the Democratic National Committee.

Twice during April and early May McCord and Hunt made a "reconnaissance" of their target in the Watergate office building at 2600 Virginia Avenue, taking the elevator to the sixth floor, examining the glass doors leading to the committee offices, walking down the stair well to the basement, checking all possible entrances and exits. In May, McCord says, Hunt produced a "written step-by-step description" of the entire Watergate mission which he indicated he was going to give to Colson. McCord was impressed by his former CIA compatriot, feeling that Hunt would make it "a professional operation."

At the same time Liddy told Hunt that his "principals"—Mitchell, Dean, and Magruder—wanted a room bug planted in McGovern's campaign headquarters near Capitol Hill. So Hunt obtained from his "plant," Tom Gregory, a floor plan showing the location of electrical outlets, heating ducts, pictures, and lamps in the offices of McGovern's two top aides, Frank Mankiewicz and Gary Hart. On May 15, while Gregory was working late, McCord, passing himself off as Gregory's uncle, managed to case the place. Then he was ready to move. Hunt told Gregory to work late again one night, hide himself until everybody had left, and then let McCord in to do his work. Gregory went to work at about 3:00 p.m., typed labels or stuffed envelopes most of the afternoon and early evening, then hid in the furnace room until nearly midnight. When he emerged, a man sitting on the first floor said, "What are you doing here?" Gregory mumbled something about "the back room" and quickly left, telephoning Hunt to call off the operation.

Hunt and Liddy were rapidly developing doubts about their agent—"Things that go bump in the night bother him," Hunt remarked—and they decided to work around him, using a "pretext" operation such as the one they had first used to penetrate Dr. Lewis Fielding's office. The plan called for several of Barker's team to appear at McGovern headquarters carrying some heavy boxes, with McCord posing as their supervisor. While the Cubans unpacked the boxes, McCord would have enough time to plant his bug. But just as they were about to put the plan into operation, Gregory called to tell Hunt that there had been an attempted burglary at the headquarters, and Burns Agency guards had been hired to work around the clock.

So McCord turned his attention back to the Watergate burglary. In late April and early May he began stockpiling electronic equipment. Using the $65,000 Liddy had given him on April 12, he purchased tape recorders, transmitters, antennas, walkie-talkies, and other items from nearly a dozen different firms in Washington, New York, and Chicago. Much of the equipment could be sold quite legally over the counter, but McCord did not want to arouse suspicions by buying too much in one place—particularly a place near the target. So he purchased much of his illegal "surveillance" equipment—tiny room and telephone bugs—from Michael Stevens, a young Chicago dealer, who apparently assumed McCord worked for a law-enforcement agency. As McCord was leaving Chicago after one of those shopping trips, the bugs in his briefcase registered on the electronic detectors at the airline boarding gate, but he was able to explain them satisfactorily. On an expedition to New York, he came closer to giving the whole thing away. After buying some more equipment, he stopped by to check out a suspected tap on the telephones of the November Group, Nixon's ad agency. He apparently said something, because soon afterward a report circulated that the November Group was preparing to bug the Democratic National Committee.

Early in April Mitchell summoned McCord to his office for an hour-long discussion about CREEP's security. Among other things, Mitchell asked McCord to arrange protection for his ebullient, unpredictable wife and his young daughter. The five-man FBI team which had handled these tasks had been withdrawn after Mitchell resigned as attorney general. For a few weeks McCord personally escorted Marty Mitchell to and from school in Bethesda. Then, on May 1, he called the Society of Former Special Agents of the FBI and obtained the name of Alfred C. Baldwin III, a thirty-six-year-old graduate student at Southern Connecticut State College. That evening he called Baldwin at his home in Hamden, Connecticut, and told him that he needed to talk with him immediately, that very night if possible. Impressed with McCord's urgency, Baldwin caught the first flight to Washington.

He was less impressed when he found out the job was to be a security guard for Martha Mitchell. But he accepted after McCord said the job was temporary and could well be "a stepping stone to a permanent position" in government. McCord then took him over to CREEP, where he was formally hired by Fred La-Rue—who handed him a snub-nosed .38 revolver, saying, "You'll need this while you are with Mrs. Mitchell." That afternoon Baldwin left on a six-day trip with Mrs. Mitchell to Detroit and Westchester County, New York. But he did not impress the demanding Martha. Later, she complained that he had led her straight into a demonstration in Detroit and that he had taken his shoes and socks off in her Waldorf-Astoria suite and "walked around in front of everybody in New York City barefoot." He was, she said, "the most gauche character I have ever met." (She tried several other bodyguards, but finally selected another former FBI agent, Steve King.)

After Baldwin's abortive stint with Mrs. Mitchell, McCord asked him to do some undercover surveillance of radical activity in Washington, promising that he would be brought to Miami in August for similar work. He was assigned to watch some sit-ins on Capitol Hill and to mingle with crowds outside the office of certain members of Congress to determine which were giving gallery passes to the demonstrators. (He recalls watching the offices of Senators Kennedy, Javits, and Proxmire and Representatives Chisholm, Abzug, Koch, and McCloskey.) During that period McCord asked him to move into a room at the downtown Howard Johnson Motor Inn which had already been reserved in the name of McCord Associates. Room 419 looked out across Virginia Avenue at the façade of the Watergate office building.

That was another spring of dissent in the streets of Washington and a renewed state of siege at the White House. Both were intensified on the morning of May 2, when J. Edgar Hoover was found dead in his bed. The death of the cantankerous old man who had blocked the Huston Plan and other intelligence projects was a vast relief to the impatient men at the White House. And some apparently saw an opportunity in it.

Hoover was scheduled to lie in state in the rotunda of the Capitol the next day, and by coincidence antiwar demonstrators were planning a simultaneous rally outside the Capitol. Daniel Ellsberg, William Kunstler, Jane Fonda, and other well-known radicals were scheduled to speak and some demonstrators were expected to carry the Viet Cong flag. Chuck Colson saw an opportunity to discredit the New Left by suggesting that they had come to demonstrate against Hoover, who, while hardly beloved in the White House, was a genuine hero to most of America; and Colson sensed a particular chance to defame a prime White House enemy, Dan Ellsberg.

A few hours after Hoover's body was found, Colson called Magruder and said, "We've got to have some people there to demonstrate and some people who can tear down that damned VC flag and protect our kids if it gets rough." Magruder says he replied, "Chuck, we can't send our kids out to get into fights," and Colson, in turn, warned that the orders came direct from Nixon, and if Magruder didn't do what he was told, he would be disloyal to the President. Ultimately, Magruder says, he checked with Mitchell and they agreed to turn the assignment over to Liddy.

"No sweat," said Liddy.

That evening, Hunt recalls, Liddy came to him with a hair-raising tale—the radicals might try to overturn Hoover's catafalque in the rotunda the next day. He asked, "Do you suppose Bernie could get some fellows together to come up and try to prevent it?" Hunt telephoned Barker and asked if he would come to Washington with perhaps twelve "well-motivated" friends. Barker readily agreed, for by then he had become CREEP's Bernie-on-the-spot for such jobs.

"I was not there to think. I was there to follow orders," Bernard Barker was to say later in describing his relationship with Hunt. For most of his life, Barker had been following orders. Born of American parents in Havana, he spent his youth shuttling between schools in Cuba and the United States. As with so many

sons of mixed heritage, he became a fierce patriot. The day after Pearl Harbor, he went to the American embassy and enlisted in the Army Air Corps—"the first volunteer in the Second World War from Cuba," he proudly proclaims. When his plane went down over Germany, Captain Barker spent sixteen months as a prisoner of war. When he returned to Havana and his Cuban wife, he joined Fulgencio Batista's secret police and reported regularly on subversive activities to the FBI. Once he served as a bodyguard for Mrs. Harry Truman and her daughter, Margaret, when they made a trip to Cuba. After a few years, when Barker applied for passport renewal, the consulate told him he had lost his U.S. citizenship because he had served in the uniformed forces of a foreign country, but this rude rebuff (rectified years later) did nothing to cool his patriotic fervor. When Fidel Castro seized power in 1959, Barker switched easily from being an FBI contact inside a friendly government to his new role as CIA informer within a hostile power. For nearly a year he fed information to the agency and helped refugees escape, until the Castro government apparently began to suspect him and he too was "evacuated" to Miami. There, the CIA hired him full time to work with the Cuban exile groups; and he rose quickly within the ranks to become Hunt's chief of staff, chauffeur, and constant companion during the Bay of Pigs operation. (Hunt described him as "eager, efficient, and completely dedicated.") He remained an agency employee into the mid-1960s (during that period, according to his lawyer, he broke into New York City's Radio City Music Hall one night as part of a CIA "test" of his skills in "surreptitious entry"). On July 31, 1966, he left the agency and settled down to make money in Miami, working as an assistant store manager, studying at night to get a real-estate license, finally opening his own realtor's office—Barker Associates—with a staff of ten salesmen. He invested some of his earnings in Latin America, and when he regained contact with his old boss, "Eduardo," they began talking about several ambitious business projects with Manuel Artime, the former Cuban exile leader and

Bay of Pigs veteran who was a close friend of both men. In Miami, Barker led the life of a prosperous real-estate man. But he had another life which he kept quite separate. Later, he wrote about his two lives: "If I am asked my name on a mission, I give my operating name. That is not a lie; it is a cover. I am not Barker then. I am another person. It is a different dimension. I, Barker, would never go into a building in the dark of night, but the operator—this other guy with a false name holding his beliefs or fighting a windmill or something—could very well do this." Dean dismissed him as "the lead Cuban," but Barker had more grandiose visions of his other self. In his address book, he scrawled "Yo soy Macho! Avanti" ("I am Macho! Onward").

Late on May 2 Barker summoned Reinaldo Pico, a burly Bay of Pigs veteran, into his office and told him that "hippies, traitors, and Communists" were going to "perpetrate an outrage on Hoover." Others were told they were going on a "government mission," and a trip "to bring us together as a team." The next day, Barker and nine others—Pico; DeDiego; Martinez; Fernandez; Frank A. Sturgis; Virgilio R. Gonzalez; Angel Ferrer; Humberto Lopez, and Iran Gonzalez—flew to Washington and checked into a Holiday Inn. (Each was given $50 before leaving Miami and $50 more when they arrived in Washington.) Barker reported to Hunt at Mullen & Company, where Liddy showed him photographs of Ellsberg, Kunstler, and other dissident leaders. According to Hunt, Barker and his men were instructed to circulate through the crowds outside the Capitol, shout "Traitor" from time to time, seize any Viet Cong flag they saw, and be prepared to protect Hoover's catafalque. But, according to Fernandez, Barker ordered the men to "get" Ellsberg and Kunstler. Another says he was told to "call Ellsberg a traitor and punch him in the nose, hit him, and run."

That evening, Barker and his men went to the west steps of the Capitol, where antiwar leaders were reading a list of servicemen killed in Vietnam. They couldn't get close to Ellsberg, but Barker began arguing heatedly with a long-haired demonstrator and ultimately Pico knocked the young man down. "I thought he was going to hit Macho, who's an older man, so I slugged him on the head," Pico recalls. Sturgis also hit one of the demonstrators. Fernandez was going to hit one too, "But he stood in front of me and said, 'Peace, brother,' and I couldn't hit him. I'm not a killer." Capitol police seized Pico and Sturgis, but Pico recalls, "I saw a man in a gray suit give a signal to the policeman and one officer took us down to the street and told us we could go away." Others say the man in the gray suit explained that they were "good men" and "anti-Communists." Later, Hunt and Liddy picked Barker up and "debriefed" him as they rode around town in Hunt's car. Driving past the Watergate, Liddy said, "That's our next job, Macho."

(Before Watergate, Barker's team may have taken on some other "jobs." Investigators suspect that some of the Cuban-Americans may have been involved in burglaries at the Chilean embassy in Washington and the Chilean Mission to the United Nations that spring. They have also been mentioned in connection with a May 16 burglary of a prominent Democratic law firm in the Watergate, whose members included Patricia Roberts Harris, chairman of the credentials committee for the 1972 Democratic convention; Sargent Shriver, John Kennedy's brother-in-law; and Max M. Kampelman, a leading adviser to Hubert Humphrey.)

Meanwhile, the day after the Capitol Hill skirmish —as Barker's team returned to Miami—Nixon inveighed against lawbreaking at Hoover's funeral. Standing by the director's flag-draped coffin, he declared, "The trend of permissiveness in this country, a trend which Edgar Hoover fought against all of his life, a trend which has dangerously eroded our national heritage as a law-abiding people, is being reversed. The American people today are tired of disorder, disruption, and disrespect for law. America wants to come back to the law as a way of life."

A week later, Hunt went to Miami to make arrangements for the Watergate job and the second part of the "double mission": a break-in to plant bugs at McGovern's campaign headquarters. "Get your men in training going up and down stairs," he told Barker. "They must be in good physical shape." Hunt said they had selected the Memorial Day weekend for the entries. Barker told him Martinez would handle the photography and introduced him to one of his team, Virgilio Gonzalez, a Miami locksmith, who would handle that end of the job. Hunt said he wanted three guards, and Barker selected DeDiego, Pico, and Sturgis. (Sturgis was the only non-Cuban member of the team. Born Frank Angelo Fiorini, he was a third-generation Italian-American from Philadelphia who for two decades had been an adventurer in some of the world's hot spots. In 1957 he joined Castro in the Sierra Maestra Mountains and later accompanied him to Havana. But, even while serving with Castro, he was probably at least an informer for the CIA. Later, it is believed, he went to work full time for the agency, seeking to overthrow Castro. During that period, he met Howard Hunt and he took his pseudonym—Frank Sturgis—from a character in Hunt's novel *Bimini Run*.)

In Miami, Hunt outlined the Watergate entry plan, which was to lead them through the Continental Room, a banquet-conference room in the Watergate office building through which access could be gained to an interior corridor, and then to the DNC offices. Hunt said they needed a sponsoring organization for their pretext banquet, and Barker suggested Ameritas, an inactive corporation he had formed some years before. On his return to Washington, Hunt asked his wife to call the Watergate Hotel and reserve the Continental Room for an Ameritas Corporation banquet on the evening of May 26.

On May 22 Barker's team flew to Washington under aliases: Barker as "Frank Carter," Martinez as "Jene Valdez," Sturgis as "Joseph Di Alberto," Pico as "Joe Granada," DeDiego as "Jose Piedra," and Gonzalez as "Raoul Godoy." They checked into the Manger-Hamilton Hotel, five blocks from the White House. The next night the six men were joined by McCord, Hunt, Liddy, and Tom Gregory for a final planning session in Barker's room. For the remainder of the week, Barker kept his men busy visiting "historical sites" in the area—including the Lincoln and Washington memorials and the Naval Academy at Annapolis, where Martinez—the veteran of three hundred naval incursions of Cuba—was particularly impressed by the monument to John Paul Jones.

On the afternoon of Friday, May 26, Barker's team —outfitted with briefcases and other paraphernalia to make them "look elegant"—checked into rooms at the Watergate Hotel. That same afternoon, Hunt rented a projector and a travelogue film from a camera store on L Street and set it up before a built-in screen in the Continental Room. Everything seemed to be progressing nicely, until McCord showed up with only four of the six promised walkie-talkies (forcing Pico and DeDiego to be dropped from the operation).

Late that afternoon, Alfred Baldwin returned from a trip to Connecticut and checked back into Room 419 at the Howard Johnson Motor Inn, which he had been occupying for several weeks. But when he opened the turquoise door, he saw that his room had been transformed into an electronics studio. McCord was sitting by a Formica-topped desk fiddling with the dials on a large radio receiver. Stacked along the desk, on the couch, and in the corners were more receivers, transmitters, tape recorders, antennas, and other equipment. McCord showed Baldwin how to use some of the gear. Pointing across the street to the Watergate's gray façade, he said, "We're going to put some units over there tonight and you'll be monitoring them." McCord amused himself for the rest of the afternoon checking and rechecking a telephone tap—inserting it in the room's white telephone, then dialing a recorded message and playing it back. Then Liddy and Hunt came over to inspect the listening post. McCord had warned Baldwin that since "we're all in security work," everybody would go under their alias—Baldwin was to use "Bill Johnson"—but when Hunt and Liddy arrived, McCord became confused and introduced everybody under their real names. After the inspection, the four men strolled across Virginia Avenue to Hunt's room at the Watergate, where they conferred for a half-hour with Barker. At eight o'clock, McCord and Baldwin went back to Howard Johnson's while the other eight men went downstairs for "the banquet."

And what a banquet it was! A small bar had been set up in one corner of the L-shaped room, and for an hour the "Ameritas executives" sipped cocktails. (Martinez recalls that Hunt, who was suffering from bleeding ulcers, was "mixing his whisky with milk.") The dinner, prepared by the Watergate Hotel, cost $236—nearly $30 per man. For Hunt—who fancied fine wine and food as much as intrigue—it must have been an exquisite evening. Lingering over dessert and afterdinner drinks, they finally dismissed the waiter with a large tip, telling him that the "board meeting" was about to begin. Then, with the travelogue playing to satisfy curious passersby, they prepared for the evening's mission. At about ten o'clock, six of them filed out, leaving Hunt and Gonzalez behind. At ten-thirty, a security guard poked his head in the door and told them they would have to leave; but when he had gone they merely shut off the lights and hid in a closet. After midnight, they crept out again and Gonzalez went to work on the door leading to the interior corridor. But, despite his best efforts, the lock wouldn't yield. So, after reporting their predicament to the others via walkie-talkie, the Cuban locksmith and the epicure spy, with all that fine wine and cheese still settling in their stomachs, huddled sleeplessly in the Continental Room until dawn.

Meanwhile, the rest of the team was launching the second part of its double mission. Around midnight, Liddy and some of the Cubans left by car from Capitol Hill. A half-hour later, McCord and Baldwin followed. On First Street, S.W., about four blocks from the Capitol, they passed McGovern's headquarters, and McCord said, "That's what we're interested in, right there." An upstairs light was on and a man—evidently a campaign volunteer—was standing by the front door. Baldwin recalls that when Liddy joined them he was carrying an attaché case in which he later saw a high-powered pellet pistol wrapped in a towel. Turning up an alley near McGovern headquarters, they paused under a bright streetlight. "Shall I take that out?" Liddy asked. McCord said it wasn't necessary. (Several nights earlier, while on a "reconnaissance" mission, Liddy had shot out a light near the same spot. And two days before, while on his way to lunch with Hugh Sloan, he had fired the pellet gun into a toilet at the prim Hay-Adams Hotel.) At about 5:00 a.m., with the man still lingering around the front door, they decided to "abort the mission" and went to bed.

The next night, they had another go at the DNC—this time with a different and bolder plan of action. McCord and Barker's entire six-man team—carrying their briefcases—marched up to the Watergate office building shortly after midnight. McCord rang the bell and the guard let them in. They signed the book as if they were going to the Federal Reserve Board office on the eighth floor, rode the elevator to the eighth floor, and then walked down to the sixth. But the lock on the DNC door was an old one, and Gonzalez couldn't open it. "He says he doesn't have the right tools," Barker reported to Hunt and Liddy by walkie-talkie. Hunt sent Gonzalez back to Miami to get more tools.

Early that morning, they made one final attempt to place a bug in McGovern's headquarters, but again the mission was aborted because some volunteers were working late, and Gregory, who had been stationed outside, was asked to "move along" by a policeman.

On Sunday, Hunt went home to spend a few hours with his family. His wife sensed that things were "not going well," but—accustomed to her husband's clandestine activities—she asked no questions. Around five o'clock, Barker called to say that Gonzalez had returned from Florida with the tools he needed. (Martinez was astonished when he saw the huge pile of picks and pries. No door could hold him, he thought.)

This time they tried still another *modus operandi*. Early in the evening, Gonzalez picked the door on the B-2 garage level, and he and Sturgis went up through the stair well, taping the door latches behind them so the others could follow. On the sixth floor, Gonzalez used his new tools to twist the lock cylinder until the

DNC door at last swung open. Inside, they reported over their walkie-talkie, "The horse is in the house." Liddy and Hunt embraced "Latin-style." Soon, Barker and Martinez joined the other two in the DNC headquarters. From his balcony at Howard Johnson's, McCord could see the pinlights from their pencil flashlights moving about like fireflies in the darkened offices. Hunt called McCord on his walkie-talkie to say, "My people are in; you can go in now." At about 1:30 a.m., McCord crossed the street, went through the basement door, and up the stair well to the back door, where one of the Cubans let him in. Getting quickly to work, McCord put one tap on the phone of Fay Abel, a secretary who sat directly outside Larry O'Brien's office and shared several extensions with him. He put another on the phone of R. Spencer Oliver, executive director of the Association of State Democratic Chairmen. Then he tested both taps with a small pocket receiver. They worked.

Meanwhile, Barker says, he was following Hunt's instructions to "look for documents indicating contributions from Cuba or from leftist organizations and those inclined to violence." Quickly sampling files from several cabinets, he could find nothing of the sort. So he took documents "where names or persons were involved," others where there were "notations of numbers," and one involving security for the Democratic National Convention. He gave these to Martinez, who photographed them with a 35 mm. camera under a large light steadied by two other men. (Martinez recalls photographing thirty to forty documents.) The mission was swiftly completed, and the team returned to Hunt's room at the Watergate. Although Hunt says he and Liddy were surprised and chagrined by the briefness of the operation and its meager results, Liddy slapped Barker on the back and said, "Macho, this has been a good job."

But it wasn't—as McCord and Baldwin found out later on Monday when they began to monitor the taps. Both transmitters, McCord says, were "deliberately low powered in order to avoid detection." After a long search with a "highly sophisticated receiver," they were able to pick up signals from the tap on Spencer Oliver's telephone, coming in on 118 megacycles. But they couldn't find the Abel-O'Brien tap on 135 megacycles. McCord tried switching antennas. Still nothing. He then asked Baldwin to get another room higher in the motel in hopes that would improve the reception. That afternoon, they moved up to Room 723. Still nothing. McCord finally concluded that either the O'Brien tap was faulty or there was too much shielding in O'Brien's office. (In April 1973, when the tap was discovered, it was still operating, but apparently without enough power to reach the Howard Johnson listening post.)

That week Baldwin settled down to monitoring the one working tap. "I would keep an eye on the little TV-type screen on the monitoring unit," he recalls. "A constant line ran across the screen when the tapped phone was not in use. When someone started using the phone, the line would scatter and I would quickly put on the earphones." At first Baldwin transcribed the conversations by hand on a yellow legal pad. Then McCord brought him an electric typewriter (borrowed from Hunt), and he would type "almost verbatim" transcripts in duplicate. When something caught McCord's eye in the transcript he would sit down and type up a memo from information in the logs, beginning the memo, "A confidential source reports . . ."

But there was very little of such importance. Of the two hundred calls Baldwin estimates he monitored over the next few weeks, some dealt with "political strategy," but many covered "personal matters." Baldwin says several secretaries used Oliver's phone because they thought it was the most private one in the office. They would say, "We can talk; I'm on Spencer Oliver's phone." Some of the conversations, Baldwin recalls, were "explicitly intimate." A federal prosecutor later described them as "extremely personal, intimate, and potentially embarrassing." Ehrlichman, after debriefing Magruder, reported, "What they were getting was mostly this fellow Oliver phoning his girl friends all over the country lining up assignations." So spicy were some of the conversations on this phone that they have given rise to unconfirmed reports that the telephone was being used for some sort of call-girl service catering to congressmen and other prominent Washingtonians.

McCord gave Baldwin's typed transcripts to Liddy, who had his secretary, Sally Harmony, type some of them on special stationery, headed "Gemstone," with spaces for the date and "source." As the source for the Watergate transcripts, Liddy told her to use the code name "Crystal." (Mrs. Harmony used this same stationery to type up reports from "Ruby I" and "Ruby II"—the Wyatt-Buckley team and Tom Gregory—who, as their code names indicate, were considered part of the Gemstone operation.)

On June 10, Hunt flew to Miami carrying two rolls of Kodak Tri-X film, which had been shot at the Watergate. At lunch he turned them over to Barker for developing, and Barker took them to Rich's Camera Shop at 1600 West Flagler Street. The shop was about to close—it was a Saturday—and the owner, Michael Richardson, said there would be a $40 surcharge for processing the film that day. Barker told him to go ahead, and several times in the next few hours he called from the restaurant urging speed. By three o'clock, Richardson had produced thirty-eight seven-by-ten glossy prints, which showed gloved hands holding documents against a shag rug (later determined to match the rug in Room 419 of the Howard Johnson Motor Inn, suggesting that the burglars had taken at least some of the documents back there to photograph). Richardson says some of the documents had an emblem and were headed "Chairman Democratic National Committee." Most were typed, a few were short handwritten notes. One document mentioned either Robert or Edward Kennedy. "It's real cloak-and-dagger stuff, isn't it!" Richardson exclaimed. Barker nodded, sped to the airport, and handed the prints in an envelope to Hunt, who took off immediately for Washington and gave the photographs to Liddy.

According to Ehrlichman, Liddy prepared three "rather obscure synopses" of what had been heard on the taps, attributing the information to "a confidential informant" or "a sophisticated political source." He forwarded these and the photographs—in two batches

—to Magruder. The first batch of synopses came in around June 8. Magruder recalls that he was unimpressed and decided to wait for the second installment. He noticed one provocative conversation between Spencer Oliver and CREEP's own Harry Flemming. For a moment, Magruder thought, My God! Flemming's a double agent! But a closer examination of the transcript showed that Flemming and Oliver were both members of a bipartisan group called Young American Political Leaders and were merely discussing one of its activities.

Because of the "sensitive nature" of the materials, Magruder says, he did not send them by messenger to Strachan at the White House as he had done with previous information on the operation. Instead, he asked Strachan to come over and examine them in his office. He says Strachan read them and said something like, "This idiot is just wasting our time and money." Strachan denies that he ever saw the materials.

Magruder showed the transcripts and photographs to Mitchell at their regular eight-thirty meeting the next morning. Magruder says Mitchell studied the material briefly and then, frowning, snapped, "Get Liddy in here."

As Magruder describes the scene, Liddy appeared a few moments later, and Mitchell told him, "This stuff isn't worth the paper it's printed on," not to speak of the money that had been paid to get it. He called the wiretap reports "shitty."

Liddy explained, "There's a problem. One of the bugs isn't working. And they put one of them on O'Brien's secretary's phone instead of O'Brien's phone. But I'll get everything straightened out right away."

Mitchell denies that these conversations ever took place, calling Magruder's version "a palpable, damnable lie," but most investigators seem to believe Magruder.

Liddy evidently talked to McCord, because on June 12 McCord walked into the listening post, handed Baldwin a $100 bill, and said, "You are going to have a ball this week." He asked Baldwin to visit the DNC headquarters under an alias and make sure where O'Brien's office was. Familiar with the party's officials in his home state, Baldwin decided to masquerade as the nephew of John Bailey, Connecticut State Democratic Chairman and former Democratic National Chairman. The Democrats were very happy to show such a dignitary around and assigned him as a guide Ida "Maxie" Wells, Spencer Oliver's secretary, whose intimate phone conversations he had been listening to with such interest. Baldwin could barely stifle a grin as Maxie led him into O'Brien's office and said, "This used to be your uncle's office." Baldwin noted its location overlooking the Potomac River, then went back to the motel and drew a diagram for McCord.

On the afternoon of June 14, Hunt recalls, Liddy came to his office at Mullen & Company and, while Hunt's radio blared, told him, "We've got to go into DNC headquarters again." Hunt says he protested, since O'Brien had largely moved his base of operations to the Fontainebleau in Miami Beach in preparation for the Democratic convention. If there was to be another burglary, he said, "The Fontainebleau's the place, not here." Moreover, it was McCord who had "fouled up" his side of the operation and Barker's team shouldn't be asked to risk their necks again to get him in. Hunt says Liddy agreed to present these arguments to his "principals," but later that day he reported back that they were adamant.

Hunt says he then walked over to the Executive Office Building and, using the secure phone in Room 16, called Barker in Miami. He asked whether he could reassemble the "entry team"—Barker, Martinez, Gonzalez, and Sturgis—and come to Washington on Friday, June 16.

Liddy had told Hunt that while Barker's team was around they might as well "have another go" at McGovern headquarters. Hunt was scheduled to meet Tom Gregory at noon on Friday in the lobby of the Roger Smith Hotel. So he brought McCord along to discuss the details of the weekend's operation. But when they met, Gregory told Hunt he was quitting. "This is getting too deep for me," Gregory said. McCord watched him go and then told Hunt, "We might be better off without Gregory. The last time I was in the headquarters with him I noticed he was sweating. I don't think he was cut out to be an agent." (The operation at McGovern's Washington headquarters was scrubbed. But Magruder says that plans went ahead for bugging the senator's suite at the Doral Hotel during the Democratic convention. At a brief meeting in early June, he says, Liddy told Mitchell and Magruder that the suite Mitchell was to occupy at the Doral during the Republican convention would first be assigned to McGovern at the Democratic convention a few weeks earlier. They discussed bugging the suite and, according to Magruder, Mitchell said, "Just make sure you get the bugs out before I move in.")

On the afternoon of June 16 Barker's team arrived at National Airport. In the terminal, Sturgis ran into an old acquaintance, Jack Anderson, who had once written a column about him as a "soldier of fortune." Anderson asked what he was doing in Washington, and Sturgis told him brusquely, "Private business." The team rented an Avis car and on the ride into town engaged in some gallows humor about the automobile, which reminded Martinez of a hearse. When they reached the Watergate Hotel, Barker and Martinez checked into Room 214 and Sturgis and Gonzalez into Room 314. At $38 a night, they were the cheapest rooms the luxury hotel had to offer, though elegantly turned out with gold carpets, gold bedspreads, and red-trimmed gold drapes.

But they didn't have much time to enjoy the accommodations. "There was no time for anything," Martinez recalls. "It was all rush." McCord, too, remembers the sense of urgency that night. Hunt and Liddy, he says, were "very anxious to get the operation over with. The instruction was 'hurry up and go.'" At five o'clock they went downstairs for a lobster dinner in the Terrace Restaurant overlooking the broad sweep of the Potomac. Barker ate too much and felt ill. Martinez wasn't feeling very well, either. His divorce had come through that day; he had gone from the court to the airport; and somehow, he felt, "the whole thing was bad."

Hunt had dinner at home with his son St. John and his daughter Lisa (his wife and other two children had left for a European vacation). Then he drove his Pontiac Firebird to the Watergate, parked it in the underground garage, and went up to Room 214—where Liddy, McCord, and Barker's team were gathered for a final planning session. For this operation, they had purchased a second Minolta camera, and for a while Barker and Martinez practiced their routine: one photographing documents, while the other loaded the spare camera, then exchanging cameras and repeating the operation. McCord had brought three walkie-talkies: he gave one to Barker, one to Liddy, and kept the third for himself. Hunt took each man's wallet and identification and put them in his briefcase. He gave Sturgis his CIA identification in the name of Edward J. Hamilton and McCord another, in the name of Edward J. Warren. He also gave each man two $100 bills to use as a bribe in case they were caught.

Although Gonzalez and Sturgis had taped the doors during the Memorial Day weekend entry, McCord for some reason volunteered to do it this time. He says he expected Hunt to do the taping and volunteered only after Hunt appeared unwilling. McCord walked past the guard in the office-building lobby, rode the elevator to the eighth floor, and then began walking down, taping six or eight doors leading from the floor corridors into the stair well so that they could be opened from either side. He taped three more doors on the subbasement garage level to provide access to the stair well. McCord apparently put the tapes horizontally across the latches, leaving swatches visible on either side of the doors—instead of the approved method, apparently used by Gonzalez and Sturgis, with the tape placed vertically down the latch so that it would be hidden by the door frame. (Other members of the Watergate team—Hunt and Martinez in particular—have criticized McCord for this and other blunders during the operation. They hint broadly that the CIA's former chief of physical security was either incompetent or a double agent working for the Democrats.)

After the taping was completed, McCord reported the situation to the men in Room 214, then went back across the street to the listening post in Howard Johnson's. For a while he tested a room bug—disguised as a "smoke detector"—which he intended to install in O'Brien's office. Later, he went out and bought a shopping bag full of screwdrivers, wires, batteries, and soldering irons, and for several hours he and Baldwin worked on the equipment, testing it on the phone and the television set. Near midnight, Hunt called McCord from Room 214 and asked how the Democratic committee looked across the way. McCord told him one man was still working there. (It was Bruce Givner, a Columbia University freshman who was working as a summer intern at the committee. Givner had stayed late to finish up some work and then decided to use the committee's WATS line to call friends in Ohio, where he had grown up. The boyhood friends chatted on as the burglars fumed.) A few minutes later, Liddy and Hunt went out on the avenue to see for themselves. But the light was still burning, so they went into the Watergate restaurant for a snack. Hunt moved his car from the garage to a spot in front of the Watergate Hotel— where it would be more convenient for a quick getaway. Then he rejoined Liddy in Room 214, where they nervously sipped Cokes and watched the late movie on television while awaiting further word from McCord.

At midnight, a new security guard came on duty at the Watergate office building. He was Frank Wills, a twenty-four-year-old black high-school dropout, who, after drifting from a defunct Job Corps training program in Fort Custer, Michigan, to Detroit to Washington, had finally landed a job with General Security Services, the company which had the security contract for the Watergate. Around 12:45 a.m., Wills began his first round of the building.

At about that time Baldwin was returning from the Howard Johnson restaurant, where he had eaten a chocolate sundae. He found McCord on the phone with Hunt, puzzling over the lights which still burned in the DNC headquarters. Just then, Baldwin saw a man get up from a desk in the committee office and turn off the lights. He alerted McCord, who told Hunt, "It looks all right." Hunt told him to come over. McCord dumped his wallet, papers, and change on the bed, and unhooked a walkie-talkie from his belt, telling Baldwin, "Any activity you see across the street, you just get on this unit and let us know."

At about one o'clock, Wills was completing his round when he found a piece of tape over the latch on one of the garage-level doors. "I took the tape off, but I didn't think anything of it," he said later. "I thought maybe the building engineer had done it."

Bruce Givner rode down the elevator. In the lobby, he found Wills, who had just returned from his tour, and asked where he could find a restaurant. Wills told him about the Howard Johnson's, and together they strolled across to the restaurant, where Givner had a cheeseburger, a shake, and french fries while Wills ordered the same, to go.

Meanwhile, McCord was crossing Virginia Avenue in the opposite direction. But here the participants' stories begin to diverge widely. McCord says he checked the garage-level door and found the tape still there. Hunt makes no mention of this. (One is inclined to side with Hunt; for how could McCord have seen the lights go off in the committee and get across the street in time to find the tape still there if Wills had pulled the tape off before getting upstairs to see Givner come down in the elevator?) McCord says Barker and Martinez went back to Room 214 to report their predicament to Hunt and Liddy; Gonzalez tried to pick the door, and McCord went back to Howard Johnson's, where he got a call from Hunt saying that Gonzalez had the door open and the operation was proceeding. But Hunt says McCord came up to Room 214 and argued Liddy into letting him proceed with the operation. Martinez also says McCord came to Room 214, but that Liddy and Hunt retired to a room together and apparently called someone before Hunt emerged to say that the operation would continue. Thus each major participant blames someone else for the decision to go ahead at this point.

But go ahead they did. Gonzalez picked the downstairs lock and retaped the latch. The entry team went up to the sixth floor, where Gonzalez went to work on the DNC door. The lock was rusty and would not give.

The concrete stair well echoed like a cave to the clanging of the locksmith's tools. And the static from Barker's crackling walkie-talkie made so much noise that Barker turned it off.

By now, Wills had returned from Howard Johnson's and was making his second tour of the building. At about 1:50 a.m., he found the tape replaced on the outer garage-level door. This time he called the police.

Upstairs, the burglars had given up on the rusty lock. Instead, they hammered the pins out of the hinges and lifted the door out. Gonzalez quickly went to work on the glass door leading into O'Brien's suite. Barker and McCord began rifling the files in the Youth Division.

Alerted by Wills, the metropolitan police dispatcher radioed Officer Dennis P. Stephenson and told him to go to the Watergate. Stephenson, who had just arrived at the Second District, begged off, pleading a lack of gas and a pile of paperwork to complete. The dispatcher put out the call again at 1:52 a.m.

"Is there any TAC unit in the area?"

Cruiser 172, an unmarked sedan from the casual-clothes squad of the Second District Tactical Squadron, replied, "We are a TAC unit and we have a sergeant on board." Sergeant Paul Leeper and Officers Carl Shoffler and John Barrett had completed their 4:00 p.m.-to-midnight shift, stopped off for a couple of drinks at a Georgetown after-hours spot, and were cruising along K Street when they got the call. Within three minutes they pulled up in front of the Watergate.

Standing on the balcony of his room admiring the "beautiful night," Baldwin saw an unmarked car pull up to the Watergate. Three men got out and went into the building. But Baldwin thought nothing of it.

Wills showed the policemen the taped door. He also reminded them that burglary attempts had recently been made on the eighth and sixth floors. The policemen told Wills to stay in the lobby and watch for anyone trying to escape. Then they ran up the stairs to the eighth floor, where they were joined by a Federal Reserve Board guard. Turning on the lights, they searched the floor.

When Baldwin saw the lights go on, he grabbed the

walkie-talkie and said, "Base headquarters, base one, to any unit, do you read me?"

A voice he recognized as Hunt's said, "I read you. Go on. What have you got?"

"The lights went on on the entire eighth floor," said Baldwin.

"We know about that," Baldwin says Hunt responded. "That is the two-o'clock guard check. Let us know if anything else happens."

On the sixth floor, Barker turned his walkie-talkie back on and reported that they were inside the committee offices. According to McCord, Hunt replied, "Be advised that the guard is making his two-o'clock rounds on the eighth floor." Falsely reassured, the team went to work, removing the ceiling panels from O'Brien's office to install a room bug.

Finding nothing on the eighth floor, the policemen widened their search. Barrett went up to the ninth floor while Leeper and Shoffler began working their way down. When they found tape on the sixth-floor door, Leeper called Barrett down, and the three began searching the DNC offices. As they entered each room, they turned on the lights. Finding a door to a balcony propped open with a chair, Leeper and Shoffler searched the terrace. Shoffler noted Baldwin standing across the street on his seventh-floor balcony. Since they were not in uniform and Shoffler had his service revolver in one hand and a flashlight in the other, the policemen feared the onlooker might misunderstand the situation. "Do you think he'll call the police?" Shoffler asked.

Baldwin saw the two men clearly outlined against the lighted offices. Leeper was wearing light blue slacks, a light blue T shirt, a golf cap, and a dark-blue windbreaker emblazoned "George Washington University." Shoffler wore a short Army jacket and a pair of slacks. And Baldwin could see still a third figure in the office beyond who was carrying a gun and looking behind desks. He whispered into his walkie-talkie, "Base one to unit one."

Howard Hunt's voice responded, "What have you got?"

"Are our people dressed casually or are they in suits?"

"What?" shouted the astonished Hunt.

Baldwin repeated the question.

"Our people are dressed in suits."

"Well, we've got a problem," said Baldwin. "We've got some people dressed casually and they've got guns. They're looking around the balcony and everywhere, but they haven't come across our people."

At that, Baldwin recalls, Hunt went "a bit frantic."

Hunt says it wasn't he going frantic, it was Liddy. He recalls Liddy shouting into his walkie-talkie, trying desperately to raise the entry team in the Watergate: "One to two. . . . Two, come in. . . . There are lights on your floor. Any trouble? . . . One to two. . . . Come in. . . . This is an order. Repeat. Come in!"

Leeper and Shoffler rejoined Barrett in the corridor and the three policemen began opening office doors, switching on lights, and shouting, "Come out! Police!"

Crouched with the other four behind a wood-and-frosted glass partition around a secretary's desk, McCord realized they were trapped. There was nothing to do but wait, and hope that the police would not make a thorough search.

As Barrett approached the secretary's cubicle, he saw part of an arm rub against the cloudy glass at the top of the partition. "Hold it!" he shouted. "Come out!" Leeper jumped up on a desk and drew his gun.

"Be careful, you got us," said one of the men.

Barker turned up his walkie-talkie long enough to croak, "They've got us."

A moment later, McCord asked, "What are you people? Are you metropolitan police or what?"

When the police said, yes, that is what they were, the five men raised their hands sheathed in blue surgical gloves. "They were probably five of the easiest lockups I ever made," Leeper recalled later.

In Room 214, Hunt and Liddy began throwing McCord's surplus electronic gear and other "operational litter" into suitcases. The long automobile antenna they had used to give their walkie-talkie extra range wouldn't fit in any of their bags, so Hunt thrust it down one of his pants legs.

Into the walkie-talkie, Hunt said to Baldwin, "Are you still across the street?"

"Yes, I am," Baldwin replied.

"Keep your lights out and stay out of sight. I'll come over as soon as I can. We're signing off."

From his balcony, the crouching Baldwin could see "all kinds of police activity" below him on Virginia Avenue, "motorcycles and paddy wagons driving up and guys jumping out of patrol cars and running up to the Watergate." Then he saw Hunt and another man carrying suitcases out of the Watergate Hotel. They jumped into a car and drove away.

"My jeep's up the street," Liddy told Hunt.

"I'll take you there."

"What about him?" Liddy said, gesturing toward Baldwin's balcony.

Hunt said he'd take care of that.

Dropping Liddy near his jeep, Hunt made a U-turn and parked two blocks from the motel ("within pistol range of the police cars," he reflected later). Soon afterward, there was a furtive knock on Baldwin's door. Baldwin opened it and Hunt burst in. According to Baldwin, Hunt crouched behind a table, whispering hoarsely, "What is going on, what is going on?"

"C'mon and see," Baldwin said.

"I have got to use the bathroom," Hunt said as he scuttled toward the toilet.

8

COVER-UP

*The cover-up began that Saturday when we
realized there was a break-in. I do not think
there was ever any discussion that there would
not be a cover-up.*

—Jeb Magruder,
testimony to the Senate Select Committee
on Presidential Campaign Practices, June 14, 1973

When Howard Hunt came out of the bathroom, he
told Al Baldwin to pack up all his "gear" and get it out
of there. Baldwin says Hunt told him to take it to
Jim McCord's house in Rockville, Maryland. Hunt insists he said that was "the last place to go"; Baldwin
should dump it in the river or anywhere else, he should
just get it out of there. "We will be in touch," he said.
"You will get further instructions."

As Hunt rushed down the hallway toward the elevator, Baldwin cried after him, "Does this mean I won't
be going to Miami?"

There was no answer.

Baldwin quickly packed up everything in the room
—tape recorders, receivers, electric typewriter, walkie-
talkies, McCord's wallet—and took it all down to the
Dodge panel truck McCord had purchased for the occasion with the money Gordon Liddy supplied him.
After calling Mrs. McCord to say something had "gone
wrong," he drove the truck to her house. She and her
two daughters then brought Baldwin back to his car,
and he drove through the dawn to his home in Connecticut.

There is no agreement on when the CIA first learned

of the arrests. According to Carl Rowan of the *Washington Star-News,* Richard Helms was awakened before dawn by a telephone call from someone at the agency who told him about the events at the Watergate. Andrew St. George, a free-lance writer who has written frequently about the intelligence community, says the "watch officer" at CIA headquarters first alerted Helms shortly before 7:00 a.m. and their conversation went something like this:

HELMS: Ah, well. They finally did it.

WATCH OFFICER: It's a pity about McCord and some of those guys.

HELMS: Well, yes. A pity about the President, too, you know. They really blew it. The sad thing is, we all think, that's the end of it, and it may be just the beginning of something worse. If the White House tries to ring me through central, don't switch it out here, just tell them you reported McCord's arrest already and I was *very* surprised.

But, according to the CIA's own records, the first call it received on the matter came from a *Washington Post* reporter at 5:00 p.m.—a full fourteen and a half hours after the arrests. After that, in quick succession, came calls from the Secret Service and the FBI. At 8:45 p.m., when it became clear that McCord and Hunt had been involved, the news was relayed to Director of Security Osborn, who called Helms at 10:00 p.m.

Two days later Lee R. Pennington, Jr., a CIA operative who worked on a $250-a-month retainer under Howard Osborn, was dispatched to McCord's house. Pennington, a man in his seventies, described by one investigator as looking like "a kindly old gentleman," either destroyed or watched Mrs. McCord destroy incriminating material. McCord says the rest of his equipment remained in his van or his house until July, when he buried some of it in the woods and threw the rest in the Potomac River.

Still before dawn on June 17, Hunt drove from Howard Johnson's to the Executive Office Building, where he went to his third-floor office and stashed a black briefcase containing more of McCord's electronic equipment in his safe. From the safe, he took $10,000 in cash which Liddy had given him earlier for "emergencies." Then he called C. Douglas Caddy, a Washington lawyer who had once worked in the Mullen & Company offices while serving as Washington representative of General Foods, a Mullen client. Hunt says he told the sleepy Caddy that he had a "tough situation" and needed to talk with him immediately. Caddy told him to come on over. (There have been persistent reports that Caddy once worked for the CIA and may have been assigned beforehand to represent the Watergate burglars in case something went wrong. If so, he may have been the one who tipped off Helms.)

Leaving the EOB, Hunt walked across the street to 1700 Pennsylvania Avenue, where Mullen & Company had its offices. To disguise his movements, he signed in at the guard's desk under the name "Bob Wait," the man who had succeeded Caddy as General Foods' Washington representative. In his office, Hunt called Bernie Barker's wife, Clara, in Miami, told her that her husband had been arrested, and suggested that she go to a pay phone and call Caddy to request formally that he represent Barker and the others.

Then Hunt drove to Caddy's apartment house at 2121 P Street, where he arrived at about 3:40 a.m. Quickly explaining the situation, he gave Caddy $8500 in cash and asked him to bail the five men out of jail. Caddy explained that he wasn't a criminal lawyer, but he and his hastily alerted partners (at Gall, Lane, Powell & Kilcullen) made a spate of predawn phone calls to other attorneys. Most of those they reached were less than enchanted with the prospect. At four-thirty, Frank H. Strickler, a prominent Washington criminal lawyer, was awakened at his vacation house in Bethany Beach, Delaware, and growled, "You think I'm going to interrupt my vacation and represent anybody like that? You're crazy!" Finally, they found Joseph Rafferty, Jr., to handle the bail procedure. Confident that he had the situation under control, Hunt drove home, took a sleeping pill, and, as the sun came up over the Potomac, fell into a deep, untroubled sleep.

But Hunt—accustomed to the full support of a clandestine agency—underestimated the trouble he and his colleagues were in. Sergeant Paul Leeper says he realized immediately from the five men's dapper business suits and sport coats and their cool demeanor that he was not dealing with ordinary burglars. He was impressed, too, by the sophisticated equipment the men were carrying—blue Playtex surgical gloves, two eavesdropping devices, lock picks, door jimmies, short-wave receivers for monitoring police calls, a walkie-talkie, forty rolls of unexposed film, two 35 mm. cameras, three pen-sized gas guns, and $1754 in cash—$1300 of it in $100 bills. "We felt that it was just a little bigger than the average burglary," Leeper said.

When the five men were booked at the Second District station house and later at Metropolitan Police Headquarters, Barker's team gave the same aliases they had used all weekend—Frank Carter, Jene Valdez, Joseph Di Alberto, and Raoul Godoy. In addition, Sturgis was carrying Hunt's identification in the name of Edward J. Hamilton. McCord, who gave the alias "Edward Martin," was also carrying Hunt's identification in the name of Edward J. Warren. Two of the men were carrying keys to Rooms 214 and 314. The police obtained search warrants, and at two-thirty on Saturday afternoon, Sergeant Leeper, Officer Carl Shoffler, Detective Robert Dennell and Don Cherry of the Mobile Police Laboratory searched the rooms. They found some more electronic equipment, more surgical gloves, several suitcases, and $3566.58 in cash ($3200 in sequentially numbered $100 bills). In Room 314, where Sturgis and Gonzalez had stayed, they found two pieces of lined yellow paper, one addressed to "Dear Friend Mr. Howard" and another to "Dear Mr. H.H." In Room 214—the command post which had been occupied by Barker and Martinez—they found a stamped unmailed envelope containing a check for $6.36 made out by E. Howard Hunt to the Lakewood Country Club in Rockville. They also found Barker's little black address book and Martinez' flip-top telephone directory. Barker's book contained an entry for "H.H." followed by a dash and the initials "W.H." with a telephone number (which turned out to be Hunt's number in the EOB.) Martinez was even less circumspect. His directory listed "Howard Hunt" and gave the same telephone number marked "W. House."

While Hunt lay in drugged sleep, Gordon Liddy was wide awake and frantic. At nine-thirty Saturday morning, in a corridor at the finance committee, Hugh Sloan met a very agitated Liddy who told him, "My boys got caught last night. I made a mistake. I used somebody from here, which I told them I would never do. I'm afraid I'll lose my job." A few minutes later, Liddy ran into Rob Odle, CREEP's director of administration, and asked him where he could find a paper shredder. Odle directed him to the second floor and soon Liddy was shoveling a foot-thick pile of papers into the shredder—among them his collection of hotel soap wrappers (which would have traced his travels as surely as a road map) and even some of the telltale $100 bills he had been issued by Sloan.

At about eleven-thirty, Liddy put through a call to Jeb Magruder at the Beverly Hills Hotel. The day before, CREEP's top echelon—Mitchell, Mardian, La-Rue, Magruder, and Porter—and their wives had flown to Los Angeles for a series of meetings with California Republican leaders, to be topped off by a "Celebrities for Nixon" party. They had taken over an entire wing of the elegant hotel and were asleep there when the burglars were arrested at the Watergate. (Martha Mitchell claims that her husband learned about the burglary at 7:00 a.m. Pacific time in a phone call from Haldeman—but this is not corroborated by anyone else.) At about eighty-thirty, the Magruders, LaRues, Porters, and Mardians were eating breakfast in the Polo Lounge. The lounge was one of Magruder's favorite places in Los Angeles, in part because it was one of the few places he could get kippered herring. He was eating kippers when a waiter told him he had a call and brought a telephone to the table. It was Liddy, and according to Magruder the conversation went something like this:

LIDDY: You've got to get to a secure phone.

MAGRUDER: A secure phone? I don't know where a secure phone is, Gordon.

LIDDY: There's one at a military base at El Segundo, about ten miles from your hotel.

MAGRUDER: I haven't got time to go to a military base. What's so important?

LIDDY: Our security chief was arrested in the Democratic headquarters in the Watergate last night.

MAGRUDER: What? Do you mean McCord?

LIDDY: That's right. Jim McCord.

At that point, Magruder realized that he did, indeed, need a secure phone. Turning to LaRue, he said something "confidential" had come up and he needed a secure phone, adding, "I think maybe last night was the night they were going into the Democratic National Committee." LaRue said a pay phone should be secure enough. "What's your number?" Magruder asked Liddy. "I'll call you back."

On the pay phone outside the lounge, they spoke again. By now Magruder was angry, and he berated Liddy for using McCord and thus linking CREEP to the break-in. Liddy said they hadn't given him enough time: he needed someone to handle the electronics, and McCord was the only one he could get. After filling Magruder in on the arrests, he said, "Don't worry. My men will never talk." But Magruder was worried. "I've got to talk with Mitchell," he said. "Stay by the phone. We'll get back to you."

Magruder went back to the breakfast table and joylessly spooned up the rest of his kippers. At the first opportunity, he drew LaRue aside again and told him what had transpired, moaning "Oh God, why didn't I fire that idiot Liddy when I had the chance? How could we have been so stupid?"

LaRue rushed into Mitchell's suite to break the news, and when he told Mitchell of McCord's arrest, he recalls, the former attorney general exclaimed, "That's incredible!"

Magruder and Mardian were then summoned for a full-dress strategy session. The four men quickly agreed that McCord was the heart of their problem because he could provide investigators with a direct link from the Watergate to CREEP and thus to the White House. But they remained confident he could be removed from jail and spirited away. "After all," Magruder recalls, "*we* were the government." Ultimately, they decided that somebody should call Liddy and have him tell Deputy Attorney General Kleindienst to arrange for McCord's release. Magruder says Mitchell ordered Mardian to make the call because he was friendly with Liddy.

"When things are going great, they ignore me; when things get screwed up, they lean on me," Robert Charles Mardian once told a friend. In the aftermath of the Watergate break-in, Mitchell and others at CREEP leaned heavily on Mardian to get them out of trouble, and he resented it. Muscular, aggressive, often belligerent, Mardian had been passed over twice for key jobs under his friend John Mitchell—once as deputy attorney general and then as deputy director of CREEP. The CREEP job had gone to Jeb Magruder, and now Mardian found it particularly humiliating to ride to the rescue of the fresh-faced kids who had scorned his services. At the time, he told friends that he was "damned upset" at being fobbed off with the title of "political coordinator," and later he said, "My role was political organization. I knew a lot of people in a lot of states. But I had to spend most of my time arguing with a bunch of dumb kids with demographic charts." Magruder returned the distaste: "You just couldn't deal on a rational basis with Mardian. If you asked his advice on something, he'd take that as a sign of weakness and try to take over whatever it was. If you had a disagreement, he'd fly into a rage, pace around the room, and start shouting that he knew what was right and you didn't know anything."

Mardian had lost out for the jobs he wanted, in part because of a reputation for right-wing extremism. He was close not only to Mitchell but to Kleindienst—probably his best friend—and to Kleindienst's mentor, Barry Goldwater. Mardian's brother, Sam, had been mayor of Phoenix and a stalwart of Arizona conservative Republicanism. Bob Mardian managed Goldwater's 1964 Presidential campaign in the western states; played the same role for Nixon in 1968; and was rewarded with the job of general counsel to the Department of Health, Education, and Welfare, where he earned a reputation for consistently trying to scuttle school-desegregation guidelines. A fierce advocate of Mitchell's Southern Strategy, Mardian drew the animosity of liberals within the department. Once he told them bluntly, "Look, you might as well recognize that you're in politics. There are two kinds of people in the world—winners and losers. I knew a loser once and he was a queer," adding, "That's a joke." In late 1970 he moved over to become assistant attorney general in charge of the Internal Security Division and within a few months he had rejuvenated the long-moribund division, which had almost faded away after the Communist-hunting 1950s. Mardian beefed up the staff and went after draft-resisters and radicals of all stripes, specializing in broad conspiracy prosecutions (of the Harrisburg 6, the Camden 28, the Seattle 7, the VVAW 8), most of which the department lost. He was a great admirer of White House aide Tom Charles Huston and wanted to hire him as his deputy, but even Huston found Mardian overly zealous. Later he remarked, "Mardian didn't know the difference between a kid with a beard and a kid with a bomb." But his extremism never hurt Mardian all that much in the White House circles where such hard-line views were appreciated. Kleindienst once called him "a prodigious worker, a brilliant lawyer, and great believer in America. He knows what freedom ain't."

Mardian denies making the telephone call to Liddy. But Liddy received the instructions. For, as Kleindienst ate lunch at the Burning Tree Golf Club in Bethesda, Liddy came through the door accompanied by Powell A. Moore, a CREEP information officer. Kleindienst recalls that Liddy was "very agitated," beckoned to him in "a rather furtive" manner, and said he needed to speak to him privately. Since there were sixty or seventy men eating lunch in the club's main dining room prior to a member-guest golf tournament, Kleindienst ushered his unexpected guests into an adjacent locker room. According to Kleindienst, Liddy said, "Mitchell has sent me out here to talk to you and he wants those five people who were arrested last night released from jail"—adding that some of the burglars might have had some connection to either the White House or CREEP. Powell Moore later told Mardian that he stood behind Liddy and motioned to Kleindienst—whom he knew well from prior service at the Justice Department—not to believe Liddy. Evidently, Kleindienst did not believe the order came from Mitchell. His first move was to pick up a nearby phone and call Henry E. Petersen, the assistant attorney general in charge of the Criminal Division, who at eight that morning had already informed Kleindienst of the Watergate arrests. In this second conversation from the locker room, Kleindienst says he told Petersen he wanted the Watergate defendants treated just as anybody else would be. (But he did not tell Petersen— or anybody else—about Liddy's unorthodox, and illegal, request.)

Meanwhile, back in Los Angeles, the CREEP officials left the Beverly Hills Hotel for scheduled meetings of state Republican leaders at the Airport Marina Hotel. They did their best to keep up a good face, but between meetings they held whispered conferences about each new scrap of information they received. Bart Porter recalls one gathering of Mitchell, LaRue, Mardian, and Magruder in a large, empty banquet hall, during which he was instructed to stand guard some fifty yards away. Martha Mitchell—who had been told nothing—remembers walking into a room and seeing "all of them with their heads down. I said, 'For God's sake, what's the matter with all of you? I came

out here to have a good time.' And they all dispersed."
Later, she walked into still another conference and
asked, in exasperation, "What in the world is going
on?"

The circuits to Washington droned with apprehension. Around three o'clock California time, Magruder
called his office and instructed Robert Reisner to remove the Gemstone file and several other "political
folders" from his desk for the weekend, supposedly as
a security precaution against a retaliatory raid by the
Democrats. Reisner took some of the files, but when
his briefcase filled up, Odle took the Gemstone file—a
light gray folder about four inches thick—and put it
in a cupboard with his golf clubs.

The circuits were also busy at the White House,
where the mounting fears focused less on McCord than
on Hunt. The police had finally deciphered the references to Hunt in the burglars' address books, and that
afternoon, Al Wong, special agent in charge of the
technical services division in the White House, called
Alexander Butterfield, the Haldeman aide who handled
liaison with the Secret Service, and told him Hunt's
name had been traced to the White House. Butterfield said he knew of nobody by that name. Wong said
he thought Hunt might be a consultant to Colson. Butterfield asked his staff secretary, Bruce Kehrli, who
confirmed that Hunt did work for Colson but that
"Haldeman told me not to list him." So when an FBI
agent called Butterfield at five o'clock to ask how to
find Hunt, Butterfield could tell him. A little while
later, two FBI agents went to Hunt's home and asked
to talk with him. Hunt would do no more than verify
that the check to the Lakewood Country Club was his.
He said he would have to confer with his attorney
before going any further.

Toward dusk, Lilburn "Pat" Boggs, assistant chief
of the Secret Service, called John Ehrlichman with
much the same information about Hunt. Ehrlichman
passed it on to Ron Ziegler, who was with the Presidential party in Florida. (Nixon, just returned from
his trip to the Soviet Union, was spending the weekend on Walker's Cay, the northernmost island in the

Bahama chain, which belonged to his close friend Robert H. Abplanalp.) Apparently at Ziegler's suggestion, Ehrlichman called Chuck Colson to check on Hunt's current status at the White House. Colson said he didn't know but would find out. When Ehrlichman got home he got still another call—this one from John Caulfield. Caulfield told him about McCord's arrest and, as he recalls, their conversation continued like this:

CAULFIELD: John, it sounds like a disaster of some type.
EHRLICHMAN: My God, I can't believe it. I guess I better call Mitchell.

But Ehrlichman apparently didn't reach Mitchell. For that evening, still bravely keeping up appearances, the CREEP officials were off at the Celebrities for Nixon party at the Bel Air home of Taft Shreiber, vice president of Music Corporation of America and a major contributor to the Nixon campaign. Even by California standards, it was a lavish affair—held at poolside, with a dance band, songs by Vicki Carr, lots of food, wine, and a galaxy of Hollywood stars drawn by the aphrodisiac of power into the Nixon firmament: John Wayne, Zsa Zsa Gabor, Jack Benny, Terry Moore, John Gavin, even Charlton Heston, a Democrat being passionately wooed by the Republicans. Magruder tried to keep the conversational ball bouncing with his dinner partner, one of Rory Calhoun's ex-wives, but his heart wasn't in it. In the early morning hours of Sunday, the CREEP officials convened once more back in Mitchell's suite, where Mitchell decreed that Mardian should return to Washington later that day to take charge of the deteriorating situation.

Some hours later, when Haldeman called Magruder, he quickly countermanded that order, explaining that the President had no confidence in Mardian. Haldeman, still at the Key Biscayne Hotel in Florida, had been briefed earlier by Ehrlichman about Hunt's and McCord's role in the break-in. Now he told Magruder to get back to Washington himself and take charge of the situation. Magruder caught a commercial flight for

Chicago, but had to charter a plane from Chicago to Washington and didn't arrive until late Sunday evening. Meanwhile, John Dean returned to the country that morning, after a four-day trip to the Philippines (where he had delivered a lecture on drug abuse). Landing at San Francisco airport, he called his assistant Fred Fielding, and learned for the first time about the arrests at the Watergate. He caught the first flight for Washington, arriving about the same time as Magruder.

By Sunday, the press was beginning to demand a comment from Mitchell about McCord. On Saturday his aides—assisted by Cliff Miller, a Los Angeles public-relations man—had drafted a statement for him; but although McCord and the other burglars had given their real names at the arraignment that day, nobody had yet traced McCord to CREEP. On Sunday, however, an enterprising Associated Press reporter compared the names of those arrested with a list of CREEP employees and found McCord's name on both lists. In response to an AP query, Mitchell issued a statement that grossly understated McCord's relationship to CREEP: "We have just learned from news reports that a man identified as employed by our campaign committee was one of five persons arrested at the Democratic National Committee headquarters in Washington, D.C., early Saturday morning. The person involved is the proprietor of a private security agency who was employed by our Committee months ago to assist with the installation of our security system. He has, as we understand it, a number of business clients and interests and we have no knowledge of those relationships. We want to emphasize that this man and the other people involved were not operating either in our behalf or with our consent. . . ."

But Martha Mitchell knew exactly who Jim McCord was and had grown fond of him during the weeks in early spring when he had served as her security guard and then provided other guards for her. Her awareness of McCord's role at CREEP worried John Mitchell, who told his aides to prevent her from seeing press accounts of the arrests. On Sunday afternoon the entire

CREEP party drove from Beverly Hills to Newport Beach, the ocean resort halfway between downtown Los Angeles and the Western White House at San Clemente. Newport Beach—that bastion of Southern California Nixonism, the home of Herb Kalmbach and of Donald Nixon, and headquarters of the Lincoln Club, was also the site of the Newporter Inn, a favorite watering spot for the Nixon people. That afternoon the Mitchells checked into one of the inn's detached cottages—dubbed the Villa Roma—and the rest of the party dispersed to surrounding villas. In the evening they all attended a "Mexican fiesta" at the nearby home of Mrs. Donald K. Washburn, widow of the former president of 7-Up. The cocktail-buffet, for about fifty major campaign contributors and "prime prospects," was marred by a heated argument between John and Martha Mitchell. As he led Martha away, Mitchell told some guests he was leaving early to attend "a very important meeting." The argument may have been over his decision to leave Martha behind in California while he returned to Washington. She says he told her, "Since you're so tired, why don't you stay out here for a few days, get some sun and swim." The next morning Mitchell, Mardian, and LaRue left for Washington aboard a corporate jet belonging to the Gulf Oil Company and arriving late on Monday afternoon. Martha remained in the Villa Roma with her eleven-year-old daughter, Marty; her secretary, Lee Jablonsky; and her security guard, Steve King (the ex-FBI man who had replaced the "gauche" and barefoot Al Baldwin).

That Monday morning, California papers had carried large photographs of McCord. Mrs. Mitchell recalls Mardian joining the other CREEP officials around the pool "looking like a newspaper boy, with papers under his arm." After they had left, she looked for the papers but couldn't find one. She finally got hold of one and found reports of both the arrests and McCord's subsequent dismissal from CREEP. "Jesus Christ!" she recalls, "I jumped out of bed like a sheet of lightning." Reaching for the telephone, she tried to call her husband, but he was still in the air. So she called Jeb Magruder at CREEP headquarters to ask, "Why are you firing Jim McCord? Why are you throwing him to the wolves?" Later, she reached Mitchell at their Washington apartment, where he was meeting with the CREEP high command, and he told her that "somebody tried to create this problem for us, there's nothing to it and don't worry about it." Convinced that they were trying to keep her quiet and out of Washington so they could hold secret meetings in her apartment, she began to brood. For three days King kept her from making any more outside calls. But at 9:00 p.m. Thursday, while pretending to be asleep, she managed to place a call to her longtime confidante, Helen Thomas of United Press International. According to Ms. Thomas, Mrs. Mitchell sounded "subdued and somewhat sad" until the Watergate matter came up, when she became agitated and said, "That's it. I've given John an ultimatum. I'm going to leave him unless he gets out of the campaign. I'm sick and tired of politics. Politics is a dirty business." Suddenly, Mrs. Mitchell became very "excited" and shouted, "You just get away—get away!" Then the line went dead. Later, Mrs. Mitchell explained that at that moment King had burst into her bedroom and ripped the phone out of the wall.

When Ms. Thomas tried to call back, the operator told her, "Mrs. Mitchell is indisposed and cannot talk." Ms. Thomas promptly telephoned John Mitchell in Washington for a comment on his wife's strange call. He did not seem concerned.

"She's great," he said. "That little sweetheart. I love her so much. She gets a little upset about politics, but she loves me and I love her and that's what counts."

But the Battle of Villa Roma went on. At eight the next morning, other guests heard a loud noise from the villa. Mrs. Mitchell had put her hand through a plate-glass patio door, apparently during another struggle with King. Herb Kalmbach was summoned to the villa, and he in turn summoned his personal physician, Dr. Dan Romaine Kirkham. When he got there, Dr. Kirkham says, Mrs. Mitchell was "hysterical," shouting, "I'm being held a political prisoner" and "I know information, so I can't inform anyone." He says he gave her a "shot" that would keep her sedated for four to six hours. He concedes that she had to be forcibly "restrained." (Mrs. Mitchell puts it differently: "They threw me down on the bed—five men did it—and stuck a needle in my behind." She also claims that King threw her to the floor and kicked her.)

Kalmbach wanted Dr. Kirkham to sew up the severe cut on Mrs. Mitchell's hand right there, but the doctor balked, insisting that she be taken to a hospital. Finally, Kalmbach relented, although he insisted that she be checked into the hospital emergency room under the name Dorothy Kalmbach. But the cover was blown when the doctor who examined her turned out to be Dr. Clark McGaughey, who had treated her earlier in the week when she burned her hand on a matchbook. "For God's sake, Martha," he said, "what are you doing here?" Kalmbach was "beside himself, pacing the floor."

The next day, friends accompanied Mrs. Mitchell to New York, where she checked into the Westchester Country Club in Rye. On Sunday morning she called Ms. Thomas again, saying, "I have been through so much. Martha isn't going to stand for it. I love my husband very much. But I'm not going to stand for all those dirty things." About the week's events, she said, "I'm black and blue. They left me in California with absolutely no information. They don't want me to talk." Then she mumbled something about "McCord."

Mrs. Mitchell remained in seclusion for months, except for one telephone call in which she pleaded with Ms. Thomas, "If you don't hear from me, call the police." But even the police couldn't see her. Acting FBI Director L. Patrick Gray III testified later that Mitchell refused to let agents interview his wife. "Mr. Mitchell said that Mrs. Mitchell's stories and the things that were in the press were not so, and we were not going to interview Mrs. Mitchell . . . and that was that," Gray reported. Republican officials broadly hinted to reporters that "Martha is imbibing," even suggesting that she was in Silver Hill, a private psychiatric hospital in Connecticut specializing in the treatment of alcoholics. Mrs. Mitchell insists her problem wasn't drinking—it was what she knew about the Watergate affair and particularly the demands for total secrecy emanating from the White House.

A t the White House that Monday, June 19, with the President and Haldeman still in Florida, John Ehrlichman had been put in charge of containing the burgeoning scandal. He, in turn, delegated much of that job to John Dean, asking him to find out what he could as quickly as possible and report back. Dean, who had attended the first two Gemstone planning sessions, knew that the man to see was Gordon Liddy. He reached Liddy at the finance committee and they took a walk down 17th Street toward the Corcoran Gallery. As Dean recalls it, Liddy conceded that the Watergate burglars were his men but blamed Magruder for "pushing him into it." He said he had used McCord only because Magruder had cut his budget so sharply. Then he turned apologetic, saying that he was "a soldier," he would "never talk," and "if anyone wished to shoot him on the street, he was ready." Dean reported all this back to Ehrlichman, telling him also about his earlier meetings with Mitchell and Magruder.

Later that afternoon, Dean says, Ehrlichman told him to call Liddy and have him instruct Hunt to "get out of the country." Dean concedes that he telephoned Liddy to pass on these orders but insists that soon afterward "I realized that no one in the White House should give such an instruction," and persuaded Ehrlichman to rescind it. Dean says he again called Liddy, who said he had already given Hunt the message.

Hunt recalls that Liddy first telephoned him around four and asked to meet him at the corner of Pennsylvania Avenue and 18th Street. When he got there, Liddy was leaning up against the United States Information Agency building reading a newspaper, but he casually fell in step with Hunt as they walked down 18th Street. According to Hunt, Liddy told him urgently, "They want you to get out of town. . . . They want you to get moving and fast." He reluctantly agreed to go, but urged Liddy to find him a lawyer. *"Adiós, amigo,"* Liddy said as he strode away. Hunt went home and began to pack. He says Liddy then telephoned again to tell him, "The orders have been changed. You don't have to leave town." But Hunt says he decided to go anyway. He flew to New York, spent the night in a motel, then flew on to Los Angeles, where he took refuge with a former CIA colleague, Morton B. "Tony" Jackson, a lawyer who lived in a house "high on a crest in Beverly Hills, handsomely furnished in teak acquired in Bangkok."

On Monday afternoon, Hunt had been the main topic in still another discussion between Ehrlichman and Dean, who this time were joined by Chuck Colson and Ken Clawson. They first discussed Hunt's employment status. Colson, who was becoming defensive about his connection with Hunt, insisted that Hunt's consultant role at the White House should have been terminated on March 31, 1972. But Bruce Kehrli was told to bring Hunt's records up to the meeting, and they showed no such termination.

Colson then urged that Hunt's safe in Room 338 be cleared out as quickly as possible. (Dean says Colson and Hunt had discussed the safe problem over the weekend, but Colson denies this. Still, he was certainly well aware of the dangers that lurked within the safe because that very morning Hunt had been in to check it and afterward had stopped off in Colson's office. Colson hadn't yet arrived, but Hunt told his secretary, Joan Hall, to tell her boss, "That safe of mine upstairs is loaded.") Ehrlichman quickly agreed that the safe should be unloaded and told Dean to take custody of the materials inside. Kehrli arranged for the General Services Administration staff to move the safe up to Room 522, a GSA storeroom. There, a team of safe specialists drilled it open. Kehrli and Fred Fielding were summoned to take charge of the contents. They emptied the two drawers into several boxes and took them to Kehrli's office, where they were stored over-night.

Meanwhile, Mitchell, Mardian, and LaRue had arrived from California, and Magruder and Dean were summoned to Mitchell's apartment at the Watergate for another strategy session. When Magruder got there, shortly after six o'clock, he found the others drinking and talking "in bitter, despondent voices." Magruder could see "a long evening of booze and self-pity shaping up," and when he got a telephone call from the Vice President's appointments secretary asking him to round out a tennis foursome later that evening, he accepted with alacrity. Just before he left, Magruder recalls, he asked Mitchell what he should do with the Gemstone file which he had retrieved from Odle that morning.

He says Mitchell responded, "Maybe you ought to have a little fire at your house tonight."

Magruder nodded and went off to the Linden Hill indoor courts in Bethesda. At first, he had read no particular significance into the Vice President's tennis invitation that night. But after he and the appointments secretary had beaten Agnew and a man from the State Department, Agnew drew him aside. According to Magruder, their conversation went like this:

AGNEW: Jeb, what the hell is going on?
MAGRUDER: It was our operation. It got screwed up. We're trying to take care of it.
AGNEW (*frowning and looking away*): I don't think we ought to discuss it again, in that case.

Arriving home about midnight, Magruder went to the kitchen for a glass of milk. Then he took the Gemstone file out of his suitcase, went into the living room, and built a fire in the big fireplace. Sitting cross-legged by the hearth, he took papers one by one out of the folder, glanced at them, and fed them into the blaze. Reading transcripts of the DNC bug, he couldn't help but chuckle at the graphic details of the secretaries' private lives. The photographs taken by Barker and his men blazed brightly like a Christmas tree. Suddenly, there was a rustle at the doorway and Magruder turned to see his wife, Gail, standing there.

"What in the world are you doing?" she asked. "You're going to burn the house down."

"It's all right," he said. "It's just some papers I have to get rid of." And they went off to bed.

As Magruder burned the Gemstone papers, Nixon was arriving back at the White House after his long weekend in the south. The President's first reactions to news of the Watergate break-in and arrests have been shrouded in the fogs which occasionally wash the white beaches of Bob Abplanalp's private island. All Saturday (and perhaps part of Sunday) Nixon had remained on Walker's Cay with Abplanalp. Even Haldeman, the President's most trusted lieutenant, was a hundred and fifty miles away in Key Biscayne. According to his logs, the President spoke with Haldeman from 10:58 to 11:02 a.m. on Saturday (some nine hours after the arrests). Nixon later told Colson that when he first learned of the break-in—perhaps during this first call with Haldeman—he was so "furious" and "outraged" that anybody connected with CREEP should have been implicated that he threw an ashtray across the room.

Colson was the man the President called most frequently in those first days after the break-in—no less than three times for a total of one hour and forty minutes between 3:00 p.m. Sunday and noon on Monday. Several White House aides have testified that when they first heard about the break-in they presumed that Colson was somehow involved. Evidently Nixon thought so too. Colson recalls that when the President called the first time, "he asked me what I knew about what was going on," to which, Colson says, "I merely explained that I had no idea what had happened." But that would hardly have consumed an hour and forty minutes. We do not know just what Colson told the President.

Nor do we know what Haldeman may have told Nixon. On Monday morning Nixon talked to Haldeman twice on the telephone and then met with him for about an hour and fifteen minutes around midday at Key Biscayne. By then, Haldeman almost certainly knew a great deal about the break-in and the arrests. He had talked with Ehrlichman, Colson, and Magruder. Magruder recalls that all Saturday he had dreaded a call—"I feared the wrath of Haldeman"—but when it finally came on Sunday morning it was short and businesslike. "I spoke with the assumption that he knew about the break-in and nothing he said indicated he did not." Similarly, Strachan recalls that he "expected over the entire weekend Mr. Haldeman to call me and ask me what I knew, if I knew anything why I had not reported it to him, the usual very tough questions he would ask." But the call never came, and Strachan concluded that either "he didn't expect me to report to him" or "he knew."

At 7:48 p.m. Monday, Nixon and Haldeman boarded the *Spirit of '76* and conferred for another fifty-five minutes on the flight back to Washington. As they sped north, watching the lights of Jacksonville, Atlanta, and Richmond sliding beneath the big jet's wings, they almost certainly talked about the break-in and arrests. We do not know what they said to each other. But they must have realized that the weekend's events had jeopardized their futures, which, like their pasts, were so tightly joined.

As a young advertising man just out of USC, Harry Robbins Haldeman followed Richard Nixon's vigorous prosecution of the Alger Hiss investigation in 1948–49 much the way young people twenty-five years later became obsessed by another political scandal. Young Haldeman was a true believer in the Crusade against Communism. His paternal grandfather, a Los Angeles pipe-supply man, had founded the Better America Foundation, an early forerunner of the John Birch Society. As a campus politician, Haldeman expressed alarm at Communist infiltration of student organiza-

*tions and once tried to purge the USC student news-
paper of "Red" influence. So when Richard Nixon
emerged in the late 1940s as a leader of the national
purge, Haldeman became a fervent admirer. The two
men did not meet until 1951 and Haldeman did not
work for Nixon until 1956, when he served as an
advance man in the Vice Presidential campaign. In
those years, Haldeman was still chiefly concerned with
building a career in advertising. Beginning as a researcher at Foote, Cone & Belding, he soon switched
over to the mammoth J. Walter Thompson. After brief
tours in San Francisco and New York, he settled into
the agency's Los Angeles office, where he remained off
and on for sixteen years, eventually as a vice president
supervising the Walt Disney, 7-Up, and Black Flag
accounts. Single-minded and intense, he seemed utterly
lacking in a sense of humor. (Later, he conceded, "I
cannot remember anything funny that happens. It's a
failing of mine. Even when I was an advertising salesman and I needed jokes, I couldn't remember one.")
Gradually, the political interruptions grew more frequent. In 1960 he served as chief advance man for
Nixon's losing Presidential campaign, and two years
later he managed his abortive race for the California
governorship. The two men became especially close in
those dark days of defeat when Haldeman sat for hours
listening to Nixon's bitter recriminations and then
helped frame them into the book* Six Crises. *Indeed,
what set Haldeman apart from Nixon's other early advisers was his willingness to submerge his own preferences in total loyalty to his leader. Over the years he
became an extension of Nixon's will, an ever-ready
instrument for the accomplishment of Nixon's purpose. But he was no passive tool. During the 1960
campaign he became convinced that the loose organization had dissipated Nixon's energies and subjected his
natural volatility to undue pressures. So as White
House chief of staff, installed just a hundred feet down
the gold carpet from the Oval Office, he built up a
tight protective barrier (soon nicknamed the "Berlin
Wall"). Even cabinet officers and the Joint Chiefs of
Staff had to persuade Haldeman that they deserved en-*

tree to the President and they didn't take kindly to his curt rebuffs. But Haldeman said bluntly, "Every President needs a son-of-a-bitch and I'm Nixon's. I'm his buffer and I'm his bastard. I get done what he wants done and I take the heat instead of him." Crew-cut, austere, and puritanical, Haldeman set the pace for his eager, humorless staff (dubbed the "Beaver Patrol"), communicating with them through brisk, impersonal memos, scribbling acerbic remarks in the margins. (One aide got a memo back with TL² penned in one corner. When he asked what that meant, Haldeman growled, "Too little, too late.") Haldeman's system seemed to work, but his total loyalty contained one overriding flaw—a lack of autonomous judgment that might have checked Nixon's worst instincts.

With Nixon and Haldeman back in Washington, the cover-up moved into a second stage on the morning of Tuesday, June 20. After three days of drift and improvisation, the President's men sought to regain control of the slippery situation. At nine, Haldeman convened the first truly top-level strategy session on the matter, attended by Ehrlichman, Mitchell, and, later, Dean and Kleindienst. While this meeting went on, Nixon remained alone in the Oval Office taking and receiving no telephone calls. Then, from 11:26 to 12:45 Haldeman met with the President, apparently to brief him on the earlier discussions and to devise a course of action. Haldeman's notes of his talk with the President reflect a particular concern with public relations: "What is our counterattack? . . . PR offensive to top this . . . hit the opposition with their activities . . . pt. out libertarians have created public . . . do they justify this less than stealing Pentagon Papers, Anderson files, etc. . . . we shld be on the attack—for diversion—"

But the first step in the still embryonic White House cover-up plan was the continued destruction of any documents that might link the President or his assistants to the break-in. Already Liddy had shredded virtually his entire files; Hunt had evidently destroyed certain "incriminating material" at his home; Magruder had burned the Gemstone file; Reisner had destroyed other "sensitive material" in Magruder's files; Mardian and LaRue had directed a "massive housecleaning" of CREEP's remaining files; and Colson had one of his aides destroy all pages in a White House telephone directory which showed Hunt as his "consultant." Now Strachan surveyed Haldeman's files and found several items which he realized could be embarrassing if they came to light, particularly his own Political Matters Memo 18, sent to Haldeman in early April, which reported CREEP's establishment of a "sophisticated intelligence system with a budget of 300." After the Tuesday morning meeting, Strachan went into Haldeman's office, still "scared to death" of what Haldeman might say. As he recalls it, the conversation went like this:

HALDEMAN (*almost jokingly*): Well, what do we know about the events over the weekend?

STRACHAN (*showing Haldeman Memo 18*): Well, sir, this is what can be imputed to you through me, your agent.

HALDEMAN (*turning to a tab covering the activities of "Sedan Chair II," Michael McMinoway*): "I should have been reading these, these are quite interesting."

(*Pause.*)

HALDEMAN: Well, make sure our files are clean.

Strachan got the message. He went downstairs and shredded a pile of documents, including Memo 18; an April 4, 1972, "talking paper" that he had prepared for Haldeman and Mitchell; a memo from Jeb Magruder to Mitchell on Donald Segretti's activities.

That same Tuesday morning another "cleansing" operation was under way in a nearby office. Fielding had the two boxes containing the contents of Hunt's safe brought into Dean's office, and there the two White House lawyers began sorting through them. Among other things, they found:

• a .25-caliber automatic Colt revolver;
• a clip for the revolver, containing live ammunition;

- a holster;
- McCord's black attaché case, containing a tear-gas cannister, two microphones, two earphones, antennas, jack wires, and harnesses;
- a tan folder filled with papers on Daniel Ellsberg, including the CIA's psychological profiles;
- six brown envelopes filled with classified material on the Pentagon Papers;
- two clothbound notebooks;
- a pop-up address book;
- a folder containing material on Hunt's interview with Clifton DeMotte and other investigations of Edward Kennedy;
- a large pile of State Department cables on Vietnam, including the two cables fabricated by Hunt;
- a memo to Colson on Hunt's talk with William Lambert about the forged cables; and
- a folder containing memos from Hunt to Colson about various Plumbers' operations.

When they had finished, the counsel to the President turned to the associate counsel to the President and said, "Holy shit!"

Dean and Fielding decided that much of the material could be very embarrassing, particularly during an election year. Dean went to Ehrlichman's office to report what he had found. He says Ehrlichman told him to shred the documents and "deep six" the briefcase. He asked him what he meant by "deep six," and Ehrlichman replied, "You drive across the river on your way home at night, don't you?" When Dean said he did, Ehrlichman said, "Well, when you cross over the bridge on your way home, just toss the briefcase into the river." Dean says he replied jokingly that he would bring Ehrlichman the materials, and he could take care of them because he, too, crossed the bridge at night. "No thank you," said Ehrlichman.

Dean thought about the proposal for a few days. Then, on the twenty-sixth, he told Ehrlichman that too many people had seen the materials removed from the safe—among them, a Secret Service man, Fielding, and Kehrli. Therefore he suggested another plan: they would hand the nonsensitive materials to FBI agents and give the sensitive ones directly to Patrick Gray. Thus, if he were ever under oath, Dean could testify that everything found in the safe had been turned over to the FBI.

On the twenty-seventh, FBI agents Daniel C. Mahan and Michael J. King came to the White House and collected two boxes filled with nonsensitive materials. The next day Ehrlichman told Dean that Gray was coming to his office that afternoon and he should bring the sensitive materials over. Just before Gray was due, Dean brought in two white manila legal folders—containing the fake cables, the materials on Ted Kennedy, the Ellsberg documents, and the memos to Colson about Lambert and the Plumbers' operation—and placed them on the coffee table in Ehrlichman's office. (For some reason, Dean held back Hunt's pop-up address book and his two notebooks. Hunt had purchased the black, clothbound Hermès notebooks while working with the CIA in Paris and over the years he had filled them with names, aliases, telephone numbers, code words, and other details of his clandestine operations —a groaning board of goodies for a hungry investigator. Dean says the notebooks contained information about people Hunt had worked with in the burglary of Dr. Lewis Fielding's office—a very good reason to keep them from falling into the wrong hands, even Gray's. Dean says that in late January 1973 he threw the address book into the waste basket, shredded the notebooks, and "hoped the problem would go away.")

Gray, who arrived at around six-thirty, recalls the following conversation. After the opening greetings, Ehrlichman said, "John has something that he wants to turn over to you." Dean, gesturing toward the two folders, said they contained Howard Hunt's classified papers which had "national security" implications but no bearing on the Watergate investigation. Either Dean or Ehrlichman said that the files should not be allowed to muddy the Watergate case. Dean said they were "political dynamite" and "clearly should not see the light of day." Gray later testified that although neither Ehrlichman nor Dean had expressly instructed him to destroy the files, "the clear implication of the substance and tone of their remarks was that these two files were to be destroyed and I interpreted this to be an order from the Counsel to the President of the United States issued in the presence of one of the two top assistants to the President of the United States." Gray took the folders home and placed them under a pile of shirts on a closet shelf. A few weeks later he returned them to his office and put them in his safe. In early October he brought them to his home in Stonington, Connecticut, where—after glancing at a few of the contents— he burned them along with the holiday wrapping paper a few days after Christmas.

"Aye, aye, sir," was the watchword of his career, the ex-Naval officer later explained. A Navy man for twenty years, Louis Patrick Gray III retained the grooming, demeanor, and habits of thought accumulated during that service. He still asked his neighborhood barber to cut his hair every two weeks "to military length—maybe a little tighter." He exercised every morning, attended early mass every day, and didn't drink or smoke. And he firmly believed in following orders passed down to him through the chain of command. Pat Gray got used to taking and giving orders very early when he was made a submarine commander while still in his mid-twenties, leading the USS Steelhead *on five combat patrols in the Pacific during World War II. After the war, he was selected over hundreds of other applicants to attend the George Washington University Law School. Graduating in 1949, he became a Naval legal officer and rose to become military assistant to the chairman of the Joint Chiefs of Staff and special assistant to the secretary of defense, in which capacity he attended meetings of the National Security Council and the cabinet. Gray liked what he saw there and, he recalled later, "I wanted to get in." So in 1960 he forfeited his Naval retirement and other benefits to go to work for a man who he thought could get him "in"—Richard M. Nixon, that year's Re-*

*publican candidate for President. The two men had
met thirteen years before at a Washington cocktail
party when Gray was studying law and Nixon was
garnering headlines with his investigation of Alger Hiss.
Gray handled campaign logistics for Robert Finch, director of Nixon's campaign staff. When his candidate
lost, Gray joined a law firm in New London, established a small investment company, and made enough
money to buy a large, modern A-frame house with an
impressive view of Stonington harbor. But he stayed in
close touch with Nixon during the 1960s and worked
for him in the 1968 campaign. His reward was modest
at first—executive assistant to his old boss, Finch, who
became Nixon's first secretary of health, education, and
welfare. But as his administrative skills drew attention,
Gray moved gradually upward, first to assistant attorney general and then to appointment as deputy
attorney general. Before that appointment could be confirmed by the Senate, J. Edgar Hoover died on May 2,
1972. The next day the President named Gray acting
FBI director, explaining that he would not fill the post
permanently until after the November elections. Gray's
first weeks at the bureau were good ones as he moved
quickly to loosen the rigid bonds Hoover had imposed
during his forty-eight years as director. He opened the
bureau to women, made himself accessible to press and
public, and allowed agents to wear longer hair and
colored shirts. "The agents thought they had died and
gone to heaven," one veteran recalls. But soon disillu-
sionment set in as Gray went off on speaking tours for
Nixon—more than twenty speeches between May and
November—often spending several days at a time, a
habit which earned him the nickname Two-Day Gray.
Some agents thought him too malleable, too responsive
to Presidential pressure. And ultimately the President
concluded that Gray was "a little bit on the stupid
side."*

At the start, before he realized the depth of the
White House involvement in the Watergate affair, Gray

and his agents performed conscientiously. Their most significant early discovery involved the $4500 in $100 bills found on the burglars and in their hotel rooms. Within five days they had traced the bills—by their consecutive serial numbers—through the Federal Reserve Bank in Atlanta to Barker's bank account in Miami's Republic National Bank and thence to the four Mexican checks (totaling $89,000) and the $25,000 check from Kenneth Dahlberg. It was only a matter of time before they traced them back to the Finance Committee for the Re-election of the President. The White House determination to raise a massive campaign war chest, CREEP's surreptitious "money-washing" operations, and the sheer chance that led Hugh Sloan to pick out of his safe the very cash which Liddy had laundered for him through Barker—all this had left a tell-tale trail of green from the break-in straight to the President's re-election campaign.

Gray, who had been in California over the break-in weekend, got his first briefing on the investigation at four o'clock on Tuesday from Assistant Director FBI Director W. Mark Felt, Jr.; Assistant Director Charles Bates, who was to head up the Watergate investigation; and Robert Kunkel, special agent in charge of the Washington field office. Kunkel advanced a theory that the break-in was "in furtherance of the White House efforts to locate and identify 'leaks' "—a remarkably quick recognition that the burglary was an outgrowth of the Plumbers' operation. According to a memo written by Bates, Gray stressed that possible White House involvement should not hamper the investigation, "that this was most important, that the FBI's reputation was at stake and that the investigation should be completely impartial, thorough and complete." That day, the bureau knew about the Mexican checks. At 10:25 the next morning, Bates first informed Gray about the discovery of the Dahlberg check.

In one of several conversations on Wednesday and Thursday, Gray passed on the FBI's information about the checks to John Dean, whom Ehrlichman had designated as the bureau's White House liaison on the Watergate investigation. Dean told Mitchell, Ehrlichman, and others—with predictable results. Sometime during those first weeks, Mardian told Dean, "For God's sake, John, somebody's got to slow Pat Gray down. He's going like a crazy man."

So the White House began a new phase of the cover-up—an effort to throw the protective shield of "national security" over the Mexican and Dahlberg checks and, by extension, over the entire Watergate affair.

This strategy apparently grew out of several quite innocent conversations which Gray held on Thursday, June 22. At 5:23 p.m. that day Gray telephoned Richard Helms to tell him "of our thinking that we may be poking into a CIA operation" and to ask if Helms could confirm or deny this. According to Gray, Helms replied that "he had been meeting on this every day with his men, that they knew the people, that they could not figure it out, but that there was no CIA involvement."

Just where Gray got the notion that Watergate might be a CIA operation is not clear. It may have come from Assistant Director Bates, with whom he had spoken just minutes before. Certainly, there were good grounds to suspect some CIA involvement, since by then the FBI knew that both McCord and Hunt were former CIA employees and that Barker's team had strong CIA connections.

At six-thirty, Gray told Dean about several "theories" the FBI had developed to explain the break-in: "that the episode was either a CIA covert operation of some sort simply because some of the people involved had been CIA people in the past, or a CIA money chain, or a political money chain, or a pure political operation, or a Cuban right-wing operation, or a combination of any of these."

Later on Thursday evening, at a meeting in Mitchell's office, Dean recounted these remarks. Apparently, the canny Wall Street lawyer realized that the CIA could be used to stifle the FBI investigation. Mitchell suggested that Dean explore the idea with Haldeman and Ehrlichman. Either that evening or the next morning, Dean passed the idea on to Haldeman, and at

10:04 a.m. on June 23 Haldeman and the President discussed it, as follows:

HALDEMAN: Now, on the investigation, you know the Democratic break-in thing, we're back in the problem area because the FBI is not under control, because Gray doesn't exactly know how to control it and they have, their investigation is now leading into some productive areas because they've been able to trace the money . . . and it goes in some directions we don't want it to go. . . . Mitchell came up with yesterday, and John Dean analyzed very carefully last night and concludes, concurs now with Mitchell's recommendation that the only way to solve this, and we're set up beautifully to do it . . . is for us to have Walters call Pat Gray and just say, "Stay to hell out of this—this is ah, business here we don't want you to go any further on it." That's not an unusual development, and ah, that would take care of it.

NIXON: What about Pat Gray—you mean Pat Gray doesn't want to?

HALDEMAN: Pat does want to. He doesn't know how to, and he doesn't have, he doesn't have any basis for doing it. Given this, he will then have the basis. He'll call Mark Felt in, and the two of them—and Mark Felt wants to cooperate because he's ambitious—

NIXON: Yeah.

HALDEMAN: He'll call him in and say, "We've got the signal from across the river to put the hold on this." And that will fit rather well because the FBI agents who are working the case, at this point, feel that's what it is.

Later on in the conversation the President enthusiastically endorsed Haldeman's plan, telling him, ". . . When you get in (*unintelligible*) people, say 'Look, the problem is that this will open the whole, the whole Bay of Pigs thing, and the President just feels that ah, without going into the details—don't, don't lie to them to the extent to say no involvement, but just say this is a comedy of errors, without getting into it, the President believes that it is going to open the whole Bay of

Pigs thing up again. And, ah, because these people are plugging for (*unintelligible*) and that they should call the FBI in and (*unintelligible*) don't go any further into this case period!"

After talking to the President, Haldeman summoned Helms and Helms's deputy, Vernon A. Walters, to the White House. At about one-thirty they met with Haldeman and Ehrlichman in Haldeman's office. In a memo written for the files five days later, Walters described the meeting:

"Haldeman said that the 'bugging' affair at the Democratic National Committee Hqs at the Watergate Apartments had made a lot of noise and the Democrats were trying to maximize it. The FBI had been called in and was investigating the matter. The investigation was leading to a lot of important people and this could get worse. He asked what the connection with the Agency was and the Director repeated that there was none. Haldeman said that the whole affair was getting embarrassing and it was the President's wish that Walters call on Acting FBI Director Patrick Gray and suggest to him that since the five suspects had been arrested that this should be sufficient and that it was not advantageous to have the enquiry pushed, especially in Mexico, etc. Director Helms said that he had talked to Gray on the previous day and had made plain to him that the Agency was not behind this matter, that it was not connected with it and none of the suspects was working for, nor had worked for the Agency in the last two years. He had told Gray that none of his investigations was touching any covert projects of the Agency, current or ongoing. Haldeman then stated that I could tell Gray that I had talked to the White House and suggest that the investigation not be pushed further. Gray would be receptive as he was looking for guidance in the matter. The Director repeated that the Agency was unconnected with the matter. I then agreed to talk to Gray as directed. . . ."

Walters recalls that when he and Helms got downstairs, they talked briefly by their car and Helms said, "You must remind Mr. Gray of the agreement between the FBI and the CIA that if they run into or appear to expose one another's assets they will notify one another."

Helms has testified that he agreed to go along with the White House plan—despite his repeated denial of a CIA role in the burglary—because "I had to recognize that if the White House, the President, Mr. Haldeman, somebody in high authority, had information about something in Mexico which I did not have information about, which is quite possible—the White House constantly has information which others do not have— that it would be a prudent thing for me to find out if there was any possibility that some CIA operation was being—was going to be affected, and, therefore, I wanted the necessary time to do this."

It is difficult to imagine how the White House would know about a CIA operation if the director of that agency did not, and one suspects that Helms simply found it "prudent" not to disobey Nixon. (That day, the President told Haldeman, "Well, we protected Helms from one hell of a lot of things," and Haldeman says he told Helms that the Watergate investigation "tracks back to the Bay of Pigs and it tracks back to some other, the leads run out to people who had no involvement in this, except by contacts, and connections, but it gets to areas that are liable to be raised. . . . So at that point he got the picture. He said we'll be very happy to be helpful.")

Moreover, Helms knew he would not have to make the strange *démarche* himself. The White House had selected Walters to carry the message to Gray for reasons of its own. An old friend of Nixon's, Walters had served as his interpreter while he was Vice President and had accompanied him on his tumultuous trip to Venezuela in 1956, an ordeal which undoubtedly drew the two men together. Dean recalls Ehrlichman saying that Walters was "a good friend of the White House" who had been "installed so they could have some influence over the agency."

At two-thirty, Walters went to see Gray. As Gray recalls it, he said he had just talked with "senior staff members" at the White House and "we were likely to uncover some CIA assets or sources if we continued our investigation into the Mexican money chain." Gray said he understood this to mean that "if the FBI persisted we would uncover CIA covert operations and that the CIA had an interest in Messrs. Ogarrio and Dahlberg and in the $114,000 involved." Gray said he would handle the investigation "in a manner that would not hamper the CIA," adding that this was "a most awkward matter to come up during an election year and he would see what he could do."

What he did was to call Bates and order him to hold up his interview of Manuel Ogarrio (although he says he permitted certain other inquiries about Ogarrio and Dahlberg). For the time being, the FBI's active investigation of the money chain was halted. Indeed, the only real investigation of the telltale checks that Friday took place at CREEP headquarters, where Stans, LaRue, and Mardian were meeting with Kenneth Dahlberg, who had answered their summons to detail his role in the transaction.

But over the weekend Walters developed qualms about the whole undertaking. He checked with the agency's Latin American specialists who told him there was no way that the Watergate investigation could jeopardize any CIA operation in Mexico. And Walters repeated that conclusion when Dean summoned him to the White House on Monday morning. But Dean "pressed and pressed," Walters recalls, seeking "some way I could help him." Dean said some of the accused were "wobbling" and he asked Walters whether the CIA could pay their bail and their salaries. Walters says he told Dean:

"Mr. Dean, any attempt to involve the agency in the stifling of this affair would be a disaster. It would destroy the credibility of the agency with the Congress, with the nation. It would be a grave disservice to the President. I will not be a party to it and I am prepared to resign before I do anything that would implicate the agency in this matter."

But Dean would not give up. He summoned Walters back to the White House the next day and the day after, pressing for the CIA to "help the White House out." Walters insists he stood firm. (Curiously, while the "political" appointee resisted, the "career" man—Helms—seemed quite willing to help out. On June 28 he wrote Walters a memo saying, in part, ". . . we still adhere to the request that they [the FBI] confine themselves to the personalities already arrested or directly under suspicion and that they desist from expanding this investigation into other areas which may well, eventually, run afoul of our operations.")

Meanwhile, Gray was under heavy pressure from some of his subordinates who felt he was caving in to the White House. Warning that a "cover-up" operation was under way, they wanted to interview Ogarrio and Dahlberg. For much of that week, Gray was pinioned between countervailing forces, unable to move decisively in either direction. On the afternoon of June 28 he told Bates to go ahead with the two interviews; but hours later, after Dean called to plead "national security" again, he reversed the orders.

Finally, over the Fourth of July weekend, the discontent within the bureau became too great. Many agents were seething at Gray ("Nobody likes to work for a political hack," said one) and were leaking information to the press. Gray tried to stem the leaks, but he realized he could delay the investigation no longer. On July 5 he told Walters he would order the interviews completed unless the CIA gave him a written request to the contrary. Walters declined to discuss the matter on the telephone, but he came to see Gray at ten the next morning and told him he could not possibly write such a letter. According to Walters, he said, "I had a long association with the President and was as desirous as anyone of protecting him. I did not believe that a letter from the agency asking the FBI to lay off this investigation on the spurious grounds that it would uncover covert operations would serve the President. Such a letter in the current atmosphere of Washington would become known prior to election day and what was now a minor wound could become a mortal wound." Again, according to Walters, Gray said he would "prefer to resign" rather than suppress the investigation and "he did not see why he or I should jeopardize the integrity of our organizations to protect some middle-level White House figures who had acted imprudently. . . . He felt it important that the President should be protected from his would-be protectors." The two men parted, congratulating each other on their frankness and integrity.

The next thing Gray did was to order the Ogarrio and Dahlberg interviews carried out immediately. (Dahlberg was interviewed that very day—July 6—Ogarrio four days later.) Then he sat at his desk mulling over the conversation with Walters. "I was confused, uncertain and uneasy," he recalls. "I was concerned enough to believe that the President should be informed." So he called San Clemente and told a campaign official that he wanted to speak with Nixon about White House pressure on the Watergate matter.

Some thirty-seven minutes later, the President telephoned him. As Gray recalls the conversation, Nixon began by congratulating him on the FBI's handling of an attempted hijacking of a Pacific Southwest Airlines plane the day before, during which FBI agents had shot and killed two armed hijackers. Gray thanked the President and then "blurted out" what was on his mind. He says the conversation went like this:

GRAY: Mr. President, there's something I want to speak to you about. Dick Walters and I feel that people on your staff are trying to mortally wound you by using the CIA and FBI and by confusing the questions of CIA interest in, or not in, people the FBI wishes to interview.

(*Slight pause.*)

NIXON: Pat, you just continue to conduct your aggressive and thorough investigation.

Then the President hung up. Although Gray thought his warning had been "adequate to put him on notice," he expected Nixon to ask for more details. Yet no further inquiry came. On July 12, and again on July 28, Gray asked Walters whether he had heard from the President. Walters said he hadn't. Finally, Gray began to feel that perhaps he and Walters had been "alarmists."

Meanwhile, over at CREEP, Mitchell and his aides

were trying another method of obscuring the fatal money chain. Assuming that the FBI would eventually trace the Ogarrio and Dahlberg checks to the Nixon campaign, they began fabricating a cover story to explain what had happened to the money.

As a first step, Jeb Magruder went to Hugh Sloan. Both men agree Magruder warned that Sloan "might have a problem" with the money and might have to find some other version of what had happened. "You mean commit perjury?" Sloan asked. "You might have to," said Magruder. (Since then, Magruder has insisted that was only a casual remark, that what he really wanted from Sloan was a firm figure on the money he had given Liddy, that he wanted a figure as low as possible but that he could have lived with anything. But he says Sloan persistently refused to provide a figure—saying that he hadn't calculated it yet or that he had to talk with Stans first.) Sloan tells a very different story. He says that from the start Magruder pressed hard for a figure of $75,000–$80,000—far less than Sloan had actually given Liddy—and that he flatly refused.

On June 22 Sloan got word that two FBI men were waiting to see him. He says Fred LaRue suggested he ought to see Mitchell first. Sloan recalls that he felt that "the campaign literally at this point was falling apart before your eyes, nobody was coming up with any answers as to what was really going on. I had some very strong concerns about where all of this money had gone. I essentially asked for guidance."

Mitchell merely leaned back in his chair, took a puff on his pipe, and growled, "When the going gets tough, the tough get going."

Sloan left Mitchell's office a very angry man. Surprisingly, the FBI interview went easily: the agents were only interested in Al Baldwin's employment records. (Three days later Baldwin—the barefoot bodyguard—began talking volubly to the FBI. Granted immunity from prosecution, he became the bureau's first important informant on the Watergate operation.)

That evening, while they were all at a cocktail party on the Presidential yacht *Sequoia,* Sloan complained somewhat vaguely about the pressures on him to

Dwight Chapin and Kenneth R. Cole, Jr., Ehrlichman's assistant on the Domestic Council. Chapin asked Sloan to come to the White House at noon the next day, and Cole called on June 23 to set up a two-o'clock appointment with Ehrlichman. Sloan got little satisfaction from either man. When he told Chapin that "a tremendous problem" existed at CREEP "and something had to be done," the President's appointments secretary suggested that he was tired and should take a vacation. Trying again with Ehrlichman, Sloan said, "Someone from the outside should come in and look at the whole thing," but Ehrlichman chose to interpret his problem as a purely personal one. He offered to help Sloan find a lawyer, but said, ". . . do not tell me any details; I do not want to know. My position would have to be until after the election that I would have to take executive privilege."

Later that day, Sloan made a final report to Stans on disbursements of pre-April 7 funds, showing that payments to Liddy totaled $199,000. He gave Mardian a similar report. At Kalmbach's urging, he destroyed the cash book used to prepare the report. Then he left with his wife for a vacation in Bermuda.

By then, Sloan had become the single greatest menace to the cover-up. He was like a modest little dinghy broken loose from its mooring in a storm and threatening to punch holes in the proud hulls of some much larger but terribly vulnerable ships. It would be very difficult to show that Liddy had been given $199,000 for purely legal purposes; $40,000 yes; $80,000, perhaps; but $199,000! Panic began to set in at CREEP. Whether Sloan's act of independence stemmed from conscience, as he says, or the survival instinct, as Magruder charges, it was imperiling the entire campaign superstructure and perhaps the very re-election of Richard Nixon.

On July 5, Sloan's first working day after his vacation, Magruder invited him to have a drink at the Black Horse Tavern, a quiet restaurant at 1236 20th Street, N.W. According to Sloan, he said, "You know, we have to resolve this Liddy thing," and then suggested they go to U.S. Attorney Harold Titus and tell him

Liddy had received $40,000 or $45,000. Sloan said he would think about it, but the next morning he insisted he would, if asked, tell Titus the truth about what Liddy got. Magruder abruptly dropped the whole idea. On July 7 the increasingly disaffected Sloan talked to Kenneth W. Parkinson and Paul L. O'Brien, the two Washington attorneys who had been hired on June 22 to represent CREEP in the Watergate matter, and told *them* the full story. The lawyers didn't seem at all comfortable with the information. They urged Sloan to leave town immediately, a suggestion reinforced a few hours later by an urgent telephone call from LaRue in California. At LaRue's insistence, Sloan went to California and stayed there until July 12. When he got back, he resigned from CREEP, retained a lawyer, and went to the U.S. attorney's office to tell his story.

But the week's delay had been just long enough for the CREEP high command to refine its cover story. As early as June 20 Mitchell and his aides had discovered the full extent of the scandal which the trail of money could uncover. On that day Mardian and LaRue met with Liddy at LaRue's apartment on the third floor of Watergate West. While the usual protective radio blared, Liddy told them what he and Hunt had been up to during the past months—not only the break-ins at the Democratic National Committee but the attempted bugging of McGovern's campaign headquarters, the burglary of Dr. Fielding's office, and Hunt's expedition to hush up Dita Beard in Denver. Mardian and LaRue rushed over to Mitchell's $325,000 duplex in Watergate East and filled him in. All three men say they were appalled by the sheer scope of what Mitchell later called the "White House horrors." Something had to be done to prevent the Dynamic Duo's footprints from tracking all that dirt to the very doorstep of the Oval Office.

On June 28, CREEP cut the most embarrassing link —to Liddy himself. Two FBI agents, who had turned up Liddy's name in Martinez' address book, came to the finance committee that afternoon and asked to interview him. When he refused to answer even rudimentary questions, Stans fired him. Nobody wanted

Gordon around any more. And two days later another key link was severed when Mitchell abruptly resigned from CREEP. The White House released a letter to the President in which Mitchell said his wife had told him to choose between her and politics. Mitchell said he could no longer devote his full energies to the campaign and "still meet the one obligation which must come first: the happiness and welfare of my wife and daughter." Clark MacGregor, a former Minnesota congressman then serving as director of congressional relations, was named to succeed him.

Mitchell's concern about his wife was probably real enough: he had spent three days that week with Martha at the Westchester Country Club. But there were undoubtedly other considerations. As early as June 20 the President talked with Mitchell and that evening reported on a Dictabelt, "He is terribly chagrined that the activities of anybody attached to his committee should have been handled in such a manner, and he said that he only regretted that he had not policed all the people more effectively. . . ." Three days later Nixon asked, "Well what the hell, did Mitchell know about this?" and Haldeman replied, "I think so. I don't think he knew the details, but I think he knew." As the month ran out, it became increasingly clear that Mitchell—either because of his failure to supervise, or because of overdiligence, or simply because the burglars had been arrested with CREEP cash in their pockets—was becoming a severe embarrassment to Nixon's campaign.

On June 30, a few hours before Mitchell submitted his resignation, the President, Haldeman, and Mitchell met at the White House. Much of their discussion seems to have focused on the public-relations advantages to be gained by having Mitchell resign then for "personal reasons" rather than waiting and perhaps having to resign under direct pressure over Watergate.

HALDEMAN: Well, there maybe is another facet. The longer you wait the more risk each hour brings. You run the risk of more stuff, valid or invalid, surfacing on the Watergate caper. . . .

NIXON: Well, I'd cut the loss fast. I'd cut it fast. If we're going to do it I'd cut it fast . . . if you put it in human terms—I think the story is, you're positive rather than negative, because as I said as I was preparing to answer for this press conference . . . it'd make anybody else who asked any other question on it look like a selfish son-of-a-bitch, which I thoroughly intended them to look like. . . .

MITCHELL: (*unintelligible*) Westchester Country Club with all the sympathy in the world.

NIXON: That's great. That's great. . . .

HALDEMAN: You taking this route—people won't expect you to—be a surprise.

NIXON: No—if it's a surprise. Otherwise, you're right. It will be tied right to Watergate. . . .

Mitchell's move across the hall from CREEP to the Washington office of his old law firm probably gained him some sympathy, but it did not significantly alter his contribution to the cover-up. If anything, he had more time now to devote to the artful reconstruction of the past. For the next few weeks Mitchell, Magruder, and LaRue—sometimes joined by Mardian and Dean—met regularly in Mitchell's office to work out the story. Magruder recalls the businesslike air of those meetings: "We did not discuss the Watergate affair in terms of perjury or burglary or conspiracy. We would refer, rather, to 'handling the case' and 'making sure things don't get out of hand.'" But things often threatened to get out of hand and there were moments of urgency, even of panic. Dean says that one day, while Hurricane Agnes roared through the mid-Atlantic states, he was trying to keep the floodwaters from his doorstep. He learned that the Potomac was cresting at twenty-one feet, nine feet above his living-room floor. At that very moment, Mardian called and told him "For Christ's sake, get back here . . . this is more important than what you're doing." The CREEP officials often felt the tidal wave of Watergate was about to crest at their doorstep.

Rather quickly they recognized that they could not hope to conceal that Liddy had been authorized

$250,000—and paid $199,000—for intelligence-gathering purposes. Instead, they decided to claim that these activities had been entirely legal. To make this cover story more plausible, they took tasks that Liddy had indeed been assigned, such as surveillance of radicals planning to demonstrate at the Republican convention—but greatly exaggerated the funds paid him for such purposes so as to cover the money actually spent on the Watergate break-in. Magruder would cover about $150,000 himself by testifying he had given that much to Liddy for investigations of Jack Anderson and others. But they needed somebody else to cover the other $100,000 and to corroborate the story. Time and again they came back to Herbert Porter—because he had indeed made some payments to Liddy; because he was attractive, articulate, and would make a persuasive witness; because he was intensely loyal, a "team player," and because, everything considered, he was one of the people most likely to commit perjury for the cause.

"He's a little fish who got caught in the net," Ehrlichman recalled months later. The net was a long time aweaving. In 1946, when Bart Porter was only eight, his parents took him to a black Baptist church to hear the Republican candidate for Congress in California's 12th District. The only whites in the audience, the Porters remained after the speech to meet Dick Nixon and they talked with the young candidate for the best part of an hour. Later, Mr. Porter became a local campaign chairman and young Bart spent weekends with his father handing out Nixon leaflets in shopping centers and pasting bumper stickers on cars. Father and son worked for Nixon again in 1948 and 1960, proudly sporting Nixon buttons on their lapels. Later, Bart Porter was to say, "I felt as if I had known this man all my life—not personally, perhaps, but in spirit. I felt a deep sense of loyalty to him. I was appealed to on this basis." Porter went to the University of Southern California with Chapin, Strachan, Ziegler, and Segretti; served in the Marine Corps; and by 1970 was an executive with a small computer company in Phoenix.

One day that fall he got a call from an old USC friend in Washington, telling him that the President was coming to speak in Phoenix and asking him to help with the arrangements. Porter served as an advance man for the strident Phoenix speech in which Nixon called the demonstrators "violent thugs," the speech which was rebroadcast with such disastrous results on election eve. But that wasn't held against young Bart. He had impressed the President's men, and a few days later he was asked to come to Washington. He didn't find the decision difficult. "To begin with," he recalls, "I had been in love with the city for years—the exhilaration, the feeling of excitement, the sense of history, the aura of mystery. Things happened that I wanted to know about." Porter spent his first few months in Herb Klein's communications office, helping to "sell" the President's programs. Then he moved over to CREEP, where he became director of scheduling, with particular responsibility for the "surrogate" speakers program, in which dozens of cabinet officers, senators, and congressmen crisscrossed the country speaking for the President while he tended to the nation's business. Although Porter was disliked by several White House aides—among them Dwight Chapin and Larry Higby—he got along with Jeb Magruder. Their wives and children saw a lot of each other and the two families went on trips together. But Magruder sized up his friend with cool realism: "Porter was extremely ambitious, both socially and politically. Unlike most of the young men at the White House and CREEP, he cared a lot about Georgetown dinner parties and the Washington social scene. And we were all well aware that Porter had a consuming desire to get ahead in the Nixon administration. He'd been in the White House and gotten a taste of the limousines and all the other amenities, and he wanted eagerly to have them for his own . . . and knew that his future in the administration might depend on the kind of support I gave him."

On June 29 Magruder called Porter into his office and told him that Liddy had been fired, assured him that nobody else in CREEP had any connection with the Watergate break-in, but said, "We still have a problem about the money." Specifically, he asked whether Porter would be willing to tell the FBI that $100,000 had been paid to Liddy for infiltrating radical groups that could endanger the safety of Porter's "surrogate" speakers. Porter agreed that such a program could easily have cost $100,000 if ten college students had been hired as informants for ten months at $500 a month and $500 expenses, each. Without much further ado, he agreed to tell this story to investigators. And he did—to the FBI in July, to a grand jury in August, and later to a jury.* Even if they could make the investigators believe that the payments to Liddy had been intended for purely legal purposes, Liddy had used them for quite illegal purposes. They also had to persuade the investigators that Liddy and Hunt had taken the money and gone off on their own—on some kind of weird ex-agents' binge—to commit the Watergate and other burglaries. They had to establish that no other ranking member of CREEP or the White House knew anything about such bizarre activities.

At one point early on, Magruder volunteered to "take the heat," to tell the investigators that he had authorized the break-in. For a time, Ehrlichman thought that was quite a nice idea. But soon everybody realized it wouldn't work. Magruder didn't have the authority to give Liddy the money he got. Once the stain reached Magruder it would lead to Mitchell and then to the President. So the watchword of the cover-up became: "The buck stops with Liddy."

To make sure the Watergate investigators didn't get beyond Liddy, the President's men had to monitor and—if possible—control the investigations. Almost

---

*Porter eventually pleaded guilty to a charge of making false statements to the FBI, was sentenced to thirty days in prison, and served twenty-seven days.

from the start, they tunneled deep into the supposedly sacrosanct FBI and grand jury inquiries, extracting chunks of valuable information and exercising restraint over the investigations. Dean later told the President, "I was totally aware what the bureau was doing at all times. I was totally aware what the grand jury was doing. I knew what witnesses were going to be called. I knew what they were going to be asked."

One of the most successful tunneling operations managed to restrict severely the information the FBI got from Kathy Chenow, the former secretary to the Plumbers. The FBI had stumbled across Miss Chenow in checking out the phone numbers listed for Howard Hunt in Barker's and Martinez' address books: Hunt's private phone in the Plumbers' office was listed by the telephone company in Miss Chenow's name. She was vacationing in England in late June, and when agents called on her former roommate, the roommate alerted David Young. Young in turn warned Dean that Miss Chenow, if caught off guard by the FBI, might disclose a lot about the Plumbers' operations, perhaps including the burglary of Dr. Fielding's office. On June 28 Dean called Pat Gray and asked him—on the now familiar "national security" grounds—to postpone the Chenow interview. Gray promptly agreed. Dean then explained the situation to Ehrlichman and suggested that someone fly to England and caution Miss Chenow not to reveal any of the Plumbers' operations. With Ehrlichman's approval, Dean dispatched his assistant, Fred Fielding, who caught the first plane, found the astonished secretary in London, and brought her home. In Washington, Dean and Fielding briefed her carefully for her FBI interview—which they both attended.

Indeed, by then Dean and Fielding were sitting in on all FBI interviews of White House personnel questioned about Watergate—a most unusual procedure. Dean had simply informed Gray that he would do this in his official capacity as counsel to the President and Gray had acquiesced. And CREEP's attorneys, Parkinson and O'Brien, did the same for virtually all campaign personnel. Not surprisingly, their very presence proved intimidating. An FBI summary report that summer said several CREEP staffers had "contacted the FBI Washington Field Office and requested to be further interviewed away from committee headquarters and without the knowledge of committee officials. These persons advised that the presence of the attorney during the interview prevented them from being completely candid." But despite FBI complaints the practice persisted.

The lawyers couldn't accompany their clients into the grand jury room, but they found other methods of frustrating the work of the jury, which began hearing evidence on the Watergate break-in during late June. Dean persuaded Henry Petersen, the assistant attorney general now in overall charge of the Watergate prosecution, that White House staff members should not have to appear in person before the jury because of the harmful publicity they would attract if newsmen saw them entering the federal courthouse. So the prosecutors—Principal Assistant U.S. Attorney Earl J. Silbert and his colleagues, Seymour Glanzer and Donald E. Campbell—interviewed White House officials under oath in Petersen's office at the Justice Department, again a most unusual procedure which deprived the jurors of a chance to assess the witnesses' credibility at first hand. Krogh, Young, Colson, and Colson's secretary, Joan Hall, were heard this way.

When Maurice Stans was subpoenaed in late July to appear before the grand jury, he flew into a rage, demanding that he get the same consideration as White House officials. Dean relayed this demand to Petersen, but Petersen said the grand jury wanted to hear Stans directly. When the President heard about this, Ehrlichman recalls, he said that "a man who was a former cabinet officer and so on should not be subjected to that kind of a situation." So Ehrlichman called Petersen, complained that Silbert was "acting like a local prosecutor"—which, of course, is exactly what he was—and told him to stop "harassing" Stans. When Petersen again demurred, Ehrlichman complained to Kleindienst that Petersen "refused to follow instructions." The next day Kleindienst, Petersen, and Silbert met and decided to let Stans testify privately at the Justice Department—which he did on August 2.

But all this was preliminary skirmishing, the contestants feeling each other out for the deadly combat that was to follow. The decisive question was this: Could the White House hold the line at Liddy and prevent the prosecutors from piercing their cover story and uncovering the role of Magruder, Mitchell, Dean, and others? For the time being, the burglars, Hunt, and Liddy were holding firm. Therefore, the struggle turned increasingly on the grand jury appearance of Magruder, the next man up the pecking order from Liddy.

Magruder's first appearance before the grand jury came on July 5, but it was brief and rather perfunctory. If the White House and CREEP were still framing their story, the prosecutors were still feeling their way. Moreover, Magruder had not yet been interviewed by the FBI. So, on this occasion, the prosecutors limited themselves to organizational questions.

But the showdown was approaching. Later that week, three FBI agents came to see Magruder and started probing at crucial links of the "money chain." In turn, Magruder and Porter gave the finishing touches to their cover story and, at Parkinson's request, put it in writing. In early August the prosecutors informed CREEP's lawyers that Magruder was officially a target of their investigation, a warning they were required to give. If the White House had not known before, it knew then just what Magruder's role had been. Dean, Mitchell, and Ehrlichman had talked about it early in August and Ehrlichman had reported back to Nixon. Magruder says Mitchell asked him to tell the grand jury the "limited role" Mitchell played in the campaign and the major role Magruder played. Not surprisingly, Magruder began to feel cornered, fearing that he might yet be made the scapegoat for the whole operation. He knew that Sloan had given his full story to the grand jury —including the allegation that Magruder had asked him to commit perjury. And he knew that damaging material was coming to the FBI from several female employees of the finance committee (among them, Judith Hoback, an assistant to Sloan, whom Dean described as a disgruntled Democrat).

But the President's lawyers had a pipeline into that material, too—through confidential FBI reports on the investigation. Shortly after the break-in, Dean asked Kleindienst whether he could see such reports, known in the bureau as FD 302s. Kleindienst refused, but Dean simply made an end run around the attorney general to Pat Gray. On July 28 Gray gave Dean eighty-two of these reports, which Dean shared with Parkinson, O'Brien, and Mardian, who used them to brief officials before their FBI interviews or grand jury appearances.

Magruder's second grand jury appearance was set for August 16 and a preliminary session with the prosecutors for August 15. On the fourteenth, Mitchell went through his testimony with him for half an hour. The next morning Dean rehearsed him meticulously, firing the toughest questions he could think of, particularly on the money and Liddy's job at CREEP. All this preparation left Magruder in good shape to handle the prosecutor's questions. He had the answers when he needed them and when he didn't he was beautifully vague. Later, Earl Silbert summarized Magruder's effective line in this fashion:

Q. Well, did you get any accounting from Liddy for this two-hundred-and-fifty-thousand-dollar authorization?

A. Not really.

Q. Why not?

A. He was the expert in these matters. I was interested in advertising. That was my skill. If you ask me about advertising, how money was spent, I kept close tabs on that because I know and I am familiar with it. But investigations, intelligence, I don't know anything about that. That was Mr. Liddy's expertise or area of expertise and he and I didn't get along, I was afraid of him, we operated on a different premise, we didn't communicate that well, and two hundred and fifty thousand dollars was not that important to me. I was dealing with thirty-five million dollars, ten million for advertising. . . .

Silbert recalls that he found the vagueness "disturbing" but says, "We had nothing substantive to counteract it, to show that it was wrong, to show it was false or it was inaccurate."

Magruder left the jury room feeling that he had given a "successful performance." The next day Dean got a call from Higby who said that Haldeman wanted to know how Magruder had done. So Dean telephoned Petersen and Petersen called Silbert. According to Petersen, Silbert said Magruder was "an articulate young man who made a good appearance, good witness in his own behalf, but nobody believes the story about the money." According to Dean, Petersen reported a few hours later that Magruder had "made it through by the skin of his teeth." When he relayed this to Haldeman, the President's chief of staff was "very pleased because this, of course, meant that the investigation would not go beyond Liddy." Magruder was pleased too. He and LaRue celebrated that night by getting "roaring drunk" at Billy Martin's Carriage House Restaurant in Georgetown.

But the celebrations were short-lived. In the last week of August the grand jury subpoenaed Magruder's office diary and indicated it would summon him to testify again. This stirred fresh panic at CREEP because the diary's entries for January 27 and February 4 showed something like "AG's office—w/Dean and Liddy." These would link Liddy directly to Mitchell, breaching the crucial Liddy defense line.

When Magruder, Dean, and Mitchell conferred, they briefly considered erasing the pencil entries for those days, but dropped the idea when they realized the FBI would have means of detecting such erasures. Ultimately, they hit on another scheme. Magruder would testify that the January 27 meeting had been canceled at the last minute and rescheduled for February 4, when they had introduced Liddy to Mitchell and discussed the new campaign finance law. Magruder says Dean asked at one point whether he couldn't be removed from the meeting altogether, but Magruder said that wouldn't work because too many people knew he had been there.

At noon on September 13 Magruder, Dean, and Mitchell met once again in Mitchell's office to rehearse this story. An hour and a half later Magruder made his third appearance before the grand jury. He sailed through; his neat little story went virtually unchallenged.

Two days later the grand jury handed down indictments for conspiracy, burglary, and violation of federal wiretapping laws against seven men: Barker, Martinez, Sturgis, Gonzalez, McCord, Hunt, and Liddy. John W. Hushen, the Justice Department's director of public information, said the investigation into the Watergate case was over. "We have absolutely no evidence to indicate that any others should be charged," he said.

That afternoon Nixon and Haldeman met with Dean, who had done so much to implement the White House "containment" policy. As Dean walked into the Oval Office, the conversation went like this:

NIXON: Well, you had quite a day today, didn't you. You got, uh, Watergate, uh, on the way, huh?

DEAN: Quite a three months.

HALDEMAN: How did it all end up?

DEAN: I think we can say "Well" at this point. The press is playing it just as we expect. . . .

HALDEMAN: Five indicted . . .

DEAN: Plus two White House aides.

HALDEMAN: Plus, plus the White House former guy and all that. That's good. That takes the edge of whitewash really—which—that was the thing Mitchell kept saying that—

PRESIDENT: Yeah.

HALDEMAN:—that to those in the country, Liddy and, and, uh, Hunt are big men.

DEAN: That's right.

PRESIDENT: Yeah. They're White House aides.

DEAN: That's right.

HALDEMAN: And maybe that— Yeah, maybe that's good.

Later in the conversation, they congratulated themselves on keeping the President free of any taint during
his re-election campaign.

DEAN: . . . certainly it had no effect on you. That's
the good thing.

HALDEMAN: It really hasn't.

NIXON: (*unintelligible*).

HALDEMAN: No, it hasn't. It has been kept away
from the White House almost completely and from the
President totally. The only tie to the White House has
been the Colson effort they keep trying to haul in.

DEAN: And now, of course—

HALDEMAN:—that's falling apart.

Indeed, they were so confident now they could barely contain their contempt for the whole investigation, which Dean reported had been larger than the
one conducted after John Kennedy's assassination.

HALDEMAN: . . . Isn't that ridiculous though?

NIXON: What is?

HALDEMAN: This silly-ass damn thing.

NIXON: Yeah.

HALDEMAN: That kind of resources against—

NIXON: Yeah for Christ's sake (*unintelligible*).

HALDEMAN: Who the hell cares?

NIXON: Goldwater put it in context, he said "Well,
for Christ's sake, everybody bugs everybody else. We
know that."

And the President was feeling so cheerful that when
the conversation was interrupted by a call from Clark
MacGregor, he signed off with a jaunty quip:

". . . get a good night's sleep and don't bug anybody
without asking me. Okay?"

John Dean undoubtedly deserved the President's congratulations for holding the Liddy Line; but many people feel he should share the credit with two men from the Justice Department: Henry Petersen and Earl Silbert.

Certainly, Petersen seems to have shown undue deference to the White House. As early as June 19 or 20, Dean says, he told Kleindienst and Petersen that "I did not know what would happen if the investigation led into the White House, but that I suspected that the chances of re-electing the President would be severely damaged." A few minutes later, he told Petersen, "I did not think the White House could withstand a wide-open investigation." Petersen does not recall those words, but he remembers "some concern about this ought not to be an excuse in a political year to run a general probe of the White House." And, he says, "I had no problem agreeing with that. I certainly didn't conceive the occurrence . . . as an excuse for me to run a general investigation of the White House and all its activities. I assured them there would be no fishing expedition as far as White House activities were concerned." He seemed to understand the White House problems quite well when he permitted the White House officials to testify privately rather than before the grand jury. And he steered the investigation along a very narrow path. Dean told the President that Petersen had sought to "make sure that the investigation was narrowed down to the very, very fine criminal thing, which was a break for us." And Petersen concedes he told Silbert, "Keep your eye on the mark . . . we're not investigating the whole damn political thing."

Specifically, the initial investigation largely bypassed two seemingly important aspects of White House activity: Don Segretti's dirty-tricks operation, and Herb Kalmbach's fund-raising and dispensing. A few days after the break-in, the FBI traced some of Hunt's calls to Segretti, who immediately alerted Chapin and Strachan.

They put him in touch with Dean, who briefed him on how to handle the FBI interview. In interviews on June 26 and 28 Segretti managed to avoid mentioning Strachan, Chapin, or Kalmbach. Following those interviews, Dean says he explained to Petersen the embarrassment that could be caused by linking Segretti to any of those people and Petersen said he did not believe the prosecutors would need to get into those areas before the grand jury. (Silbert recalls getting a telephone call from Petersen in which the assistant attorney general mentioned both Segretti and Kalmbach.) Indeed, when Segretti appeared before the grand jury on August 22, the prosecutors asked no questions "in that area," and only a curious juror forced him to reveal Chapin's and Kalmbach's roles in recruiting and paying him. But Silbert apparently did not lend much significance to these revelations about the President's appointments secretary and the President's lawyer. His attention was riveted on the burglary and, he later explained, "None of Segretti's activities were related to the Watergate bugging and burglary."

Even on the Watergate burglary itself, Silbert, Glanzer, and Campbell—and the FBI investigation team under Angelo Lano, whose efforts Silbert directed—curiously failed to follow some important leads. Although FBI agents had supposedly conducted a thorough search of the Democratic National Committee offices right after the break-in, they failed to detect the taps on the telephones used by Larry O'Brien's secretary and by Spencer Oliver. Even after Baldwin told the agents about them on July 10, no effort was made to retrieve them. The tap on O'Brien's phone wasn't discovered until April 1973. The Democrats themselves discovered the Oliver tap on September 13, 1972, when his secretary heard a "crackling" sound on the line and a telephone company repairman was called. The tap was removed that evening by the FBI, which for some reason waited more than a month before testing it and discovering that it transmitted on the frequency on which Baldwin said he had picked up the tapped conversations. Instead, the FBI said it regarded the wiretapping as a separate offense unrelated to the burglary. Justice Department officials even intimated that the Democrats had placed the tap themselves to further embarrass the Republicans and the FBI launched an extensive investigation along those lines. (In his September 15 conversation with the President, Dean reported this investigation and then chortled, "If we can find that the DNC planted that, the whole story is going to—the whole—just will reverse.")

There were other curious omissions. In the first days after the break-in, Silbert did not ask the court for a search warrant for McCord's house. He has said since that "mere suspicion is not enough to obtain a search warrant. We had no specific grounds necessary to ask a magistrate for such a warrant." By July 10 he had those grounds, for Baldwin had told the FBI that he trucked all the electronic equipment from Howard Johnson's to McCord's house, but even then Silbert sought no warrant. He has argued since that by then McCord had been released on bail and undoubtedly had hidden the material. McCord had, indeed, buried the equipment in the woods (along with wiretap logs, $18,000 in $100 bills, carbon copies of wiretap logs, a letter from Mitchell to McCord, and notes mentioning Mitchell, Dean, and Magruder meetings on the burglary). But a thorough search might have turned up some of it—or perhaps some other incriminating evidence that McCord, Mrs. McCord, or CIA operative Lee Pennington, Jr., had failed to destroy. Only after the indictments were handed down in September did Silbert threaten to indict McCord's wife as an accessory to the burglary. With that, McCord dug up the equipment and handed it over.

Perhaps more important, neither the FBI nor Silbert interviewed Robert Reisner, Magruder's administrative assistant, during this first phase of the investigation. Since Magruder was supposed to be a major target of the investigation, this seems a most peculiar omission. And it was a critical one. For Reisner knew Magruder reported on Gemstone projects to Mitchell and he knew that Mitchell and Magruder had approved the Liddy plan at their Key Biscayne meeting in March. Silbert's explanation seems a lame one: that Reisner was never interviewed "because his name was never brought to our attention from any of the innumerable interviews conducted by the FBI at CREEP, in the grand jury testimony of CREEP personnel, or from any other leads that developed." And the prosecutor adds that if Reisner really possessed so much information "there was nothing of which we are aware preventing him from coming forward and disclosing this information to the FBI, grand jury, or the prosecutors."

Finally, some critics wonder why the prosecutors didn't grant immunity to one of the defendants—presumably McCord—to get information on higher-ups. When asked about this, Petersen merely denounced McCord: "He was no witness! He's the biggest phony of the bunch." Silbert spells it out a little more: "We did consider it [immunity] very soon for McCord, but he was a basically uncooperative witness. We concluded that Gordon Liddy was in charge of the operation and we had grave reservations that McCord had any special knowledge because he reported to Liddy." Later, in October, the prosecutors did make an offer of partial immunity to McCord, but he rejected it.

Silbert says that from the start he believed other more important figures were involved in the case but that the indictments were brought against the seven underlings because "we ran up against a stone wall in trying to get the cooperation of Gordon Liddy, James McCord, and Howard Hunt. We got turned down stone-cold. We couldn't get any insiders."

Even then, he insists, they had a plan. The prosecutors knew that the closer a man gets to the clang of the prison gate, the more willing he is to talk. Silbert says that throughout that fall and winter they were still looking to crack one of the seven. "Our strategy was to indict, convict, and then immunize the conspirators so that we could reconvene the grand jury and get more information."

Silbert didn't know that by then the White House had taken steps designed to assure that none of the defendants would provide such information. In the ancient tradition of clandestine operations, someone had evidently assured the burglars and their chiefs before the break-in that they would be "taken care of" if they were caught. Many people associated with the Watergate affair have spoken of such a "commitment," although nobody seems sure just who made it. But when Liddy met with Mardian and LaRue on the evening of June 20, he wasted no time in reminding them that "certain commitments had been made and subsequently passed by him to the other people involved" regarding bail, legal expenses, and maintenance of their families. Mardian and LaRue promptly passed this message on to Mitchell. Three nights later Mardian—with Mitchell's approval—suggested that the CIA might provide the men's bail and salaries, and Dean persistently but unsuccessfully explored this proposal with General Walters.

When the CIA refused to participate in any such scheme, Mitchell turned to CREEP's most faithful and productive source of cash. He asked Dean to see whether the White House would authorize use of Kalmbach to raise the money. (Kalmbach had resigned as deputy finance chairman of Nixon's campaign on April 7, the day the new campaign law went into effect, and Haldeman and Ehrlichman had promised to protect him from further demands by Stans or Mitchell.) On June 23, Dean recalls, Mitchell drew him aside and said that Ehrlichman, in particular, "should be very interested and anxious to accommodate the needs of these men." Dean assumed he was referring to "activities that they [Hunt and Liddy] had conducted in the past that related to the White House, such as the Ellsberg break-in." Indeed, Mitchell feared that if the "White House horrors" became public knowledge they would jeopardize Nixon's re-election, and he has testified that this fear above all led him to support the cash payments to the defendants. He chose to ignore a more private fear —that Hunt and Liddy might have exposed his own approval and supervision of the Gemstone program. But clearly the money was more than just bail or legal and living expenses. It was designed to put wraps on the White House horrors, the CREEP horrors, and any other horrors that might be lurking around the corner. It was hush money.

Haldeman and Ehrlichman evidently feared the horrors too, for they promptly approved an emergency appeal to Kalmbach. On June 28 Dean telephoned him in Newport Beach and asked him to come to Washington immediately for "a very important assignment." Kalmbach caught the "red eye" from Los Angeles, arrived just after dawn on the twenty-ninth, and checked into the Statler Hilton. Without pausing for sleep, he called Dean and offered to come right over to his office. As Kalmbach recalls it, Dean replied, "No, you are at the Statler. I am here at the Executive Office Building. Why don't we both start walking and meet in front of the Hay-Adams Hotel?"

When they got there, Kalmbach suggested they have coffee in the hotel's comfortable dining room, but again Dean demurred. "No," he said, "let's just walk in the park."

They began to stroll through Lafayette Park, across the street from the White House. Dean put his foot up on a bench and suggested that Kalmbach do the same, warning him with gestures that somebody might be watching. So the President's public lawyer and the President's private lawyer stood there with their feet on a park bench in full view of the President's official residence and discussed payoffs to the burglars. Only that wasn't how Dean put it. He said, "We would like to have you raise funds for the legal defense of these defendants and for the support of their families," an entirely proper and legal procedure, he assured him. Kalmbach asked Dean why a public committee couldn't be formed to raise the money, and Dean said there wasn't time. And he stressed the importance of "absolute secrecy," warning that if the payments became known they might be misinterpreted and thus jeopardize the re-election campaign. He told Kalmbach "everything I knew about the case at the time" and then suggested that Tony Ulasewicz be called in to deliver the cash.

Kalmbach knew Ulasewicz. They had first met almost exactly two years before, when Kalmbach agreed to channel him cash for his White House gumshoeing. After the rejection of Caulfield's Operation Sandwedge, Ulasewicz had been phased out of White House activities. But Kalmbach knew he was "someone that could be trusted," so he called him in New York and told him to come back to Washington for another "special assignment." Meanwhile, Kalmbach called Maurice Stans, told him he would need some cash, and within hours Stans brought $75,100 in $100 bills to the hotel. He and LaRue also met, agreed that the defendants should be reached through their attorneys, and arranged to deal with each other in the future through the code name "Bradford."

The following day Ulasewicz arrived from New York and the two old associates worked out a procedure which Kalmbach later described as "a James Bond scenario." They decided to communicate through aliases—"Mr. Rivers" for Ulasewicz, "Mr. Novak" for Kalmbach (to be on the safe side, they agreed on some back-up aliases too: "Tom Kane," "John Ferguson," and "Tommy Smith"). Howard Hunt would be "the Writer" and his wife "the Writer's Wife." If Kalmbach or Ulasewicz wanted to speak to each other, one was to telephone and give his alias, then the other would go to a predesignated telephone booth and await a call-back after half an hour. When they had completed their arrangements, Ulasewicz put the $75,100 in a hotel laundry bag and took it back to New York. From then on, the money was known as "the laundry," and the vault in which Ulasewicz kept it was called "the icebox." (Kalmbach would ask, "Do you have sufficient laundry in the icebox to take care of this?")

But delivering the laundry did not prove easy. Twice, on Kalmbach's instructions, Ulasewicz called

Washington attorneys who might serve as intermediaries, asking "what the script for the play would cost and how much the actors wanted." But neither lawyer—Douglas Caddy or Paul O'Brien—wanted any part in this play. Ulasewicz got tired of carrying his "cookies" around wrapped in a paper bag tied with some old string. Then, some days later, Mrs. Howard Hunt went to O'Brien's office and demanded to know what was being done for her husband. When O'Brien said he didn't know, Mrs. Hunt said there were "serious implications" in this for the White House and "people over there better get on the ball."

On July 3, after weeks as a quasi-fugitive in Los Angeles and Chicago, Hunt returned to Washington, made contact with a former high-ranking Justice Department lawyer named William O. Bittman, and arranged to meet with the prosecutors (taking the Fifth Amendment on most questions). By this time Liddy had assured Hunt that "everything would be taken care of 'Company style.'" "The Company" is a common euphemism for the CIA, and Hunt assumed that this meant the White House would handle the case as the CIA would in similar circumstances: "Heroic efforts to right the situation, financing legal defense if it came to that and certainly income replacement for those of us who had lost or would lose our jobs as a result of the unflattering publicity."

Now, with Parkinson's assurance that it was all right to talk to "Rivers," Bittman told the White House emissary that he wanted a down payment of $25,000 on his legal fees. On July 6 Ulasewicz placed the money in a brown envelope on a shelf by a bank of telephone booths in the lobby of Bittman's office building. Then he called Bittman from one of the booths and watched while the lawyer came down and collected the money. Ulasewicz stationed himself across the lobby to make sure that nobody else picked up the envelope. If someone had, Ulasewicz later testified, "I would separate them very quickly from the envelope. I would obtain it in some manner."

In mid-July, on Kalmbach's instructions, Ulasewicz

called Hunt and went through his spiel about a "script" and "actors' fees," but Hunt refused to play. Through intermediaries, it was agreed that Mrs. Hunt should handle all future dealings with Ulasewicz. One evening Ulasewicz called her and told her to go to a phone booth in nearby Potomac Village, where he would call her a half-hour later. In the second call he told her to get an estimate of monthly living costs and lawyers' fees from all seven defendants. So she called Liddy, McCord, and Barker (representing the Miami delegation) and relayed the estimates to McCord at an appointed time the following day from another phone booth. According to Hunt, Ulasewicz then said, "Well, let's multiply that by five to cut down on the number of deliveries." Mrs. Hunt asked him why "five," and he said it was an easy number for him to deal with. But when his wife told him this, Hunt immediately noted that five months of payoffs would carry the cover-up safely through the election.

Judging by his testimony, Ulasewicz didn't much care for "the Writer's Wife." He makes her sound like a strident, constantly complaining yenta who "injected herself continually and early, feeling that I would pass a message on . . . no matter how many times I would try to stop her she would continue in with that. . . . She started with herself, the fact that she had lost her own job due to this, and that should be taken into consideration, and that hospitalization and whatever benefits might be there, that had been lost . . . that Mrs. Liddy was undergoing some psychiatric treatment, or might be undergoing, and that she was a schoolteacher and that she probably would not be able to work as a result of this." He says she warned him that "if Mrs. Liddy goes, she might blow everything," the entire Watergate story.

But ultimately he got the five-month budget which included $3000 a month in salary for Hunt, McCord, and Liddy; $700 a month "family support" for Barker, Martinez, Gonzalez, and Sturgis; a separate $23,000 for Barker, comprising $10,000 bail, $10,000 "under the table," and $3000 for "other expenses"; $25,000 apiece to cover the legal fees of Hunt, McCord, Liddy, and Barker; $10,000 each for the other three defendants' legal fees, and $5000 for Mrs. Hunt's personal expenses, including air fares to deliver the money to "the people down South." In all, the budget came to nearly $450,000.

This was an imposing sum, far exceeding the meager $50,100 he had left, but Ulasewicz quickly arranged a "down payment" of $40,000 to Mrs. Hunt. On July 17 he left the money, stuffed in a blue plastic airlines travel bag, in a locker at Washington's National Airport and Scotch-taped the key underneath the coin box of a phone booth across from the Northwest Orient ticket counter. He watched as Mrs. Hunt (who had told him she would wear her hair pulled straight back in a "pony tail") arrived on the prearranged dot of noon, found the key, and picked up the money. In the following days, Mrs. Hunt distributed the cash to Liddy, McCord, and "the people down South."

On July 19 Kalmbach came back to Washington, picked up $40,000 from LaRue (part of the finance committee's $81,000 cash surplus that Stans had given to LaRue), and delivered it to Ulasewicz at the Regency Hotel in New York. On the same trip, Dean told him they were virtually out of cash in Washington and asked him to start raising money for the Watergate defendants. At this, Kalmbach began getting nervous about the propriety of what he was doing. He wanted reassurance from someone at the White House. On July 26 he met with John Ehrlichman and their conversation, as he recalls it, went something like this:

KALMBACH: John, I'm looking you right in the eye and I know Jeanne and your family, and you know Barbara and my family, and you know that my family and my reputation mean everything to me. And you've got to tell me here and now that this is something that is proper that I should go forward with.

EHRLICHMAN: Herb, this is proper. It's for those fellows and their attorneys' fees and their families. Herb, you are to go forward with this.

But then he added that, although the operation was proper and legal, it had to be carried out with the utmost secrecy. If the press learned about it, Ehrlichman said, "They'd have our heads in their laps."

For some reason, this satisfied Kalmbach. He went back to work, relaying $30,000 more from LaRue to Ulasewicz, then raising $75,000 in new money from Thomas V. Jones, chairman of the Northrop Corporation. (Jones thought this was merely an additional contribution to the Nixon campaign, part of the $150,000 in Northrop's corporate gifts for which the corporation has been convicted and fined.) Kalmbach told Ulasewicz to come to California and collect the $75,000. On August 3 he picked him up at the Orange County Airport and drove him a few miles until they found a safe spot where Kalmbach could hand over the packet of cash. By this time Ulasewicz was brooding too about all the secrecy and the increasing payments. "Something here is not kosher," he warned, but it seemed to Ulasewicz that his Yiddish vernacular "went a little over his head." So he tried again with a bit of Ebbetts Field *patois:* "It's definitely not your ball game, Mr. Kalmbach." But even then the Polish cop wasn't sure he was getting through to the sun-tanned lawyer. "He was a world apart from me," he recalls. "I being a policeman from New York and him the President's attorney, it is difficult to explain to a man of that stature what you are thinking and have on your mind."

Despite his multiplying doubts, Ulasewicz kept up his cash-delivery service that summer, lugging packets of $100 bills onto the Eastern shuttle between New York and Washington, ducking in and out of phone booths, his bus conductor's changemaker clanking with change. His favorite delivery technique remained the locker-and-phone-booth gambit at the National Airport. On July 31 he left $8000 there for Liddy (after Liddy assured him on the telephone, "I am a stand-up guy. I'm all right and you can ask any of my friends and they will assure you that"); the same day, $43,000 for Mrs. Hunt; on August 9, $18,000 for Howard Hunt, subbing for his "indisposed" wife.

After picking up his money that day, Hunt was so

moved that he wrote a short note to Chuck Colson, ending, "Let me say that I profoundly regret your being dragged into the case through association with me, superficial and occasional though the association was. What small satisfaction I can dredge up at the moment is the knowledge that I was not responsible for the affair or its outcome. All this pales, of course, beside the overwhelming importance of re-electing the President and you may be confident that I will do all that is required of me toward that end"—which seemed to promise exquisite discretion until Nixon was back in the White House for four more years.

Colson appreciated Hunt's delicacy and asked his secretary, Joan Hall, to telephone him and pass on this message: "Mr. Colson received the letter and obviously cannot be in touch with him. As soon as the election is over, Mr. Colson plans to be in touch with Mr. Hunt and will do everything he can to help him on a personal basis. As far as Mr. Colson is concerned, he is really royally angry at whoever used Mr. Hunt—if in fact he was used. Mr. Colson said he will make it a crusade in life to get even with the s.o.b. who got Mr. Hunt involved in the matter. Mr. Colson appreciates enormously Mr. Hunt's loyalty and feels terrible at what happened. He is sorry he ever recommended Mr. Hunt for a job at the White House, but that Mr. Hunt should not be discouraged because he is positive it would turn out all right." When Miss Hall read him the message, Hunt said he would probably go to prison, but "my lips are sealed."

On September 18 Ulasewicz made his final cash delivery to the defendants—$53,500 for Mrs. Hunt.* That same day, on Kalmbach's instructions, he left his remaining $29,900 for LaRue on a ledge in the lobby of the Howard Johnson Motor Lodge, the same motel which had served as the Watergate burglars' listening post. For, by then, Kalmbach had decided he could no longer participate in what he now realized was "an illegal activity." On August 29 he advised Dean and

---

*Ulasewicz, who failed to report his income from Kalmbach, was indicated for filing fraudulent income-tax returns in 1971 and 1972.

LaRue of his decision. On September 21 he met both men in Dean's office. From his wallet he took a small slip of paper on which he had written an accounting of receipts and disbursements ($220,000 taken in, $187,500 paid to the defendants). He read the figures to LaRue, who was to take over the assignment. Then they all watched solemnly as Kalmbach burned the slip in an ashtray on Dean's desk.

As soon as the financial wand was passed from Kalmbach to LaRue, the Hunts began complaining that the "commitments" were not being kept. Hunt's attorney, Bittman, relayed these complaints repeatedly to Parkinson, the CREEP attorney, during clandestine meetings in parked cars and at an art gallery. Parkinson checked with Dean, who—with an eye on the approaching elections—told Parkinson to assure Bittman that the commitments would be honored. Finally, on Mitchell's instruction, LaRue flew to Key Biscayne on October 12 and picked up a sum variously described as "between $25,000 and $30,000" and "about $50,000" from Bebe Rebozo—half of which was allocated to Lee Nunn, the Republican senatorial candidate in Kentucky and half to the Watergate defendants. On October 20, using the alias Baker, LaRue arranged to pass $20,000 on to Bittman. This time the delivery was more straightforward—a messenger merely brought the cash to Bittman's office in a package marked "personal and confidential."

Hunt happened to be in Bittman's office that afternoon and was angered when he saw that the package contained "far less than what was owed my attorney and . . . nothing for family support for myself or for Liddy, McCord, or the Miami men." Two days later Dorothy Hunt called Joan Hall at home to say: "I am sorry to have to bother you but there is no one else to call. . . . There are commitments that have not been met . . . all of this is creating a terrible amount of frustration. I cannot go through regular contacts at the committee to find out an answer. They kept saying I would receive a telephone call and I sat by the phone every day since the first of September. I received not one call. This makes for a very bad situation. Everyone wants to hold firm, but——"

Despite the grumblings, the defendants did hold firm. The cover-up held together. And, on November 7, Richard M. Nixon was re-elected President of the United States over George McGovern with 60.7 per cent of the vote—second in history to Lyndon Johnson's 61.1-percent landslide in 1964. Nixon's numerical margin—47,165,234 to 29,168,110—was the greatest in history. True to John Mitchell's Southern Strategy, Nixon carried the entire South. Indeed, he carried the entire North and West and all the East too except Massachusetts and the District of Columbia. It was an awesome reward for CREEP's mighty labors, a stunning personal vindication for Richard Nixon. In his election-night statement, Nixon called it "one of the great political victories of all time."

Nixon's re-election hardly reassured the seven Watergate defendants. Quite the contrary. Now that the President was safely back in office for four more years, they feared he would have much less concern about what they might disclose and therefore little reason to assist them. But the new atmosphere cut both ways, for it freed the defendants from the pre-election constraints. On November 13 Hunt telephoned Colson's office for the first time in months. The still cautious Colson had a secretary tell him to call back at noon the next day. On the fourteenth, after congratulations on the election results and Colson's self-serving insistence that he knew nothing about the Watergate affair and didn't want to know (he was taping the call), the conversation went like this:

HUNT: The reason I called you was . . . because of commitments that were made to all of us at the onset, have not been kept. And there's a great deal of unease and concern on the part of seven defendants and possibly, well I'm quite sure, me least of all. But there's a great deal of financial expense here that has not been covered and what we've been getting has been coming in very minor dribs and drabs. And Parkinson, who's been the go-between with my attorney, doesn't seem to be very effective and we're now reaching a point at which . . .

COLSON: Okay. You've told me that—don't tell me any more. . . .

HUNT: . . . and I thought that you would want to know that this thing must not break apart, uh, for foolish reasons.

COLSON: I agree. Yeah. Oh no. Christ no. Everybody gets . . .

· Then Hunt started getting tough:

HUNT: All right, now, we've set a deadline now for close of business on the twenty-fifth of November for the resolution, the liquidation of everything that's outstanding.

COLSON: Um hmm.

HUNT: And this is—I'm now talking about promises from July and August.

And he kept hammering:

HUNT: And, uh, the election's out of the way, uh, initial terror of a number of people has subsided, some people have already left the administration, and that's all to the good.

COLSON: Um hmm.

HUNT: So now its pared down to the point where a few people ought to be able to really concentrate on this, get the goddamn thing out of the way once and for all . . .

And threatening:

HUNT: After all, we're protecting the guys who were really responsible. But now that's . . . a continuing requirement, but at the same time, this is a two-way street . . . and, as I said before, we think that now is the time when some moves should be made and, uh, surely your cheapest commodity available is money . . .

Finally, Hunt said he would "lay" a memorandum on Parkinson, and then he let up a little on his friend Colson:

HUNT:. . . uh, I don't want to, uh, bore you with what it's been like, but it hasn't been pleasant for any of us.

COLSON: Oh, Jesus Christ, I know it. I hope you're doing some writing to keep yourself busy. . . .

HUNT: Oh, I am. Yeah, I am. I don't know if anything'll ever come of it, but it's a good—uh, well, it keeps my mind from my plight.

Hunt's perceived plight—the indifference of those who should have been taking care of him—remained very much on his mind, even at the typewriter. In November he was finishing up a novel he called *The Berlin Ending*. On its last page, he wrote this exchange between Apelbaum, the Israeli intelligence agent, and Thorpe, the former CIA man:

" 'All of us,' said Apelbaum, 'did what we thought was right. But Werber was always the Soviets' man. And they take care of their own. Believe me, I know.'

" 'Unlike C.I.A.,' Thorpe said thinly. 'Damn them, too.' "

But if Hunt was agitated, so were the President's men when they heard Hunt's veiled and not-so-veiled threats. Colson gave his tape of the conversation to Dean. Dean had it transferred to a cassette, which he played for Haldeman and Ehrlichman on November 15 at Camp David, where he also warned them about the increasing and now threatening demands for money being passed to the White House by Bittman. The President's lieutenants told Dean to "tell Mitchell to take care of all these problems." That afternoon, Dean flew to New York for a prearranged meeting with Mitchell at the elegant Metropolitan Club. Dean played the cassette for Mitchell and relayed the White House request that he take care of the problem. But Mitchell merely nodded and puffed on his pipe.

Meanwhile, Hunt put aside his novel for a few hours and rapped out a memo summing up the defendants' complaints, a blistering nine-hundred-word indictment of how the White House had handled the Watergate affair.

The defendants, he charged, had gone ahead with

the burglary "against their better judgment" and despite a pattern of "diminishing funding coupled with increasing demands by those who conceived and sponsored the activity." Since the burglary, he wrote, the White House had been guilty of:

• "Indecisiveness at the moment of crisis";

• "Failure to quash the investigation while that option was still open";

• "Allowing Hunt's safe to be opened and selected contents to be handed over to the F.B.I.";

• "Permitting an F.B.I. investigation whose unprecedented scope and vigor caused humiliation to families, friends, and defendants themselves";

• "Failure to provide promised support funds on a timely and adequate basis; continued postponements and consequent avoidance of commitments"; and

• "An apparent wash-hands attitude now that the election has been won, heightening the sense of unease among all defendants who have grown increasingly to feel that they are being offered up as scapegoats ultimately to be abandoned."

Then Hunt weighed in with some pointed threats, noting that:

• "Mitchell may well have perjured himself";

• "The Watergate bugging is only one of a number of highly illegal conspiracies engaged in by one or more of the defendants at the behest of senior White House officials. These as yet undisclosed crimes can be proved";

• "Immunity from prosecution and/or judicial clemency for cooperating defendants is a standing offer"; and

• "Congressional elections will take place in less than two years."

Hunt extended the deadline he had given Colson by two days—until five o'clock, November 27—but he said the defendants would meet on November 25 "to determine our joint and automatic response to evidence of continued indifference on the part of those in whose behalf we have suffered the loss of our employment, our futures, and our reputations as honorable men. The foregoing should not be interpreted as a threat. It is among other things a reminder that loyalty has always been a two-way street."

But, of course, the White House recognized Hunt's memo as just what it was—a threat. On November 20 Bittman read the memo to Parkinson, who passed the message on. A few days later Bittman gave Parkinson a folded slip of paper—apparently a list of the defendants' specific needs—which Parkinson passed on to Dean and La Rue.

During the last week of November Mitchell finally responded. He told Dean that to satisfy the defendants' new demands he would have to use some of the $328,000 remaining in Haldeman's $350,000 secret fund (the money transferred from CREEP to Haldeman in April 1972, and then passed by Alex Butterfield to his friend Leonard Lilly, who kept it in a safe-deposit box in Arlington). Dean was reluctant to have White House funds used for the payoffs, but it was the only cash available. Early on the morning of November 28 Strachan rushed into Butterfield's office and said, "We need that money today, we must have it today, so I hope your friend is in town, I hope he is not traveling." Butterfield met Lilly later that morning in the lobby of the Key Bridge Marriott Motor Hotel, retrieved his briefcase, and rushed back to the White House. That afternoon Strachan packed $50,000 in $100 bills into two envelopes and took them to LaRue, who had it delivered to Bittman. A short while later LaRue asked for more money, and Haldeman told Dean to give him "the entire damn bundle, but make sure we get a receipt." Strachan took the rest of the money to LaRue at his Watergate apartment. Before taking the stacks of bills out of the box, LaRue carefully donned a pair of gloves. Strachan blanched, realizing that his own fingerprints were all over the bills. He asked for the receipt, but LaRue flatly refused. "You'll have to talk to John Dean about that," he said. "I never saw you."

Frederick Cheney LaRue had good reason to be leery of financial hanky-panky. Years before, his father,

*Ike, had gone to prison in Texas for banking viola-
tions. A first cousin of oil tycoon Sid Richardson, LaRue
Senior decided he'd try oil himself when he got out of
jail. Backed by Texas money, he went drilling in
Mississippi and in 1954 got his first strike at Bolton,
twenty miles west of Jackson. The LaRue family company corked the field for several years until they sold
it for $30 million in 1957—the same year Fred shot
and killed his father in a Canadian duck-hunting accident. Some say the LaRues never controlled their oil
fortune, others say they lost it in imprudent invest-
ments. But Fred—known to other good old boys as
"Bubba"—spread plenty of money around Mississippi
in the next couple of years and quickly became a
political power in the state (and a Republican national
committeeman). In 1964 he contributed heavily to
Barry Goldwater's Presidential campaign and three
years later he became an early contributor to Nixon,
whom he had first met in 1965 at a Republican conference in Albuquerque. Quickly, LaRue became one
of John Mitchell's confidants and a key implementer of
the Southern Strategy. "Nixon's dilemma," he explained
later, "was that he had to win the nomination basically with the same forces Goldwater had in 1964 but
without associating with them or being associated."
Shy, a "mumbler," homely behind his Coke-bottle
lenses, LaRue had neither the personality nor the inclination for a public role in the administration. But
he was a skilled behind-the-scenes operator, and in
September 1969 he was brought into the White House
as the quintessential backstage man—with no title, no
salary, not even a listing in the White House directory.
His chief function was to hold the South in line for
Nixon—and he did this by keeping in close touch with
Southern Democrats, particularly his friend James O.
Eastland, Mississippi's senior senator. (Eastland consistently supported the President's unpopular Supreme
Court nominations and in 1972 LaRue made sure the
White House withheld support from Eastland's Republican opponent.) In January 1972 LaRue moved over
to CREEP as an assistant to Mitchell, but again
with no clear-cut assignment. He shared a suite with*

Jeb Magruder and, though six years his senior, quickly established a "teacher-pupil" relationship with the younger man, becoming so close that some CREEP staffers called them "Magrue." (Magruder calls his friend "likable, sincere, and politically astute.") In the following months, LaRue stuck closely by Mitchell and Magruder—passing messages, briefing witnesses, delivering cash—the indispensable jack-of-all-missions. He may also have used his position for personal benefit. Federal investigators have looked into charges that he intervened with the Agriculture Department on behalf of the now bankrupt Stirling Homex Corporation, whose vice president paid him $200 a month for occasional use of LaRue's apartment at the Watergate. And LaRue and Mitchell used a Homex jet on their trip to Florida the week Mitchell approved the Watergate burglary.

On December 8 Dorothy Hunt boarded United Airlines Flight 553 for Chicago. In his book, Hunt says his wife was on her way to deliver Christmas presents to her cousins Harold and Phyllis Carlstead (with whom Hunt had spent his last fugitive days in July). But she was carrying something else too: $10,000 in $100 bills. Hunt insists this money was to have been their investment in Hal Carlstead's motel-management company, which controlled two Holiday Inns and a third one under construction in Chicago. But this seems a peculiar use for the family's dwindling cash reserves. Dean later told the President that Mrs. Hunt had gone to Chicago "to pass that money to one of the Cubans, to meet him in Chicago and to pass it to somebody there." And, after all, Mrs. Hunt had been ferrying just such packets of $100 bills here and there around the country for more than four months.

The former Dorothy de Goutière had met Hunt in 1948, in Paris, where she worked as one of Averell Harriman's secretaries at the Economic Cooperation Administration, married Hunt the next year, and followed him on the rest of his "Company" assignments. After the Watergate burglary, she lost her job in the

Spanish embassy, where she had been employed four hours a day translating speeches and documents from Spanish to English. Barker recalls that after her husband's arrest, she quickly and enthusiastically took up her role as a clandestine courier, using Howard's old code words, admonishing Barker to stick to Company rules. Fondly recalling her untiring efforts to bring him cash, Barker thought she was "a very wonderful woman."

At 2:27 p.m. the Boeing 737 was nearing Chicago's Midway Airport through drizzle and fog. Instructed to make another approach, the plane suddenly nose-dived into a neighborhood of one-story bungalows a mile and a half short of runway 31L. Forty-three of the fifty-five people on board were killed, including Mrs. Hunt. Policemen sifting through the wreckage found her purse filled with $100 bills. This stirred allegations that the plane had been sabotaged to erase evidence of the Watergate payoffs. Sherman Skolnick, a free-lancing investigator in Chicago, has charged that air controllers and high government officials conspired to bring about the crash and then disguise the cause of the disaster. However, several official investigations and many press inquiries have failed to turn up evidence of any sabotage.

Whatever caused it, the crash sent Howard Hunt's spirits plummeting too. At one point in those first few days, he recalls, he contemplated suicide. When Barker saw him a few days later, he seemed "a broken man" and "looked eighty years old." Barker says Hunt told him then, "Well, you do what you want, but I am going to plead guilty."

"Why, Howard?" asked Barker.

"We have no defense," said Hunt. "The evidence against us is overwhelming."

Until late fall Hunt had believed he might be acquitted. Bittman thought he could demolish the government's case against Hunt with a motion to suppress the evidence taken illegally (without a warrant) from his safe. Bittman assumed that Silbert had built the case against Hunt with the use of the two highly informative notebooks he had left in the safe. But when the motion to suppress was first heard in October, and later, when Hunt was permitted to examine the seized materials, the notebooks were not there. Silbert insisted he had never seen them (as indeed he had not, since Dean had retained them and was to destroy them the following month).

But there were other ingredients to Hunt's decision. In his book about Watergate, he says that after his wife's death he knew he "could not stand the stress of a four to six week trial . . . I decided to plead guilty in the hope that leniency would be accorded me." Increasingly, the idea of leniency, clemency, pardon played a lead role in Hunt's thinking about the future. He asked Bittman to begin exploring the idea with Colson, but to no avail. Colson would not see him.

On the last day of 1972—the year which had started with Hunt and Liddy exuberantly toasting the Gemstone in their future—Hunt sat down and wrote a melancholy, almost desperate letter to Colson. It read, in part:

"I had understood you to say that you would be willing to see my attorney, Bill Bittman, at any time. After my wife's death, I asked him to see you, but his efforts were unavailing. And though I believe I understand the delicacy of your overt position, I nevertheless feel myself even more isolated than before. My wife's death, the imminent trial, my present mental depression, and my inability to get any relief from my present situation, all contribute to a sense of abandonment by friends on whom I had in good faith relied. I can't tell you how important it is, under the circumstances, for Bill Bittman to have the opportunity to meet with you, and I trust that you will do me that favor.

"There is a limit to the endurance of any man trapped in a hostile situation and mine was reached on December 8th. I do believe in God—not necessarily a Just God but in the governance of a Divine Being. His Will, however, is often enacted through human hands, and human adversaries are arraigned against me."

On January 2 Colson sent a copy of the letter to Dean

with a stark covering note: "Now what the hell do I do?"

Dean, who had spent the Christmas holidays with other White House staffers in California, was about to board *Air Force One* in Los Angeles on January 2 when he got an urgent call from Paul O'Brien in Washington, saying "Mr. Hunt is off the reservation." When Dean got back to Washington that evening, O'Brien spelled it out: Hunt was "quite upset," wanted to plead guilty but would do so only if he got a White House promise of executive clemency. O'Brien said that Hunt would take the assurance only from Colson but that Bittman had been trying to reach Colson without success.

When Dean reached his office on the morning of January 3 he found Hunt's letter and Colson's covering note. Now he recognized the full seriousness of the situation. The White House wanted Hunt to plead guilty, thus avoiding a public airing of the case against him which could always lead to further disclosures. And it certainly wanted to avoid any real disaffection that might induce Hunt to blurt out everything he knew. So Dean spoke with Colson, who was still trying desperately to hoist his cuffs above the mud and did not want to meet with Bittman. But Dean then took the matter to Ehrlichman, who told Colson to find out what was on Bittman's mind.

At the first Colson-Bittman meeting—which took place that same day—all agree there was no promise given. Indeed, Hunt says Bittman got only "banalities" from Colson. But afterward, Dean recalls, Colson came to a meeting with him and Ehrlichman looking "extremely shaken" and arguing that it was "imperative that Hunt be given some assurance of executive clemency." According to Dean, Ehrlichman said he would have to take the matter up with the President. The next day, Dean recalls, Ehrlichman told him he had given Colson "an affirmative regarding clemency for Hunt" and that Colson had relayed that to Bittman.

Colson insists that at the second meeting he told Bittman only to "reassure Howard that I as an individual felt real grief over Howard's circumstances, that I would always be a friend, regardless of what he did," but as for anything more specific "there was nothing anyone could do."

But Dean says that on January 5 Colson met with him and Ehrlichman again and reported that he had indeed given Bittman a "general assurance" that Hunt would get clemency. Dean asked Ehrlichman whether such a commitment applied to all the defendants, and he says Ehrlichman replied that "if Hunt was going to get an assurance for clemency, the others could understand that it applied to all."

Hunt's recollections coincide with Dean's. At the January 4 meeting, he says, Bittman pressed hard for clemency and Colson replied that if Hunt were to get a long sentence, "Well, Christmas comes around every year." Hunt regarded that as a firm promise of clemency at least by Christmas 1973. He notes that Bittman, while at the Justice Department, had prosecuted Jimmy Hoffa and that Colson had been chiefly responsible for getting Hoffa clemency at Christmastime 1971, so Colson knew his message would not be lost on Bittman or his client.

Four days later, on January 8, Colson and the President spoke by telephone about clemency for Hunt:

NIXON: . . . I, uh, question of clemency. . . . Hunt's is a simple case. I mean, after all, the man's wife is dead, was killed; he's got one child that has . . .

COLSON: Brain damage from an automobile accident.

NIXON: That's right.

COLSON: (*unintelligible*) one of his kids.

NIXON: We'll build, we'll build that son-of-a-bitch up like nobody's business. We'll have [William] Buckley write a column and say, you know, that he, that he should have clemency, if you've given eighteen years of service. (Ironically, Buckley was by then one of the few men outside the White House who knew the truth about Hunt's role in Watergate and his relationship to the President's men. About ten days after his wife's death, Hunt had telephoned Buckley—who was a former colleague in the CIA, the godfather of his three oldest children, and now the alternate executor of his wife's estate. In two hours at Buckley's New York apartment, he told the columnist "the story of Watergate—as far as he knew it." But Buckley, considering that the story had been given to him "in confidence," kept his friend's secret.)

A bit later in his January 8 conversation with Colson, Nixon indicated that clemency would not necessarily be offered to the other defendants.

NIXON: . . . I would have difficulty with some of the others.

COLSON: Oh, yeah.

NIXON: You know what I mean.

COLSON: Well, the others aren't going to get the same . . . the vulnerabilities are different.

NIXON: Are they?

COLSON: Yeah.

NIXON: Why?

COLSON: Well, because Hunt and Liddy did the work. The others didn't know any direct information—

NIXON: Uh, well, I think I agree.

COLSON: See, I don't give a damn if they spend five years in jail—

NIXON: Oh, no . . .

COLSON: They can't hurt us. Hunt and Liddy: direct meetings, discussions are very incriminating to us. More important that those . . . they're both good healthy right-wing exuberants.

On January 11 when the Watergate trial began, Hunt stood in the well of Washington's United States District Court—tense, pale, almost gaunt from the fourteen pounds he had lost since his wife's death.

DEPUTY CLERK: Mr. Hunt, in Criminal Case No. 1827–72, do you now wish to withdraw the plea of not guilty which was entered previously and now enter a plea of guilty to Counts One, Two, Three, Four, Five, and Eight of the indictment?

HUNT: I do.

Outside the courthouse, reporters asked Hunt whether "higher-ups" in the Nixon administration had been involved in a broader Watergate conspiracy and he replied, "To my personal knowledge there was none."

Four days later, on January 15, Barker, Martinez, Sturgis, and Gonzalez followed suit. The columnist Jack Anderson says this decision resulted from heavy pressures put on them by the White House and by Hunt, followed by a "cut off" in their hush-money payments. Anderson also claims that he was in an adjoining room in mid-January when the four Miami defendants met at the Arlington Towers, an apartment hotel across the Potomac from the Watergate, to debate whether they should give in to this pressure. After a "heated discussion," he says, they decided to plead guilty.

In court, Judge John J. Sirica questioned the four men closely on whether "higher-ups" had pressured them to change their pleas. They replied with emphatic "noes" and vigorous shakes of their head. They also denied that Hunt had induced them to follow his lead. Hunt later denied it too, and given the intense loyalty they still felt for "Eduardo," he probably hadn't had to push too hard. In his book he recalls that Bernard Barker told him, "If you're pleading guilty, then that's enough for us." If Hunt was going to march into his cell with lips sealed, then so would the four "freedom fighters" from Miami.

That left only McCord and Liddy to stand trial. Liddy—who months before had been ready to let himself be assassinated for the cause—was just as ready to go off to jail, though out of stubborn pride he declined to plead guilty. But McCord was quite another matter.

If Hunt had briefly strayed off the reservation, McCord had been climbing the fences for months. Between July 30, 1972, and January 5, 1973, he wrote seven letters to officials of the CIA warning that the White House was wrongly trying to picture Watergate as an agency operation. The first, on July 30, was merely a cover note to Helms saying, "From time to time I'll send along things you might be interested in from an info standpoint. This is a copy of a letter which went to my lawyer." The note was unsigned, but the accompanying letter was signed "Jim," and from the context Helms could certainly have discerned that McCord was the author.

The other letters went to Paul Gaynor, a friend from McCord's old CIA security office. The letters to Gaynor intensified in frequency and urgency as McCord's trial approached, reaching their shrillest pitch after McCord met twice with his lawyers in late December. At the first conference—a December 21 lunch with attorneys Gerald Alch and Bernard Shankman at Washington's Monocle Restaurant—Alch had just come from a meeting with Hunt's lawyer, Bittman, and seemed to be relaying a request from Bittman (and presumably Hunt). According to McCord, Alch suggested he claim that Watergate was a CIA operation and contend that he had been recalled from retirement specifically for the mission. James R. Schlesinger, who by then had been designated to replace Helms as CIA director, "would go along" with this story, Alch indicated. Five days later in Alch's Boston office, McCord says, the lawyer continued to press him on the CIA cover story, but McCord responded that "even if it meant my freedom I would not turn on the organization that had employed me for nineteen years, and wrongly deal such a damaging blow that it would take years for it to recover from it." Alch, a partner of the prominent Boston attorney F. Lee Bailey, has denied McCord's allegations, claiming that he only wanted to know if the CIA was involved. (F. Lee Bailey was a close personal friend of Mitchell's, and suspicions persisted that Alch was implementing a strategy designed, in part, by Mitchell. Later McCord said Dean had admitted to him that there was a "conduit system" from Alch to Paul O'Brien to Mitchell. "O'Brien knew almost everything you were thinking," Dean is said to have told McCord.)

Following his meetings with Alch, McCord sent Gaynor letters with warnings like these:

• December 22—"There is tremendous pressure to put the operation off on the Company. Don't worry about me no matter what you hear. The way to head this off is to flood the newspapers with leaks or anonymous letters that the plan is to place the blame on the Company . . ."

• December 29—"I am convinced that the fix is in on Gerry Alch and Bernie Shankman. Too many things don't add up. . . . They are trying to put the blame for the operation on CIA and McCord, or both, shifting the focus away from the White House [Liddy and Hunt]."

• Undated but probably late December—"The pressure is still on. They can go to hell."

• Undated but probably early January—". . . When the hundreds of dedicated fine men and women of CIA can no longer write intelligence summaries and reports with integrity, without fear of political recrimination—when their fine director is being summarily discharged in order to make way for a politician who will write or rewrite intelligence the way the politicians want them [sic] written, instead of the way truth and best judgment dictates, our nation is in the deepest of trouble and freedom itself was never so imperiled. Nazi Germany rose and fell under exactly the same philosophy of governmental operation."

McCord claims that he was merely trying to protect the CIA, that he was not seeking anything for himself. But mixed in with the warnings to the agency were some remarks well calculated to grab the attention of anyone in the White House who might hear about them. For example, on December 29 he wrote to Gaynor, "I have the evidence of the involvement of Mitchell and others, sufficient to convene a jury, the Congress and the press."

And sometime during late December he wrote a letter which was sure to reach the White House—this one to his old friend John Caulfield, by then acting director for Enforcement of the Alcohol, Tobacco, and Fire-arms Division of the Internal Revenue Service (the very division which the White House had wanted him to head in 1970). The letter read:

"Dear Jack:
"I'm sorry to have to write you this letter, but felt you had to know. If Helms goes and the Watergate operation is laid at CIA's feet, where it does not belong, every tree in the forest will fall. It will be a scorched desert. The whole matter is at the precipice now. Just pass the message that if they want it to blow, they are on exactly the right course. I'm sorry that you will get hurt in the fallout."

This time the message got through. Although unsigned, the letter had been postmarked in Rockville, and Caulfield suspected it came from McCord. He read the letter over the telephone to Fielding and later gave it to Dean, who passed word to Mitchell. Abruptly, Alch and Bittman abandoned their efforts to construct a CIA cover story. And Mitchell issued instructions that McCord should get the same promise of executive clemency Hunt had gotten.

On January 8 Caulfield was attending a drug conference in San Clemente when Dean telephoned and told him to relay the message to McCord. Caulfield realized he was being asked to do a "very dangerous thing" and told Dean he didn't want to do it. When Dean persisted, Caulfield said he would ask Tony Ulasewicz to handle the job. Ulasewicz didn't want to do it either. But he'd been doing a lot of very dangerous things the past few months and one more wouldn't make much difference.

So at 12:30 a.m. January 9, McCord received a telephone call at his home telling him to go to a pay phone near the Blue Fountain Inn on Route 355 in Rockville and wait for another call. McCord drove to the inn ("Specializing in Choice Steaks—Live Entertainment"), found the pay phone in the parking lot, and waited until the same unfamiliar voice told him:

"Plead guilty. One year is a long time. You will get executive clemency. Your family will be taken care of and when you get out, you will be rehabilitated and a job will be found for you. Don't take immunity when called before the grand jury."

Although Ulasewicz reported McCord's apparent satisfaction with this, Dean told Caulfield to pass the message in person. So Ulasewicz instructed McCord to drive to the second overlook on the George Washington Parkway at 7:00 p.m. on January 12, and there Caulfield and McCord talked for half an hour in Caulfield's car. According to McCord, Caulfield said he carried the clemency message from "the very highest levels of the White House," that the President would be apprised of the meeting, and "I may have a message to you at our next meeting from the President himself." (Caulfield says he didn't mention the President in that first meeting, but when he reported to Dean the next day, Dean said he could use the "highest levels" phrase. Could he say that the offer came from the President himself? Dean replied, "No, don't do that. Say that it comes from way up on top.")

McCord told Caulfield he wasn't interested in clemency. He said he had another plan which would prevent him from going to jail at all. During the autumn he had placed two calls to foreign embassies—the Israeli embassy on September 21 and the Chilean embassy on October 10—whose telephones he knew were wiretapped by the FBI. On both occasions he said he was someone involved in the Watergate scandal and, without giving his name, inquired about obtaining visas for those countries. Now, McCord told Caulfield, if he could get the government to concede that he had been overheard, the prosecutors would face the embarrassing prospect of admitting in open court that the embassies of two friendly countries were being wiretapped. Therefore, McCord urged, the government should drop the case against him rather than jeopardize its foreign relations.

The two men met again at the same spot on Sunday afternoon, January 14, and this time they got out of their cars and clambered down a path leading from the overlook toward the Potomac. Caulfield told McCord that the government was still studying the wiretap question. But, he assured him, even if that didn't work out he would receive clemency after ten or eleven months (presumably the same Christmas pardon Hunt had been promised). McCord was indignant. He said that some of those involved in Watergate were going to be convicted, while others like Mitchell, Dean, and Magruder (who was "perjuring himself") were being "covered for." That, he said, was not his idea of "American justice." So Caulfield emphasized the gravity of the situation, telling his old friend, "The President's ability to govern is at stake. Another Teapot Dome scandal is possible and the government may fall. Everybody else is on track but you. You are not following the game plan. Get closer to your attorney."

The two men talked twice more that month on the telephone and met again, on the twenty-fifth, at the highway overlook. But they were unable to resolve their differences. Caulfield kept pressing McCord to accept clemency. McCord kept threatening to blow the whole thing open. Ultimately, Caulfield warned his friend, "Jim, I have worked with these people and I know them to be as tough-minded as you and I. When you make your statement, don't underestimate them."

For the time being, though, McCord stuck with the game plan. Magruder and Porter followed the plan too —smoothly telling the same false story they had given the grand jury the summer before. And LaRue played his role, passing $20,000 to Liddy's attorney and $60,000 more to Bittman. Summing up the government's case at the trial, Silbert called Liddy "the leader of the conspiracy, the money man, the boss" and argued that higher-ups were not involved because McCord and Liddy "were off on an enterprise of their own, diverting that money for their own uses." On January 30 the jury of eight women and four men needed only ninety minutes to find McCord and Liddy guilty as charged.

The cover-up had held again. But at least one man was not convinced. On February 2, setting bond for the two men at $100,000 apiece, Judge Sirica declared sternly, "I am still not satisfied that all the pertinent facts that might be available—I say *might* be available —have been produced before an American jury."

9

UNCOVER

*All that crap, you're putting it in the paper?
It's all been denied. Katie Graham's gonna get
her tit caught in a big fat wringer if that's published. Good Christ! That's the most sickening
thing I ever heard.*
          —John Mitchell to Carl Bernstein,
                    September 28, 1972

On June 10, 1969, Alexander Butterfield, deputy assistant to the President, wrote a memorandum to John
Ehrlichman:

"The President read in a recent news summary that
many of his critics complain about the Administration's not being 'as open as promised.' His only comment, addressed to you, appears below:

" 'John—Tell Herb and Ron to ignore this kind
of criticism. The fact of the matter is that we are
far *too* open. If we treat the press with a little more
contempt we'll probably get better treatment.'
"cc. Mr. Klein
    Mr. Ziegler"

For decades, Richard Nixon treated the press with
a contempt that lightly disguised roiling resentment.
William Safire, the former public-relations man who
served as a White House speechwriter, recalls Nixon's
saying over and over again, "The press is the enemy."
Indeed, if the Kennedy clan was the first of "them"
and Dan Ellsberg later a close second, the press was

the source of their special power to wound him. John
Kennedy, in particular, had positively glimmered in the
mirror of an adoring press, which never wearied of
describing his "grace," "charm," "easy wit," and
"boyish good looks." But to Nixon, the small-town
boy who grew up listening to train whistles in the night,
Kennedy was a rebuke to everything he stood for: hard
work, perseverance, preparation, the old-style virtues
which earned you rewards in the American system.
As Nixon saw it, Kennedy never had to work for what
he got; he just fooled the press into giving it to him.
And Nixon, to whom nothing ever came easily, loathed
the press for never trusting or loving him too.

Another man, settling luxuriously behind the desk in
the Oval Office, might have abandoned or at least relaxed this grim vendetta. But not Nixon, particularly
not after the fall of 1969 when the press pummeled his
appointment of Clement F. Haynsworth, Jr., to the
Supreme Court, assailed his hard line on Vietnam, and
ridiculed his November 3 appeal to "the great Silent
Majority of my fellow Americans." Instead, he gave
the go-ahead for a speech Spiro Agnew gave on November 13 in Des Moines which blistered the "dozen
anchormen, commentators, and executive producers
[who] . . . decide what forty to fifty million Americans will learn of the day's events in the nation and
in the world . . . read the same newspapers . . . draw
their political and social views from the same sources
. . . talk constantly to one another, thereby providing
artificial reinforcement to their shared viewpoint." Safire says Nixon went through the speech line by line in
advance with its author, Pat Buchanan, toughened it
in a few places, and then chortled, "This really flicks
the scab off, doesn't it?"

For the next two and a half years Nixon kept up his
campaign of intimidation against the press. He rewarded a few friendly reporters with exclusive interviews or tips, while ordering his aides to avoid all contact with critical journals like *The New York Times* or
St. Louis *Post-Dispatch*. Reporters who dared to ask
tough questions at news conferences—like Stuart
Loory of the *Los Angeles Times*—abruptly found

their access to White House officials cut off. All administrations do this kind of thing from time to time, but there was a special animus, a special glee in Nixon's determination to bring the press to heel.

Not surprisingly, then, one of the President's first steps following the Watergate break-in was to discuss with Bob Haldeman on June 20 ways of keeping the true story from the press and diverting their attention with a "PR offensive to top this." The day before, his press secretary, Ronald Ziegler, had refused to comment on what he called "a third-rate burglary attempt." On the twentieth, John Mitchell declared that CREEP had not authorized the Watergate burglary and therefore was "not legally, morally, or ethically accountable for actions taken without its knowledge and beyond the scope of its control." At a news conference on June 22 the President echoed these statements, insisting that "the White House has no involvement whatever in this particular incident." And on August 29 these early denials were capped when the President announced that John Dean had conducted "a complete investigation" of the Watergate affair—an outright fabrication, for there had been no such investigation—and determined that "no one in the White House staff, no one in this administration presently employed was involved in this very bizarre incident."

Some White House officials tried to mislead reporters by suggesting that the burglary was the work of anti-Castro Cubans—out to prove that the Democrats were getting contributions from Castro. The Washington *Evening Star,* which often followed the White House lead, went for the Cuban Connection completely, reporting in its July 7 edition that the break-in had been financed by "a right-wing group" of Cuban exiles. And *The New York Times* assigned the Watergate story at first to its Latin American specialist, Tad Szulc, who spent valuable days tracking down the ties Bernie Barker and his men had to Cuban exile groups in Miami.

Meanwhile, over at *The Washington Post* the story was being handled chiefly by two young metropolitan desk reporters, Carl Bernstein and Bob Woodward.

"Woodstein"—as the reporting team came to be known—was a bizarre hybrid, a kind of journalistic centaur with an aristocratic Republican head and runty Jewish hindquarters. Bob Woodward was a tall, good-looking Yale graduate whose face Vogue magazine was later to call "as open as a Finnish sandwich." The son of a Midwestern judge, he had been a Naval officer for five years, drove a 1970 Karmann Ghia, and reminded Bernstein of "lawns, greensward, staterooms, and grass tennis courts." Bernstein was a rumpled, pock-marked, shaggy-haired dropout from the University of Maryland who occasionally wrote about rock music for the Post and reminded Woodward of "those counterculture journalists [he] despised." When they found themselves sharing the Watergate story in the days after the break-in, they were mutually suspicious and resentful. But soon they found that they worked well together: Woodward supplying the establishment credentials, the informed sources within government, a well-honed intelligence, and dogged diligence; Bernstein providing the writing skill, cunning, combativeness, and an almost feral intensity. They had other advantages for this kind of story. Woodward had recently been divorced, Bernstein was separated from his wife, so neither had a family life to prevent them from working twelve to eighteen hours a day, seven days a week. Both were ambitious young men—Woodward was twenty-nine, Bernstein was twenty-eight—who felt their talents were not fully recognized or utilized by the Post. (Woodward, on the paper barely nine months, had been relegated to minor police stories; Bernstein, in six years with the Post, had worked himself up from copyboy to the not terribly exalted job of Virginia political reporter.) Most important, they were outside the well-grooved orbit of big-time National Journalism, which seduced so many of its practitioners into a cozy rapport with their sources and a slothful delectation of their prestige and perquisites. Woodstein was a hungry animal that prowled through the back alleys of Washington journalism, feeding on the scraps and gutter detritus, ignored by the well-tailored denizens of the National Press Club bar and the Sans

Souci restaurant. Woodward had one supersource whom he called "Deep Throat" and met in drafty parking garages (and whom many believe to have been W. Mark Felt, Jr., then deputy associate director of the FBI). But most of their information was gleaned from less glamorous founts—bank records, telephone bills, crisscross directories, and the hazy recollections of secretaries, clerks, and minor officials whom they tracked through endless telephone calls and waited for on doorsteps in the middle of the night. "You know," a Post *reporter told Timothy Crouse of* Rolling Stone, *"if that story had been given to our national staff, we probably would have lost it. These were two city-side guys with nothing to lose and they just worked their asses off."*

At first, their labors brought only a meager harvest of minor exclusives—Hunt's consultant status at the White House or his interest in Ted Kennedy. Then they began bringing down some riper fruit—snatched from a growing roster of disaffected sources: Hugh Sloan, the renegade campaign treasurer; a finance committee bookkeeper who realized ruefully that "something is rotten in Denmark and I'm part of it"; a few FBI agents fed up with Pat Gray; or Justice Department officials dismayed at the cover-up.

And from August through October, Woodstein produced a spate of "scoops" which changed the shape of the Watergate story for good: August 1—the Dahlberg check and the financial link between CREEP and the Watergate burglary; September 16—the "secret fund" controlled by Maurice Stans and CREEP aides; September 17—Jeb Magruder's and Bart Porter's withdrawals from the fund; September 29—Mitchell's control of the fund; and on October 10 a blockbuster which wove together the various strands of their investigation into a story which began: "F.B.I. agents have established that the Watergate bugging incident stemmed from a massive campaign of political spying and sabotage conducted on behalf of President Nixon's re-election and directed by officials of the White House and

the Committee for the Re-election of the President."
In that and subsequent stories they also revealed Donald Segretti's activities; his ties to Dwight Chapin, Gordon Strachan, and Herb Kalmbach; and Ken Clawson's alleged admission that he had written the "Canuck" letter.

The President took the *Post*'s reporting as a personal affront. On September 15 Dean told him, ". . . the *Post,* as you know, has got a real large team that they've assigned to do nothing but this," and Nixon said, "The *Post* is going to have damnable, damnable problems out of this one. They have a television station." (They had several stations, all subject to license challenges before the Federal Communications Commission. Within months, three challenges had been filed against WJXT in Jacksonville, and another against WPLG in Miami. Both stations were owned by the *Post.* The challenges were not successful, but there is strong evidence to indicate that they were instigated by the Nixon administration.)

The administration fought back more publicly too, with scathing denunciations of the *Post*'s stories: "a collection of absurdities," "a senseless pack of lies," "shabby journalism," "unfounded and unsubstantiated allegations," "mud-slinging," "guilt by association," "a political effort by *The Washington Post,* well conceived and coordinated, to discredit this administration and individuals in it," "using innuendo, third-person hearsay, unsubstantiated charges, anonymous sources, and huge scare headlines, the *Post* has maliciously sought to give the appearance of a direct connection between the White House and the Watergate."

Woodward and Bernstein did make several errors: one, an October 6 story which reported that Al Baldwin had delivered Gemstone memos to Rob Odle, Bill Timmons, and J. Glenn Sedam, a CREEP lawyer; another, their October 25 report that Sloan had told the grand jury that Haldeman was authorized to make payments from the secret fund. Edward J. Epstein, a press critic, has contended that the two reporters also erred in lumping Segretti and the other dirty-tricksters together with Watergate in one massive spying operation.

Indeed, it could be argued that their October 10 story went a step too far in seeing Watergate "whole," in not differentiating between competing power centers within the administration. But this was a minor distortion compared to the Petersen-Silbert line, which pictured Watergate as a mere burglary carried out by some berserk agents. Epstein is right in contending that much of the *Post*'s material came from official investigators, but only Woodward and Bernstein during the fall and winter of 1972–73 were putting that material together in a comprehensible and, ultimately, accurate whole.

Indeed, their reporting should have had a substantial effect on the Presidential campaign. It didn't—primarily because the White House had largely isolated the *Post*. With few exceptions—Sandy Smith of *Time* magazine; Jack Nelson and Ron Ostrow of the *Los Angeles Times;* and, sporadically, *The New York Times, Newsday, Newsweek*—the major institutions of the American press did not support their embattled colleague with any solid investigative reporting that summer and fall. Most newspapers dismissed the Watergate burglary as a joke; their favorite word for it that fall was "caper." Ben Bagdikian, writing later in the *Columbia Journalism Review,* reported that of the 433 reporters in the 16 largest newspaper bureaus in Washington, fewer than 15 reporters were assigned full time to the Watergate story. The average Washington bureau had no one on the story full time. "It is possible," Bagdikian wrote, "that more man-hours of investigative journalism were put into the 1962 rumor (never confirmed) that John F. Kennedy had been secretly married in 1947 than were assigned to investigate the Watergate affair." And most newspapers, magazines, and television networks devoted relatively little attention to Watergate in the months before the election.

In part, this was what Russell Baker of *The New York Times* has called "the tendency to piss all over the other guy's story, to hope that the story will go away because it makes you look bad for missing it." But this was not just a missed story, it was a dangerous story, a story sure to arouse the ire of the Biggest

News Source of Them All. The press shied away from it in large part because the administration's three-year campaign of intimidation had succeeded—beyond its wildest expectations. The television networks in particular—because of the great powers of the Federal Communications Commission and the persistent writ-rattling of the White House office of Telecommunications Policy—feared a head-on confrontation with the President. Newspapers and magazines were beset by irresolution and self-doubt, half believing that they really were part of some coterie of effete Eastern intellectuals out to get the President. Agnew's Des Moines speech, echoed time and again by the President and his aides, put the press on the defensive precisely when it should have been most vigilant, and when news generated by the *Post* or *Times* did percolate into the heartland, it was often disregarded simply because it came from sources that Agnew and Nixon had effectively discredited. (As usual, most newspapers around the country supported the Republican candidate for President—but this time, by an even larger margin. According to a poll by *Editor & Publisher,* 753 daily papers endorsed Nixon, while only 56 endorsed McGovern.)

The press' impotence gravely undercut George McGovern's efforts to expose and exploit the Watergate issue. As early as June 20, the Democratic National Committee filed a $1-million civil damage suit against CREEP, and depositions for the suit proved an effective means of bringing some facts into the open. McGovern spoke frequently about Watergate, denouncing "criminal activity and political subversion that is operating from deep inside the White House itself," branding it "the kind of thing you expect under a person like Hitler," and asking such pertinent questions as: "Who ordered this act of political espionage? Who paid for it? Who received the memoranda of the tapped telephone conversations?" But the issue never caught fire, partly because reporters—shunned by the aloof, unavailable Nixon—focused instead on the easy, available stories about McGovern's staff troubles; his positions on amnesty, abortion, and marijuana; and his first running mate's shock treatments. Small wonder that a few weeks before the Nixon landslide the Gallup Poll found that 48 per cent of Americans had never heard of the Watergate affair.

In their telephone conversation one week after the election, Howard Hunt and Chuck Colson chortled over how flat the issue had fallen:

COLSON: . . . but the Democrats made such an issue out of the whole goddamn . . .

HUNT: Well, on the other hand, it kept them from addressing themselves to the real issues.

COLSON: Well, I always thought when I write my memoirs of this book—of this campaign—that I'm gonna say that the Watergate was brilliantly conceived as an escapade that would divert the Democrats' attention from the real issues, and therefore permit us to win a landslide that we probably wouldn't have won otherwise.

HUNT and COLSON: (*laughter*).

COLSON: . . . Dumb bastards were on an issue that the public couldn't care less about—really.

C ongress was almost as inert as press and public. Twice in the fall of 1972 congressional investigations were launched into the Watergate affair—by the General Accounting Office, an investigative wing of Congress; and by the House Banking and Currency Committee.

The GAO investigation outraged the President and on September 15 he, Dean, and Haldeman discussed means of turning it off. When Dean reported that Speaker of the House Carl Albert was behind the investigation, Haldeman said, "Well, goddamn the Speaker of the House. Maybe we better put a little heat on him . . . because he's got a lot worse problems than he's going to find down here." The President agreed, citing reports by "the police department" (presumably on scrapes Albert was known to have gotten into while drinking). Haldeman concluded, "What we really ought to do is call the Speaker and say, 'I regret to see you ordering GAO down here because of what it's going to cause us to require to do to you.' " But the White House apparently never followed through with this political blackmail scheme. The GAO continued its probe into the financial aspects of Watergate, producing only meager results.

The White House was more determined—and more effective—in blocking the House Banking and Currency Committee investigation. Under the feisty leadership of Chairman Wright Patman, a seventy-nine-year-old Texas populist, the committee's inquiry could have proved a constant source of embarrassment to Nixon in the months before the election. On September 15 Dean told the President of plans to stop the investigation, ". . . we're looking at all the campaign reports of every member of that committee because we are convinced that none of them have probably totally complied with the law either. And if they want to get into it, if they want to play rough, someday we better say, 'Well, gentlemen, we think we ought to call to your attention that you haven't complied A, B, C, D, E, and F and we're not going to hold that a secret if you start talking campaign violations here.' " But, eventually, the White House followed a more traditional route, bringing heavy political pressure to bear on committee members through Michigan Representative Gerald R. Ford, Jr., the House minority leader, and others. Buttressed with a letter from Henry Petersen saying that a public investigation at that time could jeopardize the rights of the Watergate defendants—a questionable doctrine—the committee voted 20–15 against issuing the necessary subpoenas. The fulminating Patman was reduced to lecturing empty witness chairs and, Dean recalls, "another sigh of relief was made at the White House that we had leaped one more hurdle in the continuing cover-up."

But the stifling of Patman provoked Senator Edward Kennedy into his own private inquiry. Using the staff of his Subcommittee on Administrative Practices and Procedures, he developed enough evidence between

October and January to persuade the Senate Democratic leadership there was basis for a public investigation. (All Nixon's worst fears were fulfilled. Once more he fled his own relentless demons—the omnipresent Kennedys. He told Dean, "I guess the Kennedy crowd is just laying in the bushes waiting to make their move.")

By early February 1973 Democrats eager to revenge the past fall's humiliation joined forces with Republicans resentful of Nixon's "to-hell-with-the-party" campaigning. On February 7, by a 77–0 vote, the Senate established a Select Committee on Presidential Campaign Activities. Senator Sam J. Ervin, Jr., Democrat of North Carolina, was named chairman of the committee, which was composed of three more Democrats (Daniel K. Inouye of Hawaii, Joseph M. Montoya of New Mexico, and Herman E. Talmadge of Georgia) and three Republicans (Howard H. Baker, Jr., of Tennessee, Edward J. Gurney of Florida, and Lowell P. Weicker, Jr., of Connecticut).

That weekend Haldeman, Ehrlichman, Dean, and Richard Moore met in California to develop their "game plan" against the select committee. On Saturday morning, February 10, they gathered in Ehrlichman's office in the Western White House. But that afternoon they moved for the rest of the weekend to Haldeman's "villa" at Rancho La Costa, thirty miles down the coast. La Costa is a 5600-acre resort—condominiums, theater, hotel, golf course, tennis courts, and health spa—frequented by Hollywood celebrities (Frank Sinatra, Dean Martin, Desi Arnaz), athletes (Sandy Koufax), politicians, gamblers, and gangsters. The $100-million project was built with money from the Teamsters pension fund and the banking interests of Nixon's old friend C. Arnholt Smith. Haldeman and his guests were in Nixon country now, and they donned slacks and open-necked sport shirts as they lounged in the sun with "talking papers" and memos spread out before them.

From the start, Dean says, they recognized that they were up against a much tougher situation than they had been with the Patman committee. Because of the Select Committee's composition, because of the resolution's scope and because "the Senate was a hostile ground for the White House," it was going to take an "all-out effort" to contain its investigation. Analyzing the committee member by member, they concluded that only Gurney could be counted on to support the White House—and perhaps Baker, if he was handled properly. The Republican staff for the committee would therefore be especially important, and Haldeman stressed that it must be headed by "a real tiger, not an old man or a soft-head." Ehrlichman suggested J. Fred Buzhardt, Jr., then general counsel in the Defense Department. (But the job eventually went to one of Baker's protégés, Fred D. Thompson, a former assistant U.S. attorney in Tennessee.)

Dean says the quartet agreed on a strategy for handling the committee: "The White House will take a public posture of full cooperation but privately will attempt to restrain the investigation and make it as difficult as possible to get information and witnesses. A behind-the-scenes media effort would be made to make the Senate inquiry appear very partisan. The ultimate goal would be to discredit the hearings and reduce their impact by attempting to show that the Democrats have engaged in the same type of activities."

Late on Sunday afternoon Ehrlichman asked what Dean called the "bottom-line" question: "Would the seven defendants remain silent through the Senate hearings?" They all agreed that the strategy depended on continued silence, but Dean reported that the defendants were making new demands for hush money. (The payments had continued during the late fall and winter, but at a diminished rate. After his wife's death, Hunt had funneled $21,000 to Manuel Artime, his old friend from Bay of Pigs days. Artime had earlier formed an informal committee to aid the Miami defendants; as a leader of the Cuban exile community and the godfather of Hunt's youngest son, he was an ideal man to assume this role. When Artime came to Washington in December, Hunt gave him $12,000 in a manila envelope for distribution to Barker and his men. Later Hunt arranged to have three envelopes containing $3000 each left in Artime's mailbox. In February Fred LaRue passed $12,000 more to Artime. That same month LaRue put $60,000 in Bill Bittman's mailbox, intending it for Hunt, and gave Gordon Liddy's attorney $20,000. But again LaRue, Dean, and Mitchell feared they would soon run out of cash. Once more they asked Kalmbach to get back into the fund-raising business, but he predictably refused. So LaRue assumed the job himself, armed with a list of four "hot prospects" supplied by Maurice Stans. One of those LaRue spoke with about the unidentified "White House project" was Carl H. Lindner, board chairman of the American Financial Corporation and chairman of the *Cincinnati Enquirer*. Lindner was willing to contribute $50,000–$100,000 but wanted to know what he was giving for. LaRue consulted Mitchell, who said they obviously couldn't tell him what it was for. So that source too was abandoned.)

As the La Costa meeting broke up, Moore was assigned to tell Mitchell that it was his responsibility to raise some more money from his "rich friends." On February 15 Moore flew to New York and reported to Mitchell that the White House had nominated him as the new fund-raiser—to which Mitchell snarled, "Tell them to get lost."

Mitchell was cranky in his Wall Street exile—making lots of money again, but harassed by Martha, who desperately missed being at the center of things, as Mitchell did too at times. But he didn't want any part of the assignments the White House kept thrusting at him. Nixon, in turn, was wary of Mitchell, keeping his distance for fear of the Watergate taint on him.

Once the second inaugural was over, the President distanced himself from some others stained by Watergate. Chapin, once like a son to Nixon but terribly vulnerable because of his tie to Segretti, resigned as Presidential appointments secretary in February to join United Airlines. Colson—tarnished by his friendship with Hunt and his "wild man" reputation—left the White House on March 10 to set up the firm of Colson & Shapiro, taking with him the lucrative Teamster account. (Nixon planned to use him as a freelance troubleshooter, telling aides that "Colson can be more valuable out than in.") Egil Krogh, Jr., the ex-Plumber, was shunted over to the Department of Transportation in January as undersecretary. Strachan, who knew all about Gemstone, left Haldeman's staff to become counsel to the United States Information Agency. Sloan had resigned in July. Bob Mardian had returned to California shortly after the election. LaRue went quietly back to Mississippi. David Young, the other ex-Plumber, resigned from the White House in mid-March. Bart Porter got a job in New York.

One tricky personnel problem remained: What to do with Jeb Magruder? Magruder was deeply implicated in Watergate, but he had lied repeatedly to protect the President and his continued silence was essential to the cover-up. He hoped eventually to run for governor of California and wanted to enhance his visibility with another government job. But Sloan, still steaming at Magruder's pressure on him to perjure himself, warned the White House that if Magruder were ever appointed to a position that required Senate confirmation, he would testify against him. Even without Sloan's testimony, such hearings would provide Senate Democrats with a forum to reopen Watergate just as the Kleindienst hearings had served to reopen the ITT affair. Yet, the White House desperately wanted to keep Magruder happy. So—until Watergate "blew over" and they could hand him a riper plum—he was named to a $38,000-a-year job as director of policy planning at the Commerce Department.

With all these departures, and with the ever-growing problems of containing Watergate, John Dean abruptly emerged as a central figure at the White House. Despite his impressive title, the counsel to the President of the United States had met with the President only three times during 1972 before his September 15 meeting —once to go over Nixon's tax returns, again during a Rose Garden "photo opportunity" for National Secretaries Week, and again to have the President sign various legal documents. But between February 27 and March 23, 1973, Dean suddenly plunged into a series of thirty-one meetings and telephone calls with Nixon in barely three weeks. Although these meetings dealt at great length and substance with Watergate, there are those who discern quite another reason for the sudden spate of consultation. Sometime in February Dean had warned Ehrlichman that if he were called as a witness he probably couldn't invoke executive privilege because he had never discussed Watergate with the President or dealt directly with him on it. By suddenly getting so close to his hitherto obscure young counsel, the President may have been establishing a claim of executive privilege, or lawyer-client privilege, to prevent Dean from testifying as a witness—and a potentially dangerous witness at that.

"He was a pilot fish—you know the little fish who follows beside the sharks," says a former colleague. Many of those who worked with John Wesley Dean 3d over the years recall him as a young man following at a discreet distance from the big fish—very deferential, very affable, very eager to "please the boss." But he changed bosses frequently, always using the last one to boost him to the next level of his ever-escalating career. From the start, Dean traded on good connections. His father, a middle-level executive at the Firestone Tire and Rubber Company in Akron, Ohio, provided him a privileged childhood and then sent him off to Staunton Military Academy in Virginia. As a star on the school swimming team, he became very friendly with another swimming star—Barry M. Goldwater, Jr., the son of the Arizona senator, who was to be helpful in years to come. He went to Colgate University but soon switched over to Wooster College—at the urging of Charles McDermott, his father's business associate who was a Wooster trustee. Away for a semester at American University in Washington, he met Karla Hennings, a daughter of Missouri's late Democratic Senator Thomas C. Hennings, Jr., and he married her in 1962. After three years at Georgetown Law School (where he struck one classmate as "the cleanest, prettiest guy in the class"), he was promptly hired by Welch & Morgan, a Washington law firm specializing

in communications law, because, as one member put it, "he was Tom Hennings' son-in-law" and a senior partner in the firm was an old friend of the senator's. After only six months with the firm, he was dismissed for "unethical" conduct—while preparing an application for a St. Louis television station he had been secretly working on a rival application with a friend. But, as always, Dean landed on his feet. Through Representative William M. McCulloch of Ohio, a prominent Wooster College alumnus, he became minority counsel to the House Judiciary Committee, on which McCulloch was the ranking Republican. (McCulloch recalled Dean as "an able young man, but he was in a hell of a hurry.") On the Hill, Dean got to know Representative Richard H. Poff of Virginia and when Poff became vice chairman of the National Commission on the Reform of Federal Criminal Law he took the bright, ambitious young lawyer along as associate director. (He later recalled Dean as "bright, smooth, likable, very ambitious and very flexible; he adapts.") In his spare time Dean worked on position papers for Nixon's 1968 "law and order" campaign, and, after the election, Poff recommended Dean to his good friend John Mitchell, who brought him into the Justice Department. There, as associate deputy attorney general, he helped negotiate parade routes and permits with antiwar demonstrators planning Washington protests in 1969. And the chain of helpful boosts was completed in 1970, when Mitchell recommended him to replace Ehrlichman as Presidential counsel. Along the way, Dean shed Karla and married Maureen Kane, a strikingly attractive former airline stewardess. They lived in a $72,500 town house in Alexandria, owned a twenty-foot sailboat on the Chesapeake Bay, and drove a maroon Porsche 911, in which Dean—still crisp and pretty in his $200 Brooks Brothers suits —cruised down to the White House. There, he impressed the President's men as he had all his other bosses along the way. He would do almost anything they asked him to do, take almost any position—"just like we were selling Wheaties," as he later put it. On September 15, 1972, Haldeman glowingly described

Dean's role in the Watergate cover-up, "John is one of the quiet guys that gets a lot done. . . . He turned out to be tougher than I thought he would." And later, Dean described his own role to the President, "I was all over this thing like a wet blanket. I was everywhere —everywhere they look they are going to find Dean."

Dean's first meeting with the President in 1973 came on February 27. As he recalls it, Nixon summoned him into the Oval Office that afternoon and said Watergate was taking too much of Haldeman's and Ehrlichman's time, that they were "principals in the matter," and Dean could be more "objective." Henceforth, the President said, Dean should report directly to him on Watergate.

At 9:12 a.m. the next day the President summoned Dean to the Oval Office again, for a much longer conversation in which they ranged through all the Watergate-related problems, particularly the Ervin committee investigation.

DEAN: . . . Well, I think . . . these hearings are going to be hot, and I think they are going to be tough. I think they are going to be gory in some regards, but I'm also convinced that if everyone pulls their own oar in this thing, . . . that we can make it through these, and minimal people will be hurt. And they may even paint themselves as being such partisans and off base, that they are really damaging the institutions of government themselves.

NIXON: I frankly would say that I perhaps rather that they be partisan—that they get to be partisan . . . I'd rather have that, rather than for them to have the façade of fairness and all the rest, and then come out—'cause Ervin, in spite of all this business about his being a great Constitutional lawyer—Christ, he's got Baker totally buffaloed on that—I mean Ervin is as partisan as most of our Southern gentlemen are. They are great politicians. They're just more clever than the minority. Just more clever.

So Nixon's first instinct was to strike back politically—to show that the Republicans were no worse than the Democrats (what he called the "you're another" strategy). "The need," he told Dean later, "is to broaden the scope of the damn thing. [We've got] nothing on the Democrats and nothing on what the previous three administrations did." This had been part of Nixon's strategy since the third day after the burglary, when he told Haldeman to "hit the opposition with their activities." And on September 15 he told Dean, "Goldwater put it in context. He said, 'Well, for Christ's sake, everybody bugs everybody else. We know that.'" But it accentuated in February 1973 as the White House mobilized to deal with the assault from Capitol Hill. On February 10 Haldeman instructed Dean to "get our people to put out the story on the foreign or Communist money that was used in support of demonstrations against the President in 1972. We should tie all 1972 demonstrations to McGovern and thus to the Democrats as part of the peace movement."

On February 28 and at subsequent sessions, Nixon and Dean discussed how they could prove the Democrats had bugged Republicans and misused the FBI for political purposes. Nixon recalled something J. Edgar Hoover had said in 1968, when he visited the victorious Republican candidate in his suite at the Pierre Hotel in New York. Eager to ingratiate himself with the President-elect, Hoover told him that, a few weeks before, President Johnson had used the FBI to investigate Nixon and Agnew.

This investigation had focused on the activities of Mrs. Anna Chennault, the Chinese-born widow of Lieutenant General Claire Chennault, an American hero of World War II. A dedicated Republican, who gave heavily to the party and threw elaborate bashes at her apartment in the Watergate, Mrs. Chennault was known in some circles as "Dragon Lady" (after the cartoon character in *Terry and the Pirates*) because of her good looks and her penchant for international intrigue. In the fall of 1968 she had plunged into intrigue with a vengeance, lobbying vigorously with her friends in the South Vietnamese government to prevent their participation in the Paris peace talks until after the election. Under the code name "Little Flower" she was in close touch with her friend Bui Diem, the Vietnamese ambassador to the United States who was serving as an observer in Paris; Senator John G. Tower of Texas, chairman of Nixon's Key Issues Committee; and Richard V. Allen, Nixon's first national security adviser.

Mrs. Chennault's activities had aroused the suspicions of the Washington intelligence community, and a plethora of agencies seemed to be watching her closely. According to published reports, the FBI tapped her telephone and put her under physical surveillance; the CIA tapped the telephones at the South Vietnamese embassy and conducted a covert investigation of Richard Allen. Then, a few days before the election, the National Security Agency—which routinely monitors traffic to and from foreign embassies in Washington —intercepted a cable from the Vietnamese embassy to Saigon urging delay in South Vietnam's participation in the Paris peace talks until after the elections. Indeed, on November 1, her efforts seemed to have paid off when President Nguyen Van Thieu reneged on his promise to Lyndon Johnson and announced in Saigon, "The government of South Vietnam deeply regrets not to be able to participate in the present exploratory talks."

According to one report, Mrs. Chennault was overheard on November 2, 1968—three days before the election—telling a high-ranking South Vietnamese official in Washington that his government should resist all efforts from Johnson for a change of heart before the election, because Saigon would get a better deal from Nixon if he were to be elected. When the official asked Mrs. Chennault whether Nixon knew what she was doing, she replied, "No, but our friend in New Mexico does." That very day Spiro Agnew was in Albuquerque.

Whether Mrs. Chennault was acting as Nixon's agent in all this is difficult to determine. She repeatedly implied that she was. Clearly, he knew about it. Richard Allen kept him informed through a series of memos, and Tower too may have reported to him. William Safire, in his account of the events, concludes that she was acting on her own but had "not been restrained" by anybody in the Nixon camp.

Lyndon Johnson was not inclined to be so charitable. He clearly suspected that the Dragon Lady was acting at Nixon's behest. Any sort of peace settlement by Election Day would have greatly assisted the Democratic candidate, Hubert Humphrey; Johnson—who played an uninhibited brand of politics himself—expected Nixon to do everything he could to block it. But when the FBI reported Mrs. Chennault's activities on November 6, Johnson called Nixon in Los Angeles to berate him angrily for meddling with U.S. foreign policy. Then he ordered the bureau to find out whether Agnew and Mrs. Chennault had talked on November 2. Agents examined telephone company records on thousands of long-distance calls and finally determined that Agnew had made five toll calls that day—three from his campaign plane and two from a portable telephone that had been plugged into the plane during the stop in Albuquerque. None of these had gone to Mrs. Chennault, but Johnson remained convinced that the Republicans had sabotaged the peace talks.

Although clearly the FBI examined Agnew's telephone records, there is no evidence that it tapped his or Nixon's telephones, or other communications. Yet, whenever Nixon told his aides about Hoover's report on the 1968 investigation, he invariably spoke of wiretapping. On September 15, 1972, he told Dean and Haldeman, "We were bugged in sixty-eight on the plane," an apparent reference to Agnew's plane. On February 28, 1973, he told Dean, "Hoover told me, so, uh—and he also told Mitchell, personally that this had happened. . . . I'm talking about the sixty-eight bugging of the plane." And as that winter wore on, Nixon grew ever more determined to break that story out as a counterpoise to the Watergate bugging.

The White House knew that Cartha DeLoach, a former assistant to Hoover, was the man who had

passed Lyndon Johnson's request on to the FBI. De-
Loach had left the bureau in July 1970 and was working for Donald Kendall, board chairman of PepsiCo,
Inc., and one of Nixon's closest confidants. The White
House had sought information from DeLoach, apparently without much success. So on February 10
Haldeman told Dean, "Mitchell should probably have
Kendall call DeLoach in and say that if this project
turns up anything that DeLoach hasn't covered with us,
he will, of course, have to fire him." Mitchell did talk
with DeLoach, who let him review his files on the 1968
operation. But, according to Dean, the files were not
very helpful and DeLoach either couldn't or wouldn't
add much from his memory. "This is DeLoach protecting his own hide," Dean told the President.

So, increasingly, they looked to yet another former
FBI official—one with whom they had had profitable
dealings before. William Sullivan had once been a
trusted confidant of Hoover's and had harbored ambitions to succeed him. But he fell out with the director
in the late 1960s and pinned his hopes on an alliance
with the White House. He played a major role in drafting the so-called Huston Plan; funneled information to
the White House through his friend Robert Mardian;
eventually, in July 1971, gave Mardian the logs of the
secret "national security" wiretaps. At this, Hoover determined to force Sullivan out. In late July he named
Mark Felt to the new position of deputy associate
director, dropping Sullivan to the number-three spot in
the bureau. On August 28 Sullivan wrote Hoover a
long, bitter memo warning that he was "harming [him-
self] and the organization." Sullivan went on vacation
September 13. When he got back, he found that he
had been replaced. Sullivan still resisted, so Hoover had
his name plate removed from his door and the lock
changed. Sullivan resigned a few days later.

But the White House took care of its friends. Delighted to have such a well-informed ally, it found
Sullivan a job—as director of the Justice Department's
Office of National Narcotics Intelligence—and waited
for a time when it could make use of him.

That time came in the winter of 1973. In mid-February Dean went to see Sullivan on another matter, and Sullivan told him some stories about how other administrations had used the FBI for political purposes. On February 28 Dean told the President that Sullivan had "a world of information that may be available," and Nixon indicated he would like to have it. Sometime in early March Dean went back to Sullivan: "Bill, I would like, for my own use, to have a list of some of the horribles that you're aware of." On March 12, Dean says, he got a note from Sullivan promising the "horribles" shortly and assuring him, "John, I am willing at any time to testify to what I know if you want me to." The next day Dean reported to the President that what Sullivan knew was "dynamite" which could "destroy Hoover's image . . . [and] tarnish quite severely some of the FBI and a former President." To that, the President said "Fine." They discussed what *"quid pro quo"* they could offer Sullivan for this information:

DEAN: . . . What Bill Sullivan's desire in life is, is to set up a national or domestic national security intelligence system, a plan, a program. He says we're deficient . . . since Hoover lost his guts several years ago. . . . That's all Sullivan really wants. Even if we just put him off studying it for a couple of years, we could put him out in the CIA. . . .

NIXON: Put him there; we'll do it.

(Sullivan says he was never offered any *quid pro quo* for the information. "If anyone had offered me a job as a payoff, it would have been a violation of the law and I'd have turned him in. I'd have taken steps to have him arrested. I didn't want a damned thing from them.")

The President kept pressing Dean to get the information from Sullivan. On March 17 he reminded him that he needed Sullivan's list quickly. On March 21 he asked, "Any further word on Sullivan?" When Dean replied that Sullivan was coming over to see him that very afternoon, Nixon said, "As soon as you get that, I'll be available to talk to you. . . . I'd like to just see what it is."

That afternoon, or on some subsequent occasion, Sullivan gave Dean a memo outlining the FBI "horribles" he could remember. The memo has never been made public, but, according to news accounts, it focused heavily on Lyndon Johnson's and Franklin Roosevelt's use of the FBI. Among other things, it discussed Johnson's orders for the establishment of special FBI teams at the 1964 and 1968 Democratic conventions, nominally to gather intelligence on "militants" but actually to produce a wide range of political and other intelligence for Johnson. (In 1964 the squad placed bugs and wiretaps in a hotel suite occupied by Martin Luther King, Jr., and in a storefront used by civil-rights groups, and these taps picked up conversations with Attorney General Robert Kennedy and other Democratic politicians.) The memo also reported Johnson's efforts to discover Communist ties to Arkansas Senator J. W. Fulbright and other members of the Senate Foreign Relations Committee, and efforts to trace Republican involvement in a 1964 homosexual incident involving Johnson's aide Walter Jenkins. Similarly, President Roosevelt was reported to have ordered the bureau to call off an investigation of his under-secretary of state, Sumner Welles, who had been accused of homosexual behavior; to have used the bureau to dig up dirt on his enemies; and to carry out some "unusual requests" for Mrs. Roosevelt. According to various other reports, the memo said Robert Kennedy had ordered the bureau to tap the phones of suspects in the Bobby Baker case in order to turn up information embarrassing to Johnson, and Johnson had asked the FBI to dig up "dirt" on Goldwater in 1964.

No prompt or effective use was made of this memo (although six months later some of the same material was obtained by the *Chicago Tribune* and by the Scripps Howard newspapers), perhaps because there was such confusion in the White House about how to disseminate it. Dean and Nixon talked about the dangers in openly "pissing on Johnson." They agreed that the disclosures must not be linked to the President, but they feared that any leak would be traced back to them anyway. "I don't know how the Christ to get it down there [Capitol Hill]," Nixon once exclaimed in exasperation. He and Dean talked about giving the story to a friendly newsman—"a jackass like Mollenhoff" (Clark Mollenhoff, who had left his administration job to return to the *Des Moines Register*)—or the ever-amenable Washington *Evening Star*. On March 21 they were still debating. Nixon's eagerness to get the stories out may also have diminished when he realized that Sullivan's memo did not bear out his most cherished contention—that he and/or Agnew had been bugged in 1968. But, essentially, such diversionary tactics were overtaken by events. By mid-March the skin was starting to peel off the cover-up apple, exposing more dark patches of White House involvement every day.

The new exposure came in an unexpected forum— the Senate Judiciary Committee's confirmation hearings on Pat Gray's nomination to be FBI director. The hearings began innocuously enough on February 28 with lavish praise from Connecticut's two senators: Lowell Weicker assuring the committee that Gray was "a man of absolute integrity" and Abraham A. Ribicoff promising that he would "perform his tasks on a completely nonpartisan basis." But before the first day was over, there was reason to doubt both contentions. There was also reason to doubt Gray's political savvy. For, without solicitation or undue prodding from the senators, he volunteered some startling new information about the Watergate matter: that as early as July 1972 he had started turning data on the investigation over to Dean, had discussed the progress of the inquiry on numerous occasions with Dean and Ehrlichman, and had allowed Dean to sit in on FBI interviews with Watergate figures.

By the second day of the hearings Dean's conduct had become as much an issue as Gray's competence. The Presidential counsel, whose name had been scarcely known to most Americans and who had never been linked in any incriminating way with Watergate, suddenly became a central figure. Senator John V.

Tunney of California said he thought Dean should be called to testify.

On March 2 Nixon—citing "executive privilege" —said, "No President could ever agree to allow the counsel to the President to go down and testify before a committee." From the start, the President and his counsel were agreed that Dean could not testify: too much could come out that would damage both men and perhaps crack Watergate open for good. But their tactics on the Gray hearings quickly merged with their strategy on the Ervin committee. Over the next few weeks the two men—occasionally joined by Haldeman and others—evolved a theory of "executive privilege" which they hoped would allow Dean and other White House aides to avoid direct testimony before any congressional committee.

The President told Dean to draft a statement on executive privilege and to issue it quickly—before he was officially invited to appear before the Judiciary Committee—so that it would not seem to be a direct response to the committee. They recognized that their position might well involve them in a protracted legal struggle with either or both committees, and that the Gray nomination might be left hanging until that struggle was resolved. But that didn't bother them, for already they had privately abandoned Gray. (A few days later the President told Dean that Gray should "not be head of the FBI" and would "not be a good director," less because of any flaws in character than because the hearings had hampered his capacity to cooperate with the White House and might compel him to prove his independence.) So, minutes after Ehrlichman told Gray on March 6, "Keep up the good work, my boy. Let me know if I can help," he told Dean, "I think we ought to let him hang there. Let him twist slowly slowly in the wind."

Their first position, as Dean and the President discussed it on February 28, was to insist on "written interrogatories." Later Dean told Nixon, "You know, as a lawyer that you can handle written interrogatories where cross-examination is another ball game," and the President said, "I know." But they knew that the senators knew that too, and therefore, as Nixon said, "They will never probably accept, but it may give us a position, I mean it'd be reasonable in the public mind." Their fall-back position, then, was to let the two ranking members of the committee—Senators Ervin and Baker—come to the White House alone and question certain witnesses in closed session. Since most senators rely on their counsel and aides to master the details of an investigation and to carry the brunt of the questioning, such sessions would be unlikely to produce tough, informed interrogation. (Nixon hoped that Baker could be induced to accept some such compromise formula and could use influence on Ervin. Baker had come to the White House for a secret meeting with the President late in February and had left him with the impression that he wanted to cooperate. But, according to Nixon, Baker wanted to avoid further direct contact with the White House and asked to keep in touch through Kleindienst. The President urged Kleindienst to serve as "our Baker hand-holder" and work out some sort of compromise. But these efforts never paid off.)

In his conversations with Dean, the President constantly invoked the precedent of the Alger Hiss case to buttress his argument for executive privilege. On February 28, for example, he recalled that even the FBI had refused as an executive agency to help the congressional investigation of Hiss. "Hoover himself, who was a friend of mine even then, said 'I'm sorry. I have been ordered not to cooperate.' And they didn't give us one goddamn thing. I conducted that investigation with two stupid little committee investigators—they weren't that stupid—they were tenacious. One had been fired by the FBI. He was a good, decent fellow, but was a drunk. And we got it done. But we broke that thing without any help." And Dean said, "Funny, when the shoe is on the other foot, how they look at things, isn't it?" (But that remark applied equally to Nixon. As a congressman Nixon had vigorously challenged President Truman's invocation of executive privilege in refusing to hand over an FBI report to Congress. In a speech on the House floor, he thundered against Truman's proposition that "the Congress has no right to question the judgment of the President. I say that the proposition cannot stand from a constitutional standpoint or on the basis of the merits." At a meeting on March 1 Dean reminded the President of this speech. At Nixon's request, Dean got a copy and together they discussed "how it could be differentiated from the present situation.")

But when the President issued his statement on executive privilege on March 12 it gave no evidence of such doubts. It advanced a bold, sweeping construction of the President's right to withhold information and witnesses from Congress. It said the "well-established" doctrine of executive privilege was "designed to protect communication within the executive branch in a variety of circumstances in time of both war and peace." Coming to the current circumstances, it said:

"Under the doctrine of separation of powers, the manner in which the President personally exercises his assigned executive powers is not subject to questioning by another branch of government. If the President is not subject to such questioning, it is equally appropriate that members of his staff not be so questioned, for their roles are in effect an extension of the Presidency. This tradition rests on more than Constitutional doctrine: It is also a practical necessity. To insure the effective discharge of the executive responsibility, a President must be able to place absolute confidence in the advice and assistance offered by the members of his staff. And in the performance of their duties for the President, those staff members must not be inhibited by the possibility that their advice and assistance will ever become a matter of public debate, either during their tenure in Government or at a later date. Otherwise, the candor with which advice is rendered and the quality of such assistance will inevitably be compromised and weakened. What is at stake, therefore, is not simply a question of confidentiality but the integrity of the decisionmaking process at the very highest levels of our Government."

Finally, the statement held that no member of the President's staff could be compelled to testify before a congressional committee. And it extended that claim to two other breeds never before included under an executive privilege umbrella: "former members" of the President's staff and those cabinet members who held dual appointments as "Presidential counselors," insofar as they were being questioned in that capacity (this latter category was presumably designed to cover Mitchell and Stans, both of whom had served as Presidential counselors while in the cabinet).

This seemed a sweeping claim of privilege, but a few weeks later it was broadened still further when Attorney General Kleindienst, appearing before a joint congressional panel, argued that Congress had no power to order any employee of the executive branch to testify if the President prohibited such testimony. Thus, the Nixonian doctrine of executive privilege would potentially have embraced some 2.5 million people.

But even without the Kleindienst Corollary, the Nixon doctrine came in for quick, scathing criticism from a broad spectrum of legal and lay opinion. Critics noted that executive privilege was an implicit rather than an explicit Presidential power. It was not even mentioned in the Constitution and its limits were therefore difficult to chart. Nixon, the critics said, had exploited precisely this vagueness in attempting to enshrine with unchallenged authority an unprecedented claim for absolute privilege. The most authoritative rebuttal of the President's claim came from Raoul Berger, Charles Warren Senior Fellow in American Legal History at the Harvard Law School. Berger, then writing a book on the subject, declared that "executive privilege—root and branch—is a myth, without constitutional basis." Nixon had "chosen to build his right to withhold information from Congress on the doctrine of separation of powers . . . [but] the separation of powers does not grant power: it merely protects power elsewhere conferred. And since the [Constitutional] Convention did not confer on the Executive the power to refuse information to the legislature, a Congressional requirement of information from the Executive does not encroach on powers confided to the Executive; it does not violate the separation of powers."

For the time being, though, such legal sallies hardly fazed the President. Behind the imposing fortress of executive privilege, he seemed unabashed, even cocksure. On March 13 he told Dean that after about three weeks the Ervin committee hearings would begin to "peter out." Noting that some people were starting to talk about "the great crisis in the confidence of the Presidency," he asked:

"How much of a crisis? I mean, it'll be in a newspaper, but the point is that everything is a crisis . . . it'll be a crisis among the upper intellectual types, the ass holes, you know, the soft heads, soft—our own too—Republicans, Democrats, and the rest. Average people won't think it is much of a crisis unless it affects them."

And a few minutes later, he described the growing clamor about Watergate as: ". . . the last gasp of . . . our partisan opponents. They've just got to have something to squeal about . . . but that will end. . . . They're having a hell of a time, you know. They got the hell kicked out of them in the election. . . . They're going to Watergate around in this town, not so much our opponents, but basically it's the media, uh, I mean, it's the Establishment. The Establishment is dying and so they've got to show that after some rather significant successes we've had in foreign policy and in the election, they've got to show 'Well, it just is wrong because this is—because of this.' In other words, they're trying to use this to smear the whole thing."

Indeed, there was something jaunty in their parting that day, the salutation of two men who had gone through some tough times together but were coming out of it now.

NIXON: It's never dull, is it?
DEAN: Never.

But a few days later it started getting more exciting —and more dangerous—than John Dean had ever bargained for, and he began backing out of his strange partnership with Richard Nixon.

Judge Sirica had set March 23 for sentencing of the Watergate Seven. For Howard Hunt—the only defendant out on bail—it was "a date whose finality conditioned my every move and thought." Hunt says that since his wife's death on December 8 he had received no family "support money" (despite the $60,000 which LaRue had paid to Bittman during February). Facing a prison cell, Hunt says, he desperately needed money to cover mortgage payments, insurance premiums, college tuition for two daughters, private school for David, plus salary for the children's former governess whom he had brought from Argentina to care for the family while he was in prison.

Hunt asked Bittman to arrange a meeting with Paul O'Brien, the CREEP lawyer, so he could "review the financial situation." On Friday, March 16, Hunt went to Hogan & Hartson, Bittman's law firm, and met with O'Brien in a small room down the hall from Bittman's office. Hunt—who struck O'Brien as "agitated and disturbed"—told the lawyer that he had only a few days left to get his affairs in order, but that "commitments" made to him had not been kept. He said he needed $132,000—$60,000 in attorneys' fees already owed and $72,000 to provide two years of "family support" (at $3000 per month)—and he needed it before he went to prison, so that he could make "prudent disposition among members of my family." He told O'Brien to take a message to Dean at the White House: that Hunt had done "a number of seamy things" for Ehrlichman and that if he didn't get his money he would have to "review his options."

O'Brien says he was stunned: "I had never had anyone make a personal demand on me for over a hundred thousand dollars." So he told Hunt, "Chuck Colson is your friend. Why don't you write him a memorandum?" Regarding O'Brien as "a Mitchell man," Hunt interpreted this remark as a power play

—designed to shunt responsibility for the payoffs to Colson—and he resented it. Indeed, when he asked O'Brien why he should get in touch with Colson, Hunt claims O'Brien replied, "Because some of us feel it's time Colson got into it—got his feet wet like the rest of us." That got Hunt's back up even further and he told O'Brien frostily, "On the other hand, Chuck hasn't been involved so far. I don't see any reason to involve him now."

Of course, Colson had been very deeply involved and, as soon as O'Brien left, Hunt told Bittman he wanted to see Chuck again. Bittman called Colson's office and then told Hunt he could see David Shapiro, Colson's new law partner, which Hunt assumed was just a way of disguising a meeting with Colson. But when he got to the lawyer's office, Shapiro told him the meeting *was* with him and nobody else. Finding Shapiro's manner "both arrogant and offensive," Hunt gave him the same message he'd given O'Brien, but sharpened his threat this time with a new warning: that if the commitments to him were not kept, the Republicans would lose the 1974 and 1976 elections. Then he stomped angrily out of the office.

On Monday, March 19, Shapiro reported Hunt's remarks to Colson but advised him not to tell anyone at the White House because he might "unwittingly become a party to an obstruction of justice." Colson talked to the President by telephone that day, but insists he didn't mention Hunt's threat.

The message got to the White House anyway a few hours later—passed by O'Brien to Dean, as Hunt had requested. When he finished recounting Hunt's warnings, O'Brien recalls, the usually cool, contained young counsel suddenly erupted: "I am tired of being put in the middle! I am going to bust this goddamn thing up. You and I are being screwed as conduits in this case. We can get stuck with an obstruction of justice."

That evening Dean was supposed to go to a reception honoring Chuck Colson. This struck Dean as rather ironic, for one of Colson's assignments when he left the White House was to "hold Mr. Hunt's hand and to take care of his problems." Obviously, Colson hadn't done his job very well and now Dean was damned if he'd go to any reception for him. Instead, he went directly home and had "more than one Cutty Sark" brooding about the bind he was in.

Dean's mood had shifted sharply within days. On February 28 he had told the President, "I'm convinced we're going to make it the whole road and put this thing in the funny pages of the history books rather than anything serious." On March 13 he had warned, "There are dangers, Mr. President, I'd be less than candid if I didn't tell you." But as late as March 17 he was telling the President that the March 2 news conference had helped: "as a result of your press conference, that the forward momentum that was going and building, stopped and . . . again we're in this breathing space."

But now it was getting very hard to breathe. The money demands, particularly Hunt's, were getting out of hand. Dean realized it could cost them a fortune over the next couple of years. How could they keep up that kind of "continual blackmail operation"? Sooner or later somebody was bound to "blow." And once one of the principals began talking, it would be like a line of dominoes (what the President had so graphically described as: "Sloan starts pissing on Magruder and then Magruder starts pissing on who, even Haldeman"). Dean had already begun to notice how everyone was hiring his own lawyer, the lawyers were intervening more, everybody was looking to "cover his own ass." Worst of all, his own "cover" had been blown during the Gray hearings; he was more and more out front, in the newspapers, increasingly vulnerable, ripe to be made the scapegoat. Drenched in Cutty Sark and apprehension, he dragged himself off to bed.

The next day, March 20, Dean recounted Hunt's threat to Ehrlichman. According to Dean, Ehrlichman tried to "give the impression that he wasn't particularly concerned." The two men had never felt comfortable with each other and Dean thought Ehrlichman always played it "close to the chest" with him. But in fact, as Ehrlichman recalls, he was "shaken by this, because

Dean put it in terms that this was a threat aimed at me on a personal basis." Both men were shaken because they knew just exactly what Hunt was threatening to expose—the burglary of Dr. Lewis Fielding's office which could be traced at least to Ehrlichman and perhaps to Nixon.

Just what and when the President knew about the Fielding burglary remains something of a mystery. At 3:03 p.m., September 8, five days after the burglary and a few hours after Egil Krogh and David Young reported on it to him, Ehrlichman met with Nixon privately in a session that lasted for forty-seven minutes. But, although Ehrlichman says he kept the President up to date on all Plumbers' operations, he insists he did not tell him about the break-in then. Nixon says he didn't find out about it until March 17, 1973, and the transcript of his conversation with Dean that day seems to bear him out. When Dean told him about the burglary under Ehrlichman's auspices, Nixon exclaimed, "What in the world, what in the name of God was Ehrlichman having something (*unintelligible*) in the Ellsberg?" And a few minutes later he said, ". . . the first time I ever heard of this . . . Jesus Christ!"

But, if the President was just discovering it then, nonetheless some dangerous clues to the Ellsberg operation had been rattling around for months and Ehrlichman had been seeking to bottle them up. On November 27, 1972, William E. Colby, then the CIA's third-ranking official, had met with the prosecutors. When Earl Silbert asked which White House official had authorized the agency to supply Hunt with false credentials, Colby recalls, he "danced around the room several times" before identifying Ehrlichman. This identification was based on the recollection of former CIA Deputy Director Robert Cushman, and during the next few months, Ehrlichman sought to persuade Cushman that he was wrong. On January 10, 1973, under heavy White House pressure, Cushman changed his mind and said he couldn't recall who had requested assistance for Hunt.

Meanwhile, on December 5, 1972, the CIA had given the prosecutors Xerox copies of the photographs the agency had developed for Hunt and Liddy during their "reconnaissance" trip to Dr. Fielding's office (since August 27, the copies had been kept in the safe of the acting chief of the Technical Services Division and removed only after the Watergate burglary). One of the photographs showed Liddy lighting a cigar outside the office and another showed the doctor's parking space with the sign marked "Dr. Fielding." These photographs had been enough for the CIA to conclude that Hunt was involved in some sort of surreptitious break-in, but Petersen and Silbert could make nothing of them (although the materials removed from Hunt's safe had contained several references to Fielding, including a copy of an FBI report on an agent's attempt to interview him). "Mr. Silbert and I did discuss it," Petersen recalls. "We were trying to rationalize Mr. Liddy's conduct. He is a very bizarre individual . . . [so] photographs of himself didn't seem at all unusual." But Ehrlichman was very worried about the photographs. Fearing they might lead investigators to the burglary, he asked Dean to have the CIA recover the pictures. On February 9, 1973, Dean passed this request on to the new CIA director, James Schlesinger, but the next day, the agency respectfully declined to interfere.

Not surprisingly then, when Ehrlichman heard about Hunt's threats, he feared this might be the long-feared crack which would expose the Fielding break-in (and presumably the other White House "horrors" Hunt had been involved in). Ehrlichman spun into action, rushing off to see the President, then calling ex-Plumber Egil Krogh to tell him about the threat. But Ehrlichman's chief hope that evening was John Mitchell. Ehrlichman told Krogh that Mitchell was "responsible for the care and feeding of Howard Hunt." And Dean says Ehrlichman told him to inform Mitchell.

Dean telephoned Mitchell at home that night and briefly recounted Hunt's threats. He was very cautious because LaRue had warned him that if you called Mitchell at home, Martha would often pick up the extension and listen in. So, discussing how they might raise some money quickly, the former attorney general and the counsel to the President resorted to code. According to Dean, the conversation went like this:

DEAN: Did you talk to the Greek?
MITCHELL: Yes, I have.
DEAN: Is the Greek bearing gifts?
MITCHELL: Well, I want to call you tomorrow on that.

The "Greek" was Thomas A. Pappas, a Greek immigrant to the United States who had returned to his native land in the 1960s to build an oil, shipping, and chemical empire. Pappas had been a major financial backer of his *landsman* Spiro Agnew, while Agnew was still governor of Maryland, and has been credited with a prime role in the selection of Agnew as Nixon's running mate. Friendly with both the Greek junta then in power and the CIA—"I have worked for the CIA anytime my help was requested," he once boasted—Pappas became virtually the official host for U.S. dignitaries visiting Athens in the early 1970s. He spent much of 1972 shuttling between Greece and the United States, helping to raise money for Nixon; and he himself contributed more than $100,000 before the April 7 deadline. Sometime during the winter of 1973, Dean says, LaRue told him to ask Pappas for $250,000–$300,000—as a *quid pro quo* for some import quotas Pappas needed to construct two crude-oil conversion plants in the United States or Canada. Both Mitchell and LaRue spoke with Pappas. On March 21 Dean told the President, "Pappas has agreed to come up with a single amount I gather from Mitchell." (Later in the spring Nixon said, "Good old Tom is raising money. . . ." But Pappas insists he made no such contribution and there is no evidence that he did.)

After he spoke with Mitchell, Dean got a call from the restless President. For hours, Dean had agonized over the "blackmail" attempt and its implications. He had discussed his dilemma with his friend Richard Moore, who urged him to tell the President the whole story. Now, he seized the opportunity to ask Nixon for some time "to examine the broadest, broadest implications of this whole thing and, you know, about thirty minutes of just my recitation to you of facts so that you operate from the same facts that everyone else has . . . we have never really done that. It has been sort of bits and pieces. Just paint the whole picture for you, the soft spots, the potential problem areas." Nixon said "Right," and they set the briefing for ten o'clock the next morning.

Dean was operating on the assumption that the President still did not know the full, coherent story of Watergate and its ancillary operations. The President did nothing to challenge that assumption, but he was not being entirely frank with Dean. Nineteen minutes before their telephone conversation, he had finished a seventy-minute telephone call with Haldeman in which the two men went through much, if not all, of the material Dean was planning to present the next day. If the President had not known before—and there are signs that he knew some things much earlier—he certainly knew most of the Watergate story by 7:10 p.m., March 20.

In their conversation that evening Haldeman and Nixon gradually sorted the burgeoning scandal into four categories:

• The Segretti dirty-tricks operation. Here Haldeman quickly conceded that with his "concurrence" Chapin and Strachan had recruited their old college friend, that Kalmbach had paid him, and that Segretti "did go a little far on the tricks," a little beyond what they had intended. But both of them felt that didn't hurt the White House much. Haldeman mused, "I can say it was bad judgment on Chapin's part to let the guy go as far as he did, or Chapin can say it was bad judgment on Segretti's part to do some of the things he did." The President dismissed it all: "Horseshit! That's so inconsequential!"

• The Watergate break-ins and wiretapping. This, they agreed, wasn't inconsequential and "it isn't a question of bad judgment." Haldeman reported, "Strachan's job was to know, was to keep on top of everything that was going on . . . he knows what happened over there . . . and I possibly got reports on some of that stuff . . .

if I did I didn't know it, but Strachan did know because he gave me, you know, stuff that thick and I never looked at it." Moreover, Haldeman said, "What they're after is Colson on criminal—they think he's the highest guy they can get on criminal in the White House and Mitchell on the outside. . . ." And they agreed that Mitchell probably was involved. As Nixon said, "You can't figure Magruder did it by himself." Haldeman said things weren't so good "if Mitchell was the authority as attorney general of the United States. . . ." To which Nixon added ruefully, "And the President's campaign manager. That's pretty goddamn bad. That's damn near as bad as it is out here."

• The burglary of Dr. Fielding's office and other White House horrors. "Oh Jesus!" exclaimed Haldeman. "You got Ehrlichman. John knows a hell of a lot." The President put in quickly, "He does know a hell of a lot, but not about this case, not about Watergate. . . . He ran the other thing. He ran, you know, that damn stuff about . . ." Haldeman helpfully supplied, "Ellsberg . . . Teddy Kennedy . . ." And the President groaned, "Uh, I don't like it."

• The secret fund. Haldeman conceded that "there was $350,000 transferred out of the campaign fund over to a separate holder and it was under Strachan's control. It was, in a sense, transferred to me. . . . And that has been transferred back to the re-election committee." The President shrugged and said, "Well . . . boxes in every campaign." Haldeman didn't say anything specifically about the hush money, but something was bothering him: "Not that it worries me, not that it's ever worried me and I—and maybe there's more to it, than I, there's something to it, than I've found. . . ." The President said, "Sure," and laughed.

The more they talked about it all, the more they saw how one part led to another. They agreed that the "Segretti thing" wasn't so bad, you could "let that one hang out." Haldeman said they ought to be able to turn that part of it off, "but the problem is the price of turning it off may hurt the people on the Watergate side." And the President said, "Yeah, the people on the Watergate side unfortunately are also our friends."

So, Haldeman said, "The problem is—can't the truth stop at the truth . . . or does the innuendo come then so hard on top of it that you can't turn it off? . . . There's no question that they're going to keep building the innuendo that will lead into the White House and will be able to come to some proof, what they'll call proof. . . ."

They didn't want anybody tracking into the White House after that kind of proof. "We just can't allow that sort of thing to come out," the President said. But he wasn't entirely satisfied with Dean's outright "containment, keep-it-in-the-box" policy either, because it had begun to "look now that I am just doing that as a thumb-your-nose, screw-off" policy, and that way "you've got the story of cover-up."

The President concluded, "I think we have to find a way to make statements . . . any kind of a statement . . . as general as possible . . . just so somebody can say that . . . a statement has been made through the President upon which he has based his statement to the effect that he has confidence in his staff. . . . I didn't do this, I didn't do that, da da da da, da da da da, da da da da, da da da da. Haldeman didn't do this. Ehrlichman didn't do that. Colson didn't do that."

HALDEMAN: I wouldn't say that this is the whole truth.

NIXON: Yeah.

HALDEMAN: I'd say in relation to the charges.

So when Dean entered the Oval Office at ten the next morning, March 21, for his showdown meeting, the President already knew most of what Dean was going to tell him and had largely mapped out his new cover-up strategy. He listened politely to Dean's lengthy account, which probably included some details he didn't know, and to his young counsel's heartfelt warning: ". . . there's no doubt about the seriousness of the problem we've, we've got. We have a cancer—within—close to the Presidency, that's growing. It's growing daily. It's compounding itself."

But he reacted sharply only when Dean reached

Hunt's specific "blackmail" demand, which, he said, would cost them more than $120,000 now and much more in years to come.

NIXON: How much do you need?
DEAN: I would say these people are going to cost a million dollars over the next two years.
NIXON: We could get that.
DEAN: Uh huh.
NIXON: You, on the money, if you need the money, I mean you could get the money. Let's say—
DEAN: Well, I think that we're going—
NIXON: What I mean is, you could get a million dollars. And you could get it in cash. I know where it could be gotten.

Dean had come into the President's office that morning determined to argue against any more payoffs—indeed, against continuing the cover-up of which he had been the major architect. And he tried: "It'll cost money. It's dangerous. . . . People around here are not pros at this sort of thing. This is the sort of thing Mafia people can do: washing money, getting clean money, and things like that. We just don't know about these things, because we're . . . not criminals and not used to dealing in that business. . . ."

And again: "What really bothers me is that this growing situation, as I say, is growing because of the continued need to provide support for Watergate people who are going to hold us up for everything they've got and the need for some people to perjure themselves as they go down the road here. If this thing ever blows and we're in a cover-up situation, it'd be extremely damaging to you. . . ."

And still again: "I am not confident we can ride through this. I think there are soft spots . . . some people are going to have to go to jail. . . . It's something that is not going to go away . . . I think it's at the juncture that we should begin to think in terms of how to cut the losses."

But the President didn't want to hear this kind of talk. ". . . You say we're going to go down the road, see if we can cut our losses and no more blackmail and all the rest, and the thing blows and they indict Bob and the rest. Jesus, you'd never recover from that, John. . . . It's better to fight it out instead . . . and not let people testify, so forth and so on. . . ."

Time and again, Nixon came back to the money for Hunt. "Don't you, just looking at the immediate problem, don't you have to handle Hunt's financial situation damn soon? You've got to keep the cap on the bottle that much in order to have any options . . . at the moment, don't you agree that you'd better get the Hunt thing? I mean, that's worth it, at the moment . . . you better damn well get that done, but fast."

And when Dean still seemed hesitant, the President said, "Well, for Christ's sake get it. . . ."

All of a sudden, Dean recalled later, "I was back in the cover-up, going along." The President was determined. So was Haldeman (who, very worried about Hunt talking, told Colson, "We can't let that happen"). Dean, the compleat acolyte, slipped uneasily back into his old role.

After the meeting Dean called LaRue and told him that Hunt was urgently demanding $135,000 in legal fees and living expenses. According to Haldeman, La-Rue was dismayed at the prospect of more payoffs and told Dean, "This whole thing is ridiculous now. If I were in charge of this now what I would do is I'd get a large bus and I'd put the President at the wheel and I'd throw everybody we've got around here in it and I'd drive up to the Senate and I'd have the President open the door and I'd say, 'You all get out and tell everything you know and I'll be back to pick you up when you're through.' " LaRue was particularly dismayed at the amount of money Hunt was asking for, far more than he'd ever handed out in a single payment. He asked Dean whether he should pay it, but Dean—who was trying to remain aloof from the payoffs—said he was just relaying the message. LaRue said he couldn't make a payment unless someone authorized it; so Dean suggested he get in touch with Mitchell. LaRue called Mitchell and told him Hunt wanted $75,000—the amount he guessed Hunt needed for legal fees (he apparently omitted the rest because he wasn't sure he had enough cash). Mitchell, who had earlier spoken with Haldeman, instructed LaRue to pay it.

That evening LaRue invited a few friends over for dinner at his Watergate apartment: his secretary, Laura Fredericks; Manyon M. Millican, the marketing director of a West Virginia snow-shoe company who was serving as CREEP's director of canvassing; and Sherman E. Ungar, a Cincinnati lawyer who happened to be in town for the day. The dinner got off to a bad start when the exhaust fan in LaRue's fireplace malfunctioned, filling the apartment with smoke, but the four old friends laughed through it. At about ten o'clock, while the others chatted gaily in the living room, LaRue took Millican into the bedroom and asked him to deliver an envelope to Bittman—a service the snow-shoe man had performed twice before under similar circumstances. When Millican readily agreed, LaRue gave him an eight-and-a-half-by-eleven-inch manila envelope filled with $75,000 in $100 bills— apparently from the remainder of Haldeman's secret cache of $350,000. Millican drove to Potomac, and stuffed the envelope into Bittman's mailbox. At about eleven-thirty, alerted by a telephone call from LaRue under the name "Baker," Bittman came out to retrieve the money. The next morning he telephoned Hunt, who lived only a mile away and came over to get the unopened envelope. This was the last of the "hush-money" payments, and it brought the total paid out to the seven defendants to $429,500.*

Hunt says he was angry when he discovered the envelope contained barely three-fifths of what he had demanded. (He has complained publicly that by this time his funds were "long since exhausted." Yet, he had received $260,000 in flight insurance from his wife's death and, hours before he collected the $60,000 on March 21, he bought $109,872 worth of stock. His lawyer says the stock was purchased with some of the

---

*LaRue later pleaded guilty to conspiracy to obstruct justice and was sentenced to six months in prison.

insurance money by a brokerage firm to which Hunt had given discretionary power and that Hunt was "sore as hell" when he heard about it. But a March 20 letter to Hunt from the firm indicates that Hunt discussed at least one of the purchases with his broker. The $75,000 was kept in Hunt's home for a time and later put into a safe-deposit box by his daughter Kevan. Bittman was paid by check sometime in April—a check drawn on the insurance money.)

At a White House meeting with Haldeman, Ehrlichman, and Dean on the morning of March 22 Mitchell reported that Hunt was "not a problem any more." Afterward, Ehrlichman called Krogh to report that Hunt was "stable" and that he should "hang tough."

"**H**ang tough" was the watchword around the White House in those days after Nixon's decision to pay Hunt's demands. The President's men were more committed than ever to the cover-up, and everyone was talking tough. Once, in a hurried conversation outside the President's office, Haldeman and Dean discussed "drawing the wagons around the White House" (an apt metaphor, considering the buses which had so often ringed the White House to protect it from hostile demonstrators).

But not everyone was to be allowed within the protective security of that wagon circle. The President, of course; Haldeman and Ehrlichman, certainly; Dean, for the time being. They were "White House." But Magruder was slated for sacrifice now. And Mitchell— once the President's closest confidant, the "big enchilada" of Nixon's first administration—was also being readied for the Indians.

When the President and Haldeman talked on March 20 Nixon said, "Our real concern is Mitchell." But then he mused, "Maybe they're going to get him anyway." The next afternoon, after Dean and the President talked, Haldeman, Ehrlichman, and Dean met in Ehrlichman's office and Haldeman said, "I wonder if we are taking all this anguish just to protect John Mitchell." Dean says the conversation went further and all three began to feel that "Mr. Mitchell should be the one to step forward and stand responsible for the entire Watergate matter and that, if he did, the problems that had occurred after June 17 would dissipate. . . . In other words, a big enough fish would have been caught that the problem would have been resolved." And a few hours later, when the trio met with Nixon to continue making strategy, Ehrlichman tried out his idea on the boss: "Suppose Mitchell were to step out . . . and make some kind of disclosure." But the President wasn't sure: "What the hell is he going to disclose that isn't going to blow something?"

Practicalities aside, the President wasn't comfortable with the idea of abandoning his old friend. At the end of a March 22 meeting, Mitchell stayed behind in the Oval Office and the two former law partners and drinking companions had a long chat. Not surprisingly, the situation reminded Nixon of an old wound—the way Eisenhower had made him suffer over his piddling little secret fund in 1952, demanding that he be "as clean as a hound's tooth." Now he told Mitchell, "That's what Eisenhower—that's all he cared about. He only cared about—Christ, 'Be sure he was clean.' Both in the fund thing and the [Sherman] Adams thing. But I don't look at it that way. And I just— that's the thing I am really concerned with. We're going to protect our people, if we can." And so he told his old friend, though at that stage he preferred a somewhat more subtle policy of limited "cooperation" with the investigators, he would back him to the hilt if he wanted to fight all the way: "I don't give a shit what happens, I want you all to stonewall it, let them plead the Fifth Amendment, cover-up or anything else, if it'll save it—save the plan."

Some of the President's men—notably Ehrlichman —still hoped to dump the blame for Watergate on Mitchell's hunched and hardened shoulders. They discussed it enough so that Martha Mitchell's sensitive antennae picked it up and she called *The New York Times* to say, "I fear for my husband. I'm really scared.

I have a definite reason. I can't tell you why, but they're not going to pin anything on him. I won't let them." And, for the time being, neither would the President.

Instead, Nixon and his aides turned their attention to another possible scapegoat—John Dean. The strategy this time was subtler and evolved more slowly. Haldeman and others began warning the President that the total "stonewall" executive privilege line was hurting him with the public. "They think you clanged down an iron curtain here and you won't let anybody out of here, ever, that have ever worked here, scour lady on up," Haldeman said. "The guy sitting at home who watches John Chancellor . . . says, 'What in the hell's he covering up? If he's got no problem why doesn't he let them go and talk?'" And Nixon began "thinking of how the President looks" and realized that it would all look much better if "the President makes the move." So they began talking again about a statement.

By mid-March—only days after he took his stand on executive privilege—Nixon knew it would not be enough to block the investigators. On March 17 Nixon began pressing Dean to write a different kind of report: one which "basically clears the President" and says that "no one on the White House staff is involved." He suggested that Dean could "make self-serving goddamn statements," could specify that he had "never heard any discussions of bugging," and could argue that CREEP's intelligence system was "not only legal . . . but totally necessary because of the violence." It was not what the President doubtfully called the "hangout" approach; not even what Haldeman called a "limited hang out," but what Ehrlichman finally dubbed "the modified limited hang out."

All through March 20, 21, and 22 the President and his men kept pressing the reluctant Dean to write such a report. They suggested that he owed it to the President. On March 21 Ehrlichman told him, "The Presidency is in a stronger position later if he can be shown to have justifiably relied on you at this point in time." And when Dean objected that that didn't clean out "the cancer," Ehrlichman replied, "Doesn't it permit the President to clean it out at such time as it does come up, by saying 'Indeed, I relied on it. And now this later thing turns up, and I don't condone that. And if I'd known about that before, obviously I wouldn't have done it. And I'm going to move on it now.'"

Dean had been through this once before, in August 1972, when the President announced that Dean had thoroughly investigated Watergate and determined nobody at the White House was involved. But that had been a total fabrication, an investigation that was never carried out, an oral report that was never made. This time it would be a real report, on paper. And when things began "blowing"—as Dean was sure they would—the President would be there with a "Dean Report" to say, "There. Look. This is what I relied on."

No wonder Dean was reluctant. He dawdled, diddled, dallied until, on the afternoon of March 22, Haldeman told him to "hole up for the weekend" and write the report, "put an end to your business and get it done!" And the President suggested, "Why don't you go up to Camp David?" (the Presidential retreat in Maryland's Catoctin Mountains). Dean could delay no longer. The next day he and his wife left for Camp David.

But before they reached the city limits, Dean's worst fears had come to pass. McCord had "blown." McCord's defection came as no real surprise to the White House. Through Caulfield, the President's men knew how restless, unhappy, and resentful the former CIA man was, how unwilling he was to go to jail to protect the "higher-ups." Indeed, the transcript of the President's conversation with Haldeman on the evening of March 20 contains some curious, garbled remarks by Nixon which suggest that he may have had some specific warning: "McCord didn't want to go to jail (*unintelligible*) jail sentence (*unintelligible*) decided to talk. I said, 'What the hell's he doing?'" On March 21—the day the President ordered the last installment of hush money to keep Hunt quiet— McCord tried to deliver a sealed letter to Judge Sirica, who refused to accept it, fearing that it might contain money or something else which could embroil him in a scandal. He ordered McCord to give the letter to his probation officer, James D. Morgan.

In a sense, Morgan had provoked McCord's letter. For Sirica had instructed the probation officers who prepared the presentencing reports to ask the defendants certain questions about motivation, intention, and other mitigating circumstances. When those questions were posed to Hunt, he regarded his officer with ill-disguised contempt as "a cautious, rather oily bureaucrat" and resented his efforts to "weasel from me fresh information about Watergate." Stiffened by the hush money and promises of clemency, he flatly refused to cooperate.

But when McCord got the same questions from Morgan, he felt "whipsawed" by conflicting pressures. On the one hand, his answers might be used against him in future appearances before the Ervin committee, in a civil suit, or at some future trial. On the other hand, he realized that failure to answer the questions would "appear to be noncooperative" and might bring him "a much more severe sentence." And McCord, more than any of the other defendants, wanted to avoid a lengthy sentence. Liddy was a martyr to his own compulsions. Barker and his men were loyal soldiers in the fight for a Free Cuba. Hunt by then was a beaten man, with little to live for. But McCord, despite his years in the CIA and his abiding loyalty to the organization, was much less the clandestine operator than Liddy or Hunt, much less the true believer than the Miami men. Deeply rooted in his church, his community, and his family; still married to his college sweetheart; the father of three children, one of them a retarded girl for whom he felt great responsibility, McCord had compelling reasons to cooperate with the judge. So he wrote the brief letter which Sirica now read to an astonished courtroom:

". . . in the interest of restoring faith in the criminal justice system, which faith has been severely damaged in this case, I will state the following to you at this time which I hope may be of help to you in meting justice in this case." Then he made several revelations, including:

"There was political pressure applied to the defendants to plead guilty and remain silent.

"Perjury occurred during the trial in matters highly material to the very structure, orientation and impact of the Government's case, and to the motivation and intent of the defendants.

"Others involved in the Watergate operation were not identified during the trial, when they could have been by those testifying.

"The Watergate operation was not a C.I.A. operation. The Cubans may have been misled by others into believing that it was a C.I.A. operation. I know for a fact that it was not."

McCord asked to talk privately with Judge Sirica in chambers after sentencing, noting that he would "not feel confident" talking in the presence of FBI agents, Justice Department attorneys, or "other government representatives." (He said he feared "retaliatory measures will be taken against me, my family, and my friends should I disclose such facts . . . either publicly or to any government representative.") The judge said he would hear McCord under oath and with a stenographer present, though he warned that he would make no promise that "my lips will be sealed" regardless of "what he [McCord] might tell me." He postponed sentencing McCord until after their meeting.*

With this "preliminary matter" out of the way, Judge Sirica began handing out sentences to the other six defendants. He proved worthy of his courthouse nickname, "Maximum John." To five of the defendants he gave the maximum terms permissible under the law—forty years each to Bernard Barker, Eugenio Martinez, Virgilio Gonzalez, and Frank Sturgis, thirty-five years to Howard Hunt. But he made those sentences "provisional" and said he would review them after three months and after the defendants had had an opportunity to cooperate with other investigators. Al-

---

*Eventually, Sirica sentenced McCord to one to five years in prison, but he served only three months and twenty-one days.

though the crimes they had committed were "sordid, despicable, and thoroughly reprehensible," he said, they might mitigate their sentences "if you testify openly and completely regardless of what the implications are to yourself or to anyone else" before the Ervin committee and the grand jury. "You must understand that I hold out no promise or hopes of any kind. But I do say that should you decide to speak freely I would have to weigh that factor in appraising what sentence will be finally imposed in each case."*

To warn the five men what might happen if they did not cooperate, Judge Sirica gave Gordon Liddy an extraordinarily severe sentence, this one with no provision for review. The mustachioed gun collector had remained impassive and utterly uncooperative throughout the trial and the judge plainly intended the sentence—a minimum of six years eight months and a maximum of twenty years—as a stern example of the justice he was prepared to mete out. Unlike Hunt, who made a stirring plea for mercy ("Since the Watergate case began, I have suffered agonies I never believed a man could endure and still survive. . . . My fate—and that of my family—my children—is in your hands"), Liddy declined to address the court and he took his medicine the way he took everything, with a stiff little grin. But later he was to say, "I really can't be too critical of John Sirica because John Sirica and I think alike. He believes that the end justifies the means. He puts that into practice. He does what is necessary."

Some civil libertarians made exactly the same point. Joseph L. Rauh, Jr., former national chairman of Americans for Democratic Action, has found it "ironic that those most opposed to Mr. Nixon's lifetime espousal of ends-justifying-means should now make a hero of a judge who practiced this formula to the detriment of a

---

*Judge Sirica imposed final sentences in November 1973. He gave Gonzalez, Martinez, and Sturgis each one-to-four-year terms, but later ordered them released after they had served a little more than a year. Barker received an eighteen-month to six-year sentence, but Judge Sirica ordered him released after he had served one year. Hunt was given a thirty-month to eight-year sentence and a $10,000 fine.

fair trial for the Watergate Seven." Chesterfield Smith, president of the American Bar Association, is "concerned about a federal judge—no matter how worthy his motives or how much we may applaud his results—using the criminal sentencing process as a means and tool for further criminal investigation of others." And Monroe Freedman, dean of the law school at Hofstra University, says, "Sirica deserves to be censured for becoming the prosecutor himself." To such complaints, Judge Sirica calmly replied, "I don't think we should sit up here like nincompoops. The function of a trial court is to search for the truth." And search he did. During the Watergate trial, he often became so exasperated at the prosecutors' performance and the defendants' evasive answers that he took over the questioning himself. "Don't pull any punches—you give me straight answers," he told the four Miami defendants when they pleaded guilty. And he often refused to accept the answers he got. When Barker said he didn't know who had sent him expense money in a plain envelope, he snapped, "Well, I'm sorry, but I don't believe you." He did not have much respect for the niceties of courtroom behavior. When Liddy whispered in his lawyer's ear, Judge Sirica said sarcastically, "I see you're getting some good legal advice from your client, the former attorney." The lawyer jumped up and objected to the implication that Liddy had already been disbarred, but the judge said brusquely, "All right, he's still a lawyer admitted to the bar. I'll grant you. Now let's get on with it." By birthright and training, Sirica was a fighter. His childhood was spent wandering through Florida, Louisiana, Ohio, Virginia, California, and Washington, D.C., as his father, a tubercular Italian barber, searched for work. "It was an uphill fight against poverty, poverty, poverty," he recalls. Helping to support the family by greasing cars, waiting on tables, and selling newspapers, he never attended college and had a hard time in law school. At George Washington University, he "couldn't understand anything they were talking about, so I quit." A year later he tried Georgetown University, but had trouble with the Latin terminology and left again.

Finally, he tried Georgetown once more and stuck with it. He worked part time as a boxing coach for the Knights of Columbus and, after getting his law degree in 1926, became the sparring partner for Jack Britton, the former world welterweight champion. He fought a few "smoker" bouts himself, prompting one paper to call him a "great little mitt artist" (he is only five-foot seven). Turning from ring to bar, he remained combative, jumping up once to shout at a judge, "It ain't fair! It ain't fair!" Long active in Republican politics, he was appointed to the federal bench by Eisenhower in 1957. Never regarded as one of the intellectual lights of the bench, Sirica was reversed by appeals courts more often than any other judge in the District. But that didn't seem to bother him. "A reversal record doesn't mean that they're right and you're wrong," he said. "It just means they've got the last word on you." Watergate clearly angered him and he was determined to get at the truth even at the risk of another reversal. Jack Dempsey, an old friend from his boxing days, remarked, "He's a better fighter now than he ever was."

In the rustic retreat used by six Presidents, John Dean brooded over the events in Washington. He and his wife "Mo" strolled through the Catoctin woods, still flecked with patches of dirty snow. He tried to write his "report," scrawling in longhand on a yellow legal pad, and even summoned his secretary up from the White House to begin typing it. But he couldn't get much done: would anyone believe it any more? On Monday, the *Los Angeles Times* reported that McCord had told Senate investigators that both Dean and Magruder had advance knowledge of the Watergate burglary. In Key Biscayne, Ron Ziegler announced that, despite the story, the President had "absolute and total" confidence in Dean and had told him so in a telephone call. But Dean had received no call from the President, and when he heard of Ziegler's announcement he sensed that he was "in some obscure way being set up." Feeling increasingly cornered, he told Mo that he had only one choice: to go to the prosecutors. She wept, but agreed. He called his lawyer, Tom Hogan, who suggested they get in touch with a hard-nosed criminal lawyer named Charles Shaffer.

On Haldeman's instructions, Dean returned to Washington on March 28, his report still largely unwritten. On Friday, March 30, he engaged Shaffer. That afternoon Dean told Hogan and Shaffer the whole story. They continued meeting all weekend and again on Monday morning. On Monday afternoon, April 2, Hogan and Shaffer told the prosecutors that Dean was ready to cooperate. After some preliminary fencing over immunity, Dean began gingerly telling his story to Silbert and his colleagues on April 8. That day Dean telephoned Haldeman to let him know that he was going to the prosecutors, and Haldeman cautioned him, "I think you ought to think about it, because once the toothpaste is out of the tube, it's hard to get it back in."*

But by then the toothpaste was coming out of the tube for good. In part, this was because Dean's other prediction had come to pass. The Nixon "team" which had held together so well for months was falling apart now, day by day. In Magruder's words, it was "every man for himself." The President himself had set the tone for this disintegration. Although he could celebrate loyalty and trust—notably in his March 22 chat with Mitchell—he more often breathed contempt for such treacly principles: on March 13 he told John Dean, "Bullshit: Nobody is a friend of ours"; and on March 21, when informed that Colson, Kalmbach, and Chapin were retaining lawyers, he snapped, "Well, let's not trust them." By April nobody trusted anybody in the Nixon camp. Haldeman, Ehrlichman, and Dean were routinely taping their conversations with each other and any potential witness. Lawyers warned their clients not to talk freely with their former colleagues. And soon the men who had lied so long to grand jury,

---

*John Dean pleaded guilty to obstruction of justice and defrauding the United States and was sentenced to one to four years in prison. He was released after serving about four months.

jury, FBI, and press were racing each other to get to the prosecutors.

With the cards finally falling their way, the prosecutors at last began to play their hands with some shrewdness. On March 26 they reconvened the federal grand jury and in following days got orders from Judge Sirica granting the Watergate Seven immunity from further prosecution in return for testimony before the grand jury. The prosecutors played a particularly clever game with Liddy. Stubborn to the end, Liddy refused to tell the grand jury anything, but Silbert kept him sitting in an anteroom for hours; when his attorney angrily told reporters he was saying nothing, this only strengthened suspicions that Liddy was at last spilling his guts. (This increased the pressure on Dean. Only after Dean's attorneys went to the prosecutors on April 2 did Silbert go back to Judge Sirica and get Liddy cited for contempt of court, with eight to eighteen months added to his sentence.) Hunt did talk extensively to the grand jury, although much of what he told it was later shown to be untrue. And McCord, with his sentence now postponed until June, began testifying on April 5.

The pressures generated by the grand jury and Ervin committee investigations were accentuated by a suddenly revived press corps. Washington newsmen— again with the exception of the relentless Woodstein and their competitors at the *Timeses* of New York and Los Angeles—had largely dropped the Watergate story after Nixon's re-election. But with the pyrotechnics of March and April, they were suddenly everywhere, swarming over officials' lawns and back porches, sticking microphones in faces which had barely swallowed their morning eggs. And the more resourceful reporters managed to dig out secret testimony naming big names, high places, and titillating machinations. Ziegler denounced these "irresponsible leaks in tidal-wave proportions," but the stories were often leaked by the participants for their own reasons, and they kept coming—lapping at every doorstep, intensifying the pressures to get your office mate before he got you.

Indeed, it was from a newspaper story published on March 30 that Jeb Magruder realized that his months-long bluff was about to be called. Woodstein that day quoted Senate sources as saying that the Ervin committee had subpoenaed his former administrative assistant Robert Reisner. Magruder knew that Reisner —who had inexplicably slipped through the prosecutors' net the summer before—could tie Magruder firmly to the planning for Gemstone. Desperately, he picked up the telephone and tried to arrange a meeting with Reisner, but the canny young man declined. Nearly hysterical now, Magruder implored, "Bob, what are you doing? . . . Aren't you going to cooperate? Everybody else is cooperating. It isn't just me. If this gets out of hand they're going to impeach the President."

But everybody else wasn't cooperating, and Magruder knew it all too well. Two days before, he had met with Mitchell and Dean at the White House to get their assurance that they would stick by the story they had all agreed on the summer before—that they had held only one meeting with Liddy and that one merely to discuss the new campaign-finance law. He got a ready pledge from Mitchell (who had earlier promised Magruder that he would make sure he got legal fees, family support, and eventually even clemency if he went to prison sticking to his story which, incidentally, also protected Mitchell). But Dean—who had already told the President the true and very different story of the Liddy meetings—steadfastly refused to give Magruder any promise.

As the ground slipped from under Magruder's feet, he scrambled for safety. On March 30 he and his wife flew to Bermuda to see James Bierbower, a prominent Republican lawyer who had been recommended to him and who was attending a bar association conference on the island. After a preliminary talk in the sun—during which Magruder stuck to his cover story—Bierbower agreed to represent him. The Magruders won a section of the mixed-doubles tennis tournament at the Coral Beach Club, then returned to Washington and cold reality on April 3.

For a week longer, Magruder maintained his story.

But Jim Sharp, a former U.S. attorney in Maryland who had recently joined Bierbower's firm, did not believe him and kept urging him to come clean before it was too late to claim some immunity from prosecution. Increasingly nervous, drinking too much, and unable to sleep at night, Magruder finally could see no reason for continuing to protect Mitchell and others at his own expense. On April 10 he told Sharp the full story of Watergate as he knew it. On April 12 Sharp and Bierbower opened negotiations with the prosecutors for the best immunity bargain they could strike. On the thirteenth they got a deal they couldn't refuse—a one-count felony indictment (punishable with a maximum of five years in prison) in exchange for Magruder's full cooperation. The former deputy director of the President's re-election campaign grabbed it.*

But part of striking a good deal for your client in those days was making sure nobody else's client got to the prosecutors first and grabbed the deal you wanted. Jim Sharp knew the game from his days in the Baltimore U.S. attorney's office and he played it with consummate skill. On April 11 Magruder had called Bart Porter—the young CREEP aide he had persuaded to lie the summer before—and warned him that he ought to come down from New York and talk to the prosecutors. Magruder suggested that Porter see Paul O'Brien, and have O'Brien set up an appointment with the prosecutors. Porter came to Washington on April 13, but O'Brien stalled him much of the day and finally sent him over to see Sharp. Sharp had already sealed Magruder's deal with the prosecutors, but Magruder hadn't been to see them yet and Sharp didn't want any last-minute disruptions. So when Porter told him he wanted to confess all, Sharp exclaimed:

"My God, you are an ant! You are nothing. Do you realize the whole course of history is going to be changed?"

When Porter bridled a bit, Sharp abruptly changed

---

*Jeb Magruder pleaded guilty to conspiracy to obstruct justice, defrauding the United States, and wiretapping the DNC headquarters. He was sentenced to a prison term of ten months to four years, and was released after serving seven months.

his approach. If Porter was adamant about going to the prosecutors, the lawyer said, why of course Magruder would give him the "courtesy" of going down first. Porter thanked him.

But as soon as Porter was out of the office, Sharp called Silbert and set up an appointment for Magruder at eight-thirty the next morning, April 14. Magruder met with the prosecutors then, and in the afternoon, at Ehrlichman's invitation, he went to the White House, and reported on the gist of what he had told the prosecutors. Walking back from the White House at about five, he ran into Porter outside St. John's Episcopal Church. "It is all over," he told Porter, "the President has directed everyone to tell the truth." And then he mentioned that he had been to see the prosecutors that morning. Porter, remembering Sharp's proffered "courtesy" of the day before, was "rather stunned."

Ehrlichman had summoned Magruder to the White House that afternoon in his new role: since March 30 he had taken over Dean's assignment as chief of Watergate "containment." At first Ehrlichman did his best to hold on to all the unraveling strands; but soon he could do little more than keep track of who was telling what to which investigator.

The day before he saw Magruder, Ehrlichman had received some alarming news. Chuck Colson and his law partner, David Shapiro, told him that Hunt was going to testify before the grand jury the following Monday, that he would corroborate most of McCord's testimony and would deeply implicate Mitchell, among others, in the planning of Watergate. As Ehrlichman told Nixon the next morning, Colson thought "the next forty-eight hours are the last chance for the White House to get out in front of this and that once Hunt goes then that's the ball game." Therefore, Colson had urged Ehrlichman to "smoke out" Mitchell and force him to "take responsibility for it [Watergate] and end this thing."

Colson and Mitchell had never gotten along. They resented each other's influence on the President and suspected each other's motives and methods. Colson says that as early as mid-January he began warning

Nixon that Mitchell and Magruder must have been involved in Watergate and that if he didn't act against them the scandal could spread into the White House. "I was somewhat resentful of the fact that Mitchell was sitting up in New York coining money in his law practice while my friend Hunt was going to go to jail," Colson recalls. Now, as the whole scandal seemed to be cracking open, the Colson faction and the Mitchell faction struggled on the brink of the chasm trying to nudge the other over the edge and scamper to safety. Throughout April, as the groups jockeyed for position, Nixon warned his aides, "I don't want people on the staff to divide up and say, 'Well, it's this guy that did it, or this guy that did it.'" But that's just what was happening. Colson and his allies passed word that Mitchell and Magruder were trying to "lay off" responsibility for Watergate on the White House. These reports strengthened Haldeman's and Ehrlichman's hand as they tried anew to place the blame on Mitchell.

On April 13 Larry Higby, Haldeman's chief administrative assistant, telephoned Magruder to determine just what he was up to. Without Magruder's knowledge, Higby taped the call—presumably to preserve evidence that could later be used in Haldeman's defense. Higby opened with an angry accusation based on Colson's report to Ehrlichman. "I've just picked up a story here that really bugs the shit out of me," he told Magruder. "Ehrlichman just called down here and says that he's received word that you have talked to two reporters and given the story out with regard to Watergate . . . that you'd talked to Haldeman regarding the bugging in general and the Watergate specifically."

Magruder vehemently denied "that kind of crap. Jesus Christ! I mean that just makes me sick, Larry." Magruder, of course, had originally been brought into the White House by Haldeman and had later been sent over to CREEP as Haldeman's chief agent. He had established cordial relations with Mitchell, which made him suspect in some circles, but now Magruder proclaimed his loyalty to his old boss. "Do you think I would turn on Bob?"

Then Magruder took the offensive: "Look, you

know damn well that there's a rumor that they're going to dump everything on me. . . . The rumor's all over town on that basis. That Magruder is the pigeon and he's going to take it—all the gas."

And he exploded at the man who, Higby had said, was badmouthing him: "Well, you just tell Ehrlichman to go to hell. For me. I mean, you just tell him. I'm tired of this bullshit. You know, we're not playing games any more. I is going to go to jail, Larry. . . . I've committed perjury so many times now that I'm, you know, I've got probably a hundred years on perjury alone. . . . Our lives are ruined right now anyway. You know, most of ours. Mine is certainly and so will many others before this is over. I think we ought to realize that."

He grew pensive: "I cannot lie any more. I've protected John Mitchell. I've protected the President when it was important. The story is going to come out. I have to do what I have to do now to protect whatever I can."

Higby began pressing to find out just what Magruder was going to tell the prosecutors.

HIGBY: Well, if you tell the story, I don't think Haldeman has anything to worry about.

MAGRUDER: Nothing to worry about. Now you—

HIGBY: 'Cause you never discussed this goddamn thing with him.

MAGRUDER: Larry, there's no problem. . . . Haldeman will have no problem with those facts.

HIGBY: Huh.

MAGRUDER: John Mitchell will. John Dean will. And Gordon [Strachan] will, probably.

Now Higby had what he wanted on tape—an exculpation for Haldeman—and suddenly he turned very friendly: "Well, my friend, if there's anything I can do, let me know." Soon, he was calling Magruder "Jebber" and Magruder was calling him "Lar" as they chatted about the case.

MAGRUDER: You visit me, kiddo?

HIGBY: Huh! I'll do more than that.

What he did was to play the tape for Haldeman, who reported on the conversation when he and Ehrlichman met with the President for a marathon strategy session the next morning. There was a sense of urgency at the White House that Saturday, a feeling they had to do something over the weekend before Hunt spilled the whole story to the grand jury on Monday. From 8:55 to 11:31, all that Nixon and his two chief aides talked about was Watergate. As Ehrlichman said, "This week there's no other subject."

Apparently, Colson was not the only one trying to shift all responsibility to Mitchell. Ehrlichman reported that Dean had suggested a "scenario" for such a move. "The President calls Mitchell into his office on Saturday. He says, 'John, you've got to do this and here are the facts: bing, bing, bing. . . .' And Mitchell stonewalls you. So then John [Mitchell] says, 'I don't know why you're asking me down here. You can't ask a man to do a thing like that. I need my lawyer. . . .' So the President says, 'Well, John, I have no alternative.' And with that the President calls the U.S. attorney and says, 'I, the President of the United States of America and leader of the Free World, want to go before the grand jury on Monday.' "

"I won't even comment on that," Nixon said. "That's like putting Bob on national television."

"With Dan Rather," said Haldeman, and they all dropped Dean's little scenario.

But John Connally—whose political savvy Nixon respected—was also urging that the blame be pinned on Mitchell. Haldeman relayed Connally's warning: that Mitchell was "the one man you couldn't afford to let get hung on this" because "he's the epitome of your hard line"—"unless," Connally warned, "it's the President himself who nails Mitchell."

And, as if Haldeman and Ehrlichman had coordinated their strategy beforehand, Ehrlichman hammered home this lesson with some speculation about what the news magazines might read like a week from then. On the one hand, he suggested, the lead story might read like this:

"The White House main effort to cover up finally

collapsed last week when the grand jury indicted John Mitchell and Jeb Magruder. Cracking the case was the testimony of a number of peripheral witnesses, each of whom contributed to developing a cross-triangularization and permitted the grand jury to analyze it. The final straw that broke the camel's back was an investigator's discovery of this and that and the other thing. The White House press secretary, Ron Ziegler, said that the White House would have no comment."

Or, he said, the story might read like this:

"Events moved swiftly last week after the President was presented with a report indicating for the first time that suspicion of John Mitchell and Jeb Magruder as ringleaders in the Watergate break-in were in fact substantiated by considerable evidence. The President dispatched so and so to do this and that and these efforts resulted in Mitchell going to the U.S. attorney's office on Monday morning at nine o'clock asking to testify before the grand jury. Charges of cover-up by the White House were materially dispelled by the diligent efforts of the President and his aides in moving on evidence which came to their hands in the closing days of the previous week."

It was a telling parable for a President so intensely aware of how the press would play the story, and indeed Nixon quickly said, "I'd buy that."

So the President finally accepted the "Mitchell scenario" which Haldeman and Ehrlichman had broached in late March, but which Nixon had shrunk from then because it reminded him too much of "hound's tooth" Eisenhower. But it had to be done. As he said that Saturday morning about John Dean, "Give 'em an hors d'oeuvre and maybe they won't come back for the main course." Dean and Mitchell could both be hors d'oeuvres—little mincemeats stuck on skewers. Quickly the discussion turned from "Whether" to "How" and particularly to "Who." For Nixon couldn't bring himself to approach Mitchell personally. The decision, he told his assistants, was "goddamn painful" and Mitchell should be told that it was "the toughest decision he'd made . . . tougher than Cambodia, May 8 [the mining of Haiphong harbor] and December 18 [the "Christ-

mas bombing" of North Vietnam] put together . . .
harder than firing [Walter J.] Hickel . . . and that he
just can't bring himself to talk to you about it. Just
can't do it."

They ran through a pack of candidates to speak to
Mitchell but quickly dismissed them all: Richard
Kleindienst; Henry Petersen; Secretary of Defense Elliot L. Richardson; Kenneth Rush, deputy secretary of
state; Leonard Garment, special consultant to the President; John H. Alexander, the tax specialist in Mitchell's
law firm. Ehrlichman argued that Secretary of State
William Rogers, as dean of the cabinet and a former
attorney general himself, was the man for the job. But
Nixon noted that Mitchell "hates Rogers," and Haldeman warned, "Mitchell will wind him around his finger. . . . Mitchell will say, 'Bill, you're out of your
fucking mind.' "

Suddenly, the President turned to Ehrlichman and
ordered, "John, go see Mitchell." Ehrlichman was the
man, Nixon concluded, because "somebody has to talk
to him who knows the facts." Ehrlichman and Mitchell
had never liked each other, and Ehrlichman seemed to
relish the prospect of thrusting at his old adversary's
jugular. Only a few days before, he had said, "The
interesting thing is, would be, to watch Mitchell's face
at the time I recommend to Magruder that he go down
and ask for immunity and confess." Now Magruder
was on his way down to confess and Ehrlichman would
get to watch Mitchell's face as he broke the news.

But, whether he relished it or not, Nixon declared,
"the Message to Garcia has got to be carried." The
Message to Mitchell, they all agreed, should be—in
Ehrlichman's words—"The jig is up, John. I've listened
to Magruder and he's gonna blow. And that's the last
straw. . . . And the President strongly feels that the only
way that this thing can end up being even a little net
plus for the administration and for the Presidency and
preserve some thread is for you to go in and voluntarily
make a statement [and admit] 'I am morally and legally responsible.' "

Ehrlichman said, "If he asks me, 'What do you want
me to do?' I am going to say, 'If you would do what

I ask you, what I would suggest, you would pick up the phone or you would allow me to pick it up and call Earl Silbert and make an appointment today and go over and talk with the U.S. attorney about this case with counsel. . . .' Today is probably the last day that you can take that action, if you're ever going to take it [to] do the President a bit of good."

Nixon liked that idea. Everybody ought to protect the President. "That has got to be the attitude of everybody because it isn't the man, it's the goddamn office."

"Sure, sure," said Haldeman.

At times that morning, the President took on a desperate tone: ". . . the boil has to be pricked. . . . We have to prick the goddamn boil and take the heat. Now that's what we are doing here." He told Ehrlichman to tell Mitchell, "The President has said let the chips fall where they may. We are not gonna cover for anybody."

But no such housecleaning was contemplated at that point. The President was still determined to protect the White House inner circle and, of course, himself. So, late in the session, he suddenly was assailed by guilt over what he was doing to Mitchell. Ruefully, he told Ehrlichman, "What I am doing, John, is putting you in the same position as President Eisenhower put me in with Adams." (In 1958 Ike had sent Nixon and then Attorney General William Rogers to tell his chief assistant, Sherman Adams, that he was fired.)

Then he perked up. "But John Mitchell, let me say, will never go to prison. I agree with that assumption. I think what will happen is that he will put on the goddamnedest defense that . . ."

His voice trailed off. Suddenly, it hit him. That wasn't the strategy at all. ". . . the point, you have, your suggestion," Nixon said to Ehrlichman, "is gonna be he *not* put on a defense. You're suggesting he go in and say, 'Look, I am responsible here. I had no knowledge but I am responsible. And uh, I, uh, I, and nobody else had, and uh, that's it. I *myself*. That's it. And I want to plead, uh, this, this has got to stop—innocent people are being smeared in this thing.' "

"He will understand," Ehrlichman said reassuringly.

But John Mitchell didn't understand. Not at all. Summoned to Washington by Haldeman, he caught a shuttle from New York and met with Ehrlichman in his office at 1:40 p.m., only to be told by his old antagonist, "Some people thought that their silence served his [the President's] purpose at this point. Now obviously you're in a situation of jeopardy. . . . This is just very hard for him and that's the reason I am talking to you. And he just didn't want anybody to labor under the misapprehension that there was any overriding consideration in his interest of anybody remaining mute. . . . The President now feels his interest institutionally—not individually necessarily—but the institution of the Presidency is better served by having this thing aired, disposed of, and put behind us so to speak. . . . Jeb Magruder has decided to make a clean breast of things and to take a guilty plea. So that pretty well starts to work from the middle in all directions. . . . The time remaining to do anything which will in any way, uh, put pluses on the side of the Presidency is rapidly running out, obviously."

MITCHELL: What's his first proposed action?
EHRLICHMAN: He hasn't any right to tell you what to do, uh—
MITCHELL: Oh, I'm not talking about telling me.
EHRLICHMAN: Yeah.
MITCHELL: No, no, no, no. What is brother Dick doing about that?

Mitchell knew just what Ehrlichman was suggesting and he wasn't having any part of it. He slapped the ball back in the President's court, where Ehrlichman took it on a nasty hop.

EHRLICHMAN: . . . What in the world does he do? What do I do?
MITCHELL: Well, there's, uh, obviously two things: to take care of his own house in an appropriate way.
EHRLICHMAN: Right, right. That's under way.
MITCHELL: That's the one thing.
EHRLICHMAN: Yeah.

MITCHELL: And the other thing is, uh, certainly not to impinge upon anybody's rights.

"Well," Ehrlichman stuttered, "I would certainly not attempt to tell you what to do." From then on he never tried to. All the tough talk he had charted with Nixon and Haldeman—about getting Mitchell to call Silbert, confessing that he was morally and legally responsible, the sole authority for Watergate—all this was meekly shelved in the face of Mitchell's bluff stonewall. Instead, the former attorney general told the President's man what he was going to do.

MITCHELL: Well, let me (*clears throat*) tell you where I stand. There is no way that I'm going to do anything except staying where I am because I'm too far, uh, far out. The fact of the matter is that I got euchred into this thing, when I say, by not paying attention to what these bastards were doing, and uh, well you know how far back this goes—this whole genesis of this thing was over here [at the White House]—as you're perfectly well aware.

EHRLICHMAN: No, I didn't know that.

This was just what Ehrlichman, Haldeman, and the President had feared—Mitchell was "laying off" on the White House. And he kept it up. He flatly denied any responsibility for Watergate: "I didn't authorize the bastards. . . . I have had no contact with Liddy. I've never seen Hunt and, as far as Jeb and all of the dirty-tricks department, I never knew a goddamn thing about it"—strongly implying that these were all White House projects. As far as the "cover-up" was concerned, Mitchell said he was only "trying to keep the lid on it until after the election and, in addition to that, to keep the lid on all the other things that were going on over here that would have even been worse, I think, than Watergate."

After a little more of this, Ehrlichman had had enough. "I have another visitor," he said. "I'm running kind of a musical chairs game here today."

"All righty," said Mitchell.

Ehrlichman said the President would be happy to see his former attorney general and campaign director "if there were any reason that you wanted to see him."

But Mitchell, recognizing a hollow gesture when he saw one, said, "I don't want to embarrass him."

As Mitchell left, Ehrlichman ushered someone named "Suzie" into his office and complimented her on her dress ("That's quite something!"). Fourteen minutes later he re-entered the President's office, where Nixon and Haldeman were anxiously awaiting him.

NIXON: All finished?

EHRLICHMAN: Yes, sir. All finished. He is an innocent man in his heart and in his mind and he does not intend to move off that position.

Ehrlichman reported in detail on what Mitchell had told him, emphasizing his accusations against the White House.

NIXON: His throwing it off on the White House isn't going to help him one damn bit. . . . He shouldn't throw the burden over here, Bob, on you. Now frankly Colson I understand, but, 'cause Colson certainly put the heat on over there. I don't think John would seriously have believed that you put him up to this thing.

HALDEMAN: I told you I didn't. He knows I didn't. No question of that.

NIXON: I should think he knows it. He let it all happen himself (*pause—banging on desk to beat of music*). . . . You know he'll never go to prison (*twenty-second pause*). What do you think about that as a possible thing—does a trial of the former attorney general of the United States bug you? This goddamn case!

The afternoon of Saturday, April 14, was a frantic one at the White House, as the President's men scurried about trying to find out just how much of the story was getting out. Haldeman talked by telephone with Magruder, who summarized what he had told the prosecutors that morning and then warned, "I really think, Bob, you should realize that you know, the whole thing is going to go . . . there isn't anybody now that is going to hold . . ." and ended with a rather pathetic apology, "I'm sorry things didn't work out, Bob." A few hours later Magruder came in to see Ehrlichman and outlined his testimony in greater detail. Dean also met with Haldeman and Ehrlichman; pulling a sheet of yellow legal paper from his pocket, he said, "My lawyer has analyzed this whole situation very closely and I think that the following people are involved in potential obstruction-of-justice problems" and might be indicted. The breath-takingly long list included, with various checks and question marks: Mitchell, Magruder, Strachan, Dean, LaRue, Mardian, O'Brien, Parkinson, Colson, Kalmbach, Ulasewicz, Bittman, Stans—and Haldeman and Ehrlichman.

"Needless to say," Dean recalls, "that got their attention very much."

At 5:15 p.m. Haldeman and Ehrlichman rejoined Nixon in his office and discussed the day's events for more than an hour. Ehrlichman told the President what he had learned from Magruder, and they all agreed that they were on a very "sticky wicket." The case was cracking wide open, and they somehow had to show that they were the investigators, not the targets. They decided that Ehrlichman should call Attorney General Kleindienst immediately to demonstrate that "the White House conducted its investigation and turned it over to the Justice Department before the indictments," or—in the President's words—that "we weren't drug kicking and screaming into this thing."

Kleindienst had spent the afternoon playing his usual

Saturday game of golf at Burning Tree Golf Club. But in midafternoon he had been alerted by Ehrlichman's secretary that her boss might want to speak to him later. So at five-thirty he was waiting at home when Ehrlichman, perched on a couch in the President's office, made his call.

"Hi, general," he began casually. "How are you? How was the golf?" Then he dropped his bomb. "The President has had me trying to gather together, as you know, a certain amount of law and facts to be in a position to kind of substitute for Dean, and to advise him on the White House involvement, but even broader involvement in this whole transaction. Yesterday I gave him my summary and, admittedly, it was hearsay, but some of it pretty reliable. . . . One of the things I told him was that I had encountered people who appeared to be reticent to come forward because they somehow felt that the Presidency was served by their not coming forward. So he had me today, in a series of conversations with people, to straighten them around on that point. The first one I talked to was your predecessor. Then I talked to Magruder and . . . well, as it turns out I was just a little late in talking to Magruder because he had just come back from telling everything to the U.S. attorney. He has decided to come clean. . . . And he implicates everybody in all directions up and down in the Committee to Re-Elect." He told Kleindienst that Magruder's testimony was "dramatically inconsistent" with what he had told the grand jury; that there was a substantial case of perjury against Mitchell and Magruder; that Magruder and Mitchell were "principals" in the conspiracy; that Dean, Mardian, and Porter were also implicated and LaRue was involved "from stem to stern."

Ehrlichman went on: "My purpose and intent was to advise you of this when I got finished with this process and tender this information for whatever purpose it would serve, recognizing that up until just a few minutes ago it was almost entirely hearsay. Magruder has just unloaded on me the substance of his conversation with the U.S. attorney—informal conversation. And I find that I now have very little to add to what Magruder had already given the U.S. attorney. I felt that I should go forward and at least advise you of this."

Kleindienst was hearing all of this for the first time, and he was stunned. But he recovered quickly, warning Ehrlichman to "be very careful what you do from here on out. . . . Yours is a very goddamn delicate line as to what you do to get information to give the President and what you can do in giving information to the Department of Justice."

Ehrlichman assured him he was being very careful. "That is why I am calling you, my dear. . . . You are my favorite law-enforcement officer. . . . Okay, my boy, I just wanted you to have a nice time this evening."

Kleindienst swore under his breath. After what Ehrlichman had told him, he wasn't going to have much of a time that evening. But, still, he wanted to attend the annual White House Correspondents' Association Dinner, which always gave him "an opportunity to gig back members of the press after they have been gigging me all year." The President, Haldeman, and Ehrlichman were also scheduled to be there, and it would be an awkward occasion for them, particularly because Woodward and Bernstein were scheduled to get several awards for their Watergate coverage. (Later Nixon told Ehrlichman he found it "terribly painful" to even show up at the affair.) But they went; the President arrived in the International Ballroom of the Washington Hilton Hotel at 9:04 p.m.—after the Worth Bingham and Raymond Clapper awards had been presented. Ted Knap of Scripps-Howard presented him with an eighteenth-century silver globe for his efforts toward world peace. Among the twenty-five hundred black-tied diners were some sixty White House staff members, fifty senators and congressmen, and a posse of judges, generals, and other officials. In his remarks, the President struck a lofty note which, at the same time, suggested his own indispensability. Americans, he said, had embarked "on a great adventure together—building a peace that will last. No other nation can provide the leadership for peace in the world. . . . Others have good intentions, but only America has the power." (Brave words from a man who had never felt so powerless to stave off his relentless enemies.)

He stayed barely an hour at the dinner, leaving shortly after ten to return to the White House. At 11:02 he was on the telephone with Haldeman and at 11:22 with Ehrlichman, suggesting to both that they find some way of tipping off Colson about what Magruder was saying so that Colson wouldn't go into the grand jury cold and draw a "perjury rap."

After the dinner, Woodstein cornered Kleindienst in the hotel lobby and the attorney general confided, "The Watergate case is going to blow up," and agreed to meet them the next morning and fill them in. But Kleindienst still didn't know the half of it.

While the reporters went upstairs to party, Kleindienst returned to his home in McLean. At about twelve-thirty he received a telephone call from Henry Petersen, who said, "It is important that we get together with you tonight." All evening, Petersen had been meeting with the prosecutors—U.S. Attorney Harold Titus and his assistants, Earl Silbert and Seymour Glanzer—who had been telling him what they had learned that day from Magruder and what they had extracted from Dean over the past week (including several documents handed over that afternoon). The prosecutors had concluded that there was a "putative" case against Mitchell, Mardian, LaRue, Magruder, Dean, Ehrlichman, and Haldeman. They wanted to inform the attorney general immediately.

Kleindienst told them to come out right away. Petersen, Titus, and Silbert arrived at about one-thirty in the morning, and for the next three and a half hours they outlined the case in some detail to the increasingly distraught attorney general. Kleindienst remembers this as "the most shocking day of my life. . . . I don't think since my mother died when I was a young boy that I ever had an event that has consumed me emotionally with such sorrow and sadness." Two of the men with evidence now building against them—Mitchell and Mardian—were "two of the closest friends" Kleindienst ever had. As the prosecutors made their case, the attorney general wept.

Then he borrowed some of his wife's personal stationery and made "rather copious notes" of what they told him. When his visitors finally left, at about five in the morning, Kleindienst caught three hours' sleep and was on the telephone to the White House at eight-thirty asking to see the President. Nixon returned his call at 10:13 and told Kleindienst to come down to the White House worship service at eleven-thirty and he would see him afterward. By the time Woodstein arrived at the attorney general's home that morning for their promised meeting, Kleindienst had left for the White House. There, he listened to a sermon by the Reverend Edward V. Hill, pastor of Mount Zion Missionary Baptist Church in Los Angeles, and some hymns by the Rochester Male Chorus of Rochester, Minnesota; then he joined the Presidential party for a reception in the State Dining Room.

As Kleindienst prepared to meet with Nixon, he felt he was bearing terrible tidings which would shock the President. He was not the first official to labor under this delusion. On July 5, 1972, Pat Gray had warned Nixon that his White House aides were trying to "mortally wound" him, but the President was not surprised. On March 21, 1973, John Dean had told him a "cancer" was growing on the Presidency, but the President was not surprised. Now, when Kleindienst met with Nixon in his office at 1:21 p.m., he told him that his two closest assistants, Haldeman and Ehrlichman, might be implicated in the Watergate scandal. Kleindienst was still unsure whether there was sufficient evidence to bring an indictment, but the evidence "could raise a very serious question with respect to both of them. That is my primary reason for talking to you."

Again the President was not surprised. "Sure, sure," he said. Patiently, he listened as his agitated attorney general read from the notes on his wife's stationery. Now and again, he would ask questions to which he already knew the answers, so that Kleindienst would not think he was personally involved. Then, when he had heard him out, Nixon said, "We've got to just ride it through, Dick. Do the best we can. Right? We don't run to the hills on this and so forth. The main thing is to handle it right."

Kleindienst had handled things right before. A year earlier, in congressional testimony, he had stubbornly stuck to his bogus story that the White House had never pressured him on the ITT affair. And, although Gordon Liddy told him on June 18, 1972, of a White House–CREEP involvement in the Watergate break-in, he had never passed this information on to the prosecutors in his own department.

Now, the President easily manipulated his attorney general once again. When Kleindienst suggested that Nixon might ask Haldeman and Ehrlichman to resign —or at least to take leaves of absence pending resolution of their cases—the President skillfully maneuvered him into agreeing that that would "find them guilty before they have a chance to prove their innocence." Then Kleindienst said that, because of his close friendship with Mitchell and other potential defendants, he would disqualify himself from supervising the Watergate investigation. He urged that the President name a special prosecutor—preferably Barnabas Sears, an attorney who had served with distinction in that capacity in his native Chicago. But the President rejected this notion, saying that it would be "too much of a reflection on our system of justice and everything else." Instead, he suggested Deputy Attorney General Joseph Sneed should take over Kleindienst's Watergate functions. Kleindienst objected: Sneed was a Presidential appointee who would presumably be loyal to the President. He counterproposed Henry Petersen, "the first career assistant attorney general I think in the history of the department." With seeming deference to his attorney general, the President accepted Petersen—very possibly the man he had wanted all along.

Three weeks before, on March 21, John Dean had told Nixon how helpful Henry Petersen was being. "Why did Petersen play the game so straight with us?" Nixon asked. "Because Petersen is a soldier," Dean explained. "He kept me informed. He told me when we had problems, where we had problems, and the like. He believes in you. He believes in this administration. This administration has made him." Indeed, until Nixon moved into the White House, Henry Petersen had been a relatively unknown bureaucrat at the Justice Department—in charge of the organized crime and racketeering section of the criminal division. His rise to that spot had been long, arduous, and anonymous. Born in Philadelphia, he served as a staff sergeant with the Marine Corps in the South Pacific, and after World War II, went through Georgetown University and Catholic University law school on the GI Bill. In 1947, while still at law school, he went to work for the FBI as a clerk and four years later switched over to the Justice Department. He remained there for the next twenty-six years. Rising slowly through the antitrust and criminal divisions, he became, in 1966, the top civil servant in charge of prosecuting mobsters, gamblers, and Mafiosi. But it was only with John Mitchell's arrival in 1969 that Petersen moved up into the leadership echelon of the department. Although a registered Democrat, Petersen thought a lot like Mitchell (and Nixon). A hawk on Vietnam and a tough "law-and-order" man, he believed criminals had often been coddled in previous administrations and he praised Mitchell as "a man of high integrity and a tough prosecutor—he's such a refreshing breath of air after Ramsey Clark." Mitchell, in turn, gave Petersen additional authority—first as deputy to Will R. Wilson, the new assistant attorney general in charge of the criminal division, and then, when Wilson became implicated in a Texas stock-fraud scandal and resigned, as his successor. Although some of his colleagues praised him as "tough," "candid," "decent," and "a thoroughgoing pro," others questioned Petersen's judgment. In 1970 and 1971 he signed Wilson's name to hundreds of letters authorizing wiretaps, and when an aide signed Mitchell's name to the authorizations, the bogus signatures upset hundreds of prosecutions in what one official called "the biggest goof-up we've ever had." And he twice helped Harry Steward keep his job as U.S. attorney in San Diego, though Steward had been charged with blocking investigations into illegal political contributions made by influential Republicans, including Nixon's friend C. Arnholt Smith. But Petersen displayed his worst judgment after he began supervising the Watergate investigation in June 1972. In the months to come, he kept the investigation relentlessly focused on the actual burglary; ordered the prosecutors to stay away from the Kalmbach, Chapin, and Segretti matters; fed grand jury testimony and other information to Dean; permitted administration witnesses to testify in camera; helped kill the Patman inquiry; and issued press releases extolling the investigation. Later, he conceded, "We were snookered," and admitted he may have shown "too much restraint." But he defended his general approach: "If I am going to err I am going to err on the side of restraint. . . . I hope justice is not blind. I do not apply it blindly. . . . While I recognize that everybody is equal before the law, I also recognize that not everybody can be treated equally and that applies to senators and congressmen and government officials—not because of the person but because of the office. . . . There are many, many concessions that are made because of the office. . . . We don't deal gently, but I do deal with restraint and I am conscious of the political connotations of my actions. I don't expect to ruin political reputations." And when such statements led to more unflattering allegations about his performance, Petersen grew indignant and shouted, "I am not a whore!"

That Sunday afternoon Petersen was doing some work on his twenty-six-foot boat, preparing it for a summer of cruising on Chesapeake Bay, when he got a telephone call from Kleindienst asking him to come down to the office. Dressed in a dirty T shirt, jeans, and tennis shoes, he rushed to the Justice Department, where Kleindienst informed him that they were going to see the President. This was the first time Petersen had met Nixon, except for ceremonial occasions or large briefings on legislation, and he was terribly "embarrassed" about calling on the chief executive in such attire. But Kleindienst cleared it with the White House and at four o'clock they went to see Nixon and stayed for an hour and a quarter.

Petersen briefed the President in some detail on the evidence building up against Haldeman and Ehrlichman, and he recommended that Nixon dismiss the two men immediately. He couldn't guarantee that criminal indictments would be brought against them, but he could guarantee that "these people are going to be a source of vast embarrassment to the Presidency." Petersen recalls that Nixon "exhibited a lack of shock" that surprised him. "Here I was recommending that two people whom he had known and worked with for years be dismissed. . . . I would have been cussing and fuming," but Nixon was "calm and collected," in "immense control of himself." Nixon "spoke well of Haldeman and Ehrlichman," reserving his criticism for Dean, who had supplied so much of the damaging evidence. He suggested that Dean was "simply trying to exculpate himself" and asked whether he shouldn't force Dean's resignation. "My goodness, no," Petersen recalls saying. "Now here is the first man who has come in to cooperate with us, and certainly we don't want to give the impression that he is being subjected to reprisal because of his cooperation. So please don't ask for his resignation at this point." Instead, Petersen recommended, the President should talk with Dean to learn directly what he was telling the prosecutors rather than getting it second- or third-hand. The President said he would.

Nixon and Dean hadn't talked since March 23, the day Dean left for Camp David. In the intervening three weeks, they had dealt with each other at sword's length, only through intermediaries (chiefly Haldeman and Ehrlichman), and with mounting mutual suspicion. Neither was sure just what the other was up to. Dean wasn't sure what he was up to himself. He had begun talking to the prosecutors on April 8, seeking immunity from prosecution, and was willing to tell them just what he needed to, but no more. Tentatively, he offered them tidbits of the story—evidence on Mitchell, then on Ehrlichman, then on Haldeman. Each time, the prosecutors said that wasn't enough for immunity. They agreed that until some deal was struck, the prosecutors couldn't use what he was telling them. Dean was feeling his way.

And so was Nixon. By early April he knew that Dean had established some sort of contact with the prosecutors, but he wasn't sure whether Dean was talking to them directly and, if so, how much he was saying. If Dean were merely implicating Mitchell and Magruder, that would serve the President's purposes. But perhaps he was going further. Intimations filtered into the White House: Dean was talking about this, Dean had "blown" that. The President's men brought what pressures they could to bear on Dean. Ehrlichman got Dean's personnel folder from his assistant, Fred Fielding, to establish that Dean had been dismissed from his first law firm—and made sure that Dean knew he had this information. And Nixon told Ehrlichman to see that Dean realized that "there's only one man that could restore him to the ability to practice law in case things still go wrong." By Saturday, April 14, the President knew Dean was talking to the prosecutors and was ready to dismiss him, but Ehrlichman warned against it, arguing that the grand jury and the Ervin committee would treat Dean more gingerly if he were still the President's counsel than if he were merely a private citizen. Once he was out, Haldeman said, Dean would be "defrocked"—unprotected by the last shreds of "executive privilege" or Presidential mystique. Now Petersen was warning that Dean's forced resignation would be seen as a reprisal for his cooperation with the prosecutors. The President was trapped with an informer in his house (or "an asp at your bosom," as Colson put it).

After Petersen advised the President that he ought to meet directly with Dean to learn what he was telling the prosecutors, Ehrlichman tried to set up an appointment with the wayward counsel. On the advice of his attorneys and Petersen, Dean refused to meet with Ehrlichman. But, recognizing that the President now knew what he was doing, he telephoned a message through Larry Higby to Nixon. It read:

"1) I hope you understand that my actions are motivated by total loyalty to you & the Presidency. If that is not clear now, I believe it will become clear.

"2) E has requested to meet with me tonite, but I believe it is inappropriate for me to meet with him at this time.

"3) I am ready & willing to meet with you at any time to discuss the matter.

"4) You should take your counsel from Henry Petersen, who I assure you doesn't want the Presidency hurt."

Within forty-five minutes the White House operator called to say that the President wanted to see him at 9:00 p.m. The meeting was the first of three—totaling more than two hours—the two men held within the next twenty-four hours. The discussions were much the same, with Dean now very ill at ease, the President superficially cordial but asking leading questions designed to establish his own innocence. Nixon warned Dean that he should not tell the prosecutors about their private conversations or about any of the "national security" matters Dean knew about. Over and over, he tried to get Dean to agree that decisive Presidential action had uncovered Watergate. "We triggered the whole thing," he said. "What got Magruder to talk? I would like to take credit for that." Dean said Magruder had talked because he knew Dean was talking, but the President plowed ahead, telling Dean he should testify that "as a result of the President's action the thing has been broken." It was vital, he said, that "the President should stay one step ahead of this thing. Shit, I'm not going to let the Justice Department break this case . . . and say, 'Look, we dragged the White House in here.' I've got to step out and do it."

In their second meeting—at ten on Monday morning—the President tried to get Dean to resign. He handed him a manila folder containing two unsigned letters. The first read:

"Dear Mr. President. In view of my increasing involvement in the Watergate matter, my impending appearance before the grand jury and the probability of its action, I request an immediate leave of absence from my position on your staff."

The second read:

"Dear Mr. President. As a result of my involvement in the Watergate matter, which we discussed last night and today, I tender you my resignation, effective at once."

The President said he wouldn't release anything then, that he would hold both letters, and, if and when necessary, would release the appropriate one. Dean coolly declined to sign either, saying he would draft his own letter. When they met again, at 4:07 that afternoon, he presented his version, which read:

"Dear Mr. President. You informed me that Bob Haldeman and John Ehrlichman have verbally tendered their request to give them immediate and indefinite leave of absence from the staff. So I declare I wish also to confirm my similar request that I be given such a leave of absence from the staff."

It was a shrewd riposte, Dean's way of saying—as he put it a few minutes later—"There is a problem for you [with] the scapegoat theory." Dean had no intention of becoming a scapegoat. If he went, Haldeman and Ehrlichman were going too. The rest of their conversation that afternoon was jerky, almost incoherent, as the two men appeared to have lost all rapport. It was the last face-to-face meeting between Nixon and Dean.

Indeed, as the crisis deepened, Nixon narrowed his consultations, meeting only those with whom he felt most comfortable. On April 17 Ehrlichman said Colson wanted to see him, but the President declined, saying, "I don't want Colson to come in here. I feel uneasy about that, his ties and everything." Leonard Garment, who had taken over much of Dean's legal work, asked to see him, but Nixon tried to avoid a meeting, complaining that "Len always reacts to things" (at which Haldeman exclaimed, "Len is the panic-button type. If we had reacted in Garment's way in other things we wouldn't be where we are"). Ultimately, the President granted Garment sixteen minutes and, indeed, he did react—urging that everybody directly connected with the Watergate scandal be dismissed. One man Nixon did seek out several times that week was Secretary of State Rogers, an old friend whose judgment Nixon obviously respected. On Monday evening Nixon and Rogers dined together on the Presidential yacht while Nixon outlined the situation "with the bark off." He was using the *Sequoia* a lot those fragrant spring evenings. The night before he had cruised up the Potomac with Bebe Rebozo.

But most of his time around these critical ides of April was spent "game-planning" with the only two men he really trusted by then—Bob Haldeman and John Ehrlichman. Hour after hour was consumed talking with one, with the other, or with both: six hours and twenty-seven minutes on April 14; four hours and twenty-one minutes on April 15; two hours and thirty-one minutes on April 16; four hours and four minutes on April 17. Occasionally, they were joined by Petersen on legal matters and Ziegler on press and public relations. The only real subject by then was public relations; how to get the White House "out front" on Watergate quickly, before some other institution—*The Washington Post, The New York Times,* or the Justice Department—seized the initiative.

They were like a Latin American junta in the calm just before another *coup d'état*—every hour brought some fresh intimation of disaster. "Ziegler has just left my office," Ehrlichman told the President at 9:50 on Monday morning. "He feels we have no more than twelve hours. He's got some input from the *Post* and he estimates unless we take an initiative by nine o'clock tonight it will be too late." At about 2:45 p.m. Nixon said, "I've got to get [it] out and I've got to get it out today." Ten minutes later, he exclaimed, "I'm so sick of this thing! I want to get it done with and over, and I don't want to hear about it again!" But they couldn't get anything ready on Monday, and by Tuesday morning the air of imminent apocalypse was even more intense. At 9:47 a.m. Haldeman told the President, "Colson for instance called Ehrlichman this morning and said that his sources around town, department sources and everything, say that we've got one more day to act on our own initiative." A few minutes later he said, "The White House has got to move . . . we have to get out in front in some way." The President complained, "It is breaking so fast." And at two o'clock he exclaimed, "Everything is likely to blow around here!"

The problem, of course, was just what kind of story would they "get out"? Ehrlichman talked of going "full breast on it," but there was never any serious consideration given to a clean-breast disclosure of everything they knew. Instead, they bounced around a number of "scenarios," until, finally, a plausible story began to emerge. At a meeting Monday morning, Nixon rehearsed it with Haldeman and Ehrlichman.

NIXON: How has the scenario worked out? May I ask?

HALDEMAN: Well, it works out very good. You became aware some time ago that this thing did not parse out the way it was supposed to and that there were some discrepancies between what you had been told by Dean in the report that there was nobody in the White House involved, which may still be true.

NIXON: . . . I would say I was not satisfied that the Dean Report was complete and also I thought it was my obligation to go beyond that to people other than the White House.

EHRLICHMAN: Ron [Ziegler] has an interesting point. Remember you had John Dean go to Camp David to write it up. He came down and said, "I can't."

NIXON: Right.

EHRLICHMAN: That is the tip-off and right then you started to move.

NIXON: That's right. He said he could not write it.

HALDEMAN: Then you realized that there was more to this than you had been led to believe.

NIXON: Then how do I get credit for getting Magruder to the stand?

EHRLICHMAN: Well it is very simple. You took Dean off of the case right then. . . .

NIXON: Why did I take Dean off? Because he became involved. I did it, really, because he was involved with Gray. . . .

HALDEMAN: The scenario is that he told you he couldn't write a report, so obviously you had to take him off.

NIXON: Right, right.

EHRLICHMAN: And so then we started digging into it and we went to San Clemente. While I was out there I talked to a lot of people on the telephone, talked to several witnesses in person, kept feeding information to you, and as soon as you saw the dimensions in this thing from the reports you were getting from the staff . . . you began to move. . . .

NIXON: Go ahead. And then—

EHRLICHMAN: And then it culminated last week—

NIXON: Right.

EHRLICHMAN:—in your decision that Mitchell should be brought down here; Magruder should be brought in; Strachan should be brought in . . . you should say, "I heard enough that I was satisfied that it was time to precipitously move. I called the attorney general over, in turn Petersen."

That was it. It didn't bear much relationship to the truth, but it had a nice air of decisiveness and action and Presidential determination to clean his own house. So at 4:42 p.m., Tuesday, April 17, the President strode onto the stage of the White House press room, where he read a brief statement:

". . . On March 21st, as a result of serious charges which came to my attention, some of which were publicly reported, I began intensive new inquiries into this whole matter.

"Last Sunday afternoon, the Attorney General, Assistant Attorney General Petersen, and I met at length in the EOB to review the facts which had come to me in my investigation and also to review the progress of the Department of Justice investigation.

"I can report today that there have been major developments in the case concerning which it would be improper to be more specific now, except to say that real progress had been made in finding the truth. . . ."

He said any indicted official would be suspended and anyone convicted would be dismissed; opposed granting of immunity to any major official; called on everyone to cooperate with the investigation; backed away from his executive privilege doctrine in announcing that White House officials would testify before the Ervin committee (though initially in executive session and reserving the right to invoke privilege on specific questions); and condemned "any attempts to cover up in this case, no matter who is involved."

Although Nixon had stepped "out front" of the Justice Department investigation, he continued to monitor it closely through Henry Petersen. During the last two weeks of April the President and Petersen met or talked on the telephone twenty-five times. Nixon encouraged Petersen to report to him any time he had something new: "If anything comes up, call me even if it's in the middle of the night, okay?" On April 16 he told Ehrlichman and Ziegler, "I've got Petersen on a short leash." And, indeed, Petersen seemed awed by all this attention from the nation's chief executive. "Damn," he said on April 17, "I admire your strength, I tell you." The President shrewdly exploited that admiration: flattering Petersen, cajoling him, telling him he was now "the President's special counsel," asking if he would like to be director of the FBI. Petersen responded as the President had hoped he would—with undiluted loyalty to the Oval Office and an eagerness to be helpful in any way he could. Soon, he was reporting secret grand jury testimony to the President, just as he had to John Dean the summer before.

The President abused his confidence on this. Late on the evening of April 16 he had telephoned Petersen at home to get new information.

"Of course, you know anything you tell me, as I think I told you earlier, will not be passed on because I know the rules of the grand jury," he told the assistant attorney general.

"I understand, Mr. President," said Petersen. He then proceeded to tell the President about LaRue's testimony at the grand jury that day which, he said, had been "rather pitiful"—LaRue breaking down in tears on the stand, admitting to obstruction of justice. Petersen also informed Nixon that Kalmbach had been involved in paying hush money to the defendants; that Dean had said Haldeman authorized Kalmbach to raise this money; and that Kalmbach would soon be called before the grand jury. At 9:47 the next morning —barely twelve hours later—Nixon relayed Petersen's account to Haldeman. "Get John [Ehrlichman] and yourself," the President went on, "and sit down and do some hard thinking about what kind of strategy you are going to have with the money. You know what I mean?" And he added, "Look, you've got to call Kalmbach . . . be sure Kalmbach is at least aware of this, that LaRue has talked very freely. He is a broken man."

Petersen still believes it was proper for him to disclose this information to the President—particularly since he had no reason to suspect that his interests and those of the President diverged. That they might, in fact, diverge was "an unthinkable thought" which he was not prepared to entertain. "You can only indulge that possibility if you reach the conclusion that the President was, to some degree, corrupt. And I was not willing to do that in the absence of evidence. . . . I think that one has to treat public officials, in the absence of evidence to the contrary, as being people who are prepared to discharge their duties and responsibilities. I was prepared to do so and I was not prepared to conclude that the President would do anything less."

But even Petersen, the good soldier, found a few things hard to stomach. One was the burglary of Dr.

Fielding's office. Evidence of the burglary finally found its way to the Watergate prosecutors on April 15—not from Howard Hunt, as the President's men had feared, but from John Dean. Still unsuccessfully seeking immunity, Dean had upped the ante that day with information on the Hunt-Liddy operation at Dr. Fielding's office. On April 16 Silbert whipped off a memo to Petersen. The next day Petersen ordered a Department of Justice investigation to determine if any information obtained from Dr. Fielding's office had gotten to the prosecutors at the espionage trial of Daniel Ellsberg and his associate, Anthony J. Russo, Jr., then under way in Los Angeles. He was told that the prosecutors knew nothing about the burglary and, so far as they knew, had no evidence emanating from it. But a check of the FBI files disclosed that agents had once tried to interview Ellsberg's psychiatrist, a Dr. Lewis Fielding. The Watergate prosecutors recognized that name. It was one they had puzzled over before—on the parking space in the pictures from Hunt's Tessina camera turned over to the investigation by the CIA. At last, the mysterious pictures made sense.

On April 18 Petersen relayed all this to Nixon. As he recalls it, their conversation during a telephone call that afternoon went something like this:

NIXON: What else is new?

PETERSEN: I got this report that Liddy and Hunt burglarized Ellsberg's psychiatrist's office.

NIXON: I know about that. That's a national-security matter. Your mandate is Watergate. You stay out of that.

PETERSEN: Well, I have caused a check to be made and we don't have any information of that nature in the case. Do you know where there is such information?

NIXON: There's nothing you have to do.

For weeks Nixon had feared just this, but he and his assistants had carefully prepared their fall-back position—a claim that the burglary was a "national-security matter," off limits to a criminal investigation. Moreover, they had taken steps to prevent documentary evidence on the operation from falling into the wrong hands. In late March Ehrlichman had ordered David Young to bring him the Plumbers' files on the Pentagon Papers investigation. On March 27, Young says, Ehrlichman told him that Hunt might "go public" about the Fielding burglary and therefore he had decided to retain certain memos from the file that were "a little too sensitive and show too much forethought." When Ehrlichman returned the files to Young, two important memoranda linking Ehrlichman to the burglary were missing. (Later Ehrlichman instructed Young to turn all his files on the matter over to the President and to refuse to discuss the burglary with anyone, on grounds of "national security.")

Then, concerned that the Fielding burglary might surface at the Ellsberg trial, Nixon intervened directly in the judicial process. On March 21 Ehrlichman had warned Nixon that the burglary was an "illegal search and seizure," which, if disclosed, would be "sufficient at least [to declare] a mistrial." One way to prevent that would be to bring pressure to bear on Judge William Matthew Byrne, Jr., who was presiding at the trial. A forty-two-year-old bachelor, widely respected in the law-enforcement community, Matthew Byrne had served as U.S. attorney in Los Angeles and as director of the President's Commission on Campus Unrest. On March 31 Haldeman, Ehrlichman, and Kleindienst discussed offering Judge Byrne the FBI directorship. Acting Director Gray had never been confirmed, and it was becoming clear that he never would be. (Indeed, Nixon withdrew the nomination on April 5 and Gray resigned as acting director on April 27.) On April 4 Ehrlichman called Judge Byrne and invited him to San Clemente for a discussion he said was unrelated to the trial. The next afternoon the two men strolled out toward a bluff overlooking the Pacific and Ehrlichman asked the judge whether he would like to be FBI director. Ehrlichman says Judge Byrne expressed a "very strong interest," but Judge Byrne insists he told Ehrlichman that he "could not and would not give consideration to any other position until this case is concluded." Just then, Nixon came out of the house and he and Byrne shook hands and exchanged greetings. The tentative job offer was left hanging. The next day Judge Byrne requested another meeting with Ehrlichman, and on April 7 the two men took a walk through Palisades Park in Santa Monica. Ehrlichman says Judge Byrne "restated his very strong interest in the job." Judge Byrne again tells a sharply different story: that he restated his firm decision not to even discuss such an appointment until the trial was over.

Nixon and Ehrlichman have strenuously denied that the approach to Judge Byrne was meant to influence his conduct of the Ellsberg trial or his handling of possible disclosure of the Fielding burglary. But the importance of the judge's rulings on such matters was underlined just a few weeks later.

For Henry Petersen was having second thoughts. When Nixon ordered him on April 18 to stay away from the Ellsberg matter, he dutifully passed the instruction on to Silbert, saying, "The President said stay out of it, Earl, and that is it." But during the next week he began to wonder whether evidence of the burglary itself wasn't exculpatory material that should rightly be turned over to the Ellsberg defense. Although legal opinions differed, he decided this was not the case in which to test the issue. So, on April 25, Petersen took his misgivings to Kleindienst, who, after soliciting more legal opinions, concluded that he was right. That very afternoon Kleindienst went to the White House and told the President they ought to disclose the information to the prosecutors at the Ellsberg trial immediately. Kleindienst recalls that the President was "very provoked . . . very upset about it," and promptly agreed that the Justice Department memoranda on the matter should be dispatched to Los Angeles.

Even then, some Justice Department officials believed—and hoped—that Judge Byrne might examine the material *in camera,* conclude that it was irrelevant to the trial, and never inform the defense. On April 26 David Nissen, chief prosecutor at the trial, filed the memos *in camera.* But the next day Judge Byrne refused to accept an *in camera* filing and ordered the material turned over to the defense in open court. He then read Silbert's memo to Petersen out loud—the first public disclosure of the Fielding burglary.

The revelation, of course, set off an uproar—both in the courtroom and in the press. (It also caused deep consternation at the CIA, where—after a cursory investigation—Director William Colby ordered destruction of some records of the agency's illegal domestic activities.) The storm grew on April 30 when the Washington *Evening Star* revealed that Ehrlichman had met with Judge Byrne about a high-level government appointment. And it grew still further on May 10 when Judge Byrne, now demanding full disclosure of all government surveillance of the defendants, extracted an FBI admission that Ellsberg had been overheard on a wiretap of Morton Halperin's telephone —but that the tapes and logs of the conversations had mysteriously disappeared from the files of both the FBI and the Justice Department.

This last disclosure tipped the cautious judge off his precariously neutral perch. Angered at the government for repeatedly misleading him and for tainting his own reputation with an improper approach, Byrne dismissed the charges against both defendants on May 11. His face flushed, stumbling at times over words, he read from a statement written out on a yellow legal pad, "The disclosures made by the government demonstrate that governmental agencies have taken an unprecedented series of actions with respect to these defendants. . . . The conduct of the government has placed the case in such a posture that it precludes the fair, dispassionate resolution of these issues by a jury. . . . The totality of the circumstances of this case . . . offend 'a sense of justice.'" Daniel Ellsberg—Nixon's Enemy No. 2—embraced his wife, pledged to "make love in every climate on earth," and concluded, "the President has led a conspiracy against the American public."

Indeed, the Watergate investigation was by then at last beginning to focus on Richard Nixon himself. Dean had realized that not even his disclosure to the prosecutors of the Fielding burglary would earn him immunity. In part, the President himself was responsible for this. In his conversations with Petersen, he repeatedly opposed granting immunity to Dean, clearly because he was afraid that his former counsel would continuously expand his charges in exchange for escaping prosecution. But the very elusiveness of his goal may at last have goaded the desperate Dean into carrying his charges to the very door of the Oval Office.

The President had never really believed that Dean would dare disclose "national security matters" like the Fielding burglary or private conversations with him which, Nixon believed, were protected by executive privilege. "I don't think Dean would go so far as to get into any conversation he had with the President—even Dean I don't think," he told Haldeman on April 17. But Dean could and did.

At first it came only from his attorney, Charles Shaffer, who began warning that unless Dean were given immunity, "We are going to try Ehrlichman, Haldeman, Nixon and this whole administration, that's going to be our strategy." Petersen reported these threats to the President on April 16, warning, "It's a goddamn poker game . . . guts poker." This caught the President's attention and he kept coming back to it. "I'm a little concerned about Dean or his lawyer, that he's going to attack the President and so forth," he told Petersen. Later he told Ehrlichman about it, and Ehrlichman exclaimed, "But what can he say?" And Nixon said, "That he's informed the President and the President didn't act? He can't say that, can he? I don't think. I've been asking for his damned report, you know." The next day, he returned to it again with Rogers, complaining ruefully, "They probably think the President can cover up. If I wanted to, I sure haven't done it very well, have I?"

Nixon's concern peaked on April 27, after Seymour Hersh of *The New York Times* got wind of Dean's threats and began calling around town to check them out. That afternoon the President summoned Petersen to the White House in a white heat. "Sit down, sit down," he said hurriedly as the assistant attorney general came in the door. "We have gotten a report that, ah, that really we've got to head off at the pass. Because it's so damn—so damn dangerous to the Presidency in a sense. There's a reporter by the name of Hersh, of *The New York Times*, you probably know . . . who told Bittman who told O'Brien that they have information . . . indicating that Dean has made statements to the prosecuting team implicating the President. . . . The [*Washington*] *Post* has heard similar rumors. Now, Henry, this I've got to know."

Petersen went into the Cabinet Room to call the Watergate prosecutors and a few minutes later came back to explain what the new flap was all about. On April 23 Shaffer had made a new threat: "We will bring the President in—not this case but in other areas." The prosecutors didn't know exactly what that meant, but the President probably had a pretty good idea: the Plumbers' activities; the investigations carried out by Caulfield and Ulasewicz; the 1969–71 wiretaps; and all the other things which John Mitchell dubbed "the White House horrors." Moreover, Nixon was very worried that Dean would talk about the hush money, particularly the March 21 conversation in which he had authorized the final $75,000 payment to Hunt. Now he told Petersen, "My purpose [at the March 21 meeting] was to find out what the hell had been going on before. And believe me, nothing was approved. I mean as far as I'm concerned, I turned it off totally. . . . Henry, it won't stand up for five minutes because nothing was done. . . . I have broken my ass to try to get the facts of the case. . . . You've got to believe me. I'm after the truth, even if it hurts me. But, believe me, it won't."

Confronted with Dean's threats, Nixon reacted with fierce determination. He told Ziegler to "take a hard line," "totally knock down" the story Hersh and Woodstein were working on, "kill it, kill it, hard," tell them "they better watch their damn cotton-picking faces." And he told Petersen, "If there's one thing you have got to do you have got to maintain the Presidency out of this. I have got things to do for this country." Then, a note of self-pity crept in as he exclaimed, "I sometimes feel like I'd like to resign. Let Agnew be President for a while. He'd love it."

By now Petersen was in a bit of a bind himself, which made it difficult for him to help Nixon. As the Watergate trail led the prosecutors ever closer to the President, they became increasingly irritated at the close relationship Petersen was maintaining with Nixon. On the evening of April 25 they had it out. As Petersen told Nixon later, the prosecutors were "concerned and scared" about "my reporting to you." They told him that since he would be a potential witness against Dean (because of the two men's close contacts the summer before) he should not be so deeply involved now. Petersen reassured them he was acting under "very specific instructions" from the President. Petersen told Nixon it was "a kind of crisis of confidence." Others have described the meeting as a "bad shouting match . . . awful, just awful."

The next day Petersen went to U.S. Attorney Titus and told him, "We have to draw the line. We have no mandate to investigate the President. We investigate Watergate." As a result, the prosecutors cut off all their contact with Petersen and the Justice Department, carrying on their investigation as secretly as possible to prevent Petersen from carrying further reports to Nixon.

Petersen remained confident he was doing the right thing. He did not believe he had any right to investigate the President. "If it came to that," he told Nixon on April 27, "I would have to come to you and say, 'We can't do that.' The only people who have jurisdiction to do that is the House of Representatives, as far as I am concerned." And toward the end of their conversation Petersen related a little domestic parable—designed perhaps to indicate that although others were beginning to develop doubts about the President he, at least, remained loyal. ". . . Mr. President, my wife is not a politically sophisticated woman. She knows I'm upset about this and you know, I'm working hard and she sees it. But she asked me at breakfast. She —now I don't want you to hold this against her if you ever meet her, because she's a charming lady. She said,

'Doesn't all this upset you?' And I said, 'Of course it does.' She said, 'Do you think the President knows?' And I looked at her and said, 'If I thought the President knew, I would have to resign.' . . . Mr. President, I pray for you, sir."

Yet no personal expression of loyalty could still the President's premonitions of disaster. As April wound down, he and his closest aides released their anxieties in private maledictions at the traitor, John Dean. Dean was "not un-American and anti-Nixon," said Haldeman, but "I must admit the guy has really turned into an unbelievable disaster for us." Later Ehrlichman said everybody in the White House should be warned that Dean was a "piranha." Nixon said, "This is an evil man, you know. . . . I at least have treated him decently, in fact more decently than he deserves. On the other hand, he may become totally intractable. If he does, you're going to have one hell of a pissing contest." And a few minutes later he resolved, "If he's going to have this pissing contest, all right, bring it out and fight it out and it'll be a bloody goddamn thing."

If anything, Haldeman and Ehrlichman were more vitriolic than Nixon in their denunciations of Dean. "At some point, like you do on anything else," Haldeman advised Nixon, "you gotta face up to the fact that the guy is either a friend or a foe or a neutral. If he's neutral you don't have to worry about him. If he's a friend you rely on him. If he's a foe you fight him and this guy—it seems at this point—is a foe." John Dean was Enemy No. 3.

But there was one problem with flatly dismissing Dean. "If you break it off with him, then he could go out and say, 'Screw the ———.'" The President was still trying to find some way of dumping Dean without arousing his ire even more. Gradually, he recognized that he could only fire Dean if he fired Haldeman and Ehrlichman at the same time. Dean was refusing to be made the scapegoat and if he were dismissed alone he would merely redouble his attack on Haldeman and Ehrlichman—and on the President, too. "You see," Nixon said, "if I say, 'Dean, you leave today,' he'd go out and say, 'Well, the President's covering up for

Ehrlichman and Haldeman.' " The only way to take the heat off the President was to clean house all at once.

As Nixon broached the idea ever so gently, Haldeman and Ehrlichman fought desperately to keep their seats at the President's right hand. On April 17 Ehrlichman argued, "If Dean says, 'What about Haldeman and Ehrlichman?' You say, 'John, I'm talking to you about you. Now I'll take care of them my own way. I'm not going to have you bargaining with me. . . . I'll go if they go!' Supposing I said, 'I won't go unless Henry Kissinger goes!' Yeah, it's ridiculous. . . .'"

At one point, Ehrlichman seemed to be trying something very close to blackmail of the President. "Obviously, if we are put in a position of defending ourselves, the things that I am going to have to say about Dean are: that basically that Dean was the sole proprietor of the [cover-up] project, that he reported to the President, he reported to me only incidentally."

"Reported to the President?" Nixon exclaimed.

"Yes, sir, in other words——"

"When?" challenged Nixon. Not until March, he seemed to be saying, not until very late.

"But you see," Ehrlichman persisted, "I get into a very funny defensive position vis-à-vis you and vis-à-vis him, and it's damn awkward."

"Of course, he didn't report to me," the President shot back. "I was a little busy, and all of you said, 'Let's let Dean handle that and keep him out of the President's office.' "

The two aides also argued that they should not be forced out on the basis of uncorroborated allegations. Both said they would leave voluntarily if charged with a criminal offense. Until then, Ehrlichman urged Nixon to say, " 'This is a town that is so full of wild charges that if I operated on any other basis, even of those who were brought to me by twenty Bishops and an attorney general, I couldn't be suspending people around here or the place would look like a piece of Swiss cheese. . . .' "

Eventually, it was Nixon's own vulnerability that forced him to get rid of his two closest confidants. As public suspicion of the President's involvement in Watergate grew almost daily, other advisers warned him that the continued presence of Haldeman and Ehrlichman in the White House only damaged him further. "I think they have made you very, very vulnerable," Petersen warned. "I think they have made you wittingly or unwittingly very, very vulnerable. At least in public forums they eroded confidence in the office of the Presidency." Leonard Garment said Haldeman and Ehrlichman would be nibbled away "tidbit by tidbit" if he didn't dismiss them then. William Rogers told the President flatly, "I think John and Bob ought to resign."

Nixon seemed genuinely distressed at the prospect of losing them. "I know that as far as you're concerned, you'll go out and throw yourselves on a damned sword. I'm aware of that," he told the two men. "I'm trying to think the thing through with that in mind because damn it, you're the two most valuable members on the staff. I know that. The problem is you're the two most loyal and the two most honest. We don't have to go into that. You know how I feel about that. It's not bull—it's the truth."

Late on Tuesday, April 17, the three men got together for a long talk in the President's office, and a tacit agreement emerged that Haldeman and Ehrlichman would probably have to resign. The two Presidential assistants had more or less accepted their fate— Ehrlichman told David Young around this time that his resignation would be like "throwing a block for the President"—but they were still a trifle bitter. "I think we've just about had it," said Ehrlichman. He was particularly concerned about being disbarred—a prospect which made his wife, Jeanne, "furious." Well, jibed Haldeman, "you can always handle traffic cases." Then Haldeman too grew morose, noting that even if they "beat the rap" they would be "damaged goods," unable to get back into government. "You are not damaged goods as far as I am concerned," Nixon said, suggesting they both might work half time for the Nixon Foundation, which, he said, "is going to be a hell of a big thing, it's bound to be." Haldeman said he might be interested in the foundation, but what he really wanted to do was to "get funding for the ability to clear my name and spend the rest of my life destroying what some people like Dean and Magruder have done to the President."

At this and subsequent meetings, Nixon offered his two assistants between $200,000 and $300,000 in cash, nominally for legal fees and family support, but presumably also to guarantee their continued silence on matters which could damage him. Not surprisingly, given their "hush-money" experience, they rejected the offer. Haldeman said, "That compounds the problem. That really does."

On April 19 John J. Wilson and his associate, Frank H. Strickler—the lawyers engaged by Haldeman and Ehrlichman—made a final attempt to stave off the inevitable. At an hour-long meeting in the President's office, they warned that his assistants' resignations would harm him more than they would help him. "I feel that resignations now by these two gentlemen will be a tremendous reflection on the Presidency," said Strickler. "If they stepped out at this point there is going to be a public feeling that this is an admission of guilt." Nixon had kind words for his old friends: "They're great, fine Americans. And they tell the truth too. . . . I just hope we can save them."

It was too late. On the evening of April 27 Nixon went up to Camp David accompanied only by his Irish setter, King Timahoe, and his speechwriter, Raymond K. Price. That night he brooded alone in Aspen Lodge, the Presidential residence. But the next morning, helicopters began landing and taking off like medevac teams at Da Nang. First, Ron Ziegler arrived to help draft some impending statements. Then came Nixon's confidant, William Rogers. On Sunday, April 29, Haldeman and Ehrlichman arrived, and in separate conversations the President told them they would have to resign. According to Ehrlichman, Nixon broke down and cried as he told him it was "very painful" and he "regretted very much having to take this step." When Ehrlichman again rejected cash for his attorneys' fees, Nixon asked whether there was anything else he could do for him. Ehrlichman said, "Sometime I'd like you to explain to our children . . ."

Another helicopter that day brought Attorney General Kleindienst to Camp David. By then, Kleindienst had decided to resign, which was just what Nixon wanted him to do. In part, the President's decision may have grown from a lingering resentment over Kleindienst's role in forcing revelation of the Fielding burglary and, thus, the dismissal of charges against Daniel Ellsberg. But Nixon had other good reasons for wanting Kleindienst out. With the Watergate scandal now lodged squarely inside the White House, he needed to demonstrate a jut-jawed determination to bring all wrongdoers to justice. Kleindienst could be of little help in this regard, because his close friendship with Mitchell, Mardian, and other potential defendants had already forced him to withdraw from supervising all Watergate matters. So, for a new attorney general to personify vigor, honesty, and integrity to a deeply suspicious press and public, Nixon chose Secretary of Defense Elliot Richardson. That same Sunday Nixon summoned Richardson to Camp David too, and told him of his intention.

At noon on Monday, April 30, Ziegler announced the resignations of Haldeman, Ehrlichman, Kleindienst, and—at long last—John Dean, and the appointment of Richardson.* That evening Nixon discussed the day's developments in a television speech.

Two weeks before, Nixon had told Haldeman that Kleindienst was urging him to "go out and make a Checkers Speech at nine o'clock at night. I told him, 'Now, Dick, I am not going to do that,' " and Haldeman replied, "Oh, I think that would be crazy, I sure do." But that is precisely what the President now proceeded to do. His speech that night was not unlike

---

*Haldeman and Ehrlichman were later indicted—along with Mitchell, Mardian, Colson, Parkinson, and Strachan—on charges that included conspiracy, obstruction of justice, and lying under oath. Haldeman, Ehrlichman, and Mitchell were found guilty and each was sentenced to a prison term of twenty months to five years. They are appealing those sentences. Mardian was convicted of obstruction of justice and was sentenced to ten months to three years. Parkinson was acquitted. The charges against Colson were dropped after he pleaded guilty to a charge of obstructing justice in the Ellsberg case. The charges against Strachan were dismissed by the government.

the famous 1952 Checkers Speech in which Nixon had
defended himself against charges that he had made improper use of a "secret fund" set up for him by California businessmen. Again, he cleverly twisted the facts
to awake sympathy for him and his associates.

The acceptance of Haldeman's and Ehrlichman's
resignations, he said, was "one of the most difficult decisions of my Presidency" and carried with it "no implication whatever of personal wrongdoing on their
part." Indeed, he still regarded them as "two of the
finest public servants it has ever been my privilege
to know." Kleindienst, he said, had "no personal involvement in the matter." The President offered no
such disclaimer for Dean, leaving the strong implication that he was deeply involved.

Flanked by a bust of Lincoln and a photograph of
his family, Nixon abandoned the tone of outraged
innocence which had characterized his earlier remarks
on Watergate, but he continued to pose as a chief
executive so busy with momentous matters of war and
peace that he had no time to supervise the minor business of his own re-election campaign.

". . . As the 1972 campaign approached," he said,
he had decided that "the Presidency should come first
and politics second. To the maximum extent possible,
therefore, I sought to delegate campaign operations,
and to remove the day-to-day campaign decisions from
the President's office and from the White House. . . .

"The easiest course would be for me to blame those
to whom I delegated the responsibility to run the campaign. But that would be a cowardly thing to do.

"I will not place the blame on subordinates—on people whose zeal exceeded their judgment, and who may
have done wrong in a cause they deeply believed to
be right.

"In any organization, the man at the top must bear
the responsibility. That responsibility, therefore, belongs here in this office. I accept that."

It was a cunning formulation, suggesting that he was
utterly innocent of any involvement in Watergate, but
too principled to ask subordinates to shoulder the blame.
In fact, that is precisely what he intended to do. "And

I pledge to you tonight," he went on, "that I will do everything in my power to ensure that the guilty are brought to justice, and that such abuses are purged from our political processes in the years to come, long after I have left this office." Such purging, he said, would be carried out by Elliot Richardson, "a man of unimpeachable integrity and rigorously high principle." Nixon said he had given Richardson "absolute authority to make all decisions bearing upon the prosecution of the Watergate case and related matters. I have instructed him that if he should consider it appropriate, he has the authority to name a special supervising prosecutor for matters arising out of the case."

When the cameras were off, Nixon brushed tears from his eyes and remarked to the television technicians, "It wasn't easy." Then he took another step that could not have been easy. He marched into the White House press room and standing in the shadows behind Ziegler's lectern spoke to a group of fifteen reporters and photographers, "Ladies and gentlemen of the press. We have had our differences in the past, and I hope you give me hell every time you think I'm wrong. I hope I'm worthy of your trust." Then he turned and walked upstairs to his living quarters.

But if Nixon had expected the day's peace offerings to awaken new trust in press and public, they did not. There was some praise for his housecleaning from some all too predictable sources. Senator Hugh Scott, the Senate minority leader, hailed the speech as evidence that Nixon was "determined to see this affair thoroughly cleaned up." And when the President strode into a cabinet meeting the next day, the members of his official family rose as one and applauded him. "I want you to know that Republicans everywhere are strongly supporting you," said Republican National Chairman George Bush. "I know that the American people are with you," said Secretary of State Rogers.

But the American people were not with him. A Gallup Poll taken soon after the President's speech showed that fully half of those responding believed that Nixon had personally participated in the Watergate cover-up. In a regular Gallup Poll several weeks later, those disapproving the President's performance in office (45 per cent) outnumbered those approving (44 per cent) for the first time since Nixon had entered the White House. Most of the public, press, and Congress did not believe the President had leveled with them. Senator Mark O. Hatfield, Republican of Oregon, summed up many people's feelings when he demanded that Nixon produce "the truth, the whole truth, and nothing but the truth."

For a few more weeks Nixon temporized. During much of May he was preoccupied with reshuffling his high command to meet the difficult days ahead. Appropriately enough for the now embattled White House, Haldeman's spot as second-in-command went to a military man—General Alexander Haig, Army vice chief of staff and formerly Kissinger's chief aide. Nobody was named immediately to fill Ehrlichman's job. Most of his duties were assumed by Kenneth Cole, his assistant on the Domestic Council, until early June, when Melvin Laird, the former secretary of defense, became Nixon's new domestic affairs adviser. Leonard Garment replaced John Dean as counsel to the President, but legal problems relating to Watergate were entrusted to J. Fred Buzhardt, Jr., who had been general counsel to the Defense Department and was now a special counsel to the President. The White House staff was further augmented with the appointment as unpaid special adviser of John Connally, the former secretary of the treasury, who had switched from the Democratic to the Republican party a few days before; and of Bryce Harlow, who resumed his role as Presidential counselor. James Schlesinger, CIA director, replaced Elliot Richardson as secretary of defense; and his place at the CIA was taken by William Colby, the agency's deputy director for operations. William D. Ruckelshaus, head of the Environmental Protection Agency, succeeded Pat Gray as acting FBI director.

But probably the most important appointment of

the month came when Elliot Richardson, trying to persuade the Senate Judiciary Committee that he would be an independent attorney general, selected his former law professor, Archibald Cox of Harvard, to be special Watergate prosecutor. Testifying before that committee on May 21, Cox said he would not "shield anybody and I don't intend to be intimidated by anybody." He said that if the trail were to lead him there, he would pursue the investigation into the Oval Office. (Silbert, Glanzer, and Campbell tried for a time to work under Cox's supervision, but, seeing his appointment as a reflection on their independence and integrity, they resigned on June 29.)

Cox's determination to dig out the full Watergate story undoubtedly contributed to Nixon's decision that week to issue another long statement on Watergate. The four-thousand-word statement released on May 22 resembled the report Nixon had once pressed John Dean to write: long but incomplete; detailed in some areas, vague in others; truthful on inconsequential matters, false or misleading on important ones; damning to some of the President's subordinates but exonerating Nixon himself.

He said he had no "prior knowledge" of the Watergate burglary; never authorized illegal campaign activities; never took part in or was aware of the cover-up; never tried to implicate the CIA in Watergate; never authorized any executive clemency offer to the defendants; did not know of the money paid to the defendants or of the Fielding burglary until he began his "own investigation" in mid-March. Nixon conceded that he had tried to prevent uncovering of certain "covert national security activities"—the term he now used to describe the Fielding burglary, the 1969–71 wiretaps, and many of the Caulfield-Ulasewicz operations. Moreover, he said, he had recognized that "since persons originally recruited for covert national security activities had participated in Watergate, an unrestricted investigation of Watergate might lead to an exposé of those covert national security operations." He denied that he tried to restrain the Watergate investigation himself, but admitted, "It now appears that there were persons who may have gone beyond my directives, and sought to expand on my efforts to protect the national security operations in order to cover up any involvement they or certain others might have had in Watergate." Finally, he said, "With hindsight, it is apparent that I should have given more heed to the warning signals I received along the way about a Watergate cover-up and less to the reassurances."

For all its concessions and admissions, Nixon's May 22 statement added up to just another reassurance—that whatever else may have gone wrong those past few years, whatever "horrors" had been perpetrated, the President himself was not involved. Yet it was precisely this which much of the press and public was no longer willing to accept. And it was precisely this which the Senate Select Committee on Presidential Campaign Activities began challenging when it opened its hearings on May 17, 1973.

The strategy of Chairman Sam Ervin and his chief counsel, Sam Dash, was a simple one: to begin with the foot soldiers—the secretaries, the CREEP functionaries, the former New York cops—and move relentlessly upward in the ranks through the subalterns to the mighty commanders of Nixon's forces. So the first witnesses who paraded through Room 318 of the Old Senate Office Building (the Senate Caucus Room) were little known to the gaping spectators or the millions more who watched on television: Rob Odle of CREEP; McCord; Caulfield; Ulasewicz; Barker; Baldwin; Liddy's secretary, Sally Harmony; Reisner; Sloan; Porter. Only after nine days of hearings and seventeen witnesses, did the committee reach a nationally known figure—Maurice Stans. And not until June 14 did it reach a man—Jeb Magruder—who could provide testimony incriminating the upper ranks of CREEP and the White House.

But even Magruder was only a piquant appetizer for the main dish soon to be set steaming and sizzling before the committee members and a ravenous nation. The nervous anticipation with which John Dean had been awaited was only intensified when the committee voted to postpone his testimony a week so as not to

poison the Washington atmosphere any more than
necessary during the state visit of Party Secretary
Leonid I. Brezhnev of the U.S.S.R. During the
"Brezhnev recess," though, the White House took the
offensive—leaking its own account of the Nixon-Dean
meetings that spring; disclosing that Dean had "borrowed" $4000 from a campaign cash fund to finance
his Florida honeymoon with Mo; and impugning his
motives. (Senator Hugh Scott told reporters, "Nothing
is so incredible that this turncoat will not be willing to
testify to it in exchange for a reward.")

Finally, on Monday, June 25, Dean took the witness
chair beneath the crystal chandeliers and Corinthian
columns, and began to read: "To one who was in the
White House and became somewhat familiar with its
interworkings, the Watergate matter was an inevitable
outgrowth of a climate of excessive concern over the
political impact of demonstrators, excessive concern
over leaks, an insatiable appetite for political intelligence, all coupled with a do-it-yourself White House
staff, regardless of the law." And so it went through
the 245-page statement on which Dean had been
laboring since April—facts, dates, reconstructed conversations, all delivered with the cool dispassion of a
bemused owl.

Nixon countered again—this time with a memo from
Fred Buzhardt, his new Watergate counsel. Intended
only for the senators' "background" information, the
memo was read into the record by Senator Daniel
Inouye, and thus the President's bold strategy was
publicly disclosed: to pin the blame on Dean, "the
principal actor in the Watergate cover-up," and even
on John Mitchell. Ron Ziegler hurriedly disavowed
the memo, but the episode only added to the impression
of a panicky President desperate to lay blame wherever
he could. This lent new significance to the solemn
question which Senator Howard Baker asked of virtually every witness: "What did the President know and
when did he know it?" As the hearings droned through
the dog days of the Washington summer, this question increasingly preoccupied the nation.

10

HOUSES IN THE SUN

The President does not like ice cubes with holes in them.
—Commander Ronald Jackson,
White House Mess Chief,
May 21, 1970

On February 28, 1973, John Dean told Nixon that investigators had subpoenaed the records of his personal attorney, Herbert Kalmbach, and warned his boss, "Herb's got records that run all over hell's acre on things for the last few years."

NIXON: Now, his records, that is, with regards to the campaign. They can't re— they can't get his records with regard to his private transactions.
DEAN: No, none of the private transactions. Absolutely—that is privileged material.
NIXON: That's right.
DEAN: Anything to do with San Clemente and, and the like—that is just so far out of bounds that, uh—
NIXON: Yeah. Did they ask for that?
DEAN: No, no, no. No indication.
NIXON: Good. Oh, well, even if it is, I mean—
DEAN: Well, it's just none of their—you know, that's really none of their business.

What the President and his counsel thought was none of the public's business was the way Nixon had purchased and developed his two houses in the sun—at San Clemente, California, and Key Biscayne, Florida. Many recent Presidents have had a sunny refuge somewhere to which they could escape from the rigors of

Washington. These have been borrowed (like Eisenhower's cottage at the Augusta National Golf Club); or existing government property (like the Key West naval base that Harry Truman used), or their own, pre-Presidential homes (like Lyndon Johnson's ranch). Yet within seven months of his election—while still a man of relatively modest means—Nixon had purchased two expensive and elaborate new homes.

The press and public paid little attention to the announcement in April 1969 that the President was buying a fourteen-room Spanish-style *hacienda* and roughly five acres of surrounding waterfront land in the scenic little town of San Clemente, about halfway between Los Angeles and San Diego. A brief press statement five months later said only that Nixon would pay $100,000 to the owner, a ninety-year-old widow named Mrs. Henry Hamilton Cotton, and would assume a $240,000 mortgage. The White House said the portion of the Cotton estate not purchased by the Nixons was being held in trust by the Title Insurance and Trust Company of Los Angeles until the President could find a buyer—perhaps the Richard Nixon Foundation, which would soon be looking for a library site. Those few reporters who bothered to look deeper into this transaction met only blank stares at the White House.

Then, in October 1972, Senator Edward Kennedy's Subcommittee on Administrative Practices and Procedures began looking into irregularities in Nixon's re-election campaign. Jim Flug, the subcommittee's chief counsel, and Carmine Bellino, its chief investigator, concentrated on Donald Segretti's contacts with the White House and the payments he received from Kalmbach. They flew to the West Coast and, in the words of another investigator, began "handing out subpoenas like traffic summonses." Some of those subpoenas were for Kalmbach's bank and telephone records. This was the investigation Dean told the President about on February 28. It had turned up nothing on San Clemente.

Indeed, by February, Kennedy's subcommittee was ending its staff investigation and turning its findings over to Sam Ervin's Select Committee. In March Bellino moved over to become an investigator for the Ervin committee and late that month he accompanied Terry F. Lenzner, an assistant chief counsel, on a trip to California, where they interviewed Kalmbach extensively. After Lenzner returned to Washington, Bellino stayed on, interviewing Kalmbach's secretaries and examining his financial records. But the focus had now switched to Kalmbach's role in the Watergate cover-up, and committee sources can recall no evidence turning up on San Clemente at that time.

Yet, on May 14 the *Santa Ana Register,* a small daily newspaper in a community twenty-nine miles up the coast from San Clemente, reported that Senate investigators had found evidence indicating that funds left over from the 1968 Nixon campaign had been used to purchase the San Clemente property. According to the article by *Register* reporter John Blackburn, the investigators had "stumbled across" the possibility while looking into the fund Kalmbach maintained at the Newport Beach branch of the Bank of America.

It was a curious story. No other newspaper has ever turned up evidence to support it. But it was by no means pure fantasy. The rumor was in the air. In September 1971 Hank Greenspun had heard almost the same thing—that campaign contributions in 1969 and 1970 had gone to furnish San Clemente, although he specified that the money had come from Howard Hughes. His casual mention of this story to Herb Klein had been enough to send Kalmbach winging to Las Vegas to talk with the maverick publisher. If word of the article had reached Dean—as it almost surely must have—it would account for his anxious mention of San Clemente in his conversation with the President.

In any case, the *Santa Ana Register*'s story attracted wide attention—in part because the *Register* was an unlikely paper to be muckraking the Nixon White House. Until then, it had hardly been known for investigative reporting, and it generally reflected the conservative, often reactionary, politics of Orange County. But the editors had been nettled by *New York Times* and *Washington Post* reporters tearing up their turf, so they had turned Blackburn loose. He paid for it with a spate of hate mail from the county's Nixon loyalists.

("You goddamn filthy bunch of Communist bastards. Your newspaper is a lousy, filthy lying rag which isn't fit for people to wipe their ass on. If I was President I would sue your goddam filthy paper. You can take your Ellsburg [*sic*]—that Jew Communist thief—and Ted Kennedy, that murderer, and all the Democrats, and stick them all up your cancerous ass.")

The *Register* story aroused a more temperate but equally outraged reaction at the White House. By the time it came clattering over the wire-service tickers in the press room late on the afternoon of May 14, most reporters had left for the day. Adam Clymer, the Baltimore *Sun*'s White House correspondent, recalls, "Ron Ziegler was furious. He called anyone still in the press room into his office and delivered a tirade against the *Register,* calling the piece 'totally false and malicious.' " But Clymer and Norman Kempster of United Press International kept needling Ziegler about the holes in the official version on the financing of San Clemente until the press secretary promised to release a detailed explanation within the next few days.

On April 15 Ziegler announced that the President still owed $630,000 on the San Clemente property—a figure that seemed inconsistent with what was known about the scope of the President's purchase—and promised a full accounting within a day or so. Over the next ten days the document was rescheduled for release three times and each time failed to appear. Then, on May 25, Elliot Richardson was sworn in as attorney general in the East Room of the White House. When reporters returned from the ceremony, they found a written statement on San Clemente stuffed in the distribution racks in the press office. It held a lot of surprises.

The statement told the following story. In the spring of 1969 the President had wanted to buy the Cotton House and surrounding 5.9 acres. But the owner insisted that the 27.732-acre estate be sold as a unit and was asking $1.4 million for it. Unable to raise that much, the President hoped that some "compatible" buyer would purchase the other 22 acres. The Nixon Foundation backed out—apparently because the site was too small for a Presidential library—and no other buyer could be found by the July 15 closing date. Temporarily, then, the President had to purchase the entire tract. To make the larger down payment, Nixon got a $450,000 loan from his friend Robert Abplanalp, and put $400,000 of it down on the property, assuming a $1-million mortgage for the rest. In October 1969 Nixon picked up an adjacent 2.934 acres (the Elmore property) for $20,000 down and an $80,000 mortgage —bringing the total cost of the 30.666 acres to $1.5 million. In both cases, the purchases were made and formal title retained by the Title Insurance and Trust Company, thus disguising the actual owner. Finally, on December 15, the unwanted portion of the property was sold to an investment company headed by Abplanalp for $1,249,000—accomplished by Abplanalp's canceling his own loans to the President, which then totaled $625,000, and his company's assuming the $64,000 mortgage on the Elmore property and $560,000 of the remaining $900,000 on the Cotton property. In return, Abplanalp's company was assigned an interest in the trust.

White House staffers declined further comment on the statement, which, they said, "spoke for itself." If it spoke for itself, then it stuttered badly. What was the name of Abplanalp's investment company? Who were the other investors? Where did the money come from? Reporters asked these questions, but they got little help from the White House and none from the trust company, where the files on the Nixon property were held far more closely than other documents. "A man can get his arm broken just asking for them," one employee said.

But the inquiries continued, and on August 27 the White House finally released a still more detailed analysis prepared by Coopers & Lybrand, an international accounting firm. Among other things, this disclosed that for several years, until Abplanalp bought him out, Bebe Rebozo had been a silent partner in the investment company, which was known as the B & C Investment Company. The audit also revealed that the company had purchased the Elmore parcel and most of the Cotton property, leaving Nixon the 5.9 ocean-

front acres he had always wanted, along with the villa
and its outbuildings: a garage, guest cottage, shed,
"view house," and three gazebos. A White House
spokesman said he hoped that this statement would put
the San Clemente question "to rest once and for all."

But it didn't. Reporters noted that—despite the sale
of an interest in the trust—Orange County records still
didn't show any division of the property. A wall, paid
for by the federal government, ran around the entire
tract. An $85,000, three-hole golf course, built for the
President by a group of patriotic businessmen called
The 76 Club, occupied two and a half acres. A path-
way and a bridge crossed the property from the golf
course to the beach. For all intents and purposes,
Nixon retained use of all 30.666 acres. And, what
with the sales, loans, and resales, he had gained control of property worth at least $1.5 million for a
capital obligation of $356,000 or—if interest payments
are included—$532,000.

Investigators have found nothing illegal in all of this.
But several questions of propriety have been raised.
One is whether the President of the United States
should have been so heavily and secretly in debt to two
millionaires and ultimately to one—Robert H. Abplanalp.

*Pfft. Pfft. Pfft. Each year, some 3 million aerosol
cans squirt hair spray, weed killer, whipped cream,
paint, starch, toothpaste, rust remover, and deodorant
in homes throughout the world. About half of those
cans bear valves manufactured by the Precision Valve
Corporation of Yonkers, New York, whose president,
chairman, and sole owner is Robert Abplanalp, sometimes known as "the father of modern aerosols." In
1969 he got an honorary degree from Villanova for his
invention of the valve which "made life simpler, easier,
safer, and healthier for millions of people." Of late, the
propellant used in aerosols has come under attack by
ecologists as a threat to the ozone layer that shields the
earth from the sun's rays ("Nonsense!" snorts Abplanalp). The "pfft man" was born in the Bronx of*

Swiss parents (their name, in Swiss-German, means "from flat mountain"). His father, Hans, was a machinist and taught him the trade at an early age. "I could run a lathe when I was seven," Bob recalls. After studying mechanical engineering at Villanova for three years, he dropped out to open his own machine-jobbing shop. One day, a customer asked for a reliable aerosol valve. Abplanalp developed one and took out patent No. 2,613,814, which has earned him a personal fortune of more than $100 million. Precision Valve has spawned several subsidiaries, including a trout preserve and hatchery in the Catskills and several fishing resorts. Fish are Abplanalp's private obsession. As a boy, he would go dangling for porgies with his father in Long Island Sound. Today, he would "rather fish than eat"; owns a fifty-five-foot yacht called Sea Lion II; and once caught a 535-pound marlin after a seven-hour battle. He has taken a ninety-nine-year lease on a dozen coral keys in the northern Bahamas, among them the hundred and twenty-five-acre Grand Cay and the hundred-acre Walker's Cay, on which Nixon frequently stayed. Abplanalp first met Nixon in 1963, when he went over to him in a Manhattan restaurant and told the then Wall Street lawyer that he had been "robbed" in the 1960 election. That same year, Precision Valve retained Nixon's law firm, chiefly to keep the government out of its hair. ("We didn't want them to know what we were doing," the company's former president says. "We were afraid they'd steal our ideas.") The two men soon became such close friends that Nixon considered buying a house next door to Abplanalp's split-level home in Bronxville, New York. Although the friendship is based more on a shared enthusiasm for fishing, sports, playing cards, and drinking beer with a group of cronies, the burly, six-footer is a longtime supporter of conservative causes, among them the Tell It to Hanoi Committee. He has been called "a hard-hat without venom."

There is no evidence to show that Abplanalp received anything—besides camaraderie and a certain renown—from his relationship with Nixon. But it appears that Nixon gained in more than one way from his relationship with Abplanalp. The $1.5 million which Nixon paid for the 30.666 acres at San Clemente works out to $48,901 per acre. But the $1,249,000 which B & C paid for the 24.6 acres it bought in 1970 works out to $50,777 per acre—even though the fourteen-room villa and other improvements are on the portion of the land which Nixon retained. Thus, Abplanalp and Rebozo purchased the less valuable land from the President at a price that appeared to give him a substantial capital gain on the transaction.

Arthur Blech of Los Angeles, Nixon's regular tax accountant, determined that there had been no profit on the sale. Following his advice, Nixon paid no capital-gains tax on it. But the transaction drew close scrutiny from congressional investigators and journalists. Eventually, the Joint Congressional Committee on Internal Revenue Taxation determined that Nixon had indeed realized a large capital gain—$117,836—and he was ordered to pay taxes on half of it.

In comparison to San Clemente, the purchase of Nixon's Key Biscayne establishment was relatively simple. But it too was a major undertaking, for it involved not one but a cluster of five one-story stucco houses —a compound that immediately provoked comparisons with the Kennedy compound in Hyannis Port.

Richard Nixon had been vacationing in Key Biscayne on and off for almost twenty years. Just twenty-six miles across a causeway from downtown Miami, the Key has been called "Fair Lawn, New Jersey, with palm trees." The homes which cluster in the middle of the island are sand white and flamingo pink with lots of patios, gardens, and swimming pools. The larger ones sell for more than $300,000. Overwhelmingly white, largely WASP, the residents included a phalanx of corporate executives, among them Samuel C. Johnson, president of Johnson's Wax; Larry MacPhail, president of the New York Yankees; and Harold Geneen, ITT's board chairman.

After his election in the fall of 1968, Nixon stayed for a while on Bay Lane, a pleasant road running along the blue waters of Biscayne Bay. His retreat— 500 Bay Lane—was a beige brick-and-stucco ranch house that belonged to his old friend Senator George A. Smathers of Florida. Nixon liked it so much that on December 20 he bought it for $125,527. On one side of his new house, at 490 Bay Lane, lived another of the President's old friends, Bebe Rebozo. On the other side, at 516 Bay Lane, lived Manuel Arca, Jr. Arca didn't want to move but when approached by Rebozo, he agreed to sell the home he had bought for $145,000 to Nixon for $127,800. ("The President of the United States wanted it," he said later. "What could I do?") Perry and Lucy O'Neal, who lived at 478 Bay Lane, didn't want to sell, either. "We decided to sell because they [the Secret Service] were deviling us to death," Mrs. O'Neal said. "My friends couldn't come in [to the compound] or anything. They were turned away until someone came to vouch for them. My husband couldn't go to the golf course without signing out and saying when he'd come back." And nobody offered the O'Neals the deal given to the man who bought their house. Bob Abplanalp bought it for $150,000 and promptly leased it right back to the Secret Service at $18,000 a year—a deal which would have brought him $144,000 if the President had remained in office for eight years. The government leased the fifth waterfront house for a communications facility in a deal similar to Abplanalp's. The owner, through a trust, was A. Edward Campbell, a stockholder in Rebozo's Key Biscayne Bank. Soon the compound was ringed with high hedges and fences laced with loudspeakers and electronic sensing devices. A gatehouse blocked the road into the compound, and a Coast Guard boat patrolled the bay, keeping sightseers away.

By the spring of 1973 another aspect of the President's real-estate transaction was drawing scrutiny and producing a still more tortuous chain of explanations and accountings by federal agencies. It all began on May 26, the day after the White House admitted Abplanalp's interest in the San Clemente property. Noting that the President claimed to have spent $123,514 of his own money for improvements on the property—he later raised that figure to $187,977—*The New York Times* and Associated Press correspondents on duty at the White House that weekend asked what federal funds had been spent on the San Clemente estate. Gerald L. Warren, the assistant press secretary, gave the figure as $39,525, which, he said, had been spent on "security measures."

But reporters began checking building permits, and soon they turned up construction totaling more than $100,000. Local tradesmen told of government work done on walls, fences, walkways, and a heating system. The General Services Administration (GSA), the government's housekeeping agency, began revising its calculations almost daily: $185,000 on June 11; $423,000 on June 13; $460,312 on June 14; $703,365 on June 21. Ultimately, a House subcommittee concluded that the San Clemente and Key Biscayne enterprises had cost the taxpayers $17.1 million—$10 million for fixed improvements and $7.1 in personnel costs over five years.

This total included many improvements clearly related to the President's official duties. Unlike previous Presidents who used their second homes for occasional vacations in the sun, Nixon was a private, reclusive, restless man who often holed up for weeks on end at one of his palm-fringed refuges or shuttled between them and Washington as the spirit moved him. Thus, San Clemente and Key Biscayne—quickly dubbed the Western and Southern White Houses—had to be converted into full-scale Presidential complexes with all the offices, communications nets, and security precautions required by a mid-century chief executive. So the government spent $6 million to construct and maintain the Western White House office building on the Coast Guard base adjoining the San Clemente home; $412,000 for a helicopter pad and boat-docking facility at Key Biscayne; $127,719 for a Secret Service command post at Key Biscayne; and $5100 for road repairs at Key Biscayne to make it easier for the Secret Service to control vehicles entering the compound.

The White House and the GSA insisted there were equally compelling reasons for the money spent directly on the President's houses and grounds—$701,-000 at San Clemente and $575,000 at Key Biscayne. "All the work the government did was at the express request of the Secret Service for security reasons," a White House official said.

But as reporters and other investigators probed further, they found that many projects paid for by the government originated not with the Secret Service but with the President or his representatives. This was particularly true at San Clemente, where many of the work orders came from Herbert Kalmbach. As the President's on-site representative there, Kalmbach paid some construction costs out of an account in the Newport Beach branch of the Security Pacific National Bank. (This may have given rise to the rumors that he was using 1968 campaign funds, because some campaign funds were kept in Kalmbach's account in that bank.) Kalmbach frequently received instructions from John Ehrlichman on which part of the San Clemente costs should be borne by Nixon and which by the government. Sometimes, improvements billed to the government had nothing to do with the President's security.

Ultimately, the Joint Congressional Committee on Internal Revenue Taxation found that at least $66,614.03 of the work done at San Clemente and $25,684 done at Key Biscayne did not relate to security, should have been paid for by Nixon himself, and thus constituted taxable income to the President. These projects included:

• Installation of a fireplace exhaust fan at San

Clemente. On January 11, 1971, Kalmbach wrote a memorandum to his secretary, Marilyn Correa, noting that "Mr. Rebozo says the President feels the fireplace in the library doesn't draw well—there is smoke in the room." He asked Miss Correa to have the contractor, Warren Sturtevant, "go there, start a fire in the fireplace, do what is necessary to see that it draws right, and write me a note so I can send a reply to Mr. Rebozo." After making the test, Sturtevant reported that "there were only two occasions out of about ten possible times used where there was a smoking problem." Nevertheless, Sturtevant installed a small exhaust fan in the chimney and billed Kalmbach $388.78. Kalmbach requested that the bill be forwarded to the GSA. But on June 8, Ernest Garbarino, a GSA buildings manager at San Clemente, called Miss Correa taking exception to the bill and arguing that Kalmbach should pay it. On June 25 Miss Correa wrote Sturtevant reporting that "Ken Iacovoni informed me that SS [Secret Service] would pay for the installation after I informed him that it definitely was placed for security purposes and how would he like it if you know who was asphyxiated ever because there was a certain wind condition which caused the draft to come downwards and cause the smoke to come into the room. He finally agreed with me." GSA later paid the bill "per Mr. Kalmbach."

• A new electric heating system at San Clemente. From the start, the President's contractor intended to replace an antiquated wall heating system which he regarded as inadequate to heat the house. The Secret Service too was determined to replace the system, but for safety considerations. The contractor favored a gas-fired system. The Secret Service wanted an electric system—again for safety reasons. The Secret Service won out and the GSA paid $18,493 for the electric system. But the joint committee found that the government should have paid only the difference between the cost of the electric system and the $12,988 which the gas system would have cost.

• Four new windows in the President's second-story den at San Clemente. During a "walk-through" of the house in June 1969, Harold Lynch, the President's architectural consultant, sat down in Nixon's desk chair in his den and noticed that he could not see the ocean. He thought the President would like such a view and requested that the GSA have the windows enlarged. The Secret Service approved the request, specifying that bulletproof glass be installed. The GSA paid $1600 for the work.

• Handrails at San Clemente. The Secret Service ordered new handrails installed down the stone steps to the beach. Subsequently, Lynch inspected the rails, found them drab, and ordered Sturtevant to stain the redwood and decorate it with hand carvings. At the same time, he ordered new wrought-iron handrails to replace railings on a path to the gazebos. The cost of these improvements was $998.50, and the joint committee decided that they were "not for security purposes."

• A shuffleboard court at Key Biscayne. When a Secret Service command post was constructed on the President's property, a concrete slab shuffleboard court was partially destroyed. The court was replaced by a black, white, and green terrazzo court at a cost of $2000. The joint committee held that the President should have paid the difference between that and the cost of a new concrete court—$1600.

In addition to those projects which the joint committee found to constitute taxable income to Nixon, a whole range of other items have been questioned by other investigators:

• A forty-foot Fibreglas flagpole with a six-inch gold-leaf ball installed in Key Biscayne for $587.

• Twelve brass lanterns at the entrance of San Clemente and five light standards at the pool, costing $5300.

• A bulletproof, transparent shield on the ocean side of the President's San Clemente pool—costing $13,000. The government said the shield was necessary to prevent someone from shooting at the pool from a boat at sea. Others have suggested that its main purpose was to protect the sunbathing President from the gusty winds that blow off the Pacific. Indeed, during a news conference, Arthur F. Sampson, the general services administrator, referred to it as a "wind screen."

• Furniture for the President's second-story den at San Clemente—$4834.50. Sampson argued that the study was just another Presidential office and should therefore be furnished at government expense, even though a $1.7-million Western White House facility had already been constructed for him at the Coast Guard base, only three hundred yards away. Invoices show that the den furniture—which included $68 for decorative pillows—came from the same Los Angeles decorating firm that did the rest of the house.

• An automatic ice maker at Key Biscayne, costing $621. GSA officials originally said the ice maker was solely for the use of Secret Service and military personnel stationed there. But a GSA memo revealed that Commander Ronald Jackson, the White House mess chief, had visited Key Biscayne on May 21, 1970, and, noting that the only ice maker on the premises was one which produced little ringlets, said, "The President does not like ice cubes with holes in them." The new machine was installed five days later. A Secret Service agent subsequently conceded that the ice maker was for Nixon's use and said it was "to insure that the President was not using poisoned ice."

(Only once did the GSA balk outright at a Presidential request. On January 16, 1970, Kalmbach released Mrs. Christensen, the full-time housekeeper at San Clemente. He told the GSA building manager that the President wanted the GSA to take over housekeeping duties at the residence during his absences. Kalmbach said GSA employees were to assume the following duties: cover all upholstered furniture; remove all potted plants from the patio and the residence to the greenhouse; dust all furniture once a week; lightly clean the house once a week. The building manager would be given twenty-four hours' notice before each Presidential visit, so that he could remove the furniture covers, replace the potted plants, and set up the lawn furniture. The GSA flatly refused to perform these housekeeping duties at the Nixons' private home. Navy mess stewards were then assigned to ready the residence a few days prior to each Presidential visit.)

The General Accounting Office concluded that many of the expenditures—particularly at San Clemente—improved the value of Nixon's property. The San Clemente villa, which Nixon renamed La Casa Pacifica (the House of Peace), was an impressive building from the start, with its fourteen rooms built around a square courtyard in which a cupid sits atop a pyramid fountain decorated with Spanish tiles. But the house, built in 1925, had badly deteriorated under its previous occupants. Some critics have suggested that the government, in effect, restored the dilapidated estate for the Nixons.

The President rejected that interpretation. In answer to a question at his September 5, 1973, press conference, he said, "As a matter of fact, what the government did in San Clemente reduced the value of the property. If you see three Secret Service gazebos and if you see some of the other fences that block out the rather beautiful view to the hills and the mountains that I like, you would realize that what I say is quite true; it reduces its value as far as a residential property is concerned."

But investigators disagreed—among them Representative Jack Brooks, chairman of the House subcommittee looking into Nixon's real-estate transactions. When a GSA official echoed the President's contention that the expenditures had detracted from the house's value, the Texas Democrat said, "Anytime you want to desecrate my property with all that money you just come on down to Texas and do it."

B y the summer of 1973 Richard Nixon not only had two spacious, well-appointed homesteads in the sunny enclaves of the very rich, he was very rich himself. In May of that year his net worth had reached $988,522—more than three times what it had been when he entered the White House four years before. By midsummer he was almost certainly a millionaire. People began asking where all the money had come from so quickly.

It was, indeed, a Horatio Alger story to warm the hearts of every true believer in the American system. Nixon's childhood had been positively Dickensian in its drab and dreary poverty. His father, Frank, was a streetcar motorman in Columbus, Ohio, when he struck out for the Gold Rush state. There, he tried his faltering hand as a farmhand, oilfield roustabout, carpenter, and lemon rancher—finally eking out a skimpy living with a general store and gas station in Whittier. The Nixon boys wore hand-me-down clothes ("I wore my brother's shoes and my younger brothers were handed down mine," the future President recalled). At ten, young Dick worked as a part-time farm laborer; at fourteen, he was a fortune-wheel barker for the Slippery Gulch Rodeo. Even when Dick married Pat, the only vacation they could afford that first year was on a United Fruit boat from California to New Orleans. ("We had the worst cabin in the boat . . . right down there in the hold with the sound of the engines and the smells. So when we came to New Orleans, we decided to eat one meal in a good restaurant. We came to Antoine's and we ordered one Oysters Rockefeller for the two of us, and one pompano-in-a-bag.") During the war, he scraped together a small stake playing poker with his Navy buddies, then promptly blew it on an abortive orange-juice–bottling venture called Citra Frost.

Hard times bred a frugal, parsimonious young congressman. When Rose Mary Woods joined him as a secretary in 1947, she was impressed by his tidy bookkeeping and modest expense accounts. The $18,235 "secret fund" established by California businessmen for him in 1952 was less a mark of his corruption than evidence of his relative penury. He shrewdly exploited that in his "Checkers speech," telling his radio audience that he owned only "a 1950 Oldsmobile car; a three-thousand-dollar equity in my house in California in which my parents were then living; a twenty-thousand-dollar equity in my house in Washington; four thousand dollars in life insurance, plus a GI term policy, which would expire in two years; no stocks or bonds; no interest in any other property or business." This scant catalogue was balanced by his debts: "Ten thousand dollars on the California house; twenty thousand on the Washington house; forty-five hundred to the Riggs National Bank of Washington; thirty-five hundred to my parents; five hundred on my life insurance." The most potent political symbols of that election year were the gift the Nixons were going to keep—a little black-and-white cocker spaniel called Checkers; and Pat's "respectable Republican cloth coat."

Even after eight years as Vice President, Nixon's net worth probably did not exceed $100,000. Two years later, after the defeat by Pat Brown, he was living in a showcase home in Trousdale Estates near Los Angeles, around the corner from Harpo and Groucho Marx, but he was deep in debt. Only when Nixon moved to New York in 1963 did he begin to make some real money—between $100,000 and $250,000 a year from his law practice and about $250,000 from his book, *Six Crises*. He bought a co-op apartment at 812 Fifth Avenue, the same building where Nelson Rockefeller lived (the Rockefellers never invited him to dinner), and he ventured gingerly into the Big Apple's moneyed circles: dining at Mercurio's with Abplanalp, going to the opera, having drinks with his Wall Street colleagues at the Links Club. After his election in 1968, he sold his apartment for $312,500 and his stock market holdings for $371,782. In January 1969 his net worth was $307,141. "I wasn't a pauper," he recalls.

Nixon's attitude toward money was ambivalent. He professed disdain for the "old money" people of the Eastern Establishment (who had never accepted *him*, either). "I have seen those who have nothing to do— I could be one of them if I wanted—the people just lying around at Palm Beach," he told the writer Garry Wills. "Nothing could be more pitiful."

But the "new money" people, the brash, vigorous

men on the make who had earned their fortunes in electronics, plastics, airlines and aerospace, oil and natural gas, retailing and real estate—they were Nixon's kind of men. They were men "in the arena," not lying around at the beach. His original twelve-man cabinet included no less than seven millionaires, all of them "self-made": Winton M. Blount, postmaster general; Walter J. Hickel, secretary of the interior; David M. Kennedy, secretary of the treasury; William P. Rogers, secretary of state; George W. Romney, secretary of housing and urban development; Maurice H. Stans, secretary of commerce; John A. Volpe, secretary of transportation. In subsequent years, still more self-made millionaires joined the Nixon team: Roy Ash, director of the Office of Management and Budget; George Bush, chairman of the Republican National Committee; William Clements, deputy secretary of defense; John Connally, secretary of the treasury; Frederick B. Dent, secretary of commerce.

Nixon money was not only new, active, entrepreneurial—it was also drawn heavily from what Kirkpatrick Sale has called "the Southern Rim, the sun belt that runs from southern California through Arizona and Texas down to the Florida Keys." Bush, Clements, and Connally were from Texas; Fred Dent from South Carolina; Blount from Alabama; Ash from California. The pattern of "Southern Rim" influence pervaded Nixon's world, whether among his personal cronies—Kalmbach (California), Abplanalp (the Bahamas), Rebozo (Florida); the money men who supported his campaigns—Jack Drown, Thomas V. Jones, Henry Salvatori, C. Arnholt Smith (all from California); Robert Allen, Walter T. Duncan, William Liedtke, the Murchisons, H. Ross Perot (all from Texas); Anthony Rossi (Florida), Robert Vesco (the Bahamas); or on the White House staff—Harry Dent and Fred Malek (South Carolina), Fred LaRue (Mississippi), Bryce Harlow (Oklahoma), Bill Timmons (Tennessee), Dean Burch (Arizona) and Chapin, Chotiner, Elbourne, Finch, Haldeman, Higby, Klein, Porter, Mardian, Strachan, and Ziegler (all from California).

These were men with whom Nixon felt at home: men without the sophistication, the Ivy League education, and the clubby manners that so humbled and humiliated him. Most of them had risen through the Depression years, made the system work for them, emerged with few intellectual pretensions, and loved the good life which could best be found in the sun belt—fishing, boating, golfing, or just sitting around drinking vodka tonics with a bunch of good old boys. No wonder then that Nixon had established his two outposts at the poles of the Southern Rim—southern California and the Florida Keys.

No wonder, either, that long association with such men should have left Nixon with a profound appreciation of the good things money could buy. If, as Rebozo insists, Nixon "never cared about money" before, as President he realized the opportunities which lay before him. Just as he determined to use "the powers of the incumbency" to assure his re-election, so he used those same powers to assure that he would leave the White House a wealthy man.

In his first year as President, rumors began circulating in Washington about Nixon's taste for high living. In August 1969 the "Washington Beat" column in the *Evening Star* said, "Inside Washington political salons, the curious and the gossips are trying to figure out how President Nixon could possibly afford to spend all the money he is lavishing on himself and his family." But not until the summer of 1973 did persistent reporters and congressional investigators begin asking seriously where Nixon got all that money while serving as President.

In part, it came from avoiding—or evading—taxes. During his White House years Nixon managed to salt away most of his $200,000 salary and some of his $91,000 expense allowance by dodging the taxes most ordinary citizens had to pay.

He paid no state or local income taxes. The law exempts federal officials from paying income tax to the District of Columbia, where they are presumably only temporary residents. But Nixon paid no taxes in California, either, even though he was a registered voter there and once claimed the state as his legal residence. When he made a \$142,912 profit on the sale of his New York apartment in 1969, he avoided paying a capital-gains tax by saying that he was applying the profit to the purchase of his new "principal residence" in San Clemente. But his lawyers persuaded California officials that the President was not liable for state taxes by arguing that he occupied San Clemente "for brief periods of time [that] would not aggregate more than a few weeks in each year" and that his principal residence was actually the White House. California's senators and representatives all pay state taxes although they, too, live in Washington. Nixon's critics argued that San Clemente either was or wasn't his prime residence. If it was, they said, he should pay California taxes; if it wasn't, he should have paid capital gains on the sale of the New York apartment. (Eventually, the California Franchise Tax Board ruled that Nixon was not a California resident for tax purposes, because, although he had his principal residence there, his absence from the state was not "temporary or transitory." Nevertheless, he was billed \$5052.26 in back taxes, penalties, and interest for that portion of his income earned in California during visits to the state. Finally, the California legislature passed a law which closed any possible loophole and retroactively made all Nixon's 1974 income taxable in California.)

Then, in early autumn 1973, the nation learned with some incredulity that during much of his tenure in the Presidency Nixon had paid virtually no federal income taxes either. Working from the figures available in the Coopers & Lybrand audit of the President's finances, first the Baltimore *Sun* on September 11 and then *The New York Times* on September 12 reported that Nixon had enough tax deductions in 1970 and 1971 to have wiped out all of his taxable income. Then an IRS employee at the National Computer Center in Martinsburg, West Virginia, got a read-out of the President's taxes and sent them off to reporters on the Providence *Journal-Bulletin* (Providence was the employee's home town). The paper was on strike at the time, but three weeks later—on October 3—the

Journal provided the precise figures: Nixon had paid $792.81 in federal income tax for 1970 and $873.03 in 1971. (He paid $4298 in 1972.) The IRS employee who supplied the figures later quit under pressure; but Nixon confirmed his data. The President's taxes for those years were about what would have been paid by a family of three earning between $7500 and $8500.

Nixon's low taxes were due to whopping deductions taken on a staggering variety of items, many of them improvements and expenses that seemed more personal than professional. But evidently this was a policy, decided quite early. On June 16, 1969, Ehrlichman relayed the President's view to Frank DeMarco, Jr., a member of Kalmbach's law firm, who had become Nixon's tax lawyer in March: "The President holds the view that a public man does very little of a personal nature. Virtually all of his entertainment and activity is related to his 'business.' He wants to be sure that his business deductions include all allowable items. For instance, wedding gifts to congressmen's daughters, flowers at funerals, etc."

The President's tax returns over the next four years reflected this theory. The IRS later disallowed many of these items including:

• A $32,167.86 deduction for 25 per cent of operating costs at San Clemente, including such household expenses as $168.42 for linens, $677.70 for refrigerator repairs, and $22.50 for cleaning Mrs. Nixon's bathroom rug. Nixon even charged for watering the three-hole golf course on his property, even though those costs were reimbursed to him by the golfing friends who installed the course. The President argued that these expenses were deductible because he used San Clemente as an office about 25 per cent of the time. The Joint Committee on Internal Revenue Taxation and the IRS rejected this claim, noting that adequate office facilities were available at the Coast Guard base and the government even supplied golf carts to take the President and his staff back and forth between his home and office.

• A $24,787.11 deduction for 100 per cent of operating costs for the business use of one residence

(500 Bay Lane) at Key Biscayne. The IRS and joint committee noted that the government would have provided the President with an office at Key Biscayne if he had asked for one.

• A $3331.56 deduction for depreciation of Nixon's own furniture: a cabinet table at the White House and a credenza in the Key Biscayne office.

• A $47,765.89 deduction for miscellaneous "expenses incurred in the performance of official functions as President of the United States," including $6750 for Christmas cards, $5391.43 for Tricia Nixon's "masked ball" in May 1969, and food furnished to the first family and their guests at San Clemente, Key Biscayne, Camp David, and aboard the yacht *Sequoia*.

Most of the President's tax deductions, though, came in two large chunks: the substantial interest paid to finance the purchases of San Clemente and Key Biscayne; and the donation of his pre-Presidential papers to the National Archives. The interest deductions were quite proper, but most of the papers gift— and therefore the deduction—was later declared bogus.

Nixon says he first learned about this form of tax shelter when he paid a courtesy call on Lyndon Johnson at the White House late in 1968. "He told me he had given his Presidential papers, or at least most of them, to the government. . . . And he said, 'You ought to do the same thing.' I said, 'I don't have any Presidential papers.' He said, 'You have got your Vice-Presidential papers.' " Johnson or one of his aides gave the President-elect the name of Ralph G. Newman, a Chicago-based Lincoln scholar who has appraised the papers of every President since Herbert Hoover. Late in December Nixon signed a formal deed for the gift, valued by Newman at $80,000, of which $70,552.27 was deducted on Nixon's 1968 taxes and the remainder carried over. This was a perfectly proper donation and deduction.

Nixon hoped to get a similar deduction the next year. A February 6, 1969, memo from Ehrlichman to the President said, "We contemplate keeping the papers as a continuing reserve [of tax deductions] which we can use from now on to supplement other gifts," to which Nixon scrawled, "Good." What intervened was a congressional move to close this tax loophole. Some say this was a punitive measure aimed by Democratic congressmen at Nixon. Others say it was aimed at Lyndon Johnson, who, it was rumored, intended to make a series of gifts that would free him from federal taxes for the rest of his life. In any case, the House Ways and Means Committee announced on May 27, 1969, that it was considering eliminating the charitable deductions for "all gifts of works of art, collections of papers, and other forms of tangible personal property." A bill containing a similar provision was approved by a conference committee on December 22 and signed by the President on December 30.

All fall, the effective date of the prohibition had fluctuated. First it was set at December 31, 1968—which would have ruled out any gift by the President in 1969. Bryce Harlow, then a White House aide, pushed hard to move the deadline one year forward. Ultimately, the conference committee split the difference, setting the deadline at July 25, 1969. Any gift made after that date would bring the donor no deduction.

The congressional debate had posed a problem for Nixon. Not knowing when the cutoff date would be, he did not want to donate his papers (later valued at $2,012,000) to the National Archives unless he was assured he would qualify for tax benefits. Thus, he tried to keep his options open, waiting for Congress to resolve the problem. During the first months of 1969, a large body of Nixon's pre-Presidential papers were stored in the Old and New Executive Office Buildings. Daniel Reed, assistant archivist for Presidential libraries, agreed to inventory them there, but found the space inadequate and suggested that the papers be moved to the archives. On March 26 and 27, 1176 boxes were brought there. (They included 173 boxes of invitations for speaking engagements, with carbons of Nixon's replies; 56 boxes of invitations to social events and Nixon's responses; 826 boxes of general correspondence; and others containing thousands of newspaper clippings and some unclipped newspapers.)

This transfer to the National Archives did not, in itself, constitute a gift to the nation. The archives not only receives gifts of papers and objects but provides courtesy storage of materials for Presidents, members of Congress, and certain others. The GSA says that on the July 25 deadline, Nixon's papers remained in a courtesy storage area and had been neither sorted nor formally valued. Originally, Newman claimed to have started sorting the papers comprising the 1969 gift on April 8, 1969. But when confronted with contrary testimony from an archives employee who accompanied him, he conceded that he had worked only with the 1968 gift that day. Newman did not begin sorting the 1969 gift until November 3, 1969. When Congress passed its new law setting the July 25 deadline, the Chicago appraiser assumed Nixon had missed the opportunity to make a gift that year. "I thought he'd blown it," Newman recalls.

But on March 27, 1970, DeMarco told Newman that the President had indeed made a bulk gift of papers in 1969, accomplished by moving them to the archives. DeMarco asked for a list of papers worth about $500,000. Newman said he had selected some papers the previous November but would require some additional items. This he did by telephone with an archives employee. On April 6 or 7 Newman sent an appraisal document to DeMarco. The lawyer claims that he had prepared a deed for the gift on April 21, 1969, and now merely had it retyped to match the type and paper of the newly prepared gift schedule. On April 10, 1970, DeMarco took the new deed to the White House office of Edward L. Morgan, deputy counsel to the President (not to be confused with Edward P. Morgan, Howard Hughes's counsel). DeMarco says he asked Morgan to "re-execute" the retyped deed—dated March 27, 1969—and Morgan promptly did so on behalf of the President. At 12:15 p.m. DeMarco and Kalmbach took the President's 1969 tax returns into the Oval Office for his signature.

DeMarco explained the major items and when he got to the deduction for the papers, Nixon said, "That's fine."

Fine it was for Nixon. The gift produced a total deduction of $576,000. Nixon took $85,298 of that in 1969 and carried over the rest as follows: $123,959 in 1970; $128,668 in 1971; $134,093 in 1973; leaving $93,982 for subsequent years.

Since then, the joint committee and the IRS have invalidated the deductions because the donation was not made before the July 25 deadline. Edward Morgan conceded that the deed had been "back-dated" to March 27, 1969, to sneak in under the deadline.*

When all these deductions were disallowed, the IRS found that Nixon—who had paid only $78,615.10 on roughly $1.2 million of income during 1969–72— owed back taxes (and a 5 per cent penalty) for those years totaling $434,787.13. With interest, his tax bill came to about $467,000. Nixon agreed to pay all of it (including $148,080.97 for 1969, which he was not required to pay because the statute of limitations had run for that year).

But the underpaid taxes did not fully explain Nixon's new wealth. Some of his money came from lucrative land deals made with the help of his moneyed friends—several of them in Florida.

In 1967, for example, Nixon purchased 199,891 shares in one of Bebe Rebozo's companies which controlled Fisher's Island, between Miami Beach and Key Biscayne. Rebozo and his associates had purchased the undeveloped 213-acre island in the 1950s, intending to develop it as an exclusive resort community, but the

---

*Morgan, who had moved from the White House to become assistant secretary of the treasury, resigned his treasury post. He pleaded guilty to engaging in a criminal conspiracy to create a fraudulent tax deduction and was sentenced to four months in prison. Ralph Newman and Frank DeMarco were indicted for conspiracy to commit fraud and lying to IRS agents. Newman was found guilty and fined $10,000. The case against DeMarco was dismissed and is being appealed by the government.

group's plans had been balked by the city's unwillingness to build a causeway to the island. Nixon paid a dollar a share. Subsequently, he sold 14,000 of his shares at a dollar per share to Rose Mary Woods; Pat Buchanan; and his valet, Manolo Sanchez. Despite the corporation's ill fortunes, in 1969 Rebozo and the other investors bought back the President's remaining 185,891 shares at $2 a share—nearly doubling his investment.

Also in 1967 Rebozo arranged for Nixon to pose for publicity pictures at a Key Biscayne subdivision built by the Cape Florida Development Company. In return for the favor, Rebozo's friend Donald Berg, a developer, sold Nixon two choice lots for a total of $53,100—although similar lots were selling for about $50,000 apiece at the time. In December 1972 the President sold the lots for $150,000 to William E. Griffin, the corporate secretary of Abplanalp's Precision Valve Company—nearly tripling his investment. (Nixon borrowed $20,000 of the original purchase price from his daughter Tricia. The money came from the proceeds of a trust fund set up for her in 1958 by Elmer H. Bobst, then chairman of the Warner-Lambert Pharmaceutical Company, as the Senate was preparing for hearings on drug prices.)

But even these deals did not seem to explain all of Nixon's new money. Some investigators suspected Nixon was getting a flow of cash from still another—undisclosed—source. Such suspicions frequently focused on the millionaire who was Richard Nixon's closest friend—Charles Gregory "Bebe" Rebozo.

"Nixon likes to be alone, and with Bebe along, he is," a Miami wag once remarked. From the start, the friendship between the two intensely private, secretive men has been strangely uncommunicative. It began in 1950, when, weary from his successful Senate campaign, Nixon went to Miami for a rest, and their mutual friend Senator George Smathers suggested Rebozo "show him a good time." Rebozo asked the new senator out on his $18,000 houseboat, but later recalled, "I

*doubt if I exchanged a dozen words with the guy."
Rebozo assumed that Nixon hadn't enjoyed himself,
but soon he got a warm thank-you note, and many
more trips followed. Paul Keyes, former producer of
Laugh-In and a friend of both men, says, "Every President needs someone who demands nothing of him,
who is good company—a trusted friend with whom he
can sit in a room and talk when he wants to talk and
think when he wants to think and have the other man
understand it. Bebe needs nothing, he wants nothing.
He is the kind of man who can afford a President."
They would go for long, silent walks on the beach; listen to show tunes on the hi-fi; watch football games;
dine in expensive restaurants, or go for cruises on Rebozo's boat, Cocolobo II, during which, Bebe said,
"We do some fishing, some swimming, and a lot of
sunbathing. We work, too. Dick takes his briefcase and
I take mine." The briefcases were an important link,
for both men are methodical plodders who worked
hard to rise in the world. The youngest child of an immigrant Cuban cigar-maker, Rebozo hustled through
a score of jobs—airline steward, chauffeur for a tourist
limousine, filling-station operator, tire salesman. Then
Florida plunged into a wild land boom. Rebozo
bought some beachfront property cheap, sold it for a
big profit, bought more, sold again. Today, he has vast
real-estate holdings, office buildings, a title company,
coin laundries, and is board chairman, president, and
principal stockholder of the Key Biscayne Bank (for
which Richard Nixon broke ground with a gold shov-
el). By his own accounting, Rebozo's wealth increased
sevenfold—from $673,000 to $4.5 million—during the
five years of the Nixon Presidency. Rebozo has always
thrived on his good connections. Swarthily handsome
(he was voted the best-looking boy in the Miami High
School class of 1930), he is a suave ladies' man. He
was twice married to his high-school sweetheart and
twice divorced, the last time in 1950. Since then, he
had escorted some of the most beautiful women in
Florida and moved easily in Miami society. One valuable contact was George Smathers, who grew up with
Rebozo in Miami's Buena Vista section. Their paths*

parted for a while, then crossed again just as Smathers was beginning his political career. When he reached Congress, he began sending some of his new colleagues down for rest and relaxation tours with Bebe. Rebozo was a genial host, serving his guests tall, tinkly tropical drinks, broiling steaks on his back-yard grill, whipping up Spanish-style picadillo. *Since Smathers was a Democrat, most of those early visitors were Democrats: Senators Russell, Long, Symington, Jackson, Magnuson, and a big man from Texas named Lyndon Johnson. (Rebozo still has an engraved wristwatch given to him by Lady Bird.) Then came Nixon, and Rebozo switched political allegiances. He was the only "outsider" with the Nixon family in the Ambassador Hotel in Los Angeles on the night of November 8, 1960, when Nixon lost the Presidency to John Kennedy, and it was in Rebozo's house that Nixon made his final decision to enter the 1968 race. He became virtually a sixth member of the Nixon family (Rose Mary Woods counted as the fifth); joining them for Thanksgiving, Christmas, and other holidays; serving as a genial Latin uncle to Julie and Tricia; a brother to Nixon. One White House aide recalls seeing the two men playing a game called King of the Pool at Key Biscayne. It was late at night. The two men had been drinking. Nixon mounted a rubber raft in the pool while Rebozo tried to turn it over. Then, laughing and shouting, they changed places and Nixon tried to upset Rebozo.*

Rebozo is intensely protective of Nixon. "He doesn't want anything to embarrass the President," a friend says. Ironically, then, Rebozo has proven something of an embarrassment to his friend, in several ways:

• A loan he received from the Small Business Administration in 1962 for his Key West title company. One man who helped the loan along was Thomas A. Butler, a Miami SBA official who was a friend of Rebozo's and a stockholder in his bank.

• Decisions that assured Rebozo's Key Biscayne Bank a monopoly in the affluent community. A federal bank examiner recommended that another, competitive bank be chartered for the island. But federal officials have twice refused such a charter while a group of Rebozo's friends and business associates gained approval to open a savings-and-loan association there.

• Charges that Rebozo knowingly sold $91,500 worth of stolen stock in 1969. The stock was stolen from the New York brokerage firm of E. F. Hutton & Company in 1968. Later, Charles Lewis, an Atlanta businessman, turned up at Rebozo's bank and offered the stock as collateral for a loan. Rebozo accepted, then quickly sold the stock. An insurance investigator has said that he told Rebozo the stock was stolen before he sold it, although Rebozo denies this. The Justice Department says the sale would not have been an illegal act in any event.

• The employment—as vice president in charge of his bank's trust department—of Franklin DeBoer, who less than a year earlier was barred by the SEC from being a stockbroker because of falsifying records and selling unregistered stock. DeBoer resigned from the bank when he became the subject of a Federal Deposit Insurance Corporation investigation.

• Close connections with gambling interests in the Bahamas, particularly on Paradise Island, site of one of the world's largest and most profitable casinos. Investigators have looked into allegations that profits "skimmed" from the gaming tables there found their way through Rebozo's Key Biscayne Bank into Nixon's campaigns—or even into his pockets.

But most embarrassing of all was Rebozo's acceptance of the $100,000 from Howard Hughes in 1969 and 1970. Not only was the money an apparent *quid pro quo* for the Justice Department's revised ruling on Hughes acquiring the Dunes Hotel, but there are indications that much of the money eventually went to Nixon, his family, and his close associates.

Although the money was nominally a campaign contribution (Richard Danner says for the 1970 congressional campaign, Rebozo says for 1972), Rebozo insists he put the two $50,000 installments in safe-deposit box 224 in the Key Biscayne Bank and held it there untouched until June 1973, when he returned the money to a Hughes representative. He retained the money initially, he says, because the Nixon campaign had "no campaign manager or no finance director at the time and I was waiting for him to be named." However, Kalmbach was already functioning as the unofficial campaign finance chairman early in 1969. Although he did not begin actively soliciting 1972 campaign funds until late 1970, Kalmbach was accepting contributions for the President's re-election at least a month before Rebozo got the first $50,000 from Danner in mid-September 1969.

Even after Maurice Stans was formally named to head Nixon's fund-raising efforts in February 1972, Rebozo says he held on to the money because of the fight then raging within the Hughes empire. "I didn't want to risk even the remotest embarrassment of Hughes's connection with Nixon," he recalls. "I was convinced that [the Hughes loan to Donald Nixon] cost the President the 1960 election and didn't help him in 1962 in California." Fearing that the increasingly bitter dispute between Hughes and Robert Maheu could force a disclosure of the Hughes contribution, Rebozo says he "just thought it better not to use that money for the 1972 campaign and try to see if things cleared up and to hold it for 1974 or 1976, some point where I could turn it over to the properly appointed authority. But matters went from bad to worse with the Hughes organization." The other Nixon fund-raisers were not so cautious about Hughes. Just days before the 1972 election the finance committee asked him for and got $100,000.

Rebozo insists that the only person he told about the Hughes money before the 1972 election was his longtime friend Rose Mary Woods. Only after the election, Rebozo says, did he explain "the whole picture" to Nixon, but the President offered no advice then about what to do with the money. Nixon and others apparently began urging that the money be returned to Hughes when they became aware that the IRS was looking into the Hughes contribution.

The IRS was slow off the mark on this investigation, evidently fearing Rebozo's political clout. It first learned of the Hughes-Rebozo connection from Danner in May 1972. Almost immediately, field agents asked permission to interview Rebozo, but these requests were denied by Johnnie Walters, the IRS commissioner, who says a top-level decision had been made not to interview sensitive political figures during the campaign year (although the investigation of Larry O'Brien—in which the White House had a strong interest—continued full force all year). Finally, on February 23, 1973—nearly ten months later—Walters informed Secretary of the Treasury George Shultz that an interview with Rebozo was necessary. Shultz approved the interview on April 7, and John Ehrlichman told Rebozo that month that the IRS would soon approach him. The interview—a brief and innocuous one—took place on May 10.

Meanwhile, Rebozo began frantically conferring about the money. Sometime in April, during a weekend at Key Biscayne, he took the matter up again with Nixon. He says he suggested that the $100,000 be returned to Hughes, and the President agreed. During the next few weeks, while Nixon and his men tried desperately to contain the Watergate scandal, the problem of the Hughes money bubbled on a back burner. On April 30—the very day Nixon announced the resignation of Haldeman and Ehrlichman—Rebozo conferred on the money with Kalmbach, who urged him to give it back. On May 3 Rebozo met in Florida with William E. Griffin, Abplanalp's corporate secretary. After studying the problem, Griffin told him he should get an "independent individual" to count the money in the safe-deposit box, identify the bills, and arrange for its return.

On Friday, May 18, Rebozo and Danner met at the Madison Hotel in Washington to discuss the return of the money. (Danner evidently wanted no part of it.) On Saturday Rebozo joined the President at Camp David and on Sunday he invited Danner to come up, too. In that sylvan setting, Danner and Rebozo went over the money problem still again, but both men insist the subject did not come up when they met with the President that afternoon. Instead, they say, they discussed "political feelings on the West Coast concerning Watergate."

But General Haig talked about the Hughes money with Nixon a few days later and then telephoned Rebozo to recommend that he get in touch with Kenneth Gemmill, a Philadelphia tax lawyer and an old friend of Nixon's. Gemmill advised Rebozo to go to the bank and—with a government representative present—count the money. On June 18 Rebozo called Kenneth Whitaker, a friend who was the special agent in charge of the FBI's Miami office, and asked him to come to the bank. There, Rebozo; his lawyer, Thomas H. Wakefield; and Whitaker counted the money and listed the serial numbers (an extra $100 bill had somehow been added, making $100,100). Finally, on June 25, William Griffin delivered the money to the Marine Midland Bank in New York, where Walter Glaeser, a Hughes representative, accepted it.

Rebozo insists he returned the very same bills he had put in the safe-deposit box more than three years before (he cannot explain the extra $100 bill). But Ervin committee investigators turned up evidence strongly suggesting that at least some of the original cash had been removed and used for purposes unrelated to Nixon's re-election.

Substantial evidence indicates that Rebozo controlled a fund of cash available for Nixon's private purposes. When Nixon had been in the White House ony a month, he asked Rebozo to contact J. Paul Getty, the multimillionaire oilman, "regarding major contributions." A memo from Haldeman to Ehrlichman said these funds would "go to some operating entity other than the national committee, so that we can retain full control of their use." On April 29, 1969, Rebozo wrote Kalmbach, "Over the weekend, I spoke with John Ehrlichman and explained to him that it had been decided that the larger balance which I mentioned to you will be kept here in order to take care of frequent administration-connected costs which arise from time to time." Rebozo seems to have retained some surplus 1968 funds, but evidently he had other substantial sources. Larry Higby has testified that Haldeman told him about a $400,000 "secret fund" controlled by Rebozo which could be used for legal fees. This is apparently the fund to which Nixon referred on April 17, 1973, in talking with Haldeman and Ehrlichman: "Let me ask you this, legal fees will be substantial. But there's a way we can get it to you and, uh—two or three hundred thousand dollars, huh? . . . No strain. Doesn't come out'a me. I didn't, I never intended to use the money at all. As a matter of fact, I told Bebe, basically be sure that people like, uh—who have contributed money over the contributing years are, uh, favored and so forth in general. And he's used it for the purpose of getting things out, paid for in check, and all that sort of thing."

The cash available to Rebozo came from two major sources: the $100,000 from Hughes, and $50,000 delivered to Rebozo in early 1972 by Artemus Darius Davis, the sixty-eight-year-old vice-chairman of a southern supermarket chain called Winn-Dixie Stores, Inc. Davis has testified that he delivered the money to Rebozo in $100 bills on April 5—in time to make the April 7 deadline. Rebozo has said he handed the money over to Fred LaRue in Miami on April 7. But LaRue says he did not pick up any money from Rebozo until some six months later—in mid-October—and his travel vouchers support this. LaRue originally testified that he then picked up $25,000–$30,000, which was subsequently passed to Lee Nunn's Kentucky campaign for the Senate. Later he said it could have been as much as $50,000. Senate investigators were unable to determine whether Rebozo indeed gave some or all of the Davis money to LaRue or whether he retained it, as he did the Hughes money.

In any case, at least $23,500 in cash—all in $100 bills—was deposited in four trust accounts established under the name of Thomas H. Wakefield, Rebozo's attorney. And this money—along with other funds—was used to pay some of Nixon's private expenses. In all, Senate investigators concluded that between 1968 and 1972 Rebozo paid at least $50,000 of Nixon's personal bills.

According to Herb Kalmbach, Rebozo told him on

April 30, 1973, that he had given portions of the Hughes money to Rose Mary Woods; the President's two brothers, Donald and Edward; and "unnamed others." Kalmbach says Rebozo told him that the President had asked that he consult with him on the problem. When Kalmbach suggested that Rebozo explain everything to the IRS, Rebozo replied, "This touches the President and the President's family, and I just can't do anything to add to his problems at this time, Herb." Miss Woods and the two Nixon brothers have all denied that they received any money from Rebozo. But there is hard evidence that Rebozo did spend money from some cash source on other intensely personal matters for the President and his family.

For example, $4562.38 in surplus 1968 funds went for the purchase of diamond-studded earrings which Nixon gave his wife for her sixtieth birthday in 1972. On March 17, 1972, a set of platinum earrings containing eighteen pear-shaped diamonds and two tapered baguette diamonds were delivered to the White House by Harry Winston, a prominent New York jeweler. The full cost of the earrings was $5650. Of this, $4562.38 came from an account maintained by Wakefield for the 1968 Florida Nixon for President Committee. On June 28, 1972, Wakefield withdrew the $4562.38 and deposited it in another trust account in his name at the Key Biscayne Bank. Later that day he transferred $5000 from that account to still another of his trust accounts at the First National Bank of Miami. Then he withdrew it again in a $5000 cashier's check. This complex, four-stage process was evidently designed to disguise the fact that the President of the United States had purchased diamond earrings for his wife with money contributed to his 1968 campaign.

In addition, Rebozo paid $45,621.24—chiefly from the same trust accounts—for improvements and furnishings at the President's two Key Biscayne properties: 500 and 516 Bay Lane. These included $2076.65 for architects' fees and models; $1654 for tile repairs; $11,978.84 for conversion of a garage at 516 Bay Lane into a living room, bedroom, and bath; $243.57 for an "Arnold Palmer Putting Green"; $3586 for a fireplace; $1138.80 for a pool table; $6508.11 for extension of a roof; and $18,435 for a twenty-by-forty-foot swimming pool at 500 Bay Lane and various pool "accessories" (heater, windscreen, pool carpet, and furniture). These expenditures were withheld from the Coopers & Lybrand audit of spending on the President's houses. In August 1973, the month the audit was issued and two months after Rebozo had returned $100,000 to Hughes, Nixon reimbursed Rebozo $13,-642.52 for a portion of the swimming-pool costs. (Federal law does not directly prohibit the use of campaign funds for personal purposes, but it does require that such funds be declared to the IRS as taxable income —which was not done.)

Asked about these expenditures under oath, Rebozo said, "I'm not going to nit-pick with the President. If there's something I think he should have, I might just go ahead and do it without even him knowing about it. He just doesn't concern himself at all with financial problems; never has."

But there is ample evidence that the President and the men around him were very worried indeed about the persistent reports that campaign funds had been spent on his personal properties. In October 1971 Kalmbach had rushed to Las Vegas to persuade Hank Greenspun that there was no truth in the story he had heard. In March 1972 John Mitchell had authorized burglaries of Larry O'Brien's and Greenspun's offices —apparently at least in part to determine what they knew about the Hughes payments to Rebozo. In May 1973 Ron Ziegler had angrily denied the report in the *Santa Ana Register* which, like Greenspun, suggested that the money had been spent on San Clemente. The Ervin committee's investigation suggests that Greenspun and the *Register* were very nearly right. If the committee's conclusions are correct, then Nixon and his associates must have lived in perpetual dread that someone somewhere would put the evidence together and realize that they simply had the wrong house in the sun.

11

TAPES

I don't think it should ever get out that we taped this office, Bob.
—Nixon to Haldeman,
April 26, 1973

One Ervin committee stenographer brought a four-leaf clover to work that day. A young lawyer joked with colleagues outside the hearing room about walking under a ladder workmen were using to replaster a ceiling. It was Friday the thirteenth of July 1973—an unfortunate day for Richard Nixon, a day that many would later recall as the start of the Unmaking of a President.

That afternoon, as the committee grilled special White House counsel Richard A. Moore beneath banks of television lights in the Senate Caucus Room, across the street in the Dirksen Senate Office Building committee staffers were interviewing a prospective witness. Ranged around a conference table in Room G-334 were Donald Sanders, a lean, former FBI agent who was now the committee's deputy minority counsel; Gene Boyce, a courtly North Carolina lawyer serving as an assistant majority counsel; Scott Armstrong, a Harvard Law School dropout who had worked for a time as a car salesman and was now one of the committee's most valuable investigators; and Marianne Brazer, a staff assistant. Across the green felt surface sat Alexander P. Butterfield, a brisk, crisp former deputy assistant to the President who was now chief of the Federal Aviation Administration.

500

For three hours Armstrong questioned Butterfield in painstaking detail about the President's office routine: record-keeping, filing, appointments, staff assignments. At one point, he handed him a memo—provided by special Presidential counsel Fred Buzhardt—which summarized the conversations between John Dean and the President. The committee had asked Buzhardt only for the dates on which Nixon had met with Dean, but for once, Buzhardt had been overly cooperative. He had provided remarkably detailed summaries of what the two men talked about in each conversation. For example, about the critical March 21, 1973, talk, it said, in part: ". . . Dean gave the President his theory of what had happened. He still said no prior June 17 White House knowledge, that Magruder probably knew, that Mitchell possibly knew, that Strachan probably knew, that Haldeman had possibly seen the fruits of the wiretaps through Strachan, that Ehrlichman was vulnerable because of his approval of Kalmbach's fund-raising efforts. . . . He stated Hunt was trying to blackmail Ehrlichman about Hunt's prior Plumbers' activities unless he was paid what ultimately might amount to $1 million. . . ."

As soon as he read that, Butterfield knew exactly where all the information had come from. But in the absence of a direct, specific question from Armstrong, he wasn't volunteering anything. Sure, that was a lot of detail. Yes, the President's memory was good, but not that good. No, Nixon generally didn't take notes at such meetings. If he wanted notes taken he would have a staff member sit in, but nobody else was present during most of his conversations with Dean.

At about five-thirty Armstrong ended his interrogation. It was time to give the minority staff a chance. Don Sanders was an experienced interrogator, having served as chief counsel and staff director of the House Internal Security Committee, the successor to the House Committee on Un-American Activities. "All afternoon," he recalls, "a suspicion had been growing in the back of my mind. The summaries of the Dean conversations were simply too detailed for anyone to have recalled unless there was a more definitive record, probably a verbatim transcript. Moreover, I recalled that Dean himself testified that at the end of his April 15 meeting the President had gotten up, gone into the corner of his office, and told Dean in a barely audible voice that he was probably foolish to have discussed Hunt's clemency with Colson—making Dean suspect that Nixon was trying to avoid being overheard by a tape recorder."

For a few minutes Sanders asked Butterfield about other matters, but the suspicion nagged and tugged at him. Finally, he asked the question that had been trembling on several lips that afternoon—Gene Boyce says he would have asked it when his turn came if Sanders hadn't. To Sanders' best recollection—the session was not recorded—the exchange went like this:

SANDERS: John Dean has testified that at the end of one conversation with the President he was taken to a corner of his office and addressed by the President in a very soft voice. Do you know of any basis for the implication in Dean's testimony that conversations in the President's office are recorded?

BUTTERFIELD: I was hoping you fellows wouldn't ask me about that. I've wondered what I would say. I'm concerned about the effect my answer will have on national security and international affairs. But I suppose I have to assume that this is a formal, official interview in the same vein as if I were being questioned in open session under oath.

SANDERS: That's right.

BUTTERFIELD: Well . . . yes, there's a recording system in the President's office.

Then, in a calm but troubled voice, Butterfield went on to explain. For more than two years, he said, on the President's express instructions, hidden tape recorders had picked up virtually everything that Nixon and his aides or guests had said in the Oval Office, the President's EOB office, the Cabinet Room, the Lincoln Sitting Room on the second floor of the White House, and the Aspen Lodge at Camp David, as well as over the telephones in all but the Cabinet Room.

"Butterfield seemed torn between loyalty to the President and honesty with us," Boyce recalls. "I remember he said, 'This is something the President doesn't want revealed, but I don't have any other choice.' He behaved admirably. I thought he was one of the finest public servants I'd ever met."

Loyalty was handed down with the swords and medals in the Butterfield family. Alex was a third-generation military man—his grandfather was a West Pointer, his father a Navy pilot—and he grew up under the screech of aircraft from the Pensacola Naval Air Station in Florida. Not surprisingly, he aimed for Annapolis; but he failed the eye test and instead attended UCLA before entering the Air Force aviation cadet program in 1948. A year later, he was commissioned a second lieutenant and—most important—a pilot. Ever since, his grand passion has been flying. "Essentially," he recalls, "I was in the fighter business." But he also became a qualified parachutist and flew for the Air Force stunt team called the Sky Blazers, which won the acrobatic prize at the 1953 Paris Air Show. Singled out early as a young man of unusual promise, Butterfield served as an aide to an array of top officials: the commander of the Fourth Allied Tactical Air Force in Europe; the commander in chief of the U.S. Pacific Air Forces; and ultimately Joseph Califano, special assistant to Secretary of Defense Robert McNamara (one of the other military aides in the same office was Alexander Haig). In 1968 he was selected for the National War College, a training ground for those with a future. But he remained a pilot at heart: in Vietnam, he commanded a low-level reconnaissance squadron, and won the Distinguished Flying Cross; and as an instructor at the Air Force Academy, it is said, he would take an F-80 jet up to thirty-five thousand feet and put it on automatic pilot to get himself in the proper mood for grading student papers. No wonder that Butterfield was a trifle bored when, in 1967, he was dispatched to Australia with the imposing title of Commander in Chief Pacific/ Representative/

Australia but the most mundane of duties: supervising the dependents' school program, arranging "R and R" for American soldiers in Vietnam, inspecting lamb that went to U.S. servicemen. Therefore, he was in a receptive mood when he got a telephone call on January 12, 1969, from an old friend of UCLA days, Bob Haldeman. The two men had become friendly at college because their girl friends—Joanne Horton and Charlotte Mary Maguire—were sorority roommates. The four double-dated and eventually Joanne became Mrs. Haldeman and Charlotte Mrs. Butterfield. They had gone different ways, but the wives exchanged Christmas cards every year. Haldeman had received Butterfield's file during the search for an aide to Henry Kissinger. That job had gone to Butterfield's old Pentagon sidekick, Haig, but now Haldeman thought of him for another job: his own principal line assistant. So he asked on the telephone call halfway around the world, "How would you like to be part of all this?" It was a difficult decision for Butterfield. "I was a serious career officer," he recalls. "It had never entered my mind that I might leave before my thirty or thirty-five years were up." Haldeman said he couldn't give him much time to make up his mind; the President wanted to begin with an entirely new staff on January 21. Butterfield thought about it overnight. He called back the next day to say it would be "a great honor," left Australia two days later, and was sworn in as a deputy assistant to the President on Inauguration Day. Soon, Butterfield was functioning as the assistant chief of the White House staff. After a year, when Nixon wanted Haldeman to be more of a strategic planner, Butterfield took over Haldeman's office, immediately adjoining the President's, and many of his day-to-day responsibilities. Yet, gradually, he tired of the relentless routine. In March 1973 he gladly accepted appointment as administrator of the Federal Aviation Administration. He had never lost the instincts of a flier alone in the sky. Confronted with a difficult decision in Room G-334, he made it.

The impact in the room was palpable. "It tended toward the speechless," recalls Boyce. "We were all struck with the enormity of the matter," says Sanders. Though it was six-thirty by then, the interrogators excused Butterfield, then huddled around the table to decide on their next move. Quickly, they agreed to tell only two people: Majority Counsel Samuel Dash and Minority Counsel Fred Thompson. Armstrong and Boyce found Dash leaving his office with a pile of books under his arm. He told them he didn't have time to talk: his wife, Sarah, would be angry if he were late for dinner. They persisted. When Dash heard the news, he said, "I'd better call Sarah and tell her I'll be late."

Fred Thompson had left for the day, but Sanders traced him to the bar of the Carroll Arms Hotel across the street, where he was having a beer with two reporters from the *Evening Star* and the *Chicago Tribune*. "Naturally, I couldn't tell Fred right then and there that the President of the United States had been recording his telephone and other conversations, so I ordered a beer myself. After a few minutes I asked Fred if he could step away. 'Sure,' he said, 'let's go outside.' We went outside, and on the corner there, right across from the Dirksen building, I told him the story about the President's tape system." Thompson promptly called Senator Howard Baker, the ranking Republican on the committee, while Dash informed the chairman and ranking Democrat, Sam Ervin.

Butterfield was scheduled to go to Moscow on July 17. As he left the committee room, he had asked Armstrong whether he should send someone else. Armstrong said he didn't think that would be necessary. On Saturday, July 14, Butterfield flew to Nashua County, New Hampshire, for the dedication of a new air traffic control center there. Returning home that night, he found a message from Armstrong; when he returned the call, the young investigator said he was recommending that Butterfield be called to testify publicly on Monday. Astonished and angry, Butterfield telephoned Senator Baker and went over to see him at 2:00 p.m. on Sunday, urging him to consider the "ramifications" of public testimony on the taping, particularly from a peripheral figure like himself. But Baker said there was no way they could keep it quiet. "Everything leaks," he said. "I'll be surprised if it keeps for the weekend."

Then Butterfield telephoned Leonard Garment, Dean's successor as counsel to the President. He was out of town, but returned the call that evening. When Butterfield gave him the news, Garment—who had not previously known about the taping—exclaimed, "Jesus Christ!"

On Monday morning Butterfield was having his hair cut at the Sheraton Carlton Hotel—in the shop run by the man who cut Nixon's hair—when James Hamilton, an assistant majority counsel, telephoned to say he was to be the committee's next witness. "I won't appear," Butterfield snapped angrily. Twenty minutes later Hamilton called back to say, "I whispered your message in Ervin's ear and the senator said, 'If he's not in my office at twelve-thirty, I will have law-enforcement officers come and get him.'"

During the noon recess Butterfield met with Ervin and Baker to apologize for his testiness. Then, shortly after two o'clock, a startled press corps and a flabbergasted national television audience watched as the unscheduled witness slid behind the witness table in the Caucus Room and abruptly told the world what barely a dozen men had known until then.

THOMPSON: Mr. Butterfield, are you aware of any listening devices in the Oval Office of the President?

BUTTERFIELD: I was aware of listening devices; yes, sir.

It was not the first time that White House conversations had been recorded. According to one account, Franklin Roosevelt stationed stenographers in a specially constructed cubicle beneath his office to eavesdrop on his guests. After Butterfield's testimony, Nixon's staff alleged that Lyndon Johnson had routinely taped proceedings in his office. This was heatedly denied by former Johnson aides—"a damned outrageous smear, a total smear, on a dead President," said

Joseph Califano—but some five hundred transcripts of Presidential telephone conversations are preserved in the Johnson Library in Austin. (Nixon has since claimed that he installed his taping system at Lyndon Johnson's suggestion, after Johnson passed word through Don Kendall that his tapes had proved to be "exceedingly valuable in preparing his memoirs.") President Kennedy's archives also contain sixty-eight recordings of his telephone conversations and one hundred twenty-five tapes of Presidential meetings, though the director of the Kennedy Library contends that the participants in all these conversations knew they were being recorded.

These were sporadic, haphazard undertakings compared to Nixon's. Yet, there is no agreement about why Nixon was so intent on a wholesale, systematic recording effort.

Butterfield says the tape machines were installed for "historical purposes." He believes the President was "preoccupied with history and the place his Presidency would have in history. . . . He would write little notes on precisely what time he finished handwriting a portion of a speech—'3:14 a.m.' He made it known to me in various ways that he wanted to be sure that '3:14 a.m.' got some place, got logged. . . . He was wholly taken up with history."

William Safire takes that one step further. Nixon, he says, was "convinced left-leaning historians would try to deny him his place in history," just as radical journalists were trying to deny him his place in the present. So while he appealed over the heads of the press, using the electronic media to speak directly to the people, he would use the technology of the tape recorder to appeal to history over the heads of the historians. The tapes would guarantee him the honored place in history he so craved.

Of course, they would also be an invaluable aid to his own writing of history. Like all recent Presidents, Nixon knew he was going to write his memoirs—both as a means of producing revenue after he left office and as a way of justifying his actions in office. The recordings would make such a project easier, quicker, more accurate—and they would give him an immense advantage over others who were writing about the same events.

But there is one problem with all of these explanations. Nixon's taping system was not installed until February 1971—more than two years after he entered office. Indeed, in February 1969, Nixon had ordered the Army Signal Corps to rip Lyndon Johnson's old taping system out of the White House. Theodore White says Nixon told Bob Finch that month that nobody should be bugged in the President's office. When the taping was begun, no machines were installed at San Clemente or Key Biscayne, where the President spent much of his time. This does not sound like a man primarily concerned with recording history. Two valuable years of history—including some of the most dramatic and important decisions of his administration—passed before Nixon ordered the tapes to start whirring.

What intervened to change his mind? One possibility presents itself immediately. In December 1969 Congress passed the Tax Reform Act, which eliminated tax deductions for gifts of papers. Some two months later, on March 5, 1970, Ralph Newman, the Chicago appraiser who had been valuing Nixon's documents, wrote a letter to Frank DeMarco, Nixon's tax lawyer, which read in part:

"Now that we are in 1970 and you have had an opportunity to study the Revised Reform Tax Bill of 1969, I wonder what the procedure will be with reference to the Nixon Papers and other material.

"As I mentioned over the telephone, the President has a considerable amount of material in the National Archives that qualifies as gift material under this bill. This includes books, trophies, plaques, artifacts, and other items not covered by Section 514, which relates to personal papers."

Newman doesn't say anything about tapes, because there were no Nixon tapes at that time and even if they were being contemplated it is unlikely that Newman would have known this. DeMarco had no knowledge of tapes or contemplated tapes either. But Newman's letter may well have reminded him that Section 514 of the 1969 Tax Reform Act eliminated a deduction only for "a copyright, a literary, musical or artistic composition, a letter or memorandum, or similar property." The law is clear that when such exceptions are made they are to be read literally. Thus any other object —certainly a tape recording—would not be affected by the congressional action.

There is no evidence of anyone drawing this conclusion with respect to tapes or passing it along to the White House. But it may well have occurred to De-Marco, Kalmbach, or one of Nixon's other lawyers. If so, the President may well have been persuaded to institute a taping system on these grounds. For if a few pre-Presidential letters and memos had brought him a $576,000 tax deduction, then tape recordings of his entire Presidency would almost certainly guarantee that he would never pay another substantial tax bill for the rest of his life. In any case, the first recording equipment was installed in the White House in February 1971—eleven months after Newman's letter.

One morning that month Larry Higby, Haldeman's assistant, told Butterfield that the President wanted a tape-recording system set up in the Oval Office and the Cabinet Room. Higby said, "Make sure that you don't go to Signal"—the Army Signal Corps, which normally handled most communications and electronics matters at the White House (they had installed and dismantled Lyndon Johnson's system). "Have the Secret Service do it," Higby said. "And do it right away."

So Butterfield called in Al Wong, Jim McCord's friend who was chief of the Secret Service's Technical Security Division at the White House (a separate group altogether from the Service's Presidential Protective Division, which, as its name suggests, guards the President). When Butterfield told Wong what had been ordered, Wong shook his head "as if to say here we go again," and said he hoped they wouldn't do it. But when Butterfield told Wong "there was no choice," he called in his "experts," who said they could handle it. The machines were installed over the next week, chiefly at night when the staff was not there.

This kind of technology was nothing new in the

Nixon White House. Indeed, the President and his men seemed intrigued by all sorts of space-age gimcrackery. Haldeman, Ehrlichman, Chapin, and Ziegler, in particular, were utterly fascinated by the walkie-talkies on which they crackled back and forth during motorcades, rallies, or other complex logistical enterprises, always under their Secret Service code names: "Wisdom" (Ehrlichman), "Watchdog" (Haldeman), "Whaleboat" (Ziegler). They rarely strayed very far without their "beepers," which could summon them from concerts, dinner parties, or ball games with an insistent "beep-beep-beep." Nixon, of course, increasingly put his faith in the magic powers of television and his schedules were often drawn up to coincide with America's viewing habits (his arrival in Peking was scheduled for prime time in the four zones back home—10:30 p.m. in New York, 7:30 p.m. on the West Coast). Haldeman was a camera bug, tracking the President with his expensive movie camera, recording him for "history" just as the hidden tapes did. And Haldeman, Ehrlichman, Higby, and Colson, among others, routinely taped their conversations with unsuspecting callers.

The first segment of Nixon's recording system was installed by three Secret Service electronics specialists —Raymond C. Zumwalt, the team's chief; Charles Bretz; and Roger Schwalm. They imbedded five microphones in the President's Oval Office desk to record conversations between Nixon and his aides, who generally gathered around the desk for conferences. At the other end of the office, where Nixon entertained all state visitors, two microphones were hidden in wall light fixtures near the cluster of chairs and couches around the fireplace. The three telephones in the office —all on Extension 500—were also tapped. In the Cabinet Room, microphones were placed in the bases of several lights.

Two to four months later, on Higby's instructions, four microphones were placed in the desk of Nixon's EOB office (and a tap on Extension 504); and other microphones and telephone taps were installed in the

Lincoln Sitting Room and at the Aspen Lodge at Camp David.

The recording devices had unusually sophisticated triggers, of which the Secret Service team was especially proud. The telephone taps were activated when the President lifted the receiver, thus dropping the voltage from 49 to 12. The room bugs were triggered by the "Presidential Locator System," a network of lights in his assistants' offices which informed them where he was at any time. Each of the six lights indicated a different location—Oval Office, West Wing, South Grounds, East Wing, EOB, or "out." As the President moved through the White House, the Secret Service would telephone his location to the police at the switchboard who, in turn, would flick on the appropriate light. This would alert the corresponding recording system, so that it could be "voice-activated" —meaning the tapes would then start to record within one-quarter to one-half a second after the first voice in the room.

Only the Cabinet Room tap was manually controlled. Originally, the Secret Service installed two buttons by the President's chair at the cabinet table: one marked "Butterfield" turned the recorder on; the other marked "Haldeman" turned it off. Other buttons were already there—one for Stephen Bull, Butterfield's assistant; another for the White House mess stewards— so the new buttons weren't conspicuous. But Nixon told Butterfield he didn't want to push any buttons. So the Secret Service installed a button on Butterfield's telephone in the room—he was by then cabinet secretary—which activated the recording system.

The taps and bugs all fed into a series of Sony 800B recorders hidden in closets around the White House and the EOB. Each five-inch reel held 1800 inches of tape, enough for six hours and twenty-two minutes of conversation when recorded at 15/16 of an inch per second. Each room's microphones and each telephone tap fed into a two-recorder system with an automatic timer, which switched the sound from one machine to the other at midnight. Agents changed the reels every day, Monday through Saturday. (On Sundays the reels were rarely changed, since agents authorized to deal with the tapes generally did not work then and the offices and telephones were not used much; agents concede that with heavy use the tapes might have run out.)

Some experts have expressed mild surprise at the mediocre quality of the White House equipment. Nixon later admitted it was "no Apollo system." Al Wong testified that the whole system had cost only $2500–$3000, in part because the Secret Service used equipment on hand, some of which had been employed in "stakeouts around the country." The Sony 800B—which retailed for about $199 at the time—is described as a "middle-quality" recorder. "It is hardly the type of equipment one would have expected the President of the United States to use," said Ed Myers, president of Myers-Emco and a member of the Acoustical Society of America. Similarly, Harold Lipset, a former investigator for the Senate Watergate committee and a technical consultant for *The Conversation,* a film on bugging, called the Sony 800B "adequate but not professional." Lipset said the White House equipment did not compare with the highly sophisticated machines James McCord used to bug the Watergate. One weakness was that the Sony used only monaural, or single-track, tape. A more sophisticated recording system would have permitted the use of four-track tape, so that every voice could be recorded on a different track. This would have reduced the number of "inaudibles" and "unintelligibles" which generally resulted when two or more people spoke at once.

Nevertheless, most experts agree that the system should have been adequate to record almost everything said in the President's offices or over his telephones. Raymond Zumwalt, who designed the system, testified later, "We ran tests. . . . Anyone talking in a low voice, it would pick it up." Butterfield, who had overall responsibility for the system, says he tested the recording quality shortly after the machines were installed. He listened to two tapes—one between the President and his friend Donald Kendall, the other between the

President and John Connally. "I could hear everything very well," he says. "Even low tones were picked up very well, very clearly."

Butterfield recalls only one occasion when the recording system malfunctioned during his time at the White House. "The fellow that put the tape on put it on inverted or something. At any rate, it did not record and we missed on that occasion—which was an Oval Office tape—we missed a morning, a half day. . . . Mr. Wong felt bad. They were not accustomed to making mistakes like that and he promised that it would never happen again." Later, Butterfield says, "Mr. Wong assured me that the taping equipment was checked daily. He said daily. I took that to mean precisely what he said."

The very existence of the tapes was a closely held secret at the White House. The tapes—in little cardboard boxes—were stored in filing cabinets in Room 175½ of the EOB. The room was kept locked and secured by an alarm. Only the four or five men in the Secret Service tapes detail had access. Butterfield told the Senate Watergate committee that, besides these Secret Service men, knowledge of the taping system was initially restricted to him, his secretary, Nixon, Haldeman, and Higby. Later, Haig was informed when he replaced Haldeman, and Steve Bull was let in on the secret when he replaced Butterfield.

Butterfield said it was his "guess" that Ehrlichman and Dean "definitely did not know" about the tapes. Ehrlichman testified that he first heard about the tapes when Butterfield revealed their existence before the committee. But the tapes themselves show that Ehrlichman knew about them nearly three months before.

On April 25—with his own time at the White House rapidly running out—Ehrlichman told the President they ought to determine whether "you committed a crime." He said the only legal process against a President was impeachment and that could be brought to bear only if he had committed a crime. "I think we have to think about that," he said, "and see . . . how serious it is, and would Dean [be] a threat, and what we do about it. My own analysis is that what he has falls far short of any commission of a crime by you. So far as I know. . . . [But] I don't know what you may have talked about with him in those ten or twelve hours you and he spent there in the months of February and March. You get down to a point where you've got John Dean prancing in there and saying, 'The President said this and the President said that,' and having somebody in your behalf come back and say, 'No, the President didn't say that and that's ridiculous.' Uh and so you get a kind of credibility thing. . . . And I think really the only way that I know to make a judgment on this is for you to listen to your tapes and see what actually was said then, or maybe for Bob to do it, or, or, somebody."

Translated, that would seem to mean: You are about to fire me. That's okay, but now I'd like to know more about what you've been up to. Dean keeps saying you are guilty of this, that, or the other. You keep proclaiming your innocence. It's difficult for the rest of us to know who is telling the truth. Now, I know all about your tapes. The only way to settle this is for somebody—perhaps me—to listen to those tapes and find out the truth.

Not surprisingly, this conversation made the President very nervous. The next morning, as he and Haldeman were discussing the Dean problem, Nixon abruptly switched subjects:

NIXON: With regard to the tapes . . . I don't think it should ever get out that we taped this office, Bob. Have we got people that are trustworthy on that? I guess we have.

HALDEMAN: I think so.

NIXON: If it does, the answer is yes. We only, but we only taped the national security, uh, information. All other, all other, all other information is scrapped, never transcribed. Get the point? That's what I want you to remember on those, if you will. . . . I think that's very important, very important. You never want to be in a position to say the President taped it, you know. I mean taped somebody.

HALDEMAN: Well, the whole purpose of this was for national security. . . .

NIXON: I know, but I just don't want this to be—I just don't want that tape, for example, I don't want you to, I don't want to disclose that to Ehrlichman or anybody else, I mean that's just something—I know what you can tell Ehrlichman. Just say you went over it and it's about the same as . . .

HALDEMAN: I've already, what I said to him is that the tape—he knows I went over it, of course. Uh, I said, "It basically says what the President recalled."

"It" was apparently the critical March 21 tape, which Nixon had asked Haldeman to listen to in late April. Translated, Nixon was now saying: I trust you to listen to the tapes, but I don't trust Ehrlichman. Don't let him anywhere near those tapes. Just tell him they support my position.

What made Nixon most nervous of all was the possibility that Dean might have been taping some of their conversations himself. A few hours after his conversation with Ehrlichman on April 25, the President talked with Haldeman about the prospect of impeachment.

NIXON: I don't see the Senate or any senators starting an impeachment of the President based on the word of John Dean.

HALDEMAN: That's right.

NIXON: That's all it is, you know, and, ah, I mean, John Dean says that this and that and the other thing happened.

HALDEMAN: And there's no way he can support it. I mean, there's no way to make a case.

NIXON: Well, except he could be, recorded his conversation . . .

HALDEMAN: Still his word unless he's got a tape recording . . .

NIXON: I don't know, ah, a tape recording is, ah, I can't believe that he could have walked in there with a tape recorder that day, because that day, I mean I'm not trying to be wishful thinking, that particular day [probably March 21] he wasn't really out to get the President, I don't think. . . . Unless he tape-records every, does he, does he, does he tape-record everything that he comes in?

HALDEMAN: No, no.

NIXON: Does he, you're sure of that?

HALDEMAN: No, I'm not sure of it, but I am convi —never had any reason to believe that he did.

NIXON: Mmmm, mmmm.

HALDEMAN: And the way, you know, he dresses uh just casual enough in his clothing and all, that I can't imagine you'd . . . he'd have [a] tape recorder, yah, it's bulky and you gotta get it in your pocket somewhere and all that. It isn't all that easy to do.

NIXON: Right, right, right.

But the President still wasn't satisfied. Less than an hour later he called Haldeman back.

NIXON: Is there any, uh, way that, uh, even surreptitiously or discreetly or otherwise I mean, that, ah, way you could determine whether this matter of whether Dean might have walked in there with a recorder on him? I don't know.

HALDEMAN: No, I don't think there is any way. . . .

NIXON: Well, we've gotta, I mean it's . . . but the point is that that's ah, that's a real bomb, isn't it? . . . That's what may be his bomb. In other words, he put that on the desk with Henry Petersen and says, "I gotta recording of the President of the United States and here's what he said."

HALDEMAN: Well, that would be very hard. . . .

NIXON: I didn't look at him that closely, but you were there, goddamn, I mean, I'd think that it's a little, it's, even the smallest ones are bulky enough that you mean, with a fellow like Dean you'd sort of see that wouldn't ya, where do you carry them, in your hip pocket or your breast pocket?

HALDEMAN: Oh, under your arm, you know, where they carry a pistol holster or something.

NIXON: Um, hmmm, ya. Well . . .

HALDEMAN: I really don't think it's—it's so remote as to be almost beyond the realm of possibility.

NIXON: In this matter nothing is beyond the realm of possibility.

That was confirmed on Friday, July 13, when the "bomb" Nixon had so feared from John Dean was dropped by one of his own men, Alex Butterfield.

The revelation was indeed a bombshell. The notion of a President bugging his unsuspecting guests—including foreign heads of state—was repugnant to many people. (The President, it seems, even lied outright to some of his guests. On March 23 he assured representatives of the milk industry, "Oh, I won't go that far. [*Laughter.*] Matter of fact the room is not tapped. [*Laughter.*] Forgot to do that.") The use of a telephoning device without a beeper to alert the other party was an outright violation of FCC regulations. Both drew expressions of outrage. George Meany, president of the AFL-CIO, called it "so fantastic as to be almost beyond belief." Former Interior Secretary Walter Hickel said, "America will be sick at heart."

But the implications of Butterfield's testimony went beyond such improprieties. "I don't have to draw the line underneath and add it up," Sam Dash told reporters. What the tapes added up to was the first concrete, irrefutable evidence that could resolve the dispute over what had happened at the White House during the months before and after the Watergate burglary. It could settle who said what in the disputed Nixon-Dean conversations and could go far toward determining the President's guilt or innocence.

Butterfield's revelation had come at a most opportune time for the committee. Following Dean's startling charges in June, the staff had been unable to provide any corroboration, and the hearings had begun to lag a bit. Moreover, the committee had reached an impasse with Nixon over the release of relevant White House documents and a Presidential appearance before the committee. On July 6 Nixon had flatly refused to permit either. In a letter to Ervin, the President said his decision, in both cases, was "based on my Constitutional obligation to preserve intact the powers and prerogatives of the Presidency." His stand was reminiscent of the hard "executive privilege" line he had taken in early April on the committee's requests that his aides testify. In May he had relaxed that stand, but now he seemed to be reverting to his hard line by drawing a distinction between public testimony and delivery of papers. "While notes and papers often involve a wide-ranging variety and intermingling of confidential matters, testimony can, at least, be limited to matters within the scope of the investigation." Release of any Presidential papers, he said, would "move us from proper Presidential cooperation with a Senate Committee to jeopardizing the fundamental Constitutional role of the Presidency. This I must and shall resist."

The committee had sought to avoid a constitutional confrontation with Nixon, instructing Senator Ervin on July 12 "to meet with the President to ascertain whether there is any reasonable possibility of working out any reconciliation." Later that day Ervin telephoned the President to request a face-to-face meeting. Nixon was in an "emotional state" during their fourteen-minute conversation. At one point he told Ervin he would not provide the papers because the committee was "out to get me." They agreed to meet anyway, but a few hours later the President entered Bethesda Naval Hospital amid rumors that he was having a nervous breakdown (his doctors soon diagnosed viral pneumonia). Nixon was still in bed when Butterfield dropped the bomb; from his supine position, he orchestrated moves to halt further congressional inquiries on the tapes.

At noon, on July 17, Senators Ervin and Baker and committee counsel had just begun a meeting with Secret Serviceman Al Wong when they were interrupted by three other Secret Service officials, accompanied by

Edward L. Morgan, the former deputy counsel to the President (who had signed the deed of Nixon's papers to the National Archives) and now an assistant secretary of the treasury. They bore a letter from Nixon to Secretary of the Treasury George Shultz ordering that "no officer or agent of the Secret Service shall give testimony to Congressional committees concerning matters observed or learned while performing protective functions for the President or in their duties at the White House." The officials said the letter prevented any further interviews with Wong, and they led him away.

The committee again opted for conciliation rather than confrontation. It voted to ask the President for "all relevant documents and tapes under control of the White House that relate to the matters the Select Committee is authorized to investigate." And it added a personal note: "The committee deeply regrets your illness and hopes for you a speedy recovery."

For the next week the White House maintained a stolid silence on the committee's request and on a similar letter from Special Prosecutor Archibald Cox (though a skillful prankster on July 19 momentarily persuaded Senator Ervin, and through him the nation, that the White House had capitulated). On July 20 Nixon emerged from the hospital in a feisty mood. Denouncing suggestions that he might resign—"just plain poppycock"—he told two hundred reporters and members of his staff in the White House Rose Garden, "What we were elected to do, we are going to do, and let others wallow in Watergate." (His staff quietly acknowledged that the taping system had been disconnected on July 18—not because it was improper but merely because it had become a political "embarrassment.") After his Rose Garden speech, Nixon and Bebe Rebozo left for a weekend at Camp David, where the President worked on his reply about the tapes.

On Monday, July 23, the answer came: a firm "no" to both Ervin and Cox. In his letter to Senator Ervin, Nixon said he based his refusal on the same constitutional principles of "separation of powers" and "executive privilege" enunciated in his July 6 letter concerning the Presidential papers. "Indeed," he wrote, "the special nature of tape recordings of private conversations is such that these principles apply with even greater force to tapes of private Presidential conversations than to Presidential papers." Finally, he said, the tapes would not settle anything anyway, because, though they were "entirely consistent with what I know to be the truth," they contained comments that "persons with different perspectives and motivations would inevitably interpret in different ways."

This brought a skeptical snort from Ervin, who told an appreciative audience in the Caucus Room that afternoon, "The President says he has heard the tapes or some of them and they sustain his position. But he says he's not going to let anybody else hear them for fear they might draw a different conclusion."

Given Nixon's determination to keep the tapes from those who might draw their own conclusions, one wonders why he did not destroy all the incriminating reels during those ten days following Butterfield's revelations. Indeed, he was urged to destroy at least some of them in a passionate memorandum from Pat Buchanan on July 25. "Can the President be certain of the final disposition of those tapes, that only sympathetic or objective historians will ultimately inspect them?" the memo asked. "Unless the President can guarantee this into perpetuity, then, in my judgment, the President should exercise now selectivity over which tapes are preserved and which are not. If there are conversations with confidential aides, such as Charles Colson or Bob Haldeman (exclusive of the so-called Watergate tapes) that are better left confidential forever—what then is the sense of their preservation? Perhaps the President should be provided with a day-by-day log of his tape library, and himself separate the wheat from the chaff—from his own recollection—and have the latter burned. If such a program is undertaken, it should be announced, not in advance, but as a *fait accompli*."

Buchanan's proposal—perhaps for cosmetic reasons—seems to exclude the Watergate tapes. But it might have applied to them too. Had Nixon announced that the tapes were burned to spare anyone "embarrassment" there undoubtedly would have been a spate of outrage, of thundering denunciations from *The New York Times* and *The Washington Post,* of calls for impeachment from Democrats in Congress. But after a while the storm probably would have abated and when it did there would have been no hard evidence left on which to build an irrefutable case against the President. Why did Nixon not choose this course?

First, Nixon apparently believed that he had almost as much to gain from the tapes as he had to lose. On April 25 he had told Haldeman, "I always wondered about that taping equipment, but I'm damn glad we have it, aren't you? . . . It's helpful because while it has some things in there that, ah, we prefer we wouldn't have said, but, on the other hand, we also have some things in there that we know we've, that I've said that weren't, that were pretty good, I mean."

In addition to such "exculpating" evidence, he and Haldeman may have thought that some of the material on the tapes could be used to threaten, intimidate, or punish their enemies or to keep their former colleagues loyal. The tapes might themselves be potent weapons in Nixon's fight for political survival.

Then, if Nixon had indeed started the taping to give himself a whopping tax deduction, he might have been reluctant to destroy the materials which offered him financial security for the rest of his life. (If he had given the tapes to the National Archives at some later date, he could presumably have edited them as he liked and deleted any incriminating material.)

Finally—and probably most important—Nixon was evidently convinced that he would never have to surrender the tapes. His lawyers, relying on high-sounding principles like "separation of powers" and "executive privilege," told him he was safe. Nixon—whose legal experience did not include constitutional law—believed them, probably because he wanted to believe them.

In any case, by the afternoon of July 23, it was too late. For an hour and a half the seven senators met in Ervin's office down the hall from the Caucus Room.

Then at three-thirty they filed out and took their places at the hearing table. The television lights flashed on. A hush fell over the room. Ervin read the President's letter of refusal on the tapes. Then he announced that the committee had voted to subpoena five tapes of conversations between the President and Dean. The country, Ervin said, was more interested in finding out what had really happened in the Watergate matter than in "abstruse arguments about the separation of powers or executive privilege." And he concluded, "I think that Watergate is the greatest tragedy this country has ever suffered. I used to think the Civil War was the country's greatest tragedy, but I do remember some redeeming features in the Civil War in that there was some spirit of sacrifice and heroism displayed on both sides. I see no redeeming features in Watergate."

That same afternoon Archibald Cox issued his own subpoena for nine tapes. Both subpoenas were hand-delivered to the White House before nightfall. With the acceptance of the two documents, the tapes became potential evidence. To destroy them would be a criminal offense and a strong count in any bill of impeachment. As if to remind the White House of the impending constitutional crisis, Rufus L. Edmisten, the deputy majority counsel who delivered the committee subpoena, presented the President's lawyers with one of the blue-covered pocket editions of the Constitution which Sam Ervin liked to hand out to his constituents.

"The finest thing to come out of the mind of man," *is the way Sam Ervin describes the United States Con-* *stitution. It is one of his three basic texts—along with* *the King James Version of the Bible and the Collected* *Works of William Shakespeare—and Ervin is a funda-* *mentalist about all three. He is a text man, a strict* *constructionist, a conservative who believes the words* *in those documents mean exactly what they say. Sam* *Ervin's reverence for the Constitution is quintessential-* *ly Southern and helps resolve the prime paradox of his* *senatorial career: his passionate commitment to First* *Amendment liberties and his equally passionate op-*

position to racial civil rights. A leader of Southern
filibusters against such bills, he argued that they would
grant Negroes' rights at the expense of states' rights.
"We will not fool history as we fool ourselves when we
steal freedom from one man to confer it on another,"
he warned. "When freedom for one citizen is diminished it is in the end diminished for all." In the 1950s
and early 1960s, when civil-rights legislation was the
focus of national debate, liberals generally regarded
Ervin as a hopeless mossback. In the mid-1960s, when
Vietnam became the central issue, he reinforced this
reputation by his stanch support for the war. But at
the end of the decade, as many liberals worried about
government encroachment on citizens' rights, Ervin
suddenly emerged as the Senate's most eloquent champion of individual liberties. As chairman of the Government Operations Committee and of three subcommittees
of the Judiciary Committee, he fought against Presidential impoundment of funds, efforts to compel newsmen to reveal their sources, military surveillance of
antiwar dissidents, preventive detention, and unrestricted wiretapping. So, when Senator Mike Mansfield
of Montana banned all Presidential aspirants from the
Watergate committee, the seventy-six-year-old Ervin
seemed the logical choice for chairman. "Sammy was
the only man we could have picked on either side of
the aisle who'd have had the respect of the Senate as a
whole," Mansfield said. At the start, even the White
House felt it could do business with him. On March
22, 1973, Dean told Nixon he thought Ervin could be
handled: "I've dealt with him for years and have
reached accord with him on legislation. . . . Ervin,
away from his staff, is not very much, and I think he
might just give up the store himself and lock himself
in." Ervin's drawling Tarheel accent, rustic manner-
isms, cracker-barrel yarns, and eyebrows which flap
like blackbirds' wings may have lulled the White House
into believing he could be handled. "I'm an old country
lawyer," he would say and everyone would grin. But
soon the President and his men realized he was not
quite the simple country lawyer he pretended to be. A
graduate of Harvard Law School, Ervin had served for

six years as a county judge and for seven more years on the North Carolina Superior Court. A veteran of two decades of North Carolina politics and eighteen years in the Senate, he knew politics too. His hill-country tales and Biblical allusions were shrewd political weapons which nettled the White House witnesses like the banderillas *spiked into a bull's neck. When Ervin reminded John Ehrlichman of the parable of the Good Samaritan, Ehrlichman snarled, "I read the Bible, I don't quote it"—a remark not likely to earn him much good will with a nationwide television audience. Mary McCarthy has compared Ervin to an old Shakespearean character actor specializing in "common-sense rustics" and representing, as such characters did in the Bard's plays, the "low" reality principle. His down-to-earth common sense set off for all to see the fancy footwork of Wall Street lawyers and double-entry bookkeepers. When Maurice Stans told the committee he had destroyed most records of campaign contributions and insisted that this was "very simply for the reason—" Ervin cut in, "It is too simple for me to understand, really." Stans tried again, "Mr. Chairman, for the reason that we were seeking to protect the privacy, the confidentiality of the contributions on behalf of the contributors." Simple Sam thought he finally understood: "In other words," he drawled, "you decided that the right of the contributors to have their contributions concealed was superior to the right of the American citizens to know who was making contributions to influence the election of the President of the United States."*

As expected, the President rejected the subpoenas on July 26, and both the committee and the special prosecutor moved to take the battle to court, thus setting off an unprecedented four-way struggle among the President, the Congress, the courts, and the special prosecutor.

Within a week, though, the struggle had become largely triangular. For quickly it became evident that the courts—heeding the separation of powers—would probably not take jurisdiction over a legislative suit for executive documents. Although Judge John Sirica did not resolve this question until mid-October, by early August attention had shifted almost entirely to the special prosecutor's suit. Not only was Cox unhampered by the separation-of-powers argument—he was part of the executive—but he had a grand jury investigation under way, and thus a compelling need for the best available evidence which the courts would be inclined to honor.

The special prosecutor's case was further strengthened when Haldeman, testifying before the Watergate committee, said he had refreshed his recollection of two critically important conversations (September 15, 1972, and March 21, 1973) by listening to the tapes. Only days before, a Presidential lawyer had said, "It is very difficult to make any claim of privilege for material that is no longer confidential." Some lawyers argued that the President might have waived his "executive privilege" when he gave even one tape to a man no longer employed by the White House (Haldeman had listened to the September 15 tape at home in July, well after his resignation).

To further blunt any claim of "executive privilege" or "national security," the special prosecutor's subpoena also asked for several memoranda—a notice transferring Howard Hunt from the White House staff to CREEP, and copies of Gordon Strachan's "political matters memoranda." These were clearly political materials which by no stretch of the legal imagination could be included in a Presidential privilege.

But the central issue remained the tapes. By mid-August the legal battle had resolved into a contest over nine tapes of Presidential meetings or telephone conversations that the special prosecutor felt would either substantiate or disprove charges against Nixon or his aides:

• June 20, 1972, 10:30 a.m.–12 noon (approximately) —A conversation, three days after the Watergate break-in, between Nixon, Haldeman, and Ehrlichman, shortly after the two Presidential assistants had met with Dean and Mitchell.

• June 20, 1972, 6:08–6:12 p.m. —A brief telephone conversation between Nixon and Mitchell.

• June 30, 1972, 12:55–2:10 p.m. —A talk at lunch between Nixon, Haldeman, and Mitchell, one day before Mitchell's resignation from CREEP.

• September 15, 1972, 5:27–6:17 p.m. —The President's discussion with Haldeman and Dean on the day the seven Watergate defendants were indicted.

• March 13, 1973, 12:42–2:00 p.m. —Nixon's conversation with Haldeman and Dean at which they considered the involvement of White House and CREEP staff in Watergate.

• March 21, 1973, 10:12–11:55 a.m. —The President's discussion with Dean at which the $1-million hush-money demand was discussed.

• March 21, 1973, 5:20–6:01 p.m. —Nixon's talk with Haldeman, Ehrlichman, Dean, and Ziegler at which the hush money was discussed again and clemency considered.

• March 22, 1973, 1:57–3:43 p.m. —A long discussion among Nixon, Haldeman, Ehrlichman, Mitchell, and Dean about how to get "out front" on Watergate.

• April 15, 1973, 9:17–10:12 p.m. —A meeting between Nixon and Dean at which Nixon allegedly tried to exculpate himself.

But the President was determined to resist. "He's digging in," one aide told *Newsweek*. "He's saying they're not going to get those goddamn tapes." In midsummer Nixon was grappling with another of those periodic crises which studded his career. "Crises," he once wrote, "can indeed be agony. But it is the exquisite agony which a man might not want to experience again—yet would not for the world have missed." He had always been most fully alive during a crisis.

Yet Garry Wills has suggested that Nixon's truly exhilarating crises required a well-defined enemy with whom to do battle: Alger Hiss, Venezuelan rioters, Nikita Khrushchev, John Kennedy, Dan Ellsberg. This time there was no external force to fight. Nothwithstanding the massive "enemies list" drawn up at the White House, the President's worst enemies came from within his own inner circle and, ultimately, from inside himself. The greatest danger that summer were his own words wound on the reels in the White House basement. Perhaps that is why his midsummer attacks were generally directed not so much at any concrete personal enemy as at the very material itself, the grimy stuff of the scandal that would not go away.

The President's response to the special prosecutor's suit, filed on August 7, reflected the same tone of unfocused rage at an ill-defined enemy. Drafted largely by Fred Buzhardt and a new Presidential lawyer—Charles Alan Wright of the University of Texas—the thirty-four-page brief contended:

"The present proceeding, though a well-intentioned effort to obtain evidence for criminal prosecutions, represented a serious threat to the nature of the Presidency as it was created by the Constitution, as it has been sustained for 184 years, and as it exists today. If the Special Prosecutor should be successful in the attempt to compel disclosure of recordings of Presidential conversations, the damage to the institution of the Presidency will be severe and irreparable. The character of that office will be fundamentally altered and the total structure of government—dependent as it is upon a separation of powers—will be impaired. . . . The issue here is starkly simple: Will the Presidency be allowed to continue to function."

Six days later Cox volleyed back with a sixty-eight-page rebuttal: "The President has an enforceable legal duty not to withhold material evidence from a grand jury. The grand jury occupies a fundamental position in the administration of public justice. There is no exception for the President from the guiding principle that the public, in the pursuit of justice, has a right to every man's evidence."

While the lawyers exchanged lofty abstractions, John Dean's concrete accusations still hung heavily in the muggy midsummer air, preoccupying the capital and much of the nation beyond. In late July and early August John Ehrlichman and H.R. Haldeman took their turns before the Ervin committee and did their best to discredit Dean and his testimony. But all of Ehrlichman's disdainful defiance ("Mr. Chairman, you interrupted me—you have a delightful trial-room practice of interrupting something you do not want to hear") and Haldeman's stolid denials ("The President had no awareness of any such acts") could not still doubts about the President's role. Pressures grew on Nixon to answer the charges himself.

In early August the President made at least three trips to Camp David to prepare a public response to questions about Watergate. Every Nixon crisis included a period of solitary withdrawal—not unlike religious retreats of ritual purification and self-discipline—in which he pondered his next move and gathered strength. Increasingly, during the Watergate ordeal, the President took refuge on the remote hundred-foot peak in the Catoctin Mountains, surrounded by two steel cyclone fences, coils of barbed wire, ferocious watchdogs, and Secret Service men with carbines. At the Aspen Lodge—from which the taping equipment had now been removed—he could swim in the new $150,000 pool outside the front door, gaze over the dense western Maryland forests from the living-room picture window, or brood at night by the big stone fireplace. He loved the isolation, the transcendence of workaday Washington concerns. "The clouds are right around you," he said once. "When it's like that you may think you were in space."

On August 15 Nixon came down from his mountaintop and went before a nationwide television audience for his long-awaited address to the nation. For a time, his staff had worked to prepare a point-by-point reply to the accusations against him, but this was soon abandoned as "politically unproductive." Some of the President's aides were leery of his appearing to respond to every charge from the grubby political pit. They noted that his earlier, partial responses—the statements of April 30 and May 22—had done him more harm than good. "Every time he opens his mouth," one aide said, "he risks rebuttal from a witness." So the August 15 speech—and the supplementary statement handed to reporters—contained few direct answers. "It would not be right for me to try to sort out the evidence, to refute some specific witnesses, to pronounce my own judgments about their credibility."

Instead, Nixon urged his audience to transcend the grimy scandal and turn their attention to more lofty matters. "After twelve weeks and two million words of televised testimony, we have reached a point at which a continued, backward-looking obsession with Watergate is causing this nation to neglect matters of far greater importance to all of the American people. . . . The time has come to turn Watergate over to the courts, where the questions of guilt or innocence belong. The time has come for the rest of us to get on with the urgent business of our nation. . . . I ask for your help to insure that those who would exploit Watergate in order to keep us from doing what we were elected to do will not succeed."

The President and his advisers had concluded that nothing he could say would change most people's presumptions about his guilt or innocence. They decided he could live with suspicion for a time, meanwhile working to dispel the national preoccupation with Watergate. The next day White House officials expressed confidence that strategy was beginning to work. Mrs. Nixon, through her press secretary, conveyed "the feeling that Watergate is behind all of us now."

But the feeling was hardly universal. Two of the most significant reactions came from Republican senators—Edward Brooke ("The American people want the facts. The President gave us rhetoric") and Barry Goldwater ("In my opinion, the President did not add anything to his other speeches that would tend to divert suspicion from him"). And a Gallup Poll commissioned by *The New York Times* showed that 44 per cent of those who watched the speech found it "not at all" convincing, while only 28 per cent were convinced "completely" or "quite a lot."

This wave of skepticism evidently dismayed Nixon,

plunging him into a sour and combative mood. All summer he seemed to swing back and forth between extremes: at times brooding and suspicious, at other times apparently confident, even cocky. On August 20 his anger flared publicly for a moment during a quick trip to New Orleans to address the national convention of the Veterans of Foreign Wars. The trip was an apparent effort to counteract the negative poll results by bringing the President before a friendly audience and large crowds his advance men promised to produce in the streets of the southern city. But as his jet landed, the Secret Service announced that it had detected a "possible conspiracy to assassinate the President" and his motorcade was diverted through back streets where only small clusters of people saw him. At the auditorium, the veterans and their wives gave the President an enthusiastic welcome, but he put on a curious performance—stumbling over his words, pacing nervously about the stage, waving his arms in broad, exaggerated gestures. Perhaps the most revealing incident of the day occurred just before he entered the convention hall. As Ron Ziegler and the White House press corps trooped after him, Nixon abruptly grabbed Ziegler by the shoulders and shoved him toward the reporters, saying, "I don't want any press with me. You take care of it."

The President's shove was but the latest indignity heaped on the husky shoulders of the former fullback from Dixie Heights High. Melvin Laird and John Connally had both called for his dismissal. A committee of the staid National Press Club had declared that Ronald Ziegler "misled the public and affronted the professional standards of the Washington press corps." And White House reporters had been griping for years about his talents for obfuscation (he was quickly nicknamed "Zigzag" and his answers labeled "Ziegles"). They pointed to classics such as his reply when asked whether allied troops were preparing to invade Laos: "The President is aware of what is going on in Southeast Asia. That is not to say that anything is going on in Southeast Asia." Or his response when pressed to explain what he meant by the President's "least unlikely" decision: "You should not interpret by my use of 'least unlikely' that ultimately, or when the final decision is made, that that may not be the decision, but what I'm saying is that it is only one of the matters under consideration and the decision has not been made." But the reporters' irritation escalated to indignation over Ziegler's bluff stonewalling on Watergate, a subject on which he seemed to follow the maxim, "When in doubt deny everything." But probably nothing brought more scorn down on Ziegler's head than his acceptance of a reporter's phrasing on April 17, 1973. After Nixon announced "major developments" in the Watergate case that day, Ziegler told reporters that this was the President's "operative" statement. R. W. Apple of The New York Times *asked whether that meant "that the other statement is no longer operative, that it is now inoperative." After fencing with Apple for a while, Ziegler finally gave in: "The President refers to the fact that there is new material; therefore, this is the operative statement. The others are inoperative." The next day Clark Mollenhoff of the* Des Moines Register, *a former Presidential assistant who felt burned by his very association with Nixon, thundered at Ziegler, "Do you feel free to stand up there and lie and put out misinformation and then come around later and say it's all 'inoperative'? That's what you're doing. You're not entitled to any credibility at all." Relations between Ziegler and the press became so embittered that White House officials declined to appear in the White House press room, calling it a "poisoned forum." Even a gracious apology to Woodstein—whose stories he had once labeled "shabby journalism"—did not earn Ziegler any good will. So gradually he relinquished the briefings to Assistant Press Secretary Gerald L. Warren (a former newsman) and went on to more majestic matters. Part of Ziegler's problem with the press was that he had never been a reporter. Growing up in Covington, Kentucky, he became a star running back in high school, where his kindergarten sweetheart (and future wife)*

*was the football queen and led Z-I-E-G-L-E-R cheers
for him. He won a football scholarship to Xavier University
in Cincinnati, but soon followed the sun west
to Los Angeles, where he got a job for the summer
piloting the "jungle cruise boat" at Disneyland and
giving the same spiel thirty-three times a day: "Welcome
aboard, folks. My name's Ron. I'm your skipper
and guide down the River of Adventure. Before we
pull away from the dock, please turn around and take
a good look. You may never see it again. . . . On the
left, the natives on the bank. The natives have only
one aim in life and that is to get a-head." He liked
California so much that he transferred to USC, where
he was a B— marketing major, Signa Chi social chairman,
and active Young Republican. When Nixon
came to USC in 1960 for a campaign speech, Ziegler
handled press arrangements for the visit. He worked
in the disastrous 1962 campaign, but impressed the
campaign manager, Bob Haldeman, who recruited him
for J. Walter Thompson. In his five years there, Ziegler
became an account executive for Disneyland, Sea
World, 7-Up, and Blue Chip Stamps. Haldeman took
him into the 1968 Presidential campaign and then into
the White House, where he first held the lowly title
of "press assistant." Later he got the full "press
secretary" title, and when Haldeman, Ehrlichman,
Colson, et al. left the White House in the spring
of 1973, Ziegler suddenly found himself Nixon's last
link to a lost past. On June 6 the President gave him
complete responsibility for all White House communications
matters and the additional title of assistant to
the President. As summer wore on, Ziegler joined
Haig and Kissinger in the new "inner circle" of advisers.
Nobody knew what Ziegler advised the President
on. "He doesn't know anything but PR," said
one aide. "So it must be PR."*

Ziegler was at the President's side on August 22
when Nixon held his first news conference in five
months on the sun-splashed lawn of the Coast Guard
complex adjoining San Clemente. Clearly nervous and

strained, the President lashed out at the press, which was now increasingly the "enemy" his crisis required. When Dan Rather of CBS said he wanted to state his question with "due respect," the President replied scornfully, "That would be unusual." Asked to explain his August 15 remark that some people were seeking to "exploit" Watergate, he readily identified them: "Some political figures, some members of the press, perhaps, some members of the television . . . people who did not accept the mandate of 1972. . . ." Late in the news conference, the increasingly combative Mollenhoff lumbered to his feet: "Where is the check on authoritarianism by the executive if the President is to be the sole judge of what the executive branch makes available and suppresses?" he asked. "And will you obey a Supreme Court order if you are asked and directed to produce the tapes or other documents for the Senate committee or for the special prosecutor? And if this is not enough is there any limitation on the President, short of impeachment, to compel the production of evidence of a criminal nature?" His own rage barely under control, Nixon replied, "This administration has, I think, gone further in terms of waiving executive privilege than any administration in my memory." But, as for what he would do in response to court decisions, the President said he would wait for the judgments and then make his "determination."

That very morning Charles Alan Wright and Archibald Cox finally confronted each other from behind identical walnut tables in the high-ceilinged courtroom of the U.S. district court. First up was Wright, the hulking constitutionalist from Texas, who declared that the President was "beyond the process of any court." To hold otherwise, he warned Judge Sirica, would be to give four hundred federal district judges the right to compel disclosures of Presidential conversations on the most confidential matters, even those relating to national security. "That, I submit, sir, is a frightening prospect." Then Cox, looking sternly over his half-moon spectacles, said privilege didn't apply when there was reason to suspect criminality and now there was "strong reason to believe that the integrity of the executive office has been corrupted." Quoting the thirteenth-century English author Henry de Bracton, he said, "The King ought not to be under any man—but he is under God and the law."

From his red leather chair high on the bench, Judge Sirica pondered the arguments. After two and a half hours he adjourned the session and went into seclusion with his law books. For three days he read Anglo-Saxon jurisprudence, the *Federalist Papers*, and the minutes of the Constitutional Convention. He examined citations from eighteen different Supreme Court cases spanning a hundred and seventy years. Over the next weekend he began drafting his decision, then spent a day revising it. Unable to sleep that night, he got up at one in the morning to make some changes, up again at four o'clock to pencil in some more. At noon, on August 29, his law clerks were still hustling fresh pages to the typist. At three o'clock mimeographed copies of the judge's decision were distributed to reporters.

Essentially, Judge Sirica upheld Cox's contention that the President was not above the law. "In all candor," he wrote, "the Court fails to perceive any reason for suspending the power of courts to get evidence . . . simply because it is the President of the United States who holds the evidence." But the judge did not go quite as far as the special prosecutor had asked. Instead of ordering that the tapes be handed over directly to the grand jury, he directed the President to make them available to him for his own private examination in chambers. Only then, Sirica said, could he rule on the claims of executive privilege. If there was privileged material in the tapes, he would excise it before handing the unprivileged portion to the grand jury.

The first reaction from the President, still vacationing at San Clemente, was enigmatic: a terse statement saying that Nixon would not comply with the judge's order and that he was considering the possibility of appeal or "how otherwise to sustain the President's position." Nixon had said earlier that he would obey a "definitive ruling" by the Supreme Court, but had refused to define what he meant by "definitive." His statement now suggested that he might choose simply to defy Judge Sirica rather than let the Supreme Court reach a definitive decision. But the next day, after the President met for an hour with his lawyers, the White House announced that he would appeal. Cox, too, appealed the ruling, asking that the President be ordered to give the tapes directly to the grand jury, with no prior judicial screening.

The stage was set for a protracted legal struggle through the Court of Appeals to the Supreme Court, a struggle which might take three or four more months to resolve. The legal complexities were mind-boggling to most laymen, and there were signs that the public was getting a bit bored by the endless wrangling.

Nixon played to this boredom, urging time and again that his critics in the press and Congress move beyond Watergate and let him get to work on "the business of the people." By early September the counterattack he had begun in mid-August was starting to rack up some points. Some senators and congressmen returning from the summer recess reported heavy pressure from their constituents to restrict the Watergate hearings. Although by August the televised hearings had zoomed to the top of the daytime Nielsen ratings ("Ervin & Co. Soaking the Soaps" was the *Variety* headline), many viewers still begrudged the interruption of their regular programing. Callers to ABC said, "We're sick of nothing but Watergate, Watergate" and "Us housewives are bored with it." A Harris Poll showed that, by 50 to 44 per cent, Americans thought: "The press and television have given Watergate more attention than it deserves."

The President made some progress in his efforts to drive Watergate off center stage during another news conference in Washington on September 5. More at ease than he had been in San Clemente, he delivered only an occasional snipe at the press, particularly at the "leers and sneers of commentators." The White

House press corps—which the President had chided for its disproportionate interest in Watergate two weeks before—now devoted only six of fourteen questions to the subject.

The shifting mood had a heavy impact on the Ervin committee. After thirty-seven spectacular days on national television, the senators had recessed August 7, planning to resume on September 10 with prolonged public sessions on the "dirty tricks" and "campaign financing" portions of their inquiry. But in mid-September these grandiose plans were sharply cut back —to eighteen days of hearings scheduled to end November 1. Partly, the change of plans stemmed from staff and budgetary limitations that hampered preliminary investigations. But the prime reason was the senators' fear that further prolonged hearings might produce a public backlash against the committee and increased sympathy for those implicated in the Watergate scandal. This concern was accentuated on September 26 when the White House scored its first public-relations victory of the hearings: Pat Buchanan deftly fielding most of the committee's ill-researched questions and ridiculing its inquiry as a "foolish exercise."

Thus, by early autumn, the President had hit upon a strategy that seemed to be working. By avoiding a point-by-point response to the charges against him, by dribbling out his answers over many months, by discrediting those who continued to ask the same boring old questions, and by keeping the matter of the tapes bogged down in endless legal arguments, he appeared to be winning his war of attrition against the public preoccupation with Watergate. Once more, as so often in the past, Richard Nixon seemed to be riding out a crisis.

12

AGNEW

The man is the goddamn Vice President of the United States! What are you trying to do? Get him to crawl on his belly?
—Henry Petersen to Barney Skolnik,
September 15, 1973

Abruptly, in midsummer, Richard Nixon turned World Statesman. In the space of only ten days he received four foreign heads of government, calling at the Court of Washington like barons paying homage to Charlemagne. First came His Imperial Majesty Mohammed Reza Shah Pahlavi, Shahanshah of Iran, accompanied by his elegant wife, Empress Farah, for a round of state dinners, cocktail parties, receptions, and discussions focusing on the acquisition of Grumman F-14 fighter planes for the Iranian Air Force. Then came Australia's acerbic, unpredictable Prime Minister Edward Gough Whitlam. Only two months before, Whitlam had sought an invitation to the White House but had been snubbed in apparent retaliation for his criticism of American bombing in North Vietnam. Now he was received like an old friend. Then it was Japan's Prime Minister Kakuei Tanaka, whom the President welcomed on the South Lawn "as an equal partner, working for a cause to which we are equally devoted, the cause of progress for the whole world and peace for the whole world." Finally, on August 2, came Alfred-Bernard Bongo, president of Gabon.

Bongo's visit was the most instructive of all. His eight-day trip was a private one, sponsored by large

American corporations which did business in the tiny West African republic. In Los Angeles he was the guest of Bethlehem Steel, which had a large iron concession in Gabon. In Pittsburgh, his host was U.S. Steel, which operates a giant manganese mine in Gabon. In San Francisco, the check was picked up by Gulf Oil, which had tapped into Gabon's vast oil reserves. (CREEP, at least, knew all about Gabon's oil; Ashland Oil's illegal corporate contribution to Nixon's campaign had been laundered through its Gabon subsidiary and the company—which had close ties to the CIA—gave $200,000 in under-the-table "contributions" to Gabonese officials, including $150,000 to none other than Alfred-Bernard Bongo.) When the White House learned that Bongo was coming, it insisted that he pay a call on the President. There were no burning issues between Gabon and the United States, nothing that demanded a heart-to-heart talk. But Bongo was another "world leader" to add to Nixon's impressive midsummer roster.

What one might call the Bongo Stratagem had worked well for Nixon before. Through most of the 1972 campaign—while his agents were burglarizing the Watergate and sending unordered pizzas to Muskie —he was off in Peking and Moscow seeking a "generation of peace." This was more than mere stratagem, of course. The rapprochement with China and the continuing détente with the Soviet Union were long-overdue items on America's world agenda; and Nixon had always felt more comfortable charting bold steps in foreign policy than wrestling with unemployment or urban redevelopment. Nevertheless, he knew full well that his "peace-maker" image had been the best antidote to his Watergate problems and now—tangled in the telltale tapes—he invoked that old magic again. Toasting Prime Minister Tanaka on August 1, Nixon said a nation should not "be remembered only for the petty, little, indecent things that seem to obsess us. . . . Let others spend their time dealing with the murky, small, unimportant, vicious little things. We have spent our time and will spend our time in building a better world."

But scarcely four days after he had chatted with Alfred-Bernard Bongo about world trade and African unity, another visitor arrived in the Oval Office bearing word of a matter much closer to home. On the morning of Monday, August 6, Elliot Richardson came to tell Nixon that his Vice President, Spiro Agnew, was under investigation for accepting payoffs from Maryland architects and engineers.

The President had heard intimations of the new scandal from his aides. But this was his first detailed briefing, and he was aghast. Later, according to one assistant, he "hit the ceiling." For a few hours, Nixon may have hoped that this scandal—like Watergate in its early stages—could be contained. But within twenty-four hours *The Wall Street Journal* and *The Washington Post* had both printed major stories on the "far-ranging criminal investigation."

The Agnew affair must have been particularly depressing for Nixon that muggy, miserable August. Just when he had hoped to soar into the ethereal realm of mega-politics, he had been brought back to the murky, vicious little things of American micro-politics. He was being dragged into the kind of local scandal usually reserved for mayors and county commissioners and members of zoning boards. Moreover, it was a scandal with its roots in real-estate transactions, a subject on which he felt personally vulnerable. Although the new scandal was only indirectly related to Watergate, it tainted the administration with an element of old-fashioned graft which could only weaken Nixon's position further. And it subjected his embattled Presidency to a bewildering variety of new pressures.

The scandal had been building quietly for almost eighteen months, ever since an Internal Revenue Service team turned its attention to Baltimore County, that arc of go-go suburbia exploding around Baltimore city. The county had more than doubled its population since 1950. This meant acres of new tract housing that needed sewer, water, and road connections; towering apartment buildings that required rezoning; expressways and bridges that needed engineering studies. All this, in turn, required an army of architects, engineers, road builders, consultants, real-estate agents, contractors, and subcontractors. Operating on the assumption that "where the action is, the corruption is sure to follow"—and fueled with a couple of anonymous tips—the IRS team began looking into the relationship between these men-on-the-make and county officials.

The revenue men weren't quite sure what they were looking for, but by the winter of 1972–73 they had generated enough intriguing rumors and hints to call U.S. Attorney George Beall into the case. On December 5 a federal grand jury was impaneled with the double assignment of looking into police corruption in Baltimore city and political corruption in Baltimore County. On January 4 Beall's office subpoenaed a hundred and twenty filing cabinets' worth of documents from the county government and stacks of other material from the twenty-seven firms doing the most business with the county. Most of these were construction companies, but one was an architectural firm —Gaudreau, Inc. And there, in Gaudreau's books, the IRS team found what it was looking for: suspicious traces of cash. The company ledgers showed that when Gaudreau got payments for county work, it would invariably issue a check to a corporate officer for about 5 per cent of that payment. Such bonuses were an ideal way of generating free cash. (Greyhound, Carnation, and other companies used the system to develop cash for their corporate contributions to political campaigns.) The agents concluded that the company was probably kicking back 5 per cent of its fees to the county, a time-honored Maryland custom but one rarely documented by records. Paul Gaudreau, the company president, promptly admitted that he had been paying off William E. Fornoff, the county's administrative officer, in exchange for contracts.

Recognizing that the paydirt might lie with architectural and engineering firms rather than construction outfits, Beall's men issued another wave of subpoenas on January 11. One of these went to a firm called Matz, Childs and Associates. Neither John Childs nor Lester Matz was at work that day, but on Monday, January 15—the day the five Watergate burglars were pleading guilty in Washington—Matz got his subpoena and rushed to his lawyer, Joseph H. H. Kaplan, in the distinguished old Baltimore firm of Venable, Baetjer & Howard. Matz told Kaplan that he too had been kicking back 5 per cent of his fees. Kaplan reassured Matz that he was not the target of the investigation: clearly the prosecutors were after bigger game. Kaplan advised his client to cooperate.

MATZ: Do I have to tell them everything I know?
KAPLAN: Yes, you do.
MATZ: In that case, I can't cooperate.
KAPLAN: Why not?
MATZ: Because I have been paying off the Vice President.

The young lawyer sat stunned as Matz told him that he had begun paying off Spiro Agnew in 1962, the year Agnew became Baltimore County executive; that those cash payments—in exchange for engineering contracts—had continued when Agnew became Maryland's governor in 1967; and that he had kept up the payoffs even after Agnew became Vice President.

At his client's insistence, Joe Kaplan kept his explosive secret for the next few months. But rumors were already circulating in Baltimore that Beall's investigation was now focusing on Agnew. From a political standpoint, this seemed unlikely. Not only was George Beall a Republican, he was the younger brother of J. Glenn Beall, Jr., the Republican junior senator from Maryland. It seemed inconceivable that the younger Beall would launch an investigation of a Republican Vice President. In fact, Beall and his IRS team had nothing on Agnew at that time. If they had a specific target it was the logical political one—Dale Anderson, a Democrat then serving as Baltimore County executive.

Yet the rumors persisted. On February 6 Beall drove to Washington to assure Attorney General Richard Kleindienst that they were false. Three days later Spiro Agnew telephoned Kleindienst to say that the Baltimore investigation might embarrass him if the press got ahold of it. He warned that one of Beall's assistants —Barnet D. Skolnik—was politically motivated. (Skolnik had worked in Ed Muskie's campaign.) Kleindienst passed Agnew's concerns on to Beall, who, in turn, told his three young assistants: Skolnik, Russell T. "Tim" Baker, Jr., and Ronald S. Liebman. When Baker heard this, he told his colleagues, "We're going to get Agnew." The others guffawed.

Through the early spring Beall and his assistants pressed for more evidence from engineers and architects in Baltimore County. They used an old prosecutorial technique known in the trade as "dealing up." Starting with minor figures in the scandal, the prosecutor promises a degree of immunity in return for information that can help convict higher-ups. Implicit in this technique is the warning that the government needs only so much information; when it gets what it wants, no more deals will be available. The Baltimore office had a notable record of convicting corrupt politicians with this method: Speaker of the Maryland House A. Gordon Boone, Congressman Thomas Johnson, U.S. Senator Daniel B. Brewster. Some years before, the lawyers in the office joked about drawing up a coat of arms: "deal up" in Latin with a stool pigeon on a field of yellow. And, down through the years, they liked to make their point with a striking metaphor. "The boat is at the dock. Passengers are boarding. But nobody knows how many seats are left or when the boat will leave. Those who don't get on board now may be left behind." Sometimes they said, "The train is at the platform." Sometimes they said, "The plane is at the gate." But generally—perhaps because they lived on the Chesapeake Bay, which is filled with pleasure boats every weekend—they preferred, "The boat is at the dock."

But Matz, Childs and Jerome B. Wolff, another Baltimore engineer, resisted such pressures. So Barney

Skolnik transferred his full attentions to William Fornoff. If they could "turn" the county's administrative officer, the other witnesses would fall like ripe fruit off a branch. The battle for Fornoff was a classic. For his lawyer was Stephen Sachs, Beall's predecessor as U.S. attorney and a master at precisely this kind of "dealing up." Indeed, Skolnik had learned much of his technique from Sachs and so theirs was a struggle between the master and his most talented pupil. At the start Sachs demanded total immunity for his client; Skolnik flatly refused. For weeks they fenced and feinted. Finally, on the afternoon of May 4, the door to Beall's office opened a crack and a hand appeared—waving a handkerchief. It was Sachs's surrender signal. Fornoff had been "turned."

Meanwhile, Baker and Liebman continued negotiations with the others. The stakes were getting higher. On May 18—during an otherwise routine call to Baker —Joe Kaplan finally played his strongest card.

KAPLAN: Mr. Matz, of course, has information about the Vice President which I assume you don't want to hear about or pursue.

BAKER: What do you mean? How can you say that?

KAPLAN: Well, I assumed that since Beall is a Republican he wouldn't want to hear something about a Republican Vice President. . . .

BAKER: Well, you're wrong. That's an insult to George and an insult to this office. Go back and tell your client that we want his information whether it's on Agnew or the Pope.

For several weeks they heard no more from Kaplan. Then, on June 4, Fornoff appeared in court and pleaded guilty to one count of "impeding the enforcement" of federal law by paying off a public official. The boat was clearly filling up. The next morning Kaplan called to say, "My client had decided that it is in the national interest for him to cooperate."

Several more weeks elapsed before the terms of the plea-bargaining with Matz and Childs were set. Finally, on June 21, Kaplan and another Baltimore attorney,

Arnold Weiner, met with the prosecutors to recite their clients' full story. It was quite a story.

Matz had become friendly with Agnew in 1960, when the future Vice President was still only chairman of the Baltimore County Zoning Board of Appeals. Over the next four years Agnew introduced him to J. Walter Jones, an Annapolis banker, and the three of them joined in business transactions. One was the purchase of a 107-acre tract in Anne Arundel County which was to be the site of a new Chesapeake Bay bridge. Agnew was also a director of Jones's bank—the Chesapeake National Bank—and several of his partners in the land deal were also directors. After Agnew's election as county executive, Jones told Matz that the two of them were going to make a lot of money. A short while later he asked Matz to prepare a chart showing how much money engineers could be expected to kick back on contracts. Matz came up with the 5 per cent figure. Jones then told Matz he would be expected to pay 5 per cent on engineering contracts and 2.5 per cent on surveying contracts. From then on, Matz would tell Jones what contracts he wanted and would hand him the requisite kickbacks. Later Matz began to suspect Jones of skimming money off the top and arranged with Agnew to make his payments directly: Agnew agreed. But Matz fell far behind in his payments. Trying to catch up, he made a large cash payment—$20,000—to Agnew at the State House in Annapolis in July 1968. In 1969 he delivered another $10,000 in Agnew's office in the basement of the White House, a visit that left Matz "shaken" because he had just made a payoff to the Vice President of the United States. In 1971 he paid Agnew another $2500 in return for a federal contract. In 1972 Jones pressed Matz for yet another $10,000. When Matz complained to Agnew, the Vice President said, "Say you gave at the office." (Jones has steadfastly denied Matz's version of his role.)*

---

*Walter Jones has never been indicted for his role in the Agnew case. However, he has been charged in a nine-count indictment involving a $10,000 corporate campaign contribution from the Singer Company to the 1972 Nixon-Agnew re-election campaign.

All that spring of 1973 Agnew got warnings of the trouble brewing in Baltimore. Matz and Wolff passed some alarms through an intermediary. Other warnings came—again through an intermediary—from I. H. "Bud" Hammerman II, a real-estate developer and investment banker who had also served as a conduit for many of the payoffs to Agnew. These men hoped the Vice President could somehow turn off the investigation. (Agnew never tried to halt the entire inquiry —that would have reeked of political favoritism—but he did what he could to take the heat off himself.) In April, realizing that he needed a lawyer, Agnew turned to Chuck Colson, who had left the White House a month before to resume the private practice of law. The two men had become friendly during the previous few years—they shared a natural pugnacity—but Colson was busy preparing his own legal defense on Watergate. So he suggested one of his partners, Judah H. Best. All during the spring and summer, Best kept pestering George Beall to find out what the Baltimore prosecutors had on the Vice President. Beall kept saying they had nothing—which was true until Matz got on board in mid-June. Then, on July 10, Beall told Best that he had nothing more to say: when and if the U.S. attorney's office had any news it would be in touch. This was a clear signal that Best's client was, at last, a prime target of the investigation.

By early June the case against Agnew was building so rapidly that Beall felt he had to inform the new attorney general, Elliot Richardson. On June 12 he went to Washington and told Richardson briefly about the investigation. After Matz's lawyers spilled their full story on June 21, Beall—this time accompanied by his three assistants—went back for a much longer session on July 3.

The attorney general was a preoccupied man that day. He kept rushing out to take telephone calls from the Western White House. That morning, the *Los Angeles Times* had carried a story saying that the special prosecutor's office was looking into Nixon's real-estate transactions, particularly the $1.5 million used to purchase San Clemente. First, Haig called from San

Clemente to say that the President was furious about the story. When Richardson asked Cox about it, the special prosecutor explained that he had merely asked his press officer to collect newspaper clippings on San Clemente after he was asked about it at a press conference (the press officer requested clippings from the *Los Angeles Times,* which apparently triggered the story). Richardson relayed this information to Haig, who said that Cox ought publicly to deny the story. At Richardson's suggestion, Cox drafted a denial. But when the attorney general called Haig back, the President's chief of staff said the proposed denial was inadequate. At that point, Nixon himself broke in to demand an unequivocal statement from Cox within an hour. (Cox later issued a denial. Ziegler—reflecting Nixon's mood—branded the original story "malicious, ill-founded, and scurrilous." The President's fury was another indication of his extreme sensitivity on anything relating to the financing of his real-estate transactions.)

The constant harassment of the attorney general by the White House that day made it difficult for the Baltimore prosecutors to get Richardson's attention. But finally they seized it. When Beall and Baker reviewed the evidence against Agnew, it was clear that whatever was going on with San Clemente and Key Biscayne, here was explicit, concrete evidence pointing to corruption in the highest levels of the federal government. The attorney general maintained his surface cool, but inside he felt "sick." He told Beall to press ahead with the investigation but to check with him before he granted any witnesses immunity from prosecution. Then he asked the question they had all been waiting for: "Do you think I ought to tell the President?" The Baltimore prosecutors were against it, because they feared the information would get back to Agnew, who could begin covering his tracks. Richardson, in turn, had just been given ample proof of Nixon's agitated state of mind and his extreme preoccupation with his own problems. The attorney general agreed to sit on the scandal for the time being.

Twice more during July the Baltimore team met with

Richardson, each time reporting new progress. (Two more prime suspects—Jerome Wolff and Allen Green, another Baltimore engineer—hopped on board during this period.) After their second meeting—on July 27 —Richardson felt he could no longer keep his information from the White House. He sketched out the situation briefly for Haig and asked for an appointment with Nixon. And on August 1 the prosecutors formally notified Judah Best that Agnew was under investigation for tax evasion, bribery, and extortion.

After Richardson met with the President on August 6, Agnew went to see Nixon and assured him of his total innocence. That same day, the President—who could never fire anyone in person—sent Haig to suggest to Agnew that he might consider resigning. But Agnew was having none of that. On August 8 he called a news conference. Some two hundred reporters jammed into the auditorium on the fourth floor of the EOB. All three networks covered it "live." Agnew began by labeling the reports of his corrupt activities as "damned lies, false and scurrilous and malicious." Asked by one reporter whether he had "ever received money for your personal use from any person, contractor, doing business with the state of Maryland or the federal government," the Vice President answered unblinkingly, "Absolutely not." He said he had "nothing to hide" and promised full cooperation with the investigators.

It was an impressive performance and contrasted sharply with the stance of the President, burrowed into defensive isolation from the press. Nixon had not held a news conference for nearly five months. When a reporter asked Agnew why he was willing to meet them when the President was not, he replied, "The best answer I can give you to that is that President Nixon hasn't received a letter from the United States attorney telling him he's under investigation. . . . And I think the matter of how President Nixon is going to respond to the matters that are being discussed currently regarding him is a matter for his own determination, and I want to repeat I have absolutely total confidence in him, and the fact that his response is going to be entirely satisfactory." It was a curious turnabout—the beleaguered Vice President expressing "total confidence" in the President, a backhanded way of reminding the world that if he was in trouble then so was his boss. And it only underlined the contrast between the darkly suspicious, furtive President and the disarmingly frank, straightforward Vice President.

From the start, that had been one of Spiro Agnew's charms—the notion that he was somehow different from other politicians. "Agnew says what a lot of politicians are thinking and are afraid to say," a Pittsburgh lawyer told the Gallup Poll. "I wish I had the guts to say the things he does," said an Idaho maintenance man. And the Cherokee Nation inducted him as "the Chief Who Speaks Straight." Some of his fabled frankness may have been no more than the license accorded the administration's hatchetman: "he can deliver a knee to the groin while the President can only give the back of his hand," one Republican leader noted. And some may have been sheer insensitivity, which permitted him to call a Nisei newsman a "fat Jap" or compare "querulous" American black leaders unfavorably with African dictators. But, more than his critics liked to admit, Agnew's strident voice often turned out to be the vox populi. *He spoke for many ordinary Americans, because—far more than the tortured Nixon—Spiro Agnew was a relentlessly ordinary man. Born in Baltimore city, he moved as a young veteran to Loch Raven in Baltimore County, a quintessential postwar suburb, and he remained a suburbanite in outlook, habits, and tastes. He liked pizza, James Michener's books, Duke Ellington's records, sing-along sessions around the piano with songs from* The Sound of Music, *and visits to the Baltimore Colts locker room, where, one Colt said, "he knows everybody by their first name and generally has a word for most of the guys." When he became governor in 1967, he built a Loch Raven style "club basement" in the governor's mansion, where he played billiards with his bodyguards. When he became Vice President and could socialize with just about anyone he liked, he chose Frank Sinatra and Bob Hope. He frequently stayed at Sinatra's Palm Springs house, playing golf, tennis, and "horsing around." Hope had his writers produce jokes for Agnew and drew him into "the circuit"—a small group of the comedian's closest friends whom he called at one or two in the morning with the latest gags. One circuit member concedes that most of the jokes that hummed along those night lines were "what you'd call dirty; Bob loves a good dirty joke and so does the Vice President." Like Howard Hunt, he was soon to pour his secret fantasies into a novel: in which the son of Theofraste Anagnostopoulos was transformed into Vice President Porter Newton Canfield, a "wealthy and aristocratic Ivy League politician" who has an affair with the lithe, luscious thirty-four-year-old secretary of health, education, and welfare ("she was a forbidden chocolate candy—one he found more and more difficult to resist"), and was duped by Iranian militants determined to trigger a Soviet-American confrontation. But his real indiscretions were more mundane. Bud Hammerman and J. Walter Jones—Agnew's Rebozo and Abplanalp—showered him with expensive gifts. Jones built a wine cellar into the basement of the governor's mansion. Hammerman bought him suits, a new car, even jewelry to give a secretary. The Sheraton Park Hotel (owned by ITT) gave him a substantial "celebrity discount" for his suite, and Joseph Rash, an executive of Food Fair Stores, Inc., sent him 273 weekly shipments of groceries. Those who knew Agnew well say these and the more serious transgressions for which he would soon be charged were less signs of his overweening pride and ambition than evidence that his priorities had not changed much since his days in Baltimore County. "The Veep isn't interested in being President," one of his aides told Richard Whalen in 1970. "He's interested in making money. He feels that he owes his kids an estate and that he'd better start making some real dough soon."*

The day before Agnew's press conference Henry Petersen testified to the Senate Watergate Committee.

Fresh from a vacation aboard his boat on the Chesapeake Bay, the assistant attorney general was in a tough, combative mood, determined to defend his performance during the Watergate investigation. "I've got to get something off my chest," he shouted at the senators. "I resent the appointment of a special prosecutor. Damn it, I think it's a reflection on me and the Department of Justice. . . . We would have broken that case wide open."

Thus, Petersen was determined to prove himself when Richardson told him Nixon wanted him to assess the Agnew investigation. This came as no surprise. Nixon regarded Petersen as the one man in the entire Watergate matter who had dealt with him fairly ("Petersen, bless his soul, has been a valuable man to us," he told Ziegler on June 4). Others, of course, believed Petersen had been more than fair. But Petersen was a proud man who felt he had been at the Justice Department "too long to jeopardize my reputation for anyone." So he plunged into a full review of the Agnew inquiry, interviewing the lawyers, arranging for Matz and Wolff to undergo lie-detector tests (they passed). On August 17 the case against Agnew was strengthened still further when Bud Hammerman came aboard with new, highly damaging material. Soon the evidence began leaking into the press, climaxed by an August 27 *Time* magazine story which quoted a Justice Department official as saying, "The evidence is so strong that the case must be taken to trial."

Just as Nixon had used leaks from the Ervin committee and the FBI to discredit the Watergate investigations, so Agnew seized on these new leaks to charge that he was being railroaded by the Justice Department. At a news conference on August 21 Agnew called it a "clear and outrageous effort to influence the outcome of possible grand jury deliberations." He demanded that Richardson halt the leaks and punish the leakers. If anything, Richardson was even angrier than Agnew, for he was determined that his inquiry not be sabotaged. The Baltimore prosecutors, in turn, suspected that the leaks were coming from Agnew's own camp, in an effort to discredit the investigation.

Others believed that it was Nixon forces who were leaking information to force Agnew out of office. For by then the President clearly wanted the tainted Vice President to resign. He was treading carefully in public, for fear of antagonizing Agnew's conservative constituency—which Nixon would need in his own Watergate battles. (At his August 22 news conference, he stuck publicly with his Vice President: "My confidence in his integrity has not been shaken and in fact has been strengthened by his courageous conduct.") And for a time, some at the White House argued that the new scandal at least provided a diversion from Watergate and the struggle over the tapes. "As long as they're talking about Agnew they're not talking about Nixon," one aide remarked. But by Labor Day Nixon had concluded that the Vice President was far more an albatross than a decoy. Agnew had to go—and quickly.

But Nixon still couldn't deliver the message himself. That was left to Al Haig and Fred Buzhardt, who called on the Vice President on September 10 and this time left nothing to his imagination. The message got through. The next day Buzhardt let Richardson know that Agnew's lawyers were ready to start talking. Within a few hours Beall told his assistants to prepare for "the most momentous plea bargaining in United States history."

The bargaining, which began in earnest on September 13, was an intricate balancing of multiple self-interests. Agnew's chief concern was to stay out of prison. He was a proud man—proud of the way he had climbed in the world, proud of his nice clothes, his good grooming, his well-placed friends. Prison not only would strip him of all this, it would be the ultimate shame, a disgrace too mortifying to contemplate. Very early he made clear to his lawyers that he would do almost anything to avoid it.

The Baltimore prosecutors had various priorities. Some pressed for a prison term ("Agnew is a bad man," argued Baker. "He must go to jail"). Others wanted a maximum admission of guilt. All wanted desperately to hold on to the case, to keep it from being appropriated by the attorney general or, worse yet, by the special prosecutor. For them, the chase had become a personal one; they wanted to get their man.

Henry Petersen craved vindication. He wanted to show the world that he was a tough, honest prosecutor who could be trusted with momentous matters. At times, he was deeply suspicious of Agnew's lawyers (even believing that Judah Best was a double agent, reporting on the negotiations to Colson and Nixon). But, ultimately, he could not shake the career bureaucrat's deference to authority. Alone of all the prosecutors, he believed the President should be told whatever he wanted to know about the case (despite fears that he would pass it on to Agnew, as he had passed secret grand jury data to his aides the spring before). And Petersen was prepared for greater leniency than the others, out of respect for the office of the Vice President. "The man is the goddamn Vice President of the United States!" he shouted at Skolnik one day. "What are you trying to do? Get him to crawl on his belly?"

Elliot Richardson wanted one thing above all else: Spiro Agnew's resignation. Having seen at close hand how unstable Nixon was, Richardson believed that Agnew had to be removed immediately from the line of succession. "The President is under tremendous strain," he would say. "Anything could happen. Do you want a Vice President whose honesty is under open attack to succeed him?" He was willing to sacrifice almost anything—prison, admissions of guilt, or other sanctions—to get Agnew out of office. But there were other considerations, too. Elliot Richardson was an ambitious man who clearly wanted to be President himself one day. He and his trio of close aides—J. T. Smith, Richard G. Darman, and Jonathan Moore—were determined to avoid any misstep that might sap his growing stature. In an administration soiled by a widening stain of arrogance and deception, Richardson had to keep himself "clean." Yet he could not show himself too eager to remove Agnew—for fear that he would seem to be clearing his own way to the Presidency in 1976. He had to strike a delicate balance between prosecutorial zeal and judicious moderation.

These differing perspectives clashed in a seven-hour strategy session at the Justice Department on September 15. Through that hot Saturday the arguments raged among the ten-man working group which had now taken charge of the Agnew affair (Richardson, Deputy Attorney General William Ruckelshaus, Petersen, Smith, Darman, Moore, Beall, Skolnik, Baker and Liebman). Finally, the group reached a rough consensus: that if Agnew resigned, he might be let off with a simple guilty or *nolo contendere* (not contested) plea to one count of income-tax evasion, as long as he admitted accepting the payoffs.

But when this position was relayed to Agnew, he balked at admitting his role in the bribery. On September 20 he complained bitterly to Nixon that Richardson was being vindictive. That afternoon Buzhardt and Haig warned Richardson that his "tough" terms could not be allowed to stand in the way of Agnew's quick departure. Richardson discussed the terms again with his aides and the next day called Buzhardt back to say he was standing firm: it was the minimum the Justice Department could live with. Richardson expected an explosion from the Oval Office, but instead Haig telephoned back to say that Nixon now agreed. Apparently the beleaguered President decided he could not afford a break with his attorney general.

Then, on September 22, Agnew found a convenient excuse to break off the negotiations. That morning *The Washington Post* ran an article reporting that the Vice President and the Justice Department were engaged in what "could be described as plea bargaining." Agnew was "livid," convinced that the Justice Department had leaked the story to weaken his position. Under other circumstances, he might have swallowed his anger. But, confronted with an implacable Richardson, he decided to take the offensive, hoping to make his opponents back down.

Three days later Agnew launched phase one of his offensive. In a letter to Speaker Carl Albert, he asked the House of Representatives to conduct a full investigation of the allegations against him. It was a shrewd move—appealing over the heads of the Baltimore grand jury to a forum likely to be far more understanding of his actions; after all, many House members had accepted "campaign contributions" from companies that wanted favors from them. Moreover, it was a cunning challenge to Nixon himself. For, without even mentioning the horrid word, it raised the specter of impeachment. This posed an unfortunate precedent for the White House. Once the creaking legal machinery had been geared up for use against the Vice President, Congress might find that it still worked quite well and could be used against the President. Carl Albert promptly turned down the Vice President's request, but the threat of "the impeachment track" was to haunt Richard Nixon.

On September 28 Agnew launched the second phase of his offensive, which worried the President and his lawyers just as much. A day after the prosecutors began calling witnesses before the Baltimore grand jury, the Vice President's lawyers filed a motion asking the federal district court there to prohibit the Justice Department from presenting any more evidence to the jury. The motion was based on two grounds: that news coverage of the investigation had deprived Agnew of "all hope of a fair hearing on the merits"; and "the Constitution forbids that the Vice President be indicted or convicted in any criminal court." The first ground was a bold one, but it was the second which worried Nixon's men. By raising the question of the indictability of a sitting Vice President, it implicitly raised the question of whether a sitting President might be indicted, too. With the tapes wending their way through the courts, this was not an issue Nixon wanted to see posed now.

The third punch in Agnew's frenetic flurry came the next day in Los Angeles. Speaking to the National Federation of Republican Women, the Vice President focused on the news leaks and particularly those which he traced to the Justice Department. He named no names, but his chief target was clearly Henry Petersen, who had been quoted by Fred Graham of CBS as saying, "We've got the evidence [on Agnew]; we've got it cold." Now Agnew told the Republican women that "conduct of high individuals in the Department of Justice, particularly the conduct of the chief of the criminal investigation division of that department, is unprofessional and malicious and outrageous. . . . Individuals in the upper professional echelons of the Department of Justice have been severely stung by their ineptness in the prosecution of the Watergate case. They have been so severely stung that the President and the attorney general have found it necessary to appoint a special prosecutor and they are trying to recoup their reputation at my expense. I'm a big trophy. And one of those individuals has made some very severe mistakes, serious mistakes. . . . He needs me to reinstate his reputation as a tough and courageous and hard-nosed prosecutor. Well, I'm not going to fall down and be his victim, I assure you."

The Republican women loved it. Frank Sinatra loved it. Agnew's staff loved it. Old Spiro was socking it to them again. His press secretary, J. Marsh Thomson, predicted more of the same when Agnew spoke to a $125-a-plate dinner of the United Republican Fund in Chicago on October 4.

But a funny thing happened to the Vice President on his way to Chicago. He finally realized there was no way out. The message came in several ways. First, the President publicly supported his old ally Henry Petersen, telling reporters that the assistant attorney general was "an individual who has served both administrations with distinction for many, many years." Then, Haig passed a warning to Arthur Sohmer, Agnew's right-hand man: no more attacks on Petersen and other administration officials or there could be no deal. Lastly, despite the applause in Los Angeles and the encouragement of his aides, his fighting speech aroused no widespread support. The Agnew Defense Fund had drawn only $310 in a week.

So when Agnew addressed the gathering of Midwest Republicans in the Imperial Ballroom of the Conrad Hilton on October 4, his speech was anything but the rousing polemic that had been expected. Turning to the large delegation of national reporters, he told them, "Tonight is not going to be an X-rated political show. It's just going to be PG. So if you have to go someplace, go." And then he added a line which was to puzzle and intrigue reporters and politicians for days to come:

"A candle is only so long before it burns out."

If Agnew's fighting spirit had not already burned out, it certainly did the next day when he returned to Washington only to discover that the Justice Department had cut the last link between his own fate and the President's. That morning Solicitor General Robert H. Bork filed a response to Agnew's suit, arguing that although a President could not be indicted while in office, a Vice President could. If upheld by the courts, this argument would have put Nixon and Agnew in two separate boats and would have left the President little reason to bail out the Vice President.

This may have been the brief that broke Agnew's back. He and Judah Best agreed they had no choice but to resume the plea bargaining. Best telephoned Buzhardt who was at Key Biscayne, and that evening flew to Florida for a conference. The next morning Best told Richardson that Agnew was ready to accept essentially the same deal the Justice Department had offered two weeks before. Meanwhile a meeting was arranged for Monday, October 8, at which Agnew's attorneys and the Justice Department team could seal the deal with Judge Walter E. Hoffman. The meeting took place in Room 208 of the Olde Colony Motor Lodge in Alexandria.

(For a scandal that takes its name from a hotel-apartment complex, it is perhaps appropriate that so many of Watergate's gripping scenes were played out in motels, hotels, restaurants, and airport lounges. Much of the action, of course, took place across the street at the Howard Johnson Motor Lodge. Magruder heard of the break-in while eating breakfast at the Polo Lounge of the Beverly Hills Hotel. Martha Mitchell was held captive at the Newporter Inn in the days after the break-in. Haldeman, Ehrlichman, and Dean met at the La

Costa Resort Hotel to plan the cover-up. Liddy and Hunt—who traveled widely and stayed first-class wherever they went—lived at the Beverly Wilshire Hotel while they masterminded the burglary of Dr. Lewis Fielding's office. It was in a room there that they discussed the break-in at Hank Greenspun's office with Ralph Winte. Kalmbach met Greenspun at the Sahara Hotel in Las Vegas to discuss the Hughes money, which was probably paid as a *quid pro quo* for a revised Justice Department ruling on purchase of the Dunes Hotel. Kalmbach almost always stayed at Washington's Madison Hotel, where Chotiner and Nelson met him to reaffirm AMPI's $2-million pledge to the Nixon campaign; where Ulasewicz came to arrange his alias and *modus operandi* with Kalmbach; and where Rebozo and Danner talked about returning the Hughes money. John Dean couldn't remember whether he met Kalmbach in the Mayflower Hotel or the Mayflower Coffee Shop of the Statler Hilton Hotel. Kalmbach and Raine passed money for Governor Brewer's campaign against Wallace to couriers in the lobby of New York's Sherry-Netherland Hotel. Andreas passed cash to Dahlberg on the golf course of the Sea View Hotel in Bal Harbour. Hunt and Liddy met Segretti at the Frolics Motel in Miami Beach, and later Hunt conferred with Segretti at the Sheraton Four Ambassadors Hotel in Miami. Butterfield and Lilly met twice to pass a briefcase full of cash in the lobby of the Key Bridge Marriott Motor Hotel—J. Willard Marriott was a major contributor to Nixon's campaign and twice chairman of his inaugural committee. ITT's pledge for the 1972 convention in San Diego was contingent on Nixon's use of the new Harbor Island Hotel as his headquarters. Ulasewicz left hush money in lockers at Washington's National Airport for Liddy and Mrs. Hunt, who was allegedly carrying money for investment in Chicago Holiday Inns when her plane crashed. Ehrlichman hired Caulfield in the American Airlines VIP lounge at La Guardia Airport. Paul Alagia met the AMPI leaders at 4:00 a.m. in the lobby of the Louisville Airport. And the day after the Watergate break-in, Liddy shredded his treasured collection of hotel soap wrappers. Evidently, Watergate was not the kind of thing you wanted to bring home to wife or mother.)

Judge Hoffman sat at the head of the coffee table in Room 208. Best and Agnew's other two lawyers—Jay H. Topkis and Martin London—sat on chairs on one side of the table and Petersen, Beall, and Skolnik on the couch across from them. For several hours they reviewed the elements of the deal. The one major point that remained to be resolved was the sentence. Richardson wanted to avoid a Justice Department recommendation against prison if possible—he preferred that to be the judge's decision. But Agnew's lawyers wanted a commitment, and the judge wouldn't give it without a recommendation from Richardson. Ultimately, at an October 9 meeting in the Justice Department, Richardson agreed to make the recommendation.

At 2:05 p.m., on October 10, the Vice President's resignation was delivered—as the law required—to Secretary of State Henry Kissinger. "Dear Mr. Secretary," it read. "I hereby resign the Office of Vice President of the United States, effective immediately. Sincerely, Spiro T. Agnew." A few minutes later, Spiro Agnew stood before Judge Hoffman in Baltimore district court, pleaded no contest to one charge of income-tax evasion, and accepted a sentence of three years of unsupervised probation and a $10,000 fine.*

In selecting Agnew's replacement, Nixon made a show of soliciting advice from Republicans around the country, but apparently his list was a short one from the start: John Connally, Governor Ronald Reagan of California, New York Governor Nelson Rockefeller,

---

*Some of the other participants in the Agnew affair received much stiffer sentences than the Vice President did. I. H. Hammerman pleaded guilty to obstructing tax laws and was sentenced to eighteen months in prison (he is appealing). Allen Green pleaded guilty to the same charge, was sentenced to twelve months in prison, and was released after serving four months. Eugene Y. Hsi, another Baltimore engineer, pleaded guilty to lying to a grand jury about the payoffs. He was sentenced to six months in prison. Hsi said he had lied because "I knew it was going to lead to Mr. Agnew. In June 1973, when I lied, he was my political idol. He was Vice President of the United States."

Elliot Richardson, and House Minority Leader Gerald Ford. Richardson quickly took himself out of the running—the executioner could not replace his victim—and that left four.

On the evening of October 12 Nixon summoned Washington dignitaries—the cabinet, congressional leaders, members of the diplomatic corps—to the East Room of the White House. Chamber music rang through the brightly lighted rooms while the guests chatted excitedly in front of the darting television cameras. There was a curious air of celebration; Governor Tom McCall of Oregon called it "a hoedown, a shivaree." The President maintained the air of unreality in his speech, never once mentioning the departed Agnew or the events which had driven him from office. Then he announced—though television had already relayed word of his intention—that he was nominating Gerald Ford as Vice President of the United States.

He had just climbed out of the backyard pool and the dinner steaks were on the grill when the telephone rang with word that he was the President's choice. There was a muscular normality about Jerry Ford which many found reassuring after the bizarrerie of the past two years. He reminded many Americans of the husky young athlete who sat next to them in their high-school geometry class—none too bright but honest, hard-working, and brimming with good-natured vigor. Indeed, Ford had started as an athlete—a star center for the University of Michigan's undefeated national championship teams of 1932 and 1933 (he was called "Junie" because he darted about the field like a June bug). His sterling performance in the East-West Shrine Game of 1935 won him a bid to play professional ball for Curly Lambeau's Green Bay Packers, but, instead, he accepted an offer from Yale University to be assistant line coach, junior varsity coach, and coach of the Yale boxing team. Then he set to work seeking admission to Yale Law School. The faculty there was not enthusiastic about taking a football coach, but they let him try two courses. Ultimately, Ford graduated in the top third of his class. After serving in the Navy during World War II, he practiced law for two years in Grand Rapids, Michigan, before Senator Arthur H. Vandenberg, the Republican party's leading internationalist, encouraged him to challenge his district's isolationist Republican congressman in the primary. Ford beat the incumbent, then handily defeated his Democratic opponent. As he won re-election repeatedly, he became a ranking member of the House Appropriations Committee and the leading Republican expert on defense budgets (he favored big ones). Following the crushing Republican defeat in the 1964 congressional elections, Ford deposed the aging House minority leader, Charles A. Halleck, and soon proved himself a hard-nosed partisan. He scrapped repeatedly with Lyndon Johnson, but he supported Richard Nixon even when many other Republicans deserted him: on the Vietnam war, construction of the supersonic transport, bans on school busing, and the nominations of Haynsworth and Carswell to the Supreme Court. In retaliation for Carswell's defeat, he led the 1970 crusade for the impeachment of Justice William O. Douglas, largely on the grounds that he had let parts of his controversial book Points of Rebellion *appear in* Evergreen *magazine. "For a Supreme Court justice to be reprinted in that magazine!" he told a reporter. "Have you seen* Evergreen? *Several pages prior to his article there is as much hard-core pornography of a man and woman as you can get."*

That same week, a satisfied Elliot Richardson, looking back on his maneuvering in the Agnew affair, told Al Haig, "This reminds me of the first hard decision I had to make after D-Day. A guy stepped on an antipersonnel mine behind the doom line on the beach. Somebody had to go in after him. The sand was blown and drifted and there was no way of knowing when a mine might blow up under you. So you put your feet down gingerly. It was a very delicate maneuver."

Within two weeks, Richardson would have reason to recall those blithe words and wonder how he could ever have been so foolhardy as to go wandering through an uncharted mine field.

13

FIRESTORM

Your perception of national interest is so different from mine.
—Nixon to Richardson,
October 20, 1973

There was a clanking and a rumbling, the sense of monumental forces shifting underfoot, shaking the legal bedrock of the land. All summer and early fall the marbled halls and courtrooms of Washington rang with echoes of Montesquieu, Bentham, and Locke, the clang of lofty doctrines like "separation of powers" and "due process," the weight of precedents like *Brady* v. *Maryland* and *Marbury* v. *Madison*. But through it all ran a kind of dread, the lawyers' recoil from ultimate measures, a fear of the constitutional apocalypse.

Seated in their black, padded chairs beneath white marble statues of Moses, Hammurabi, Solon, and Justinian, seven judges of the Court of Appeals for the District of Columbia heard Archibald Cox and Charles Alan Wright reargue the tapes case on September 11. Both lawyers were challenging Judge John Sirica's August 29 ruling that the nine tapes sought by the special prosecutor should first be handed over to Judge Sirica for excision of privileged material. But Wright soon demonstrated the depth of their differences. He spoke so softly that the judges had to crane forward to hear him, but what they heard was almost unprecedented in an American courtroom. The President's lawyer clearly suggested that Nixon might not heed an adverse judicial decision. "The tradition is very strong that judges should have the last word" on production of evidence, he said, "but in a government organized as ours is, there are times when that simply cannot be the case."

Two days later the Court of Appeals tried to draw back from the abyss. In a unanimous memorandum the judges urged the President and the special prosecutor to seek an out-of-court compromise. It proposed that the President voluntarily submit "portions" of the tapes to lawyers for each side who would agree between themselves what relevant material would go to the grand jury. The vaguely worded proposal left unclear whether the President himself would have carte blanche in deciding what material to exclude, or whether the special prosecutor would participate in that initial screening to make sure no vital evidence was suppressed. Fred Buzhardt and Cox met on September 17, 18, and 19 in an effort to hammer out a compromise. At one point, Cox did propose a plan under which a "third party" would play a role in verifying transcripts of the tapes—a suggestion that would soon come back to haunt him. But the negotiations foundered, and on September 20 both sides reported their failure to the court.

By then, the impasse between the President and the special prosecutor was more than merely legal. Nixon had never much cared for the idea of a truly independent prosecutor. He had resisted the concept when it was pressed on him by Richard Kleindienst in April. "The special prosecutor thing can only open other avenues potentially," he told John Erlichman, on April 14, who chimed in quickly, "I think it is folly." The next day Nixon said a special prosecutor would feel free to "tear the hell out of the place," that his appointment would "just put another loose cannon right there rolling around the deck." But after Kleindienst talked with him again about the plan, Nixon began to see some advantages in it. What appealed to him was not the concept of an independent prosecutor following the investigation wherever it might lead, but the idea of a respected figure who could validate what Nixon's own men in the Justice Department were doing. He explained all that to Bob Haldeman that afternoon:

NIXON: This is not to prosecute the case. A special prosecutor to look at the indictments to see that the indictments run to everybody they need to run to, so that it isn't just the President's men, you see.

HALDEMAN: In other words, he is above Silbert rather than replacing Silbert.

NIXON: Oh no. Silbert runs the case and that's all. But he is just in there for the purpose of examining all this to see that the indictments cover everybody.

HALDEMAN: Uh, huh. Well that does protect you a lot, because if they don't indict some of us then you have a cover-up problem. If you have a guy, then you have a basis—

NIXON: Then he goes out and says, "I have examined all of this, and now let's stop all this. These men are not guilty and these men are not indictable and these are."

HALDEMAN: Yeah.

And later in the same conversation, Nixon saw still another advantage: "The special prosecutor thing helps in another way," he said. "It gets one person between me and the whole thing." In other words, the special prosecutor would be a glorified Henry Petersen, posing as a buffer between the President and the case, seeming to guarantee a disinterested investigation, but actually keeping the reins on Earl Silbert and his men, preventing them from straying too far afield, and defending the narrow findings they brought in.

This remained Nixon's view of the job, when, in naming Elliot Richardson attorney general on April 20, he said, "I have instructed him that if he should consider it appropriate, he has the authority to name a special *supervising* prosecutor for matters arising out of the case" (author's italics). But Richardson apparently saw it quite differently. On May 7 he announced that, if confirmed, he would appoint a special prosecutor and give him "all the independence, authority, and staff support needed to carry out the tasks entrusted to him."

For a time, the different conceptions of the job were papered over—apparently because the Senate quickly made approval of an independent special prosecutor a condition for Richardson's confirmation. On May 21 Richardson submitted a statement on "Duties and Responsibilities of the Special Prosecutor" to the Senate Judiciary Committee. It said, among other things, "The Special Prosecutor shall have full authority for investigating and prosecuting offenses against the United States arising out of the unauthorized entry into Democratic National Committee Headquarters at the Watergate, all offenses arising out of the 1972 Presidential Election for which the Special Prosecutor deems it necessary and appropriate to assume responsibility, allegations involving the President, members of the White House staff, or Presidential appointees and any other matters, which he consents to have assigned to him by the Attorney General." It also provided that the special prosecutor would "have the greatest degree of independence that is consistent with the Attorney General's statutory accountability for all matters falling within the jurisdiction of the Department of Justice. The Attorney General will not countermand or interfere with the Special Prosecutor's decisions or actions. The Special Prosecutor will determine whether and to what extent he will inform or consult with the Attorney General about the conduct of his duties and responsibilities. The Special Prosecutor will not be removed from his duties except for extraordinary improprieties on his part." Nixon seemed to acquiesce in this statement, announcing on May 22 that Richardson had his "full support" in his effort to "see the truth brought out" through the special prosecutor.

In fact, Nixon's reservations about a truly independent prosecutor remained as strong as ever and were only intensified by Richardson's selection of Archibald Cox to fill the job. Almost from the start, Cox and Nixon seemed to be on collision course. Part of the difficulty was a gulf in heritage and taste so vast that it produced an almost chemical incompatibility (at long range, for their paths had rarely crossed over the years). True to his promise, Nixon had given Richardson a free hand in choosing a special prosecutor. The attorney general had tried several other well-known lawyers, but when they declined he had naturally turned to his former professor at the Harvard Law School. Within a few weeks the White House knew a mistake had been made. One of the President's men said later, "I can hardly imagine two guys less likely to hit it off than Dick Nixon and Archie Cox."

To a California storekeeper's son who grew up listening to those train whistles in the night, Archibald Cox must have seemed the very personification of the Eastern Establishment (the St. Paul's School, Harvard College, Harvard Law School, the Harvard Law Review, *a clerkship with Judge Learned Hand, three years with the Boston law firm of Ropes, Gray, Best, Coolidge & Rugg). A professor at Harvard Law School at thirty-four, rising to become Williston Professor of Law, though with repeated leaves for government work (member of the National Defense Mobilization Board, associate solicitor in the Department of Labor, chairman of the Wage Stabilization Board, and, later, solicitor general in the Kennedy administration). From a long line of lawyers and married to Phyllis Ames, descendant of another distinguished legal family ("What a powerful legal combination!" Learned Hand exclaimed at their wedding). An unmistakable patrician air (long, lean, almost gaunt, hair crew-cut, and with a predilection for three-piece suits, tweeds, bow ties, nubby sweaters). Though born in New Jersey, now rooted in the New England countryside with a house at Wayland, Massachusetts, where he once served as a town selectman, and a farm on Penobscot Bay, Maine, where he loved to pitch hay and ride horses ("All of our family, we all end up with intellectual careers, but we are peasants at heart"). An indefatigable worker, whether on the farm, in the classroom, or in a government office ("The view which I hold with the greatest conviction is that Ezra Thayer was right in observing that the central tragedy of life is that there are only twenty-four hours in the day"). A professorial air even in Washington (an assistant said that, though the special prosecutor's Thursday staff meetings often dealt with material that would "blow the lid off the goddamn city if it got out," Cox ran them "like the dullest, driest seminars back at Harvard"). Flexible on political matters (perhaps stemming from his years as a specialist in labor law and as a mediator in the textile and railroad industries). But tenacious on matters of principle and questions that he believed infringed on "the majesty of the law" (as solicitor general he refused to argue a case involving the right of government officials to search automobiles brought to police headquarters, because he believed the government's position was unjustified). Perhaps a bit arrogant (one lawyer recalls an appearance before the Supreme Court in which he "lectured the justices like they were nine law students"). Above all, a great sense of the fitness, the propriety of things (an aide recalls a dinner at which Phyllis Cox said something that her husband thought was indiscreet, and he looked at her "as though he had just bitten halfway through a lemon").*

Cox's ties to the Kennedy family did nothing to endear him to Nixon. He had known the family for years; had become close to John when they worked together on revisions to the Taft-Hartley Act; served as a key member of his "brain trust" in the 1960 campaign; became solicitor general under Robert at the Justice Department. Both Ethel and Edward Kennedy attended his swearing-in ceremony, and to the Nixon men present they stood out like Amos and Andy at a klavern of the Ku Klux Klan.

The President's suspicions were exacerbated still further by the staff Cox selected. Of the thirty-seven lawyers he ultimately recruited, all but one were Ivy Leaguers, eighteen of them from Harvard; most were Democrats; many had worked in the Justice Department under Robert Kennedy or Nicholas deB. Katzenbach. The only Republicans in the top echelon were Joseph J. Connolly, head of the ITT "task force," and Philip Lacovara, the chief counsel, who had been chairman of Students for Goldwater at Columbia University in 1964.

The staff's homogeneity worried some of Cox's advisers and they urged the appointment of at least one prominent, eminently visible Republican. The only one seriously considered was William Ruckelshaus, who completed his short tour as acting director of the FBI in early July. Cox was impressed with Ruckelshaus, but there were problems. A man of his stature would have to be brought in as Cox's top deputy, thus displacing the current number-two man, the able and trusted Henry Ruth. While they were still wrestling with such considerations—and before the idea had even been broached to Ruckelshaus—Richardson named him as deputy attorney general. And the special prosecutor's office remained relentlessly Democratic.

One night that summer Cox tossed restlessly on his bed in Georgetown, fretting over the approaching confrontation with the President over executive privilege. In the morning he told one of his aides about his insomnia.

"If you think you had a bad night," the aide said, "imagine what a night he must have had."

"I suppose you're right," Cox chuckled. "Maybe we ought to meet at three a.m. at the Lincoln Memorial and talk this whole thing over" (a reference to the early-morning hours of May 9, 1970, when a sleepless Nixon talked with antiwar demonstrators at the Lincoln Memorial).

By then, there was scant chance of accommodation between Nixon and Cox—if, indeed, there ever had been.

As early as July 25 Buchanan had warned Nixon that Cox was the head of a "Fifth Column . . . dominated by McGovern-Kennedy types." In that memo, he outlined a strategy which was to come to fruition in October. The public focus, he suggested, should be switched "from a question of whether the President 'knew' of the cover-up where 70 per cent of the nation is against us—to a question of whom do you wish to govern this nation—the President or the men who would destroy him. Our adversaries do not simply wish to show Nixon's involvement, they wish to castrate the President, to strangle the New Majority in its crib, to reverse the democratic verdict at the polls in November. The Left has an enormous stake in Watergate; they have really nothing else; and they fully intend the exploitation of this scandal to cancel the Nixon Counter-Revolution. . . . If we have to drift into demagoguery so be it—we owe them a few."

The first indication Cox got of the White House attitude toward his investigation was its resistance to handing over many of the documents he needed. In pledging full cooperation with the special prosecutor on May 22, Nixon had promised that executive privilege would be waived "as to any testimony concerning possible criminal conduct or discussions of possible criminal conduct, in the matters presently under investigation, including the Watergate affair and the cover-up." Three days later, however, Nixon told Richardson that this did not apply to documents. And soon he was stonewalling Cox's efforts to obtain relevant White House logs and memoranda. Occasionally the President's lawyers flatly refused—as they did when Cox requested an inventory of the files of former Nixon assistants. More often they simply stalled. Among the documents for which the special prosecutor waited in vain were notes Ehrlichman had made of his conversations, and logs of meetings between the President and key Watergate figures. Sometimes, when Cox sought papers from a White House official, they were transferred from personal files to the files of "Presidential Papers," so that privilege could be claimed.

Finally, on July 10—six days before Alexander Butterfield publicly revealed the existence of the tapes—Cox wrote to Buzhardt, "I am much disturbed by the lack of progress in obtaining answers to my several requests with respect to access to papers in the White House files . . . the delay is now hampering our investigation. . . . Review of our correspondence shows that I have been very patient—perhaps too patient —in seeking voluntary cooperation. . . . Further delay would be so prejudicial to our work, however, that I must insist upon a prompt, categorical response to each of my prior requests."

Buzhardt did not reply until July 21, and then he made clear that the delay was coming primarily from Nixon himself. "Virtually all of your requests raise questions that can only be resolved by the President of the United States. The precedents are clear that a decision to claim or to waive executive privilege is one that must be made personally by the President. In the period in question the President has had the summit meeting with Mr. Brezhnev. He has also been hospitalized for seven days. These are in addition to all of the usual burdens that any President bears. You will surely understand that, under these circumstances, obtaining a decision from the President on sensitive questions that only he can decide is often not a speedy process."

One area in which Cox met particular resistance was his investigation of the Plumbers' activities. On August 23 he wrote to Buzhardt asking for records, logs, and other materials on the activities of Hunt, Liddy, Krogh, Young, Colson, and Ehrlichman; data on their conversations with the President; and documents relating to the Pentagon Papers, Dan Ellsberg, and Dr. Lewis Fielding. None of these documents were ever given to Cox. Nevertheless, by mid-September, the special prosecutor was about to bring indictments on the Fielding burglary when Buzhardt suddenly warned Cox that the trial might jeopardize national security because of other sensitive matters in which the Plumbers had been involved. White House aides said privately that the Plumbers' prosecution could breach security in four ways: by revealing a nuclear-targeting plan, which officials once believed Dan Ellsberg might hand over to the Russians; by compromising the Soviet double agent who informed the CIA that the Pentagon Papers had been turned over to the Soviet embassy; by further endangering a CIA informant within the Indian government; and by disclosing that the United States had been eavesdropping on Soviet leaders' radio-telephone conversations, some of which were referred to in an unpublished volume of the Pentagon Papers. Investigators later concluded that the fears were largely illusory and that the White House warnings were designed to spare the President and his former aides embarrassment and/or prison. But, for the time being, Cox agreed to tread carefully and the indictments were postponed. (Nixon evidently used "national security" as a shield even against his own lawyers. Charles Alan Wright has testified that the President had told him one of the nine subpoenaed tapes contained material "so highly sensitive that he does not feel free even to hint to me what the nature of it is.")

Nixon and his men were outraged at Cox's invasion of other areas which they claimed were totally outside his charter. They were not happy about his examination of ITT, milk money, or campaign financing. Inquiries on the President's personal finances or his real-estate purchases stirred genuine indignation. And Nixon exploded when he heard that the prosecutor was looking into Bebe Rebozo's finances, particularly the Howard Hughes money. "Cox wasn't containable," a White House aide explained later. "He was constantly expanding, so that he would be with us for three and a half years, dividing the executive branch against itself."

Moreover, the President must have been deeply concerned by Cox's success in striking deals with medium-level figures in the Watergate case. One after another, they trooped into court and pleaded guilty to limited indictments in exchange for agreements to testify against other defendants. On June 27, it was Fred LaRue; on August 16, Jeb Magruder; on September 17, Donald Segretti; on October 19, John Dean himself. It was the classic "dealing up" strategy which had accumulated the evidence against Spiro Agnew. The White House could not fail to see the implications for other major figures in the case—even for Nixon himself. If sufficient evidence could be gathered against Haldeman and Ehrlichman, they might be induced to testify against the President. This was one reason Nixon never wavered from his description of them as "two of the finest public servants it has ever been my privilege to know."

In midsummer the special prosecutor's staff learned that certain Presidential assistants—who were proper and polite enough in person—were privately referring to them as "the Cox-suckers." And Cox got a series of more overt messages from the White House, most of them sent via Elliot Richardson. On July 3 Haig and Nixon himself had expressed outrage over the *Los Angeles Times* story about Cox's alleged investigation of San Clemente. On July 23 Haig again telephoned Richardson to complain, this time about a questionnaire that the special prosecutor's office had sent to all government agencies capable of wiretapping. One went to the Secret Service, which promptly protested to the White House. Cox later agreed that the questionnaire, prepared by one of his assistants, was too broad, and he revised it. But not before Haig had warned that Nixon wanted "a tight line drawn with no further mistakes," and that "if Cox does not agree, we will get rid of Cox." The President's chief of staff warned Richardson, "If we have to have a confrontation, we will have it." Finally, on September 27, as they concluded a conversation about the Agnew case and walked toward the door, Nixon told Richardson, "Once we get this problem cleared up, we can go ahead and get rid of Cox."

This was the President's mood when, on October 12, the Court of Appeals handed down the ruling nearly everyone had anticipated. By a 5-to-2 vote, it ordered the President to turn the tapes over to Judge Sirica for his examination. "Though the President is elected by the nationwide ballot, and is often said to represent all the people, he does not embody the nation's sovereignty," the court said. "He is not above the law's commands." The court stayed its own order for five working days—until October 19—to permit the appeal to the Supreme Court that nearly everyone assumed was inevitable.

At the White House, though, some minds turned to an article by Professor Alexander M. Bickel of the Yale Law School which had appeared in the September 29 issue of *The New Republic*. When it first appeared, the article had attracted little attention among the press or public, but it was read carefully at the White House—and now it was read again. Entitled "The Tapes, Cox, Nixon," it said: "Mr. Cox has no constitutional or otherwise legal existence except as he is a creature of the Attorney General, who is a creature of the President. . . . To the extent, therefore, that the President's adversary is Mr. Cox, the President is litigating with himself. He is suing himself and defending himself against himself, putting on the guise of Charles Wright from one side of the counsel table, and the guise of Archibald Cox from the other. . . . And the President runs no risk. For if he loses in the guise of Charles Wright, he can discard his mask of Archibald Cox. He can discharge Mr. Cox and appoint someone else in his place—perhaps Mr. Wright if he chooses—who will follow his directions to abandon the demand for the White House tapes."

What was hence called "the Bickel option" had an obvious appeal. For, to borrow the professor's elegant phrase, the President had lost in the guise of Charles Wright. And his legal advisers, who earlier had doubted that the Supreme Court would issue a "definitive" ruling against him, now began to warn him that the Court might do just that. The President could not afford outright defiance of the highest tribunal—that would almost certainly shove a reluctant Congress into impeachment proceedings. But neither could he afford full disclosure of the tapes under terms the Supreme Court might order. The time was ripe for a move that would avoid either of those distasteful alternatives—providing the President an opportunity to "discard his mask of Archibald Cox."

Early in the afternoon of Saturday, October 13, Nixon helicoptered to Camp David, accompanied by his wife, his daughter Julie, and his son-in-law David

Eisenhower (for whom the Maryland retreat was named). It had been one of his most demanding weeks. On Wednesday Spiro Agnew had resigned. On Friday—the day of the Court of Appeals decision—Nixon had announced his appointment of Gerald Ford. And all week long, the new Middle East war had raged—with America's ally, Israel, largely on the defensive. The Soviet Union had heavily supplied the Arabs this time and had even alerted three of its own airborne divisions. Détente seemed to be collapsing and a direct collision between the Americans and the Russians in the Middle East seemed possible. On Friday Henry Kissinger had warned that the war carried the "potentialities for getting out of hand." Kissinger had tried to signal Washington's determination to Moscow by heavily reinforcing Israel, but the airlift had been hampered by a bureaucratic impasse. At 10:30 a.m., Saturday, Nixon had summoned an emergency meeting at the White House to resolve the impasse. When Secretary of Defense James Schlesinger began explaining about delays in chartering civilian aircraft, Nixon had shouted, "To hell with the charters! Get the supplies there with American planes! Get moving! I want no further delays!"

Barely two hours later—in this imperious and agitated mood—he left for Camp David. At Aspen Lodge, that afternoon and evening, he brooded over the Court of Appeals decision and the October 19 deadline for a Supreme Court appeal. By Sunday morning he had made up his mind. He would make what he liked to call "the big play," a bold, dramatic move that cuts quickly through the tangle of a crisis and transforms it to one's advantage.

At ten o'clock on Sunday he came down from Camp David to attend the first White House worship service in six months—almost as if he were seeking divine guidance for the week ahead. Sometime that afternoon Haig called Richardson and asked him to come to the White House the next morning, implying that the President wanted to consult him about the Middle East crisis. But when Richardson arrived, at about nine-thirty on Monday, he found that his meeting was with Haig and Buzhardt, not Nixon. Haig did talk for a while about the war, showed Richardson the latest cable from Brezhnev, and hinted that the attorney general could play an important part in resolving the crisis.

Flattered by these attentions, the former secretary of defense and undersecretary of state said, "I'm ready. I'll go home and pack my bags. Where do you want me to go?"

"Now wait a minute," Haig said. "That's not exactly what I had in mind."

Feeling rather foolish, Richardson abruptly realized that he was not being asked to deal with the Egyptian tank tracks on the Sinai desert but with the telltale tracks on the White House tapes. Haig then sketched out the President's "big play." He would not appeal the tapes decision to the Supreme Court. Nor would he obey it. Instead, Nixon would follow the "Bickel option"—firing Cox and thus "mooting the case," since there would be nobody left to subpoena the tapes. Then he would submit his own summary of the nine disputed tapes to Judge Sirica.

Now Richardson felt more than foolish. He was angry. He reminded Haig that he had solemnly promised the Senate that Cox would not be removed "except for extraordinary improprieties." Since there had been no such improprieties, Richardson could not fire Cox. If pressed to do so, he would resign.

Evidently, Richardson's warning scotched that plan. For, after he returned to the Justice Department, Haig telephoned at 12:10 to assure him that Cox would not be fired. Instead, he put forward a proposal that he identified as his own. What would Richardson think of having Senator John Stennis of Mississippi—instead of the President—prepare a verified version of the tapes? The idea of "third-party verification" was by no means a new one. Richardson had discussed it with Haig and Buzhardt in July, and with Cox later. Cox had entertained a variation on the idea during the September search for a compromise (at that time, simply a proposal that former Solicitor General J. Lee Rankin arbitrate the conflicting claims on "national security" and "executive privilege"). Now Richardson told Haig it was "an idea that deserved to be considered." Haig said he would try to "sell" it to the President.

At one-fifteen Haig telephoned again to say that after a long discussion he had finally persuaded the President to accept the "Stennis plan." But, in return, Haig said, Nixon would insist that Cox agree "this was it"; once he got those "verified" tapes, there would be nothing more. And the President would expect Richardson to dismiss Cox if he refused that compromise.

After putting down the telephone, the attorney general discussed the new proposal with two of his assistants, J. T. Smith and Jonathan Moore. At three-twenty he told Haig he would support the Stennis plan but would not agree to fire Cox.

That afternoon Haig and Buzhardt rushed up to Senator Stennis's office on the Hill to urge him to accept the job. The seventy-two-year-old senator reminded the men from the White House that he was not in the best of health. Still recovering from a gunshot wound inflicted eight months before by a mugger outside his home, Stennis said he couldn't listen to all those tapes himself. Fred Buzhardt gallantly offered to help him and Stennis gratefully accepted the offer. Nevertheless, the senator said he wanted to sleep on the proposal. Stennis and Haig differ on just what the proposal was. The senator says he thought he was merely to authenticate transcripts for the Senate Watergate committee, not for Judge Sirica. "There was never any mention about the court," he insists. "I wouldn't have done it if there was. No, no, no. I was once a judge and the courts can ask for what they want."

A few minutes after four, Richardson went back to the White House for a meeting with Haig and Buzhardt, and promptly agreed to try to sell the Stennis plan to Cox. The attorney general accepted the assignment with a confidence bred partly of his success in negotiating Agnew's resignation just the week before. Although some had denounced him for letting the Vice President off without a jail term, Richardson's astute handling of the Agnew affair had draped him in a new mystique. On the day the Court of Appeals handed down its tapes decision, *The Wall Street Journal* ran a long front-page article which began, "It seems the worse things get, the better things go for Elliot L. Richardson, the serene, self-assured Attorney General who nailed Spiro Agnew. . . . Indeed, under his leadership the [Justice] department is assuming a unique position of power and independence within the Nixon administration." William Safire, Nixon's former speechwriter who had recently been named a *New York Times* columnist, called him "the most Solomon-like compromiser since Henry Clay." Later Richardson was to regret his self-assured serenity. But as he received Cox at six that afternoon, he did feel a bit like the administration's Solomon—a cool, Olympian accommodator of seemingly irreconcilable interests. If he could resolve the Agnew tangle, surely he could work things out with his old law professor. So, as he donned his evening clothes for a White House dinner, Richardson explained the proposal. Cox listened politely, expressed some doubts, but agreed to think about it overnight.

At seven-thirty Richardson was back at the White House for the third time that day—for a dinner honoring former Secretary of State William Rogers, who had been displaced by his old antagonist, Henry Kissinger, in August. But while Nixon and Richardson honored one outgoing official, they missed another's farewell address. That evening Spiro Agnew appeared on nationwide television to explain that he had resigned not because he was guilty but to "still the raging storm." Agnew's storm was over. But another—soon to be called "firestorm"—was about to begin.

First thing the next morning, Tuesday, October 16, a worried Archibald Cox summoned his senior staff into his office and asked what they thought of the Stennis plan. The reaction was largely negative. Some staffers focused on Stennis himself, deriding the Southern conservative and staunch Nixon supporter. "We'll never get a fair shake from that guy," one aide warned. But Cox knew he could not argue on such personal grounds. In some Washington circles, Stennis was very nearly a demigod; in others, he was a demon. Cox didn't want to get caught in the trap of accepting or rejecting the senator himself. He wanted to respond to the plan.

Cox relayed his reservations to Richardson at a ten-o'clock meeting in the attorney general's office. By all accounts, this conversation—like the others between the two men that week—was marked by the warm rapport and understanding for each other's problems that had long since developed between the law professor and his former student. This mutual respect was nurtured by a striking similarity of experience—both had gone to Harvard College and Harvard Law School, both had been elected to the *Harvard Law Review*, clerked for Learned Hand, worked for Ropes & Gray, and served with the Justice Department. Moving now with lawyerly precision, they divided the subject into two areas: those that were negotiable and those that were not. Finally Cox said he could respond to the proposal better if he could see the Stennis plan in writing. Richardson agreed to write it up for him.

Then the attorney general left to dedicate New York City's new police headquarters. Addressing the massed policemen at the ceremony, Richardson quoted some famous lines from Gilbert and Sullivan's *The Pirates of Penzance*:

> When constabulary duty's to be done,
> The policeman's lot is not a happy one.

On the flight back to Washington, the nation's chief law-enforcement officer began drafting the Stennis plan for Cox.

Wednesday morning, Richardson finished up his memorandum and early that afternoon Buzhardt picked it up. By three-thirty he was back at the Justice Department with several changes that apparently came from the President himself. Most important, Buzhardt wanted to remove an entire section called "Other Tapes and Documents," which specified that the proposed arrangement would cover "only the tapes heretofore subpoenaed." Buzhardt said the paragraph was being deleted only because it was redundant— the Stennis plan was never intended to deal with future eventualities. This proved to be a short-lived assurance.

Late that afternoon Cox received the final Stennis plan proposal. In it, Richardson said the plan's objective was to provide an accurate account of the subpoenaed tapes "insofar as the conversations recorded in those tapes in any way relate to the Watergate break-in and the cover-up of the break-in, to knowledge thereof on the part of anyone and to perjury." He said the "verifier" would be given the tapes themselves and a preliminary transcript prepared by the White House, with conversations in the third person and with long irrelevant portions deleted. The verifier would listen to the tapes, making additions to the transcript as he saw fit. He could paraphrase language that might be "embarrassing to the President" and could paraphrase or omit references to sensitive defense or foreign-relations matters.

Cox and Richardson discussed the Stennis plan twice on Wednesday and once on Thursday. At midafternoon, Thursday, the special prosecutor gave the attorney general his written reply. It stressed that the idea of nonjudicial verification was "not unacceptable." Since "there should be no avoidable confrontation with the President," he would be "glad to sit down with anyone in order to work out a solution along this line if we can." But Cox went on to raise eleven "highly important objections," among them: the transcripts should cover not only Watergate but other crimes within his jurisdiction; the public should not confide such a task to "one man operating in secrecy, consulting only with the White House"; any persons entrusted with the job ought to be named "special masters" of the court; the standards for omitting "national security" and other data should be tightened; the third-person transcripts should include the names of all speakers and those mentioned, if they were under investigation; if the trial court refused to accept a partial transcript, the White House should provide the evidence in any form the court prescribed, including the original tapes if necessary; the proposal should include the Presidential papers included in the subpoena and thus establish the special prosecutor's right to "other evidence."

Though framed in diplomatic language, Cox's response made clear that the two positions were rather far apart and a great deal remained to be negotiated. But, by the White House's schedule, time was running out. Haig and Buzhardt insisted that a decision must be reached and announced by Friday midnight, the deadline for Nixon's appeal to the Supreme Court. Richardson felt that was desirable, but not essential. Cox felt, as he later told the Senate, that these matters were "far too important and far too serious for us to do it overnight." Richardson concedes that he never communicated to Cox "quite the degree of urgency I was getting from the White House." He believes that "if Cox and I had been left to pursue the matter along our own lines, we might have arrived at something." But the White House was getting impatient—as was evident at a meeting hurriedly assembled at 6:00 p.m. on Thursday in Haig's office. Present this time were Haig, Buzhardt, Richardson, and two newcomers to the negotiations—Leonard Garment, counsel to the President, and Charles Alan Wright.

Wright had just returned from Texas, where he had been drafting Nixon's appeal to the Supreme Court. (It was completed and even the check for the $100 filing fee was made out.) So the lanky Texan did not quite understand what Richardson meant when he said, "I have a response from Archie."

"Could I see the proposal that he's responding to?" Wright asked.

Then, for the first time, the President's chief lawyer for the tapes litigation saw the proposal his client was making to resolve the case. Wright had never quite understood the clamor for the tapes: "I thought it was a matter of public voyeurism, that everybody in the country would just love to be able to hear what the President of the United States is like when he has his hair down." So he felt that the President was making a remarkably magnanimous gesture: "I was astonished that the President was willing to go that far."

All the White House men chose to interpret Cox's letter as an outright rejection. They all felt he should be dismissed. Richardson says he "outlined the problems which would attach to any Cox firing and objected particularly to a suggestion that I and Henry Petersen could take over the Watergate investigation." When Wright continued to hymn the merits of the President's plan, Richardson said, "Charlie, you are very convincing. Why don't you talk to Archie? Maybe you can do better than I can."

Wright agreed to try. But the White House men were adamant on one thing: if Wright failed, then Cox would have to go.

Not having heard from Richardson by six-thirty, Cox left his office, telling Henry Ruth that he would be at his brother Louis's home in McLean. In the middle of dinner, the telephone rang. It was Ruth, telling Cox to call Wright at the White House. His five nephews and nieces were scampering all over the room, abuzz with Uncle Archie's important doings, and Cox had difficulty hearing everything the President's lawyer was saying. But he says he heard Wright begin coldly, "Here are some conditions you can't accept," and then say further conversation was useless unless Cox would agree categorically that (1) the tapes would be submitted to only one man, whom the President had already selected—Stennis; (2) Stennis would not be named a "special master"; (3) no portion of a tape would ever be provided to the court, and (4) "not to subpoena any other White House tape, paper or document." Cox said later that he felt Wright made his points "in such a way that I could not accept them," in fact, that the whole call was designed to "elicit rejection."

Wright remembers the call somewhat differently. He says he told Cox that four of the points he had raised in his memo were "fundamentally inconsistent with what the President was proposing." But he says that he never told Cox he must abandon all future efforts to get more White House evidence through the courts, that he merely refused to give an advance commitment on the matter, which was "to be left open, a matter for negotiation in the future rather than something that we were going to be resolving at this time." And Wright says he had no intention of cutting off negotiations with the special prosecutor.

At Cox's request, Wright put his end of the conversation in a letter, which was delivered the next morning. Although it does not fully confirm either man's version of the exchange, it is generally bleak in tone and ends, "If you think that there is any purpose in our talking further, my associates and I stand ready to do so. If not, we will have to follow the course of action we think in the best interests of the country. I will call you at 10:00 a.m. to ascertain your views."

Meanwhile, Richardson had left for his home in the woods of McLean, fearing that Cox would be fired on Friday and that he would have to resign. Late Thursday night, scribbling on a yellow legal pad, he drafted a document he called "Why I Must Resign." It read, in part:

"While Cox has rejected a proposal I consider reasonable, his rejection of it cannot be regarded as being as far beyond the pale as would justify my own exercise of my reserved power to fire him. He is, after all, being asked to accept a proposition that would give him significantly less than he has won in two court decisions. Besides, I really believe that in all my dealings with him he has been honest and fair.

"I believe that so far as I personally am concerned, there is need for an independent prosecutor:

"(a) because of my part in this Administration from its beginning;

"(b) because since Cox's appointment I have been serving as a middleman between Cox and counsel for the President, and this role has impaired the independence I might otherwise have;

"(c) I don't think I could effectively deal with Buzhardt *et al.* in Cox's place with the independence that a prosecutor should have;

"(d) I am in fact loyal to the President, and I am by temperament a team player, and these were the reasons originally why a Special Prosecutor was perceived to be necessary. I cannot now change spots completely enough to be perceived to be—or feel that I am—as independent as I should be."

Elliot Richardson is a team player. In five years on the Nixon team he had played each of his important positions with a cheerful recognition that his captain's requirements came before his own—even, his critics say, before principle. When he first joined the Nixon administration as undersecretary of state, Richardson was darkly distrusted by Haldeman and Ehrlichman —not only because he was an Ivy League aristocrat in a sea of southern California advertising men but because he was a favorite of Kissinger's (for months, Richardson was the only ranking man at State Kissinger trusted). But just as Kissinger soon proved he could be quite as tough as anyone at the White House, so Richardson quickly proved he could be quite as loyal. During the Cambodian invasion in May 1970, a dozen of his Harvard classmates (class of 1941) called on him. "Look, Elliot," said Eugene Nickerson, a Democratic politician from New York, "this administration is no damn good and we rely on you to do something." But, Nickerson recalls, Richardson sat there "smoking his pipe, looking like H. M. Pulham with brains, telling us, you know, that the Cambodian invasion was really a move toward peace." When he joined the cabinet a month later as secretary of health, education and welfare, Richardson showed an even greater capacity for accommodation. Following the 1971 Supreme Court decision proclaiming busing a "legitimate tool" for integrating schools, he initially announced that HEW would support busing programs across the country. But when the White House expressed its adamant opposition to busing, Richardson promptly called a news conference and reversed his field 180 degrees. And during the 1972 "Christmas Bombing" of Hanoi, when he awaited Senate confirmation as secretary of defense, he expressed private reservations but, despite friends' urgings, never voiced them publicly. Indeed, it is this finely honed political instinct which set Richardson apart from Archibald Cox, with whom he shared so many other characteristics. He could be a stern moralist—even a public scold—as demonstrated by his zealous prosecution in 1959–60 of Bernard Goldfine, the textile manufacturer who bought influence with gifts to Sherman Adams. But from the age of eight, when he was president of the Herbert Hoover Club at the Park School, he has been one of the subtlest of politicians. Working first as a legislative assistant to Senator Leverett Saltonstall— later Chuck Colson's mentor—then rising to lieutenant governor of Massachusetts and attorney general he learned the gentle art of compromise. Although he could be frosty and aloof in public, his private warmth and ebullience—he is a passionate tennis player, a joyous dancer, an enthralling dinner partner—earned him loyalty and friendship wherever he went. "The morale just seemed to jump in any office Elliot headed," one Massachusetts politician remarks. "People loved working for him." Richardson's value to Nixon was obvious. His Brahmin air of chilly rectitude was priceless coin in an administration increasingly steeped in the seamy business ethic. He was "Nixon's Harvard man"—a Kennedy-style patrician who was a constant reminder that this President too could attract men of brains, style, and breeding. No wonder that Nixon shuttled him in and out of top positions—in barely four and a half years he held four cabinet or subcabinet jobs. ("Think of the pressure," his daughter once jibed. "Only three years to go and eight more cabinet posts to fill.") But Nixon pressed his luck too far with Richardson. Convinced that he would be loyal to his last drop of blue blood, he thrust him into the one job where Richardson was unable—and unwilling—to compromise. A lawyer trained by Learned Hand and Felix Frankfurter, he would not tamper with funda-

mental rules of due process. And by fall 1973 Richardson had been dragged to Nixon's polluted well once too often. This time he would not drink.

By Friday morning even so skilled an accommodator as Richardson had run out of accommodations. As he left for the office that morning, he tucked his scribbled notes from the night before into the vest pocket of his business suit. After reading "Why I Must Resign" to Smith, Darman, and Moore, he told his secretary to type it up. At nine-fifteen he called Haig to ask about the progress of the negotiations. Haig said they were still proceeding. Richardson said that if and when they broke down, he wanted to see the President —a plain warning that he intended to resign. But a few minutes later Cox's letter arrived at the White House, saying: "I have a strong desire to avoid any form of confrontation, but I could not conscientiously agree to your stipulations without unfaithfulness to the pledge which I gave the Senate." At 9:55 Haig telephoned Richardson and told him the President would see him right away. With his freshly typed resignation statement carefully folded in his pocket, the attorney general left for the White House.

But when he got there—shortly after ten—Haig, not Nixon, met him with a sharp change of tack. "Maybe we don't have to go down the road we talked about last night," he said. "Suppose we go ahead with the Stennis plan without firing Cox." Richardson's implicit threat to resign had apparently carried the day.

At this point, Buzhardt, Wright, and Garment joined the conversation. While Haig went off to get the President's agreement to drop the dismissal of Cox, they and Richardson went over Cox's letter. Richardson quickly noted that Cox was strenuously objecting to a prohibition of future subpoenas of White House materials; where had he gotten such an idea? (Wright didn't tell Richardson that he and Cox had discussed such a restriction the night before.) At Richardson's insistence, Wright agreed to write Cox still another letter, explaining that this limitation was never part of the proposal. (The letter, delivered later that day, said the prohibition was meant to apply only to "private Presidential papers and meetings." Wright said he was making the clarification only "in the interest of historical accuracy," not to renew the negotiations. On the contrary, he wrote, "The differences between us remain so great that no purpose would be served by further discussion.")

Then, suddenly, this very prohibition which they had all just disowned did become linked to the Stennis plan. Just how that happened—and how firm the linkage was—is a matter of dispute between Richardson and the others who attended the meeting. Both sides agree that a free-ranging discussion ensued about various "scenarios" and "game plans" for carrying out the Stennis proposal and for limiting further demands for White House materials.

One of the White House officials present at the meeting offered this explanation of what happened: "Elliot must have realized that one way or another the President was determined to get rid of Cox. If Cox was fired, under any pretext, Elliot would have to resign. But if Cox could be induced to resign, Elliot might be able to stay on. I think at that point he was trying to find a way to stay. So he said, 'Why not simply order Cox to abandon all further subpoenas for White House materials?' Someone asked, 'Would that make any difference?' And Elliot said, 'Yes, I think he would resign.'"

Richardson does not remember it quite that way: "You have to realize that I'd come in there to resign. When you get ready to hurl yourself against a closed door and it turns out to be glass and you go crashing through and find yourself in a heap on the other side, you have to pick yourself up and reassess the situation. That's what I was trying to do at that meeting—realign myself to a new situation. All sorts of scenarios were being thrown around and I was trying to decide how I felt about each, one at a time. I do recall that we discussed the possibility of linking to the Stennis plan a flat order to Cox on future access to White House materials, some way of saying 'This is all you get.' Someone asked how I thought he would react to such an order and I thought he would probably resign. But I never gave any clear indication of my attitude on this. I hadn't had time to think through the implications."

Within hours—after talking with his staff over lunch in the attorney general's dining room—Richardson did think it through. He decided that linking the Stennis plan to a prohibition on future subpoenas was "clearly ill-advised."

A White House official believes two things happened that afternoon: "I think Elliot realized he was playing it too cute, trying to draw too narrow a distinction. And I think Cox probably told him he wasn't going to resign, whatever happened." A Richardson aide says the attorney general did conclude that afternoon that Cox would not resign. Shortly thereafter, he began to express his objections to the White House plan in telephone conversations with Haig and Buzhardt. But Richardson still believed some compromise could be worked out: "Remember, up to then I'd been able to defuse each situation that had arisen. I'd managed to turn off the Monday proposition. I'd managed to turn off the Thursday proposition. Friday afternoon, I went to work to turn off the Friday morning proposition."

The President's men say they do not recall Richardson clearly objecting to the plan that afternoon. In any case, it was already too late to stop it. With the midnight deadline for a Supreme Court appeal only hours away, Nixon, Haig, and Buzhardt were moving quickly to implement the new proposition.

First, they tried to nail down Stennis's participation. The senator had given his tentative assent but stipulated that Sam Ervin and Howard Baker must also accept the plan. This set off a frantic search for the senators. Ervin was located at the New Orleans airport, Baker at a symposium in Chicago. Both flew to Washington and rushed to the White House. It was an opportune time to offer a deal to the Senate Watergate committee, for just that week Judge Sirica had rejected its suit for five White House tapes. Haig apparently persuaded Baker to go along with the plan first. When Ervin arrived, the senators were swept into the Oval

Office, where for forty minutes Nixon, Haig, and Buzhardt sold Ervin the plan. Ervin says that whenever he asked how Cox felt about the proposal, Nixon or one of the others changed the subject. (Stennis too says he was never told that Cox had rejected the plan.) Ervin says he was promised verbatim transcripts, whereas the White House later said it had planned to issue third-person summaries. The Middle East crisis was invoked, with Haig arguing that the President needed a "strong hand" to resolve it. Finally, the senators agreed to recommend the Stennis proposal to the Watergate committee—further strengthening the President's position by isolating the Senate "firebrands"—like Ted Kennedy, Birch Bayh, and Walter "Fritz" Mondale—who could be expected to dissent.

By dusk the President and his top aides were convinced they had the deal wrapped up. At 6:45 Haig told Presidential aides Melvin Laird and Bryce Harlow about the plan for the first time. Laird asked whether Richardson agreed with it. "The only way this thing can float is if Elliot's on board a hundred per cent," Laird said. "Otherwise it will sink to the bottom of the sea."

Haig assured him that Richardson was "on board."

In retrospect, several participants in the week's negotiations agree that this was the major miscalculation. "The whole thing was an example of wishful thinking," a White House aide says. "We were all huffing and puffing to keep the plan up in the air, so we didn't ask all the hard questions that needed to be asked." Richardson calls it "a failure of imagination—on everybody's part." Friday morning's meeting, Al Haig later conceded, "set in train a chain of events which brought us to Saturday evening's firestorm."

A few minutes after Haig met with Laird and Harlow, the plan began to come apart. At seven Haig telephoned Richardson and read him a letter from the

President that, he said, had already been sent. It instructed Richardson to order Cox "that he is to make no further attempts by judicial process to obtain tapes, notes, or memoranda of Presidential conversations," and added, "I regret the necessity of intruding to this very limited extent on the independence I promised you with regard to Watergate when I announced your appointment."

The attorney general was furious, but he kept his anger under tight control. "Al, given the history of our relationship on this, I would have thought that you would have consulted me prior to sending any letter," he said. He had understood there was to be more discussion before any step like this were taken. Haig replied that he had twice told the President of Richardson's objections but Nixon would not yield.

All day, Cox had been waiting for the White House to respond to his letter. By six-thirty he had given up and gone home. As he walked through the door, the telephone rang. It was Richardson, who said, "I have a letter. I am going to read it to you. It is for your information." Richardson said he made "explicitly clear" that he was not transmitting the instructions to Cox, just reading them.

At eight-thirty Bryce Harlow telephoned Richardson to see how he had taken the President's letter. The attorney general said he felt he had been "shabbily treated" by the White House. He said he intended to issue a press release praising the Stennis plan but disowning all responsibility for the added prohibition on access to further material.

Meanwhile—without informing either Richardson or Cox—the President had gone public. At about eight-fifteen the White House press office issued a Presidential statement which announced steps "to bring the issue of Watergate tapes to an end and to assure our full attention to more pressing business affecting the very security of the nation." Nixon announced the Stennis plan and then said, "Though I have not wished to intrude upon the independence of the special prosecutor, I have felt it necessary to direct him, as an employee of the executive branch, to make no further attempts by judicial process to obtain tapes, notes, or memoranda of Presidential conversations."

Cox, who had hastily reassembled his staff at their K Street offices, promptly issued a defiant statement: "I cannot be a party to such an agreement." When asked by a reporter whether he would resign, he said, "No—hell, no."

Only at about nine, when Richardson and Cox talked again by telephone, did the attorney general learn of the President's public announcement. And only then did he discover that Nixon had made no mention of the letter to Richardson ordering *him* to deny further access to Cox. For some reason, Richardson had been left out of the public statement. There was no need for the press release on which he had been laboring for two hours.

At about ten the attorney general went home to McLean. There, he received another telephone call from Haig, saying he was sorry Richardson felt shabbily treated.

"Well, I'm home now," Richardson said. "I've had a drink. Things look a little better and we'll see where we go from here."

Then he sat up much of the night writing out notes for a letter to Nixon. At the top, he printed a title suggested by his wife to indicate going out in style: "The Mahogany Coffin."

The next morning Richardson reviewed his remaining options with Darman, Smith, and Moore. By then, Darman was fed up, and he drafted a letter to the President which began, "I am returning herewith your letter of October 19. . . ." That just wasn't Richardson's style. Instead, he completed a letter—based largely on "The Mahogany Coffin"—which began respectfully, "Thank you for your letter of October 19 . . ." and went on to spell out still another compromise, based on an understanding that any further attempt made by the special prosecutor to obtain tapes or memoranda through the courts would be dealt with on the Stennis plan precedent.

But there was no middle ground left. At one o'clock Cox went before television cameras at the National Press Club. Coolly, quietly, with self-deprecating humor, he explained why he could not accept the President's order:

"I read in one of the newspapers this morning, the headline, 'Cox Defiant.' I do want to say that I don't feel defiant. In fact, I told my wife this morning I hate a fight. Some things I feel very deeply about are at stake, and I hope that I can explain and defend them steadfastly. . . .

"I am certainly not out to get the President of the United States. I am even worried, to put it in colloquial terms, that I am getting too big for my britches, that what I see as principle could be vanity. I hope not. In the end, I decided that I had to try to stick by what I thought was right. . . .

"I think it is my duty as special prosecutor, as an officer of the court, and as the representative of the grand jury, to bring to the court's attention what seems to me to be noncompliance with the court's order. If the court should rule that there was satisfactory compliance, then it would be my duty in those same capacities to abide by the court's order. Of course, I would, and we would go about our business as best we can. That is what I regard as the basic adherence to our institutions of justice, which should be complied with and followed in dealing with these problems. . . .

"I do want to emphasize that the giving of instructions in this very important respect isn't important because it interferes with Archie Cox. . . . That isn't what is involved. It is that there is a basic change in the institutional arrangement that was established."

At the White House, one aide, watching the news conference on television, banged his fist on the table and called it "insubordination."

At 2:07 Garment telephoned Richardson. Because of the Middle East crisis the President wanted to avoid a chain of resignations, he said; would the attorney general be willing to dismiss Cox first, and then, if he must, resign? Richardson refused.

At 2:20 Haig telephoned Richardson and ordered him to fire Cox. "Well, I can't do that," Richardson said. "I guess I'd better come over and resign."

While the attorney general waited for a summons to the White House, he discussed the situation with Ruckelshaus and Solicitor General Robert Bork. Richardson asked Ruckelshaus what he would do if ordered to fire Cox. Ruckelshaus said he would resign. Then Richardson turned to Bork, who had been appointed before Cox, who had made no pledge to the Senate about the special prosecutor's independence, and who indeed did not think the post was necessary. Bork said he would be willing to fire Cox. "Somebody has to carry out the President's order," he said. "But then how could I stay on and be regarded as an *apparatchik?* I'd have to resign too." Richardson urged Bork not to resign. Somehow the Justice Department had to keep functioning.

At 3:20 Haig told Richardson to "come on over." As the attorney general left the office, he mumbled something about "a Greek tragedy."

Meanwhile, in the Oval Office, the President was talking about the Mediterranean, too. He was on the phone to the Defense Department demanding that it speed more C-5A transport planes to Israel. "One every fifty minutes isn't enough!" he shouted. "I want them to take off as fast as they get on the runway." Then he turned despairingly to Leonard Garment and exclaimed, "If I can't get an order carried out by my attorney general, how can I get arms to Israel?"

Garment said the attorney general felt he was being asked to violate his word to the Senate.

"Elliot isn't doing this," Nixon said. "I'm doing it."

A few minutes later Haig and Richardson entered the Oval Office. Richardson sat in a chair at the President's right hand; Haig sat at his left hand. Richardson said he had come to resign.

Invoking the Middle East crisis again, Nixon tried to get Richardson to postpone his resignation. Kissinger was then in Moscow. The Russians, Nixon argued, would interpret the resignation as a sign of crisis in

Washington. The Arab-Israeli cease-fire—perhaps world peace itself—could be jeopardized.

"Mr. President," Richardson said, "I feel that I have no choice but to go forward with this."

Nixon urged Richardson to dismiss Cox, wait a week, then resign.

"That would never be believed," Richardson said.

"Be it on your head," Nixon snapped. "I am sorry that you feel you have to act on the basis of a purely personal commitment rather than the national interest."

"I'm acting on the basis of national interest as I see it," Richardson said sharply. "There should be no mistaken impression."

"I mean your perception of national interest is so different from mine," Nixon said.

Richardson rose and, standing by the President's desk, bid him a dignified farewell. Then he turned and left the Oval Office. Later he recalled, "I don't think he was sorry to see me go."

At five-fifteen Richardson returned to his office, where all his top aides were waiting. Paraphrasing Macbeth after he killed the king, he announced: "The deed is done." The Saturday Night Massacre was under way.

A moment later a secretary said Haig was calling for Ruckelshaus. The deputy attorney general took the private elevator down to his office on the floor below. When he picked up the telephone, Haig started talking about the Middle East. They were in a crisis, he said, and the President was depending on Ruckelshaus. If it's that critical, Ruckelshaus said, why don't you wait a week?"

"No," Haig replied. "Your commander in chief has given you an order. You have no alternative."

"Politics and soldiering are very, very close," Al Haig has said. "[They're both] fields where a man lays everything on the line to win or lose. They're tested by the vote or they're tested in battle. When one

doesn't win, the results are fatal; and in the case of the military, quite fatal. So I have a great respect for politicians." Haig fought in two wars. During the Korean conflict, he waded ashore at Inchon. In Vietnam, he served as a brigade and battalion commander, earning the Distinguished Service Cross for action at An Loc. But for twenty-five years his prime talent had been at the curious intersection of war and politics. Joseph Califano, once his colleague at the Pentagon, calls Haig "one of a new breed of Army officers who know politics, international affairs, and people." Fresh out of West Point in 1947, he served as an administrative assistant in General Douglas MacArthur's office while the general was imposing a new political order on Japan. ("This wasn't test-tube stuff," Haig recalls proudly. "This was formed in the vortex of a political situation.") After gaining an M.A. in international relations from Georgetown University, he began a rapid rise through the military-political bureaucracy at the Pentagon: working first on European and Middle Eastern affairs; then becoming military assistant to Secretary of the Army Cyrus Vance; finally following Vance when he became deputy secretary of defense under Robert McNamara. In 1964–65, he was responsible for liaison between the secretary of defense and President Johnson. On his return from Vietnam, Haig was recommended by Califano to become Kissinger's military adviser on the National Security Council. Within a year, he had become Kissinger's top deputy ("Kissinger's Kissinger") and—at least on military matters—virtually his partner. "Al saved Henry's ass in that job by forcing discipline and order on the staff," one official recalls. Frequently, Kissinger would go out to a party at eight, leaving Haig with a pile of work to be finished. "When you see lights burning in Kissinger's office," Nixon once said, "it's usually Haig." A former colleague says Haig's rapid advancement under Kissinger came because he "rarely argued with Henry, in contrast to the academic types who did, and being a military man, he never questioned authority. He respectfully did what he was

*told to do and he made no waves. He never consti-
tuted a threat to Henry's position."* (One of the dirty
jobs Haig shouldered was supplying the names of wiretapping targets to the FBI.) In September 1972 Haig
reaped his reward for all that hard work. He was leap-
frogged over two hundred and forty more senior officers to four-star general and vice Army chief of staff.
Many felt that by the time Nixon left the White House
Haig would be chief of staff—and perhaps even chairman of the Joint Chiefs. (Like Generals Vernon Walters and Robert Cushman, Haig was being rewarded
for past services to Nixon and in anticipation of future
loyalty. Once, on the lawn at San Clemente, Nixon
leaned over and fingered the stars on Haig's shoulder,
as if to emphasize who had put them there.) Then,
on May 2, 1973, Haig's orderly progression in the
ranks was abruptly sidetracked. While he dined with
fellow officers at Fort Benning, Nixon telephoned to
summon him back to White House duty: as the new
Presidential chief of staff. Haig was reluctant, but Nixon insisted. He promised that the job would be temporary (six to eight weeks, Haig gathered), and that
he would have nothing to do with Watergate. But
—though he felt as if he had taken over "a battalion
that has just been overrun"—Haig performed with
such dispatch that all limitations vanished and he found
himself, as one aide put it, "Haldeman and Ehrlichman
rolled into one." Under congressional pressure he was
forced to retire from the Army ("intellectually, it
was not a tough decision; it was a problem of the
heart"). Haig—who knew "the essentiality of discipline" in war and politics—bowed his neck to Nixon
as he had to every other commander. Some say he
was a "yes man," who always told the President what
he wanted to hear. It was a habit which may have
begun when Al was only seven and told his brother,
Frank, there was no Santa Claus, but warned him
not to tell their parents and "spoil their fun." Until it
was too late, Al Haig never shattered Richard Nixon's
cherished myths.*

When Haig told Ruckelshaus he had no alternative but to obey his commander in chief, the deputy attorney general replied, "other than to resign."

Haig suggested that he fire Cox, then resign a week later—the same deal offered to Richardson minutes before. Ruckelshaus again demurred, but added that Bork felt differently. "If you really are determined to get rid of Cox, I think Bork may be your man." Haig asked if Bork was still there. Ruckelshaus said he would go get him.

Upstairs, Richardson and his staff could hear the elevator droning back again. J. T. Smith turned to the solicitor general and said, "You're next, Bob."

Bork took the call in Ruckelshaus's office, and Haig said he was sending a White House limousine for him. When the big black car arrived, Buzhardt and Garment were inside as high-level escorts, presumably to make sure that Bork did not change his mind on the short ride. At the White House, the red-bearded professor from Yale was quickly designated acting attorney general. Then he drafted a brisk two-paragraph letter of dismissal, which was sent by messenger to Cox.

Over the telephone, Cox dictated a short statement to James Doyle, a former Washington *Evening Star* reporter who was serving as his press spokesman. It read: "Whether we shall continue to be a Government of laws and not of men is now for Congress and ultimately the American people [to decide]."

Richardson called Cox to tell him of his own resignation. Judge Learned Hand had once inscribed lines from the *Iliad* on a picture of himself he had given to Richardson, and Richardson quoted them to his old friend: "Now, though numberless fates of death beset us which no mortal can escape or avoid, let us go forward together, and either we shall give honor to one another, or another to us."

At 8:25 a grim Ron Ziegler appeared in the White House press room and announced the dismissal of Cox, the resignation of Richardson, and the dismissal of Ruckelshaus (the White House had decided not to give the deputy attorney general the dignity of resignation). He also declared that "the office of the Watergate

Special Prosecution Force has been abolished as of approximately eight p.m. tonight. Its function to investigate and prosecute those involved in the Watergate matter will be transferred back into the institutional framework of the Department of Justice, where it will be carried out with thoroughness and vigor."

At 9:05 seven FBI agents arrived at the special prosecutor's office on the ninth floor of the office building at 1425 K Street, N.W. The offices were normally among the most secure in town: with no sign on the plain metal door, just a simple legend, "Push Bell"; closed-circuit television monitoring the corridor; yellow stickers on the telephones warning against bugging; drawn venetian blinds and specially coated curtains to guard against high-powered cameras that might focus on desks from neighboring office buildings. But now the agents quickly pierced all this security and took up positions at doors and in corridors. They told Cox's staff, which had begun gathering when they heard the news, that the office was being disbanded and that no files could be removed. Henry Ruth, Cox's deputy, was told by one agent that he could not remove what Ruth later described as a "love letter" from his wife. At an impromptu news conference in the tenth-floor law library, Ruth was close to tears as he read a statement: "I must say I suppose that human emotions take over because one thinks in a democracy this would not happen." On his way out, Jim Doyle stopped by his office to take a few family pictures from his desk and a framed copy of the Declaration of Independence from his wall. Angelo Lano, the FBI man who headed the occupying force, told Doyle he couldn't take anything out. But Doyle knew Lano, who had been the bureau's liaison with the special prosecutor's office. "It's the Declaration of Independence, Angie," he snapped. "Just stamp it 'void' and let me take it home." (Meanwhile, other FBI men sealed off Richardson's and Ruckelshaus's offices at the Justice Department.)

Under questioning at a news conference, General Haig later took responsibility for ordering the agents to the special prosecutor's office "because we had reports that members of the staff were leaving rapidly with huge bundles under their arms." This does not sound much like Haig. But it does sound like Nixon—particularly since the President had been enraged on May 1 when Ruckelshaus, then acting FBI director, had sent FBI agents to seal off Haldeman's and Ehrlichman's offices. The dispatch of the agents six months later may well have been the President's revenge.

On Monday, October 22, Nixon called Richardson back to the White House to find out what he was going to say at his news conference the next day. Richardson assured him that he would be "balanced and fair." And indeed he was: defending both Cox ("I would have done what he has done") and Nixon ("The President can always revise the terms on which he has appointed somebody to his administration").

But the American people were not so judicious. Within hours of Ziegler's announcement, a tidal wave of protest began thundering down on Washington. Thousands of letters, telegrams, and telephone calls poured into government offices—the most spontaneous outpouring many could remember. Dozens of Democrats in the House of Representatives readied impeachment resolutions. The AFL-CIO, meeting in Bal Harbour, called on the President to resign. Chesterfield Smith, president of the American Bar Association, said Nixon had tried to "abort the established processes of justice." And Republicans, too, began to desert the President. "The office of President does not carry with it a license to destroy justice in America," said Senator Bob Packwood of Oregon. House Republicans warned Bryce Harlow that they would not "go to the wall" to prevent impeachment proceedings.

"If our first goof was in not foreseeing Elliot's resignation," a White House official recalls, "then our second was in not anticipating the public protest. Clearly we just weren't in touch with the mood of the country." The two "goofs" added up to a staggering miscalculation—an utter misreading of the political temperature in Washington and the nation at large, all the more surprising in a man who had gained a reputation for astute gauging of the public mood. Almost overnight, the President had been thrown on the defensive again, and he recognized that drastic steps were needed to regain the initiative.

14

OPERATION CANDOR

I am not a crook.
—Richard Nixon,
to the Associated Press Managing Editors Association,
November 17, 1973

On the morning of Tuesday, October 23, the President dispatched two aides, Bill Timmons and Bryce Harlow, to test the political waters on Capitol Hill. Soon they were back with frozen toes. The House of Representatives was in turmoil. Thundering denunciations of the President's "arrogance" ricocheted through the chamber. Majority Leader Thomas P. "Tip" O'Neill, Jr., of Massachusetts referred a barrage of impeachment resolutions to the House Judiciary Committee for "speedy and expeditious consideration." Republican leaders warned Timmons and Harlow that they would not speak up for the President unless he produced the subpoenaed tapes.

When Nixon heard this he called Alexander Haig, Fred Buzhardt, and Leonard Garment into the Oval Office for a meeting which Haig later described as "very painful and anguishing." All agreed they had little choice. Charles Alan Wright—who was scheduled to argue the "Stennis plan" before Judge John Sirica at noon—was quickly summoned. The White House asked for and received a two-hour postponement in the hearing.

At two the President's Texas lawyer strode up the center aisle of the U.S. district court like Gary Cooper in *High Noon*. At the opposite table sat no fewer than eleven lawyers from Archibald Cox's staff, refusing to

600

quit, prepared to do battle. Judge Sirica entered and read his original order calling for surrender of the tapes. Then, putting down his papers, he looked sternly over his glasses and asked Wright, "Are counsel prepared at this time to file the response of the President to the modified order of the court?"

Wright rose in the hushed courtroom. "I am not prepared at this time to file a response," he said. "I am, however, authorized to say that the President of the United States would comply in all respects with the order of August 29 as modified by the order of the court of appeals."

Pausing, to let his message sink in, Wright continued, "It will require some time, as your honor realizes, to put these materials together, to do the indexing and itemizing as the court of appeals calls for."

Judge Sirica, who had entered court that day prepared to cite the President for contempt, was clearly stunned. He broke in, "As I understand your statement, that will be delivered to this court?"

"To the court," Wright said, *in camera.*

Then—to underline what had just happened—Wright declared, "This President does not defy the law."

Barely seventy-two hours after firing Cox for insisting on access to the tapes and other White House materials, Nixon had reversed himself 180 degrees. It was the start of a new phase in the Watergate saga —a period in which the President tried to give the impression that he was bowing to the courts, cooperating with the investigators, and speaking candidly to the public.

But, never one to bargain from weakness, Nixon was eager to erase the memory of this capitulation. And, as luck would have it, within hours of the humiliating concession, he was presented with a striking opportunity to demonstrate his strength and resolution.

On October 23—barely twelve hours after a Middle East cease-fire had gone into effect—Israeli forces completed their encirclement of Egypt's 20,000-man III Corps on the east bank of the Suez Canal. At three o'clock on October 24, President Anwar el-Sadat called for a joint Soviet-American task force to supervise the cease-fire. The United States rejected the plea. At eight Soviet Ambassador Anatoly F. Dobrynin delivered a message from Soviet Party Secretary Leonid Brezhnev to Henry Kissinger calling for such a force. After conferring with the President by telephone, Kissinger again rejected the proposal, explaining that it could be disastrous to involve both superpowers in such a tense situation (privately, American officials suspected that the Russians were using the proposal as a pretext to get a large Soviet force into the Suez area). At 10:40 p.m. Dobrynin brought another Brezhnev message to Kissinger. This one was blunter, warning that if the United States refused to act jointly with the Soviet Union, "we should be faced with the necessity urgently to consider the question of taking appropriate steps unilaterally." This time Dobrynin did not wait for an answer.

The warning—plus intelligence reports of Soviet troop movements and alerts—alarmed Kissinger. He immediately telephoned the President, who was in his living quarters at the White House. Together, they agreed on a firm political response, backed up by a military signal. Nixon left the details to Kissinger.

At 11:00 p.m. Kissinger and Secretary of Defense James Schlesinger met in the map-filled Situation Room in the White House basement. Later, both men described this as an "abbreviated" National Security Council meeting. If so, it was one of the most curious NSC meetings in history. The records maintained by the NSC staff make no mention of a council meeting that night. Of the council's four statutory members, only two were present. The President remained upstairs. The Vice President did not exist (Gerald Ford had not yet been confirmed). Admiral Thomas Moorer, chairman of the Joint Chiefs of Staff—not a council member—was there as military adviser. CIA Director William Colby—also not a member—was called in belatedly as intelligence adviser. Kissinger, of course, was there in two capacities—secretary of state and the President's assistant for national security affairs. "In effect," one aide said, "the meeting consisted of Kissinger, Kissinger, and Schlesinger."

In any case, Kissinger and Schlesinger swiftly decided to put U.S. forces on "Defense Condition 3," which is defined by the Pentagon as "an order to stand by for further orders that may come." It is the middle stage in a scale of five alerts; the top two have never been used. After Admiral Moorer transmitted the orders to the service chiefs at eleven-thirty he and James Schlesinger discussed the situation for another two hours. Then they drove back across the Potomac, where Schlesinger bolstered the alert by ordering the aircraft carrier *John F. Kennedy* with her A-4 fighter bombers from the Atlantic to the Mediterranean and telling the 15,000-man 82nd Airborne Division at Fort Bragg, North Carolina, to prepare to board transport craft.

At 3:00 a.m. Kissinger walked upstairs to the President's private quarters, where Nixon had remained throughout the night, and got "ratification" of all the moves. Then they went to bed.

The next day, after news of the alert leaked out to the news media, the "crisis" was quickly resolved. That afternoon the United States and the Soviet Union both supported a Security Council resolution establishing a United Nations peace-keeping force in the Middle East.

Two days later, at a news conference, Nixon described this as "the most difficult crisis we've had since the Cuban confrontation of 1962." He also dramatized his own role in the matter, suggesting that he had been in active charge of the American response: "When I received that information, I ordered shortly after midnight on Thursday morning, an alert for all American forces around the world."

Some commentators—noting the President's curious isolation on the critical evening—expressed disbelief. They suggested that there had been no crisis at all, merely a potential crisis which quickly vanished. When reporters asked Kissinger whether the whole affair might have been puffed up to divert the country's attention from Watergate, he indignantly denied it, saying that the very fact that such doubts could be raised was "a symptom of what is happening to our country."

Whatever the motivation for calling the alert, Nixon certainly exploited it later to underline his role in maintaining world peace and, thus, the need to keep him in office. "Even in this week, when many thought the President was shell-shocked, unable to act, the President acted decisively in the interest of the country," he told his October 26 news conference. And he added, "I have a quality which is—I guess I must have inherited it from my Midwestern mother and father—which is that the tougher it gets, the cooler I get."

But then, amid all this bravado, he dropped the other shoe in his awkward retreat from the Saturday Night Massacre. Revoking the weeklong "abolition" of the special prosecutor's office, he announced that Acting Attorney General Robert Bork would soon appoint a replacement for Cox. The new special prosecutor would have "independence" and "total cooperation from the executive branch," Nixon said—although that cooperation would not include handing over further tapes of Presidential conversations.

On October 30 Haig put through a long-distance call to a Houston lawyer named Leon Jaworski. Would he be interested in becoming the new special prosecutor? No thanks, said Jaworski. He had received a similar feeler from Elliot Richardson before Cox's appointment, but had turned it down because he did not think the post had sufficient independence. Things had changed, Haig insisted. Wouldn't he at least come to Washington and talk it over? Haig spoke about the "revolutionary" state of the country and said, "I'm going to put the patriotic monkey on your back." Jaworski resisted some more, but finally agreed to fly to Washington on a plane Haig sent to pick him up. At the White House the next day Haig promised Jaworski that, if necessary, he could sue the President for any materials he thought essential to his task, and he could not be fired without "substantial concurrence" from the majority and minority leaders of the Senate, the Speaker and minority leader of the House, the chairman and ranking Republican on both the House and Senate Judiciary Committees. It was a hard sell, but the White House wanted Jaworski very badly. On November 1—as Senator William B. Saxbe of Ohio was nominated to be the new attorney general—Bork announced Jaworski's appointment.

To Nixon and his men, Jaworski must have seemed the docile special prosecutor they had been looking for from the start. A self-made Texas millionaire who traveled in the same Southern Rim circles as the President; a corporate lawyer who represented special, rather than public, interests; director of three banks and four corporations; a conservative Democrat long closely allied to the Johnson-Connally wing of the party; a former president of the American Bar Association (a badge of recognition from the legal establishment). In almost every respect, he seemed the antithesis of the austere Archibald Cox, and his appointment plainly dismayed Cox's young attorneys ("It looks like we're about to be sold down the Rio Grande," one groused). But such alarmists underestimated the combative obstinacy which lurked within the wizened little man from Houston. "He's a stand-up guy," said Chesterfield Smith, the new president of the ABA. "If he's shoved, he will shove back." And an old friend warned, "He's a real, soft-spoken, gentle, tough s.o.b." Leon Jaworski's special brand of gentle-toughness was bred in the hard-scrabble hill country of northern Texas. His Polish father and Austrian mother were "poor as church mice" when they brought up their four children in Waco. But an old family friend recalls their third child's extraordinary drive: "Leon didn't court success, he swept her off her feet." At nineteen, he *was the youngest student ever to graduate from Baylor University. He earned a master's degree from George Washington University in Washington at the tender age of twenty. And soon he became the youngest licensed attorney in Texas history. From the start, he had a penchant for tough cases. His first case was defending a man accused of operating a still in bonedry west Texas. In 1962 he accepted appointment by then Attorney General Robert Kennedy to prosecute Mississippi Governor Ross Barnett for criminal contempt in blocking the admission of James Meredith to the University of Mississippi. This drew a spate of threatening telephone calls and hate mail which compelled police to guard his home. (One banker wrote: "Every mentally mature person knows you are participating in the Mississippi affair to curry favor with the administration. I hope your daughter has a nigger baby.") The banker's charge was close to the mark on one score: Jaworski did enjoy unusually close ties with then Vice President Lyndon Johnson. In 1948 Jaworski helped win an electoral fraud case against him. Twelve years later he defended Johnson again in two suits challenging his right to run simultaneously for the Senate and the Vice Presidency. When Johnson became President, he wanted to appoint Jaworski attorney general. Sensitive to charges of cronyism, he selected another Texan, Ramsey Clark, and named Jaworski to four Presidential commissions instead. So, during the 1960s, Jaworski spent most of his time back in Texas, making lots of money (more than $200,000 a year) and practicing law with the huge Houston firm of Fulbright, Crooker & Jaworski. In that turbulent decade, he seemed to retreat into a hardline law-and-order position. In 1965 he declared that it was "illogical" to add poor people to the board of Houston's antipoverty agency, of which he was then chairman. Juris Doctor—a national magazine which speaks for many young lawyers—found "no fierce sense of moral outrage at social injustice gnawing at his gut." He was much less interested in legal theory or extensive staff analysis than Cox. "Archie ran this place like a law professor at a seminar," one aide said.*

"Leon runs it like the head of a litigation section of a major law firm." He wanted results and he wanted them quickly. "The American people are entitled to some answers without waiting forever," Jaworski said as he took office, "and I intend to get those answers."

One reason the White House wanted a cooperative prosecutor on the job became clear on October 31—the day before Jaworski's appointment was announced. That morning Fred Buzhardt revealed that two of the nine subpoenaed tapes did not exist. The June 20, 1972, conversation between John Mitchell and Richard Nixon and the April 15, 1973, talk between John Dean and Nixon, he said, had never been recorded.

These were two vital links in the chain of evidence which the special prosecutor's office had been trying to assemble. The June 20 telephone conversation was the first time Nixon and Mitchell talked following the Watergate burglary. Both men had been briefed by their aides that day: Nixon had spoken with H. R. Haldeman and John Ehrlichman at length; Mitchell had received a report from Bob Mardian and Fred LaRue after they debriefed Gordon Liddy. Presumably the two men had plenty to say to each other, though they talked for only four minutes—from 6:08 to 6:12 p.m. Nixon says he called Mitchell to "try to cheer him up," but that the attorney general was "terribly chagrined that the activities of anybody attached to his committee should have been handled in such a manner, and he said that he only regretted that he had not policed all the people more effectively." Mitchell says he told Nixon only about the five burglars and nothing about the involvement of "higher-ups." Since Mitchell knew all about the roles of Liddy and Hunt —not to mention Magruder, Dean, and himself—the prosecutors wanted to hear the tape of that conversation.

The April 15 meeting was the first of three which Dean and Nixon held within twenty-four hours in the crisis days of mid-April. Earlier that day the President had been briefed extensively on the burgeoning scan-

dal—including Dean's testimony to the prosecutors
—by Richard Kleindienst and Henry Petersen. Meanwhile, Dean had met with the prosecutors again and
told them for the first time about Hunt's and Liddy's
role in the Fielding burglary. By the time Nixon and
Dean met at the White House—from 9:17 to 10:12
p.m.—they were very near an open break. But each
was still feeling the other out, trying to determine what
his intentions were. According to Dean, at this meeting
the President said in nearly inaudible tones—apparently to avoid the microphones—that he had been foolish
to discuss Howard Hunt's clemency with Chuck Colson, and that he had been joking when he said it
would be easy to raise $1 million in hush money for
the Watergate defendants. The President's notes of the
meeting indicate that he asked Dean what Herbert
Kalmbach had been told about the purpose of the
"hush money" and Dean replied that he had briefed
Haldeman and Ehrlichman every inch of the way. The
prosecutors needed this tape to chart the course of the
cover-up.

Buzhardt's startling revelation about the missing
tapes was made first at a private session with Judge
Sirica and representatives of the special prosecutor's
office on the morning of October 31. The judge
promptly summoned both sides into open court, where
he announced that he would conduct hearings on the
matter. But the more he tried to unsnarl the issue, the
more tangled it became.

At first, Buzhardt said the June 20 conversation had
not been recorded because it was made from a phone
in the West Hall of the White House which was not
hooked up to the tape recorders, and that the April
15 meeting had not been picked up by a malfunctioning recorder. Buzhardt repeated these explanations in
court the next day, presenting a Secret Service agent
who testified that a timer that should have switched on
the machines on April 15 had not worked. But on
November 2 the White House revised this explanation,
contending that a six-hour tape had run out before
the Nixon-Dean conversation could be recorded. And
as Judge Sirica continued his fact-finding inquiry, em-

barrassing new revelations emerged every day: tapes had been removed from a White House safe without being logged back in; record-keeping for the tapes proved to be surprisingly informal, with one log kept on the back of a paper bag; and, finally, the President had known the tapes did not exist on September 29, more than a month before his lawyer informed the court.

But substantial evidence suggested that the tapes had once existed or, that if they had somehow disappeared, the President would have known about it much earlier than September 29. The most compelling evidence concerned the April 15 tape. Henry Petersen has testified that on April 18 Nixon offered to let him listen to that conversation ("I have it on tape if you want to listen to it") but later said he had no such tape, only a Dictabelt recording of his own recollections of the meeting. (Later still he told the special prosecutor that even the Dictabelt had disappeared.) Moreover, the President conceded that on June 4, 1973, he listened to certain tapes of his conversations with Dean; Stephen Bull says Haig gave him a list of conversations the President wanted to hear and he got twenty-six tapes from the Secret Service; the Secret Service record of the tapes checked out to Bull suggests that the tapes of the April 15 conversations were among them. If a tape of the Dean conversation did not exist, the President presumably would have known about it then. Bull also testified that on June 25, 1973, Nixon ordered a tape flown to San Clemente, but that no courier flight could be arranged. At first Bull said the tape he was prepared to send west was of the April 15 Dean conversation; after he had been "educated" by White House officials, he changed his mind and said it was of a March 20 meeting with Dean.

Many people simply did not believe the White House explanations about the missing tapes. Senator James Buckley, the New York Conservative-Republican, said, "As of this moment, President Nixon has the clear burden of satisfying the American people that he has been speaking the truth. If he fails in this, then we are faced with a political crisis of the most profoundly disturbing proportions." Senator Mark Hatfield, the Oregon Republican, said, "The startling revelation that certain key tapes of the President's conversations do not exist—the very tapes that have been fought over to the brink of a constitutional crisis—dramatically escalates the problems of the administration's credibility."

If the firestorm had primed the charge, the "missing tapes" triggered it—setting off a chain reaction of new demands for the President's resignation. First, they came from predictable quarters: John Gardner of Common Cause ("He sits in the midst of wreckage. He cannot govern. He should resign"), and Democratic Senators John Tunney and Daniel Inouye. But then the President's former friends and supporters joined the attack: Senator Edward Brooke ("I do not think that the country can stand the trauma that it has been going through for the past months"), the conservative columnist Joseph Alsop ("The President has been crippled"). In their editions of Sunday, November 4, *The New York Times,* the *Detroit News,* the *Denver Post,* and the *Atlanta Journal* all called for Nixon's resignation. They were followed by *Time* magazine which, in its first editorial in fifty years, said "he has irredeemably lost his moral authority, the confidence of most of the country, and therefore his ability to govern effectively."

Others—as diverse as the columnists James J. Kilpatrick and Anthony Lewis, Senator George McGovern and Clare Boothe Luce—argued that resignation was the easy, and wrong, way out. Each for his own reasons believed that only impeachment could determine the President's guilt or innocence and restore the people's faith in the governmental process.

By November 7—one year after the President's landslide re-election—confidence in Nixon had dropped precipitously. That very day, Congress handed him a serious legislative defeat by overriding his veto of the War Powers Bill, which limited the President's authority to wage undeclared war. The stock market, hard hit by fears of a growing "energy crisis," continued a steep decline. And that same week, the Gallup Poll showed that only 27 per cent of those questioned thought the President was handling his job well, against 60 per cent who did not—almost precisely reversing the results of a year before, when 62 per cent approved of his performance and 28 per cent did not. "Let's face it," a White House aide told *Newsweek*. "Our backs were to the wall. We had to go public."

On November 6 Gerald Warren, the deputy press secretary, said the President had a "complete and full understanding" of the credibility problem he faced on Watergate and "intends to meet this matter head on" and "deal with it in a forthright way." The next evening Nixon formally opened his counterattack with a nationally televised address on the energy crisis that he closed on a personal note: "I have no intention whatever of walking away from the job I was elected to do. As long as I am physically able, I am going to continue to work sixteen to eighteen hours a day."

The counterattack, which came to be known as Operation Candor, actually began on October 31 when Al Haig went to Capitol Hill to brief anxious Republican leaders and assured them that the tapes were "exculpatory." Specifically, he promised that the March 21, 1973, tape would show that was the first time Nixon learned of the Watergate cover-up.

Operation Candor gathered force during early November when the President personally took his case to Congress. In both scope and tenor the effort was unprecedented: a series of eight meetings in six days, during which the President met with nearly all of the two hundred and thirty-four Republicans in the House and Senate—and forty-six Democrats as well. Over corned-beef hash at breakfast, and hot hors d'oeuvres and cocktails in the evening, he appealed for support from the representatives who might one day vote on his impeachment and from the senators who would then have to pass on his guilt or innocence. The exercise brought a stinging rebuke from House Majority Leader O'Neill, who accused Nixon of trying to "curry favor with his prospective grand jurors." But most of those invited felt they should at least go and hear their President out.

The gatherings usually began with a Nixon monologue. He appealed for sympathy in his Watergate travails ("seven months of pure hell"), attacked John Dean's credibility ("I'm not saying he's a liar. I'm just saying he's mistaken"), defended himself against charges of personal corruption ("If I wanted to make money, I would not be in this business. If I wanted to cheat, I wouldn't do it here"), accused Cox and Richardson of double-dealing ("Elliot didn't tell the truth about what happened"), and warned that he had to stay in office ("If you cut the legs off the President, America is going to lose").

Some of his listeners were awed (Representative Dan Kuykendall of Tennessee exclaimed, "My God, I wish ten reporters had been there! The candor, the obvious straightforward honesty of his answers!"), and some were impressed by his sheer determination to survive ("You just have to struggle back up hill and that's what he apparently intends to do," said Representative Barber B. Conable of New York). But others—chiefly senators—were less respectful and reticent. Senator Brooke told the President, "I have reluctantly come to the conclusion, as painful as it is to me, that you should resign." Barry Goldwater said, "The only time you get us down here is when you get your ass in a crack and want us to get it out for you."

The frankest of all was Senator Bob Packwood. At forty-one, in the fifth year of his first term, Packwood was one of the most independent Senate Republicans and had already distanced himself somewhat from Nixon. His first open break with the President had come when Nixon nominated Clement Haynsworth to the Supreme Court. While he was still undecided about how to vote on the nomination, Packwood had been summoned to the Oval Office for a thirty-minute "one-on-one" session with Nixon. After listening to his reservations—chiefly concerning Haynsworth's stand on civil rights and civil liberties—the President put his arm around the young senator and said, "Bob, I understand all that, but I'd like you to do me a personal favor and vote for Haynsworth." Packwood thought, Boy, this is the most pressure I've ever been under. But he voted against Haynsworth. The President never quite forgave him.

A year later, Packwood was "carrying the ball" for the administration on a transportation strike bill designed to deal with the nationwide paralysis caused by a months-long longshoremen's strike. "I'd been working on the bill for six or seven months, ten or twelve hours a week. We were right up to the final vote when Larry Silberman, the undersecretary of labor, called up to say that the administration no longer felt the bill was 'appropriate or timely.' I said, 'Larry, what are you doing?' He said, 'I can't tell you any more now. You'll understand this afternoon.' That afternoon the Teamsters endorsed Nixon for President. It was pretty clear that dropping the bill had been part of the deal. That left a lasting impression on me."

From the start Packwood had suspected the President's disclaimers on Watergate. A close friend of William Ruckelshaus, he was outraged by the Saturday Night Massacre. So, when the President invited him and ten other Republican senators over for a chat, he sat down and prepared an outline for a six- or seven-minute statement.

At five o'clock on November 15 he and the other senators were ushered into the White House solarium, recently renamed the "California Room." The President strode in wearing a subdued sport coat and slacks, and over drinks joked nervously with them about being too "sportily" dressed. When they were all seated in a large oval, Nixon made a few opening remarks and then called on one senator after another. Most of them were discreet and decorous. Some of the senators were solid "Nixon men": Strom Thurmond of South Carolina, Peter H. Dominick of Colorado, William L. Scott of Virginia. Others were relatively junior senators like Robert T. Stafford of Vermont and Richard S. Schweiker of Pennsylvania, without the seniority or self-confidence generally required to challenge the President.

One of the few questions with any sting came from Schweiker, who asked, "Mr. President, are there going to be any more surprises about the tapes?"

"No, absolutely not," Nixon said.

Senator Scott brought the conversation back to more parochial matters. He asked Nixon about an appointment in Virginia that had not been cleared with the Republican state chairman.

When Packwood heard that, he was more determined than ever to make his statement. "I'm as much in awe of the White House, of the office of the Presidency, as anybody else," he recalls. "But somebody had to tell the President what the country was feeling. I was determined to go ahead come hell or high water."

When Nixon turned to him, Packwood said he had a statement to make and he'd prefer to go through it without interruption. The room grew hushed and he could sense the others thinking, Oh God, what's he going to say! What's he going to do? But he plunged ahead.

"All of us, Mr. President, whether we're in politics or not have weaknesses. For some, it's drinking. For others, it's gambling. For still others, it's women. None of these weaknesses applies to you. Your weakness is credibility. This has always been your short suit with the news media and the general public. The problem with the public is that they no longer believe you. They no longer trust the integrity of the administration," Packwood said.

As for Congress, he went on, many members believed Nixon had broken his word to them by firing Cox. "Congress has come to expect that many people who testify before it lie. It's an entirely different matter, however, when one person gives his word to another. That is a bond which those of us in politics revere highly. Those who breach that bond suffer an incalculable loss of credibility."

Packwood then broke away from his outline to deal with a remark the President had made earlier in reply to a question from Senator Stafford. Nixon had said he would not resign because he had not been convicted of any crime. "That just struck a nerve with me," Packwood recalls. "It hit me that that was the crux of the whole Watergate thing."

So he told the President, "For too long, this administration has given the public the impression that its standard of conduct was not that it must be above suspicion but that it must merely be above criminal guilt. Mr. President, that is not an adequate standard of conduct for those who have been accorded the privilege of governing this country."

Throughout the long statement, Nixon looked toward the young senator, but not at him. "He seemed to be looking right through me," Packwood recalls. "He wasn't focusing. I don't think he wanted to focus on what I was saying. When I was finished he said, 'Thank you,' and moved on to the next man."

Nixon was not interested in reassessing his standards or his approach to government. It was too late for that. He was engaged in a public-relations operation. Indeed, from the start, the President had approached Watergate essentially as a public-relations problem. Haldeman's notes of a conversation with Nixon three days after the break-in show that the President's first reaction was to order a "PR offensive to top this."

This was Nixon's approach to most problems. As Jonathan Schell has pointed out, he was preoccupied with "the appearance of things." Alexander Butterfield testified that "The President often, of course, was concerned whether or not the curtains were closed or open; the arrangement of state gifts—whether they should be on that side of the room or this side of the room, displayed on a weekly basis or on a monthly basis. . . . He was deeply involved in the entertainment business—whom we should get, for what kind of group, small band, big band, black band, white band, jazz band, whatever. He was very interested in meals and how they were served. . . . He was very interested in whether or not salad should be served and decided that at small dinners of eight or less the salad course should not be served."

He concentrated relentlessly on the image, rather than the substance, of policy.

Surrounding himself with men whose background had been in advertising or marketing, he sought to bring those soft-soaping techniques to bear on the intractable stuff of politics. His first reaction to many issues was not "Is it right?" but "Will it sell?" This may be true of many politicians, but Richard Nixon was distinguished by his utter absorption with merchandising techniques. Jeb Magruder, one of those brought in to handle PR, recalls, "The most sophisticated student of public relations in the White House was neither Haldeman nor Klein, but the President himself." Early in his administration, he bombarded his assistants with memos complaining about the White House public-relations operation. On September 22, 1969, for example, he wrote to Haldeman, "In memoranda in the future, I shall use the letters PR whenever I am referring generally to a project I want carried out in the PR front. Until we get a full-time man I think we need in this field, you have full responsibility for seeing that these decisions are implemented. What is particularly important is that I be informed as to what action has been taken and, if action is not taken, why the decision has been made not to take it."

His aides took these strictures seriously. Witness this memo by Jeb Magruder, explaining how to reach the youth of America: "Who better than Marty Anderson [another Presidential assistant] can 'turn on' young people about draft reform. Young Metro-America won't listen to Mel Laird, but they will to Marty Anderson, not because Marty's any more liberal (he's probably less liberal than Laird) but because he's got more *hair,* a Ph.D., a sexy wife, drives a Thunderbird, and lives in a high-rise apartment." Haldeman agreed. "Absolutely," he scrawled in the margin. "Really work on this."

Nixon knew how fickle the public could be. "I'm a proponent of the idea, 'buy a good headline for a day,' " he told Haldeman and Ehrlichman on April 14, 1973. He knew that a bombshell in Washington was often a weak firecracker in Iowa. On April 16 he said, "Well, in the country it is not that big. It is just a little bit in the evening news and it should be handled as a news story." He knew people's memory was short. On April 17 Haldeman said, "You know where the Watergate story is in *The Washington Post* today? Page nineteen," and Nixon replied, "I know. And it'll be page nineteen five months from now if we handle it right." Day in and day out he asked, "How do you handle that PR-wise?" And he constantly reminded his assistants that they were not fighting primarily a legal battle, not even a narrowly political battle. "What we're fighting," he said, "is a public-relations battle."

On November 15—the day he met with Packwood —Nixon began carrying Operation Candor to the people. In a hastily arranged address to four thousand members of the National Association of Realtors, he mixed pledges of probity ("The President has not violated his trust and he isn't going to violate his trust now") with patriotic bravura ("I believe in America and I believe in America's real estate"). And the next day he set out on a five-day swing through the South, a barnstorming trip reminiscent of his political campaigns. He chose the South because it was the only region in which he retained even a shred of his former popularity. White House aides conceded that audiences were carefully selected to show him in his best light.

The first stop was Disney World. The Magic Kingdom in Orlando, Florida, is a masterful blend of fantasy and reality. Visitors suspend disbelief as they traipse through Cinderella's Castle; the Mickey Mouse Revue; Frontierland; Tomorrowland; Adventureland; Fantasyland; the Country Bear Jamboree; Main Street, U.S.A.; and the Hall of Presidents, in which life-sized "Audio-Animatronic" figures of thirty-six Presidents —including Richard Nixon—nod, blink, gesticulate, and orate.

Walt Disney's vision of Disneyland and Disney World was of a "controlled environment which would have everything I dreamed of doing as a kid—and couldn't." Now, Disney World provided the beleaguered President his own form of controlled environment—the annual meeting of the Associated Press Managing Editors Association. The President had long tried to go over the heads of the working press to editors, publishers, and broadcast executives, who were further from the news and less inclined to ask the hard questions. Herb Klein had carefully cultivated this tailored constituency, inundating them with documents and inviting them to cozy Presidential "briefings." The managing editors' meeting offered Nixon an ideal opportunity to stage the appearance of a news conference without its substance. White House correspondents who accompanied the President on his Southern blitzkrieg —but were prohibited from asking questions at Disney World—warned their editors that they were being had. Some of the editors took these warnings to heart and did their best to prepare.

But most of their questions were like soft lobs at the net for Rod Laver. John Quinn of Gannett, the association's president, asked, "Can we keep the Republic, sir?" Richard Smyser of Oak Ridge, Tennessee, asked: to what extent did the President's heavy responsibilities "explain possibly how something like Watergate can occur?" (George Packard, editor of the *Philadelphia Bulletin,* concluded ruefully, "The President should have been walking into a den of lions, but what he found instead was a Disney World where the animals have no teeth.") At times Nixon seemed delighted with these puffballs, complimenting the editors on their "very good questions and very appropriate ones." But once he seemed to chide them for not asking tougher ones: "Since you haven't raised some of the subjects, I'll raise them myself. ITT, how did we raise the price of milk—I wish somebody'd ask me that." And he found time for one of his most memorable disclaimers: "People have the right to know whether or not their President is a crook. Well, I am not a crook."

His next step was Macon, Georgia, where he paid tribute to a Democrat—former Representative Carl Vinson—on his ninetieth birthday and got a warm response from the predominantly Democratic audience. Then, on November 20, he flew to Memphis for a meeting with the nation's nineteen Republican governors. In a Holiday Inn overlooking the Mississippi, he wooed the governors with rare contrition: "If I have added to your burden, I am sorry for it." The governors, many of them anxious about Watergate's backlash, seemed cheered by the President's performance. "All of us are going home feeling better," said Governor Ronald Reagan of California. They were particularly reassured when Governor Tom McCall of Oregon asked a question that had been on many of their minds: "Are we going to be blindsided by any more 'bombshells'?" and the President responded, "If there are any more bombs, I'm not aware of them."

Nixon did know of one item, however, that sounded very much like a bomb when it dropped onto the Washington battlefield the next day. On November 21—in a private session in Judge Sirica's chambers —Fred Buzhardt said, "Judge, we have a problem." Then he disclosed that the tape of the June 20 conversation between Nixon and Haldeman had a shrill buzz which blocked out some eighteen minutes of the conversation. Buzhardt asked Sirica to withhold the news, "because disclosure would be devastating." Jaworski objected, noting that obstruction of justice could be involved. Judge Sirica sided with the special prosecutor, and a few minutes later Fred Buzhardt dropped the new bomb into a stunned courtroom.

In early 1973 Judge Matthew Byrne discovered that for nearly a year the government had been withholding reports showing that release of the Pentagon Papers did not compromise national security. The reports had been written in the office of J. Fred Buzhardt, Jr., general counsel to the Department of Defense. Moreover, there was testimony that high Defense Department officials had ordered the reports suppressed so as not to jeopardize the prosecution of Daniel Ellsberg. But when Buzhardt was called to testify at Ellsberg's trial on January 30, he insisted he could not recall anything about the exculpatory reports or about suppressed evidence. Three months later Buzhardt was named special counsel to the President with particular responsibility for Watergate. In midsummer he took responsibility for the sensitive White House tapes. Dur-

ing the next year—as suspicious gaps and missing conversations kept cropping up in the tapes under Buzhardt's control—many people wondered what had led Nixon to place a man like this in charge of his Watergate defense. But they ignored one startling possibility: that the President knew precisely what he was doing when he brought in a lawyer trained to withhold —rather than disclose—information. Fred Buzhardt came to Nixon's defense out of the military establishment and the Southern Strategy. Born in Greenwood, South Carolina, he served in the Army Air Corps in 1942–43, then entered West Point, where he compiled a mediocre academic record, graduating 510th in a class of 875. He resumed his Air Corps career, but in 1950—at the age of twenty-six—he was forced to give up flying because his delicate ears could not take the pressure. So he went home to South Carolina, got a law degree, and for the next six years practiced law with his father (he still likes to call himself a "country lawyer"). Buzhardt senior was a close friend and former law partner of Senator Strom Thurmond. In 1958 Thurmond brought his old friend's son to Washington, where, for the next eight years, he worked on the senator's staff. In 1966 Buzhardt went back to South Carolina to practice law. But after Nixon took office—with Strom Thurmond's enthusiastic support —the senator found his protégé a place in the new administration: special assistant to the assistant secretary of defense for administration. At home in the military world, he moved up quickly. Soon, he became chairman of a panel which proposed major cutbacks in the department's bureaucracy. In August 1970 he was promoted to general counsel and, in that capacity, became one of Secretary Melvin Laird's closest advisers. The secretary listened to him, one colleague recalls, "on everything from civil rights to dropping bombs." When the press began publishing the Pentagon Papers in June 1971, Buzhardt became deeply involved in the investigation and in the administration's efforts to exploit the situation for political purposes. He and Robert Mardian met with leaders of the House Armed Services Committee to prepare for hearings which, they hoped, would portray Ellsberg as part of a major radical conspiracy. When Elliot Richardson became secretary of defense he too found Fred Buzhardt useful. "He is a man who finds solutions," Richardson said. "In Fred's case, there is always a way to get there from here, and it's always a legal way." His reputation spread. In January 1973, when the White House was trying to install "a real tiger" as minority counsel to the Ervin committee, Ehrlichman suggested Buzhardt for the job, which eventually went to Fred Thompson. When he reached the White House, Buzhardt's performance drew contempt from some (one colleague called him a "bubblehead") and fury from others (Joe Kraft said he was a "shyster lawyer" who specialized in "misrepresentation, corner-cutting, deceit, obstructions"). He was the most anonymous of officials, the quintessential "inside man." But after he left office, he talked a bit about his philosophy of government. Warning against "expecting public officials to deal effectively with the nation's problems if restricted by an inflexible moral code," he told an interviewer, "You can make a strong argument that for a President in this day and time you don't want a babe in the woods. He's got to deal with some pretty rough-and-tumble people. Would you rather have a competent scoundrel or an honest boob in office?"

The June 20 meeting was presumed to be one of the most important in the Watergate cover-up. The night before, Nixon and Haldeman had returned from Key Biscayne and Walker's Cay where they had been during the Watergate break-in. From 9:00 to 10:30 a.m. Haldeman met with Ehrlichman, Mitchell, Dean, and Kleindienst to go over the weekend's events; Ehrlichman went in to see the President at 10:30 but they did not discuss Watergate. Then, from 11:26 to 12:45, Haldeman met with Nixon, and his notes make clear that after some preliminaries, they began talking about Watergate, chiefly the "public-relations" problems it raised.

The timing of the buzz is suspicious. The first three

minutes and forty seconds of the conversation, given over to preliminaries, are preserved on the tape. The last audible exchange is about a trip west, including a mention of Ely, Nevada, Mrs. Nixon's birthplace. According to Haldeman's notes, this was the last topic discussed before they moved on to Watergate. The buzz then covers the next eighteen and a half minutes, which apparently coincide almost precisely with the portion of the conversation which dealt with Watergate. The tape becomes audible again as Nixon and Haldeman began to talk about the Senate Foreign Relations Committee hearing on SALT—according to Haldeman's notes, the first subject they got to after Watergate.

At a hearing before Judge Sirica on November 26, Rose Mary Woods testified that she had caused the buzz by pressing the wrong button on her tape recorder while she was transcribing the tape—although later she insisted she could only have been responsible for five of the missing eighteen and a half minutes.

According to testimony given at subsequent hearings, the President had decided on September 28 to review the contents of the nine tapes subpoenaed by Cox. He asked Miss Woods to go to Camp David to transcribe the tapes and Steve Bull to accompany her to "cue" them up. The next morning—Saturday, September 29 —they took eight to twelve tapes to the Maryland retreat and began transcribing the first tape listed on Cox's subpoena as "1-A Meeting of June 20, 1972, in the President's Executive Office Building ('EOB') Office involving Richard Nixon, John Ehrlichman, and H. R. Haldeman from 10:30 a.m. to noon (time approximate)."

Haig has testified that early that morning Bull told him he could not find the tape for the Nixon-Haldeman meeting. Haig says he called Buzhardt, who told him that Cox was confused about that item and that what the special prosecutor really wanted was a conversation between Nixon and Ehrlichman that lasted from 10:30 to 11:25 a.m. (although an August 13 memo from the special prosecutor had clarified the original subpoena, making clear that the conversations with Ehrlichman and then Haldeman lasted until 12:45 p.m.). Haig passed this message on to Miss Woods, who worked until the early hours of Sunday morning, then all Sunday (a total of twenty-nine hours) transcribing the Ehrlichman portion of the tape. Once, Nixon wandered into the Dogwood Cabin, where she and Bull were working, "listened to different parts of the tape, pushing buttons back and forth," then sympathized with them on their "terrible" job. One reason the job was so terrible, Miss Woods testified, was that the Sony had no foot pedal for stopping, reversing, and restarting the tape. So the Secret Service was instructed to purchase a machine with a foot pedal.

On Monday, October 1, Miss Woods continued work on the tape in her office at the White House, this time with a new Uher 5000 recorder supplied by the Secret Service. According to her later testimony, this is what happened. Around two o'clock she finished the Ehrlichman portion and was listening to the start of the Haldeman section—merely to make sure that Ehrlichman had left the room. Just as she heard the remark about Ely, Nevada, the telephone rang. As she answered it, she must have pressed the "record" button on the unfamiliar machine instead of the "stop" button. (In a court appearance before the eighteen-minute gap was revealed, she said scornfully that she was as careful as she needed to be about accidental erasures. Asked what precautions she took, she replied, "I used my head. It was the only one I had to use.") Technicians explained that the Uher machine could have erased the tape if she had pressed the "record" button while keeping her foot on the pedal. Asked if she had done this, Miss Woods said she "must have." But a photograph taken of her re-enacting this feat at the White House made her look—as Jimmy Breslin pointed out—as if she were sliding into third base. And when she ran through it again in court, with the same tape recorder, she reached back to take the phone —and her foot came off the pedal.

Miss Woods says she was on the telephone for at

most five minutes. Then she began listening to the tape again and heard the "shrill" buzz (a reporter who heard the tape later said the buzz sounded like "a television set after a station has signed off for the night"). Miss Woods says she "practically panicked," and when the President was free rushed in to tell him she had made a "terrible mistake." (The President's logs show that his doctor, Major General Walter R. Tkach, was with him when Miss Woods entered and remained there for the two minutes she was with him.) Miss Woods says Nixon took the matter very calmly. "There is no problem," he said, "because that is not a subpoenaed tape."

Haig says he learned that it was indeed a sub-poenaed tape only on November 14. Fred Buzhardt told him he had re-examined the subpoena after discovering that the buzz was eighteen minutes, not five minutes as he had originally thought. Haig waited another twenty-four hours before relaying both these developments to the President, because he did not want to bother Nixon just before he spoke to the realtors. When he did tell him, Haig says, the President was "very, very disturbed" and "almost incredulous." This was at about 4 p.m. An hour later Nixon joked with Bob Packwood and the other senators about his sporty clothes. When asked by Schweiker whether there were any more surprises about the tapes, he said, "No, absolutely not."

The White House waited still another week to inform Judge Sirica. Haig says they delayed in an effort to discover the cause of the buzz. On the evening of November 20—while Nixon was meeting with the Republican governors in Memphis—Buzhardt told Haig that he could find "no innocent explanation," and concluded that the buzz had come from "some outside source of energy" rather than a malfunctioning of the tape recorder. Haig says he and other Presidential assistants suspected that night that the buzz had been caused by "some sinister force."

As November slipped into icy December, a subtle battle developed between Rose Mary Woods and Nixon's lawyers over who that sinister force might be. At her first court appearance on November 8—over the "missing tapes"—Miss Woods had been accompanied by Buzhardt and Garment. But when she appeared on November 26, she had retained her own lawyer, Charles Rhyne, a friend and former law-school classmate of the President's. Rhyne says Haig had called him to say that "White House lawyers had arrived at the conclusion that Rose had erased the tape and they were not going to defend her." Later, he says, Garment and Buzhardt told him, "She did it. No question about it." Soon Rhyne and the men from the White House were scrapping openly. "They're throwing her to the wolves," he told a friend. Nixon's men often did seem to be saddling Rose Mary with blame for the full eighteen minutes, not merely the five. They suggested that the buzz had been caused by her high-intensity lamp or her typewriter. "I've known women that think they've talked for five minutes and then have talked for an hour," Haig said pointedly.

It hardly seems possible that this was not putting a strain on Miss Woods's relations with Nixon. As she left court one day, a reporter asked her whether she still regarded the President as an honest man. "That is a rude, impertinent question," she snapped. "And the answer is yes."

"Rose would die for him," says a friend. "She would just lay down her life and die for him." Even in the worst of the tapes dispute, she seems never to have wavered an inch in her savage support for the man she called "the boss." Indeed, as the palace guard was decimated by resignations and defections, Rose Mary Woods stood as one of the last true loyalists and probably the President's fiercest defender. "She's a little like the choir member in the Baptist church who falls in love with the minister," says one White House aide. "It's the classic Christian fantasy of the virgin and God—and obviously a part of the fantasy is that nothing ever happens. It just remains a kind of worship." Rose Mary never married, but once, it is said, she had a real love. Back in Sebring, Ohio, she was infatu-

ated with the high-school basketball star. They were supposed to get married after graduation, but he died of spinal meningitis. Armed with a high-school prize for shorthand, Rose Mary moved to Washington in 1943 to join the army of young women working for the swollen wartime bureaucracy. After the war she joined the staff of a House committee (studying the Marshall Plan) of which Nixon was a member. The freshman congressman impressed her because he was the only member of the committee who turned in an expense account "titled, totaled, signed, and all properly done." Nixon must have been impressed too, because when he went to the Senate in 1951 he asked her to be his secretary. Over the next twenty years, she became Nixon's "gatekeeper," through whom everyone had to go to reach "the boss." Accumulating a vast store of names and faces, she sorted them into "friends," whom she rewarded with ready access, and "enemies," for whom she harbored a deep, abiding grudge. Leonard Hall, who had been Nixon's campaign manager in 1960, worked for Governors Romney and Rockefeller in 1968. When Nixon was nominated that year, Hall made the traditional call to offer his congratulations. Rose Mary answered the phone and cut him dead with a frosty "Don't call us, we'll call you." And after Butterfield disclosed the taping system to the Ervin committee, Rose Mary telephoned him to say, "You dirty bastard. You have contributed to the downfall of the greatest President this country ever had. You are on the other side." Not surprisingly, Bob Haldeman resented Rose Mary's longtime association with the President—she was one of the last old-timers left—and particularly her proximity. In the "Berlin Wall" he was erecting around the President, with Nixon's wholehearted support, there could be only one gatekeeper: Haldeman himself. So the chief of staff sent Rose Mary a dozen roses, then began maneuvering her out of her strategic location at the doorway to the Oval Office. He even tried for a time to move her over to the Executive Office Building, but eventually settled for a transfer down the West Wing Hall, where, with a staff of three secretaries, she han-

dled the personal side of Nixon's life: invitations, Christmas cards, letters to and from his supporters. For a time, it is said, the despondent Rose Mary turned to drink. And Haldeman, who had driven her to it, promptly told the President she was an unreliable drunk. For these many injuries, she put Haldeman very near the top of her own "enemies list" and seethed inwardly until the moment he resigned. After his departure, she was rewarded with the additional title of "executive assistant" and regained much of her old influence (though not her old office). Even during her professional exile, she had never lost her personal ties to the Nixon family. Known to some as "the Fifth Nixon," to Tricia and Julie as "Aunt Rose," she joined them for Christmas and Thanksgiving dinners, swapped clothes with Pat (they are both size 10), and passed messages back and forth from his relatives (Nixon's mother, Hannah, once told her son that Rose Mary was "our kind of people"). And even during the bad times, she retained a warmth and gaiety largely missing in the rest of the White House. She lived in a duplex at the Watergate decorated with mementoes from her travels with the President. "She doesn't cook," a frequent escort says, "but she's good with ice cubes." A music lover, there is nothing she would rather do than dance. Late one evening, at a reception in San Clemente, a three-piece Mexican band was playing and there on the deserted floor was Rose Mary doing an expert tango—alone.

In late November Judge Sirica announced the appointment of a six-man panel—selected jointly by the White House and the special prosecutor—to study "the authenticity and integrity" of the tapes. On January 15 the experts reported that the eighteen-and-a-half-minute gap had been caused by at least five and perhaps as many as nine separate erasures—"almost surely" on the Uher 5000 machine used by Miss Woods on October 1. They said the erasures had resulted from separate hand manipulations of the controls and not by a single accidental pressing of the wrong button, as the

White House had suggested. The panel declined to say whether the erasures had been deliberate or accidental, but they said the evidence found was "consistent" with the traces left by a deliberate erasure.

Three days later Judge Sirica found "a distinct possibility of unlawful conduct on the part of one or more persons" and asked the special prosecutor to take the matter before a grand jury. The White House pledged full cooperation with this new investigation, but at the same time Nixon's aides began attacking the six experts. In February they hired their own technical expert—Dr. Michael Hecker of the Stanford Research Institute—who soon began impugning the panel's judgments. And Charles Rhyne called the experts' report a "hundred-thousand-dollar boondoggle" prepared by "professors who don't know what they're doing."

But the experts stuck with their conclusion in a final report submitted later that spring. And their conclusions narrowed the search for the person or persons responsible for the erasures. Since they concluded that the erasures had almost certainly been made on the Uher machine purchased on October 1, investigators focused on determining who had access to both that machine and the tape itself between October 1 and November 21. This seemed to eliminate all but five persons: Miss Woods; Stephen Bull; Fred Buzhardt; Haig's deputy, Major General John C. Bennett; and Richard Nixon himself. On January 16 a White House reporter asked Gerald Warren, "Did the President erase the tape?" Warren said, "No." (Despite a thorough investigation, the grand jury has returned no indictments in this area.)

Meanwhile, Judge Sirica was sorting out the seven tapes turned over to him by the White House on November 26. Early in December he gave the special prosecutor four tapes on which the White House had claimed no executive privilege. Then he and his law clerk began listening to the other three. On December 19 the judge ruled that nearly all of two tapes and part of a third were covered by executive privilege and would not be turned over to the prosecution. He said there was no discussion of Watergate in most of the June 20 conversation involving Nixon, Haldeman, and Ehrlichman (he could not rule, of course, on the eighteen minutes of buzzing) and most of the June 30 conversation among Nixon, Haldeman, and Mitchell, except for two sections adding up to less than five minutes. And he said that fifteen minutes of the fifty-minute September 15 conversation among Nixon, Haldeman, and Dean had nothing to do with Watergate. It was the President's first victory in the protracted battle over the White House tapes—a small one, albeit, but still a victory.

On most other fronts, though, the President was fighting a grim, rear-guard battle for his political survival. On December 6 the House of Representatives completed congressional confirmation of Gerald Ford as Vice President and he was sworn in an hour later, with the President standing right behind him. No sooner had the vacancy been filled—and a Republican again placed in direct line of succession—than many Republicans again began talking seriously about impeachment. "It makes impeachment thinkable," said one GOP congressman. "It really hasn't been an acceptable alternative up to now." Ford, they argued, was a conservative Republican whose accession to the Presidency would not violate the 1972 mandate. Moreover, he had the low profile and reputation for quiet integrity many people would now welcome in an interim President.

On December 8 Nixon made the most dramatic gesture of Operation Candor. He released the most complete financial statement ever issued by an American President, a massive dossier of documents, audits, and tax returns that Nixon hoped would "lay to rest" the allegations about his personal finances. And he made two announcements designed to take the sting out of two of the most questionable transactions. He said he would donate the San Clemente estate to the nation after he and his wife died. And he said he would allow the Joint Congressional Committee on Internal Revenue Taxation to decide whether the gift of his Vice-Presidential papers to the National Archives met the criteria for tax deductions and whether there had been any capital gain on his sale of San Clemente land.

But the financial statement did not work out quite as the White House had hoped. First, the joint committee decided not to limit its inquiry to the two issues the President had specified but to examine every aspect of Nixon's tax returns for his Presidential years. The public reacted to the disclosures with continued skepticism and new questions that enraged the President. One day, Nixon bitterly asked several aides if he would next be expected to undress in front of the press.

The public mood of disbelief led the White House to reconsider the efficacy of Operation Candor. The financial statement had originally been conceived as the first in a series of "white papers" designed to answer all the charges against the President. The second installment was to have been detailed summaries of the seven tapes already turned over to Judge Sirica. In a meeting with Republican senators and congressmen on November 9 the President had promised to make such summaries public. But in late December the White House said this decision had been reversed.

Presidential assistants traced this reversal to two "irresponsible" actions by Nixon's opponents. First, they cited an incident on December 17, in which William A. Dobrovir, a lawyer for the consumer advocate Ralph Nader, played a copy of a White House tape—obtained in a lawsuit—at a Georgetown cocktail party. The other factor was the Senate Watergate committee's December 19 subpoena of some five hundred White House tapes and documents. The committee acted after Congress passed a new law giving the courts jurisdiction over congressional subpoenas of the President. The White House called the new subpoenas "irresponsible, ridiculous in their scope, extreme, and utterly incredible," and the President flatly refused to comply. A Presidential spokesman, explaining how these two actions influenced Nixon's thinking on release of the tape summaries, said, "There comes a time to examine the motivation of people seeking this material. When there is excess, when the atmosphere becomes entirely partisan, on the basis of any logic there must be reconsideration. It's hard to respond responsibly to irresponsibility."

But there is substantial evidence to suggest that the Dobrovir incident and the committee subpoena had very little to do with Nixon's decision about the tapes. At most, they were convenient excuses for a conclusion reached on quite different grounds. For months a debate had been raging within the White House on whether release of the summaries would help or hurt the President's cause. Some aides—like the speechwriter Pat Buchanan—had argued that the taped material could only improve Nixon's position. Admittedly, much of it was ambiguous and could be interpreted in different ways by different people. A majority of the American public already believed the President was deeply implicated in the cover-up. By releasing summaries of the tapes, these aides argued, Nixon would get credit for openness, and if most Americans came away with a sense of "ambiguity," at least that was better than a certainty of guilt. Others argued just as strongly that the material on the tapes was so damaging that "most of the public and the news media would conclude that the President was involved in a conspiracy." At a minimum, they said, the tapes showed there was an organized effort to deceive the public and "contain" Watergate because it represented a threat to Nixon's re-election. To many, they would demonstrate much worse. The decision to withhold the summaries was apparently made on the evening of December 14— three days before the Dobrovir incident and five days before the committee's subpoenas—at the meeting in the Roosevelt Room of the White House attended by Haig, Buzhardt, Ziegler, Garment, Buchanan, Harlow, and several others. Chuck Colson says that on December 18 the President told him he would resign rather than release all the White House tapes. "He said he would not sit and preside over the destruction of the Presidency," Colson recalls.

The last gasp of Operation Candor came on January

8, with the President's release of statements on his role in the ITT and milk episodes. In the milk matter, the President acknowledged that he took "traditional political considerations" into account when he ordered the 1971 increase in price supports, but he denied that the increase had been a direct *quid pro quo* for the milk trusts' pledge of $2 million to his campaign. Likewise, he denied that the settlement of the government's suits against ITT had anything to do with the corporation's pledge of $400,000 to underwrite the Republican National Convention. He had intervened in the ITT matter, Nixon said, merely because he opposed the Antitrust Division's philosophy that "bigness per se is bad."

More revealing than the statements themselves was the White House cancellation of an earlier plan to release supporting documents. "In view of the fact that the documents and tapes are on file with the special prosecutor," a press release said, "it should be clear that the accounts published today are consistent with the basic facts contained in those documents and tapes." Clearly, Nixon again preferred that the public not see the evidence itself.

By the turn of the year, then, the President had reversed course once again. Stung by public skepticism, angered by the perpetual prying of the press, chastened by warnings that further disclosures would only weaken his position, Nixon abandoned his effort to fight the case in public and reverted to a tight-fisted, close-to-the-chest stance with heavy emphasis on a tenacious legal defense. This tactical shift was signaled on January 4 by the appointment of James D. St. Clair to replace Fred Buzhardt as the President's chief Watergate lawyer.

*"Nixon just got the best trial lawyer in the country,"
Boston's mayor, Kevin White, remarked when he
heard the news. As he dug in for what promised to be
a long legal battle for survival, the President—on
Chuck Colson's advice—had reached out for a man
with a formidable reputation for protecting his clients'*

interests. Those clients spanned a broad ideological spectrum. St. Clair had represented bankers accused of embezzling and a business charged with bank fraud; but he had also gained acquittal for William Sloane Coffin, Yale's chaplain, in his celebrated trial for conspiracy to encourage draft evasion. He had defended the Boston school committee in its long struggle against mandatory school desegregation; but he prosecuted a Boston municipal court judge charged with lying under oath and unethical conduct. His career betrayed no pattern of personal commitment or substantive concerns. "The trouble with St. Clair is that he is all case and no cause," said his former client Coffin. George V. Higgins, the author and former assistant U.S. attorney in Boston, calls him "a hired gun." But few legal authorities have ever faulted James St. Clair on his knowledge or use of the law. After he won a major antitrust suit against the National Cranberry Association, Judge Charles E. Wyzanski called St. Clair's performance "a model not likely to be surpassed" for its "thoroughness of preparation, economy of effort, and that indefinable distinction which breathes excellence." Though now the model of a Boston lawyer—known in State Street circles as "the Silver Fox," because of his handsome shock of gray hair—St. Clair came from the rough rubber town of Akron, Ohio. After graduating from the University of Illinois, he entered Harvard Law School. After three years out for wartime service in the Navy, he completed his legal training and then joined the prestigious Boston firm of Hale & Dorr. St. Clair first gained public distinction as the chief assistant to Joseph N. Welch, special counsel for the U.S. Army in the televised Army-McCarthy hearings of 1954. Others credit him with an important behind-the-scene role in the struggle which helped destroy Senator Joseph McCarthy. In subsequent years, St. Clair won a particular reputation for meticulous trial preparation. "Jim can accumulate and absorb an incredible amount of information," says one Boston attorney. He carried into every courtroom a thick, black loose-leaf notebook from which he could extract at a moment's notice any fact relevant to his client's defense. But soon he discovered that representing the President of the United States was different from representing most clients. Some of his former students suggested he would do well to consult a paragraph in Robert E. Keeton's Trial Tactics and Methods, *a book which St. Clair used in a course in trial techniques he taught at Harvard Law School: "Your client may be lying to you. Or he may be grossly, though honestly mistaken. . . . You must check on everything he says . . . unless because of your own extensive association with the client you are willing to stake your own reputation on his being right. If you do not follow this rule, you will sooner or later find yourself in the embarrassing predicament of having your client's falsification exposed to your surprise during trial."*

The day after Christmas, Nixon and a party of twenty-five slipped out of the White House and, under cover of rain and fog, boarded United Airlines Flight 55 for Los Angeles. Only hours before, Gerald Warren had denied that the President would be going to California; in a sharp break with precedent the White House press corps was not informed of the trip until after the plane's departure and no press pool accompanied him. Later Warren said his plans had been kept secret for "security reasons," and he explained that the President's extraordinary use of a commercial flight instead of *Air Force One* was designed to "set an example for the rest of the country during the current energy crisis." But it was also the start of a strange eighteen-day stay at San Clemente, marked by an almost furtive burrowing away from the press, public, and even much of his own administration.

In part, the President's seclusion may have been a response to the atrocious weather which descended on the San Clemente area as soon as he arrived. Nixon's favorite House in the Sun was a desolate refuge in a storm those weeks as the sun disappeared behind slate clouds for days on end and record rains, the highest tides in three hundred years, and even a minor earthquake battered the deserted beaches. On many days he would not even walk the three hundred yards from the house to his office, preferring to remain in his study, telephoning instructions to his staff at the Coast Guard base. Apart from Haig, Ziegler, and Kissinger—his new triumvirate of advisers—during his entire stay he received only three other callers on substantive business. Others cooled their heels for hours and were finally fobbed off on aides. Roy Ash, head of the Office of Management and Budget, flew out to discuss the new budget figures with the President, but was never admitted to Nixon's presence and had to deal with Haig instead. Withdrawn and pensive, Nixon took solitary walks along the beach, read Elton Trueblood's *Abraham Lincoln: Theologian of American Anguish*, watched the football playoffs on television, and sometimes rose in the middle of the night to play the piano in a darkened room. "The President doesn't want to see anyone," a White House official said, "and no one really wants to see the President."

At times, Nixon would suddenly be overcome with an urge to "drive somewhere, anywhere." In violation of the long-standing agreement with the wire services to inform them of Presidential travel plans, he ordered aides not to tell reporters about these trips. Then, he and Bebe Rebozo would sneak off in an unmarked Lincoln and prowl the slippery freeways, trailed only by a single carload of Secret Service men.

On January 9, 1974—Nixon's sixty-first birthday—his staff and family tried to cheer him up with a surprise party. They walked into his office carrying sixty-one roses and wheeling a yellow, blue, and white cake with "Happy Birthday, Mr. President" traced on top. The President stood by his desk, weariness showing on his puffy face, but he ventured a smile as the cake was placed before him.

"Hey, King, want a little lick?" he asked his red Irish setter, King Timahoe.

In the confusion, he leaned against the cake and got icing all over his hands and jacket.

"Let King lick it off," someone shouted.

The President sat down and let his dog clean him up.

Even on his birthday, Nixon was restless. So he, Pat,

and Tricia drove eighty-five miles to the Palm Springs home of Walter H. Annenberg, the ambassador to the Court of St. James. They found the heavily guarded retreat-from-a-retreat so satisfying that they stayed until they were ready to return to Washington on January 13.

On January 21 Congress returned from its Christmas recess and the House Judiciary Committee slowly mounted its impeachment investigation. Nixon withdrew again—this time to Camp David for prolonged work on his State of the Union message.

On the evening of January 30 he appeared before a joint session of Congress and announced his ten-point program to deal with the energy crisis, check inflation, reform domestic programs, and promote world peace. Then, he said he wanted to add "a personal note" about Watergate.

"I recognize that the House Judiciary Committee has a special responsibility in this area, and I want to indicate on this occasion that I will cooperate with the Judiciary Committee in its investigation." But, he said, there was one limitation: "I will follow the precedent that has been followed by and defended by every President from George Washington to Lyndon B. Johnson of never doing anything that weakens the office of the Presidency of the United States."

Moreover, he said, "I believe the time has come to bring that [impeachment] investigation and the other investigations of this matter to an end. One year of Watergate is enough."

Many Republicans rose and gave the President a standing ovation. But most of the Democrats sat with their hands on their knees. And a dozen or so actually hissed the President of the United States.

15

IMPEACHMENT

If, in fact, President Nixon, or any President, has had a central part in planning and executing this terrible deed of subverting the Constitution then I shall do my part as best I can to bring him to answer before the Congress of the United States for this enormous crime.

—John Doar,
July 19, 1974

On February 6 Tom Railsback sent his regrets to the White House. He could not attend the meeting of the Chowder and Marching Club to be held that evening in the executive mansion. The young congressman from downstate Illinois was sorry about that. He enjoyed the weekly gatherings of his legislative fraternity, and particularly their occasional meetings at the White House which had become a tradition during the Nixon years. After all, how many of America's voluntary associations could claim the President of the United States as one of its charter members?

The Chowder and Marching Club grew out of the frustration that many younger members of Congress feel when they try to buck the legislative riptides on Capitol Hill. In March 1949, two young Republicans —Glenn R. Davis of Wisconsin and Donald L. Jackson of California—felt the leadership had "rammed" a veterans' pension bill through the House Committee on Veterans Affairs. Jackson suggested they "get some of the fellows together and see what might be done." They went right out to the Speaker's Lobby and agreed on thirteen of their Republican colleagues (including a young freshman from California named Richard Nixon). All accepted and they gathered at five o'clock the next Wednesday in Jackson's office.

Over the years the group continued to meet at the same time every week, the role of host rotating among the members. They heard reports from each House committee represented, then drifted into wide-ranging discussions of politics and legislation which they lumped under "the good of the order." On ceremonial occasions they would wear chef's hats and aprons to conform with their whimsical title. Membership was augmented at the start of each new Congress with the admission of at least one freshman; and, unlike similar groupings on the Hill, members who left the House remained in the club and often attended meetings.

Indeed, these graduate members soon became the club's greatest ornament. Like the Dallas Cowboys of the National Football League, Chowder and Marching developed a reputation for making shrewd draft choices, carefully picking young talent that would ripen into stardom. By the late 1960s many of its original members had gained seniority in the House, Senate, or elsewhere in government. And when Nixon entered the White House, he brought a formidable array of his Chowder and Marching colleagues into office with him: Melvin Laird as secretary of defense; Hamer H. Budge as chairman of the Securities and Exchange Commission; Donald Jackson as a member of the Interstate Commerce Commission; David Dennison as a member of the Federal Trade Commission; Rogers Morton as chairman of the Republican National Committee, and later secretary of the interior; Clark MacGregor as director of Congressional Relations and then as head of CREEP; Kenneth B. Keating as ambassador to India; John D. Lodge as ambassador to Argentina. Later, of course, Gerald Ford became Vice President. Meanwhile, Ed Gurney, Bill Brock, and Norris Cotton had become administration stalwarts in the Senate. (Charles E. Goodell, a Chowder and Marching member who had fallen out with the President, lost his Senate seat from New York in 1970, largely through the efforts of his old clubmate.)

No wonder, then, that Chowder and Marching's members should have found themselves honored guests at the White House: for regular club meetings when it was Nixon's turn; for stag parties, dinners, or other special events. In March 1969—the club's twentieth anniversary—Nixon gave a dinner party at the White House. The next evening, at yet another Chowder and Marching party, he described the club as "the most ill-organized, disorderly organization I know. It has no constitution, no bylaws, and no president and—I learned last night—no respect for any President." That wasn't what he meant, of course. He meant they were brimming with respect for the President, even awe at their proximity to him, but that they sometimes expressed it in the joshing, irreverent locker-room style which had become the club's trademark.

By early 1974, though, things had changed. Many members of Chowder and Marching had little respect left for the President. Some lamented his indiscretions. "There's a lot of grieving that one of our own has been wounded," said Representative Clair W. Burgener of California. Others—Melvin Laird, John Byrnes, Charles Goodell—already formed part of Gerald Ford's "shadow cabinet." Two members—Tom Railsback and Trent Lott, a young congressman from Mississippi—were on the House Judiciary Committee, studying the President's impeachment. At the weekly Chowder and Marching meetings, Railsback and Lott started giving reports on the progress of the Judiciary Committee's work.

Lott was a down-the-line loyalist, one of the surest votes the President had on the committee. But Railsback was quite a different matter. "Rails"—as his friends call him—had early been tagged as a "comer" in the House. Cautious, deliberate, eager to remain on good terms with his powerful friends in leadership positions, yet a moderate Republican with good instincts, he was not committing himself either way on the impeachment issue. Precisely because of his "centrist" position, he was destined to play a key role in the committee's deliberations. Recognizing this, Bill Timmons and Bryce Harlow had invited him to lunch at the White House mess in December 1973 to get a sense of where he stood and what the committee was up to. Railsback insists that the meeting was "totally innocent —they didn't try to pressure me or anything." But afterward he concluded that he ought to keep his distance from the White House.

When he got the President's invitation to the February 6 Chowder and Marching meeting, Railsback was strongly tempted to go. Lott was going. It was too large a meeting for any pressure to be put on them. But that very day the House of Representatives voted 410–4 to give the Judiciary Committee broad powers to investigate the President and to subpoena anyone, including Nixon himself. "Things were getting pretty serious," Railsback recalls. "I realized that I might soon be facing the President across a hearing table. At the very least, I would soon be voting on an impeachment resolution. In light of all that, I decided it would be better if I didn't go to Chowder and Marching that week."

Until then, few members of Congress—and probably few Americans—had taken the prospects for impeachment very seriously. There had been talk of it for almost a year—ever since April 1973, when the cover-up came apart and spilled a stream of dirty stories into the public trough. On July 31—while the Ervin committee hearings were coming to a close—Democratic Representative Robert F. Drinan of Massachusetts submitted a resolution to impeach Nixon, not for Watergate but for the illegal bombing of Cambodia and, specifically, for lying to Congress about it. The Jesuit priest and law professor from Boston College marshaled a compelling case: that Nixon had ordered some 3700 bombing raids over Cambodia while telling the Congress, "We have scrupulously observed the neutrality of Cambodia for the last five years." Drinan, known to his colleagues as the Mad Monk, was a brilliant, impetuous cleric, impelled by passionate commitment to his principles. But even those who shared

Drinan's outrage over Cambodia and hoped to drive Nixon from office saw his resolution as premature and as a threat to eventual impeachment. For if the matter came to a vote in the late summer of 1973, it certainly would be voted down by a thunderous majority, making a subsequent impeachment effort harder to mount. The White House dallied with the idea of forcing a vote on the resolution, but then decided it would only give the notion greater credence.

During the late summer and early fall, as the President fought with some minor success to regain the initiative on Watergate, the prospect of impeachment receded still further in the public consciousness. To many people, it seemed a remedy so drastic, a precedent so dangerous that it could not be contemplated except in the most bizarre circumstances. Few Americans knew that twelve men had been impeached by the House of Representatives in 185 years—one President, a U.S. senator, a secretary of war, nine federal judges—and four convicted by the Senate. Those who knew anything of this history recalled the impeachment of President Andrew Johnson in 1868, but that precedent only discredited the process further. The Radical Republicans who had sought to drive Johnson from office had been so partisan, hyperbolic, unrestrained, and vicious that they had led historians to cast impeachment into the junkyard of history along with such national experiences as secession and appeasement. The conventional wisdom in academic and legal circles was that the procedure—though a legal last resort—was divisive, disruptive, and futile.

But following the Saturday Night Massacre in October, the idea suddenly seemed less preposterous. Nixon's extreme measures seemed to call for extreme remedies. Early the next week, twelve impeachment resolutions were dropped into the House hopper, co-sponsored by thirty-seven congressmen (thirty-six Democrats and one Republican, Paul McCloskey of California). Seventy-six other congressmen sponsored thirteen other resolutions calling for inquiries into possible impeachment or studies of the President's misconduct.

On Monday, October 22, the Democratic leaders of the House met to survey the various demands for impeachment and quickly agreed to launch a formal inquiry. Some of them favored turning the matter over to a special—or select—committee, comparable to the Ervin committee in the Senate. Others warned that this would cause unnecessary strife over the committee's composition. Ultimately, Speaker Carl Albert decided that the assignment should go to the House Judiciary Committee. That evening he summoned the committee's chairman, Representative Peter W. Rodino, Jr., a Democrat of New Jersey, and handed him the assignment. Shortly before noon the next day Albert held a crowded press briefing to announce that he would refer all impeachment resolutions to the Judiciary Committee. Barely three hours later, word reached the Hill that Nixon had capitulated on the tapes. But a spokesman for Rodino's committee said the President's action would not halt the investigation. Impeachment was on track to stay.

"From that day, we knew we had a job to do," says Paul S. Sarbanes, a Maryland Democrat who is a former Rhodes scholar, a thoughtful student of government, and one of the most earnest, dedicated members of the committee. "Congress is very good at not taking up an issue if it doesn't want to. Sometimes that's the way to handle an issue—just bury it with inaction. But once you refer it to a committee for a formal investigation, you can't do that. When we got handed the impeachment thing in October, we had no choice but to take it seriously. You had to do it thoroughly, because otherwise you could be faulted for not doing your job."

For a time, though, impeachment had to take a back seat to the confirmation of Gerald Ford, which was also before the Judiciary Committee. From mid-October until November 29 the committee was preoccupied with filling the Vice Presidency. Only in December did it begin grappling with the possibility of emptying the Presidency—and then only with the housekeeping details involved in mounting a major investigation: appropriations, office space, staff. On December 20 Rodino named his chief counsel: John M. Doar, a nominal

Republican who had led the Justice Department's Civil Rights Division during the Kennedy and Johnson administrations. On January 7 the Republicans selected Albert E. Jenner, Jr., a widely respected Chicago attorney, as counsel to the minority. The staff—which eventually grew to forty-four lawyers and sixty investigators, clerks, and secretaries—was installed in the House Office Building Annex (formerly the Congressional Hotel), across the street from the Rayburn House Office Building.

But by then Congress was into the Christmas recess and, although some senior committee members stayed around Washington to help organize the investigation, little progress had been made when Congress reconvened January 21. For weeks thereafter, a chorus of complaints was raised both on and off the committee about its painfully slow pace.

Senator George D. Aiken, the Vermont Republican, had told the House as early as November 7 either to impeach the President or to "get off his back." On December 19, as Melvin Laird announced his resignation from the White House staff, he criticized the committee's delays and urged that the matter be brought to a vote in the House by March 15. Republicans on the committee pressed for more "expeditious action," suggesting that much of the early work be turned over to a nine-member subcommittee. Republicans in and outside the House charged that the Democratic majority was, in effect, trying to keep Richard Nixon twisting slowly, slowly in the wind so as to influence the outcome of the 1974 congressional elections.

Many liberal Democrats were just as irritated by the pace and style Rodino and Doar were setting. One committee member groused privately, "At this rate, they never would have crucified Jesus Christ." But mainly this impatience was reflected in the press, where liberal columnists chafed at the committee's plodding progression. On January 21 Jack Anderson complained that the tight security imposed by Doar was hiding only the committee's "inaction and lack of direction." Joseph Kraft called for somebody on the committee to step into "the role played by Edmund Burke in the impeachment of Warren Hastings—the role of laying out the broad outlines of the case. That job is going begging because the men managing the impeachment proceedings have deliberately avoided any suggestion of acting as prosecutors. . . . Mr. Rodino is having his brush with history. He is determined to do everything right. He wants to avoid the slightest hint of partisanship and to be fairness itself. Mr. Doar reinforces the chairman's personal bent. He is what some people call a man of the highest rectitude and what others call a bit of a Christer."

Doar and Rodino refused to be hurried. They determined to proceed deliberately, building a solid footing for each subsequent step. In January and February the chief counsel put his staff to work on the first and fundamental problem: what constituted an impeachable offense? The constitutional provision was spare: "The President, Vice-President and all Civil Officers of the United States, shall be removed from Office on Impeachment for, and Conviction of, Treason, Bribery, or other high Crimes and Misdemeanors." No two lawyers agreed on what "high Crimes and Misdemeanors" were—and all thirty-eight members of the committee were lawyers. Some said they had to be criminal offenses; other said they didn't. Rodino and Doar decided not to force a decision on this question by the committee itself, which would only bog it down in bruising debate (and ultimately would not bind anyone, since each member was free to cast his vote as he wished). Instead, they settled for a staff report that would guide the members in their deliberations.

On February 21 Doar presented a report entitled "Constitutional Grounds for Presidential Impeachment," which set forth a definition of impeachable offenses well beyond ordinary crimes. It said, in part:

"Impeachment is a constitutional remedy addressed to serious offenses against the system of government . . . in the English practice and in several of the American impeachments the criminality issue was not raised at all. The emphasis has been on the significant effects of the conduct—undermining the integrity of office, disregard of constitutional duties and oath of office, arrogation of power, abuse of the governmental process, adverse impact on the system of government. Clearly, these effects can be brought about in ways not anticipated by the criminal law. Criminal standards and criminal courts were established to control individual conduct. Impeachment was evolved by Parliament to cope with both the inadequacy of criminal standards and the impotence of courts to deal with the conduct of great public figures. . . . Not all presidential misconduct is sufficient to constitute grounds for impeachment. There is a further requirement—substantiality. In deciding whether this further requirement has been met, the facts must be considered as a whole in the context of the office, not in terms of separate or isolated events. Because impeachment of a President is a grave step for the nation, it is to be predicated only upon conduct seriously incompatible with either the constitutional form and principles of our government or the proper performance of constitutional duties of the presidential office."

Many Republicans on the committee did not accept this position. Representative Edward Hutchinson of Michigan, the ranking minority member, said he would continue to demand that "criminality" be demonstrated. And a few days later this position was buttressed in a White House brief. Not surprisingly, the President's lawyers took the strictest possible construction of the constitutional provision. "High Crimes and Misdemeanors" meant just what they said—crimes. And, Nixon's men concluded, "If there is any doubt as to the gravity of an offense or as to a President's conduct or motives, the doubt should be resolved in his favor. This is the necessary price for having an independent Executive."

On February 25 Nixon hammered home this interpretation at his first news conference in four months. "You don't have to be a constitutional lawyer to know that the Constitution is very precise in defining what is an impeachable offense." And he expressed confidence that when the House came to vote it would find no impeachable offense. "I do not expect to be impeached," he declared.

Nixon's confidence must have dimmed four days later when the grand jury handed up its long-awaited indictments on the Watergate cover-up. Seven men—H. R. Haldeman, John Ehrlichman, John Mitchell, Charles Colson, Gordon Strachan, Robert Mardian, and Kenneth Parkinson—were accused on twenty-four counts of conspiracy, lying, and obstructing justice. But there was worse news yet for the President. It was soon revealed that the grand jury had found Nixon himself deeply implicated in the cover-up, had considered indicting him, and when advised by Leon Jaworski that a sitting President could not be indicted, had decided to turn its evidence on the President over to Judge John Sirica for possible transmission to the congressional impeachment inquiry. (Only in June was it revealed that the President had also been named in the indictments as an unindicted co-conspirator, a legal technique which enabled his conversations to be introduced in evidence against his former assistants.) When Vladimir Pregelj, the grand jury foreman, handed the "sealed report" to Judge Sirica, a member of Jaworski's staff gave the judge a large, brown briefcase containing supporting evidence. For weeks the "bulging briefcase," as it came to be known, rested in Judge Sirica's safe—intriguing the press, tantalizing the Judiciary Committee, and undoubtedly tormenting Richard Nixon in his sleepless nights.

On March 6—at Nixon's second news conference in ten days—a reporter asked him, "Would you consider the crimes returned in the indictments last week—those of perjury, obstruction of justice, and conspiracy—to be impeachable crimes if they did apply to you?"

It was one of the bluntest questions asked of Nixon since he entered the White House, and at first all he could say was, "Well, I have also quit beating my wife."

The time had come for another Presidential counter-attack. Since returning from San Clemente, Nixon had once again regained his combative edge. "There is a time to be timid," he told one congressional delegation. "There is a time to be conciliatory. There is a time to fly and there is a time to fight—and I'm going to fight like hell."

And in that cold, blustery winter of the nation's discontent, Nixon carried his fight principally to the South. From the start, of course, the Southern Strategy had been the big play in his political game plan. Determined to woo Wallace voters into the "New Majority," he had done his best to slow school desegregation, appointed one grossly unqualified Southerner and another who was barely qualified to the Supreme Court, and when the Senate rejected both of them, had railed against "regional discrimination." All this had gained him little in the 1970 midterm elections and its effect in the national sweep of 1972 was difficult to estimate. Now he was trying a variation on the old theme.

In March the Gallup Poll showed that approval of Nixon's performance had sunk to 25 per cent—an all-time low for this or any other President. But there were regional variations. In the East, only 20 per cent thought Nixon was doing a good job; in the Far West, 23 per cent; in the Midwest, 26 per cent; and in the South, 31 per cent. The last bastion of hard-core Nixon support seemed to lie somewhere below the Mason-Dixon Line (or the "Mason-Nixon Line," as one editorial writer called it). With impeachment wending its way toward a probable showdown on the House floor, the President decided to maximize his remaining strength. If fifty to sixty Southern Democrats could be won over, then, with more or less solid support from his own party, Nixon might survive an impeachment vote in the House.

His wooing of the Southland resumed in February, when he shared the platform at an "Honor America Day" rally in Huntsville, Alabama, with his old rival, Governor George Wallace. Forgotten for now were Nixon's efforts to force Wallace out of the 1972 race, his covert funneling of $400,000 to Governor Brewer, and the IRS investigation of Wallace's brother. Introducing his guest, the governor was lavish in his praise: "God bless you, Mr. President, and I submit that you are among friends." Nixon responded in kind, embracing the entire South in the warmth of his rhetoric: "I thank you all for reminding all of America that here in the heart of Dixie we find that the heart of America is good, the character of America is strong."

Then, in mid-March, he made another plunge into the warm, welcoming bosom of Dixie: to Nashville for dedication of the Grand Ole Opry's new home, then to Houston for a question-and-answer session with the National Association of Broadcasters. But it was the Nashville visit which epitomized Nixon's fervent appeal to Southern loyalties. In the Tennessee Air National Guard hangar at the airport, Republican officials handed out little American flags and pro-Nixon banners to a crowd of invited well-wishers. When Nixon arrived, the throng sang a song called "Stand Up and Cheer for Richard Nixon" to the tune of "Okie from Muscogee":

> I'm sick of what I'm reading in the papers,
> I'm tired of all that trash on TV,
> Stand up and cheer for Richard Nixon
> I've been hearing talk about impeaching
> The man we chose to lead us through these times
> But talk like this could weaken and defeat us
> Let's show the world we're not the quitting kind.

Down at the $15-million Opryland, new home of the forty-eight-year-old country-music radio show, Nixon joined Johnny Cash, Roy Acuff, and Minnie Pearl on stage for a razzle-dazzle performance which calculated to tug at every Southern heartstring. He played the piano while the Opry Chorus sang "Happy Birthday" to Mrs. Nixon on her sixty-second birthday. Then he played "My Wild Irish Rose," explaining that Pat's Irish father always celebrated her birthday on St. Patrick's Day. And he finished up by leading the clapping, stomping audience of forty-four hundred in a rousing rendition of "God Bless America."

Nixon told the crowd that he'd heard the only thing stronger than country music was country moonshine. "Country music radiates a love of this nation—patriotism," he said. "Country music is America. The peace of the world for generations, maybe centuries, may depend not just on our military might or wealth but on our character, our love of country, our willingness to stand up for the flag, and country music does that."

Ignoring a man who held up a sign, "He Ain't Country, He's Crooked," Nixon reached into his pocket and pulled out a bright yellow yo-yo. Everybody laughed, for the yo-yo had long been the trademark of Roy Acuff, "the King of Country Music." Now the President of the United States—hoping to please the simple country folk before him—tried to bounce the yellow yo-yo up and down. But it wouldn't work. It just hung there at the end of the long string.

The Sixth District of Georgia may have been the most "pro-Nixon" district in the nation. In 1972 it went 79.6 per cent for the President. Only five other districts in the land produced bigger margins for Nixon, headed by Trent Lott's Mississippi Fifth, with 85.2 per cent. But in 1973 the old Sixth was redistricted, adding still more supporters of the President. Democratic Congressman John J. Flynt, Jr., lost six rural, starkly conservative, but traditionally Democratic counties. In their place, he gained the southern suburbs of Atlanta —Fairburn, Red Oak, Stonewall, and Palmetto— whose tract houses and garden apartments were filled with middle-class whites who had fled the city where they had become a minority. Fearful of blacks, fiercely antibussing, passionately pro "law and order," this was Archie Bunker country with a drawl. And, statistically at least, it was Nixon country with a vengeance. But Nixon had never been truly loved in Georgia. In 1968 the state had gone for George Wallace. In 1972 there hadn't been any choice: McGovern wasn't the Democratic candidate, he was the anti-Christ. At best, for the past six years, Nixon had been an imperial figure who happened to serve Southern interests. Now that he was deeply stained by scandal, many Georgians were torn between their ideological affinity for him and their repugnance for what he had done. John Flynt was torn, too. At the start, he had looked to Nixon for a Northern version of his own starchy Southern conservatism. The President, in turn, had cultivated the powerful eight-term congressman. On Flynt's office wall hangs a photograph of a 1971 meeting showing a relaxed Nixon chatting with Flynt and Representatives Richard H. Ichord of Missouri, David E. Satterfield III of Virginia, O. C. Fisher of Texas, and Joe D. Waggonner, Jr., of Louisiana—all conservative Democrats closely aligned with the President. But gradually Flynt soured a bit on Nixon. Balking at his unbalanced budgets, he concluded that the President was by no means the fiscal conservative he pretended to be. And he lost faith in Nixon's conduct of the Vietnam war. A soldier at heart, Jack Flynt was educated at the Georgia Military Academy, served in World War II, remained active in the Army Reserve, and for eleven years served on the Board of Visitors of the Air Force Academy. A powerful member of the House Appropriations Committee, he had generally supported any level of spending the Defense Department requested. But precisely this loyalty to the American fighting man led Flynt to his greatest crisis of conscience: his break with Nixon over the war. What eroded Flynt's support for the war effort was not any doubt about the morality of U.S. intervention but a growing horror at the "no-win policy" and particularly at the untenable position in which it placed the fighting man. His final breach came in April 1971 following the conviction of First Lieutenant William L. Calley, Jr., for his role in the massacre of Vietnamese at My Lai. The trial took place at Fort Benning ("The Home of the Infantry") in Columbus, Georgia, and pro-Calley sentiment was very strong in the Sixth District. Flynt saw Calley being sacrificed on the altar of "limited war." With great re-

luctance, he determined to vote against the bill extending the draft for another two years. "My conscience will not let me vote to continue to conscript young Americans to fight a war which most Americans do not want and a war which the U.S. government apparently lacks the courage to either win or stop," he told the House on April 1. Flynt's stand was supported the same day by his fellow Georgian, Representative Phil Landrum. Their defection was described on the front page of The New York Times as "a break in the once solid Southern flank" of support for the war. John Flynt was very proud of this "conscience vote." Close friends predicted that he would relish the idea of voting his conscience again on impeachment. But what Flynt did on the war was less to choose between "conscience" and "politics" than to sense, almost intuitively, which way his district was moving and then to define the issue in such a way that conscience and political reality coincided. Now, faced with a strong challenge from a bright young Republican in November, he had to make a similar calculation on impeachment. One day that spring, something happened in his home town of Griffin which helped bring conscience and politics together for him. Late one afternoon C. T. Parker abruptly left his office at the Commercial Bank and Trust Company of Griffin. A few hours later, his secretary found his body on the floor of a lakeside cabin with a bullet in the head. A .22-caliber rifle lay nearby. The next morning the Griffin Daily News ran a page-one editorial mourning the death of "the leading businessman of this community and among its very top leaders in almost every constructive field." Two days later eleven hundred persons jammed the First Baptist Church for the funeral, the largest in Griffin's living memory. C. T. Parker was known as "Cool 'Tater" to some and "Mr. Griffin" to others. In a few years he had boosted his bank's resources from $12 million to over $100 million and was buying up four smaller banks in neighboring towns. He was chairman of the Board of Education; chairman of the Board of Deacons of the First Baptist Church; and longtime chairman of the campaign committee for his good friend John Flynt. But

*within a few days of his death, disturbing rumors were
circulating in town. The police indicated that the
wound had been "self-inflicted." Later the coroner's
jury was informed that minutes before Parker left the
bank, examiners had discovered "irregularities" in the
bank's books. "Parker's death rocked this town and I
think it rocked Jack Flynt," said one of Griffin's leading citizens. "First, we learned that the man we elected
to the nation's highest office by an overwhelming majority was at best not very admirable and at worst a
crook. Then, we discover that our top civic leader was
very probably robbing the deposits of the people who
trusted him completely. A lot of folks around here are
asking themselves these days: Who can you trust, who
in the world can you have faith in?"*

Some of the answers to these questions—insofar as
Richard Nixon was concerned—lay in the brown briefcase handed to Judge Sirica on March 1. But, for the
time being, the briefcase remained locked in the
judge's safe and there were legal obstacles to obtaining
it. The decision to hand the material to Judge Sirica
had been Leon Jaworski's response to regulations
which appeared to prevent the special prosecutor from
giving secret grand jury evidence to Congress. Rule 6
(E) of the Federal Rules of Criminal Procedure, buttressed by recent court decisions, clearly required that
grand jury proceedings be kept secret. On January 12
Jaworski had said he could "see no way at the present
time" to make any of his materials available to the impeachment inquiry. But Rodino warned that if his
committee could not get access to Jaworski's materials,
the impeachment inquiry could be delayed perhaps a
year. At this point, Jaworski devised the technique of
giving the materials to Judge Sirica and letting the committee seek them from him.

The next legal obstacle came not directly from Nixon himself but from his seven aides indicted in the
Watergate cover-up. The President feared that an
attempt to block the transfer would look as if he were
simply seeking to protect himself. Instead, lawyers for

the cover-up defendants went to court, arguing that release of the materials to the House would generate publicity prejudicial to their trials. On March 18 Judge Sirica ruled that the materials should be turned over to the committee, noting that "the person on whom the report focuses, the President of the United States, has not objected to its release to the committee." Three defendants carried the case to the Court of Appeals, which upheld the judge. Finally, on March 27, John Doar picked up the briefcase in Sirica's chambers and —closely guarded by police—took it to the ex-Congressional Hotel, where Rodino and Hutchinson spent three hours examining its contents. Afterward, they refused comment to reporters, except to say that the materials were "relevant" to their inquiry.

But there were other relevant materials which the Judiciary Committee needed, and much time during the next few months was consumed in a convoluted struggle with the White House over access to that evidence.

In mid-February Jaworski had given the committee a list of all the materials—nineteen tapes and some seven hundred documents—which the special prosecutor's office had received to date from the White House. On February 25 Doar wrote James St. Clair asking for those materials plus some forty-two other tapes covering the period from February 20 to April 18, 1973. On March 6 St. Clair replied, saying the White House would be happy to supply the committee with all the tapes and documents it had given Jaworski. But, he said, the President believed that these materials were "more than sufficient to afford the Judiciary Committee with the entire Watergate story . . . [and] to resolve any questions concerning him." Although St. Clair did not flatly refuse to supply the other forty-two tapes, he strongly implied they would not be forthcoming.

To buttress this resistance, St. Clair tried to use one investigator's words against another. He said the Judiciary Committee should be satisfied with what Jaworski had been given because "the special prosecutor himself has confirmed in the public press that the grand jury now knows the whole Watergate story." That day, in his press conference, the President hammered home the same point, stressing that he had given the special prosecutor "enough material that Mr. Jaworski was able to say that he knew all, and that the grand jury had all the information that it needed in order to bring to a conclusion its Watergate investigation."

In these remarks, Nixon was exploiting a curious and still-disputed incident. On February 26 Jaworski, accompanied by his press spokesman, Jim Doyle, had lunched at Washington's F Street Club with three members of the *New York Times* Washington Bureau: Clifton Daniel, the bureau chief; Robert Phelps, Daniel's deputy; and Anthony Ripley, the reporter who covered the special prosecutor's office. The next day, an article by Ripley appeared on page one of the *Times* saying that Jaworski believed his office "now knew the full story of the Watergate affair." Doyle telephoned Phelps, angrily charging that the discussion had been off-the-record. Phelps insists it was on-the-record. Doyle says that Ripley's story also took the remark somewhat out of context. What happened, he says, is that somebody asked, "Do you think we'll ever know the story of what happened?" and Jaworski said, "Oh, we know the story." But none of the *Times*men took notes and the remark—not a direct quote—came out somewhat differently in the paper. The White House, of course, gleefully picked up the comment as published and for weeks to come used it to justify continued refusal to give more materials to the special prosecutor or the Judiciary Committee.

Whatever Jaworski said at lunch that day, he certainly did not know "the full story of Watergate" because the White House had refused to give him the tapes and documents which told it. In fact, relations between the President and the special prosecutor had deteriorated very rapidly. For a few weeks after Jaworski's appointment, as Nixon sought to dispel memories of the Saturday Night Massacre, they enjoyed a brief "honeymoon." The President promised "full cooperation" and even handed over some materials on the milk and ITT cases. Then, in mid-December, Jaworski began meeting with Al Haig and Fred Buzhardt to discuss his gaining access to Watergate material, and finally he requested some twenty-five tapes of Presidential conversations. Sometime in December Nixon told Haig he should give "nothing more" to Jaworski. And, according to Attorney General Saxbe, aides to the President repeatedly asked him to intervene with Jaworski and have him "stop this type of activity, this infringement of executive privilege." Finally, in his State of the Union message on January 30, 1974, the President declared that he had given Jaworski "all the material that he needs to conclude his investigation and to proceed to prosecute the guilty and to clear the innocent." This was a signal. The next day St. Clair said he hoped the President could continue to cooperate with Jaworski, but "there has to come an end at some point." The end came three days later, when St. Clair informed the special prosecutor that the President had rejected all outstanding requests for tapes and documents. Suddenly Jaworski found himself facing just what Archibald Cox had confronted the fall before: a White House stonewall.

As some of his friends had predicted, the corporate lawyer from Texas did not cave in. He shoved back. In mid-March Jaworski subpoenaed a batch of documents relating to campaign contributions. This time, Nixon gave in and sent them over in a brown envelope. But on April 16 the special prosecutor went to court again, now asking for sixty-four conversations between Nixon and seven others—Haldeman, Ehrlichman, Dean, Ziegler, Colson, Kleindienst, and Petersen —for use in the cover-up trial. On April 18 federal marshals delivered a subpoena to the White House. If the President refused to comply—as seemed likely— he would be locked once more into a legal struggle with a special prosecutor. This time it could lead to far more than a firestorm.

Meanwhile, the Judiciary Committee was pursuing many of the same materials along its separate track (of the sixty-four conversations subpoenaed by Jaworski, twenty-four were on the committee's list). But the White House continued to stall, refusing to give an answer one way or the other. Instead, it derided the committee in increasing contemptuous terms. Ken Clawson said the committee wanted "carte blanche to rummage through every nook and cranny in the White House on a fishing expedition." Ron Ziegler said, "The mere fact of an impeachment inquiry does not give Congress the right to back up a truck and haul off White House files" (Nixon later elaborated that a bit, making the truck a "U-haul"). And Bryce Harlow said the committee was "in the position of a lot of children in homes all over the United States. When you are at meals and you want seconds, you have to clean up your plate first."

Some Democrats on the committee—the same who had earlier grown impatient with Doar's slow pace—now were furious at Nixon's lofty disdain. Father Drinan said something had to be done to show that "we're not going to be pushed around" by the White House. One day, Representatives Jerome R. Waldie of California, John Conyers of Michigan, and Charles B. Rangel of New York charged into Rodino's office saying "we can't take this lying down" and demanding that the committee subpoena the tapes from the President.

But Rodino, Doar, Jenner, and other cooler heads urged patience. They thought they could detect a deliberate White House plan to provoke the committee into a rash and premature confrontation. Paul Sarbanes, one of those counseling caution, put it this way: "Nixon and his people were being so provocative, so scornful in their position that it looked like a setup. So we asked ourselves: what are they up to? And the way it looked to us, they were trying to make us rise to the bait, make us subpoena him, then cite him for contempt or something. Then they'd have us locked into a procedural battle. He could appeal it to the courts, arguing that we didn't have the right to the tapes and documents. We concluded that we ought not to go to the mat with him on procedural questions without the substance of our inquiry. Therefore, we were determined not to be provoked, to keep our cool."

The cooler heads prevailed. Rodino told reporters,

"The Judiciary Committee does not view itself as being engaged in a lawsuit with the President. It has been authorized and directed to conduct a thorough inquiry, and we will do that. We expect and will continue to expect full cooperation from all persons. The Constitution permits nothing less."

But the committee's forbearance had a limit. On April 4, after waiting thirty-eight days for a reply, it gave the President five days to decide whether or not he would turn over the tapes. "We have been respectfully patient," Rodino declared. "The courts were patient. The House has been patient. The people have been patient for a long, long time. But the patience of this committee is wearing thin."

Hours before the deadline, St. Clair asked for an extension until April 22, the day Congress returned from its Easter recess. At that time, he said, the White House would furnish materials that "will enable the committee to complete its inquiry properly." Although St. Clair hinted that some tapes might eventually be turned over, he also seemed to reserve the right to choose which tapes were relevant.

On April 11 the committee scheduled a meeting to consider its next step in the battle of nerves. At 9:57 a.m.—just thirty-three minutes before the committee was to go into session—St. Clair telephoned Doar to say the tape review could be completed in "a day or two," and that he could then "try" to provide tapes in four of the six categories requested by the committee. Would that be acceptable? Doar couldn't speak for the congressmen, but said he would relay the offer. Not surprisingly, the committee was unimpressed. "It's a little late to make a deal," said Representative Robert W. Kastenmeier, a Wisconsin Democrat. "The course has been set, and it has been set by the White House. They have had forty-five days in which to reply, and an eleventh-hour offer is unacceptable." The committee then voted 33–3 to issue a subpoena, giving the President until April 25 to provide the tapes. It was the first time in history that a committee of the House had subpoenaed a President. (Eight days later the committee underlined its point by making still another request for tapes—this time for 142 conversations dealing with the Watergate cover-up, ITT, and milk matters. It seemed to be telling the President, "All your delays and diversions have earned you nothing. We intend to keep asking for the materials we need and if we do not get what we need one way, we will subpoena it.")

On April 23 St. Clair asked for still another extension—five more days. This time, the committee gave it to him by a vote of 34–4. Having gone that far with the President, Rodino said, "We want to grant him this one last request." The word "last" echoed in the marble chamber.

By then, the President was edging up on a decision to "end-run" the committee by publishing his own version of the tapes. This option—not unlike the Stennis plan of six months before—was considered in mid-April during a weekend that Nixon spent with his advisers at Key Biscayne. It had some obvious advantages. Facing nearly simultaneous subpoenas from the special prosecutor and the Judiciary Committee, the President could not afford full compliance with either. Among the tapes being sought by Jaworski, for example, was the June 23, 1972, conversation in which Nixon told Haldeman to have the CIA tell the FBI "Don't go any further into this case period!" There were others—or portions of others—that were almost as damaging. But with the impeachment inquiry proceeding through the House, he couldn't afford to "stonewall" either. Publication of selected tapes, edited as he saw fit, would strike a mean between the two extremes.

Moreover, the White House knew that the Judiciary Committee had an unexpurgated version of the March 21 tape—one of nineteen tapes which the President had already provided the special prosecutor and which, in March, he had agreed to give the committee. One assistant to the President said, "The March 21 tape loomed very big in our thinking. We knew it would be shoved in our face sooner or later." Another White House aide recalls, "Everyone assumed the tapes they had would be leaked and leaked selectively in the way most harmful to the President. So the best thing was to go ahead and dump them. They were going to be broadcast willy-nilly. So it was best to put them out and let the President take the credit. And put a White House twist on what the tapes showed."

This had the flare of the "big play," which always appealed to Nixon. It seemed like the PR inspiration which could transform the situation and convert all the President's debits into assets. All of a sudden he would be the frankest President in history, washing all his dirty linen in public, holding nothing back, letting it all hang out. Some of the President's advisers had their doubts, warning that there was very damaging material on the tapes. But the lawyers argued that there was no evidence of a crime. Much of the public expected just that. To them, the tapes would be reassuring. And the President had always believed that on balance—with several major exceptions, like the June 23 conversation—the tapes didn't hurt him much. On June 4, 1973, after reviewing several reels, he told Ziegler, "Don't you think it's interesting though to run through this? Really, the goddamn record is not bad, is it?" He had an enormous capacity to deceive himself.

For weeks in April, a team of White House stenographers had been transcribing the subpoenaed tapes, working under tight security in an office recently vacated by Haig's former deputy, John Bennett. Fred Buzhardt—to whom Nixon had entrusted chief responsibility for the tapes—read the transcripts and marked portions of them to be deleted. But Nixon made the final decisions. "As far as I know," Buzhardt said later, "he read the entire package and he had the final say on it all." For a time there was a spirited argument over whether to include some of the saltier expressions. The lawyers argued that they should stay in, that they would give the transcripts greater verisimilitude and would avoid undue deletions. But Ziegler said they could only damage the President's image. They came out. (Later, unexpurgated versions of some tapes showed that the deleted "expletives" were relatively mild by longshoremen's standards: "bastards," "son-of-a-bitch," "ass hole," "balls," "pissed off," "pissed on.") Other cuts were made for "national security" and for "lack of relevance." Some sections were marked "inaudible" or "unintelligible." Ultimately, the White House assembled partial transcripts of forty-six tapes, some of them from the Judiciary Committee's list, some from Jaworski's list, some from neither. (Buzhardt later contended that eleven of the conversations on the committee's subpoena had never been recorded.)

The extended deadline for the Judiciary Committee's subpoena was April 30. On the weekend of April 27–28, Nixon retired to Camp David—an eerie replay of that weekend six months before when he had gone there to contemplate his "big play" on Cox's subpoena. At about 1:00 p.m. on Sunday, the twenty-eighth, a jury of nine men and three women filed into a courtroom in the U.S. District Courthouse in New York's Foley Square. After twenty-six hours of deliberation spread over four days, they were ready with their verdict in the Mitchell-Stans trial. In the hushed courtroom, Sybil Kucharski, a twenty-one-year-old bank clerk from Westchester County, called out "Not guilty" to each of the fifteen counts. Maurice Stans covered his eyes and wept softly. John Mitchell leaned back in his chair and sighed. When the news was relayed to Nixon at Camp David, he was described as "very pleased for the two men and their families." Presumably, he was pleased for other reasons. It was the first legal victory the White House had scored in the whole Watergate saga. Although the Vesco case was not properly speaking a Watergate matter, Stans and Mitchell were both intimately involved in Watergate, Mitchell was a defendant in the upcoming cover-up trial, and their acquittal had undoubtedly provided a tremendous morale boost to the President on that critical weekend. Perhaps more important, the verdict to some extent discredited John Dean, whose testimony at the trial clearly had not convinced the jurors. Since Dean was the principal witness against Nixon, too, the acquittal certainly emboldened the President and may have encouraged him to make his bold play on the tapes.

Understandably, Al Haig discounts such speculation. According to Haig, Nixon telephoned him on Sunday morning—hours before the Mitchell-Stans verdict—to say, "We're going ahead. We're going to go ahead." Haig caught a helicopter to Camp David and met with the President in Aspen Lodge at 11:30 a.m. At 1:06 p.m., Haig's aide, George Joulwan, called from the White House with the trial verdict. The President and Haig conferred for another twenty minutes, and Haig then helicoptered back to the White House.

At 2:45 the next morning two White House aides scurried through darkened streets to deliver the type-written transcripts of the edited tapes to the Government Printing Office, where printers worked nonstop for almost two days to grind out the 1254 pages and bind them into blue books. Later that Monday morning Haig "pretested" the text of Nixon's address, drafted by speechwriter Ray Price, on several presumably friendly audiences. First, he showed it to Republican congressional leaders, who liked much of it but objected to three pages attacking the media, the Judiciary Committee, and its staff. Nixon agreed to drop this portion. Then Haig ran it past the cabinet, even playing a brief snippet of tape for them to demonstrate how inaudible the "inaudibles" really were. The reaction there was more positive.

Finally, at nine that evening, April 29, the President sat down at his desk in the Oval Office and told the American public of his decision. The thirty-five-minute television address was a masterfully orchestrated show. Stacked on a table near the President's desk was a tall pile of green loose-leaf binders. One of the binders was propped against the others, plainly showing the gold Presidential seal stamped on its front. As the camera lingered on the notebooks, it gave the impression of a massive mountain of evidence. In fact, there were fifty notebooks, each containing an average of only about twenty-five pages. The book of transcripts published the next day—marked pretentiously "Submission of Recorded Presidential Conversations to the Committee on the Judiciary of the House of Representatives by President Richard Nixon"—was about the size of the Manhattan telephone directory. But that wouldn't have looked as impressive on television.

The President, too, had been artfully prepared for his performance. His hair had been freshly trimmed, leaving just enough gray at the temples to lend him a distinguished, elder-statesman look. He was dressed in an Oxford gray suit and gray tie. The thermostat in the Oval Office had been turned down, to keep him from sweating.

And Nixon rose to the occasion with one of his smoothest performances—probably his best speech of the Watergate ordeal. Cool, self-contained, without the trembling and hesitation of recent months, he played the role of a chief executive "leveling" with the people:

". . . I spent many hours during the past few weeks thinking about what I would say to the American people if I were to reach the decision I shall announce tonight. And so my words have not been lightly chosen. I can assure you they are deeply felt. . . .

"In these folders that you see over here on my left are more than twelve hundred pages of transcripts of private conversations I participated in between September 15, 1972, and April 27 of 1973. . . .

". . . everything that is relevant is included—the rough as well as the smooth, the strategy sessions, the exploration of alternatives, the weighing of human and political costs.

"As far as what the President personally knew and did with regard to Watergate and the cover-up is concerned, these materials, together with those already made available, will tell it all.

"I shall invite Chairman Rodino and the committee's ranking minority member, Congressman Hutchinson of Michigan, to come to the White House and listen to the actual full tapes of these conversations so that they can determine for themselves beyond question that the transcripts are accurate. . . .

"Because this is an issue that profoundly affects all the American people, in addition to turning over these transcripts to the House Judiciary Committee, I have directed that they should all be made public, all of those that you see here. . . ."

But not right away. Public release of the transcripts was delayed for hours, so that full press attention could focus on a fifty-page brief by St. Clair which interpreted them to the President's best advantage. St. Clair stressed the lack of hard evidence of a crime. "In all the thousands of words spoken, even though they are unclear and ambiguous, not once does it appear that the President of the United States was engaged in a criminal plot to obstruct justice," he wrote. The White House public-relations experts—augmented that week by Herb Klein, the former communications director— had hoped that the wire services would lead their stories that day with St. Clair's self-serving document. But some of the Democrats on the Judiciary Committee— who already had their transcripts—thumbed immediately to the March 21 conversation and released the juiciest slices to the press. The wires jumped on them and the White House public-relations scheme backfired.

Indeed, as reporters and investigators studied the transcripts, they noticed some peculiar things about them. One was the extraordinary number of gaps. According to one count, there were 1787 portions marked "inaudible" or "unintelligible" and another 35 sections of unspecified length labeled "material unrelated to Presidential action." Moreover, the inaudibles came in suspicious circumstances. There were nearly twice as many in Nixon's conversation as in all other speakers combined. The breaks came most frequently when the President was talking with Haldeman and Ehrlichman, and least frequently when he was talking with Dean. One nine-minute conversation with Haldeman and Ehrlichman was speckled with 54 "inaudibles," 29 of them by Nixon. (Later, Seymour Hersh of *The New York Times* reported that those who had heard tapes of the Nixon-Dean conversations on February 28 and March 20 recalled that the President had made disparaging remarks about Jews and called Judge Sirica a "wop," but that these and other "ethnic slurs" had been removed from the transcripts. Buzhardt denied that any such language appeared on the tapes.)

But the Judiciary Committee had a still better way to check the transcripts. It had copies of tapes of eight conversations for which White House transcripts had now been issued. Moreover, it had some highly sophisticated electronic equipment, capable of "keying up" one voice, then another. The committee also had a tapes expert on its staff and even made use of a blind person whose hearing was more highly developed than normal. Using these facilities, the committee detected some curious discrepancies between the transcripts made public on April 30 and the tapes in its possession. Although some of these discrepancies could have been due to the superior equipment used by the committee, most of them seemed to fall into a pattern. In most cases, the White House transcripts gave a version less damaging to the President than the committee's version. For example:

Committee Transcript, March 22, 1973	*White House Transcript*
NIXON: But now—what—all that John Mitchell is arguing, then is that now, we, we use flexibility. DEAN: That's correct. NIXON: In order to get on with the cover-up plan.	NIXON: Well, all John Mitchell is arguing then is that now we use flexibility in order to get off the cover-up line.

Committee Transcript, March 21, 1973	*White House Transcript*
DEAN: Uh, we don't, it doesn't— NIXON: Including Ehrlichman's use of Hunt on the other deal?	DEAN:—And we don't, it doesn't. NIXON: (unintelligible) for another year

Committee Transcript, March 21, 1973	*White House Transcript*
NIXON: As far as what happened up to this time, our cover there is just going to be the Cuban Committee did this for them up through the election.	NIXON: Those fellows though, as far as what happened up to this time, are covered on their situation, because the Cuban Committee did this for them during the election.

Committee Transcript, March 21, 1973	*White House Transcript*
NIXON: Yeah, yeah—I just have a feeling on it. But let's now come back to the money, a million dollars, and so forth and so on. Let me say that I think you could get that in cash, and I know money is hard, but there are ways. That could be (*unintelligible*). But the point is, uh, what would you do on that. Let's look at the hard facts.	NIXON: I just have a feeling on it. Well, it sounds like a lot of money, a million dollars. Let me say that I think we could get that. I know money is hard to raise. But the point is, what we do on that— Let's look at the hard problem—

Committee Transcript, March 22, 1973	*White House Transcript*
EHRLICHMAN: A case in point: the issue of whether or not I had a phone call reporting the burglary. DEAN: Right.	HALDEMAN: In case of that the committee would issue a warrant on our phone calls. Bully! DEAN: That's right.

The committee made two other significant discoveries. Large chunks had been removed from two conversations in the White House transcripts with no indication that anything was missing. In the September 15, 1972, transcript, the White House had deleted a section in which Haldeman and Nixon discussed how Dean was "moving ruthlessly on the investigation of McGovern people, Kennedy stuff, and all that" and another in which Haldeman, Nixon, and Dean discussed giving "damnable, damnable problems" to *The Washington Post* and its lawyer, Edward Bennett Williams. Similarly, a twenty-five-hundred-word section of the March 22, 1973, transcript had been removed, including a passage in which Nixon told Mitchell, "I don't give a shit what happens. I want you all to stonewall it, let them plead the Fifth Amendment, cover-up, or anything else, if it'll save it—save the plan." Confronted with this deletion, White House aides said Nixon himself had ordered the section removed because it was of "dubious relevance" to his role in the case.

The public responded first to what was in the transcripts, not what was deleted. Initially, readers depended on snatches of the most sensational material picked up by newspapers or television. But the wire services soon transmitted all of the estimated 350,000 words and some 50 newspapers—including such bastions of "Middle America" as the *Chicago Tribune,* the *Houston Chronicle,* the *Denver Post,* and the *St. Petersburg Times*—printed all of it in massive inserts or supplements. CBS television did a dramatic ninety-minute reading à la *Don Juan in Hell.* National Public Radio staged a marathon reading of the entire transcript over its 164 noncommercial stations. When Bantam Books and Dell Paperbacks both rushed out paperback volumes, they became instant best-sellers, with some 3 million copies in print within a week. Many bookstores reported that the transcripts were the hottest selling item since *The Exorcist.* One publisher exclaimed, "We didn't realize the extent to which this book touched some kind of nerve in the American public."

Within a week it was clear that the tapes' release had been a massive miscalculation by the President, an unqualified disaster which ranked with the Saturday Night Massacre in its impact on his standing in the country. Although some Americans gave him credit for candor, most were horrified by the tone and content of the tapes. Presidential Counselor Dean Burch, in a letter to the *Chicago Tribune,* argued, "What emerges from the transcript is life as it is. It is life in government and politics, life in industry and business—and, yes, life in the editorial offices of every newspaper. It is how things actually are, warts and all." But most Americans either did not accept that picture of themselves or demanded higher standards from the President, the man sworn to uphold the Constitution and the laws of the United States. "It is almost as if the public had been admitted to the most private plotting within a felon's lair," said William P. Thompson, chief executive of the United Presbyterian Church. Rabbi Alexander Schindler, president of the Union of American Hebrew Congregations, said the Presidential conversations "reek with the stench of moral decay." Even those friendliest to the President were stunned. "Sheer flesh-crawling repulsion. The back room of a second-rate advertising agency in a suburb of hell," fulminated the columnist Joseph Alsop. Nixon was "a man totally absorbed in the cheapest and sleaziest kind of conniving," said William Randolph Hearst, Jr. The evangelist Billy Graham could "not but deplore the moral tone." And, perhaps most significantly for the President's chances on Capitol Hill, Senator Hugh Scott of Pennsylvania, the Senate minority leader who had excused Nixon's worst iniquities, called the transcripts "deplorable, disgusting, shabby, immoral."

"It's not the side of Nixon I know or like," said Jerry L. Pettis. "I abhor the kind of profanity I find in the transcripts. I am appalled and distressed at many of the things that I have read went on down there. But that doesn't mean it's necessarily grounds to impeach him." Pettis, the congressman from the Thirty-seventh District of California, was in a particular bind that spring: he had probably known Richard Nixon longer and better than any other member of the House. He had first met him in 1945, when Nixon was preparing to run for Congress against Jerry Voorhis. "He was still in uniform. A friend asked me to help raise money for him, and I did. I remember most how sincere Nixon was. He was really Mr. Totally Committed. The world needed changing. He was on his anti-Communist kick then." Four years later, when Nixon ran for the Senate against Helen Gahagan Douglas, Pettis —a skilled pilot—flew him around the state. "For much of that campaign I was his private pilot. I can't say I got to know him all that well, but we exchanged pleasantries in the air. I was still very impressed by him." So impressed that, in 1963, when Pettis decided to run for Congress himself, he went to Nixon—then a Wall Street lawyer—for advice. There was a natural affinity because Pettis' district (east of Los Angeles) included part of Nixon's old congressional district, including the town of Ontario, where Nixon had given

his first political speech in November 1945 and where he traditionally ended all his campaigns. "He said, 'If there's anything I can do, just let me know,' and one day that summer he came down to make a speech for me. I was a neophyte. He was the old pro. He coached me how to stand in the right place, what kind of media I should use, the virtues of hard work. A pep talk. He also raised some money for me. I haven't forgotten that." But when Nixon entered the White House, Pettis had difficulty getting through to him. "I spent more time with Johnson when he was President than I did with Nixon, because Johnson was the kind of guy who liked to have people around him, including Republicans. Nixon is kind of a loner. He does very well in public ceremonies and then he can turn the light off or pull down the curtain and shut you out." Pettis understood that, but he particularly resented an incident at the end of the 1972 campaign. He had been redistricted that year—taking over a huge swath of the Mojave Desert—and at a White House bill-signing, Nixon asked him if the Republicans could hold on to his former district. The Republican candidate was Howard Snider, the mayor of Ontario, and Pettis said, "You're going to have to do something a little extra, like putting your arm around this guy." The President turned to Haldeman and said, "Let's see what we can do." Later, Pettis tried to remind Nixon, "This is going to be a real cliffhanger," but he couldn't get through. And when the President arrived in Ontario on the last day of the campaign he was utterly absorbed in the drama of "the last speech I will ever give as a candidate for office." Pettis, several other local congressmen, and Snider were seated in the farthest bleachers. "They had a bunch of movie stars, comedians, and disc jockeys up on the platform instead. When Haldeman got there, we tried to explain how important it was that Snider be up with the President. Haldeman was cold as ice. He brushed us off and went back to his walkie-talkie. That infuriated me. But I didn't blame it on Nixon so much. I said to myself, Haldeman is the real snake in the grass." From such experiences, Pettis concluded that the President often didn't know what his aides were up to and, therefore, he doubted that one could hold him responsible for the acts of his subordinates. But what bothered him was Nixon's failure to act decisively once some of those acts were uncovered. "When he said he was going to carry out his own investigation, I thought, Oh, boy, there are going to be some heads rolled, because he could roll heads and he was a tough guy. But then nothing happened and I began to get suspicious." He was particularly distressed by Nixon's apparent finagling with his taxes and public expenditures on his homes. Pettis himself was a classic product of the Southern Rim: a southern California citrus rancher and electronics executive who became a self-made millionaire. But he was also a Seventh-Day Adventist—the only one·in Congress—and he took his religion very seriously indeed. Most of those who knew Jerry Pettis regarded him as a man of the utmost personal probity. When he decided to run for Congress, he put all his financial holdings in an irrevocable trust with the church, from which he received $65,000 a year. He was one of the first members of Congress to make full disclosure of all his campaign contributions, and he is meticulous in his accounting and tax procedures. "At first, when questions were raised about the President's taxes, I thought, He's so busy and not an expert on these things he probably took somebody's word for it. Then I thought, Why did he hire those people? I've never heard of the people he had doing his taxes. The top people in the country would be delighted to advise him. Here am I, a garden-variety businessman, and I get one of the top outfits in the nation. I pay a pretty fancy price for it, but I get results. I've never had a question or a quibble from the IRS. Why wouldn't the President do the same thing?" Despite all this, Pettis could not shake his lingering respect for the President: "I respect him for his grasp of foreign affairs. I respect him for having disengaged us from a tragic war in Southeast Asia and for having found a good secretary of state and giving him full *rein." But, by late spring, he had to face up to a stunning possibility: that he might vote to impeach his old friend.*

If the transcripts dismayed Nixon's friends and enraged his enemies, they came like a wet towel in the face to the House Judiciary Committee. "To respond to a lawful subpoena by going on television was not a decent thing to do," said Representative John F. Seiberling, Democrat of Ohio. "To give us sanitized, cleansed transcripts of conversations just won't wash," said Representative Edward Mezvinsky, Democrat of Iowa. But Peter Rodino expressed it best: "The President has not complied with our subpoena. We did not subpoena an edited White House version of partial transcripts of portions of Presidential conversations. We did not subpoena a Presidential interpretation of what is necessary or relevant to our inquiry. And we did not subpoena a lawyer's argument presented before we have heard any of the evidence."

Rodino still had to deal with members of his own committee, some of whom now demanded that contempt proceedings be brought against the President. But the chairman and the chief counsel again soothed the firebrands. After all, they argued, there was no way to enforce a contempt finding against the President. No judge would sentence him to jail. The sergeant-at-arms could not be sent to the White House to seize the tapes. "How can we enforce a subpoena?" asked Representative Don Edwards of California. "He has a bigger army than we do." Ultimately, at a long evening session on May 1, the Democrats were persuaded to take a subtler tack. That had been Law Day and the President had issued a proclamation, saying, "The law retains its value and force because every person knows that no man or woman is above the requirement of the law." The committee decided to remind Nixon that not even he was above the law. It voted 20–18 to reject the transcripts and to send the President a letter reading simply:

"Dear Mr. President: The Committee of the Judiciary has directed me to advise you that it finds as of 10 A.M. April 30 you have failed to comply with the Committee's subpoena of April 11, 1974. Sincerely, Peter W. Rodino, Jr., Chairman"

The vote was virtually along party lines. (Democrats Waldie and Conyers voted against the motion because they thought it was too weak, while Representative William S. Cohen, a Maine Republican, joined the other Democrats in supporting it.) In that respect, the vote was a triumph for Nixon. For weeks, Rodino had sought to prevent party politics from dividing his committee. Now, the polarization had come—not so much on the transcripts' acceptability (most Republicans agreed they were inadequate) but on reprimanding the President for "noncompliance."

All spring and early summer the test of wills over the tapes went on. Within days, the White House served notice that it would release no more tapes or other Watergate materials. "The President has now put out for public assessment what we consider to be all the relevant information on the Watergate story," said Haig. But on May 15 the committee ignored these warnings and issued two new subpoenas: one for diaries of Nixon's White House meetings in 1972–73; the other for eleven tapes covering Presidential conversations on April 4, June 20, and June 23, 1972 (June 23, of course, was the date of the supersensitive conversation on the use of the CIA to block the FBI investigation—a tape already subpoenaed by Jaworski). On May 22, in his most sweeping statement yet, Nixon said he would refuse to comply with the two new subpoenas and "such further subpoenas as may hereafter be issued." In a letter to Rodino, the President wrote that "constantly escalating requests" for materials "constitute such a massive invasion into the confidentiality of Presidential conversations that the institution of the Presidency would be fatally compromised." The President's position surprised even some of his most fervent supporters, for it violated a long-standing assumption by legal scholars that an impeachment inquiry was entitled to whatever information it required to reach a judgment.

Eight days later the committee responded with a letter far stiffer than its mild little note of May 1. The President's refusal was "a grave matter," it said, and such defiance "might constitute a ground for impeachment." And it warned that if he continued to withhold evidence, it might feel justified in drawing "adverse inferences"—that the withheld tapes were incriminating to Nixon. The President's stonewall had sharply eroded his support in the committee. The new letter was approved 28–10, drawing support from all the Democrats except Conyers—who again demanded tougher action—and eight of the seventeen Republicans. As if to underline the gravity of its warning, the committee issued another subpoena—this one for forty-five more Watergate-related tapes. On June 10 the President again refused to comply and the committee —now firmly staking out its new ground for impeachment—came right back with four more subpoenas for forty-nine tapes (bringing the total it had subpoenaed to one hundred and forty-seven).

Meanwhile, Jaworski continued his battle for the sixty-four tapes he had subpoenaed on April 18. After releasing the transcripts, Nixon went to court on May 1 to quash Jaworski's subpoena. Four days later the special prosecutor tried a bold ploy. At a meeting with Haig and St. Clair, he warned that in a court fight he would probably have to disclose that the grand jury had named the President as an unindicted co-conspirator in the cover-up case. Jaworski offered to spare Nixon that embarrassment if the President would let him have only thirty-eight of the sixty-four tapes —twenty which the President had already released partial transcripts of on April 30, plus eighteen new ones. On May 6 and 7 Nixon listened to sixteen of the newly subpoenaed tapes and on the afternoon of May 7 turned down the special prosecutor's compromise. But he didn't tell St. Clair why. He just said, "I've got better things to do than listen to tapes. Let's go to the court." Evidently, he preferred to take his chances in court than hand over the damaging tapes.

So Judge Sirica heard the motion to quash. At a closed hearing, St. Clair argued that Jaworski, as an employee of the executive branch, had no right to subpoena Presidential tapes or documents. This, of course, violated the assurances that Haig had given Jaworski before he was appointed. Jaworski wrote to the Senate Judiciary Committee—which had asked him to report any efforts to infringe his independence —warning that such a doctrine would "make a farce of the Special Prosecutor's charter." On May 20 Judge Sirica upheld Jaworski's argument, refused to quash the subpoena, and ordered Nixon to turn the sixty-four tapes over to the court. When the President took the case to the Court of Appeals, Jaworski appealed all the way to the Supreme Court, arguing that the issue was of "such imperative public importance" as to require "immediate settlement." On May 31 the Supreme Court agreed to hear the case immediately, setting the stage for a definitive judgment on the President's right to withhold evidence.

While the struggle for new White House materials dragged on, the Judiciary Committee began hearing the available evidence. On the afternoon of May 9 the members filed into Room 2141 of the Rayburn House Office Building and up onto the two-tiered mahogany dais under the oil paintings of their illustrious predecessors. At 1:10 Rodino banged the gavel six times to open the committee's fact-finding stage. "For some time," he told the nationwide television audience, "we have known that the real security of this nation lies in the integrity of its institutions and the trust and informed confidence of its people. We conduct our deliberations in that spirit." Edward Hutchinson, the ranking Republican, said, "The power of impeachment is one of those great checks and balances written in our Constitution to ameliorate the stark doctrine of the separation of powers. But impeachment of a President is most drastic, for it can bring down an administration of the government." Then the committee voted 31–6 to conduct the rest of its fact-finding behind closed doors. After only seventeen minutes, the room was cleared of both spectators and cameras, and the committee withdrew from public view to begin its labors.

The thirty-eight members behind the black and white name plates on the dais were hardly a cross-section of the House. Two were women, three were black, six were under forty and half under fifty, eleven were freshmen, six were first elected in 1970, nearly half had served less than four years in the House. The Judiciary Committee had undergone a startling transformation in the previous decade, reflecting the social changes abroad in the land. Never considered a committee of the first rank—like Ways and Means, Rules, and Appropriations—it had not generally attracted men of top caliber. For years, it had been dominated by a coalition of Southern Democrats and conservative Republicans. But in the 1960s—as civil rights, open housing, criminal justice, women's rights, and privacy became burning public issues—liberal Democrats began clamoring for a place on it. By the early 1970s the Democrats on the committee were well to the left of their colleagues in the House ("These aren't Southern gentlemen like Sam Ervin," warned one Republican. "These guys are out for blood"). In turn, the Republicans on the committee were somewhat to the right of their party. These two camps seemed destined to lock in bruising partisan combat, particularly since the committee's leadership was new and untried.

Emanuel Celler—the crusty Brooklynite who had been chairman for twenty years—was defeated in 1972 by a thirty-one-year-old Harvard Law School graduate named Elizabeth Holtzman, who took his place on the committee. At the same time, William McCulloch of Ohio retired, and the second-ranking Republican, Richard Poff of Virginia, became a state supreme court justice. On the surface, the new leadership did not impress. Peter Rodino was a dapper, silver-haired legislator representing Newark's "Little Italy," whose greatest achievement to date had been his revision of the immigration laws and his sponsorship of legislation making Columbus Day a national holiday. Ed Hutchinson was a constitutional scholar, but bland, timid, and old beyond his years. Some members of Congress bluntly suggested that the Judiciary Committee was not up to its task.

In early spring Rodino had shown surprising finesse in keeping his committee together on the tortuous procedural issues. But now he faced a tougher job: trying to get some rough consensus out of a committee sharply divided on the evidence. Although few of the members had flatly declared themselves, one could sort them into six rough categories:

• *Democratic Firebrands,* certain to vote for impeachment: Jack Brooks of Texas; Conyers; Drinan; Edwards; Holtzman; Kastenmeier; Rangel; Waldie.

• *Democratic Probables,* likely to vote for impeachment: George E. Danielson of California; Harold D. Donohue of Massachusetts; Joshua Eilberg of Pennsylvania; William L. Hungate of Missouri; Barbara Jordan of Texas; Mezvinsky; Wayne W. Owens of Utah; Rodino; Sarbanes; Seiberling.

• *Democratic Possibles,* who might be persuaded: Walter Flowers of Alabama; James R. Mann of South Carolina; Ray Thornton of Arkansas.

• *Republican Possibles:* M. Caldwell Butler of Virginia; Cohen; Hamilton Fish, Jr., of New York; Robert McClory of Illinois; Railsback; Henry P. Smith III of New York.

• *Republican Doubtfuls,* unlikely to vote for impeachment: Harold V. Froehlich of Wisconsin; Lawrence J. Hogan of Maryland; Hutchinson; Wiley Mayne of Iowa.

• *Republican Diehards,* almost certain to vote against impeachment: David W. Dennis of Indiana; Delbert L. Latta of Ohio; Lott; Joseph J. Maraziti of New Jersey; Carlos J. Moorhead of California; Charles W. Sandman, Jr., of New Jersey; Charles E. Wiggins of California.

Until May 9, none of the committee's members except Rodino and Hutchinson had had access to the confidential evidence being compiled by Doar, Jenner, and their staff. Although still lacking some essential White House tapes and documents, the staff had drawn together a huge collection of data from a wide variety of sources: the grand jury's "bulging briefcase," the Senate Watergate committee, the Joint Committee on Internal Revenue Taxation, the Internal Revenue Service, other congressional fact-finding committees, and private individuals with relevant knowledge. This information was compiled in thirty-six black loose-leaf notebooks, each dealing with a specific topic in the committee's inquiry: "Events Following the Watergate Break-In" (a euphemism for "cover-up," which the Republicans naturally regarded as a loaded term), "White House Surveillance Activities"; "The 1971 Milk Price Support Decision"; "Department of Justice /I.T.T. Litigation" and the like. Each notebook presented a series of numbered "statements of information" (originally, they were to be called "statements of fact," but some Republicans argued that assumed too much certitude). Under each statement came a list of the supporting evidence, and in the following pages the staff reproduced that evidence. For example, Statement 30 in the book on White House surveillance activities read like this:

"30. In June 1971 Dwight Chapin, the President's Appointments Secretary, and Gordon Strachan, an aide to H. R. Haldeman, recruited Donald Segretti to disrupt the campaigns of candidates for the Democratic presidential nomination. Shortly thereafter, Haldeman met with Herbert Kalmbach and authorized Kalmbach to pay out of political funds Segretti's salary and expenses, which totaled $45,000 during the next year.

30.1 Donald Segretti testimony, 10 Senate Select Committee 3980
30.2 Gordon Strachan testimony, 6 Senate Select Committee 2502

30.3 H. R. Haldeman testimony, 7 Senate Select Committee 2877

30.4 Herbert Kalmbach testimony, *United States v. Chapin,* April 2, 1974, 386–88

30.5 Herbert Kalmbach deposition, *Democratic National Committee* v. *McCord,* July 31, 1973, 23–26

30.6 Dwight Chapin testimony, Watergate Grand Jury, April 11, 1973, 16–17

30.7 Checks issued to Donald Segretti by Herbert Kalmbach, Senate Select Committee Exhibit 223

During the committee's closed sessions in Room 2141, Doar would read each "statement of information" and then cite supporting evidence, sometimes quoting from one of the documents to reinforce a point. To avoid the slightest editorial bias, he deliberately read in a droning monotone which put some members to sleep. Later, trying to relieve the tedium, Rodino asked one of the other lawyers to read the statements to which Doar would then offer explanations. Members were supposed to interrupt only to ask brief, clarifying questions, but that rule was honored chiefly in the breach. (St. Clair, after much wrangling, had been permitted to sit in on the sessions. But he could not intervene in the discussion—except on procedural issues and then only with the chairman's permission. Most of the time, he sat quietly at his table and took notes.) Now and again, everyone would don earphones to hear one of the committee's nineteen White House tapes. But most of the time it was a dry recitation of documentary evidence—hour after hour, day after day.

"Damned dull!" Bob McClory reported. "Sometimes it's hard to stay awake," said Delbert Latta. "If these meetings were ever televised the country would impeach us," quipped another member. As the hours droned by, John Seiberling counted all fifty-five feathers in the white-and-gilt eagle on the opposite wall.

Many members complained about Doar's deadpan presentation, which simply laid out the evidence with little interpretation and no sign of where all this mass of data was supposed to lead. "John believes you arrive at the truth by accumulating little facts and fitting them together," said one staffer. A committee member exclaimed, "This isn't an investigation, it's a compilation!"

This impatience was greatest among those who kept searching for "the hand in the cookie jar" or "the smoking gun"—that single piece of evidence which would conclusively show that the President was guilty of a crime, or at least a broader "impeachable offense."

By May, this search had zeroed in on the events of March 21, 1973—the day Dean told Nixon about Hunt's new demands for $132,000 in hush money and the President told him to "get it." From early in the summer of 1973, Nixon had recognized the critical importance of this meeting, and his own versions had shifted according to the exigencies of the moment. On August 15, 1973, he had acknowledged that Dean told him that "funds had been raised for payments to the defendants, with the knowledge and approval of persons on the White House staff and at the re-election committee." But, he insisted, "I was only told that the money had been used for attorneys' fees and family support, not that it had been paid to procure silence from the recipients." When that account aroused skepticism in the press, he modified it at a news conference a week later, saying, "Basically, what Mr. Dean was concerned about on March 21 was not so much the raising of money for the defendants but the raising of money for the purpose of keeping them still—in other words, so-called hush money." But throughout, he kept insisting that he had never authorized Dean to raise the money for Hunt, in fact that he had specifically said, "it would be wrong."

Then, in the March 1, 1974, "cover-up" indictments, Haldeman was charged with lying when he quoted the President as saying "it would be wrong" to raise hush money for Hunt. Clearly, the grand jury had listened to the March 21 tape and the President knew that the Judiciary Committee had the tape, too. So at a news conference on March 6 he changed his story once again. Now, Nixon conceded the statement "it is wrong" applied not to hush money but to clemency. But then he tried to show that the effectiveness of the hush money depended on clemency, because "no individual is simply going to stay in jail because people are taking care of his family or his counsel as the case might be." Thus, he said, "it is wrong" applied to "the whole transaction," including the hush money. (This tortured interpretation is not borne out by the tape, in which hush money and clemency are discussed as two separate items and in which the President plainly approves raising the money.)

Nixon changed his story again on March 6: admitting for the first time that Dean had told him that "payments had been made for defendants for the purpose of keeping them quiet." This represented a major shift from August 15 and even from August 22, when Nixon had said only that Dean was raising such money. Now he conceded that as of March 21 he knew that "hush money" had already been paid to the defendants. This stirred questions about why the President had not reported the payoffs to federal prosecutors, since they constituted a serious crime. A few days later St. Clair came to his defense, saying that Nixon had no legal obligation to report a crime to anybody, since "the President is the chief law-enforcement officer in the country."

Knowing that the transcript would ultimately be made public, Nixon now conceded that it was subject to different interpretations. "When individuals read the entire transcript of the [March] 21st meeting or hear the entire tape where we discussed all these options, they may reach different interpretations. But I know what I meant and I know, also, what I did."

To the President's lawyers, the fascination with the March 21 conversation provided—as Dan Ellsberg once had—both a danger and an opportunity. The danger was clear and present: it could confirm Nixon's participation in a conspiracy to obstruct justice. But the opportunity was just as great: because the tape was indeed ambiguous, it did not seem to provide the "smoking gun" that some legalists were looking for. The White House lawyers set out to prove a narrow legal point: that nothing the President did at the meeting had prompted the payments to Hunt. They tried to show that, at worst, Nixon had condoned payments already initiated by others and that even the $75,000 paid to Hunt the next day was made as a result of a chain that Dean alone had set in motion. If they could demonstrate that, they might save the President yet.

The stress on the "smoking gun" was accentuated by incessant pressure from the press for a daily "angle" or "news break." It was a tough story to cover. For hours on end, some of the ablest members of the Washington press corps learned—in the words of one Philadelphia veteran—to "lurk with dignity" in the marble corridors. When the committee broke for a quorum call, lunch, or at the end of the day, eighty to a hundred reporters thundered down the hallway after their favorites, begging for a scrap of data—a quote, a date, an assessment of the evidence. When they got something, they would huddle with their colleagues trading a snippet here for a snatch there. "I'll trade a good Hungate," one would proffer. "How about a Wiggins?" another would venture. Like a pair of Armenian rug merchants they would scurry around a corner to exchange merchandise. Paul Sarbanes had another metaphor: "The press treated the hearings like a baseball game. Every day you were supposed to walk out and give them the score—inning by inning, play by play. Well, it wasn't a baseball game. You couldn't make judgments that way. We were trying to lay it all out, the whole landscape. We were trying to see what it looked like and how it fitted together and what it meant."

It was hardly the best way to assemble a news story —as the results frequently showed. The most partisan committee members were generally the most talkative. (The first out the door every evening was Joseph Maraziti—soon nicknamed the "Streaker"—who ran to the microphone and pronounced Nixon innocent.) A reporter's story often depended on whom he had managed to buttonhole in the corridor. One day a headline in *The New York Times* proclaimed: "Nixon Tape Is Said to Link Milk Price to Political Gift," while *The Washington Post*'s story was headlined: "Tape Provides No Nixon Link to Milk Funds." After the committee heard the March 21 tape, members differed widely on what Nixon had said to Dean about the hush money for Hunt. Waldie heard it as: "Well, for Christ's sake, get it." Conyers heard: "Goddamn it, get it." A Republican remembered: "Jesus Christ, get it." (Waldie was right.)

But the corridor stampede was only the first wave of the press onslaught. More determined and resourceful reporters cultivated members of the committee who, in the privacy of their offices or over a drink in a quiet bar, could often be induced to brief them more fully or even show them Doar's books of evidence. In mid-June this produced yet another furor over "leaks"—the perennial issue which seemed to crop up during every stage of the Watergate investigation. Once again, the White House seized on the issue, this time to portray the Democrats on the committee as "out to get" the President. Ken Clawson said the leaks were part of a "purposeful effort to bring down the President with smoke-filled-room operations by a clique of Nixon-hating partisans." Pat Buchanan talked of "nameless, faceless character assassins." Gerald Warren said "selective leaking of prejudicial and unfair material" was daily violating "fairness and due process."

Often, as in Warren's remark, the White House implied that the leaks were infringing on the President's legal rights, as though he were a defendant in a criminal trial. This was the source of much confusion. To be sure, comparisons were frequently drawn between the House impeachment inquiry and a grand jury: each body determined whether there was probable cause to send a matter up for trial. But there the comparison broke down. For, plainly, impeachment was as much a political as a legal process. The members of the Judiciary Committee were politicians whose judgments were inevitably influenced by the view of their constituents at home and thus by their own prospects for re-election. The President understood this very well and took full advantage of the nonjudicial character of the proceedings. His refusal to respond to subpoenas, his public release of edited transcripts, his White House chats with his congressional "jurors," his frequent use of television and public speeches to argue his case—all were techniques plainly inappropriate for a defendant in a criminal trial. Clearly, then, one could not expect the congressmen to apply the procedures of a criminal process to a quasi-political undertaking. And who had ever heard of anything remaining secret more than twenty-four hours after it had been handed to thirty-eight politicians?

One source of the leaked information was a series of memos written by William P. Dixon, a veteran Judiciary Committee aide (though not on the special impeachment staff). Perplexed and irritated by Doar's rigorously objective presentation, several Democrats —among them Waldie and Kastenmeier—had asked Dixon to prepare memoranda which put the evidence in greater perspective. Dixon wrote thirteen such reports, which were distributed to Democrats on the committee. In mid-June they suddenly began appearing in the press, principally the *Los Angeles Times*. One of them detailed differences between the White House and committee transcripts, noting that Nixon had said on March 21 "we should buy time" by making the hush-money payment, and on April 16 that he was "planning to assume some culpability" for the payments. Another suggested that the President had begun meeting regularly with Dean in February 1973 to give Dean an excuse to claim executive privilege. The first of the Dixon memos came from a Democrat on the committee, but the others were leaked by a Republican, who hoped to show the partisan bias of the other side.

More explosive than the Dixon memos, though, were several leaks which cast doubt on Henry Kissinger's disclaimers about his innocence in the 1969-71 wiretapping of seventeen officials and newsmen. On June 6 Laurence Stern of *The Washington Post* reported that a section of the February 28, 1973, Dean-Nixon meeting, deleted from the White House transcripts, showed that the President said Kissinger "asked that it [the wiretapping] be done." That afternoon, fresh from a triumphant round of negotiations in the Middle East, Kissinger held a news conference at the State Department. Clearly expecting questions on his diplomatic achievements—and probably awed deference, too—he was obviously stunned by some rough journalistic gang-tackling about the wiretaps. The first question came from Walter Peckarsky, the one-man Washington bureau of *Tech*, the student newspaper at the Massachusetts Institute of Technology. Noting several conflicts in Kissinger's previous testimony on the wiretapping matter, Peckarsky asked the secretary of state "whether or not you have consulted or retained counsel in preparation for a defense against a possible perjury indictment?" Flinching noticeably, Kissinger said he had not retained counsel, he was "not conducting my office as if it were a conspiracy," and he would "answer no further questions on this topic." He hadn't reckoned with Clark Mollenhoff. Like an enraged bull, Mollenhoff shouted: "Mr. Secretary, on that question—what you have engaged in here, it's been a matter of evasion and failure to recollect, and some other patterns that we've seen over a period of weeks through the Watergate period. I wonder why you cannot answer the direct question—if you had any role in initiating the wiretaps on your subordinates." When Kissinger continued to sidestep, Mollenhoff kept shouting, "Did you recommend that they be wiretapped? Can't you answer that direct question? Did you make those recommendations?" until finally Kissinger said, "I did not make a direct recommendation."

That night a reporter found Kissinger "fuming and resentful" at a White House dinner. On Sunday *The New York Times* reported in a page-one story that General Haig, while serving as Kissinger's deputy, had ordered the FBI to terminate the eight wiretaps in effect in February 1971—thus contradicting Kissinger's testimony that his office had only indirect contact with the wiretapping program after May 1970 and no role in ending it. That day the newly enraged Kissinger telephoned Senator William Fulbright, chairman of the Senate Foreign Relations Committee, demanding that it reopen hearings into the matter.

On Monday, June 10, the President and his secretary of state left for Salzburg, Austria, on the first stage of a nine-day trip to the Middle East. The next day, reporters were summoned to an extraordinary news conference in the ornate Kavalierhaus Schlosshotel, part of the old palace complex in which Nixon's party was staying. When the secretary of state appeared, old Kissinger hands immediately recognized that something was very wrong. He entered frowning and engaged in none of his usual banter with reporters as he planted himself heavily in front of a tapestry portraying a medieval forest.

"It seems to me," Kissinger declared, "that our national debate has now reached a point where it is possible for documents that have already been submitted to one committee to be selectively leaked to another committee without the benefit of any explanation, where public officials are required to submit their most secret documents to public scrutiny, where unnamed sources can attack the credibility and the honor of senior officials of the government without even being asked to identify themselves. . . .

"I do not believe it is possible to conduct the foreign policy of the United States under these circumstances when the character and credibility of the secretary of state is at issue. And if it is not cleared up, I will resign."

It was a threat bred more of anger and fatigue than of calculation. But, suddenly, Kissinger had posed an intriguing question: Could he not only drive his own critics to cover but throw his great prestige into the Watergate scales on the President's side? He seemed to be saying: "Look, see what you have done. You have brought your great secretary of state, the Nobel Prize-winning peace-maker, to the brink of resignation.

If you force him over the edge, then won't you be sorry. So you better control yourselves and recognize the overriding issues of world peace that are at stake in all this." Yet there was a risk, too: that in calling such dramatic attention to his own vulnerability, Kissinger had severely tainted not only his own image but the one remaining policy area in which most Americans still valued the President, foreign affairs.

At first, it seemed as if the gamble would pay off handsomely for both Kissinger and Nixon. Senator Barry Goldwater called for an end to the "incessant nit-picking" over what Kissinger had done. Senator Edmund Muskie called the secretary a "brilliant servant," who deserved "the support of his countrymen until there is a record to show the contrary." And on June 13—long before the Foreign Relations Committee could begin its review which eventually cleared him —no fewer than fifty-two senators had signed a resolution expressing full confidence that Kissinger's "integrity and veracity are above reproach."

But the furor cooled quickly, and soon it was evident that the President had gained little, if anything, from Kissinger's bold gambit. The erosion of the country's respect for Nixon had gone too far to be repaired by that old World Statesman magic he and the secretary of state had worked so many times before.

This became particularly clear during the next two weeks as the President barnstormed through the Middle East and the Soviet Union, doing his best to conjure up memories of his spectacular summitry two years before. As he boarded his plane in Washington, the President had described his trip as "another journey for peace," the term he had used for his 1972 trips to Moscow and Peking. Arriving in Salzburg, he struck the same theme: "Every nation in the world has a stake in maintaining peace in the Middle East and we trust that this journey, as that of two years ago, will contribute to peace not only in that area but throughout the world."

The ensuing week-long tour through five Middle East countries did very little for world peace, but it provided Nixon with his best PR in more than a year.

As television beamed his every move in living color back to the United States, the President was welcomed in Cairo by 300,000 exuberant Egyptians waving American flags and a pulchritudinous belly-dancer named "the Ambassadress of Love" who rotated within inches of his nose; in Saudi Arabia, by Bedouin tribesmen festooned in black bandoleers and by King Faisal, who urged the American people to "stand behind you, to rally around you, Mr. President"; in Syria by four Soviet-built MIGs, which met *Air Force One* at the border and escorted it to the capital, where a sign announced "Revolutionary Damascus Welcomes President Nixon"; in Jerusalem, where the Israelis cleared out the 250-bedroom King David Hotel for the Nixon party, but where for the first time he encountered echoes of Watergate (one sign warned, "You can't run from justice"); and finally in Jordan, by embattled King Hussein, who escorted the President in a silver Lincoln Continental Mark IV surrounded by fifteen armored vehicles each carrying six soldiers with automatic weapons and a machine gun (a Jordanian aide assured reporters, "It's not protection, it's a guard of honor").

Then, after only five days at home, Nixon embarked on the second stage of his "impeachment diplomacy" —the return to Moscow. In fact, it was the third annual meeting between the President and Soviet Party Secretary Leonid Brezhnev. Ironically, for one who had gotten his start in national politics by vitriolic attacks on communism in general and Soviet communism in particular, Nixon probably felt more at home now in the familiar walls of the Kremlin than he did on Capitol Hill. These Russians, at least, were men who understood the uses of power, who realized that at times one had to act toughly, even brutally, in one's own self-interest. They were not bleeding-heart civil libertarians who threw the Constitution at you all the time, and they knew how to keep reporters and dissidents in their place. Over the years, Nixon and Brezhnev had struck up a bluff, hearty, jovial relationship, full of nudges and belly laughs. At their first summit, in 1972, Nixon had presented auto buff Brezhnev with a Cadillac. At their second meeting he gave him a

Lincoln Continental. Now he brought a Chevrolet Monte Carlo, which the Soviet leader had specifically requested after reading that it was *Motor Trend* magazine's "car of the year."

But such rapport could carry Nixon just so far in the steely-eyed *Realpolitik* of modern Russia. Although Brezhnev broke protocol precedent by coming to Moscow's Vmukovo Airport to meet him, subtle strains soon began to show. The President's desperate haste to get to the summit while impeachment still hung in the balance meant that both sides were ill-prepared for any very substantive discussion. The best they could come up with was some limited agreements on nuclear relations, which fell far short of the hoped-for breakthrough on limiting offensive missile systems. But Nixon tried to exploit their modest agreements, stressing that they had been made possible "because of a personal relationship that was established between the General Secretary and the President of the United States." And he added, "Because of our personal relationship, there is no question about our will to keep these agreements and to make more." But the Russians clearly did not want to balance détente on Richard Nixon's rickety future. Once, *Pravda* struck the term "close personal relationship" from the text of a Nixon toast, changing it to "relations between us." And, at the final banquet, Brezhnev pointedly alluded to the American people and the American Congress—a reminder that the Kremlin wanted to go on doing business with Washington even after Nixon was gone.

Undaunted, Nixon determined to make the most of his world travels at home. Even before he got back to Washington, he grabbed off some prime time in Caribou, Maine. At seven-thirty on July 3, his sleek blue-and-white plane swooped out of the evening sky over the tiny Maine village and landed him at Loring Air Force Base precisely on schedule for a television and radio speech to the nation. Some five thousand people —chiefly Air Force personnel and their families— gathered in a huge hangar at the Strategic Air Command base to welcome the President home. The Caribou High School Band, with plumed hats and a

Viking mascot symbol on their maroon jackets, struck up martial tunes. When the President entered the hangar, the crowd whistled, stamped, and cheered as the cameras ground. Then, Nixon, his voice hoarse from too many toasts, said, "It's always good to come home to America. That is particularly so when one comes home from a journey that has advanced the cause of peace in the world."

The next day was the Fourth of July, and across the country legislators went home to test the political winds ("A lot of guys," one congressman said, "have wet fingers sticking out of their heads"). They munched the annual picnics, marched in the parades, watched the fireworks, and often delivered that staple of a congressman's summer—The Fourth of July Speech. But, if they were Republicans, they generally dodged the question of impeachment. Asked what he was going to tell his county-fair audience about the President, Representative William G. Bray, a seventy-one-year-old Republican from Indiana, replied, "If a fish kept his mouth shut he wouldn't get caught."

That summed up the attitude of many Republicans in the summer of 1974. Whatever they did they were in trouble, so for the time being they tried to do nothing. From midwinter on, many of them had wanted to see the President resign, simply disappear; then they wouldn't have to grapple with the impeachment issue at all. In January Barry Goldwater tried to nudge the President in that direction, warning, "It's going to be goddamn tough for any Republican to get re-elected, including myself. I can sense a strong feeling right here on the Hill—and you're going to see it more and more as the weeks go on—that many Republican members of Congress would like to run this year without Mr. Nixon." Goldwater's analysis was borne out by a bone-rattling series of Republican defeats in five special elections held in February, March, and April to fill vacancies in the House. The Republicans won only one—a safe California seat where the Democrats were splintered seven ways. They lost four—one each in Pennsylvania and Ohio and two in Michigan. One of the Michigan seats was Jerry Ford's old Fifth District, held by Republicans since 1910. The Vice President said the loss made him "very upset," but the other Michigan loss was even more ominous. Nixon had spent a day in April campaigning for James M. Sparling, Jr., the Republican candidate. Six days later, Sparling went down to a decisive defeat, the first time since 1932 that a Democrat had carried the district. "Nixon is an albatross around our necks," one Republican moaned. "Isn't there some small Quaker university that needs a president?"

In early May, following release of the edited transcripts, Washington had been rife with rumors that the President would indeed resign. On May 10 a senior administration official was quoted as saying that Nixon would leave office "within forty-eight hours." But this seems to have been chiefly wishful thinking. The next day the President told a crowd of more than 25,000 in the Oklahoma State University football stadium, "I've got the old Okie spirit and I've got it down deep inside. We never give up." Gradually, Republicans concluded that he really meant it. Dean Burch warned the Republican National Committee that they were stuck with Nixon and better learn to live with him. "Richard Nixon is our President and the leader of our party. Our hopes and our goals and fortunes are as one. His record of accomplishment is our record. The President's record is a platform for Republican candidates."

By July 4, most Republican congressmen found themselves impaled on a very spiky fence. Nixon's popular approval stood at 26 per cent in June and that, as Senator Bob Dole of Kansas remarked, was "seven degrees below freezing." A vote for impeachment might gain a Republican some support from the other 74 per cent. But that was a risky calculation. In most districts the anti-Nixon majority was made up largely of Democrats who wouldn't vote for a Republican candidate anyway. The 26 per cent approving the President were a hard core of Nixon loyalists who would never forgive a Republican for abandoning the President in his hour of need. And they, as Senator William Brock of Tennessee pointed out, were "the people who work the precincts, the bedrock of the party." House Minority Leader John J. Rhodes of Arizona warned, "Any Republican who thinks he can win a congressional election without that hard-core support is more optimistic than I am." If, by some chance, a Republican managed to get re-elected in November with Democratic and independent support, the loyalists were almost sure to get him in the next primary. "It's an impossible dilemma," said Dole, the one-time chairman of the Republican National Committee. "One guy gives me hell for betraying Nixon. The next guy comes up to me and says, 'I'm for you, Bob, but you've got to get Nixon off your back.' No way to stay on that tightrope very long."

Golf carts were lined up like white swans in front of the Loch Ledge Country Club as guests in dinner jackets and long gowns began arriving for the "Salute to Ham Fish Dinner" one evening in early summer. It should have been a splendid occasion for the young congressman from the Twenty-fifth District of New York, but it turned out to be a rather awkward one. The Hudson River gentry who paid $75 a plate for roast beef and oratory were still largely Nixon supporters who expected "Hammy" to stick with the President. But down at the club gate, closely watched by a line of Yorktown Heights police, were several hundred demonstrators who jeered at the entering limousines and brandished placards reading "Ham is not kosher," "A vote for Fish is a vote for Nixon," and "Did we elect a Fish—or a clam?" A spokesman for Westchester People to Impeach Nixon said they were there to protest Fish's "aristocratic diffidence" on impeachment. But back at the clubhouse, Fish was anything but diffident. He was feeling "trapped between Scylla and Charybdis." For the dinner was to be graced with the presence of Vice President Gerald

Ford, who was touring three Republican districts in upstate New York that day. At nine-thirty the toastmaster on the dais announced, "Ladies and Gentlemen, the Vice President of the United States." Grinning broadly, Ford rose: "I'm here to pay tribute to one of the good troops I had when I was in the House. I can say that when the going was tough and the chips were down, Ham Fish was the kind of man I wanted on my side. As you all know, Ham is on the Judiciary Committee which has to decide whether the President is guilty of an impeachable offense, and I know we can all count on Ham to make that decision fairly and not on the basis of the indirection, innuendo, and leaks that, in the past few weeks, have so undercut the achievements of our great President who has done more for peace than any other President in our history." Sitting at the Vice President's side, Fish gritted his teeth and tried to look as if he were smiling. By that time, he was caught not only in the standard Republican dilemma but in the vise of a distinctive family tradition. For he was the fourth consecutive Hamilton Fish to sit as a Republican in Congress. His great-great-grandfather, who served as secretary of state in the Grant administration, was first elected as a Whig in 1842 but became a Republican in 1856 at the party's first national convention. His son served a single term in the 61st Congress, lost a race for the 62nd as a Bull Mooser, and sired another Hamilton Fish who served in the House from 1920 to 1945. This third was the Ham Fish immortalized by Franklin Roosevelt's excoriation of "Martin, Barton, and Fish," all superisolationists who opposed America's entry into World War II; by his decade-long feud with Roosevelt, who came from Fish's own district but was never able to carry it; and by his chairmanship of the first congressional committee to investigate Communist activities in the United States. Now eighty-five, Ham Fish, Sr., was a fervent backer of Richard Nixon. He was president of "Operation Freedom," which ran large ads in The New York Times *and elsewhere attacking the committee on which his son served. "Can there be fair and impartial justice among the left-*

winged Democrats on the House Judiciary Committee who received large campaign contributions from organized labor? Will they impeach the President . . . using minor, inconsequential and partisan issues? Let any Democrat or Republican without sin cast the first stone." Ham Fish, Jr., didn't think he was without sin. Indeed, he was deeply embarrassed by his passing association with one of the central Watergate figures. Gordon Liddy, while an assistant district attorney in Poughkeepsie, had challenged Fish in the 1968 primary. At the behest of local Republican leaders—but clearly with Fish's enthusiastic approval—Liddy bowed out of the race with the assurance that if Nixon won he would be found an appropriate job in Washington. After the election, Fish wrote three letters of recommendation for Liddy which ultimately helped get him a job at the Treasury Department. *"Later,"* Fish conceded, *"I wondered what would have happened if I'd never helped Gordon get to Washington."* No, Fish was not without sin, but for months now he had conscientiously studied Richard Nixon's transgressions and he was edging very close to an impeachment vote. Until well after the Watergate burglary, he had been a consistent supporter of Nixon: during 1972 he voted with the President 76 per cent of the time, compared to a Republican average of 64 per cent. But the Saturday Night Massacre hit him *"right in the gut."* He was disturbed not so much by Cox's dismissal as by the resignations of Richardson and Ruckelshaus. *"They were people with whom I had more affinity than others in the administration. If they had to get out, I knew something must really be wrong."* His distress deepened that fall as tapes turned up missing or pocked with gaps. *"It was terrible sitting up on the Hill that winter with the thud, thud, thud of new revelations marching down Pennsylvania Avenue."* In December Fish asked his staff to cull the thousands of letters which had poured into his office since the Cox firing and give him a dozen of the most deeply felt to answer personally. He took them home and began scrawling answers on a legal pad, *but the letters were so troubling to him that he could not frame adequate responses. One which bothered him particularly was composed only of questions: "Is Mr. Nixon utterly amoral? Or does he know the difference between right and wrong, but firmly believes that a lie repeated often and loud enough can fool all of the people all of the time?" The polls showed his constituents divided almost 50–50 on impeachment. Ultimately, Fish decided, "that was a break for me, because politically I had nothing to gain either way, so I had to decide the issue on only three grounds: the Constitution, the evidence, and my conscience."*

By early summer the Judiciary Committee seemed almost certain to recommend impeachment. The Democrats alone had the votes. But Rodino and his advisers had long recognized that the House itself might not impeach Nixon—and the Senate certainly would not convict him—if the committee divided along party lines. The chairman was determined to pick up enough moderate Republicans so that the impeachment resolution would be perceived as the product of a broad bipartisan majority. Just how many was "enough" was a matter of some dispute among Democrats. Assuming that all twenty-one Democrats voted for impeachment, one Republican was certainly too little. Two wouldn't quite do it. Three was probably the most realistic goal. Four would be helpful. Five would be splendid. Anything over that was gravy. From May on, Rodino expected Bill Cohen of Maine to vote for impeachment. By June, Ham Fish was regarded as a possible second vote. Tom Railsback was the critical third vote. The fourth and fifth might be picked up from among Henry Smith, Robert McClory, and M. Caldwell Butler.

But if the Democrats knew all this, then so did the White House. Its strategy for blocking impeachment was to harden the political lines in the committee, hold as many of the middle-of-the-road Republicans as possible, and portray the result as a partisan vendetta by Democrats and a few GOP renegades. All its efforts —and those of its allies within the committee—were bent in that direction.

On June 21 the committee completed its closed hearings on the evidence. In the six weeks since May 9 it had reviewed 650 "statements of information" and more than 7200 pages of supporting documents. Now it moved on to the next stage, the testimony of live witnesses. But the determination of how many witnesses it would hear provoked the first major battle along party lines.

Under the committee's rules for St. Clair's participation, he could suggest witnesses and question those that were called. In late June he proposed six witnesses —John Dean, John Mitchell, H. R. Haldeman, Fred LaRue, Bill Bittman, and Paul O'Brien—all of whom were involved in the $75,000 "hush-money" payment to Howard Hunt. The committee staff and members suggested four other witnesses: Alexander Butterfield, Herbert Kalmbach, Henry Petersen, and Chuck Colson. On June 26 the Democratic majority won a narrow victory when it decided to call only two of St. Clair's witnesses and five in all—Butterfield, Kalmbach, Petersen, Dean, and LaRue. The Democrats decided that the others should be questioned by the committee staff and summoned before the full committee only if it appeared that they could give crucial testimony. Bitter wrangling ensued. "This is not going to be a circus or a trial, and we're not here for the purpose of delay," snapped Peter Rodino. Delbert Latta taunted the Democrats: "Why not call the witnesses? What are they afraid of? What are they afraid to hear?" And an outraged Trent Lott declared, "Any hope of nonpartisanship is gone."

The White House gleefully heaped fuel on the fire. Dean Burch called the Democrats "a partisan lynch mob." The Reverend John McLaughlin, a Jesuit priest serving as a special assistant to the President, said the Democrats were trying to "deny Mr. Nixon his day in court." The polarization continued on June 28 when the *Los Angeles Times* reported that Rodino had said all twenty-one Democrats would support impeachment.

Rodino rushed to the House floor to "unequivocally and categorically" deny the story. But the author, Jack Nelson, stuck by his version and won support from Sam Donaldson of ABC-TV who said he had been there when the chairman made the statement. Rodino seemed to be exercising a politician's prerogative—to deny his own words when they proved embarrassing. But no denial could prevent the White House from exploiting the indiscretion. Ken Clawson reminded reporters that he had warned against Rodino's "partisanship" for weeks. "Now we have our worst fears confirmed out of Rodino's own mouth. I'm confident that the American people will now once and for all realize that President Nixon is the subject of a witch hunt."

Suddenly, Rodino found his central strategy—the search for a bipartisan majority—in jeopardy. On July 1 he backed down on the witnesses, agreeing to call all six on St. Clair's list. But this did not appease the aroused opposition. That same day the Republicans blocked an effort to waive a House rule guaranteeing each member the right to question each witness. "A gag rule!" cried Trent Lott. "Parliamentary suicide!" David Dennis protested. The committee split nearly along party lines—23–15—in voting to examine all witnesses in closed session. The Republicans had pressed for open hearings, charging that selective news leaks were unfairly damaging the President's position. Increasingly now, the two parties were digging into the trenches. Each morning the Republicans would gather in Robert McClory's office (Edward Hutchinson was in the hospital for minor surgery), sometimes joined by House Minority Leader John Rhodes. When Albert Jenner refused to argue against impeachment, the Republicans fired him as minority counsel and replaced him with his assistant, Samuel A. Garrison III (Jenner remained with the staff as Doar's associate counsel). "The honeymoon is over," one member conceded ruefully.

Ultimately, though, the White House pushed its divide-and-rule strategy too far. Though Rodino had miscalculated a few times, he had generally been generous to a fault with the opposition, treating them with great courtesy and deference. So when Ron Ziegler called the committee a "kangaroo court" and Dean Burch assailed its proceedings as "a black spot on jurisprudence," the Republicans—who were secretly rather proud of the committee's performance—rallied to Rodino's support. "The chairman has done a good job," said McClory. "By and large, it's been fair," said Wiggins. Once again, the President's tactics had backfired.

During the first two weeks of July the committee heard ten witnesses go over much the same ground it had been treading for months. Little new evidence was produced, but the witnesses put flesh on the bare bones of the written evidence and the members assessed their credibility. To Paul Sarbanes, Kalmbach came across as "a well-meaning man who got caught up in something terrible and knew it was terrible," while Colson seemed to be "twisting and dodging." Most important was John Dean's performance. For hours, St. Clair hammered at the former White House counsel, trying to shake his story. "A real bloodletting," one member called it. But Dean held firm, impressing most members with his stubborn consistency.

On July 8 St. Clair shifted his defensive positions a few hundred yards across Capitol Hill and erected them again in the Supreme Court chamber, where Jaworski's suit for the sixty-four tapes was to be argued, along with the President's countersuit contesting the grand jury's right to name him an unindicted co-conspirator in the cover-up. The very names on the Court docket signaled the momentous forces colliding there: *United States of America* v. *Richard Nixon, President of the United States. Richard Nixon, President of the United States* v. *United States of America.*

On the marble plaza outside, two hundred people had waited all night to win seats in the courtroom. By nine-thirty, the line had doubled. Applause mixed with boos as St. Clair arrived. A few minutes later Leon Jaworski marched up the steps to cheers and shouts of "Save the Constitution" and "Go U.S.A.!" Inside the chamber, the front seats were filled with a Watergate roster: Bob Haldeman, Sam Dash, Leonard

Garment, Robert Bork, Henry Petersen, and three members of the Judiciary Committee—McClory, Cohen, and Railsback.

Despite the complex legal issues involved, the major question was classically simple: who was to decide whether a President must obey a subpoena—the courts or the President himself? Standing stolidly in the well of the court, Jaworski warned, "This nation's constitutional form of government is in serious jeopardy if the President, any President, is to say that the Constitution means what he says it does and that there is no one, not even the Supreme Court, to tell him otherwise." High on the bench, eight justices leaned forward in their black padded chairs. (Justice William Rehnquist, a former assistant attorney general, had disqualified himself, presumably because of his close association with John Mitchell—though he had been ridiculed by Nixon, referred to on the tapes as part of a "group of clowns . . . Renchburg and that group.") Making his first appearance before the Supreme Court, St. Clair declared, "The President is not above the law. Nor does he contend that he is. What he does contend is that as President the law can be applied to him in only one way, and that is by impeachment."

Back in Room 2141, the committee's deliberations were finally drawing to an end. On July 18 St. Clair made his final argument for the President, relying heavily on the lack of a "smoking gun." He argued that neither on March 21 nor in any other conversation had the committee turned up positive proof of Nixon's participation in the cover-up. To support this point, St. Clair then tried to introduce an excerpt of a March 22 conversation which the committee had subpoenaed but the President had refused to provide. (The excerpt quoted Nixon as saying, "I don't mean to be blackmailed by Hunt—that goes too far.") This was a major blunder. Outraged members—Republicans and Democrats alike—charged that the President was playing games with them, holding back material when it could be embarrassing, then throwing them scraps which might benefit him.

The next day John Doar presented a 306-page

"Summary of Information" and 29 proposed articles of impeachment, covering a wide range of approaches. At Rodino's urging, Doar then abandoned his air of discreet neutrality, becoming at last the impassioned advocate many members had long sought. The central question, he argued, was not whether the President had committed one heinous act but whether his "pattern of conduct was designed not to take care that the laws be faithfully executed but to impede their faithful execution, in his political interest and on his behalf." As an individual, Doar said, "I have not the slightest bias against President Nixon. I would hope that I would not do him the smallest, slightest injury. But if in fact, President Nixon, or any President, has had a central part in planning and executing this terrible deed of subverting the Constitution, then I shall do my part as best I can to bring him to answer before the Congress of the United States for this enormous crime." And, Doar concluded, "reasonable men acting reasonably would find the President guilty."

On July 22 Sam Garrison made his pitch. It was a very different argument than the one St. Clair had presented only four days before. Garrison did not deny that some powerful evidence had been accumulated against the President. The central question, he said, was "whether the public interest would be served or disserved by his removal from office." The committee, Garrison concluded, had a "political" judgment to make.

The next day, one of the Republicans for whom Garrison had spoken made his political judgment. Representative Lawrence Hogan was a candidate for the Republican gubernatorial nomination in Maryland. His reputation had been tarnished a bit by disclosures that he had hired John "Fat Jack" Buckley—the former CREEP spy—to investigate Governor Marvin Mandel and his associates. Hogan was a conservative who had a "zero" rating from Americans for Democratic Action. But he was also a former FBI man who had been deeply disturbed by Nixon's misuse of the bureau.

When word spread that he planned to announce his

position, several White House aides and Vice President Ford telephoned his office. Hogan did not return the calls from the White House. Out of courtesy, he spoke with Ford, but did not tell him what he was going to do.

Then, stepping before microphones in a Rayburn Building hearing room, Hogan announced, "After having read and reread, sifted and tested the mass of information which came before us, I have come to the conclusion that Richard M. Nixon has, beyond a reasonable doubt, committed impeachable offenses which, in my judgment, are of such sufficient magnitude that he should be removed from office."

Hogan's declaration on July 23 surprised his colleagues on the committee. He had not been regarded as a likely impeachment vote, certainly not a pathbreaker. Moderate Republicans were mildly miffed, suspecting that he had stolen a march on them to grab off publicity for his campaign. Nixon loyalists were angry, suggesting that Hogan was "playing politics" with his vote. (Hogan said he didn't expect the decision to win him any votes in Maryland, and, in fact, he later lost the primary.) The White House was stunned. Hogan's decision clearly indicated that a substantial number of Republicans on the committee might vote for impeachment (he predicted there would be at least four others). George Will, the conservative columnist, compared the effect on the President's men to "being slugged on the base of the skull with a sock full of wet sand."

16

RESIGNATION

If I were to become an ex-President, I'd have no ex-Presidents to pal around with.
—Richard M. Nixon,
August 7, 1974

The next day, the President was hit with the other sock.

When the Supreme Court announced that it would meet July 24, *cognoscenti* knew there were only two cases on which the justices had heard arguments but had not rendered judgments: the tapes' suit and the Detroit busing case. Reporters had urged the Court not to announce both decisions the same day. But only seven persons in the audience that morning knew for sure which it would be. At nine, someone at the Court had telephoned the White House and the special prosecutor's office to suggest that they send counsel to the chamber that morning. Jaworski and three assistants were there, as were three young lawyers from St. Clair's office.

At seven, California time, the President got the word at San Clemente—where he had been in semiseclusion since July 12. He telephoned Fred Buzhardt in Washington, where it was shortly after ten. "There may be some problems with the June 23 tape, Fred," Nixon said, and suggested the lawyer listen to it. Buzhardt went down to the closely guarded storage vault and checked out the June 23 tape. As the Supreme Court chamber began filling up, he went back to his office, clamped earphones on his head, and listened to the President and Haldeman making strategy six days after the Watergate break-in.

At 11:03 the burgundy velvet drapes behind the bench parted and the justices filed in. A marshal cried, "Oyez! Oyez! Oyez! All persons having business before the Honorable the Supreme Court of the United States are admonished to draw near and give their attention for the Court is now sitting. God save the United States and this Honorable Court!"

The Court was seated. At that moment, several reporters noticed that only eight justices were on the bench. The seat farthest to the right—Justice William Rehnquist's—was vacant. Since Rehnquist had disqualified himself in the tapes' case, that meant they were about to hear a decision in *United States of America* v. *Richard Nixon, President of the United States*.

Chief Justice Warren E. Burger spoke for a few moments about his predecessor, Earl Warren, who had died a few days before. Then he picked up the papers in front of him and began to read a condensed version of his thirty-one-page opinion.

Citing the landmark case of *Marbury* v. *Madison*, Justice Burger declared: "The judicial power of the United States vested in the federal courts by the Constitution can no more be shared with the executive branch than the chief executive, for example, can share with the judiciary the veto power, or the Congress share with the judiciary the power to override a Presidential veto."

He conceded that there were "Constitutional underpinnings" for the Presidential claim to executive privilege, but, he said, such privilege "cannot prevail over the fundamental demands of due process of law in the fair administration of criminal justice. The allowance of the privilege to withhold evidence that is demonstrably relevant in a criminal trial would cut deeply into the guarantee of due process of law and gravely impair the basic function of the courts. Without access to specific facts, a criminal prosecution may be totally frustrated. . . . The President's broad interest in confidentiality of communications will not be vitiated by disclosure of a limited number of conversations preliminarily shown to have some bearing on the pending criminal case."

Still reading in dry, professorial tones, the chief justice ordered the President of the United States to turn over the sixty-four tapes subpoenaed by the special prosecutor "forthwith" to Judge Sirica, who would screen them for any information relevant to the cover-up trial.

The decision was unanimous: 8–0.

It was a devastating blow to the President's position in Congress as well as in the courts—all the more so because of the Court's unanimity. Three of those joining in the decision—Burger himself, Justices Harry A. Blackmun and Lewis F. Powell, Jr.—were Nixon appointees, who, with Rehnquist, had formed a deeply conservative bloc on the Court. When joined by one or both of the "swing" justices—Byron R. White and Potter Stewart—the bloc frequently became a majority. Yet on this issue, so crucial to Nixon's future, all of them had now joined with the "liberal" faction—Justices William O. Douglas, William J. Brennan, Jr., and Thurgood Marshall.

Justice Burger's opinion had the ring of a heavily "negotiated" settlement. Admirers of the Supreme Court frequently suggest that its decisions are reached through some ethereal distillation of legal scholarship and pure reason. In fact, the justices are intensely aware of the political consequences of their actions. They know that in cases of far-reaching social impact —such as the 1954 school desegregation case—their decision will have more moral weight if it is unanimous. The question generally is: What price has to be paid for unanimity? In this respect, the negotiations among the justices were not unlike those going on within the Judiciary Committee. At that stage, unanimity seemed out of the question on the committee, but many members were working to develop a position that could be supported by a bipartisan majority. Both justices and congressmen had to decide how much they were willing to give up to win over their colleagues.

By tradition, the Supreme Court never discloses what goes on inside its conferences. But it is known that on July 9—the day after the justices heard arguments in the 'tapes' case—the eight participating justices met for six hours in the large conference room outside Burger's chambers. At the meeting, Burger assigned himself to write the decision. This was the only formal conference they held on the case. There is no evidence that any justice ever expressed a desire to write a dissenting opinion. But that does not mean that all eight justices reached full agreement on July 9. As Burger wrote his decision, he circulated drafts to his colleagues, who made additions, deletions, or objections. Even Douglas—who went home to Goose Prairie, Washington, in mid-July—sent his comments in by mail and telephone.

One point on which there was very likely some tugging and pulling was the Court's acceptance of the doctrine of "executive privilege." This came as something of a surprise. Not only was the doctrine a questionable one—derided by many legal scholars—but it wasn't necessary to the Court's decision. Normally, the justices try to "make" as little law as possible; they could have dismissed Nixon's claim to executive privilege in this case, without considering its applicability in other matters. Instead, they enshrined the principle in the constitutional pantheon. In all probability, this was one of the prices for unanimity: a condition for getting some of the wavering justices to go along.

Another negotiating point may have been the President's own countersuit, challenging the grand jury's right to name him as an unindicted co-conspirator in the cover-up. In striking contrast to its willingness to rule on executive privilege, here the Court simply reneged on its promise to review the question, a promise it said had been "improvidently granted" in the first place.

According to Court officials, the chief justice spent forty-one consecutive days—including Saturdays and Sundays—on the tapes' case. He began reviewing briefs by both sides in mid-June. Burger and his two law clerks—Timothy Kelly and Kenneth Ripple—sometimes worked from eight in the morning until well into the evening, eating picnic lunches prepared by Mrs. Burger. The Court's cleaning crews were permitted to enter the chief justice's chambers only once a week, a day that all the papers related to the case were locked away.

Burger finished reading his condensed opinion about 11:20 a.m.—or 8:20 in San Clemente. The first bulletins came clattering across the news tickers at the Western White House about five minutes later. Haig, St. Clair, Ziegler, Price, and Clawson—the top echelon of Presidential aides in California—delayed for another twenty minutes or so before informing Nixon. "There's no use bothering the President with something he can't do anything about," Haig mumbled. Someone suggested sending King Timahoe in with a sign around his neck that read "8 to 0." Finally, Haig walked from the office complex to La Casa Pacifica and up to the towerlike study. Nixon, sunk in an armchair, was gazing out across the ocean; behind him on the wall hung a poem written in Julie Eisenhower's girlish script ("Handsome and kind/ always on time/ Loving and good/ Does the things he should"). When Haig gave him the wire copy, the President exploded, cursing the man he had named chief justice, reserving a few choice expletives for Blackmun and Powell, his other appointees.

Meanwhile, two members of St. Clair's staff—Jerome J. Murphy and Michael A. Sterlacci—had grabbed a copy of the full opinion at the Court, rushed back to the White House, and dispatched it by telecopier to San Clemente, where it arrived around nine. St. Clair took another thirty minutes to digest the document, then met with the President for several hours.

At first Nixon seriously considered defying the Court. For months he had refused to commit himself to obey an order to turn over the tapes. As far back as July 26, 1973—ten days after Butterfield publicly revealed the tapes' existence—Gerald Warren had said the President would obey a "definitive decision of the highest Court," but neither Warren nor the President would ever define what "definitive" meant.

The question became moot after the President fired Cox and handed the seven tapes over to Judge Sirica, but was raised again after the Supreme Court agreed to hear Jaworski's appeal. On June 3 Warren said he could "not deal with such a hypothetical question." Leonard Garment refused to engage in "idle speculation." In the oral arguments before the Court on July 8, Thurgood Marshall asked St. Clair whether he was "leaving it up to this Court to decide it?" St. Clair said, "Yes, in a sense." When Marshall asked, "In what sense?" St. Clair replied, "In the sense that this Court has the obligation to determine the law. The President also has an obligation to carry out his constitutional duties." The justices did not press him on the point, but the next day reporters did. St. Clair said Nixon would abide by an order to hand over the tapes if he determined "it is in the public interest to do so." As late as July 22—two days before the Court was to rule—St. Clair said the President had still not made up his mind about obeying an order: "I don't see how he can until he gets the decision, reads the opinion, and consults with counsel."

The President may simply have been buying time. If he were determined to resist a Court order, he would not announce it prematurely, for fear it would be converted into a count of impeachment. On the other hand, if he expected the Court to rule in his favor, he would have hoped never to face the prickly issue. But, by then, not even Nixon could have fooled himself into thinking he would win. More likely, he had pinned his hopes on a sharply divided Court, so he could claim the decision was insufficiently "definitive" for a matter of this magnitude. A President who could nominate a Carswell or a Haynsworth for a seat on the Supreme Court plainly had little respect for the institution and may have believed the men he *had* appointed would stick by him no matter what. Chuck Colson says the President counted on all three of his appointees. Others say he was sure of "the Minnesota Twins"—Burger and Blackmun. But, of course, he got none. Significantly, his greatest fury seems to have been directed not at the decision itself but at the three justices who "deserted" him. It was the Court's seamless unity which made defiance so difficult.

When his rage subsided, the President went on grasping at drifting sand. Was there "any air" in the decision, he asked St. Clair, any way around it? No, his lawyer told him, there was "no air." The more frantically the President sought an avenue of escape, the more emphatic St. Clair became. He warned that the country would not understand an outright defiance of the Supreme Court, and that it would merely assure his impeachment by the House and his conviction by the Senate. Finally, St. Clair said, legal "ethics" might compel him to withdraw from the case if the President persisted on this path. It was not an outright threat to resign, but it had the same effect.

It must have been an excruciating moment for Nixon. His lawyer warned him he could not defy the Court. But he knew he could not afford to comply. That is why he had asked Buzhardt to listen to the June 23 tape—to see whether he agreed it was too damaging to release.

Buzhardt agreed. Sitting there—three thousand miles away—listening to the scratchy voices over his earphones, he thought the tape was catastrophic. He listened to three conversations between Haldeman and the President—one from 10:04 to 11:09 a.m., another from 1:04 to 1:13 p.m., and the third from 2:20 to 2:45. Cumulatively, they portrayed the President at his least attractive: refusing to focus on serious matters of state, the international monetary situation, for instance ("I don't give a [expletive deleted] about the lira!"); using the same phrase to denounce the press ("I don't give a [expletive deleted] about the newspapers!"); looking for narrow political advantage from legislation ("There ain't a vote in it"); examining his ratings in the polls ("Well, Johnson, of course —sixty-six, forty-five, fifty-six . . . Except his negatives were higher—forty-two, forty-four, forty-one —our negatives have never been that high"); deriding his old friend Herb Klein ("He just doesn't have his head screwed on"); joking about homosexuals embar-

rassing the Democrats at Miami Beach ("ha, ha");
warning that his daughter Tricia should stay away
from museum and art functions ("They're Jews,
they're left wing"); worrying about his women's hair-
dos ("Pat raised the point last night that probably
she and the girls ought to stay in a hotel on Miami
Beach. . . . The moment they get [on] the helicopter
and get off and so forth, it destroys their hair");
and urging Haldeman to go for the jugular ("Play it
tough! That's the way they play it and that's the way
we are going to play it").

What made the tape so damaging was not, of course,
these jibes and sneers and maledictions but the plain,
irrefutable language which showed that six days after
the Watergate burglary the President of the United
States knew a great deal about the break-in, realized
that Liddy and Hunt had been involved, recognized
Mitchell's probable complicity, personally ordered a
cover-up of the facts, and used the CIA and the FBI
to protect his personal political interests. The tape
flatly contradicted most—if not all—of Nixon's disclaimers about participation in the cover-up, and
provided ample evidence that he had engaged in systematic obstruction of justice for more than two years.
Here, at last, was the "smoking gun" the Judiciary
Committee had been seeking—a weapon so redolent of
powder, so smeared with prints that no defendant
could hope for acquittal.

After two hours with his tape recorder, Buzhardt
had heard enough. Around 12:30 p.m. Washington
time (9:30 a.m. in San Clemente), he telephoned Haig
and St. Clair at the Western White House to report
that the tape was devastating. "I told them that in my
judgment it was all over," he recalls. "The June 23
tape clearly contradicted material we had submitted
to the House Judiciary Committee. I told Al that in my
opinion the tape was conclusive evidence. It was no
longer a question of the President leaving office, but
how he was leaving."

The two men at the California end of the line do not
seem to have taken the warning very seriously. They
may have discounted Buzhardt's assessment in part

because of personal friction that had developed during the preceding months. Just as Haldeman had once found Garment an alarmist, so Haig found Buzhardt too gloomy. The friction between St. Clair and Buzhardt was more serious. Although the barrister from Boston had replaced the South Carolina attorney as Nixon's chief Watergate lawyer six months before— Charles Alan Wright was back in Texas—Buzhardt had continued to play an important role behind the scenes. St. Clair was the "outside man"—the articulate, charming, smooth-as-silk courtroom advocate. Buzhardt was the "inside man"—the tough, pragmatic, military figure who specialized in blocking investigations. But the balance of power may have been on Buzhardt's side: because he alone controlled access to the White House tapes and documents. Cecil Emerson, a loquacious Dallas lawyer who worked on St. Clair's staff for several months, resigned in mid-March with a blast. "Buzhardt is in the driver's seat," he said. "Buzhardt is the political person. St. Clair is the professorial, nonpolitical, private practitioner, but he has to involve Buzhardt because he is the only one who knows everything that is going on." Even after Buzhardt suffered a mild heart attack in June, he hung on to his key functions. He remained the only man in the White House whom the President permitted to listen to the tapes. On several occasions, he and St. Clair had harsh words. So it was not surprising that St. Clair should not fully grasp the import of his rival's warning.

When he got off the telephone with Haig and St. Clair, Buzhardt went to lunch with Garment, Timmons, and Burch in the elegant White House Executive Dining Room. It was a gloomy meal. Timmons and Burch felt the Supreme Court decision had dealt the President a death blow. Timmons, who had been sounding congressional opinion all week, thought the Court ruling gave Nixon the perfect opportunity to resign on a matter of principle: that he would take no step which would weaken the Presidency in the future. Garment thought resignation was probably inevitable, but favored a waiting game. Buzhardt, hardly a loquacious man, was particularly silent. Noticing his lugubrious air, Garment asked, "What's up?" Buzhardt mumbled, "There's some bad stuff."

Meanwhile, in San Clemente, Haig and St. Clair presented Buzhardt's grim assessment to the President. Nixon's reaction was strange. Having suggested that Buzhardt listen to the "problem" tape, he now suggested that his reaction was exaggerated. Perhaps the President was still not willing to let his own chief of staff and his principal courtroom defender know what was on the worst of the tapes.

For the next few hours Nixon, Haig, St. Clair, and Ziegler reviewed their "options"—one of the President's favorite terms. Haig, who had spoken with Timmons, broached his resignation scenario without comment. Another White House aide suggested that the President might simply destroy all the tapes and challenge the House to impeach him—which it certainly would have. But ultimately the President and his assistants concluded that they had no real choice.

Eight hours went by while the men at the Western White House debated their response and framed a statement. The silence prompted many in Washington to conclude that Nixon was preparing to defy the court. But from midafternoon on, all he was preparing was another "PR" ploy. By holding St. Clair's announcement until four o'clock San Clemente time, the President timed it to coincide with the seven o'clock start of network television news on the East Coast. So on that critical day—when the Supreme Court had ruled against him and the Judiciary Committee was about to begin its public debate—the President maneuvered two of the networks into opening their newscasts with live pickups from California, shifting the emphasis from the decision to the response. (CBS refused to cave in to the White House strategy. It began its news with Walter Cronkite on the Supreme Court steps, reporting the Court's decision and the public reaction. Then, and only then, did it play a videotape of St. Clair's statement.)

There, at the Surf and Sand Hotel in Laguna Beach, was the President's lawyer—all earnest and solemn

—reading a statement from Nixon which said, in part, "While I am, of course, disappointed in the result, I respect and accept the Court's decision, and I have instructed Mr. St. Clair to take whatever measures are necessary to comply with that decision in all respects." For his own part, St. Clair said the task of reviewing the tapes for transmittal to Judge Sirica would be a "time-consuming" one. But he said, "As we all know, the President has always been a firm believer in the rule of law, and he intends his decision to comply with the Court's ruling as an action in furtherance of that belief."

Minutes after St. Clair went off the air, the Judiciary Committee came on. At 7:45 p.m. it convened in Room 2141 for the start of its formal debate before a hundred and twenty-five reporters, seventy-five friends, family, and spectators, and 40 million Americans in the television audience. The President's effort to snatch away the public's attention had been in vain. The nation was watching that night as Peter Rodino banged his gavel and began the debate with a solemn admonition: "Make no mistake about it. This is a turning point, whatever we decide. Our judgment is not concerned with an individual but with a system of constitutional government. It has been the history and the good fortune of the United States, ever since the Founding Fathers, that each generation of citizens and their officials have been, within tolerable limits, faithful custodians of the Constitution and the rule of law. For almost two hundred years every generation of Americans has taken care to preserve our system and the integrity of our institutions against the particular pressures and emergencies to which every time is subject. . . . Let us leave the Constitution as unimpaired for our children as our predecessors left it to us."

After Edward Hutchinson delivered his own warning—"ours is more of a political than a judicial function"—the word passed by seniority to Harold D. Donohue, the seventy-two-year-old Democrat from Massachusetts, due to retire in January after twenty-eight years in the House, a massive, chalky personage whom James Naughton of *The New York Times* likened to "James Cagney rolled in baby powder." To Donohue had been accorded the honor of introducing the Articles of Impeachment, the product of days of frantic drafting and redrafting by the staff, and by several committee factions. In the harsh accents of working-class Worcester, he intoned, "I move that the committee report to the House a resolution together with articles of impeachment, impeaching Richard M. Nixon, President of the United States."

The committee then moved into its ten-hour general debate, with each member allocated fifteen minutes. For months it had shunned this kind of public exposure, in part because Rodino had feared that premature television debate would commit members to positions they could not later alter, in part because he and others believed that interminable review of the evidence would put the country to sleep. Even now there were those who warned that most of the members were simply not up to sustained public debate on the issues, that they would betray the shallowness of their perceptions, the pettiness of their motivation, the mean and narrow minds of parochial politicians. But such warnings proved unfounded. Instead of sinking to their lowest common denominator, most of them pitched their remarks on the high plateau of constitutional imperatives and the broad sweep of the national interest. Most recognized that this was probably the most important vote of their lives, that whatever else they did they would be remembered best for what they were to do in that room during the next few days. As they spoke, they addressed themselves less to their colleagues than to their constituents at home, to the American people gathered before their television sets across the land, and—most of all—to the pages of history yet to be written.

Even so partisan a politician as Jack Brooks—an old crony of Lyndon Johnson—tried to set an elevated tone for the proceedings. "If ever there was a time to put aside partisanship now is that time. There would be no Democratic gain from removing a Republican President and having him replaced by another Republican who could represent, and might well receive a great outflowing of support from our people. We must now report to the House of Representatives and the American people our conclusions as to whether there is sufficient evidence that Mr. Nixon, while serving as President, has violated his oath of office and has thereby jeopardized our constitutional system of government. This is not a pleasant duty, but it is our constitutional duty. Its performance may mean ignoring personal and political relationships of long standing. But we as well as the President are on trial for how faithfully we fulfill our constitutional responsibility."

Robert McClory, the second-ranking Republican, took a similar tack. "I have heard it said by some that they cannot understand how a Republican could vote to impeach a Republican President. Let me hasten to assert that that argument demeans my role here. It would infer that no matter what high crimes and misdemeanors might have been committed that, if attributable to a Republican President, then I as a Republican am foreclosed from judging the merits of the case. I cannot and do not envision my role in that dim light. As a purely partisan matter, would it enhance our Republican party if, despite the evidence and the weight of constitutional law, we as Republicans on this side of the aisle decide to exonerate a Republican President accused of high crimes and misdemeanors simply because he and we are Republicans? I see that as leading to Republican party disaster."

Then it was Tom Railsback's turn. Unlike most of the members, he had no prepared text. For seventeen minutes—his own fifteen and two yielded by a colleague—he tried to lay out the evidence which had caused him so much anguish. Much of it came out a hash of dates, places, names, and meetings. But at the end he managed to croak—in a voice worn thin from endless debate—a heartfelt appeal to his fellow Republicans: "I am concerned and I am seriously concerned. I hope that the President—I wish the President could do something to absolve himself. . . . Some of my friends from Illinois . . . say that the country cannot afford to impeach a President. Let me say to these people, many of whom are good supporters and friends, I have spoken to countless others including many, many young people, and if the young people in this country think that we are not going to handle this thing fairly, if we are not going to really try to get to the truth, you are going to see the most frustrated people, the most turned-off people, the most disillusioned people, and it is going to make the period of LBJ in 1968, 1967, look tame. So I hope that we just keep our eye on trying to get the truth. Thank you."

"Rails," a bemused colleague exclaimed one day, "you've got more moves than Gypsy Rose Lee!" Of all the committee's Republicans, Railsback was the most accomplished politician—a nifty dancer to the shifting rhythms of public opinion, able to keep time to the bang of the drum while swiveling his hips to the syncopated sax. In his four terms representing the Nineteenth District of Illinois, Railsback had managed to please three widely divergent constituencies. In the rich black loam land of Fulton, Carroll, and Henderson counties along the east bank of the Mississippi, he was regarded as a stolid and solid Midwest Republican; in Moline and Rock Island, where Deere and Co. and International Harvester employed thousands of blue-collar Democrats, he was viewed as a liberal young legislator sympathetic to the workingman (he even won endorsements from the United Auto Workers); and in Washington, whether playing paddle ball in the House gym or playing politics on the House floor, he struck his associates as a rising young star, destined for either a leadership role in the House or elevation to the Senate. But that was all B.I.—Before Impeachment—as his young secretaries called it. Suddenly, Railsback found all his bright prospects in jeopardy. For months, he hoped the issue would simply go away,

so he wouldn't have to vote on it. Then, for a time in midwinter, he thought the impetus for impeachment might fade—if only the President would make a clean breast. In May he came up with another temporary escape—to take the President to court on the committee subpoenas—but most of the committee members were unwilling to let the courts resolve a battle between the legislature and the executive. Then, Railsback joined the vain search for a smoking gun. On June 8 he read an article by Walter Pincus in The Washington Post *which pointed toward one suspicious-looking weapon: evidence that Nixon had violated the grand jury process by passing on secret testimony he had received from Henry Petersen to Bob Haldeman. For a while Railsback went around showing the Pincus piece to his colleagues, but then he decided it wouldn't do, either. His worst time came in late June and early July—after the committee had heard all the evidence but before the live witnesses. Since he wouldn't buy James Madison's "superintendency" theory—that a President could be held responsible for the acts of his subordinates—he kept searching for "direct Presidential knowledge or involvement in substantial wrongdoing." But he couldn't find any. "It was terrible," Railsback recalls. "I'd go down to the old Congressional Hotel and spend hours listening to the tapes. I couldn't sleep. I'd wake up at three a.m. and lie there thinking: We just don't have anything serious enough, anything the people at home will understand." He began to emerge from his dark tunnel of indecision on July 11 —the day John Dean testified before the committee in closed session. Railsback listened as Doar and St. Clair took the President's former counsel through his familiar paces. When his turn came, he asked Dean about the President's efforts to intimidate his political opponents by having the IRS audit 490 contributors to the McGovern campaign. "Did the President also say that if you needed any help that he would be willing to help you accomplish your purpose?" Railsback asked. "That is correct," Dean replied. For Railsback that was what he had been looking for: Nixon's use of the IRS—later the CIA and the FBI too—for his own political purposes. A few hours after Dean testified, committee Republicans held one of their periodic caucuses. When Hutchinson pressed for publication of a minority report, Railsback suddenly objected that "Some of us may not agree with the minority position." Plainly taken aback, Hutchinson exclaimed, "Do you mean to say you would vote to impeach a Republican president!" and Railsback shot back, "I would vote to impeach any President I thought was subverting my government." From then on, Railsback pretty well knew where he was headed. But still he had to deal with his district. Twice in mid-July he went back to Moline to try his new position out on party stalwarts. He didn't say flatly that he would vote for impeachment but he indicated that he might and asked for their support whatever he did. Some men who had once been his most fervent supporters were furious. "He's a dog as far as I'm concerned," said Wayne Overstreet, a Henderson county commissioner. Carroll County chairman Bill Linker threatened to support a conservative candidate against Railsback in 1976 (he had never had a primary opponent). "Good Republicans are like elephants," Linker warned. "They never forget." And one state legislator drew the congressman aside and said in hushed tones, "Tom, down in Springfield some of the guys are asking, 'What's happened to Tom Railsback?'" In Washington, too, the pressures were intense. One of his closest friends in Congress told him that if he voted for impeachment he would never be a U.S. senator. But Railsback was very close to a decision. On the weekend of July 20–21 he went off with his wife, his four daughters, and a huge stack of committee documents. They had planned to go to the Lake Geneva Playboy Hotel in Wisconsin, but couldn't get a reservation, so they stayed instead with his wife's parents in Western Springs, a Chicago suburb. Except for a few hours watching a golf tournament at the La Grange Country Club and a Sunday-night family dinner at the Pizzeria Duo, the congressman holed up in his father-in-law's study with John Doar's 306-page summary. All of a sudden, he found a compelling case not only in the abuse of the federal agencies but in the Watergate cover-up. Flying back to Washington on Monday, Tom Railsback knew that if the right articles of impeachment were drawn, he would vote to impeach the President of the United States.*

For weeks it had been clear that if the "undecideds" joined forces, they could largely shape the Judiciary Committee's decision. "It's the guys who have the problems who have the leverage," Railsback says. "They needed us. They had to have us or the vote wouldn't carry much weight in the House. So we were in the driver's seat and we knew it."

But it took some time for the guys with the problems to get together. In April, May, and early June it seemed as if Bill Cohen might be the only Republican rat to leave Nixon's foundering ship. Then, on June 29, Ham Fish went down to the Congressional Hotel to go over the volumes of evidence. "I looked particularly at the events of March 21, the hush money and all that," he recalls. "For hours I went over and over the books and then I realized that what had occurred before March 21 and after March 21 was just as important as what happened on that day. For so long we'd been zeroing in on whether the President actually ordered Dean to pay hush money that we forgot the context. Whatever happened that day, the President had long known his aides were funneling money to the defendants, had done nothing at all to stop it, had in fact clearly acquiesced in it, and well into the spring had conspired with Haldeman and Ehrlichman to contain the scandal, to keep the truth from getting out. Suddenly, I saw March 21 as just another day in a pattern of events. At that point, I was very close to voting for impeachment."

Fish wasn't sure where Cohen stood. "I never asked Bill whether he was going to vote for impeachment and he never volunteered anything." Then, one July evening, Sam Donaldson of ABC-TV cornered Fish and Cohen together in the parking garage. They began discussing the loyalists' argument that the country would be much worse off if the House voted to impeach, but the Senate, by a narrow margin, found the President not guilty. "That shows a definite lack of confidence in Mr. Cohen and myself as managers of the House case," Fish quipped. When Donaldson asked whether he could use that, Cohen's eyes rolled to the sky. But then he smiled at Fish. "That's all there was," Fish recalls. "But from then on I think Bill and I had a tacit understanding that we were in this together."

For weeks, though, they feared that they might be in it alone—that they might be the only two Republicans out on the end of the creaking limb. "It was a very queasy feeling," Fish says. "If it had ended up that way, with only two of us, I don't know what I would have done. I'd have been reluctant to put my judgment up against everybody in my party, knowing they knew as much as I did."

During the next few weeks Cohen and Fish met several times. On Sunday, July 14, they spent five hours at Cohen's house in McLean, with two members of the minority committee—Richard Cates and Frank Polk—going over the Watergate part of the case, from the break-in through the cover-up. (The next Sunday Cates and Polk went to Fish's house to brief him on "abuse of power.")

The first hint they had that Railsback might be crawling out on the limb too came on July 11—the day Railsback questioned Dean and then rebuffed Hutchinson at the caucus. Afterward, Cohen, Fish, and Railsback talked about the "disturbing implications" of Hutchinson's demands for Republican unanimity.

On the evening of July 15 Railsback and Cohen had dinner together. All along, Railsback had been deeply influenced by the younger man. They had been close friends ever since Cohen came to Congress in 1972 and particularly since he joined the Judiciary Committee's third subcommittee of which Railsback was the ranking Republican. "We worked very closely on newsmen's privilege and penal reform," Railsback says. "We visited prisons together and socialized together. It's a very close, mutually respecting friend-

ship." The two men were very different. A Latin
scholar and a poet, Cohen once gave this definition of
impeachable conduct: "It's like Robert Frost on love.
It's indefinable and unmistakable—I know it when I
see it." Railsback was not at ease with poetry, or even
with words. He wore loud sport jackets, clashing ties,
and an air of small-town bonhomie. But he was intrigued by Cohen's erudition, and through the spring
and early summer the two congressmen often had
lunch and dinner together to talk about the issues.
"Bill was very morally indignant about the whole
thing," Railsback said. "That isn't my normal style.
But gradually his indignation seeped in. I got angrier
and angrier."

Railsback was also close to Walter Flowers, the
young Alabamian who sported an American flag in his
lapel, wore red, white, and blue saddle shoes, and had
originally come to Congress as a supporter of George
Wallace. "Walt and I have a deep friendship. We had
genuine mutual concerns. We both had Nixon leanings;
both of our districts had gone heavily for the President.
But we were genuinely undecided. I knew Flowers
was standing up at Democratic caucuses, refusing to be
pushed around. So he had a certain credibility with me
that no other Democrat would have had. For example,
I wouldn't have trusted Jim Mann, because I knew
from a trip with him that he didn't like the President.
I think he'd prejudged the case. I think Ray Thornton
had too. Likewise, I don't think Walt would have dealt
with a Bill Cohen, a liberal from Maine, in the same
way he did with me. Flowers was a key guy for me. I
think I was a key guy for him."

Rodino, too, knew Flowers was a key man. He knew
that impeachment stood no chance in the Senate if
it appeared to be the work of zealots like Waldie or
Conyers. "The decision has to come out of the middle
of the committee," he would say. So he treated Flowers, Mann, and Thornton—the three southern Democrats—with the utmost courtesy and deference; too
much deference for some of the northerners, one of
whom was heard to grouse that the chairman didn't
need to "carry those guys on a velvet pillow." But the

chairman knew what he was doing. In mid-July he gently, very gently suggested to Flowers that he might think about getting the "men in the middle" together.

On July 22—the day Railsback got back from his in-laws' house in Western Springs—the committee met to hear Sam Garrison's argument for the "minority." After the session, Railsback and Flowers walked down the corridor together, and Flowers said, "I have a couple of guys. Why don't you get your guys and we'll get together and talk about it."

Flowers' guys were Thornton and Mann. Railsback's guys were Fish, Cohen, and Caldwell Butler, the sad-eyed freshman from Roanoke, Virginia. At eight-thirty the next morning, the seven congressmen convened in Railsback's office, Room 218 of the Cannon Building. Also sitting in on the meeting were Bill Hermelin, Railsback's administrative assistant, and Tom Mooney, a minority counsel to the committee who had worked closely with Railsback on penal reform and other matters ("Mooney is my chief adviser and right arm," Railsback says). Over coffee and Danish pastry, the group began feeling each other out.

For a few minutes they talked about substituting a censure resolution for impeachment, but Flowers asked whether "the punishment fit the crime" and they dropped that idea. Then they went through the matters they would not want in Articles of Impeachment —the bombing of Cambodia, impoundment, illegal corporate contributions, ITT, the milk fund, public expenditures on San Clemente and Key Biscayne, the President's taxes. "Many of these were serious enough," Fish recalls, "but for one reason or another we didn't think they rose to the level of impeachable offenses. Many congressmen had received illegal corporate contributions. The milk thing was out because sixteen members of the Judiciary Committee had received money from the milk trusts. The President had lied to us about Cambodia, but we couldn't shoulder him with responsibility for a war many congressmen had supported. It was hard to show any direct *quid pro quo* on ITT. The President had played fast and loose with his taxes, but tax evasion was too private a crime.

For impeachment, we demanded an offense against the political process or the constitutional system of our country."

Turning to such matters, they suddenly found themselves in remarkable agreement. Gone was the search for the smoking gun. Instead, they all seemed to be focusing on patterns of conduct, lines of behavior which undermined the constitutional system. In a matter of minutes, all seven said they would vote for narrowly drawn articles in two areas: the Watergate cover-up and abuse of power. They were astonished by their unanimity. "I was very relieved to find that our thoughts were parallel," says Fish. "It was a very moving moment," Flowers recalls. From that moment the seven congressmen became a unit: known to some as the Unholy Alliance, to others as the Terrible Seven, to still others as the Magnificent Seven, and to themselves as the Fragile Coalition.

The coalition quickly agreed that the Articles proposed by Doar the week before were too incendiary, too filled with emotive words like "malicious" and "deliberate." Railsback warned that the wording must not be overdone so that "it not look as if we are trying to pour it on the President." Mann volunteered to redraft the articles, with help from Tom Mooney.

Rodino had already appointed a four-man Democratic drafting committee—Brooks, Sarbanes, Conyers, and Edwards—which was meeting in a small subcommittee room on the second floor of the Rayburn Building. After lunch, Flowers and Mann went over to see them. Not surprisingly, the drafters promptly agreed to consider whatever the Fragile Coalition came up with. "They were calling the shots at that point," recalls Sarbanes. "We weren't about to say them nay."

In the steamy cauldron of the next few days, tensions did develop between the two groups. Conyers bridled when Flowers urged northern Democrats not to mention Cambodia in their speeches. And Kastenmeier led an outright revolt when the coalition insisted that the articles be voted on all at once, so that they would not be forced to commit themselves in full view of their constituents day after day. Charging that the

Terrible Seven were getting their way too often, the liberals mustered a 21–16 majority to require separate debate and votes on each article. (Flowers was furious for a few hours, but cooled down.)

All day on Wednesday, July 24, the two drafting groups met separately—the coalition in Railsback's office, and the Democrats in the Rayburn Building. Sometimes they conferred by telephone; sometimes Mann shuttled between the two. By 7:00 p.m.—a half-hour before debate was to begin—they agreed on a rough draft which, though far from satisfactory, would do for the time being. These were the articles shoved in front of Harold Donohue just in time for him to introduce them.

The drafting continued on Thursday while the committee resumed its public debate. The speeches that day ranged from the controlled fury of Jerome Waldie ("You cannot look at this case without feeling a deep sadness but a deeper anger, a deeper anger that this country was jeopardized to the extent it has been in the past two years") to the arid legalisms of Charles Wiggins ("My guess, Mr. Doar, is that you can put all of the admissible evidence in half of one book. Most of this is just material. It is not evidence and it may never surface in the Senate because it is not admissible evidence").

But the day belonged principally to the southerners, whose remarks breathed a sense of history, a worship of the Constitution and of the institutions it enshrined. "What if we fail to impeach?" asked Walter Flowers of Alabama. "Do we ingrain forever in the very fabric of our Constitution a standard of conduct in our highest office that in the least is deplorable and at worst impeachable?" And James Mann of South Carolina intoned, "We have built our country on the Constitution. That system has been defended on battlefields and statesmen have ended their careers on behalf of the system and have either passed into oblivion or immortality." And Barbara Jordan, a formidable black woman from Houston, Texas, took off on a flight of brilliant rhetoric: "Earlier today we heard the beginning of the Preamble to the Constitution of the United

States. 'We, the people . . .' It is a very eloquent beginning. But when that document was completed on the seventeenth of September in 1787 I was not included in that, 'We, the people.' I felt somehow for many years that George Washington and Alexander Hamilton just left me out by mistake. But through the process of amendment, interpretation, and court decision I have finally been included in 'We, the people.' Today, I am an inquisitor. My faith in the Constitution is whole, it is complete, it is total. I am not going to sit here and be an idle spectator to the diminution, the subversion, the destruction of the Constitution."

But perhaps the most dramatic pronouncement of all came from M. Caldwell Butler, the last of the Fragile Coalition to make up his mind. Butler's Sixth District of Virginia—stretching from the eastern slope of the Blue Ridge to the Alleghenies—was a nest of Republican sentiment in the cradle of the Confederacy. In 1972 it had given Nixon his biggest margin in the state—72.7 per cent. The weekend of July 20–21— while Railsback was at his in-laws' house and Fish was studying "abuse of power"—Butler was playing host to Vice President Ford, whose presence in the district could only be construed as not so subtle pressure on the congressman. But Butler was being nudged by others too—among them his wife, who had long since opted for impeachment and who read him portions of Woodstein's *All the President's Men* before they went to sleep. Butler knew he was risking voter retaliation. At the Tuesday morning meeting in Railsback's office, Flowers leaned over and whispered in his ear, "You better be careful, Caldwell. Every pick-up in Richmond could be here by nightfall."

But by Thursday night Butler had resolved any last-minute doubts. Peering owlishly through thick lenses, he paid tribute to Richard Nixon's "significant accomplishments," acknowledged his "many kindnesses and courtesies," and was "not unmindful" of the loyalty he owed both Nixon and the Republican party. But he warned, "For years we Republicans have campaigned against corruption and misconduct. . . . But Watergate is our shame. Those things have happened in our house and it is our responsibility to do what we can to clear it up. It is we, not the Democrats, who must demonstrate that we are capable of enforcing the high standards we would set for them. . . . In short, power appears to have corrupted. It is a sad chapter in American history, but I cannot condone what I have heard; I cannot excuse it; and I cannot and will not stand for it. . . . Mr. Chairman, while I still reserve my final judgment, I would be less than candid if I did not now say that my present inclination is to support articles incorporating my view of the charges of obstruction of justice and abuse of power. But there will be no joy in it for me."

By Friday, there was no joy in it for anybody. Exhausted, jittery, surfeited with evidence, hoarse from debate, and many of them suffering from a stomach virus, the members plowed through another day of argument. In the early afternoon Sarbanes introduced the revised version of Article I, which now became known as the "Sarbanes substitute." It charged that the President had "prevented, obstructed, and impeded the administration of justice, in that . . . using the powers of his high office, [he] made it his policy, and in furtherance of such policy did act directly and personally and through his close subordinates and agents, to delay, impede, and obstruct the investigation of [the Watergate burglary]; to cover up, conceal, and protect those responsible; and to conceal the existence of other unlawful covert activities. . . . In all this, Richard M. Nixon has acted in a manner contrary to his trust as President and subversive of constitutional government to the great prejudice of the cause of law and justice and to the manifest injury of the people of the United States. Wherefore, Richard M. Nixon, by such conduct, warrants impeachment, trial, and removal from office." (The article also included nine subparagraphs detailing the operation of the cover-up.)

Abruptly, the Republicans launched a ferocious counterattack. It began with Charles Wiggins, the shrewd, tough Californian, who—in the absence of leadership from the lackadaisical Hutchinson—had increasingly become the point man for the Republican loyalists.

WIGGINS: Now, the heart of this matter is that the President made it his policy to obstruct justice and to interfere with investigations. Would you please explain to this member of the committee and to the other members, when, and in what respect, and how did the President declare that policy? And I wish the gentleman would be rather specific, since it is the heart of the allegation.

SARBANES: Well, of course, the means by which this policy has been done are the ones that are set out subsequent to the second paragraph.

WIGGINS: If the gentleman could confine himself to the question, when was the policy declared?

SARBANES: . . . Well, the policy relates back to June 17, 1972, and prior thereto, agents of the committee committed illegal entry, and it then goes on and says subsequent thereto, Richard M. Nixon, using the powers of his high office, made it his policy, and in furtherance of such policy did act directly—

WIGGINS: I can read the article, but I think it is rather important to all of us that we know from you, as the author of the article, exactly when this policy was declared, and I hope you will tell us.

Of course, the committee had no evidence that the cover-up had ever been officially proclaimed as Presidential policy; Nixon and his men had simply acted from the start as if it were understood. So Sarbanes found himself squirming and shifting under Wiggins' assault.

But if Wiggins was the minority's rapier, slicing at the soft spots in the majority argument, then Charles W. Sandman, Jr., of New Jersey was their blackjack, thudding relentlessly around his opponent's head and shoulders.

SANDMAN: Do you not believe that under the due-process clause of the Constitution that every individual, including the President, is entitled to due notice of what he is charged for? Do you believe that?

SARBANES: I think this article does provide due notice.

SANDMAN: You are not answering my question.

SARBANES: Well, I think I am answering your question.

SANDMAN: Well, let me ask you this, then. As I see this, you have about twenty different charges here, all on one piece of paper, and not one of them specific. . . . How does he answer such a charge? This is not due process. Due process—

SARBANES: I would point out to the gentleman from New Jersey that the President's counsel entered this committee room at the very moment that members of this committee entered the room and began to receive the presentation of information, and that he stayed in the room—

SANDMAN: I do not yield any further.

SARBANES:—Throughout that process.

SANDMAN: I do not yield any further for those kind of speeches. I want answers, and this is what I am entitled to. This is a charge against the President of the United States, why he should be tried to be thrown out of office, and that is what it is for. For him to be duly noticed of what you are charging him, in my judgment, he is entitled to know specifically what he did wrong, and how does he gather that from what you say here?

Quickly, other loyalists took up Sandman's bludgeon. "A common jaywalker charged with jaywalking any place in the United States is entitled to know when and where the alleged offense is supposed to have occurred," said Delbert Latta. "Is the President of the United States entitled to less?"

For the rest of the afternoon the Republicans kept up their persistent demand for "specificity"—dates, times, and events to support each allegation in the article. Caught off guard—unable to pronounce the tongue twister, much less respond to it—the Democratic majority and their allies in the Fragile Coalition fell back in confusion. Some said the problem was not too little evidence but too much ("We really have so much that we do not have any," said Butler). Some argued that the articles themselves would be supported by a committee report chock-full of details. Still others explained that the article had been phrased broadly so as to cover additional evidence that might become available before the Senate trial (chiefly from the new tapes to be turned over to Jaworski). But the Republicans struck back with ridicule. "Isn't it amazing?" rasped Sandman. "They are willing to do anything except make these articles specific. It is the same old story, you know, when you don't have the law on your side, you talk about the facts. If you don't have the facts on your side, you just talk, and that is what a lot of people have been doing today."

The discomfiture was greatest among the coalition. Northern Democrats were confident that their constituents understood the case against the President—or would support it even if they didn't understand it. But the southern Democrats and moderate Republicans feared that if they did not make the case clear, if they seemed to be indicting the President without precise and specific evidence, the retaliation would be all the swifter and surer.

That evening the Fragile Coalition—augmented now by Hogan and, surprisingly, Harold Froehlich of Wisconsin—met for dinner at the Capitol Hill Club, a Republican gathering spot. "We all agreed it had been a bad, bad day," Railsback recalls. "The specificity thing had hurt a great deal, and we were not doing a good job laying out the evidence. We talked about what to do, and there was strong sentiment for postponing debate until Monday so we could prepare our case more carefully. But I knew Rodino wouldn't buy that. So we decided to meet it head on."

During the evening session Sandman moved to strike the first subparagraph of Article I for lack of "specificity"—warning that he would try to strike each of the succeeding eight subparagraphs on the same ground. At 11:30 p.m. his motion lost 27–11—a portent of things to come—but everyone expected a protracted struggle the next day. Staff lawyers worked late—some of them the whole night—to gird for the battle.

At an early morning caucus the contested items were divided up among the Democrats and moderate Republicans, and each was supplied with the relevant material prepared overnight by the staff. But, when the committee convened, Sandman executed a rapid about-face. Recognizing that the votes were now massively against him, he abandoned his motions to strike. Flowers promptly picked them up—not because he opposed the article but because he thought the case for it had not adequately been made and he wanted more time to lay it out. Railsback went over to Flowers on the dais and said, "Walter, let's get off this kick. As long as they [the loyalists] were getting in their licks, we had to fight back. But if they don't want to push it, let's vote." Flowers said he'd think about it, conferred with Rodino, and agreed to a compromise—a limited, twenty-minute debate on each item.

Later Railsback came up with an amendment which strengthened the article. He moved to strike the word "policy"—which had given them all so much trouble the day before—and substitute "course of conduct or plan." Everyone agreed it was a big improvement.

Just before 7:00 p.m. they were ready to vote. In deference to the delicacy of his position, Flowers was granted the last word. "There are many people in my district who will disagree with my vote here," he said mournfully. "Some will say that it hurts them deeply for me to vote for impeachment. I can assure them that I probably have enough pain for them and me."

Then the clerk called the roll on the key vote—the motion to replace the Donohue article with the Sarbanes substitute. One by one, the Democrats responded "Aye," most of them with an air of great solemnity, eyes downcast, heads bowed. Then, marching along the top tier of Republicans, the roll reached Railsback.

"Mr. Railsback."

"Aye."

"Mr. Wiggins."

"No."

"Mr. Dennis."

"No."

"Mr. Fish."

"Aye."

"Mr. Mayne."

"No."

"Mr. Hogan."

"Aye."

"Mr. Butler."

"Aye."

"Mr. Cohen."

"Aye."

"Mr. Lott."

"No."

"Mr. Froehlich."

"Aye."

Six Republicans had voted for impeachment—far more than anyone had predicted only a week before. When the call ended with Rodino's hoarse "Aye," the vote was 27–11. Quickly they ran through another roll call to adopt the Sarbanes substitute. The vote was the same. At 7:05 p.m. the committee adjourned until Monday. Just then, Kenneth R. Harding, the House sergeant at arms, rushed up to Rodino and said, breathlessly, "A plane has just left National Airport. We had a call that it's a *kamikaze* flight that's going to crash into the Rayburn Building." Rodino ordered the hearing room cleared. Several members stood at windows to watch for the *kamikaze,* which never appeared. Others, the chairman among them, went into adjoining offices, closed the doors, and cried.

A s the committee voted, Nixon was walking with his daughter Tricia and her husband, Edward Cox, on Red Beach near his San Clemente home. Staff members at the Western White House waited about twenty minutes—as they had when the Supreme Court ruled—before informing the President via a telephone on the beach. Later that evening Ziegler issued a statement which said, "The President remains confident that the full House will recognize that there simply is not the evidence to support this or any other article of impeachment and will not vote to impeach. He is confident because he knows he has committed no impeachable offense."

According to Ziegler, Nixon did not watch any of the committee's debates on television, although his aides monitored them carefully on a set in the Western White House conference room. In his two weeks at San Clemente, the President did his best to show that he was ignoring the events on Capitol Hill. Unlike his winter visit there—when he seemed too distracted to work— he spent part of each day on the nation's business. Several long meetings were devoted to the deteriorating economy. Kenneth Rush, the President's new economic adviser, was pleasantly surprised when Nixon allowed one meeting to run an hour and a half over its allotted time. On July 25—the first full day of committee debate —he helicoptered to Los Angeles to deliver a nationally televised address on the economy before four California business groups. (Billed as the kickoff to a "great crusade" against inflation, the speech turned out to be a rather pedestrian primer on supply and demand.) On July 26 he spent two hours with Secretary of State Kissinger and West Germany's foreign minister, Hans-Dietrich Genscher. On Saturday, July 27—the day the committee voted—he met for twenty-five minutes with James T. Lynn, secretary of housing and urban development. Lynn told reporters that the President had "concentrated totally" on housing issues and "did not seem at all distracted" by the impeachment process.

As usual, the private Nixon was very different from the cardboard figure his aides tried to erect. Not surprisingly, he was very much distracted by impeachment, indeed obsessed by it. If he could really keep himself from watching the debates on television—which seems unlikely—he could hardly avoid them in the newspapers he read every day: the Los Angeles Times, which played the story prominently on page one, and the Copley papers in San Diego, which once had buried news unfavorable to Nixon but now recognized the growing inevitability of the events in Congress. "There was scarcely a waking moment out there when he wasn't thinking about impeachment, brooding about it," one aide says. "He'd put on this mask even for us, trying to concentrate on the prime rate or Greek politics or housing starts. But whenever he was off guard you would catch him gazing out the window at the ocean with this haunted look in his eyes, the look of a man who knew he was going to die. And don't think it wasn't death. For Richard Nixon, leaving the White House was like going six feet under. He could feel the cold already."

Perhaps that is why he hardly left the compound during the entire two weeks. Except for the trip to Los Angeles for the economic speech, his only night out was for a dinner party with a hundred and fifty California friends and supporters at the lavish Bel Air estate of Budget Director Roy Ash, a house once owned by W. C. Fields. (In a speech that night, Nixon said, "I can assure you that no man in public life—and I have studied history rather thoroughly—has ever had a more loyal group of friends.") Not once did he slip out for a meal at his favorite Mexican restaurant, nor go for a ride down the San Diego freeway. He spent hours immersed in a biography of Napoleon, perhaps reflecting a change in mood from his winter vacation, when he read a book about Lincoln. One reason for his self-imposed seclusion was the absence of Bebe Rebozo, his companion on many such ventures. Nixon is believed to have had several long telephone talks with Rebozo and also with Bob Haldeman, his other former confidant. But among his current aides, only Ron Ziegler had anything like the personal relationship with Nixon that those two men enjoyed. Increasingly, during those last weeks, it was Ziegler—the former account executive for 7-Up and tour guide at Disneyland— from whom the President of the United States sought counsel in his darkest hours of doubt.

Early on the afternoon of Sunday, July 28, Nixon boarded *Air Force One* for the flight back to Washington. On the plane Haig, the former four-star general, conceded to reporters that the President had taken "very heavy losses."

At the Rayburn Building, committee members in their Sunday sports clothes were gathering for caucuses on Article II. First, Rodino and Mann met with McClory, who had drafted his own version of the article. The second-ranking Republican on the committee, McClory had vacillated for months, flapping with the prevailing winds like the big flag on the Capitol dome. He had voted against Article I, but now that he was willing to vote for Article II, the Democrats would do almost anything to accommodate him. The day before, the Fragile Coalition had largely adopted McClory's approach, which hinged the second article on the requirement—in Article II of the Constitution—that the President "take care that the laws be faithfully executed." This dovetailed nicely with the coalition's insistence that all articles tie wrongdoing directly to the President. One could subsume a grab bag of offenses under the umbrella charge that Nixon had failed in his constitutional obligation to make sure that the laws were faithfully executed. Among these offenses, the coalition would have preferred to include the President's refusal to honor the committee's subpoenas for evidence. But another condition of McClory's support was that this should be made a separate article. Reluctantly, at the morning meeting, Rodino and Mann went along. Then they gained approval for the compromise from a caucus of eighteen Democrats.

After the caucus, Bill Hungate of Missouri went to a movie (*Blazing Saddles*) to unwind the "impeachment kinks" in his head, but he was so exhausted he slept through most of Mel Brooks's horse-opera bouffe. Then he went home and had a beer. At about nine-thirty Rodino called to ask whether he would introduce Article II. "The Hungate substitute has been born and I wasn't even present at the accouchement," he told his wife in mock dismay. The chairman wanted a Southerner to introduce the article, but it was one thing to ask Mann, Flowers, and Thornton to support it, another to ask them to put their name on it for all time. So the chairman selected Hungate, who represented the "Little Dixie" section of Missouri.

At eight the next morning Hungate met with Doar and Mann to go over the supporting material. Then, at 11:35, he took the microphone in Room 2141 to introduce "the Hungate substitute," which read, in part: "Using the powers of the office of President of the United States, Richard M. Nixon, in violation of his constitutional oath faithfully to execute the office of the President of the United States and, to the best of his ability, preserve, protect, and defend the Constitution of the United States, and in disregard of his constitutional duty to take care that the laws be faithfully executed, has repeatedly engaged in conduct violating the constitutional rights of citizens, impairing the due and proper administration of justice and the conduct of lawful inquiries, or contravening the laws governing agencies of the executive branch and the purpose of these agencies. . . . In all of this, Richard M. Nixon has acted in a manner contrary to his trust as President and subversive of constitutional government, to the great prejudice of the cause of law and justice and to the manifest injury of the people of the United States." (The article included five subparagraphs, which specified Nixon's misuse of the FBI, CIA, Secret Service, and the IRS, among other agencies.)

For seventy-six of the past seventy-eight years, the Ninth District of Missouri had been represented in Congress by only three men. From 1897 to 1921, the congressman was Champ Clark, who served as Speaker of the House for nine years and was almost nominated for President in 1912. After an inexplicable Republican interlude of two years, the seat was held for the next forty-two years by Clarence Cannon. Beginning as Clark's secretary and as House parliamentarian, Cannon went on to serve as chairman of the House Appropriations Committee for twenty years and became

*one of the body's great patriarchs. On Cannon's death
in 1964 he was succeeded by Bill Hungate, who is
profoundly aware of the glorious tradition in which he
treads. "You couldn't grow up in Bowling Green, Missouri, without being aware of it," he says. "Living in
Champ Clark's home town, walking by his statue on
the way to school, seeing his son—Bennett Clark—
come back to town for a torchlight parade as U.S.
senator, watching Mr. Cannon around the courthouse
—this all had to have an impact on you, particularly
Mr. Cannon's role. I can remember, as a young man,
going to a political meeting out to the Pike County
Country Club. First, they'd introduce Governor Dalton
and he'd make a speech. Then they'd introduce Senator
Symington and he'd make a speech. Then he'd introduce the real speaker of the evening to whom everybody
else paid due deference—Mr. Cannon. Very early, I
realized that real power could be exercised in the House
of Representatives because Mr. Cannon had it and he
exercised it. It was Mr. Cannon who kept the Congress
there until Christmas one year because Senator [Carl]
Hayden [of Arizona] insisted the House come to the
Senate side for a conference and Mr. Cannon said he
wouldn't do that, the House originated appropriations
and so the Senate should come to the House side. Mr.
Cannon wasn't easily impressed, not even by Presidents. He'd cut Jack Kennedy's appropriations bills
and Kennedy would call him to talk it over. But old
Clarence was pretty tough. He wouldn't go to the
phone. There may be an element of plain stubborn
pride in all this, but there's also insistence on the
prerogatives of the lower House which appeals to me
very much. The House is the body closest to the people.
In a system based on the sovereignty of the people,
it's ultimately the most sovereign of all our institutions.
That's why I got so mad when the President defied our
subpoenas. He lost me irrevocably on that. At some
point, you have to stand up and say 'We are the representatives of the people and here is what we require
of you, Mr. President.' " Not surprisingly, there is one
President to whom Hungate feels very close—Harry
S Truman, the Man from Missouri. "You know, peo-*

ple say old 'Give 'Em Hell' Harry was pretty tough and they ask what's the difference between the stuff he did and the stuff Nixon did. I'll tell you the difference. Mr. Truman was an open man. What he said, he said out in public. That's what got him in trouble so much of the time. He didn't send secret memos around telling the agencies to do this and that. Mr. Truman wasn't a sneak. Moreover, he always remembered that he was a temporary occupant of the office. He often said that 'many men would make a better President than I, but by God, I'm the President.' He realized that he didn't take on any additional attributes by virtue of being President. In Nixon's case, it seems like he felt it made him bigger than life." What a lot of people like about Bill Hungate is that he doesn't feel that being a six-term member of Congress makes him bigger than life. He retains a puckish sense of humor that keeps bubbling up at moments that more solemn people find inappropriate. In that respect, he feels very close to still another man from his district—Mark Twain. Hannibal has deteriorated into a tawdry little town, with junky souvenir shops catering to the tourists. But Twain's sly, irreverent mirth lived on in Missourians like Hungate. During high school and college, he played clarinet and saxophone in an assortment of bands, and later he became an inveterate song writer, penning little ditties on matters of public interest. On Palm Sunday, 1973, while the Watergate scandal was cracking open, he went to the piano and wrote out a song called "Down at the Old Watergate," which went, in part, "Come, come, come and play spy with me/ Down at the old Watergate/ Come, come, come love and lie with me/ Down at the old Watergate/ See the little German band/ Ehrlichman und Haldeman/ Don't Martha Mitchell look great?" As soon as he wrote it, he knew he had "a winner." The Democratic National Committee had a telephone service on which they would play any congressional message of less than a minute. So Hungate recorded his song, accompanying himself at the piano, and it became so popular that most of the time all you could get on the line was a busy signal. Some editorial writers at home denounced him as

*insufficiently serious and when the Judiciary Committee
began hearing evidence on impeachment, some people
said the author of "Down at the Old Watergate" ought
to disqualify himself from voting. But Hungate just
chuckled and said, "I have never thought a sense of
humor needed to destroy your sense of responsibility,
and in my case I felt it better to have a sense of humor
than no sense at all." And he kept it up. When the
committee debated whether "inferences" could be
drawn from the evidence against Nixon, Hungate said,
"I'll tell you, if a guy brought an elephant through that
door and one of us said, 'That is an elephant,' some of
the doubters would say, 'You know, that is an inference. That could be a mouse with a glandular condition.'" And when others cautioned that no President
had ever been removed from office in 198 years and
we ought not to start now, Hungate replied, "They tell
the story about Mark Twain's uncle in an itty-bitty
Missouri town after the Civil War. A big troop of
soldiers came through and one of them went to wash
his hands. He came back and said, 'Hey, I want to tell
you, that roller towel you've got back there is the
filthiest thing I've ever seen.' And Twain's uncle said,
'I don't know what you mean. There's two hundred
fellas used it and you're the first one that complained.'
Well, that's where we may be with the Presidency. The
towel's finally got to be changed."*

Despite Hungate's occasional levity the debate on
Article II was more elevated, more serious, and ultimately more important than the debate on Article I.
For the committee was now discussing the most elemental of public issues: the limits which a democracy
should place on its leaders, the balance between the
powers of the state and the rights of the individual.
Bill Cohen cautioned, "When the chief executive of the
country starts to investigate private citizens who criti-
cize his policies or authorizes his subordinates to do
such things, then I think the rattle of the chains that
would bind up our constitutional freedoms can be heard,
and it is against this rattle that we should awake and

say no." And Jim Mann warned, "If there be no accountability, another President will feel free to do as he chooses. But the next time there may be no watchman in the night." At 11:20 on that Monday night, the committee voted 28–10 for Article II (with McClory's vote swelling the Republican defectors to seven).

That was the high-water mark of the impeachment tide. The next day the committee adopted McClory's Article III, which charged the President with failing "without lawful cause or excuse to produce papers and things, as directed by duly authorized subpoenas issued by the Committee on the Judiciary" on April 11, May 15, May 30, and June 24, 1974. The article won support from the hard-line Democrats, but the Fragile Coalition at last broke apart. Some of its members may have heeded Republican warnings that the article would drastically weaken the Presidency in its future relations with Congress. Some may have acted less on principle than on a need to hedge their political bets. Some "no" votes and some "responsible" speeches wouldn't hurt at home. "Perhaps we've been too infused with our newfound power," warned Flowers. "Please, reconsider what you're doing here." In all, seven coalition members—Flowers, Mann, Railsback, Fish, Butler, Cohen, and Froehlich—voted with the Republican loyalists ("It's been a long time, Tom," Wiggins whispered to Railsback). Only McClory, Hogan, and Thornton voted with the majority. The article squeaked through: 21–17.

Later that day, two more proposed articles—on the bombing of Cambodia and the President's taxes—lost by identical votes of 26–12. At 11:08 p.m., on July 30, the committee completed its work and adjourned.

Even as the committee's drumroll of judgments echoed along the Potomac, the White House began to comply with the Supreme Court's earlier judgment. On July 25 St. Clair had flown back from San Clemente to begin processing the subpoenaed tapes. In court the next day, Judge Sirica told St. Clair and Jaworski to work out a timetable for their delivery. During a head-on conference behind closed doors, the two lawyers agreed that by July 30 the White House would turn over the twenty conversations which had been only partially included in the edited White House transcripts. The following Friday—August 2—was set as the deadline for delivery of the remaining forty-four conversations, or as many as possible.

A few minutes later, in open court, the judge posed one question which clearly shook the President's lawyer.

"Have you personally listened to the tapes?" he asked.

St. Clair mumbled something about being "a poor listener."

"You mean to say the President wouldn't approve of your listening to the tapes?" Judge Sirica said. "You mean to say you could argue this case without knowing all the background of these matters?"

The answer to both questions, of course, was "yes." But it was a matter which had already caused St. Clair so much grief that he could not bring himself to reply directly. So Judge Sirica simply ordered him to listen to the tapes and prepare an analysis for the court of those sections on which the President still claimed some privilege.

St. Clair did say that Nixon wanted to listen to all the tapes himself before they were turned over: "The President feels quite strongly that he should know what he is turning over." Nixon began these listening sessions on the following Monday, July 29. Alone in the Lincoln Sitting Room, that favorite hideaway in the White House living quarters, he played the tapes on a machine whose erase mechanism had been rendered inoperable (an unnecessary precaution, since he listened to copies made by the Secret Service, while St. Clair, in his office, listened to the originals). As the Judiciary Committee voted on Articles II and III, Nixon sat there reliving the events which had brought him to the brink of impeachment.

The President had already listened to the twenty tapes included in the edited transcripts. So he authorized St. Clair to turn them over on schedule that Tuesday afternoon. A husky aide carried a large suitcase, containing eleven reels of tape, into court that afternoon at 3:48, just twelve minutes before the deadline. "I'm going to have to ask your honor for a receipt," St. Clair said with a smile. Judge Sirica suggested that he settle for a transcript of the hearing and St. Clair agreed.

Richard Ben Veniste, an assistant special prosecutor, asked St. Clair if any part of the conversations was missing.

"Not to my knowledge," St. Clair said. "These were copied mechanically and I have had no reports of abnormalities."

But the next day, a somewhat sheepish St. Clair reported still another gap in a White House tape. He told Judge Sirica that five minutes and twelve seconds of the April 17, 1973, conversation between Nixon, Haldeman, and Ehrlichman had never been recorded —because a machine ran out of tape. (The gap began about 4:20 p.m., only twenty-two minutes before the President went to the White House press room to announce "major developments" in the Watergate case.) On Friday, when St. Clair gave Sirica thirteen more tapes, he admitted that another whole conversation was missing—the June 21, 1972, talk between the President and Colson, which St. Clair now said had never been recorded, because Nixon made the call from a telephone in the White House living quarters which was not hooked up to the taping system. (And on August 7, the White House reported that nine more of the subpoenaed conversations were not available on tape —seven because they had never been recorded, and two which could simply not be found.)

Six months before, these gaps would have been new "bombshells" on the Watergate battlefield. Now they were mere pistol shots which rattled harmlessly by the ears of the distracted armies. By then, the White House was preoccupied with a far graver matter: the June 23 tapes.

On Tuesday, July 30, the President was still en-

sconced in the Lincoln Sitting Room, slumped in a
favorite brown armchair. He had heard the June 23
tapes before—on May 6 and 7, when he considered,
then rejected, the compromise with Jaworski. Now he
listened to them again, then called Buzhardt in and
asked the gloomy lawyer to go through them again too
and reconsider his judgment. Buzhardt called St. Clair
and suggested that he come into his office and listen too.
The two lawyers—so often antagonists but now equally swept along by the rush of events—clamped earphones on their heads and sat down to listen to the
evidence their client had been withholding.

For Buzhardt, this second hearing merely confirmed
his initial impression, and he so reported to Nixon
late that afternoon (apparently infuriating the President, for he refused to speak with Buzhardt again that
week). For St. Clair—who had not heard the tapes
before—their effect now was cataclysmic. The week
before, he had partly discounted Buzhardt's warnings
about the tapes; only when he heard them for himself
did he recognize how devastating they were to the
President's case. Aides who saw him a few minutes
later say he looked "demolished, wiped out."

On Wednesday morning St. Clair gave Haig transcripts of the June 23 tapes, and at long last the President's chief of staff realized the gravity of the situation.
His first instinct was to consult his old mentor, the
man for whom he had initially worked at the White
House and to whom he still felt very close: Henry
Kissinger. Quickly ordering his limousine, he sped to
the State Department and told Kissinger of the latest
developments. The secretary of state had become increasingly irritated with Nixon's inability to focus on
foreign affairs, the area which had once absorbed his
most productive energies. Now, with a war raging in
Cyprus, a cabinet crisis in Italy, skirmishes along the
Indian-Pakistani border, and new fighting in South
Vietnam, the President did not even have time to read
the daily cable traffic. Moreover, in most world capitals, the President's credibility had been virtually
demolished by the Judiciary Committee's actions on
impeachment. Kissinger had already concluded that

Nixon should probably resign, and Haig's news merely reinforced this conclusion. But he warned his former assistant that the transition should be as smooth and dignified as possible—Henry Kissinger always insisted on dignity—so as to reassure America's allies and give its enemies no encouragement.

By now Haig was acting largely on his own, convinced that Nixon was not seeing his own situation clearly. On Thursday the chief of staff decided it was time to tip off Gerald Ford. For months, the Vice President had been trying to balance his conflicting obligations—to the President and to the truth. At the start his confidence in Nixon had seemed boundless. "I know that the President was not involved," he declared in January. But then his friends urged him to stop campaigning for the President, or at least to hedge his support, lest it destroy his effectiveness if and when he became President himself. He began to qualify his statements, saying that "the preponderance of the evidence" showed Nixon was innocent. But as the Judiciary Committee began voting articles of impeachment, Ford once more proclaimed his total faith in Nixon. On July 24 he told a crowd in Muncie, Indiana, "I can say from the bottom of my heart that the President of the United States is innocent."

That kind of thing, Haig recognized, could indeed destroy a future President's credibility. So at his meeting with Ford on Thursday morning in the Vice President's EOB office, he warned that such sweeping declarations could be dangerous, particularly in light of new evidence on the tapes to be turned over to Judge Sirica the following Monday. Haig said the new evidence, when disclosed to the House, would almost certainly tip the balance there in favor of impeachment; but he did not tell the Vice President what that evidence was.

During the next few hours Haig studied the June 23 transcripts more carefully and decided that he should be more forthright with Ford. At noon he telephoned to request another meeting with the Vice President. When they met again at three-thirty, Haig summarized the new revelations for Ford and said they would be "devastating, even catastrophic, insofar as President Nixon was concerned." He asked Ford whether he was ready to take over the Presidency "within a very short time," and whether he had any recommendation to make to Nixon, any suggestions on how to accomplish an orderly transfer of power. Ford was "shocked and stunned," as much by the realization that he was about to become President as by the new evidence itself.

Haig said opinion within the White House staff was sharply divided. Some favored "riding it out," letting impeachment take its course through the House, but making a last-ditch fight against conviction in the Senate. Others believed resignation was inevitable, although views differed on when and how it should take place. Among the options then being considered by the staff, Haig said, were:

• Nixon could simply delay resignation until further along in the impeachment process, hoping that something would crop up to save him.

• Under provisions of the Twenty-fifth Amendment, he could step aside temporarily and let Ford serve as President until the Senate reached a verdict.

• He could try to persuade the House to settle for a vote of censure.

• He could pardon himself before resigning.

• He could pardon various Watergate defendants, then pardon himself, and then resign.

• He could be pardoned by his successor after resignation.

Evidently, Haig was preoccupied with the question of pardon. In this, he presumably reflected Nixon's own concern during his last days in office that he avoid criminal prosecution once he was no longer President. Haig may also have seen a promise of pardon as his best lever for persuading the President to resign. In any case, it formed a major part of his conversation with Ford that day. The Vice President caught on quickly and asked just what a President's pardon power was. Haig said one White House lawyer had informed him that a President could grant a pardon even before a criminal action had been brought against an individual.

Ford has denied that he made any "deal" with the President to pardon him after he resigned.* But even if there was no explicit agreement, there may well have been an implicit understanding between Ford and Nixon, relayed through Haig. The mere mention of one option—that Nixon pardon himself and other Watergate defendants before resigning—may have served as a form of political blackmail on the Vice President. Ford could hardly fail to recognize the disastrous repercussions such a step would have on the Republican party and on his own Presidency. Haig and Ford could presumably agree that *anything* would be better than that; they would not have to spell out the alternatives.

Haig may also have been bringing pressure on the Vice President when he stressed the "urgency" of the situation. According to Ford, the two men discussed the terrible impact of a prolonged Senate trial, "the handling of possible international crises, the economic situation at home, and the marked slowdown in the decision-making process within the federal government." If the nation's economy—and even world peace —were at stake, could a mere pardon be allowed to stand in the way of resolving the crisis?

Ford says he refused to make any recommendation to Nixon, indicating that he needed "time to think," to talk with his wife, and also to consult with St. Clair. At eight the next morning St. Clair came to Ford's office for a discussion of the legal situation. The President's lawyer said he agreed with Haig that the new evidence was so damaging that impeachment in the House was a certainty and conviction in the Senate highly probable. They discussed the various options which Haig had mentioned the day before, but St. Clair said he was not the White House lawyer who had given advice on the Presidential pardon power.

After considering the problem further, Ford con-

---

*He ultimately did pardon Nixon on September 8, 1974.

cluded that he could make no recommendation on Nixon's course of action or on problems of transition (although informal planning for the transition had been under way for some months under the direction of his close friend Philip W. Buchen). "I had consistently and firmly held the view previously that in no way whatsoever could I recommend either publicly or privately any step by the President that might cause a change in my status as Vice President." So on Friday he called Haig to say, "I wanted him to understand that I had no intention of recommending what President Nixon should do about resigning or not resigning, and that nothing we had talked about the previous afternoon should be given any consideration in whatever decision the President might make." Since Ford insists he made no recommendation or commitment the afternoon before, it is unclear what he was talking about in this telephone conversation.

During the next few days, while touring Mississippi and Louisiana, Ford gave no hint that he knew of the new evidence against the President. Fearing that any change in his position would imply that he now wanted to see Nixon resign, he continued to proclaim his full faith in the President's innocence.

Late on Thursday afternoon, Haig called a meeting of White House political and public-relations staffers, ostensibly to plan strategy for the coming impeachment fight. He ordered the formation of "defense teams" to lead the battle against each article of impeachment: Ray Price headed one; Charles Lichtenstein, an assistant to Counselor Dean Burch, headed the second; Pat Buchanan and David Gergen, another speechwriter, led the third.

But the operation was largely internal public relations—designed to keep most of the staff from knowing what was really going on in the inner circles. Indeed, only a few minutes after the meeting broke up, Haig summoned Ray Price back into his office. "Now, Ray," Haig said, "it's time you knew what's been happening." Whereupon, he told the President's most trusted speechwriter the substance of the June 23 conversations. Then he ordered him to begin writing a resignation speech, working toward a deadline of Monday, August 5, when Haig indicated the President would probably resign.

On Friday morning, word reached the White House that Judge Sirica had sentenced John Dean to one to four years in prison. It was the third legal action involving a former member of the White House staff within five days. On Monday John Connally had been indicted for perjury, obstruction of justice, and accepting bribes in the milk-pricing case. On Wednesday John Ehrlichman was sentenced to twenty months to five years in prison for his role in the burglary of Dr. Fielding's office. The three decisions resounded like the raps of a judge's gavel on the White House door, reminding all within that justice was very near at hand.

Deciding the time had come for action, Haig made a bold move—worthy of Richard Nixon himself, who had once relished such "big plays." Like a fullback who often carries the ball directly at the other team's strength, so Haig decided to take his new evidence to the one man who would be hardest to persuade of the President's guilt. After all, Charles Wiggins had put his own prestige on the line for days in front of a vast national television audience, proclaiming the President's innocence against all comers. If Wiggins could be persuaded, who could resist? At two, St. Clair invited Wiggins to the White House. A half-hour later the congressman was ushered into Haig's office—where he had never been before—and found Haig and St. Clair waiting for him.

For a few minutes the three men chatted lightly. Haig complimented the silver-haired Californian on his skilled and vigorous defense of the President. Then, getting straight to the point, Haig said that within the past few days they had come across some new evidence which bore directly on the President's role in Watergate. He slid several typed pages of transcript across the coffee table, and Wiggins began to read. He read them once. He read them again. He felt betrayed. "The guys who stuck by the President were really led down the garden path, weren't we?" he said bitterly. He meant himself and the other loyal Republicans on the

Judiciary Committee. But the remark applied as well to Haig and St. Clair, and they nodded morosely.

Then Wiggins said the President had only two alternatives: to plead the Fifth Amendment or to surrender the tapes immediately to the Judiciary Committee. St. Clair assured him that the tapes would be delivered to the committee. Wiggins read the transcript a third time and said that if the President didn't release them, he would. Haig and St. Clair nodded, but urged him to do nothing until Monday, and Wiggins agreed. Wiggins wondered what the President had up his sleeve now. "Does he have another 'Checkers speech' on him?" he asked bitterly.

Then, very reluctantly, he said it would be "wholly appropriate to consider the resignation of the President." The President's men did not argue. St. Clair said only that it would be "inappropriate" for the President's lawyer to tell him to resign. Haig said it would be "very difficult for a staff member to go to his boss and suggest something of that magnitude." It was clear to Wiggins that they had set out through more circuitous means to force their boss to resign.

Numb with rage, Wiggins returned to his office. His desk was piled with briefs and arguments for the President which the congressman now began balling up one by one and tossing into the wastebasket. He had intended to use some of these papers in a series of pep talks with 180-odd congressmen, but now he told his secretary to call all of them back and cancel the sessions.

Meanwhile, Haig was reaching other Nixon loyalists. He had already warned Senator James Eastland of Mississippi, chairman of the Senate Judiciary Committee. Now he telephoned Senator Robert P. Griffin of Michigan, the minority whip in the Senate and one of Vice President Ford's closest friends. Haig summarized the tapes for Griffin and told him of Wiggins' reaction. The senator pondered the new developments during a late flight to his home in Traverse City. After a largely sleepless night, he called his Washington office on Saturday and dictated a letter for immediate delivery to the White House. Written as if Griffin knew nothing of the June 23 tape, the letter told the President that he had barely enough votes to survive in the Senate. And, he warned, the Senate would have to subpoena his tapes for the trial. "If you should defy such a subpoena," Griffin wrote, "I shall regard that as an impeachable offense and shall vote accordingly." The warning could not have failed to rock the President—particularly since he had no reason to suspect that Griffin knew what was on those tapes.

Haig also began telephoning cabinet members. Secretary of Health, Education, and Welfare Casper W. Weinberger got a call which went something like this:

HAIG: Now there is this further thing. There is this tape. The President did have knowledge of this from the beginning. After it had happened.

WEINBERGER: That's the absolute end, Al. There is no possibility of avoiding impeachment with that.

HAIG: That's right.

WEINBERGER: What's being done?

HAIG: Well, I think we're going to be able to persuade the President that that is the case and that he would serve the country better if he would step aside.

Late on Friday evening, Haig showed the transcripts to Ray Price and Pat Buchanan. Both men, savvy veterans of White House infighting, quickly recognized that the game was up. The night before, in ordering Price to begin work on a resignation speech, Haig had told him the substance of the transcripts. "At that time," Price recalls, "I thought Al might be overreacting. But when I saw the actual conversations on Friday evening I thought they were even worse than he'd told me. I knew the case was lost. I thought the President ought to resign as quickly as possible and I asked Al to relay that conclusion to him. It would be nice to claim great moral outrage, but I didn't feel it. In fact, I felt the President had done me a favor in not telling me about this. Not—as some people have suggested —because it was easier for me to write his speeches for him, but because I think that if the President had told me what was really going on, I might have joined the cover-up and gone to jail. Like others at the White House, I felt that Nixon was engaged in a very delicate process designed to establish a new structure of world peace. I thought it was very important that he prevail. And I might well have concluded that obstruction of justice was a lot less serious than nuclear war."

Price's reaction was very different from that of a middle-level White House official who saw the transcripts about the same time and told John Osborne of *The New Republic,* "I was sick. I was shocked. I told myself I couldn't believe it although I had to believe it. He had *lied* to me, to all of us. I think my first thought, before that sank in, was of those Republicans on the Judiciary Committee—Wiggins, Sandman, those men who had risked their careers to defend him. He had lied to them! You won't believe it, I guess, but at some point that afternoon, when I first read the transcript of those tapes, I said to myself that this has to be some sort of ghastly joke. I actually laughed aloud. I laughed and laughed."

The President was still in the Lincoln Sitting Room, spinning his tapes. At about seven, after the rest of the family had dined without him, he summoned them into the room: Pat, Julie, Tricia, David Eisenhower, and Bebe Rebozo (son-in-law Edward Cox was flying down from New York and arrived while the meeting was still going on). Seated in the brown chair, the President launched into a disjointed monologue which lasted nearly two hours. Gathered in a semicircle around him, the family members exchanged troubled glances as Nixon darted from subject to subject, sometimes lucid and logical, at other times veering into wild conjectures and bursts of anger at "the people who won't rest until they get me."

His daughters and their husbands wanted to see the troublesome transcripts, so the President told Haig to send them over. Nixon's valet, Manolo Sanchez, brought them in and the two young couples went into the West Wing Living Room to read them. The two husbands—one a lawyer, the other a law student—immediately recognized that the President was guilty of obstructing justice. David Eisenhower, then in his second year at George Washington Law School, recalls, "My day-to-day exposure was with law students. I was far more pessimistic than the people involved in the everyday political atmosphere." But his wife—just as political and combative as her father—wasn't ready to give up. At midnight she called Pat Buchanan at home where he was soaking his bruised feelings in a pitcher of martinis. She had to see him the next morning.

Assisted by her sister, Julie was seeking someone on the White House staff to lead the last-ditch battle for survival. By then, their choice was severely limited. One aide whom Julie consulted gave her a profoundly ambiguous message for the President, a line from Dryden: "I will lay me down for to bleed a while/ Then I'll rise and fight with you again." The band of true loyalists had dwindled down to a precious few: Rose Mary Woods, of course; Ken Clawson; Bruce Herschensohn, one of Clawson's staffers. At times, Ron Ziegler seemed to side with him, but his heart wasn't in it. Buchanan seemed a likely prospect: tough, loyal, deeply conservative, a gut fighter from way back. But the June 23 transcripts had been too much even for his well-callused sensibilities. When he met with the President's daughters in the White House solarium on Saturday morning, he told them quietly but firmly that their cause was hopeless: if their father didn't resign, he would be impeached and convicted. Why put the nation through the trauma of a Senate trial when the result would be the same? But Julie and Tricia persisted. So Buchanan bought time, suggesting that they all wait for the public reaction to the new evidence.

By Saturday noon the President had evolved a similar strategy: to release the transcripts of the June 23 tapes on Monday and go on television to appeal for public support as he had so often before (the Checkers speech Wiggins had anticipated). After transmitting this decision to Ziegler, Nixon helicoptered to Camp David with his family and Rebozo. The key staff members were to follow on Sunday to help draft the television speech.

That afternoon Haig, St. Clair, and Price met at the

White House. None of them liked the President's decision. All thought the fighting television speech was a terrible mistake. But they recognized that they would never change Nixon's mind by arguing with him. Nobody could—perhaps nobody should—persuade the President to resign. Events had to persuade him.

At one-thirty on Sunday, a helicopter landed at Camp David carrying five men: Haig, St. Clair, Ziegler, Price, and Buchanan. They set up shop in Laurel Lodge, the camp's main dining room, while Haig walked over to Aspen Lodge, where the President sat alone by the cold fireplace. When he returned, Haig said the President had changed his strategy again. There would be no television speech, just a brisk statement to accompany the release of the transcripts. Price went off to Hawthorne Lodge to draft the statement while the others conferred in Laurel. Later, Haig took the draft over to Nixon, who penciled in changes, and Price revised it accordingly. St. Clair and Haig insisted that the statement make unequivocally clear that they had known nothing about the June 23 conversations. By seven, the statement was largely complete and the Presidential party "choppered" back to Washington.

Late on Sunday Haig telephoned John Rhodes, the House minority leader, who had scheduled a news conference the next morning to announce his position on impeachment. Haig urged him "very strongly" to postpone the news conference. When Rhodes asked why, the President's chief of staff said only, "You will know all you need to know tomorrow." Rhodes developed a quick but crippling case of laryngitis.

But elsewhere in Washington that Monday, others —utterly unaware of the new developments inside the White House—were hard at work preparing for the impeachment vote in the House and the subsequent trial in the Senate. That very morning, House members began listening to the nineteen tapes already available to them in four heavily guarded rooms in the Cannon and Rayburn buildings. Until then, the tapes had been heard only by members of the Judiciary Committee, but now, with transcripts in front of them and earphones on their heads, congressmen crowded around the long tables. "It just confirms what I've been hearing from other sources all along," Representative Edward I. Koch, a New York Democrat, said afterward. "There are a lot of low-class people in that White House."

Other congressmen were drafting the rules under which the House would carry out its second impeachment debate in history. Leaders of both parties had tentatively agreed that the debate would begin on August 19 under a "closed rule" that would permit no amendments. After some fifty-five hours of general debate and thirty-two hours on motions from the floor, the articles of impeachment were expected to come to a vote before Labor Day. The leadership had also agreed to permit "gavel-to-gavel" television coverage.

For months, a White House "defense group"—a successor to Chuck Colson's "attack group"—had been meeting at nine every morning to plan the President's response to whatever boils and locusts were then afflicting him. Headed by Dean Burch—and including Ken Clawson, Bill Timmons, and Pat Buchanan—it directed all congressional lobbying, press, and public-relations efforts. Its efforts notwithstanding, the White House had done surprisingly little lobbying during the Judiciary Committee's deliberations. A few of the crucial "swing" men were invited out for cruises on the *Sequoia,* but had declined to go. Others got telephone calls or letters from major Republican backers in their districts—which may have been inspired by Nixon's men. But as the battle moved to the floor, the "defense group" began mobilizing for all-out war. Recognizing that they faced an "uphill struggle" in the House, they settled on the only strategy left to them: somehow to hold down the margin for impeachment so they could eke out a bare "one-third plus one" vote in the Senate. Someone at the White House came up with a bizarre conception: a direct telephone line from the White House to the minority staff room of the House Judiciary Committee so that St. Clair, watching the debate on television in his office, could deliver orders directly to the President's defenders on the front line.

The official White House effort was augmented by at

least three other groups of down-the-line loyalists. The first—Americans for the Presidency—was a quasi-official outfit which had the President's full blessing and stayed in close touch with him. Indeed, Nixon had chosen its leader—his old friend Donald Kendall, board chairman of PepsiCo. In March Kendall had begun assembling an impressive board of directors, filled with the President's cronies: former Deputy Secretary of Defense David Packard; former Secretary of Housing and Urban Development George Romney; Mrs. Mamie Eisenhower; the Reverend Norman Vincent Peale; and Bob Hope. Later in the spring these directors and others lent their names to full-page newspaper ads in more than a hundred and fifty newspapers around the country urging support for Nixon.

The second line of defense was manned by an Orthodox rabbi from Taunton, Massachusetts, named Baruch M. Korff. Although Nixon didn't meet the rabbi until 1973, he welcomed the little old man with the heavy Ukrainian accent, granted him exclusive interviews, and permitted him to serve as an unofficial ambassador to the "little people" who still had faith in the President. Korff responded with the zeal of the Maccabees, denouncing the Judiciary Committee as an "impeachment gang," other opponents as a "lynch mob," and the press as "assassins." His National Citizens Committee for Fairness to the Presidency—a national umbrella group for two hundred and thirty local chapters—ran a newsletter, placed ads, lobbied in the halls of Congress, and one night in late July marched by candlelight to the Lincoln Memorial.

But Nixon's most visible supporters in Washington that month were the "Moonies"—members of the Reverend Sun Myung Moon's Unification Church of America. For three days during the Judiciary Committee's debates, three hundred and fifty crew-cut, well-scrubbed acolytes held a public fast and prayer ceremony on the steps of the Capitol, each with a sign around his neck reading "I am praying for [a member of Congress]." They heard speeches from several of the President's most fervent congressional supporters and one day a messenger arrived with a statement from

Nixon himself: "The world has always known the shrill voices of anger and frustration, but what has saved mankind even in the darkest hours of our civilization has always been the voices that are raised in prayer and a spirit of love for one another." When the fast ended, the Moonies filled Washington restaurants, stuffing down fried eggs and apple pie. And now on Monday, August 5, they were back in the House corridors lobbying for love, forgiveness, and Richard Nixon.

As a Wesleyan undergraduate, Edward G. "Pete" Biester, Jr., majored in classics. Now, as a Republican congressman from Pennsylvania, he often perceived somber parallels between events in Washington and the timeless themes of Greek mythology. In early summer, as the pressures for impeachment gathered force, Biester had dark intimations of impending tragedy. "What is the traditional role of kings?" he asked a visitor to his office one June afternoon. "To rule?" the visitor ventured. "No," Biester said. "To die, so as to bring about catharsis, a purging of fear and pity. And that's what I'm afraid we could be getting into here. We've already destroyed our last two Presidents: we killed Jack Kennedy, we hounded Lyndon Johnson out of office. Now we're on the verge of impeaching Nixon. Impeachment—almost as much as assassination—is a twentieth-century expression of that old, atavistic urge to kill the king and thereby to bring about a reunification and rebirth of the people. God knows we need some rededication to our founding principles, but killing the king is a terribly fragile basis on which to achieve it. As Aeschylus warned us, the killing of one king sets off a cycle of vengeance and retribution that is very hard to stop and that ultimately leads to madness." Biester took a book down from his shelf and traced the bloody tale of the House of Atreus: the kidnaping of Helen, the sacrifice of Iphigenia, the ax murder of Agamemnon, the slaying of Clytemnestra, then of Aegisthus, and finally the descent into madness of Orestes and Electra. Breathless from his recitation of murders, Biester paused for a moment, then plunged on: "What marks the line between the whole classical period and the Christian era is the sacrifice of Christ, the last king figure to be killed. Through his crucifixion, Christ signals to mankind: 'I am the final sacrifice. You don't have to do this any more. Or at least you can do it in ritual form, through the mass. You don't have to actually kill any more kings.' And out of that flowed a different ethos—of forgiveness instead of vengeance, of tolerance rather than the old, brittle, supermoralism. Well, frankly, I'm worried that this great urge to impeach Nixon is a reversion to the old ethic. By doing that we could set off a cycle of vengeance which could be with us for years. The next round would be the Republicans saying 'We'll get the people who got him'; then the people who got them will be gotten in turn. No President would be safe from the vengeance of the allies of the last fallen President. That way lies the destruction of our system as we know it, a politics of blood, violence, and God knows what else." Late in June the visitor returned to Biester's office, where, for the first time, he noticed the two pictures above his couch—of Abraham Lincoln and Cotton Mather. "I keep them there to remind me of the two great threads in American thought," he said. "Self-righteous, Platonist puritanism as symbolized by Mather, and tolerant, forgiving humility as exemplified by Lincoln. Certainly there has to be a balance struck between the two, but for our society I tend to think the Lincolnian is the more useful. I want to make very sure that, in this impeachment process, Congress doesn't act like a set of Cotton Mathers, engaging in witchhunts, setting extraordinarily high standards for other people, though not always for themselves." In early July Biester began reading Antonia Fraser's biography of Oliver Cromwell. "Cromwell was more or less a British Mather. Like most revolutionaries, he had supreme confidence in his own convictions and wasn't willing to check them against the law. I want to make sure I don't start behaving like either a Cromwell or a Mather in all this." In mid-July, over dinner at a downtown steakhouse, the congressman continued his ruminations: "You know, I've been thinking, we may kill the king and not even get the catharsis we all seem to be seeking. Remember, Aristotle said that to produce catharsis in the audience, a tragedy had to have a certain unity and rhythm. All Greek tragedies followed Aristotle's formula, more or less—but this great impeachment drama hasn't. It's dragged on for six months already, and if you want to count the earlier dramas in the cycle—the Saturday Night Massacre and Watergate itself—it's been going on almost two years. It has lost all unity or rhythm. It's the longest third act in history. And we may end up with the audience bored beyond all patience, walking out of the theater before the play is over, before the king is killed. What purpose would it all have served then?" But by the start of August Biester had resolved his doubts. "I went home to Bucks County last weekend and talked to all sorts of people," he reported. "I went to a Republican picnic at a country club. I went to a labor union picnic on a baseball diamond. I spoke with neighbors and friends. Most of them were bored by the whole impeachment thing. They weren't slavering for Nixon's blood. They just wanted to get him out of there, get the whole thing over with so they could get back to the important things in their lives. Well, that night I was driving back to Washington and suddenly it hit me. That boredom which had worried me so much a few weeks ago was the best thing that could have happened. It meant we weren't getting a big emotional catharsis out of this. We weren't really even killing a king. We were affirming that we will permit no king to rule here. Remember—although those plays were about kings—they were presented to democratic audiences in Athens. To such audiences, the tragedies said: one-man rule is necessarily rich with error and produces tragic consequences. The kings make those tragic errors because they believe they are above the law. Hubris and all that. In America, as in Athens, we may elevate a person to leadership, but he does not thereby become a majestic or kinglike figure. He is still subject to all the laws of society. And when he violates those laws, he has to go."

At eight-thirty on Monday morning Charles Wiggins remembered that John Rhodes was supposed to announce his position on impeachment that day. He telephoned him at home to warn that he had seen "devastating" new evidence against Nixon. At last Rhodes understood the cryptic message he had received from Haig the day before. He kept his silence.

But by then Bob Griffin could remain silent no longer. Flying home from Michigan the night before, he had scribbled a statement on a pad of yellow paper. That morning, at a meeting of the Senate Rules Committee, he kept pulling the papers from his pocket. On his way out of the meeting, he encountered some reporters and, on an impulse, read them the statement calling on the President to resign "in both the national interest and his own interest." He still didn't say anything about the transcripts.

Haig and St. Clair put through a call to Leon Jaworski at his home in Houston. They said they had just learned that the June 23 tape contained incriminating evidence which they planned to turn over to Sirica and make public. "If I were you I wouldn't let any grass grow under my feet," Jaworski warned.

On his way to work, Bill Timmons heard on the car radio that most of his colleagues had been at Camp David the day before. When he reached the White House he asked Haig what was going on. Haig told him. Timmons went into Burch's office for the nine-o'clock "defense group" meeting and a few minutes later Buchanan brought in transcripts of the June 23 tape. For the first time, Timmons, Clawson, and Burch read them. Burch broke out a bottle of scotch and everyone had a belt. Then they divided up the labor for what was to be one of the busiest days any of them had ever spent.

Burch was assigned to go with Fred Buzhardt to John Rhodes's house to brief the minority leader. They called George Bush, chairman of the Republican National Committee, and asked him to meet them there. Over lunch, the two men from the White House showed the transcripts to the GOP stalwarts.

At 3:15 p.m. another two-man team—St. Clair and Timmons—went to the office of Leslie Arends, the House minority whip, who had assembled eight of the ten Republican loyalists on the House Judiciary Committee (Trent Lott and Wiley Mayne were unable to attend). "Gentlemen," St. Clair said, "I'm sorry to say it, but I'm not the bearer of good tidings." When he told them what was on the tape, they felt to a man betrayed. "We were just dumbfounded," says Delbert Latta. "We'd put our trust in the President. We felt he was telling us the truth. I think every American has that right—to put his trust in the President. It was a terrible let-down feeling." St. Clair told the congressmen he had considered resigning, but Dave Dennis assured him that nobody blamed him because "we know you've been led down the primrose path too." Then Wiggins revealed that he had seen the evidence on Friday, that it was just as "devastating" as St. Clair said it was, and that he was now ready to vote for Article I on the Watergate cover-up. One by one, the others agreed. They briefly considered issuing a joint statement, but then decided this was a decision so personal and painful that every man had to explain it for himself.

As the congressmen rushed off to frame their *volte-face,* St. Clair and Timmons walked across to the Senate side of the Capitol where a group of Republican leaders were gathered in Hugh Scott's office: among them, Wallace Bennett (Bob Bennett's father); Norris Cotton; Bob Griffin; John Tower of Texas. Although less publicly committed to the President than the House Judiciary Committee members, the senators were no less stunned. "It's the worst thing we've had," said one. (Later that afternoon the transcripts and a copy of the President's statement were handed to Barry Goldwater in the Senate cloakroom. When he read them, the President's last best hope for significant support in the Senate knew the game was up.)

Meanwhile, Haig had summoned some hundred and fifty staffers to the fourth-floor auditorium in the EOB. Mounting the platform, he told them what was about to happen, and read the President's statement, which

Price had just finished. Then he asked them for their support in the days to come—if not for the President, then for the country. "You may feel depressed or outraged by this," he said, "but we must all keep going for the good of the nation." As he left the room, the secretaries, staff assistants, and senior aides—many of them in tears—gave him a standing ovation.

Just after four o'clock aides in the White House press room handed out copies of the June 23 transcripts and the President's two-page statement to a clamoring mob of reporters. Nixon's comments were a rather strange *mea culpa,* confessing improprieties with no real sense of remorse. He seemed to be saying: Technically I may be guilty, but I didn't really do anything wrong. He admitted that the June 23 tapes were "at variance with certain of my previous statements," that he had known this at least since early May when he had listened to the tapes, and that he had not informed either his counsel or members of the Judiciary Committee. "At the time," he said, "I did not realize the extent of the implications which these conversations might now appear to have. As a result, those arguing my case, as well as those passing judgment on the case, did so with information that was incomplete and in some respects erroneous. This was a serious act of omission for which I take full responsibility and which I deeply regret." The President conceded that impeachment in the House was "virtually a foregone conclusion" and that the new evidence would further damage his case. But he urged that in the Senate trial "the evidence be looked at in its entirety and the events be looked at in perspective. Whatever mistakes I made in the handling of Watergate, the basic truth remains that when all the facts were brought to my attention, I insisted on a full investigation and prosecution of those guilty. I am firmly convinced that the record, in its entirety, does not justify the extreme step of impeachment and removal of a President. I trust that as the constitutional process goes forward, this perspective will prevail."

A few weeks before, Ken Clawson had told an interviewer, "There aren't any more bombshells and there won't be any more bombshells." He was right.

This wasn't a bombshell. It was a nuclear explosion that ripped across the Washington landscape, destroying the last vestiges of support for the President. Most loyalists left standing by earlier blasts were now brought down.

One of the first to rush to the waiting microphones was Wiggins, who had the advantage of prior knowledge. While the transcripts were being released across town, he stood before the cameras with eyes brimming and voice cracking to say that the facts had now changed. "With great reluctance and deep personal sorrow I am prepared to conclude that the magnificent career of public service of Richard Nixon must be terminated." Wiley Mayne and Joseph Maraziti also announced that they were ready to vote for impeachment. Most of the other Republicans on the committee said they were reassessing their positions. The Republican leadership caved in. Representative John B. Anderson, chairman of the House Republican Conference, said, "This goes to the very heart of the first article. The President's own words seem to convict him." Barber Conable, Jr., chairman of the House Republican Policy Committee, announced that he was ready to vote for impeachment, adding, "I don't approve of leaders who mislead." John Rhodes, in a statement from his home, said, "The fact that the President's veracity is put in question by this disclosure is a tragedy." Representative Earl F. Langrebe of Indiana, one of the last Republicans to stick with Nixon, seemed stunned: "It's like a mutiny on a ship. A sort of madness has set in."

Elsewhere, the reaction was much the same. On the Senate side, Senator Jesse A. Helms, a deeply conservative Republican from North Carolina, said "Honesty is the best policy. Some people learn it early, some people learn it late." And John Tower quoted the Greek tragedies: "And now a wave of melancholy tranquillity settles over Thebes." In Tuscaloosa, Alabama, Mayor C. Snow Hinton—who only a week before had called the Judiciary Committee hearings "disgusting"—now said the President "would do the nation a service by resigning." In California, Jim Dean, executive editor of the *Orange County Register,* an organ of the Nixonian heartland, said, "The illusion has been dissipated. Maybe lawyers can continue to haggle about his guilt or innocence, but, for the layman, yesterday's revelations should settle it." The columnist George Will wrote, "If the current impeachment process were a boxing match, the referee would stop the fight."

Nixon wasn't acting like a boxer on the ropes. That evening he went off for a dinner cruise on the *Sequoia* with Pat, the Eisenhowers, the Coxes, and Rose Mary Woods (Bebe Rebozo had returned to Key Biscayne). After dinner they sat in a big semicircle on the upper deck as the yacht steamed toward Mount Vernon. In mid-trip, Haig telephoned to report the defections on the Judiciary Committee. The President tried hard to maintain an air of gaiety, but as the boat headed back toward Washington he fell silent.

At eleven Tuesday morning, the cabinet convened at the White House. The aides who normally crowded the seats along the wall were excluded this time: only the cabinet secretaries, Haig, and Bush sat there. The President spun out a forty-minute monologue, recounting his diplomatic triumphs in Moscow and Peking, his ending of the Vietnam war, his efforts to bring peace to the Middle East. It was these foreign-policy achievements, he explained, that had led to his problems on the domestic front. "One thing I have learned is never to allow anybody else to run your campaign," he joked feebly. Turning to his current troubles, he said he had considered resigning but had decided against it. "The Constitution makes no provision for resignation," he said. "I believe in following the Constitution."

Gerald Ford, seated across the big oval table from Nixon, broke in to say that he did not believe the public interest would be served by his making any further statements on behalf of the President.

"I understand," Nixon said. Then—as though that

took care of that—he launched into a discussion of the "number-one problem in the world today"—inflation. He said he was determined to go forward with the economic "summit meeting," proposed by Senate Majority Leader Mike Mansfield.

"Mr. President," implored Attorney General Saxbe, "can't we just wait a week or two to see what happens?" George Bush supported Saxbe's plea.

Glaring angrily at them, Nixon snapped, "No, this is too important to wait."

One participant told Lou Cannon of *The Washington Post,* "It was a most curious meeting. Nixon assembled the cabinet not to ask for advice but to announce a decision that he would not resign. He had a sort of eerie calm about him. The mood in the room was one of considerable disbelief. Because if you had any realism about what was happening, you knew the place was about to fall down, and he was sitting there calmly and serenely and vowing to stay on. You began to wonder if he knew something you didn't know—if he had some secret weapon that he hadn't disclosed yet."

After the meeting, Secretary of State Kissinger stayed behind for a chat with the President in the Oval Office. By all accounts, Kissinger at last weighed in with his own quiet, cautious argument for resignation. Kissinger reminded Nixon of all they had done together, but stressed that foreign negotiations had to be carried on from a position of strength at home. A President couldn't work for peace if his domestic base had been destroyed. Moreover—as demonstrated by the public skepticism toward the October 1973 alert —the country might no longer trust the President if the time came when military force had to be used. (Over at the Pentagon, this problem had already occurred to Defense Secretary Schlesinger. Determined to stay in Washington until the Presidential crisis had been resolved, he gave orders that the armed forces were to accept no commands from the White House without his countersignature. This would protect not only against the President's starting a war somewhere to distract attention from the events at home but against the use of any military unit in the domestic power struggle.)

When Kissinger left, Bill Timmons came in with more disheartening news about the erosion of support on the Hill: the President could count on no more than twenty votes in the Senate. Nixon asked him to check out five specific senators.

At noon the Senate Republican Policy Committee, joined by some other Republican senators, met for lunch. The senators were in a rebellious mood. "There are only so many lies you can take and now there has been one too many," Barry Goldwater growled. "Nixon should get his ass out of the White House—today!" During the meeting, Goldwater was called to the telephone to take a call from Haig. How many senators would stand by the President? Twelve to fifteen, Goldwater said (five to eight less than Timmons had estimated minutes before).

Ford arrived to brief the senators on the cabinet meeting, and what he told them only made them angrier. "Is that *all* the President had to say?" asked Maryland Senator J. Glenn Beall, Jr. And Goldwater jumped to his feet: "I'm not yelling at you, Mr. Vice President. But I'm just getting something off my chest. The President should resign!" Things got so hot that the Vice President excused himself. The senators began discussing how they could get their message through to Nixon.

That discussion continued at a three-thirty meeting in Scott's office attended by the senior Republican senators: Scott, Cotton, Tower, Brock, Bennett, Griffin, Goldwater, and Javits. It was determined that Goldwater should be the group's emissary to the President. During the next twenty-four hours, a flurry of telephone calls passed between Scott and Goldwater on the Hill and Haig, Timmons, and Burch at the White House to arrange such a meeting.

Meanwhile, the President was busy with other matters. At three-thirty, he received Baruch Korff and told him he was considering resigning. Bitterly, Nixon complained to the sympathetic rabbi about his enemies: "I know these people. When they detect weakness somewhere they would not hesitate to harden their po-

sition. If they want to put me behind bars, let them."
The usually voluble Korff left the White House by a
side door to avoid reporters. But when one persistent
newsman followed him, he said, "Yes, the President
has weaknesses. He's a human being. So he waited
three months before disclosing the information. So
what? He's still the greatest President of this century."

By late afternoon the demands for resignation had
swelled to a deafening chorus. From California came
the voice of Governor Ronald Reagan. All ten Republican loyalists on the Judiciary Committee had chimed
in. (But when one of them asked Rodino whether he
would reopen the voting in the committee, the chairman snapped—in an echo of the Baltimore plea-bargaining—"The train has left the station.") Only a
handful of zealots stuck by the President: Senators
Bennett, Cotton, William Scott of Virginia, Carl Curtis
of Nebraska ("This country will become a banana republic if we start forcing Presidents out of office"),
Representative Otto E. Passman, a Louisiana Democrat
("To err is human, to forgive divine") and Earl
Langrebe ("I'm sticking by my President even if he
and I have to be taken out of this building and shot").

Haig and Timmons outlined the deteriorating situation to the President. "They told him it was all over,"
one aide recalls. A few minutes later Haig urged Price
to get working on that resignation speech—this time
in earnest.

Wednesday was National Student Government Day,
and one of the President's first acts that morning was
to issue a proclamation: "One of the foundation blocks
in the American democracy is the civic responsibility
which every American accepts as part of his obligation." He also nominated five members to the Board
of the Corporation for Public Broadcasting, a body
which his aides had often criticized in the past.

Haig put through a telephone call to Ford—catching him in his car on the way to a breakfast meeting of
the Chowder and Marching Club—and asked him to
come to the White House as quickly as possible.
Couldn't it wait, Ford asked with a touch of irritation.
No, it couldn't. The Vice President turned around and

drove to the executive mansion, where Haig told him that if all went according to schedule he would be President of the United States by Friday.

In midmorning George Bush delivered a letter to Nixon's office. It was an extraordinary missive for the chairman of the Republican National Committee to write to the leader of his party. It asked him to resign. "I expect in your lonely embattled position this would seem to you an act of disloyalty from one you have supported and helped in so many ways. My own view is that I would now ill serve a President, whose massive accomplishments I will always respect and whose family I love, if I did not give you my judgment. Until this morning resignation has been no answer at all, but given the impact of the latest development, and it will be a lasting one, I now firmly feel resignation is best for this country, best for this President."

For several hours that day, Price conferred with the President on the resignation speech. "As far as I could tell," Price says, "he had already made up his mind to resign—probably as early as Tuesday evening. By Wednesday, in any case, he showed me no sign of indecision. He was very businesslike, very much in command of himself, very concerned with doing it the right way, but resigned to resignation, you might say."

At midday, Bob Haldeman tried to telephone the President. Haig had anticipated such a call. Nixon and Haldeman had spoken frequently in recent months, but Haig now instructed the White House switchboard to transfer all Haldeman's calls to him. Now Haldeman told Haig that he wanted a pardon before Nixon left office. He suggested that either the President pardon all his indicted aides (and perhaps himself) or announce a "national reconciliation" amnesty which would include deserters and draft resisters. John Ehrlichman had put in his bid for a pardon too, going through Rose Mary Woods and, later, Julie Eisenhower. According to one report, Haig—and later Nixon himself—resented the tone of both Haldeman's and Ehrlichman's pleas, and interpreted Haldeman's as "threatening" and tantamount to "blackmail." The implication, according to one White House official, was that Haldeman had threatened that "he'd send Nixon to jail if he didn't get a pardon." Even before relaying Haldeman's request to Nixon, Haig told his predecessor that it was "out of the question." Nixon apparently rejected both requests out of hand. Haig and St. Clair—fearing that the very discussion of the question could be regarded as part of the continuing cover-up—later informed Jaworski of the pardon appeals.

Outside the White House that day, crowds had begun gathering on the sidewalk, standing three, four, five deep, their faces pressed against the iron fence in a kind of deathwatch. Behind them, on the green reach of Lafayette Park, stood several hundred more people. James L. Johnson of Baltimore had come to Washington to look for a job, but now he joined the crowd in the park. "It's a historic moment," he said. "Something you ain't gonna see too much in a lifetime."

By Wednesday virtually the only fierce resistance to resignation was coming from Julie Eisenhower; and, out of loyalty to her and her father, from other members of the family. Haig asked Buchanan—whom the family trusted—to deal with this problem. That afternoon he met with David Eisenhower and Edward Cox, trying to dissuade them from further battle. "Their heart wasn't really in it," says one aide familiar with these discussions. "Julie was the fighter. She was so much like her father—a real, tough, little battler—that at times that week I think she lost touch with reality. And that just fed her father's illusions."

Just how out of touch with reality was Richard Nixon in those final days? This is a difficult question. One shrinks from long-range "psycho-journalism," the reading of bitter tea leaves at the bottom of his cup.

There is no lack of such analysis, much of it probably accurate. Many qualified observers have noted Nixon's paranoia, his need to vent aggression against "enemies," his exaltation of strength and his fear of passivity. James David Barber of Duke University, in his 1972 book *Presidential Character,* sees Nixon constantly fluctuating between "moves to protect himself against doubts of his goodness and doubts of his manliness." Bruce Mazlish of MIT sees much the same pattern, noting that "he is extremely ambivalent about his aggressive impulses and tends to deal with them by projection onto others."

Certainly, much of Nixon's behavior during his last year in office was, at the very least, unorthodox: his sweating, trembling, and stuttering at news conferences; his obsessive attention to detail; his nocturnal piano playing; his high-speed dashes along the California freeways; his shoving of Ziegler in New Orleans; his seclusion from all but family and a shrinking circle of advisers. And during July and August he often acted even more strangely. One aide recalls passing him in a hallway and hearing him muttering to himself what sounded like, "The bastards! The bastards!" Others say his conversations rambled, at times became almost incoherent. One assistant compares Nixon in August 1974 to Captain Queeg, the erratic commander in Herman Wouk's *The Caine Mutiny:* "Like Queeg, he was given to sudden rages, to wild suspicions, terrible doubts about everybody." And there are other stories, stranger yet, which one is reluctant to report because they are so difficult to confirm.

Is this really all so surprising? Nixon had been under excruciating strain for two years. One sympathetic assistant says, "The President was not immune to these pressures. Very few people could bear up under them. I know I couldn't." The prolonged strain may have helped to bring on the physical ailments which beset him during his last year in office: the viral pneumonia which struck him in July 1973; the phlebitis which invaded his left leg in June 1974. Such tensions could well produce erratic, even bizarre, behavior.

But, of course, Nixon's troubles were largely self-induced, even lusted after. The great irony of his life is that after seeking ultimate power for three decades, once he finally achieved it he remained overwhelmed by a sense of powerlessness. Even in the Oval Office, he still felt the outsider, snubbed and spurned by the real elites. So he fought back with all the means at his disposal—and as President they were many and potent. Nothing was off limits for a man who had suffered what he had suffered. "We owe them a few," Buchanan prompted. Yet this was a cycle that once begun could not easily be checked. As his perversions of power multiplied, he could only maintain some sense of his own morality by stoking the fires of grievance which had fed him for so long. So he courted new enemies, new humiliations, new mortifications of the spirit. And ultimately, the enemies who had once been largely his own private demons became very palpable foes who tracked him down and destroyed him. That is the dark streak that snakes through the Nixon years. It is for others, better qualified than I, to say if it is madness.

His former aides differ on how clearly the President saw his situation in those last days. Ray Price, for example, insists that Nixon was in full command of the situation, that Haig and others were merely carrying out his strategy as they tested the political waters and determined whether he could carry on. Others say Haig and his accomplices were compelled to demonstrate the situation to him, gently but relentlessly, until he bowed to the inevitable. By either interpretation, the testimony of the congressional leaders became critically important.

On Timmons' advice, the Goldwater meeting was expanded to include Scott and Rhodes. It was scheduled first for the morning, then pushed back several times until late afternoon. Haig asked Timmons to brief the two minority leaders on the President's state of mind and did the same with Goldwater over lunch. Just before five, Rhodes's limousine pulled up at the White House; Goldwater and Scott followed in another. Haig intercepted the trio on their way to the Oval Office, warning them explicitly this time not to call for Nixon's resignation. "The President is up and down on this thing," Haig said. "Please give him a straight story—if his situation is hopeless, say so. I just hope you won't confront him with your demands. He's almost on the edge of resignation, and if you support it he may take umbrage and reverse."

Nixon greeted the delegation at the door to his office and for a few minutes they exchanged perfunctory small talk. "He seemed anxious to put us at ease,"

Scott said later, "because I'm sure he knew we weren't." Nixon reminisced about the Eisenhower years and confided that the last time he had cried was at Ike's death. "If I were to become an ex-President, I'd have no ex-Presidents to pal around with," he complained with a bitter little smile.

That was the first hint of what he had in mind. "I have a decision to make," he added. "What I need to do is get your appraisal of the floor."

"Mr. President," said Goldwater, "if it comes to a trial in the Senate, I don't think you can count on more than fifteen votes."

"And no more than ten in the House, John?" Nixon asked.

"Maybe more, Mr. President," Rhodes said, "but not much more."

"And I really campaigned for a lot of them," Nixon said. "But that's all right. That's politics. Hugh, what's your assessment of the Senate?"

"I'd say twelve or fifteen, Mr. President," Scott answered. "Gloomy."

"Damned gloomy," said Nixon.

"Yes, sir."

That was all. The President did not ask for their advice. They offered none. As they said good-bye at the door, Scott murmured, "These are sad times, Mr. President."

"Don't you bother about that, Hugh," said Nixon. "Do your duty and God bless you."

At that very hour, some of Nixon's closest friends and associates were already hard at work preparing the Ford Presidency. They gathered at five o'clock at the home of William G. Whyte, the chief lobbyist for United States Steel Corporation, on Rockwood Parkway. Attending the secret meeting were Philip Buchen, who was directing the "transition planning" for Ford; former Representative John Byrnes of Wisconsin, a longtime member of the Chowder and Marching Club; Senator Griffin; Bryce Harlow; former Governor William W. Scranton of Pennsylvania, who had been a law-school classmate of Ford's at Yale; and Clay T. Whitehead, who had just resigned as head of the White

House Office of Telecommunications Policy. The men had cocktails, ate steaks grilled by Mrs. Whyte, and then talked about the shape of the Ford administration until nearly midnight. (Griffin had been delegated to get Chief Justice Burger back to Washington to swear in the new President. On vacation in Holland, he sent word through his assistant that he didn't think he should return until there was "something official." Ultimately, he had to be rushed back on a military transport.)

Sometime in the early evening, Nixon apparently brushed aside the last traces of indecision and informed Haig of his final, irrevocable decision to resign on Thursday. Nixon told his family over dinner in the solarium. The bright yellow and green room was the family's favorite; they all realized that was probably the last time they would gather there. After dinner, the President wanted some pictures to commemorate the occasion and he summoned Ollie Atkins, the White House photographer. It was obvious to Atkins that Pat, Tricia, and Julie had been crying, but the whole family put on a brave face, forming a line with their arms linked, the President in the middle with one hand tightly gripping his wife's, the other holding Tricia's. And they smiled—oh how they smiled—right into the camera. It was "the President's idea of what a picture should be," Atkins said, and he dutifully took it. "I used a flash because the available light would have made it even more pathetic with the tears." Then, at David Eisenhowers's request, he took it again. "I'm a blinker," David said.

As the tight little line broke up, Julie burst into tears and her father put his arms around her. Atkins snapped a picture which was to become the most memorable record of those last hours.

Afterward, Nixon summoned Henry Kissinger to the White House, and for two hours they talked of their past triumphs and diverging futures. Even after Kissinger left, Nixon could not sleep. He made repeated telephone calls to Ray Price, as the speechwriter prepared the final version of the resignation speech.

At 9:00 a.m. on Thursday, Haig informed the White

House inner circle of the President's decision. Timmons called congressional leaders and some of the President's most faithful supporters on the Hill, inviting them to farewell sessions that afternoon.

At 11:03 Nixon received his successor in the Oval Office. Ford recalled later, "He was the most controlled person. I wondered how anybody could be that controlled under those circumstances. And as I recollect the first statement, he said, 'Jerry, you'll do a good job.' What do I say then? I asked for any suggestions." Then, for nearly seventy minutes, they had what Ford described as a "very practical, very helpful discussion about foreign policy, very high level." Nixon lavishly praised Henry Kissinger and "strongly" urged that Ford retain him.

Late that morning Haig sent an aide to pick up Leon Jaworski and take him to Haig's house. Jaworski says they met there "because the White House was surrounded by reporters, and if I was seen entering everybody would have said the President and I were plea-bargaining." The special prosecutor insists there was no such bargaining. In fact, he says he began the conversation that morning by saying, "Al, do we have an understanding that we're not going to have any understanding."

At 12:20 Ziegler appeared before a herd of impatient reporters in the White House press room. With tears glistening in his eyes, he said, "I am aware of the intense interest of the American people and of you in this room concerning developments today and over the last few days. . . . Tonight, at nine o'clock, the President of the United States will address the nation on radio and television from his Oval Office."

Nixon conferred twice that day with Price to go over his speech. He met briefly with Buzhardt, talking fatalistically about a jail sentence and remarking that men like Gandhi and Lenin had done some important political writing in their cells.

That afternoon the President vetoed a $13.5-billion appropriations bill for environmental, consumer, and rural assistance programs. He also appointed three federal judges, and accepted the resignations of an assistant secretary of transportation, a deputy director of the National Science Foundation, and a member of the Atomic Energy Commission.

During the day some of the President's most personal belongings—including his private collection of porcelain birds and the family pictures which he kept in the Oval Office—were removed and packed by family members and household staff. The family spent the day upstairs, packing and attending to other last-minute duties. Mrs. Nixon's staff were unable to communicate with her. Notes sent to the family quarters went unanswered. Telephone calls from longtime friends were not accepted.

Bob Haldeman, still pressing for a pardon, telephoned Haig again that day to renew his appeal. Shortly after his call, St. Clair telephoned the Washington office of Haldeman's lawyers—John Wilson and Frank Strickler—to ask whether they had some papers for him. The documents proved to be a two-and-a-half-page brief on Presidential pardon powers and alternative messages outlining Haldeman's two pardon plans. (The plans were virtually identical, except that one would simply pardon all Watergate figures—including those involved in the ITT, milk, Plumbers', wiretapping and related cases—while the other would extend the pardon to draft resisters and deserters. Since there would have been nothing left for the special prosecutor to do, his office would be closed.) Included with the lawyers' documents was a memo from Haldeman to the President, entitled "Notes for Consideration." It read, in part:

"On personal basis—better to close the chapter now than to have to sit by helplessly for the next several years and watch trials and appeals.

"Historically—would be far better to grant the pardon and close the door to such process than to let it run and have the trials become a surrogate impeachment. Also, history will look kindly on loyalty and compassion to subordinates caught in the web.

"Solves problems of potential prosecutor access to files and tapes by eliminating basis for further prosecution—also solves problem of defense forcing access to files.

"The only way to wipe the slate clean is to shut down the prosecution totally. As long as it is there, there is a possibility of other things. . . ."

At 7:30 p.m., Thursday, the President walked from the White House to the EOB. Some of the crowd outside the gates waved flags and sang "America." Others shouted "Jail to the Chief" and less polite phrases. Newsmen were locked in the White House press room to keep them from "harassing" the President. In his EOB office, Nixon met with five congressional leaders: Carl Albert, James Eastland, Mike Mansfield, John Rhodes, and Hugh Scott. They sat around a coffee table while the President briefly explained why he had decided to resign. "I don't know when I'll come back to Washington—if ever," he said sadly. Then he turned to Mansfield and said, "I'll miss our breakfasts, Mike." It was all over in twenty minutes.

The President walked back to the White House, where forty-six old supporters from Congress—twenty senators and twenty-six representatives—were gathered in the Cabinet Room. The first meeting had been a formal obligation—the leader of the executive branch bidding farewell to the leaders of the legislative branch. This was different. These were Richard Nixon's old comrades-in-arms, many of them Republicans from the Chowder and Marching Club, others crusty southern Democrats who had so often rallied behind him. The room was filled with friends, faces that brought back recollections of better days, old memories floating there above the oval cabinet table. And the President's farewell was a deeply personal one, sometimes rambling, sometimes incoherent, as he ranged back across the years. He thanked them all for helping him to end the Vietnam war and to make appointments to the Supreme Court which ended the "leftist" domination of that body. He said he would have preferred to fight it out. But that was impossible. One had to think of the nation Then, suddenly, his tight composure deserted him. "I just hope," he said in a half-sob, "I just hope that you don't feel that I let you down." He choked. His face ran with tears. He stumbled backward and nearly fell over a chair. Some of his friends pressed around trying to comfort him. Goldwater hugged him. Then, with aides clearing the way, he left the room, his head bowed, his shoulders shaking.

Somehow, he put back the mask of state. Twenty minutes later he was seated at his desk in the Oval Office in a blue suit, blue tie, and American flag pin in his lapel. The office was empty except for the television technicians and Ollie Atkins, moving quietly about, recording the moment for history. Watching the photographer, Nixon jibed, "Ollie will wait until I'm picking my nose and then he'll take the picture."

At 9:00 p.m. the red light on the camera went on, and the President looked into the lens with that same earnest gaze which Americans had come to know so well during the past five years.

"This is the thirty-seventh time I have spoken to you from this office in which so many decisions have been made that shape the history of this nation. . . . Throughout the long and difficult period of Watergate, I have felt it was my duty to persevere; to make every possible effort to complete the term of office to which you elected me. In the past few days, however, it has become evident that I no longer have a strong enough political base in the Congress to justify continuing that effort. . . . I would have preferred to carry through to the finish, whatever the personal agony it would have involved, and my family unanimously urged me to do so. But the interests of the nation must always come before any personal considerations. . . . I have never been a quitter. To leave office before my term is completed is opposed to every instinct in my body. But as President I must put the interests of America first. . . . Therefore I shall resign the Presidency effective at noon tomorrow."

It was six years almost to the hour since he had stood before the Republican National Convention in Miami Beach to accept his party's Presidential nomination and told the cheering partisans: "America is in trouble today not because her people have failed but because her leaders have failed."

After his farewell speech, the President had dinner with his family, then he and Pat took a last sentimental walk around the White House. He met once more with Kissinger that night, and then stayed on the telephone into the early-morning hours, calling old friends and colleagues, saying good-by. One of those who received a call was Senator Harry F. Byrd, Jr., of Virginia. Byrd was awakened at 1:00 a.m. by an operator who said, "Just a minute, Senator Byrd, the President would like to speak with you."

"Harry," Nixon said. "I'm sorry to call you so late, but I've been kind of busy tonight. I just wanted to know if you feel I took the proper course."

"Mr. President," Byrd said, "I feel confident you did what you thought was in the best interests of the country, and I think you made the proper decision."

After less than five hours' sleep, Nixon rose for the last time in the White House. He said good-by to the household staff. He signed the simple letter of resignation to Henry Kissinger which Haig would deliver to the secretary of state when Nixon's plane was over Jefferson City, Missouri ("Dear Mr. Secretary: I hereby resign the Office of the President of the United States. Sincerely, Richard Nixon"). At nine-thirty he went downstairs to the East Room. The cabinet and their families were there; Al Haig, James St. Clair, Leonard Garment, Bill Timmons, J. Fred Buzhardt, all the men who had skillfully maneuvered Nixon to that moment; and many secretaries, clerks, and lower-ranking aides.

Standing on the low platform, with his wife and family ranged behind him, Nixon—sometimes overcome with emotion—began to speak of personal things.

He spoke of his father: "I think they would have called him sort of a little man, common man. He didn't consider himself that way. You know what he was? He was a streetcar motorman, first, and then he was a farmer, and then he had a lemon ranch. It was the poorest lemon ranch in California, I can assure you."

He spoke of his mother: "Nobody will ever write a book, probably, about my mother. Well, I guess all of you would say this about your mother—my mother was a saint. And I think of her, two boys dying of tuberculosis, nursing four others in order that she could take care of my older brother for three years in Arizona and seeing each of them die, and when they died, it was like one of her own. Yes, she will have no books written about her. But she was a saint."

He spoke about the White House: "I was thinking of it as we walked down this hall, and I was comparing it to some of the great houses of the world that I have been in. This isn't the biggest house. Many, and most, in even smaller countries are much bigger. This isn't the finest house. Many, in Europe, particularly, and in China, Asia, have paintings of great, great value, things that we just don't have here. . . . But this is the best house. . . . This house has a great heart and that heart comes from those who serve."

He spoke about his background: "As you know, I kind of like to read books. I am not educated, but I do read books."

He spoke about sorrow: "We think that when someone dear to us dies, we think that when we lose an election, we think that when we suffer a defeat, that all is ended. . . . Not true. It is only a beginning, always."

And he spoke about hatred: "Always remember others may hate you, but those who hate you don't win unless you hate them, and then you destroy yourself."

A NOTE ON SOURCES

The central problem in researching this book was not a shortage of information but a glut. Perhaps no segment of our national history is so amply documented as the last years of Richard Nixon's time in the White House. The difficulty is in sifting the truth from this surfeit of incomplete, self-serving, and conflicting data.

Although the press was late in comprehending these events, once it began to catch on it made up for lost time. Between March 1973 and August 1974 it deluged its readers with an unprecedented flood of coverage. But the flood came in a succession of ever-larger waves—reflecting the material available at each stage in the unfolding story. Every event went through many versions, with the broad outlines remaining the same, but details and nuances shifting according to who was recounting the story and how much he knew. (In what follows, I omit references to thousands of daily newspaper stories and news-magazine articles that I used during all phases of my research—except for a few major investigative pieces and lengthy wrap-ups which were particularly useful. I relied most heavily on *The New York Times* [which allowed me to use its morgue and computer services], *The Washington Post*, and the *Los Angeles Times*. I also consulted the *Boston Globe*, the *Chicago Tribune*, *Newsday*, the Providence *Journal-Bulletin*, the St. Louis *Post-Dispatch*, *The Wall Street Journal*, and the Washington *Star-News*.)

Parallel with—and heavily contributing to—the press accounts were the official investigations: by the FBI, the Justice Department, the Watergate grand juries, the Special Prosecutor's office, the General Accounting Office, the Senate Foreign Relations Committee, the Joint Committee on Internal Revenue Taxation, the Senate Select Committee on Presidential Campaign Activities, and the House Judiciary Committee. These last two committees published not only their reports and recommendations but vast accumulations of supporting data—30 volumes totaling 16,912 pages by the Senate Select Committee, 43 volumes totaling 18,126 pages by the House Judiciary Committee.

Then, another source became available—an unusual one, rich in detail and flavor, but also rich in problems for the conscientious journalist or historian. The White House tapes that were painfully extracted from a resisting President provided a verbatim record, unavailable to those who have written about earlier administrations. But they demanded great care because of the selectivity of their release; the gaps, deletions, and self-serving editing; and, again, successive and conflicting versions.

Finally, of course, there have been many other books on aspects of this same story. Some of the prime figures have written memoirs. Other authors have recounted parts of the story or addressed themselves to particular issues. A few attempts have been made to tell the whole tale—though none, I think, so comprehensive as this one.

After surveying this wealth of material, I concluded that little purpose would be served by attempting to duplicate most of the original investigations. The central characters in the story have now been questioned by relays of investigators: first the FBI, then the committee staffs, then members of the committees, then —in many cases—prosecutors. Moreover, the Senate and House committee volumes contained masses of documentation which most writers have not had time to absorb. I decided to concentrate my efforts first on assimilating and ordering this available evidence.

Once this was largely completed, I identified nine or ten problem areas—aspects of the story on which there seemed to be a serious paucity of information, or on which the documentation appeared deeply contradictory. Among these were the role of Robert Bennett and Mullen & Company, the 1969–71 wiretapping, the Hughes-Nixon relationship, the Saturday Night Massacre, and the role of the Fragile Coalition in the House Judiciary Committee. I concentrated my new research and interviews in these areas, trying to resolve the problems as best I could.

In the following, I have listed the most important sources used in writing each chapter. Where appropriate, I have also discussed the value of certain materials or the problems which arose in using them.

Chapter 1. FEAR OF LOSING

Books: Rowland Evans, Jr., and Robert D. Novak, *Nixon in the White House: The Frustration of Power,* Random House, 1971. Gary Wills, *Nixon Agonistes,* Houghton Mifflin, 1971. Jeb S. Magruder, *An American Life: One Man's Road to Watergate,* Atheneum, 1974. Kevin Phillips, *The Emerging Republican Majority,* Arlington House, 1969. The Ripon Society and Clifford W. Brown, Jr., *Jaws of Victory: The Game-Plan Politics of 1972, the Crisis of the Republican Party, and the Future of the Constitution,* Little Brown, 1974. Reg Murphy and Hal Gulliver, *The Southern Strategy,* Scribner's, 1971. Richard M. Scammon and Ben J. Wattenberg, *The Real Majority: How the Silent Center of the American Electorate Chooses Its President,* Coward-McCann & Geoghegan, Inc., 1970. Richard J. Whalen, *Catch the Falling Flag: A Republican's Challenge to His Party,* Houghton Mifflin, 1969. Jules Witcover, *The Resurrection of Richard Nixon,* Putnam, 1970. **Articles:** John Osborne, "The Nixon Watch: Love that Pap!" *The New Republic,* November 28, 1970. Jonathan Schell, "The Time of Illusion," *The New Yorker,* June 2, June 9, June 16, June 23, June 30, and July 7, 1975. Various articles by R. W. Apple and Robert Semple in *The New York Times* for November and December 1970. *Time* and *Newsweek* for the same period. **Interviews:** R. W. Apple, William Safire. **Remarks:** Wills's book is the classic interpretation of Nixon. Witcover and Whalen have produced helpful political analyses. Magruder's memoir—ghosted by Patrick Anderson, a Washington journalist—is probably the best written of the Watergate memoirs and contains much valuable detail, but it is consistently self-serving.

Chapter 2. STATE OF SIEGE

Books: Magruder, *An American Life*. Victor Marchetti and John D. Marks, *The CIA and the Cult of Intelligence*, Knopf, 1974. Dan Rather and Gary P. Gates, *The Palace Guard*, Harper & Row, 1974. **Articles:** Taylor Branch and George Crile II, "The Kennedy Vendetta," *Harper's*, August 1975. Bo Burlingham, "Paranoia in Power," *Harper's*, October 1974. Robert Fink, "The Unsolved Break-ins," *Rolling Stone*, October 10, 1974. Douglas A. Hallett, "A Low-level Memoir of the Nixon White House," *The New York Times Magazine*, October 20, 1974. Seymour Hersh, series of articles on domestic programs of the CIA beginning in *The New York Times* on December 22, 1974. Paul Meskil, "Secrets of the CIA," series of five articles in the New York *Daily News*, April 21–25, 1975. Andrew St. George, "Confessions of a Watergate Burglar," *True*, August 1974. Tad Szulc, "How Nixon Used the CIA," *New York*, January 1975. Sanford J. Ungar, "The FBI File: Men and Machinations in the Court of J. Edgar Hoover," *Atlantic*, April 1975. **Documents:** Senate Select Committee, Chapter 1, Part I. House Judiciary Committee, Volumes VII and VIII. Report to the President by the Commission on CIA Activities within the United States, June 1975. Report by William E. Colby, director of the Central Intelligence Agency, to President Gerald Ford, December 24, 1974. Report on the Special Services Staff of the Internal Revenue Service by the Joint Committee on Internal Revenue Taxation, May 1975. **Other:** I am indebted to the Special Prosecutor's staff for certain materials on Robert Bennett, and to Nicole Szulc for unpublished materials on Mullen & Company. Also to Mike Wallace's interviews with H. R. Haldeman on March 23 and March 30, 1975. **Remarks:** The CIA's activities in domestic surveillance remain one of the murkiest sections of this story. Sy Hersh broke this open with his reporting in December 1974. In the months that followed, the CIA and its allies in Washington did all they could to discredit Hersh's accounts. Ultimately, the Presidential Commission, headed by Vice President Nelson A. Rockefeller, largely verified Hersh's reporting. However, even this report has left much of the story untold. One hopes that forthcoming books by Hersh and by Taylor Branch and George Crile will answer some of the remaining questions.

Chapter 3. LEAKS AND TAPS

Articles: Joseph Kraft, "On Being Bugged," *New York Review of Books,* October 4, 1973. John D. Marks, "The Case Against Kissinger," *Rolling Stone,* August 1, 1974. **Documents:** Senate Select Committee, Chapter 2, Part I. House Judiciary Committee, Volume VII, Statement of Information on Behalf of President Nixon, Minority Memorandum on Facts and Law. Hearings Before the Committee on Foreign Relations, U.S. Senate: Dr. Kissinger's Role in Wiretapping, 1973–74. Joint Hearings Before the Subcommittee on Administrative Practices and Procedures and the Subcommittee on Constitutional Rights of the Committee of the Judiciary, and the Subcommittee on Surveillance of the Committee on Foreign Relations, U.S. Senate, Warrantless Wiretapping and Electrical Surveillance, April/May 1974. **Interviews:** Daniel Davidson, Fred Emery, Max Frankel, Morton Halperin, Hedrick Smith. **Remarks:** The version of the 1969–71 wiretapping which emerges from the committee reports tends to accept Kissinger's explanations at face value. Only after I talked with Morton Halperin and Dan Davidson did I reach the view of the wiretapping expressed in this chapter. (The House Judiciary Committee reports are impossible to understand unless one knows the FBI letter code for the wiretap targets. For the convenience of future researchers, here it is: A.—Sullivan; B.—Sonnenfeldt; C.—Sneider; D.—Smith; E.—Sears; F.—Safire; G.—Pursley; H.—Pedersen; I.—Moose; J.—McLane; K.—Lord; L.—Lake; M.—Kalb; N.—Halperin; O.—Davidson; P.—Brandon; Q.—Beecher.)

Chapter 4. PLUMBERS

Books: E. Howard Hunt, *Undercover: Memoirs of an American Secret Agent,* Berkley, 1974; *The Berlin Ending,* Berkley, 1973; *Give Us This Day,* Popular Library, 1974; as David St. John, *The Coven,* Weybright & Talley, 1972. Richard M. Nixon, *Six Crises,* Doubleday, 1962. Peter Schrag, *Test of Loyalty,* Simon & Schuster, 1974. Tad Szulc, *Compulsive Spy: The Strange Career of E. Howard Hunt,* The Viking Press, 1974. Sanford J. Ungar, *The Papers and the Papers,* E. P. Dutton, 1972. **Articles:** Michael Getler, "The Yeoman and the Admirals: What Brass!" *The New Republic,* March 9, 1974. G. Gordon Liddy, "A Patriot Speaks," *Harper's,* October 1974. Walter Pincus, "Impeachment Issue: Did the President Conceal Wiretap Records?", *The Washington Post,* April 27, 1974; "The Duping of Richard Helms," *The New Republic,* February 15, 1975. **Documents:** Senate Select Committee, Chapter 1, Part II. House Judiciary Committee, Volume VII and Appendix III. Senator Howard H. Baker's report on CIA activities in Watergate, Chapter 11 of the Senate Select Committee's final report. **Interviews:** Daniel Ellsberg, Leslie Gelb, Morton Halperin, Neil Sheehan, William Van Cleave. **Remarks:** Walter Pincus's articles in *The New Republic* and *The Washington Post* were consistently thoughtful and provocative. Howard Hunt's account of his role as a Plumber—in *Undercover*—must be treated with considerable care. After the book was published, Hunt admitted that he had knowingly falsified several sections. His publisher later circulated a sheet of corrections, and Hunt now stands behind everything in the book. I remain skeptical. He has changed his testimony so frequently that one suspects he no longer knows what is true. Nevertheless, his book is full of intriguing detail, and, from time to time, I have quoted portions which seem plausible. In each case, I have explicitly attributed the account to Hunt and leave it to the reader to judge the material's credibility.

Chapter 5. DIRTY MONEY

Articles: George Crile, "Our Man in Jamaica," *Harper's*, October 1974. **Documents:** House Judiciary Committee, Volume VI. Senate Select Committee, Chapters 4, 5, 6, and 8, and Volumes 20–24. Deposition of Herbert Kalmbach in suit filed by Democratic National Committee against CREEP. **Interviews:** David Dorsen, Ken Guido, James Polk. **Remarks:** For most of the events covered in this chapter, the Senate Select Committee is most complete and authoritative. Particularly valuable is its extensive treatment of the Hughes-Rebozo connection. Jim Polk, formerly of the *Washington Star-News,* has done the best reporting in this area.

Chapter 6. DIRTY TRICKS

Documents: Senate Select Committee, Chapter 2; House Judiciary Committee, Volume VII. **Remarks:** I am particularly indebted to John Crewdson of *The New York Times,* who shared with me some materials on Donald Segretti's activities.

Chapter 7. BREAK-IN

Books: Lewis Chester, Cal McCrystal, Stephen Aris, William Shawcross, *Watergate,* Ballantine, 1973. Stephen Fay, Lewis Chester, Magnus Linklater, *Hoax: The Inside Story of the Howard Hughes–Clifford Irving Affair,* The Viking Press, 1972. Hunt, *Undercover.* John Keats, *Howard Hughes,* Random House, 1966. James W. McCord, Jr., *A Piece of Tape, The Watergate Story, Fact and Fiction: Reference Handbook to the Watergate Cases.* Washington Media Services Ltd., 1974. Magruder, *An American Life.* Lawrence F.

O'Brien, *No Final Victories: A Life in Politics from John F. Kennedy to Watergate,* Doubleday, 1974. David B. Tinnin, *Just About Everybody vs. Howard Hughes,* Doubleday, 1973. Steve Weissman, ed., *Big Brother and the Holding Company: The World Behind Watergate,* Ramparts Press, 1974. Theodore H. White, *The Making of the President 1972,* Atheneum, 1973. Bob Woodward and Carl Bernstein, *All the President's Men,* Simon & Schuster, 1974. **Articles:** Bernard Barker, "Mission Impossible: The Watergate Bunglers," *Harper's,* October 1974. Jerry Landauer, "Investigators Believe Hughes Case Provides Motive for Watergate," *The Wall Street Journal,* May 6, 1974. Eugenio Martinez, "Mission Impossible: The Watergate Bunglers," *Harper's,* October 1974. Ron Rosenbaum, "What Were They Hoping to Hear on Larry O'Brien's Phone?" *The Village Voice,* August 8, 1974. **Documents:** Senate Select Committee, Chapter 1. House Judiciary Committee, Volume I. Unpublished staff report to Senate Select Committee by Terry Lenzner *et al.* **Interviews:** Richard Gerstein, Hank Greenspun, Mark Lackritz, Terry Lenzner, Jim Phelan. **Remarks:** For the central theory behind the Watergate and Greenspun burglaries, I am deeply indebted to Terry Lenzner and his colleagues on the staff of the Senate Select Committee.

Chapter 8. COVER-UP

Books: William F. Buckley, Jr., *Execution Eve—And Other Contemporary Ballads,* Putnam, 1975. Hunt, *Undercover.* Magruder, *An American Life.* Barry Sussman, *The Great Cover-Up: Nixon and the Scandal of Watergate,* Thomas Y. Crowell, 1974. Theodore H. White, *Breach of Faith: The Fall of Richard Nixon,* Atheneum, 1975. **Articles:** George V. Higgins, "The Judge Who Tried Harder," *Atlantic,* April 1974. Walter Pincus, "A Promotion for Earl Silbert?" *The Washington Post,* July 22, 1974. Donnie Radcliffe, "Martha Mitchell: Two Long Years After Watergate," *The Washington Post,* June 16, 1974. **Documents:** Senate Select Committee, Chapter 1, Part II. House Judiciary

Committee, Volumes II and III. Hearings Before the Committee on the Judiciary, U.S. Senate, Nomination of Earl J. Silbert to be U.S. Attorney for the District of Columbia, April–May 1974. **Interviews:** Terry Lenzner, Christopher Lydon, Helen Thomas. **Remarks:** Barry Sussman's book is badly organized and incomplete. George Higgins' work is consistently interesting and helpful, particularly on the role of the prosecutors (although I differ with him on interpretations).

Chapter 9. UNCOVER

Books: Frank Mankiewicz, *Perfectly Clear: Nixon from Whittier to Watergate,* Quadrangle, 1973. Mary McCarthy, *The Mask of State: Watergate Portraits,* Harcourt, Brace, Jovanovich, 1974. William Safire, *Before the Fall: An Inside View of the Pre-Watergate White House,* Doubleday, 1975. White, *Breach of Faith.* **Articles:** Ben H. Bagdikian, "The Fruits of Agnewism," *Columbia Journalism Review,* January/February 1973. Marjorie Boyd, "The Watergate Story: Why Congress Didn't Investigate Until After the Election," *Washington Monthly,* April 1973. Edward J. Epstein, "Did the Press Uncover Watergate?" *Commentary,* July 1974. George V. Higgins, "The Friends of Richard Nixon," *Atlantic,* November 1974. Charles Peters, "Why the White House Press Didn't Get the Watergate Story," *Washington Monthly,* August/September 1973. Walter Pincus, "Did Mr. Nixon Mislead the Prosecution?" *The Washington Post,* June 8, 1974. Eric Redman, "Pre-Watergate Watch: Did Nixon Legally Win the 1968 Election?" *Rolling Stone,* March 13, 1975. Sanford Ungar, "The FBI File: Men and Machinations in the Court of J. Edgar Hoover," *Atlantic,* April 1975. **Documents:** Senate Select Committee, Chapter 1, Part II. Senate Judiciary Committee, Hearings on the Nomination of Earl J. Silbert, etc. House Judiciary Committee, Volumes III and IV. Submission of Recorded Presidential Conversations to the Committee on the Juciary of the House of Representatives by President Richard Nixon, April 30, 1973, and other transcripts turned over to various investigators by the White House. **Remarks:** As indicated earlier, the White House transcripts present serious problems for any researcher. Four major categories of tapes and transcripts are presently available: (1) seven tapes which Nixon turned over to Judge Sirica in November 1973 following the public outrage at the Saturday Night Massacre; (2) twelve more turned over to the Special Prosecutor's office in the winter of 1973–74 (later, all nineteen tapes in these two groups were made available to the House Judiciary Committee and—carefully transcribed by its staff—formed the base of its impeachment case against the President); (3) forty-six partial and heavily edited transcripts released by Nixon on April 30, 1974; (4) thirty-six tapes subsequently obtained by the Special Prosecutor after the Supreme Court upheld its suit against the President (and later made public at the cover-up trial). These transcripts vary greatly in completeness and reliability. In general, the least reliable are those in Group 3 and the most reliable are the nineteen transcripts of Groups 1 and 2 prepared by the House Judiciary Committee. The Special Prosecutor's transcripts submitted at the cover-up trial are also good. Since the four groups overlap considerably, it is important for the researcher to use the best available transcript of any given tape. The transcripts present other problems. In several tapes during the spring of 1973, Nixon seems to be consciously speaking for the recording machines, making his own historical record. Such comments should obviously be treated with great caution. But there may be other, less obvious, occasions when Nixon is using the tapes to establish his innocence or to perpetuate a false version of events; so all the transcripts should be used with an eye to this danger.

Chapter 10. HOUSES IN THE SUN

Articles: John Blackburn, "S.C. White House Buy with GOP $ Probed," *Santa Ana Register,* May 13, 1973. John Blackburn, "Getting the Goods on San Clemente," *The Nation,* November 20, 1973. Robert W. Greene and others, Special Report, *Newsday,* October 6, 7, 9, 11, 12, and 13, 1971. Kirkpatrick Sale, "The World Behind Watergate," *New York Review of Books,* May 3, 1973. Jack White, "Nixon's Income Tax Bill $1670 for Two Years," *Providence Journal,* October 3, 1973. **Documents:** House Judiciary Committee, Volumes X and XII. Examination of President Nixon's Tax Returns for 1969 through 1972. Joint Committee on Internal Revenue Taxation, April 3, 1974. Senate Select Committee, Chapter 8, Part X. **Interviews:** Adam Clymer, David Dorsen, Jim Flug, John Kaplan. **Remarks:** I am particularly indebted to Kirk Sale's important analysis in his *New York Review* article, later expanded into his book, *Power Shift,* Random House, 1975.

Chapter 11. TAPES

Books: Jimmy Breslin, *How the Good Guys Finally Won,* The Viking Press, 1975. Sussman, *The Great Cover-Up.* White, *Breach of Faith.* **Articles:** Aaron Latham "There Is a Tape in the Oval Office," *New York,* June 17, 1974. Lloyd Shearer, "The Little-Known Man Who Asked the Big Watergate Question," *Parade,* June 30, 1974. **Documents:** House Judiciary Committee, Volume IX. Alexander Butterfield's testimony to the Senate Select Committee and the House Judiciary Committee. Deposition of Richard M. Nixon in *Richard M. Nixon* vs. *Administrator of General Services, et al.,* July 25, 1975. **Interviews:** Eugene Boyce, Donald Sanders.

Chapter 12. AGNEW

Books: Richard M. Cohen and Jules Witcover, *A Heartbeat Away: The Investigation and Resignation of Vice President Spiro T. Agnew,* The Viking Press, 1974. **Articles:** Aaron Latham, "Closing in on Agnew: The Prosecutor's Story," *New York,* November 26, 1973. James M. Naughton, "How Agnew Bartered His Office to Keep from Going to Prison," *The New York Times,*

October 23, 1973. **Interviews:** George Beall, Joseph H. H. Kaplan, Elliot Richardson, Stephen Sachs, Barney Skolnik. **Remarks:** The Cohen-Witcover book is the definitive work on the Agnew episode and, indeed, one of the best books yet written on any aspect of the Nixon Presidency. Aaron Latham, too, has done valuable work in this area.

Chapter 13. FIRESTORM

Books: White, *Breach of Faith.* **Articles:** Alexander Bickel, "The Tapes, Cox, Nixon," *The New Republic,* September 29, 1973. Aaron Latham, "Seven Days in October," *New York,* April 29, 1974. **Documents:** House Judiciary Committee, Volume IX. **Interviews:** Richard Darman, Leonard Garment, Melvin Laird, Jonathan Moore, Henry Petersen, Elliot Richardson, William Ruckelshaus, Henry Ruth. **Remarks:** This chapter was written chiefly from my own reporting in the fall of 1973. Latham's article was also helpful.

Chapter 14. OPERATION CANDOR

Articles: David Binder, "An Implied Soviet Threat Spurred U.S. Forces' Alert," *The New York Times,* November 21, 1973. **Documents:** House Judiciary Committee, Volume IX. **Interviews:** Senator Robert Packwood. **Remarks:** This chapter was written largely from the available news reports on the President's activities in the fall and winter of 1973.

Chapter 15. IMPEACHMENT

Books: James D. Barber, *The Presidential Character: Predicting Performance in the White House,* Prentice-Hall, 1972. Breslin, *How the Good Guys Finally Won.* Frank Mankiewicz, *U.S. vs. Richard M. Nixon: The Final Crisis,* Quadrangle, 1975. John Osborne, *The Last Nixon Watch,* The New Republic Book Company, 1975. White, *Breach of Faith.* **Articles:** Elizabeth Drew,

"A Reporter in Washington, D.C.," Parts I and II, *The New Yorker*, October 14, October 21, 1974. **Documents:** House Judiciary Committee, final report. Comparison of White House and Judiciary Committee Transcripts of Eight Recorded Presidential Conversations. **Interviews:** Jim Doyle, Representative Hamilton Fish, Representative John Flynt, Representative Jerry Pettis, Raymond K. Price, Representative Tom Railsback, Representative Paul Sarbanes. **Remarks:** This chapter draws heavily on the material which I gathered during the summer of 1974 for a third *New York Times Magazine* Watergate issue—which never appeared because of the President's resignation. Elizabeth Drew's articles were helpful in keeping the complex sequence of events straight.

Chapter 16. RESIGNATION

Books: Osborne, *The Last Nixon Watch*. The Staff of *The New York Times, The End of a Presidency*, Bantam, 1974. The Staff of *The Washington Post, The Fall of a President*, Dell, 1974. White, *Breach of Faith*. **Articles:** Lou Cannon, "The Last Seventeen Days of the Nixon Reign," *The Washington Post*, September 29, 1974. Elizabeth Drew, "A Reporter in Washington, D.C.," Part III, *The New Yorker*, October 28, 1974. James M. Naughton, "How a Fragile Centrist Bloc Emerged as House Panel Weighed Impeachment," *The New York Times*, August 5, 1974. "Nixon Slide from Power: Backers Give Final Push," *The New York Times*, August 12, 1974. "The Change in Presidents: Plans Began Months Ago," *The New York Times*, August 26, 1974. William Safire, "Last Days in the Bunker," *The New York Times Magazine*, August 18, 1974. I. F. Stone, "Mr. Ford's Deception," *New York Review of Books*, November 14, 1974. Loudon Wainwright, "The End of a Presidency—Seventeen Days in Summer," *Life*, Special Report, "The Year in Pictures," Winter 1975. Also full issues of *Newsweek* and *Time* for the week of August 19, 1974. **Interviews:** Representative Edward G. Biester, Representative William Hungate, Barrett McGurn, John Osborne, Representative Tom Railsback. **Remarks:** Again, this chapter draws heavily on the reporting for my third but abortive *New York Times Magazine* article. The Cannon, Drew, Naughton, and Wainwright articles and the Osborne book were also particularly helpful.

INDEX

ABOUT THE AUTHOR

J. ANTHONY LUKAS was born in New York City and graduated from Harvard College. After four years on *The Baltimore Sun,* he joined *The New York Times,* serving successfully as a foreign correspondent in Africa, India, Australia, Japan and Korea; roving national correspondent; and staff writer for the Sunday *Magazine.* His reporting on the political and social upheavals of the late 1960s won him virtually all of journalism's top prizes: the Pulitzer Prize, the George Polk Memorial Award, the Mike Berger Award and the Page One Award of the New York Newspaper Guild. Mr. Lukas is the author of *The Barnyard Epithet and Other Obscenities,* a book about the Chicago Conspiracy Trial, and *Don't Shoot—We Are Your Children!* A co-founder and contributing editor of *More,* he presently writes for various periodicals on subjects that range from politics to sports.

Programming JavaScript for Netscape 2.0

Tim Ritchey

New Riders Publishing, Indianapolis, Indiana

Programming JavaScript for Netscape 2.0

By Tim Ritchey

Published by:
New Riders Publishing
201 West 103rd Street
Indianapolis, IN 46290 USA

Printed in the United States of America 1 2 3 4 5 6 7 8 9 0

CIP data available upon request

Warning and Disclaimer

This book is designed to provide information about Java. Every effort has been made to make this book as complete and as accurate as possible, but no warranty or fitness is implied.

The information is provided on an "as is" basis. The author and New Riders Publishing shall have neither liability nor responsibility to any person or entity with respect to any loss or damages arising from the information contained in this book or from the use of the disks or programs that may accompany it.

Publisher
Don Fowley

Marketing Manager
Mary Foote

Publishing Manager
Jim LeValley

Managing Editor
Carla Hall

Development Editor
Suzanne Snyder

Production Editor
Clifford Shubs

Copy Editors
Chris Cleveland
Sarah Kearns
Catherine Manship

Assistant Marketing Manager
Tamara Apple

Acquisitions Coordinator
Tracy Turgeson

Publisher's Assistant
Karen Opal

Cover Designer
Karen Ruggles

Book Designer
Sandra Schroeder

Production Manager
Kelly Dobbs

Manufacturing Coordinator
Brook Farling

Production Team Supervisor
Laurie Casey

Illustrator
Jerry Blank

Production Analysts
Jason Hand
Bobbi Satterfield

Production Team
Heather Butler, Angela Calvert, Kim Cofer, Tricia Flodder, David Garratt, Glenn Larsen, Erika Millen, Erich J. Richter

Indexer
Cheryl Dietsch

About the Author

Tim Ritchey received his Honors B.S. from Ball State University in physics and anthropology and is currently working toward his Ph.D. in archaeology from Cambridge University, England. He has worked on artificial intelligence, high-performance parallel architectures, and computer vision. His honors thesis was the development of an inexpensive 3D scanner using structured lighting. Present interests include aritificial intelligence, distributed computing, VRML, and, of course, Java. Besides computing and archaeology, he enjoys scuba diving, flying, and riding his Harley Davidson motorcycle. His Ph.D. thesis includes adapting non-linear dynamics and artificial intelligence techniques to archaeological theory.

Trademark Acknowledgments

Dedication

This book is dedicated to my parents, Jim and Bonnie, for their loving care, patience, and dedication for the past 24 years—a much harder job than writing a book.

Acknowledgments

Writing a book doesn't seem to get any easier, so I still have many thanks for everyone who helped on this one. I would like to thank all of the New Riders Publishing staff for their help in getting this book finished: Suzanne, Cliff, Jim, Steve, Chris, Sarah, Catherine, and all the production and development staffers who worked overtime on this. Thanks to Kristin for letting me take over her apartment when I was in Lexington, to Don, for someone to look at and say, "Well, at least I'm not THAT busy!" To Howard for feeding me (Bengal tonight?), and to Judy and Leon for providing entertainment on those long drives to Little Mexico (do we get the quilt now?). There are undoubtedly people I have forgotten to mention. To all of those who have helped me along the way so far, a heartfelt thanks. All the errors in this book are, of course, my own.

Contents at a Glance

Table of Contents

3 Control Flow and Functions in JavaScript   77

10 Objects in Java—The Class   301

A JavaScript Object Hierarchy Reference   435

Introduction

This book shows you two of the most dramatic changes to come to the world of Internet browsers since the very first NCSA Mosaic program was introduced—JavaScript and Java. Netscape brings the first two platform-independent development languages for the Internet to every desktop in the new Navigator 2.0. By incorporating the JavaScript and Java run-time engines into their widely popular Web browser, Netscape has enabled application and Web page developers to write to a single Java specification that will run on almost all the platforms Navigator 2.0 is available for.

As a Web developer, you want to get your site up to speed with the newest technology as soon as possible. This book takes you through *both* of these exciting and powerful new languages and gives you the advantage of creating dynamic and interactive Web pages immediately. This is possible because JavaScript is built upon the Java language, and the two use similar syntax. For you, this means that after you have learned JavaScript, picking up Java will be much easier. You can learn JavaScript first and use it to begin developing interactive dynamic sites without delay. At the same time, the Java sections of the book take advantage of your JavaScript knowledge and use it to teach you Java by pointing out similarities and differences between the languages. Then, when you have finished Java, you can begin to incorporate Java applets into your Web pages to create a total site package for dynamic interaction using JavaScript or Java wherever the two are appropriate to your needs.

The Purpose of This Book

This book was written to lead you through the JavaScript and Java programming languages to provide you with the skills you need to develop scripts and applets for your Web pages.

If you are a Web page developer wanting to move your sites up to the full capability these languages provide, this book teaches you how to program JavaScript into your pages to allow them to interact with the user and their client-side environment. By moving all of your scripting to the client machine, you can do away with bothersome CGI scripting, which means maintaining not only your Web documents, but also the program files and directory structure on the server machine. With JavaScript, you can program into a single document, encapsulating your entire document into a single point of maintenance. If you want to change something, you can simply load up your editor and change it just like any other HTML document. After you have learned the intricacies of JavaScript, you can take your knowledge and move on to the more complicated, but more powerful, world of Java applets.

If you are an experienced programmer wanting to learn about these two new languages that you undoubtedly hear about, then this book will guide you through these languages and point out comparisons to and differences from other languages such as C/C++. Because Java and JavaScript are loosely based upon the C++ language, you should have no problems getting up to speed quickly and moving through both sections on Java and JavaScript, allowing you to start writing programs as soon as possible.

If you already know only a little bit, or have done any programming in JavaScript or Java, then this book can provide you with a single handy reference to both of these languages. The special reference section in the back of the book should prove especially helpful when you are writing out that long script and can't remember the name of a method or the arguments it takes.

The Organization of This Book

This book is divided into two sections. The first section, Chapters 1 through 7, present the JavaScript language, and the Netscape Navigator objects that JavaScript can interact with.

1. Introduction to the Java Family

2. JavaScript Fundamentals

3. Control Flow and Functions in JavaScript

4. Using and Creating Objects in JavaScript

5. JavaScript Built-In Objects

6. Netscape Navigator Objects: The document Object

7. The forms, window, history, and location Objects

Chapters 8 through 13 present the Java language and several of the Java application programming interfaces provided with the Java Development Kit.

8. Moving On to Java

9. The Java Fundamentals

10. Objects in Java—The Class

11. Understanding Threads and Exceptions

12. The Java Language, Utility, and I/O Class Libraries

13. Using the applet and awt Class Libraries

The Appendix provides several references for the JavaScript language and objects.

Conventions Used in This Book

Before you begin to read, you should be aware of several different types of print that are used.

➤ Print that looks like this is program code.

➤ Print that uses *italics* in programming code indicates the word is a variable—the actual word varies according to you and your situation.

➤ Italics are also used to indicate *new words* that are followed by a definition.

Also used in this book are icons that illustrate notes, tips, and warnings. The author made an effort to set these aside for your added information.

A note includes extra information that you will find useful. It complements the discussion rather than being a part of it.

A tip provides quick instructions for getting the most from Java.

A warning cautions you to be aware of certain dangerous situations that can arise during a particular step in a process. Make sure you read these carefully.

With these special fonts, bullets, and icons in mind, you will be able to read through this book with less trouble and more productivity.

Before You Begin

For the JavaScript sections of this book, you will need only the Netscape Navigator 2.0 browser and a plain text editor. You can check out Netscape's site at **http://home.netscape.com** for downloading instructions. After you move on to Java, you will need Sun's Java Development Kit, or any other Java compiler/ interpreter combination, such as Metrowerk's Code Warrior or Native Intelligence's Roaster.

Java is a language at the cutting edge of Internet technology. It has already been widely introduced into the Virtual Reality Modeling Language (VRML) efforts, and many companies have announced products either based on or tools for the Java language. It is an exciting time to be learning such a language, so be sure to stay abreast of all the most recent developments.

Good luck and smooth programming.

Timothy Ritchey
Cambridge, England

Chapter 1

Introduction to the Java Family

Welcome to the Java language family. The Java family is comprised of Java, Sun Microsystems' development environment and language, and JavaScript, an HTML (HyperText Markup Language) scripting tool developed by Netscape. These two languages support the development of dynamic content for the World Wide Web, and are built into the Netscape Navigator 2.0 browser. Because you are reading this book, you are obviously interested in what Java can do for you, and what it can do for your Web presence. In short—and forgive the dramatics—the Java family brings your Web pages to life. Whether by means of a Java applet or JavaScript function, many static, CGI script-based HTML pages are now being replaced by pages that provide dynamic content and automatic reaction to the client actions without recourse to server-side scripting.

The World Wide Web (WWW) is one of the fastest growing media for the transportation of multimedia information in today's technology-driven industry. What was an arcane subject for computer gurus a year ago, is now almost universally advertised. Many newspaper, magazine, and television ads now include WWW Uniform Resource Locators (URLs) for home pages of businesses. With this increase in usage comes the demand for more advanced presentations. The day of the text-based terminal is over. Full-motion video and interactive virtual reality in stereo sound are the holy grails that are being sought by Internet-savvy companies these days. Much development work is also geared toward standardizing such media protocols as VRML and MPEG II. In the midst of the fray comes Java—a new programming language that promises to make much of the potential of the Internet a little closer to reality.

The following sections provide a brief synopsis and comparison of HTML, JavaScript, and Java, including what they bring to the Web, and how they compare with each other. These three languages provide an entire package for developing dynamic, interactive Web page content—from the layout of the page, to the scripting of events and execution of full-blown applications. By understanding where to most effectively execute each language, you can create a powerful presence for those who view your Web page, as well as reduce overall development time.

Netscape provides a unified environment for dealing with the problems of creating dynamic client-side HTML pages with its integration of Java and JavaScript in a Web browser. Therefore, in addition to dealing with the language specifications that define ways to write programs for Java and JavaScript, this chapter discusses specific implementation details of these languages in Netscape Navigator 2.0 and ways that these features relate to running Java applets and JavaScript scripts.

The World Wide Web and HTML

The World Wide Web and HTML are a subset of the medium generally known as the Internet. The Web is popularly viewed as being synonymous with the Internet, because it is the most frequently used Internet protocol. In actuality, it is only one of many protocols used to deliver information over the Internet. A *protocol* in Internet terms is an agreed-upon format for transmitting information. These protocols specify the exact format of the data and how it is transmitted. Examples of such protocols are ftp, gopher, http (the World Wide Web), and e-mail. In order to understand the role of JavaScript and Java as client-side execution languages, it is also important to understand the HTML protocol, and the way it relates to the formatting and presentation of Web pages in a browser.

HTML is the first thing with which a Web developer should be thoroughly familiar when learning how to create a WWW presence. It is beyond the scope of *Programming JavaScript for Netscape 2.0* to cover the entire HTML language in depth; therefore, if you don't already know how to create HTML pages, it is imperative that you pick up a comprehensive HTML book—such as Ian Graham's *The HTML Sourcebook,* published by John Wiley and Sons, Inc.—and study it before attempting to take on JavaScript or Java. *Programming JavaScript for Netscape 2.0* will show you by example how the HTML elements work whenever there is an instance in which Java or JavaScript interacts with the HTML language. If you are familiar with HTML, you might already be acquainted with some elements of the introduction to the Internet that follows. Those of you who are unfamiliar might be interested in the historical background of the Internet, World Wide Web, and HTML.

History of the Internet

In 1957, the U.S.S.R launched the Sputnik satellite, much to the surprise of the U.S. government. In response, hoping to catch up and shrink the wide gap in the space race, the U.S. government created ARPA—the Advanced Research Projects Agency. The purpose of this agency was to research advanced technologies that were too risky for private enterprise to undertake, but were seen to be important steps in a technology-driven time. In 1969, the Department of Defense commissioned the ARPAnet to be created for research into networking protocols. Early on, it was realized that this network of computers would need a standardized protocol, so the TCP/IP protocol was created in 1973 to fulfill this need. This is the same protocol that still drives the transport of information over the Internet.

The TCP/IP protocol, or Transmission Control Protocol/Internet Protocol, is a collection of protocols that enable divergent networking platforms to interchange information. In today's computing environment, the standard for routing network data is Ethernet; however, when TCP/IP was developed, there was no standard for networked computers. TCP/IP should be considered a hardware-independent protocol that is carried along, on top of whatever hardware-based protocol is being used. This means that you can use Ethernet, ATM, or whatever new hardware methods for transmitting data that are in use, or might be developed.

However, it wasn't the standardization of the protocol that popularized TCP/IP. In 1983, the University of California at Berkeley released a version of their Unix operating system that incorporated the TCP/IP protocol. Because Unix was running on many of the computers connected to ARPAnet, the TCP/IP protocol became the de facto standard for connecting to the ARPAnet. It is interesting to note that this scenario is very similar to the current relationship between Java and Netscape. Alone, Java might be a difficult sale, but by Netscape's inclusion of the Java run-time engine in one of the World Wide Web's most popular browsers, developers and supporters of the language have a guaranteed audience.

In 1983 there were 500 Internet hosts. In 1986, the National Science Foundation entered the fray, by creating NSFnet, a backbone spanning five supercomputing centers around the country running at 56 Kbps. By the end of the year, there were 5,000 Internet hosts. In 1989, with more than 100,000 hosts on the Internet, NSFnet was upgraded to a 1.5 Mbps T1 line. The next year, the role of the Advanced Research Projects Agency in the Internet was finished and ARPAnet ceased to exist, with all of its functionality being subsumed by the larger NSFnet and Internet in general. What was once a purely academic research project was now suddenly the next big thing on campuses and large corporations.

Although it took 20 years for the original ARPAnet to reach the 1,000,000 hosts mark in 1992, within one year of reaching that mark the number of hosts doubled.

By 1992 there were more than 1,000,000 hosts on the Internet, and it was just beginning its meteoric rise. By the end of 1994, the Internet had over 4,000,000 hosts connected and in 1995, the NSF decommissioned the NSFnet. The role of the government in starting this fledgling technology was over, and private industry was expected to take up the slack. In March of 1995, the official number of com, or business addresses, passed that of edu, or educational addresses, for the first time, signaling the true beginning of a commercial model for the future of the Internet.

Development of the WWW

When the Internet began, it was widely perceived as an arcane and mysterious network useable only by Unix gurus and the strong-willed. In many cases this was true. The protocols and commands were a dizzying array of cryptic codes for sending bits of information this way and that. However, there were attempts at making the Internet more useful, and applications such as e-mail and newsgroups increased the everyday use of the Internet by nontechnical users in the early eighties. Of course, these applications were all passive—the files being transmitted were static documents or images that were set once by the creator and typically did not change that often without significant work. The e-mail file was just an electronic version of a letter, and newsgroups were simply electronic bulletin boards. As more and more users began to get onto the Internet, the demand for more useful programs grew.

In 1990, Tim Berners-Lee, from the European particle research laboratory CERN, developed a protocol for delivering different kinds of files over the Internet using a common protocol. This protocol was the beginning of the World Wide Web. At that time, the Web still had a text-based interface, and while popular, it didn't become the major force it is today until the National Center for Supercomputing Applications (NCSA) in Illinois developed a graphical interface for the Web. This interface was known as Mosaic.

Overnight the Web was the golden child of the Internet. It was impossible for Net surfers not to be swept away by its formatted text and fancy graphics—a far cry from what the Internet had been just a few years before. The text-based commands were gone, in fact, the command prompts themselves were gone! It was simply point, click, and poof, there it was—like magic. Of course, it wasn't magic. Pretty soon, you were including more than just GIF images or audio sounds, and once you got away from the files that the browser could handle, you were searching the Net for a program that could display the latest BIG THING on your computer platform, only to discover that your platform wasn't supported. Despite these inconveniences, navigating the Web with Mosaic or one of the many other graphical browsers was worlds easier than before, and browser developers were constantly including more functionality. Even though it was just point and click, you were still the one doing all of the work. The content being provided was still as passive and static as ever—it was just getting easier to make it do what you wanted.

Features of the HTML Language

The new language that drove the World Wide Web was the HyperText Markup Language (HTML). This language is a series of tags and directives inserted into a plain text file. These tags and directives indicate how the elements of the page are to be displayed. With HTML, you can do the following:

➤ Create platform independent documents

➤ Create links to other documents on the Internet

➤ Include graphics and multimedia

➤ Link to additional resources on the Internet

The first, and most important feature of the World Wide Web and HTML is that both are platform independent. This means that the designer of the Web page can create one file that will work on all of the PCs, Macs, and Unix boxes attached to the Internet. Because of the heterogeneous nature of the Internet, this feature was of primary importance. Because Web authors could not be sure what computer their file would be displayed on, to depend upon platform-specific implementations would be too burdensome.

The ability to link to other documents is where the term "hyper" comes into play. *Hypertext* refers to the ability to create links in a document that send the reader to related information at the push of a button. This nonlinear approach to document design is intended to aid learning, and increase interest in a subject by allowing readers to follow the paths they prefer, instead of forcing upon them the linear approach that has dominated instruction since the advent of writing.

In addition to displaying standard text in the browser window, HTML provides methods for including multimedia such as sounds, images, and movies. In addition, Netscape provides the capability to embed additional programs inside the browser window so that it can display more advanced media such as VRML and Shockwave Director files. By doing so, the HTML file is able to extend its functionality beyond the mere text representation used to create the HTML files.

The HTML language is also capable of implementing any new protocols that are added in the future. Because it uses a text tag format, any new tag can be ignored by a browser that cannot handle it. This feature enables different Internet protocols to be called in the HTML file, thus adding to the extensibility of the language.

HTML has proved to be a highly extensible and versatile language for creating documents and presentations over the Internet. When HTML was first created, the Internet and the World Wide Web were still text-based media, and many of the first Web browsers were text-only programs such as Lynx. In fact, in many pages you can see a "text only" link that enables users of these kinds of browsers to view HTML files that don't depend upon visual media such as image maps. It wasn't until Marc Andreesson, who later went on to start Netscape Corporation with Jim Clark, developed Mosaic at the NCSA that the Web was seen as a graphical medium. For a language to make the transition from simple text files to complex multimedia presentations as HTML has done is certainly a feat.

Today, there is very little text left in the resulting HyperText Markup Language documents. Sure, the tags and directives are still there to tell the browser *how* to display the page, but they are more often displaying pictures, running animation files, or calling up embedded inline programs such as WebFX or Macromedia's Shockwave. However, as complicated as modern Web pages can get, they are still based on the text-based HTML language that was used to create the simple text-based pages that got the WWW off the ground.

Hello, World! Page in HTML

Since the publication of Kernighan and Ritchie's *C Programming Language* book, a little program known as Hello, World! has been used to introduce individuals to new programming languages. In that tradition, as HTML, Java, and JavaScript are introduced, Hello, World! will be used in *Programming JavaScript for Netscape 2.0* to show the reader the differences and similarities of each language. In the case of the version of the Hello, World! program in this text, a few extras will be added to further display the features of each language.

HTML works by telling the client browser, such as Netscape or Internet Explorer, how to display not only the text, but the inline images, sounds, and other files that browsers and their helper applications now support. HTML performs this magic by using tags. Because you are most likely familiar with developing HTML pages, the details of how these tags work should not be necessary. Suffice it to say that these tags are interpreted by the browser, and instruct it how to display the page. The following code is a simple HTML page that displays the words "Hello, World!"

```
<HTML>
<TITLE>Say Hello:</TITLE>
<BODY>
<A HREF="http://www.mcp.com/~newriders">Hello, World!</A>
<IMG ALIGN=MIDDLE SRC="images/planet.gif">
<HR>
Send me some mail: <A HREF="mailto:tdr20@cus.cam.ac.uk">
<IMG ALIGN=MIDDLE SRC="images/mail.gif" BORDER=0></A>
</BODY>
</HTML>
```

This file can be found on the CD in the /JavaScript/HTML/
directory as Hello, World!.html. You should see the following
picture on your screen in Netscape 2.0:

Figure 1.1

The Hello, World! program as an HTML file.

This short program displays each of the four main features of the
HTML language that were talked about in the previous section:

➤ It is portable

➤ It uses media other than text

➤ It links to another site on the Internet

➤ It invokes a non-World Wide Web protocol

The first thing this HTML file proves is that HTML is completely portable. This book will return to this issue again and again in dealing with technologies that will direct the future of the Internet. It is essential that these technologies be able to run on the diverse platforms that are available to users and that are connected and running on the Internet. Such is the case with HTML files. Files are saved in a standard ASCII format that is portable across all computer and operating systems. The tags themselves are defined by an international committee, and as long as you stick to the specifications, you can be confident that your document can be displayed on any platform that implements the correct browser standards. If, as in the case of JavaScript and Java, you are not using the standard tags that all browsers are equipped to handle, there are methods this book covers later on that hide from unequipped browsers newer elements such as scripts and applets.

 It is important to keep in mind individuals who don't have the means to view or execute the latest protocols, and design your Web page accordingly, whether you are inserting JPEG images, VRML worlds, or JavaScript programs.

Second, the Hello, World!.html file brings in two images from the /images subdirectory and tells the browser to display them in the document. In other words, the file deals with multimedia, and has the capability to direct browsers how to display it. It is important to notice that in the case of the HTML language, you don't need to know anything about the actual image itself. HTML only defines how to display the image, and depends upon the browser to understand the niceties of decoding GIF images and displaying them. In fact, the HTML language doesn't even deal with the data at all—it simply indicates where the files can be found. You will see later on that the Java language overcomes this limitation, and can perform the data manipulation and display what is required for more complex behavior such as image drawing. You will also see that JavaScript falls somewhere between the HTML and Java languages. JavaScript is actually more akin to the scripting qualities of HTML, although it retains the capability to call upon a more advanced programming syntax. At the same time, JavaScript is unable to implement Java's more advanced low-level behavior, such as direct display drawing.

The Hello, World! program also illustrates a third point about HTML. When you look at the Hello, World! page in your Web browser, you may notice that the Hello, World! words are highlighted. You should be very familiar with the hypertext link that takes viewers to a new spot on the Web. This spot could be a target in the same page, a new page on the server, or a completely different site altogether. By using Uniform Resource Locators (URLs), HTML can dictate any file in the Web as a target as long as the file is accessible through the Internet. This is the hyper portion of HTML.

JavaScript and Java both use tags similar to the HTML's HREF and IMG tags to indicate files to load into the browser. In the case of Java, these files are compiled programs—called *classes* in Java parlance—which load and then run on the client machine. In future releases, JavaScript will have a similar option for loading scripts by using an URL. The ability to load scripts from the server and execute them on the client machine is a major element in the distribution of these new technologies. Instead of having the executables or scripts either running on another computer, with the results being sent to you (as in the case of CGI scripts), or already existing on the client and running there, the Java and JavaScript files can be brought to the client over the Internet dynamically, and then executed locally.

Finally, in the case of the Hello, World! program, there are two images. The planet is a stand-alone image, while the envelope is a link to send an e-mail message. The HREF tag used to send the e-mail message does not use the HTTP protocol, which is the transport method used by the World Wide Web. Instead, if you are using a mail-enabled browser such as Netscape, a mail composition window appears, and you can speed off an e-mail to the address indicated. This e-mail message is then transported using the traditional e-mail methods without using the HTTP protocol that runs the Web. This process keeps HTML from becoming overburdened with feature-itis, as some refer to the ever increasing size and functionality of modern applications. There was no reason for HTTP to implement its own mail system—it had one in place it could easily use. In many ways, this economy of features sums up the entire philosophy of the HTML language. The syntax itself is built around directing the display of many different media, without regard for the implementation-specific problems itself.

The Java Language

In April, 1991, a small group of Sun employees moved off campus to Sand Hill Road, breaking direct LAN connection and most communication with the parent company. Settling on the name Green for their project, work began on what they considered a move into commercial electronics. In May, 1995, Sun officially announced Java and HotJava at SunWorld '95. Over this four-year period, the Green group moved through consumer electronics, PDAs, set-top boxes, and CD-ROMs to emerge as the most likely contender to become the ubiquitous language of the Internet in the next decade. What follows is a history of how the Java language came to be.

When the Green group was first envisioned as a foray into selling modern software technology to consumer electronics companies, it was realized early on that a platform-independent development environment would be needed. The public was not interested in what processor was inside their machines, as long as it worked well; in other words, developing for a single platform would be suicide. James Gosling began work by attempting to extend the

C++ compiler, but soon realized that C++ would need too much work for it to succeed. Gosling proceeded to develop a new language for the Green project—Oak. The name came to Gosling when he saw a tree outside his window as he was entering the directory structure for the new language. After failing a trademark search, however, the name came to be known as Java.

Originally four elements—Oak, an operating system known as the GreenOS, User Interface, and hardware—were put together into a PDA-like device known as *7 (star seven), named for the telephone sequence used to answer any ringing phone from any other in the Sand Hill offices. The small handheld device was good enough to impress Sun executives, but they were uncertain what the next step should be.

The technology in *7 was at first envisioned by the Green team as a marketable product that could be sold to consumer electronics manufacturers who would place the company logo on the front of boxes: a similar concept to what Dolby Labs had been doing for years. However, in early 1993 the Green team, now incorporated as FirstPerson, Inc., heard that Time-Warner was asking for proposals for set-top box operating systems and video-on-demand technology. These boxes would be used to decode the data stream that entertainment companies would be sending to consumers all over the country for display on television sets.

Ironically, at the same time FirstPerson heard about and began to focus on the set-top box market of interactive television, NCSA Mosaic 1.0, the first graphical Web Browser, was released. Even as the Green technology was being developed for one market—set-top boxes, the field in which it would gain the most acceptance was just getting started itself. The Web had, of course, been around for several years by this time, developed at CERN by Tim Berners-Lee in 1990. Up to this point, however, the Web had still retained the text-based interface which reminded people too much of Unix and lingering DOS—a text-based interface that was quickly becoming obsolete in the new graphical user interface environment of software development. NCSA's Mosaic changed the face of the Internet by enabling graphics and text to be merged into a seamless interface from what had been a cryptic and confusing system of protocols and commands.

Java and the Web were both developed at the beginning of the decade, an ocean apart. It would take three years for the potential of the Web to be realized in Mosaic, and another two years before Java was made available to the wider Internet community.

At the time of Mosaic's release, FirstPerson was bidding on the Time-Warner TV-trial, where hundreds of homes would be fitted out with experimental video-on-demand hardware for testing. In June of 1993, Time-Warner chose Silicon Graphics, Inc. over Sun. By early 1994, after a near deal with 3DO fell through, and no new partners or marketing strategy was forthcoming, FirstPerson's public launch was canceled. Half of the staff left for Sun Interactive to work on digital video servers, and FirstPerson was dissolved. However, with the remaining staff, work continued at Sun on applying FirstPerson's technology to CD-ROM, online multimedia, and network-based computing.

At the same time that FirstPerson was losing the race for interactive television, the World Wide Web was winning the bandwidth race on the Internet. There was no doubt about it—the Web was big and getting bigger. In September of 1994, after realizing the potential of Oak and the World Wide Web, Naughton and Payne finished WebRunner, later to be renamed HotJava. Soon, Arthur Van Hoff, who had joined the Sun team a year before, implemented the Java compiler in Java itself, whereas Gosling's original compiler had been implemented in C. This showed that Java was a full-featured language, and not merely an oversimplified toy.

On May 23 in 1995, the Java Environment was formally announced by Sun at SunWorld '95.

Java took four years, and an evolution of purpose, to make it into the Internet mainstream. With Netscape Communications— maker of the popular Web browser Netscape Navigator—

incorporating Java into its software, 3D standards such as VRML possibly using Java for interactive behavior, and Java's potential in future applications such as intelligent agents, it is almost certain that Java is destined to be the most overreaching technology of the Internet in the next decade.

Of course, Java's infusion on the Internet is not the end of the Java mission. Sun sees Java's success on the Internet to be the first step in employing Java in interactive television set-top boxes, handheld devices, and other consumer electronics products—exactly where Java began four years ago. Its portable nature and robust design allow it to be used for cross-platform development in stringent environments such as consumer electronics.

Features of the Java Language

The Java language changes the passive nature of the Internet and World Wide Web by allowing architecturally neutral code to be dynamically loaded and run on a heterogeneous network of machines such as the Internet. Java provides this functionality by incorporating the following features into its architecture. These features make Java a promising contender for being the major protocol for the Internet.

> **Portable.** This means that it can run on any machine that has the Java interpreter ported to it. This is an important feature for a language to be used on the Internet where any platform could be sitting at the business end of an Ethernet card.

> **Robust.** The features of the language and run-time environment make sure that the code is well-behaved. This comes primarily as a result of the push for portability, and the need for solid applications that won't bring down a system when a user stumbles across a home page with a small animation file.

> **Secure.** In addition to protecting the client against unintentional attacks, the Java environment must protect it against intentional ones as well. The Internet is all too familiar with

Trojan horses, viruses, and worms to allow just any application to be downloaded and run.

➤ **Object-oriented.** The language is object-oriented at the foundations of the language, and allows the inheritance and reuse of code both in a static and dynamic fashion.

➤ **Dynamic.** The dynamic nature of Java, which is an extension of its object-oriented design, allows for run-time extensibility.

➤ **High performance.** The Java language supports several high-performance features such as multithreading, just-in-time compiling, and native code usage.

➤ **Easy.** Because the language itself could be considered a derivative of C and C++, it is familiar. At the same time, the environment takes over many of the error prone tasks from the programmer such as pointers and memory management.

The job of providing dynamic content for the Internet is daunting, but the protocol that succeeds will become as universal as e-mail or HTML is today.

Java is Portable

The Java programming language provides portability in several ways. Two of these ways are

➤ The Java language is interpreted. This means that every computer it wants to run on must have a program to convert the Java codes into native machine code.

➤ The Java language does not allow a particular machine to implement different sizes for fundamental types such as integers or bytes.

By executing in an interpreter environment, the Java code does not have to conform to any single hardware platform. The Java compiler that creates the executable programs from source code, compiles for a machine that doesn't exist—the Java Virtual

Machine. The Java Virtual Machine is a specification for a hypothetical processor that can run Java code. The traditional problem with interpreters has always been their performance, or rather their lack of it. Java attempts to overcome this by compiling to an intermediate stage, converting the source code to bytecode, which can then be efficiently converted into native code for a particular processor.

In addition to specifying a virtual machine code specification to ensure portability, the Java language also makes sure that data takes up the same amount of space in all implementations. C programming language data types, on the other hand, change depending upon the underlying hardware and operating system. For example, an integer that occupied 16 bits under Windows 3.1, now takes up 32 bits on Windows 95. The same problem exists across processor platforms, where some computers, like the DEC Alpha, are 64 bits, while others, such as Intel's 486, are only 32 bits. By creating a single standard for data size, Java makes sure that programs are hardware-independent.

These are some of the features that ensure that Java is capable of running on any machine for which the interpreter is ported. This way, once a single application has been ported, the developer and user have the benefit of every program written for Java.

Java is Robust

The Java environment is robust because it gets rid of the traditional problems programmers have with creating solid code. The Java inventors looked at extending C++ to include the functionality required by a distributed program, but soon realized that it would be too problematic. The major problems in making C++ a portable program are its use of pointers to directly address memory locations, and its lack of automatic memory management. These features allow the programmer to write code that is syntactically and semantically correct, and yet still proceeds to crash the system for one reason or another. Java, on the other hand, ensures a robust environment by eliminating pointers and providing automatic memory management.

Because the whole point of the Java programs is to automatically be able to load and run, it would be unacceptable for there to be a chance that one of those applications might have a bug that could bring down the system by, for example, writing over the operating system's memory space. For this reason, Java does not employ the use of pointers. Memory addresses cannot be dereferenced, and a programmer cannot employ pointer arithmetic to move through memory. Additionally, Java provides for array bounds checking so that a program cannot index address space not allocated to the array.

Java provides automatic memory management in the form of an automatic garbage collector. This garbage collector keeps track of all objects and references to those objects in a Java program. When an object has no more references, the garbage collector tags it for removal. The garbage collector runs as a low priority thread in the background, and clears the object, returning its memory back to the pool either when the program is not using many processor cycles, or there is an immediate need for more memory. By running as a separate thread, the garbage collector can provide the ease of use and robustness of automatic memory management without the overhead of a full-time memory management scheme.

Java is Secure

The necessities of distributed computing demand the highest levels of security for client operating systems. Java provides security through several features of the Java run-time environment.

➤   A bytecode verifier

➤   Run-time memory layout

➤   File access restrictions

When Java code first enters the interpreter, before it even gets a chance to run, it is checked for language compliance. Even though the compiler only generates correct code, the interpreter checks it again just to make sure, because the code could have been intentionally or unintentionally changed between compile time and runtime.

The Java interpreter then determines the memory layout for the classes.

The *class* is Java's basic execution unit—equivalent to an object in OOP parlance.

This means that hackers cannot imply anything about what the structure of a class might be on the hardware itself and then use that information to forge access. Additionally, the class loader places each class loaded from the network in its own memory area.

Even then, the Java interpreter's security checks continue by making sure that classes loaded do not access the file system except in the specific manner they are permitted by the client or user. Altogether, this makes Java one of the most secure applications for any system. Although site administrators may squirm in their seats at the idea of programs automatically loading and running, the Java team has made every effort to assure administrators that their worst fears, such as an especially effective virus or Trojan horse, will never become reality.

Java is Object-Oriented

Java's most important feature is that it is a truly object-oriented language. The Java designers decided to break from any existing language and create one from scratch. Although Java has the look and feel of C++, it is in fact a completely independent language, designed to be object-oriented from the start. This provides several benefits, including the following:

➤ Reusability of code

➤ Extensibility

➤ Dynamic applications

Java provides the fundamental element of object-oriented programming (OOP)—the object—in the class. The class is a collection of variables and methods that encapsulates functionality into a reusable, and dynamically loadable object. This means that once the class has been created, it can be used as a template for creating additional classes that provide additional functionality. For example, a programmer might create a class for displaying rectangles on the screen, and then decide that it would be nice to have a filled rectangle. Instead of writing a whole new class, the programmer can simply direct Java to use the old class, with a few extra features. In fact, the programmer can do so without even having the original source code.

After a class has been created, the Java run-time environment allows for the dynamic loading of classes. This means that existing applications can add functionality by linking in new classes that encapsulate the methods needed. For example, you might be surfing the Net, and find a file for which you don't have a helper application. Traditionally, you would be stuck looking for an application that could deal with the file. The Java browser, on the other hand, can ask the server with the file for a class that can handle the file, dynamically load it in along with the file, and display the file without ever losing a beat.

Java's High Performance

Typically the cost of such portability, security, and robustness is the loss of performance. It is unreasonable to believe that interpreted code can run at the same speed as native code; however, Java has a few tricks that reduce the amount of overhead significantly.

➤ Built-in multithreading

➤ Efficient bytecodes

➤ Just-in-time compilation

➤ The ability to link in native C methods

One way Java overcomes the performance problems of traditional interpreters is by including built-in multithreading capability. It is rare for a program to be constantly using up CPU cycles.

Instead, programs must wait for user input, files, or network access. These actions leave the processor idle in single-threaded applications. Instead, Java uses this idle time to perform the necessary garbage cleanup and general system maintenance that causes interpreters to slow down many applications.

Additionally, the compiled Java bytecodes are very close to machine code, so interpreting them on any specific platform can be very efficient. In cases where the interpreter isn't going to be enough, the programmer has two options: compiling the code at runtime to native code or linking in native C code. Linking in native C code is the quicker of the two, but places additional burden on the programmer and reduces portability. Compiling at runtime means that code is still portable, but there is an initial delay while the code compiles.

Java's Ease of Use

Finally, the Java language is easy. The Java language is simple and effective because of its well-thought-out design and implementation. The three most important elements that make it an easy language to use are:

➤ It is familiar because it is fashioned after C++

➤ It eliminates problematic language elements

➤ It provides powerful class libraries

Java is consciously fashioned after the C++ language, providing a look and feel that most programmers are comfortable with. At the same time, Java eliminates problematic elements of C++ such as pointers and memory management. This means that programmers can spend less time worrying about whether code will run, and more time developing functionality. Java also has a powerful set of class libraries that provide much of the basic functionality needed to develop an application quickly and effectively.

Hello, World! as a Java Applet

As can be seen, the Java language is a far cry from the limitations of HTML. Java is a full-fledged language in its own right, and can provide functionality unavailable to plain old HTML. The following source code implements the Hello, World! program again. This time, the additional images have been left out, and the program merely displays the text "Hello, World!" in the document. This simple program exhibits many of the features of the Java language.

```java
import java.awt.Graphics;

public class HelloWorld extends java.applet.Applet {
   public void init() {
           resize(150,50);
   }
   public void paint(Graphics g) {
           g.drawString("Hello, World!", 50, 25);
   }
}
```

Of course, this is not the only code we need. Notice the second line of the code:

```java
public class HelloWorld extends java.applet.Applet {
```

This code is saying to the compiler to create a class named HelloWorld that is a subclass of Applet. All applets expect to run in a particular environment, which is typically provided by a browser such as Netscape 2.0. This means that an applet needs to be called from an HTML file. The following listing is the HTML file that loads the Hello, World! applet.

```html
<HTML>
<HEAD>
<TITLE>Hello, World!</TITLE>
</HEAD>
<BODY>
Say Hi to Everyone:
<APPLET ALIGN=MIDDLE CODE="HelloWorld.class" WIDTH=150
HEIGHT=50></APPLET>
```

```
</BODY>
</HTML>
```

This file can be loaded into Netscape from a local disk by entering the path to the file with a leading file: directive such as:

```
file:///D:/Java Examples/Hello, World!/Hello, World!.html
```

Figure 1.2

The Hello, World! program as a Java applet and HTML file.

Additionally, you can browse the disk by using the File, Open File menu option and selecting the HTML file Hello, World!.html.

Pretty exciting, eh? Okay, so maybe it is a little less snazzy than the previous pure HTML page, but because the purpose of this example is to show the main features of each language, it wasn't meant to be snazzy.

The fact that this particular Java applet does not draw pictures gives a good indication of one feature of Java—as a language, it is very low-level. Whereas with HTML, a simple tag pointing to the image file is enough to get it to display; with Java, since it is working at such a lower level, in order to program that behavior from scratch, it takes a much larger example than belongs in an introductory chapter. At the same time, the features of the Java language enable you to build upon the work of others easily, while not limiting yourself to a particular browser implementation. When the HTML Hello World picture was loaded using the HTML file, all of the functionality was subsumed by the browser. As Web page developers, we depend upon the features we expect everyone's browser to have, such as the ability to display GIF and JPEG images. With Java, dependence upon these features is not the case. As an exercise, point Netscape 2.0 to the file java/demo/ Animator/example.html on the CD. What you see (and hear) running is an animation file written and compiled in Java. Running an animation file is not a feature of Netscape, it is an entirely new feature created by the Java programmer. Of course, if you care to look at the Animator.java file in the same directory that holds the source code for the applet, you will notice that it is 883 lines long. The power of Java comes at the expense of complexity.

Figure 1.3
The Animator applet from the Sun Java Development Kit.

Even though Java is complex, it is easy for the end user of a Java applet in an HTML page. Take a look at the HTML file example.html in the java/demo/Animator directory of the CD:

```
<title>The Animator Applet</title>
<hr>

<applet code=Animator.class width=100 height=200>
<param name=imagesource value="images/Duke">
<param name=endimage value=10>
<param name=soundsource value="audio">
<param name=soundtrack value=spacemusic.au>
<param name=sounds
value="1.au¦2.au¦3.au¦4.au¦5.au¦6.au¦7.au¦8.au¦9.au¦0.au">
➥<param name=pause value=200>
</applet>

<hr>
<hr>
<a href="Animator.java">The source.</a>
```

As you can see, once the class file is created, it can be used in eight lines of HTML code, as compared to the 883 lines needed for the class file itself. The page author simply provides the images and sounds, and tells the applet what to do. For the end user, Java class files are as easy to use as any other media. In fact, the main transmission protocol for delivering Java applets to a client machine is the HTTP service running on the Web sites that deliver the HTML pages containing the Java applets.

This book's coverage of Java will focus solely on its role in the area of applet creation and use, and how this role can be tied in with the JavaScript language. Java has a wider functionality associated with stand-alone programs, but for the Web page designer, this feature will be less important than the Applet functionality which is implemented by the Netscape 2.0 browser. It is for this reason that the stand-alone functions of Java will not be considered.

The biggest feature of the Java language to keep in mind is its object-oriented nature. In the program listing for Hello, World! you should have noticed some organizational features of the program. In essence, you have a class, which is Java's representation of an object declared by the statement:

```
public class HelloWorld extends java.applet.Applet {
...
}
```

The declaration `public class HelloWorld` tells the Java compiler to create a new class, or object, that is based upon the Applet object. Later on, Chapter 10, "Objects in Java—The Class," provides a more in-depth discussion of objects and object-oriented programming in Java. Suffice it to say for now that Java is an object-oriented programming language to the core, and all programs are required to follow this methodology. Thus, our Hello, World! program must define itself as an object. Everything inside the outside braces are what defines our Hello, World! applet, and this is the basic building block for any Java class.

Inside the object definition, you can see two additional blocks defined by the curly braces:

```
public void init() {
        resize(150,50);
}

public void paint(Graphics g) {
        g.drawString("Hello, World!", 50, 25);
}
```

These two statements are known as *methods* in Java. In addition to methods, Java objects, or classes, can also have variables, or containers, for information. When we look at JavaScript, we will see that JavaScript objects have the same properties. However, where in Java, objects are a requirement, JavaScript is much more lenient, and will allow more standard procedural styles of programming.

The JavaScript Language

Of course, the new arrival in the Java family is JavaScript. This scripting language has been implemented for the first time in the 2.0 version of Netscape, and aims to provide a small, dynamic, object-based language that is used to both create dynamic stand-alone scripts that can be embedded in HTML pages to create client-side interaction, and to interact with Java applets, linking together objects in a page. In addition, JavaScript will be available for server-side scripts in much the same way as Common Gate-way Interface (CGI) programs are used today. This functionality will provide HTML authors the flexibility to create powerful presentations without relying on a complicated system of CGI programs and server calls in order to process user input.

JavaScript, while linked with Sun's Java programming language, was actually created at Netscape, and is a completely separate language from Java. In its first Beta release, the language was referred to as LiveScript—relating the language to the LiveWire server protocol that Netscape was developing for its line of HTTP products. Soon, it became apparent that Java was poised to take over much of the job being performed by server-side scripts and programs, and that a client-side scripting tool would be useful. Because LiveScript fit that bill nicely, Netscape—in partnership with Sun—renamed the language JavaScript, and began to market it as the companion scripting tool for the Java language. The main connections between Java and JavaScript are the similar syntax, and the capability of JavaScript to access the public members of a Java class. JavaScript is a very useful lan-guage on its own, and can be used to create complex programs that can interact with the user without relying on network trans-mission for the running of CGI programs.

The JavaScript language is an interpreted script that is embedded or integrated in the standard HTML file. When the file is loaded, the Netscape 2.0 browser interprets the Script, and performs the operations specified. JavaScript only works on browsers that implement the JavaScript engine, and right now Netscape 2.0 is the only program that does this. Netscape has been a strong leader in the browser market, and the role that JavaScript fills in relation to the Java language is an important one. Therefore,you can expect other companies to bring JavaScript into their browser implementations as well.

Features of the JavaScript Language

The development of JavaScript necessitated a balance between a full-blown language such as Java, and a simple scripting language for controlling browser functionality such as HTML. Of course, the JavaScript developers did not want to compete with either of these standards, and instead made their language do a good job of filling in the necessary jobs that fall between these two implementations. The JavaScript language has several important features that make it a powerful addition to client-side Web page development.

> **Simple.** JavaScript is simple, and is based upon the syntax of Java, which makes the language easy to learn for those who are used to Java or C++ already. It is also a good stepping stone for those wishing to learn Java after JavaScript.

> **Dynamic.** JavaScript is dynamic, and can react to user and client system input without recourse to server-side programs, such as CGI scripts.

> **Object Oriented.** JavaScript is object-based, which means it can implement its own objects. It can also interact with objects in the browser and plug-in objects. In future releases, JavaScript will be able to interact with Java applets that are loaded on a page-by-page basis.

The combination of features upon which JavaScript is built define it in relation to the HTML and Java standards that have either already set themselves as the de facto standard for Web page development (HTML) or have come a long way towards achieving that goal (Java). It is important to understand these features, and be able to incorporate them into your own requirements when designing, building, and maintaining a Web presence.

JavaScript is Simple

The JavaScript language can be seen as a simple and compact design that takes on the basic syntax and control flow structure of Java in order to facilitate a quick transition between the languages. For example, all of the control flow statements that JavaScript uses are present in Java such as if...else, while, and for loops. In addition, all of the expressions for arithmetic, logical, and string statements are present in JavaScript from Java. This means that programmers are able to use a common language set for creating both Java applets and JavaScript scripts.

JavaScript is not a strictly typed language, and therefore variables are not declared as in Java. In Java, whenever you create a variable to hold a value, you must tell the compiler what kind of variable it is. From then on, the compiler will check to make sure that the variable stays as that type. This is known as *strict type checking*. For example, the following code creates two variables in Java. The third line generates an error because the two kinds of variables are not the same.

```
int number = 10;   // create a variable which holds a number
➥such as 1, 5, 100, 32,056 …
String text = "20"; // create a variable which holds a String
➥such as "Hello, World!"
number = letter;    // this line would produce an error
```

This kind of strict type checking is not present in JavaScript; a variable can be freely associated with any kind of data. When declaring variables, there is no need to indicate what kind of variable it is to be. This freedom has both benefits and drawbacks, but for most scripting, the strict type checking of Java would be unnecessary.

```
number = 10              // create a variable and assign it
➥the number 10
text = "20"   // create a variable and assign it the string
➥"this is a test"
number = text            // this would convert
```

In addition to loose type checking, JavaScript does not enforce the creation of classes and an object-oriented paradigm. This enables the programmer to use the language in the most efficient way possible without resorting to more complicated class hierarchies and inheritance. Instead of creating a class, member methods, and variables for a very simple function, the programmer can simply write the function itself, and call the function when the proper event occurs. This behavior will be detailed in Chapter 3, "Control Flow and Functions in JavaScript."

JavaScript is Dynamic

One great benefit of JavaScript is its capability to handle dynamic events in its environment elegantly. By interacting with the form input built into HTML and the Netscape objects available to JavaScript, the programs created can react to user input in an event-driven manner. This capability is an important benefit in developing client-side behavior without too much complexity and without reliance on server-side network calls.

JavaScript is Object-Based

While not a truly object-oriented programming language in the strict sense, JavaScript can be considered object-based—that is, much of its functionality comes from the interaction of the scripts with objects that have exposed methods to the scripting environment. These objects include the window, location, history, and document objects that Netscape provides, any applet objects that are loaded in a page, and any inline programs that have been integrated with the Netscape browser. By interacting with these objects, the JavaScript language is able to incorporate more powerful functions that these advanced programs can provide.

The JavaScript version implemented in Netscape Navigator 2.0 does not allow interaction with Java applets. However, future releases are expected to have this functionality.

The objects provided by Netscape to the JavaScript interpreter enable programmers to gather information about the execution environment, and alter the way in which documents are displayed accordingly. For example, you can access the document history of the browser session, and control where to go next depending upon where the user has been. Additionally, you can control the display characteristics such as the background color. Whereas with HTML you are stuck with one setting per file, with JavaScript you can enact these changes immediately without calling up a new page from the server.

In addition to built-in objects, you will also be able to access applets and inline programs that might be loaded by an HTML document. For example, you could load an animator applet, and call its stop() or start() method, depending upon events occurring in a form. You could alter the animation file an applet was playing depending upon which form item had the focus—displaying pertinent information for that control. This enables you to use the simple form creation methods available in HTML, and link them to a more complicated behavior provided by the Java applet. You wouldn't necessarily even have to know how the Java applet worked beyond the functions you called to get the behavior you desired. This capability to script together objects in an easy fashion is one of the more powerful features of the JavaScript language. As mentioned before, this is a feature slated for incorporation in future releases. For now, you can still dynamically load applets to be run in a page, but you cannot interact with them in any way beyond what it already available with standard HTML tags.

Hello, World! as a JavaScript Function

The following code implements the Hello, World! program in JavaScript style, and shows off the dynamic capability of the language.

```
<HTML>
<HEAD>
<TITLE>Say Hello:</TITLE>
</HEAD>
<SCRIPT LANGUAGE="JavaScript">
<!-- this line hides the script from old browsers
   function helloWorld() {
          alert("Hello, World!")
   }
// this is the end of the script and comment structure-->
</SCRIPT>
<BODY>
<FORM>
<INPUT TYPE="button" VALUE="Say Hi:" ONCLICK="helloWorld()">
</FORM>
<HR>
</BODY>
</HTML>
```

As you can see, the code is integrated into the HTML file. In a way, JavaScript can be considered a kind of HTML, but the behavior it invokes is much more complicated. Notice the creation of a function known as helloWorld, which makes a call to a function named alert. The helloWorld function can then be used anywhere in the HTML file to enact the behavior specified in the function declaration. In this case, the button created by the HTML code calls the function helloWorld when it is pressed. The helloWorld function then calls the method alert, which brings up a dialog box with the string indicated in the method call. The following screenshot shows the resulting display.

Figure 1.4

The Hello, World! program as a JavaScript function.

In the next chapter, "JavaScript Fundamentals," you will begin right away by going into the specific details of how a JavaScript program is put together, and how to begin using code in your own HTML pages.

A Comparison of Java and JavaScript

Now that you have gone over each of the languages in general terms, there are more specific implementation details that can be seen when comparing Java and JavaScript. The following table shows the different ways in which Java and JavaScript have been implemented.

Table 1.1   A Comparison of Java and JavaScript

Feature	Implementation
Execution	**Java:** Java source code is compiled before it is sent to the client to be executed. There still has to be an emulator or interpreter in order to execute the file on a specific platform.

continues

Table 1.1   Continued

Feature	Implementation
	JavaScript: JavaScript is not compiled at all before it is sent to the client, rather, it arrives as a plain text file, to be interpreted line by line in the browser.
Object methodology	**Java:** Java is a truly *object-oriented* programming language, and the programmer is required to develop objects for even the simplest programs.
	JavaScript: JavaScript is an *object-based* language that does not have classes or inheritance. However, objects of a sort can be created, and the language can interact with objects created in other programming languages.
Use in HTML	**Java:** Java is a separate format from HTML, and must be loaded like an inline image or sound file.
	JavaScript: JavaScript is plain text, and can be either integrated into the HTML file directly, or embedded, and loaded dynamically. Either way, the resulting code is still in a text format.
Variable declaration	**Java:** Java uses strong type checking, and all variables must be declared at compile time before they are sent to the client machine.
	JavaScript: JavaScript uses loose type checking in that the interpreter evaluates the data type at runtime and makes the appropriate assignments.
Object references	**Java:** Java object references must be available at compile time in order for the compiler to be able to implement strong typing. This is referred to as static binding.
	JavaScript: JavaScript object references are left to be checked at runtime. This is because without compilation there is no way to implement object reference checking. This is considered dynamic binding.

In addition to the previous features, it is worth noting that both Java and JavaScript implement a strong security philosophy, and neither are allowed to access the local hard disk.

Netscape 2.0 and the Java Family

Java and JavaScript are currently only implemented in Netscape Navigator 2.0, but many companies have indicated support for these standards. Java is in a much more mature state than JavaScript, and has therefore much more support in the development community. Companies such as Oracle, Microsoft, Borland, Quarterdeck, Symantec, and others are all busy developing Java-enabled browsers and development tools. By the time you read this there may be other companies which have released versions of browsers that are Java-enabled. Of course, Sun is working on its own browser, HotJava, which will support Java and JavaScript.

Because JavaScript is in a much earlier stage, there are no firm commitments yet by companies promising to implement JavaScript in their browsers. As the role of Java burgeons on the Internet, so too will the need for such a scripting language, and it can be expected that JavaScript will take on a similar importance. For now, Netscape 2.0 is the only game in town for implementing both Java and JavaScript.

Built-In JavaScript Interpretation

The JavaScript engine is built into Netscape 2.0 for every platform from PC to Mac to Unix. If you are running Netscape 2.0, you can run JavaScript programs. Netscape's JavaScript implementation is the de facto standard for the language now. The JavaScript specification is being placed before Internet committees in an attempt to position it as an open standard on the Internet. This means that other companies will be likely to implement it since they are freed from licensing fees to Netscape.

Built-In Java Run-time Engine

The Java run-time engine-enabled Netscape 2.0 is currently only available in 32-bit Windows (Windows 95 and Windows NT) and Unix versions. It does not support 16-bit Windows (Windows 3.x) and the MacOS. Although there is not expected to ever be a 16-bit version for Windows, work is underway at several companies, including Sun, to get out a Macintosh version. Unfortunately, the

Macintosh Operating System architecture is much closer to the cooperative multitasking environment of 16-bit Windows, which makes it very difficult to port a preemptive multitasking engine to it. Work is underway though, and a Macintosh version should be available by the end of the year.

Summary

The functionality and versatility of Java and JavaScript for the Web site developer are bound to make them a cornerstone of the next generation of Internet development. Each language brings unique features to the Web and to the development of dynamic, distributed applications that will bring the Web alive.

Java is a powerful and feature-rich specification that attempts to overcome the many hurdles in the way of distributed, object-oriented computing. Java has attained the portability, security, and robustness necessary, while at the same time keeping the language easy-to-use and at a high-performance level. Java, from its beginning more than four years ago in consumer electronics, is a powerful tool that predicted many of the advancements of computing in recent years. Object-oriented, dynamically extensible, multithreading and robust—Java fits in well with the emerging realities of the Internet and personal computing systems.

JavaScript supports the object-oriented features of Java and other Netscape plug-ins, and provides the means to stitch together diverse components in order to create a complex online presence. In addition, JavaScript is capable of powerful behavior itself, and can bring HTML documents to life by incorporating event-driven scripts. The ease of use of the language also means that anyone who can already do HTML can migrate to JavaScript easily, and then on to Java itself.

It is the aim of this book to take the competent HTML author from learning the rudiments of JavaScript to writing Java applets. Because of the close integration of the language, there is little overlap in the fundamentals, and what you learn in the first half of the book is (with only a few exceptions) applicable in the second half of the book. In the next chapter, the fundamentals of the JavaScript language will be presented. This takes you through the syntax of the language, and prepares you for implementing JavaScript in your own HTML documents. In later chapters you will use this information to bring in more JavaScript functionality. In the second half of the book, you will use what you have learned about JavaScript to begin coding actual Java applets.

Chapter 2

JavaScript Fundamentals

The first chapter of this book introduced the reader to both the Java and JavaScript languages, their development, purpose, and design. It is important to understand these issues when picking up a new programming language for the first time, because maximizing the usefulness of new technologies means using them for the right job. Of course, JavaScript is a derivative of Java, so many of the lessons you learn here are applicable when you move on to Java in later chapters. The different roles of the Java and JavaScript languages do play an important part in what you learn in this chapter; however, it is always a good idea to keep in mind where you want to go as you pick up new features of the language.

This chapter focuses on the fundamental programming lessons for learning JavaScript. In order to program in JavaScript you must know how to get JavaScript programs to run by doing the following:

➤ Learning how to integrate JavaScript into your HTML code

➤ Learning the syntax and general structure of the JavaScript language

After you become familiar with what a JavaScript program looks like and have learned how to place it into your HTML documents, you are ready for this chapter, which covers the following elements:

➤ The creation of variables

➤ How to use variables in different expressions

➤ How to use operators

Knowing how to create variables, form expressions, and use operators, as well as understanding the basic elements of style, provides you with all of the building blocks you need to begin coding useful JavaScript statements that can be incorporated into more complicated scripts in later chapters.

In many of this book's sections, you will run across places where elements of style in programming are discussed. Elements of style are not imperative to programming a JavaScript or Java program, but they become more and more important as you look toward code reusability and maintenance. High-level languages such as Java and JavaScript are designed to be easily read and understood by programmers (at least in comparison to older low-level languages, such as Assembler). Even so, creating easy-to-read code is more the result of a programmer's coding habits than of any language's features. Hopefully, you will find the style advice useful, and portable to any language to which you may move in the future.

JavaScript and HTML

JavaScript is interpreted from HTML files that are loaded into the Netscape 2.0 browser. This means that in order to use JavaScript in your Web documents, you must be able to integrate your JavaScript code with the rest of the HTML code. There are two ways to include JavaScript code in a document:

➤ Embed the code within the document

➤ Load the code from a separate file

In addition, you need to learn how to use HTML to hide JavaScript code from older Web browsers that cannot handle it. You also need to understand the order in which JavaScript code is executed.

Embedding a Script

In order to embed a JavaScript program into your HTML file, use the <SCRIPT></SCRIPT> tag, and place all of your code between the beginning (<SCRIPT>) and end (</SCRIPT>) tags. Although the <SCRIPT> tag will take several options in future releases, for embedding JavaScript, you only need to specify what scripting language is being used. In this case, it is JavaScript:

```
<SCRIPT LANGUAGE="JavaScript">
</SCRIPT>
```

After you have created the tags, any code inside is interpreted by the JavaScript interpreter. For example, the following HTML file uses JavaScript for all of the text output to the screen.

```
<HTML>
<HEAD>
<SCRIPT LANGUAGE="JavaScript">
<!--
document.write("<HR>")
document.write("This is a test of the JavaScript
functionality of Netscape.")
document.write("<HR>")
// -->
</SCRIPT>
</HEAD>
<BODY>
</BODY>
</HTML>
```

In this example, the JavaScript source is placed in the <HEAD> </HEAD> tags of the HTML document. This is not necessary; placing the <SCRIPT></SCRIPT> tag in the body will work just as well. However, unless you are trying to mix in JavaScript output with regular HTML when you are creating functions, and calling them with event handlers, your code will be more robust if you define the functions in the head of the HTML document. Doing so ensures that the functions are read before any HTML code that attempt to access it. If you are using the JavaScript code to format the page, you may need to place it in the body; otherwise, try to keep everything in the head portion of an HTML file.

Loading Script Source Files

Another useful way to load JavaScript source code into a page is by loading a file that holds the JavaScript source code. In order to load the source file instead of writing JavaScript source code directly into the HTML file, you can provide the URL to the file that holds the source code:

```
<SCRIPT LANAGUAGE="JavaScript" SRC="JavaScriptCode.js">
</SCRIPT>
```

There are two things you should remember when importing JavaScript code:

> ➤ The extension to the source code file should be .js

> ➤ The LANGUAGE attribute is not necessary if you indicate the source type in the extension

Therefore, the following code is equivalent to the previous:

```
<SCRIPT SRC="JavaScriptCode.js"></SCRIPT>
```

The advantage to using source files instead of embedding the code inside your HTML files is that you can update the source code without changing the HTML file at all. You simply replace the old .js file with the replacement copy. Of course, you must be careful that the new copy will work with the original HTML file. Although this feature is documented in the JavaScript guides, it is currently not implemented in the Netscape 2.0 browser.

Commenting out JavaScript Source Code

You may have noticed two codes that were inside the <SCRIPT>
</SCRIPT> tags, but outside the actual scripting code:

```
<!--
// -->
```

These two lines are HTML comments that hide the JavaScript
source code from browsers that are not able to interpret the
<SCRIPT></SCRIPT> tag. Everything between the comment tags
will be ignored by these older browsers. You should note the two
forward slashes (//) before the end comment tag (-->). These are
actually JavaScript comments that hide the end HTML comment
tag from the JavaScript interpreter. Why they are necessary will be
covered shortly. It is useful to mark these lines with explanatory
comments.

```
<SCRIPT LANGUAGE="JavaScript">
<!-- this line hides the JavaScript source from older
➥browsers
document.write("Hello, World! - try this on older browsers
➥with and without HTML comments")
// this is the end of the HTML comment tag -->
</SCRIPT>
```

Additional HTML Considerations

There are additional considerations when dealing with the
Netscape Navigator 2.0 edition of JavaScript and HTML files.
While these are not features of the language, they arise from the
interaction of JavaScript with the Navigator environment and
mean that typical HTML code might require some special attention.

First, <IMG> tags in HTML files can cause problems if they do not
have their WIDTH and HEIGHT attributes set. To avoid these
problems always set the width and height values for images you
use in your program. Including a <SCRIPT> tag after the last
image tag will also fix the problem.

Second, nested tables and forms can cause problems with JavaScript, so if you use tables to organize your forms, you might want to rethink the layout of your tables if you have created a nested hierarchy you want to use. In Chapter 8, "Moving On to Java," forms are covered in more detail, but because you probably already have HTML files you want to incorporate JavaScript into, you may need to begin to think of how the HTML will fit in with the JavaScript structure.

Third, there are several functions in JavaScript that enable you to send text output to the screen, including returns, tabs, and spaces. Traditionally, HTML browsers ignore any formatting information of this kind unless they are surrounded by the <PRE></PRE> or <XMP></XMP> tags. Be sure to use these wherever you have JavaScript output.

Processing Order

JavaScript code is interpreted within the HTML page after the entire page loads, but before the page is actually displayed. When you use source files, and call them in as SRC attributes in the <SCRIPT></SCRIPT> tags, this code is evaluated as if it were script container content. This evaluation occurs before any embedded scripts are executed.

Later on, when the use of functions is discussed, this book presents a more in-depth look at when scripts are evaluated. The reason for this postponement of the execution is because functions are stored, but not executed until they are called by an event handler. This can create interesting behavior that can work either for or against you. Be sure to check out the section on processing order and event handlers in Chapter 3, "Control Flow and Functions in JavaScript."

JavaScript Architecture and Writing Code

The JavaScript architecture is based on tokens that the interpreter extracts from the source file and executes. The following list contains JavaScript's basic tokens:

➤ Comments

➤ Literals

➤ Identifiers

➤ Separators

➤ Operators

These elements of the JavaScript language provide the basic building blocks of all code you will ever write. You can imagine all of these elements as different elements in a building that can be placed together in an infinite number of ways. It is knowing how each of these elements functions in relation to the others that enables you to write successful programs. How good your building—your program—is depends upon how good you are with the material you must work with.

This chapter contains the kind of syntax you will use when typing JavaScript code for things such as numbers, variables, function names, comments, and so forth. Many errors you will run into later when creating your own programs will come from typos and forgetfulness. The problem is that most of the information provided is relatively easy, and you might be tempted to gloss over it. You should still take time to read and understand everything. Your programming exercises in later chapters of this book will be be much more enjoyable if you have retained the material presented in the earlier chapters, so you won't have to keep flipping back and forth in the book to remind yourself of something.

Comments

When writing code in any language, it is important to remember to include written comments about what each line or group of statements is doing. In order to keep the JavaScript interpreter from trying to execute this text, you must hide it behind comment characters. Comments in JavaScript come in two styles. Table 2.1 presents the two kinds of comments available in JavaScript.

Table 2.1	The Different Comments in Java
Comment Type	**Description**
// comment	All characters after the // to the end of the line are ignored.
/ comment */*	All characters between /* and */ are ignored. These comments can extend onto multiple lines.

The older (/* */) style was originally used in the ANSI-C standard and is carried on in Java and JavaScript. The text that comes between the front comment marker (/*) and back comment marker (*/) is hidden from the interpreter upon execution. The /* */ comment is useful for multiple-line comments found at the beginning of a code fragment such as the one that follows:

```
/* The following JavaScript function converts
   from Fahrenheit to Celsius.
   created 11-Jan-95                              */
function fahrToCel(fahrTemp) {
    celsTemp = (fahrTemp-32)*5/9
    return celsTemp
}
```

If you need to comment out only a single line, there is a more useful syntax. The // comment method was added to C++ as an easier way than the older C style comment (/* */) to comment out individual lines, and it is retained in JavaScript and Java. You can either use this to comment out an entire line:

```
// this line returns the Celsius temperature
return celsTemp
```

or just the last portion of a line:

```
return celsTemp   // return the Celsius temperature
```

If a line of code does something important, it is useful to call attention to it with a short comment. It is always considered good programming to provide comments for all your code in order to help future readers of the code (including yourself) understand what's happening.

Which type of comment you use and for what purpose you use it is entirely up to you.

Two styles of commenting programs use the Sun and Microsoft styles for implementing comments in code. Most of the Sun documentation uses the following style for multiple lines because it is useful with the automatic document generator that comes with the Java Development Kit.

```
/**
 * this is a multi-lined comment
 * for the following function
 */
```

The /** tag on the first line is used to direct the document generator to use the comments as text in the resulting HTML file that it creates automatically from source code. This kind of comment is not used in JavaScript, but if you are moving on to Java, it is nice to get into the habit of using it. It doesn't affect the comment, but when you begin coding Java applets and want to comment a line, when you use the automatic document generator, your comments will be used to generate the text of the resulting HTML file. As with the standard comment, */ closes the comment block.

Microsoft program documentation uses the // comment in code, especially code that is associated with the Visual C++ environment. The following code is an example of a multi-lined comment in Microsoft documentation.

```
///////////////////////////////////
// this is a multi-lined comment
// for the following function
```

Again, the choice to use either style is up to you. If you are planning to use Java extensively in the future, and are using JavaScript as a stepping stone to learning Java, you should probably use the Sun form for comments, because it will be helpful when you make the transition to Java later on. If you intend to use only

JavaScript, the // comment is easier to use because it simply comments out the rest of the line, and you don't have to keep track of the beginning (/*) and end (*/) tags.

Including comments in code is an important habit to get into. Even though it seems as though everything is perfectly clear when you are writing your code, someone else who wants to use the code might have great difficulties in determining exactly what certain lines of your code are supposed to accomplish. Using comments also saves you many headaches later when you decide to update a JavaScript function that you spent weeks creating, only to find that you can't figure out how to work in new code without disrupting what you've done. In this object-oriented programming world, using comments is perhaps the easiest, cost-effective, and most powerful method for ensuring that code is readable and reusable.

Literals

Literals, which are used when entering explicit values into your code, such as 5 or x, refer to the basic representation of two types of data in the JavaScript language:

➤   Numbers

➤   Strings

Number literals can be categorized into two subtypes: *integers* (numbers without a decimal point) and *floating points* (numbers with decimal values). In addition, there is a special literal known as the boolean. A boolean variable can either be true or false. The boolean literal is included under numbers because in C there is no true boolean literal, instead, the integers 1 and 0 are used for true and false, respectively. Although boolean is being categorized as a number here, it should really be considered its own fundamental type. The string literal is any character sequence that is placed between single (') or double (") quotes. So things like "hello," "testing, one, two, three," and 'a' are all string literals.

Literals are closely linked with types, which are discussed in the section on declaring variables. The difference between types and literals is that literals are explicit values entered into the code of your program, whereas types refer to the kind of internal representation and storage that the JavaScript interpreter assigns to certain kinds of data.

Think of the small child's toy that has different pegs to put into the right shaped hole. It has round, square, triangle, and star-shaped pegs, and a set of holes to match. The holes that can accept the different pegs are the equivalent of types—they are the variables that hold the data. Literals are the equivalent of the pegs, or data, actually placed in those holes, or variables.

Integer Literals

The first literal is the integer. This literal, the most common of literals, comes in three guises: *decimal, hexadecimal,* and *octal* format. The decimal, or base 10 integer, is the most familiar, and appears in the way that you would expect. The important thing to note about the decimal integer is that it does not have a leading zero. The hexadecimal, or base 16 integer, is typically used as a binary shorthand, each digit grouping four binary ones and zeros. Hexadecimal integers are represented by the digits 0–9 and the upper- or lowercase letters A–F, which represent the numbers 10–15. These integers are preceded by 0x or 0X. Octal, or base 8 integers, are represented by the presence of a zero (0) in front of the digits. Table 2.2 gives examples of several numbers in the different formats.

Table 2.2 Decimal, Octal, and Hexadecimal Representations of Integers

Decimal	Octal	Hexadecimal
0	0	0x0
2	02	0X2
63	077	0X3f
83	0123	0x53
631	0771	0x3F1

The numbers used earlier in the equation for the fahrToCels function (found in the previous "Comments" section) are examples of using integer literals in a script. In this case, the integer literals are used to convert a Fahrenheit temperature to Celsius.

```
CelsTemp = (fahrTemp-32)*5/9
```

Floating Point Literals

Floating-point literals represent decimal numbers with fractional parts such as 1.5 or 43.7. They can be in either standard or scientific notation. Following are some examples:

3.1415, 0.1, .3, 6.022e23, 2.997E8, 1.602e-19

If in the temperature conversion you didn't want to first multiply by five and then divide by nine, you could use a floating point number, and just multiply by a single number:

```
celsTemp = (fahrTemp - 32)*0.5555556
```

Although carrying out only one operation instead of two appears to be more efficient, try typing in the following code, and replacing the line that does the calculation with the two previous examples.

```
<HTML>
<HEAD>
<TITLE>Say Hello:</TITLE>
<SCRIPT LANGUAGE="JavaScript">
<!--  this line hides the script from old browsers
    /**
     * function to convert a Fahrenheit
     * temperature to Celsius
     */
    function fahrToCels(fahrTemp) {
        celsTemp = (fahrTemp-32)*5/9    // this does the
➥conversion
        return celsTemp                 // this returns the
➥Celsius number
    }
```

```
        document.write("The boiling point of water in Celsius
➥is: ")
        document.write(fahrToCels(212))
// this is the end of the script and comment structure-->
</SCRIPT>
</HEAD>
<BODY>
<HR>
</BODY>
</HTML>
```

When you run both of these what do you notice? The resulting
value for the equation using the floating-point number should
not be exactly 100. In this case, there is less precision because we
have to round off the floating-point number instead of using an
infinite number of fives. On many computers, the storage and
calculation of integers is much more efficient than with floating
point numbers. It is better, therefore, to represent things with
integers, rather than floating point numbers.

Boolean Literals

The Boolean literal has two states—true and false—which are
represented by the keywords true and false. This value represents
the state of something that can have only one of two values. The
values are typically used as flags for determining whether to take
a certain action or not. The Boolean value is a true literal, and not
a representation of the integers zero or one as in C or C++. The
following code shows how you use Boolean literals.

```
flag = true
if(flag) {
    document.write("This line will print")
    flag = false
}
if(flag) {
    document.write("This line will not print")
}
```

The if statement is covered in greater depth in the next chapter. For now, all you need to know is that the if statement checks to see if the statement in the parentheses is true or false. If the statement is true, it executes the statements between the curly brackets.

String Literals

The term *string literal* refers to any number of characters enclosed in double (") or single (') quotation marks. Table 2.3 gives examples of some strings and their printed output.

Table 2.3 Examples of Valid Strings	
The Declaration	**The Result**
""	
"\'"	'
"Your Ad Here"	Your Ad Here
"Multiple\nLines"	Multiple Lines

If you would like to see what some strings look like on-screen, you can take our Hello, World! script and change the string in the line.

```
document.write("place your String here")
```

Reload the HTML page from the Hello, World! example after you have changed the string, and see how it has changed.

The backslash (\) is used to represent non-printing or conflicting characters. Table 2.4 lists the various non-printing control character combinations JavaScript accepts. These characters provide formatting of text that is not provided for in an easy way on a standard keyboard, and so must be implemented with a control code. They can be used in both string literals and variables.

Table 2.4   Special Character Representations

Description	Standard Designation	Sequence
Continuation	\<newline\>	\
New-line	NL(LF)	\n
Horizontal tab	HT	\t
Backspace	BS	\b
Carriage return	CR	\r
Form feed	FF	\f
Backslash	\	\\
Single quotation mark	'	\'
Double quotation mark	"	\"

Identifiers

Identifiers are the names given to variables and functions to identify them to the interpreter. Identifiers used in previous examples of JavaScript code include helloWorld, text, and number. What makes a valid identifier? In JavaScript, all identifiers must begin with a letter or the underscore character (_). All subsequent characters can also include digits (0–9). Letters are considered the upper- and lowercase alphabet from A to Z.

In addition, those words designated as *keywords* in the following section are unusable. Table 2.5 gives examples of valid and invalid identifiers in Java.

Table 2.5   Valid Identifiers

Valid	Invalid	Valid, but Not Recommended
watts	wattage #	WATTS
lightOn	light-on	lighton
monthsWith_31_days	5dogs	_number
x	abstract	$_243_fubar

In the case of the invalid identifiers above, the following rules apply:

➤ **wattage #.** There can be no white spaces within an identifier.

➤ **light-on.** The hyphen (-) is an invalid character.

➤ **5dogs.** Cannot use a number to start an identifier.

➤ **abstract.** Abstract is a keyword.

Of course, unless you have a non-American standard keyboard, using anything other than the "_" and "A"–"Z" letters would merely create difficulties in editing, so you shouldn't have any problems following those standards. Unless you have good reason, it is advisable to only use the "_" in the middle of identifiers (between words) to improve readability. This practice is of most use to Java programmers, but getting into the right habit now will help the transition later. Using descriptive names should provide you with all the flexibility you need. As a rule of thumb when you create identifiers, make all the letters lowercase except the beginning of words that appear in the middle of an identifier (such as in lightOn).

In C and C++, the standard is to name #define identifiers with all uppercase letters. JavaScript does not implement a #define, so for ease of transition, all-uppercase identifiers should not be used. This is not a requirement; however, this rule will come in handy when you are using Java, and it is good to not get into the habit of using all uppercase early on.

Keywords

Keywords are identifiers used by the JavaScript language, and cannot be used in any other way than that defined by the JavaScript language. You won't be able to remember every single keyword, so if you are having a problem with an identifier that is a single lowercase word, be sure to check out the keyword list in table 2.6.

Table 2.6	List of Reserved JavaScript Keywords		
abstract	double	int	super
boolean	else	interface	switch
break	extends	long	synchronized
byte	false	native	this
	final	new	
case	finally	null	throw
			throws
catch	float	package	transient
char	for	private	true
	function		
class	goto	protected	try
			var*
const*	if	public	void
continue	implements	return	while
default	import	short	with
	in		
do	instanceof	static	

* Reserved keywords, but currently unused by JavaScript

Separators

In JavaScript, the spaces, tabs, and newlines between characters are known as *separators*. These are essentially removed by the interpreter; therefore, how you use them is primarily a matter of aesthetics. For example, the following code fragments are all spaced differently, but they are all equally valid sentences.

```
celsTemp =  (fahrTemp - 32) * 5 / 9
celsTemp=(fahrTemp-32)*5/9
celsTemp    =    (fahrTemp-32)*5/9
```

How you choose to write your code is up to you. It is easier to read the first example with spaces between everything, but sometimes you will want to make sure everything fits on one line, so the second version may be more useful. If you are listing items, it is sometimes useful to line up statements over several lines, so inserting spaces helps.

```
name    = "Billy Bob"
address = "401 Chicken Holler Road"
city    = "Clinton"
```

```
state   = "Indiana"
zip     = 47804
```

Whatever the situation, remember that they are there to make the code easier to *read,* not to run, so go for what looks good and makes sense to a programmer reading it later on.

Declaring Variables

Variables are used to store data values in named holders that can be referenced later. For example, in the fahrToCels function used in previous examples, fahrTemp and celsTemp were variables that held the Fahrenheit and Celsius temperatures, respectively. One of the first things you do in most programming languages is declare variables based on what kind of data you want them to hold. This is typically done for more efficient code compilation, and also for strong type checking. *Strong* type checking means the compiler or interpreter checks to make sure that each variable must declare what kind of data it can hold, and then it is checked to make sure that no other kind is placed in it. Because JavaScript uses a loose type-checking architecture, there is no need to declare what kind of value each variable will hold. *Loose* type checking means that a variable can hold any type of data without the need to declare a specific type. Later, when we move on to Java, which is a strong typed language, you will need to learn how to declare variables.

There are two main reasons for implementing a strongly typed language: storage optimization and robustness. If the compiler knows beforehand what type of data a variable can hold, then it can set aside enough memory and not worry about it anymore. If it doesn't know and has to constantly adjust the amount of memory a variable has, many processing cycles are used, which can make a program run inefficiently. To use such an optimization, the compiler must be able to detect when the programmer is trying to fit data into a variable without enough memory. Otherwise, programmers could lose valuable information. In JavaScript, a variable can be adjusted automatically to make room for the larger data size. In Java, you would lose the data that overhangs.

For now, all you need to do is the following, and you should be okay:

1. Use a valid name, as defined by the section on identifiers in the previous section.

2. Be sure not to use a JavaScript keyword.

If you are familiar with languages, and the idea of declaring variables before you use them, keep that concept in mind because it will be useful later on. For now you can create variables wherever you need them. The act of assigning a value to a variable is what declares them in JavaScript. You use the equal (=) sign to assign a value to a variable, just as you have done in previous examples.

```
number = 10
name = "Steve"
cost = 10.99
isLightOn = false
```

One good piece of advice—try to declare all variables, and assign a value to them at the beginning of code blocks where they are used. This makes the function easier to read since you can see all the information you will be using right away.

It also is a good habit to make sure that all your variables exist in a known state before program execution enters a complex section of code. This means that if you have to go in looking for a bug, you at least know where all of the information is coming from. When you move on to a more strict object-oriented programming language like Java, this advice becomes even more useful.

Using 'var' for Variables

Of course, now that you have been told to go create variables wherever it pleases you, it's time to bring some order back to things. One problem with the dynamic interpretive feature of JavaScript is that it is very difficult to catch errors in code, especially in terms of variable naming. For example, you may bring in a JavaScript source file using the SRC attribute that uses the same variable name as a function you are embedding directly in the HTML page. Which one takes precedence? If you use the keyword var when creating your variable inside the block of code, this variable will be used instead of any other global variables that have the same name.

The following code shows how the var statement can affect the execution of a script. Try running this, and look at what happens:

```
<HTML>
<HEAD>
<SCRIPT LANGUAGE="JavaScript" >
<!-- hide script from old browsers

function test() {
  flag = true

  document.write(flag + " ")
  test1()
  document.write(flag + " ")
  test2()
  document.write(flag + " ")
}

function test1() {
  var flag = false
  document.write(flag + " ")
}

function test2() {
  flag = false
  document.write(flag + " ")
}

// end script hiding -->
</SCRIPT>
</HEAD>
<BODY>
<SCRIPT LANGUAGE="JavaScript" >
<!-- hide script from old browsers
test()
```

```
// end script hiding -->
</SCRIPT>
</BODY>
</HTML>
```

If you run this in Netscape 2.0, you will notice that the output comes out as

```
true false true false false
```

when what you might expect is either this:

```
true false false false false
```

or

```
true false true false true
```

What is happening is that the two functions that are used by the first function use the same name for flag. The function test1 is a friendly function and uses the var statement to ensure that it doesn't affect any global variable of the same name in existing code. Function test2, on the other hand, declares the variable flag without regard to any other code that might be trying to use the same name. Although this is a simple example, and you might think that a programmer should be able to keep track of this, in today's distributed computing environment, you never know where code can come from.

A similar situation could happen if some functions you needed were loaded using the SRC attribute, to which you then added your own code. You might know how to call the functions you imported, but you might not know what the guts of the scripts were. If the programmer was unkind, and didn't use var, and there was a variable that matched, you could have a function alter variables in ways that could be difficult to track down.

For this reason, whenever you create a variable, be sure to use var in front of it to ensure that it doesn't conflict with any global variables that might have the same name.

Creating Expressions and Using Operators

After you have created your variables, you must be able to assign them values, make changes to them, and perform calculations. These are the roles of the operators. Table 2.7 lists the operators, from highest to lowest precedence.

Table 2.7		Operators from Highest to Lowest Precedence									
.	[]	()									
++	--	!	~								
*	/	%									
+	-										
<<	>>	>>>									
<	>	<=	>=								
==	!=										
&											
^											
|											
&&											
||											
?:											
=	+=	-=	*=	/=	%=	<<=	>>=	>>>=	&=	^=	|=
,											

Precedence refers to the order in which multiple operations are computed. Operators on the same level have equal precedence. For example, the following calculation

```
a=b+c*d/(c^d);
```

proceeds by working from left to right on all binary operations (those involving two variables), computing those operations at

the top of the list and working down. In this case, because the ()
operator has higher precedence than anything else, the c^d
would be computed first. Next, the c*d would be computed and
that result divided by the result of the first operation. Finally, all
this would be added to b and the result placed in a.

Whenever you are in doubt about the order in which something is
calculated, be sure to use the parentheses () to specify to the compiler
the way to do things.

Out of this list, the first operator you need to know is the assignment operator (=). This does exactly what you think it does. It
takes the values on the right side of the equal sign and places
them into the variable on the left side of the equal sign. Even
though this is the easiest operator, it can get you into lots of
trouble. Later on, you will look at the == operator, which compares two values, *but does not change either one.* Instead, it
returns whether they are equal at the time of the operation. It
does not alter the right hand operand to equal the left hand
operand as in the = operator.

Casting Variables

JavaScript attempts to convert data from one type to another type
when needed, but sometimes it is unable to. This is a unique
problem to a dynamic language such as JavaScript. Because there
is no compiler to check whether assignments are correct before
they run, the programmer must be very careful when writing
scripts.

One example where JavaScript might not convert is when trying
to make a string into a number. As long as the string *represents* a
number already, the conversion works. If the string represents a
series of letters, the conversion will fail with an error. The following table (2.8) lists the results of almost all conversions.

Table 2.8	Conversions between Types				
		Target Data Type			
Data Type	function	object	number	Boolean	string
function		function	error	error	decompile
object	error		error	true	to String
Null object	funobj OK		0	false	"null"
number (non-zero)	error	Number		true	to String
number (0)	error	null		false	"0"
Error (NaN)	error	Number		false	"NaN"
+ infinity	error	Number		true	"+Infinity"
- infinity	error	Number		true	"-Infinity"
false	error	Boolean	0		"false"
true	error	Boolean	1		"true"
string (non-null)	funstr OK	String	numstr OK	true	
null string	error	String	error	false	

Some of these results might not make sense to you now. As you cover more of the language and begin to use objects and functions, come back to this list and compare how different objects convert to each other to make sure you understand what is going on in examples where conversions take place.

Arithmetic Expressions

Now that you have learned how to create variables, you probably would like to know how to use them. JavaScript has several operators that can be used on variables—some of which are specific to certain kinds of variables, and return specific kinds of values. Some of these values we saw in table 2.8. There are essentially three kinds of operators: arithmetic, logical, and string. The last three sections of this chapter present these different operators and their common usage.

Arithmetic operators come in two flavors: binary and unary. The binary operators require two variables to work on, while unary operators operate on a single variable. Table 2.9 lists the unary operators.

Table 2.9	Unary Integer Operators
Operator	**Operation**
-	Unary negation
~	Bitwise complement
++	Increment
--	Decrement

The *unary negation* changes the sign of a number. *Bitwise complement* changes each bit of the variable to 1 if it is a 0, and to 0 if it is a 1. *Increment* increases the value of the variable by one, and *decrement* decreases the value of the variable by one. Following is an example:

```
i = 0;
j = 10;
for(i = 0; i<10; i++) {
    j--;
    document.write(i+"\t"+j)
    document.write("<p>")
}
```

This script runs increasing numbers in one column and decreasing numbers in the other. Note the use of ++ and --. Each time these occur, the system either raises or lowers the value of the operand by one. This is how unary operators work—they change the value of the variable they are used on. For the negation and bitwise complement, the variable is not changed; for the increment and decrement, the variable is changed. The following code gives an example of the way this works:

```
i = 10, j = 10, k = 10, l = 10
    document.write(i+"\t"+j + "\t" + k + "\t" + l)
    document.write("<p>")
j++
i--
~k
-l
document.write(i+"\t"+j+"\t"+k+"\t"+l)
document.write("<p>")
```

Notice that j and i have been changed, and print out their new values, but k and l have reverted to their original values. When you use the unary negation and bitwise complement in a compound operation, you actually use a temporary variable that holds the new value of the operand. The increment and decrement operators are both prefix and postfix—that is, they can be placed before (++x) or after (x++) the operand. If they are used in compound statements such as

```
i=x++
```

or

```
i=++x
```

then the first line increments x *after* assigning its value to i, and the second line increments x and then passes the new value on to i.

The second type of integer operator is the binary operator. These operations do not change the values of the operands. They return a value that must be assigned to a variable. Table 2.10 lists the binary number operators

Table 2.10   Binary Integer Operators

Operator	Operation
+	Addition
-	Subtraction
*	Multiplication
/	Division
%	Modulus
&	Bitwise AND
|	Bitwise OR
^	Bitwise XOR
<<	Left shift
>>	Right shift
>>>	Zero-fill right shift

The following program prints the values of some operations:

```
i = 5
j = 10
document.write(i+"\t"+j)
document.write("<p>")
j = j + i
document.write(i+"\t"+j)
document.write("<p>")
j = j * i
document.write(i+"\t"+j)
document.write("<p>")
j -= i
document.write(i+"\t"+j)
```

Notice the last operation. It is a combination of the binary operator and the assignment operator. This is equivalent to writing j=j-i. This can be done with all the binary operators, and is a common form of shorthand to get used to. If the operator is

```
x [op]= y
```

then the expression is equivalent to

```
x = x [op] y
```

Take the time to place your own equations into the code. Add variables and try different combinations.

Here are some further notes on the integer operations. First, division of integers rounds toward zero. Second, if you divide or module by zero, you will have an exception thrown at runtime. If your operation exceeds the lower limit, or underflows, the result will be zero. If it exceeds the upper limit, or overflows, it will lead to wrap-around. Moving past the upper limit will place you at the very bottom value—approximately –2.1 billion.

There are also additional relational operators that produce boolean results. These operators are shown in table 2.11.

Table 2.11	Relational Integer Operators that Produce Boolean Results
Operator	Operation
<	Less than
>	Greater than
<=	Less than or equal to
>=	Greater than or equal to
==	Equal to
!=	Not equal to

The equal-to operator (==) can cause you endless suffering. Sometimes I still replace the double equal sign with just a single equal sign when I mean to compare two values instead of assigning the value of the right operand to the left. Make sure that you use the double equal sign for comparison. Try this application:

```
i = 0;
j = 10;
while(i<j) {
    document.write(i)
    i++;
}
```

Here, the control statement while checks the values of i and j. While the statement i<j is true, it runs the code fragment that prints i and then increases it by one. As soon as i<j is false, the program drops out of the while loop and finishes. You will cover while loops in Chapter 3.

Logical Operators on Boolean Types

The boolean type adds several new operators for logical computation. These operators are listed in table 2.12.

Table 2.12   Boolean Operators

Operator	Operation
!	Boolean negation
&	Logical AND
|	Logical OR
^	Logical XOR
&&	Evaluation AND
||	Evaluation OR
==	Equal to
!=	Not equal to
&=	AND assignment
|=	OR assignment
^=	XOR assignment
?:	Ternary

If you consider the boolean value to be the equivalent of either 1 for true, or 0 for false, the operators act the same as those for the integer operators if they are working on a single bit. Negation (!) is the equivalent of the integer bitwise complement (~) and is a unary operation. Table 2.13 lists the results of the operations.

Table 2.13   Results of Boolean Operations

AND			OR			XOR		
Op1	Op2	Result	Op1	Op2	Result	Op1	Op2	Result
true	true	true	true	true	true	true	true	false
true	false	false	true	false	true	true	false	true
false	true	false	false	true	true	false	true	true
false	false	false	false	false	false	false	false	false

The &, |, and ^ operators evaluate both sides of the argument before deciding on the result. The && and || operators can be used to avoid evaluation of right-hand operands if the evaluation is not needed.

The ?:, or ternary, operator works as shown here:

Operand1 ? Statement1 : Statement2;

Operand1 is evaluated for its truth or falsity. If it is true, *Statement1* is completed; if it is false, *Statement2* is completed. The following code provides an example of this operation:

```
i = 10
j = 10
test = false
test ? (i = 0) : (j = 0)
document.write(i+"\t"+j)
test = true
test ? (i = 0): (j = 0)
document.write(i+"\t"+j)
```

Note the parentheses. They are not needed in this example, but if you use more complicated statements, you might want to include them.

In addition to these operators, &=, |=, and ^= work as assignment operators on boolean values just as they do for numerical values.

Operators on Floating-Point Numbers

The traditional binary operations work on floating-point values (-, +, *, and /), as well as the assignment operators (+=, -=, *=, and /=). Modulus (%) and the modulus assignment operator (%=) are the floating-point equivalent of an integer divide. Also, the increment and decrement operators (++, --) increase or decrease the value of the variable by 1.0.

Operators on strings

Strings can be concatenated using the + operator. If any of the operands are not strings, they are converted to strings before being concatenated. In addition, the += operator works by placing the concatenation of two strings into the left-hand operand. You used the + operator in the previous examples when you wanted to print several items on one line. Try using the document.write() function and the + operator to make different combinations of output with the interpreter.

The left-hand operand in a += string operation must already have a value in order to work in Netscape 2.0. For example:

```
string2 = "Hello"
string1 += string2
```

does not work because string1 is not defined. However,

```
string1 = ""
string2 = "Hello"
string1 += string2
```

does work.

As far as using JavaScript for computations goes, you have now covered all the basic operations that can be performed on variables. You should spend time with the information presented and try experimenting with your own programs. Of course, even in the examples here, you used several control-flow statements to make the programs really do something. Control flow provides the basic engine that makes your calculations work. In the next chapter, you learn the control flows available in JavaScript.

Summary

This chapter covered the basic architectural components of the JavaScript language. These components included how to place JavaScript code into HTML pages, the concept of keywords, the declaration of variables, and issues of general syntax, in addition to a discussion of the operators that can be used to build up the computational aspects of a JavaScript program. In many ways, the material you learned in this chapter provides the basic engine for doing computations in JavaScript, along with the set of parts that is available when you begin to add more frills later on. There were several tips on how to format your code, and what is considered good coding practice.

What you have been provided with is where the real computational aspect of computers occurs. In the next chapter we will begin to delve into the organizational and control-flow aspects of the language where we can really begin doing some full-blown programs. The importance of these methods has already been shown in some of these early examples—for instance, it is difficult to do anything beyond the most trivial operations without control flow.

After you have the concept of control flow down, it will be time to get into functions and event handlers, where much of JavaScript's functionality lies. You will be able to handle events from form input controls and create functions that react to user input without resorting to CGI scripts on a server. The chapter you have just completed and the next will prove to be the most used aspects of the language, because they provide what is required for any programming you want to do.

Chapter 3

Control Flow and Functions in JavaScript

So far, the JavaScript language fundamentals have been covered, but beyond the most trivial applications, there is not much more you can do. In order to add real functionality to your program, you need to begin using control-flow statements and functions. These enable you to create complex actions that respond to the execution state of the script based upon either computational results or input from the system or user. *Control-flow statements* allow programs to pick execution paths depending upon certain conditions.

Control-flow statements are the basic organizational tools used in programming languages. JavaScript provides several control-flow statements that can be used to do the following:

➤ Iterate through code blocks

➤ Make branch decisions

➤ Return from function calls

➤ Allow the path of execution to be altered dynamically

Functions in JavaScript can be declared as stand-alone routines that can be called from additional embedded scripts or from event handlers in the HTML code, such as form buttons. In this respect, JavaScript differs from Java in that functions are not required to be parts of an object, although they can be, as will be seen in Chapter 5, "JavaScript Built-In Objects."

Functions in JavaScript enable you to do the following:

➤ Encapsulate often-used code into a simple routine

➤ Allow the use of event handlers in HTML pages that can create certain behavior based upon user input.

Besides the functionality provided by function declarations, declarations also provide an organizational benefit for code blocks that are executed more than once.

After you have finished this chapter, you should have all of the basic tools necessary for creating useful JavaScript scripts that extend beyond mere trivial behavior. In the next chapter, "Using and Creating Objects in JavaScript," you will begin to look at the areas in which JavaScript really excels—the use of objects provided by the Netscape environment and created from scratch in JavaScript code. This object-based capability enables JavaScript to access exposed methods and properties of objects, such as document, window, location, and history, along with built-in JavaScript objects for utilities such as date and math functions. Later on, this same capability is used to access plug-ins and Java applets in order to script together diverse components to build truly object-oriented Web pages.

Control Flow in JavaScript

Control flow is the method used to make your program move through the steps needed in the correct order with the least amount of fuss. JavaScript provides several control-flow expressions, as shown in table 3.1. Control flow is the heart of the JavaScript program, providing it with direction. Rarely does a program go through a single series of steps in order to produce its output. In order to have interaction, programs must be able to react to input and calculations, and make decisions about what code to execute next. In addition, if you need to repeat a code fragment several times in a row, it is a waste of effort to type in the same code block several times—instead, you can tell the JavaScript interpreter to repeat the code block. JavaScript provides control-flow methods for these and other situations.

Table 3.1	Control-flow Expressions
Type	**Expression**
if-else	if(boolean) statement
	else statement
break	break [label]
continue	continue [label]
return	return expression
for	for(expression1 ; expression2 ; expression3) statement
for-in	for(expression1 in expression2) statement
while	while(boolean) statement

In the next few sections, the if-else, break, continue, for, and while control-flow structures are discussed. The return and for-in control-flow statements, which are particular to objects and functions, are covered in their respective sections in the last half of this chapter, and in the next chapter. To begin with, a short statement about blocks and comments will help make your reading and writing of code much easier. Incorporating comments into your code early helps you get used to the idea and accustomed to reading comments along with the code fragments they belong to.

Using Blocks and Comments to Organize Code

The basic organizational method for grouping code uses the curly braces to define the beginning ({) and end (}) of code blocks. You may have noticed these braces in the function definitions from the previous chapter's examples. The following is an excerpt of that code:

```
Function functionName( arguments ) {
...
}
```

It is not important to understand the exact nature of the function statement right now. What is important to look at is the use of the braces to tell where the function statements begin and end. The use of braces enables the interpreter to know how to organize and execute the different lines, and how to associate them with the proper control-flow statements and function declarations. You will also run into these code blocks when you have more than one statement after a control statement. The following example shows how a single statement works with the for loop. Don't worry about the exact syntax of the for loop yet; it is enough to understand that the command tells the interpreter to repeat the statements that follow 10 times.

```
<HTML>
<HEAD>
</HEAD>
<BODY>
<SCRIPT LANGUAGE="JavaScript" >
<!-- hide script from old browsers
for(i=0;i<10;i++)
        document.write("for loop " + i + "<br>")
// end script hiding -->
</SCRIPT>
</BODY>
</HTML>
```

Run the preceding code and view the output. You should see a column of statements saying for loop 0, for loop 1, ... for loop 9. Now, what if you wanted to add an additional statement to be executed in the loop? Your first impression might be to add the new line that you wanted. Try it:

```
<HTML>
<HEAD>
</HEAD>
<BODY>
<SCRIPT LANGUAGE="JavaScript" >
<!-- hide script from old browsers
for(i=0;i<10;i++)
    document.write("for loop " + i + "<br>")
    document.write("second line of for loop " + i + "<br>")
// end script hiding -->
</SCRIPT>
</BODY>
</HTML>
```

Instead of printing out the new output on each line, the code causes it to place the output on the end. This occurs because the interpreter is not able to tell how many more statements it should run in the loop, so it just runs one. Otherwise, where would it stop? Two lines? Four? Ten? The way to guarantee that the interpreter knows how many lines to execute with the for statement is to use the braces.

```
<HTML>
<HEAD>
</HEAD>
<BODY>
<SCRIPT LANGUAGE="JavaScript" >
<!-- hide script from old browsers
for(i=0;i<10;i++) {
    document.write("for loop " + i + "<br>")
    document.write("second line of for loop " + i + "<br>")
}
// end script hiding -->
</SCRIPT>
</BODY>
</HTML>
```

You will run across blocks of code like the preceding in all sorts of statements, especially when organizing objects and functions, along with control-flow statements. If you imagine them as setting off a series of statements that act as a single unit, you should be able to follow the program structure.

Using Indentation for Clarity

One thing you might have noticed is the use of indentation in the code examples. Indentation enables the reader to fit statements in a block together at a glance without searching for beginning and end braces. Because spaces and tabs are ignored by the interpreter anyway, they are simply there for the program reader's convenience. Indentation is one of the most common elements of style used in programming, and you should definitely follow it.

The standard for indentation and block usage is to indent the code within a block, but to leave the braces at the indentation level of the previous code, as follows:

```
statement1 {
    statement2 {
        statement3
        statement4
    }
    statement5 {
        statement6
        statement7
    }
}
```

The preceding code is much easier to keep track of than the following, in which there is no indentation:

```
statement1 {
statement2 {
statement3
statement4
}
```

```
statement5 {
statement6
statement7
}
}
```

In this last case, you would be searching for braces, trying to match them up with each other, and generally having a hard time of it.

There are many good editors for HTML out on the Web that support all of the tags available, and help keep track of additional media such as inline images and sounds. A special text editor for writing your JavaScript code is useful, however—one that supports automatic indentation, picks out matching brackets so you can find the beginning and end of code blocks, and makes sense out of expressions that use several layers of parentheses. A good program is a shareware text editor known as Text Pad. This program is available as a 32-bit program for Windows NT and Windows 95 from Helios Software Solutions, and can be downloaded from many archives on the Internet, including www.shareware.com.

Another block statement concern is that of where and how frequently to place explanatory comments in the code. Programmers who are placing comments in code in order to document it often wonder how much documentation is necessary. For example, should each line be commented? Probably not, because this makes the source files ungainly to actually read, a move that is too far in the other direction from the typically under-documented file.

Start by placing your comments before all control blocks. Typically, all the information you need to provide someone is best presented in a block-by-block fashion; therefore, placing comments before blocks is a good rule of thumb to follow. Knowing what each block is supposed to do makes it easier for someone to check the code. More comments are not usually worth the added effort, unless a line does something particularly unusual or important.

Using If-Else Statements to Make Decisions

The if-else branch is the basic control-flow expression in the JavaScript language. Simply put, *if* something is true, you execute the first statement; *else*, do the other statement. For example:

```
if(a < b) a = b
else b = a
```

Note

Note that the expression evaluated is a *boolean*, not a number—unlike C, in which 0 = false and any other number is true. You must make some relational statement in order for JavaScript to evaluate the if statement. Because JavaScript automatically changes types to match the variable target, however, the zero and non-zero numbers are changed to false and true respectively. This is *not* the case in Java, so beware.

If you don't want to do anything if the statement is not true, you can simply leave off the `else`. If you want to have your program do more than one thing for each statement, surround the statements with curly brackets {}, as follows:

```
if(!lightOn) {
    wattage = 0
    roomDark = true
}
else {
    wattage = 60
    roomDark = false
}
```

In addition, if you want to string together a series of tests, you can do so as shown here:

```
if(boolean) statement
else if(boolean) statement
else if(boolean) statement
...
else statement
```

In this case, the boolean expressions at each stage are evaluated. If one is found to be true, it is executed; otherwise, the final `else` is executed.

Be sure to use the curly braces for your statements if it is unclear in which order statements should be executed. Here's an example:

```
if(x > 0)
    if(x == z) a = z
else a = x        //this else would be associated with the
inner if.
```

The preceding example produces an incorrect result if you want a to equal x only if x <= 0. Instead, block notation should be to make it explicit:

```
if(x > 0) {
    if(x == z) a = z
}
else a = x
```

You now have enough pieces together to write a program that does something beyond just sending text to the screen. The following is an example of a function that, depending upon the button pressed, outputs a different message:

```
<HTML>
<HEAD>
<SCRIPT LANGUAGE="JavaScript">
<!-- hide script from old browsers
function pickAWinner(number) {
    if(number == 1)
        alert("You win a Car!")
    else if(number == 2)
        alert("You picked the goat")
    else if(number == 3)
        alert("You get to keep your 100")
    else alert("incorrect entry")
}
// end script hiding -->
</SCRIPT>
</HEAD>
<BODY>
<FORM>
```

```
<INPUT TYPE="button" VALUE="Curtain #1"
➥onClick="pickAWinner(1)">
<INPUT TYPE="button" VALUE="Curtain #2"
➥onClick="pickAWinner(2)">
<INPUT TYPE="button" VALUE="Curtain #3"
➥onClick="pickAWinner(3)">
</FORM>
</BODY>
</HTML>
```

Obviously, the program doesn't do that much—unless you are on a game show—but you can see the way in which you can use the if-else statement to control the flow of the program, depending on the condition of certain variables. Figure 3.1 shows the result of the JavaScript code.

Figure 3.1

The if-else control in action.

The 'for' Loop for Repeating Code

The for loop is a powerful tool for looping through a series of instructions until some limit has been reached. The format of the for statement uses a variable to compare with a certain limit. When the limit is reached, the loop is broken, as follows:

```
for( i=0 ; i<10 ; i++) ...
```

The format of the argument (*ex1* : *ex2* : *ex3*) is explained next.

1. The first expression, i=0, tells the for loop where to start the variable and is known as the *initial* expression. In this case, i is set to zero.

2. The second expression, i<10, tells the for loop when it should stop and is called the *conditional* expression. In this case, the statement is true (that is, the loop should continue) for all values 0–9.

3. The last expression tells the loop what to do to the variable each time, and is known as the *update* expression. In this example, the i++ tells the JavaScript interpreter to increase the value of i by 1 each time the loop is run. This causes i to go from 0 to 9 through all of the intervening integers.

You could use a statement like the following to address the members of an array (that will be covered in the next chapter) in order:

```
for( i = 0 ; i < 10 ; i++) a[i] = 0;
```

The preceding code would fill the array with integers of zero.

The last expression in the for statement (i++) can be omitted, but be sure to do something with the variable in your statement—if the conditional expression was true the first time, you will be in an endless loop because nothing will change that status. The following code changes the state of the i variable not in the for statement itself, but in the code block:

```
for(i = 10; i >= 0 ; ) i--
```

An example of using the for loop would be to print a conversion from Celsius to Fahrenheit in five-degree increments, as follows:

```
<HTML>
<HEAD>
<SCRIPT LANGUAGE="JavaScript">
<!-- hide script from old browsers
for(cels = 0; cels <= 100; cels += 5) {
    fahr = cels * 9 / 5 + 32
    document.write(cels + " " + fahr + "<br>")
}
// end script hiding -->
</SCRIPT>
</HEAD>
<BODY>
</BODY>
</HTML>
```

Warning

Be careful if you use the variable that is being used as the index for the for loop (such as `cels` in the previous example) within the actual block of code. If you change the number somewhere within the for statement block, it could alter the number of times the loop executes. In addition, this might not occur in the most obvious manner, so tracking down the bug could be difficult.

You can use for loops in many places—for array indexing, anywhere a series of numbers is needed, or anytime something has to execute a specific number of times, such as a time delay. You will understand why arrays are useful in the next chapter.

Using Conditional While Loops

```
while(condition) statement
```

The statement is identical in format to the for and if-else loops in that either single statements, or multiple statements surrounded in a block, can be used. You can mimic the behavior of a for loop using while as seen in the following code.

```
i = 0;
while(i < 10) {
    i++
    document.write("loop " + i)
}
```

The for loop is more compact, and makes for easier reading when dealing with a series of numbers. The while loop is better equipped for establishing the condition of more complicated statements, such as the following:

```
while(intruderInHouse && !policePresent) {
    soundAlarm()
    intruderInHouse = checkForIntruder()
    policePresent = checkForPolice()
}
```

Typically, you will need to check for some external change in the state of a variable, such as `intruderInHouse`, in order to reevaluate each conditional variable that would need to change. The important thing with while statements is ensuring that you can actually get out of them, meaning that the code you execute in the while block must actually change the state of the expression you are checking in the statement itself.

Using 'break' and 'continue' to Control Loops

The break statement is used when you need to exit a looping statement such as while or for immediately. The break statement continues execution at the first statement past the closing brace. You might want to use a break statement to test for a possible error condition before a computation. The following code checks to make sure the denominator in a division operation is not zero before proceeding:

```
for(i=0;i<20;i++) {
    if(denominator == 0) break
    result[i] = numerator/denominator
    // update numbers
}
```

In this case, the for loop runs until either i is 19, or the denominator equals zero. Because you don't want to divide by zero, you have the loop break so that it doesn't throw an error.

The continue statement is used when you don't want to execute any of the statements from that point to the end of the block, but want the loop to carry on with the next iteration. In the case of the previous example, if a denominator was zero, then the loop would break, and the rest of the array would not be filled. Instead, you can use continue, which not only skips the actual process of updating the array, but skips past the calculation that would throw an error. The following code allows the for loop to continue, but skips any divisions where the denominator is zero:

```
for(i=0;i<20;i++) {
    if(denominator == 0) continue
    result[i] = numerator/denominator
    // update numbers
}
```

Both of these statements can be used with the for and while loops to either break out of the loop completely when it might otherwise fail, or skip the remaining code in the loop block, and continue with the rest of the loop.

Warning

Make sure you attempt to catch all problems (such as division by zero) before they become an issue to the user. Because these programs will be running on remote systems, it is important that they be as robust as possible. In Java, a more complex system for catching exceptions is used, but this system is not available in JavaScript. Getting into the habit of looking for such problems now can get you in a good position for handling exceptions later.

Creating Functions in JavaScript

The use of functions in JavaScript serves several purposes. JavaScript functions can be used to organize blocks of code that recur several times in a JavaScript program. By placing this code in a function, the programmer can encapsulate behavior and use a single command to invoke complex actions without the repetition of typing in long code every time it is needed. In addition to the greater readability and ease in programming that functions create, they also help in the actual programming of the code inside the functions—the programmer can concentrate on the actions required by the function code in isolation from the rest of the program. This modular programming idiom is the basis for much of the increased functionality of object-oriented programming.

JavaScript functions also are the basis for creating *event handlers*, which allow a JavaScript-enhanced Web page to react to user events without relying on server-side scripting and network calls. This is one of the most important requirements of the JavaScript function as it pertains to the extension of HTML capabilities. You have already seen examples of functions used as arguments for event handlers, so you should be familiar with this idea. In the next section, you will go through a step-by-step process of creating functions and using them as event handlers.

In order to create a function in JavaScript, you must declare it by using the function statement:

```
function functionName(arguments) {
…
}
```

This statement creates a function that can be called using the following statement:

```
functionName(arguments)
```

For example, say you want a function that will convert between Fahrenheit, Celsius, and Kelvin. The first thing you need to ask yourself is what this function needs in order to perform this calculation. In this case, it needs to know what the temperature to convert is, what scale that temperature is in, and what scale to convert to. Therefore, your function needs to take three arguments: temp, fromScale, and toScale. The function statement would look like the following code:

```
function tempConvert(temp, fromScale, toScale) {
...
}
```

This defines the function. Once it has been established what the function needs to do, and the arguments it takes, the body of the function can be created, as follows:

```
function tempConvert(fromTemp, cType) {
    var toTemp = 0
    cType.toUpperCase()
    if(cType =="CK")
        toTemp = temp + 273.15
    else if(cType == "CF")
        toTemp = temp * 9 / 5 + 32
    else if(cType == "FK")
        toTemp = ((temp - 32)* 5 / 9) + 273.15
    else if(cType == "FC")
        toTemp = (temp - 32) * 5 / 9
    else if(cType == "KC")
        toTemp = temp - 273.15
    else if(cType == "KF")
        toTemp = ((temp - 273.15) * 9 / 5) + 32
    else {
        alert("Error - arguments incorrect")
        return fromTemp
    }
    return toTemp
}
```

In this version of the conversion function, it takes a temperature, which can either be an integer or a floating-point number, and a string, which indicates which conversion should be done. Then, using this information, the conversion is made, and returned to the calling statement.

A note of advice: It is optimal if you can place all of your function declarations inside the <HEAD></HEAD> tag, because this is read and interpreted before the rest of the Web page. This makes sure that any functions that might be called in the main HTML document are loaded into memory.

Using the 'return' Statement in a Function

You may have noticed two statements that use the return keyword. These statements are used to send values back to the statement that called the function. For example, say you wanted to convert the temperature of 100 degrees Celsius to its equivalent in Fahrenheit. You might call the function in a JavaScript later on in the page by invoking the function as follows:

```
newTemp = tempConvert(100,"CF")
```

In this case, newTemp would now be equal to 212. Notice that instead of requiring that you write the equation for the conversion every time, you only need to provide the necessary information for the function to return the correct value. In addition to sending back the correct answer, if the conversion type is unknown, then an alert dialog box opens up, and the original temperature returns to the calling statement.

Using 'var' in Functions

You may have noticed the use of the var statement in front of the variable declaration for toTemp. You can use the var statement when you want to make sure that the variable is completely local. In the case of the toTemp variable, you don't know if that variable has already been used somewhere else. Because you don't want to inadvertently change data in a global variable, you should make sure that all variables declared and used in a function are declared as var to ensure protection of possible variables sharing the same name.

Using var is a good habit to get into, and increases the safety and reliability of your code.

One related issue: In addition to ensuring that you don't inadvertently alter global variables by using the var statement, it is also important from a design standpoint that you refrain from altering global variables intentionally. Whatever variables you need should be created as local vars, or sent as arguments that can be used by the function. This way, you are assured that your functions will be portable to other HTML pages, and that they can be mixed in with scripts without requiring that you know the implementation details, or have to worry about how the variables might conflict.

Allowing for Variable Argument Lengths

You might want to have a function that can take several numbers of arguments. In this case, how do you know how many arguments have been passed to your function? In this case, you can use the arguments variable, which is an array that holds the values of all of the arguments passed to the function. You might, for example, have a function that takes four arguments, but only requires one:

```
function setNumber(number, areaCode, countryCode, extension)
{
...
}
```

The number of arguments passed is stored in the variable arguments.length. By checking the number stored in arguments.length, you will know how many have been passed to the function.

```
function setNumber(number, areaCode, countryCode, extension)
{
    argc = setNumber.arguments.length;
    number = number;
    if(argc.length > 1)
        areaCode = areaCode;
    if(argc.length > 2)
        countryCode = countryCode;
    if(argc.length > 3)
        extension = extension;

// then do something with the number
...
}
```

In this case, the function could store the values of the phone number depending upon which were given. Because only the first number would necessarily be given, it can check to make sure that it has information to deal with each type of number be it long distance, international, or to a local exchange.

Arguments are actually arrays. Although most languages have built-in array types for holding variables, JavaScript does not, except for those provided by the language environment such as arguments and elements you will see later. For more information on arrays, see Chapter 4, "Using and Creating Objects in JavaScript."

Using Functions and Events

In order to use functions, you must either call them in a script or as an event handler. Calling functions in scripts is a rather simple affair, and requires only that you call the function by using the name and include the required arguments. The tempConvert function, for example, can be used to create values for a temperature conversion table, as follows:

```
<HTML>
<HEAD>
<SCRIPT LANGUAGE="JavaScript">
<!-- begin hiding of script
function tempConvert(fromTemp, cType) {
    var toTemp = 0
    cType.toUpperCase()
    if(cType =="CK")
        toTemp = fromTemp + 273.15
    else if(cType == "CF")
        toTemp = fromTemp * 9 / 5 + 32
    else if(cType == "FK")
        toTemp = ((fromTemp - 32)* 5 / 9) + 273.15
    else if(cType == "FC")
        toTemp = (fromTemp - 32) * 5 / 9
    else if(cType == "KC")
        toTemp = fromTemp - 273.15
    else if(cType == "KF")
```

```
            toTemp = ((fromTemp - 273.15) * 9 / 5) + 32
      else {
          alert("Error - arguments incorrect")
          return fromTemp
      }
      return toTemp
}
// end script hiding -->
</SCRIPT>
</HEAD>
<BODY>
<PRE>
<SCRIPT LANGUAGE="JavaScript">
<!-- begin hiding of script
document.write("Celsius\tKelvin\tFahrenheit\n")
for(i=0;i<100; i+=5) document.write(i + "\t" +
➥tempConvert(i,"CK") + "\t" + tempConvert(i,"CF") + "<br>")
// end script hiding -->
</SCRIPT>
</PRE>
</BODY>
</HTML>
```

Figure 3.2 shows the resulting output of the JavaScript code in an HTML page. You should notice the use of the <PRE></PRE> tags before and after the <SCRIPT></SCRIPT> tag. These enable you to use the text formatting characters such as tabs, spaces, and newlines in order to format the display of text on-screen without resorting to HTML tags.

Triggering Functions Using Event Handlers

Of course, there is another way in which functions can be used, and that is as an event handler for objects. The use of forms and handling events will be discussed in more detail in Chapter 7, but because you have already used event handlers before in the example code which used form buttons, it is worth mentioning them here.

Figure 3.2

The tempConvert method in action.

Table 3.2	Events that JavaScript Can Handle
Event	**Object**
Focus	Text fields, text areas, selections
Blur	Text fields, text areas, selections
Change	Text fields, text areas, selections
Click	Buttons, radio buttons, check boxes, submit buttons, reset buttons, links
Select	Text fields, text areas
MouseOver	Links

In order to process an event for a field, an event handler attribute must be added to the tag for the field. You can cause a button to invoke a dialog box using the following tag:

```
<FORM>
<INPUT TYPE="button" VALUE="Test" onClick="alert('This is a
test')">
</FORM>
```

The onClick attribute tells the interpreter what JavaScript code to run when the designated event occurs. In this example, the alert function is built into the JavaScript language, but you can also substitute new functions. One item to note is the use of single quotes in order to demarcate HTML tag attributes from function arguments. The limitations of text in HTML dictate that quotations being sent to JavaScript functions or variables are of a different quote style than that used to indicate what is to be executed for the event handler. For this reason, if you use onClick=" ... ", you must use single quotes inside, as in the following code fragment. If you use onClick=' ... ', you must use double quotes for any statements inside. Of course, you don't have to call a function. You can also place plain JavaScript code in this attribute tag, separating statements using a semicolon (;):

```
<FORM>
<INPUT TYPE="button" VALUE="Test" onClick="i++; buttonPressed
= 'Test'">
</FORM>
```

The use of a single function makes this code much more modular by allowing changes in the code to be made in one place, not to mention the fact that a single function call makes the event handler easier to read.

The next chapter provides a more in-depth discussion of event handlers, and presents form objects and examples of the events they handle. For now, it is important to see how functions can be used in relation to the event handler, and to get a feel for the overall usability of the function declaration.

Note

Later on, as you begin to look at the objects provided by the JavaScript language, such as form elements, you will be able to access the event handler of these elements directly. Although HTML enables you to set the event handler by calling onClick, ONCLICK, or onclick, because of the way the JavaScript symbols are stored, if you want to refer to an event handler by name, you must use all lowercase letters, such as onclick.

Summary

The use of control-flow and function statements are simple yet powerful means for creating smooth-flowing, modular, easy-to-maintain scripts for HTML pages. These features of the language will be used time and again in the first half of this book, and many of them will be used in Java. In fact, almost all programming examples will include at least one of these items in order to allow behavior complex enough that doing anything with it is worthwhile.

In the next chapter, the JavaScript basics will be moved aside for more complicated matters. It is time to begin looking at objects: how to create them in JavaScript, how to use them, and what objects are available in the basic Netscape environment. Of all the chapters on JavaScript in the book, the next chapter is the most important. Be sure that you understand all of the basic tenets of the language before moving on, because quite a bit of this background information is required in order to develop object-based scripts for your HTML pages.

Chapter 4

Using and Creating Objects in JavaScript

One of the most important features of the JavaScript language is its ability to create and use objects. These objects enable the programmer to implement powerful models for application development. These models not only ease design and implementation details of complex programs, but also allow you to bring together previously created objects for use in current projects. Chapter 10, "Objects in Java—The Class," provides a more in-depth look at object-oriented programming, and the ways in which JavaScript and Java implement the object-oriented paradigm.

JavaScript's implementation of objects is not considered fully object-oriented because it does not provide many of the basic functions of object-oriented languages such as abstraction, inheritance, and encapsulation. Because of this limitation, JavaScript is not able to create objects like those available in the Java language. Its capability to *use* objects that have been created in other more traditional *object-oriented programming* (OOP) languages such as Java has lead JavaScript designers to call JavaScript an object-based language. For JavaScript to implement the full object-oriented paradigm would be considered overkill, and would miss the main point of the language: to script simple programs for execution in HTML pages that can tie together objects that exist in the browser environment, such as Java applets. A fully object-oriented programming language already exists in Java. It is JavaScript's job to pull together the more complex objects created in languages such as Java into a unified structure. JavaScript does this by providing an HTML-based language that can easily be implemented by Web page developers.

Although Java's object-based language architecture does not provide many of the most common features of OOP languages such as inheritance, encapsulation, and abstraction, it does provide a means of creating objects that can have properties and methods, much like those found in the Java class structure. The benefit of using objects in a JavaScript program is that once you create the object implementation, you can reuse the class in much the same way as you are able to reuse the functions created in the previous chapter. Besides creating objects, you can also use the object structure to create the JavaScript equivalent of an array. In addition to objects that you can create yourself, JavaScript and the Netscape environment provide several objects that can be used in your JavaScript programs. Chapters 5 through 7 will cover these objects in more detail. For now, this chapter covers objects in two respects:

➤ Techniques for using objects that already exist

➤ Creating your own objects

After you have learned how to interact with objects and create your own, you have learned the fundamentals of JavaScript. The next three chapters merely provide you with information about built-in functionality that you can use in your JavaScript programs.

Using Objects in JavaScript

In order to use objects in JavaScript you must understand their basic structure, as well as the elements with which you need to interact to utilize the functionality of the objects. In essence, there are two kinds of elements in a JavaScript object:

➤ **Properties.** A JavaScript object property is the same thing as a JavaScript variable. It is a holder for information that the object needs in order to perform its required behavior.

➤ **Methods.** A JavaScript object method is essentially a JavaScript function associated with a particular object. These methods allow the objects to be manipulated and carried out in the desired behavior.

In order to use objects you must create instances of them. Except for static objects, which will be discussed later, the definition of an object is just that—a definition. It can be considered a mold for the final object needed. To actually use the object, you need to create an object out of the template. If you want to create a copy of an object that has already been defined, you use the new operator:

```
birthday = new Date("August 24, 1972")
```

Notice that the Date function takes a single argument—the date itself. The function that has the same name as the object is considered the *constructor* (described later in this chapter), and its arguments generally set the properties of the object. This concept goes for all of the objects that are built into the JavaScript language and the Netscape environment. After you have created a new copy of the object this way, you can go about using the methods and properties that are defined for it by using the name you have created for it. For example, anywhere you wanted to use the Date birthday, you would simply use the new name:

```
yearBorn = birthday.getYear()
```

The advantage to this model is that you can create several instances of an object, which—although they possess different names and different properties—each have the same methods so that they all behave identically.

```
Christmas = new Date(December 25, 1995)
idesOfMarch = new Date(March 15, 1995)
month1 = Christmas.getMonth()
month1 = idesOfMarch.getMonth()
```

After you have created these objects, the next thing you will want to do is gain access to their properties and methods.

Object Properties

Object properties are the variables by which objects hold information that is either being held for the program in general, or necessary for the execution of the objects' methods. One of the most common uses for objects is the storage of often-used information and the particular methods that act on this data. Let's say you have an object that holds URLs and creates a hierarchical arrangement based upon information you provide to create a graphical interface for browsing a Web site. In order to create the hierarchical list, you must first be able to store information about each URL. For example, if the URL object includes information such as name, size, type, and modification date, in addition to the URL itself, the object then consists of the following properties:

Object:	URLEntry
Properties:	name
	size
	type
	modDate
	URL

Of course, the first method used to assign values to object properties is typically in the constructor itself, as shown in the following line:

```
homePage = new URLEntry("New Riders",2234,"folder","January
➡16, 1996 12:00:00", "http://www.mcp.com")
```

This particular constructor—URLEntry(...)—takes all the function arguments and creates the object with all the properties set to the given argument values. Later on, when the creation of objects is covered, how constructors take their arguments and make objects will be covered in more datail.

Assuming that the object already exists and is named homePage, you can access each of its properties in three ways.

First, you can use the dot operator (.) to access the properties, exactly as you do in Java. The following code can be used to assign values to each of the member properties:

```
homePage.name = "New Riders Publishing"
homePage.size = 22345
homePage.type = "folder"
homePage.modDate = new Date("January 16, 1996 12:00:00")
homePage.URL = "http://www.mcp.com/newriders"
```

This format enables you to access each of the properties, set them, and use them later. This is the standard method for accessing properties in Java, and using it gets you accustomed to the syntax of Java objects. There are two more ways of accessing JavaScript properties that may be more flexible in a dynamic environment. These methods entail accessing the member properties as array indices, and can be used when the exact name of the property needed is not known until runtime.

Second, you can access each property based upon its index:

```
homePage[0] = "New Riders Publishing"
homePage[1] = 22345
```

```
homePage[2] = "folder"
homePage[3] = new Date("January 16, 1996 12:00:00")
homePage[4] = "http://www.mcp.com/newriders"
```

Accessing the property based upon its index enables you to use control-flow statements, such as for loops, to cycle through all of the properties of an object. For example, you can use the following code to list all of the properties of an object:

```
function showProps(object) {
    for(var i = 0; i <5; i++)
        document.write(object[i])
}
```

In this case, you must know exactly how many property elements there are in an object to use such a function. Fortunately, JavaScript provides a control-flow statement that cycles through all of the properties in an object by name. It is the for-in statement. We can redo the previous example using this method:

```
function showProps(object, name) {
    for(var prop in object)
        document.write(name+"."+prop+" = "+object[prop]+"\n")
}
```

In the case of our homePage object, the output would be:

```
homePage.name = New Riders Publishing
homePage.size = 22345
homePage.type = folder
homePage.modDate = January 16, 1996 12:00:00
homePage.URL = http://www.mcp.com/newriders
```

The advantage of using the for-in control-flow statement is that you do not need to know the number and names of the methods beforehand.

For the third method of accessing properties, notice the reference to the object property in the document.write statement: the array index uses the prop variable, which when used by itself is a string providing the property name for output. In the same way that the variable prop is a string, you can use strings to access object properties.

```
homePage["name"] = "New Riders Publishing"
homePage["size"] = 22345
hoemPage["type"] = "folder"
homePage["modDate"] = new Date("January 16, 1996 12:00:00")
homePage["URL"] = "http://www.mcp.com/newriders"
```

This way, you can access properties without knowing their names at runtime. This enables you to dynamically address object properties in a script without knowing what the property names might need to be. For example, you could use information from a textfield to determine which properties the user wanted to see.

Object Methods

In addition to being able to store properties, objects can also have *methods* associated with them. These methods are essentially JavaScript functions that are associated with an object and are used to carry out behaviors that the object encapsulates. In order to use a method that an object has built in, you must call it using the method reference. For example, in order to call the sin() method of the Math object that is built into JavaScript, you would call it:

```
Math.sin(3.14)
```

The method is sin(), which requires a number and is a member of the object Math. Many of the JavaScript and Netscape objects have methods associated with them, and the next three chapters are presentations of these different objects, including the properties and methods that they contain.

From the example of the URLEntry (discussed in the previous section about object properties), the showProps function:

```
function showProps(object, name) {
  for(var prop in object)
      document.write(name+"."+prop+" = "+object[prop]+"\n")
}
```

might be a method of URLEntry, renamed to toString. The only difference would be that instead of printing out the object property itself, the method might return a string, which can then be used by the programmer to be printed to the screen, or whatever else is needed.

```
  for(var prop in this)
      document.write(prop+" = "+object[prop]+"\n")
}
```

If the object name is newURL, you can get it to output the text by using the following call:

```
document.write(newURL.toString())
```

Some sample output from such a call is shown in figure 4.1. Notice that the function definition for the toString method is also listed. Moreover, if you used the call:

```
document.write(newURL)
```

you would get the exact same output. A call to document.write using any object invokes its toString function if it exists. This means that if any object you are using has a toString() method, you can send the object itself to document.write() for output. If it is an object of your own creation, you need to create your own toString() method, which is covered in the next section on creating objects.

Accessing Properties of Static Objects

There are several objects in which you do not need to create an instance of the object in order to use the methods and properties it contains. Such objects are considered *static*, and you can access their properties by using the object name itself and the property or method required. A perfect example of a static object is Math. When using the Math object, you do not need to create a new Math object with a new name. Instead, you can simply use the Math name, appended with the property or method you need.

area = Math.PI*Math.pow(r,2)

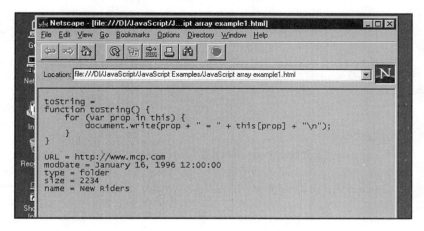

Figure 4.1
The toString method for the URLEntry object.

Throughout this book, every attempt has been made to indicate whether an object is a static object or whether an instance of the object needs to be created.

Using the with Statement to Refer to Objects

In addition to the standard use of methods, there is an important way to tell JavaScript which object you are referring to when calling methods and accessing properties. The statement to use is

```
with object {
...
}
```

All of the statements inside the `with` brackets act as if *object* was appended to the front. For example, you could use several method properties and methods without explicitly saying Math.*member* each time.

```
with Math {
    positive = (b+sqrt(4*a*c+pow(b,2)))/(2*a)
    negative = (b-sqrt(4*a*c+pow(b,2)))/(2*a)
}
```

If you did not use the `with` statement, you would be required to place Math in front of all of the method calls such as sqrt() and pow().

Using this

In JavaScript and Java there is a keyword that refers to the current object—this. An example of using `this` in JavaScript can be observed in the toString method for the URLEntry object.

```
function toString() {
    for(var prop in this)
        document.write(prop+" = "+object[prop]+"\n")
}
```

Notice that in the for-in statement the object whose properties are being traversed is `this`. In the case of the toString method, the for loop needs to know which object's properties to traverse; therefore, the this variable is used. You will see the use of `this` in many places as you move further into the use of objects.

 Whenever an object needs to refer to itself, the `this` variable is used.

Creating Objects

Although using objects that exist in the language and browser environment is a very powerful, time-saving tool, much of JavaScript's power comes from its ability to create new objects that carry out the jobs required for your Web pages. JavaScript's object model is somewhat different than Java's, as mentioned before; therefore, creating objects in JavaScript uses a much different methodology.

The JavaScript object is based around a constructor function that holds all of the properties and links to method functions. The JavaScript object does not provide any means for encapsulation in relation to property or method hiding, nor does it support abstraction or inheritance as in Java. While this is a limiting factor in terms of an object-oriented paradigm, the purpose of JavaScript is focused on a utilitarian view of objects. If the JavaScript developers had attempted to build in all of that functionality, they would have made the language too complex for the job it was designed for.

The Constructor Function

In order to create a JavaScript object, you create a function that has the same name as the object you want to create. In the case of our URLEntry object, the constructor function is:

```
function URLEntry(name, size, type, modDate, URL) {
    ...
}
```

This function definition can then be used to create instances of the object:

```
homePage = new URLEntry("New Riders",512,"folder","January
➡16, 1996 12:00:00", "http://www.mcp.com")
homePage = new URLEntry("Netscape",512,"folder","January 16,
➡1996 12:00:00", "http://home.netscape.com")
```

Adding Properties to Objects

Of course, in order to do anything with the arguments that the constructor function takes, you must create properties that can store data for the object. To add the variables that the arguments of the constructor function provides, you must assign the variables to member properties.

```
function URLEntry(name, size, type, modDate, URL) {
    this.name = name;
    this.size = size;
    this.type = type;
    this.modDate = new Date(modDate);
    this.URL = URL;
}
```

Notice the use of the Date object to hold the modification date of the URLEntry object. In addition to the standard variables, you can also have other objects as properties. The this variable name is used to indicate that the object to which the property being assigned is the object to which the constructor function belongs. Now, when the new URLEntry() constructor is called, the arguments passed to it by the programmer will be assigned to the properties of the object.

Adding Methods to Objects

In addition to adding properties to objects in the constructor, you need to add methods for the object so that it can actually do something. This is also carried out in the constructor function for an object. The URLEntry object, for instance, needs to be able to return a string representing the properties of the object. The function we need to add, therefore, is:

```
function toString() {
    for(var prop in this)
        document.write(prop+" = "+object[prop]+"\n")
}
```

In order to add this function as a method of URLEntry, you can employ a statement similar to that used for properties.

```
this.toString = toString()
```

Now, you can use the toString() function as a method of the URLEntry object. When you call an object of URLEntry type with the toString() method, it returns a string that holds all of the properties of the object instance.

There is now enough code to present an object that holds information and provides a string representation of itself when needed.

```
<HTML>
<HEAD>
<PRE>
<SCRIPT LANGUAGE="JavaScript">
<!-- begin hiding
function URLEntry(name, size, type, modDate, URL) {
    this.name = name;
    this.size = size;
    this.type = type;
    this.modDate = new Date(modDate);
    this.URL = URL;
    this.toString = toString;
}

function toString() {
    for(var prop in this)
        document.write(prop + " = " + this[prop] + "\n");
}

newURL = new URLEntry("New Riders",2234,"folder","January 16,
➥1996 12:00:00", "http://www.mcp.com");
document.write(newURL);

// end hiding -->
</SCRIPT>
</PRE>
</HEAD>
<BODY>
</BODY>
</HTML>
```

Notice in the lines of the previous code that each of the statements ends with a semicolon. The semicolon is not a requirement of the JavaScript language, but is a requirement of Java. It doesn't matter whether you leave them off in JavaScript; however, in order to get used to the idea of using these end-of-statement markers in Java, it is a good idea to incorporate them into your JavaScript code.

Creating Arrays

Most programming languages include a variable type known as an array. *Arrays* are collections of data under a single variable that are accessed using an index. Although JavaScript has no explicit array data type as is found in C/C++ or Java, you can create an array structure by defining an object makeArray. By doing so, you can create properties for your object to hold the data you need. The function declaration is:

```
function makeArray(n) {
    this.length = n;
    for(var i = 1; i <= n; i++)
        this[i] = 0;
    return this
}
```

You call the makeArray function with the number of elements you want the array to hold. You can then assign values and access the individual properties of the makeArray object using the *identifier[n]* statement. The following code creates an array of three items, and then prints them out on the display:

```
<HTML>
<HEAD>
<SCRIPT LANGUAGE="JavaScript">
<!--
function makeArray(n) {
    this.length = n;
    for(var i = 1; i <= n; i++)
        this[i] = 0;
    return this
}

testArray = new makeArray(3);
testArray[1] = "hello\n"
testArray[2] = "this\n"
testArray[3] = "is\n"
document.write("<PRE>");
for(i=1;i<=3;i++)
    document.write(testArray[i]);
```

```
document.write("length = " + testArray.length);
document.write("</PRE>");
// -->
</SCRIPT>
</HEAD>
<BODY>
</BODY>
</HTML>
```

In addition to the standard variable types, you can also hold objects in arrays. As with all JavaScript statements, there is no need to expressly declare the kind of data you want the variable to hold, so the array can store all types.

One problem with the declaration of arrays as defined in the JavaScript beta documentation is that it sets a standard whereby arrays are indexed from 1 to n, where n is the number of elements in the array. Unfortunately Java, C/C++, and most languages start indexing arrays at 0 and run to n–1. Because JavaScript objects store *all* properties in the array structure so that they can be indexed (as mentioned in the previous section on objects), the property length takes up this first (0) position; therefore, the data in the array must be placed in 1 to n.

You can reverse the order in the makeArray function between the for statement and the creation of the length property to make sure that the data indices fall from 0 to n–1, so that it conforms with the other language standards. You do this by moving the length property from the beginning of the constructor function to the end. This is how it would look:

```
<HTML>
<HEAD>
<SCRIPT LANGUAGE="JavaScript">
<!--
function makeArray(n) {
    for(var i = 1; i <= n; i++)
        this[i] = 0;
    this.length = n;
    return this
}
```

```
testArray = new makeArray(3);
testArray[0] = "hello"
testArray[1] = "this"
testArray[2] = "is"
for(i=0;i<3;i++)
    document.write(testArray[i]);
document.write("length = " + testArray.length);
// -->
</SCRIPT>
</HEAD>
<BODY>
</BODY>
</HTML>
```

Of course, using the indexing from 0 to n–1 enacts a trade-off in robustness in your code. The advantage to leaving the length property at the beginning of the property list is that if you attempt to index past the end of the array, you will receive an error when the program runs, and you can catch the problem before it gets out onto the Web—this is an essential element to robustness. This procedure is known as *bounds checking*, and by placing the length property at the beginning of the property list, JavaScript can catch this kind of error instead of passing incorrect data along. If you use the makeArray function, which indexes from 0 to n–1, then accidentally go over by one when you are indexing the array, it will send the length property as a valid value. While this will not crash the program immediately, it will send incorrect data to sections of code later on, and either crash those portions of the code, or cause erratic behavior in your program. In addition, because there is no bounds checking, it makes it very difficult to determine later on where the problem might be.

In all of the examples, this book uses the former method of indexing that runs from 1 to n. Although you might have to relearn it the other way for Java later on, and all of the arrays are provided with built-in objects, it provides a much more robust environment for debugging code.

Creating a Directory for a Web Page

There is now enough material to show how to bring all of the object elements together into a full-blown JavaScript program. In this instance, the purpose of the script is to provide an explorer-like directory structure that can be used to organize a home page. The example shows some of the potential available with JavaScript, and its ability to automate and enhance Web pages. Figure 4.2 shows what the final script provides.

Figure 4.2

The Directory JavaScript program.

The first function in the code is the makeArray() function, which creates arrays in JavaScript, as described in the previous section.

```
/**
 * this is used to create arrays in JavaScript
 */
function makeArray(n) {
    this.length = n;
    for(var i = 1; i <= n; i++)
        this[i] = 0;
    return this
}
```

As you can see, the 1 to n indexing is used because it presents a much more robust object to deal with, even though it takes some getting used to if you are an experienced C or Java programmer.

The next function is the constructor function for the URLEntry object. This object is the basic element in the directory structure. Besides a few additional helper functions, all of the necessary behavior is coded into this object.

```
/**
 * this is the constructor function for the URLEntry object
 */
function URLEntry(name, size, type, modDate, URL, objectName)
{
    this.name = name;
    this.size = size;
    this.type = type;
    this.modDate = modDate;
    this.URL = URL;
    this.objectName = objectName;
    this.URLEntry = new makeArray(0);
    this.display = displayURLEntry;
    this.addURLEntry = addURLEntry;
    this.toggle = toggle;
}
```

When an object is created, it takes several parameters. The following list indicates the uses for these parameters:

➤ **name.** This is the name displayed for the URLEntry in the directory.

➤ **size.** This is the size of the file the link points to. This parameter can be used to indicate to users how long it might take to download the file. Of course, with some kinds of URL entries there is no file size such as FTP and Malto.

➤ **type.** This parameter indicates the type of entry, such as whether it is an HTML document, FTP site, folder, and so on. This string is used to indicate which GIF file should be loaded as the icon for the entry. The property is also displayed as text at the end of the entry. This value is used to hold the state of folder URLEntries. Also, if the type is "folder," then it can be toggled to "open folder" with the onClick event handler.

➤ **modDate.** This is the last modification date of the link, and is displayed on the URLEntry line in the directory.

➤ **URL.** This is the actual URL that the link points to, and is used as the target of an HREF tag when the URLEntry is selected.

➤ **objectName.** This is used to hold the actual name of the object when it is created. JavaScript doesn't have a built-in method for exposing an object's name, so in order to refer to it by name you must direct it to store its name before referencing it. It is necessary to have an object's name in order to call the object's method from an event handler, such as onClick or onMouseOver.

➤ **URLEntry.** This is an array, initially set for zero elements, that will hold the children URLEntries of this URLEntry. When it comes time for a URLEntry to display itself, after doing so, it will instruct its children to display themselves. This displaying of children occurs only with folder URLEntries that are currently set as open folders.

In addition to the standard properties, the URLEntry object also has three methods that are assigned to it.

1. The first method is display(), which in this case of the previous constructor function code is assigned to the function displayURLEntry(). This method tells the object to display itself.

2. The second method, addURLEntry(), adds children to folder URLEntries. Of course, you can always add children to non-folders, but they will never be displayed.

3. The final method of the URLEntry object is toggle(), and is the event handler method called when an item is clicked. If the URLEntry object is a folder, toggle() either opens or closes the folder based upon its current state.

Each of these methods will now be covered in more detail. The following function displays the URLEntry object in the directory structure window.

```
/**
 * this is the display function for the URLEntry object
 */
function displayURLEntry() {

    frames[0].document.write("<TR>");
    frames[0].document.write("<TD WIDTH=200>");
    for(var i = 0; i<this.level; i++)
        frames[0].document.write("<IMG ALIGN=LEFT
        ➡SRC=\"blank.gif\">");
    frames[0].document.write("<A HREF=\"" + this.URL + "\"
    ➡");
    if(this.type == "folder" || this.type == "open folder")
      frames[0].document.write("TARGET=\"DIRECTORY_WINDOW\"");
    else
        frames[0].document.write("TARGET=\"DOCUMENT_WINDOW\"");
    frames[0].document.write("onClick=\"parent."
    ➡+this.objectName+".toggle()\">");
    frames[0].document.write("<IMG ALIGN=LEFT BORDER = 0
SRC=\"" + this.type + ".gif\">");
    frames[0].document.write(this.name + "</A>");
    frames[0].document.write("</TD><TD WIDTH = 50>");
    frames[0].document.write(this.size);
    frames[0].document.write("</TD><TD WIDTH = 200>");
```

```
frames[0].document.write(this.modDate);
frames[0].document.write("</TD><TD WIDTH = 100>");
frames[0].document.write(this.type);
frames[0].document.write("</TD></TR>");
if(this.type == "open folder") {
    for(var i = 1; i <= this.URLEntry.length; i++)
        this.URLEntry[i].display();
}
}
```

The first thing you should notice is all of the frames[0] objects to which the document.write() method refers. This script is in the overall HTML file that creates the directory structure frame and display frame, and later on in the code you will see where these frames are created. Since there are now essentially two subdocuments in the main window, it is necessary to indicate which document receives the text. The text being sent to the document is HTML code for the creation of a row in a table. Later on in this chapter, you will see the code that creates the beginning and end tags for the table.

Frames are a new specification for Netscape 2.0 and are not included in the HTML 3.0 standard. Check out Netscape's site for more information on how to implement frames in a document.

The first column in the table row is set at 200 pixels wide, and is used to hold the icon and name of the URLEntry object. Before the icon and entry name are displayed it is necessary to indent them, depending upon the level of the hierarchy in which they occur. The first for loop creates a blank.gif image tag for every level of index. Next, if the URLEntry object is a folder, then the URL to which it points needs to update the frame holding the directory structure and not the document window. If the URLEntry object points to anything else, then the target of the URL to which it points will need to be updated in the lower document window.

The TARGET HTML argument is a new feature of Netscape 2.0. For more information on how to implement targeting in an HTML document, refer to Netscape's Web site.

The next lines create the HTML HREF tag so that you can create a link out of the URLEntry name. The tag is then used to initiate and update the directory structure whenever any of the URLEntry objects receive a mouse click. Notice the use of the double quote backslash control character (\") used to send a double quote to the HTML document page.

In addition to the normal HTML tag accoutrements, the HREF tag has an extra argument: onClick. This argument tells what JavaScript statements are executed when the Click event occurs for this link object. The URLEntry object passes its own name to the HTML document, appending the method toggle() to the end—a procedure that causes the event handler to call the toggle statement from the correct instance of the object. This process is an important element of the program and one you should understand and experiment with.

It is important that the objects you want to call in a statement such as onClick are available to the event handler from the point of view of the document. If the onClick method had been this.toggle(), how does the event handler know what 'this' is, and how do you put 'this' into a string for an HTML document? By allowing the object to have a copy of its own name, it can pass the name on to the HTML document easily.

Following the construction of the HREF link, which controls the behavior of the directory structure, the next several lines create the rest of the table row. This row includes information about size, type, and modification date. The last three lines of the display function check to see if the URLEntry is an open folder. If it is, then all (if any) of its children are told to display themselves.

```
/**
 * this function is used to add an entry to the folder type
➥of URLEntry
 */
```

```
function addURLEntry(newURLEntry) {
    newURLEntry.level = this.level + 1;
    var tempArray = this.URLEntry;
    this.URLEntry = new makeArray(this.URLEntry.length+1);
    for(var i = 1; i <= this.URLEntry.length; i++)
        this.URLEntry[i] = tempArray[i];
    this.URLEntry[this.URLEntry.length] = newURLEntry;
}
```

The addURLEntry function is used to add entries to the URLEntry object and is specifically meant to be used with a folder object type. The function takes a URLEntry object as its argument. First, it sets the level to one higher than that of the previous URLEntry object level. If, for example, the folder to which you were adding was on level 2 of the directory hierarchy, then anything placed in it would be on level 3. This technique was used in the previous display method to provide indentation as a visual clue. Secondly, the next four lines take the original URLEntry array in the object, place it in a temporary array, enlarge the original array by one, and then move each entry back into place. Finally, the last line adds the new URLEntry to the newly created end of the list.

The following method is called by the onClick event handler in order to change the state of a folder.

```
/**
 * this function toggles the folder from open to closed and
➥vice versa
 */
function toggle() {
    if(this.type == "folder")
        this.type = "open folder";
    else if(this.type == "open folder")
        this.type = "folder";
}
```

The function simply checks the state of the URLEntry object. If the object is in a folder state (closed), then it sets it to open. If it is open, then it resets it to a closed state. If the object is not a folder, it simply falls through the method. After the toggle method is called, the link for the HREF tag is called. If the object is a folder, then the target becomes the directory window itself. The link is a document called clear directory.html. This file is an HTML file with only the necessary headers and a single function, which is to displayRoot(). This essentially blanks the window, and calls the displayRoot() function to redraw the screen, enabling the directory with the updated folder structure to be seen. The clear directory.html file is as follows:

```
<HTML>
<HEAD>
</HEAD>
<BODY BGCOLOR="#FFFFFF">
<SCRIPT LANGUAGE="JavaScript">
<!--
parent.displayRoot();
// -->
</SCRIPT>
</BODY>
</HTML>
```

Notice that the displayRoot() method call is directed at the parent object. In this case, the parent is the entire window that holds the two frames. It is the parent of these frames that is holding all of the JavaScript code, and where objects in this case need to be referenced.

```
/**
 * This is the declaration for the root URLEntry which starts it all
 */
root = new URLEntry("Root", 0, "folder","January 16, 1996
➡12:00:00","clear directory.html","root");

/**
 * this is the function called to create the table, and direct each of
 * the URLEntries to display themselves and their children
 */
function displayRoot() {
    frames[0].document.write("<HTML><BODY BGCOLOR=\"#FFFFFF\">");
```

```
frames[0].document.write("<TABLE BORDER=0>");
root.display();
frames[0].document.write("</TABLE>");
frames[0].document.write("</BODY></HTML>");
}
```

The previous two sections of code are used to create the root object that holds all of the URLEntry objects (and is a URLEntry object itself) and to begin displaying the entire tree. The construction of the root entry is like any other object constructor, and provides all of the arguments the entry needs in order to create the object. There is one piece of code that is essential, however, and that is the URL itself. It is important that this URL point to the clear directory.html file that is used to clear the screen and trigger a redraw.

The displayRoot() function is necessary in order to get the URLEntry hierarchy going. It is necessary to create the beginning and end tags for the table that the display() method provides the rows for. Note that the displayRoot() function is not attached to any object, and is invoked as a method for setting up the table and triggering the display of the hierarchy—which, once started, traverses the tree of URLEntries and displays them as directed.

The following function, as noted in the reminder code, is used to create the two frames that hold the directory and document windows.

```
/**
 * this function creates the directory and document frames in which
 * everything is displayed
 */
function createFrames() {
    document.write("<FRAMESET ROWS=\"150,*\">");
    document.write("<FRAME SRC=\"clear directory.html\"
➥NAME=\"DIRECTORY_WINDOW\">");
    document.write("<FRAME SRC=\"clear document.html\"
➥NAME=\"DOCUMENT_WINDOW\">");
    document.write("</FRAMESET>");
}
```

The frames are created and two source files are used in order to provide clear windows on loading. Of course, the clear directory file also calls the function displayRoot() that causes the window to be updated.

This is essentially all of the code you need to create and control the directory. Now, all that is necessary are some URLs to the URLEntry object. The following code includes the constructors used in building up the directory shown in figures 4.2 through 4.4.

```
/**
 * this is the beginning of the creation of the directory structure
 * note: all of these entries are dummies, and you can change them to
 * your own.
 */

//add companies Folder to root
compFolder = new URLEntry("Companies","--","folder","January 16,
➥1996 12:00:00","clear directory.html","compFolder");
root.addURLEntry(compFolder);

//add New Riders url to companies folder
newRidersURL = new URLEntry("New Riders",22436,"http",
➥"January 16, 1996 12:00:00","http://www.mcp.com/newriders/
➥","newRidersURL");
compFolder.addURLEntry(newRidersURL);

//add Netscape folder to companies
netscapeFolder = new URLEntry("Netscape","--","folder","--
➥","clear directory.html","netscapeFolder");
compFolder.addURLEntry(netscapeFolder);

//add Netscape WWW to Netscape folder
netscapeURL = new URLEntry("Netscape WWW",34067,"http","January 17,
➥1996 12:00:00", "http://home.netscape.com/","netscapeURL");
netscapeFolder.addURLEntry(netscapeURL);
```

```
//add Netscape ftp to Netscape folder
netscapeFtpURL = new URLEntry("Netscape FTP","--
➥","ftp","January 17, 1996 12:00:00", "http://
ftp.netscape.com/","netscapeFtpURL");
netscapeFolder.addURLEntry(netscapeFtpURL);

//add Netscape ftp2 to Netscape folder
netscapeFtp2URL = new URLEntry("Netscape FTP2","--
➥","ftp","January 17, 1996 12:00:00", "http://
ftp2.netscape.com/","netscapeFtp2URL");
netscapeFolder.addURLEntry(netscapeFtp2URL);

//add Netscape ftp3 to Netscape folder
netscapeFtp3URL = new URLEntry("Netscape FTP3","--
➥","ftp","January 17, 1996 12:00:00", "http://
ftp3.netscape.com/","netscapeFtp3URL");
netscapeFolder.addURLEntry(netscapeFtp3URL);

//add Microsoft url to companies folder
microsoftURL = new URLEntry("Microsoft",48243,"http","January
➥16, 1996 12:00:00", "http://www.microsoft.com/
","microsoftURL");
compFolder.addURLEntry(microsoftURL);

//add Sun url to companies folder
javaURL = new URLEntry("Sun's Java
➥Page",24925,"http","January 16, 1996 12:00:00", "http://
➥java.sun.com/","javaURL");
compFolder.addURLEntry(javaURL);

//add mailto: url to root folder
mailURL = new URLEntry("Send Mail", "--", "mailto","--
➥","mailto:tdr20@cus.cam.ac.uk","mailURL");
root.addURLEntry(mailURL);
```

The final bit of code invokes the createFrames() function to start
the whole thing in motion. When createFrames() is called, it
creates the two frames in the window. The document frame sits
idle, while the directory frame issues a call to the displayRoot()
function. This function creates a table tag, and calls on the root
object to display itself, which in turn tells all of its children to

display themselves, and so on, until all URLEntries that should be drawn are drawn. After the display is finished, the displayRoot() method ends the table tag, and the whole document is displayed. When one of the folder entries is hit, it triggers the toggle() method, which switches the state of the folder. At the same time, the URL of the pointer reloads the clear directory.html file that issues the call to displayRoot() to update the display. If an entry besides a folder is selected then the URL is sent to the document window for display.

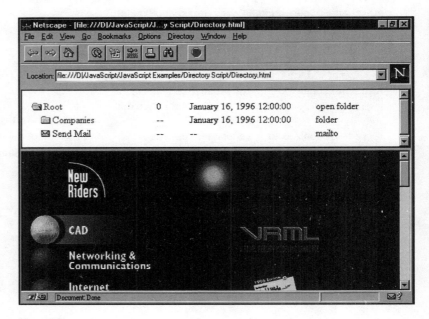

Figure 4.3

The Directory Script with a collapsed folder.

Figure 4.4

The Directory Script with an expanded folder.

The entire file, once it is placed in the HTML tags looks like the following:

```
<!--
    File: Directory.html
    Description: This script creates a directory structure for a web
        page that can be automatically expanded and collapsed
    Author: Tim Ritchey
    Date: 16 January, 1996
    Note: This Script is freely available for download and use. Please
        indicate where you got it from, and I would be grateful.
-->
```

```
<HTML>
<HEAD>
<SCRIPT LANGUAGE="JavaScript">
<!-- begin hiding

/**
 * this is used to create arrays in JavaScript
 */
function makeArray(n) {
    this.length = n;
    for(var i = 1; i <= n; i++)
        this[i] = 0;
    return this
}

/**
 * this is the constructor function for the URLEntry object
 */
function URLEntry(name, size, type, modDate, URL, objectName)
{
    this.name = name;
    this.size = size;
    this.type = type;
    this.modDate = modDate;
    this.URL = URL;
    this.objectName = objectName;
    this.level = 0;
    this.URLEntry = new makeArray(0);
    this.display = displayURLEntry;
    this.addURLEntry = addURLEntry;
    this.toggle = toggle;
}

/**
 * this is the display function for the URLEntry object
 */
function displayURLEntry() {

    frames[0].document.write("<TR>");
    frames[0].document.write("<TD WIDTH=200>");
    for(var i = 0; i<this.level; i++)
```

```
            frames[0].document.write("<IMG ALIGN=LEFT SRC=\"blank.gif\">");
        frames[0].document.write("<A HREF=\"" + this.URL + "\" ");
        if(this.type == "folder" || this.type == "open folder")
            frames[0].document.write("TARGET=\"DIRECTORY_WINDOW\"");
        else
            frames[0].document.write("TARGET=\"DOCUMENT_WINDOW\"");
      frames[0].document.write("onClick=\"parent."+this.objectName+".toggle()\">");
        frames[0].document.write("<IMG ALIGN=LEFT BORDER = 0 SRC=\"" +
➡this.type + ".gif\">");
        frames[0].document.write(this.name + "</A>");
        frames[0].document.write("</TD><TD WIDTH = 50>");
        frames[0].document.write(this.size);
        frames[0].document.write("</TD><TD WIDTH = 200>");
        frames[0].document.write(this.modDate);
        frames[0].document.write("</TD><TD WIDTH = 100>");
        frames[0].document.write(this.type);
        frames[0].document.write("</TD></TR>");
        if(this.type == "open folder") {
            for(var i = 1; i <= this.URLEntry.length; i++)
                this.URLEntry[i].display();
        }
}


/**
 * this function is used to add an entry to the folder type of URLEntry
 */
function addURLEntry(newURLEntry) {
    newURLEntry.level = this.level + 1;
    var tempArray = this.URLEntry;
    this.URLEntry = new makeArray(this.URLEntry.length+1);
    for(var i = 1; i <= this.URLEntry.length; i++)
        this.URLEntry[i] = tempArray[i];
    this.URLEntry[this.URLEntry.length] = newURLEntry;

}

/**
```

```
 * this function toggles the folder from open to closed and vice versa
 */
function toggle() {
    if(this.type == "folder")
        this.type = "open folder";
    else if(this.type == "open folder")
        this.type = "folder";
}


/**
 * This is the declaration for the root URLEntry which starts it all
 */
root = new URLEntry("Root", 0, "folder","January 16, 1996
*_12:00:00","clear directory.html","root");


/**
 * this is the function called to create the table, and direct each of
 * the URLEntries to display themselves and their children
 */
function displayRoot() {
    frames[0].document.write("<HTML><BODY BGCOLOR=\"#FFFFFF\">");
    frames[0].document.write("<TABLE BORDER=0>");
    root.display();
    frames[0].document.write("</TABLE>");
    frames[0].document.write("</BODY></HTML>");
}



/**
 * this function creates the directory and document frames in which
 * everything is displayed
 */
function createFrames() {
    document.write("<FRAMESET ROWS=\"150,*\">");
    document.write("<FRAME SRC=\"clear directory.html\"
➥NAME=\"DIRECTORY_WINDOW\">");
    document.write("<FRAME SRC=\"clear document.html\"
```

```
NAME=\"DOCUMENT_WINDOW\">");
    document.write("</FRAMESET>");
}


/**
 * this is the beginning of the creation of the directory structure
 * note: all of these entries are dummies, and you can change them to
 * your own.
 */

//add companies Folder to root
compFolder = new URLEntry("Companies","--","folder","January 16, 1996
➥12:00:00","clear directory.html","compFolder");
root.addURLEntry(compFolder);

//add New Riders url to companies folder
newRidersURL = new URLEntry("New Riders",22436,"http","January
➥16, 1996 12:00:00",
"http://www.mcp.com/newriders/","newRidersURL");
compFolder.addURLEntry(newRidersURL);

//add Netscape folder to companies
netscapeFolder = new URLEntry("Netscape","--","folder","--","clear
➥directory.html","netscapeFolder");
compFolder.addURLEntry(netscapeFolder);

//add Netscape WWW to Netscape folder
netscapeURL = new URLEntry("Netscape WWW",34067,"http","January
➥17, 1996 12:00:00",
"http://home.netscape.com/","netscapeURL");
netscapeFolder.addURLEntry(netscapeURL);

//add Netscape ftp to Netscape folder
netscapeFtpURL = new URLEntry("Netscape FTP","--","ftp","January
➥17, 1996 12:00:00",
"http://ftp.netscape.com/","netscapeFtpURL");
netscapeFolder.addURLEntry(netscapeFtpURL);
```

```
//add Netscape ftp2 to Netscape folder
netscapeFtp2URL = new URLEntry("Netscape FTP2","--","ftp","January
➡17, 1996 12:00:00","http://ftp2.netscape.com/","netscapeFtp2URL");
netscapeFolder.addURLEntry(netscapeFtp2URL);

//add Netscape ftp3 to Netscape folder
netscapeFtp3URL = new URLEntry("Netscape FTP3","--","ftp","January
➡17, 1996 12:00:00", "http://ftp3.netscape.com/","netscapeFtp3URL");
netscapeFolder.addURLEntry(netscapeFtp3URL);

//add Microsoft url to companies folder
microsoftURL = new URLEntry("Microsoft",48243,"http","January
➡16, 1996 12:00:00",
"http://www.microsoft.com/","microsoftURL");
compFolder.addURLEntry(microsoftURL);

//add Sun url to companies folder
javaURL = new URLEntry("Sun's Java Page",24925,"http","January 16,
➡1996 12:00:00", "http://java.sun.com/","javaURL");
compFolder.addURLEntry(javaURL);

//add mailto: url to root folder
mailURL = new URLEntry("Send Mail", "--", "mailto","--
➡","mailto:tdr20@cus.cam.ac.uk","mailURL");
root.addURLEntry(mailURL);

createFrames();
// end hiding -->
</SCRIPT>
</HEAD>
<BODY>
</BODY>
</HTML>
```

Summary

This chapter covered the basics of object creation in JavaScript, and showed you how to use built-in objects, as well as how to create your own. The script used to create the directory frame in a Web page is a fairly complex script that depends upon many features and objects built into the scripting language, and provides a good example of what can be done to enhance your own pages beyond the standard HTML standard using JavaScript. The next two chapters will cover the functions and objects that are built into the JavaScript language and the Netscape environment. Because JavaScript exposes many of the low-level features of displaying Web pages, by utilizing these features you can wring the most out of plain HTML without requiring CGI scripts or multimedia authoring tools to get the job done.

Chapter 5

JavaScript Built-In Objects

The previous chapters present the groundwork for developing powerful Web-based documents that can dynamically adjust to environment and user events. Chapter 1 presents an introduction to the language features of Java and JavaScript and discusses the different ways in which each language provides support for client-side execution of code in Web documents. Chapter 2, "JavaScript Fundamentals," provides the fundamental look and feel of the JavaScript language and focuses upon the overall architecture of writing JavaScript programs. Chapter 3, "Control Flow and Functions in JavaScript," presents more advanced features of the language, including control flow and the use of functions. The previous chapter, Chapter 4, "Using and Creating Objects in JavaScript," discusses the most powerful feature of the JavaScript language—its object-based approach to script design and creation. The Directory Script shown at the end of that chapter is an excellent example of how an object such as URLEntry can provide functional interfaces for Web documents.

The real power in object-oriented computing is, of course, the ability to use already existing objects to extend the functionality of your programs without the need to code everything from scratch. Even with the basics of the JavaScript language behind us, it was necessary in previous chapters to resort to using objects and methods we hadn't discussed before in great detail because in order to do anything in a complex environment, such as the Netscape browser, it would be difficult to program every feature you needed from scratch. This chapter and the next two focus on the objects that the JavaScript language and Netscape browser provide in order to expand the capabilities of the JavaScript language. One of the best examples is the document object used to control the actual HTML content being displayed with its write() method.

The objects available for use in Web page scripts can be divided into two types:

➤ objects built into JavaScript itself

➤ objects provided by the Netscape environment

Objects which are built into the JavaScript language include String, Math, and Date. In addition, JavaScript provides three stand-alone functions: eval, parseInt, and parseFloat. This chapter focuses on these built-in objects and functions. Chapter 6, "Netscape Navigator Objects: The document Object," deals with objects provided by the Netscape environment that can be used in JavaScript programs. These objects include the window objects, such as parent and frames, document and form objects, as well as the history and location objects.

Built-In Objects and Functions

JavaScript provides several objects that are considered a part of the standard language and are available in all run-time environments. These include the String, Math, and Date objects. In addition to full objects, JavaScript also provides several built-in, stand-alone functions such as eval, parseInt, and parseFloat. The String, Math, and Date objects are used in JavaScript to provide extended data type functionality for common formats of information not provided by the basic types such as characters, numbers, and Booleans. In addition, the Math object provides methods for arithmetic functions not provided by the standard operators. The eval, parseInt, and parseFloat functions all return the numerical values for strings representing numerical values. These can be important when using values returned from form items such as text areas.

Unlike the Netscape Navigator objects that are discussed in Chapter 6, the objects provided by the JavaScript language are available automatically in every document. The Netscape Navigator objects are document dependent and might change depending upon the HTML environment.

Besides the standard objects related to HTML pages, a Netscape environment might run different plug-ins or applets, which provide even more objects with which JavaScript will be able to interact in the future. These plug-in– or applet-associated objects are currently unavailable in the JavaScript version embedded in Netscape 2.0, but they are promised to be available for future releases.

In addition, if JavaScript is taken up by other Web browsers, it is possible that elements that represent different browser features may be exposed to the Web document author and may be available for control in JavaScript. As object-oriented technology becomes more pervasive in application development and Web site creation, JavaScript's functionality can expand to incorporate these new objects into its realm of control. This means that you can apply your time investment in learning JavaScript's object control method to new Web elements in the foreseeable future.

The String Object

The most common object used in JavaScript is the String object. This is because the String object does not need new statements to create an instance of the object. Anytime you place text between two quotation marks and assign it to a variable or property, you create a String object. Each of the following lines create new String objects:

```
name = "John Doe";
URLEntry.type = "folder";
```

Additionally, the use of a string literal creates an instance of the String object.

In order to use a string property or method, you append the dot and method or property name as in all objects.

```
stringLength = name.length;
tempString = URLEntry.type.toUpperCase();
```

One item to notice is that the dot property is cumulative and works from left to right, evaluating each statement and treating the next operation as if it were appended to the result. The preceding statement could also have been written:

```
tempString = URLEntry.type;
temp2String = tempString.toUpperCase();
```

The evaluation works from left to right so that the method or property in question refers to a valid argument. In the preceding case, the URLEntry object property type is assigned to the variable tempString, which is then converted to all uppercase letters using the toUpperCase() method of the String object. This is essentially what happens with the statement that strings all the dot operations together.

You do not need to use a variable name for invoking methods or properties of strings. You can simply append the method or property name to the end of the string.

```
tempNumber = "Hello, World!".length;
tempString = "Hello, World!".toUpperCase();
```

Of course, the previous code is more of a theoretical example to show you how literal strings can be used rather than to show you anything of practical importance. It is theoretical because you would never want to perform a function on a literal string when you could precompute the result and not invoke the overhead of the function call at runtime. Just figure out what the result should be and use that. Relying on methods at runtime, where they are not needed, is a waste of computing cycles, particularly in an interpreted environment where it is important to optimize scripts.

String Object Properties

The String object has a single property known as length. This property holds the number of characters in the string, including all white spaces and special characters. The following code uses the length property of the string object to line up different columns of text:

```
<HTML>
<HEAD>
<PRE>
<SCRIPT LANGUAGE="JavaScript">
<!-- begin hiding
function spacer(string,n,type) {
    space = ""
    for(var i = 0; i < (n - string.length); i++)
        space += " ";
    if(type == "L")
        return string + space;
    else return space + string;
}

document.write(spacer("New Riders Publishing", 25, "L"));
document.write(spacer("WWW Home Page", 15, "L"));
document.writeln(spacer("http://www.mcp.com/newriders", 30, "R"));

document.write(spacer("Netscape", 25, "L"));
document.write(spacer("FTP site", 15, "L"));
document.writeln(spacer("ftp://ftp.netscape.com", 30, "R"));
```

```
// end hiding -->
</SCRIPT>
</PRE>
</HEAD>
<BODY>
</BODY>
</HTML>
```

Notice the use of the <PRE></PRE> tags to format the text. Notice also the use of the writeln() method at the end of each row to include a carriage return. The spacer function uses the length property of the string to compute how many spaces to add to the beginning or end of the string to make sure they line up.

String Methods

In addition to the single length property, the String object has several methods associated with it. We have seen a couple of the methods, such as toUpperCase() and toLowerCase, but what follows is an exhaustive list of all the string methods:

➤ **anchor(*nameAttribute*).** The anchor method creates an anchor out of the string using nameAttribute as the anchor NAME tag. The following code is equivalent to using this method, and produces the same HTML output:

```
document.write("<A NAME=\"anchor_point\">Hello, World!</
➥A>");
document.write("Hello, World!".anchor("anchor_point"));
```

➤ **big().** The big method returns the string surrounded by the <BIG></BIG> tags that display the text in a big font relevant to the base font size.

➤ **blink().** The blink method returns the string surrounded by the <BLINK></BLINK> tags. This causes the string text to blink in the resulting HTML document.

➤ **bold().** The bold method returns the string surrounded by the <B></B> tags that display the string in bold in the resulting HTML document.

➤ **charAt(*index*).** The charAt method returns the character in the string at the specified index.

➤ **fixed().** The fixed method returns the string surrounded by the <TT></TT> tags that display the string in a fixed pitch font in the browser window.

➤ **fontcolor(*color*).** The fontcolor method surrounds the string with the color tag and causes the browser to display the string in the specified color. You can specify the red, green, and blue colors with the hexadecimal "rrggbb" color declaration or use one of the predefined colors. The resulting tag is <FONT COLOR="*color*"></FONT>.

➤ **fontsize(*size*).** The fontsize method surrounds the string with the <FONTSIZE=*size*></FONTSIZE> tag. You can use an absolute value between 1 and 7 or use a +/– in front of the number to indicate a relative font to the base font size declared in the BASEFONT tag. The default base font size is 3.

➤ **indexOf(*character*, [*fromIndex*]).** The indexOf method searches the String object for the first occurrence of the character and returns that index. The fromIndex argument is optional and indicates where to begin the search. You can find the index values for all of the same characters by starting after the previous index.

```
while(index < text.lastIndexOf("a"))
    index = text.indexOf("a", index + 1);
    document.writeln(index + "\t");
```

➤ **italics().** This method surrounds the string with the <I></I> tags that display the text in italic font.

➤ **lastIndexOf(*character*, [*fromIndex*]).** The lastIndexOf method is identical to the indexOf method except that it searches through the string backwards for the character starting at fromIndex.

➤ **link(*URL*).** The link method is similar to the anchor method except it creates an HREF tag that points to the URL provided. The resulting tag is <A HREF=*URL*>*text*</A>.

➤ **small().** This method is similar to the big method, except that it causes the string to be surrounded by the <SMALL> </SMALL> tags that display the text in a smaller font relative to the base font.

➤ **strike().** The strike method displays the string with a strikeout through the middle and surrounds it with the <STRIKE></STRIKE> tags.

➤ **sub().** The sub method displays the string in subscript by appending the tags to the beginning and end of the string.

➤ **substring(*startIndex,endIndex*).** The substring method returns the string that runs from startIndex to the character right before endIndex. If startIndex is larger than endIndex, the method acts as if the two are in each other's positions. If the two indexes are equal, it returns an empty string.

➤ **sup().** The sup method returns the string with the tags appended to the beginning and end of the string. This displays the string in superscript.

➤ **toLowerCase().** The toLowerCase method returns the string with all characters changed to lowercase.

➤ **toUpperCase().** The toUpperCase method returns the string with all characters changed to uppercase.

Figure 5.1 shows what these methods produce respectively in the Hello, World! text.

The script that follows produces the document.

```
<HTML>
<HEAD>
</HEAD>
<BODY BGCOLOR="#FFFFFF">
<PRE>
<SCRIPT LANGUAGE="JavaScript">
<!--
text = "Hello, World!";
```

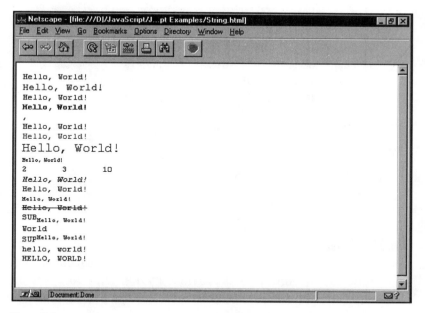

Figure 5.1

Results of the String methods on "Hello, World!"

```
document.writeln(text.anchor("text"));
document.writeln(text.big());
document.writeln(text.blink());
document.writeln(text.bold());
document.writeln(text.charAt(5));
document.writeln(text.fixed());
document.writeln(text.fontcolor("red"));
document.writeln(text.fontsize(5));
document.writeln(text.fontsize(-2));
index = 0;
while(index < text.lastIndexOf("l"))  {
    index = text.indexOf("l",index + 1);
    document.write(index +"\t");
}
document.write("\n");
document.writeln(text.italics());
document.writeln(text.link("http://www.mcp.com/newriders"));
```

```
document.writeln(text.small());
document.writeln(text.strike());
document.writeln("SUB" + text.sub());
document.writeln(text.substring(7,12));
document.writeln("SUP" + text.sup());
document.writeln(text.toLowerCase());
document.writeln(text.toUpperCase());

// -->
</SCRIPT>
</PRE>
</BODY>
</HTML>
```

The Math Object

The Math object provides standard mathematical constants and functions beyond what is provided by the standard operators for addition, subtraction, division, multiplication, and so on, where a single character represents the function to be carried out. The Math object is considered *static*; that is, there does not need to be an instance of the object in order to use the Math object's properties and methods. There is no need to use the *new* statement to create a copy of the Math object; instead, refer to the Math object directly.

```
area = Math.PI*Math.pow(radius,2);
```

The Math object is a perfect example of when to use the with() { ... } statement. If you are using several Math functions and constants together, it will be more convenient to declare a block as being with(Math) so that you can refer to the properties and methods of Math without prefixing the Math object name to every call. The following two code blocks are equivalent to each other.

```
With(Math){
area = PI*pow(radius,2);
}

area = Math.PI*Math.pow(radius,2);
```

Math Properties

The Math object provides six properties. These properties hold fundamental constants—constants that are often used in mathematical functions. These properties follow:

➤ **E.** This property holds the value for Euler's constant, which is approximately 2.718

➤ **LN10.** This property holds the natural logarithm of 10, which is approximately 2.302

➤ **LN2.** This property holds the natural logarithm of 2, which is approximately 0.693

➤ **PI.** This property is the constant that holds the ratio of a circle's circumference to its diameter. The value is approximately 3.1415

➤ **SQRT1_2.** This property holds the square root of one half (1/2), approximately 0.707

➤ **SQRT2.** This property holds the square root of 2, which is approximately 1.414

Figure 5.2 shows all the values displayed using the following script:

```
<HTML>
<HEAD>
</HEAD>
<BODY BGCOLOR="#FFFFFF">
<PRE>
<SCRIPT LANGUAGE="JavaScript">
<!--
with(Math) {
document.writeln(E);
document.writeln(LN10);
document.writeln(LN2);
document.writeln(PI);
document.writeln(SQRT1_2);
document.writeln(SQRT2);
}
```

```
// -->
</SCRIPT>
</PRE>
</BODY>
</HTML>
```

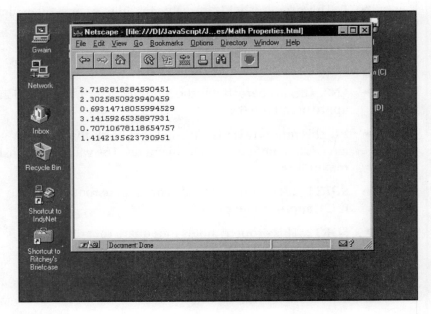

Figure 5.2
The Math properties.

Math Methods

In addition to the properties built into the Math object, several methods perform calculations. These include the following:

➤ **abs(*number*).** This method returns the absolute value of the number provided. If the number is zero (0) or positive, the method returns the number unchanged. If the number is negative, the method returns the number without the negative sign.

➤ **acos(*number*).** This method returns the arc cosine of *number*. *Number* should be from -1 to 1, and acos() returns the value in radians, which run from 0 to Pi radians. If *number* is outside the -1 to 1 range, the method returns 0.

➤ **asin(*number*).** This method returns the arc sine of *number*. *Number* should be from -1 to 1, and asin() returns the value in radians, which run from -Pi/2 to Pi/2 radians. If *number* is outside the -1 to 1 range then the method returns 0.

➤ **atan(*number*).** This method returns the arc tangent of *number*. *Number* should be the tangent of an angle, and atan() returns the value in radians, which run from -Pi/2 to Pi/2 radians. If *number* is outside the -1 to 1 range, the method returns 0.

➤ **ceil(*number*).** This method returns the integer that is the next integer further away from zero than *number*. Ceil(32.5), for example, would become 33, and ceil(-24.8) would become -25.

➤ **cos(*number*).** This method returns the cosine of an angle (*number*), which is represented in radians. The result will run from -1 to 1.

➤ **exp(*number*).** This method returns *e* to the power of *number*.

➤ **floor(*number*).** This method returns the integer closest to *number* toward zero. For example, 32.5 would become 32, and -24.8 would become -24.

➤ **log(*number*).** This method returns the natural logarithm of the value *number*.

➤ **max(*number1, number2*).** This method returns the greater of two numbers.

➤ **min(*number1, number2*).** This method returns the lesser of two numbers. For example, min(45, 23) would return 23.

➤ **pow(*base,exponent*).** This method returns the value of base to the power of exponent. For example, pow(2,3) would return 8.

➤ **random().** This method is only available on X-platforms, which are essentially any Unix operating systems. It returns a pseudo random number between 0 and 1.

➤ **round(*number*).** This method rounds the value of *number* to the nearest integer. If the decimal portion of the number is .5, the number rounds up.

➤ **sin(*number*).** This method returns the sine of an angle (*number*), which is represented in radians. The result will run from -1 to 1.

➤ **sqrt(*number*).** This method returns the square root of the value of *number*. The value of *number* must be non-negative; otherwise, the function always returns zero. If you want to deal with complex numbers, you have to use the a + bi notation where the real and imaginary components are separated.

➤ **tan(*number*).** This method takes an angle in radians as its argument and returns the tangent to the angle.

The following script shows an example of each of these functions in use. The results provided are shown in figure 5.3.

```
<HTML>
<HEAD>
</HEAD>
<BODY BGCOLOR="#FFFFFF">
<PRE>
<SCRIPT LANGUAGE="JavaScript">
<!--
with(Math) {
document.writeln("abs(-9): " + abs(-9));
document.writeln("acos(0): " + acos(0));
document.writeln("asin(-1): " + asin(-1));
document.writeln("atan(-2): " + atan(-2));
document.writeln("ceil(32.5): " + ceil(32.5));
document.writeln("cos(2): " + cos(2));
document.writeln("exp(1): " + exp(1));
document.writeln("floor(32.5): " + floor(32.5));
document.writeln("log(10): " + log(10));
```

```
document.writeln("max(10,20): " + max(10,20));
document.writeln("min(10,20): " + min(10,20));
document.writeln("pow(2,3): " + pow(2,3));
//document.writeln("random(): " + random());
document.writeln("round(23.4): " + round(23.4));
document.writeln("sin(1.624): " + sin(1.624));
document.writeln("sqrt(3): " + sqrt(3));
document.writeln("tan(2.5): " + tan(2.5));
}
// -->
</SCRIPT>
</PRE>
</BODY>
</HTML>
```

Figure 5.3

Results of the Math methods.

A simple example of one of the Math methods in action is shown in figure 5.4. In this case, an array of rows is looped, each representing a value from 1 at the top to -1 at the bottom. As the script moves along the columns, it moves progressively through the radian measurements in 0.1 radian increments. If the value of sin at that point is less than the row value, a pound sign (#) is printed. The code that carries out this wave is as follows:

```html
<HTML>
<HEAD>
</HEAD>
<BODY BGCOLOR="#FFFFFF">
<PRE>
<SCRIPT LANGUAGE="JavaScript">
<!--
with(Math) {
for(var i = 0; i < 20; i ++) {
    for(var j = 0; j < 7; j += 0.1) {
        if((10 + sin(j)*10) > (20 - i)) {
            document.write("#");


        }
        else {
            document.write(" ");
        }
    }
    document.write("\n");
}
}
// -->
</SCRIPT>
</PRE>
</BODY>
</HTML>
```

The Math functions in JavaScript, when dealing with double precision floating point numbers, are liable to platform dependent accuracy bugs when numbers get close to boundary conditions such as +/– Inf, and NaN. Be aware of these problems when using the Math methods.

The Date Object

As with the String object, JavaScript does not have a native Date type, so it provides the programmer with an object that encapsulates information about a date and time and provides methods for handling this information. The Date object is similar to the Java Date object in that it stores the date as the number of milliseconds since January 1, 1970 00:00:00. Because of this format, there is no way to store dates prior to January 1, 1970.

Figure 5.4

A sine wave using JavaScript.

Date Constructors

In order to use Date methods, you must first create an instance of a date with the value you want. There are three ways of constructing a Date object.

```
tempDate = new Date();
```

This constructor method creates a new date and stores the current date and time as the value for the object.

```
tempDate = new Date("month day, year hours:minutes:seconds");
```

This constructor takes a string such as "January 22, 1996 06:32:00" and creates a date. Omit any of the time values, and they will be set to zero automatically.

```
tempDate = new Date(year, month, day, hours, minutes,
➡seconds);
```

This constructor uses comma-separated numbers instead of a string and sets the Date object accordingly. Again, you can omit any of the time values and zero will be substituted.

Date Methods

The Date object does not have any properties that can be set or accessed directly. Instead, it provides several methods with which to interact with Date values.

The first group of methods enables you to set information about the date.

Table 5.1

Method	Range of Valid Values
setDate(*dayOfMonth*)	1–31
setHours(*hours*)	0–23
setMinutes(*minutes*)	0–59
setMonth(*month*)	0–11
setSeconds(*seconds*)	0–59
setTime(*milliseconds*)	0 and up
setYear(*year*)	1970 and up

The setDate methods enable you to control the value of Date objects after they are created. Each method takes an integer in the range specified in the preceding table. Most of the methods are staightforward, except for the setTime method. This method takes the time as the number of milliseconds after January 1, 1970 00:00:00. Obviously, this is not a convenient notation to use. This method is intended for use in conjuction with the getTime method to set the time from an already established Date object.

In addition to the setDate methods, there are also several getDate methods for returning the values of different elements of a Date.

For all of the set functions, there exist identical get functions. These get functions return the integers that represent the values specified in the preceding table.

Table 5.2

Method	Return Value
getDate()	Returns the day of the month
getDay()	Returns the day of the week
getHours()	Returns the hour of the day
getMinutes()	Returns the minutes in the hour
getMonth()	Returns the month
getSeconds()	Returns the seconds in the minute
getTime()	Returns milliseconds since 1.1.1970
getTimezoneOffset	Returns the offset from GMT
getYear()	Returns the year—post 1970

In addition to the standard get methods, there are two methods—getDay and getTimezoneOffset—that return values that cannot be set directly through the Date object. The getDay method returns the day of the week that is determined by the other Date values, so there is no need to set this number explicitly. The getTimezoneOffset method returns the offset from Greenwich Mean Time in minutes of the client's computer locale. This is information set by the operating system, not the programmer.

In addition to the set and get methods, the Date object has five other methods. Two of these methods—parse() and UTC()—are static and are implemented using the Date.*method()* syntax rather than being appended to an actual instance of an object.

➤ **parse(*dateString*).** This method parses the string representation of Date and returns the number of milliseconds from January 1, 1970 00:00:00. The date is expected to be in local time. The Timezone offset of the computer will be used unless a GMT stamp is placed on the end of the string, for example, "GMT-0330." Notice that the GMT offset is in hours and minutes (hhmm), not total minutes.

➤ **UTC(*year, month, day* [, *hours*] [, *minutes*] [, *seconds*]).** This method returns the number of milliseconds since January 1, 1970 00:00:00 based upon Greenwich Mean Time (GMT) or Universal Coordinate Time (UTC). Use this method if you have a date based upon GMT instead of local time.

There are also three methods for producing string output of the Date. These are:

➤ **toGMTString().** This method returns the Date in GMT using Internet conventions.

➤ **toLocalString().** This method returns the Date in local time, using the mm/dd/yy hh:mm:ss format.

➤ **toString().** This method returns the Date in local time, using the Internet standard of Month, day year hh:mm:ss.

Figure 5.5 shows the get methods and toString methods for the Date object produced by the following source code.

```
<HTML>
<HEAD>
</HEAD>
<BODY BGCOLOR="#FFFFFF">
<PRE>
<SCRIPT LANGUAGE="JavaScript">
<!--
today = new Date();
today.setTime(Date.parse("January 26, 1996"));
document.writeln(today);
document.writeln(today.toString());
```

```
document.writeln(today.toLocaleString());
document.writeln(today.toGMTString());
document.writeln("Date: "+today.getDate());
document.writeln("Day: "+today.getDay());
document.writeln("Hours: "+today.getHours());
document.writeln("Minutes: "+today.getMinutes());
document.writeln("Month: "+today.getMonth());
document.writeln("Seconds: "+today.getSeconds());
document.writeln("Time: "+today.getTime());
document.writeln("Offset: "+today.getTimezoneOffset());
document.writeln("Year: "+today.getYear());
// -->
</SCRIPT>
</PRE>
</BODY>
</HTML>
```

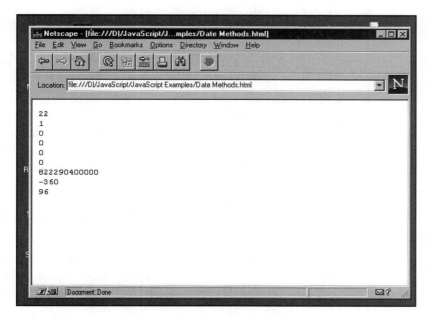

Figure 5.5

Output from several of the Date methods.

The eval, parseInt, parseFloat, escape, unEscape, and isNaN Functions

The final area of built-in functionality in JavaScript is the eval, parseInt, parseFloat, escape, unEscape, and isNaN functions. Unlike the objects discussed previously, these functions are stand-alone methods that are not attached to any object. Therefore, they can be called without reference to any one particular instance or static reference to an object.

➤ **eval(*statement*).** The eval function takes a string and returns the numerical equivalent of any operations represented by the string. For example, this line:

```
result = eval("2+6/2");
```

would return the number 5. This function is important in form elements such as textfields, where you are provided with a string representing the function you need to evaluate. You might, for example, have a spreadsheet script in which you need to evaluate arithmetic expressions in a cell represented by a text input field. You could then take the string from the text field and return the numerical equivalent.

➤ **parseInt(*numberString, radix*).** This function returns the numerical equivalent of the integer string based upon the integer *radix* provided. *Radix* represents the base of the number to convert to, such as 10 for decimal, 8 for octal, and 16 for hexadecimal. Because parseInt expects an integer, it truncates any decimal portion of a number without rounding. If the method cannot parse the string, it truncates the number wherever it ended. If it cannot parse even the first character, it returns 0.

➤ **parseFloat(*floatString*).** This function returns the floating point equivalent of the number represented by *floatString*. The parseInt function can handle floating-point numbers in both decimal and scientific notation.

➤ **escape(*character*).** This function returns the ASCII encoding of the argument in the ISO Latin-1 character set. For example, escape("&") returns "%26."

➤ **unEscape(*string*).** This function returns the ASCII character for the encoded string argument. For example, unEscape("%26") returns "&". Both escape and unEscape can be used to encode characters which would not normally be understood by a file type. In Chapter 6, these functions are used for the document.cookie property.

➤ **isNaN(*number*).** This function is only available on Unix platforms and tells you whether a number is of type NaN, or not a number.

Summary

The built-in function of the JavaScript language provides a useful set of features that programmers can use to develop powerful scripts quickly. Most programmers have become accustomed in today's advanced development environments to the kind of built-in support that these objects provide for JavaScript. The next two chapters cover the objects that are built into the client-side browser environment of Netscape. These include the document, window, history, and location objects, as well as the assorted member objects of each of these classes. You need to understand the hierarchical relationship between all of these elements in order to get the most out of your JavaScript-enabled Web pages.

Chapter 6

Netscape Navigator Objects: The document Object

After you get beyond the objects built into the JavaScript language, the Netscape Navigator program provides several objects that enable the scripter to interact with HTML documents. The main objects that fall into this category are the document and form objects. These objects enable the user to control and respond to events in the Navigator environment. In fact, the document and form objects are at the bottom of the Navigator object hierarchy, which is why they are the first, and easiest objects that can be used in a JavaScript program without extensive knowledge of the Navigator hierarchy. You encountered the document object in the very first chapter of this book, when its write() method was used to send text to the HTML document for display in the Navigator window.

Introducing the Navigator Object Hierarchy

The Navigator object hierarchy is shown in figure 6.1, and depicts the relationship among objects provided by the Netscape

Navigator environment. Many of these objects are dependent upon what the HTML source actually generates. For example, if your HTML file does not include any forms, then there are no form objects present. If there are no links created, then there are no link objects present. In this way, the object hierarchy is very dependent upon the current environment.

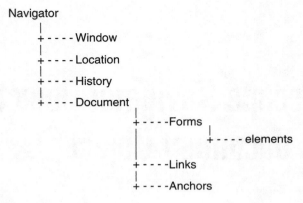

Figure 6.1

The Netscape Navigator object hierarchy.

At the top of the hierarchy is the window object. This object is the encapsulation of the Netscape Navigator window in which the document is being displayed. This object, in addition to window properties, also holds several other objects that can be considered members of the window. These objects include the following:

➤ Any frames that have been created

➤ The location and history objects that hold information about the current URL, and URLs forward and backward in the link history

➤ The document, or documents (if there is more than one frame), is encapsulated

The window object, along with the location and history objects, are covered in more detail in Chapter 7, "The forms, window, history, and location Objects."

Introducing window Object Properties

The window object's first property in the hierarchy includes several similar objects that all refer to windows, or frames within windows that are being displayed by the Netscape Navigator program. The parent object is used when calling functions or object methods that reside in the window object, and are being called from a frame that exists as a child of the window. There are also two more named objects that are used to refer to windows: self and top objects encapsulate window objects that refer to the current window and the original window that was brought up when Netscape was first loaded, and from which all child windows were produced. Finally, the window object includes each frame that populates the screen space. Therefore, if there are two frames, there will be two frame objects. All these objects are dependent upon the HTML code that is passed to the Navigator program from the source file, whether it is code generated on-the-fly or static HTML tags.

Two objects that do not depend upon the HTML code are the location and history objects. Although the content of these objects changes depending upon the environment, their existence is static. The location object refers to the current URL of the source file creating the HTML source code. Because the Navigator 2.0 JavaScript specification does not implement the SRC= attribute for the <SCRIPT></SCRIPT> tag, the file URL for the script and the HTML document are the same. In the future, when the SRC= attribute is included in the <SCRIPT></SCRIPT> tag, it is the parent HTML document to which this object will refer. The history object holds information about the links a user has visited, the links being identical to the links shown in the Go menu item of the Navigator window.

The document object is the final and most important object in the Navigator hierarchy. Its importance is seen in its immediate use in even the most rudimentary JavaScript examples, such as Hello, World!. You will undoubtedly need to use the document object if you want the end user to see the results of anything you do. The document object itself has several objects as properties. The three most important of these are the following:

➤ link object

➤ anchor object

➤ form object

The link and anchor objects are dependent upon there being links or anchors in the document's HTML code. Otherwise, they are not created. The form object is also dependent upon the existence of form tags in your HTML code.

The link object refers to <A HREF=></A> tags that link an element such as text or an image to a specific URL. The link object is not useful on its own, but exists as a property of the document object itself. When links exist, they can be referenced as an array property of the document object. The anchor object refers to any <A NAME=></A> tag that exists in the HTML code. Like the link object, the anchor object exists as an array property that holds all the anchors in a document. Both of these objects are covered in more detail in this chapter.

The form object is also included as a property of the document object, and like the link and anchor objects, exists as an array that holds each of the forms as a single element. For example, the first form on the page would be document.forms[0], document.forms[1], and so on. In addition, each of the forms in a document has properties relating to each of the elements in the form itself, such as buttons and text areas. These elements can then be accessed through the document object. The forms property can be used to control the validation of forms before they are sent to a server side CGI program or other protocol to be handled, thus saving much of the networking overhead that is presently a persistent element of much HTML interaction. The forms object will be covered in more detail in Chapter 8, "Moving On to Java."

The Netscape Navigator object hierarchy is quite extensive, and the number of levels the programmer is expected to work through in order to use a specific object can be quite tedious. In order to ensure that the correct objects are being used, however, and to create as flexible a tool as possible, the object hierarchy becomes a useful device for implementing complicated scripts that rely on several frames or windows to carry out their tasks. In addition, by using the hierarchical structure, JavaScript stays closer to the object-oriented design principles upon which it is based, and keeps the programmer thinking along these lines as well.

The document Object

The document object as just presented exists in the middle of the Navigator object hierarchy between the higher level windows and frames, which are used to partition off screen real-estate, and the lower level individual elements that together comprise the entire document presented to the end user. The document object's job is to bring together all these elements and expose them to the programmer for use in their JavaScript code. This object-oriented approach to the encapsulation of HTML elements is central to the JavaScript implementation, and many of the objects are designed to allow interaction with different elements of the HTML language.

The HTML Equivalent of the document Object

The document object itself actually refers to the body of the HTML document that is defined by the <BODY></BODY> tag. The body of an HTML document takes several optional attribute tags. The following code defines all these options:

```
<BODY
    BACKGROUND="background image"
    BGCOLOR="background color"
    FGCOLOR="foreground color"
    LINK="unfollowed link color"
    ALINK="activated link color"
    VLINK="followed link color"
    onLoad="event handler code"
    onUnLoad="event handler code">
</BODY>
```

All these options, except for the background image, are included as properties of the document object and can be referenced by the document.*property* naming convention. In addition to the standard attribute properties, the <BODY> tag can also include the onLoad and onUnLoad event handlers that execute the enclosed code the same as all event handlers do when the action of loading or unloading the document occurs.

When creating HTML documents, it is important to take into account the browsers that do not support the JavaScript standard, or older versions of browsers that do. If you are looking for a specific color scheme, be sure to use the standard HTML <BODY> tag to define these preferences. Then, if you want to enhance the page, you can use the document object's properties to override these settings.

Understanding the order in which document attributes are assigned when using both the object properties and the HTML tags is important. In the following code, both the JavaScript code and the HTML tag set the background color. The document object property, however, is used when the page is actually displayed.

```
<HTML>
<HEAD>
<SCRIPT LANGUAGE="JavaScript">
<!--
document.bgColor = "blue";
function change() {
    document.bgColor = "red";
```

```
}
// -->
</SCRIPT>
</HEAD>
<BODY BGCOLOR="white">
<FORM>
<INPUT TYPE="button" NAME="red" VALUE="RED"
➥onClick="change()">
</FORM>
</BODY>
</HTML>
```

Two things are important to note. First, the document property setting overrides any HTML tag settings in the body statement itself. It does not matter that the assignment of the color blue to the document.bgColor property occurs in the <HEAD></HEAD> before the body statement. It carries through in this case. Second, the background color can be updated dynamically. Even though the screen display has been completed, the change in the bgColor property that occurs as a result of the change() function call in the red button's onClick event handler causes the screen to update immediately. The bgColor property is the only property to update immediately. Try the following code that changes several of the document properties to see how changing the document property values changes the colors of the links:

```
<HTML>
<HEAD>
<SCRIPT LANGUAGE="JavaScript">
<!--
document.bgColor = "blue";
document.vlinkColor = "white";
document.linkColor = "yellow";
document.alinkColor = "red";
function change() {
    document.bgColor = "red";
    document.vlinkColor = "blue";
    document.linkColor = "green";
    document.alinkColor = "blue";
}
// -->
</SCRIPT>
```

```
</HEAD>
<BODY BGCOLOR="white">
<A HREF="http://www.cam.ac.uk/">University of Cambridge</A>
<A HREF="http://www.microsoft.com/">Microsoft</A>
<FORM>
<INPUT TYPE="button" NAME="red" VALUE="red"
➥onClick="change()">
</FORM>
</BODY>
</HTML>
```

Notice that the various link color properties are updated internally, but until the link is activated, the changes do not take effect.

Be sure to note that the default behavior of mixing JavaScript and HTML source code is not at all obvious or straightforward. This is due mainly to the ordering in which items are evaluated and which elements of the display are updated at what time. Be sure to check out the behavior of your particular script before assuming that it will act as you intend. Because JavaScript and HTML can be intermixed quite freely, it is difficult to define exactly how the two will behave in each instance. The Netscape 2.0 version of JavaScript still has a few quirks that should be fixed in the next release, slated as version 2.1.

The next two sections detail the properties, methods, and event handlers that are part of the document object as defined in the Netscape Navigator 2.0 specification.

The document Object Properties

The properties of the document object are listed here:

- ➤ alinkColor
- ➤ anchors
- ➤ bgColor
- ➤ cookie
- ➤ fgColor

➤   forms

➤   lastModified

➤   linkColor

➤   links

➤   location

➤   referrer

➤   title

➤   vlinkColor

This list of properties can be divided into two groups, with properties such as alinkColor and bgColor falling in one group, and properties such as forms and links falling in another. The properties in the first instance exist regardless of what is actually contained in the actual <BODY> tag or created by document.write() methods. These properties hold information about attributes that always exist, such as the background color (bgColor) or the color of a visited link (vlinkColor). These properties are nearly equivalent to the attributes that can be set in the standard HTML body tag, and therefore are considered the document object's attribute properties. The properties that fall into the second category are dependent upon the existence of their respective elements in the document's <BODY> tag. These include arrays such as links and forms and the *cookie* string, which is used to hold data on the client machine between browser sessions. Because these properties are created by the elements that make up the body of the document, they will be referred to as the document object element properties.

The Document Attribute Properties

The document attribute properties include the following variables:

➤   alinkColor

➤   bgColor

➤ fgColor

➤ lastModified

➤ linkColor

➤ location

➤ title

➤ vlinkColor

Of all these properties, only the location and lastModified variables are not definable in the <BODY></BODY> HTML tag. Each of the other properties directly relates to one of the attribute tags shown in the previous section.

The Color Properties

The color properties include the alinkColor, bgColor, fgColor, linkColor, and vlinkColor properties. These properties control the color formatting of the page in reference to the condition of the HREF links, if any in the document, and the background and foreground colors. The color value provided is a string that is of the form:

```
alinkColor = "#RRGGBB";
```

The RR, GG, and BB represent the red, green, and blue channels that make up the color spectrum and run in value from 0 to 255, represented in hexadecimal values. For example, the basic colors are:

red = "#FF0000"

blue = "#0000FF"

green = "#00FF00"

white = "#FFFFFF"

black = "#000000"

By mixing different values for the red, green, and blue channels, you can control the exact color. Of course, this is not at all intuitive, so JavaScript and the HTML code can accept names for colors. These names are listed in the appendix and provide almost any combination you could reasonably want. If you are trying to match an RGB value, it may be easier to use the exact numbers.

➤ **alinkColor.** This property controls the color of an active link. This is the color that a link changes to as the user depresses the mouse button over it before the actual link is selected. Notice that when selecting buttons or links, it is not the lone act of pressing the mouse down that selects the item. Rather, it is the combination of pressing *and* releasing the mouse button over the object that selects it. If you move the mouse away from the object before releasing the mouse button, it will not be selected. This attribute is updated for the next time the user selects a link in the document.

➤ **linkColor.** This property controls the color of the standard HTML link created in an <A HREF=*"URL"*>*text*</A> tag. This color attribute is not automatically updated if it is changed once the document has been displayed. As soon as a link in the document is selected, however, all the link colors are updated to show the new color.

➤ **vlinkColor.** This property is similar to the linkColor property, except that this color is used for links that the Navigator has stored as being previously visited. Like the linkColor property, and unlike the bgColor property, this property is not reflected in the displaying of the document until after a link has been selected.

➤ **bgColor.** This property holds the value for the background color of the document. This property is immediately updated in the display.

➤ **fgColor.** This property holds the value for the foreground text color in the display. It does not appear to be changeable after the color is set and the document has been parsed by the browser.

The title, location, and lastModified Properties

These three properties are strictly not members of the <BODY> tag, but are considered attributes of the document in general.

➤ **title.** This property holds the value of the title of the document as created in the <TITLE>*document title*</TITLE> tag. This title is displayed in the title bar of the browser window, and is the name given to the URL in the Bookmarks menu if the user adds it as a bookmark. This value cannot be changed after the document has been created.

➤ **location.** This property holds the full URL of the file holding the document source code. Because the Netscape 2.0 JavaScript specification has not implemented the capability to import JavaScript files by using the SRC= attribute of the script tag, the URL provided is the file from which the document source code comes.

➤ **lastModified.** This property holds the date the file was last modified. In conjunction with the document cookie, this could be used to inform the user that modifications have been made since they last visited the site. The cookie property will be discussed in more detail in the next section.

The Document Element Properties

The document properties that reflect the elements present in the HTML document are the following:

➤ anchors

➤ cookie

➤ forms

➤ links

The anchors, forms, and links properties are arrays that have an entry for every element of that kind existing in the <BODY></BODY> portion of the HTML code. The JavaScript programmer can then use these arrays to refer to the individual element objects by indexing through the array. The cookie property is a string representing the persistent file cookie.txt. This file holds what are known as cookies, which enable HTML pages to store a limited amount of information on the client machine.

The anchors document Property

The anchors document property contains all the anchors in a document in an array structure. The order of the items in the anchors array is dependent upon the order in which the anchors appear in the document. Unlike the standard array structure created with the makeArray() function created in Chapter 4, "Using and Creating Objects in JavaScript," the anchors, and all the element properties of the document object, begin indexing at zero (0) through one less than the total number of objects (n–1). Therefore, the first anchor in the document is at document.anchors[0], the second at document.anchors[1], and so on. Like the standard array, the total number of elements in the array is held in the length property of the array, and the total number of anchors in a document would be document.anchors.length. The following code prints out the number of anchors in the document.

```
<HTML>
<HEAD>
</HEAD>
<BODY BGCOLOR="white">
This is a test:<P>
<A NAME="ANCHOR 1" HREF="http://www.cam.ac.uk">University of
➥Cambridge</A><P>
<A NAME="ANCHOR 2">Microsoft</A><P>
<PRE>
<SCRIPT LANGUAGE="JavaScript">
<!--
document.writeln("This document has " +
➥document.anchors.length + " anchors.");
// -->
</SCRIPT>
</PRE>
</BODY>
</HTML>
```

Notice that anchors also refer to HREF links. The anchors tag refers to the existence of the NAME= attribute in the <A></A> tag that provides a hypertext target for a URL to move within the page.

The links document Property

The links document property is quite similar to the anchors property, except that instead of looking at all the instances of the NAME= attribute in <A></A> tags, the links property lists all the <A></A> tags with HREF= attributes. The links array begins indexing at zero (0) and goes through one less than the total number of object link elements (n–1). Therefore, the first link in the document is at document.links[0], the second at document.links[1], and so on. The total number of anchors in a document would be document.links.length. The following code is identical to the preceding, except this time it counts only the links in the document.

```
<HTML>
<HEAD>
</HEAD>
<BODY BGCOLOR="white">
This is a test:<P>
<A NAME="ANCHOR 1" HREF="http://www.cam.ac.uk">University of
➥Cambridge</A><P>
<A NAME="ANCHOR 2">Microsoft</A><P>
<PRE>
<SCRIPT LANGUAGE="JavaScript">
<!--
document.writeln("This document has " + document.links.length
➥+ " links.");
// -->
</SCRIPT>
</PRE>
</BODY>
</HTML>
```

The forms document Property

The forms document property is an array of objects that corresponds to all the named forms in a document. These forms are indicated by using the <FORM></FORM> tag, and can have several additional elements, depending upon what form input elements are included with them. The following code, like the two previous examples, counts the number of forms in a document.

```
<HTML>
<HEAD>
</HEAD>
<BODY BGCOLOR="white">
This is a test:<P>
<FORM NAME="FORM 1">
<INPUT TYPE="text" NAME="form1Text" VALUE="hello" SIZE=10>
<INPUT TYPE="button" NAME="form1Button" VALUE="test">
</FORM>
This is the second form:
<FORM>
<SELECT NAME="form2Select" SIZE=3 MULTIPLE>
<OPTION>Microsoft
<OPTION>Netscape
<OPTION>Sun Micro
</SELECT>
</FORM>
<PRE>
<SCRIPT LANGUAGE="JavaScript">
<!--
document.writeln("document has " + document.forms.length + "
➥forms");
// -->
</SCRIPT>
</PRE>
</BODY>
</HTML>
```

The following chapter details the form object and how it can be used in JavaScript programs.

The cookie document Property

The cookie property is perhaps one of the most interesting yet complicated features of the Netscape environment. A *cookie* is an entry in a text file called cookies.txt that resides in the Netscape directory. This file has typically been used by server-side CGI scripts to keep information on the client machine for whenever they might visit again. JavaScript enables the programmer access to this file to store recurring information. It is important to recognize two things about cookies. First, the Netscape environment may create only 300 cookies in total, thus limiting the capability of a site to swamp users' hard disks with information they do not necessarily want. In addition, each of these cookies is limited to 4KB in size. This effectively limits the file to about 1.2MB. Moreover, a single site may only have 20 cookie entries, and sites are limited to accessing cookie entries to those that match the same domain. The full cookie entry appears as the following:

```
NAME=VALUE; expires=DATE; path=PATH; domain=DOMAIN_NAME;
secure
```

The name is the name given to the cookie as an identifier, and the value is the value of the cookie itself. The expires date indicates how long the cookie should remain on the client. If this is not provided, it will only remain for the current session. The entry format for the expires entry is:

```
Wdy, DD-Mon-YY HH:MM:SS GMT
```

The path and domain entries are there for specifying which URLs can access the cookie entry. If the URL of the document attempting to access the cookie does not match the domain name and path, it is not allowed to view the cookie. If two sites are in the same domain (for example catal.arch.cam.ac.uk and juno.arch.cam.ac.uk) and a common domain is given in the cookie (arch.cam.ac.uk), both will have access to the cookie. Typically, at least three entries separated by two periods are needed in order to qualify the domain name. If the site is one of the major types of: "com," "edu," "net," "org," "gov," "mil," or "int," then the domain only needs two periods; any other needs three. A site can only specify a domain entry if it is in that domain. If the path or domain are not provided, they default to the exact URL values of the document creating the cookie. The secure keyword is used when you only want the cookie sent if there is a secure connection. If this is not specified, the cookie will be transferable over non-secure links.

The cookie property of the document object is a string that holds values for the cookie entry of the document. This value is altered by adding string expressions to the cookie. For example, you could have a function that places a string and an expiration date in a cookie:

```
function setCookie(name, value, expires) {
    document.cookie = name + value + ";" + "expires=" +
expires + ";";
}
```

Several functions have been developed and are in the public domain for working with cookies. The following, written by Bill Dortch, enable the user to set and examine cookies in a very flexible fashion. The following functions could be placed at the beginning of a file and used throughout your code to work with cookies. The cookie set does not use any white-space, semicolon, or comma characters, so these must be encoded. The following cookie functions use the escape() and unEscape() functions built into JavaScript to convert standard characters to their ISO Latin-1 equivalents such as '%26' for '&'.

This first function is used by the others as an internal method for accessing the items in the cookie.

```
function getCookieVal (offset) {
  var endstr = document.cookie.indexOf (";", offset);
  if (endstr == -1)
```

```
      endstr = document.cookie.length;
  return unescape(document.cookie.substring(offset, endstr));
}
```

This function returns the value of the cookie element specified by the string name. If there is no entry by that name, then it returns null.

```
function GetCookie (name) {
  var arg = name + "=";
  var alen = arg.length;
  var clen = document.cookie.length;
  var i = 0;
  while (i < clen) {
    var j = i + alen;
    if (document.cookie.substring(i, j) == arg)
      return getCookieVal (j);
    i = document.cookie.indexOf(" ", i) + 1;
    if (i == 0) break;
  }
  return null;
}
```

The following function can be used to create cookie entries. Only the first two arguments are used, and any additional arguments are optional. If you skip an argument, and provide an argument that occurs later in the list, you must use null as a placeholder. If the arguments being skipped come at the end of the argument list, with none provided after, then you do not need to provide anything.

```
function Setcookie (name;value) {
  var argv = SetCookie.arguments;
  var argc = SetCookie.arguments.length;
  var expires = (argc > 2) ? argv[2] : null;
  var path = (argc > 3) ? argv[3] : null;
  var domain = (argc > 4) ? argv[4] : null;
  var secure = (argc > 5) ? argv[5] : false;
  document.cookie = name + "=" + escape (value) +
    ((expires == null) ? "" : ("; expires=" +
➥expires.toGMTString())) +
    ((path == null) ? "" : ("; path=" + path)) +
    ((domain == null) ? "" : ("; domain=" + domain)) +
    ((secure == true) ? "; secure" : "");
}
```

This function enables the user to delete a cookie by name.

```
function DeleteCookie (name) {
  var exp = new Date();
  exp.setTime (exp.getTime() - 1);  // This cookie is history
  var cval = GetCookie (name);
  document.cookie = name + "=" + cval + "; expires=" +
exp.toGMTString();
}
```

A possible scenario for using the cookie is as follows. When a page is first loaded, it first checks to see whether its cookie exists. If it does, it then uses the information stored in the cookie to set up the page to the same state it was in when the user left it. If the cookie function returns null, then the page knows that the user is there for the first time or the cookie has expired. In this case, it could provide a default, or novice page. When the page is completed, for example on an unLoad call, the cookie could be updated with the last state of the page before exit. As you can see, the cookie provides a powerful means of creating dynamic, personalized documents for the Web.

The document Object Methods

The following five document methods exist so that the programmer can control certain aspects of the document.

➤   clear()

➤   close()

➤   open()

➤   write()

➤   writeln()

The last two methods, write() and writeln(), are already familiar, and have already been used extensively to create the output of many example HTML pages. The clear(), close(), and open() methods, however, are new methods, and provide a powerful means for creating documents from scratch.

The document.write() and document.writeln() Methods

The document.write() and document.writeln() methods have been used extensively, and you should be familiar with their behavior. The only difference between the two is that the writeln() method inserts a newline character at the end of the line being displayed.

In most cases, the write() and writeln() methods are being sent to a document that is being interpreted at HTML text. Of course, in HTML newline characters are ignored, and it is the line break tags such as <p> that designate when a new line should be created. Two tags exist that indicate to the browser that the text has been preformatted and that spaces and newlines should be kept intact. These are the <PRE></PRE> tags and the <XMP></XMP> tags. This allows the output from the write() and writeln() methods to be displayed correctly on-screen. Of course, the document to which the write() and writeln() methods are sending their values does not have to be of the text/html MIME type. Instead, documents can be written to any of the following types:

➤ text/html

➤ text/plain

➤ image/gif

➤ image/jpeg

➤ image/xbm

➤ x-world/*plug-in*

If you know the specification for a file type of GIF or JPEG format, you can use the write() method to dynamically create your own image document. The plug-in type is any plug-in that Netscape supports. You could, for example, create a VRML world on-the-fly depending upon user input.

The open(), close(), and clear() document Methods

These three methods, open(), close(), and clear(), enable the programmer to create new documents, close documents, and clear documents from windows and frames. When document.write() is called, its default behavior is to write to the current document. If there is no document for the current window, then the write() method opens a new document of type text/html and writes to this document. Of course, in the default window of the Netscape browser, there is already a document open—the file in which the JavaScript is embedded. For this reason, there is no need to open a new document for output. As you will see in the next chapter, however, it is possible to open a window without a document. In this case, document.open() is required to begin the text stream that the browser interprets at the HTML file. After you have finished writing to the document, you use the document.close() method to close the stream and display the file.

JavaScript and Netscape can become unstable if you call
document.close() in the middle of a document. Thus, using
document.close() is not recommended in the main window before all the
HTML code has been displayed because typically scripts occur in the
middle of surrounding <HTML></HTML> tags. You can call document
close() safely from an event handler because these are not evaluated
until after the main document stream has closed anyway.

The following code opens up a new browser window without a
document. It then proceeds to send several documents to the
window that create a flashing sign effect. Notice that each time
the for loop is entered, it opens a new document in the
msgWindow and closes it before it leaves.

```
<HTML>
<HEAD>
</HEAD>
<BODY BGCOLOR="white">
<SCRIPT LANGUAGE="JavaScript">
<!--
/**
 * this is used to create arrays in JavaScript
 */
function makeArray(n) {
    this.length = n;
    for(var i = 1; i <= n; i++)
        this[i] = 0;
    return this
}

text = new makeArray(5);
text[1] = "Hello, World!";
text[2] = "Welcome";
text[3] = "To";
text[4] = "My";
text[5] = "Page!";

// This creates the new window with no toolbars and sets the
➥width and height
```

```
msgWindow = window.open("","Hello",
➥"toolbar=no,width=200,height=100");

//this loop send the different documents based upon the text
➥array to the msgWindow
for(var j = 1; j <= text.length; j++) {
msgWindow.document.open();
msgWindow.document.write("<H1>" + text[j] + "<H1>");
msgWindow.document.close();
for(i=0;i<10000; i++){}
}

// -->
</SCRIPT>
</BODY>
</HTML>
```

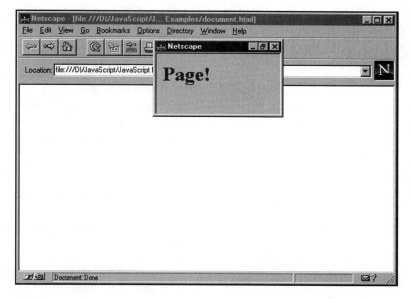

Figure 6.2

Creating new documents in a window.

Here is a breakdown of each of these methods:

➤ **open("*mimeType*").** This method is used to open a new
document stream. You can optionally specify what MIME

type the document should be by providing the mimeType argument. The browser will then assume that the data being sent to it from the write() or writeln() methods are of that format. The list of valid mime types are:

➤ text/html

➤ text/plain

➤ image/gif

➤ image/jpeg

➤ image/xbm

➤ x-world/*plug-in*

➤ You can use the write() method to create any of the previous types that Netscape can interpret itself or through one of its plug-ins. The plug-in type is any plug-in that Netscape supports. You could, for example, create a VRML world on-the-fly. If no mime type is given, then the default text/html is chosen.

By using the capability of the document.open() command to open streams to Netscape plug-ins, it is possible to detect the presence of a plug-in on a client machine. For example, to detect whether the Macromedia Shockwave plug-in for director files exists on a machine, you could call the following function:

```
var haveShockwavePlugin = false
var tiny = window.open("", "teensy", "width=1,height=1")
if (tiny != null) {
    if (tiny.document.open("application/x-director") != null)
        haveShockwavePlugin = true
    tiny.close()
}
```

Note that if the document.open command returns a non-null object, then the plug-in exists.

➤ **close()**. This is the method used to close the document stream created with the open method. If you wish to create more than one document object, as in the flashing sign example, you will need to call close() before opening another document.

➤ **clear()**. This method clears the contents of the open document and empties the contents of the document window. This functions similarly to closing and opening a new document in a window, as in the flashing sign example from the open method definition.

The document Object Event Handlers

The document object has two event handlers:

➤ **onLoad=*statement*.** This event handler executes the statement when the page is loaded. A useful action for an onLoad event handler is checking the value of a cookie when the page is first loaded and assigning it to a JavaScript variable that can then be used throughout the JavaScript code.

➤ **onUnLoad=*statement*.** This event handler causes the statement or statements to be executed when the document is unloaded. This event could be used to cause the page to update the persistent cookie before it is unloaded.

Summary

This chapter has provided the basis for using the document object in your JavaScript code. The document object is the central object in the Navigator Object Hierarchy, and provides many built-in functions for creating dynamic Web pages. Instead of depending upon static HTML tags, you can generate documents on the fly. The next chapter includes the last sections of the JavaScript language to be covered. These are the form object, the location object, and the history object. They can be used to both control the hypertext links in your document and enable you to begin populating your document with more complicated input devices in the guise of form elements.

Chapter 7

The forms, window, history, and location Objects

By now you have been presented with the meat of JavaScript programming. You have covered the foundations of the language itself, and learned about all of the individual syntactical elements, and how to use them in concert to create a functioning JavaScript program. In addition, the basic objects provided with the language have been covered, including the String, Math, and Date objects. Finally, the central object to the JavaScript paradigm—the document—was presented in the last chapter.

Of course, with all these tools at your disposal, there are still several more topics to discuss before wrapping up the JavaScript language and moving on to Java in the next chapter.

In the discussion the document object, one property was left off the list: forms. Forms enable the client user to pass input to JavaScript programs, which can then be used to dynamically alter the behavior of a document. In addition to forms, there are three Navigator objects that exist at the same level or above the document object:

➤ The location object

➤ The history object

➤ The window object

The window object enables you to control the actual screen real estate of a document, and provides access to dialog boxes and frames in addition to the standard Navigator window. The location and history objects enable the encapsulation of link information that provides JavaScript programs with the capability to react to information concerning how they were arrived at, and their Internet origins. By using these objects, the JavaScript programmer can enhance the basic document object with a diverse and dynamic range of interaction with the client user.

Using the forms Object

Perhaps the most immediately useful aspect of the document object is its capability to access forms contained in HTML documents. The form object enables the programmer to interact with the different form elements and the client user. In addition, it is also possible to access forms in a page by name.

The forms object is an encapsulation of the HTML codes that are used to create forms for HTML documents. The structure of the form tag is:

```
<FORM
    NAME="form name"
    TARGET="target window"
    ACTION="form handling URL"
    METHOD=GET¦POST
    ENCTYPE="encoding type"
    [onSubmit="JavaScript code"]>
</FORM>
```

The form tag is used to declare several attributes of the individual form:

➤ **NAME** is used to store the name of the form itself. It can be used to access the form object in JavaScript code.

➤ **TARGET** is used to specify which window the response of form submission should go to. You can also designate a frame in the <FRAMESET> tag as the target of the form response. In addition to these standard targets, you can specify special frames named _top, _parent, _self, and _blank. The targets enable you to specify targets that correspond to the JavaScript Navigator window hierarchy.

➤ **ACTION** is used to specify the URL of the program that accepts the data sent by the form. This is typically some kind of CGI script on the server machine in the cgi-bin directory.

➤ **METHOD** has two possible values: GET or POST. By specifying GET, the form information is appended to the end of the URL, which is placed in the environment variable QUERY_STRING. This can then be accessed by the CGI script to act upon the form data. This is the default attribute setting. POST sends the data to the CGI script through stdin where its length is stored in CONTENT_LENGTH. This value will be particular to whatever CGI programs you are using on your system.

➤ **ENCTYPE** indicates how the form is encoded. The two possible values are: "application/x-www-form-urlencoded" or "multipart/form-data."

Properties

As with many JavaScript objects that reflect HTML tags, the list of attributes that follows is stored in the form object's property list. The properties that a form object has follow:

➤   action

➤   elements

➤   encoding

➤ method

➤ target

All these properties, except for elements, reflect the state of the form tag's corresponding attributes. For example: the action property stores the value of the ACTION attribute.

The encoding property is unlike the other form properties in that it does not store the individual attributes of the form HTML tag. Instead, it is an array that stores the values of the individual form elements inside the FORM declaration. These elements can include buttons, textareas, checkboxes, and other features. Form elements are created in a FORM tag as follows:

```
<HTML>
<HEAD>
</HEAD>
<BODY>
<PRE>
<SCRIPT LANGUAGE="JavaScript">
<!--
// -->
</SCRIPT>
</PRE>
<FORM NAME="test">
Username:
<INPUT TYPE="text" NAME="text1" VALUE="" SIZE=20><BR>
Password:
<INPUT TYPE="password" NAME="password1" VALUE="" SIZE=10><BR>
<HR>
Choose all that apply:<P>
<INPUT TYPE="checkbox" NAME="checkbox1" VALUE="internet">
Use the Internet<BR>
<INPUT TYPE="checkbox" NAME="checkbox2" VALUE="music">
Listen to music<BR>
<INPUT TYPE="checkbox" NAME="checkbox3" VALUE="games">
Play video games<BR>
<HR>
<INPUT TYPE="radio" NAME="Sex" VALUE="Male">Male
<INPUT TYPE="radio" NAME="Sex" VALUE="Female">Female
<BR>
What kind of computer do you own:<BR>
```

```
<SELECT NAME="select1" MULTIPLE>
<OPTION>PC
<OPTION>UNIX
<OPTION>MAC
<OPTION>OTHER
</SELECT><BR>
<TEXTAREA NAME="textarea1" ROWS=10 COLS=20>comments
</TEXTAREA><P>
<INPUT TYPE="submit" NAME="submit1" VALUE="submit">
<INPUT TYPE="reset"  NAME="reset1" VALUE="reset">
</FORM>
</BODY>
</HTML>
```

These elements then reside at test.elements[0], test.elements[1], and so on. If you access the form through the document object as the first form in the HTML code, then you can also access the individual elements by using document.forms[0].elements[0], document.forms[0].elements[1], and so on. Figure 7.1 shows the resulting form.

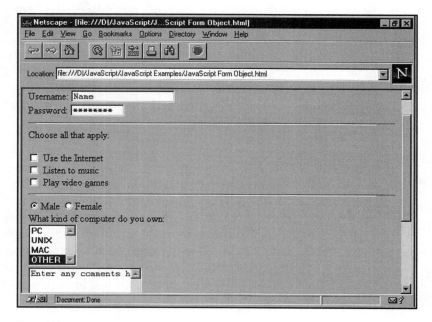

Figure 7.1

The Example Form page.

In the next section, the properties, methods, and event handlers for each of the form elements will be discussed.

form Object Methods

The only method available for the form object is the submit() method. Invoking this method is exactly like the user pressing the submit button on the form. This can be used to automatically send the form information after some action has occurred in a JavaScript program. If you wish to cause the test form shown above to be submitted, you can either call:

```
document.test.submit();
```

or

```
document.forms[0].submit();
```

 The submit() method has parentheses behind it. It is a common mistake to forget the parentheses when calling a method. This is in fact, a reference to a property, which in the case of the form object does not exist, and causes an error.

To say that the submit method is the only method of the forms object does not take into account all of the different methods that each element will have. The next section discusses each of the types of elements in the test form and their respective methods, properties, and event handlers.

Accessing form Information

As mentioned before, there are several ways to access the form objects created by HTML code in a document page. Because the document's HTML form tags are what creates the forms in the first place, it is only fitting that forms be a property of the document object itself. In a similar manner to other document properties such as links and anchors, you can access the form objects through the forms array. You can access the test form presented in the previous example with the following command:

```
document.forms[0]
```

If there are multiple forms in a document, you can access them in the order in which they occur by increasing the index of the array:

```
document.forms[1]
document.forms[2]
...
```

Remember that the array indexing of objects provided by the Netscape and JavaScript environments goes from zero to the number of objects minus one (0 to n–1). This is unlike the arrays that have been created with the makeArray function in JavaScript you were shown in Chapter 4, which index from one to the number of objects in the array (1 to n).

In addition to accessing the form objects that reside in the HTML document through the document forms array, it is also possible to refer to the form objects by name if the name is provided in the form tag attributes. For example, referencing the test form above by name appears as follows:

```
document.test
```

Notice that the test form must be accessed as a member property of the document object. What the document object essentially provides is two ways of accessing a form object: either through its name, or through its array index.

In order to refer to a form, the form must already have been created in the document. The following code, which refers to the form below it in the document, causes a run-time error to be called:

```
<HTML>
<HEAD>
<SCRIPT LANGUAGE="JavaScript">
<!--
document.test.elements[0].value = "Hello, World!";
// -->
</SCRIPT>
</HEAD>
<BODY>
<PRE>
</PRE>
<FORM NAME="test">
```

```
Username:
<INPUT TYPE="text" NAME="text1" VALUE="" SIZE=20><BR>
...
<INPUT TYPE="reset"  NAME="reset1" VALUE="reset">
</FORM>
</BODY>
</HTML>
```

The following code accesses the form successfully:

```
<HTML>
<HEAD>
</HEAD>
<BODY>
<PRE>
</PRE>
<FORM NAME="test">
Username:
<INPUT TYPE="text" NAME="text1" VALUE="" SIZE=20><BR>
...
<INPUT TYPE="reset"  NAME="reset1" VALUE="reset">
</FORM>
<SCRIPT LANGUAGE="JavaScript">
<!--
document.test.elements[0].value = "Hello, World!";
// -->
</SCRIPT>
</BODY>
</HTML>
```

The only change is that the reference to the form occurs after the form has been created in the document. Because event handlers are only called after the entire document has been loaded, you can place the call to the form in the <HEAD></HEAD> of the document in a function, which is called later on by an event handler.

In addition to the placement of the references to forms, there are two additional important items to mention: changing the value of form items and form persistence. Form *persistence* means that when the users or programmer place data into a form element, Netscape retains that information, and if the page is reloaded into the same session (that is, without Netscape being closed) then the form elements will retain their same values.

If you noticed in the above example, the JavaScript statement accesses the value statement of the form's text element. When this value changes, it appears in the text box itself. This enables you to change the data in these boxes on a dynamic basis. For example, you can create a marquee for displaying a line of text. One way to do this is to create an array that holds all of the characters (including blank spaces) for the text, and cycle through a portion of the characters you wish to show at the same time on the screen. The following code creates such a marquee:

```
<HTML>
<HEAD>
<SCRIPT LANGUAGE="JavaScript">
<!--

var buffer = "                                 ";
var text = "Welcome to my Web Page, I hope you enjoy
➥yourself!";
var marqueeString = buffer + text + buffer;
var marqueeRunning = false;
var timeoutID = null;
var position = 0;
var sLength = marqueeString.length;

function stopMarquee() {
    if(marqueeRunning)
        clearTimeout(timeoutID);
    marqueeRunning = false;
}

function startMarquee() {
    stopMarquee();
    updateMarquee();
}

function updateMarquee() {
        document.marquee.elements[0].value =
```

```
➥marqueeString.substring(position++%sLength,position+39%sLength);
        timeoutID = setTimeout("updateMarquee()", 50);
        marqueeRunning = true;
}

// -->
</SCRIPT>
</HEAD>
<BODY onLoad="startMarquee()" onUnLoad="stopMarquee()">
<PRE>
</PRE>
<FORM NAME="marquee">
<INPUT TYPE="text" NAME="textBox" VALUE="" SIZE=40><BR>
</FORM>
</BODY>
</HTML>
```

Notice the use of the timeout method that causes the updates to the windows to be called every twentieth of a second. This method is part of the window object, which is presented later in the chapter. The single most important line is:

```
document.marquee.elements[0].value =
➥marqueeString.substring(position++%sLength,position+39%sLength);
```

This line updates the value of the form element. The substring method grabs a portion of the string in order to place it in the text input box. The substring method also has two arguments: a beginning index and an end index. The beginning index is given as:

```
position++%sLength
```

This statement indicates that after the index position is used, it should be updated by one (position++). The rest of the statement indicates that the actual index used is the modulus of the index with the string length. Using the modulus operator guarantees that position is always between zero and the length of the string. Figure 7.2 shows the marquee after it has begun scrolling out of the box.

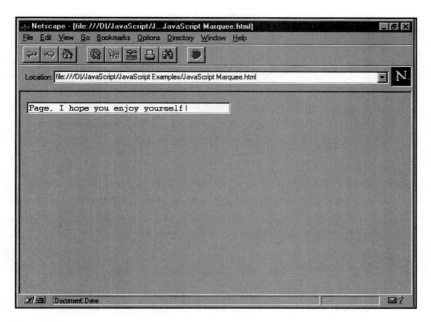

Figure 7.2
The Marquee text form.

The Marquee form represents the diversity that can be achieved with the use of HTML forms. The idea that HTML forms should only be used for sending information *from* the user *to* the server ignores the potential of these objects. It is better to think of the form object as an interface between the user and your JavaScript programs that works in in *both* directions.

In addition to JavaScript's capacity to take advantage of the update-ability of the form object, there is an additional feature that should be mentioned. Form elements retain their values in the Netscape browser between document loadings. If you have ever filled out a form, received a confirmation after submission, and then gone back to the form, you will notice that all of your old entries are still there. This is called *persistence* and can be used to store information in a document when it might be left temporarily. There may occur a situation where a form needs to be reloaded, or it might be left alone for a while, and you might want it to retain its final configuration when the user returns to it within the same session. If this is the case, you can create a text element or hidden form element, and use it to store information. Whenever the page is loaded, you can check the contents of this field, and rebuild the page according to the information in the form text or hidden element. Of course, if you want to retain information between sessions, when Netscape might be closed or your pages are removed from the cache, you will need to store this data in a "cookie," which is discussed in Chapter 6.

Elements of a form

The test form given as an example at the beginning of the chapter has examples of all the form elements for which JavaScript has provided objects. These objects include:

➤ buttons

➤ checkboxes

➤ passwords

➤ radios

➤ reset

➤ select

➤ submit

➤ text

➤ textarea

The next few sections present the properties, methods, and attributes of these objects, as well as the form of their HTML tags.

In order to reference these elements in your JavaScript code, you must provide the element's array index for the specific element of the specific form in the document where the element exists, or use the element's name:

elementName.propertyName

elementName.methodName()

formName.elements[*index*].*propertyName*

formName.elements[*index*].*methodName*

If you know the element name beforehand, it is much easier and clearer to use the name itself instead of an index. At the moment, because you cannot import JavaScript code using the SRC= attribute in the <SCRIPT> tag, all of your JavaScript code will exist on the same page as your HTML document. This means that using the actual names of form and form elements isn't a problem. However, when SRC attributes are allowed, the code you bring in could belong to a generic script, which can figure out the overall structure at runtime via the array indexing and length properties of arrays, without being hardwired for any particular HTML document. These kinds of JavaScript modules—which page developers merely call into their code to work—depend upon the more obtuse array indexing.

The button Element

The button element provides a single trigger event that can be used for anything from submitting forms to calling up dialog boxes or changing the background color of the document. The HTML code for a button element is:

```
<INPUT
    TYPE="button"
    NAME="button name"
    VALUE="button text"
    [onClick="JavaScript code"]>
```

The button object has the following members:

➤ **name.** The name property is equivalent to the NAME attribute in the button HTML tag.

➤ **value.** The value property is equivalent to the VALUE attribute in the button HTML tag.

➤ **click().** The click() method simulates the button being clicked; however, this does not call the onClick event handler. If you are trying to invoke the onClick action, you should call the JavaScript code in the handler directly. For example, if the onClick event handler were to call the stop() function, instead of simulating the event by *buttonName*.click(), you could simply call the stop() function directly.

➤ **onClick.** The onClick event handler is called when the button is pressed by the user. The JavaScript code indicated in the String is executed by the interpreter.

The checkbox Element

The checkbox element provides a single box that can be either selected or unselected. You can think of this as being either true or false. If you have several checkboxes, they can all be independently selected or deselected without affecting each other. This is different from the radio element, which ensures that only one element in the group is selected at a time. The HTML code for the checkbox is:

```
<INPUT
    TYPE="checkbox"
    NAME="checkbox name"
    VALUE="checkbox value"
    [CHECKED]
    [onClick="JavaScript code"]>
text displayed next to checkbox
```

The checkbox object has the following members:

➤ **checked.** This property reflects the state of the box, whether it is checked (true) or unchecked (false).

➤ **defaultChecked.** This property determines what the default state of the checkbox is. True for checked and false for unchecked.

➤ **name.** The name property is equivalent to the NAME attribute in the checkbox HTML tag.

➤ **value.** The value property is the equivalent to the VALUE attribute in the check HTML tag.

➤ **click().** The click() method simulates the checkbox being selected, which toggles its state to the opposite of what it was before the click; however, this does not call the onClick event handler. If you are trying to invoke the onClick action, you should call the JavaScript code in the handler directly.

➤ **onClick.** The onClick event handler is called when the checkbox is selected by the user. The JavaScript code indicated in the String is executed by the interpreter.

The hidden Element

The hidden element is a text field that is not displayed in the onscreen document. This provides the JavaScript programmer with a persistent storage medium for a document without resorting to the cookie property of a JavaScript document object. If you recall from earlier in the chapter, form elements retain their values between loading in a Navigator session. If you fill out a form document, leave the page and then return, the information in the form is retained. In addition to storing information that might be needed later on when the user returns to the page in the same session, you may also want to submit information to the server that the user would not need to see in a form element (such as a regular text field). By using the hidden element, you can store the information and submit it just like any other form information. The hidden HTML tag is:

```
<INPUT
    TYPE="hidden"
    NAME="hidden name"
    [VALUE="hidden text"]>
```

The hidden element does not have any methods or event handlers. However, it does have three properties:

➤ **defaultValue.** This property holds the default value that the hidden element stores if no other data is provided.

➤ **name.** This property is the NAME attribute of the hidden HTML tag.

> ➤ **value.** This property holds the value of the hidden text field and is equivalent to the VALUE attribute of the hidden HTML tag.

The password Element

The password element is similar to the text element, except it hides the actual text entered by replacing all the letters with an asterisk (*). This is the typical behavior for fields that accept passwords users would not want anyone looking over their shoulder to be able to see. The HTML tag for a password object is:

```
<INPUT
    TYPE="password"
    NAME="password name"
    [VALUE="password text"]
    SIZE=integer>
```

The password element has three properties, three methods, and no event handlers:

> ➤ **defaultValue.** The default value is similar to the defaultValue in the hidden object in that it provides the default String that the password object takes if none is provided.

> ➤ **name.** This property is the NAME attribute of the password HTML tag.

> ➤ **value.** This property holds the value of the password text field and is equivalent to the VALUE attribute of the password HTML tag.

> ➤ **focus.** This method causes the focus to shift the password object so that it can accept user input.

> ➤ **blur.** This method removes the input focus from the object. Input focus is required in order for the field to accept characters entered at the keyboard.

> ➤ **select.** This method will cause the text in the password field to be highlighted.

The radio Element

The radio element is a radio button object that enables the user to select one button at a time out of a group of objects. This can be used for mutually exclusive items. To define a radio group, you provide them all with the same radio name:

```
<INPUT
    TYPE="radio"
    NAME="group name"
    VALUE="button value"
    [CHECKED]
    [onClick="JavaScript code"]>
    radio button text
```

Each individual radio object can be indexed in the elements array like any other form element; however, in addition to these methods, the radio group can be referenced by the group's name as an array.

groupName[index].property

The radio element has six properties, one method, and one event handler:

➤ **checked.** This property holds the boolean value for the state of the radio button; true for checked, false for unchecked.

➤ **defaultChecked.** This property indicates whether this is the default button to be checked out of the radio button group.

➤ **index.** This property indicates which element this radio button is in the current group.

➤ **length.** This property indicates the number of radio buttons in the group.

➤ **name.** This property holds the name of the radio element and is equivalent to the NAME attribute of the radio HTML tag.

➤ **value.** This property holds the value radio element and is equivalent to the VALUE attribute of the radio HTML tag.

➤ **click().** The click() method simulates the radio button being selected, which will toggle its state to the opposite of what it was before the click; however, this does not call the onClick event handler. If you are trying to invoke the onClick action, you should call the JavaScript code in the handler directly.

➤ **onClick.** The onClick event handler is called when the radio button is selected by the user. The JavaScript code indicated in the String is executed by the interpreter.

The reset Element

The reset element provides a single trigger event that causes the form to clear all user entries, and resets the form to its original state. Otherwise, it is much like the regular button element. The HTML code for a reset element is:

```
<INPUT
    TYPE="reset"
    NAME="reset name"
    VALUE="reset text"
    [onClick="JavaScript code"]>
```

The reset object has the following members:

➤ **name.** The name property is equivalent to the NAME attribute in the reset HTML tag.

➤ **value.** The value property is the equivalent to the VALUE attribute in the reset HTML tag.

➤ **click().** The click() method simulates the button being clicked; however, this does not call the onClick event handler. If you are trying to invoke the onClick action, you should call the JavaScript code in the handler directly.

➤ **onClick.** The onClick event handler is called when the button is pressed by the user. The JavaScript code indicated in the String is executed by the interpreter.

The select Object

The select object is perhaps the most complex form object you will have to deal with. It provides a means for creating a list of selections available to the user. These selections can be in either scrolling or static windows, and the user can be restricted to the number of items that can be picked from the list. Because of this complexity, the HTML code is more involved. Additionally, the properties, methods, and event handlers are more complex as well. The HTML code for the selector is:

```
<SELECT
    NAME="selector name"
    [SIZE="integer"]
    [MULTIPLE]
    [onBlur="JavaScript code"]
    [onChange="JavaScript code"]
    [onFocus="JavaScript code"]>
    <OPTION [SELECTED]> selection option
    [<OPTION> additional selections]
</SELECT>
```

The test form at the beginning of the chapter had a select form in it for choosing which computers the user owned:

```
<SELECT NAME="select1" MULTIPLE>
<OPTION>PC
<OPTION>UNIX
<OPTION>MAC
<OPTION>OTHER
</SELECT>
```

The MULTIPLE attribute controls the number of options available at one time. The SIZE attribute indicates how many options are visible at one time. The select object has nine properties, no methods, and three event handlers:

➤ **length.** This property is equivalent to the SIZE attribute in the select HTML tag.

➤ **name.** This property is equivalent to the NAME attribute in the select HTML tag.

➤ **options.** This is an array of the different options available to choose from. The array runs from options[0] for the first option to options[n–1] for the last option.

➤ **selectIndex.** This property indicates which item is selected in the select list. If the MULTIPLE attribute is set, then changing the selectedIndex value will clear all other selections since the index only refers to a single option.

Of course, the options array is actually an array of objects also, which have their own properties. Each of the individual options in a select element has the following properties:

➤ **defaultSelected.** This is a boolean value indicating whether the option is automatically selected or unselected when it comes up.

➤ **index.** This indicates where in the options list the current option is located.

➤ **selected.** This indicates whether the option is currently selected and is equivalent to the HTML SELECTED tag.

➤ **text.** This holds the text shown for each option.

➤ **value.** This property holds the data sent to the server from the select list when the submit button is pressed.

In order to access the individual option elements in a select element, you can either use the select object's name

```
selectName.options[index].property
```

or use the form name:

```
formName.elements[index1].options[index2].property
```

Notice that the select object has its own array in the document object, and can be accessed in a manner similar to forms.

The select object has three event handlers that enable the form to react to user input:

➤ **onBlur.** This event handler is called when the select element loses the focus. This typically occurs after the user has selected items in the list and then clicked on another element.

➤ **onChange.** This event handler is called when one of the options changes states in the select list. This can be from the user selecting or deselecting an item.

➤ **onFocus.** This event handler is called when the user clicks on the select object and begins choosing items from the list.

The submit Element

The submit element provides a single trigger event that causes the form data to be sent to the URL specified in the HTML tag. Otherwise, it is much like the regular button element. The HTML code for a submit element is:

```
<INPUT
    TYPE="submit"
    NAME="submit name"
    VALUE="submit text"
    [onClick="JavaScript code"]>
```

The submit object has the following members:

➤ **name.** The name property is equivalent to the NAME attribute in the submit HTML tag.

➤ **value.** The value property is equivalent to the VALUE attribute in the submit HTML tag.

➤ **click().** The click() method simulates the button being clicked; however, this does not call the onClick event handler.

➤ **onClick.** The onClick event handler is called when the button is pressed by the user. The JavaScript code indicated in the String is executed by the interpreter.

The text Element

The text element enables the user to input short character sequences such as numbers, words, or a sentence. The text field was used in the marquee example to create a scrolling field in which the programmer provided the input to the field. The text object is defined in the HTML document as follows:

```
<INPUT
    TYPE="text"
    NAME="text name"
    VALUE="text value"
    SIZE=integer
    [onBlur="JavaScript code"]
    [onChange="JavaScript code"]
    [onFocus="JavaScript code"]
    [onSelect="JavaScript code"]>
```

In addition to the standard TYPE, NAME, and VALUE attributes, the SIZE attribute indicates how many characters the field can hold. The text element has three properties, three methods, and four event handlers.

➤ **defaultValue.** This property holds the default value string for the text element.

➤ **name.** This property is equivalent to the NAME attribute in the text HTML tag.

➤ **value.** This property is equivalent to the VALUE attribute in the text HTML tag.

➤ **focus().** This method is used to move the input focus to this text element, causing the user's keyboard input to be directed to the text element.

➤ **blur().** This method is used to cause the input focus to move away from the text element, causing the user's keyboard input to no longer be directed to the text element.

➤ **select().** This method highlights the text in the text element.

➤ **onBlur.** This event handler is called when the text element loses the focus. This typically occurs after the user has selected items in the list, and then clicked on another element.

➤ **onChange.** This event handler is called when the value of the text element changes states. This is typically called when a user alters the entry in a text field. The event is called when the user leaves the field.

➤ **onFocus.** This event handler is called when the user clicks on the text object.

➤ **onSelect.** This event handler is called when the text in the text element is highlighted.

The textarea Element

The textarea element enables the user to input longer entries typically used for messages and comments that may span more than one line of text. The textarea object is defined in the HTML document as follows:

```
<TEXTAREA
    NAME="textarea name"
    ROWS=integer
    COLS=integer
    [onBlur="JavaScript code"]
    [onChange="JavaScript code"]
    [onFocus="JavaScript code"]
    [onSelect="JavaScript code"]>
    Text displayed
</TEXTAREA>
```

Notice that instead of being a normal <INPUT> element, the textarea (like the select element) has its own name. In addition to the standard attributes, textarea also has ROWS and COLS. These attributes indicate how many lines deep, and how many characters wide the textarea should be, respectively.

➤ **defaultValue.** This property holds the default value string for the textarea element.

➤ **name.** This property is equivalent to the NAME attribute in the textarea HTML tag.

➤ **value.** This property is equivalent to the VALUE attribute in the textarea HTML tag.

➤ **focus().** This method is used to move the input focus to the textarea element, causing the user's keyboard input to be directed to the textarea element.

➤ **blur().** This method is used to cause the input focus to move away from the textarea element, causing the user's keyboard input to no longer be directed to the textarea element.

➤ **select().** This method highlights the text in the textarea element.

➤ **onBlur.** This event handler is called when the textarea element loses the focus. This typically occurs after the user has selected items in the list, and then clicked on another element.

➤ **onChange.** This event handler is called when the value of the textarea element changes states, such as when a user alters the entry in a textarea field. The event is called when the user leaves the field.

➤ **onFocus.** This event handler is called when the user clicks on the textarea object.

➤ **onSelect.** This event handler is called when the text in the textarea element is highlighted.

Event Handlers in form Object Elements

Using the event handlers in the form object elements is perhaps the most useful function JavaScript entails. You have already seen the event handlers for forms used in many of the examples, in addition to event handlers for other objects. However, as a final example of the form object, it is important that you see how a JavaScript program might verify user input before it is sent to the server.

Using JavaScript to Verify Forms

In order to verify entries in a form, it is necessary to check to see what the user has entered before it is sent to the server. To do this with text elements, anytime the user changes the text in the field, you can check to see if it satisfies the requirements for the entry. Take the following form, for example:

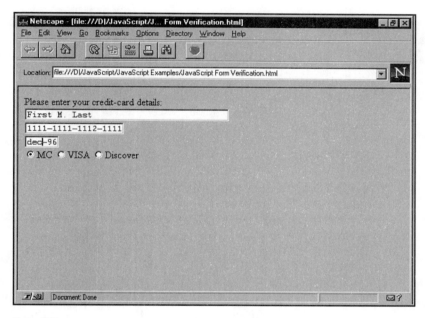

Figure 7.3

A sample Credit Card form.

If you wanted to make sure that everyone filled in the credit card number using the correct four-digit sequences with dashes in between you could create the following form and script:

```
<HTML>
<HEAD>
<SCRIPT LANGUAGE="JavaScript">
<!--
function checkNumber(number) {
    if(number.indexOf("-") != 4 || number.indexOf("-",5) != 9
```

```
➥|| number.indexOf("-",10) != 14) {
        alert("not correct card number format");
        return false;
    }
}

// -->
</SCRIPT>
</HEAD>
<BODY>
<PRE>
</PRE>
<FORM NAME="data">
Please enter your credit-card details:<BR>
<INPUT TYPE="text" NAME="Name" VALUE="First M. Last"
➥SIZE=40><BR>
<INPUT TYPE="text" NAME="cardNumber" VALUE="xxxx-xxxx-xxxx-
➥xxxx" SIZE=19 onChange="checkNumber(this.value)"><BR>
<INPUT TYPE="text" NAME="expires" VALUE="mmm-yy" SIZE=6><BR>
<INPUT TYPE="radio" NAME="cardType" VALUE="MC">MC
<INPUT TYPE="radio" NAME="cardType" VALUE="VA">VISA
<INPUT TYPE="radio" NAME="cardType" VALUE="DR">Discover
</FORM>
</BODY>
</HTML>
```

The onChange event handler for the cardNumber element causes
the checkNumber function to be called. This results in the
number being checked for the correct dashes. If a user attempts
to leave the field with an incorrect entry, he or she receives the
warning shown in figure 7.4.

Figure 7.4

The Alert dialog box from Form Verification.

There are unlimited possibilities to what you can do with the form elements in a document. This is one of JavaScript's strong points. Be sure to take the time to try out several of the event handlers and form element properties.

Controlling window Objects

At the top of the Navigator object hierarchy is the window object. This object represents the browser window that exists on the client machine, and can be used to control the screen real estate for your documents. The document object consists of several properties, methods, and event handlers that can be used to control varied aspects of how the browser window is displayed, along with dialog boxes, frames, and timeouts. You have used many of these in example programs before, so you should already have seen most of these constructions.

There are two HTML tags that correspond to elements of the Netscape window object. These are the <BODY></BODY> and <FRAMESET></FRAMESET> tags. In particular, in the HTML body tag, the onLoad and onUnLoad event handlers are properties of the window object. The frameset tag is reflected in the frames property array that holds an element for every frame in the window. The onLoad event handler was used for the marquee example in the beginning of the chapter, and the frames property was used in the Directory example from Chapter 5, "JavaScript Built-In Objects."

The window object does not need to be directly referenced in a JavaScript call, so

```
window.alert("don't do that!");
```

would be redundant, and as shown in previous examples, only

```
alert("don't do that!");
```

is necessary.

The following three sections list the properties, methods, and event handlers for the window object, and provide reference to examples that have used them.

The Properties of the window Object

In a windowed environment like Netscape Navigator, the possiblility exists to have multiple targets for document calls that can either be additional windows or frames within windows. For the most part, the properties of the window object hold references to these additional windows and frames that might exist in the Navigator environment.

➤ **defaultStatus.** This property is a string that holds the default message displayed in the status bar of the window being referenced. In many cases you will want to change the message in the status bar during an onMouseOver event, where it changes depending upon what object the mouse is over at the time. In order to do this, you must make sure the event handler returns true in order for the status to be updated.

➤ **frames.** The frames property is an array that holds all of the frames of the window. These are stored from 0 to the number of frames. The frames property refers to the frames in the order they are in the <FRAMESET> HTML tag. You can then direct your method calls to the particular frame you need. The frame object itself is a kind of window, inheriting all of the properties and methods that the window object has, so referencing window.frames[0].defaultStatus refers to the default status text displayed when the mouse is in the first frame of the window.

➤ **parent.** This refers to the window in which the frames being referenced reside. If you recall from the Directory example at the end of Chapter 5, in order to have a document in a frame refer to a function in the overall window, it has to be prefixed with a parent:

```
<HTML>
<HEAD>
</HEAD>
<BODY BGCOLOR="#FFFFFF">
<SCRIPT LANGUAGE="JavaScript">
<!--
parent.displayRoot();
// -->
</SCRIPT>
</BODY>
</HTML>
```

➤ **self.** This refers to the current window. This is not normally needed; however, sometimes it makes code easier to read if you refer to the current window as self.

➤ **status.** This property holds the current text in the status frame of the document window. You can set this status text to prompt the user when they move the mouse over a link or object that uses the onMouseOver event handler. Remember, you must return true from the onMouseOver event handler to set the status text correctly:

```
<A HREF="http://home.netscape.com/"onMouseOver=
➥"self.status='Home of JavaScript!'; return true">
```

➤ **top.** This property holds the window used to create all sub-windows. If you notice in the File menu item in Netscape, you can open a new browser window. You can do the same thing using the window.open() method, which will be covered in the next section. This was the function used to create the flashing billboard from Chapter 6. When you create new windows like this and open documents in them, the documents can refer to the topmost window used to create any child windows such as the one the document is being displayed in.

➤ **window.** This property refers to the current window and is identical in usage to the self property.

Methods of the window Object

➤ **alert().** The alert method creates a dialog box with a single OK button. In the dialog itself, the programmer can specify what he or she wishes the alert to say.

```
alert("Don't go there!");
```

This method has been used several times in previous code.

Figure 7.5
The Alert dialog box.

➤ **close().** The close method is used to close the window and should not be confused with the document.close() method, which closes the document stream.

➤ **confirm().** The confirm method is similar to the alert in that it creates a dialog box with the text that the user provides. However, this dialog box has two buttons: OK and Cancel. If the user selects OK then the method returns true if the user selects Cancel, then the method returns false.

Figure 7.6
The Confirm dialog box.

➤ **open().** The open method, not to be confused with the document.open() method, is used to open a new window. The default arguments that the method takes are:

```
window.open("URL", "window name", ["window features"])
```

The URL and window name provide the document and name of the new window to be opened. The window features argument is a string that holds the number of arguments seperated by commas with no spaces about how the window is to be opened. In the case of the Document example from Chapter 6, the method call was:

```
msgWindow = window.open("","Hello",
➥"toolbar=no,width=200,height=100");
```

Notice the use of the "toolbar=no,width=200,height=100" string to set the parameters of the window. These parameters can only be set for new windows being opened, and will not affect the parent, or top window. The full list of valid property arguments are:

```
toolbar=yes¦no
location=yes¦no
directories=yes¦no
status=yes¦no
menubar=yes¦no
scrollbars=yes¦no
resizable=yes¦no
width=pixels
height=pixels
```

➤ **prompt().** The prompt method provides an additional element to the Confirm dialog box, in that it enables the user to input a value. In order to call the Prompt dialog box, you must provide the message and an option default value for the input field:

```
prompt("Incorrect date, please enter new year:", 1996);
```

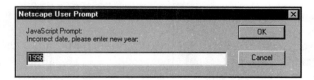

Figure 7.7

The Prompt dialog box.

➤ **setTimeout().**

➤ **clearTimeout().**

These two methods provide a means for calling a JavaScript statement after a certain time period has elapsed. If you recall the marquee example from the beginning of the chapter, the timeout methods were used to control the updating of the text element.

```
<HTML>
<HEAD>
<SCRIPT LANGUAGE="JavaScript">
<!--

var buffer = "                                   ";
var text = "Welcome to my Web Page, I hope you enjoy
➥yourself!";
var marqueeString = buffer + text + buffer;
var marqueeRunning= false;
var timeoutID = null;
var position = 0;
var sLength = marqueeString.length;

function stopMarquee() {
    if(marqueeRunning)
        clearTimeout(timeoutID);
    marqueeRunning = false;
}

function startMarquee() {
    stopMarquee();
    updateMarquee();
}

function updateMarquee() {
document.marquee.elements[0].value =
➥marqueeString.substring(position++%sLength,position+39%sLength);
timeoutID = setTimeout("updateMarquee()", 50);
        marqueeRunning = true;
}

// -->
```

```
</SCRIPT>
</HEAD>
<BODY onLoad="startMarquee()" onUnLoad="stopMarquee()">
<PRE>
</PRE>
<FORM NAME="marquee">
<INPUT TYPE="text" NAME="textBox" VALUE="" SIZE=40><BR>
</FORM>
</BODY>
</HTML>
```

Event Handlers in the window Object

The window object can handle two event handlers:

➤ onLoad

➤ onUnLoad

These event handlers were used in the marquee example to start and stop the updating of the text element when the document was loaded and unloaded, respectively.

Using the history and location Objects

The history and location objects provide a means for accessing URL links that the user has recently been to or currently occupies. This gives the JavaScript programmer the ability to make his or her script "environmentally aware." This means the scripts can tell where they are (the location object), and where they have been (the history object). By using these objects you can create a powerful tool for navigating through your site based on where a user is, and where he or she has been.

The history Object

The history object provides the JavaScript programmer with the ability to select URLs from the Go menu, which consequently loads them. This ability provides you with your own forward and back controls in documents from your site, based on where the user has actually been.

Of course, the ability to access the link history should be used carefully, especially when you begin to look at where people have been besides your own server. Since it is possible to load the information from the history list into hidden text forms and send them to a server, it is possible to gather information about how people are reaching your site. However, if you download information about places that the user wouldn't necessarily want people to know he or she had been to, then you can start to raise a few hairs. If you decide to use the history information for anything more than allowing them to skip back and forth easily, be sure to get permission first. Have an introduction document warning people that their link history will be looked at. This also goes for downloading any kind of information from a client machine that JavaScript may expose.

Properties in the history Object

The only property in the history object is length. This provides the number of links in the history object. Remember, the history list goes both backward and forward.

Methods in the history Object

There are three methods in the history object:

➤ **back().** The result of calling the history.back() method is identical to the user selecting the back arrow on the toolbar in Netscape.

➤ **forward().** The result of calling the history.forward() method is identical to the user selecting the forward arrow on the toolbar in Netscape.

➤ **go(int).** The go method takes an integer (positive or negative) and loads the link that is that many places forward or backward in the history list. For example, history.go(-3) moves the user to the link he or she was at three clicks ago.

The location Object

The location object is used to store information about the current URL. You can use the property names to get at the relevant information in the URL that you need such as the host, protocol, or pathname. The location object is a static object that you cannot change the values of. It merely stores the relevant information from the current URL. If you want to change the location information, you must use the document.location property, which is a different object than the stand alone location object. The location object enables you to break down the URL into its constituent components.

URLs can be divided into several sections. For example, take the following URL:

```
http://www.mcp.com:80/newriders/index.html#start
```

The URL can be parsed as follows. The http section of the URL is called the protocol. Other protocols besides http include mailto and ftp. The www.mcp.com represents the hostname. This can also be a series of numbers indicating the IP address of the server. 80 is the port number that the server is listening to. /newriders/index.html is the pathname, while #start is the hash. In addition to the hash, which refers to an anchor in a document, you can also have ?query=no, which would be a search for a server-side CGI program.

All of these different values are stored in the location properties.

➤ **hash**

➤ **host.** This is a combination of hostname:port.

➤ **hostname**

➤ **href.** This represents the entire URL.

➤ **pathname**

➤ **port**

➤ **protocol**

➤ **search**

Summary

This chapter has provided you with a look at almost all of the remaining JavaScript objects you can use in your HTML documents. You started out in this book by learning the fundamentals of the JavaScript language and how to place scripts within HTML documents. The chapters then moved on to cover the basic foundations of the language, and on to more complicated topics such as functions and objects. Once past that stage, the last few chapters have merely been a tour of the different JavaScript objects you can employ in your Web documents, with examples to show you what is possible. At this point, you are ready to begin diving into JavaScript on your own. Take the examples and try altering them, or try creating your own. It is the process of practicing, and getting to know the ins and outs of the language that make efficient programmers. A word of caution: JavaScript still has a few minor bugs that did not work themselves out in the first release, and it is far from a complete package. Several of the features advertised, such as the ability to interact with Java Applets, and the Navigator plug-ins have not materialized in the 2.0 release, so don't be surprised if something doesn't work like you expect.

Of course, once you have finished with JavaScript, you still have the next chapter to start. It is now that we break away from the confining restrictions of JavaScript and move on to its big brother—Java.

Chapter 8

Moving On to Java

The Java environment is a portable, robust, high-performance, advanced language that offers the ease of use and functionality that object-oriented languages have always promised, but never quite attained. By providing a portable, dynamic, multithreading language, programmers can develop advanced applications across heterogeneous networks such as the Internet. At the same time, the class libraries impart the ease of use and functionality of more open platforms while providing a secure environment for distributed systems. These features in combination are sure to make Java the dominant technology of the Internet in the next decade.

With this information in mind, understanding the ways in which to both use and serve Java content becomes imperative. For most users, the primary use of Java will be either as stand-alone applications or as extensions and applets in a browser environment. In fact, end users will most likely not even know that they are using Java—it will become as widespread as e-mail or HTML, appearing in all aspects of computing on the Web. The site administrator, however, has a new job with Java. Setting up clients and servers, providing Java content in addition to the many other networking protocols, and helping users develop or include Java content in their own documents will all be required. In addition, although Java provides a secure environment and many safety features, distributed applications invariably bring to mind viruses, Trojan horses, worms, and worse—making site administration and security a top priority. This work pays off in the end, however, by providing a more seamless incorporation of content and protocols for both client-side and server-side computing.

Up to now, this book has covered how to employ the JavaScript language to create dynamic Web sites and control the display of Web documents. While JavaScript provides a powerful tool for Internet development, there is still a drawback to its approach—you are still using the basic elements that all Web pages can have, you are simply providing them with a means to interact with their environment. Java, on the other hand, provides a completely new framework upon which you can build innovative and powerful content that is not available in the standard HTML toolkit. In fact, Java enables you to create your *own* tools, and incorporate new tools that others have created.

This chapter provides a basic introduction to programming in Java. First, you will set up your hardware and software for programming. At this point, you should be on either a Sun SPARCStation running Solaris 2.3 or later, an Intel x86 running Windows NT/95, or a Macintosh with the Roaster Development environment. If you are using Netscape's Browser, you need to get the correct software for compiling and running Java from Sun. This software is the Java Development Kit, which is supplied with the CD in the back of the book.

After the system is set up, you will cover the fundamentals of creating applets and stand-alone applications in Java. You will implement the "Hello, World!" program introduced in the first chapter as both an applet and a stand-alone application. This example is a good place to become familiar with the programming environment and the fundamentals of the programming language, while enabling you to create a framework for the more detailed explanations that will come in later chapters. Specifically, this chapter covers the following:

➤ Setting up the development environment

➤ Introduction to classes

➤ Creating the HelloWorld applet

➤ Creating the HelloWorldApp stand-alone program

➤ Troubleshooting your code

If, by some misfortune, you have problems, you can refer to the last section in the chapter, which covers troubleshooting the compiler and interpreter. Hopefully, this section won't be needed, but it is inevitable that something will go wrong at some point. A quick guide to the most common problems should address most of the errors that arise, and get you up to speed on dealing with more difficult problems if they appear.

Setting Up Your System for Programming in Java

The first step in developing for the Java language is getting the programming environment up and running. You need the javac compiler, the Java interpreter, and a Java-enabled browser for this stage and for the next few chapters. The compiler and interpreter as well as the appletviewer are all included in the Sun release. If you have already properly installed the software, you are all set to go; otherwise, this next section provides an overview of the environment. This information is not meant to be exhaustive; because many companies are coming out with development environments, software platforms could have changed quite dramatically between the time this was written and the time in which you are reading this chapter. For this reason, only the Java Development Kit (JDK) will be covered, and while it only provides command-line programs, these can do everything you need, and are the common denominator for any development environment.

The current release is the JDK 1.0, which is available at Sun's Web site: www.javasoft.com. The self extracting archive of this release is provided on the CD-ROM in the back of the book, so you should be able to simply transfer the directories to your disk. Of course, check the Sun site for updates of the JDK. The Development Kit is distributed so that it unpacks in a directory called java. You should place this root java directory wherever you want. For example, you could place it in:

```
c:\dev\
```

After you have set this directory, and unpacked the files into it (note: the archive will create the java directory for you), you need to set the environment variables for your system. Setting environment variables is different on every machine, so you need to check your system's documentation for proper procedures. In Windows 95, the environment variables are set in the autoexec.bat file. There are three variables you will need to set:

➤ PATH

➤ HOME

➤ CLASSPATH

The PATH statement should be set to the \java\bin directory. For example:

```
PATH=C:\dev\java\bin
```

This allows you to run the Java compiler and appletviewer from other directories. The HOME directory should be set to wherever your user files are located. On a single-user machine, you can set this to the java directory:

```
HOME=C:\dev\java
```

This value is used by the appletviewer when looking for the .hotjava directory to store user preferences. The CLASSPATH file should be set to the java\lib directory:

```
CLASSPATH=.;C:\dev\java\lib
```

In addition to the Java programs, you need to have a TCP/IP connection to the Internet in order to take advantage of some of Java's features, specifically the Web-browsing features of Netscape and the network connections of the appletviewer. You can still use the interpreter and appletviewer for viewing Java programs you have on your system, but you won't be able to bring up other Web pages from the Internet. Most likely, you already have Internet connectivity, but if you don't, you should note the following: Windows NT and Sun SparcStations have built-in TCP/IP connectivity, but setting up a connection will be different for each situation. If you are on a network, check with your system administrator about gaining Internet access. If you want to use it from home over a modem, check with your local service provider to get connected.

Using Stand-Alone Applications with the Interpreter

After you have completed installing the Java components on your system, you should be ready to run the Java interpreter. The Java interpreter is used to execute stand-alone Java applications. By compiling applications for Java, programmers know that their programs can run on any system for which the Java interpreter has been ported. This gives them the flexibility to worry about the content of their applications, rather than specific implementations for all the different platforms they want it to run on.

You have undoubtedly experienced the problem of trying to find a specific utility or application on the Internet. You can usually find a program to do what you want, but it often might be for the wrong system. With Java, a developer can write a single program and automatically gain the full compatibility for all platforms that Java provides. As long as there is an interpreter for the platform, you can use it.

The interpreter is not needed for Netscape 2.0. Because you are only beginning to look at the Java language, you will find that it is easier to compile and run Java applications under the interpreter than with all the overhead of the applet environment. For this reason, you should understand how the interpreter works.

The command for running the interpreter is as follows:

```
C:\> java classname
```

When the Java compiler produces the bytecode file, it appends the extension class to the original filename. When you run the Java interpreter, you only need to provide it with the class name, not the whole filename. In other words, drop the .class extension when running a program.

On the disk are several stand-alone applications that can be used with the Java interpreter. Change to the /applications/ HelloWorldApp directory on the disk and run the HelloWorldApp class. You do so by entering:

```
C:\> java HelloWorldApp
```

You should see the output of the HelloWorld class just under the command line (see fig. 8.1).

There are several other stand-alone applications on the disk, which are covered in the programming sections in later chapters. You can run any of the classes if you want to get a better handle on using the Java interpreter. Otherwise, you have run your very first Java application—that is all there is to it!

Note that the command is not `C:\> java HelloWorldApp.class`. Simply drop the extension from the filename. You should also see filenames with a JAVA extension. These are the source code files for the compiler that will be covered in the sections on programming in Java.

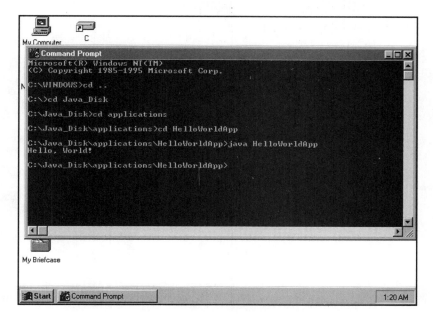

Figure 8.1

Running the stand-alone HelloWorld application.

The Java interpreter also accepts a host of command-line options.
A formal presentation of the java command line is:

```
java [ options ] classname <args>
```

Some of the options are listed in table 8.1. The arguments (args)
are passed on to the class when it executes.

Table 8.1	Java Command-Line Options
Command	**Purpose**
-cs, -checksource	Looks at the Java source file to ensure it hasn't been modified since the last compile. If the source is newer, the interpreter recompiles the code and loads the renewed class. It only works if the source code is available.

continues

Table 8.1   Continued

Command	Purpose
-classpath	Tells the interpreter where to look for the class file. The format is -classpath .:path[:optional paths]. Each new path is separated by a colon. This option overrides the CLASSPATH environment variable.
-v, -verbose	Causes Java to print a message every time a class is loaded.
-verbosegc	Prints a message anytime the automatic garbage collection feature of the Java interpreter frees memory.
-verify	Runs the verifier on all code, regardless of where it came from.
-verifyremote	This option runs the verifier on all code (default) that is loaded into the system by the class loader.
-noverify	Causes the interpreter to ignore verification of any code. This could be used if you were only running code that you knew was safe.
CLASSPATH	This is not a command-line option, but rather an environment variable that you can set to tell Java where your classes are. It uses the same parameter as the -classpath option: .:path[:optional paths] If this variable is not set correctly and you try to import a class from outside the default settings, Java gives an error, saying the class has violated access restrictions.

Note   If you are using options regularly, you can save time typing by creating a batch file for Java. To do so, open your favorite editor and type in the command options you want to use following Java. Where you would normally enter the class name and command-line arguments, place %1, %2, and so forth, up to %9. For example:

```
java -verbose -verbosegc -verify %1 %2 %3 %4 %5 %6 %7 %8 %9
```

Save the file under a name that will identify it to you, with the BAT extension (that is, javav.bat). Place the file in your /hotjava/bin directory. To run the batch file, enter your new name plus the class name and any arguments you want sent to the class. In order to run a class *classname* with *arguments* you could enter:

```
javav classname arguments
```

The %*n*s enable you to enter up to eight command-line arguments to be sent to the class, in addition to the class name itself.

You can now use the Java interpreter to run any program that you find on the Internet in Java, knowing that it will be running in a secure, robust environment. When developers begin to use Java regularly, you can expect new utilities and shareware programs to automatically work on your system. It will save you time in finding, and peace of mind in using, new programs from the Internet.

Using the appletviewer

The appletviewer provides a Java run-time environment where Java applets can be tested. The appletviewer takes HTML files that refer to the applets themselves and runs them in a window. As an example, change to one of the demos in the demo directory in the JDK release and enter the following command:

```
e:\users\tdr20\java\demo\moleculeviewer\appletviewer
➡example1.html
```

The result should be as that shown in figure 8.2. In this case, the applet is a molecule viewer that takes XYZ format molecule data and presents a three-dimensional model of the molecule.

If you look at the HTML file example1.html that is sent to the appletviewer, you can see the format for entering applets into HTML pages.

```
<title>MoleculeViewer</title>
<hr>
<applet code=XYZApp.class width=300 height=300>
<param name=model value=models/HyaluronicAcid.xyz>
</applet>
```

```
<hr>
<a href="XYZApp.java">The source.</a>
```

Figure 8.2

The MoleculeViewer applet.

The <applet ...></applet> tag is used to tell the browser that it should load a Java applet. The <param ...> tag is used to pass arguments to the applet at runtime. This is a different format than that used in the Alpha release of Java. At the end of the chapter is a fuller explanation of how to use the applet tag.

The appletviewer has several options under the Applet menu option.

➤ **Restart.** This command runs the loaded applet again.

➤ **Reload.** This command reloads the applet from disk, and is useful if the .class file has changed since it was loaded.

➤ **Clone.** This command creates a new appletviewer window based upon the command-line arguments for the first.

➤ **Tag.** This command shows the <applet> tag used in the HTML document to start the applet (see fig. 8.3).

➤ **Info.** This command provides any information about the applet that is available (see fig. 8.4).

Figure 8.3

The Tag dialog box in the appletviewer.

➤ **Properties.** This command allows the different network and
security configurations to be set for the appletviewer (see
fig. 8.5). The first four entry boxes allow the appletviewer to
be run using an HTTP proxy and firewall proxy. Both the
proxy address and the port number are required. You
should be able to get this information from your site administrator. The network access selector allows several levels of
security, including no network access, only access to the
applet's host, and unrestricted access. The class access
selector allows you to designate either restricted or unrestricted access to classes on the machine.

The appletviewer is a rudimentary tool as far as HTML content
goes. It does nothing but display the Java applet itself. For testing
applets this is enough. However, Java applets will be only one
part of an overall Web page, so it is important to see how an
applet will fit in with the rest of an HTML document. In this case,
a full-fledged Web browser must be used, such as Netscape or
HotJava.

Figure 8.4

The Info dialog box in the appletviewer.

Figure 8.5

The Properties dialog box in the appletviewer.

Netscape 2.0

Because Netscape 2.0 implements the Beta 2 version of the Java language, and does not support all of the Java functionality, not all applets will run under Netscape. Most of the limits to Java functionality have to do with security, and will be added later as Netscape more fully implements the Java run-time environment. The current version of Netscape 2.0 is in its initial release (see fig. 8.6).

There is little you have to do to use Netscape to view Java applets. In fact, Netscape is set up to run Java applets as its default behavior. If you wish to disable Java applets in Netscape, choose

Options, Security Preferences..., and you should see the dialog
box in figure 8.7.

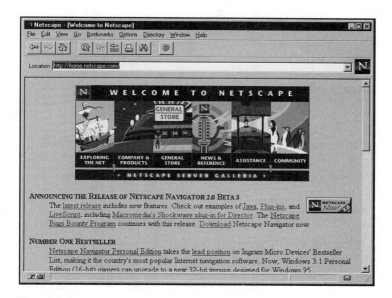

Figure 8.6

The Opening Netscape 2.0 screen.

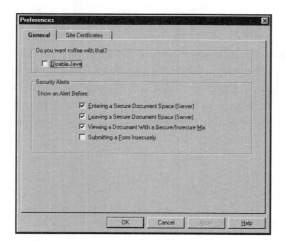

Figure 8.7

Netscape's Security Preferences dialog box.

Netscape limits the loading and functions of applets in order to ensure tight security. For example, Netscape will load applets or native code from a local hard disk, but won't allow applets loaded over the Net to write to the local hard disk. Additionally, Netscape 2.0 does not allow applets to use sockets anywhere but the host machine from which they came.

Table 8.2 The Netscape Security Restrictions	
Allows	**Doesn't Allow**
Applets to be loaded from the Net	Applets to access any machine other than the host it came from
Applets to load local classes	Applets to write or read any other files on the local disk

In order to test out Netscape, you can point it to one of the demonstration applets in the JDK directory java\demo. The animator directory has several HTML files that you can use to test to see if Netscape is set up correctly. The status bar at the bottom of the Netscape screen provides information about the status of applets that are being loaded from pages. For example, as you load Sun's Java page, the applet will place a message in this area as the individual images are being loaded.

For more information about the execution of Java applets in Netscape, the Java Console can be used (see fig. 8.8). Any run-time errors encountered will be placed here. In order to see the Java Console, select Options, and check the Show Java Console option. Be sure to then select Save options from the same menu in order for your changes to remain between sessions.

Figure 8.8
The Netscape Java Console.

Providing Applets

There is one last topic to cover before you move on to writing your own applets—providing your own content. If you want to include Java applets in your own HTML documents, there are two simple steps you should follow:

1. The first step to placing Java content in an HTML page is to create the a directory available to the Web server. Unlike the Alpha release, the class files no longer have to be in a subdirectory of the directory holding the HTML file. In any case, make sure that the directory structure is available to those browsing your Web site. Talk with your system administrator to find out where to place these directories.

2. Next, you must create your HTML file and include the Java `<applet ...>` directive. The `<applet>` directive works like any other HTML directive, and tells the browser to format the

included information in a specific way. The `<applet>` directive tells a Java-equipped browser to load the executable designated by the `code` attribute and run it. Whichever Java applet you want to include, the bytecode file ends with the extension .class. There are many options you can provide when placing an applet in an HTML page; however, here is the simplest command:

```
<applet code="applet.class" width=100 height=140></applet>
```

That is all there is to it! You will now have a Java applet in your Web page. The HelloWorld applet document in the applets/ HelloWorld directory on the book's disk looks like the following:

```
<HTML>
<HEAD>
<TITLE>Hello, World!</TITLE>
</HEAD>
<BODY>
Say Hi to Everyone:

<applet code="HelloWorld.class" width=100 height=
➥100></applet>
</BODY>
</HTML>
```

Try using some of the applets included on the disk under the /applets directory. Move them into your own HTML directory and see how they look in your pages, or bring up the HTML files directly on the disk.

The `<applet>` directive has several options that configure how HotJava and other browsers will display the applet.

```
<APPLET
    CODEBASE=class URL
    CODE=class filename
    ALT=alternate text
    NAME=applet name
    WIDTH=width
    HEIGHT=height
```

```
    ALIGN=alignment
    VSPACE=vertical spacing
    HSPACE=horizontal spacing

>
<PARAM NAME=attribute name VALUE=attribute value>
<PARAM NAME=...>
[alternate HTML]
</APPLET>
```

The following table presents each optional value:

Table 8.3 <APPLET> Tag Options	
Option	**Effect**
CODEBASE	This is an optional attribute that indicates the URL where the .class file can be found. This can be either an absolute URL or a relational reference to the HTML directory.
CODE	This is a required attribute that indicates the name of the class file of the applet to load.
ALT	If this optional attribute is present, browsers that recognize the applet tag, but are unable to actually handle Java programs, can display the text provided.
NAME	This is an optional attribute that provides the applet with its own name, which can be used by other applets on the same page to communicate with each other.
WIDTH	This is a required attribute that provides the browser with the width in pixels that the applet needs.
HEIGHT	This is a required attribute that provides the browser with the height in pixels that the applet needs.
ALIGN	This is a required attribute that tells the browser how to align the applet. The possible values are: left, right, top, texttop, middle, absmiddle, baseline, bottom, absbottom.
VSPACE	This is an optional attribute that tells the browser how much vertical space in pixels to allow between the applet and any other elements on the page.
HSPACE	This is an optional attribute that tells the browser how much horizontal space in pixels to allow between the applet and any other element on the page.

In the Alpha release of Java, in order to pass arguments to the applet at runtime, the argument name and value were used in the <APP> tag. However, this allowed the tag to have an unknown number of options, and did not conform to SGML standards. The new method for passing arguments to the applet is to use the <PARAM> tag.

The final release version of Java has changed the style of the <APP> tag used in the Alpha versions. Instead, the <applet ...> tag is now used to designate where an applet should be placed in an HTML document. The tag was changed because for the applet tag to be SGML-compliant, it could not use an unlimited number of tag attributes, which is what the older <APP> tag used.

```
<PARAM NAME=argument name VALUE=argument value>
```

This tag is used in between the <applet ...> and </applet> tags, and can be used as many times as needed in order to pass the necessary arguments to the applet. The following HTML code sends several arguments to an applet:

```
<applet codebase="e:\users\tdr20\java\demo\Animator"
code=Animator.class width=200 height=200>
<param name=imagesource value="Frames">
<param name=endimage value=10>
<param name=soundsource value="audio">
<param name=soundtrack value=sound.au>
<param name=sounds
value="1.au¦2.au¦3.au¦4.au¦5.au¦6.au¦7.au¦8.au¦9.au¦0.au">
<param name=pause value=200>
</applet>
```

Additionally, the <blockquote> tag can be used to indicate HTML source that should be displayed if the browser cannot handle Java applets. In the following example, a single frame from the animation file can be displayed in place of the full animation file.

```
<applet codebase="e:\users\tdr20\java\demo\Animator"
code=Animator.class width=200 height=200 align=right>
<param name=imagesource value="Frames">
```

```
<param name=endimage value=10>
<param name=soundsource value="audio">
<param name=soundtrack value=sound.au>
<param name=sounds
value="1.au¦2.au¦3.au¦4.au¦5.au¦6.au¦7.au¦8.au¦9.au¦0.au">
<param name=pause value=200>
<blockquote>
<img align=right src="Frames\T1.gif">
</blockquote>
</applet>
```

All HTML code between the <blockquote> and <\blockquote> tags will be ignored by Java-enabled browsers. This allows for page designs that can be used across many different browsers without the need for you to worry about what the page would look like without it. It is always good practice to check out Web pages on several browsers to ensure that even if everyone doesn't have the latest browser, the pages will maintain the correct layout.

Your First Java Program—Hello, World!

By now you should have the Java environment up and running correctly without too much suffering. You are finally ready, therefore, to start coding your first programs. The next two sections cover general ideas about programming in Java, detail what you need in order to get a program to run, and demonstrate the "Hello, World!" program as both an applet and a stand-alone program.

Your first Java program will be a simple one. It will print the words Hello, World! on-screen. Although the result of the program is not that fantastic, what actually goes on in the background to get it to do what it does *is*. The source code for the HelloWorld class is relatively short, and displays the built-in power of the Java language classes. It also provides an opportunity to demonstrate some of the features of Java.

If you flip ahead to the source code for Hello, World!, you will notice that there are several words such as import and extends. These declarations are fundamental to implementing the object-oriented nature of Java, and bring us to a basic problem in teaching the language. The problem revolves around classes—Java's representation of an object. An object-oriented language can be approached in essentially two ways:

➤ By learning about classes first and the rest later

➤ By learning about declaration, types, and control flow first, and classes later

For those coming to a new language without any experience, it is generally believed that teaching the way that classes work first is fundamental to creating good habits and programmers from the start. The problem with this approach is that classes are a more difficult concept than the basic structure, and an understanding of the fundamental types and control flows is necessary to properly demonstrate programs. However, if you learn the basics of classes and objects early, creating good object-oriented code later becomes easier.

The second method—teaching the fundamentals of the language first, and then introducing classes later—is the method I have chosen in this book for two reasons. First, I believe that most people attempting to tackle Java will not be new to programming, but will have at least some programming experience. Programmers who already have a good idea of what is in a language will be able to use the next two chapters as a quick guide comparing the environments and languages of C/C++ and Java. Toward this end, I have included comments on similarities and differences between the languages. Second, although tutorials on classes and objects would require understanding some of the fundamentals such as types, expressions, and control-flow, a single class will encapsulate the ideas presented in these two chapters and enable us to get the basic housecleaning chores out of the way before you begin to get into the meat of the Java language.

However, it is not worthwhile to ignore the whole class issue until you are ready for more detailed coverage. Java as a language requires the use of classes from the beginning; however, the necessary class structure can be kept to a minimum, and an explanation of the object-oriented techniques will provide a good impression on which to begin learning the language. If you understand classes, or are an experienced programmer and will be using these two chapters only as a general overview before diving into Java, feel free to skip to the next section.

Introducing the Concept of Classes

First and foremost, you should notice that the HelloWorld application is called a *class.* That is exactly what it is. In fact, the output of the compiler is HelloWorld.class. Java is an object-oriented language to the extreme. All aspects of the language revolve around classes of objects. When you run either the interpreter or the browser, it implements a class—not a file.

Although JavaScript has stand-alone functions and statements, Java programs must always exist within a class structure. This is perhaps one of the biggest differences between the two.

A class is, generally speaking, composed of two kinds of items:

➤ Instance variables

➤ Methods

Instance variables are what describe an object. For example, if you have an object such as a lightbulb, you need to store its state, such as on or off, or perhaps its wattage. These values—on or off, and wattage—are stored in the instance variables. An important idea to remember is that these instance variables are typically *encapsulated.* This means that only the objects themselves can change the variables.

Of course, such things as the lightbulb knowing whether it is on or off, and being able to turn itself on and off, are well and good, but how does anything else tell it what to do? This is where *methods* come in. The lightbulb would provide methods for turning itself on and off, such as TurnLightOn() and TurnLightOff(). Just as you cannot directly force the electrons to stop flowing through the tungsten filament in a bulb and must use the light switch, other objects must turn the light on and off using the light's methods. A method is identical to the methods you have learned in JavaScript and are functions that are tied in with objects giving them the capability to complete a task. However, Java does not have the equivalent of a stand-alone function as does JavaScript—all functions are methods, and must be members of a class.

The imaginary lightbulb might look something like this:

```
class LightBulb {
    boolean LightOn;
    int Wattage;
    public void TurnLightOn(){
        LightOn = true;
    }
    public void TurnLightOff() {
        LightOn = false;
    }
    public void ExpelPhotons() {
        if(LightOn) //do something to draw a lit bulb on
                        the screen
        else //do something to draw an unlit bulb on the
                screen
    }
}
```

Of course, this is an incomplete example—it doesn't explain the way in which the bulb actually lights up, for instance. But this example does give a good picture of the kinds of class definitions you will be looking at. If you don't understand the format, or specific lexical issues, don't worry; they will be explained in later sections. The idea here is to get an idea of what a class looks like, and the general way in which it works.

You need to know about one other thing to write our HelloWorld applet and application: inheritance. Say you really like your lightbulb, but think it is a little boring. You decide to include a little bell that goes off every time it is turned on to really get the attention of the user. Do you have to throw away all the code you have just worked so hard to produce? Not at all. You can use the extends modifier to show that our new class LightBulbWithBell is an extension of the old class. Our new class might look something like this:

```
class LightBulbWithBell extends LightBulb {
    public void ExpelPhotons() {
        if(LightOn) {
            ...//do something to draw a lit bulb on the
                screen
            SoundBell();
        }
        else //do something to draw an unlit bulb on the
            screen
    }
}
```

You have added functionality to the ExpelPhotons() function to make it sound a bell. Again, the exact details of the way in which it lights up, or sounds the bell, don't matter. The important idea is that you can *inherit* objects and their features and update them. The specific type of updating performed is called *overriding*, because you override the previous declaration of ExpelPhotons(). You can also add new methods and instance variables if needed. This capability to inherit properties from previously coded classes is just one of the many powerful features of object-oriented computing. This leaves you with two important points needed for studying the Java language:

➤ All Java variables and methods must be members of a class.

➤ Classes encapsulate these members and provide methods for inheritance.

A general understanding of classes at this point will make reading the code easier in the future, because so much of it revolves around the creation of classes. For this chapter and the next, however, you will be dealing with only a single class instance.

 A deeper investigation of objects and classes can be found in Chapter 10, "Objects in Java—The Class."

With this brief introduction to classes behind you, you are now ready for your first Java program.

HelloWorld as an Applet

For most users of Java, the goal of programming in the language is to provide applets over the Internet to be used by Java-enabled browsers. Therefore, our first incarnation of the HelloWorld class will be just that—an applet. Using the browser environment requires using some of the class libraries that deal with the windowing environment. In particular, you will be using the awt (Another Windowing Toolkit) class to control the appearance of our applet on-screen. You will override the paint() method of the java.awt.Graphics class in order to place the text "Hello, World!" in the window.

All applets are inheritances of the base class java.applet.Applet. You will override the init() method of this class in order to resize the window before you display the text. You will depend on the base classes to receive window calls, repaint themselves when the window is uncovered or resized, and in general provide for all housekeeping chores. All in all, our code will be only 10 lines, and half of those are there merely because of aesthetics and readability. Not a bad return for such little work on our part.

Setting Up the Environment

The first step in creating your HelloWorld class is to create the directories where the files will reside. It is important to make sure that the java\bin directory is in your path statement, and that the directories that you are using to hold your files are accessible to the Java compiler and appletviewer. For example, you might want to create a directory java\workingfiles to store all of your Java files.

```
e:\users\tdr20\> mkdir java\workingfiles
```

The directory structure used in these examples is for local machine use only. If you want to make your applet pages available to the wider Internet, you should talk with your system administrator about where you can place your files for world access. Be sure to find the correct directory structure to use, and the resulting URL necessary to find the document externally.

The Source Code for the HelloWorld Class

When you have the directory structure finished, you can begin to code the HelloWorld class. First, you must create a file called HelloWorld.java in the classes directory. The .java extension is the standard method for indicating a Java source code file. In Windows NT/95 you can either use the Edit command or use the Notepad in the Windows environment. In Solaris, you can either use a command-line editor, such as vi or emacs, or use an OpenWindows editor, such as the TextEditor. Refer to the software documentation for details about creating a plain ASCII text file for your environment. Whichever editor you use, make sure that you are familiar with all the editing features. Correcting a typo in a command-line editor can be the most frustrating problem in the world when you don't know the commands.

There is a very useful utility on the disk called JavaMaker, written by Choi Hee Chang, which provides an editor and compile environment for the JDK release under Windows NT/95.

The program is on the CD in the JavaMaker directory. View the readme file that is in the directory for installing the program. This is what is used to edit, compile, and run the code in this book (see fig. 8.9).

Figure 8.9

The JavaMaker program.

Using either the JavaMaker editor, or an editor of your own choosing, here is the source code you need to enter:

```
import java.awt.Graphics;
public class HelloWorld extends java.applet.Applet {
  public void init() {
        resize(150,50);
  }
  public void paint(Graphics g) {
        g.drawString("Hello, World!", 50, 25);
  }
}
```

When you have finished typing the code, save it as HelloWorld.java.

Look at what you have line by line. First, you have the following:

```
import java.awt.Graphics;
```

This line tells the compiler that you will be using the Graphics classes and to be ready to use them. In fact, the compiler will bring in the class definitions and include them with the source code you have written.

```
public class HelloWorld extends java.applet.Applet {
```

This line declares a new class, HelloWorld, and tells the compiler that it is a subclass of (extends) the java.applet.Applet class.

```
public void init(){
```

This line overrides the init() function of the applet class. *public* means that objects outside of this class can invoke it, and *void* means that the method returns no value. The empty parentheses show that this method also takes no arguments. When the applet is created, methods in the superclass applet will call this function, invoking the next line:

```
resize(150,50);
```

This line tells the browser to resize the window to 150 by 50.

```
public void paint(Graphics g) {
```

This line is another overriding method. It is overriding the method paint from the Applet class. When the applet is told to paint itself, this is the method it calls. Again, the method is public and has no return value. You do, however, have an argument. When paint() is called, it needs to be sent an object of class Graphics; in this case, the method refers to it as g. Therefore, g is sent by the methods you don't see in the superclass Applet that handles Graphics objects.

```
g.drawString("Hello, World!", 50, 25);
```

In this line, the Graphics object g is told to invoke its method drawString() with the arguments Hello, World!, 50, and 25. This tells the method to print the text Hello, World! at location 50, 25.

When the applet has completed running, the automatic garbage methods of the Java environment ensure that memory allocated is freed and generally makes sure that the program exits cleanly.

Compiling

After you have written the source file, and saved it into the classes directory, you are ready to compile the code. The command for compiling in both Solaris and Windows NT/95 is this:

```
C:\> javac HelloWorld.java
```

If compilation succeeds, you should have a file named
HelloWorld.class in the same directory as the HelloWorld.java
file. If you have any problems, make sure that you have typed all
commands correctly. If you still can't get the file to compile,
check out the section at the end of the chapter on troubleshooting the compiler.

If you are using the JavaMaker program, you can compile the
current file by choosing Tools, Compile, or by using the compile
button on the toolbar. A compiler output window will pop up and
provide information about the state of the compilation
(see fig. 8.10).

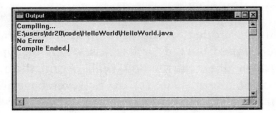

Figure 8.10

The compilation window of JavaMaker.

Creating the HTML File

After you have completed the compilation steps and created the
HelloWorld.class file, you are ready to place it into an HTML
document. Again, in your editor, create a plain ASCII text file in
the working directory called HelloWorld.html. The file will be a
standard HTML file that includes the <applet> directive. For more
information on writing HTML documents that include applets,
refer back to page 237 under the section titled "Providing
Applets." For our purposes, you need only the basic structure:

```
<HTML>
<HEAD>
```

```
<TITLE>Hello, World!</TITLE>
</HEAD>
<BODY>
Say Hi to Everyone:
<applet align=center code="HelloWorld.class" width=150
height=100></applet>
</BODY>
</HTML>
```

As mentioned in the beginning of the chapter, the <applet code=class_file> directive tells the browser to load and run the class class_name from the classes subdirectory in the HTML file logical directory. Save the file with an html extension (such as example1.html).

Loading the Applet

After you have completed a program and compiled it correctly, you are ready to view the applet using the appletviewer or Netscape 2.0. You can either invoke the appletviewer from the command line

```
e:\users\tdr20\java\code\>appletviewer example1.html
```

or run the appletviewer from JavaMaker from the menu item Tools, Appletviewer, or by choosing the appletviewer button on the toolbar. Make sure that you have set the Tools, Environment menu selection that indicates the path to the JDK files, and the name of the HTML file to run the appletviewer with (see fig. 8.11).

Figure 8.11

The Environment dialog box for JavaMaker.

When you run the appletviewer from either the command line or the JavaMaker program you should be presented with the window shown in figure 8.12. If you are having any problems, refer to the troubleshooting section at the end of the chapter.

Figure 8.12

The HelloWorld applet in the appletviewer.

Congratulations! You have finished your first applet and have completed all the steps necessary for creating your own Java applets for the Internet. Obviously, there is much more to programming more complicated applets, but in essence, you have learned all there is about the process, illustrated in the following steps:

1. You develop the code, compile it, and check for compile-time errors.

2. You develop your HTML pages, including the new applets.

3. You test the pages with the appletviewer or Netscape 2.0.

If the HTML file is loaded into Netscape, it will display the full HTML file as in figure 8.13.

Figure 8.13

The HelloWorld applet in Netscape 2.0.

Of course, that is not all that the Java language is good for. By using the Java interpreter, you can write stand-alone applications in addition to browser applets. To help you understand the differences between creating an applet and creating an application, you will recode the HelloWorld class as a stand-alone application to be run on the interpreter.

The HelloWorld Class as a Stand-Alone Application

The HelloWorld class can also be run as a stand-alone application using the Java interpreter. Although most Java work will be seen as applets, and, as you will see later, as handlers for types and protocols, the language can also be used to create stand-alone programs. Of course, these programs are not stand-alone in the true sense of the word because you still need the Java interpreter on your system to run them. To differentiate our applet from our application, you will refer to the new class as HelloWorldApp.

For the HelloWorldApp class, you will not require the classes used in the applet form of the program. Instead, you will create a new class from scratch. If you look ahead at the code, you will notice that our program does not *extend* any other class. In fact, this is misleading; you are in fact extending the class Object.

When a class is defined without specifying the inheritance class, the class Object is taken as the default.

Note

Thus, even though you seem to be creating a new class, you can still use many powerful features built into Java. In fact, all classes are derived from the Object class, as discussed in Chapter 10. Suffice it to say that the Object class provides the garbage collection and system utilities basic to all Java implementations.

Our HelloWorldApp class this time is only five lines long, half the length of the applet version, and still much of that is spacing for aesthetics and readability. For that, you get a program that will run on any platform the Java language has been ported to, along with all the features of the language.

Setting Up the Environment

Your HelloWorldApp does not require creating any special directory structure for holding the class files. Instead, you can work in any directory you choose. For now, create a directory HelloWorldApp to hold your work. In this directory, create a file named HelloWorldApp.java. Using any editor you choose, or the JavaMaker program, create the file in plain ASCII text.

The Source Code for the HelloWorld Class

The source code for the HelloWorldApp is relatively simple:

```
class HelloWorldApp {
    public static void main (String args[]) {
        System.out.println("Hello, World!");
    }
}
```

After you have finished typing the code and ensured that it is correct, save the file to the HelloWorldApp directory.

Again, let's go over the source line by line.

```
class HelloWorldApp {
```

As mentioned before, this line declares the class as HelloWorldApp. The declaration does not specify what class HelloWorldApp extends, so the default is taken as Object. Again, every class, except Object, has a superclass. In other words, every class is an inheritance of another class, except Object. This line could also have been written like this:

```
class HelloWorldApp extends Object {
```

Writing it the first way is easier, however, and the Object extension can always be assumed.

```
public static void main (String args[]) {
```

This line has several new features not in the applet:

➤ The modifier static appears. This keyword tells the compiler that this method refers to the class itself, not to a specific instance of the class. This enables the method to be invoked without a HelloWorldApp object having been created first. This topic is covered in Chapter 10.

➤ Notice that the method takes an argument, args[], that is an object of String. In fact, this object holds the arguments typed after a command when it is entered.

➤ Notice the name of the method itself-main(). This method, as in C and C++, is required of all applications to tell the interpreter where to start. The interpreter is what calls the main() method and passes the command-line arguments to it. The main method is not required in Applets, since the browser calls the applet's init() method to run. This is one of the easiest ways to distinguish between the two kinds of Java programs.

```
System.out.println("Hello, World!");
```

This line outputs the text Hello, World! to the standard output, usually the screen. In this case, the class System has the method out, which in turn has the method println, which outputs the argument to the screen. Notice that the call uses the dot (.) operator as in C and C++.

Compiling

By now you should have completed the HelloWorldApp.java file and saved it to the HelloWorldApp directory. As before, you need to compile the class using the javac compiler.

```
C:\> javac HelloWorldApp.java
```

The compiler should create the class file HelloWorldApp.class in the directory HelloWorldApp. Additionally, you can use JavaMaker to compile the file. If you have any problems, check for typing errors, and if they still persist, check the troubleshooting guide at the end of this chapter.

Running the Interpreter

After you have completed the compilation and javac has created the class file, it is time to run the application. You invoke the interpreter with the Java command. Java refers to the class, not the compiled file. To run HelloWorldApp, enter this:

```
C:\> java HelloWorldApp
```

If all goes well, you should see the output shown in figure 8.14.

Figure 8.14
Output from the HelloWorldApp and Java interpreter.

JavaMaker does not provide a means for invoking the Java interpreter from inside the program, so you will have to get to a command prompt. Of course, those using Solaris will be in the command prompt anyway.

Again, congratulations! You have completed your first stand-alone Java application. In many ways, the process is easier than creating applets. You don't have to mess around creating an HTML page with <HEAD>, <TITLE>, or <APP> declarations, or run HelloWorldApp through Netscape. Very quickly, you create a sophisticated program capable of running on many different systems. Although HelloWorldApp doesn't seem all that sophisticated, in fact, the Java language is hard at work in the background delivering a robust, high-performance application.

In the next few chapters, you will begin to piece together the fundamental aspects of the Java language needed for developing your own ideas into Java classes.

Troubleshooting

Presented here is a list of errors you might confront and solutions you might find helpful when running the Java compiler javac and Java interpreter. This is not an exhaustive list, but it should enable you to work through most of the error messages that appear as you try to compile and run the examples and your own code.

Compiling Errors

This list of compile-time errors covers the most common mistakes made during program compilation. Anytime the compiler outputs an error message, it will not output the .class file. If you are trying to compile a program and don't seem to be getting the .class file, the compiler is most likely encountering an error somewhere in your code. Most of these mistakes are typographical errors, but they are not always easy to find. Be sure to check your code carefully, especially for semicolons at the ends of statements. Semicolons are used to tell the compiler where a statement ends; however, sometimes it is not clear if you should use a semicolon at the end of some lines. In the next chapter, as the language is discussed, the usage of semicolons is covered. For now, think of them as the equivalent to periods at the end of sentences.

➤ `javac: Command not found`

This error occurs on Unix systems when the path isn't set properly. Make sure that your path statement includes the directory where the Java binaries are kept. This is typically the hotjava/bin directory. Use setenv or a similar command to set your path variable to the javac directory. A sample path statement might be the following:

`PATH=C:\hotjava\bin;C:\users\Ritchey\hotjava\classes;`

Check with your shell documentation for the specifics of your configuration.

➤ `filename:linenumber: ';' expected`
`    some line of code`
`                  ^`

`  n error(s)`

You receive this error when you have forgotten to include the semicolon (;) at the end of a statement or declaration. This error message occurs only if the compiler figures out what you were trying to do. Many times, however, the compiler cannot guess what is missing and might output strange error messages, such as Invalid type expression or Invalid declaration, on the following lines of code. If the lines in which the compiler finds an error look correct, check the lines immediately preceding those with the errors for missing semicolons.

➤ `filename:linenumber: Variable variable_name may not have`
`↪been initialized.`
`        variable`
`              ^`

`    n error(s)`

Anytime a variable is used without first being initialized, the compiler throws an error message and the .class file is not created. Make sure that all variables are initialized. Initialization is the way you tell the compiler what kinds of variables you will be using.

Interpreter Errors

Many times, programs will compile, yet still not run under the Java interpreter. The interpreter commonly issues two types of errors:

➤ `Can't find class classname.class`

This error is produced when the user tries to run a class by giving the interpreter the class filename rather than the class name. Be sure to drop the .class extension when running classes through the interpreter. For HelloWorldApp, you should enter java HelloWorldApp not java HelloWorldApp.class.

➤ `In class classname: void main(String argv[]) is not`
`↪defined`

This error occurs when a class does not have a main() method defined. All applications must have a main() method defined in order to give the interpreter a place to start execution.

Summary

You have learned the basics of developing Java code into either an applet or an application. By now, you should be comfortable using the Java compiler and interpreter, as well as using applets in HTML pages. Spend time with the Hello, World! applet and application. Change lines to get error messages, and see what the compiler and interpreter do. Try to see whether you can reproduce the errors shown in the troubleshooting section. Also, try to change the arguments used in resizing and placing text, or try outputting multiple lines of text. The best way to learn is by trial and error. Of course, the goal here is to help you get all the trial, with as little of the error as possible.

Now that you have mastered the Hello, World! application, what now? In the next chapter, you learn the basics of the language, such as declaring and using the basic types, numbers, strings, and arrays with operators. In addition, the guts of a program—control flow—are presented. This section covers all the ways to control the movement of the program.

In later chapters, you start learning more advanced topics. Classes and the ways in which to use them to their full extent are presented. You learn threads, exceptions, and the use of the standard class libraries. Eventually, you look at developing content in more detail, including the more graphical, and network based features of the Java standard objects.

The Hello, World! examples are intended to show the ways in which Java provides a powerful environment for developing applications. The portability allows for a single compile environment while allowing distribution across a heterogeneous network. The robust, high-performance execution means that the performance hit for such portability is kept to a minimum. In addition, the built-in security features enable easy development of innovative content. Most of all, these examples should give you a feel for what developing in the Java environment is like. Although this book focuses on the command-line method of creating applets for Netscape, this is only because it is the common denominator on most platforms. By the time you read this, there may well be several integrated development and visual environments in which to create applets. Be sure to watch the Internet for new information about what is available.

Chapter 9

The Java Fundamentals

Now that you have written and compiled your own code and seen it run, you should feel familiar enough with the javac compiler and Java interpreter to begin working on more substantial projects. Of course, to begin working on more complicated programs, you will need to learn more about the Java language itself. This chapter aims to familiarize the reader with the foundations of the language types, expressions, and control flow. These items are essentially the guts of any program, and are basic to any programming language.

For those who are familiar with programming, especially C and C++, the following chapter will be quite familiar. Except in a couple of places where Java sticks more closely to the object-oriented paradigm, almost all the C fundamentals are the same. Those who are coming at Java as their first programming language should read this chapter carefully. This chapter's topic is deceptively simple; and, although a cursory read might impart the feeling that you know the material, as rare as natural programmers are, photographic memory is even rarer. Be sure to go over the examples. Spend time with the code to make sure you understand what is going on. A detailed understanding of the basic structures makes later programming easier and much less frustrating.

In the preceding chapter, you learned the rudimentary skills needed for producing applets and applications. In addition, you learned the basics of the class structure of Java. An understanding of these topics is necessary for working through this chapter. In particular, knowing how to use the javac compiler and the run-time interpreter for Java is important to complete the exercises presented in the following sections. For this chapter, you primarily use the interpreter and stand-alone applications for development, rather than the browser and applets. The reason for this choice is that the overhead of writing code for the interpreter environment is much less than that for writing applets for HotJava or Netscape. Also, for the simple examples that are presented in this chapter, it is much easier to forego the overhead of writing for the browser environment. If you felt comfortable with getting the HelloWorldApp class running, you should have no problems running the examples in this chapter.

This chapter presents the fundamental data type, expressions, operators, and control-flow declarations of the Java language. In addition, the standard input and output are covered for reasons of program usage. For our programs in this chapter to be at least correct, if not precise, you must do three things. First, you must encapsulate them in a class structure. What you learned in the preceding chapter is more than enough to provide a rudimentary class for the examples here. Second, our programs must be able to output the results of their work to the user so that you know whether they have worked. In this case, you will use the method System.out shown in the preceding chapter. Third, you need to provide our program with information at runtime. This will be accomplished by using the System.in method. You could, of course, provide any data you needed in the program itself; however, if you want to test under different situations, you will need to recompile the code every time. Instead, by using the standard input methods, you determine whether the application works for a range of input variables without recompilation. These methods are not available to you when writing applets for Netscape, and are only used in console applications.

After you develop the basic structure of the programs, you will use them to learn the fundamental aspects of the language. Types such as numbers, characters, and arrays will be defined, along with operators, declarations, and expressions. These elements could be called the calculating engine of Java. They provide the means for solving equations and testing or changing the state of a variable. In addition, control-flow will be discussed. This aspect of the language provides the methods for making decisions based on the calculation portion of the code. In essence, this is where the real computing goes on. These elements exist in every programming language, and are the basis of modern computing. Because all languages share these common elements, having a good understanding of the way in which they work not only makes an understanding of the rest of the Java language simpler, but also makes learning a new programming language easier.

Many aspects of the fundamentals of JavaScript and Java are the same. You can refer to a single chapter for all the information you need instead of flipping back and forth between the JavaScript and Java sections of this book, Java items that are similar to JavaScript are repeated here, and the same overall chapter structure is used, enabling you to build upon what you already know of JavaScript.

The information in this chapter does not tell you everything there is to know about programming in Java. Even though these programs will run and do what you ask them to do, it is important to realize that they are produced in a synthetic environment in order to discuss certain features of the language. After you have completed these fundamentals, you can use the framework you have developed to build the complete picture of the Java language. When you have finished this chapter, you should be ready to learn more about the class elements of the Java language, including instance variables, methods, constructors, and inheritance, along with more advanced features such as threads and class libraries. Doing so will enable you to begin implementing full-blown applets for the Netscape browser.

The Architecture of Java Code

When you write a program in Java, you create at least one file with the extension .java that holds your source code. This file is called a *compilation unit*. All Java programs are composed of at least one, and typically more, of these units. Each unit comprises combinations of four different elements:

➤ Package statements

➤ Import statements

➤ Class declarations

➤ Interface declarations

For our programs in this chapter, you mainly use the class declaration. The other declarations are covered in more detail in Chapter 10, "Objects in Java—The Class."

The class declaration is composed of variables and methods, which can be of either the static or instance types. The variables are equivalent to the properties in JavaScript parlance, while methods are of the same name. The difference between Java methods from JavaScript is that the methods are defined within the code block of the class itself. All stand-alone applications must have a main() method defined, which is where the interpreter starts to run the program. This is only a requirement of the stand-alone Java program, and not a requirement of an applet. Altogether, the basic elements of the stand-alone programs will look as shown here:

```
class ClassName {
    public static void main (String args[]) {
        //add code here
    }
}
```

This is the basic structure of the Java code you will be working on. All the examples in this chapter add code to the main() method. Recall the earlier discussion of the main() method in Chapter 8, "Moving On to Java." The method must accept the command-line arguments from the interpreter (String args[]), and does not return any variables (void). The method is the same for all instances of the class (static) and can be invoked by any other class (public).

In addition to the class declaration, you can also use the import statement to allow the program the use of certain classes provided with the Java environment. If the code requires the use of a class' method, it will appear as shown here:

```
import ClassName

 class ClassName {
     public static void main (String args[]) {
          //add code here
     }
 }
```

Any imported functions will be explained in the text along with the code examples.

The Java Token Set

The javac compiler takes the code written in the Unicode format that you give it, and extracts individual elements known as tokens. These tokens, each of which will be discussed shortly, can be divided into five types:

➤ Identifiers

➤ Keywords

➤ Literals

➤ Operands

➤ Separators

In addition, the compiler removes comments and white spaces (spaces, tabs, and line feeds) that are not a part of the token set.

The Unicode character set replaces the standard ASCII set, expanding the number of bytes from 8 for ASCII to 16 for Unicode. Unicode extends the character set to provide support for many non-Latin language characters.

After the compiler has extracted the tokens from your code, it proceeds to create the machine-independent Java bytecode, which is capable of execution in either the interpreter or the browser environments. All of your programs will be written using the five previously mentioned types—identifiers, keywords, literals, operators, and separators—in addition to the non-token comments.

Comments

Comments in Java come in three styles. These styles are the same comments that are used in JavaScript. The older /* */ style was originally used in the ANSI-C standard. This comment format is useful for multiple-line comments, for example, at the beginning of a code fragment:

```
/* The following class will output the
   words Hello, World! to the screen
   when run on the interpreter        */
class HelloWorldApp {
...
```

The // comment method was added to C++ as an easier way to comment out individual lines. If a line of code does something important, it is always useful to make a short comment. Here's an example:

```
System.out.println("Hello, World!");  //note the use of
quotation marks
```

The /** */ comment, which is the third style, is a new addition to Java, and is used by the javadoc automatic document creator. The full set of comment types is shown in table 9.1.

Table 9.1   The Different Comments in Java

Comment Type	Description
// comment	All characters after the // to the end of the line are ignored.
/* comment */	All characters between /* and */ are ignored. These comments can extend onto multiple lines.
/** comment */	All characters between the /** and */ are ignored as in the /* */ comments; however, these comments should be used only before declarations, because they will be used by the javadoc tool in creating automatic documentation.

Including comments in code is an important habit to get into. Even though it seems that everything is perfectly clear when you are writing your code, someone else who wants to use it might have great difficulties determining exactly what you are trying to do. It will also save you many headaches later when you decide to update a class that you spent weeks creating, only to find that you can't figure out the way to insert new code without disrupting what you've done. Comments are perhaps the easiest and most powerful method for ensuring that code is reusable.

Identifiers

Identifiers are the names given to variables, classes, and methods to identify them to the compiler. HelloWorldApp, main, and LightOn are all examples of identifiers used in previous Java code. What makes a valid identifier? In Java, all identifiers must begin with a letter, the underscore character (_), or the dollar sign ($). All subsequent characters can also include digits (0–9). Letters are considered all the upper- and lowercase alphabet from A to Z, and all Unicode characters with numbers above hex 00C0. This enables non-Latin characters such as "Ç" and "ø" to be used in names; however, characters such as "¶" are not included.

In addition, those words that are designated as keywords in the next section are unusable. Table 9.2 gives examples of valid and invalid identifiers in Java.

Table 9.2   Valid Identifiers

Valid	Invalid	Valid, but Not Recommended
watts	wattage #	WATTS
lightOn	light-on	lighton
monthsWith_31_days	5dogs	_number
x	abstract	$_243_fubar

Of course, unless you have a non-American standard keyboard, using anything other than the "_", "$", and "A"–"Z" letters would merely create difficulties in editing. Unless you have good reason, it is not advisable to use the "$" at all, and only to use the "_" in the middle of identifiers (between words) to improve readability. One reason for this guideline is that later, when you are linking in C code, the "_" and "$" are typically used by library routines. Not using them in your code helps to quickly narrow down problems to specific libraries. Using descriptive names should provide you with all the flexibility you need. The standard is to make all letters lowercase except for the beginning of words that appear in the middle of an identifier (such as in lightOn).

In C and C++, the standard is to name #define identifiers with all upper-case letters. Java does not implement a #define, so for ease of transition, all uppercase identifiers should not be used. This rule will come in handy when you are linking in C code later.

Keywords

Keywords are identifiers used by the Java language that cannot be used in any other way than that defined by the Java language. You won't be able to remember every single keyword, so if you are having a problem with an identifier that is a single lowercase word, be sure to check out the keyword list in table 9.3.

Table 9.3	List of Reserved Java Keywords		
abstract	else	int	static
boolean	extends	interface	super
break	false	long	switch
byte	final	native	synchronized
byvalue*	finally	new	this
case	float	null	threadsafe
cast*	for	operator*	throw
catch	future*	outer*	transient
char	generic*	package	true
class	goto*	private	try
const*	if	protected	var*
continue	implements	public	void
default	import	rest*	while
do	inner*	return	
double	instanceof	short	

* Reserved keywords, but currently unused by Java

Literals

Literals, which are used when entering explicit values into your code such as 5 or x, refer to the basic representation of two types of data in the Java language:

➤ numbers

➤ characters

The number literals can be categorized into two subtypes:

➤ integers (numbers without a decimal point)

➤ floating-point (numbers with decimal values)

The character literal refers to a single value of the Unicode character set, whereas strings refer to collections of characters. In addition, there is a special literal known as boolean. The boolean literal is included in the numbers category because the C language did not have a boolean literal, instead, the integers 1 and 0 were used for true and false, respectively.

Literals are closely linked with types, which are discussed in the next section. The difference between types and literals is that literals are explicit values entered into the code of your program, whereas types represent an amount of memory large enough to hold that information. Think of a small child's toy that has round, square, triangle, and star-shaped pegs, and a set of holes to match. The holes that can accept the different pegs are the equivalent of types. They are an indication of the kind of data that can be stored. Literals are the equivalent of the pegs, or data, actually placed in those holes.

Integers

The first literal is the integer. This literal, the most common, comes in three guises: *decimal*, *hexadecimal*, and *octal* format. The decimal, or base 10, integer is the most familiar, appearing as you would expect it. The important thing to note about the integer is that it does not have a leading zero. The hexadecimal, or base 16, integer is typically used as a binary shorthand, each digit grouping four binary ones and zeros. Hexadecimal integers are represented by the digits 0–9 and the upper- or lowercase letters A–F, which represent the numbers 10–15. These integers are preceded by 0x or 0X. Octal, or base 8, integers are represented by the presence of a zero (0) in front of the digits. Table 9.4 gives examples of several numbers in the different formats.

Table 9.4	The Decimal, Octal, and Hexadecimal Representations of Integers	
Decimal	**Octal**	**Hexadecimal**
0	0	0x0
2	02	0X2
63	077	0X3f
83	0123	0x53
631	0771	0x3Fl

Integer literals are stored in the int data type, which provides support for 32 bits of information. This limits the range of values from (decimal) −2,147,483,648 to 2,147,483,648. If for some reason you need to represent a larger number, the long integer type is 64 bits in size, which should be adequate. If you want to force an integer to be stored as a long, you can append an l or L to the end. The section on types discusses the storage of values in more detail.

Floating-Point

Floating-point literals are used to represent decimal numbers with fractional parts such as 1.5 or 43.7. They can be in either standard or scientific notation. The following example shows some floating-point literals:

3.1415, 0.1, .3, 6.022e23, 2.997E8, 1.602e−19

The standard storage of a floating-point literal is called the *float* for single precision, and takes up 32 bits of space. There is also a 64-bit *double* for double precision. You can specify which type you want with the f/F or d/D suffix:

3.1415f, 6.022e23d, 2.997E8F, 1.602e−19D

Boolean

The boolean literal has two states: true and false. These states are represented by the keywords true and false. This value is used to represent the state of something that can have only one of two values. The values are typically used as flags for determining whether to take a certain action. The boolean value is a true literal, and not a representation of the integers zero or one as in C or C++.

Character

The character literal is a character enclosed in single quotation marks (such as 'x'). It can be any character from the Unicode character set. In addition, the backslash (\) is used to represent nonprinting or conflicting characters. Table 9.5 lists the various nonprinting control character combinations Java will accept.

Table 9.5	Special Character Representations	
Description	Standard Designation	Sequence
Continuation	\<newline\>	\
New-line	NL(LF)	\n
Horizontal tab	HT	\t
Backspace	BS	\b
Carriage return	CR	\r
Form feed	FF	\f
Backslash	\	\\
Single quotation mark	'	\'
Double quotation mark	"	\"
Octal bit pattern	0ddd	\ddd
Hex bit pattern	0xdd	\xdd
Unicode character	0udddd	\udddd

String

String literals are any number of characters enclosed in double quotation marks. Strings are in fact implemented by the class String, not as an array of characters as in C++. Each String literal creates a new instance of the class String. Don't worry about the fact that Strings are classes. Because of the very nature of classes, you don't need to worry about how to implement them—they take care of themselves. Mentioning the fact that Strings are classes here is merely for the sake of correctness. Table 9.6 gives examples of some Strings and their printed output.

Table 9.6	Examples of Valid Strings
The Declaration	The Result
""	
"\'"	'
"Your Ad Here"	Your Ad Here
"Multiple\nLines"	Multiple Lines

If you would like to see what some Strings would look like on-screen, you can take our HelloWorldApp and change the String in the line:

```
System.out.println("place your String here");
```

Compile the file as before, and run it through the interpreter. You should be able to check out all the nonprinting characters and the Unicode set.

Operators and Separators

Many characters and character combinations are used in Java as operators and separators. *Operators* are used to perform some type of computation on objects, whereas *separators* are used to tell the compiler where groups of code are divided and arranged. Table 9.7 presents all the valid operators and separators.

Table 9.7   A List of Operators and Separators

+	-	!	%	^	&	*	|
~	/	>	<	(	)	{	}
[	]	;	?	:	,	.	=
++	—	==	<=	>=	!=	<<	>>
>>>	+=	-=	*=	/=	&=	|=	^=
%=	<<=	>>=	>>>=	||	&&		

You have now seen all there is to the Java language. The previous sections presented all the possible character sequences you can use to create a Java application. Of course, this doesn't help you when it comes to learning the way to program in Java. The correct combination of the previous elements is what creates the application you want to run. You should be able to recognize which functions specific elements have before trying to figure out what they are doing in combination. As you proceed through the language, you will refer to these basic types. You need not have them memorized, but you should at least be familiar with the different classes of tokens so that when you refer to operators or identifiers, you will know what to expect.

Declaring Variables

To store a value in Java, it must be contained in a variable. For a variable to be used, it must have two items associated with it: a type and an identifier. You assign these in the declaration statement:

```
type identifier [, identifier];
```

This statement tells the compiler to create a variable with the name identifier of type type. Note the semicolon telling the compiler that this is the end of the declaration; also, the optional identifier in square brackets indicates optional declarations. In this case, you can string together the declaration of several variables with the same type by separating their names with commas. After you have created a variable, you can assign values to it or perform calculations on the value it holds with operators.

Note

If you think back to when JavaScript was being presented earlier in this book (Chapter 2), you will remember that it said that a difference between JavaScript and Java is that Java is considered a strongly typed language. This means that for all variables, the compiler must be told what *kind* of variable they are. This allows the compiler to optimize the program for memory and speed, and check to make sure that correct assignments are being made with the variables. This is not the case with JavaScript, which is a loosely typed language. Declaring variables is much different in JavaScript than Java.

The type, as mentioned in the section on literals, determines what kinds of values variables can hold, what can be done to those variables, and what these actions do to the variables. In Java, there are two kinds of types. At the first level are the types that are called *simple*. They are not built on any other type. The integer, floating-point, boolean, and character types are all of this kind. They are as basic as you can get. In addition, Java defines what are known as *composite types.* These are built on the simple types, and consist of arrays, classes, and interfaces. You will learn about the array type in this chapter and save the class and interface types for Chapter 10.

The Java type, unlike C, C++, and many other strongly typed languages, does not actually affect its memory allocation. Instead, the type controls the variable's arithmetic properties and the legal range of values. If the variable is outside of the legal range, it is divided by the range, and the remainder is used.

Declaring Integer Types

There are four integer types, each referring to variables with different bit lengths. The shortest is the byte integer, which is 8 bits long. Next is the short integer, which is 16 bits long. The int type integer is 32 bits long, and the long integer is 64 bits. All types are signed. Following are some sample integer declarations:

```
byte x;
short numberOfChildren;
int wattage;
long WorldPopulation;
int x, y, z;
```

Note the use of the commas in the last example declares three variables, x, y, and z—all of type int.

Declaring Floating-Point Types

The floating-point type is declared using either the float or the double keyword. The float keyword stores the variable as a 32-bit single-precision floating-point number, as defined by IEEE 754. The double keyword stores the variable as a 64-bit double-precision, as defined by IEEE 754. Here's an example:

```
float pi;
double avagadroNumber;
```

Declaring Character Types

Because Java uses Unicode, which is a 16-bit character set, the Java char type is a 16-bit unsigned integer. Char variables are used to store single characters, not entire strings, which is done by the String class. Following is an example:

```
char c;
```

Declaring Boolean Types

The boolean type holds the logical values true and false. This type is typically returned by methods that want to indicate the success of their operation. In addition, the logical operators return values of type boolean. Here's an example:

```
boolean lightOn;
```

The boolean type is a type all its own. It is not like Boolean in C or C++, where it is an enumeration representing the integers zero and one. For this reason, boolean values cannot be converted into numbers by casting.

Declaring Arrays

Arrays are special types in Java. Unlike JavaScript, where you must create your own function to create arrays, the array is a fundamental type in the Java language. Arrays hold a list of objects that can be referenced by indexing. In addition, you can have arrays of arrays. Following are some examples:

```
int i[];       //one-dimensional array
char c[][];   //two-dimensional array
float[] f;
```

Notice that you do not include the number of variables to be held in the array, and notice also the optional placement of the square brackets. Allocation of an array must be explicit using the new operator, which is discussed in the next section.

Unlike C and C++, Java does not use pointers; therefore, boundary-checking problems that are so common on these platforms do not occur in Java. Because of this, the array must be allocated explicitly with the new command.

Scope

When you declare a variable, it is introduced into a scope. The name can be used only in that specific part of the program. The scope of a variable is from the point it was declared to the end of the block it is in. A block is defined by the two curly braces { }. For example:

```
class App { // beginning of class App block
    public static void main(String args[]) { // beginning of
    main
        int i;                              // method block
        ...
    }                           // end of main method block
    public void method1() { // beginning of method1 block
        char c;
        ...
    }                           // end of method1 block
}                               // end of class App block
```

`int i` has been declared in the method main. Because main's block does not include the method1 block, any reference to `i` in method1 would be an error. The same would go for char `c`.

Scope is automatically assigned in Java by the location where the variable is declared instead of using the JavaScript var statement. There is no need to use the var statement, which does not exist in the Java language.

In one special situation, a variable can be hidden by other variables. This is the case in which a variable is declared in a block; then, another scope is created within the original block, and a variable with an identical name is declared. While the program is in the second block, the first variable is hidden from use. This situation occurs in the following code:

```
class App {
    public static void main( String args[] ) {
        int i;
        boolean test = true;
        // int i is in scope
        while( test ) {
            int i;
            // the first i is now hidden, and the second i
            // always referred to
        }
        // the second i has fallen out of scope, and you
        // are now back to our original i
    }
}
```

Warning

Be careful when you are declaring variables, and keep track of what you have done. This is one reason it is important to use comments and descriptive names. You will be able to tell the difference between variables, and the problem of hidden variables will be less frequent.

Operators

After you have created your variables, you must be able to assign them values, make changes to them, and perform calculations. These are the roles of the operators. Table 9.8 lists the operators, from highest to lowest precedence.

Table 9.8	Operators from Highest to Lowest Precedence			
.	[]	()		
++	—	!	~	instanceof
*	/	%		
+	-			
<<	>>	>>>		
<	>	<=	>=	
==	!=			
&				
^				

&&

||

?:

=   op=

,

Precedence refers to the order in which multiple operations will be computed, and works the same as in JavaScript. Operators on the same level have equal precedence. For example, the calculation

```
a=b+c*d/(c^d);
```

proceeds by working from left to right on all binary operations (those involving two variables), computing those operations at the top of the list and working down. In this case, because the () has higher precedence than anything else, the `c^d` would be computed first. Next, the `c*d` would be computed, with that result being divided by the `(c^d)` result. Finally, all this would be added to `b` and the result placed in `a`.

Whenever you are in doubt about the order in which something is calculated, be sure to use the parentheses () to specify to the compiler the way to do things.

Of course, the first operator you need to know is the assignment operator (=). This does exactly what you think it does. It takes the values on the right side of the equal sign and places them into the variable on the left side of the equal sign. Even though this is the easiest operator, it can get you into lots of trouble. Make sure that the left-hand variable is big enough to hold the results of anything that occurs on the right-hand side. This is not a problem with JavaScript, and was not encountered before. Look over the information on literals at the beginning of the chapter again to see how much memory each holds. It will be important when dealing with characters and integers in some operations, where the value returned is a 32-bit integer that needs to go into a 16-bit character. The following sections list the rest of the Java operators.

Operators on Integers

Operations on integers fall into two categories:

➤ Unary

➤ Binary

Unary operators act on one variable at a time. Binary operators act on two variables at a time. For operations resulting in an integer, if any of the variables—or *operands*—is long, the result is a long; otherwise, the result is an int. Even if the operands in question are byte, short, or char, the result is an int. Table 9.9 lists the unary operators.

Table 9.9	Unary Integer Operators
Operator	**Operation**
-	Unary negation
~	Bitwise complement
++	Increment
--	Decrement

The *unary negation* changes the sign of an integer. *Bitwise complement* changes each bit of the variable to 1 if it was a 0, and to 0 if it was a 1. *Increment* increases the value of the variable by one, and *decrement* decreases the value of the variable by one. Following is an example:

```
class Unary {
    public static void main (String args[]) {
        int i = 0;
        int j = 10;
        for(i = 0; i<10; i++) {
            j--;
            System.out.println(i+"\t"+j+"\n");
        }
    }
}
```

This application runs increasing numbers in one column and decreasing numbers in the other. Note the use of ++ and --. Each time these occur, the system either raises or lowers the value of the operand by one. This is the way in which unary operators work—they change the value of the variable they are used on.

For the negation and bitwise complement, the variable is not changed; for the increment and decrement, the variable is changed. The following code shows how this works:

```
class Unary {
    public static void main (String args[]) {
        int i = 10, j = 10, k = 10, l = 10;
        System.out.println(i+"\t"+j+"\n");
        j++;
        i--;
        ~k;
        -l;
        System.out.println(i+"\t"+j+"\t"+k+"\t"+l+"\n");
    }
}
```

Notice that j and i have been changed, and print out their new values, but k and l have reverted to their original values. When using the unary negation and bitwise complement in a compound operation, you are actually using a temporary variable, holding the new value of the operand. The increment and decrement operators are both prefix and postfix—that is, they can be placed before (++x;) or after (x++;) the operand. If they are used in compound statements such as

```
i=x++;
```

or

```
i=++x;
```

then the first line increments x after assigning its value to i, and the second line increments x and then passes the new value on to i.

The second type of integer operator is the binary operator. These operations do not change the values of the operands. They return a value that must be assigned to a variable. Table 9.10 lists the binary integer operators.

Table 9.10	Binary Integer Operators
Operator	**Operation**
+	Addition
–	Subtraction
*	Multiplication
/	Division
%	Modulus
&	Bitwise AND
|	Bitwise OR
^	Bitwise XOR
<<	Left shift
>>	Right shift
>>>	Zero-fill right shift

The following program prints the values of some operations:

```
class Binary {
    public static void main (String args[]) {
        int i = 5;
        int j = 10;
        System.out.println(i+"\t"+j+"\n");
        j = j + i;
        System.out.println(i+"\t"+j+"\n");
        j = j * i;
        System.out.println(i+"\t"+j+"\n");
        j -= i;
        System.out.println(i+"\t"+j+"\n");
    }
}
```

Notice the last operation. It is a combination of the binary operator and the assignment operator. This is equivalent to writing
j=j-i;. This can be done with all the binary operators. Take the
time to place your own equations into the code. Add variables
and try different combinations.

Some further notes on the integer operations. First, division of integers
rounds toward zero. Second, if you divide or modulo by zero, you will
have an exception thrown at runtime. If your operation exceeds the lower
limit, or underflows, the result will be a zero. If it exceeds the upper limit,
or overflows, it will lead to wrap-around. Moving past the upper limit will
place you at the very bottom value—approximately -2.1 billion.

There are also additional relational operators that produce
boolean results. These operators are shown in table 9.11.

Table 9.11   Relational Integer Operators Producing Boolean Results

Operator	Operation
<	Less than
>	Greater than
<=	Less than or equal to
>=	Greater than or equal to
==	Equal to
!=	Not equal to

I will point out again that the equal-to operator (==) will cause you
endless suffering, just as in JavaScript. I still replace the double
equal sign with just a single equal sign when I mean to compare
two values instead of assigning the value of the right operand to
the left. Make sure that you use the double equal sign for comparison. Try this application:

```
class Binary {
    public static void main (String args[]) {
        int i = 0;
        int j = 10;
```

```
        while(i<j) {
            System.out.println(i+"\n");
            i++;
        }
    }
}
```

Here, the control statement while checks the values of i and j. While the statement i<j is true, it runs the code fragment that prints i and then increases it by one. As soon as i<j is false, the program drops out of the while loop and finishes. You will cover while loops in the section on control flow.

Operators on Boolean Types

The boolean type adds several new operators for logical computation. These operators are listed in table 9.12.

Operator	Operation
Table 9.12 Boolean Operators	
!	Boolean negation
&	Logical AND
|	Logical OR
^	Logical XOR
&&	Evaluation AND
||	Evaluation OR
==	Equal to
!=	Not equal to
&=	AND assignment
|=	OR assignment
^=	XOR assignment
?:	Ternary

If you consider the boolean value to be the equivalent of either a 1 for true, or 0 for false, the operators act the same as those for the integer operators if they are working on a single bit. Negation (!) is the equivalent of the integer bitwise complement (~) and is a unary operation. Table 9.13 lists the results of the operations.

Table 9.13   Results of Boolean Operations

AND			OR			XOR		
Op1	Op2	Result	Op1	Op2	Result	Op1	Op2	Result
true	true	true	true	true	true	true	true	false
true	false	false	true	false	true	true	false	true
false	true	false	false	true	true	false	true	true
false	false	false	false	false	false	false	false	false

The &, |, and ^ operators evaluate both sides of the argument before deciding on the result. The && and || operators can be used to avoid evaluation of right-hand operands if it is not needed.

The ?:, or ternary, operator works as shown here:

```
Operand1 ? Statement1 : Statement2;
```

Operand1 is evaluated for its truth or falsity. If it is true, Statement1 is completed; if it is false, Statement2 is completed. The following code gives an example of this operation:

```
class TestTernary {
    public static void main (String args[]) {
        int i = 10, j = 10;
        boolean test = false;
        test ? (i = 0) : (j = 0);
        System.out.println(i+"\t"+j+"\n");
        test = true;
        test ? (i = 0): (j = 0);
        System.out.println(i+"\t"+j+"\n");
        }
    }
}
```

Note the parentheses. They are not needed in this example, but if you use more complicated statements, you might want to include them.

In addition to these operators, the &=, |=, and ^= work as assignment operators on boolean values just as for integer values.

Operators on Floating-Point Numbers

The traditional binary operations work on floating-point values (-, +, *, and /), in addition to the assignment operators (+=, -=, *=, and /=). Modulus (%) and the modulus assignment operator (%=) give the floating-point equivalent of an integer divide. Also, the increment and decrement (++, --) work, increasing or decreasing the value of the variable by 1.0.

Similar to the integer variables, the result is placed in the largest denominator. If the operation includes two floats, the result will be a float type. If one or more of the operands is a double, the result will be a double. When you use the relational operators (>, <, >=, <=, ==, and !=), note that floating-point variables do not behave like integers, and just because a==b is true does not mean that a<b || a>b is true! This is because floating-point values are not ordered like integers. Be careful when you are writing a program and making assumptions about floating-point values. Floating-point values also include Inf for infinity. Overflow produces an Inf underflow zero and divide-by-zero Inf.

Array Operators

Contrary to C or C++, and much like the use of the makeArray function in JavaScript, the allocation for an array always uses the new operator to create the array and assign it to the variable. Here's an example:

```
int a[] = new int[10];
```

The preceding example creates an array of 10 ints and assigns it to a. You refer to the individual variables by number: a[0], a[1], through a[8], a[9]. Note that the subscripts go from zero, the first element in the array, to the size of the array minus one. This is contrary to the standard JavaScript form that goes from 1 to the number of elements (n). Arrays are used just like any other variable. The individual members of an array can be used anywhere that a variable of that type would be used. If x = 1; is valid, then x[3] = 1; is valid. Java also supports arrays of arrays:

```
char c[][] = new char[10][10];
float f[][] = new float[5][];
```

Notice in the second declaration that only one dimension is defined. Java requires that at least one dimension be defined at compile time (that is, explicitly in the source code). The remaining dimensions can be allocated later.

Arrays are used where you would like to keep a lot of similar information in the same place and refer to it easily by number. Arrays are very powerful; they are discussed more in later chapters.

Strings

Strings can be concatenated using the + operator. If any of the operands are not Strings, they are converted to Strings before being concatenated. In addition, the += operator works by placing the concatenation of two Strings into the first. You used the + operator in the previous examples when you wanted to print several items on one line. Try using the System.out.println and the + operator to make different combinations of output with the interpreter.

As far as using Java for computations, you have covered all the basic operations that can be performed on variables. You should spend time with the information presented, and try experimenting with your own programs. Of course, even in the examples here, you broke down and used several control-flow statements to make the programs really do something. Control flow provides the basic engine for getting your calculations working. In the "Control Flow" section, you learn the control flows available in Java.

Casting Types

The System method System.in.read() returns an integer value. Typically, however, you want to use it as a character. What happens when you have an int and need to place it into a char? In JavaScript, the conversion is carried out automatically, so there is no need to convert from one to the other. This is not done in Java so you do what is called a *cast*. You cast the int into a char. The method for placing one type into another follows:

```
int a;
char b;
a = (int) b;
```

The parenthetical reference to int tells the compiler that you want to change the character into an integer and place it into a. On the other hand, if you need to go the other way, you would use:

```
b = (char) a;
```

It is important to remember how much space the ints and chars each take up. Because both ints and chars are 32 bits, you can move from one to the other without a loss of information. However, if you were to move from a long—64 bits—to an int, you might lose information because longs can hold numbers larger than 32 bits. Even if the two quantities are the same size, such as int and float (both hold 32 bits) you would lose information about fractional numbers. Java does not allow automatic casting like C or C++. When you explicitly cast something be sure that it can hold the information you are casting. The casts that will not result in a loss of information are:

➤ Byte to short, char, int, long, float, double

➤ Short to int, long, float, double

➤ Char to int, long, float, double

➤ Int to long, float, double

➤ Long to float, double

➤ Float to double

➤ Double can only be stored as a double without loss of information

Be sure to check the type of cast you want to perform. You might not always lose information if you perform a cast that is not listed here, but it would be dangerous to assume a cast of this nature will always work. For example, if you cast a long to an int, and the long number is less than the maximum storable in an int, there would not be any loss. This is because the leading zeros would be dropped, and wouldn't provide any information about the number. However, you have to be sure that the long is always less than the maximum allowable value for an int.

Control Flow

Control flow is the method used to make your program move through the steps needed in the correct order with the least amount of fuss. Java provides several control-flow expressions, as shown in table 9.14. Control flow is the heart of the program, providing it with direction. Rarely does a program go through a single series of steps in order to produce its output. In order to have interaction, programs must be able to react to input and calculations, and make decisions about what code to execute next. In addition, if you need to repeat a code fragment several times in a row, it is a waste of effort to keep repeating it, instead you can tell your program to repeat it. Java provides control-flow methods for these and other situations.

Table 9.14	Control-Flow Expressions
Type	**Expression**
if-else	if(boolean) statement
	else statement
switch	switch(expression1) {
	case expression2: statement
	...
	default: statement
break	break [label];
continue	continue [label];
return	return expression;
for	for(expression1 ; expression2 ; expression3)
	statement
while	while(boolean) statement
do-while	do statement while(boolean);
label	label:statement

The if-else Branch

The if-else branch is the basic control-flow expression in the Java language. Simply put, if something is true, you execute the first statement; else, do the other statement. For example:

```
if(a < b) a = b;
else b = a;
```

Note that the expression evaluated is a boolean, not a number. Unlike in C, you cannot place an integer here as a shortcut, in which 0 = false and any other number is true. You must make some relational statement in order for Java to evaluate the if statement.

If you don't want to do anything if the statement is not true, you can simply leave off the else. If you want to have your program do more than one thing for each statement, surround them with the curly brackets {}.

```
if(!lightOn) {
     wattage = 0;
     roomDark = true;
}
else {
     wattage = 60;
     roomDark = false;
}
```

In addition, if you want to string together a series of tests, you can do so as shown here:

```
if(boolean) statement
else if(boolean) statement
else if(boolean) statement
...
else statement
```

In this case, the boolean expressions at each stage are evaluated. If one is found to be true, it is executed; otherwise, the final else is executed.

Be sure to use the curly brackets for your statements if it is unclear which order statements should be executed in. Here's an example:

```
if(x > 0)
     if(x == z) a = z;
else a = x;        //this else would be associated with the
                   //inner if.
```

The preceding example would produce the incorrect result if you wanted a to equal x only if x <= 0. Instead, the block notation should be used to make it explicit:

```
if(x > 0) {
     if(x == z) a = z;
}
else a = x;
```

You now have enough pieces together to write a program that does something interesting. You will be introducing a new function—System.in.read(). This function enables us to read characters from the standard input, typically the keyboard. System.in.read() returns the character entered. If an end-of-input character is entered (Ctrl+D on Unix and Ctrl+Z on DOS and Windows systems) it will return a -1. In the JavaScript example of this program, the forms buttons were used for input. The following is an example:

```
class Reply {
    public static void main (String args[]) {
        char a;
        System.out.println("Enter a number from 1-3:");
        a = (char)System.in.read();
        if(a == -1)
            System.out.println("\nno character entered");
        else if(a == '1')
            System.out.println("\nYou win a Car!");
        else if(a == '2')
            System.out.println("\nYou picked the goat");
        else if(a == '3')
            System.out.println("\nYou get to keep your
            100");
        else System.out.println("\nincorrect entry");
    }
}
```

Obviously, the program doesn't do that much (unless you are on a game show), but you can see the way in which you can use the if-else statement to control the flow of the program, depending on the condition of certain variables.

The while and do-while Loop

The while loop checks to see whether an expression is true, and processes the given statement until the expression becomes false. On the other hand, the do-while loop will process a statement, and then evaluate the expression to see if the statement needs to be processed again. You used the while loop earlier to show the increment operator. You should remember that you must be changing whatever expression you are evaluating in the loop itself; otherwise, if it is true, you will enter an infinite loop because the statement will then always be true. Following is an example:

```
boolean test = true;
while(test) {
     System.out.println("Hey!, get me outta here!\n");
}
```

Try this code in one of the previous apps, but don't wait for it to finish (Ctrl+C breaks you out of the program). If you want to make sure that your statement executes at least once, even if the expression is false, use the do-while loop. Following is another example:

```
boolean test = false;
do {
     ...
} while (test);
```

This control is used much less frequently, but is sometimes necessary. It is not implemented in JavaScript as of the Netscape 2.0 release. Note the ending semicolon (;) after the while statement.

The switch Branch

The switch branch is a kind of if-else structure, but makes coding much easier than writing out if-else conditions, especially if there are several options.

The control is executed by comparing the value of the variable in the switch parentheses with the values listed for each case and executing the statement that occurs at each line.

This control-flow statement is available in C and C++, but not JavaScript.

If none of the values match, the default: case is executed. After each case, you should use the break; statement. Otherwise, all the cases after the one found will execute. This is called drop-through. Try the following example with and without the break; statements:

```
class SwitchTest {
    public static void main (String args[]) {
        char a;
        System.out.println("Enter a number from 1-3:");
        a = (char)System.in.read();
        switch(a) {
          case '1':
            System.out.println("\nYou win a Car!");
            break;
          case '2':
            System.out.println("\nYou picked the goat");
            break;
          case '3':
            System.out.println("\nYou get to keep your
            100");
            break;
          default:
            System.out.println("\nIncorrect entry");
        }
    }
}
```

Be sure to use the break; statement, and if you do not need it, make sure that you will not be dropping down onto code you don't want to.

With the while and switch statements in hand, you can proceed to write a more substantial program. This program counts the number of digits, white spaces, and other characters entered from the terminal:

```java
class SwitchTest {
    public static void main (String args[]) {
        int numberOfWhite = 0, numberOfDigits = 0,
            numberOfOthers = 0;
        char c;
        while((c = (char)System.in.read()) != -1 && c !=
            '\n') {
            switch(c) {
            case '0':
            case '1':     case '2':
            case '3':     case '4':
            case '5':     case '6':
            case '7':     case '8':
            case '9':     numberOfDigits++;
                          break;
                case ' ':         case '\n':
                case '\t':        numberOfWhite++;
                                  break;
                default:          numberOfOthers++;
                                  break;
            }
        }
        System.out.println("\nResults:\n");
        System.out.println("Number of digits = " +
        numberOfDigits + "\n");
        System.out.println("Number of white spaces = " +
        numberOfWhite + "\n");
        System.out.println("Number of others = " +
        numberOfOthers + "\n");
    }
}
    }
}
```

The while loop at the beginning of the code grabs a character from the keyboard until the end-of-input flag is sent. Then, the switch statement takes the character and compares it to all the digits first, and then to the white spaces. When it finds one, it falls through and increments the relevant counter. When the number is incremented, the break statement ends the switch. If it cannot find any matches, it increases the "other" counter. The final switch in the default statement is not necessary, but is placed there for consistency and in case extra case statements need to be added to the end.

The for Loop

The for loop is a powerful tool for looping through a series until some limit has been reached. The format of the for statement uses a variable to compare with a certain limit. When the limit is reached, the loop is broken.

```
for( i=0 ; i<10 ; i++) ... ;
```

The format of the argument (ex1 ; ex2 ; ex3) is explained next. The first expression tells the for loop where to start the variable. In this case, i is set to zero. The second expression, i < 10, tells the for loop when it should stop. In this case, the statement is true (that is, the loop should continue) for all values 0–9. The last expression tells the loop what to do each time to the variable. In this example, the for loop runs i from 0 to 9. You could use a statement like this to address the members of an array in order:

```
int i, a[] = new int[10];
for( i=0 ; i<10 ; i++) a[i] = 0;
```

The preceding code would fill the array of integers with zeros.

You can declare your variable in the for loop header, and the last expression can be omitted; but be sure to do something with the variable in your statement.

```
for(int i = 10; i >= 0 ; ) i--;
```

An example of using the for loop would be to print a conversion from Celsius to Fahrenheit in five-degree increments:

```
class TempConversion {
    public static void main (String args[]) {
        int fahr, cels;
        System.out.println("Celsius  Fahrenheit\n");
```

```
for(cels = 0; cels <= 100; cels += 5) {
        fahr = cels * 9 / 5 + 32;
        System.out.println(cels + "\t" + fahr);
    }
}
}
```

The for loops can be used in many places—for array indexing, anywhere a series of numbers is needed, or anytime something has to execute a specific number of times.

Labels

Labels provide a method for controlling loops when the simple break; method will not work. If a break is encountered in the execution of a loop statement, the loop ends, regardless of what the other control evaluations are. This is an example of how a simple break; statement works:

```
boolean test = true;
int i = 0;
while(test) {
    i++
    if(i > 10) break;
}
```

The while loop runs only 10 times, despite the fact that the expression test always returns true.

What happens when you are nested down several levels in statements and need to break out? The normal break will break out of only a single block. You can use labels to mark which statement you want to break out of.

```
char a;
outer:                  //this is the label for the outer loop
    for(int i=0; i<10 ; i++) {
        for(int j=0; j<10; j++) {
            a = (char)System.in.read();
            if (a == 'b') {
```

```
                    break outer;
              }
              if (a == 'c') {
                    continue outer;
              }
        }
  }
```

In this case, the loops accept 100 input characters from the keyboard, unless the b key is entered, at which time the break outer; statement ends both loops. Notice the continue outer; statement. This statement tells the computer to break out of the present loop and continue with the outer loop.

Java does not have a goto statement. To those C/C++ programmers who were accustomed to using goto—shame on you, you know better! Gotos are confusing and end up causing more problems than they are worth. They are generally a quick solution to a dirty problem, but increase the amount of time needed later to figure out what a program is doing.

Summary

You have learned quite a bit of material in a short amount of space. Java is a powerful programming language, and there are many ways to tackle the same problem. Learning what is the best way takes experience and much trial and error. This chapter gave a general review of the fundamentals of the Java language. You learned the Java token set, Java types, operators, and control statements. This is a very long list for a single chapter. Do not worry if you feel as though there is too much to digest. As you work through problems in the following chapters, you will continually use the basic material you learned here. You will go through many programs before you become completely comfortable with all the elements of the language. Use this chapter as a reference if you are having syntactical problems with your code. You should be able to find the answers to your questions in this chapter.

To C/C++ programmers, it should be obvious that the Java language is a product of these languages; however, be sure to note the differences. Many programmers have come to rely on dangerous shortcuts involving the use of pointers and casting. Java does not allow this kind of coding. You might think that the advantages of being close to the system are more desirable, but when you have no idea what system your code will be running on, this kind of low-level programming is impossible. What Java gives up in this area, it gains in others. You will find that the ease of use and naturally good performance of the Java environment make giving up those old habits easy. True, you will never get the same speed from a Java application as from finely tuned C code—but you wouldn't be able to run that code over the Internet anyway.

By now you should be very comfortable with using the javac compiler and Java interpreter. You should be able to work through the examples and try out different combinations of your own. Seeing what doesn't work is just as useful as seeing what does work. In the following chapters you move on to the higher-level language elements, such as classes, interfaces, and packages. All of these elements are merely containers for the guts of the system you have just learned. These containers provide powerful capabilities to our code. In the next chapter, you will see the way in which object orientation, specifically its implementation in Java, brings ease of use, portability, reusability, and robustness to your costly investment of code. This will also allow you to easily begin developing applets for the Netscape environment.

Chapter 10

Objects in Java——The Class

Using the Java programming language means learning object-oriented programming. So far the basics of classes have been discussed, and the examples provided have used the basic class structure to get you started. However, in order to utilize the full power of Java and object-oriented computing, you will need to learn how to create, import, and inherit your own and pre-built classes.

The topics covered up to this point focused on gaining an understanding of the Java environment, learning to use the Java run-time systems, providing interactive content over the Internet, and the beginnings of learning to program in the Java language. The Java environment fulfills a need in the Internet for distributed, secure, high-performance programs that will provide a level of interactivity unseen in traditional media, and provide the technology for the future of communications and information delivery. Object-oriented computing is the foundation and fundamental solution to many of these technological problems by providing the encapsulation and extensibility needed in the dynamic atmosphere expected in the future of the Internet.

The Java architecture is one based upon object-oriented methodologies. All but the most fundamental types, such as integers and floating point numbers, are objects or classes. By encapsulating the language features in classes, Java can provide an extensible environment where programmers do not have to repeat the jobs other programmers have carried out. In addition, Java provides solutions for many of the problems of object-oriented approaches in languages such as C++ by providing run-time evaluation of the class structure to overcome the fragile superclass dilemma. This allows objects to be loaded from across the room or across the country just as easily—an important element when developing code for the Internet.

The Netscape 2.0 browser provides the run-time environment to load the developed classes in the form of Java bytecodes. This enables the end user to take full advantage of the object-oriented paradigm by simply removing the common hassles of more traditional approaches. The Java browser and interpreter enables the individual to load applications and applets seamlessly into their existing environment. In the context of the World Wide Web, this means that Web page developers can build sites with applets, knowing that client users will be able to view the new content immediately without having to wait for the latest viewers to become available on their platform.

The previous two chapters introduced the fundamentals of programming in the Java language. Chapter 8 introduced the compiler, browser, and interpreter as development tools, and showed you how to get a stand-alone application and applet coded, compiled, and running. Chapter 9 provided you with the foundations of the Java language in order to allow later examples to be more readable, and to get you started as soon as possible writing code that actually did something. By now you should be familiar with the Java tokens, identifiers, types, operators, and control flow statements. This sets you up for a more advanced understanding of Java's object-oriented approach-classes.

This chapter looks at two elements of the Java language:

➤ How classes are created and used

➤ The incorporation of interfaces and packages

Classes provide the Java and JavaScript equivalent of an object. You will look at the elements of a class—variables and methods—in addition to different methods of access. The creation and destruction of objects is covered, along with inheritance and other advanced topics. Next, interfaces and packages are discussed. These two elements of the language allow the incorporation of classes into existing code and are important in using classes to their full potential.

Objects in Java

Java's implementation of an object is called a class. The *class* declaration can be seen as a template for creating objects. After you have created a class declaration, you can reuse it to create as many objects of that type as you need. Some people say that classes add new fundamental types to a language, except the programmers provide all the functionality themselves, instead of the language. For example, you can create a Rectangle class that you can treat just like an Integer or String.

Java takes object-oriented computing to the extreme in making every executable an object. When you run a stand-alone application or applet in the browser or interpreter run-time environment, Java creates an instance of the class loaded. After the object that was constructed from the class template has been created, it controls its action by either executing its own methods, creating objects of other classes, or a combination of the two.

All classes in Java are inherited from a superclass, known as Object. A class does not, however, have to be an immediate subclass of Object. You can create your new class by inheriting another class. Figure 10.1 shows the relationship between a superclass and its derived subclasses.

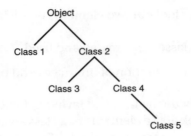

Figure 10.1
Inheritance from the Superclass Object.

In each case, the subclass inherits the properties of the superclass above it. In this way, a class can be several inheritances away from Object and still be said to be a subclass of Object. Object is the only class that does not have a superclass. In a way, it could be considered a fundamental type. If a class does not implicitly declare of which class it is an inheritance, Java assumes it is a subclass of Object.

Classes in Java

The basic declaration for a class is as follows:

```
class name {
     //class information
}
```

Note the beginning and ending curly braces, which designate the limits of the class definition. For example, perhaps you want to create a class of rectangles, and you have the following code:

```
public class Rectangle {
     ...
}
```

In this case, the class Rectangle is a subclass of the class Object, because it doesn't specifically mention which class it is derived from. Later on, you will see how to designate which superclass to use instead of Object. Also notice that the class is declared as public. This is necessary later on when it will be placed in a package to be imported. In the first few examples, it is being declared in the same file as the class that is using it, so this declaration is not needed; however, in order for it to be imported as a package, this is necessary.

Instance Variables in Java Classes

After you have created your class, you need to be able to provide it with a means of storing its own information. You do this by declaring instance variables. If you recall from Chapter 9, "The Java Fundamentals," you declare a variable by giving its type and then the identifier, or name, such as in the following example.

```
type name;
```

In this case, you might want to store information about rectangles in the rectangle class:

```
int width, height;
```

You could hold other information, but for this simple rectangle, class width and height are enough. If you needed to, you could have instances of floats, arrays, or, as you will see later, classes themselves. Up to now, the class looks as follows:

```
public class Rectangle {
    int width, height;
}
```

Of course, this object doesn't even do much; all it can do is hold its own width and height. If you want it to do anything, you have to provide it with methods.

Methods in Java Classes

A method is equivalent to a function in JavaScript; however, in order to include a method in Java, you must provide the class with more information than you do in JavaScript. This is because Java needs to check at compile time every element of your class structure before it can allow it to be run. You declare methods in Java with the following statement:

```
returnType name(parameters) {
    //function body
}
```

Again, note that you *do not* use the semicolon at the end of the method brackets as you would for normal declarations as mentioned in Chapter 9. Every method must return a value or be declared as void. Many times, methods are called to do specific calculations; in this case, they must return their result. The return type tells the compiler what kind of value to expect. In other cases, the method wants to indicate whether it has successfully completed its task. The parameters are a comma-delimited list providing the method with information it needs. As an example of the return type and parameter list, perhaps your rectangle should be able to calculate its own area:

```
int getArea(int w, int h) {
    int a;
    a = w*h;
    return a;
}
```

When the method reaches the return statement, it sends this value back to where it was called from.

It should be noted that the variables the method is passed and uses, such as w and h, are merely copies. The method does not alter the originals. For example, the following code would in fact do nothing because it is only acting on copies of the variables:

```
int width, height;
swap(width,height);
void swap(int w, int h) {
    int temp = h;
    h = w;
    w = temp;
}
```

Additionally, if you declared this function, the rectangle variables width and height would be hidden by the new variable declarations (see Chapter 9 for a discussion of hidden variables):

```
void swap(int width, int height) { ...
```

If you wanted to actually swap the width and height, you would have to do so explicitly.

In the case of the rectangle, your class would now look like this:

```
public class Rectangle {
    int width, height;
    int getArea(int w, int h) {
        int a;
        a = w*h;
        return a;
    }
}
```

Notice that the method declaration is inside the class declaration itself. If you recall in JavaScript, methods are assigned to objects by merely indicating which functions they refer to. This is not the case in Java.

In addition to being able to calculate its own area, the rectangle should also be able to draw itself. In this case, it will need another method:

```
public class Rectangle {
    protected int width, height;
    protected int getArea(int w, int h) {
        int a;
        a = w*h;
        return a;
    }
    public void drawRect() {
        for(int i=width; i>0; i-) {
            System.out.print('#');
        }
```

```
System.out.print('\n');
for(int i=height-2; i>0; i-) {
    System.out.print('#');
    for(int j=width-2; i>0; i-) {
        System.out.print(' ');
    }
    System.out.print('#\n');
}
for(int i=width; i>0; i-) {
    System.out.print('#');
}
System.out.print('\n');
    }

}
```

Note

The final line of #s is followed by `System.out.println("\n")`. This occurs because the print method does not actually output to the screen until the entire line is completed and the buffer is flushed. If you are not getting output, and you use the print method, make sure you have finished the output with a newline ("\n") character.

The new drawRect method is quite lengthy, but provides the class with a way in which to draw itself. One thing to note: this method's output is neng sent to stdout. For a stand-alone Java program being run with the Java interpreter this is the command-line screen itself. For an applet, this would be the Java console, which is not normally shown in Netscape. This will not output the text to the Navigator window.

You should also note the two additions to the method declarations: protected for getArea() and public for drawRect(). The protected modifier means that this method is only available to the Rectangle class and to any class that is derived from Rectangle. The public modifier means that drawRect() is available to any class that needs to tell the rectangle to draw itself. There is a third modifier, private, which means that only the class in which the modifier was declared can use the method; not even sub-classes of the class can use those methods. These modifiers are also relevant for variables. If you do not want other classes to be able to see the instance variables, you can declare them as private. The following line of code shows the use of the private modifier.

```
private int secretVariable;
```

It is good practice to keep member variables and methods as restricted from outside use as possible. Of course, you also want the methods and variables that subclasses might need to be available. If you do not specify the access modifier, then it is assumed to be *friendly*, or only available to classes in the same package. Packages are discussed later in this chapter. Generally, you are safe if you use the protected modifier for everything other classes don't need to see, and public for those methods that other classes need to make your object work. Notice I said *methods*. It is not good practice to make any of your variables public. If someone needs to change a variable, make them do so through a method such as this:

```
public void setWidth(int w) width = w;
```

This way you can keep track of everything that goes on in your class.

Note

Classes can also use the public modifier. If you do not use the public modifier in front of the class declaration, it will only be accessible to classes in the same package (see "Understanding Packages in Java" later in this chapter). Using the public modifier will allow all classes the capability to create instances of the class.

Overloaded Methods

What happens if you need to send the same method different kinds of information in different cases? You can *overload* the method by declaring more than one version. Essentially, you create a new method; you just give it a different parameter list, as in the following example:

```
void getArea(int w, int h);
void getArea(float w, float h);
```

In the second case, the method getArea() takes two float variables as its arguments. The compiler determines which method to call based upon how you call the method. If you provide the method with two ints, you get the first method. If you provide the methods with two floats, the second is used.

The Static Members

In addition to public, private, and protected, you can also declare members to be static. The *static* modifier indicates that a variable or method is the same for all classes. The rectangle might have a variable that you would want all rectangles to share, for instance, the version number of the class. If you declare it as static, that variable will be the same for all instances of the class.

```
static int versionNumber = 1;
```

The benefit of static methods and variables is that they can be referenced without a specific instance of the class being created. For example, the drawRect() method uses the System.out.println method, even though you haven't created a System object. Out is a static variable, which enables you to reference the variable even though you haven't created an object from the variable's class—System. Additionally, there is a final modifier that tells the compiler that the variable or method cannot be changed by a subclass by overriding. Overriding methods are covered in a later section.

Object Creation and Destruction

Java provides methods and operators for creating instances of classes. After you have created the "template" for your objects using the class declaration, and if you want to use the new class, you must create it. To create an object, it must first have a creation method. After this is complete, another class can create a copy of the object by using the new operator.

When an object is about to be deleted because it has fallen out of scope, it first looks for a finalized method, and then proceeds to be garbage collected. The Java specification does not assure the programmer that the finalize method will be called as soon as the object falls out of scope, but it is good programming practice to always use the finalize method to finish off anything that the object might leave hanging. For example, if you have opened a file, it is wise to close it before the thread completely ends.

The creation Method

The creation method in Java is a method with the same name as the class that does not return any value. Inside the creation method, you might want to initialize certain variables and get the object ready for use. The Rectangle creation method is as follows:

```java
public Rectangle(int w, int h) {
    width = w;
    height = h;
    area = getArea(w,h);
}
```

Note the use of the public modifier. Otherwise, later on, when you place Rectangle in a package, other classes won't be able to use the creation method.

You now have a completely usable class as follows:

```java
public class Rectangle {
    protected int width, height;
    protected int area;
    public Rectangle(int w, int h) {
        width = w;
        height = h;
        area = getArea(w,h);
    }
    protected int getArea(int w, int h) {
        int a;
        a = w*h;
        return a;
    }
    public void drawRect() {
        for(int i=width; i>0; i-) {
            System.out.print('#');
        }
```

```
            System.out.print('\n');
            for(int i=height-2; i>0; i-) {
                System.out.print('#');
                for(int j=width-2; i>0; i-) {
                    System.out.print(' ');
                }
                System.out.print('#\n');
            }
            for(int i=width; i>0; i-) {
                System.out.print('#');
            }
            System.out.print('\n');
        }

    }
```

The new Operator

In order for a class to be able to use the Rectangle class, it must use the new operator to create an instance of it. You might, for example, have an application class that merely creates a 3×4 rectangle and draws it to the screen:

```
public class doRect {
    public static void main(String args[]) {
        Rectangle rect = new Rectangle(3,4);
        rect.drawRect();
    }
}
```

Notice how the new operator is used in the previous example. Although you declare the variable as you do any other type (as in Rectangle Rect;), you must use the new operator to create a copy of the class to which the new variable points. By using the new method, you tell the Java compiler to create an instance of the object in the Java heap, thus allocating memory for the object. Otherwise, it only creates a reference to an object of type Rectangle. Also notice how the member method is invoked using the "." operator. The following is how you reference all class member variables and methods.

```
class.member
```

Of course, only those member variables and methods that are accessible according to the public, protected, friendly, and private modifiers are valid for referencing.

The finalize Method

In addition to the creation method, you can also provide a finalize method, like the following example.

```
void finalize() {
    //cleanup chores
}
```

This method enables you to close any files you might have open and generally makes sure that your object exits cleanly before the automatic garbage collection removes your object from memory. There is no guarantee that Java will invoke the finalize() method, so you should not depend upon the finalize method for your code to run correctly. Instead, you should think of it as an optimization of your code.

Command-Line Arguments

Now is a good time to cover command-line arguments in the interpreter environment. By now you have noticed the string args[] parameter that is in the main() method. This array of strings holds the command-line arguments entered when Java is run.

For C/C++ users, the command-line argument array does not include the call to Java or the class name itself. The array begins with the first argument after the class name.

The doRect class can take those arguments and use them to enter the width and height of the Rectangle object to create. The following code sets the width and height variables to values entered at the command line.

```
class doRect {
    public static void main(String args[]) {
        int w = Integer.valueOf(args[0]).intValue();
        int h = Integer.valueOf(args[1]).intValue();
        Rectangle rect = new Rectangle(w,h);
        rect.drawRect();
    }
}
```

The Integer class is called a *type wrapper,* along with the Float,
Long, and Double. The valueOf(String) method converts the
String number to the relevant type, and the intValue() method
returns the int represented by the Integer class. Check Chapter 12
for a more detailed look at type wrappers.

Type wrappers are classes in the Java language that are used to hold
variables and provide methods, such as valueOf(), for the different kinds
of data. They are different from the actual *types* of int, float, char, and so
forth.

You now have the necessary pieces for creating an instance of the
Rectangle class and having it draw itself. Create a file named
doRect.java with the following contents:

```
public class Rectangle {
    protected int width, height;
    protected int area;
    public Rectangle(int w, int h) {
        width = w;
        height = h;
        area = getArea(w,h);
    }
    protected int getArea(int w, int h) {
        int a;
        a = w*h;
        return a;
    }
    public void drawRect() {
```

```
        for(int i=width; i>0; i-) {
            System.out.print('#');
        }
        System.out.print('\n');
        for(int i=height-2; i>0; i-) {
            System.out.print('#');
            for(int j=width-2; j>0; j-) {
                System.out.print(' ');
            }
            System.out.print('#\n');
        }
        for(int i=width; i>0; i-) {
            System.out.print('#');
        }
        System.out.print('\n');
    }
}

class doRect {
    public static void main(String args[]) {
        if(args.length == 2) {
            int w = Integer.valueOf(args[0]).intValue();
            int h = Integer.valueOf(args[1]).intValue();
            Rectangle rect = new Rectangle(w,h);
            rect.drawRect();
        }
        else {
            System.out.println('Wrong number of
            ➥parameters');
        }
    }
}
```

Compile the file and run the application with the Java interpreter:

```
C:\> java doRect 20 15
```

You should see the output shown in figure 10.2.

Figure 10.2
Output of the doRect application.

Understanding Packages in Java

After you have created a class that you would like to use over and over again, it is useful to include it in a package. A *package* is a group of classes that all belong together. For example, Java provides packages, such as Java.io and Java.lang, which hold some of the basic classes used, such as System and String. You can create your own packages that bring together several classes that are related.

Your rectangle might be included in a general package known as Shapes. In addition to providing a simple way of referencing classes, packages also provide the scope for the friendly access modifier for variables and methods. Class members that you do not explicitly declare public, private, or protected can only be seen by classes in the same package. This allows for similar classes to have access to each other's methods, without compromising the encapsulation offered by object-oriented programming.

Declaring a Package

You declare a package by prefacing the file with the following declaration:

```
package name_of_package;
```

Typically, packages are grouped by relationships. In the case of the Rectangle class, it might be this:

```
package Shapes;
```

In this file, you might want to include classes for circles, triangles, and so forth. The package provides an easy way to associate these classes both for your own and others' benefit. The compiler creates a directory structure matching the package names. For example, javac creates the directory /Shapes/ in the target directory of the compiler. You can nest packages by using the ".", as in the following example:

```
package myclasses.Shapes;
```

This statement would create the directory structure /myclasses/ Shapes/ where it would place the Rectangle.class file.

In order for the compiler to know where to place the directory structure, indicate where you would like your packages placed with the following statement:

```
C:\> javac -d /your_path/ Rectangle.java
```

In this case, the Java compiler places the directory structure /Shapes/ Rectangle.class in the specified path. Be sure to include this path in your CLASSPATH environment variable. In the JDK release, all of the classes provided with Java are compressed in a file called classes.zip in the \java\lib directory. You might want to place your class files within this structure, that way your CLASSPATH environment variable can point to the single \java\lib directory.

Importing Other Packages

To use packages that have previously been compiled, you must import them into your source code with the import command. You can import classes in three ways:

1. By giving the full package reference before each class name:

```
Shapes.Rectangle rect = new Shapes.Rectangle(10,20);
```

2. By importing the class itself:

```
import Shapes.Rectangle;
  class doRect {
        Rectangle rect = new Rectangle(10,20);
        ...
  }
```

3. By importing the package that contains the class:

```
import Shapes.*;
class doRect {
      Rectangle rect = new Rectangle(10,20);
      ...
}
```

Note

Be sure that your CLASSPATH variable is set to the directory where the package bytecode file is located; otherwise, the Java compiler will not be able to link it in.

Creating and importing classes are important to utilizing the full functionality of Java. In later chapters, when you look at the different packages provided with Java, the use of importing classes becomes clear.

Using Inheritance in Java

Perhaps one of the most powerful tools in object-oriented programming is class inheritance. Class inheritance allows you to take an already existing class and build upon it. Say, for example, that you want to have a rectangle that would fill itself in when it was drawn on the screen. You could either start from scratch or use the old Rectangle class to build upon. The following sections will show you how to inherit the functionality of your Rectangle class, without rewriting all of the code used in the Rectangle class.

There is no equivalent to inheritance or abstraction in JavaScript. Although the lack of this functionality limits JavaScript's object-oriented appeal, as mentioned before—to try to incorporate all of these OOP features would most likely have overburdened the JavaScript language.

The extends Modifier

The way in which Java enables programmers to inherit from already existing classes is with the extends keyword. To tell the compiler and run-time system that you are inheriting the existing class Rectangle, you must import the old class and refer to it in the new class declaration as follows:

```
import Shapes.Rectangle;

class fillRect extends Rectangle {
    //New code here
}
```

Overriding Methods

In the case of the fillRect class, there are two areas in which you can improve the Rectangle class: the drawRect method itself, and the addition of a filling capability.

You are going to create a private method so that you can shrink the size of the drawRect() method. If you notice, Rectangle has to draw a series of characters based upon the width and height of the rectangle. Instead of rewriting virtually the same code over, you can create a method for a rectangle to use when it needs to draw itself.

```
private String makeString(char ch, int num) {
    StringBuffer str = new StringBuffer();
    for(int i=num; i>0; i-)
        str.append(ch);
    return str.toString();
}
```

In this case, the for loop keeps adding additional characters to the end of the string until it is filled with the necessary number of characters. Then the method returns the string that has been built up. Notice the use of the StringBuffer class. Stringbuffer is used because String only creates a static type—it can't be changed, while StringBuffer creates a string type that can be added to.

Now, the code for the drawRect method can be rewritten as follows:

```
pubic void drawRect() {
    for(int i=height; i>0; i-) {
        System.out.println(makeString('#',width));
    }
}
```

The new class must create a solid rectangle. In order to draw a solid rectangle instead of just the outline the drawRect method is *overridden*. By using the same method name, you replace the old method with the new method. In its entirety, your class now looks as follows:

```
class fillRectangle extends Rectangle {
    public fillRectangle(int w, int h) {
        super(w,h);
    }
    private String makeString(char ch, int num) {
        StringBuffer str = new StringBuffer();
        for(int i=num; i>0; i-)
            str.append(ch);
        return str.toString();
    }
    pubic void drawRect() {
        for(int i=height; i>0; i-) {
            System.out.println(makeString('#',width));
        }
    }
}
```

The size of the code has been shrunk, and the less code you have, the easier it is to keep bug-free. Notice that you no longer have to include all the code that is common between the two classes. Instead, just add the code that makes it do what you want. You do have to create a new constructor to differentiate between the two classes. In this case, the constructor is called for the superclass in order to initialize the instance variables. Notice, however, how the constructor is called with the super method name in the new constructor fillRectangle().

After you have begun creating your own set of reusable classes, the benefits of object-oriented programming become clear. You do not have to repeat many lines of code, and once you have debugged a class, you can inherit its features, knowing you only have to worry about implementing the new features you want to add.

Abstract Methods and Classes

There is a another way in which classes can be built. Java enables you to define what are known as *abstract* classes, which are made up of methods that have not been completed. It is up to the subclasses of the abstract class to override the methods. You create abstract methods with the keyword "abstract."

```
abstract returnType methodName(parameterList);
```

After you have included an abstract method in a class, the class itself is considered abstract and cannot be initialized. Only subclasses that override the abstract method can be created with the new operator. There are three kinds of methods that cannot be abstract:

➤ Constructors

➤ Static Methods

➤ Private Methods

Using Interfaces

Java provides a method for creating entirely abstract classes known as *interfaces.* You declare an interface as follows:

```
public interface interfaceName {
    //list of abstract methods
}
```

The default access is private. Variables in an interface are not expected to be changed, and are, therefore, always static and final. You do not use the abstract keyword when declaring the member methods.

You implement the interface in a class by using the implements keyword:

```
public class className extends superClass implements inter
        face [, optional interfaces] {
    //class body
}
```

Notice that a class can implement more than one interface. What is the benefit of using interfaces? By creating an interface, you can define the protocols for an abstract class without worrying about the specific implementation, leaving that until later. In addition, you can share the same interface with several classes, without worrying about how the other class is handling the methods. If you inherit the properties of the interface, other users will automatically know what the method calls are for that class. Say, for example, you want all your shapes to have a draw() method. You could create an interface and name it Shape:

```
public interface Shape {
        void draw();
}
public class Triangle implements Shape {
    void draw() {
        //draw() implementation
    }
    ...
}
```

Now, any time you use a shape, you will know that it has a draw()
method, and what parameters it takes. You can also use the
Shape class as a type itself. This enables you to create methods
and member variables that can hold any of the objects that
implement Shape.

```
Shape sh;
void rotateShape(Shape rot) {
    ...
}
```

By using a class cast, you can give the function rotateShape an
instance of type Triangle.

```
Triangle tri = new Triangle();
rotateShape( (Shape)tri );
```

Casting Classes

Casting was covered in Chapter 9, but that was for the fundamental types such as Integers and Floats. The rules for casting classes
between subclasses and superclasses is as follows:

➤ You can cast from a superclass to a subclass implicitly,
   without an explicit call for conversion, although explicit
   casts to subclasses are not an error. The following code
   shows this kind of casting.

   ```
   Triangle tri = new Triangle();
   Shape sh;
   tri = sh;
   ```

   or

   ```
   tri = (Triangle)sh;
   ```

➤ You can cast a subclass into a superclass; however, references to instance variables may change, even though they
   are of the same name. You must explicitly perform the cast
   using the parenthetical reference. The following code shows
   an example of an implicit casting of classes.

```
Triangle tri = new Triangle();
Shape sh;
sh = (Shape)tri;
```

➤ Casting between sibling classes is not allowed. You could not for example, cast between the Rectangle and Triangle subclasses of Shape.

null, this, and super Variables

There are three variables that all classes have: null, this, and super. The *null* reference points to nothing and can be used in place of an actual object to indicate that there is no instance, as in the following example:

```
Rectangle rect = null;
```

This example creates the rectangle variable, but does not create an object to place in it. It is essentially like creating an empty box of the right shape to hold a rectangle. In addition, if a method expects an object, you can use the null reference instead, as in the following:

```
rotateShape(null);
```

The *this* reference is the actual object itself. What do you do, for example, if a class needs to pass a reference to itself or to another method? The class can refer to itself using this reference:

```
class Rectangle {
 void RectMethod() {
    newClass obj = new newClass();
    obj.Method(this);
    ...
 }
}
```

The rectangle object would send a reference of itself to the newClass' Method.

The *super* variable is a reference to the superclass type of the class. You might recall from earlier that this is how the constructor for the superclass of fillRectangle was called to initialize the instance variables.

Summary

The use of classes in Java is the foundation of its object-oriented approach, and as you can undoubtedly see, is much different from how JavaScript creates objects. There is a lot of material in this chapter that is important to writing good Java code. Make sure that you are comfortable creating your own classes, importing already compiled classes, and inheritance. This will not only allow you to write cleaner, more efficient code, but it will be imperative to using many of the advanced features of Java later.

The creation of a class is the fundamental job of a Java programmer. It is the class itself that the run-time environment executes. Instance variable and member methods all combine to encapsulate the behavior of the object into a user-friendly shell. It might seem like more work to create the class in the first place, but it will save time later when you want to reuse the class. Of course, since your primary aim is most likely to create applets for Netscape, or the World Wide Web in general, it is important to get used to classes early on— because in order to create applets, you must inherit from the Applet class, as we have seen in Chapter 8. For now, we will continue to use the interpreter to create example programs for ease of explanation.

The reuse of classes through importing and inheritance is where object-oriented programming shows its true colors. As you saw with the fillRectangle example, by inheriting a class you had already created, adding new functionality was simply a matter of bringing in the new methods and overriding the relevant old methods. This will also become important in writing applets and using the class libraries. Much of the work in creating useful code has already been done for you. Learning classes now will allow you to take advantage of all that hard work.

The next chapter covers multithreading and exceptions. Both of these functions are encapsulated in classes, which means that adding threading and exception handling to your code is simply a matter of incorporating the right classes. In fact, the rest of the programming chapters deal with using specific classes in more detail, and how to add functionality to your Java programs and applets.

Chapter 11

Understanding Threads and Exceptions

Perhaps Java's next greatest strength behind its object-oriented foundation is its native multithreading capability. Multithreading—or the capability to maintain more than one concurrent execution path—is the major feature being incorporated into new releases of popular operating systems such as Windows 95 and the forthcoming Copeland MacOS. By providing native support for threads both in the language and in the class libraries, Java makes using this feature much easier.

Java also supports exception handling, a feature important for making robust programs. Whenever a run-time error occurs in a class method, it can throw an exception, which allows your code to either recover from the error or exit gracefully, without bringing down the entire system. This is important when your program is running at the same time as several other critical applications in a multitasking environment. Although the operating system might be able to close down your program without affecting others, this is not always ensured. By being prepared to handle exceptions that might be thrown, you can create a more user-friendly program.

The Java environment provides both the end user and programmer with powerful features needed to use and develop advanced media and applications. Multithreading and exception handling are two important elements that form the cornerstone of modern applications. The Java architecture incorporates multithreading at more than one level, and exception handling is built in to many of the class libraries. The end user and content provider can benefit from these features through more responsive applications and interfaces. The programmer can benefit from the ease-of-use of the multithreading and exception-handling elements of the language and class libraries by being able to quickly develop programs that incorporate these features.

The Java architecture supports multithreading at several levels, the least of which is the programming language itself, which has built-in modifiers for implementing threaded objects. In addition, the Java run-time environments in the browser and interpreter include a threaded automatic garbage collector, which cleans up unused objects after they are finished. Because Java provides all of the memory management, the programmer does not have to worry about conflicts with different threads and can concentrate on developing content in a secure, robust, and high-performance environment.

The browser and interpreter run-time environments also provide the end user and content provider with the security and performance necessary for distributed systems. The object-oriented and threaded paradigm enables the user to interact with multiple concurrent objects, each providing dynamic and extensible behavior. This functionality provides the user with a wider variety of resources over the Internet by removing the problems associated with platform-distributed software. The content provider can concentrate on content itself and not on worrying whether the potential users will have the means of dealing with it.

The previous chapters introduced the fundamentals of the Java language, from both a syntactical and organizational standpoint. By learning the fundamentals of the language, such as tokens, types, identifiers, operators, and control flow statements, you should be able to implement the computational side of the applications you want to develop. It is, however, the object-oriented paradigm that provides the Java programmer with the most functionality and power. By organizing your code along ideas of objects, you can create dynamic applications, free from the constraints of procedural code. It is important that you have a good grasp of how classes work, how to create your own, and how to implement already developed code.

This chapter covers how to implement multithreading capability into your own code and use the exception class for handling errors. Multithreading is encapsulated in the Thread and Runnable classes. The Thread and Runnable classes enable you to make classes that can run concurrently with other processes on the system and in your program, as well as detect and correct system and program errors. Exceptions are method calls made when Java encounters an error. You can handle these method calls in your own programs, allowing them either to recover from the error or close down gracefully. Threads and exceptions are the last major elements of a Java program that can be considered fundamental.

After you have finished this chapter, you will have the framework and plumbing necessary to build your own Java applications. However, your program would look pretty sparse, and it might be difficult to do everything you would like to from scratch. Java provides the necessary class libraries for adding accessories and a pretty face to your applications. These include the class libraries for input/output, and other system functions, along with the windowing class library and network protocols. Later chapters discuss how to use these predesigned elements in your own code.

Understanding Multithreading

In all of the previous examples provided, the programs have been single-threaded applications—meaning there was only one thing going on at any time in the program. In other words, you could follow what was happening with your finger (if it was fast enough). Of course, while your program was executing, everything else was waiting for it to finish. All the resources of the Java run-time system were being used to run only the single program.

Of course, this does not mean that your program is the only thing running on the whole system. In fact, Java includes its own garbage collection thread to manage memory for you, and the operating system is managing several tasks on the computer at the same time. To the Java run-time system, however, your program is the only thread running in the virtual machine.

Running a single-threaded program is fine when you only have to deal with small programs that have to do a single task, but what if you had a Web page with several applets that were all supposed to be running at the same time, or you wanted to run a calculation in the background while getting more user input? In this case, each of these applications would have to be multithreaded.

In Java there are two ways to create a class that can be multithreaded:

➤ Create a class that extends the Thread class

➤ Create a class that implements the Runnable interface

The Thread Class and Runnable Interface

The implementation of a threaded class can be either an extension of the class Thread, or an implementation of the interface Runnable. Both ways are shown in the following example.

Creating Threads

You can create a thread by extending Thread with your own class, and overriding the run() method, which is similar to overriding the main() method for a standard application:

```
class className extends Thread {
    public void run() {
        //Thread body of execution
    }
}
```

For example, you might want to compute primes in the background.

```
class primeThread extends Thread {
    boolean keepRunning = true;
    public void run() {
        int number = 10;
        int mod = 0;
        boolean flag = true;
        while(keepRunning) {
            loop:
            for(int i=2; i<number; i++) {
                if((mod = number % i) == 0) {
                    flag = false;
                    break loop;
                }
            }
            if(flag) {
                System.out.println(number);
                flag = true;
            }
            number++;
            flag = true;
        }
        System.out.println('Thread Stopped');
        System.exit(0);
    }
    public void stop() {
        keepRunning = false;
    }
}
```

In this case, the thread sets itself up in an infinite loop, printing out the prime numbers as it finds them. If you had this class and wanted to call the thread, you would create an instance of the class primeThread just like any other class:

```
primeThread getPrimes = new primeThread();
```

You would then call its start() method to cause it to run:

```
getPrimes.start();
```

The start() method invokes the thread's run() method. After the thread has been started with the start() method, the method immediately returns and the main thread of the program continues. The following example runs the prime thread, waiting for the user to press the Enter key.

```
class runPrimes {
    public static void main(String args[]) {
    throws java.io.IOException {
        primeThread getPrimes = new primeThread();
        getPrimes.start();
        char ch;
        while((ch = (char)System.in.read()) != Ô\n');
        getPrimes.stop();
    }
}
```

Note the call to the class' stop() method to exit execution of the thread. When the call to stop() is made, it changes the state of the variable keepRunning so that the while() loop in the primeThread class' run() method drops through.

In addition to extending the Thread class, you can have your class implement the Runnable interface:

```
class className implements Runnable {
    public void run() {
        ...
    }
}
```

A class that has implemented the Runnable interface can be run in a thread by passing the instance of the class to a new Thread object.

```
className instanceName = new className();
new Thread(instanceName).start();
```

The computation of primes using the Runnable interface would
be as follows:

```
class primeRunnable implements Runnable {
    boolean keepRunning = true;
    public void run() {
        int number = 10;
        int mod = 0;
        boolean flag = true;
        while(keepRunning) {
            loop:
            for(int i=2; i<number; i++) {
                if((mod = number % i) == 0) {
                    flag = false;
                    break loop;
                }
            }

            if(flag) {
                System.out.println(number);
                flag = true;
            }
            number++;
            flag = true;
        }
        System.out.println('Thread stopped');
        System.exit(0);
    }
    public void stop() {
        keepRunning = false;
    }
}

class runPrimesRunnable {
    public static void main(String args[]) {
    throws java.io.IOException {
        primeRunnable getPrimes= new primeRunnable();
        new Thread(getPrimes).start();
```

```
                              char ch;
                              while((ch = (char)System.in.read()) != Ô\n');
                              getPrimes.stop();
                      }
              }
```

Additional Thread Methods

In addition to the start() and stop() methods, the Thread class provides a number of additional methods and instance variables for controlling the execution of the thread.

There are three variables in the class Thread:

➤ MAX_PRIORITY

➤ MIN_PRIORITY

➤ NORM_PRIORITY

Although it is said that threads run concurrently, they do not actually run at the same time. Instead, each thread gets a turn to run for a short time, then lets the other running threads have a chance to process. Because the times are so short and today's processors so fast, it appears as if all the threads are running at the same time.

To make sure the required threads have the time they need to run, they are given priorities. These essentially set the amount of time each has to run before it must give up control. Threads with low priority have less time, whereas threads with high priority have more use of the processor.

MAX_PRIORITY is an integer holding the maximum allowable value for the thread's priority. MIN_PRIORITY holds the minimum priority value, and NORM_PRIORITY holds the default priority of a thread. You can set the thread's priority by using its setPriority(int) method. You pass the method an integer that indicates the priority of the thread. If you want to set a thread to its maximum priority, you would use the following:

```
Thread.setPriority(Thread.MAX_PRIORITY);
```

You can also see what a thread's priority is with the getPriority() method.

There are four constructors for the Thread class. The prime number example used two of them:

➤ Thread()

➤ Thread(Runnable)

In addition, you can name a thread when it is constructed by passing a String parameter:

➤ Thread(String)

➤ Thread(Runnable, String)

The Thread constructors create an instance of the Thread class, allowing the object to be run concurrently with other objects. When creating a thread, you can either create the thread by subclassing Thread itself; or, if you have a class that implements Runnable, pass that class to the Thread constructor, which will then create a thread out of that class. The previous four constructors provide for both of these situations. Passing a String to the constructor allows you to create references to individual threads, which can then be used as symbolic references. For example, if you have created several instances of the same thread, you could give them each a distinctive name to keep track of them.

The getName() method returns a String holding the name of the thread, and setName(String) sets the thread's name.

The following are also useful methods for determining a thread's status and controlling the execution of a thread.

➤ currentThread() returns the currently executing thread.

➤ isAlive() checks to see if the thread is active.

➤ suspend() suspends the execution of the thread.

➤ resume() resumes execution of a suspended thread.

➤ sleep(*int*) causes the thread to sleep for *int* milliseconds.

➤ yield() causes the thread to give up execution to waiting threads.

There are additional modifiers, but these are the ones most used in controlling the execution of a threaded application. For more information on Thread methods, or for methods and variables of any of the class libraries provided with Java, check out the API reference on the accompanying disk.

Using Thread Modifiers in Classes

So far, only the class implementation of Threads has been discussed. Java also includes support for synchronization and optimization of classes, variables, and modifiers at the language level. One problem in dealing with multithreading applications is controlling their access to data. In single-threaded applications, you always know in what order the program will be accessing variables and data. However, when you have multiple threads running at once, there is no way to know when any thread might be reading or writing to a variable.

The Java run-time environment attempts to control thread access to data so that conflicts don't arise out of two or more threads attempting to modify or read the same data at once. This does not mean, however, that problems cannot arise. Your program might, for example, have two threads that are accessing the same object—one is changing data in the object, the other is printing data from the object. Imagine what would happen to the Rectangle class if a function were added to change the width and height interactively.

```
public void setWH(int w, int h) {
    width = w;
    height = h;
    area = getArea(w,h);
}
```

Now, the drawRectangle class might spin off two threads, one to print the rectangle, and another to get new information about the width and height from the user.

```
class drawRectangle implements Runnable {
    Rectangle rect = null;
    Thread kicker = null;
    public void run() {
        rect.drawRect();
    }
    public void start(Rectangle r) {
        rect = r;
        kicker = new Thread(this);
        kicker.start();
    }
}

class getWidthHeight implements Runnable {
    Rectangle rect = null;
    Thread kicker = null;
    public void run() {
        int w, h;
        char ch;
        StringBuffer str = new StringBuffer();
        System.out.println('Enter Width:');
        while((ch = (char)System.in.read()) != Ô\n') {
            str.append(ch);
        }
        w = Integer.valueOf(str.toString()).intValue();
        System.out.println('Enter Height:');
        str = new StringBuffer();
        while((ch = (char)System.in.read()) != Ô\n') {
            str.append(ch);
        }
        h = Integer.valueOf(str.toString()).intValue();
        rect.setWH(w,h);
    }
    public void start(Rectangle r) {
        rect = r;
        kicker = new Thread(this);
        kicker.start();
    }
}
```

In the first thread class, drawRectangle, the call to rect.drawRect() would cause the rectangle to be printed out on the screen. At the same time, the second thread class, setWidthHeight, could be getting new width and height values. What happens if the setWidthHeight class started to change the values of width and height just as drawRectangle wanted to draw it? You might get some weird output on the screen—not the old rectangle or the new one, but a combination of both, depending on where each thread was. How can you make sure that each call to setWH() and drawRect() has completed before the other is able to run? You use the synchronized modifier.

The Synchronized Modifier

Imagine a relay race where runners have to be in possession of a baton to be able to run. Each team has only one baton, and only one runner can be running at a time; therefore, after a runner has finished his portion of the race, he hands it off to the next so that he can begin.

The Java equivalent to the baton is called a *lock*. Each class or object has a single lock that it uses to keep sections of code from running at the same time as others. By using the synchronized modifier, you are telling Java that the portion of code marked must have the lock in order to run.

In the Rectangle class, the problem of the setWH() and drawRect() methods interfering with each other can be solved by setting them as synchronized.

```
public synchronized void drawRect() {
    ...
}

public synchronized void setWH(int w, int h) {
    ...
}
```

Now, the drawRect() and setWH() methods cannot run at the same time. For each of them to run, they have to have the lock; however, there is only one lock per object, or class, so only one of them can be running at a time. This lock protocol ensures that each method has completed its work before the other can take over. Each method waits until it can acquire the lock before executing.

In addition to setting the methods as synchronized, blocks of code can be synchronized with objects. If the methods are not synchronized themselves, but you still want to make sure that they are not called at the same time, you can indicate that they should be run synchronized when they are called.

This system for setting synchronization is not recommended because a well designed object should take care of itself. However, you might want to synchronize methods from different classes. In this case, you could use the lock from one class to ensure that its method does not run until the method from the other class is finished.

In the drawRectangle class, this is the following:

```
synchronized (rect) {
     rect.drawRect();
}
```

For the setWidthHeight class, it would be the following:

```
synchronized (rect) {
     rect.setWH(w,h);
}
```

Notice the use of the object name in the parentheses. This indicates which lock the block of code should wait to acquire. Both the drawRectangle and setWidthHeight classes should wait for the rect lock to be freed before calling the method. When the method has returned, and the block of code indicated as synchronized is exited, the lock for the object is freed, and any other code waiting for the lock can execute.

Although the second system for ensuring synchronization, where methods must acquire a lock before execution, is adequate, the first system where methods are marked as being synchronized, is preferred for portability and ease of use. If you know that two class methods could interfere with each other, you should mark them as synchronized in the class declaration itself. Programmers who later use your classes then won't have to worry about making sure the objects created can handle multiple threads. Also, while synchronizing called methods is one way to use the synchronized block, you can also use it to block out specific areas of code in a method, without necessarily causing the whole method to have to wait for the lock.

```
class className {
    void method1() {
        // non synchronized code
        synchronized (this) {
            // synchronized code
        }
        // non synchronized code
    }
}
```

Notice the use of this object, referring to the class itself. By using the synchronized modifier this way, the method only requires the use of the lock for the minimum amount of time required, allowing it to be used by other threads.

The Threadsafe Modifier

If you know that a variable will never be changed by one thread while another is using it, you can mark it as threadsafe. Doing so enables the compiler to perform optimization that would otherwise cause difficulty by masking changes that might occur to the variable in one thread from being seen in another. You might, for example, have a variable that is set when the class is created, but never changed by any methods.

```
threadsafe int variableName;
```

Make sure that any variables marked as threadsafe are actually free from alterations by methods that could be invoked from different threads. Typically, static and final variables will be threadsafe.

Using Exceptions in Java

Java code can detect errors and indicate to the run-time system what those errors were. When an error occurs, Java throws an exception. Normally, a thrown exception will cause the thread to terminate, and an error message will be printed. If you want to handle the exception yourself, you can include a catch statement to trap the exception. One addition to the Java language that was not in the Alpha version is that the compiler will give a warning if methods do not indicate what exceptions they throw. If you look at the runPrimesRunnable class again, you will notice that the main() method indicates that it (or one of its functions, in this case System.in.read()) can throw a certain exception.

```
class runPrimesRunnable {
    public static void main(String args[])
    throws java.io.IOException {
        primeRunnable getPrimes= new primeRunnable();
        new Thread(getPrimes).start();
        char ch;
        while((ch = (char)System.in.read()) != Ô\n');
        getPrimes.stop();
    }
}
```

You should pay attention to the definitions of all functions in the API, and determine exactly what exceptions they can throw. If you do not indicate which exceptions a method will throw, the class can still compile, but will generate a warning. It is advisable, however, to indicate all of the exceptions that can be thrown when a method is defined.

Handling Exceptions

To handle exceptions, you must *try* the method that might throw an exception, and then catch any objects that could be thrown by the method.

```
try {
     // some code which might throw an exception
} catch (exceptionType name ) {
     // Handle the exception
 }
```

The code in the `try` block is executed and any exceptions generated are matched with the catch statement. You can, in fact, have several catch statements to cover different exceptions that might occur. Any code after an exception that is thrown in the try statement is ignored. If there is code you need executed even if an exception is thrown, use the 'finally' block (covered in a later section). When an exception is thrown, the run-time system attempts to match the exception with the relevant catch statement in the following order:

➤ The catch statement that matches the exception exactly executed.

➤ The catch statement that matches the superclass of the exception.

➤ The catch statement that is an interface that the exception implements.

For example, you can have the following code, which catches several different exceptions:

```
class exceptionTest {
    public static void main(String args[]) {
        try {
            int i = 0;
            i = i / i;
            //any other code here will not be executed
        } catch (ArithmeticException e) {
```

```
        System.out.println('Attempt to divide by
        zero');
    } catch (Exception e) {
        System.out.println('Some other error was
        thrown');
    }
  }
}
```

After the attempt to divide by zero, the run-time system throws the exception. However, if for some reason another exception were to be thrown, it would be caught by the second catch statement.

The exceptions thrown by the class libraries vary. You should check with the class library API for more information on the specific exceptions thrown by different errors. The section on run-time errors in this chapter lists the exceptions thrown by the Java interpreter.

Throwing Exceptions Around

You can also throw your own objects, which are subclasses of the exception class. To create your own exception, make a class that is a subclass of the exception class.

```
class newException extends Exception {
}
```

Now, you can throw this exception yourself:

```
void newMethod() {
    try {
        if(no error) {
            // run code
        }
        else {
            throw new newException();
        }
    } catch (newException e) {
        // handle exception
```

```
    } catch (Exception e) {
        // handle general errors
}
```

You also can have multiple levels of, or nested, exception handling. After you are finished with the exception at one level, you can throw it onto the next.

```
try {
    try {
        // Some code which generates an exception
    } catch (Exception e) {
        // Handle exception
        throw e;
    }
} catch (Exception e) {
    // Handle exception
}
```

The first time the exception is caught, it is handled and then thrown again, to be caught by the outer try statement.

Using the Finally Statement

You can use the finally statement to include code that should be executed even if an exception is thrown:

```
try {
    // code which might throw exception
} finally {
    //clean up after it
}
```

The finally block is executed no matter what happens in the try block. Even if there is a break, continue, return, or throw, the finally block will be executed.

Run-Time Exceptions

The class library APIs list all the exceptions thrown by classes. In addition, the run-time system will throw the following exceptions:

➤ **ArithmeticException.** Dividing or taking the modulus of an integer by zero.

➤ **NullPointerException.** An attempt to access a variable or method in a null object.

➤ **IncompatibleClassChangeException.** A change to a class has been made that affects references to methods or variables to that class in other objects, and those objects haven't been recompiled.

➤ **ClassCastException.** Incorrect casting of a class.

➤ **NegativeArraySizeException.** If an array is created with a negative size.

➤ **OutOfMemoryException.** New is called and there is no more memory available for objects.

➤ **NoClassDefFoundException.** A class is referenced, but the system cannot find it.

➤ **IncompatibleTypeException.** Thrown if an attempt to instantiate an interface is made.

➤ **ArrayIndexOutOfBoundsException.** Thrown if an attempt is made to reference an invalid element in an array.

➤ **UnsatisfiedLinkException.** Thrown if a native method cannot be linked at runtime.

➤ **InternalException.** This exception should never be thrown, and indicates a problem with the run-time system itself.

Summary

The use of Thread and exception classes is an important feature of robust, high-performance Java programs. By using the multithreading and exception handling features, you are able to develop code that takes full advantage of the Java environment and modern operating systems. Multithreading enables you to use the full processing power available in today's computers, while exception handling provides the robust error detection and correction that is expected in modern applications. Java provides powerful and easy-to-use threading and exception tools for incorporating these features into your programs.

The Thread class and Java language synchronized and threadsafe elements provide the programmer with a full range of options for developing multithreading applications. You should be able to write your own classes that extend the Thread class or implement the Runnable interface. In addition, the synchronized and threadsafe modifiers will enable you to optimize your code for a multithreading environment. Because Java is a multithreading environment, it is important that you begin to think of your programs in the wider context of concurrent threads.

The exception class, and try, throw, catch, and finally statements, provide you with powerful tools for detecting, handling, and recovering from errors that occur in your program. Users expect robust applications and want programs that can take care of themselves without bringing down the rest of the system. Exception handling is the most important way to deal with any problems that arise.

By incorporating multithreading and exception-handling capabilities into your Java programs, you provide a level of sophistication difficult to obtain with many other programming languages. Take advantage of the ease with which Java enables you to provide these features. In the following chapters, the class libraries and advanced features of Java are presented. Threads and exceptions are the last elements of the Java environment that could be considered fundamental to writing good Java code. In the next sections, the basic groundwork is extended to add functionality to your code by incorporating the class libraries of the Java environment.

The Java Language, Utility, and I/O Class Libraries

The Java environment provides the programmer with a host of packages that contain class libraries for useful utilities often needed by programmers. Instead of having to write the classes for these utilities yourself, you can simply import the necessary packages into your program. Doing so makes writing sophisticated, functional programs much easier.

Almost all programming languages provide standard libraries that implement basic utilities beyond what the basic language can provide. These libraries typically include file input/output, system calls such as date and time, and classic functions for math and strings.

As you learn to program in the Java language, it will become quite obvious to you that objects are everything. In the case of Java, the object is represented by the Java class. The fundamental programming skills learned in Chapter 8, "Moving On to Java," are all encapsulated in the framework of classes. Anything you want to do in Java must be done in the form of a class. Although it can be argued that object-oriented programming is more costly for the initial code creation, the encapsulation of classes allows for greater reusability in the long run. Once you have a grasp of programming with classes, the entire development process will come together. By reusing classes that you or others have developed, programming time can be cut drastically. This is exactly what these later chapters are all about—using classes developed for the Java language that provide utilities for getting solid Java programs out the door quickly and effectively.

The goal of object-oriented programming is to allow the greatest reusability of code as possible. In this light, Java includes class libraries in the form of packages, which provide methods for many basic functions of a Java program. These include file I/O, System calls, graphical user interface classes, and network protocol classes. By using these classes, you can quickly get up to speed with your Java applications.

This chapter is devoted to covering the Java class libraries, comprised of the java.lang, java.util, and java.io packages. Some of the classes have been seen in previous examples, but most are new. These classes are important no matter what kind of Java code you are writing, be it applets, stand-alone applications, or handlers.

After you finish this chapter, you will have all the ingredients for making an advanced Java program. You should pay careful attention to the lists of methods these classes provide, because they can save you time and endless suffering from attempting to code your own functions. Chances are, the basic language class libraries have a class that can handle whatever you need.

With updates in the Java release, aspects of the Language API might change. Be sure to check out the Sun Java site at `www.javasoft.com`, to find information on the latest state of the Java APIs. In addition, it is impossible to list all of the variables, methods, and exceptions of each class, or for that matter, even list all of the classes available. Check out the full hypertext version of the API that comes with the release of the Java environment. This API documentation can also be found at the Sun Java Web site.

Introduction to the Class Libraries

The class libraries provided with Java can be grouped into two broad categories—those intended for the general Java interpreter and those intended for a browser environment. Although the Java packages can be used by all Java programs, the applet classes are mainly intended for use in the environment of a browser. This is because all browsers that implement Java must support the applet API.

Java Class Libraries

The Java class libraries provide three packages for utilization of low-level system methods. These packages are java.lang, java.util, and java.io. You can import all of these libraries using standard import methods such as

```
import java.lang.*;
import java.io.*;
import java.util.*;
```

This brings in all of the basic Java class libraries. Alternatively, you can only import the packages you will specifically need.

```
import java.util.Date;
```

The lang Package

The java.lang package provides the low-level classes used to encapsulate methods for basic program functionality. These include the following:

➤ Boolean, Character, and Number type wrapper classes

➤ Math classes for basic functions

➤ String and StringBuffer classes

➤ A System class for standard I/O and low-level system information

➤ Thread and ThreadDeath classes

➤ Abstract classes for the libraries

➤ The base Object class

These classes are used for the fundamental elements of a Java program, and provide useful methods for handling the basic objects. This package will be covered in the latter half of this chapter.

The util Package

The java.util package provides additional low-level utilities that enable the programmer to have greater control over program execution, and more advanced control and storage methods. These include the following:

➤ Vector and StringTokenizer classes

➤ Stack and Hashtable classes

➤ Date class

The io Package

The java.io package contains classes for implementing input/output with the Java language. Input/output can occur between several places, including the keyboard, screen, printer, disk file, or network. Utilities are included for the following:

➤ Files

➤ Data

➤ Buffers

➤ Filters

➤ Pipes

➤ Print Streams

➤ Random Access Files

➤ A Stream Tokenizer

If you plan on doing any input/output with your program, which is imperative for interactivity, you should pay careful attention to the java.io package. It provides useful classes for almost all necessary I/O needs.

Of course, in the Netscape environment, applets are restricted in what they can do, and file access is one of those no-no's. Network access is also restricted, and applets can only create connections with the host they are from.

Warning

The applet and awt Class Libraries

These two class libraries support the more advanced functions of the Java environment in both the stand-alone and browser environments. Although the applet class library is the standard of implementation for all browsers, it can also be used to create stand-alone applications. The awt library provides the buttons, menus, and scroll bars that make up the User Interface. This library has been significantly updated since the Alpha version of the Java environment. Using these classes, programmers can develop advanced code quickly and easily, taking advantage of the true object-oriented nature of Java.

The awt Class Library

The AWT package provides classes for creating graphical user interface elements. By using these elements you can control the look and feel of your applet. Classes provided in the awt package include methods for the following:

➤ Windows

➤ Buttons

➤ Menus

➤ Fonts

➤ Images

➤ Scroll bars

Almost all programs today rely on a graphical user interface. The days of text-based DOS and Unix interfaces are on their way out. By using the AWT class, you can impart a familiar and easy-to-use shell to your applications. The next chapter will cover the awt library

The applet Class Library

The applet package includes classes for implementing Java applets in a browser run-time environment. You can control the formatting of HTML documents, in addition to including audio in your applications. In addition, the applet package includes the Applet class, which is used to create the applets included with HTML pages. Browser classes provide methods for

➤ Applets

➤ Audio

➤ Links

➤ Style

➤ Properties

In order to create an applet that runs in a Web page, you extend the Applet class, which is a member of the applet package.

The Language Foundation Class Library

The language foundation class library provides the basic functionality required by programmers at the lowest level. At the top of the hierarchy of classes is the Object class, from which all other classes are descended. The Object class is included in the language class library. Additionally, the basic types are provided with *type wrappers*, defined later in this section, that encapsulate the fundamental types into classes that can provide methods for easier manipulation. The Math class provides the basic mathematical functions required beyond the classic operators handled at the language level. The library also provides classes for string manipulation. Finally, the language library provides a System class, which includes methods for low-level operating system interaction.

The java.lang package is automatically loaded with the compiler, so there is no need to import it explicitly. Many language classes also implement their methods as static members. Because static members can be accessed without a specific instance of the class itself, there is no need to create an instance of the class in order to use the function. For example, in order to determine the absolute value of an integer, you can use the Math class' abs() method:

```
int a = -1;
a = Math.abs(a);
// a now equals 1
```

The static member method abs() of the class Math has been used without creating a new instance. In earlier examples, the methods System.out.println() and System.in.read() were used in a similar manner.

The Object Class

The Object class is at the top of the class hierarchy. Whereas all classes have a superclass—Object is *the* superclass to everything. The methods implemented by the Object class apply to all classes, because they are all derived from Object. This means that you can use these methods with your own classes, or any class you import.

There are several useful Object methods you might want to use.

> ➤ **protected Object clone().** This method makes an exact copy of the Object, and returns the copy.

```
Rectangle rect = new Rectangle(10,20);
Rectangle rectCopy = rect.clone();
```

➤ **protected void copy(Object src).** This method copies the contents of the Object passed to the method into the current Object. Both Objects must be of the same type. The contents are considered the values of the instance variables of the Object being passed to the method.

```
Rectangle rect1 = new Rectangle(10,20);
Rectangle rect2 = new Rectangle(20,20);
    rect1.copy(rect2);
    // rect1 width and height are now both 20
```

➤ **public final Class getClass().** This method returns the class definition object Class. The Class object stores information about the class name, superclass name, implemented interfaces, and additional information. For example, Class has a method getName() that returns a String holding the name of the class.

```
Rectangle rect = new Rectangle(10,10);
System.out.println("class
➥name:"+rect.getClass().getName());
```

Notice how you can append methods to other methods. The order in which the methods work is left to right, and they act upon the return type of each previous method. In this case, the rect.getClass() method returns an object of type Class, which is then appended with getName() (Class.getName()). This is a useful and compact method for applying several methods to an object at once.

The Type Wrappers

The type wrappers are used to hold information about the fundamental types—boolean, character, int, long, double, and float—in addition to providing useful methods for comparison and string output. It is important to note that the type wrappers are classes, whereas the fundamental types are not. It is easy to get confused; for example, the Boolean wrapper differs from the fundamental type by only a capital B. The type wrappers and

regular types are not interchangeable, so be sure to use the
*type*Value() method provided with each of the wrappers to get the
fundamental type from the wrapper. The classes implemented by
wrappers are the following:

➤ Boolean

➤ Character

➤ Double

➤ Float

➤ Integer

➤ Long

While each of the type wrappers implements special methods for
its specific type, there are several methods that are common to all
of the wrappers.

➤ **public ClassType(type).** All of the wrapper constructors take
a parameter that is the type they encapsulate. The following
example creates wrappers for int, char, and float:

```
Integer i = new Integer(1);
Character ch = new Character('a');
Float flt = new Float(1.234);
```

➤ **public type typeValue().** This method will return the native
type of the type wrapper created. The type wrappers are not
equivalent to the native types, so you will need to use this
method in order to process the value of the wrapper normally.

```
int x = i.intValue();
char y = ch.charValue();
float z = flt.floatValue();
```

➤ **public String toString().** This method will return the string
representation of the type held in the wrapper. This function is useful for creating string representations of types for
output.

```
System.out.println(i.toString());
System.out.println(ch.toString());
System.out.println(flt.toString());
```

➤ **public boolean equals(Object obj).** All wrappers except for the Character wrapper implement this method. Because the wrappers cannot be compared directly with the equal (=) sign, this method will return true if the two values are the same, and false if they are not.

```
Integer j = new Integer(2);
boolean bool = j.equals(i);
// bool is now false
```

The Boolean Type Wrapper

The Boolean type wrapper does not implement any methods other than the standard methods mentioned previously. The Boolean class can have two states: TRUE or FALSE. You can change the state of the object by doing the following:

```
bool = Boolean.TRUE;
```

or

```
bool = Boolean.FALSE;
```

Notice that you cannot change them by using the bool = true; statement because these two types are not equivalent.

The Character Type Wrapper

The Character type wrapper implements several methods in addition to the methods for all of the wrappers. However, Character is the only wrapper class that does not provide an equals() method. The additional methods the Character wrapper provides are all static. This means that you can use them without creating an instance of the class.

```
public static boolean isLowerCase(char ch).
```

The isLowerCase() method returns `true` if the character is lower-case, or false if it is not. You can use this method by referencing the Character class itself. With non-static methods, the only way to use the method is to create an instance of the class.

```
Character ch = new Character('a');
boolean LowerCase = ch.isLowerCase('b');
// LowerCase is now true
```

Notice that an instance of ch was created just to use the isLowerCase method. However, because it is static, the method can refer to the general Character class instead.

```
boolean LowerCase = Character.isLowerCase('b');
// LowerCase is now true
```

The following methods work the same way.

➤ **public static boolean isUpperCase(char ch).** This method returns true if the character is uppercase, or false otherwise.

➤ **public static int digit(char ch, int radix).** This method returns the integer value of the character ch. Radix is the base of the number (2 for binary, 8 for octal, 10 for decimal, and 16 for hexadecimal).

```
int x = Character.digit('a',16);
// x is equal to 10
```

➤ **public static boolean isDigit(char ch).** This method returns true if the character is a digit (0–9), or false otherwise.

➤ **public static char forDigit(int digit, int radix).** This method returns the character value for the digit in the specified radix.

➤ **public static char toLowerCase(char ch).** This method returns the lowercase equivalent of the character provided. If a lowercase character is given, it is returned the same.

➤ **public static char toUpperCase(char ch).** This method returns the uppercase equivalent to the character provided.

Again, if an uppercase character is given, it is returned the same.

Type Wrappers for Numbers

In addition to the standard methods provided by the wrappers, the number wrappers Double, Float, Int, and Long provide several common methods. The instance methods provided are the following:

➤ public int intValue();

➤ public long longValue();

➤ public float floatValue();

➤ public double doubleValue();

These methods return the relevant values for each type. For example, if you have a Double instance, and you would like the int value for that Double, you could use:

```
Double d = new Double(1.234);
int x = d.intValue();
// note that there is a loss of precision in casting from
// double to int.
```

Of course, the methods that return the same types as those of their wrapper types are safe from casting loss mentioned in Chapter 8, "Moving On to Java," but you should be aware of the precision you will lose if you use a different number type.

```
public int hashCode()
```

This method returns a hashcode value for the Double.

In addition to the previous instance methods, the number wrappers provide a static method for converting a string to the relevant wrapper type.

```
public static Type valueOf(String s)
```

This method converts the string and returns an instance of the wrapper type. The following code creates an instance of the class Long with the value 1234.

```
Long l = Long.valueOf("1234");
```

You could also convert a String to the basic type using the following:

```
int i = Integer.valueOf("1234").intValue();
```

Remember that the valueOf() method returns an instance of the type wrapper referenced in the method call, not the basic type itself.

The number wrappers also provide two variables MAX_VALUE and MIN_VALUE that hold the maximum and minimum numbers for each type. You can use these numbers to ensure that your code does not exceed the boundaries and either cause an exception to be thrown or a loss of data.

The Float Type Wrapper

The Float wrapper adds two final variables and two methods to the standard set of members implemented by the number wrappers. The two final variables are

- ➤ public final static float E   e = 2.718281...
- ➤ public final static float PI   π = 3.141592...

Notice that these numbers are regular floats. This means that you can use them directly with other types, unlike the Boolean variables TRUE and FALSE.

```
float f = Float.E;
```

Float also provides two methods for determining if Float numbers are either the special NaN or Inf. The public static boolean isNan(float f) method returns true if the float value is an NaN (not a number), or false otherwise.

The public static boolean isInfinite(float f) returns true if the float is an Inf (an infinitely large number), or false otherwise.

```
float f = 0, j = 1000;
j = j/f;
boolean bool = isInfinite(j);
// bool is true
```

Refer to the section on floating point numbers in Chapter 8 for more information on when a floating point operation might return either an Inf or a NaN.

The Integer Type Wrapper

The Integer type wrapper adds both a new constructor and several new methods to those provided by all number wrappers.

➤ **public Integer(String s).** This constructor creates an Integer instance from the string variable presented. This is different from the normal constructor, which would take an int. The radix is assumed to be 10. That is, the string is assumed to be a decimal number, rather than binary, octal, or hexadecimal.

➤ **public static String toString(int i, int radix).** This method is provided in addition to the standard toString() method. It allows you to specify the radix for the resulting string (2 for binary, 8 for octal, 10 for decimal, and 16 for hexadecimal).

➤ **public static int parseInt(String s, int radix).** This method returns the integer value of a String representation. The base of the representation is taken as radix. Notice that this is a static method, which you can use on any string, without creating an instance of the Integer object. If you do not include the radix (parseInt(String s)) then the base is assumed to be 10.

➤ **public static Integer valueOf(String s, int radix).** This method is similar to the standard valueOf() methods, except it takes radix as the base of the Integer representation.

Integers are used in almost every aspect of a computer program, and you will contsantly be using integers to keep track of control flow, mathematical equations, and user input/output. This means that you will be using the previous methods often, and it is worthwhile to play around with the Integer, and all wrapper classes.

The Long and Double Type Wrappers

The Long and Double type wrappers do not add any variables or methods other than the standard type wrapper and number members. They act as any other type wrapper, and can be used for extra precision, in the case of the Double wrapper, or for extremely large numbers, in the case of the Long wrapper.

The Math Class

The Math class provides several methods for implementing the standard mathematical functions. All of the Math member functions are static, so you do not have to create an instance of the Math class. Instead, append the method you want to use with the Math class reference.

```
Math.method(variable);
```

Be sure to note the return types and argument variables.

➤ public static double sin(double a)

➤ public static double cos(double a)

➤ public static double tan(double a)

➤ public static double asin(double a)

➤ public static double acos(double a)

➤ public static double atan(double a)

➤   public static double exp(double a)

➤   public static double log(double a)

➤   public static double sqrt(double a)

➤   public static double ceil(double a)

➤   public static double floor(double a)

➤   public static double rint(double a)

➤   public static double atan2(double a, double b)

➤   public static double annuity(double a, double b)

➤   public static double pow(double a, double b)

➤   public static int round(float a)

➤   public static int round(double a)

➤   public static void srandom(double a)

➤   public static double random()

➤   public static int abs(int a)

➤   public static long abs(long a)

➤   public static float abs(float a)

➤   public static double abs(double a)

➤   public static int max(int a, int b)

➤   public static long max(long a, long b)

➤   public static float max(float a, float b)

➤   public static double max(double a, double b)

➤   public static int min(int a, int b)

➤   public static long min(long a, long b)

➤   public static float min(float a, float b)

➤   public static double min(double a, double b)

Note that the srandom() method sets the seed for the random number generator method random(), which returns a random number between 0.0 and 1.0.

The String Classes

Java provides the programmer with two string classes—String and StringBuffer. The String class is for strings that are constant—they will not change. The StringBuffer class is for strings that are not constant and need to be altered. C and C++ do not provide any mechanism for strings at all; they are merely represented by null terminated arrays of characters. Using arrays for strings is wholly unsatisfactory in an environment like Java, where security and portability demand a much more robust approach. The danger of allowing strings to be represented by character arrays is that you always run the risk of overrunning the boundaries of the array. By encapsulating Strings in classes, you do not have to worry about this problem.

Using Strings

The String class holds constant strings that cannot be changed once they are initialized. There are several constructors for Strings, depending upon how your String data is organized. The most basic constructor is that used for the string literals. When the Java compiler encounters a String literal, it actually creates an instance of the String class for that literal. Therefore, the easiest way to initialize a String object is to use the String literal:

```
String s = "Hello, World!";
```

In addition, you can initialize the String in the traditional manner, by either including another String object, or a string literal.

```
String s = new String(someString);
```

You can also give the String constructor a character array for initialization. You can either pass the whole array,

```
public String(char value[])
```

or just a portion of the array, or subarray,

```
public String(char value[], int offset, int count)
```

Offset indicates where the subarray begins, and count indicates how long the subarray is.

Warning

Make sure that you do not alter the array after you use it to create the String. The array is not copied, and any alterations made to it will change the value of the characters in the String.

Additionally, you can use an array of bytes to initialize a String, in the same manner as an array of characters.

```
public String(byte ascii[], int hibyte)
public String(byte ascii[], int hibyte, int offset, int
➥count)
```

In the case of an array of bytes, because Java uses the UNICODE character set, you need to indicate what the upper 8 bits of the 16-bit character are. You do this by using the hibyte argument. Typically the hibyte will be zero (0) for the Latin character set.

There are many methods provided for the String class. While this multitude of options can be confusing, there is undoubtedly a way to do something you want with this class. The following is a listing of some of the more important methods for the String class:

➤ **public int length().** This method returns the number of characters in the String.

➤ **public char charAt(int index).** This method returns the character at the position index.

➤ **public boolean equals(Object o).** This method compares two String objects, and returns true if their contents are the same, and false if otherwise.

➤ **public int compareTo(String s).** This method returns an integer based upon the lexical relationship of the two strings. If s is greater than this String, then a number less than zero is returned. If the two strings are equal then a zero is returned. If the String s is less than this String, then a number greater than zero is returned.

➤ **public boolean regionMatches(int toffset, String other, int ooffset, int len).** This method returns a boolean value based upon whether it can find a region starting at toffset in the String that matches a substring of other, beginning at ooffset, of length len. If a matching region is found, it returns true; otherwise, it returns false.

➤ **public boolean startsWith(String prefix).** This method is identical to the previous method except that it looks for the prefix at the beginning of the String.

➤ **public boolean endsWith(String suffix).** This method returns true if the String ends with the same String as suffix, false otherwise.

➤ **public int indexOf(String str).** This method returns the index of the first occurrence of str in the String. -1 returned if String not found.

➤ **public String substring(int beginIndex, int endIndex).** This method returns the substring that begins at beginIndex and ends at endIndex.

➤ **public String concat(String str).** This method returns the concatenation of the two Strings.

➤ **public String toLowerCase().** This method changes all the characters in the String to lowercase.

➤ **public String toUpperCase().** This method changes all the characters in the String to uppercase.

➤ **public char toCharArray().** This method creates a new array of characters from the String.

➤ **public static String valueOf(type variable).** This method creates a String from the variable argument. String provides a method for all of the basic types including boolean, int, long, float, double char[], and Object. This method implements the toString() method of the object passed as the argument.

It would be impossible to cover every single method of every single class Java provides. To cover any one class more than another would present an unbalanced impression of the Java class libraries. In addition, because the APIs will change, you should become familiar with how to use the online API guide that Sun provides with each release. While you will be able to do most of what you will need with the methods mentioned in this book, be sure to check out the API for a more comprehensive listing. You might just find a method that does exactly what you need.

The StringBuffer Class

The StringBuffer class provides methods for implementing a modifiable string. Whereas the String class dealt with strings that weren't meant to change, the StringBuffer class is essentially an expanding buffer for characters and other types to be used in creating Strings. This class provides methods for inserting and appending data to the String. Once you are finished creating your string, you can convert it with toString() to a String object that you can then manipulate with the String class methods.

Remember to use the StringBuffer class if you want to hold strings that you know will be changing.

There are three constructors for the StringBuffer class:

➤ **public StringBuffer().** This constructor creates an empty StringBuffer.

➤ **public StringBuffer(int length).** This constructor creates a StringBuffer the size of length.

➤ **public StringBuffer(String str).** This constructor creates a StringBuffer with the string str.

The methods implemented by the StringBuffer class are meant to allow you to create Strings from combinations of incoming types such as characters, integers, floats, and objects. The following example presents a use of the StringBuffer to build up a String from keyboard input:

```
StringBuffer str = new StringBuffer();
System.out.println("Enter Width:");
while((ch = System.in.read()) != '\n') {
    str.append(ch);
}
```

Notice that the StringBuffer was initialized as empty, and that the class automatically allocated space for new characters at the end. Here are a few of the more important methods. Again, check out the online API guide if you don't seem to find what you need in this list.

➤ **public int length().** This method returns the length of the String in the buffer (not the actual space of the buffer).

➤ **public int capacity().** This method returns the amount of space available in the buffer for new characters.

➤ **public synchronized StringBuffer append(type variable).** This method adds the variable type to the end of the StringBuffer. Valid types include Object, int, long, float, double, char[], and boolean.

➤ **public synchronized StringBuffer insert(int offset, type variable).** This Method will insert the same types as append() in the location specified by offset.

➤ **public synchronized StringBuffer insertChar(int offset, char ch).** This method inserts a single character into the StringBuffer at the offset location.

➤ **public synchronized String toString().** This method converts the StringBuffer to a String.

Whenever you use the StringBuffer class, it automatically allocates more space for insertions. This way, you don't need to worry about overrunning your array of characters. You can explicitly allocate space in the buffer, and demand that a specific amount of space be set aside. Refer to the online API guide for more information on the StringBuffer class.

A Word on Arrays

Arrays in Java are a nebulous entity. They are classes, but they cannot be explicitly subclassed. As an object, the only instance variable that the array provides is length, which holds the length of the array. This is a useful variable for ensuring you are not exceeding the boundaries of the array. Even though Java will catch these mistakes, they will still throw exceptions, interrupting the execution of the program. If you catch boundary problems early, you can avoid the exceptions altogether.

The System Class

The System class provides many functions for interacting with, and getting information about not only the Java run-time system, but the computer *outside* the Java environment. All of the System variables and methods are static. This means there is no need to create an instance of the System class at all. You merely reference the methods in the same way as the Math methods:

```
System.method
```

The System class includes three variables:

➤ public static InputStream in

➤ public static PrintStream out

➤ public static PrintStream err

These variables are instances of the Input and PrintStream classes, and provide the read(), print(), and println() methods used in the examples in this book to interact with stdin, stdout, and stderr. Typically stdin is the keyboard, and stdout is the terminal or monitor. Stderr is also sent to the screen by default in the interpreter; however, in the browser stderr is sent to the file weblog in the /.hotjava/ directory created from the HOMEPATH and HOMEDRIVE environment variables when HotJava loads. Recall how the print(), println(), and read() methods were implemented:

```
System.in.read()
System.out.print(String)
System.out.println(String)
```

All of these methods were invoked from static member variables without creating an instance of System, InputStream, or PrintStream.

The methods provided by System enable interaction with both the Java interpreter and the Hardware platform itself. Here are a few of the more important methods. Check out the online API for a full listing.

➤ **public static void arraycopy(type src[], int srcpos, type dest[], int destpos, int length).** This method copies an array of type *type* from the source array src[] to the destination array dest[] starting at the srcpos index in the source array, of length *length*. The array is copied to the destpos index of the destination array. *Type* can be any one of boolean, byte, char, short, int, long, float, double, or Object.

➤ **public static int currentTime().** This method returns Greenwich Mean Time in milliseconds from some undefined epoch. This method is useful for comparing two timed events, but not for printed output.

➤ **public static int freeMemory().** This method returns the amount of free system memory in bytes. The API notes that this number is not always accurate.

➤ **public static int totalMemory().** This method returns the amount of system memory in bytes.

➤ **public static void exit(int status).** This method will cause the interpreter to exit with the exit code status.

➤ **public static InputStream execin (String command).** This method allows the program to execute a system command from within the interpreter, and send the output of the command to a FileInputStream. While this command will give you great power over the system, for obvious reasons the Java interpreter will not run this command if the code initiating it has come over a network.

➤ **public static OutputStream execin(String command).** This method will execute a system command from within the Java interpreter, and will return a FileOutputStream that is connected to the standard input of the command. Again, this will not run if loaded over the Internet.

➤ **public static void exec(String command).** This method executes a system command outside of the Java interpreter without redirecting standard input or output for the command.

➤ **public static String getenv(String var).** This method returns a String holding the value of the environment variable var. If the variable is not defined, the String is null.

➤ **public static String getCWD().** This method returns the Current Working Directory.

➤ **public static String getOSName().** This method returns the name of the Operating System upon which the interpreter is running. While getting the operating system is useful for implementing OS dependent code, remember that Java's purpose is to be portable. Using code that is OS dependent should be for optimization only, and not a default solution. Otherwise, any other system your code might be used on would not be able to run your application.

Although many of the System methods are useful for getting information about the platform and execution environment, in general, most of these methods will not need to be used, except for the in, out, and err variables.

The I/O Class Library

The java.io package provides several classes for receiving and sending data to different input and output devices on a computer. The standard input device is the keyboard, and the standard output device is the terminal or monitor. These devices can be accessed using the InputStream and PrintStream classes, and have already been used in many of the examples presented in previous chapters. The most used input/output device after the keyboard and monitor is the file system. Java provides a RandomAccessFile class, which encapsulates the essential file access methods for getting data to and from disks.

Additionally, there are classes for buffered, filtered, and piped streams, and string tokenization. The java.net packages use these abstract classes to interact with what could be considered the third class of input device—the network. By providing a range of classes with which to build input and output methods, it is simply a matter of opening the right stream, and using the predeveloped classes in order to read and write from the stream. Java also provides an AccessErrorHandler class for dealing with any problems that might arise from dealing with I/O methods.

Of course, what is presented here is a small number of the classes provided in the java.io package. Be sure to check out the online API for a comprehensive listing of all the classes and methods available. This section covers the standard input and output classes, along with the RandomAccessFile class. These classes provide fast and easy access to the keyboard, monitor, and files on a system. They might not be the optimal classes in terms of performance, but will suffice for the majority of I/O jobs a program will need to handle.

If you are developing applets that you intend to have running on Netscape over the Web, remember that Netscape does not allow any local file access. This means that you will generate a security violation if you attempt to do so. This restriction may change, as did the earlier socket restrictions for network access, so you might still want to learn how to access files.

The java.io library is not automatically loaded into the compiler as is the java.lang package. Therefore, you will need to explicitly load the package.

```
import java.io.*;
```

The * indicates that you want all of the classes in the io package to be loaded. You also can specify only the individual classes you want to load.

```
import java.io.RandomAccessFile;
```

stdin and stdout with InputStream and PrintStream

At the top of the java.io class hierarchy are two classes, InputStream and OutputStream, from which all classes in the java.io package are descended. Both of these classes are abstract, so cannot be initialized themselves, and must be extended for functionality. However, all classes that are subclasses of these two will have the same methods.

Interactions with the keyboard (stdin) and the monitor (stdout) are perhaps the most common streams programmers will have to deal with, and are encapsulated in the instance variables in and out of the System class. The instance variables in and out are of type InputStream and PrintStream, respectively. InputStream and PrintStream cannot be created with new directly. If you do not want to use System.in, or System.out, you can set your own stream objects equal to the System variables.

```
InputStream stdin = System.in;
PrintStream stdout = System.out;
```

You should try to use the System variables, because they will make your code easier for other programmers to understand. Other programmers will be familiar with the standard java.lang.System protocols.

The programs presented so far have already used three of the methods provided by the InputStream and PrintStream classes.

```
System.in.read();
System.out.print();
System.out.Println();
```

The next two sections will take a more detailed look at the methods provided by the InputStream and PrintStream classes.

InputStream

The basic job of the InputStream class is to read bytes from whatever stream it is attached to, be it the keyboard, a disk, or the Internet. There are two important attributes of the InputStream class:

1. When a call for information is made to InputStream the method employed will wait until input is available. This is known as blocking. For example, if you invoke the following, the method will wait until a byte can be processed (the user has typed something from the keyboard and pressed Return) before returning:

   ```
   System.in.read();
   ```

2. The InputStream class works with bytes, not characters. While the old ASCII format was only an 8-bit character set, the same as a byte, the newer Unicode character set is 16 bits long. This means that when receiving characters from stdin, you will not be receiving the hibyte of the Unicode character set.

Using the Read Method

The main method of the InputStream is read(). You are probably familiar with this method because it has been used in previous examples to read in characters from the keyboard.

```
StringBuffer buf = new StringBuffer();
int ch;
while((ch = System.in.read()) != -1) {
    buf.append(ch);
}
```

There are actually three overloaded methods named read. They are the following:

➤ **public abstract in read().** This method reads in a single byte from the input stream, and returns it as an integer. You will typically receive an error if you try to put the integer directly into a character, because an integer type is 16 bits larger than the character type. Notice the abstract modifier. This method is always implemented in a subclass. It is the method invoked with the `System.in.read()` call.

➤ **public int read(byte b[]).** This method takes a byte array as its argument, and places the incoming bytes into this array beginning at index 0. You can use this method to grab several characters at once from stdin. Be sure that the byte array is large enough to hold the information that the read method sends it, otherwise you will end up with an IOException being generated. Remember to also indicate that methods using java.io can throw java.io.IOExceptions.

```
class input {
    public static void main(String args[]) {
    throws java.io.IOException {
        byte buf[] = new byte[50];
        System.in.read(buf);
        String str = new String(buf,0);
        System.out.println(str);
    }
}
```

Notice the statement `String str = new String(buf,0)`. The String constructor takes a byte array, and appends the hibyte specified as the second argument to each of the bytes in the array in order to generate the Unicode character set. In almost all cases, the hibyte will be zero (0), which maps the same ASCII characters to Unicode characters.

➤ **public int read(byte b[], int off, int len).** This method is similar to the previous read() method, except that you can specify where in the byte array you would like for the input to be placed. off determines how far from the beginning of

the array the method will begin to place data, and len
indicates how many bytes to fill.

```
class input {
    public static void main(String args[]) {
    throws java.io.IOException {
        byte buf[] = new byte[50];
        System.in.read(buf, 5, 20);
        String str = new String(buf,0);
        System.out.println(str);
    }
}
```

➤ The previous method is good for ensuring that you do not
run out of array before the input is finished. By setting the
offset as zero (0) and the length as the length of the array,
the method will only fill the specified blocks in the array.

```
System.in.read(buf, 0, 50);
```

Remember when using the read() method that you should use an integer
to store the value of the returning input. This enables you to catch the end
of the file indicator, which is a -1. If you were to use a character that was
an *unsigned* number, you would not be able to tell when the end of the
input had been reached.

The System.in.read() method is useful when dealing with stand-
alone programs only using stdin and stdout. However, if you want
to use keyboard input in a graphical program, you have to implement a different method. This technique is covered in Chapter 13,
"Using the applet and awt Class Libraries." In the meantime, for
basic stand-alone programs, the System.in.read() method will
suffice.

PrintStream

The PrintStream class provides two methods for sending output
to the screen: print() and println(). Both of these methods are
overloaded with several argument parameters. The print method
sends the characters to a buffer where they are stored until the

buffer is flushed by a newline "\n" character. This means that characters will not appear on the display immediately, but rather, only after a newline is sent out with print(), or a println() call is made. The standard format for the print() method is

```
public void print(type variableName)
```

where *type* can be any one of the following:

➤ object

➤ integer

➤ long

➤ float

➤ double

➤ boolean

In addition to the previous overloaded methods for print(), there are two overloaded synchronized versions of print, where type is either String or char[].

```
public synchronized print(type variableName)
```

All of the overloaded println methods are synchronized and allow for any of the previously listed types.

```
public synchronized println(type variableName)
```

In addition, a println() with no arguments will print a newline character.

Accessing Files

In addition to accessing the screen and keyboard, the most important I/O device is the file system. The java.io package provides a file input/output class known as RandomAccessFile. This class enables you to read and write information from a file in all of the Java fundamental types. In addition, there is a File class that holds information about a specific filename and methods for getting the status of the file.

The File Class

The File class provides a system-independent method for storing information about a file, its directories, and how it can be accessed. In addition to information about files, you can create instances of the File class that represent directories. Unix file systems access everything as files, including directories. For this reason, the File class is designed to not only deal with files, but directories as well. You can create an instance of the File class in three ways:

➤ **public File(String path).** This constructor creates a File object based upon the directory structure in path. This constructor creates an object based upon the final directory. The following examples are for a file text that exists in the following directory structure:

```
c:\users\Ritchey\text\input.txt
```

If you passed the string text, the File object could be said to be the directory \text\. Note that you can either pass the directory as an absolute reference

```
File dir = new File("c:\users\Ritchey\text");
```

or as a directory relative to the directory of the executable

```
File dir = new File("text");
```

➤ The machine-specific implementation of the File class will determine how your slashes go (/ for Unix and \ for NT).

➤ **public File(String path, String name).** This constructor is used to create an instance of the File class for a specific file—not the whole directory.

```
File input = new File("text","input.txt");
```

➤ **public File(File dir, String name).** This constructor is
identical to the previous constructor, except that instead of
passing the directory as a String, you pass it as an instance
of a File class, which has been created for the directory.

```
File input = new File(dir,"input.txt");
```

It is important to realize that by creating the File class, you don't
actually create a file on the system. You only create an object that
holds references to a file or directory. The methods in table 12.1
enable you to find out more about how the File relates to the
actual system.

Table 12.1	File Class Methods
Method	Information Returned
public String getName()	The name of the file in a String. This does not include the directory structure where the file is located.
public String getPath()	The path of the file in the File class.
public String getAbsolutePath()	The filename, with the path of the executable appended to the front.
public String getParent()	The name of the parent directory if there is one, and null if it doesn't exist.
public boolean exists()	True if the file actually exists on the system, and false if the method cannot find it.
public boolean isFile()	True if the File instance is a valid and normal file, otherwise it returns false.
public boolean canWrite()	True if the file exists and is writeable, and false otherwise.
public boolean canRead()	True if the file exists and is readable, and false otherwise.
public int lastModified()	The last time the file was modified. This should only be used for comparing modification time, and not printing out a time.
public boolean renameTo(File dest)	Renames the actual file with the filename in the dest File class. The

Method	Information Returned
	method returns true if the renaming was successful, false otherwise.
public boolean mkdir()	Creates the directory in the File class relative to the current directory. This can be used if the directory does not actually exist. The method returns true if the directory was successfully made, false otherwise.
public boolean mkdirs()	Same as the previous method, except it will create the entire directory structure.
public String[] list()	Lists the contents of the directory in the File class. It returns an array of filenames except for the "." and ".." equivalents. This method only works with instances of the File class that are directories.

Example of Using the File Class

The following code accepts a directory and filename, and then outputs information about the file and directory:

```
import java.io.*;
    class input  {
            public static void main(String args[])
            throws java.io.IOException {
                    System.out.println("Enter Directory:");
                    char ch;
                    StringBuffer dirBuf = new
                    ➥StringBuffer();
                    while((ch=(char)System.in.read())
                    ➥!='\n')
                            dirBuf.append(ch);
                    File dir = new File(dirBuf.toString());
                    System.out.println("Enter FileName:");
                    StringBuffer fileBuf =
                    ➥newStringBuffer();
```

```
                    while((ch=(char)System.in.read())
                    !='\n')
                            fileBuf.append(ch);
                    File input = new File (dir, fileBuf.
                            toString());
                    if(input.exists()){
System.out.println("\nFile Found");
System.out.println("File Name:
"+input.getName());
System.out.println("File Path:
"+input.getPath());
System.out.println("Abs. Path: " +
input.getAbsolutePath());
System.out.println("Readable?:
"+input.canRead());
System.out.println("Writable?:
"+input.canWrite());
System.out.println("\nDirectory listing:");
String listing[] = dir.list();
for(int i=0; i<listing.length; i++)
    System.out.println(listing[i]);
} else {
    System.out.println("File Not Found");
}
    }
}
```

The RandomAccessFile Class

The RandomAccessFile Class provides the programmer with a
wealth of methods for interacting with a file. While there are more
basic file accessor classes such as FileInputStream, and
FileOutputStream, the RandomAccessFile class provides all the
functionality of these classes combined, with the additional
functionality of a file that can be accessed anywhere. With the
standard FileInputStream and FileOutputStream classes, the file
is accessed sequentially from beginning to end. With the
RandomAccessFile class, you can determine exactly from where
in the file you want to retrieve data.

It is important that you are familiar with the following constructors:

➤ **public RandomAccessFile(String name, String mode).** This constructor takes the filename provided by name and opens a file for either read-only or read/write. The mode depends upon the mode String, which is either r for read-only or rw for read/write. When the file is accessed it can throw an IOException if the application does not have permission to access the file in the specified manner. Note that the filename is very system-dependent; therefore, it would be better to create a File class instance, check for the existence of the file and the read/write permissions, and use a second constructor.

➤ **public RandomAccessFile(File file, String mode).** This constructor takes the file described by the File class instance file and opens it in the access mode.

Once you have created the instance of RandomAccessFile, there are several methods for retrieving information from the file. The RandomAccessFile class allows you to access the file anywhere. You are not constrained to accept the bytes as they stream in. You do this by positioning a file pointer where you want to start taking data from, or writing to. When you first open the file, the file pointer will be at the beginning of the file. Before you can start moving the pointer along, you need to know how big the file is. You can do this with the length() method. This method returns the length of the file in bytes (8-bit intervals).

```
public int length()
```

Once you know the range of where you can move the file pointer, you can do so by using the seek() method. If you need to find out where the pointer is, you can use the getFilePointer() method. The seek() method moves the file pointer to the specified position in the file. The getFilePointer() method returns the position of the file pointer in bytes (8-bit intervals).

```
public void seek(int pos).
public int getFilePointer().
```

It is important that once you have finished with a file that you close it down with the close() method. You can either close it immediately, or implement a finalize method that would close the file when garbage collection occurs. This method closes the file stream:

```
public void close().
```

```
finalize {
    fileName.close();
}
```

After you have opened the file and determined where the file pointer is, you can begin to read data from the file. The RandomAccessClass provides several methods for reading different types of data from a file. These include the methods in table 12.2.

Table 12.2 Integer and String Methods for the RandomAccessFile Class	
Method	Description
public int read()	Reads a single byte, and moves the pointer forward 8 bits.
public int read(byte b[])	Reads and fills a byte array from the file, moving the pointer as many bytes as the size of the array.
public int read(byte b[], int off, int len)	Reads an array of bytes of length len, and places them in the array at off. The pointer is moved len bytes.
public final String readLine()	Returns the entire line terminated by a "\n" or EOF (end of file) in a String.
public final String readUTF()	Return a String from a UTF formatted file.

The following methods all return a value of the type specified, and move the file pointer forward the same amount.

➤ public final boolean readBoolean()

➤ public final byte readByte()

➤ public final short readShort()

➤ public final char readChar()

➤ public final int readInt()

➤ public final long readLong()

The following code will read in a text file, and print its contents out on the screen:

```
import java.io.*;
    class input  {
            public static void main(String args[])
            throws java.io.IOException {
                    System.out.println("Enter Directory:");
                    char ch;
                    StringBuffer dirBuf = new
                    ➡StringBuffer();
                    while((ch=(char)System.in.read())
                    ➡!='\n')
                            dirBuf.append(ch);
                    File dir = new File(dirBuf.toString());
                    System.out.println("Enter FileName:");
                    StringBuffer fileBuf =
                    ➡newStringBuffer();
                    while((ch=(char)System.in.read())
                    ➡!='\n')
                            fileBuf.append(ch);
                    File input = new File(dir,
                    fileBuf.toString());
        if(input.exists()){
            System.out.println("opening file");
            RandomAccessFile file = new
            RandomAccessFile(input,"rw");
            System.out.println("File length: "
            ➡+file.length());
            System.out.println("Pointer pos: " +
            file.getFilePointer());
```

```
                    while(file.getFilePointer() < file.length())
                            System.out.println(file.readLine());
                    file.close();
            } else {
                    System.out.println("Can't read file");
            }
      }
}
```

In addition to reading a file, you can also write data to a file. Essentially, all of the read methods have a corresponding write method. It should be noted that when you write to a file, you do not insert the data. Instead, the method will write over any information already in the file with the new data.

Be aware of what you are sending to a file. Additionally, you should know where you can and can't read and write files. It is not good practice to expect to be able to read or write files on a client machine over the Internet. If you do need to read or write files in a client machine, typically the /temp/ directory is set aside as the write path. However, as mentioned before—there is no applet file access to the local storage devices in Netscape.

Here is a listing of all the write methods:

➤ public void write()

➤ public void write(byte b[])

➤ public void write(byte b[], int off, int len)

➤ public final void writeLine(String line)

➤ public final void writeUTF(String utf)

➤ public final void writeBoolean(boolean b)

➤ public final void writeByte(byte b)

➤ public final void writeShort(short s)

➤ public final void writeChar(char c)

➤ public final void writeInt(int i)

➤ public final void writeLong(long l)

In addition, the following method is used for taking a String, and outputting it as 8-bit bytes so that the resulting file will be in ASCII, not Unicode:

```
public final void writeBytes(String s)
```

You will find that the RandomAccessFile class provides all of the functionality needed to read and write files in your Java programs. Try writing and reading your own file, and playing around with the different read and write types. You should be aware that Unix and DOS systems differ widely in their formatting of text files. Be sure to check how your system creates a text file. Typically Unix will only have a newline at the end of a line of text, while DOS text files have a carriage-return/newline combination. The following code writes lines entered from the keyboard to a DOS type file (which must already exist). You end inputting by typing an end of file character (Ctrl + Z for Windows NT and Ctrl + D for Solaris) on the last line by itself and hitting Return.

```
import java.io.*;
    class output   {
            public static void main(String args[])
            throws java.io.IOException {
                System.out.println("Enter Directory:");
                char ch;
                int in = 0;
                StringBuffer dirBuf = new
                ➥StringBuffer();
                while((ch=(char)System.in.read()) !=
                ➥'\n')
                        dirBuf.append(ch);
                File dir = new File(dirBuf.toString());
                System.out.println("Enter FileName:");
                StringBuffer fileBuf = new
                ➥StringBuffer();
                while((ch=(char)System.in.read()) !=
                ➥'\n')
```

```
                              fileBuf.append(ch);
                    File input = new File(dir,
                    fileBuf.toString());
        if(input.canWrite() && input.canRead()) {
            RandomAccessFile file = new
            RandomAccessFile(input,"rw");
            System.out.println("File length:
            ➥"+file.length());
            System.out.println("Pointer pos:
            "+file.getFilePointer());
            StringBuffer line = new StringBuffer();
            while(in != -1) {
                line.setLength(0);
                while((in=System.in.read()) != -1)
                line.append((char)in);
                line.append("\r\n");
                file.writeBytes(line.toString());
            }
            file.close();
        } else {
            System.out.println("Can't read file");
        }
    }
}
```

The Utility Class Library

The java.util package has many classes for special functions.
These include dates, hashtables, vectors, locks, and stacks. This
section covers the use of the Date and Stack class. Check out the
API for more information on the other utility classes available in
the java.util package.

The Date Class

The Date class provides methods for retrieving the current date
and time, and also for computing days of the week and month.
You can create an instance of the Date class in several ways.

➤ **public Date().** This constructor places the current date and time in an instance of Date.

➤ **public Date(int year, int month, int date).** This constructor creates an instance of the Date class with the month, day, and year specified.

➤ **public Date(int year, int month, int date, int hrs, int min).** This constructor creates an instance of the Date class with the year, month, day, hours, and minutes specified.

➤ **public Date(int year, int month, int date, int hrs, int min).** This constructor creates an instance of the Date class with the year, month, day, hours, minutes, and seconds specified.

The conventions for the argument values are the following:

➤ Year—post–1900

➤ Month—0–11

➤ Date—1–31

➤ Hours—0–23

➤ Minutes—0–59

➤ Seconds—0–59

After you have created the class instance, you can use it to retrieve information about the date, as shown in table 12.3.

Table 12.3   The Date Class Methods

Method	Information Returned
public int getYear()	The year.
public int getMonth()	The month.
public int getDate()	The date (1–31).

continues

Table 12.3   Continued

Method	Information Returned
public int getDay()	The day of the week (0–6).
public int getHours()	The hour.
public int getMinutes()	The minute.
public int getSeconds()	The second.
public boolean before(Date when)	Checks the instance date against the date when. Returns true if the instance date is earlier than the when date, false otherwise.
public boolean after(Date when)	Checks the instance date against the date when. Returns true if the instance date is later than the when date, false otherwise.
public boolean equals(Object obj)	Compares the two objects, and returns true if they are equal, false otherwise.
public String toString()	This method returns a string formatted with the date convention of the host system.

Using the Date class is quite straightforward. You can generate the current date simply by creating an instance without any arguments.

```
Date today = new Date();
System.out.println(today.toString());
```

or

```
System.out.println(today);
```

Notice that the println method automatically invokes the toString method without the need to explicitly call it.

The Stack Class

The Stack class is an additional class provided by the java.util package. You could develop your own stack, but it is much easier to use the stack provided by Java. This stack allows you to store any object you need to on a *first in, last out* (FILO) basis. You can imagine a first in, last out stack like one of those spring-loaded cafeteria tray despensers. The base of the stack makes sure that the top tray is always at the same level. It lowers as more trays are placed on top, and raises as they are taken off the top (see fig. 12.1). The FILO stack works the same way. If you place an object on the stack, it is placed on the very top, and if there is any other information on the stack, it moves down one level. Then, when you need the item, you simply pop it off. However, if items have been placed on the stack after the object you need, you need to pop off all of the elements that are on top of the one you need.

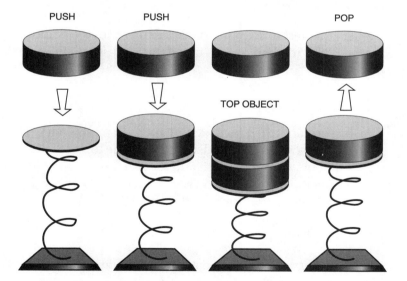

Figure 12.1
A representation of a FILO stack.

To create an instance of the Stack class, there is only a single constructor:

```
public Stack()
```

You can push Objects onto the stack using the push method, just as you can pop items off the stack.

```
public Object push(Object item)
```

```
public Object pop()
```

When you pop() an Object off the top of the stack, it is gone from the stack. If you only want to look at what is on the stack without removing it you can peek at the stack with this method:

```
public Object peek()
```

You also can test to see if the stack is empty with the empty() method. This method returns true if the Stack is empty, and false otherwise.

```
public boolean empty()
```

Finally, you can search for a particular object on the stack. The search() method returns the distance from the top of the first object that matches the search criteria. If an object is not found, a -1 is returned. The return value is essentially the number of pops necessary to bring the Object to the top of the stack.

```
public int search(Object o)
```

The following code uses two date Objects to demonstrate a Stack. Note the order in which the objects come off the stack when you run the application.

```
import java.util.*;
class stack {
   public static void main(String args[]) {
      Stack s = new Stack();
```

```
        Date today = new Date();
        Date kristinBDay = new Date(72,7,24);
        System.out.println(today);
        s.push(today);
        System.out.println(kristinBDay);
        s.push(kristinBDay);
        System.out.println(s.peek());
        while(!s.empty())
            System.out.println(s.pop());
    }
}
```

The java.net Classes

The net package provides several classes for the basic network functions needed by all protocols. Following are some of the classes:

➤ ContentHandler

➤ InetAddress

➤ ServerSocket

➤ Socket

➤ SocketImpl

➤ URL

➤ URLConnection

➤ URLStreamHandler

These classes provide the basic functionality needed to create socket connections and handle data streams to and from host computers once connections have been made. Many of the other packages and classes use these classes to implement network connections.

The InetAddress class includes several methods for storing information about an Internet host address, as follows:

➤ **public String getHostName().** This method returns the name of the host being stored by the InetAddress class (newriders.mcp.com).

➤ **public String getAddress().** This method returns the numerical address of the host (131.68.10.33) being stored by the InetAddress class.

➤ **public static InetAddress getLocalHost().** This method returns the name of the local host (the computer the application is running on). The method returns the address as an InetAddress object.

➤ **public static synchronized InetAddress getByName(String host).** This method returns the InetAddress object representing the host given as the argument of the method.

➤ **public static synchronized InetAddress[] getAllByName(String host).** This method returns an array of InetAddresses, which holds all the Internet addresses for the hostname provided as the argument of the method.

The constructor can be used along with methods to retrieve the address and port of an Internet address. For example, if you have the hostname newriders.mcp.com, you can acquire its complete address information by using the following code:

```
import java.net.*;

public class getAddress extends java.applet.Applet {
    static InetAddress addr;     static InetAddress addrList[]
    ➥ = null;
    static String ipAddress;
    static String Hostname;
    public static void main(String args[]) {
        try {               addr = InetAddress.getLocalHost();
            if(args.length > 0)
                addrList = InetAddress.getAllByName(args[0]);
        } catch(UnknownHostException e) {
            System.out.println("UnknownHostException");
            System.out.println("Exiting...");
            System.exit(1);
```

```
        }
Hostname=addr.toString().substring(0,addr.toString().indexOf(Ô/
➥'));
ipAddress=addr.toString().substring(addr.toString().indexOf(Ô/
➥')+1);
System.out.println("Local Hostname:    " + Hostname);
        System.out.println("Local IP Address: " + ipAddress);
        System.out.println("---------------");
        for(int i=0;i<args.length; i++) {
Hostname=addrList[i].toString().substring(0,addrList[i].toString()
➥.indexOf(Ô/'));
ipAddress=addrList[i].toString().substring(addrList[i].toString()
➥.indexOf(Ô/')+1);
System.out.println("Hostname:    " + Hostname);
            System.out.println("IP Address: " + ipAddress);
        }
    }
}
```

When the code is run, it probes the network for the address of the hostname given and prints out all of the relevant information. Notice the use of the toString() method to output the numerical address in a readable format. Figure 12.2 shows the output of the getAddress class.

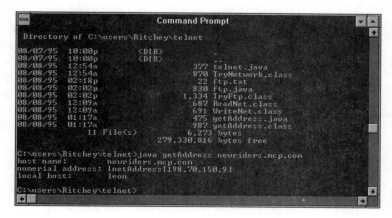

Figure 12.2

Output of the getAddress class.

The getAddress class is a useful example of how Java packages can make a programmer's task simple. In a few lines of code, the class was able to get the information from the network it needed, and present it to the user.

```
static InetAddress addr;
static InetAddress addrList[] = null;
static String ipAddress;
static String Hostname;
```

These declarations hold the information the class will gather about Internet addresses. The addr and addrList[] array will hold the address for the local host, and the addresses for the remote host being probed.

```
try {
    addr = InetAddress.getLocalHost();
    if(args.length > 0)
        addrList = InetAddress.getAllByName(args[0]);
} catch (UnknownHostException e) {
    System.out.println("UnknownHostException");
    System.out.println("Exiting...");
    System.exit(1);
}
```

This block of code implements an exception, handling a section of code that probes the network for the local host address and the remote host address provided as a command-line argument, if there is one. If the getLocalHost() method throws an exception—in this case, an UnknownHostException—the catch block will print an error and exit with a non-zero exit code indicating an error. Many systems can use the return of a program to indicate if there was an error or not.

```
Hostname=addr.toString().substring(0,addr.toString().indexOf(Ô/
➥'));
ipAddress=addr.toString().substring(addr.toString().indexOf(Ô/
➥')+1);
System.out.println("Local Hostname:    " + Hostname);
System.out.println("Local IP Address: " + ipAddress);
```

```
System.out.println("---------------");
for(int i=0;i<args.length; i++) {
    Hostname=addrList[i].toString().substring(0,addrList[i].toString().
➥indexOf(Ô/'));
        ipAddress=addrList[i].toString().substring(addrList[i].toString().
➥indexOf(Ô/')+1);
        System.out.println("Hostname:    " + Hostname);
System.out.println("IP Address: " + ipAddress);
}
```

This final block of code simply takes the InetAddress objects returned when the hostname was queried and formats it to be printed on the screen. Notice the use of the indexOf() method to grab the formatted String portions that refer to the hostname and IP address of the host. The toString() method of InetAddress returns a string with both the hostname and IP address separated by a forward slash (/).

Summary

You have now covered most of the fundamental class libraries that are common to all Java programs. These libraries provide the ease of use and functionality that is expected in a modern day high-level language. Of course, these are not the only classes and methods available—Java has many more. You should be sure to get a copy of the API, but unless you have about three reams of paper sitting around, I would not suggest printing it off in its entirety unless you cannot stand staring at a screen, reading. This chapter is merely an introduction the the many tools available to you through the Java Class Libraries. The next chapter focuses more on the applet and awt classes, and how these can be used to create graphical programs for the Web.

Chapter 13

Using the applet and awt Class Libraries

Up to this point, the examples and focus of the programming chapters has been on stand-alone applications; and while those elements are applicable to creating applets and handlers for the browser environment, the applet itself has not been looked at since the HelloWorld program in Chapter 8, "Moving On to Java." This chapter begins to look more closely at the applet and awt packages that provide encapsulation of the methods required to develop applets and graphical programs.

Most of the second half of this book so far has focused on getting the Java environment up and running, in addition to learning the basics of programming in the Java language. It has taken four chapters to present all of the background material for actually writing applets. However, now that you have covered the fundamentals of the language, and the basic class libraries included with the language, you should be equipped to start developing applets using all of this information. Without this foundation, you would have difficulties getting through the more complicated topic of the applet and awt classes. The applet package provides the classes necessary for creating applets that run under the browser environments, such as Netscape. The awt provides a fully functional window toolkit that includes many features for images, controls, and resources.

This chapter introduces the use of the awt and applet packages for creating applets that run under the browser environment. More so than with the java.lang, java.io, and java.util packages, it would be impossible to cover every aspect of the awt and applet classes and methods. The APIs themselves cover several hundred pages of material, and provide numerous methods for different functions. Therefore, this chapter focuses on a limited number of applet programming problems in order to get you up and running as quickly as possible, and to give you an idea of where to go if you want to use the full functionality of the window and applet packages.

➤ **Applet class library.** The applet section covers the Applet class, and the functions it provides (and you must override) in order to interact with the graphic environment and the user.

➤ **Another window toolkit (awt) class library.** The awt section covers some of the basic elements of the window toolkit, and shows how they are incorporated into an applet.

Once you have completed this chapter, you should have a good idea of how to use some of the classes and methods provided by the graphical packages. While every class and method will not be covered, understanding the rudiments will allow you to go on to a more comprehensive study of the APIs for the awt and applet packages.

The applet Class Library

The applet class library contains over 40 classes and interfaces for developing programs for the applet environment. The basic function of these classes is to provide methods for controlling the appearance of the browser environment as well as any applications in the environment. Classes such as BasicStyle, Document, and WRFormatter help to control the look of HTML documents and any applets that are referenced. Of course, the primary class of the applet package is Applet. As you might recall from Chapter 8, the Applet class is the superclass for all applets to be used in the browser. By extending the Applet class, the programmer is given a host of methods for running a program in the browser environment.

Extending the Applet Class

The first applet we will create is an animation file that runs through once and plays a sound when clicked. In order to create your own applet, you must extend the Applet class:

```
import java.awt.*;
import java.applet.*;
public class ClickAnimation extends Applet implements
➥Runnable {
    Thread animationThread = null;
...
}
```

The ClickAnimation class extends the Applet class, which inherits from java.awt.Panel. This makes the applet inherently graphical, and it is expected that programmers be able to use all of the awt library to enhance applets. There are two things to note about the new Applet class in Java:

1. There are no more public instance variables in the Applet class. Instead, programmers are expected to use methods to access instance variables for an applet.

2. All classes that inherit Applet must be defined as public. This allows them to be accessed outside of their own files.

Notice that the class also implements Runnable. This is not a requirement for an applet, but if you do not want your applet to interrupt other applications running, it is good practice for it to execute as a thread. For the example in this chapter, our applet will be running an animation file whenever there is a mouse click on the applet, and we do not want it stopping any other applets that might be on the page. When an applet is loaded into the browser, its init() method is called. The format for the init() method you must override is the following:

```
public void init() {
   resize(25,25);
   ...
}
```

Notice that the first method called is resize. This allows the applet to adjust its size so that the formatting of the document will be correct. It is important that you call the resize method from within the init() method. Otherwise, if you call resize() somewhere else, it can cause the entire document to be reformatted at an inopportune time. It is always good practice to set the amount of screen real-estate you want to use in the beginning. Because HTML formats the pages linearly, anything you change in one portion of the page could alter formatting in the rest of the page. The ClickAnimation class loads a 25×25 pixel image, so the applet is resized to those dimensions.

Getting Attributes

The init method is also the perfect place to load any attributes specified in the HTML <param> tag. If you recall from Chapter 8, the HTML tag for loading an applet can include programmer-defined attributes. In the case of the ClickAnimation class, the applet should be able to control how many times it runs through the sequence of frames. This attribute can be called CYCLES. In order to get the attribute from the HTML tag, you use the getParameter() method, which returns the string held in the attributes tag.

```
public class ClickAnimation extends Applet implements
➡Runnable{
Thread animationThread = null;
```

```
protected int cycles = 0;        // create an instance
                                        variable
                                 //"cycles"
public void init() {
   resize(25,25);
   String cyclesTemp = getParameter("CYCLES");
   if (cyclesTemp != null)
      cycles = Integer.valueOf(cyclesTemp).intValue();
}
```

The Integer wrapper is used to get the integer value of the cycles string. First, if the attribute exists, the String returned by getAttributes is converted to an Integer object by valueOf(), which is then in turn converted to an integer by intValue(). The attribute is included in the tag as follows:

```
<param name="CYCLES" value=3>
```

Loading Images

At the same time that the applet sets the number of cycles to run through, it should load the images it needs to run the animation file. Images are encapsulated in an awt class called Images. In the case of the ClickAnimation applet, it needs to hold 10 pictures for the animation file; therefore it needs an array 10 items long. The choice of 10 frames is purely arbitrary.

```
protected Image frame[] = new Image[10];
```

The Applet class has a method that loads an image given its URL and filename.

```
public Image getImage(URL, String name)
```

The ClickAnimation applet needs to load 10 images, so it can be done with a for loop.

```
... init() {
   ...
   for(int i = 0; i < 10; i++)
```

```
frame[i] = getImage(getDocumentBase(),
➥"frame"+i+".gif");
```

The method is given a series of filenames that should reside in the same directory as the HTML file calling the class, and the getDocumentBase() method returns the URL of the HTML file from which the applet was run. The frames of the animation are held in the GIF images frame0.gif through frame9.gif in the same directory, and so use the same URL path.

After the applet has been created and the init() method called, the next method to be run by the browser is start(). The ClickAnimation class runs the animation file the first time the class is loaded, and then only from user input. The start() method needs to spawn the animationThread in order for the animation file to run the first time.

```
public void start() {
   animationThread = new Thread(this);
   animationThread.start();
}
```

When the animationThread is started, it calls the run() method. Note the use of this designator to refer the instance of the class itself.

Painting Images

The run() method cycles through the animation frames, telling the applet to redraw itself with each new frame.

```
int cur = 0;
...
public void run() {
   for(int i = 0; i < cycles; i++) {
      for(cur = 1; cur < 10; cur++) {
         repaint();
         for(int j = 0; j < 50000; j++);
      }
      cur = 0;
```

```
        repaint();
    }
}
```

The for loop cycles instance the cur variable through the frames of the animation file, each time calling the repaint() method. When repaint is called, it updates the applet. When the browser wants the applet to draw itself, it uses the paint() method. By calling repaint(), the thread causes the applet to cycle through the frames of the animation. The cycle starts with frame 1 and ends with frame 0, so that the picture in the applet is frame 0 when not in use. The outer for loop causes the animation file to run the number of times specified in cycles, while the innermost loop places a small delay to give time for the frame to be seen before the next is drawn.

```
public void paint(Graphics g) {
    g.drawImage(frame[cur], 0, 0, this);
}
```

The paint() method takes an argument that is an awt object known as Graphics. This class has functions for drawing all of the basic graphic types, such as lines, characters, strings, and rectangles; as well as methods for clipping regions, and scaling. When the browser calls paint() it sends it the applets' graphics context to draw in. The drawImage method takes the image itself, the coordinates of where to place the image, and an ImageObserver object. In this case, the applet itself is the ImageObserver, so this can be used.

The class is now to the point where it runs. Here is the complete code:

```
import java.awt.*;
import java.applet.*;
public class ClickAnimation extends Applet implements
➡Runnable{
    Thread animationThread = null;
    protected int cycles = 0, cur = 0;
```

```
protected Image frame[] = new Image[10];
    public void init() {
        resize(30,30);
        String cyclesTemp = getParameter("CYCLES");
        if (cyclesTemp != null)
            cycles =
Integer.valueOf(cyclesTemp).intValue();
        for(int i = 0; i<10; i++)
            frame[i] =
getImage(getDocumentBase(),"frame"+i+".gif");
    }
    public void start() {
        animationThread = new Thread(this);
        animationThread.start();
    }
    public void run() {
        for(int i = 0; i < cycles; i++) {
            for(cur = 1; cur < 10; cur++) {
                repaint();
                for(int j = 0; j < 50000; j++);
            }
            cur = 0;
            repaint();
        }
    }
    public void paint(Graphics g) {
        g.drawImage(frame[cur], 0, 0,this);
    }
}
```

Create an HTML file to include the applet, and place it in a directory with the .class file. You can either use some frames that were created to test the animation file, or create your own. The applet should look like figure 13.1.

Figure 13.1

The ClickAnimation Class in Netscape 2.0.

Handling Mouse Events

Of course, the animation file only runs through the first time the applet is loaded, and it is supposed to run every time the cursor is clicked on it. Whenever events like the mouse entering the applet's area, or a button being pressed while the cursor is on the applet occur, the browser invokes the necessary method. If you have overridden the method for the specific event, you can specify what should happen.

```
public boolean mouseDown(Event e, int x, int y) {
    animationThread = new Thread(this);
    animationThread.start();
    return true;
}
```

Now, each time the mouse is clicked on the applet, it plays the animation. There are several mouse events you can deal with, so be sure to check out the API for the full list of calls the browser can send to your applet.

Dealing with Keystrokes

If you want to intercept keystrokes, you must first get the focus. This is similar to the requirement of getting the focus for form elements in JavaScript when you want the user's keyboard strokes to be sent to a specific input object. When you enter keys on a keyboard, it is difficult for the computer to know where to send the keystrokes. In order to send the keys to the right applet, the system requires that the applet be *in focus*—essentially indicating that it is the current applet receiving keystrokes. Once the applet has the focus, the browser sends keystrokes to it through the keyDown(Event e, int key) method. By overriding this method, you can deal with keystrokes however you want, for example by appending them to a stringBuffer object. If you add the following method to the ClickAnimation, and run the appletviewer so that you can see the stdout window, you should see keystrokes as you type when the applet window has the focus. If you are running JavaMaker, run the appletviewer by invoking the Tools, Appletviewer (Verbose) option. In Netscape, you can bring up the

Java Console window under the options menu to see output to stdout.

```
public boolean keyDown(Event e, int c) {
    System.out.println("keydown: "+(char)c);
    return true;
}
```

Playing Sounds

Of course, now that the applet plays an animation file, it is only proper that it also be able to play a sound. This is easily accomplished because the Applet class has methods for getting and playing .au files.

The AU file format is popular on Unix machines. However, there are several players available for creating AU files for Windows machines. There are typically AU helper apps available for different browsers, so check out your browser documentation for information on AU helper apps.

In order to load an audio file, use the getAudioClip() method, which returns an object of type AudioClip. Once the class has the AudioClip object, it can use the play() method to run the file every time the animation is run. In this case, the sound file is very short, so the loop() method of AudioClip is used to cause it to run until the animation is over. The stop() method is then invoked to stop the AudioClip from playing.

```
import java.awt.*;
import java.applet.*;
public class ClickAnimation extends Applet implements
➥Runnable{
    Thread animationThread = null;
    protected int cycles = 0, cur = 0;
    protected Image frame[] = new Image[10];
    AudioClip sound = null;
        public void init() {
            resize(30,30);
            String cyclesTemp = getParameter("CYCLES");
```

```
                    if (cyclesTemp != null)
                        cycles =
➥Integer.valueOf(cyclesTemp).intValue();
                    for(int i = 0; i<10; i++)
                        frame[i] =
➥getImage(getDocumentBase(),"frame"+i+".gif");
                    sound =
➥getAudioClip(getDocumentBase(),"sound.au");
            }
            public void start() {
                animationThread = new Thread(this);
                animationThread.start();
            }
            public void run() {
                sound.loop();
                for(int i = 0; i < cycles; i++) {

                    for(cur = 1; cur < 10; cur++) {
                        repaint();
                        for(int j = 0; j < 50000; j++);
                    }
                    cur = 0;
                    repaint();
                }
                sound.stop();
            }
            public void paint(Graphics g) {
                g.drawImage(frame[cur], 0, 0,this);
            }
            public boolean mouseDown(Event e, int x, int y) {
                animationThread = new Thread(this);
                animationThread.start();
                return true;
            }
        }
    }
```

Now, every time the animation file cycles through, it plays the associated sound.

These are only samples of the different methods available in the Applet package. Be sure to check out the API for a comprehensive listing of the classes and methods available.

The Another Window Toolkit (awt) Class Library

The awt, or Another Window Toolkit, provided by the Java environment includes over sixty classes and interfaces for creating graphical user interfaces. As with the applet, and all of the APIs, it is impossible to cover every method in every class, and they in fact deserve a book in their own right. This section presents a few of the methods from a sample of classes in order to give you a flavor of what using the awt class is like.

The Graphics Class

The Graphics class is perhaps the most important of the awt classes. It provides several drawing and clipping routines that can be used to either draw on the screen, or control how the drawing looks on the screen. You have already seen the drawImage() method in the ClickAnimation class, there are also several other methods for drawing objects on the screen.

➤ **public void drawRect(int X, int Y, int W, int H).** This method draws the outline of a rectangle of the given dimensions (relative to the applet region) in the foreground color.

➤ **public void filldrawRect(int X, int Y, int W, int H).** Same as previous method, except the entire rectangle is filled with the foreground color.

➤ **drawString(String str, int x, int y).** This method draws the String str at x, y in the current font.

➤ **public void drawLine(int x1, int y1, int x2, int y2).** This method draws a line in the foreground color from x1, y1 to x2, y2, relative to the application region.

➤ **public void copyArea(int X, int Y, int W, int H, int dx, int dy).** This method copies the region specified by the first four coordinates, and copies to the point dx, dy.

In addition to drawing methods, the Graphics class also implements several methods for changing the preferences for drawing.

➤ **public void setColor Foreground(Color c).** This method takes an object of type Color, and uses it as the foreground (drawing) color.

➤ **public void setFont(Font f).** This method takes an object of type Font, and uses it for all text output through Graphics. Fonts available on all platforms are Helvetica, TimesRoman, ZapfDingbats, Dialog, DialogInput, and Courier in point sizes 8, 10, 12, 14, 24, and 36.

An important method for animation is the clipRect() method. Because the normal call to repaint causes the entire applet to be repainted, flashing can become quite obvious for larger images in which only a small section changes. Flashing refers to when the entire image blinks on and off because the video system cannot repaint the image fast enough to fool the eyes into believing they are seeing a continuous image. In order to overcome this problem, you can clip the region in which you want painting to occur, then the rest of the image will be left alone, and only the clipping region will be changed.

In order to use the clipRect() method, you can override the update() method in the Applet class. The update method is called on a repaint() method invocation. The following is an example of an update method that clips a region of the applet area for painting.

```
public void update(Graphics g) {
   if(animating?)
      g.clipRect(x, y, W, H);  // clip to changing area
   else g.clipRect(0,0,appletWidth, appletHeight); // if
   // not animating, allow entire applet to be repainted
   paint(g); //call the paint() method with g
}
```

Color

The color class allows you to specify a color for use by the Graphics, or other class. For example, you could set the foreground color for Graphics output. You can either create a new color object by passing the red, green, and blue values of the color, or by using the static variable colors provided with the class.

```
Color MyColor = new Color(12,156,87);
g.setColor(Color.lightGray);
```

The following is a list of all static colors:

black	green	pink
blue	lightGray	red
cyan	magenta	white
darkGray	orange	yellow
gray		

Controls

In addition to drawing lines, rectangles, and Strings on the screen, you can also include control items with which the user can interact. The awt package includes classes for dialog boxes, scroll bars, text fields, radio buttons, menus, and the common button. Controls allow you to create a familiar interface for the user. Traditionally, implementing controls was a difficult process, and it is still not the easiest thing to do even with today's "Visual" compilers and libraries, although it is worlds better than it was even a few years ago.

While Java doesn't support the drag-and-drop style interface creation that many of the modern development environments do, it is still simply a matter of subclassing the provided classes with the functionality you need. There are several graphical development environments for Java being worked on and slated for release soon after this book should be in print. Borland, Sun, and others are working on integrated graphical Java Development environments which would provide the programmer with a Visual Basic or Visual C++ kind of interface. The next example shows you how to include a button in a stand-alone application.

Buttons

The button class in the awt package provides the necessary methods for creating a button that responds to being pressed. In order to create the button (see fig. 13.2), you must create a subclass of applet that handles the selection of the button for you. In this case, the subclass will be the following:

```java
import java.awt.*;
import java.applet.*;

public class Buttons extends Applet {
    boolean ImageShown = true;
    Image frame = null;
    public void init() {
        add(new Button("Try Me"));
        add(new Button("Quit"));
        frame = getImage(getDocumentBase(),"frame.gif");
    }
    public void paint(Graphics g) {
        if(!ImageShown)
            g.drawImage(frame, 100, 100, this);
        else {
            g.setColor(Color.lightGray);
            g.fillRect(100,100,100,100);
        }
        showStatus("Image updated");
    }
    public boolean handleEvent(Event evt) {
        switch(evt.id) {
            case Event.ACTION_EVENT: {
                if("Try Me".equals(evt.arg)) {
                    showStatus("updating image");
                    repaint();
                    ImageShown = !ImageShown;
                    return true;
                }
                if(("Quit").equals(evt.arg)) {
                    showStatus("Exiting...");
                    destroy();
                    System.exit(0);
                    return true;
```

```
                }
            }
        default:
            return false;
        }
    }
}
```

Figure 13.2
The application before and after the Try Me button is pressed.

There are several new items in this example that are worth talking about in reference to the awt class. This applet uses the button class, and event handling methods to display an image on the screen, and to exit. The two most important elements to the code are the add() method and the handleEvent method.

Notice the add(button("Try Me")) command in the init() method of the applet. This method is a member of the container class, which is subclassed by panel, which is in turn subclassed by applet. In this way, our subclass of applet has access to this method that adds components to a window container. Components can include several items including:

➤ buttons

➤ menus

➤ Canvas

➤ Checkbox

➤ Choice

➤ Dialog

➤ Label

➤ List

➤ Scroll bar

➤ TextField

The following example (see fig. 13.3) brings up an applet with several of the previous components, and shows how easy it is to create graphical elements with the new awt class library. Of course, none of these actually do anything, it is just a useful exercise to see how they can be created.

```
import java.awt.*;
import java.applet.*;

public class Components extends Applet {
    Frame aboutBox = new Frame("About Box");
    MenuBar menu = new MenuBar();
    Menu fileMenu = new Menu("File");
    public void init() {
        add(new Button("Try Me"));
        add(new Button("Quit"));
        add(new Checkbox("1"));
        add(new Checkbox("2"));
        add(new Scroll bar());
        fileMenu.add("Open...");
        fileMenu.add("Close...");
        menu.add(fileMenu);
        aboutBox.setMenuBar(menu);
        aboutBox.resize(50,50);
        aboutBox.show();
    }
}
```

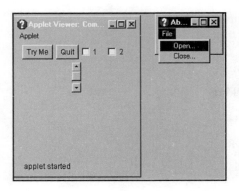

Figure 13.3

Control elements from the awt library.

In this case, a new frame is created, along with a menubar and a dropdown list. Additionally, checkbox controls were added along with a scroll bar. Once you have placed these elements, you can use the handleEvents method as in the previous example to control how your application interacts with the user.

In the case of our Try Me example, the init() method adds two buttons to the container:

```
public void init() {
        add(new Button("Try Me"));
        add(new Button("Quit"));
        frame = getImage(getDocumentBase(),"frame.gif");
    }
```

At the same time, it loads an image from the same directory of the HTML file.

```
public void paint(Graphics g) {
        if(!ImageShown)
            g.drawImage(frame, 100, 100, this);
        else {
            g.setColor(Color.lightGray);
            g.fillRect(100,100,100,100);
        }
        showStatus("Image updated");
    }
```

The applet is supposed to draw an image in the window when the button is pressed, and remove it when it is pressed again. The paint() method looks at a boolean flag known as ImageShown to see if the image is on the screen. If it is, it paints a light gray rectangle over it. If it is not on the screen, it draws the image.

When the paint() method is finished, it uses the showStatus() method to indicate to the user what state it is in. The String provided in the method call will be displayed in the status bar at the bottom of the screen.

```
public boolean handleEvent(Event evt) {
        switch(evt.id) {
            case Event.ACTION_EVENT: {
                if("Try Me".equals(evt.arg)) {
                    showStatus("updating image");
                repaint();
                    ImageShown = !ImageShown;
                    return true;
                }
                if(("Quit").equals(evt.arg)) {
                    showStatus("Exiting...");
                    destroy();
                    System.exit(0);
                    return true;
                }
            }
            default:
                return false;
        }
    }
}
```

The handle event method is the guts of an event-driven program like this applet. Whenever the applet detects that an element has been updated (such as a button pressed), it sends an Event object to a method that the programmer can implement known as a handle event. In the case of this applet, the handleEvent method tests whether the event it has been passed matches either of the two button names.

In the case of the Try Me button, it tells the user that it is updating the image in the status bar, and then calls repaint. After the image has been updated, it switches the ImageShown flag to represent its new state, and returns true. In the case of the quit button, the method sends a notice to the status bar, cleans up the applet with destroy(), and exits using the System.exit(0) method.

If you create a button named "Quit," it has the automatic behavior of exiting the window. This occurs because if the button is pressed, and the event is not handled at the level of your applet, as it gets passed up the object hierarchy it finally runs into an object that handles a quit event and exits the window.

The Try Me! example shows the ease in which graphical Java applets can be made. There are basically two steps:

➤ Create the look of the interface

➤ Handle the events that occur as the result of user interaction

Creating the Look of a User Interface

The user interface in Java is created from subclasses of the Component class. These component objects are the elements that make up a user interface. For example, the following are all considered children of the Component class:

➤ Button

➤ Checkbox

➤ Choice

➤ List

➤ MenuItem

➤ TextField

➤ Scroll bar

➤ Label

These components are then grouped together using containers such as Windows and Panels. In the case of an applet, it is already a subclass of the Panel class, so it is considered a container that can hold awt Components. The Window class can be broken down further into three groups:

➤ Dialog

➤ FileDialog

➤ Frame

These three containers are stand-alone windows that exist independently of any other windows, and allow the user to interact with the application. The Dialog container has the ability to create itself as a modal dialog box. This means that it will trap all input from the user until it is handled. This can be used for important queries that the user should not be able to ignore. The FileDialog creates an instance of the standard file open and save dialog box for the respective platform. The Frame container is the most rudimentary, but is required for most containers, including the Dialog and FileDialog containers.

The Panel container is used to group together Components with a Frame or Dialog. If you recall the earlier examples, we used the add() method of the Panel to include components in the applet's panel.

```
add(new Button("Try Me"));
add(new Button("Quit"));
add(new Checkbox("1"));
add(new Checkbox("2"));
add(new Scroll bar());
```

This is the standard method for adding new Components to a Container class such as the Panel. However, this doesn't give you any control over where components fall in the container, so the awt provides layout managers to control placement of the elements in the panel. The layout managers provided are:

➤ BorderLayout

➤ CardLayout

➤ FlowLayout

➤ GridBagLayout

➤ GridLayout

Each of these layout managers provides different means for placing elements on the screen. The following example using the BorderLayout to place the same elements used in the previous component example and places them around the edges of the panel. You can see, especially with the scroll bar component, that this is a useful manager.

```
import java.awt.*;
import java.applet.*;

public class Components extends Applet {

    public void init() {
        this.setLayout(new BorderLayout());
        add("North",new Button("Try Me"));
        add("South",new Button("Quit"));
        add("West",new Checkbox("1"));
        add("Center",new Checkbox("2"));
        add("East",new Scroll bar());

    }
}
```

Each layout manager provides different means for adjusting where elements fall, so it is useful to experiment with all of them. For all layout managers, you use the setLayout() method of the Panel class to tell it which layout manager to use. The new layout manager uses an add() method with two arguments, the Component to add, and the location to place it. In the case of the BorderLayout manager, it uses the North, South, East, West, and Center names to designate where items will go. You should note that it is possible to have panels within panels, and that they can be placed within the layout of a manager. This way, you could use, for example, the BorderLayout manager to place scroll bars along the side and bottom, and place another panel in the center that holds a graphical drawing area.

Handling Events

The previous section showed the hierarchy of the awt components and containers that are used to create a user interface. Of course, once these components are on the screen, it is necessary to handle the messages that they pass to the applet. The handleEvent() method is the easiest way to deal with this. The following code is from the example that displayed a graphic when the Try Me! button was pressed.

```
public boolean handleEvent(Event evt) {
        switch(evt.id) {
            case Event.ACTION_EVENT: {
                if("Try Me".equals(evt.arg)) {
                    showStatus("updating image");
                repaint();
                    ImageShown = !ImageShown;
                    return true;
                }
                if(("Quit").equals(evt.arg)) {
                    showStatus("Exiting...");
                    destroy();
                    System.exit(0);
                    return true;
                }
            }
            default:
                return false;
        }
    }
```

The handleEvent() method takes an argument of Event, which is sent to it by the individual components when they are used. In this example, when a button is pressed, it will send an ACTION_EVENT message, detailing which button was hit. The

Event class has an instance variable known as arg, which holds the name of the calling component in the case of the Button class. By comparing known button values with this variable, it can be determined which button was hit, and what action to take. By determining what type of Event is being caught, the programmer can initiate actions. This kind of event-driven programming is the basis for all newer Windows programs.

Creating a Tab Control

With all the tools from the awt classes, you have enough information to begin building a useful user interface element. One item that is missing from the awt, which has become standard in many interfaces, is the tabbed dialog box. The following code provides such a dialog box:

```
packege ui;

import java.awt.*;

/**
 * class that encapsulates the tab selectors and panels
 * @version 1.0 20-12-95
 * @author Timothy Ritchey
 */
public class TabControl extends Panel {

    protected TabSelectorPanel spPanel = new
➥TabSelectorPanel();
    protected TabDisplayPanel dpPanel = new
➥TabDisplayPanel();
    protected tcBorder leftBorder = new
➥tcBorder(tcBorder.tcbLeft);
    protected tcBorder rightBorder = new
➥tcBorder(tcBorder.tcbRight);
    protected tcBorder bottomBorder = new
➥tcBorder(tcBorder.tcbBottom);
    protected Dimension cSize = new Dimension();
    protected Dimension spSize = new Dimension();
    protected Dimension dpSize = new Dimension();
```

```
protected GridBagLayout cLayout = new GridBagLayout();
protected GridBagConstraints cConstraints = new
➥GridBagConstraints();

public TabControl() {
    setLayout(cLayout);
    cConstraints.gridwidth =
    ➥GridBagConstraints.REMAINDER;
    cConstraints.anchor = GridBagConstraints.SOUTHWEST;
    cLayout.setConstraints(spPanel,cConstraints);
    add(spPanel);
    cConstraints.gridwidth = 1;
    cConstraints.anchor = GridBagConstraints.NORTHWEST;
    cLayout.setConstraints(leftBorder,cConstraints);
    add(leftBorder);
    cConstraints.anchor = GridBagConstraints.CENTER;
    cLayout.setConstraints(dpPanel,cConstraints);
    add(dpPanel);
    cConstraints.gridwidth =
    ➥GridBagConstraints.REMAINDER;
    cConstraints.anchor = GridBagConstraints.NORTHEAST;
    cLayout.setConstraints(rightBorder,cConstraints);
    add(rightBorder);
    cConstraints.anchor = GridBagConstraints.CENTER;
    cLayout.setConstraints(bottomBorder,cConstraints);
    add(bottomBorder);

}

public void addTab(String name, Panel panel, int width,
➥int height) {
    spPanel.addTabSelector(name);
    dpPanel.addTabDisplay(name, panel, width, height);
    dpSize = dpPanel.getSize();
    spSize = spPanel.getSize();
    cSize.width = (spSize.width <= dpSize.width) ?
    ➥dpSize.width : spSize.width;
    cSize.height = spSize.height + dpSize.height;
    spPanel.setOverallWidth(cSize);
    leftBorder.setHeight(cSize.height);
    rightBorder.setHeight(cSize.height);
```

```
                bottomBorder.setWidth(cSize.width);
                resize(cSize);
                dpPanel.showTabDisplay(name);
        }

        public boolean mouseDown (Event e, int x, int y) {
            if(e.arg instanceof TabSelector) {
                TabSelector cSelector = (TabSelector)e.arg;
                dpPanel.showTabDisplay(cSelector.getName());
                return true;
            } else
                return false;
        }
}

/**
 * class that encapsulated the different tab panels
 * @version 1.0 20-12-95
 * @author Timothy Ritchey
 */
class TabDisplayPanel extends Panel {

    CardLayout dpLayout = new CardLayout();

    Dimension dpSize = new Dimension();

    public TabDisplayPanel() {
        setLayout(dpLayout);
    }

    public void addTabDisplay(String name, Panel panel, int
    ➥width, int height) {
        TabDisplay dDisplay = new
        ➥TabDisplay(panel,width,height);
        Dimension dSize = dDisplay.getSize();
        dpSize.height = (dSize.height > dpSize.height) ?
        ➥dSize.height : dpSize.height;
        dpSize.width = (dSize.width > dpSize.width) ?
        ➥dSize.width : dpSize.width;
        dpSize.width +=16;
        dpSize.height += 16;
```

```
        add(name,dDisplay);
    }

    public void showTabDisplay(String name) {
        dpLayout.show(this,name);
    }

    public Dimension getSize() {
        return dpSize;
    }

}

/**
 * class that encapsulates the tab panels
 * @version 1.0 20-12-95
 * @author Timothy Ritchey
 */
class TabDisplay extends Panel {

    protected Panel dPanel = null;
    protected Dimension dSize = new Dimension();

    public TabDisplay(Panel panel, int width, int height) {
        dPanel = panel;
        Dimension panelSize = new Dimension(width,height);
        dSize.width = panelSize.width;
        dSize.height = panelSize.height;
        resize(dSize);
        add(dPanel);
    }

    public Dimension getSize() {
        return dSize;
    }

}

/**
 * class that controls the selector tabs
 * @version 1.0 20-12-95
```

```
 * @author Timothy Ritchey
 */
class TabSelectorPanel extends Panel {

    /**
     * These variables hold the dimensions of the panel
     */
    Dimension spSize = new Dimension(0,0);
    Dimension spOverallSize = new Dimension(0,0);

    /**
     * this variable holds the TabSelector which is in front
     */
    TabSelector spFront = null;

    /**
     * this variable holds a Blank TabSelector which is used
       to
     * fill out the end of the panel
     */
    TabSelector spBlankEnd = new TabSelector("sBlankEnd");

    /**
     * this constructor creates an empty TabSelectorPanel;
     */
    public TabSelectorPanel() {
        setLayout(new FlowLayout(FlowLayout.CENTER, 0, 0));
    }

    /**
     * this method adds a new TabSelector to the
       TabSelectorPanel
     * @param name the name of the new TabSelector
     */
    public void addTabSelector(String name) {
        //this check to see if there are any components yet,
        //if there are, then it removes the blank component
from the end
        int nComp = countComponents();
        if(nComp > 0)
            remove(getComponent(nComp-1));
```

```
TabSelector newTabSelector = new TabSelector(name);
Dimension newSize =
➥newTabSelector.getSize(TabSelector.sFront);
spSize.width += newSize.width;
spSize.height = (newSize.height > spSize.height) ?
➥newSize.height : spSize.height;
resize(spSize);
add(name,newTabSelector);
if(spFront != null)
    spFront.setPosition(TabSelector.sBack);
spFront = newTabSelector;
spFront.setPosition(TabSelector.sFront);
if((spOverallSize.width - spSize.width) > 0)
    spBlankEnd.setEndWidth(spOverallSize.width -
    ➥spSize.width + 3);
else
    spBlankEnd.setEndWidth(3);
add("sBlankEnd",spBlankEnd);
layout();
}


/**
 * returns the size necessary for the TabSelectorPanel
 */
public Dimension getSize() {
    return spSize;
}

public void setOverallWidth(Dimension size) {
    spOverallSize = size;
    if((spOverallSize.width - spSize.width) > 0)
        spBlankEnd.setEndWidth(spOverallSize.width -
        ➥spSize.width + 3);
    else
        spBlankEnd.setEndWidth(3);
}

public boolean mouseDown (Event e, int x, int y) {
    TabSelector TabSelected = (TabSelector)e.arg;
    if(e.arg instanceof TabSelector &&
    ➥TabSelected.getPosition() != TabSelector.sBlankEnd)
{
```

```
                spFront.setPosition(TabSelector.sBack);
                spFront = TabSelected;
                spFront.setPosition(TabSelector.sFront);
                layout();
                return false;
            } else
                return false;
        }

    }

    /**
     * This class controls the tab selector component used in the
       TabControl class
     * for choosing which tab panel to display
     * @version 1.0 19-12-95
     * @author Timothy Ritchey
     */
    class TabSelector extends Canvas {

        /**
         * variable that holds the name of the Selector
         */
        protected String sName = "";

        /**
         * variable that holds the size of the selector
         */
        protected Dimension sBackSize = new Dimension();
        protected Dimension sFrontSize = new Dimension();
        protected Dimension sBlankEndSize = new Dimension();
        /**
         *
         */
        protected Font sBackFont = null;
        protected Font sFrontFont = null;

        /**
         * these member variable are constants holding the
           possible positions
```

```
 * of the selector
 */
public static final int sBlankEnd = 2;
public static final int sBack = 1;
public static final int sFront = 0;

/**
 * variable that flags for whether selector is the
   topmost
 */
protected int sPosition = sBack;

/**
 * constructor that creates a selector object
 * @param name the name of the selector to create
 */
public TabSelector(String name) {
    sName = name;
    sBackFont = new Font("Helvetica", Font.PLAIN, 12);
    FontMetrics sBackMetrics = getFontMetrics(sBackFont);
    sBackSize.width = sBackMetrics.stringWidth(sName)+24;
    sBackSize.height = sBackMetrics.getHeight()+6;
    sFrontFont = new Font("Helvetica", Font.BOLD, 12);
    sFrontSize.width = sBackSize.width + 3;
    sFrontSize.height = sBackSize.height;
    setFont(sBackFont);
    if(sName.equals("sBlankEnd")) {
        sBlankEndSize.width = 0;
        sBlankEndSize.height = sBackSize.height;
        setPosition(sBlankEnd);
    } else
        resize(sBackSize);
}

/**
 * this method returns the name of the tab
 */
public String getName() {
    return sName;
}
```

```
/**
 * this method returns the current position of the
   TabSelector
 */
public int getPosition() {
    return sPosition;
}

/**
 * this method returns the current size of the
   TabSelector
 */
public Dimension getSize() {
    switch(sPosition) {
        case 0:
            return sFrontSize;
        case 1:
            return sBackSize;
        case 2:
            return sBlankEndSize;
        default:
            return sBackSize;
    }
}

/**
 * this method returns the given size of the TabSelector
 */
public Dimension getSize(int position) {
    switch(position) {
        case sFront:
            return sFrontSize;
        case sBack:
            return sBackSize;
        case sBlankEnd:
            return sBlankEndSize;
        default:
            return sBackSize;
    }
}
```

```java
public void setEndWidth(int width) {
    sBlankEndSize.width = width;
    resize(sBlankEndSize);
}

public void setPosition(int pos) {
    switch(pos) {
        case 0:
            sPosition = sFront;
            setFont(sFrontFont);
            resize(sFrontSize);
            repaint();
            break;
        case 1:
            sPosition = sBack;
            setFont(sBackFont);
            resize(sBackSize);
            repaint();
            break;
        case 2:
            sPosition = sBlankEnd;
            setFont(sBackFont);
            resize(sBlankEndSize);
            repaint();
            break;
        default:
            sPosition = sBack;
            setFont(sBackFont);
            resize(sBackSize);
            repaint();
    }
}

public boolean mouseDown (Event e, int x, int y) {
    e.arg = this;
    return false;
}

/**
 * overrides the paint() method
 * @param g the graphics context of the selector
```

```
        */
    public void paint(Graphics g) {
        super.paint(g);

        if(sPosition == sFront) {
            g.setColor(Color.white);
            g.drawLine(0,2,0,sFrontSize.height-1);
            g.drawLine(1,1,1,1);
            g.drawLine(2,0,sFrontSize.width-3,0);
            g.setColor(Color.darkGray);
            g.drawLine(sFrontSize.width-2,0,sFrontSize.
            ➥width-2,sFrontSize.height-1);
            g.setColor(Color.black);
            g.drawLine(sFrontSize.width-1,2,sFrontSize.
            ➥width-1,sFrontSize.height-2);
            g.drawString(sName,13,sFrontSize.height-7);
        } else if(sPosition == sBack) {
            g.setColor(Color.white);
            g.drawLine(0,sBackSize.height-1,sBackSize.
            ➥width-1,sBackSize.height-1);
            g.drawLine(1,4,1,sBackSize.height-2);
            g.drawLine(2,3,2,3);
            g.drawLine(3,2,sBackSize.width-3,2);
            g.setColor(Color.darkGray);
            g.drawLine(sBackSize.width-2,2,sBackSize.
            ➥width-2,sBackSize.height-2);
            g.setColor(Color.black);
            g.drawLine(sBackSize.width-1,4,sBackSize.
            ➥width-1,sBackSize.height-2);
            g.drawString(sName,12,sBackSize.height-6);
        } else if(sPosition == sBlankEnd) {
            g.setColor(Color.white);
            g.drawLine(0,sBlankEndSize.height-
            ➥1,sBlankEndSize.width-1,sBlankEndSize.height-1);
        }
    }
}

/**
 * this class provides the borders for the panels around the
   tab control
```

```java
  */
class tcBorder extends Canvas {

    /**
     * these are the different kinds of borders
     */
    public static final int tcbLeft = 0;
    public static final int tcbRight = 1;
    public static final int tcbBottom = 2;

    /**
     * this variable hold that border it is and its size
     */
    int tcbType = 0;
    Dimension tcbSize = new Dimension(0,0);

    public tcBorder(int borderType) {
        tcbType = borderType;
        if(tcbType == tcbLeft || tcbType == tcbRight) {
            tcbSize.width = 2;
            tcbSize.height = 0;
        } else {
            tcbSize.height = 2;
            tcbSize.width = 0;
        }
        resize(tcbSize);

    }

    public void setHeight(int height) {
        tcbSize.height = height;
        resize(tcbSize);
    }

    public void setWidth(int width) {
        tcbSize.width = width;
        resize(tcbSize);
    }

    public void paint(Graphics g) {
        super.paint(g);
```

```
                    if(tcbType == tcbLeft) {
                        g.setColor(Color.white);
                        g.drawLine(0,0,0,tcbSize.height-1);
                    }
                    else if(tcbType == tcbRight) {
                        g.setColor(Color.darkGray);
                        g.drawLine(0,0,0,tcbSize.height-1);
                        g.setColor(Color.black);
                        g.drawLine(1,0,1,tcbSize.height-1);
                    }
                    else {
                        g.setColor(Color.darkGray);
                        g.drawLine(0,0,tcbSize.width-2,0);
                        g.setColor(Color.black);
                        g.drawLine(1,1,tcbSize.width-1,1);
                        g.drawLine(tcbSize.width-1,0,tcbSize.width-1,0);
                    }
                }
            }
        }
```

The TabControl object this code creates extends the panel class, and allows a programmer to create an instance of it and add tabs as needed. The following class is a test of the TabControl:

```
import java.awt.*;
import java.applet.*;
import ui.*;

public class TryTabSelector extends Applet {
    public void init() {
        Panel p1 = new Panel();
        Panel p2 = new Panel();
        p1.resize(100,100);
        p2.resize(100,100);
        p1.add(new Button("try me"));
        p2.add(new Button("this is a test"));
        TabControl tc = new TabControl();
        tc.addTab("Try Me!!",p1,90,100);
        tc.addTab("hello there",p2,90,100);
        add(tc);
        show();
    }
}
```

As you can see, after you have created an instance of the tab control, you can add tabs to it by providing it with the following three things:

1. Name of the tab

2. The panel it should display

3. The width and height of the panel

You can then add this tab control to the applet container and show it. In the case of this example, it only creates two panels with buttons on them, but you can place any panel object in the tab control. Because applets are subclasses of panels, this means you can place an applet as one of the tab selections.

It is important to notice in this example that the Panels the tab control displays must still have their events handled for the TabControl object to be a fully functioning control. However, this is something that should be done to the Panel objects before they are placed in the TabControl object. Also, the TabControl in this instance is placed in the main window, but you could just as easily add it to a dialog box instead where tab controls are more typically seen.

Hopefully the TabControl object will give you a good idea of the versatility of the awt, and what you can do with it. Granted, the classes needed to create the tab control are not trivial, and they still do not implement multiple rows of tabs, or use less than three layout managers. The overall TabControl uses the GridBagLayoutManager, while the tab selectors along the top use FlowLayoutManager and the panels being displayed use the CardLayoutManager. Otherwise, the majority of the code is spent keeping track of the state of tabs, and which panels they belong to, as well as how to draw everything in the right place. There is very little eventhandling to carry out besides checking for mouseDown events. Creating good-looking interfaces will undoubtedly become easier with the new toolkits coming out, but it is nice to see that the basic tools provided for free by Sun are still powerful enough to develop complex application user interfaces.

Summary

This chapter has given you a short introduction to developing applets, and, in general, graphical applications for the browser and interpreter environments. You should be able to write your own simple animation applets and begin to deal with mouse and keyboard events. Although this is only the simplest form of interaction an applet can have, it is the best place to start for learning the fundamentals of the browser and awt packages. Of course, there are hundreds of other classes and methods provided by these packages that are not covered in this chapter. The full API would require the devotion of an entire book. Hopefully, this introduction gives you the necessary tools to begin studying the API and incorporating them into your own programs.

As with all programming, the end of each stage simply enables you to go to the next. The previous chapters should have given you enough information to begin coding your own applets for the Netscape, and, for that matter, any Java environment. With the JavaScript and Java languages, you should have a better understanding of the complete programming tools available to you for the Netscape browser. And, as more browsers begin to incorporate JavaScript and Java, the skills you learn now will be applicable to a whole range of platforms.

Appendix A

JavaScript Object Hierarchy Reference

anchor (Client)

HTML anchors enable you to create hyperlink reference points within a document. An anchor tag names a specific index point within a document for reference via links.

JavaScript can access and take advantage of the various anchors within a document.

HTML Syntax: HTML

<A Name="anchorName">

anchor text

</A>

button (Client)

Executes an action or a JavaScript script

HTML Syntax: <INPUT TYPE="Button" NAME="objectName"
                                     VALUE="buttonText"[onClick="handlerText"]>

INPUT TYPE: The type of button or the generic "button"

NAME: A reference name for the button object

VALUE: Any text that is to appear on the button

onClick option: A JavaScript function

button

Properties

➤ name

➤ value

Method

➤ click

Event Handler

➤ onClick

checkbox (Client)

Creates and identifies a checkbox object on any HTML form.

HTML Syntax: <INPUT TYPE="Checkbox"
NAME="checkboxName" VALUE="Checked"
[Onclick="handler"]> Checkbox text

checkbox

Properties

➤   checked

➤   defaultChecked

➤   name

➤   value

Method

➤   click

Event Handler

➤   onClick

Date (Common)

The date object enables the manipulation of dates and times within HTML documents.

Syntax: objectname=new Date(Parameters)

Where Parameters =

A string of form "Month, Day, Year, Hours:Minutes:Seconds"

An integer of form Year, Month, Day, Hours, Minutes, Seconds

Date

Methods

➤   getDate

➤   getDay

➤   getHours

➤   getMinutes

- getMonth
- getSeconds
- getTime
- getTimeZoneoffset
- getYear
- parse
- setDate
- setHours
- setMinutes
- setMonth
- setSeconds
- setYear
- toString
- toGMTString
- toLocaleString
- UTC

document (Client)

Text information in the current HTML document.

HTML Syntax: Enclose the text within the <BODY> </BODY> HTML tags.

document

Properties

- alinkColor
- anchors

- bgColor
- cookie
- fgColor
- forms
- lastModified
- linkColor
- links
- location
- referrer
- title
- vlinkColor

Methods

- clear
- close
- open
- write
- writeln

form (Client)

Forms allow client data retrieval and entry and act as HTML's interface to the server.

HTML Syntax: <FORM NAME="name"
Target="windowName" ACTION="Relative Path or URL"
METHOD=GET "Post1" [onSubmit="handler"]></Form>

form

Properties

- ➤ action
- ➤ elements
- ➤ encoding
- ➤ method
- ➤ target

Method

- ➤ submit

Event Handler

- ➤ onSubmit

frame (Client)

A standard HTML frame, commonly defined as part of an HTML document.

HTML Syntax: <FRAMESET> ... </FRAMESET>

frame

Properties

- ➤ defaultStatus
- ➤ frames
- ➤ parent
- ➤ self
- ➤ status
- ➤ top
- ➤ window

Methods
- ➤ alert
- ➤ close
- ➤ confirm
- ➤ open
- ➤ prompt
- ➤ setTimeout
- ➤ clearTimeout

hidden (Client)

HTML text which is hidden from the client's view.

HTML Syntax: <INPUT TYPE= "hidden" NAME="textname" VALUE="textvalue">

hidden

Properties
- ➤ defaultValue
- ➤ name
- ➤ value

history (Client)

Syntax: history.property or history.method

history

Property
- ➤ length

Methods

➤ back

➤ forward

➤ go

link (Client)

HTML text identified as a hypertext link to another HTML document location.

Property

➤ target

Event Handlers

➤ onClick

➤ onMouseOver

location (Client)

Syntax: location.property or location.method

Properties

➤ hash

➤ host

➤ hostname

➤ href

➤ pathname

➤ port

➤ protocol

➤ search

Math (Common)

Built-in mathematical functions for use within HTML documents.

Syntax: Math.property or Math.method

Properties

➤ E

➤ LN10

➤ LN2

➤ PI

➤ SQRT1_2

➤ SQRT2

Methods

➤ abs

➤ acos

➤ asin

➤ atan

➤ ceil

➤ cos

➤ exp

➤ floor

➤ log

➤ max

➤ min

➤ pow

➤ random

➤ round

➤ sin

➤ sqrt

➤ tan

navigator (Client)

Identifies the Netscape Navigator client being used to view the current HTML document.

Syntax: navigator.property

Properties

➤ appName

➤ appVersion

➤ appCodeName

➤ userAgent

password (Client)

A form object with special hidden text properties that replace standard keystroke characters with asterisks.

HTML Syntax: <INPUT TYPE = "password"
NAME="passwordname" VALUE="textvalue" SIZE=integer>

password

Properties

➤ defaultValue

➤ name

➤ password

➤ value

Methods

➤ blur

➤ focus

➤ select

radio (Client)

Radio buttons on the current HTML form.

Properties

➤ checked

➤ defaultChecked

➤ index

➤ length

➤ name

➤ value

Method

➤ click

Event Handler

➤ onClick

reset (Client)

Identifies the RESET button on an HTML form.

HTML Syntax: <INPUT TYPE="reset" NAME="resetbuttonname" VALUE="buttontext" onClick="handler">

Properties

➤ name

➤ value

Method

➤ click

Event Handler

➤ onClick

select (Client)

A scrolling or standard selection list within an HTML form.

Properties (select)

➤ length

➤ name

➤ options

➤ selectedIndex

Properties (options)

➤ defaultSelected

➤ index

➤ selected

➤ text

➤ value

Event Handlers

➤ onBlur

➤ onChange

➤ onFocus

string (Common)

A standard string of characters. A string can be manipulated using any of the following listed methods.

Syntax: objectname.property or objectname.method

Property

➤ length

Methods

➤ anchor

➤ big

➤ blink

➤ bold

➤ charAT

➤ fixed

➤ fontcolor

➤ fontsize

➤ indexOf

➤ italics

➤ lastIndexOf

➤ link

➤ small

➤ strike

➤ sub

➤ substring

➤ sup

➤ toLowerCase

➤ toUpperCase

submit (Client)

The SUBMIT button on an HTML form.

Property

➤ value

Method

➤ click

Event Handler

➤ onClick

text (Client)

Any forms-based HTML entry field on the current HTML form.

Properties

➤ defaultValue

➤ name

➤ value

Methods

➤ blur

➤ focus

➤ select

Event Handlers

➤ onBlur

➤ onChange

➤ onFocus

➤ onSelect

textarea (Client)

Similar to the text object, this object identifies any multiline text entry field within the current HTML form.

Properties

➤ defaultValue

➤ name

➤ value

Methods

➤ focus

➤ blur

➤ select

Event Handlers

➤ onBlur

➤ onChange

➤ onFocus

➤ onSelect

window (Client)

The highest object level within the Netscape Navigator client.

Properties

➤ defaultStatus

➤ frames

➤ parent

➤ self

➤ status

➤ top

Methods

➤ alert

➤ close

➤ confirm

➤ open

➤ prompt

➤ setTimeout

➤ clearTimeout

Event Handlers

➤ onLoad

➤ onUnload

Index

W

X-Y-Z

WANT MORE INFORMATION?

CHECK OUT THESE RELATED TOPICS OR SEE YOUR LOCAL BOOKSTORE

CAD and 3D Studio

As the number one CAD publisher in the world, and as a Registered Publisher of Autodesk, New Riders Publishing provides unequaled content on this complex topic. Industry-leading products include AutoCAD and 3D Studio.

Networking

As the leading Novell NetWare publisher, New Riders Publishing delivers cutting-edge products for network professionals. We publish books for all levels of users, from those wanting to gain NetWare Certification, to those administering or installing a network. Leading books in this category include *Inside NetWare 3.12*, *CNE Training Guide: Managing NetWare Systems*, *Inside TCP/IP*, and *NetWare: The Professional Reference*.

Graphics

New Riders provides readers with the most comprehensive product tutorials and references available for the graphics market. Best-sellers include *Inside CorelDRAW! 5*, *Inside Photoshop 3*, and *Adobe Photoshop NOW!*

Internet and Communications

As one of the fastest growing publishers in the communications market, New Riders provides unparalleled information and detail on this ever-changing topic area. We publish international best-sellers such as *New Riders' Official Internet Yellow Pages, 2nd Edition*, a directory of over 10,000 listings of Internet sites and resources from around the world, and *Riding the Internet Highway, Deluxe Edition*.

Operating Systems

Expanding off our expertise in technical markets, and driven by the needs of the computing and business professional, New Riders offers comprehensive references for experienced and advanced users of today's most popular operating systems, including *Understanding Windows 95*, *Inside Unix*, *Inside Windows 3.11 Platinum Edition*, *Inside OS/2 Warp Version 3*, and *Inside MS-DOS 6.22*.

Other Markets

Professionals looking to increase productivity and maximize the potential of their software and hardware should spend time discovering our line of products for Word, Excel, and Lotus 1-2-3. These titles include *Inside Word 6 for Windows*, *Inside Excel 5 for Windows*, *Inside 1-2-3 Release 5*, and *Inside WordPerfect for Windows*.

New Riders Publishing 201 West 103rd Street ◆ Indianapolis, Indiana 46290 USA

New Riders has emerged as a premier publisher of computer books for the professional computer user. Focusing on CAD/graphics/multimedia, communications/internetworking, and networking/operating systems, New Riders continues to provide expert advice on high-end topics and software.

Check out the online version of *New Riders' Official World Wide Yellow Pages, 1996 Edition* for the most engaging, entertaining, and informative sites on the Web! You can even add your own site!

Brave our site for the finest collection of CAD and 3D imagery produced today. Professionals from all over the world contribute to our gallery, which features new designs every month.

From Novell to Microsoft, New Riders publishes the training guides you need to attain your certification. Visit our site and try your hand at the CNE Endeavor, a test engine created by VFX Technologies, Inc. that enables you to measure what you know—and what you don't!

http://www.mcp.com/newriders

PLUG YOURSELF INTO...

THE MACMILLAN INFORMATION SUPERLIBRARY™

Free information and vast computer resources from the world's leading computer book publisher—online!

FIND THE BOOKS THAT ARE RIGHT FOR YOU!
A complete online catalog, plus sample chapters and tables of contents!

- **STAY INFORMED** with the latest computer industry news through our online newsletter, press releases, and customized Information SuperLibrary Reports.

- **GET FAST ANSWERS** to your questions about Macmillan Computer Publishing books.

- **VISIT** our online bookstore for the latest information and editions!

- **COMMUNICATE** with our expert authors through e-mail and conferences.

- **DOWNLOAD SOFTWARE** from the immense Macmillan Computer Publishing library:
    - Source code, shareware, freeware, and demos

- **DISCOVER HOT SPOTS** on other parts of the Internet.

- **WIN BOOKS** in ongoing contests and giveaways!

TO PLUG INTO MCP:

WORLD WIDE WEB: **http://www.mcp.com**

FTP: ftp.mcp.com

Name _____ Title _____

Company _____ Type of business _____

Address _____

City/State/ZIP _____

Have you used these types of books before?   ☐ yes   ☐ no

If yes, which ones? _____

_____

How many computer books do you purchase each year?   ☐ 1–5   ☐ 6 or more

How did you learn about this book? _____

Where did you purchase this book? _____

Which applications do you currently use? _____

_____

Which computer magazines do you subscribe to? _____

_____

What trade shows do you attend? _____

_____

Comments: _____

_____

_____

Would you like to be placed on our preferred mailing list?   ☐ yes   ☐ no

☐ **I would like to see my name in print!** You may use my name and quote me in future New Riders products and promotions. My daytime phone number is: _____

New Riders Publishing   201 West 103rd Street ◆ Indianapolis, Indiana 46290 USA

Fax to 317-581-4670

Fold Here

BUSINESS REPLY MAIL
FIRST-CLASS MAIL PERMIT NO. 9918 INDIANAPOLIS IN

POSTAGE WILL BE PAID BY THE ADDRESSEE

NO POSTAGE
NECESSARY
IF MAILED
IN THE
UNITED STATE

NEW RIDERS PUBLISHING
201 W 103RD ST
INDIANAPOLIS IN 46290-9058

Installing the CD-ROM

This CD contains HTML-, Unix-, Windows NT-, and Windows 95-compatible files necessary for the implementation of the examples discussed in the book. Please see the book's contents and the readme files on the CD for installation information. Also note that because of the diversity in operating environments, limited information is available for any specific system installation.

Note specifically: All JavaScript examples from the book are in HTML format. You will need Netscape Navigator 2.0 or above to run the JavaScript examples contained in these files.

Specific installation information, as well as the latest release information for Java 1.0, is available from Sun Microsystems on the World Wide Web at http://java.sun.com/. The attached CD contains the latest version of Java, Java 1.0, to limit your download requirements. Please see the Sun Microsystems World Wide Web page for installation details specific to your environment.